Everything you wanted to know about the Mac

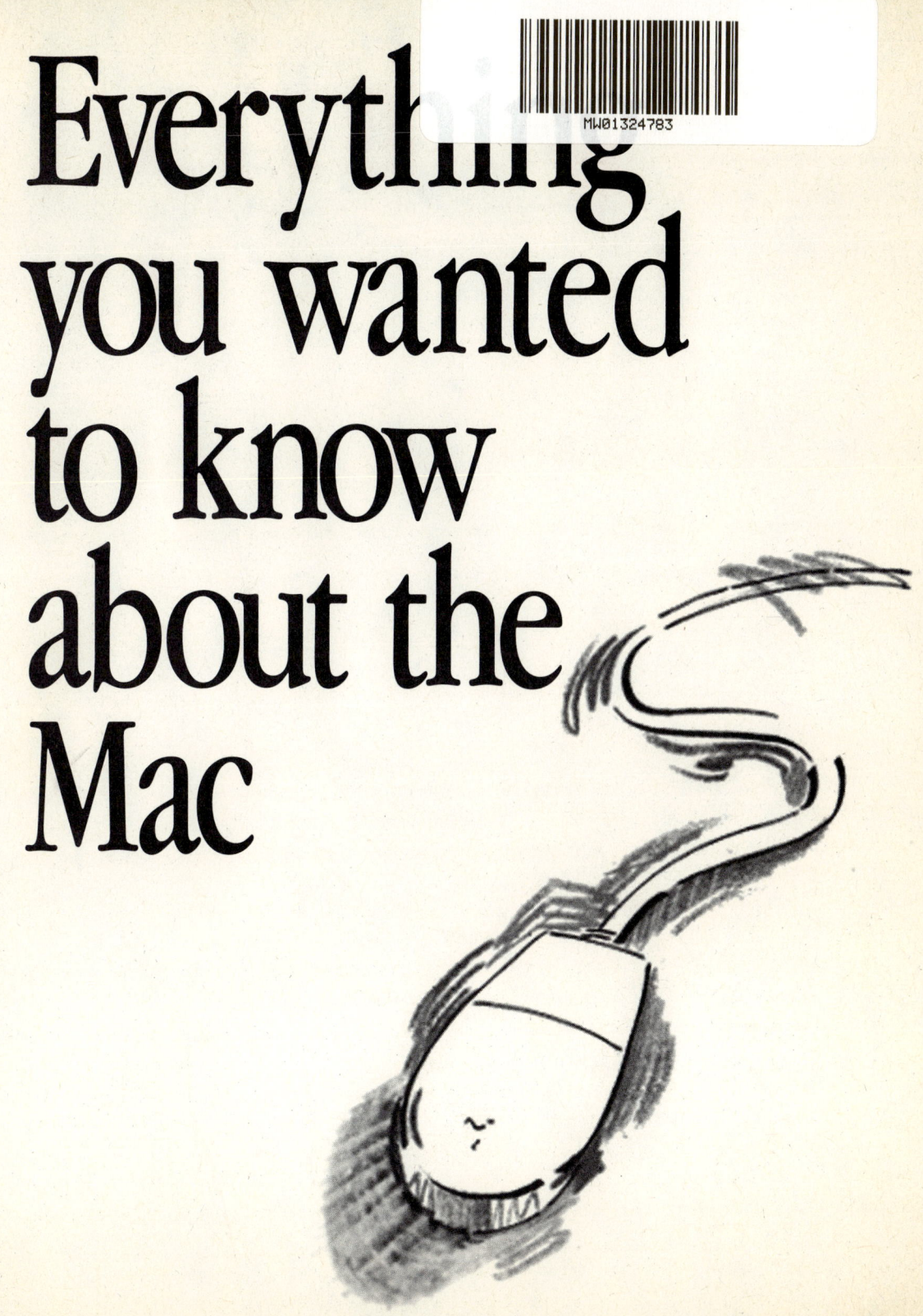

Everything you wanted to know about the Mac

Larry Hanson
and the
Dieties of Macintosh

Everything You Wanted to Know About the Mac, Second Edition

Copyright © 1993 by Hayden.
A Division of Prentice Hall Computer Publishing.

All rights reserved. Printed in the United States of America. No part of this book may be used or reproduced in any form or by any means, or stored in a database or retrieval system, without prior written permission of the publisher except in the case of brief quotations embodied in critical articles and reviews. Making copies of any part of this book for any purpose other than your own personal use is a violation of United States copyright laws. For information, address Hayden Books, 201 W. 103rd Street, Indianapolis, IN 46290.

Library of Congress Catalog No.: 93-78373

ISBN: 1-56830-058-1

This book is sold *as is*, without warranty of any kind, either expressed or implied. While every precaution has been taken in the preparation of this book, the publisher and author assume no responsibility for errors or omissions. Neither is any liability assumed for damages resulting from the use of the information or instructions contained herein. It is further stated that the publisher and author are not responsible for any damage or loss to your data or your equipment that results directly or indirectly from your use of this book.

94 93 92   4 3 2 1

Interpretation of the printing code: the rightmost double-digit number is the year of the book's printing; the rightmost single-digit number is the number of the book's printing. For example, a printing code of 93-1 shows that the first printing of the book occurred in 1993.

Everything You Wanted to Know About the Mac, Second Edition covers Apple Computer's family of Macintosh computers.

The text in this book is printed on recycled paper.

Dedication

For you.

Credits

Publisher	David Rogelberg
Acquisitions Editor	Karen Whitehouse
Project Editor	Larry Hanson
Development Editor	Dave Ciskowski
Editors	Marie-Therese Cagnina
	Matthew Ciskowski
	Marj Hopper
Technical Editor	Chuck Merkle
Publishing Coordinator	Mat Wahlstrom
Cover Designer	Jay Corpus
Interior Designers	Scott Cook
	Kevin Spear
Production Team	Angela Bannan, Diana Bigham, Katy Bodenmiller, Ayrika Bryant, Brad Chinn, Charlotte Clapp, Tim Cox, Meshell Dinn, Mark Enochs, Howard Jones, Beth Rago, Carrie Roth, Marc Shecter, Greg Simsic, C. Small

Composed in ITC Garamond, Helvetica, and MCPdigital by Hayden Books.

Contributing Authors

James K. Anders

Jim Anders is a Senior Consulting Engineer with Computer Methods Corporation. He writes and lectures on Macintosh networking, systems integration, and CAD/CAM topics in a variety of forums, such as the Mactivity networking conference and the Macintosh Summit Conference. He is the author of *Technical Drawing with Claris CAD* and *The Macintosh CAD/CAM Book,* as well as Hayden Books' *Live Wired: A Guide to Networking Macs.* He also writes reviews and articles for *MacUser* magazine. For this book, Mr. Anders contributed chapter 25, "Networking."

Jonah Benton

Jonah is a senior in Cognitive Science at the Massachusetts Institute of Technology. He has written several articles on Macintosh software and other computer related topics. A native of New York City, a skier, and a bon vivant, his interests include artificial intelligence, management science, and writing. He co-authored with Barrie Sosinsky the following chapters: 6, "Printing From Your Macintosh," 11, "Word Processors," 12, "Spreadsheets," and 26, "Macintosh and PC Coexistence." He co-authored chapter 14, "Integrated Programs," with Larry Hanson and Barrie Sosinsky. He also contributed major sections of chapter 3, "Exploring the Macintosh System," and chapter 4, "How the Macintosh Works."

Christian Boyce

Christian Boyce intended to design bridges for earthquake-prone sites after completing work at UCLA and the University of Texas at Austin. Shaky times in the earthquake engineering field led him to take a job in Southern California's aerospace industry, where he distinguished himself by championing prestressed concrete as a material for the Space Station. Christian joined the Los Angeles Macintosh Group in 1987 and soon became the Group's Director of Education. The self-described "Macintosh Consultant to the Stars," Christian specializes in helping people take advantage of the software and hardware they already own. He is the author of *Your Mac Can Do That!* and the forthcoming *Macs for Morons,* both from Hayden Books. For this book, Christian contributed excerpts from *Your Mac Can Do That!* for the Interludes: "Cool PageMaker Stuff," "Cool Word Stuff," "Cool Excel Stuff," and "Cool FileMaker Stuff," as well as for parts of chapter 2, "Macintosh Basics."

Teresa Eagan-Morrison

Teresa Eagan-Morrison is a freelance technical writer working in the Sacramento Valley area. She has more than 20 years experience in writing, editing, photography, and layout and production of technical and administrative publications, as well as the development and implementation of communications programs. A writer of non-fiction articles, which have been published in both international and local magazines, she now concentrates on user's manuals and tutorials in the computer software field. Teresa's fascination with databases began when she was introduced to a Macintosh database while cataloging a library of writer's reference materials. She is presently writing a manual for a Mac database program. Teresa wrote, fittingly, chapter 13, "Databases."

Larry Hanson

Larry Hanson is a Macintosh consultant specializing in the field of desktop publishing, an area for which he is uniquely qualified since he is also the former owner of a typesetting company and advertising agency. In addition to consulting, he uses his Mac to continue serving clients in the advertising and marketing areas with creative services, and has won several "Addy" awards for his advertising work. Hanson is an Authorized Apple Consultant and a certified trainer on more than a dozen Macintosh applications.

Larry Hanson compiled and updated the second edition, and wrote chapters 1, "Macintosh, the Computer," and 23, "Viruses and System Security;" and co-wrote chapters 9, "Fonts and Typography," 14, "Integrated Programs," and the Glossary. He also contributed major sections of the following chapters: 3, "Exploring the Macintosh System," and 4, "How the Macintosh Works."

Chuck Merkle

Chuck is a Systems Engineer at Apple Computer in Indianapolis, working primarily with Apple's K-12 customers in Indiana. Trained as a teacher, he also has a Master's Degree in Scientific Photography and has nearly completed a PhD in Instructional Technology from Indiana University. He's worked with Macintosh computers since 1984, and with his Media and Instructional Design background and a strong interest in the use of computer technologies in education, has become one of the region's Apple Multimedia Specialists. Chuck wrote chapter 19, "Multimedia on the Macintosh;" and served as Technical Editor for the entire book.

David Ramsay

David, a regular columnist for *MacWEEK*, has been a programmer for 15 years and has developed some of the best known applications on the Macintosh, including authoring MacPaint 2.0. Currently a programmer at Caere Corporation, he has been heavily involved in the development of OmniPage. His in-depth knowledge of the Macintosh and all of its capabilities led to David's writing of chapter 5, "Macintosh Hardware: A Technical Look" and chapter 28, "Troubleshooting."

Carla Rose

Carla is an advertising and magazine writer, a contributing editor of *Portable Computing,* and a member of the board of *Home and School Mac.* She is the author of *The First Book of PageMaker for the Mac* and *Mac On-Line,* and is currently researching a book about computers for the handicapped. She wrote the following chapters: 7, "Graphics," 8, "Desktop Publishing Programs," 10, "Graphic Arts Support," 16, "Education on the Mac," 20, "Macs and the Differently Abled," and 24, "Communications and Online Services." She co-authored with Jay Rose chapters 15, "Games For Fun," and 27, "The Macintosh Community." Carla also co-authored the Glossary along with Larry Hanson.

Jay Rose

Jay creates soundtracks for national advertisers including McDonald's, AT&T, and Blue Cross. He runs his studio business almost entirely in HyperCard, and has written many public-domain entertainment and educational stacks. He's author of films and training guides for high-end audio manufacturers including Bose and AKG. Jay wrote the following chapters: 17, "Sound, Music and Speech," and 18, "HyperCard and SuperCard." He co-authored with Carla Rose chapters 15, "Games For Fun," and 27, "The Macintosh Community."

Steven A. Schwartz

Steven Schwartz bought his first computer in 1978—an Apple II Plus (currently functioning as an outdoor planter at his home in Arizona). Since that time, he has written over 500 Macintosh and Apple II-related articles. He has been writing software reviews and feature articles for Macworld for the past five years. Steve is the author of Hayden Books' *The 9-to-5 Mac,* from which his contributions to chapter 2, "Macintosh Basics," were excerpted.

Kate Sherman

Kate is an independent consultant and programmer working in San Francisco. She has programmed on every type of computer from mainframes to micros over the last 15 years, and began programming on the Macintosh as soon as it was introduced. Kate wrote Chapters 21, "Utilities," 22, "Hard Disk Management," and 29, "Programming."

Barrie Sosinsky, Ph.D.

Barrie is a well-known author of more than a dozen computer books, writer of countless articles, and a much-sought-after speaker. For this book, Barrie lent his special expertise in explaining complex issues in an easy-to-understand manner. He co-authored with Jonah Benton the following chapters: 6, "Printing From Your Macintosh," 11, "Word Processors," 12, "Spreadsheets," and 26, "Macintosh and PC Coexistence." He co-authored chapter 14, "Integrated Programs," with Larry Hanson and Jonah Benton. He also contributed major sections of the following chapters: 3, "Exploring the Macintosh System," and 4, "How the Macintosh Works."

Commentators

Throughout the book, comments, asides, snipes, and so forth have been added by various well-known Macintosh dieties. In alphebetical order, they are:

Christian Boyce

As the author of the Interludes and parts of chapter 2, Christian's biography is included above. In addition, he provides his own view of what's good, what's bad, and what should be different about the software he discusses.

Guy Kawasaki

Guy Kawasaki is the former director of software product management for Apple Computer, Inc. In this position, he cajoled, coerced, and convinced software and hardware companies to create products for a computer that didn't have enough RAM, a hard disk, color, slots, an installed base, technical support, or marketing.

He has a BA from Stanford in Psychology ("the easiest major I could find") and an MBA from UCLA ("because Stanford rejected me"). While he waits for the Golden State Warriors to call him, he writes, speakes, and promotes products ("I endorse, therefore I am"). Guy is the author of several books; his comments are a sampling from *The Computer Curmudgeon,* published by Hayden Books.

Ted Landau

Ted Landau is a professor of Psychology at Oakland University in Rochester, Minnesota. He is the author of the recently published *Sad Macs, Bombs, and Other Disasters*, from Addison-Wesley, and is a frequent contributor to *Mac User*.

Bob LeVitus

Bob LeVitus was the editor-in-chief of the popular monthly periodical *MACazine* until its untimely demise in 1988. Since 1989, he has been a contributing editor/columnist for *MacUser* magazine, writing both the Help Folder and Personal Best columns each month. In his spare time, LeVitus has written nine best-selling computer books, including *Dr. Macintosh, Second Edition,* a users guide of "*How to Become a Macintosh Power User,*" *Stupid Mac Tricks, Stupid Windows Tricks,* and the recently released *Dr. Macintosh's Guide to the On-line Universe,* a hip guide to using a Mac and modem.

Bob lives in Austin, Texas with his wife Lisa, children Allison and Jacob, and assorted dogs and cats.

Mitch Ratcliffe

Mitch Ratcliffe is a co-author of *PowerBook: The Digital Nomad's Guide*. He is an Editor-at-Large for *MacWeek* and has a fondness for coyotes.

Dan Shafer

Dan Shafer is a writer and consultant specializing in microcomputer technologies and their application to real-world business problems.

Dan has written more than twenty books on microcomputer topics (including several about the Macintosh Fronties, and HyperCard) and published numerous articles in microcomputer periodicals (including frequent contributions to *MacUser, Macworld,* and *MacWEEK*). In addition, he has designed and implemented a variety of business-management and educational software products.

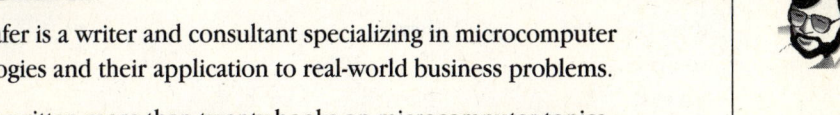

Trademark Acknowledgments

This book mentions too many companies and products to list every trademark on one page. Because we are environmentalists, and because paper is a valuable (and costly) commodity, we limit out trademark acknowledgments to the following statements:

All terms mentioned in this book that are known to be trademarks or service marks have been appropriately capitalized. Hayden Books cannot attest to the accuracy of this information. Use of a term in this book should bot be regarded as affecting the validity of any trademark or service mark.

Apple, Mac, and Macintosh are registered trademarks of Apple Computer, Inc.

We Want to Hear from You

What our readers think of Hayden Books is important to our ability to serve our customers. If you have any comments, no matter how great or how small, we'd appreciate you taking the time to send us a note.

We can be reached at the following address:

David Rogelberg, Publisher
Hayden Books
201 West 103rd Street
Indianapolis, IN 46290

(800) 428-5331 voice
(800) 448-3804 fax

Electronic Mail:

America Online:	Hayden Bks
AppleLink:	hayden.books
CompuServe:	76350,3014
Internet:	hayden@hayden.com

If this book has changed your life, we would like to hear how and why. Do you have a great book idea? Please contact us at the above address.

Acknowledgments

For the First Edition:

To Mike Britton and Karen Bluestein, for their faith and confidence. My sincere thanks for letting me work on this project and be a part of Hayden. And a big thank you to Karen Whitehouse for all your hard work and patience, and for keeping the confusing and complicated simple. Also a special thanks to Steve Poland and Chuck Hutchinson for their thorough groundwork and high levels of professionalism that preceded my involvement in this project. It made my task much easier.

For the Second Edition:

Thanks to David Rogelberg, Karen Whitehouse, and the rest of the folks at Hayden Books for their support, words of wisdom, and book contributions. Thanks to Chuck Merkle, for his superb technical review. Thanks to Jim Anders, for his outstanding efforts on behalf of the networking chapter. Thanks to Robin Williams, for her analysis. And much thanks to all the readers of the first edition, particularly those who sent in their comments, corrections, suggestions, and advice. You've made the second edition a better book.

A big hearty "Thank You!" to the production and manufacturing folks—Angela Bannan, Diana Bigham, Katy Bodenmiller, Ayrika Bryant, Marie-Therese Cagnina, Dave Ciskowski, Brad Chinn, Charlotte Clapp, Tim Cox, Scott Cook, Mishell Dinn, Mark Enochs, Beth Guzman, Larry Hanson, Marj Hopper, Howard Jones, Chuck Merkle, Barry Pruett, Beth Rago, David Rogelberg, Carrie Roth, Marc Shecter, Greg Simsic, C. Small, Mat Wahlstrom, and Karen Whitehouse. They take words and make books out of them, and do it well. Thanks also to Jay Corpus, Susan Kinola, Scott Cook again, and Kevin Spear for the wonderful book design, both outside and in.

Most of all, thanks to the many people who love the Macintosh.

Overview

Introduction xlvii

Part I Macintosh, the Computer 1

1 Macintosh, the Computer (Larry Hanson) 3
2 Macintosh Basics (Christian Boyce, Steven Schwartz) 17
3 Exploring the Macintosh System (Barrie Sosinsky,
   Jomah Benton) 55
4 How the Macintosh Works (Barry Sosinsky,
   Jonah Benton) 99
5 Macintosh Hardware: A Technical Look
   (David Ramsay) 139
6 Printing from Your Macintosh (Barry Sosinsky,
   Jonah Benton) 201

Part II What Put the Mac in Business 249

7 Drawing and Painting on the Macintosh (Carla Rose) 251
8 Desktop Publishing Programs (Carla Rose) 299
   Interlude: Cool PageMaker Stuff (Christian Boyce) 327
9 Fonts and Typography (Larry Hanson) 365
10 Graphic Arts Support (Carla Rose) 381

Part III Mainstream Mac Applications 399

11 Word Processors (Barry Sosinsky, Jonah Benton) 401
   Interlude: Cool Word Stuff (Christian Boyce) 431
12 Spreadsheets (Barry Sosinsky, Jonah Benton) 457
   Interlude: Cool Excel Stuff (Christian Boyce) 475
13 Databases (Theresa Eagen-Morrison) 507
   Interlude: Cool FileMaker Stuff (Christian Boyce) 539
14 Integrated Programs (Larry Hanson, Barry Sosinsky) 573
15 Macintosh Games (Carla Rose, Jay Rose) 587
16 Education on the Mac (Carla Rose) 617

Part IV Specialized Mac Applications 641

17 Sound, Music, and Speech (Jay Rose) 643
18 Hypercard and SuperCard (Jay Rose) 689
19 Multimedia on the Macintosh (Chuck Merkle) 747
20 Macs and the Differently Abled (Carla Rose) 809

Part V Managing Your Mac 831

- 21 Utilities (Kate Sherman) 833
- 22 Hard Disk Management (Kate Sherman) 851
- 23 Viruses and System Security (Larry Hanson) 869

Part VI Expanding Your Mac's Horizons 895

- 24 Communications and Online Services (Carla Rose) 897
- 25 Networking the Macintosh (Jim Anders) 943
- 26 Macintosh and PC Coexistence (Barrie Sosinsky, Jonah Benton) 1001
- 27 The Macintosh Community (Carla Rose, Jay Rose) 1035

Part VII For the More Technically Minded 1051

- 28 Troubleshooting (David Ramsay) 1053
- 29 Programming on the Macintosh (Kate Sherman) 1081

Glossary of Common Macintosh Terms (Carla Rose, Larry Hanson) 1109

Index 1131

Table of Contents

Part I Macintosh, the Computer 1

1 Macintosh, the Computer 3

Introduction 4
The History of Apple Computer 4
    Markulla Comes on Board 9
    More Computers Enter the Field 9
    IBM Enters the Picture 10
    The Birth of the Macintosh 10
    Sculley Joins Apple 12
    The 1984 Commercial 12
    Changing of the Guard 14
Summary 15

2 Macintosh Basics 17

Macintosh Skills 18
    Starting Up the Mac 18
    Mousing Around 19
    Dealing with Disks and Files 20
    Shutting Down the Mac 21
Words Your Mother Didn't Use 22
    Verbs 22
    Nouns 23
Mac-ing With An Attitude 25
    Being Brave 25
    Being Smart 25
    Getting Your Money's Worth 25
Built-in System Stuff 26
    Cut, Copy, and Paste 28
        Copying and Pasting between Different Kinds
            of Documents 28
    The Scrapbook 31
        Putting stuff into the Scrapbook 31
        Getting Stuff out of the Scrapbook 32
        Copying and Pasting All Over the Place ... 32

Copying from the Scrapbook and Pasting to a Control Panel	33
Copying from the Note Pad and Pasting into the Calculator	34
Copying Icons and Pasting Them Where They Don't Belong	34
Publish and Subscribe	35
Aliases	37
Making an Alias	38
The Apple Menu	40
Adding a Sound to the Apple Menu	41
Startup Items	43
Control Panels	45
General Controls	45
Sound	46
Views	47
Driving Your Mac from the Keyboard	48
Universal Command Key Equivalents	48
Other Universal Keyboard Shortcuts	49
Special Finder Shortcuts	50
Another Way to Find	52
Summary	54

3 Exploring the Macintosh System 55

The Desktop	56
Basic Macintosh Features	58
Pointers	58
Selection	59
Icons	60
Menus	60
The Apple Menu (All Programs)	62
The File Menu (All Programs)	63
The Edit Menu (All Programs)	65
The View Menu (Finder Only)	66
The Label Menu (Finder Only)	66
The Special Menu (Finder Menu Only)	67
The Balloon Help Menu (All Programs)	68
The Application Menu (All Programs)	69
Using Windows	70
The Mouse	73

    The Keyboard 74
    Dialog and Alert Boxes 76
More Basics 78
    The System Folder 78
    The System File 80
        System Resources and System 6 80
        System Resources and System 7 82
    System Enablers 83
    System Extensions 84
        The Control Panel 86
        The Start-up Order 87
        FKeys 89
    Desk Accessories 90
    Sounds 91
Recent and Upcoming System Enhancements 95
    Interapplication Communications
        and Apple Events 96
    AppleScript 97
    The Layout Manager 98
Summary 98

4   How the Macintosh Works 99

The Look and Feel (Human Interface Guidelines) 100
    The 10 Interface Commandments 100
What Is an Operating System? 101
    Driven by Events 103
How the Mac Works 105
Volumes and Files 108
    Drives and Volumes 109
    The Macintosh File System 111
        Desktop File 112
    File Attributes 114
    Resources 117
        Resource Editors 120
    The CPU 120
    Coprocessors 121
Memory: RAM, ROM, and Storage 122
    Setting Memory Allocation 124
    Installing RAM 127
    RAM Cache and RAM Disks 128

	The RAM Cache	128
	The RAM Disk	129
	Virtual Memory	130
	32-Bit Addressing	131
Buses		132
	Apple Desktop Bus	133
	SCSI	134
	NuBus and Other Slots	136
Summary		138

5 Macintosh Hardware 139

CPUs	140
Communicating with the Hardware	141
The Motorola 68000 Family	141
Mac Memory Architecture	142
Coprocessors	143
Macintosh Models	144
Lisa and Mac XL	145
Compact Macs	146
Mac 128	146
Mac 512	147
Mac Plus	147
Mac 512Ke	148
Mac SE	148
Mac SE/30	150
Mac Classic	150
Mac Classic II	151
Color Classic	151
Modular Macs	152
Mac II	153
Mac IIx	154
Mac IIcx	155
The Mac IIci	155
The IIfx	156
Mac LC	157
Mac IIsi	158
Quadra 700	159
Quadra 900	160
Quadra 950	161
Mac LCII	162

- Mac IIvx 162
- Mac LCIII 163
- Centris 610 164
- Centris 650 165
- Quadra 800 165
- Portable Macs 166
  - The Portable 167
  - PowerBook 100 168
  - PowerBook 140 and 170 169
  - PowerBook 145 170
  - PowerBook 160 and 180 170
  - PowerBook Duo 210 and 230 170
  - PowerBook 165c 171
  - PowerBook Expansion: Modems 172
- In Production 172
- Mac Internal Video 172
  - Internal Video Hardware 173
  - Macintosh LC, LCII, Classic II, and Color Classic 174
  - Macintosh IIvx 174
  - Quadra 700 and Quadra 900 175
  - Quadra 950 176
  - Centris 610 and 650, and Quadra 800 176
  - Monitor Connections 177
  - Macintosh Video Cards 179
  - Macintosh Hardware Overview Chart 180
- Memory 182
  - How Memory Works 182
  - RAM and ROM 183
  - Memory Speed and Wait States 183
  - Caching 184
  - Memory Packaging 184
  - Interleaving 185
  - 32-Bit Cleanliness 186
  - Memory: Who Uses What 187
  - Memory Problems 187
- Hard Disks 188
  - How Data Is Stored 189
  - Hard Drive Connectivity 189
  - The Boot Sequence 190

| Hard Drive Performance 190
| Performance 190
| Peripherals and Expansion 192
| The Serial Ports 192
| When Two Is Not Enough 193
| The ADB Port 194
| The SCSI Port 195
| SCSI Problems 196
| Slots 196
| Monitors 197
| Monitors for the Mac II Class 198
| 68000-Based Macs 198
| Summary 199

6   Printing from Your Macintosh 201

Introduction 202
Printing: An Overview 204
    The Printing Process 204
    Page Description Languages 205
        Postscript 205
        QuickDraw 206
        TrueImage 206
        PostScript Clones 206
        Comparing PDLs: PostScript,
           TrueImage, and QuickDraw 207
    Printers as Computers 208
    Printer Drivers 209
    Emulation 211
    Printing Engines 211
        Dot-matrix 211
        Laser and LED 213
        Inkjet and Bubblejet 216
        Thermal Transfer 218
    Dialog Box Options 219
    Print Spoolers 223
    Downloading Fonts 225
        Font Handling on QuickDraw Printers 226
        Font Handling on PostScript Printers 227
        Font Handling on TrueImage Printers 228

What to Look for in a Printer 228
    What and When to Buy 228
    Printer Speed 229
    Resolution 230
    Cost Per Page 232
    Talking to Other Computers and Printers 232
        Hewlett-Packard's LaserJets 233
    Durability 235
    Paper 236
    Color Printing 236
        Color Inks 237
        PostScript Level 2 and Color 238
Printers: Users and Manufacturers 238
    Portable 239
    Low End Dot-matrix 239
    Personal QuickDraw Printers 240
    Personal PostScript
      and TrueImage Printers 240
    Office and Work Group Printers 241
        Low-end Office Printers 242
        High-end Office Printers 242
    High-Resolution Printers 243
    Personal and Business Color 244
    High-end Color 245
    Label and Envelope Printers 246
    Plotters 247
    Fax Modems 247
Summary 248

Part I What Put the Mac in Business 249

7   **Drawing and Painting on the Macintosh 251**

Bitmapped Images and Paint Programs 252
MacPaint 253
Painting with a Mouse 255
    Painting Tools 256

- Adding Grayscales and Colors 261
- A Higher Resolution 262
  - Shades of Gray 263
- Choosing a Paint Program 266
  - Black and White Paint Programs 266
    - MacPaint II 266
    - SuperPaint 266
    - Studio/1 267
  - Low Cost Color Paint Programs 268
    - Canvas 269
    - Studio/8 269
    - DeskPaint 270
  - Professional Painters 271
    - Photoshop 271
    - Studio/32 271
    - PixelPaint Professional 271
    - Fractal Design Painter 271
- Print It! 272
  - From Screen to Paper 273
  - The Real Truth About Color 274
    - RGB 275
    - CMYK 275
    - HSV or HSB 275
- Higher Levels of Color Matching 276
  - Pantone Matching System 277
  - Separation Anxiety and How to Cure It 278
  - Spot Color and Duotone Color 280
  - Cheap Color 281
- Object-oriented Graphics 282
- Draw (Not Paint) By Numbers 283
  - The Toolbox 283
  - "Handling" Graphics 284
  - Filling Shapes and Closed Paths 287
  - Tricks with Type 289
  - Dimensions and Grids 291
- Higher Level Graphics—The Art of Illustration 291
  - Special Tools 292
  - Type Styling 295
  - Colorful Characters 296
  - Which Illustration Program Should You Buy? 297
- Summary 298

8   Desktop Publishing Programs 299

Desktop Publishing 300
Making Pages, Then and Now 301
    Pasteless Paste-up 303
    DTP Terminology 306
    Getting Started 306
    Setting up the Pages 309
    Importing Graphics 311
    Creating Graphics Within the DTP Program 312
    Placing Text 313
    Editing Text 315
    Working with Templates 318
    Printing 320
Comparing Page Layout Programs 321
    Publish It! Easy 321
    ReadySetGo 322
    Personal Press 322
    Ventura Publisher 323
    PageMaker 324
    QuarkXPress 325
Summary 326

Cool PageMaker Stuff 327

PageMaker 328
Master Pages 330
Placing 340
    Placing Text 341
    Placing Graphics 345
    Placing the Scrapbook 350
Styles 354
Buried Treasures 358
    Command-Shift Is Everything 358
    Super-Powerful Search and Replace 358
    Change Text from Upper Case to Lower Case and Back 359
    Zooming In and Out 360
    Command-Click through the Layers 360
    Set Defaults the Way You Want Them 361
    Close Multiple Dialog Boxes Quickly 361
    Kerning: A Little Is Good,
        a Lot Can Be Fun 361

  Selection Secrets 364
  Nudge Text Blocks and Graphics with Cursor Keys 364
 In Conclusion 364

9   Fonts and Typography 365

Typographical Terms 366
The Makeup of Typography 367
How Fonts and Type Work 367
 Bitmapped Fonts 368
 PostScript Fonts 369
Creating Better Quality Screen Fonts 371
TrueType's Arrival (Or, Font Wars II: The Sequel) 373
 Dumb Fonts Versus Smart Fonts 375
 TrueType and PostScript Advantages 376
Problems with Fonts 376
 Font ID Numbers and Conflicts 376
 Font Listings 377
 Finding Special Characters 378
The Future of Font Technology 379
Summary 380

10   Graphic Arts Support 381

Clip Art 382
Page Templates 385
Background Patterns and Textures 388
Utilities 390
 File Finders 391
 Font Managers 393
 Creating Your Own Fonts 393
 Font Menu Managers 395
 Putting the Best Face Forward 397
Summary 397

Part III Mainstream Macintosh Applications 399

11   Word Processors 401

Word Processing Versus Paper Processing 402

Typical Features	402
Text Editing Features	403
Layout and Formatting	405
Style Sheets	407
Page Preview	407
Index and Table-of-Contents Generation	408
Organizing	409
Graphics	410
Searching and Changing	411
Importing and Exporting	412
Mail Merge	413
Macros	414
An Evaluation of Word Processors	415
Microsoft Word	415
Nisus	417
WordPerfect	419
Taste	420
WriteNow	420
MacWrite	421
Microsoft Works	422
The Evolution of Word Processors	423
Word Processing with System 7	424
Digging Deep: The Expert User's Guide	426
Summary	430

Cool Word Stuff 431

Word Super Features	432
Styles: Ya Gotta Have Some	432
Tables: Best Invention Since Chairs	438
Print Merge: Better Junk Mail, and More	445
Print Merge Basics	446
Print Merge Specifics	447
Things That Can Go Wrong	451
In Closing	451
Buried Treasures	451
Command-Shift Is Everything	452
Customize Menus with Commands	452

Use the Apply Button 452
Adjust Margins in the Print Preview Mode 453
Open a Second Window to View Another
   Part of a Document 454
Split the Screen to View Another Part of a Document 454
Select Text Like a Pro 455
Recover Brilliantly After Typing a Paragraph with
   the Caps Lock Down 455
In Conclusion 456

12 Spreadsheets 457

Spreadsheets and Computers 458
Spreadsheet Features 459
   The Worksheet Itself 459
   Built-in Functions 460
   Graphing and Charting Capabilities 461
   Macro and Scripting Capabilities 462
   The Spreadsheet As a Database 462
   The Spreadsheet As a Presentation Tool 463
Spreadsheets for the Macintosh 463
   Microsoft Excel 463
   Microsoft Works 465
   Wingz 465
   Resolve 1.0 467
   Lotus 1-2-3/Mac 467
   MacCalc 468
Designing a Spreadsheet 468
Spreadsheet Engines and Front-ends 470
Using Spreadsheets with System 7 471
The Future of Spreadsheets: Lotus Improv 472
Resources 473
Summary 473

Cool Excel Stuff 475

Numbers For the Rest of Us 476
Styles: So Fashionable 478

Your First Style	479
Charting: It's Such Sweet Sorrow	**488**
Making a Chart	488
Formatting a Chart	493
Buried Treasures	**498**
Store Styles in Templates	498
Make a Default Worksheet	498
Command-Shift Is Everything	498
Make Borders the Cool Way	498
Insert Rows and Columns Jiffy-Quick	499
Make Columns the Right Width, Automatically	499
Use Keyboard to Do Mouse Stuff	499
Split the Screen to See Other Parts of Your Document	499
Use the Text Box Tool to Hold a Lot of Text	500
Use Repeat to Do the Same Thing Again	500
Use Fill Down and Fill Right to Save Time	500
AutoFill	501
Drag and Drop Spreadsheet Rearranging	503
Zooming In and Out	504
In Conclusion	**506**

13 Databases 507

Introduction	**507**
What Does a Database Look Like?	**509**
Files	509
Records	509
Fields	510
Subfiles/Subrecords	510
Input and Output Layouts	511
How Does a Database Work?	**511**
Flat File Database Structure	511
Relational Database Structure	512
Building a Database	**514**
Field Types	516
Field Attributes	516
Formats	516

Filters	516
Procedures and Scripts	517
Procedures	517
Scripts	518
Database Terminology	518
Selecting a Database—Requirement Versus Desire	519
Referential Integrity	519
Data Validation	519
Reviews and Demo Packages	520
Make a Checklist	521
Refine Your Requirements	522
Personal User	522
Small-Business User	523
Corporate User	523
Mac Database Programs Review	524
Double Helix 3.5	524
4th Dimension 3.0	526
FILE FORCE	529
FileMaker Pro	530
Microsoft FoxBASE+/Mac 2.01	532
Omnis 7 Plus	535
Summary	538

Cool FileMaker Stuff 539

Database Management	540
Making the Practice Database	541
Automatic Data Entry: Sure Beats Typing	545
Auto-Enter Values	545
Lookup Files	549
Scripts: Sure Beats Forgetting	553
Sharing Files over a Network: Sure Beats Walking	566
Buried Treasures	570
Flip through Records from the Keyboard	570
Change Defaults for Field Formats	570
Double-Click to Make Tools Stick	570
Choose a Default Layout	570

        Enter the Current Date Jiffy-Quick 570
        Do Calculations with Text 571
        Add Page Numbers to Layouts 571
        Add the Date to Layouts 571
    In Conclusion 572

14   Integrated Applications 573

Why Use Integrated Software? 574
When Not to Use Integrated Software 575
Product Evaluation 575
    Microsoft Works 575
    Symantec GreatWorks 577
    ClarisWorks 579
    WordPerfect Works 581
What Happens When You Outgrow the Modules? 583
The Future of Integrated Software 584
Summary 585

15   Macintosh Games 587

A Brief History of Computer Gaming 588
The Name of the Game 591
    Battle 591
    Adventure 594
    Puzzles 597
    Simulations 603
    Shareware 610
    National Home and School Mac User Group
        (The GAMER Project) 612
Gaming as a Tool 612
MacSilliness 613
    Talking Moose 613
    Flying Toasters? 614
    Insanity 614
    More Neat Toys 615
Summary 616

16   Education on the Mac 617

Toys That Teach 618
    Can You Picture This? 619
    Teaching Tools for Early Grades 621
    "By the Time I Get to Phonics" 623
    Math for All Ages 624
    Music Lessons 626
    Author, Author 627
    Going Places 628
    Go, Go, LOGO 632
For High School and Beyond 633
    Learning Languages on the Mac 633
    Physics 101 634
    "Testing, 1, 2…" 635
    Typing 637
Adult Education? 637
    Synchronicity 637
    LifeGuard 639
    MindSet 639
Summary 640

Part IV   Specialized Mac Applications 641

17   Sound, Music, and Speech 643

"Mac"ing Beautiful Music 644
    Jukebox Versus Player Piano 644
    Sound Concepts about Recording 645
        The Pressure Pitch 646
        Understanding Waves 646
        Out of Tune 648
        The Envelope, Please 649
Recording and Editing in the Mac 649
    Getting the Best Recording 649
        Apple Microphone Tips 650
        MacRecorder and Voice Impact Tips 653
    Memory and Storage Considerations 654
        Frequency Range, Sampling Rate, and Memory .. 654
        Compression and Memory 655

- Setting Compression 656
  - Predicting Memory Needs 657
- Creating Sounds Without a Microphone 658
- Editing and Controlling Sound 658
  - Modifying Sounds 660
    - Pitch Effects 660
    - Waveform Effects 662
    - Time Effects 663
    - Mixing Sounds Together 664
  - Saving Your Final Version 665
  - Professional Sound Editing on the Mac 667
  - Voice Mail on the Mac 667
- Mac, Phone Home 668
- Playlist Editors 668
- MIDI and Music Processors 669
  - The MIDI Studio 670
    - MIDI Interfaces 670
    - MIDI Cables 671
    - MIDI Setup 672
    - Advanced Setups 673
    - Framed 674
    - MIDI Messages 675
    - Clip Music 676
  - Sequencers and MIDI Software 676
    - Deluxe Music Construction Set 677
    - ConcertWare 678
    - Musicshop 678
    - Metro 679
    - Vision and Studio Vision 680
    - Performer 681
  - Other Music Software 681
    - Songworks 682
    - Music Education 682
    - Patch Librarians 683
    - Software for serious professionals 684
    - MIDI Manager and OMS 685
- Speech and Beyond 686
  - MacinTalk 686
    - Sound and ResEdit 687
- Summary 687

xxxiii

18   HyperCard and SuperCard 689

Introduction 690
HyperCard is almost MacPaint 691
HyperCard and Hypertext 692
Getting Your Hands on HyperCard 692
   HyperCard's Interpreter 693
   Compilers 694
   Which version should you run? 694
Running HyperCard 696
   Saving Your Data 697
PowerUsers and userLevels 698
   Changing the userLevel 699
   Apple's Magic Word 700
Your First Script 701
Stack Sources 702
HyperCard Structure 703
   Stack Organization 703
   Objects and Scripts 704
      HyperCard Workarounds 706
   Moving Through HyperCard 707
      Navigating with Menu Commands 707
      Using the Navigator Palette 709
      Navigating with Arrow Keys 710
      Navigating with Buttons 711
      Navigating with the Message Box
         and Scripts 712
Painting in HyperCard 712
   Where the Paint Goes 713
   Using Painting Tools and Menus 713
      Using the Painting Menus 715
   Making HyperCard Draw on Itself 717
      Using Coordinates in Drawing 717
      Dragging to Paint 719
      Using Options and Effects Not
         on the Tool Menu 722
Printing from HyperCard 723
   Printing a Single Card or Field 723
   Printing Groups of Cards 724
   Printing Reports of Data 726
Music and Sound in HyperCard 728

- Recording and Editing with the Audio Palette 728
  - Compression Pressures… 730
- Audio Alternatives 731
- Playing Sounds in HyperCard 731
  - Making Melodies 732
- Playing Pictures in HyperCard 733
- Customizing Your Stacks 733
  - No Programming Allowed 734
    - Starting a New Stack 734
    - Creating Fields 735
    - Buttons—The Easy Way 737
  - Making HyperCard Do Anything You Want 739
    - Containers 740
  - Working on Your Own 742
- Beyond HyperCard 743
  - Externals 743
    - FormsProgrammer 743
  - SuperCard 744
    - SuperCard Features 744
    - SuperCard Organization 745
  - Summary 746

19 Multimedia on the Macintosh 747

- What Is Multimedia? 748
- Basic Concepts 751
- Multimedia Uses 756
- Multimedia Engines 758
- What Is In an Interface? 760
- Multimedia Media Technologies 761
  - Visuals 762
  - Text 762
  - Still Images 763
  - Animation 764
  - Video 766
    - Video Concepts 766
    - Video Signal Types 768
- Video Media and Devices 770
- Video Into and Out of the Mac 775
- Mixing in the Mac Video Environment Versus NTSC 778

Outputting Mac Video to NTSC	780
Mac to NTSC Conversion Issues	781
Digital Video	783
Audibles	786
Sound Uses	786
Sound Sources	787
Interactables	791
Presentation and Delivery Issues	792
Planning Your Platform	793
Planning Questions	793
Configurations, Additions, and Considerations	795
Low-end Example Configuration	795
Mid-range Example Configuration	796
Upper-end Example Configuration	796
High-end and Performance-Enhancing Additions	797
Storage Considerations	797
Tools and Engines	799
Composer's Process Model	799
A Look at the Engines	802
Authoring Engines: The Continuum	803
Different Engines	803
Summary	807

20   Macs and the Differently Abled   809

Computers and the Differently Abled	810
Personalizing the Mac	811
Easy Access	811
Other Ways to Type	813
Nonrepeating Keys	814
Switches and Scanners	816
Morse Code Switches	816
Differently Abled Mice	816
Head-Controlled Mice	817
Voice Navigator	818
Alternatives to Keyboard Typing	818
Predicting More Than the Future	819
Tools for Daily Living	820
The Mac Talks Back	821

Close View	822
The Big Picture	824
outSPOKEN	825
Tactile Displays	827
Printing Braille Pages	827
Communication Disorders and the Mac	827
Sources for Help and Ideas	829
Summary	830

Part V Managing Your Mac 831

21   Utilities 833

The Tools of Computing	834
Building a Utility Toolbox	834
The Starter Kit	835
Control Panels	835
A Clock Utility	836
Chooser	836
Installer	837
Font/DA Mover	837
Virus Hunters	837
Disk Doctors	838
Screen Saver	838
Expanding the Toolbox	839
RAM Disks	839
Extension Managers	840
MS-DOS Transfer and Translation Utilities	841
Resource Managers and Editors	843
ResEdit	843
Master Juggler and SuitCase	844
Printer Utilities	845
Font Utilities	846
Keyboard Utilities	847
AppleScript	848
Disk Utilities	848
Odds and Ends	848
Utility Packages and Libraries	849
Summary	849

22 Hard Disk Management 851

Managing a Disk 852
General Principles 852
Organizing a Hard Disk 853
    Organization Utilities 854
    Partitioning a Large Disk 855
Backups 857
    Incremental Versus Volume Backups 858
    Permanent Backups 858
    Backup Utilities 859
Tuning a Disk 859
    Adjusting the Interleave Ratio 860
    Defragmenting a Disk 862
    Changing a File's Location 864
    Other Ways to Tune a Disk 865
Disk Management Utilities 866
Summary 867

23 Viruses and System Security 869

Introduction 870
What Is a Virus 870
    Worms and Trojan Horses 870
    Types of Viruses 871
Preventing a Viral Infection 872
    Virus Prevention on Networks and Other Environments 873
The Viruses 874
    The Scores Virus 874
    The nVIR Virus 876
    The INIT 29 Virus 876
    The ANTI Virus 877
    The MacMag Virus 878
    The WDEF Virus 878
    The ZUC Virus 880
    The MDEF Virus 881
    The CDEF Virus 882
    The MBDF Virus 883
    The INIT 1984 Virus 883
    The CODE 252 Virus 884
    The T4 Virus 885
    The INIT 17 Virus 886

The INIT-M Virus 886
Virus-Detecting Software 887
Keeping Up-to-Date on Viruses 893
Summary 893

Part VI Expanding Your Mac's Horizons 895

24 Communications and Online Services 897

Modems: Turning Numbers into Noise 898
    Buying a Modem 900
    Fax Modems 901
    Installing the Modem 903
Communications Programs 906
    Finding the Right Terminal Program 908
    Placing a Call 910
        Determining the Settings 910
        Getting Connected 912
        Protect Your Password! 914
    Online Work and Play 915
    Saying Good-bye 915
Choosing a Service 916
    Mail 916
    And Now the News… 917
    Going Places? 918
    Going Shopping 920
    Money, Money… 922
    Forums for All Interests 922
        Censorship? 924
    Can We Talk? 924
        Online Etiquette 926
        Conference Shorthand 926
    Come Play with Me… 927
    A Trip to the Library 930
    Downloading and Uploading 930
        MacBinary 932
    File Transfers 932
    Saving Time with Compacting Programs 934
Rating the Services 937
    The Internet 940

xxxix

What About Free Bulletin Board Systems (BBSs)? 940
Starting Your Own BBS 941
Summary 941

25 Networking the Macintosh 943

Networking Fundamentals 944
    Idea 944
    Expression 944
    Transport 944
    Medium 945
    Matching The Layers 945
Macintosh Networking: Services, Formats,
    Transports and Media 946
    Services 947
        AppleShare (AFP) 947
        File Sharing 948
        Other AFP Clients and Servers 948
        Print Services (PAP) 949
        Apple Open Collaboration Environment (AOCE) 950
        Terminal Services 950
        Data Access Language (DAL) and
            other Database Services 951
        Mail Services 951
        Service Summary 952
    Formats 952
    Protocols 953
        How does AppleTalk work? 954
        AppleTalk Phase 1 & 2 956
        Phase 1 and 2 Network Number Assignment 957
        The Importance of Dynamic Addressing 959
        AppleTalk Zones 961
        How does the Chooser work? 965
        AppleTalk Routing 966
        Routing Tables 966
        Transport Summary 968
    Media 968
        LocalTalk/Phone-type Connectors 968
        Ethernet/EtherTalk 972
        Other Cabling Systems 977
        Media Summary 982
Macintosh Networking with Other Computers 983

  Living in an Intel/DOS world 983
    AppleTalk on the PC 983
    Novell Solutions 984
    Banyan VINES 985
  UNIX Connectivity 985
    Data Access Language (DAL) 986
    File Services: FTP & NFS 986
    X-Window 987
    Terminal Services 989
  Digital VAX Connectivity 989
  IBM Connectivity 991
A Sampling of Common Mac Networking Scenarios 993
  Scenario 1: Single LocalTalk Network
    Daisy-Chain Topology 993
  Scenario 2: Single Ethernet Network
    Daisy-Chain Topology 994
  Scenario 3: Single LocalTalk Network
    Active Star Topology 995
  Scenario 4: Single Ethernet Network
    Star Topology (10Base-T) 995
  Scenario 5: Single LocalTalk Network Bridged
    Star Topology 996
  Scenario 6: Multiple LocalTalk Networks Routed
    Backbone Topology 996
  Scenario 7: Multiple Ethernet Networks Routed Backbone and
    Star Topology 997
  Scenario 8: Multiple Ethernet Networks
    with FDDI Backbone 997
  Scenario 9: Ethernet and FDDI WAN Topology 998
  Scenario 10: Structured Wiring Example 998
  Scenario Summary 999
Conclusion 999

26 Macintosh and PC Coexistence 1001

Introduction 1002
Physical Connections 1003
  Disk Drives 1003
  Local Serial Cabling 1005
Null Modem Connections 1006
  Modem Transfers 1007
  Networking 1009

AppleTalk	1009
Other Products	1011
Gateways and Routers	1012
There's a PC in My Mac!	1013
RunPC	1013
Mac86, Mac286, and Orange386	1013
SoftPC	1014
Moving Data	1016
PostScript Printers	1016
Hewlett Packard LaserJets	1017
Storage Devices	1017
Serial Peripherals	1018
Electronic Mail	1018
Internal Mail Systems	1019
External Services	1020
Translation	1020
Mac and PC Files	1020
File Formats	1022
Text Formats	1022
Graphics Formats	1024
Cell-Based Data	1025
Translation Solutions	1025
Apple File Exchange	1025
LapLink/Mac	1027
MacLinkPlus	1028
Using XTND	1029
Additional Topics	1030
File Compression	1031
Compound Documents	1031
Summary	1033

27 The Macintosh Community 1035

Sharing Macintosh Resources	1036
What You Need to Know (and How to Find Out)	1037
Be a Registered User	1037
Check Your Mailbox	1038
Magazines	1039
Hard copy magazines	1039
Electronic Magazines	1040
User Groups	1041

The Megagroups	1041
Local User Groups	1042
SIGs	1043
Independent SIGs	1043
A Macintosh Convention	1044
Stranger in a Strange Land	1045
When You Need Help	1046
Training	1048
Audio and Video Instruction	1048
Seminars	1048
Summary	1049

Part VII For the More Technically Minded ... 1051

28 Troubleshooting ... 1053

Hardware Problems	1054
The Sad Mac Errors	1054
Mac 128 Through Mac Plus	1055
ROM Errors	1056
RAM Errors	1056
Software Errors	1057
Mac SE and Beyond	1058
The Mac Portable	1061
Major Error Codes	1062
Power Manager Error Codes	1062
The Chords of Death	1063
Dead Battery	1064
Hard Disk SCSI Problems	1065
SCSI Problem Diagnosis	1065
SCSI Problem Resolution	1066
Termination	1066
Cabling	1067
The Reset Line	1068
A Final Word on SCSI	1069
Non-SCSI Hard Drive Problems	1069
Stiction	1070
Spindle Motor Failure	1070
Bad Blocks	1071

A Word About Head Parking	1071
Drive Repair	1071
Software Problems	**1072**
Common Software Problems	**1072**
INIT Conflicts	1072
Older Software	1073
Damaged System or Application Software	1074
Boot Problems	**1075**
The Boot Stages	1075
First Boot Attempt Fails, Second Works	1077
Automated Diagnostics	**1078**
Summary	**1079**

29 Programming on the Macintosh 1081

But Can I Do It?	1082
Inside a Macintosh Program	1083
Resources in a Program	1083
Creating a Macintosh Program	1085
Creating CODE Resources	1086
Compiling the Program	1087
Building the Program File	1088
Assemblers and Interpreters	1088
Interpreters	1090
Object-Oriented Versus Procedural Programming	1090
The Macintosh Toolbox	1092
Programming Languages	1093
Macintosh Pascal and Object Pascal	1093
C and C++	1094
Assembly Language	1095
BASIC	1096
Other Languages	1097
Ada	1097
APL	1097
COBOL	1097
FORTRAN	1098
FORTH	1098
LISP	1098
LOGO	1099
Modula and Modula 2	1099

- MUMPS 1099
- Prolog 1099
- Smalltalk 1099
- Special-Purpose Languages 1100
  - HyperTalk 1100
  - PostScript 1100
- Which Language Is Right for You? 1100
- Tools of the Trade 1101
  - Software for Programmers 1101
  - MPW 1102
  - Think C and Think Pascal 1102
  - ResEdit 1103
  - Resorcerer 1103
  - Rez and DeRez 1103
  - MacsBug 1103
  - TMON and TMON Professional 1104
  - Debugger V2 and MacNosy 1104
  - SADE 1104
  - PopUp Funcs 1104
  - DTS Sample Code 1105
  - AppMaker 1105
  - McCLint 1105
  - MacApp 1105
- Where to Go Next 1106
  - Universities and Colleges 1106
  - Commercial Classes and Seminars 1106
  - Self-study Programs 1106
  - Books 1107
  - Magazines 1107
  - User Groups and Developer Associations 1107
    - APDA 1107
    - SPLAsh 1108
    - BMUG and BCS 1108
    - Other User Groups 1108
- Summary 1108

Glossary of Common Macintosh Terms 1109

Index 1131

About This Book

The Macintosh computer, in any version from the original Mac 128 to the latest Quadra, has changed the way people work, think, act and react. This book is about the Macintosh, and tries to give you just what the title says—Everything you ever wanted to know about the Mac, and some things you didn't know you wanted to know!

Why This Book Is for You

This book was designed to be needed and used by just about everyone, but especially you. If you are thinking about buying a Mac, are a new user, or a grizzled Mac veteran, this book contains information covering just about everything there is about the Mac (hence the title!). It is easy to read, and parts that are very technical are labeled with icons so that you can skip them if they're too much for you, or zoom right in on those sections so you can dazzle your friends with your vast reserves of Macintosh knowledge.

What's in This Book

Chips, bits, bytes, megabytes, games, applications, programming, and more are all in this book for you! The invention of the Mac, how it operates, how it is built, and different models are covered. Chapters cover desktop publishing, graphics, fonts, word processors, spreadsheets, databases, and games. Also covered are sound, music, speech, multimedia, HyperCard and SuperCard, and applications for the differently abled.

Utilities, hard disk management, viruses, system security, communications, online services, networking, Mac and PC co-existence, and the Mac community are explored in other chapters. Troubleshooting problems with your Mac, programming, and future directions are covered in another section. And, finally, a Glossary is provided to help you define all those terms that you face with the Macintosh.

Where Do You Go From Here?

This book is so complete, the only place you can go from here is to try out some of the great things you'll learn on your own. This book will become a handy companion for your daily Mac use. As you become more of an expert on the Mac, consider sharing some of the new things you've learned and possibly become a contributing author of a future version of *Everything... About the Mac,* Write to Hayden Books at 201 West 103rd Street, Indianapolis, Indiana, 46290.

Throughout the book, comments have been added in the margins by a few of our Macintosh deities. These comments are accompanied by a caricature of the deity. The comments are there both for your enjoyment and for your information—in general, they provide a different perspective on things.

Conventions Used in this Book

The conventions used in this book have been established to help you use the book quickly and easily.

Text in **boldface type** represents menu names, menu items, button names, or other commands you see onscreen.

Text in *italics* indicates a new term.

Text in a `special typeface` indicates text you type on your computer.

Margin icons are used to call your attention to information of special interest:

 **A Closer Look**: Identifies a peek into the details of how something works, why it does what it does, or how to do something a little different from the norm.

 **Note**: Indicates an aside, a special tip, a relevant fact, or other information.

 **Warning**: Alerts you to dire consequences, potential problems, or dangerous actions.

Part I: Macintosh, the Computer

In This Part

Chapter 1: Macintosh, the Computer

Chapter 2: Macintosh Basics

Chapter 3: Exploring the Macintosh System

Chapter 4: How the Macintosh Works

Chapter 5: Macintosh Hardware: A Technical Look

Chapter 6: Printing from Your Macintosh

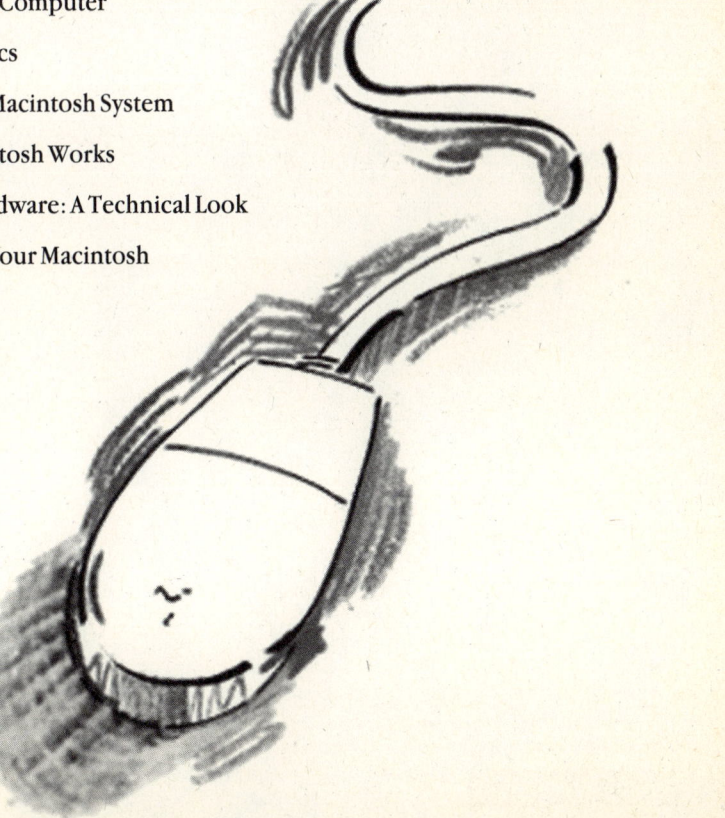

Chapter 1: Macintosh, the Computer

The Macintosh has changed the world of computing. By introducing the graphical user interface (GUI), icons, windows, and so forth, the Mac has made it possible for people to run a computer without any formal training whatsoever as to how the computer is programmed—an unheard-of situation in the beginning days of personal computers. Started by two college dropouts, Steve Jobs and Steve Wozniak, Apple

In This Chapter

- ▼ How and why the Macintosh came to be
- ▼ A short history of Apple Computer
- ▼ The birth of the Macintosh
- ▼ Sculley Joins Apple

Part I
Macintosh, the Computer

Computer has achieved a level of success unmatched by any similar venture. What began as a small venture in 1976 in Steve Jobs' garage resulted in $1 billion in sales by 1983.

Introduction

The Macintosh computer, introduced by Apple Computer, Inc. in 1984, is one of the most unique computers ever made. It forever changed the way people use computers by introducing the graphical user interface (GUI).

Prior to the birth of the Macintosh, computers used a *character-based* user interface, which required users to type instructions into a keyboard in order to make the computer perform. The Mac introduced the use of *icons* (small pictures) that appear on the screen rather than typed words to indicate an item's function. To use a Mac, one must move an arrow on the screen to point to an icon and click a button on a hand-held device known as a *mouse*.

A mouse and icons are major innovations introduced by the Mac. Another innovation is the introduction of *pull-down menus.* Instead of memorizing numerous commands to type into the keyboard, a Macintosh user merely points at a word at the top of the screen, presses the mouse button, and a menu of commands appears. Highlighting one of these commands and releasing the mouse button executes the command. Each of these important innovations is discussed in detail in this book.

The History of Apple Computer

The creation of Apple Computer truly is an amazing story of perseverance and a little luck, culminating in a dream come true. Founded by two college dropouts who had been buddies since high school, Steve Jobs and Steve Wozniak's upstart computer company forged a unique place in history.

Both men were relative loners in high school. "Woz" (as he is called by his many admirers) was a technology freak—an electronics whiz kid. Woz scrounged through rejects of the giant computer corporations that also called Cupertino, California, home to get needed parts for his home creations. For him, "hanging out" meant sitting at the library reading computer magazines

Chapter 1
Macintosh, the Computer

or touring the computer rooms of major companies. He became such a familiar face at one company that he was issued his own security pass. Steve Jobs, introduced to Woz by another high school acquaintance, was more of a dreamer. Attracted to Far-Eastern religious philosophies, Jobs was steadfastly dedicated to the concept of what technology could do for improving the world. Where Woz might be known as the ultimate computer "nerd," Jobs was a stubborn, insistent, almost antagonistic visionary. Both were somewhat the social outcasts, but for different reasons.

In the years prior to the creation of Apple, Jobs and Woz became "phone phreaks," investigating the world of "blue boxes" that enabled illegal access to the telephone company's long distance lines. Intrigued by an article they read, Jobs and Woz set out to build their own box. Without any plans, Woz was able to assemble a blue box for about $40 in parts, unknowingly outdoing the underground inventor of the illegal boxes whose cost was over $1,500 in components. Woz loved building the boxes; it was Jobs who came up with the idea of mass-producing them and selling them to fellow college students for $100 each, splitting the $60 profit with Woz.

The men's illegal business became so prosperous (and dangerous, due to FBI investigations of phone phreaks) that Jobs began to get cold feet and finally backed out. Woz tried keeping the business going on his own, but quickly discovered that he enjoyed the challenge of building and improving the boxes far more than the business of selling them and collecting the money. He, too, got out of the underground business.

Although the business was prosperous, Woz's grades were not, and he soon faced the prospect of flunking out. He decided that he delighted so much in working with technology that he decided to drop out of college and take a job with Hewlett-Packard. Jobs also dropped out of college, but more because of a disillusionment with life. He traveled to India in search of eternal truth, then moved to a commune in the Pacific Northwest United States. Finally, he wandered back to Cupertino and landed a job with a fledgling company named Atari, which was working on a video game called Pong. Both Jobs and Woz found themselves in fortunate circumstances that put them on the cutting edge of the surfacing technology of the time.

In addition to work, both Jobs and Woz spent a great deal of time involved in the "Home Brew Computer Club." Starting out with only a few members, the club soon grew to thousands. Most members were actively involved in the computer industry, and the club became a showcase of new ideas. It was also a good place for buying, selling, and trading rare computer parts (many which were of questionable origin, since so many of the members had access to the parts at their jobs). As the membership grew, it not only was a place to show off new technology, it was a good place to sell that new technology.

Part I
Macintosh, the Computer

One of the club members' preferences was almost religious: the use of Intel Corporation microprocessors in their creations. Woz was infatuated with building a small computer that could fit all the necessary components on only one board, not likely with the components available at that time. Intrigued by the challenge of his infatuation, he read with pleasure about the introduction of a new microprocessor chip by Motorola that worked differently from the Intel chips. He soon ordered several, exhausting his meager bank account. Capturing Woz's vision, Jobs knew that if he was successful, the members of the Home Brew Computer Club would be perfect customers for the one-piece board. He joined Woz in working feverishly to create their own computer board. The board took six months to design and more than 40 hours to build, but when finished, it worked (see figure 1.1).

Figure 1.1
Steve Wozniak (left) and Steve Jobs show off their original Apple 1 computer board.

With Jobs' vision that Home Brew Computer Club members would be the primary market for this board, the men fashioned a wood case for the board to protect it during transport and while on display. To get an idea of the reaction club members might have, Jobs took the board to the owner of a local computer store (who was also a club member) and they began discussing the possibilities. Rather than raving over Jobs and Woz's invention as Jobs had expected, the owner ridiculed the idea of selling just a computer board. Jobs listened, although he was discouraged by what he was hearing. Almost out of the clear blue sky, the store owner said that if Jobs could deliver 50 *complete* computers—not just boards—the owner would pay cash on delivery. He put his offer in writing and gave Jobs a target delivery date of 30 days.

Chapter 1
Macintosh, the Computer

Jobs was stunned by the unexpected order and raced out to call Woz at work. The duo originally hoped to build perhaps 50 boards, a few at a time, and use the profits to buy more materials. Where would they get the up-front money to build 50 complete computers? Still, an order in the hand is worth two in the bush (to use an old cliché), so Jobs and Woz found investment funds and suppliers who would provide the materials.

At this time, Jobs asked Ron Wayne, a middle-aged salesperson at Atari, to help set up their company structure. Wayne agreed to work for 10-percent ownership and also would create the schematics needed for the computer's manuals.

Jobs and Woz also had to create a name for their company before they could start selling their new invention. Hundreds of names were batted back and forth, but none appealed to both. Jobs, who had been on a special diet consisting mainly of fruit during his commune days, believed (erroneously so, according to some co-workers) that he could avoid taking showers by eating apples. He suggested "Apple" as a joke. The suggestion began to grow on the two men, because schools were a potential market for their new invention—an Apple for the teacher? They finally agreed on this name, and on April Fool's Day, 1976, Woz, Jobs, and Wayne signed the papers making Apple Computer official. Wayne designed the original Apple logo (see figure 1.2).

Figure 1.2
The first Apple logo was designed by Ron Wayne.

Part I
Macintosh, the Computer

All three men kept their full-time jobs but devoted evenings and weekends to manufacturing the new computers. Jobs and Woz started working in a bedroom in Jobs' house, but soon moved the operation to the garage. Paul Jobs, Steve's father, built a plywood "burn-in box" where completed boards could run safely all night. Steve's mom became the receptionist/order taker/shipper/receiver and performed other tasks as needed. Jobs' parents later joked that they paid the mortgage so they could have bedroom and bath privileges (see figure 1.3).

Figure 1.3
Here are the original Apple headquarters: a kitchen table in the home of Steve Jobs' parents.

Right on schedule, Apple delivered its first order of 50 Apple 1 computers, retail priced at $666.66 each. The price was based on Jobs' completely scientific approach to pricing known as P.F.A (Plucked From the Air). And almost immediately, Apple faced its first crisis. Convinced that the numbers were satanic, a religious group took offense at the price and launched a concerted telephone protest. The release of *The Omen*, a movie in which these numbers played a significant role as the biblical mark of the Antichrist, further fueled the controversy. Telephone lines became so flooded that the phone company had to assign Apple a special circuit, usually reserved for radio contests. Reaction died down after the price was eliminated from retail advertising for the computer.

After weathering this setback, Apple next faced major problems with lawsuits from suppliers who felt they were not being paid fast enough and minor problems in keeping up with the unexpected flood of orders. Wayne, who had failed once before in a previous business, was nervous about Apple's apparently shaky existence. He decided he wanted out. His 10-percent ownership was purchased back by Jobs and Woz for $1,700. If Wayne had kept his stock, today it would be worth millions of dollars.

Markulla Comes on Board

Amidst these severe and unexpected growing pains, Jobs and Woz realized that they needed help and needed it fast. They spent all their time going to work, coming home, building computers, and filling orders. There was no time left to sleep, let alone actually run the business. The two Steves' fledgling enterprise was suffering horribly. While searching for investors, they had been steered to a 33-year-old retired millionaire named Armas Clifford "Mike" Markulla. Markulla was impressed with the start-up company, and knew it needed help. Besides investing $250,000 in the fledgling organization, he came on board to run the business.

Formally incorporated on January 3, 1977, Apple skyrocketed under Markulla's leadership. Soon the company had sales in the millions of dollars, boasted hundreds of employees, and occupied thousands of square feet of manufacturing and office space. Part of the reason for this success was that, relieved from the daily tasks of trying to run the business, Jobs and Woz were free to blossom in their individual roles. Woz reworked the Apple 1 and created the Apple II computer. Jobs went to work as an evangelist, inspiring both customers and employees with his vision of a world set free by technology.

More Computers Enter the Field

Because of Apple's unlikely and meteoric success, other companies jumped into the foray and introduced their own personal computers; some good, most not. Each new personal computer, or PC, had its own unique "operating system." All of these different operating systems made it difficult for software companies to create common programs that worked on multiple computers. To give you an idea of how difficult this task was, compare it to the early days of railroads. Every railroad company built its own tracks with its own gauge (track width). Therefore, it was very difficult to move people or goods across the country because trains had to be switched every time the tracks changed gauge. After the Civil War, the federal government solved the problem by ordering a standard gauge. Following this analogy, computers had yet to decide on a standard "gauge" operating system, and PCs had yet to be taken seriously by companies because of this lack of standardization.

Chapter 1
Macintosh, the Computer

Part I

Macintosh,
the Computer

IBM Enters the Picture

In 1981, IBM Corporation, the mainframe computer giant, announced it was entering the personal computer marketplace. IBM promised to bring stability to the market by introducing a standard operating system for all computers.

IBM contracted with Microsoft Corporation to create the standard system. It was called *PC-DOS:* Personal Computer Disk Operating System. As part of the agreement, Microsoft would be allowed to sell *MS-DOS,* or Microsoft Disk Operating System. Available on the open market, MS-DOS would be available for any computer and would make other computers *IBM-compatible.* Any PC capable of using DOS could therefore be compatible with any other PC using DOS, whether IBM's version or Microsoft's. In a sense, all the trains would run on the same-gauge track.

Major corporations, who when they purchase machines usually purchase thousands, welcomed IBM to the personal computer market to clear up what corporations saw as a confused, almost amateurish industry. It wasn't long before any company that did not adopt the DOS operating system found itself in trouble, serious trouble. Many of the personal computer pioneers suddenly faced oblivion, bankruptcy, or both. Apple was no exception; the Apple II was ignored in favor of IBM and DOS. In fact, if it had not been for the large installed base and continued sales of Apple II computers in schools throughout the United States and the world, the company probably would have folded.

Even though the Apple II computer did not use IBM's or Microsoft's DOS, so many were in use that Apple was able to survive using its own operating system standard. But this situation was only temporary. The leaders at Apple knew they had limited time to make the decision that had already been forced on other computer companies: bow to IBM and change over to DOS, or create a new standard and try to get all other companies to adopt it.

For his part, Jobs absolutely despised IBM and their "blue suits." IBM and DOS epitomized everything Jobs wanted to overcome—distant, regimented, faceless corporations, and cryptic, hard-to-use computers. Instead, he had a vision of "a computer for the rest of us," a computer that everyone could use and would want to use. To fulfill this vision, Apple would have to set off once again on a bold new course of its own.

The Birth of the Macintosh

As Apple's director of product development, Steve Jobs single-handedly decided to buck the DOS trend and not build an IBM-compatible computer.

Chapter 1
Macintosh, the Computer

He directed a special Apple project to design a computer using a graphical user interface (GUI). This type of interface, in which a user selects little pictures, or icons, instead of typing long commands, was a dramatic departure from the character-based, code intensive interface of DOS. The GUI interface was based on research Xerox Corporation performed earlier at its Palo Alto Research Center. When Xerox decided not to pursue the new interface (which used a new device called a *mouse*) and to pursue DOS as a standard, many of its engineers and programmers left to join Apple's effort.

The first computer Apple introduced with the new interface was the Lisa—a fantastic computer originally conceived by Jobs, but transferred away from his direction in the course of an internal Apple power struggle. Without Jobs' leadership, the Lisa became a bloated, expensive computer doomed to oblivion because of its high cost (more than $10,000 compared to $1,000 for almost any IBM-compatible).

After Jobs was removed from the Lisa project, he saw his vision of a computer for the masses being sold out to chase corporate dollars. He became even more determined to create what he called the "Volkswagen of computers," a low-cost computer that would be just as easy to run and as necessary to daily living as the telephone or refrigerator.

Jobs' dream was to be realized in the Macintosh (The computer was named after a popular variety of real apple; the research department misspelled the name and Jobs decided not to correct it). He assembled the most brilliant, rebellious, dedicated individuals he could find to form his own team within Apple's corporate structure. Setting up the Macintosh team in another building across the street from one of his (and his teammates') favorite bars, the scene was far different from the typical corporate environment. T-shirts and blue jeans were standard office wear and meetings were usually held at the bar over the latest hi-tech video game.

Jobs loved everything about the Macintosh team, and with them he became almost oblivious to anything going on over at Apple, which was seriously screwing up the Apple III (almost every Apple III made had to be recalled and replaced numerous times) and had almost run the company into bankruptcy trying to invent a disk drive for the Lisa, ignoring better and less-expensive drives already on the market.

Woz helped develop certain parts of the Mac for Jobs, but the Macintosh was Jobs' "baby." By this time, Woz had become somewhat distanced from the computer world. He was busy spending his new-found wealth on humanitarian projects—and airplanes (despite narrowly cheating death when his favorite plane crashed and he suffered a form of partial amnesia for

Part I
Macintosh,
the Computer

almost 5 weeks). Woz finally decided to invest in something personally useful and returned to college full-time to get his long-delayed degree in Computer Science. He only worked on the Macintosh when Jobs pressed for help, knowing Woz would find a solution.

Sculley Joins Apple

In 1983, Markulla was ready to retire as Apple's president. Despite its setbacks with the Lisa and Apple III, Markulla had managed to transform Apple Computer, Inc. from a small garage-based business into a billion-dollar corporation in just a few years. After interviewing several candidates, Jobs made an announcement that stunned the business world: John Sculley, then 44-year old CEO of Pepsi Cola, had agreed to become the new Apple president.

Many in the business world could not imagine that the well-dressed, corporate-thinking Sculley and the long-haired, blue-jeaned Jobs could survive together. Few people realized that these two very different men shared something very important to both of them—a vision for changing the world. Sculley's claim to fame was the "Pepsi Generation" marketing campaign that began the "Cola Wars" and transformed Pepsi's image, as well as boosting its profits. Warm, fuzzy commercials showcased a new generation of cola drinkers more alive and modern than those drinking the "old-fashioned" cola. With this campaign, Sculley had proved that marketing could change seemingly locked-in attitudes, and therefore change the world.

It was Jobs' personal vision and enthusiasm for the so-called "Volkswagen of Computers" that had won Sculley over as a convert. After seeing the Lisa and then the top-secret Macintosh, Sculley was convinced by Jobs that computers could democratize business and personal lives. Jobs is quoted as asking Sculley, "Do you want a chance to change the world, or to keep selling colored sugar water the rest of your life?"

Sculley came on board just as the Macintosh went into its final phases of development, and influenced many marketing decisions that were previously under Jobs' authority alone. Sculley's input would help make the Macintosh the success Jobs had dreamed of. Ironically, it was also Sculley who soon would end Jobs' career at Apple Computer.

The 1984 Commercial

The Macintosh was released with more publicity and attention than any other computer in history. Many people to this day remember the powerful introductory commercial created by the director of the movies *Alien* and *Blade Runner*. The 1984 commercial featured a female athletic runner throwing a sledgehammer to break a screen displaying "big brother" droning endlessly to a roomful of bland, cloned figures (see figure 1.4). Apple showed the commercial only once, but it was replayed countless times on national news broadcasts and talk shows. Costing more than $500,000 to create and more than $1.5 million to show during the 1984 Super Bowl telecast ($27,500 per second of air time), the commercial was an unbelievable success and went a long way toward making the Mac's introduction a success as well.

Chapter 1
Macintosh, the Computer

Figure 1.4
Apple's landmark 1984 commercial became one of the most talked-about commercials in television history.

Personally, I would've chosen Apple's Lemmings commercial, with the IBM-like suited drone/geeks marching off the cliff. It was way sicker than 1984, which is why Apple would probably prefer it be forgotten...

Bob LeVitus

Unfortunately, the original Mac (which came to be known as the Mac 128) was too underpowered for its interface. The Macintosh 512 (or "Fat Mac") was unveiled a few short months later to remedy this problem. One of Sculley's first contributions to marketing the Macintosh was the Christmas 1984 "Test Drive a Mac" campaign, in which anyone with a major credit card could check out a Mac overnight. Sculley's thinking was that once someone got their hands on a Mac it would never come back. Unfortunately, Apple failed to reckon with the reaction of dealers who did not want to hassle with the extra paperwork at their busiest sales time of the year. Poor stocking was another problem—many dealers simply didn't have enough Macs to sell, let alone test drive. In short, the promotion was a bust.

Mac sales soared through the roof when Apple unveiled *desktop publishing* in January, 1985. Consisting of a Mac, an application called PageMaker, and the first Apple LaserWriter, high-quality printed output rivaling typesetting

Part I
Macintosh,
the Computer

could be produced on a desktop (See chapter 7, "Desktop Publishing Programs"). Businesses began purchasing Macs over other computers for this dedicated purpose, since no other personal computer could create such high-quality documents for the relatively low price of Apple's desktop publishing solution. Instead of individuals, what initially made the Mac a success was what Jobs disliked the most—big corporations.

Changing of the Guard

As Sculley plunged into his position full-force, he discovered some major flaws in Apple's corporate organization. For most practical purposes, the company functioned as two companies: the Apple II division and Jobs' Macintosh division. There was no system for tracking distribution, and as sales began to drop on all personal computers, including the Macintosh, there was no way to discover it until it was too late. Soon Apple's problems came to light, and rumors spread in the business world that John Sculley would leave and return to Pepsi.

Finally, Apple's board pushed the problem to the forefront, and asked to speak to both Sculley and Jobs, individually, in private. The result of Sculley's meeting was that he was ordered to do the job he'd been hired to do—run the company. Jobs was dressed down and told he would be replaced as head of the Macintosh division. In just a few short months, with no valid position for Jobs to fill at Apple, Sculley called Jobs and told him his services were no longer needed—he was fired.

Jobs languished for the summer, deciding what to do. He was Chairman of the Board at Apple, its largest stockholder with 11% ownership, and was 30 years old . He didn't have the votes or the money to try to retake Apple, so in September, 1985, he decided to resign and start a company of his own to be called NeXT, Inc.

But back at Apple, Jobs' brainchild, the Macintosh, had undergone major changes since his departure. He had always dictated that the Mac would be a one-piece unit with no fan, and could never be opened by anyone except authorized Apple technicians. Sculley decided that the next Mac was going to be an open architecture Mac, one which would be modular in nature and could be added to by the user. Hard disks, monitors of various sizes, external drives, and so on, would now be in Mac's realm.

The first modular Mac, the Macintosh II, was unveiled in 1986. It sported Motorola's newest power microprocessor, the 68020, and offered phenomenal performance. Jobs' original Macintosh also was upgraded. It became the Macintosh Plus, sporting increased power and memory. Both machines were beefed up to deal with the most successful area of Macintosh usage, desktop publishing.

Under Sculley's leadership, Jobs' original dream was, and is, being fulfilled. Once the Mac became legitimized in business and industry, sales climbed. As the number of Macintoshes increased, better and more powerful programs came into being. Profits were plowed back into research and development and new Macintosh units were introduced, finally leading to the PowerBook and the Color Classic. Macs are now sold at Sears and other retail consumer outlets and are well on their way to becoming the everyday appliance Jobs envisioned. Macintosh is the single largest selling brand of computer in the world, outselling every other manufacturer—including IBM. And Sculley, in a move Jobs probably would never have made, signed an alliance in October 1991 with Apple's former enemy, IBM.

In short, it can be said that Jobs was the visionary, the dreamer. Sculley captured the vision and made the dream come true.

Summary

The Macintosh, released in 1984, was the dream child of Steve Jobs, inspired by Xerox PARC's research into the graphical user interface (GUI). It was to be a needed household appliance like a stove or a vacuum cleaner.

The Lisa, another Apple project inspired by Jobs, had been released in 1983 with the graphical user interface, but it proved too expensive to be successful.

Preceded by the biggest marketing splash ever seen for a computer, the Macintosh was unveiled by a now-famous television commercial during the 1984 Super Bowl. The Macintosh has become one of the most successful computers in the world.

Chapter 2
Macintosh Basics

The Macintosh user interface is designed to make learning to use new software an enjoyable exploration rather than a tedious task. Knowing a few basics, however, is critical to being able to find your way around the system. If you are an experienced Macintosh user, this section reviews the things you first learned about using your system. For the novice, the following information is crucial. This chapter will introduce the most basic Macintosh operations and terminology, show you the "one true way" to approach your

In This Chapter

- ▼ Starting Up and Shutting Down the Mac
- ▼ Important Nouns and Verbs
- ▼ Being Brave (and Being Smart)
- ▼ Built-in System Stuff
- ▼ Cut, Copy, and Paste
- ▼ Aliases
- ▼ Driving your Mac from the keyboard

Part I
Macintosh, the Computer

Mac, and introduce you to some of the cool things that the Macintosh system can do to make your life easier.

Note: This chapter is excerpted from two Hayden books. The first section, "Macintosh Skills," is from *The 9-to-5 Mac,* by Steven A. Schwartz. *The 9-to-5 Mac* is a Macintosh business resource. The other sections are from *Your Mac Can Do That*, by Christian Boyce. *Your Mac Can Do That* is an introduction to powerful (and fun!) features of your Mac and its software—features that many people don't take advantage of.

Macintosh Skills

There are a few basic things you need to know to use your Mac. If you can turn it on, use the mouse, use disks, and turn it off, you're in business.

Starting Up the Mac

There is only one correct way to start up and shut down your Mac. Before you turn on the Mac, turn on all the devices connected to the computer. Typically, these include external hard disk drives and tape drives, but also may include a scanner or other high-speed input or output devices.

Next, locate the switch on the Mac and turn it on. Depending on your equipment, the switch typically is located on the back of the Mac; or if you have an Apple Extended keyboard, you may be able to use the power switch (the button with a triangle on it) located on the keyboard. An icon of a Mac with a smiley face then appears onscreen. Other icons may appear in the lower-left corner of the screen, and then a screen similar to the one in figure 2.1 appears. (This may take several seconds.)

This screen is referred to as the *desktop,* and it is the screen from which you can locate the files contained on your hard disk. The white bar across the top of the screen that contains an Apple in the upper left corner is called the *menu bar*.

If no symbols appear on the far right end of the menu bar, you are running the Finder under System 6. (System 6 is a version of the Macintosh operating system software.) If you see only one symbol on the far right of the menu bar, you are probably running under System 6 with MultiFinder. If a ballooned question mark and a miniature Mac appear on the right end of the menu bar, you are running under System 7.

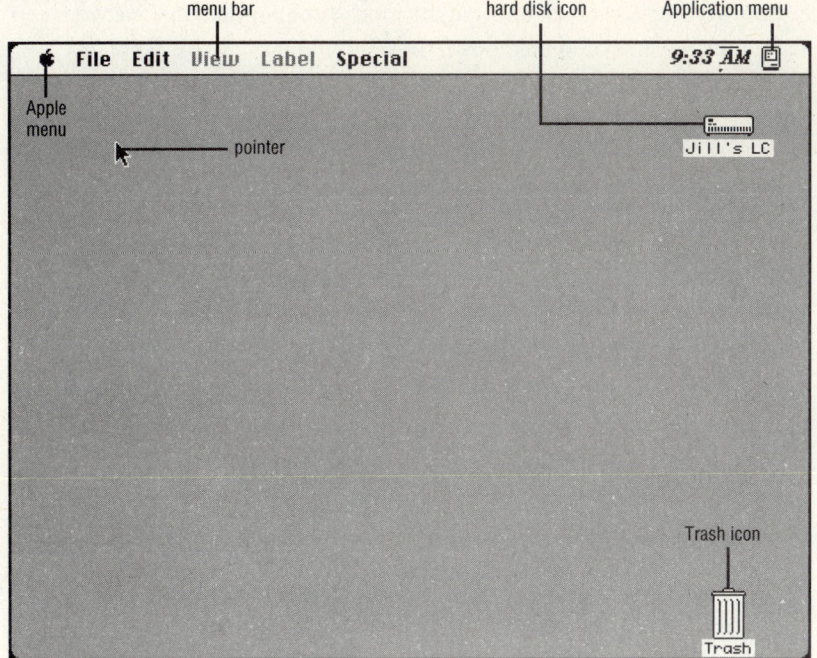

Figure 2.1
The Macintosh desktop.

Unlike a text-based environment where you must memorize a series of commands, the Mac is action-oriented. You must master four basic actions in order to successfully use the Mac. Read on to find out more about the mouse!

Mousing Around

The mouse enables you to move around on the Mac screen quickly. You can perform many functions with the mouse, but first you need to learn how to use it.

Pointing is the process of moving the mouse pointer to the position you want. By itself, pointing usually doesn't accomplish anything. It is often used as the first step in a series of actions.

Clicking consists of pressing and releasing the mouse button. It is important to hold the mouse firmly so that the mouse doesn't wiggle when you press the button. You click to select an object, insert the cursor in a particular place in a document, close windows, turn dialog box settings on and off, or to position the cursor for further action.

Dragging involves positioning the mouse pointer, pressing and holding down the mouse button, moving the pointer, and then releasing the mouse

Part I
Macintosh, the Computer

button. To drag an object, position the mouse pointer on the object you want to move. Press and hold down the mouse button. At this point, the object is selected. While holding down the mouse button, move the mouse. The object on which the pointer is positioned moves as well. After you move the object to the location you want, release the mouse button. You can drag to move objects, highlight text, and select menu items.

Double-clicking consists of clicking the mouse button twice in quick succession. The second click must occur within a predefined time period, or the system recognizes the clicks as two separate clicks rather than a double-click. You can double-click to open documents, launch programs, and select text.

Collectively, these mouse actions enable you to perform most of the necessary tasks within the Mac environment. To launch a program or open a document, for example, simply position the mouse pointer on the icon that represents the program or document you want to open, and double-click the mouse. To move a window on the desktop, position the mouse pointer on the bar that appears at the top of a window, and then drag the window to a new location.

Dealing with Disks and Files

Hard disk drives and floppy disks are the main media used for storing Macintosh data files and applications. After your Mac starts up, a column of icons appears on the right side of the desktop—one for each attached hard disk volume. As additional disks are inserted (or mounted) on the desktop, each one is represented by an icon (see figure 2.2). A selected disk (the disk on which you clicked) is represented by an icon filled with a solid color. A disk that currently is open (a disk with an open window on the desktop) is represented by an icon filled with a pattern. Floppy disk icons always look the same; they resemble a miniature floppy disk. On the other hand, there is no standard icon for hard disks. The appearance of a hard disk icon depends on the software used to initialize the disk.

There are two ways to remove a floppy disk from the desktop. First, you can eject it. To do this, you select the disk by clicking on it once, and then you select Eject from the File menu. You can hold down the Command key (the key with the symbol and/or the ⌘ symbol on it) and press E. (In short, you "press Command-E.") Because ejecting a disk still leaves an icon of the disk on the desktop, you should use this procedure when you want to keep the icon around, as when you want to copy files from one floppy disk to another on a Mac that has only one floppy drive.

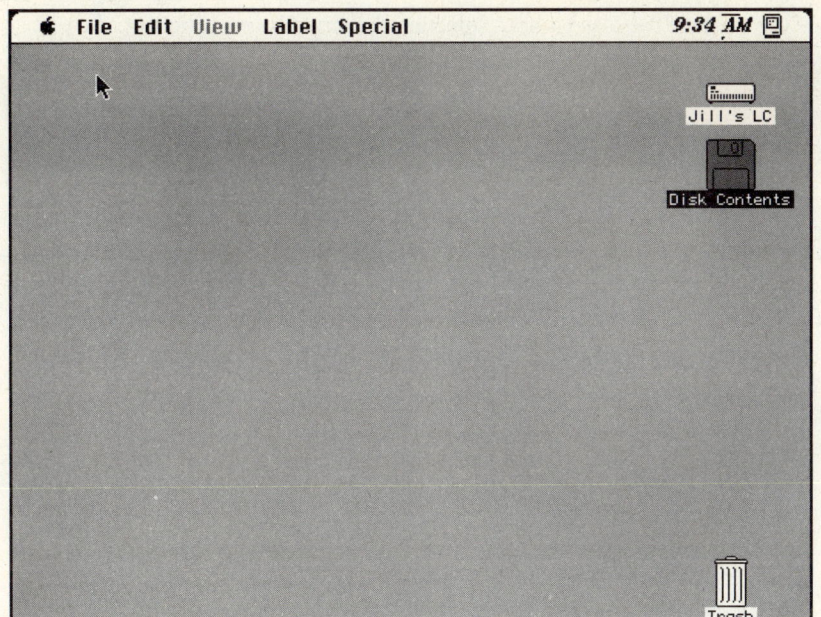

Figure 2.2
As they are mounted, or inserted, each disk is represented on the desktop by a named icon.

The second method of removing a disk from the desktop is to drag its icon to the Trash. Unlike using the Eject command to remove a disk from the desktop, dragging an icon to the Trash also removes its icon from the desktop. In addition to using this procedure with floppy disks, this also is the correct way to unmount other removable disks, such as CD-ROMs, Bernoullis, and SyQuest disks. Dragging the icons to the Trash enables you to safely remove the disk from its drive and replace it with a different one.

Disks are for storing data—any type of computer data, such as programs, documents, and program preferences. Unlike RAM (Random Access Memory) installed in your computer, data stored on a hard disk remains after you shut off the machine. RAM is used to temporarily store a program and its data files only while you are running that particular program. The contents of RAM disappear when you turn off the Mac.

Shutting Down the Mac

When you finish working with the Mac, close all programs (usually by selecting Quit from the File menu of each program), and then select Shut Down from the Special menu. Because the Mac performs clean-up work when you select Shut Down, do not turn off the power without first selecting Shut Down. The Mac notes window positions, for example, and saves this information to the hard disk.

Part I
Macintosh,
the Computer

If you turn off the Mac without selecting the Shut Down command, the desktop may need to reconstruct the next time you restart the Mac. This frequently is the cause of long delays when you restart after a crash. Worse yet, one of your programs or extensions may be trying to write information to the hard disk when you switch off the Mac. You might end up with an incomplete or corrupted data file.

After you select Shut Down, don't turn off the Mac's power switch until you see the message box that tells you to do so. (Newer Macs will not display a message. Instead, they turn off automatically when you select Shut Down.) Turn off external drives and other devices after you turn off the Mac.

Words Your Mother Didn't Use

Ten years ago, moms didn't talk about Shift-clicking, or RAM, or ROMs, especially around the children. Today, these words and others like them pop up in casual conversation, which just goes to show you how much the times have changed.

You need to know the language. Learn some terms now and the book's an easy read. Skip this section and suffer a thousand dooms.

We included the definitions of "point," "click," and so on (which you learned earlier) here to make the list complete. And just in case you weren't paying attention.

A pple uses the same words I do (maybe it's the other way around, but who's to say?). Learning things here helps you understand what Apple's talking about as well.

Christian Boyce

Verbs

"Verbs are action words." I remember this from elementary school—thanks to advanced instructional techniques in vogue at the time. You can hardly see the scars anymore.

Point   Use the mouse to position the cursor atop a target.

Click   Press the mouse button and release it.

Drag   Move the mouse while holding the mouse button down.

Double-click   Press and release the mouse button twice, quickly.

Shift-click Press and release the mouse button while holding the Shift key down.

Command-click Like a Shift-click, except you hold the Command key down.

Option-click Like a Command-click, except you hold the Option key down.

Shift-click Like an Option-click, except you hold the Shift key down (sorry!).

Nouns

Nouns are things. Objects. *Stuff*. I don't remember the exact definition from elementary school; I was probably in the nurse's office that day, recovering from the "verb" lesson.

A Closer Look In the beginning, Apple's Mac marketing focused on driving a wedge between the Macintosh computer and all other personal computers. The famous "1984" commercial (see chapter 1) started the wedge on its way. Apple drove the wedge further by snubbing IBM's computerese and inventing a unique, non-threatening vocabulary. Today's Mac manuals include both kinds of words, a sign of these "if you can't beat 'em, form a strategic alliance" times.

Applications Computer programs used to create neat stuff. Examples: Word, FileMaker Pro, PageMaker, and Excel.

Documents Things you create using an application. Examples: a letter to Dad, a customer database, a company newsletter, and a pie chart of 3rd quarter sales by region.

Documents are sometimes called "files." Unfortunately, applications are sometimes called files too. I prefer using "files" to describe things I create (documents), but not everyone agrees.

folders Analogous to folders in a filing cabinet. Folders hold things, including applications, documents, and other folders. IBM calls them "sub-directories."

Note If your filing cabinet holds a single, giant, "Everything" folder, filing things is easy. It's finding them again that's troublesome. On the other hand, too many folders makes filing a pain, so you've got to find a compromise. It's exactly the same on the Mac.

Chapter 2
Macintosh Basics

N ormal people buy applications. Brilliant people write them. Bad people steal them.

Christian Boyce

Part I
Macintosh, the Computer

You can name folders anything you want, more or less. No colons, and only 31 characters, but other than that, no restrictions. The good news is you can give folders wonderfully descriptive names like "Tax-related documents" and "My favorite games." The bad news is you can't be sure that a folder holds what its name implies. As with real folders, it's easy to misfile things.

Hardware   Computer equipment. Examples: Macs themselves, printers, modems, and scanners. Improving, or *upgrading*, hardware generally costs a lot and always involves adding or replacing parts.

Liveware   People.

RAM   Random Access Memory. Computer programs use RAM when they run; for example, when you tell Excel to add 2 and 2, it figures it out in RAM. Programs use RAM as a kind of electronic scratch pad, at times writing things down, at times reading what they've written.

> *Note:* When your Mac tells you there isn't enough memory to run an application, it's talking about RAM. People often misinterpret the "not enough memory" message, thinking it refers to hard disk space. Wrong, wrong, wrong.

If your closet were a hard disk, and your shoes were applications, your feet would be the RAM. The number of feet you have limits the number of shoes you can wear at any one time. Clearing out the closet isn't going to help you wear more shoes; the only way to wear more shoes is to add more feet. Adding RAM, unlike adding feet, is easy to do and commonly done.

ROM   Read-Only Memory. Like RAM, it's stored on a chip, but unlike RAM, all your Mac can do is read it. The instructions on the ROM chips (or ROMs) help your Mac act like a Mac.

> *A Closer Look:* Theoretically, you can upgrade a Mac by giving it new and improved ROMs. Like a hardware upgrade, it involves replacing parts, but like a software upgrade, it involves replacing instructions. ROMs are sometimes called *firmware* to reflect this dual personality.

Software   Computer programs, or instructions, in general. All applications are software (but not vice versa). Upgrading software generally costs less than upgrading hardware and involves adding or replacing instructions.

So there you have it: a tight little glossary of crucial Macintosh terms. Study them until you can toss them off confidently and without hesitation. It'll get you ready for the rest of the book.

Mac-ing With An Attitude

Chapter 2
Macintosh Basics

The Meek will inherit the Earth, but they aren't going to master the Mac. Don't be a meek Mac-er; get your hands on that keyboard and whack away with gusto.

Being Brave

You can't break a Mac by pressing the wrong key, and sometimes pressing the "wrong" key teaches you something cool. You learn by doing where the Mac is concerned, so, by all means, do.

Remember, you're using your Mac, not the other way around. Cultivate an "I'm in control, here" attitude, á la Alexander Haig. If worse comes to worse, you can always choose Shut Down.

Being Smart

You won't break your Mac by pressing the wrong keys, but there are other ways to louse things up. One way to wreck everything is to throw unfamiliar files into the Trash.

It's easy to accidentally rename a file. If an icon's selected, and you press something on the keyboard, you'll rename the icon with whichever key(s) you pressed. I dropped the phone on my keyboard once (do not try this at home!) and renamed a folder "crf."

Turning your Mac off without using the **Special** menu's **Shut Down** command is another bad move. Shutting down is gentle and good. Switching your Mac off without going to Shut Down first is like stopping your car by hitting a tree. It works but it's hard on the machine.

Finally, never, ever plug anything into your Mac while your Mac's turned on. Don't unplug anything either. Take the time to shut things down before messing with those cables. Your Mac's innards will thank you.

Getting Your Money's Worth

Are you getting your money's worth from your Mac? Most people aren't. Macs cost a lot of money, as anyone who's bought one knows, and software

The Mac world is full of secret tips and shortcuts. Maybe the programmers forget to tell the manual writers; maybe the manual writers forget to write things down. Maybe you forgot to read the manual. Regardless, you'll discover lots of cool stuff simply by clicking around. Double-click, Option-click; it never hurts to try.

Christian Boyce

Part I
Macintosh, the Computer

doesn't grow on trees. Now that you've spent the money, how can you get the most from your investment?

In the old days, you could make back your investment by charging admission to look at your Mac. People were curious—Macs were rare—and those were the Reagan years, after all. Fortunately for Apple Computer, unfortunately for you, Macintosh computers are all over the place today, so no one's going to pay to see a Mac anymore.

A better way—the right way—to get your money's worth from your Mac (and this was true in the old days as well) is to treat your Mac and your software as parts of a puzzle. Everything's supposed to fit together, and when you view the assembled collection of pieces, you see something the individual pieces only hint at. Something bigger. Something better. Something worth having.

Your Mac is just a piece of the Mac puzzle. Your word processor's another piece. So is your spreadsheet program, so is your database program, so is your page layout program, and so on and so on and so on. The pieces fit together to form The Big Picture. You don't know what the picture looks like (there's no Mac equivalent to the picture on the puzzle box), but we'll help you with the first couple of pieces. After that, as the picture takes shape, you'll do fine on your own.

Built-in System Stuff

Apple's manuals are excellent. If you want to know about everything built into the System, read your Apple manuals. However, if you want to focus on the cool stuff, the parts of the System that make you say "Yowza" and "Boy Howdy," keep reading here.

By now, I'm assuming you know the basics. If you don't, check those Apple manuals, or take the Macintosh Basics tour that came with your Mac. Wouldn't hurt to do both. Join us when you're ready.

"[Bing!]" "Welcome to Macintosh." And after a moment, the desktop, menu bar, and icons appear. It seems like magic. But it's not magic. It's your Mac Operating System at work. But that's not all the Operating System does.

Applications depend on the Operating System to translate commands like Save, Print, and Quit into instructions computer chips understand. You

Chapter 2
Macintosh Basics

depend on the Operating System to keep track of your documents, folders, and applications. When you want to customize your Macintosh environment, you depend on the Operating System again. The Macintosh Operating System is clearly an Important Thing. Question is, where is it?

Good question. The Operating System is partly in the System (on the hard disk), partly in the Finder (also on the hard disk), and partly in the ROMs (on chips inside the Mac). In theory, one Mac's System-plus-Finder-plus-ROM combination roughly equals another's; this explains why new Macs act like old Macs, only faster.

The System and the Finder are computer programs. Since they start automatically, many people think of the System and the Finder as parts of the Mac and not as pieces of software. That's fine; think of the System and Finder any way that makes sense to you. Just don't ignore them. Knowing about the System and the Finder leads to power and fun.

The System contributes to the "consistent look and feel" of Macintosh applications because the System contains font, sound, and window information that all applications use. When all applications use one set of fonts, one set of sounds, and one basic look for windows, everything on a Mac seems more or less familiar.

As you learned above, ROMs are Read-Only Memory chips. The Mac reads the ROM information automatically, and you can't help nor hinder this process. Thus, it's safe for you to forget everything you know about ROMs, freeing up space in your brain for other, more critical, facts (such as where you put the Christmas lights and how to program the VCR).

Christian Boyce

The Finder manages your files. It lets you organize files by dragging icons anywhere you want them, and it lets you delete files by dragging icons to the Trash. The Finder exemplifies the graphical interface you've heard so much about, letting you do computer work by directly manipulating objects.

A Closer Look In the beginning, personal computers were an awful lot (emphasis on the "awful") like larger computers. The IBM PC typified the "we'll do everything the same, only smaller" concept, right down to its awkward operating system. On the PC, as on its larger brothers, the operating system mattered; it was something people talked about (and something people swore about), because it was something that had to be dealt with before getting the PC to work. The Microsoft Disk Operating System, or MS-DOS, came to symbolize the unfriendliness and inaccessibility of the IBM PC it controlled. Apple, determined to make Macintosh everything the PC wasn't, strove for an operating system that didn't get in the way. The result: an operating system so well integrated with the Macintosh hardware that users felt they controlled their Macs directly, without an intervening operating system. Apple applied the finishing touch to this "invisible" operating system by not even mentioning it in the original Mac's manual.

*S*ystem 7 uses more RAM than System 6 and its Finder is slower. Some incompatibilities appeared upon System 7's introduction, but most of them were resolved via software upgrades. Upgrading from System 6 to System 7 may force you to buy more RAM and to upgrade your software. It may also make you crave a faster Mac.

Christian Boyce

Understanding the Macintosh Operating System and understanding the Macintosh go hand in hand. Two versions of the Operating System are widely used today: 1988's System 6, which is good, and 1991's System 7, which is better (and more fun). This chapter addresses System 7 in particular, but there's plenty of information that applies to System 6 as well. If a feature is missing or looks different in System 6, I'll tell you.

Cut, Copy, and Paste

The original **Cut**, **Copy**, and **Paste** commands on the Mac were revolutionary when introduced in 1984 and they're still cool today. Cut, Copy, and Paste provide a consistent mechanism for moving text and graphics, and when you understand the mechanism, you can exploit it to the max.

When you cut (or copy) something, that something gets stored on the Mac's **Clipboard** and stays there until you cut (or copy) something else. With **Cut**, **Copy**, and **Paste** in every **Edit** menu, and with a single Clipboard for the entire Mac, Apple's provided a universal facility for moving text and graphics.

Copying and Pasting between Different Kinds of Documents

Copying and pasting between two documents from different applications is cool, because often neither application can do everything you want. You can use a drawing program to draw a picture, and a word processor to do some writing, then copy the drawing and paste it into the writing. The result is a better document than either program could produce alone. Figure 2.3 shows a compound document with parts from three applications.

Figure 2.3

Compound document assembled with **Copy** and **Paste**.

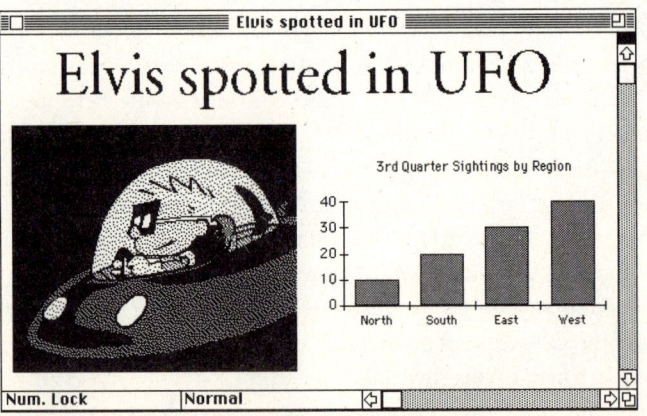

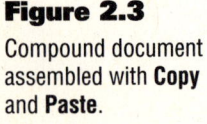

Remember, there's a single Clipboard for the entire Mac system. When you copy something, that something's stored on the Clipboard, ready for pasting anywhere. This example illustrates the "single Clipboard" concept. It also demonstrates that the Clipboard's contents aren't lost when you quit a program nor when you start another.

1. Open a drawing and select something to copy. (That is, open a MacDraw, Canvas, SuperPaint, or MacPaint document and select something to copy. If you want to get ahead of the others, you could copy a picture from the **Scrapbook**.)
2. Choose **Copy** from the **Edit** menu.
3. Choose **Quit** from the **File** menu. (**Copy** is always in the **Edit** menu. **Quit** is always in the **File** menu. Always, always, always.)
4. Open a word processing document
5. Move the cursor to where you want to paste the picture, and click.
6. Choose **Paste** from the **Edit** menu. **Paste** is always in the **Edit** menu.
7. Marvel at what you've done, and break for pizza.

The worst part about copying and pasting between different kinds of documents is the waiting: you wait for the first program to quit and you wait for the second program to launch. If you've got enough RAM you can run two programs at once; that speeds up the copy and paste routine considerably. With two programs open, you copy from one document, switch to the second document, and paste. Switching to the second document is easy: if you can see it, click on it. If you can't see the second document, use the Application menu (see figure 2.4) at the far right of the menu bar to select the second document's application. Either way, switching between two open applications is much faster than quitting from one and starting the other.

Chapter 2
Macintosh Basics

Figure 2.4

Application menu with Canvas and Word 5 running.

Your Mac's Application menu shows the applications you're running. Unless you happen to be using Canvas and Word 5, your Application menu won't look exactly like figure 2.2. Don't worry.

System 6 doesn't have an Application menu. If your System 6 Mac is using MultiFinder, there's an icon to click on but no menu comes down. Clicking the icon switches applications, cycling through all your open applications and eventually coming back to where you started. You can choose an application directly from the Apple menu; Figure 2.5 shows the Apple menu of a System 6 Mac with Canvas and Word 5 open.

Figure 2.5
Apple menu with Canvas and Word 5 running (System 6).

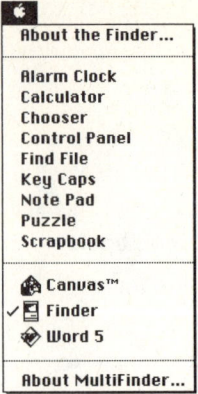

If you don't see an icon at the right end of the menu bar, your System 6 Mac isn't using MultiFinder. System 6 lets you switch between using MultiFinder (which lets you run more than one program at a time) and Finder (which lets you run just one program at a time). Use MultiFinder if your Mac has more than one megabyte of RAM (a "meg" in the jargon) and Finder if it doesn't. MultiFinder uses some RAM and a one-meg Mac doesn't have any to spare. If you used MultiFinder on a one-meg Mac you wouldn't have enough RAM left to run a program.

You can find out how much RAM your Mac has by selecting **About the Finder** from the Apple menu and noting the "Total Memory" number (which, for some strange reason, is in kilobytes, or "K"). Divide kilobytes by 1024 to get the number of megabytes of RAM in your Mac. Figure 2.6 shows an **About the Finder** window for a Mac with 8,192 kilobytes of RAM (8M).

Figure 2.6
About the Finder (System 6).

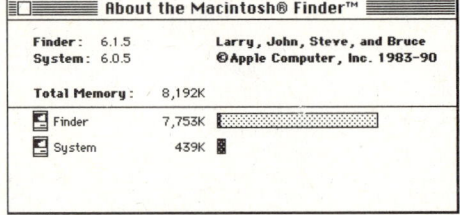

You can turn MultiFinder on and off using the **Set Startup** dialog box (see figure 2.7). Choose **Set Startup...** from the **Special** menu to obtain the **Set Startup** dialog. Choose **Finder** or **MultiFinder**, then restart your Mac to make your changes take effect.

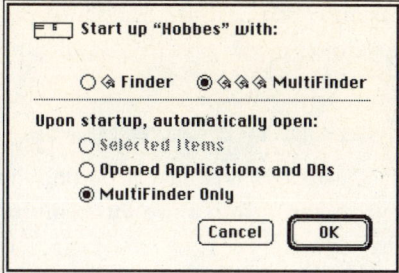

Figure 2.7
Set Startup dialog box (System 6).

The Scrapbook

Suppose you draw a logo, and suppose you want to use it day after day in your documents. Opening the logo document every time you need to copy the logo is time consuming. You need a quick and easy way to get to the logo. This is a job for the **Scrapbook**.

The Scrapbook stores pictures and text and sounds. Like the Clipboard, there's one Scrapbook for the entire Mac system. Unlike the Clipboard, the Scrapbook has pages; you can store many items in the Scrapbook, and those items are there to stay. Even through system errors and power failures. Figure 2.8 shows the Scrapbook.

Figure 2.8
The Scrapbook.

Putting stuff into the Scrapbook

As shipped, the Scrapbook holds a couple of pictures, some text, and a sound. You can put just about anything you want (more pictures, more text, more sounds) into the Scrapbook by following three simple steps:

1. **Copy** something.
2. Open the **Scrapbook** by selecting it from the Apple menu.
3. **Paste** the item into the Scrapbook.

Part I
Macintosh, the Computer

As far as I can tell, the number of Scrapbook pages is limitless. My Scrapbook has 117 pages and hasn't complained yet.

Christian Boyce

Don't worry about pasting over an existing Scrapbook page—you can't do it. The Scrapbook always creates a new page to hold what you paste.

Getting Stuff out of the Scrapbook

Getting stuff out of the Scrapbook is as easy as putting stuff in. Use **Copy** instead of **Cut**, unless you want to remove the item from the Scrapbook forever.

1. Open the **Scrapbook**.
2. Find the item you want to copy by flipping through the pages.
3. Choose **Copy**.
4. Close the Scrapbook.
5. Move the cursor to the desired position for pasting and click.
6. Choose **Paste**.

In practice, the cursor will often be in the proper location when you make your move to the Scrapbook, so you'll save a step.

A Closer Look Sad but true: occasionally, copying and pasting items between different kinds of applications doesn't work. The copying goes fine, but when you paste, nothing happens. You'll almost never see this problem when pasting things copied from the Scrapbook; basically, things copied from the Scrapbook are more "paste-able" than things copied straight out of certain kinds of documents. If a copy and paste operation doesn't work, try using the Scrapbook to smooth things over:

1. **Copy** something.
2. Open the **Scrapbook**.
3. Choose **Paste** (the items you copied are pasted into the Scrapbook).
4. Choose **Cut** (the items you pasted are cut out of the Scrapbook). **Cut** is always in the **Edit** menu.
5. Switch to the target document (the one you're trying to paste into).
6. Move the cursor to the desired position for pasting and click.
7. Choose **Paste**.

Copying and Pasting All Over the Place

You've copied and pasted between documents from different applications, and you've learned to use the Scrapbook. Still, there's more to Cut, Copy, and Paste. These last three examples show how cutting and copying and pasting opportunities turn up all over the place.

Copying from the Scrapbook and Pasting to a Control Panel

You can copy the color map from the Scrapbook and paste it into the **Map** control panel, replacing the control panel's boring black and white map. It helps to have a color Mac.

1. Open the **Scrapbook**.
2. Flip through the pages and find the color map.
3. Choose **Copy**.
4. Choose **Control Panels** from the Apple menu.
5. Find the Map icon and double-click it. Figure 2.9 shows the **Map** control panel, opened.

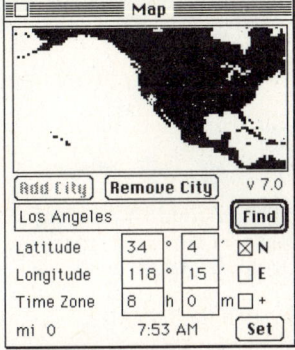

6. Choose **Paste** (and tell the Mac it's **OK** to replace the existing map picture).

> System 6 has a single Control Panel (see figure 2.8) with several control panel devices. Scroll through the list of control panel devices using the scroll bar. Click on the **Map** control panel device to produce the System 6 equivalent of figure 2.10.

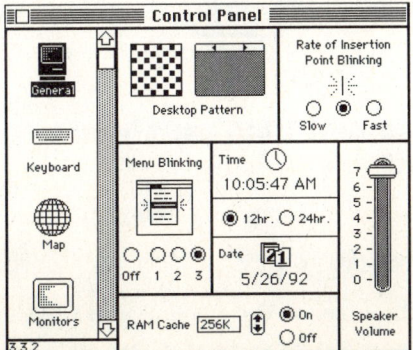

Chapter 2
Macintosh Basics

Figure 2.9
Map control panel.

Figure 2.10
Control Panel (System 6).

Part I
Macintosh, the Computer

Copying from the Note Pad and Pasting into the Calculator

This isn't something you'll use everyday. But it illustrates the universal nature of Cut, Copy, and Paste.

1. Choose **Note Pad** from the Apple menu.

2. Type **1+2+3+4+5=** (don't forget the equal sign). Figure 2.11 shows the Note Pad after step 2.

Figure 2.11
The Note Pad.

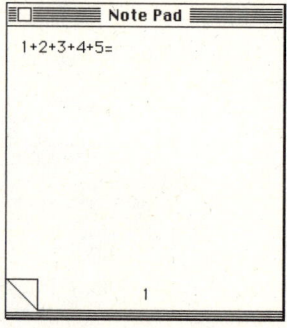

3. Select everything you typed, and choose **Copy** from the Edit menu.

4. Choose **Calculator** from the Apple menu.

5. Choose **Paste**—and watch the Calculator's buttons.

Figure 2.12 shows the Calculator after step 5. If you want to, you can Copy the answer from the Calculator, click on the Note Pad, and paste in the answer.

Figure 2.12
The Calculator.

Copying Icons and Pasting Them Where They Don't Belong

This won't hurt anything but it sure is confusing.

1. Click on any icon (for instance, a folder).

2. Choose **Get Info** from the **File** menu. Figure 2.13 shows the **Get Info** box for a folder called Fonts.

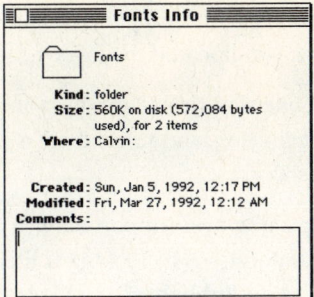

Figure 2.13
Get Info box.

3. Click on the picture of the icon in the **Get Info** box.
4. Choose **Copy**.
5. Close the **Get Info** box.
6. Click on a different kind of icon (for instance, a document).
7. Choose **Get Info**.
8. Click on the picture of the icon in the **Get Info** box.
9. Choose **Paste**.

When you're tired of being goofy, select the file with the pasted icon, and choose **Get Info**. Click on the icon's picture and choose **Clear** from the **Edit** menu. The original icon will reappear.

You're free to use any picture you want as an icon. Just copy it, open the proper Get Info box, click on the icon, and paste. Use a drawing program to create custom icons, or use pictures already in the Scrapbook. Figure 2.14 shows a window with icons that do nothing but confuse things.

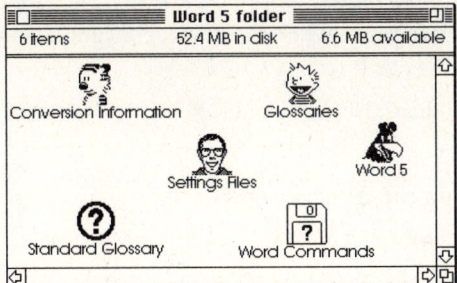

Figure 2.14
Confusing custom icons via **Copy** and **Paste**.

Publish and Subscribe

Publish and Subscribe are like Copy and Paste with a memory. Stuff you paste remembers where it was copied from, and when the original stuff changes, the pasted stuff changes too. If you published a company logo, and

Part I
Macintosh, the Computer

subscribed to it from invoices, letterhead, and business cards, you'd update the subscribees every time you updated the logo.

Copying and pasting is a one-shot deal. Publishing and subscribing is forever. Publishing is harder than copying, and subscribing is harder than pasting, but in the right situations, it's worth it.

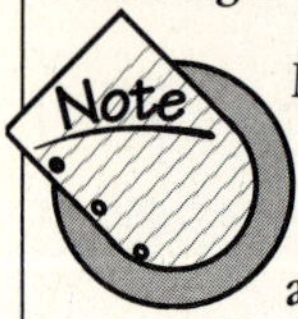

> **Note:** Many programs don't yet support Publish and Subscribe. You can check your applications by looking at their Edit menus. If you don't see "**Create Publisher**" and "**Subscribe To...**" in an application's **Edit** menu, that application can't publish or subscribe.

Publishing is similar to copying. Follow these steps to publish:

1. Select the part of a document (text or graphics) you wish to publish.
2. Choose **Create Publisher** from the **Edit** menu. Published material is stored in an Edition file. Figure 2.15 shows the dialog box for saving Editions.

Figure 2.15
Saving an Edition.

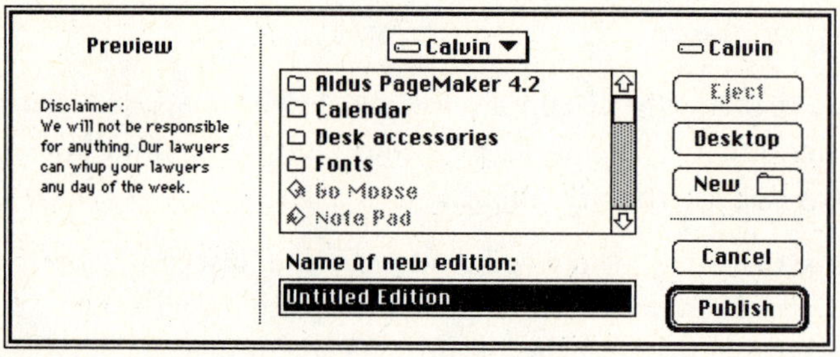

3. Name the Edition file.
4. Press the **Publish** button to save the Edition. The Edition file remembers its origins. When the original document changes, the Edition changes too.

Publishing's not so hard. Neither is subscribing. Follow these steps to subscribe:

1. Open a document (a "subscribee").
2. Move the cursor to where you want to insert the published material, and click.
3. Choose "**Subscribe To...**" from the **Edit** menu. Figure 2.16 shows the dialog box used when subscribing to an Edition.

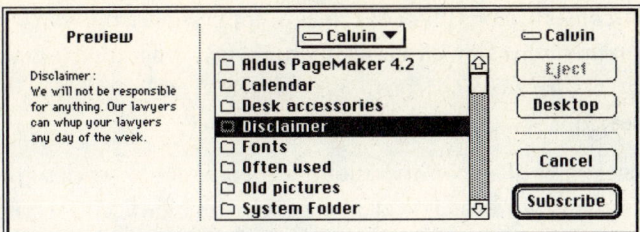

Figure 2.16

Subscribing to an Edition.

4. Select the proper Edition file from the dialog box (this may take some looking around).

5. Press the **Subscribe** button.

Your subscribing document holds a copy of the Edition. When the Edition changes (due to changes in the original document), the subscribing document changes. Subscribing links the subscribing document and the Edition file, and the link is permanent (though you can break it if you want to).

 The publishing document and the subscribing document are not directly connected. The Edition file acts as a go-between.

Publish and Subscribe aren't as useful as Cut, Copy, and Paste, partly because few programs support Publish and Subscribe and partly because Edition files are hassles to store and keep track of. Add the possibility of ruining several subscribing documents by "improving" a single publishing document and you'll see why I rarely use Publish and Subscribe. Still, the idea of links between documents intrigues me enough that I'm hoping Publish and Subscribe catch on.

Aliases

There's nothing cooler, Mac-wise, than System 7's aliases. Aliases let you store things in more than one place, which makes it easier to find things later. And, since you can store things in more than one place, you can organize your applications, documents, and folders in ways that make sense to you while simultaneously organizing things in ways that make sense to your Mac. When it comes to built-in system stuff, aliases are coolest of all. You make them, and use them, in the Finder. System 6 does not include the alias feature.

You simply must use aliases. There's no better way of customizing your Mac and making it easier to use. Ignoring System 7's alias feature is like ignoring the remote control for your TV, only ten times worse.

Christian Boyce

Part I
Macintosh, the Computer

Aliases are copies of icons (but not copies of applications, folders, or documents themselves). With aliases, then, a single application (or folder, or document) can have several icons. One icon's the "real" one, but the others (the aliases) look just the same and work just as well.

Double-clicking an alias icon does the same thing as double-clicking the "real" icon. So, if you've got an alias to an application, double-clicking it opens the application. If you've got an alias to a folder, double-clicking it opens the folder. And if you've got an alias to a document, double-clicking it opens the document. It's this "one file, many icons for opening it" that makes the alias feature so handy.

In the old days (before I dedicated every moment to writing this book), I wrote letters to Mom and stored them in a "Mom Letters" folder. Unfinished work, such as my plans to turn this book into a musical, went into an "Unfinished Stuff" folder. Problem: I couldn't figure out where to file an unfinished letter to Mom. I solved the problem by putting the real (though unfinished) letter into the "Mom Letters" folder and an alias to the letter into the "Unfinished Stuff" folder. That way, whether I look in "Mom Letters" or "Unfinished Stuff," I find an icon for the letter. "Real" or not, double-clicking that icon opens the unfinished letter to Mom. When I finish the letter I'll trash the alias. (Fortunately, throwing away an alias doesn't throw away the original file. Aliases remember where they come from until you throw them away.)

Here are some very cool ways you can use aliases:

▼ Put aliases to your favorite applications on the desktop (leaving the real applications where they belong, with their Help files and Dictionaries).

▼ Put an alias to the Trash inside your hard disk. Now you can throw things away even when you can't see the "real" Trash. Put a Trash alias on your other monitor, if you're lucky enough to have one (I'm not that lucky).

▼ Make an alias to a folder you often use, but hate to dig for. Place the alias on the desktop. Double-clicking the alias opens the folder directly, without opening intermediate folders. Dragging items to the alias places them inside the real folder. Convince yourself of this by experimenting.

Making an Alias

Making an alias is as simple as selecting an icon and choosing **Make Alias** from the Finder's **File** menu. Here's an example.

1. Open your hard disk with a confident double-click.
2. Find the **System** folder and open it.
3. View the **System** folder's contents by Icon (experiment with the **View** menu until you've got this figured out).
4. Find the Apple menu Items folder and click on it.
5. Choose **Make Alias** from the **File** menu.
6. Drag the **Apple Menu Items alias** icon onto the desktop, next to your hard disk icon.
7. Close all the windows.

Alias icons look like "real" icons, except their names are italicized and have "alias" at the end. You're allowed to change the name, but the italics are there to stay.

Close all the windows at once by holding the Option key while closing the first one.

The screen should look like figure 2.17.

Chapter 2
Macintosh Basics

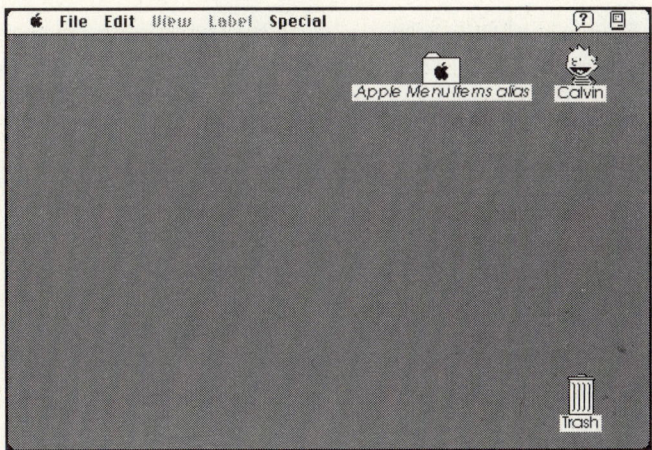

Figure 2.17
An alias to the **Apple Menu Items** folder, on the desktop.

Double-clicking the alias opens the real **Apple Menu Items** folder. Try it.

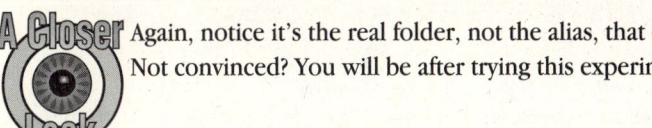 Again, notice it's the real folder, not the alias, that opens. Not convinced? You will be after trying this experiment:

Double-click your hard disk. Did you see the zooming rectangles fly out of the disk icon, signaling the opening of the hard disk's window? If you didn't,

Part I
Macintosh, the Computer

Figure 2.18
A hard disk and a hard disk alias.

close the hard disk window and try it again. Now close the hard disk window and make an alias to the hard disk. Place it far from the real hard disk icon (see figure 2.18).

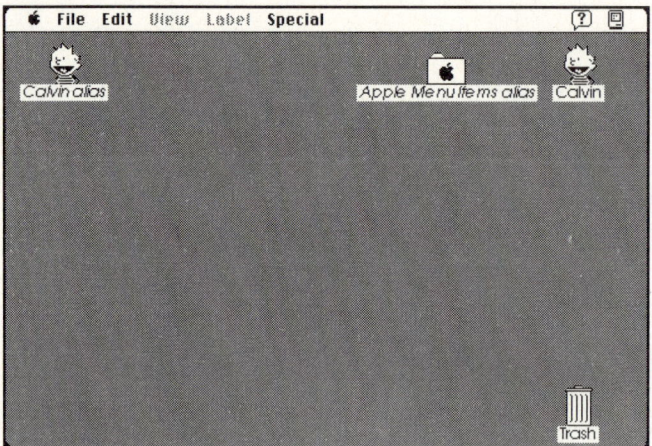

Double-click the alias. Did zooming rectangles fly out of it? No, they didn't. Zooming rectangles flew out of the real hard disk icon, not the alias. Double-clicking the alias sent a message to the real icon and opened it up. Note the shading of the real icon as compared to the alias: the real icon is gray while the alias appears unchanged. Also, whether you use the alias or the real icon, the window that opens is named after the hard disk and not after the alias. For the last time (I promise), aliases never open. They pass the "open" message to the real icon, and from there, the real icon takes over. Understanding this concept is the key to happy aliasing.

Keep that **Apple Menu Items** alias. You'll use it while customizing the Apple menu.

The Apple Menu

The Apple menu is always the first menu on the left, no matter what. Other menus come and go, depending on the application you're running, but the Apple menu persists. Constant accessibility makes the Apple menu a convenient place to access frequently used applications, folders, documents, sounds, and desk accessories.

> *Desk accessories* are small programs designed to be accessed from the Apple menu. The Scrapbook, the Note Pad, and the Calculator are examples.

System 6's Apple menu can only hold desk accessories.

Chapter 2
Macintosh Basics

Selecting an item from the Apple menu is equivalent to double-clicking an icon in a Finder window. Select an application from the Apple menu and the application opens; select a document from the Apple menu and the document opens. Select a folder and the folder opens; select a sound and the sound opens (plays).

As shipped, the Apple menu holds several desk accessories and an alias to the Control Panels folder (the real Control Panels folder is inside the System folder where it's a pain to get to). Adding items to the Apple menu is peanuts: just drag the items to the Apple Menu Items folder inside the System folder. Better yet, drag them to the Apple Menu Items alias you conveniently placed on your desktop. Everything you put in the Apple Menu Items folder, whether done directly or through the alias, shows up in the Apple menu immediately.

Note: System 6 does not have an Apple Menu Items folder. You add items to the Apple menu using the Font/DA Mover. Your *Macintosh Utilities Users' Guide* explains how to use the Font/DA Mover in great detail. The convenience of the Apple Menu Items folder makes System 7's Apple menu more easily configured.

A Closer Look: Aliases and the Apple menu are meant for each other. If you want something to appear in the Apple menu, alias the thing and put the alias in the Apple Menu Items folder. This is particularly important for applications, which typically should be stored with their dictionaries and help files for proper operation. Put an alias in the Apple Menu Items folder and leave the original where you found it. You'll be happy, and your Mac will be too.

Suppose you made an alias to the Apple Menu Items folder alias already on your desktop. And suppose you dragged this new "alias to the alias" into the alias (got that?), putting an "Apple Menu Items alias alias" into the Apple menu. What would happen if you chose "Apple Menu Items alias alias" from the Apple menu? Would your Mac go in circles, chasing its own tail as it searched for the real Apple Menu Items folder, or would the real Apple Menu Items folder open?

Why don't you try it and see? I dare you.

Adding a Sound to the Apple Menu

There's nothing like a cheerful duck to brighten your day. You should have one in the Apple menu. So should your boss. Here's how:

1. Open the **System** folder (double-click).

41

Part I

Macintosh, the Computer

Figure 2.19
The system window with **Apple Menu Items** alias.

2. Open the **System** file.
3. Rearrange and resize windows so you can see the **System** file's window and the **Apple Menu Items** alias (see figure 2.19).

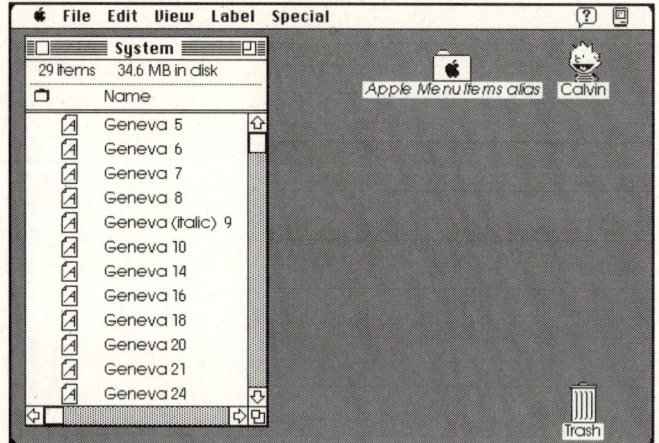

4. Scroll through the **System** file's window until you find the **Quack** sound.
5. Press and hold the Option key, then drag the **Quack** sound to the **Apple Menu Items** alias.
6. Close the **System** file.
7. Close the **System** folder.

Now look at the Apple menu. Choose **Quack**. It works!

You cannot add sounds to System 6's Apple menu.

Note: When you drag a file from one disk to a second, the file doesn't move from the first disk to the second. Rather, the file is copied to the second disk, leaving the original untouched. Dragging files from folder to folder on a single disk does move the file, unless you're using the little-known Option-Drag Technique. Holding the Option key while dragging a file makes a copy, as if you were dragging to a second disk.

In a better world, you would have made an alias to the Quack sound instead of duplicating it. Unfortunately, you can't alias things stored within the System file.

The Apple menu lists items in alphabetical order, no matter what. Rearranging the order in the menu is a matter of opening the Apple Menu Items folder and renaming the icons as needed. The Mac sorts numbers before letters, punctuation before numbers, and spaces before everything.

Two spaces come before one space, three spaces beats two, and so on. Figure 2.20 shows an Apple menu before creative ordering. Figure 2.21 shows the same menu, after.

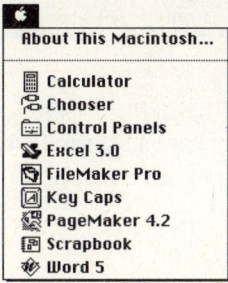

The stock System 6 Apple menu holds only 15 items. There is no built-in facility for reordering the items in the menu.

Startup Items

When I turn my Mac on, it quacks three times and opens my calendar. No, my Mac's not possessed by Type A ducks; it's just doing exactly what I asked it to. You can do this too (though you'll probably want more quacking) using the **Startup Items** folder.

The Startup Items folder is inside the System folder, as shown in figure 2.22. When you turn on your Mac, it looks to the Startup Items and double-clicks everything it finds. Applications open, documents open, folders open, and sounds open. If you want something to open every time your Mac starts up, just place that something in the Startup Items folder.

Chapter 2
Macintosh Basics

Figure 2.20
An Apple Menu (before).

Figure 2.21
An Apple Menu (after).

*O*nly the first 52 items (sorted alphabetically) show up in the Apple menu. Items 53 and higher will still be in the Apple Menu Items folder, but they won't appear in the menu. Why 52, instead of 53, or 50, or 100? Beats me.

Christian Boyce

Figure 2.22
The **Startup Items** folder (and others).

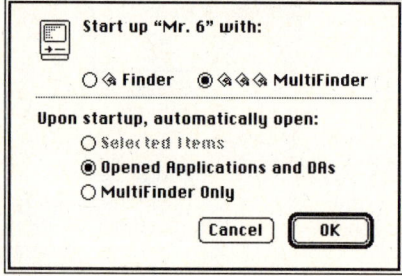

 System 6 does not have a Startup Items folder. You can use the **Set Startup** box to make a set of application open when your Mac is turned on:

1. Be sure your Mac is using MultiFinder (look for the icon at the right end of the menu bar).
2. Open each application you'd like your Mac to automatically open.
3. Choose **Set Startup...** from the **Special** menu.
4. Click the **Opened Applications and DAs** button. Figure 2.23 shows the proper choices in the **Set Startup** box.

Figure 2.23
Set Startup box (System 6).

5. Click **OK**.
6. Restart your Mac.

If, rather than simply open applications, you'd like to open certain documents at startup (still under System 6), you can do that too.

1. Be sure your Mac is using MultiFinder.
2. Move the documents you want to open at startup to the same folder.
3. Select the documents you want to open at startup.
4. Choose **Set Startup...** from the **Special** menu.
5. Click the **Selected Items** button.
6. Click **OK.**
7. Restart your Mac.

I've said it before, and here we go again: aliases are cooler than cool. I recommend using aliases in the Startup Items folder because, when you tire of your startup routine, you can trash the aliases without disturbing (or worrying about) the original files. If you place "real" files in the Startup Items folder, and you don't want them there anymore, you have to find a new place to store them. With aliases, you just toss 'em.

> Make ten or twelve aliases to the **Quack** sound in your boss's **Apple Menu Items** folder. Put the aliases in his **Startup Items** folder. Remember to duck (get it?) when the boss restarts his Mac.

Chapter 2
Macintosh Basics

Control Panels

Control panels let you, uh, control the way your Mac behaves. You change desktop patterns with a control panel, choose a beep sound with another control panel, and select a font for Finder windows with a third. Control panels are very cool, and the more you play with them, the more in control you'll feel.

> You saw the System 6 control panel in figure 2.10.

> Control panels are specialized pieces of software. They're stored in a special **Control Panels** folder, and that folder's stored in the **System** folder. Use the Control Panels alias in the Apple menu for quick and easy access. Control panel devices are loose in System 6's System folder.

Yes, that's a Control Panels alias in the Apple menu. The real Control Panels folder stays inside the System folder. Aliases don't have to be called "something alias" and they don't look italicized in the Apple menu.

General Controls

General Controls (figure 2.24) does lots of things, but changing the desktop pattern's the only cool one. You won't break anything by clicking, so feel free to experiment.

1. Open the **Control Panels** folder.
2. Double-click **General Controls**.

Control panels are fun. You can easily shoot a whole day playing with them. Don't say I didn't warn you.

Christian Boyce

Part I
Macintosh, the Computer

If you don't like the built-in patterns, you'll just have to make your own.

Christian Boyce

Figure 2.24
The **General Controls** control panel.

3. Click the arrows over the miniature desktop (right-hand box in the **Desktop Pattern** area) to cycle through the built-in patterns.
4. When you find a pattern you like, click on it.
5. Choose a color to draw with from the palette at the bottom of the **Desktop Pattern** area.

 If you don't like the colors in the palette, double-click one and choose a new color from the resulting **Color Picker** dialog box. This won't help if your Mac is black and white.

6. Click and drag in the zoomed-in, pattern editing box (left-hand box in the **Desktop Pattern** area).
7. When you're satisfied, double-click the miniature desktop.
8. Close the panel.

 It's important to double-click. A single click changes the desktop to reflect your editing, but only a double-click stores your pattern permanently.

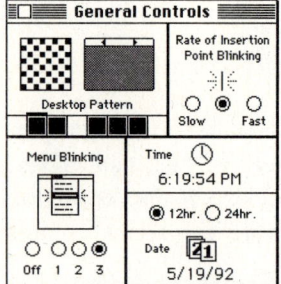

Some color Macs are shipped with the **Monitors** control panel set to black-and-white. If this sounds familiar, open the Monitors control panel and have a look around. You'll figure it out for yourself now that you know where to look. Color Macs are more fun in color. Note: the **Color** control panel controls the color of highlighted text. Do not try to use the Color control panel to change your color Mac's monitor from black-and-white to color. It won't work.

Sound

When you do something your Mac can't handle, it beeps. You can choose a different sound (my Mac quacks—what a surprise), and control the sound's volume, using the **Sound** control panel (see figure 2.25).

46

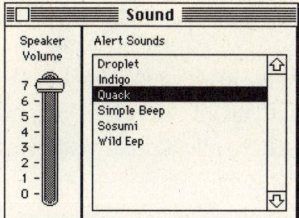

Figure 2.25

The **Sound** control panel.

1. Open the **Control Panels** folder.
2. Double-click **Sound**.
3. Choose a sound by clicking on one.
4. Choose a volume by dragging the slider up or down.
5. Close the control panel.

A Closer Look You can record your own beep sounds if your Mac came with a microphone. Start by clicking the **Add...** button in the **Sound** control panel. Then, click the **Record** button. Make your sound (up to ten seconds long), and click **Stop**. You can listen to the sound by clicking **Play**. If you like it, save it; the name you give it appears in the list of potential beep sounds.

Views

Wouldn't it be cool if the Finder used bigger letters for the names of documents, applications, and folders? You bet it would. Your Mac can use any font you've got, in any size you've got, so why use boring 9-point Geneva? The **Views** control panel (see figure 2.26) does more than just control the Finder's font, but the other stuff, while important, isn't that cool.

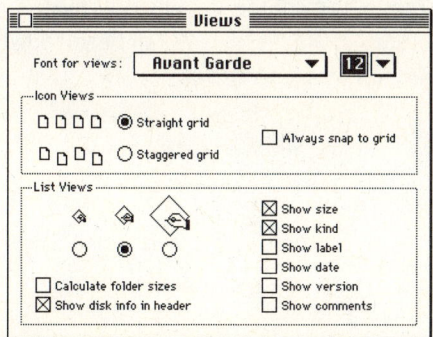

Figure 2.26

The **Views** control panel.

Part I
Macintosh, the Computer

> **Note:** System 6 has no built-in facility for changing the Finder's text from Geneva 9. However, Michael C. O'Connor's "Layout" program gives you all the Finder-changing capabilities you ever could want. Better still: "Layout" is free. Get it from a Macintosh user group, a friend, or an electronic bulletin board service.

1. Open the **Control Panels** folder.
2. Double-click **Views**.
3. Choose a font from the pop-up font menu.
4. Choose a size from the pop-up size menu.

I changed my Mac's Finder font to 12-point Avant Garde and haven't worn my glasses since. When 12-point looks small, I'll move to 14, then 18, and so on. It's cheaper than a trip to the optometrist.

Driving Your Mac from the Keyboard

In the beginning, Mac users bragged about using their mice for practically all of their work. Keyboards were considered archaic input devices. Today, even died-in-the-wool Mac-ers use keyboard commands to save time and effort.

Christian Boyce

Grab a mouse, move it around, and presto: you're running a Macintosh. At least that's what the ads tell you. Unfortunately, beginners have trouble making mice go where they want them to, and pros don't like switching from their keyboards to their mice and back. Fortunately, it's easy to drive a Mac from the keyboard.

Universal Command Key Equivalents

The basics are there in every program: Command-C for **Copy**, Command-V for **Paste**, Command-X for **Cut**, and Command-Z for **Undo**. Holding the Command key and typing the appropriate key is equivalent to making a selection from the menu. Look at the Finder's **Edit** menu (see figure 2.27); you'll see these shortcuts along the menu's right hand edge. Nearly every application uses these very same shortcuts.

Figure 2.27
Command keys in the **Edit** menu.

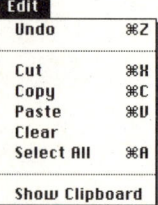

48

Other nearly-universal shortcuts include Command-P for **Print**, Command-S for **Save**, and Command-Q for **Quit**. Look at the menus in your applications to see if these shortcuts will work.

 Command-period almost always cancels whatever's going on. If your Mac seems to be in some sort of loop, Command-period might get it out. Can't hurt to try.

You'll never learn the shortcuts unless you try them. So try them.

Christian Boyce

Other Universal Keyboard Shortcuts

While Command key shortcuts provide mouseless access to many menu items, other keyboard shortcuts reduce mousing in dialog boxes (like the one in figure 2.28). Try using the Tab key to cycle through dialog box fields. It works in almost all of them.

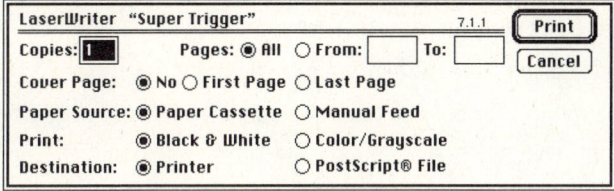

Figure 2.28

Tabbing through the fields.

1. Switch to the Finder (use the **Application** menu).
2. Double-click on the icon for your hard disk to open it.
3. Choose **Print Window...** from the **File** menu.
4. Type **2** and press the Tab key.
5. Type **1** and press the Tab key again.
6. Type **1**.
7. Click the **Print** button.

There are only three fields in the **Print Window...** dialog box, so you're done, but you could cycle through them again by continuing to press the Tab key. When you tab to a field with something already in it, you can type right over it. There's no need to hit Delete before replacing something that's highlighted.

 You can always type over things that are highlighted. When something's selected, it's ready to be replaced with whatever you type next.

Part I

Macintosh, the Computer

You could have clicked that **Print** button by pressing Return, or Enter, on the keyboard. Every dialog box has a heavily outlined button (usually offering the safest of all options, but not always), and pressing Return, or Enter, is usually the same as pressing the outlined button. I prefer the Enter key because it always works (some programs require the Enter key and won't accept Return). Also, the Enter key's got fewer keys surrounding it, meaning fewer chances for me to hit the wrong key.

Dialog boxes take a moment to appear on the screen, but you don't have to wait if you know what they look like. You'll get ahead of the Mac, but it will catch up. Meanwhile, you're doing other things.

For example, if you wanted to print three copies of the first two pages of a word processing document, you could type, as quickly as possible:

1. Command-P (to open the **Print...** dialog box).
2. **3** (for three copies).
3. Tab (to take you to the starting page field).
4. **1** (to specify that the first page should be the starting page).
5. Tab (to take you to the ending page field).
6. **2** (to specify that the second page should be the ending page).
7. Enter (to click the **Print** button).

I can run through those steps in a couple of seconds. The **Print...** dialog never shows up, but the printing works.

Special Finder Shortcuts

The Finder is loaded with shortcuts. Remember, though, if you want a complete treatment, you'll have to look somewhere else. I'm only presenting the cool stuff.

Ever open a folder, sure it holds something you want, and spend way too long finding it? The Finder's got a cure for that. Just type the first letter of the item you're looking for. This works on the desktop, in windows, and in **Open...** dialog boxes (see figures 2.29, 2.30, and 2.31). You can select things in **Save As...** dialog boxes (see figure 2.32) if you press Tab first.

You can select items in System 6's **Open...** dialog boxes by typing. The other Finder tips listed above do not work in System 6.

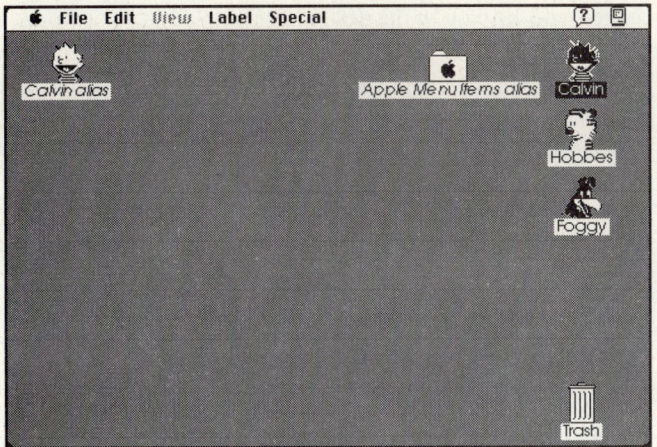

Figure 2.29
Typing **c** on the desktop.

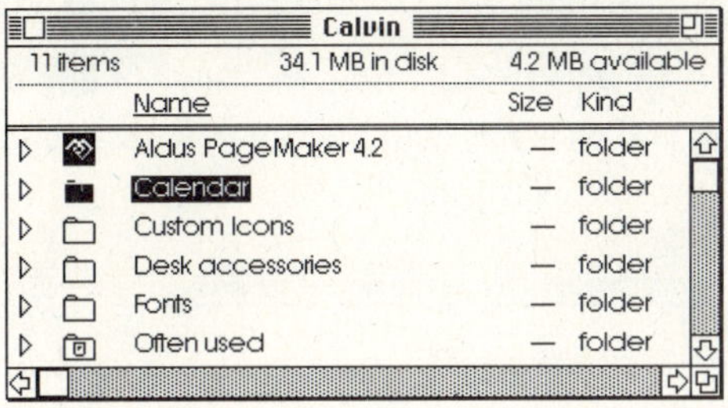

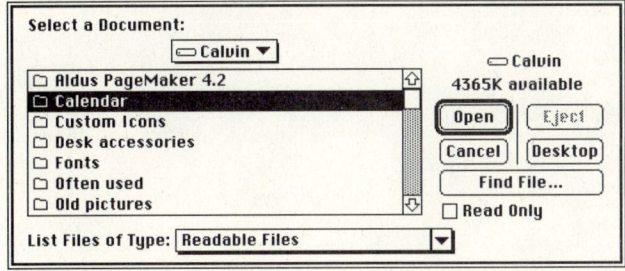

Figure 2.30
Typing **c** in a Finder window.

Figure 2.31
Typing **c** in an **Open...** dialog box.

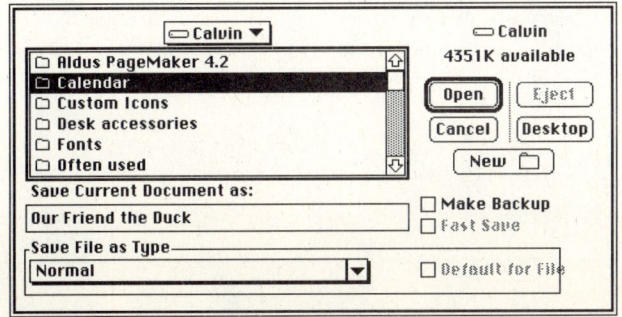

Figure 2.32
Typing Tab, then **c** in a **Save As...** dialog box.

Part I

Macintosh, the Computer

Typing a letter and zipping to the desired file is great, when it works. Sometimes it doesn't work. For instance, typing **C** selects the first file starting with "C," and you might want the second one. The obvious solution (type **C** again) doesn't work. What does work is pressing Tab. You can move alphabetically down the list, and come around again (like on a cylindrical Rolodex), by repeatedly pressing the Tab key.

 Pressing Shift while tabbing moves backward. If, while tabbing, you pass by your file, press Shift and Tab to move back up the list.

Another Way to Find

Sometimes you don't know much about a file, except that you can't find it. Typing the first letter doesn't work unless you're looking in the right place already. You need something stronger: the Finder's **Find...** feature.

Simple Finds are easy: select **Find...** from the Finder's **File** menu, type what you're looking for, and click the **Find** button. It works, but only if you know something about the lost file's name (see figure 2.33).

Figure 2.33
A Simple **Find...**

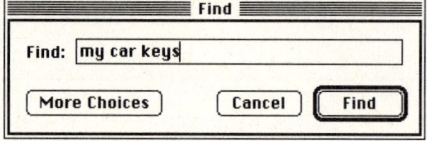

 System 6's Finder does not include a **Find...** command. However, System 6 does include the **Find File** desk accessory. Figure 2.34 shows **Find File**.

Figure 2.34
Find File desk accessory (System 6).

What if you can't remember your lost file's name? What if all you know is you're looking for a folder? No problem. You can find more stuff with the **Find** feature than most people can ever lose. The key, as usual, involves poking around a bit.

You don't have to poke very hard. All it takes is pressing the **More Choices...** button in the **Find...** box. Here's how to find all folders on your hard disk and display them all at once.

> The **Find File** DA cannot perform this kind of search.

1. Choose **Find...** from the Finder's **File** menu.
2. Press the **More Choices...** button.
3. Use the pop-up menus to define your search (see figure 2.35).

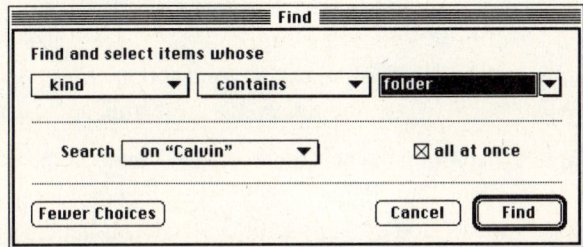

4. Check the **all at once** checkbox.
5. Press the **Find** button.

The result looks like figure 2.36. Note that aliases to folders are not selected.

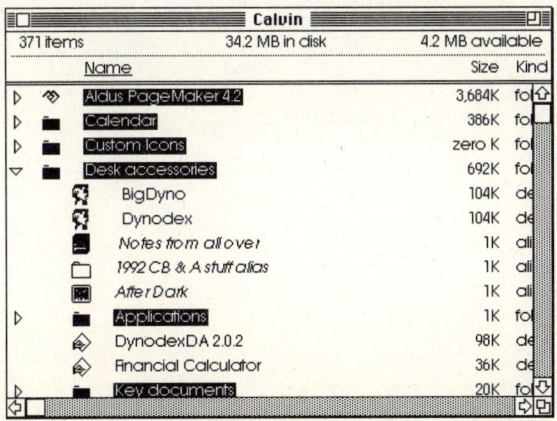

Chapter 2
Macintosh Basics

Figure 2.35
More Choices... in the Find dialog.

Figure 2.36
All folders selected at once.

53

Part I
Macintosh, the Computer

The folders stay highlighted until you select something else. If you're careful, you'll be able to scroll through the entire hard disk, looking only at the highlighted items. That's still a lot of items, but you've narrowed the search.

A Closer Look: Use **More Choices...** to search for applications, and while they're selected, choose **Make Alias** from the **File** menu. You'll end up with a bunch of highlighted aliases. Drag them into the **Apple Menu Items** alias you left on the desktop (you did leave it there, didn't you?), and you'll have easy access to each of your programs.

Summary

Right out of the box, the Macintosh System lets you and your Mac do cool stuff. You can move data between documents, share files with other computers, and make your Mac quack every time it starts. You can customize your Mac so it looks the way you want it to, and you can organize things any way, or ways, you wish. And if you're not so good at organizing, the Operating System will help you find things. It's great stuff, and it's all built-in.

The next chapter, "Exploring the Macintosh System," looks at the System in more depth. It examines some of the specifics regarding the way the Macintosh System works, and explains some of the details behind the terminology.

Chapter 3
Exploring the Macintosh System

The Macintosh is designed to be easier to use than any other computer. It accomplishes this ease of use through certain basics, including a

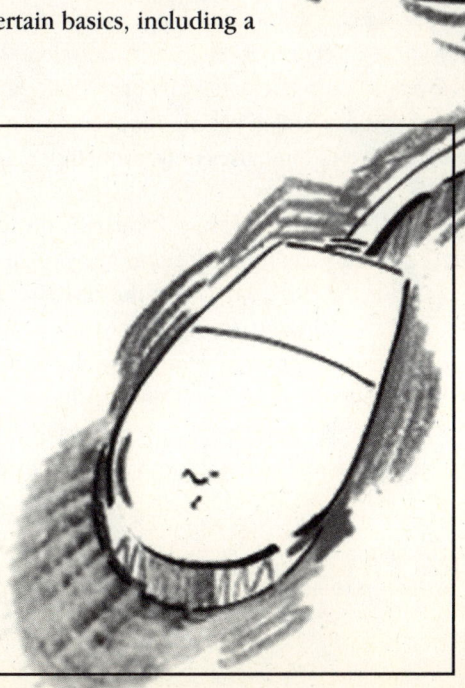

In This Chapter
- ▼ The desktop
- ▼ Pointers and cursors
- ▼ Menus and windows
- ▼ The mouse and keyboard
- ▼ Boxes and buttons
- ▼ The System folder, files, and operations
- ▼ Future improvements

Part I
Macintosh,
the Computer

user interface based on icons, menus, windows, and such. This chapter takes an in-depth look at how those individual pieces all work together to create a simple-to-use machine.

 This chapter is not, however, an introduction into using the Macintosh. Rather, it provides a look into how some of the basic Macintosh elements relate to each other. For a more introductory look at the Mac, see chapter 2, "Macintosh Basics."

The Desktop

Most people think of the desktop (the Macintosh background screen) as the Mac itself. *Desktop* is a metaphor for an electronic tabletop and is the Macintosh operating system element that the Finder organizes. The *Finder* is a program like any other Macintosh program. After you learn how to use it, you can apply the Finder's operating principles to other Macintosh programs.

The Finder uses resources such as *icons* and *cursors* and elements such as the *hierarchical file system* (HFS) contained in the System file to display a set of *windows* and elements that you can manipulate on your screen. The Finder has its own set of *menus* and *commands*. To use another program on your Mac, simply start that program and you automatically leave the Finder. If you use a version of the operating system that enables you to use MultiFinder (System 5 and later), the Finder is retained in your computer's memory so that you can switch back to it quickly while retaining other programs active in memory. System 7 uses only MultiFinder, and refers to it as the "Finder."

You will know if you are using a version of the Finder that allows multiple programs to be opened by the appearance of a program icon at the far right of the menu bar. In System 7, clicking on this icon exposes an application menu that allows you to choose the program you wish to be active. In System 5 or 6, when MultiFinder is active a tiny Macintosh computer icon appears at the right of the menu bar. To change programs in System 6, click on the program icon or select the name of the desired program from the **Apple** menu.

The concept of using an icon for available disks is common to the desktop in all versions of the System. Disk icons appear on the right side of your screen from top to bottom in order of their mounting. Your startup, or boot disk (the one with the active System folder), always appears at the top right corner (see figure 3.1). Sometimes disks are *partitioned* (split) into logical volumes; each logical volume displays an icon on the desktop.

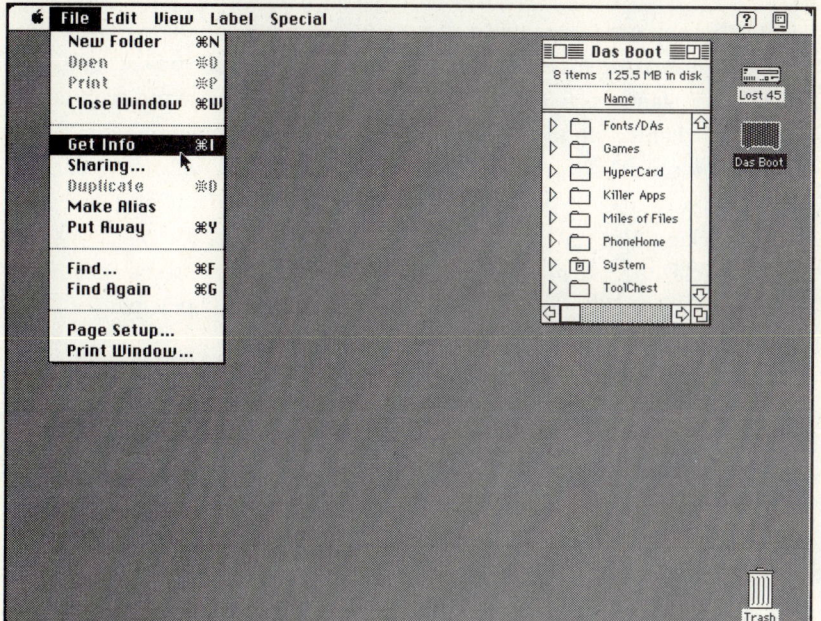

Chapter 3
Exploring the Macintosh System

Figure 3.1
The Macintosh System 7 desktop.

The Trash icon, which stores files you want to delete, also appears on the desktop. In System 6 and earlier, the Trash empties automatically during certain events (such as shutdown), but in System 7 you must choose the **Empty Trash** command from the **Special** menu to delete your files.

You can set the time and date, change the behavior of your menus and insertion point, and change the appearance of your desktop from within the General control panel in the Desktop Pattern section (see figure 3.2).

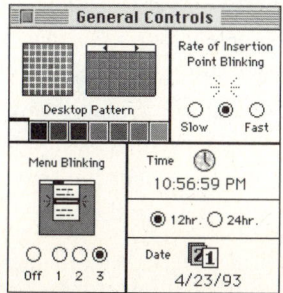

Figure 3.2
You can change the desktop pattern using the General control panel.

57

Part I
Macintosh, the Computer

If you want to put a picture rather than a pattern on your desktop, there are a number of shareware and commercial utilities that enable you to do this. DeskPicture from NOW Utilities is one such program.

Note: You can place objects that are important to you directly on your desktop for easy access. If you have a program you use constantly, placing its icon (or its *alias*, discussed in the previous chapter) on the desktop enables you to launch the program simply by double-clicking on the icon. Similarly, putting a folder for a current project on your desktop also enables you to open the folder quickly by double-clicking. You can open all objects—folders, files, and applications—by double-clicking. Placing frequently used objects on the desktop speeds up the process of accessing them because you do not have to open many different folders.

Basic Macintosh Features

This section discusses the basic features of the Mac: pointers and cursors, selection, icons, menus, windows, the mouse, keyboard, dialog boxes, and alert boxes.

Pointers

The standard *pointer* is a small arrow that you move onscreen by moving your mouse. Depending on which function your Mac is performing, your pointer may change from an arrow to another small object such as a watch. A pointer's appearance is a good clue as to what is happening at the moment. If the pointer is a watch, the computer is thinking; a paint bucket, it is painting, and so forth. All pointers have a *hot spot* that specifies one pixel that the cursor is pointing at. For a paint bucket pointer, the hot spot is at the tip of the pouring paint; for a pencil pointer, the tip of the pencil; and so on. The current location determines where the action takes place, so the paint bucket fills the object at the location of its hot spot, the pencil draws from where you place the tip of the pencil, and so on.

Selection

The Mac is designed to enable you to manipulate objects directly on your screen. You can do this using a pointing device (your mouse) or by typing on the keyboard; either way, *selection* is the key to specifying which action you want.

To select an icon in the Finder:

▼ Position the tip of the mouse pointer on the object you want to select and click the mouse button. The icon for the object highlights.

To select several objects simultaneously:

▼ Click and drag a selection *marquee* around the objects. A selection marquee is a rectangle with a dotted-line outline that appears as you hold down the mouse pointer and drag the mouse. The marquee defines the area you selected. This action is called *click-dragging*, and you use it in other actions to manipulate selected items (such as moving a window by its title bar). In System 6, you must enclose all items completely in a marquee to select them with this method; in System 7 you just need to touch an item within a marquee.

To add or remove an item (extend the range of selection):

▼ Hold down the Shift key and click on an unselected item to add it to the range of items. This action is called *shift-clicking*.

▼ Hold down the Shift key and click on a selected item to remove it from a selected range of items.

These rules of thumb apply to many situations besides the Finder, with some variations. In some lists, Shift-clicking selects everything between your first selection and the current selection, while Command-clicking enables you to select random items in the list. These variations, however, are all closely related to the basic idea: click on something if you want to work with it. A little experimentation will soon reveal the specifics in a given application.

You cannot select multiple items in different windows in System 6 and earlier systems. System 7 greatly improves object selection: it provides a method in the **Outline** view of a window (any view other than **By Icon** or **By Small Icon**) to select the objects you want in any folder (see the section, "Using Windows," later in this chapter). System 7 also enables you to change the selected icon in a window by using the Tab key to move forward and Shift-Tab to move backward. You also can

Chapter 3
Exploring the Macintosh System

use other shortcuts, such as using the arrow keys and alphanumeric keys for selection. To see a list of these, select **Finder Shortcuts** from the Balloon Help menu (the second icon from the right of the menu bar).

Icons

Icons are pictures that represent objects. An icon expresses a metaphor that makes its behavior clear. A folder icon can have items deposited in it, the Trash icon holds objects to be deleted, and so on. An icon is a resource that is attached to a file. You can change an icon in several ways: using ResEdit (an Apple programming utility) and opening the Icon template, reassigning file attributes, and using shareware programs such as ColorFinder (for System 6).

To rename an icon on the desktop:

1. Click on the icon.
2. Position your pointer over the name of the icon until the pointer changes to an insertion cursor (an I-beam)
3. Click and drag over the name to select the text.
4. Type a new name.
5. Press the Return or Enter key, or click elsewhere to deselect the icon.

If you cannot get an I-beam cursor, the file may be locked. To unlock a file, select the object, select **Get Info** from the **File** menu, and uncheck the **Locked** check box. If the icon is shared under the networking function of System 7, it also may be impossible to get the I-beam cursor. From the **File** menu, select **Sharing**, and turn off **File Sharing** (you may need to go to a higher level, such as a file or disk, to turn off file sharing). Some files just can't be renamed; the active System file is an example.

Note You also can double-click to select individual words and use the left- and right-arrow keys to move the insertion point. In System 7, you must click directly on the icon's name to select the name for modification; a box then appears around the name when you select it.

Menus

Menus are lists of actions called *commands* that you can initiate. Macintosh menus were designed by Bill Atkinson in the original Mac system, and they are referred to as *pull-down menus*. You can find menus in the menu bar in

Chapter 3
Exploring the Macintosh System

any Macintosh application; in fact, Apple specifies that every Macintosh menu bar must include at least an **Apple** menu, a **File** menu, and an **Edit** menu, in that order. Other menus can be application-specific.

The command names listed in the menu are called *menu items*. Each menu item appears in black when available and gray when unavailable. To initiate a command, click on the menu title and drag the pointer down until the menu item you want is highlighted. Then release your mouse button. The menu item blinks. (The number of blinks is controlled by the General Controls control panel; menu items can be set to blink zero, one, two, or three times.)

A keyboard equivalent appears next to some menu items. A keyboard equivalent initiates the command using a keystroke, and saves you from displaying the menu and choosing the menu item. When a menu item is followed by an ellipsis (…) symbol, choosing that command brings up a dialog box for you to make more choices. Some programs enable you to change the keystroke assigned to a menu command by either placing the command on the menu or assigning a new sequence to act as the keystroke itself (an *alias*). The process is called *keyboard remapping*. Macro programs such as MacroMaker (System 5 and 6), QuicKeys, and Tempo II also allow remapping. An example of a keyboard remapping appears in the **Edit** menu of Microsoft Word (see figures 3.3 and 3.4).

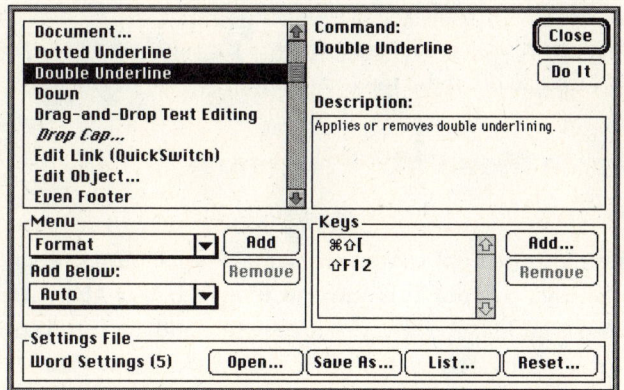

Figure 3.3
Microsoft Word's Commands dialog box enables you to remap commands.

Figure 3.4

QuicKeys can assign menu commands to keystrokes.

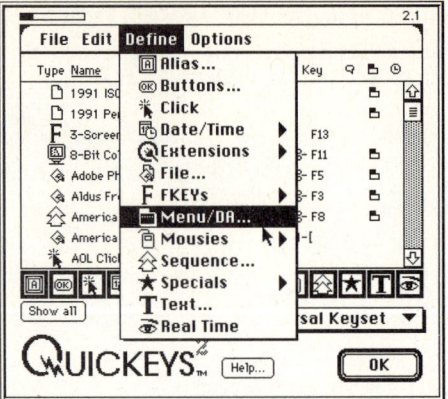

> **Note:** Menus are an attempt to organize sets of commands logically. If you have trouble remembering where to find a command, you may be working with a poorly designed program. As a first step in learning a program, examine all the program's menu items.

You often can learn a lot about the program's construction simply by experimenting.

The **Apple** menu contains desk accessories, and the **File** menu contains commands you can use for file management. System 7 has greatly expanded the use of the **File** menu to include several new functions: networking through the Sharing command, creating icons that point to programs by using the **Make Alias** command, and using a powerful and fast **Find/Find Again** command that replaces the Find File DA in past systems.

The following sections contain summaries of the standard menu commands in System 7 from left to right, top to bottom.

The Apple Menu (All Programs)

The Apple menu contains the following commands:

▼ **About This (...Application)**: Found in all applications. When you are in the Finder, **About This Macintosh** (System 7) or **About The Finder** provides information about your computer and memory usage. Many programs list a **Help** command just below the **About This (...Application)** command.

Everything else in the Apple menu is available in every application. Most Apple menu items are *desk accessories*—small applications like the Calculator and the Note Pad. In System 7, you can put anything in the Apple menu by putting that item (file, folder, or application) in the Apple Menu Items folder. Selecting an item from the Apple menu does the same thing as double-clicking its icon: selecting a folder name opens the folder; selecting an application launches that application; and selecting a file launches the application that created the file (and opens the file within that application).

The File Menu (All Programs)

The **File** menu usually contains the following items:

▼ **New Folder** (Command-N): Using this command in the Finder puts a new folder in the active window to represent a new directory in your file system. In most applications, the analagous command (usually with the same keystroke equivalent) creates a new document within the application.

▼ **Open** (Command-O): Found in almost all applications. In the Finder, this command opens a selected object such as a disk or folder. This command also launches applications from the Finder. In System 7, this command enables you to open documents by dragging them into a compatible application, even if the program is not the creator application. Applications use this command to open documents.

▼ **Print** (Command-P): In the Finder, this command prints all selected (highlighted) documents on the desktop. Each program is launched in turn, as needed, and a **Page Setup and Print** dialog box appears, enabling you to specify your desired print conditions. This is a good way to chain a set of prints together. (See chapter 6, "Printing From Your Macintosh," for more information.) In applications, this command prints the current document.

▼ **Close Window** (Command-W): This command closes the active window in the Finder. This command represents the same action as clicking in a window's close box. If you hold down the Option key before pulling down the **File** menu, this command changes to the **Close All** command, closing all windows on the desktop, which is the same as holding down the Option key and clicking in a window's close box. In applications, the **Close** command closes the current document.

▼ **Get Info** (Command-I): Generally a **Finder** command only. This command displays a dialog box that provides the following basic information about an object, a file, or an application:

Kind: Describes the type of object—disk, application, document, alias, and so on.

Size: Gives the amount of storage space allocated to this object.

Chapter 3
Exploring the
Macintosh System

Part I
Macintosh, the Computer

Where: Displays the location and path of the object in the file system or on the SCSI chain.

Created: Displays the date the disk was formatted or the application was created.

Modified: Tells when the object was last changed.

Version: Gives the current version of an application; the higher the number, the later the program. By convention, a full-number version increase (such as 7.0 versus 6.0) represents a major program improvement, whereas a smaller number change (such as 6.0.5 versus 6.0.7) represents incremental improvements.

Comments: Gives you space to type anything you want to describe the object. You now can search for comments in the Find command. When you rebuild the desktop, however, all comments are erased.

Locked: This check box, when selected, keeps you from making changes to a file. To modify a locked document, use the **Save As...** command.

Stationery Pad: This check box, when selected, locks a document so a copy opens called "Untitled."

Memory, Suggested size: Gives the developer's recommendation for a memory partition.

Memory, Current size: Tells the actual setting for an application's memory partition.

▼ **Sharing**: A Finder command only. This command sets parameters for the Mac's built-in networking capability.

▼ **Duplicate** (Command-D): A Finder command only. This command makes a copy of a selected object and its contents. In System 7, copies are labeled *XXX copy*, *XXX copy2*, and so on.

▼ **Put Away** (Command-Y): A Finder command only. This command puts the selected object back in its respective place (in its folder, for example). This command ejects a selected disk or floppy and removes its icon from the desktop (the same as dragging that icon to the Trash).

▼ **Make Alias**: A Finder command only. This command creates an alias for an application.

▼ **Find** (Command-F): A Finder command only. This command brings up a dialog box that enables you to search your disks for files by several criteria. This powerful command replaces the Find File DA.

▼ **Find Again** (Command-G): A Finder command only. This command repeats the Find command with the previously selected criteria.

▼ **Page Setup**: Found in almost all applications. This command sets the specification of the print job.

▼ **Print Window:** A Finder command. This command prints the contents of the active folder. The **Print Window** command prints the file names, not the file contents, in the active window.

To print a directory of your entire disk (under System 7):

1. Switch to an Outline view (By Name, Date, Kind, and so on) of the disk's main (root) window.
2. Click on the disk icon and press Command-Option-Right Arrow to open all folders.
3. Choose the **Print Window** command.
4. Close all folders by pressing Command-Option-Left Arrow; or switch to an icon view.

The Edit Menu (All Programs)

The **Edit** menu contains the following commands:

▼ **Undo** (Command-Z): Found in all programs. This command reverses the last action.

▼ **Cut** (Command-X): Found in all programs. This command removes selected text (or graphics) and places it on the Clipboard.

▼ **Copy** (Command-C): Found in all programs. This command copies the selected text or graphic and leaves the current selection intact. This command places a copy of the selected text in the Clipboard.

▼ **Paste** (Command-V): Found in all programs. This command places a copy of the current Clipboard contents at the insertion point or, if there is no insertion point, in the center of your window.

▼ **Clear**: Found in all programs. This command removes the current selection without changing the Clipboard.

▼ **Select All** (Command-A): Found in all programs. This command selects all objects in a window.

▼ **Show Clipboard**: Found in most programs. This command puts a window with the current contents of the Clipboard on your screen. In some applications, this command appears in the **Window** menu.

Chapter 3
Exploring the
Macintosh System

The File and Edit menus are common to all Macintosh applications. There are other menus that only apply to the Finder, however; these are the View, Label, and Special menus.

The View Menu (Finder Only)

Each window can have its own view, and some views are more useful in some instances than others. The active view is indicated by a check mark next to a command in the **View** menu, indicating the type of view. The following views are available:

▼ **By Small Icon**: Displays the contents of a window by small icon.

▼ **By Icon**: Displays the contents of a window by large icon.

▼ **By Name**: Gives the Outline view in System 7 (see the section, "Using Windows," later in this chapter). In System 6, displays only names. You can view additional information in a window by using the Views control panel.

▼ **By Size**: Lists the elements of a window by size, with the largest item at the top and the smallest item at the bottom.

In System 7, all objects are listed by size, folders and documents together. If you select the Calculate Folder Sizes option in the Views control panel, the sizes are calculated and shown. In System 6, documents are listed by size and then folders.

▼ **By Kind**: Lists items by the kind of object they are (that is, application, document, folder, and so forth).

▼ **By Date**: Lists items by their previous modification date.

The Label Menu (Finder Only)

The **Label** menu commands, which are available only in System 7, group items by an attribute that you create.

▼ **None** command: No label is assigned.

▼ **Label** command: The seven label names and their assigned colors are given default values. To change the label names and colors, use the Labels control panel (see figure 3.5). To change a color, click in the color patch to bring up the Macintosh color wheel, select a color, and then click OK. To change a label name, select a label and type a new name. You can search for items with a particular label using the Find command on the **File** menu. Some programs such as Aladdin's StuffIt SpaceSaver use labels to compress selected files.

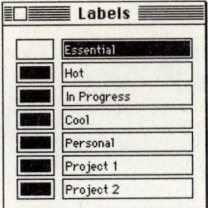

Figure 3.5
The Labels control panel.

The Special Menu (Finder Menu Only)

The **Special** menu contains the following items:

▼ **Clean Up Window**: This command aligns icons to a grid you select in the Views control panel. If icons are selected or if the Shift key is held down, the command changes to the Clean Up Selection command and only selected icons are aligned. If the Option key is held down, the menu item changes to **Clean Up by Name**—or **by Date**, or **by Kind**.... The specific cleanup type is determined by the last selection from the Views menu, excluding Icon and Small Icon.

▼ **Empty Trash**: This command deletes the contents of the Trash. A warning dialog box asks whether you want to complete this action; click **OK** to proceed. If you want to bypass the warning, hold down the Option key before selecting the command. In System 7, if you always want to bypass the warning, select the Trash icon, from the **File** menu select **Get Info**, and uncheck the **Warn Before Emptying** box in the dialog box.

WARNING! Although bypassing the warning seems convenient, you should think twice before doing so. You can avoid accidentally deleting that one important document mistakenly left in a file folder that was placed in the trash. In System 6, the Trash empties automatically at shutdown and other times without your involvement. In System 7, you must choose this command specifically to empty the Trash.

Note: **Emptying the Trash** does not erase files—it only removes the file names from the list of active files. You can often use a file recovery utility such as Symantec Utilities for the Macintosh (SUM), Norton Utilities, or Central Point Software's MacTools Deluxe to recover (undelete) files. Of course, if a new file writes over part of a trashed file, it is too late to save the original.

▼ **Eject Disk** (Command-E): This command removes the floppy disk from the disk drive but leaves the disk icon on the desktop for further

Part I
Macintosh, the Computer

manipulation. Using this command is the same as pressing Command-Shift-1 (eject the first internal floppy disk) or Command-Shift-2 (eject the second floppy disk).

▼ **Erase Disk**: This command formats a floppy disk according to the disk's maximum capacity.

▼ **Restart**: This command closes all applications, queries you about needed saves, shuts down your computer, and then restarts.

▼ **Shut Down**: This command shuts down all applications, queries you about needed saves, and then shuts down your computer.

▼ **Sleep** : This command appears on all PowerBooks. It spins down your hard drive, blanks the display, and powers down the microprocessor. Hit any key (other than the Caps Lock key) to activate all of these functions again.

The Balloon Help Menu (All Programs)

The Balloon Help menu (see figure 2.6) appears in all programs. It is represented by a balloon icon with a question mark in it. It contains the following items:

Figure 3.6
The **Help** menu.

▼ **About Balloon Help**: Contained in all programs under System 7. When activated, Balloon Help explains various features or objects. A balloon appears whenever you place your pointer or cursor above the object. Not all applications support Balloon Help.

▼ **Sh**ow **(Hide) Balloons**: Found in all programs under System 7. This command turns balloons on and off, acting as a toggle switch (see figure 3.7).

Figure 3.7
The activated Balloon Help feature.

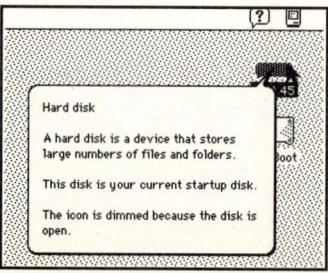

▼ **Finder Shortcuts**: Found in the Finder only. This command shows keystroke shortcuts in a window (see figure 3.8). Programs upgraded to System 7 are placing their Help menu items in this window. Figure 3.0 shows a Microsoft Excel **Help** command.

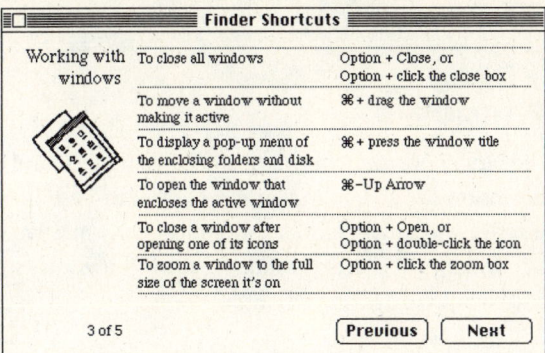

Figure 3.8
The Finder Shortcuts window.

The Application Menu (All Programs)

The Application menu is represented by the rightmost icon in the menu bar. The icon used is a small version of the Finder icon for the current active program. The following items are found in the Application menu:

▼ **Hide Finder (Application)**: Found in all programs under System 7. This command closes all opened windows of a program and switches to the next program open in the **Application** menu (alphabetically).

▼ **Hide Others**: Found in all programs under System 7. This command hides all other program windows while keeping your current application active. It cuts down on window clutter. Hidden windows are still in memory and open quickly; they also use up more memory. Closing windows releases this memory. Two shareware utilities, ZoomBar and WindowShade (both control panels), are useful for removing window clutter in System 6.

▼ **Show All**: Found in all programs under System 7. This command opens all application windows held in memory onscreen.

▼ **Application name**: Found in all programs under System 7. Listed at the bottom of the Application menu are the names of all applications currently running. The application currently in use is indicated by a check mark next to the application name (see figure 3.9). To work with a different application, select its name. If you hold the Option key before choosing another application, your Mac hides all other applications' windows.

Figure 3.9

The Application menu.

Using Windows

Windows in the Finder are your view into a disk, its folders, and documents. Elements of a window are shown in figure 3.10. You can use only one window—the active window—at a time, although many inactive windows can appear on your desktop. The active window has six horizontal stripes in its title bar; inactive windows are grayed out.

Figure 3.10

The elements of a Macintosh window.

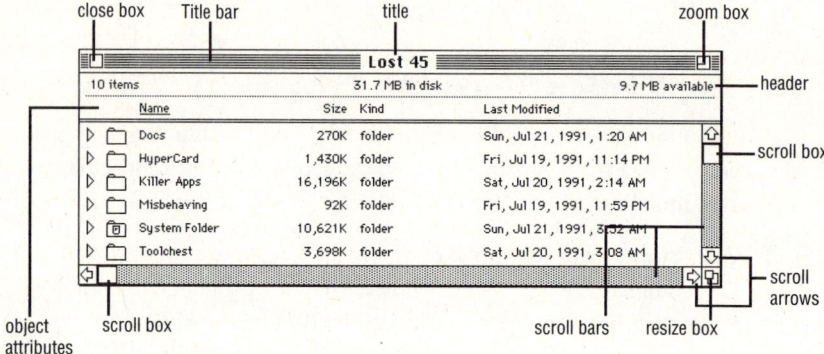

The following list explains window elements and how to use them.

▼ Title bar: Click and drag the Title bar to move a window. To move an inactive window without making it active, hold the Command key while clicking and dragging.

▼ Window title: This item is the name of the disk or folder that contains the objects in the windows.

 To see the current path of any window, hold the Command key and click the Title name. This displays a pop-up menu of all the folders that contain the current folder. You can open one of the "parent folders" by selecting its name from the pop-up menu

▼ Window header: This optional section of a window is turned on in the Views control panel. It shows the number of items in the folder and the amount of unused storage.

Chapter 3
Exploring the Macintosh System

▼ Object attributes: This header is controlled by the settings selected in the Views control panel. At the minimum, the name of the objects appear. Other attributes that can be shown are Size, Kind, Label, Date Created, (date) Last Modified, Version, and Comments.

▼ Close box: Click this close box in the upper left corner to close the active window. To close an inactive window, click the window once to activate it and then again in the close box. To close all windows on the desktop, hold the Option key and click the close box.

▼ Zoom box: Click the zoom box in the upper right corner to toggle between a larger window and a smaller one.

> **Note**
> In System 7, the smaller window size is either the size you set or the smallest size that contains all icons and data. The larger size is either the size you set or the minimum size needed to show all contents in the window. In System 6, the toggle is between the size you set and the size of your monitor.

▼ Resize box: Click and drag the Resize box in the lower right corner to resize a window.

▼ Scroll box: The scroll boxes on the right and bottom sides of the window indicate the position of the view of a window's contents. Click and drag the scroll box to move around in the window.

▼ Scroll bar: The scroll bar on the right side of the window is gray when there is additional information not shown in the window. If the scroll bar is unshaded and has no scroll box, no other information exists beyond the window. Click once above the scroll box to move the contents of the window up one windowful, or click below the scroll box to move the contents down one windowful.

▼ Scroll arrow: Click the scroll arrow at the bottom and top of the scroll bar once to move a small amount in one direction. In word processors you move a single line; in spreadsheets, a single row. If you get tired of moving up and down to use the scroll arrows, you can use the shareware program Scroll2, which puts a double-headed arrow at each corner of the window.

System 7 instituted a new kind of scrolling called *autoscrolling*. If you click and drag past a scroll bar, the window moves and scrolls for you.

In System 7, the Views control panel is the key to modifying your windows' appearance (see figure 3.11). You can control several features, including the following:

Figure 3.11

The Views control panel is the key to modifying your windows' appearance.

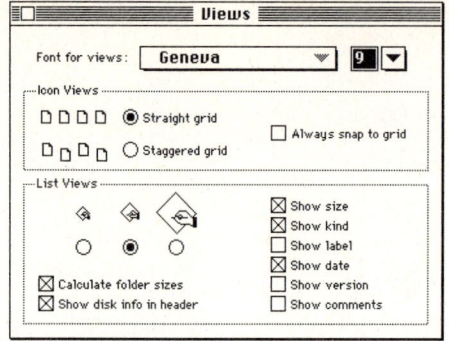

▼ Font for views: Enables you to change the font and font size used for the icon names. To enter a font size other than that shown, type it in.

▼ Icon Views: Sets a grid to align icons. When you use the **Clean Up Window** or **Selection** command from the **Special** menu, the icons align to the grid you set. If you always want icons you drag or create to align to that grid, click the **Always Snap to Grid** check box. If you want to align to the grid when Icon View is off or defeat the grid when it is on, hold the Command key while dragging.

▼ List Views: Enables you to control the types and amount of information displayed in an outline window (one shown by name, kind, size, label, or date). Click the check box next to the size of the icon you want to display.

Note: Checking the **Calculate Folder Sizes** box tells your Mac to indicate the sizes of all folders. Your Mac displays a window before all sizes are calculated but adds the sizes in the window as it calculates them, a task that occurs in the background. This calculation slows down your Mac, so turn off the feature if you do not need it and if speed is an issue. Turning off this feature can also be important when you want to improve your battery lifetime for a PowerBook. Checking the **Show Disk Info in Header** box tells you how much is stored in your disk, and how much free space you have.

The file attributes have been described in a previous section (see the section, "The **View** Menu," above). Turn the attributes on by clicking on the check box to insert an X; click again to remove the X and turn the attributes off. The more attributes that are checked, the wider the window required to contain them all.

The Mouse

The mouse was invented at the Stanford Research Institute (SRI) by Douglas Englebart in the early 1970s. However, its introduction with the Macintosh personal computer in 1984 is its strongest association in most people's minds.

The mouse is a *relative* pointing device: when you move around the screen with your mouse, your motion is relative to the location where you started to move. If you pick up your mouse, your position onscreen remains unchanged. When you put your mouse down and move it again, your motion onscreen begins in the same place but again is relative to the motion of the mouse on your desk. A graphics tablet is an example of an *absolute* pointing device because each point on the tablet corresponds to a pixel on-screen.

You can control the speed of a double-click by changing the setting in the Mouse control panel (see figure 3.12). It would be tedious to move the mouse 6 inches for every six inches the pointer moves onscreen, so different acceleration factors are applied. When you move the mouse a little, not much acceleration is applied, so you can make fine adjustments. When you move the mouse rapidly, the pointer moves faster than the mouse, which makes it easier for you to move the pointer long distances across the screen. To avoid the acceleration settings, there is a graphics tablet setting.

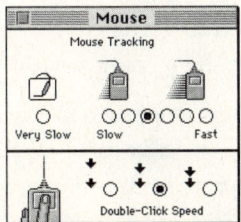

Mice with two or more buttons, without a ball (optical mice), without wires (*infrared* mice), *ergonomically* shaped (instead of shaped like a small brick), and other similar variations are available from third-party manufacturers. You generally can use a trackball—a mouse turned upside down that conserves precious desk space—for everything except detailed graphics. Trackballs are found in PowerBooks, and as Apple Desktop Bus (ADB) devices. Kensington makes a highly regarded desktop trackball for your desktop Macintosh. You can adjust the speed of motion for many third-party mice and trackballs in a control panel supplied with the device.

Chapter 3
Exploring the Macintosh System

Figure 3.12
The Mouse control panel.

Part I
Macintosh, the Computer

The Keyboard

Several varieties of Apple keyboards are available; unlike typewriter keyboards, computer keyboards feature some special keys that change the functions of alphabetic and numeric keys. Modifier keys are particularly important. There are four important keys:

▼ Command key: This key, designated with the Apple and/or Command (cloverleaf) symbol, is used for keystroke equivalents for menu items, and for other special operations.

▼ Shift key: This key serves a similar function to the Shift key on a typewriter: it creates uppercase symbols.

▼ Option key: Use this key in combination with the Command key to create special keystroke combinations. This key is also used to create special characters, such as letters for foreign languages (î, ü, and é, for instance), uncommon typographical symbols (™, ®, and ¢); and other special characters (such as • and).

▼ Control key: Rarely used on a Mac, the key is available mainly for running IBM-style programs on a Macintosh. Some keyboards lack this key.

You also can press modifier keys in combination to create new keystrokes. For example, a Command-Shift-3 combination is different from Command-3 (or Shift-3). This combination also is different from Command-Shift-Num 3, where Num 3 is the 3 key on the numeric keypad.

With so many keys, how are you supposed to remember where to find all of them? Luckily, Apple provides a desk accessory called Key Caps to help you remember. To open Key Caps, select the Key Caps command from the Apple menu. Hold down the modifier keys (Command, Shift, Option, or combinations of those keys) that you want to test. The resulting key symbols appear on the miniature keyboard in the window (see figure 3.13). (See chapter 9, "Fonts and Typography," for more information on how to use Key Caps.)

Note: One alternative to Key Caps is a shareware keyboard-mapping extension called PopChar (see figure 3.14). PopChar displays a pop-up box when you click on the upper left corner of the screen. The box shows all possible characters and symbols, and you click and drag to highlight the symbol you want to use. Norton Utilities ships with a similar character set-displaying utility.

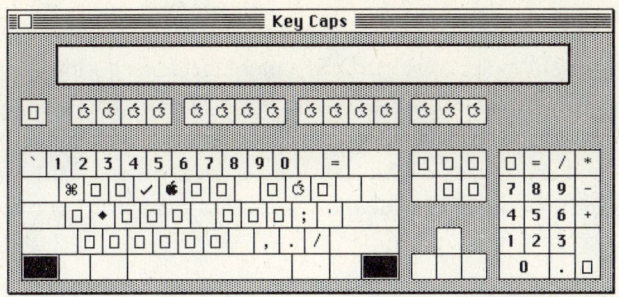

Figure 3.13

The Key Caps desk accessory, with the Chicago font selected and the Option key pressed, illustrates the special characters available.

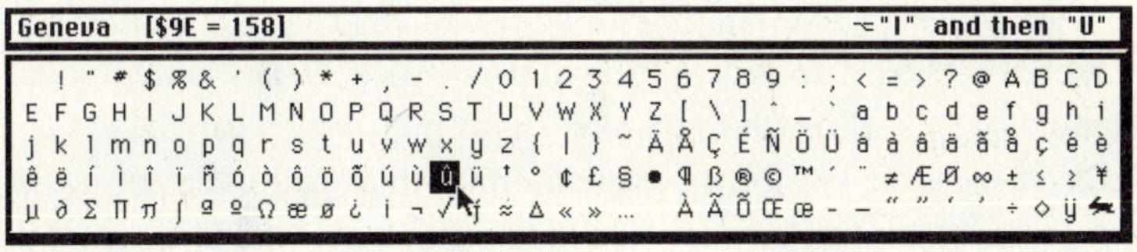

Figure 3.14

PopChar provides an alternative to Key Caps.

Other special keys exist on a Mac keyboard. These include arrow keys for moving around, the Backspace or Delete key for removing characters, and the Return and Enter keys for hard carriage returns (end of lines) and other entries.

Extended keyboards have an Esc (Escape) key at the upper left corner of the keyboard and a Power key that turns on your computer at the upper right. A set of function keys labeled F1 through F15 appear across the top of the extended keyboard. Using a macro or keyboard remapping program such as QuicKeys, or Tempo II, you can assign commands to function keys as shortcuts. A set of keys labeled Help, Del, Home, End, Page Up, and Page Down also are available for your specification, but applications such as word processors most often assign those keys specific functions related to the key names. None of these keys is found on the keyboard of the PowerBook series of portable computers.

Lastly, a numeric keypad is located on the extended keyboard. PowerBooks keyboards also lack this feature, although you can buy third party numeric keypads (ADB devices) to attach to your PowerBook. The extended keyboard sometimes is called an *AT-styled* keyboard, because it is based on a keyboard developed by IBM for the IBM AT. Alternatively, it also is referred to as the *101 keyboard* because of the number of keys.

Part I
Macintosh, the Computer

> **Note:** Some people dislike the "spongy" feel of the Apple keyboard, and wish Apple's keyboard had a more tactile feel, with a positive click and mechanical sound for each keystroke. These preferences led Apple to change the feel of the original Apple Extended keyboard to include a tactile click feel. The Datadesk Switchboard and other keyboards from Datadesk provide these features for the Mac—one also comes in a silent version.

There has been a movement underway to improve the ergonomics of keyboards to prevent repetitive stress injuries. To address this issue, Apple created the Adjustable Keyboard. This keyboard hinges in the middle—splitting the keyboard according to what hand types the key in traditional touch typing. The split enables the user to keep his hands parallel to his arms, decreasing the tension on the tendons. A third part of the keyboard, including the numerical keypad and the function keys, is separate from the rest and attaches with a short cable.

Dialog and Alert Boxes

Dialog boxes are the Mac's way of asking you to specify additional information it needs to complete a task. A good dialog box is like a form: you simply fill in the blanks. Dialog boxes use buttons, check boxes, and text boxes to request your input. Dialog boxes, by convention, always appear when a you select a command that has an ellipsis following the command name.

The elements of a dialog box are shown in figure 3.15. They include the following:

- ▼ Buttons: You click a button to perform an action ("Options"). A button that has a double line around it is the default button. You can press Return or Enter to activate the default button. Buttons with ellipses in the name lead you to another dialog box. Pressing Command-Period usually activates the Cancel button, closing the dialog box without saving or incorporating changes.

- ▼ Check boxes: Check boxes enable you turn options on or off ("Text Smoothing?"). Clicking on a check box places an X in the box, indicating that option will be used. You may click some, all, or none of the members of a set of check boxes.

- ▼ Radio buttons: A set of radio buttons indicates an exclusive choice ("Print now" or "Print later"). Radio buttons work like the buttons on a car radio—you can select only one at a time. Click on the radio button of the option you want; a dot will appear in the circle representing the button.

▼ Text boxes: You enter numbers or text in a selected text box ("Print how many copies?"). Pressing the Tab key moves you to the next text box in succession (left to right, top to bottom). The Shift-Tab keystroke moves you backward.

▼ Pop-up menus: Click and hold to display a list of choices ("Select the paper size:"). Drag down to highlight the desired choice and then release the mouse button to activate that command.

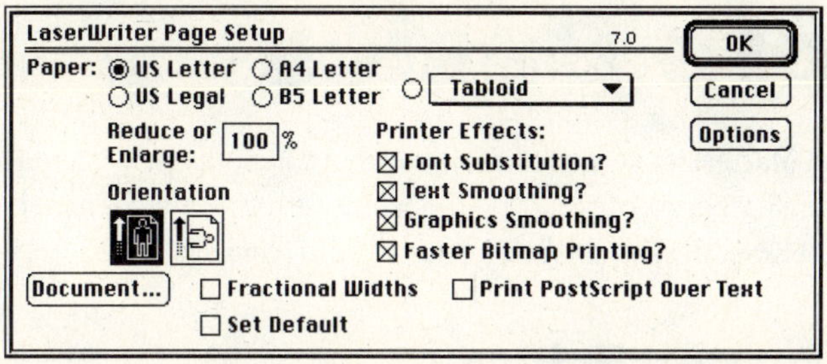

Chapter 3
Exploring the Macintosh System

Figure 3.15
The **Page Setup** dialog box offers check boxes, radio buttons, pop-up menus, and icon selections.

Most dialog boxes are *modal*:—they require you to make a choice before carrying out an action, so you are in that mode of action. When you choose the **Print** command and the **Print** dialog box appears, you can't do anything else until you deal with the Print dialog box—either Print or Cancel.

Some dialog boxes are modeless: actions can be performed while the dialog box is on-screen. You can identify a modeless dialog box by its title bar: you can drag and move it around the screen. Also, you can often work in other programs when a modeless dialog box appears on-screen (see figure 3.16).

Figure 3.16
A modeless **Copy** dialog box.

Although *alert boxes* look similar to dialog boxes, they serve a different function. Alert boxes inform you of a condition that is about to occur or is occurring and may need your attention. Alert boxes generally only offer you one or two buttons, rather than the plethora of options in dialog boxes. An alert box allows you to gracefully exit a potentially damaging action. For example, the **Empty Trash...** command displays an alert box requesting your

77

attention before it deletes files. By convention, the least damaging action is the default choice. For the **Trash** alert box, the least damaging action is to cancel the deletion; therefore, the **Cancel** button is the default button. Alert boxes are a subset of dialog boxes, and they also use the Dialog Manager.

Alert boxes are modal dialog boxes. Caution, Note, and Stop are common icons used in dialog boxes and are represented by an exclamation mark, question mark, and raised hand icon, respectively. Many alert boxes also beep or buzz when the box is displayed and when you click outside the alert box.

More Basics

Additional Mac basics you need to know about include the System folder, the System file, System resources, System extensions, the control panel, the start-up order, FKeys, desk accessories, sounds, and aliases.

The System Folder

The System folder is easy to spot because it has a small Mac icon on the folder. The active system you use to boot your Mac has an icon on it. Apple programmers refer to such a System folder as *blessed*. Only one folder can be blessed, but with System 7, all potentially useful System folders appear with the Mac icon.

Your System folder contains a number of files that are used to configure your Macintosh and make it operate properly. When your Mac boots, it looks for a folder with the word "System" in it; therefore, using the name System folder, System ƒ, or even System alone enables your Mac to function properly. However it is good practice to have only one System folder, one System file, and one Finder file on your boot drive or your Mac might get confused and become unstable.

A Closer Look If you have multiple versions of the System on your hard disk (such as if you need both System 6 and System 7 at different times), you can use the Freeware utility System Picker to select the System that will be used when you restart. Using System Picker, you can switch between different System folders as necessary; however, you will have to restart the Mac each time you switch.

Chapter 3

Exploring the Macintosh System

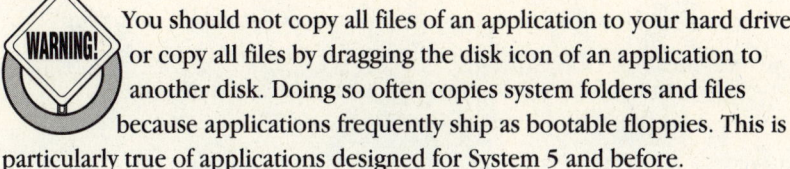

WARNING! You should not copy all files of an application to your hard drive or copy all files by dragging the disk icon of an application to another disk. Doing so often copies system folders and files because applications frequently ship as bootable floppies. This is particularly true of applications designed for System 5 and before.

Prior to System 7, all needed file additions to your system were placed at the top level of the System folder. You scrolled around a folder with a hundred or so items, looking for the file about which you needed information.

System 7 introduced a number of enhancements in the System folder's operation, including some automatic features to clean up System folder clutter. The System folder contains a set of folders to hold special files. If the special folders listed below are missing from your Macintosh upon start-up, your system software will create them automatically.

The following are special folders in the System 7 folder:

▼ **Apple Menu Items:** Any item you want to appear in the Apple menu is placed in this folder. This includes any desk accessories, applications, or aliases of applications, folders, or files you want to access. An alias placed in the Apple Menu Items folder appears in standard Chicago text on the Apple menu—not in italics as the alias would appear on your desktop.

▼ **Control Panels:** Any control panel device is placed in this folder. The alias of the Control Panels folder contained within the Apple Menu Items folder provides a convenient way to access your control panels.

▼ **Extensions:** All printer drivers, start-up documents (INITs), PostScript fonts, and other extensions are meant to reside in this folder.

▼ **Fonts:** This folder (available with System 7.1) contains the fonts that your System uses. Fonts placed in the font folder are available to any program.

▼ **Preferences:** Applications are supposed to write their *preference* files, files that keep information determining how a program works on your Mac, to files that reside in this folder. It will be a while before all applications are upgraded to take advantage of this feature, so System folder clutter lives on, at least for the near future.

▼ **PrintMonitor Documents:** This folder contains files spooled to the PrintMonitor utility. It is empty when there are no files in the print queue.

Part I
Macintosh,
the Computer

▼ **Start-up Items:** Place any program you want launched at start-up inside this folder (placing an alias of that file in this folder is more convenient). The Start-up folder replaces the Set Start-up command in Systems 5 and 6.

A Closer Look If you drag new files onto your System folder icon, your Mac attempts to determine where these files should be placed by examining the *file type* flag, which is part of every file written. RDEVs are placed in the Extensions folder, CDEVs are placed in the Control Panels folder, and so on (see figure 3.17). You can move different types of files simultaneously with the same move or copy. A dialog box appears asking your permission to allow automatic placement, and another appears after placement to tell you what was done. Your System folder now has smarts!

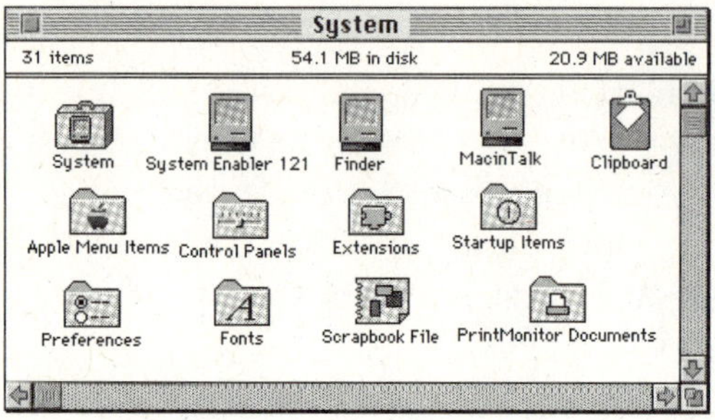

Figure 3.17
System 7's System folder is more intuitive than the System folder in previous systems.

The System File

Your System file largely serves as a repository of *system resources*. Until System 7, the only way you could get into your System file was to open it with a special program called Font/DA Mover. The System file contains fonts (before System 7.1), alert sounds, desk accessories (System 6 and before), keyboard layouts, and script systems for foreign languages. Your system requires some of these resources to operate. For example, there must always be one alert sound (or standard beep sound). Every additional resource you install makes your System file larger and makes your System take up more of your Mac's memory.

System Resources and System 6

To add or subtract system resources in System 6 and before, use utilities designed for that purpose. The Font/DA Mover adds fonts and desk accessories to the System file (Version 4.1 is the first version that properly handles TrueType outline fonts, fonts introduced with System 7). To add fonts or desk accessories:

1. Launch Font/DA Mover. A screen similar to the one shown in Figure 3.18 appears.

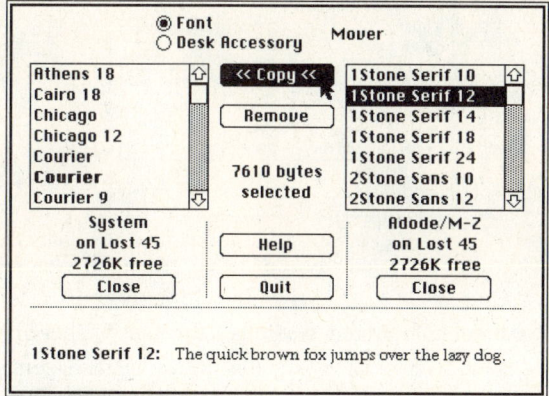

Chapter 3
Exploring the Macintosh System

Figure 3.18
The Font/DA Mover.

2. Click on the **DA** radio button to see desk accessories.
3. Click the **Open** button, navigate the Hierarchical File System, and select the file that has the resources you want to move in one window.
4. Repeat the procedure and open the file to which you want to move the resource in the other window. Keep in mind you can open not only your System file, but font, desk accessory, Suitcase, and even application files. To open an application file (or HyperCard stack), hold down the Option key before clicking the Open button.
5. Select the name(s) of the system resources you want to move. If an individual font file is selected, a sample of that font is shown for you to examine. Font/DA Mover tells you the size of the selection you have made, and the free space available on the volume(s).
6. Click the **Copy** button.
7. If you want to remove system resources, select these files and click the **Remove** button.
8. Reboot your machine for the changes to take effect.

> **Note** You can use resources outside your System file as if they were system resources by accessing them in a Suitcase file. A Suitcase file is an enclosure, like a folder, that contains either fonts or desk accessories. To access Suitcase files as if they were part of your System file, you need a type of software, called a resource manager, such as Fifth Generation's Suitcase II or AlSoft's MasterJuggler (see figure 3.19).

Figure 3.19

Suitcase II manages system resources.

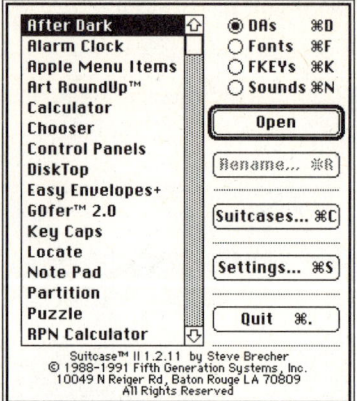

Resource manager programs were originally created to work around Apple's artificial limit of 15 fonts and 15 DAs on the System file in System versions 1 through 5. They are nearly indispensable for those systems. Resource managers keep the size of your System file small and are also more convenient for managing system resources than Font/DA Mover. These benefits have not disappeared in System 7. You can use resource managers to keep your System file to its minimum size, making it easier to manage.

System Resources and System 7

System 7 changes and simplifies the management of system resources. You add sounds (or keyboard layouts) directly to the System file by dragging them onto the System file icon. If you move sounds or keyboard layouts onto a closed System folder icon, your Macintosh asks permission to place them in the System file automatically.

You can double-click on the System file to open it and examine the resources it contains. Not all resources are viewable—only the ones you can move (see figure 3.20). Double-clicking on a sound plays that sound. Your changes take effect immediately.

You cannot move Suitcase files into a System 7 file, although you can use Suitcase in other folders with resource managers. If you double-click on a Suitcase within System 7, it opens to reveal all its enclosed font or DA files (see figure 3.21). You can then move them into your System folder—to the Apple Menu Items folder or the Fonts folder, as appropriate. You can also copy suitcase files into the Font folder within your System folder. System 7.1 knows how to use suitcases it finds in the Font folder. To create new Suitcase files, use Font/DA Mover 4.1 or make a copy using the **Duplicate** command (Command D) on the **Edit** menu.

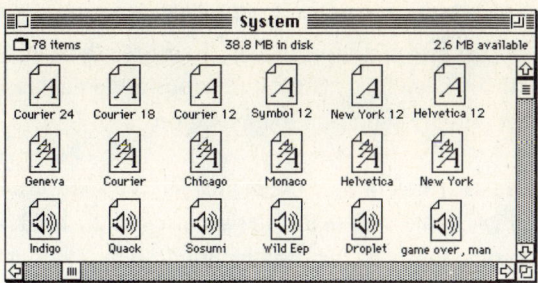

Figure 3.20
Some of the possible resources for the System file, under System 7.0.

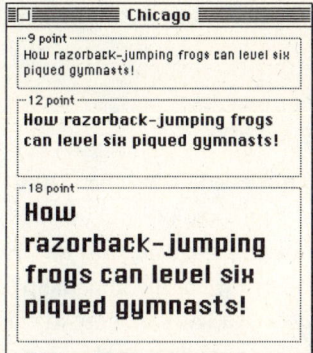

Figure 3.21
This is a sample of the Chicago outline font, as displayed when the font file is double-clicked.

System 7 requires a new sound format to work with previously recorded alert sound files. A shareware conversion utility called Sound Converter has been introduced to make the appropriate translation.

System Enablers

Prior to System 7.1, Apple introduced new versions of the system software with incremental version changes. For example, System 6.0 was followed by 6.0.1, 6.0.3, 6.0.5, and 6.0.7 to accommodate new Macintosh computers. Apple decided to begin introducing new system software components as modular pieces of software, so that you can expect to see new printing architectures, multimedia extensions, AppleScript, and other enhancements as individual products. This is done to lower the time required to bring new software advances to market.

A new system software file called the System Enabler was introduced to make your System compatible with new software modules, and to make the System file compatible with new Macintosh computers. For example, all PowerBooks other than the original 100, 140, and 170 computers require a System Enabler, as does the Mac IIvx, the Centris models, and other new Macs. The enablers are a good idea because they eliminate the slew of System software releases. When a new Mac is released, all Apple has to do is include an enabler file for that model. Unfortunately, the System Enabler files are numbered with a scheme that bears no relationship to the Macintosh computers that they are supposed to be used on.

WARNING! You can think of the System Enabler as a super-Extension file (see below). The System Enabler is placed in the top level of your System folder by the Installer application. Without that System Enabler in your System folder, you will probably get crashes, abnormal behavior, and even fatal software errors (a Sad Mac appears upon start-up). Remember, not all Macintosh computers require the use of this new system file.

System Extensions

The System file often requires additional files to customize it for individual circumstances. It would be impossible and unwieldy for Apple to accommodate all configurations that users might want. Not every person uses the same printer, the same network, or the same help files. Also, there are often small programs or *patches* that you can write to correct flaws in the system software or to add extra functionality. Apple often adds functionality as an extension file to the system first before adding it to the System file itself later. Some of these programs are placed in the Extensions folder within the System folder in System 7. Others appear in the Control Panels folder. (In System 6 and before, all system extensions appear in the top level of the System folder.)

There are actually three main types of system extensions:

▼ Chooser extensions, or RDEVs

▼ True extensions, or INITs

▼ Control panel devices, or CDEVs

These small programs are often identified by their four-letter file type, although it is more correct to refer to them by their names. Your system uses the codes to determine correct placement and behavior.

Each printer, plotter, fax/modem, etc. requires a program called a *printer driver* to translate the graphics language used for page description (QuickDraw or PostScript) to a set of codes the output device understands. Apple supplies some of these for its own printers; they are the files chosen in the Chooser. If you purchase your own third-party device, it normally comes with its own driver. Chooser-level device drivers are called RDEVs and include many types of printers, modems, faxes, network drivers, and others. As you can see in figure 3.22, these files reside in the Extensions folder.

The Chooser sets your current output device (see figure 3.23). If you remove the Chooser from the System folder, your output device cannot be changed until you return the Chooser to the System folder.

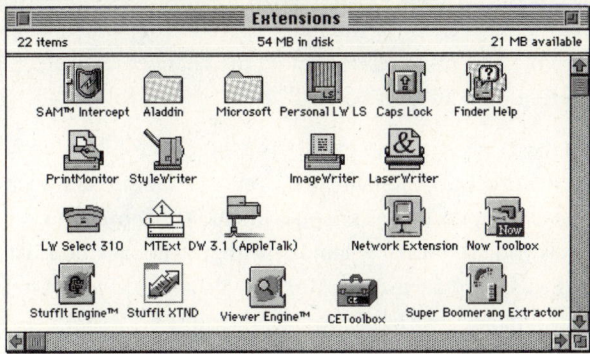

Chapter 3
Exploring the Macintosh System

Figure 3.22
The Extensions folder.

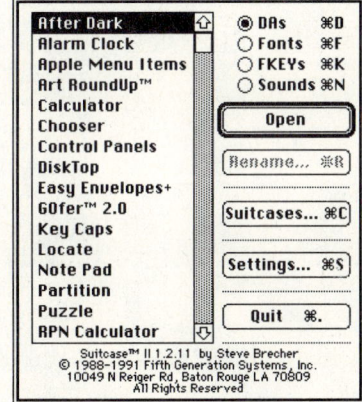

Figure 3.23
The Chooser displays the RDEVs found in your Extensions folder and allows you to select one.

> **Note:** Other peripherals such as hard drives or removable disk drives also require device drivers, particularly to mount (show up) on the desktop. If you have an INIT for this purpose and your drive still does not mount, try using SCSI Tools, SCSI Probe, or the Mount 'Em FKey. If a peripheral is still troublesome and you do not have a loose connection or other hardware problem, the problem is likely a missing or incompatible driver. Software incompatibilities are an unfortunate fact of computing life, and many times their correction is one step removed from sorcery.

In addition to drivers, you can add many small programs to the System file to customize it. Originally called INITs in Systems 6 and before, these programs reside at the top level of the System folder. They are called Extensions in System 7 and are placed in the Extensions folder.

85

Part I

Macintosh, the Computer

The Control Panel

Another extension to the System is called a control panel device, or CDEV. Control panels are like extensions, but they require user interaction to set preferences. After you make these settings, they are written to the control panel file. Sometimes changes you make to a control panel take immediate effect; sometimes you must reboot before the changes take effect. If rebooting is required, an alert box will appear to tell you so.

Control panels are generally accessed from the Control Panels folder in System 7 (see figure 3.24). Usually, the Control Panels folder is opened by selecting Control Panels from the Apple menu. Apple provides several control panels you are probably familiar with, including Color, Easy Access, General Controls, Keyboard, Map, Monitor, Mouse, Sound, Start-up Disk, and others. Control panel devices are shown in figures 3.25 and 3.26.

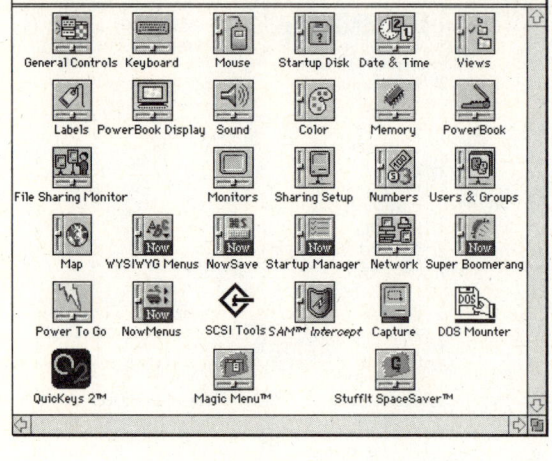

Figure 3.24
Double-click on a control panel to open it in System 7.

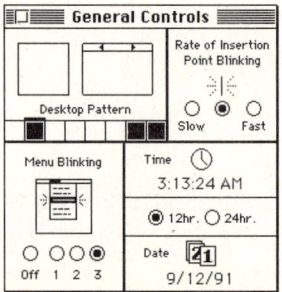

Figure 3.25
The General Controls control panel in System 7.

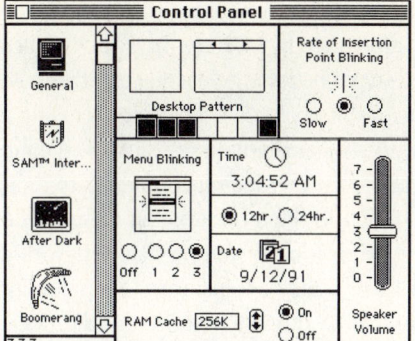

Figure 3.26
The General control panel in System 6.0.7.

There are times when you do not want anyone tampering with your Mac. If you move the General Controls out of the System folder or delete it, no one is able to change these settings. However, if you move or delete your Mouse file, your Mac does not respond to mouse movements and the pointer gets stuck in the start-up position in the upper left corner of the screen. (If your mouse pointer is frozen, the trouble can also be a loose ADB connection or, more seriously, a damaged ADB chip on the mother board—a fatal and expensive repair.)

The Start-up Order

Extensions and control panels load at start-up; many display start-up icons at the bottom of your start-up screen. Watch the order in which these icons appear on your screen: they indicate which file is being loaded at the moment. An icon with an X through it is loaded as an inactive file.

Not all extensions and control panels show start-up icons, and some allow you to choose whether an icon is loaded. Because this icon display does not affect the start-up time, it is always a good idea to display the icons so you know what is happening. Keep in mind that loading more extensions and control panels takes more time at start-up—and, more importantly, forces the System to consume more memory. Fonts, alert sounds, and other configurable System resources all consume memory.

The popular After Dark screensaver consumes memory; after all, it is a control panel. But its modules consume memory, too—even when not in use. If you have a full complement of twenty or thirty modules, After Dark can consume quite a chunk of memory. Remove any modules that you never use from the After Dark Items folder; you can always add them later if you want to.

Apple specifies rules of programming that, in principle, allow INITs to peacefully coexist. Unfortunately, *INIT conflicts* (now called Extension conflicts) are a source of considerable headaches. If your Mac exhibits strange behavior, such as unexplained crashes or refusing to start up at all, one of the first items to look at is your extensions and control panels. The recommended procedure for debugging conflicts is to remove all extensions (and control panels) and add them back one at a time. Of course, if you recently added a new extension, try adding that item with different combinations of your previously added extensions. This procedure may uncover the conflict. You may also try moving items to another location in the System folder. For example, version 2.0.1 of Adobe Type Manager and PostScript Type 1 fonts must be placed at the top level of the System folder to function properly, Sometimes the order that files load can make a difference; Boomerang requires placement at the end of your start-up sequence. Extensions load alphabetically, so change the name of an extension to change its order in the loading process.

 A control panel such as Extensions Manager (Freeware by Ricardo Bautista and available through Apple) turns extensions and control panels on and off with a double-click and enables you to troubleshoot INIT conflicts.

Collections of user-discovered conflicts can be found on electronic bulletin boards, but since these problems change often and are machine specific, such collections often cannot solve every user's problems. You can call the company that sells the product and ask for the company's help. If your offending program is shareware, check the documents that came with it. You can send a note to the author, often that person doesn't have the time to respond—after all, not many people make a living writing shareware!

With System 6, it was simple to work with the start-up order because all items load in alphanumeric order, top to bottom in the System folder. In System 7, there is a specific start-up order that makes debugging INIT conflicts a bit more difficult. In System 7, system extensions load in three groups: first, extensions in the Extensions folder; second, extensions found in the Control Panels folder; and finally, those found in the System folder itself.

The System 7 start-up order can cause some problems, especially with older programs. You can defeat this order to a degree by putting an alias of the extension in the folder in which you want to have it start up. To put items high on the list, use a space; to make an item appear at the end, use the tilde (~) symbol. Try moving control panels with spaces to the Extensions folder and those with tildes to the top level of the System folder. You can add aliases to the Control Panels folder to give you easy access to them.

FKeys

FKeys are small programs that install in your System file. Some FKeys are a standard part of the System; others are installed into the System. To run an FKey program, use a Command Shift (Number) keyboard combination. This means you can have only 10 possible FKeys, and because the Mac comes with three standard FKeys that you cannot replace, there are actually only seven available. The following are the three standard FKeys:

▼ Command Shift 1 ejects the floppy disk from drive 1.

▼ Command Shift 2 ejects the floppy disk from drive 2.

For systems such as the Mac SE with two disk drives, FKey 1 is used for the lower drive and FKey 2 is used for the upper drive. On a dual-disk-drive Mac II or IIx, FKey 1 is used for the left drive and FKey 2 is used for the right.

▼ Command Shift 3 takes a *screen shot*, a snapshot of your screen. In System 7, you hear a camera shutter action sound. The entire screen is captured to a PICT file. In System 6 and earlier, this FKey made a MacPaint file and did not work with Macs set above the 1-bit color (or black and white only).

If you take multiple screen shots, they are named Picture 1, Picture 2, etc. Use commercial or shareware products such as Capture, Exposure Pro, SnapJot or FlashIt! for partial screen shots, showing exposed menus, and creating different file formats other than PICT.

There are many FKeys in the public domain; the programs are so small that there are few to none offered for sale. Check your local BBS or the online services for a selection. The following are some FKeys you may find useful:

▼ Mount 'Em: Mounts SCSI drives.

▼ Pad Lock FKey: Sets and requires a password to display your screen. It is easily defeated by rebooting; however, it tells you if your Mac has been tampered with.

▼ Rotate FKey: Switches applications in System 7.

▼ SetSound FKey: Enables you to set the sound level of your Mac.

▼ Switch-A-Roo: Changes the colors of your monitor (see figure 3.27).

There are several ways to install FKeys. You can install them using Suitcase 2 and MasterJuggler. If you use these utilities, you have to accept the default FKey setting in that file. Two shareware offerings, FKey Mover and FKey Manager, are among the most useful programs for installing and removing FKeys from your System file. FKey Manager also enables you to assign FKey

Chapter 3
Exploring the Macintosh System

numbers and rename files. It is the utility of choice, and it works properly with System 7 (see figure 3.28).

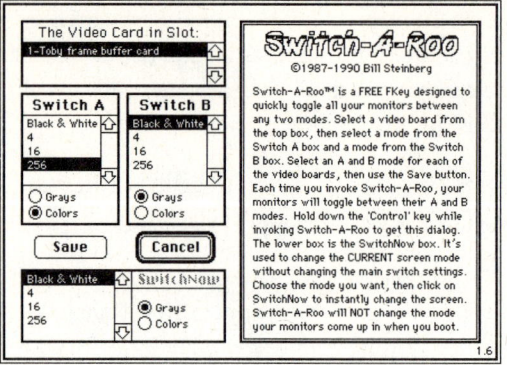

Figure 3.27

Switch-A-Roo enables you to change monitor colors with a keystroke.

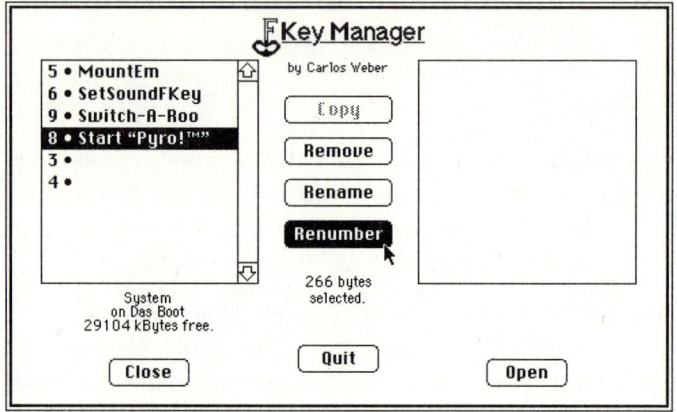

Figure 3.28

The FKey Manager.

Desk Accessories

The original concept behind desk accessories was to have a set of small programs and utilities available at all times from within the standard Apple menu. At the time the Mac was introduced in 1984, this was a novel concept that made the machine very attractive. No personal computer had a multi-tasking operating system and this was the closest thing available. Over the years, the Macintosh built up a large library of highly functional programs in the form of desk accessories; many were users' personal favorites. So, when System 7 shipped and desk accessories were basically an obsolete concept, Apple still preserved their place on the Apple menu.

Chapter 3
Exploring the Macintosh System

A Closer Look Until System 5, programs hosted desk accessories by loading them into their available memory. The Finder itself was considered a program and also hosted desk accessories. Each desk accessory was limited to 32K, the size of a programming segment. In System 6, Apple decided to improve the desk accessories' performance by insulating them in a layer of memory with the system software DA Handler program. When a DA is launched in System 6, DA Handler loads into memory. Each loaded DA gets a place on the Apple menu. DA Handler runs all DAs and provides basic **File** and **Edit** commands. This isolation provides some of the features of protected memory. With DA Handler in place, you can force a quit (Command-Shift+Escape) in a misbehaving application or DA and still keep the rest of the system up and running.

System 7 institutes a radical change in desk accessory philosophy. No longer are DAs any different from a normal stand-alone application that you double-click to launch. These programs load in the Apple menu because they are placed in the Apple Menu Items folder within the System folder. You can actually put any application (or an alias for it) in the Apple Menu Items folder; however, DAs still have a place because they often provide much of the functionality of much larger programs but use a fraction of the memory. So you can use a DA even though almost all of your Mac's memory is in use.

To use DAs in System 6 and before, you either need to install them in your System file with Font/DA Mover, as described earlier, or access them using a resource manager such as Suitcase II or MasterJuggler. In System 7, you must extract DAs found within Suitcase files. Double-click on the Suitcase, and in the resulting window, click and drag the DA out. An extracted DA has a generic application icon. System 7 still allows you to use Suitcase files with Suitcase II and MasterJuggler as before.

Sounds

One of the most beloved features of the Macintosh is its capability to play sounds. Sound is what gives the machine its personality. The Talking Moose is an early example of this capability. Today, modern Macs can serve as the nerve center of elaborate music making, editing, and synthesizing systems. The Mac is one of the favored pieces of many musicians' setup. Chapter 17, "Sound, Music, and Speech," describes in detail how to use sound and music on the Mac. In this section, you will examine a few basics.

Part I
Macintosh, the Computer

A Closer Look Early Macs used a set of routines encoded in ROM called the Sound Driver to generate sounds (essentially a device driver for the enclosed speaker). With the advent of the Mac II in 1988 and the introduction of System 6 that coincided with it, Apple introduced a set of routines called the Sound Manager to deal with multivoice stereo sound. The new Apple Sound Chip and the capability to play stereo sounds was included with the Mac II, too. System 6 provided instructions that enabled the Mac Plus and SE to take advantage of the Sound Manager.

Part of System 7 shipped early and was included as a Sound Manager enhancement in System 6.0.7. It provided

▼ A set of compression routines called the Macintosh Audio Compression and Expansion (MACE) scheme;

▼ An improved Sound control panel with a direct sound recording feature;

▼ Support for sounds in the Clipboard.

The introduction of 6.0.7 coincided with the introduction of the Mac Classic, LC, and IIsi, each of which ships with a microphone for direct sound recording. Every new Mac now ships with a mic. Prior to System 6.0.7, you needed a device such as Farallon's MacRecorder to create sound files or two MacRecorders to record in stereo. The MacRecorder can be used with the sound manage in 6.0.7 and System 7 on older Macs that lack the built-in microphone.

System 7 introduces a number of other sound enhancements to the Sound Manager, including the ability to play multichannel sound. This allows you to play one sound in the background while another sound plays in the foreground. Now, you can also use multichannel sounds to set the amount of background processing. Furthermore, a new MIDI (Musical Instrument Digital Interface) Manager that provides a standard driver for MIDI software was added to the Toolbox.

When you install a System, a basic set of alert or beep sounds is also installed. One alert sound must always remain in the System file. You can install sounds directly in the System file, like the other resources described in this chapter. In System 6 and before you can use utilities such as Sound Manager, Sound Mover, or MasterJuggler to install sounds in the System file. Sound Mover lets you modify sounds, rename them, copy all or part of the sound to the Clipboard, and more (see figure 3.29). Sound files can be large, so it does not take many to fill up your memory.

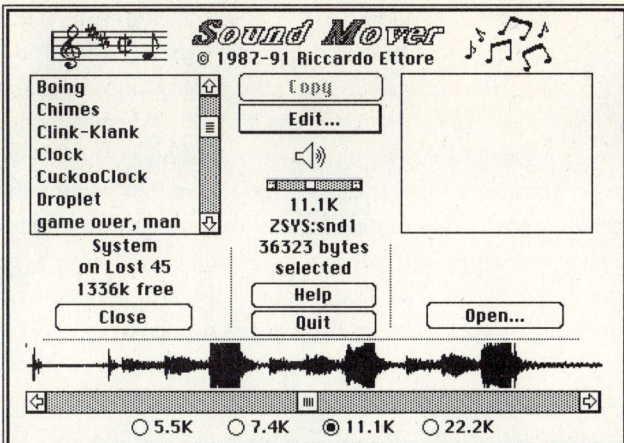

Figure 3.29
The Sound Mover.

In System 7, you can drag sounds onto the System file. However, System 6 beep sounds must first be converted into a new format; the Sound Converter shareware program does this job. In System 6, you can change system alert sounds in the general control panel or the Sound control panel. In System 7, if your Mac supports direct recording of sound through its microphone (the Classic, LC, SI, or a Mac equipped with a MacRecorder), you can change them within the Sound control panel alone.

There are two important standard sound file formats: *SND* resources (for sound) and the *Audio Interchange File Format*. SND sounds are further differentiated as Format 1 resources, which are system beep or alert sounds, and Format 2 resources, which are used within HyperCard. You need to convert between the two when you want to use Format 1 in HyperCard or Format 2 in your System file. Software such as Farallon's SoundEdit (which ships with the MacRecorder) does the job. Sound Mover can convert sounds between formats automatically.

A Closer Look For a long time, Apple distributed (unsupported) a voice and sound synthesizing system extension called MacinTalk. Most programs use MacinTalk to speak something that sounds like the English language. (It is used as the vocal chords for the popular Talking Moose feature.) MacinTalk is based on the principle of phonetic pronunciation. There are only so many unique combinations of syllables or vowel sounds, called phonemes, in a language. MacinTalk has about 40 or 50. MacinTalk is primitive by most standards but has just been overhauled. As of this writing, Apple has released a new technology called the Sound Manager which supports many different voices (including voices that use digitized phonemes).

Part I
Macintosh, the Computer

Note: Many programs allow you to put sounds into your Mac. Some are simple, such as an INIT called The Grouch. When The Grouch is placed in your system, Oscar the Grouch pops up and sings "I love trash" or "I love it because it's trash" whenever you empty the Trash Can icon. Kids love it. The ultimate kitsch utility is The Talking Moose, a cult classic. At various times, the Moose utters random phrases about the meaning of life and reads your dialog boxes to you. Adults love this one. If you miss your typewriter of yesteryear, a program called Tappy Type makes appropriate noises as you type. Last, but not least, is Sound Master, a CDEV (see figure 3.29). Sound Master lets you assign sounds to various events such as start-up, shutdown, disk insert or eject, key click, and the Return or Space keys. You can get sounds from nearly all of the online services, from most bulletin boards, and on disk from user groups and shareware distributors.

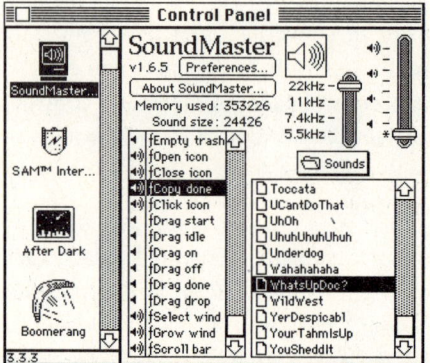

Figure 3.30
Sound Master.

A Closer Look: A project is underway at Apple to introduce Macintosh system software that recognizes speech. The software is code-named Casper. The new multimedia Macintoshes —the Centris 660AV and the Quadra 840AV—are the first release of this new product. These new Macs include an AT&T *DSP* (digital signal processor) chip that provides the extra horsepower needed for good speech recognition. Using speech recognition, you train the computer to recognize your voice. Then, when you wish to give a command, you simply speak to the computer. More capable automatic voice recognition systems which do not need to be trained are perhaps five years away from general introduction.

Recent and Upcoming System Enhancements

Chapter 3
Exploring the Macintosh System

Apple's Macintosh system software is always work in progress. Although System 7 should be around for the next two or three years, several modules to extend the system may appear in the next year or so. In this section, three of the more important modules are discussed: Interapplication Communications (IAC)/Apple Events, AppleScript, and The Layout Manager.

IAC/Apple Events was released in System 7 but is not yet widely implemented in software. It links programs together so they may share data and functionality. AppleScript is the long anticipated Apple macro language. The future also should bring The Layout Manager, which adds impressive typographical capability and advanced printing options to your Macintosh.

Apple has coined the following terms to specify an application's capability to use System 7 features:

▼ System 7-compatible: This term means the application runs in System 7 with the same degree of functionality it has in prior system software. Approximately 75 percent of Mac software was compatible at the time of System 7's release in May 1991. At the least, these programs launch and most function properly in the integrated version of MultiFinder. A program can be System 7- compatible and yet not run in 32-bit memory or while using File Sharing.

▼ System 7-friendly: To be friendly, an application must fully support System 7's integrated multitasking environment, run in 32-bit color, and offer a stationery pad feature. Any program offering these capabilities can stick a System 7 label on its box.

▼ System 7-savvy: A savvy application is one that supports System 7's Edition Manager's Publish and Subscribe functions, uses Apple Events and the Core events defined by that system, has no font size limits, and is AppleShare-compliant (shares files with servers or other Macs using File Sharing).

Part I
Macintosh, the Computer

Interapplication Communications and Apple Events

Interapplication Communications (IAC) is the process by which programs work together, cooperatively linking both data and capabilities. The potential implications of IAC are profound; it is likely to entirely change everything about the way you do your computing. Similar concepts, such as Dynamic Data Exchange (DDE) and Object Linking and Embedding are being developed in the PC world within Microsoft Windows.

Two very important changes are based on IAC. First, when programs can work cooperatively, there is no need to buy an application that does almost everything. You save money by buying only the programs with functions you need. You get what you want, pay less, and have less computing overhead. Imagine being able to work in a simple word processor or text editor, then call up an independent proofreading program, another for spell checking, and a draw, paint, or layout program as you need it!

The second change IAC will be responsible for is data sharing. This is best described as a major extension of the cut-and-paste metaphor, a sort of live copy and paste. Apple calls this process Publish and Subscribe. One program acts as a *publisher* and supplies the data, while another acts as a *subscriber* and accepts the data. You choose which data is published (and to whom) by selecting it and then choosing the **Create Publisher** (or Publish) command on the **Edit** menu to create an Edition file. Similarly, to subscribe, you select an insertion point, choose the **Subscribe To** (or simply **Subscribe**) command on the **Edit** menu, and select the Edition file from a standard dialog box. You can use the Edition file with any number of subscribers; you can choose to automatically update subscribers or update through an Options command. These processes are referred to as "hot-linked" data versus data that is "warm-linked," respectively.

You can tell which data is being published. Apple specifies it be surrounded by a medium gray (50 percent black) border three pixels thick for publishers, and a dark gray (75 percent black) border for subscribers (see figure 3.31). You only see this border when you click on the data. If you move elsewhere in the document, these borders disappear. You normally find an optional **Show Borders** command on the **Edit** menu that brings shared data into view. You can edit or change data within a publisher but not a subscriber.

Apple Events makes IAC possible by posting a message from the publisher to the subscriber. If the subscriber is open, the message is acted on according to your instructions. If not, action is taken when you next open the subscriber application and related file. Apple Events can also send messages across a network. Apple Events can store timing information as well, making it perfect for a new generation of calendars and datebooks, commonly called Personal Information Managers, or PIMs to appear. PIMs will be the next major application category as the first significant generation of Apple portable computers appears.

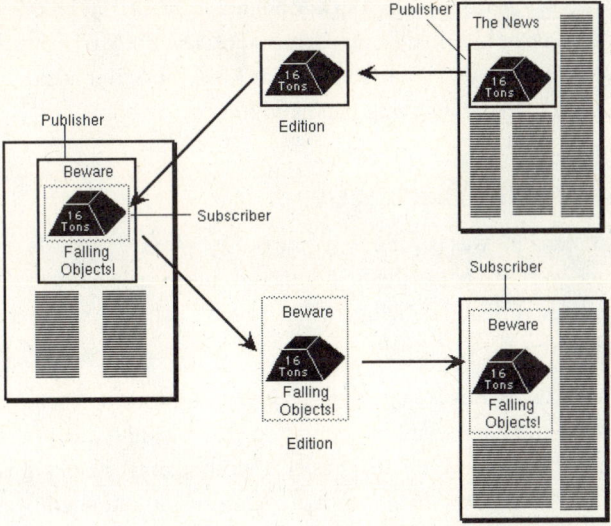

Chapter 3
Exploring the Macintosh System

Figure 3.31
Publishers, editions, and subscribers.

Apple Events stores and delivers four basic messages that are at the core of the technology, although others may be added later. To be System 7-savvy, applications must recognize as a minimum: open application, open documents, print documents, and quit application messages. There are an additional two dozen other defined Apple Events that are recommended. These include most of the standard Apple commands: close, save, undo or redo, cut, copy, and paste. Application-specific events such as show formatting codes in word processors and page layout programs can be defined, and developers can define their own proprietary messages to enhance their own sets of programs.

AppleScript

AppleScript is a scripting language that uses IAC and Apple Events. AppleScript enables you to write high-level programming code to initiate system and application events. MS-DOS has long had a similar capability, writing batch files with sets of commands that execute when the program is started.

AppleScripts are created using the Script Editor application. Scripts can be run from the Script Editor, or they can be saved as standalone applications. Scripting is not for the faint of heart—programming never is—but the capability to automate repetitive tasks will make AppleScript attractive to many. Many applications don't currently support scripting, but that will change as time passes. For more information on AppleScript, see BMUG's book *The Tao of AppleScript,* by Derrick Schneider with Tim Holmes and Hans Hansen, and published by Hayden Books. The book comes with a disk that includes the AppleScript and IAC extensions, the Script Editor, and many other useful utilities—everything you need to start scripting.

The Layout Manager

The Layout Manager was supposed to ship with System 7. Aspects of its performance were shown in the first demonstrations of the System 7, but it was not ready in time to be included. The Layout Manager is typographical control software.

For instance, The Layout Manager makes it easy to produce *ligatures*. Ligatures are letter combinations such as Æ, Œ, œ, æ, and others that are used to make the eye read the text easier. Layout manager looks at the characters and constructs the appropriate ligature without needing a special character. It also adjusts *kerning* (space between letters), *heights* of parts of a letter form based on its context, *justification*, and *fractional positioning* of characters. These are the tools well-trained typographers use with metal type to produce beautiful pages, and it represents an art form today.

Summary

The Macintosh uses a graphical user interface to translate commands given to the computer into a series of pictures and actions based on metaphors found in real life. Your screen looks like a desktop, your work is organized inside folders, items to be deleted are placed in the trash can, and so on. Menu structures, dialog boxes, and the principles of design are common to all Mac programs. This makes the Macintosh easy to use and easy to learn. It also makes new programs seem similar.

Chapter 4: How the Macintosh Works

This chapter takes an in-depth look at the Macintosh computer's operating system and how it works. Programming guidelines set out by Apple Computer create a uniform look and feel for all

In This Chapter
- ▼ Human interface guidelines
- ▼ The Macintosh operating system
- ▼ Volumes and drives
- ▼ Resources and resource editors
- ▼ CPU, RAM, and ROM

Mac programs, and these are defined. Other aspects that affect the Macintosh computing, such as memory, file construction, and so on, also are covered.

The Look and Feel (Human Interface Guidelines)

The Macintosh computer broke new ground in many respects by introducing a refined operating system with closed system architecture. The Mac contains a set of software modules called *managers* that are routines for performing functions such as drawing graphics, creating and managing windows and their functions, creating and displaying the Mac's distinctive pull-down menus, and operating storage devices. The entire set of routines and managers collectively are referred to as the *Macintosh Toolbox*, and much of the Toolbox is captured in the Mac Read Only Memory (ROM), which is permanently attached to the motherboard. When you program for the Mac, you use these routines to create your program.

This imposed uniformity has several significant implications. Most important, all Macintosh programs share common elements. When you learn how to use a window in one program, you can use a window in any other program. Standard dialogue boxes for opening or saving are also uniform. Similarly, commands such as Open, Close, Save, Cut, Copy, Clear, and Paste are common to most Mac programs.

The 10 Interface Commandments

Applications that follow the interface guidelines conform to these 10 commandments, as set out by Apple for all programmers developing software for the Mac:

1. Thou shalt use metaphors from the real world. Provide a graphical user interface.

Chapter 4
How the Macintosh Works

2. Thou shalt provide users direct manipulation. This is the event-driven environment commandment.

3. Thou shalt let users see-and-point, not remember-and-type. This is the noun-then-verb commandment; pick an object first and then specify action.

4. Thou shalt be consistent. Follow the guidelines and have no other interfaces.

5. Thou shalt be WYSIWYG (what you see is what you get). All conditions and events shall be plainly shown to you. Scholars have interpreted this to mean that what the user sees onscreen is printed to his scrolls.

6. Thou shalt allow the user, not the computer, to initiate and control all actions (a further commandment based on the event-driven environment).

7. Thou shalt keep the user informed and provide immediate feedback.

8. Thou shalt be forgiving. Users make mistakes; programs forgive them. This is the Undo command(ment).

9. Thou shalt provide perceived stability. Thou may not be stable, but thou shalt appear so to the user.

10. Thou shalt have aesthetic integrity. Looking good is being good.

What Is an Operating System?

An operating system is the software that performs low-level hardware and software computer functions. Part of the set of system operating commands called the Macintosh Toolbox is encoded in the Mac. You can think of the Toolbox as a set of bricks, lumber, pipes, and wires. The System file provides the plans and the manpower, and booting up builds the house. The Toolbox includes commands for opening and displaying windows, building and using menus and commands, drawing graphics to the screen, and handling I/O devices. Dozens of programs are in the Toolbox, including:

▼ QuickDraw: A set of graphics routines for drawing to a screen or printing.

▼ Window Manager: Displays and controls windows.

Part I
Macintosh, the Computer

▼ Resource Manager: Manipulates objects known as resources which are used by programs.

▼ Font Manager: Creates and displays characters using QuickDraw.

▼ Event Manager: Tracks input devices and system events.

▼ TextEdit: A simple set of text editing routines.

▼ File System: Creates and tracks files.

▼ Menu Manager: Creates and implements the Macintosh pull-down menus.

The Mac gets its uniform look and feel from its consistent use of the managers and resources in the Toolbox. Knowing about these managers enables you to predict the behavior of an application you have never seen previously. For example, TextEdit is a simple version of a text editor or a stripped-down word processor. You can tell when TextEdit is used because a text box supports the **Cut**, **Copy**, **Paste**, and **Clear** commands. The next time you see a standard file (Open or Save) dialog box or an application's dialog box, try cutting text from a text box and then pasting it back. That is TextEdit at work.

Have you noticed that when you keep typing and get ahead of the screen, your Mac seems to remember your keystrokes? If you type too many keystrokes too quickly, however, your Mac forgets them. That is the Event Manager at work. It establishes a queue with up to 20 events in it. Any more events are lost.

Breaking an operating system into modules is a boon to programmers. They can concentrate on learning and using just the resources they need for their projects without reinventing the wheel. For example, consider Window Manager, a set of routines for displaying and working with windows on your screen. The Window Manager creates scroll bars, close and zoom boxes, title bars, and all the other features you expect to see in Macintosh windows.

Programmers are always inventing ways to modify windows. One shareware utility called Scroll2 puts double-headed arrows at every corner of the scroll bar so you won't have to move your cursor around too much. Other utilities such as Personality! and ClickChange make even more extensive revisions to your windows. Figures 4.1 through 4.5 show the panels of Personality!, which modifies several system managers. You also can see modular programming in products such as the NOW Utilities (v. 4.0). This product is a collection of specialty programs including Super Boomerang, which modifies standard dialog boxes, and Desk Picture, which replaces your standard desktop patterns with color or black and white pictures.

Personality! is out of print. You're much better off with ClickChange from DublClick Software anyway.

Bob LeVitus

Driven by Events

The Mac differed from other computers when it was introduced because of its event-driven environment. Unlike older computers that require that you only enter information when the computer expects it, the Mac is constantly monitoring for input so that the Mac can react to your actions. Input includes keyboard entry, pointing devices such as mice or trackballs, and disk insertion. In fact, all Macintosh programs—from the System to the Finder to your favorite Macintosh software—use event-driven programming. The actual program code contains an event loop, and the program cycles in this loop until a condition occurs that requires an action.

Chapter 4
How the Macintosh Works

Figure 4.1
The control panel.

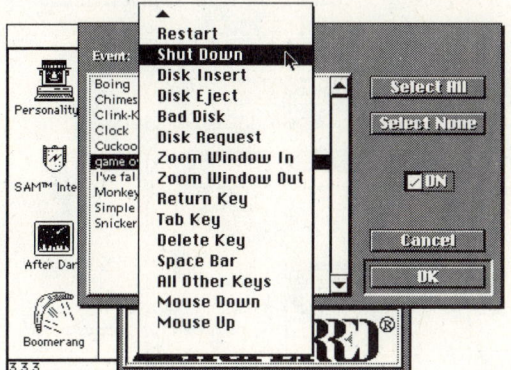

Figure 4.2
The Sound panel.

Figure 4.3
The Window panel.

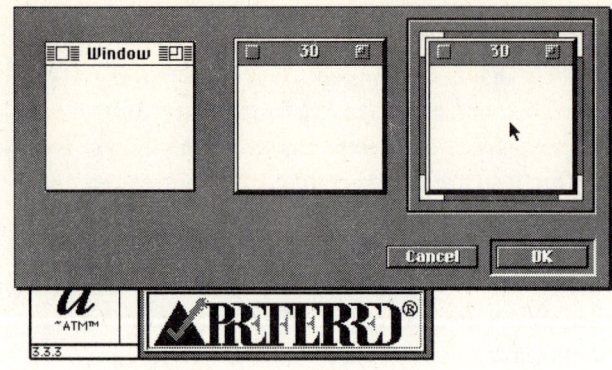

Figure 4.4
The Menu panel.

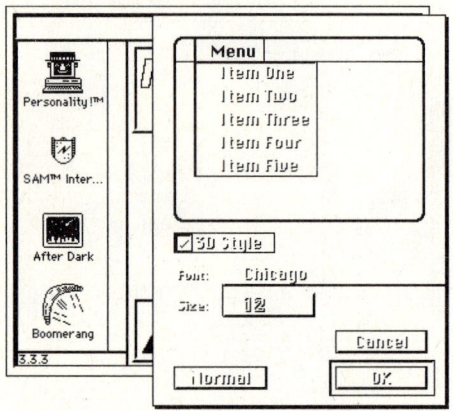

Figure 4.5
Panel for the Dialog Manager.

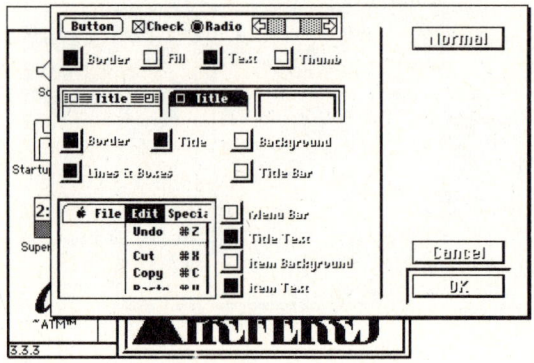

Although using the Mac is easy, programming it can be difficult. (see chapter 29, "Programming," for more information). Programmers must know which elements of the Toolbox are needed for their application, and they must anticipate all possible user input and requirements. Apple published its specifications for the Toolbox in a series of reference manuals called *Inside Macintosh*. Each book in the original five volume set represents the additional functionality of a new Mac ROM or significant system upgrade. However, many people found that they could not learn how to program a Mac from simply reading *Inside Macintosh*. A better place to start is Apple's *Programmer's Introduction to the Macintosh Family*.

> **Note** Apple totally revamped *Inside Macintosh* (published jointly with Addison-Wesley) with the introduction of a series of books that replaces this venerable old series. A total of about twenty volumes are planned, with each volume covering some aspect of Macintosh programming. Of the volumes that have appeared so far, *Files*, *Processes*, and *The Toolbox* are typical titles. The series is planned to be complete in late 1993.

How the Mac Works

When you turn on a Mac, it uses a bootstrapping procedure to start up. The Macintosh operating system is a hardware-software combination, and where you find the instructions depends on the particular model and system software. The original 128K Mac shipped with a 64K ROM. ROM upgrades occur infrequently, generally coming with the introduction of an entirely new class of machines. The Mac Plus was the first to contain the 128K ROM, whereas the Mac Classic, Mac SE, and Mac II use 256K ROMs. The latest ROMs are the 512K ROMs found in the LC, IIsi, IIci, IIfx, and Quadras.

> **Note** A start-up, or boot, disk is any logical volume that has at least a System and Finder file on it. If you boot from a disk with only these files, you are not able to use your keyboard, mouse, and other devices, or to change system settings. It is a good idea to create your own start-up disk with all your basic system files or copy your system to a floppy. This copies all the system resources and enables you to recover quickly if you corrupt your system in any way.

Chapter 4
How the Macintosh Works

In System 6.0.x, you can fit a fair-sized system onto an 800K floppy and a full system onto a 1.44M floppy. If you have trouble with your main drive, you can boot from this floppy, use a CDEV such as SCSIProbe or SCSITools to mount the drive, and run a utility such as Disk First Aid, SUM, or Norton Utilities to diagnose and fix your disk. You also can have a virus detection and repair tool on the disk. System 7 uses an enlarged system that makes it difficult to get all the necessary files onto a floppy. This approach requires a removable cartridge drive or one of the new generation of high-density floppies now coming to market.

About the best you can do with System 7 is to create an emergency startup disk using the Minimum System script of the Installer utility. This places System and Finder on a 1.44M floppy. Also place your System Enabler file on that emergency disk. Prepare a second disk with all of the required additional files such as Disk First Aid. Then, if you ever encounter a non-bootable drive you can work around the problem.

Certain ROMs restrict a machine's capabilities. A ROM upgrade is required to use a 128K or 512K Mac with a hard drive. Newer, larger ROMs contain both updated Toolbox routines and more of them. To run the operating system, the system software makes the appropriate program calls to the ROM for routines that are still applicable, but it substitutes the routines in the software when a Toolbox manager is outdated or not present.

 The operating system's hardware-software construction resulting from the combination of the System file and the ROM is the reason Apple has the ability to run new System software on nearly all Macs.

System 7 loads things in this order:

1. The System (with all its resources: desk accessories, fonts, FKeys, and sounds)
2. Control panel devices (CDEVs)
3. Extensions (INITs)
4. Programs in the top level of the System folder
5. The Finder
6. Any applications that you designated as Start-up applications

A start-up application is one active in System 6.0.x when the Set Start-up command is used. In System 7, it is a program or the alias (pointer) to a program placed in the Start-up Items folder of the System folder.

Chapter 4
How the Macintosh Works

A Closer Look: Turning on a computer's power begins a sequence of actions that readies the machine for use. The clock sends a reset signal that clears all storage circuits or registers, and it clears a special register called a program counter. The machine then begins a process called *bootstrapping,* in which the computer "pulls itself up by its bootstraps," or runs diagnostic tests and then loads some basic operating instructions found in the Macintosh ROM. This often is referred to as POST, or "power on self-tests."

On start-up, a healthy Mac performs the following steps:

1. The Mac checks basic connections such as memory and video boards.
2. If all is well, the Mac gives a distinctive electronic "boing" sound. Hardware errors are noted by three boings.
3. It loads the cursor (pointing arrow) in the upper-left corner of the screen.
4. The Mac then seeks a drive containing the System folder, which contains a System and Finder file, to use as a boot drive.
5. First, the floppy disk drive (internal) is polled. Next, the second internal floppy (if one exists) is polled, then an external floppy disk drive (if one exists). Finally, the internal hard disk is polled, followed by any external SCSI disk drives.
6. If no drive is found, a flashing floppy disk with a question mark is shown onscreen. If the start-up or boot disk has a software problem such as improperly written instructions (boot blocks), a flashing floppy disk with an X through it is shown. If there is a fatal hardware error, a "sad" Mac is displayed. The code shown explains the cause of the problem.
7. Successful start-up displays first the "happy" Mac, followed by the Start-up screen, which is normally the default Welcome to Macintosh. Any special INITs (extensions) or CDEVs may display an icon at the bottom of the screen.

    You can use any picture in a special file format called Start-up screen. By copying that file to your System file, the new picture is displayed in place of the Welcome to Macintosh screen.
8. Finally, the rest of the Macintosh operating system loads, followed by the Macintosh desktop, which is controlled by the Finder.

The start-up sequence described in "The Mac Up by Its Bootstraps" is different from the one used in System 6 and the one you may be familiar with. In System 6, steps two through four are replaced by a single step in which all CDEVs, INITs, and other executable programs in the System folder are loaded in alphabetical order. Because the loading scheme is crucial to how system extensions interact with one another, each system version requires you to work with these programs differently to resolve conflicts. (See chapter 4, "Macintosh Hardware: A Technical Look," for more information.)

A number of items load into your RAM, including:

- ▼ RAM system software: updated or new routines or managers for the Toolbox

- ▼ System extensions: INITs (extensions), RDEVs, and CDEVs

- ▼ MultiFinder: the Finder for System 6.0.x

- ▼ RAM cache: set in the Control Panel in System 6.0.x or in the Memory control panel in System 7.0

- ▼ Opened applications and desk accessories

All these programs require memory, and together they use a minimum of 300 to 400K. In a 1M Mac, you would have just enough space (600 to 700K) to run one moderate-sized program under System 6.0.x. In System 7.0, however, the increased size of the system uses a minimum of 450 to 600K of RAM. You would not be able to run a single program. Therefore, System 7 does not run on a machine with less than 2M of RAM. A fully configured system in System 7 might run from 1M to 2M in size.

Note: Realistically, you probably do not want to run a Mac with anything less than 4M these days. This amount enables you to use two or three simultaneously opened applications and gives you the opportunity to have an environment where MultiFinder can operate successfully. In System 7, MultiFinder is the only mode available to you. With the modest cost of RAM, it simply does not make sense to suffer from a RAM crunch any longer. A 4M upgrade costs less than an average-priced application and will do more for your systems' performance than any $200 investment you can make in your computer.

Volumes and Files

To understand how the Macintosh operating system functions, you need to understand how data is written and read. The following sections discuss storage technology generally. For more detailed information, see chapter 4, "Macintosh Hardware: A Technical Look."

Chapter 4
How the Macintosh Works

Drives and Volumes

A *volume* is any hard disk, floppy disk, optical disk, RAM disk, or other storage media that can show up on the Macintosh desktop. It is also possible to designate areas of a disk as logical volumes called *partitions*. A partition can be a contiguous area of a disk, but some programs enable you to create partitions that occupy several disconnected parts of a disk. You can mount and unmount logical volumes from the desktop just as though you were inserting or ejecting a floppy disk.

Note Many programs require a permanently positioned file to function properly. The file creates a partition, but often that partition does not show up on your desktop. The virtual memory swap file you create from the Memory CDEV is an example. SoftPC, the IBM PC emulator program, writes a partition to your drive so the MS-DOS data it writes does not confuse your Macintosh. The partition appears on your disk as a file icon. All of these are not considered volumes; unless you specifically direct them to, these partitions will not show up on your desktop.

Volumes are represented by an icon. Volumes have names, and your Mac also internally assigns numbers to volumes. Therefore, it is possible for your Mac to differentiate between two volumes with the same name mounted on your desktop. (However, you must give each file on the same volume a different name, since the Mac cannot distinguish between files with the same name on the same volume.)

Formatting, or initializing, a volume segments it into sections on which data can be written. Different media format or initialize in different ways. Magnetic media such as floppy disks or hard disks use a magnetically charged head that passes over a spinning disk containing magnetic particles. The head writes information by changing the *state* of these particles. The state of the particles (aligned or misaligned to the field) is read by determining their response to a weaker magnetic field.

A Closer Look Steve Wozniak designed a controller called the Super Wozniak Machine, or SWM chip, for floppy disks in your Macintosh. It slows the rotation speed as the head moves so you read a constant amount of data per unit of time no matter where you are on the floppy disk. This controller was one of the key developments that enabled the floppy disk drive to be added to Apple computers.

109

Part I
Macintosh, the Computer

WARNING! Formatting renders some of the disk unavailable for data; you cannot write to areas surrounding track and sector marks. Formatting software is provided with a hard drive purchase, but normally, drives are preformatted by the company that sells them. One of the most popular formatters, Silverlining, is shown in figures 4.6 and 4.7. Be aware: some formatting software can be incompatible with System 7 software. This is particularly true of removable SyQuest drives. If you use a formatter that is not System 7-compatible, you cannot install System 7, and you get a message that "open files" exist on the disk, preventing you from reformatting it.

Figure 4.6
Silverlining's password protection.

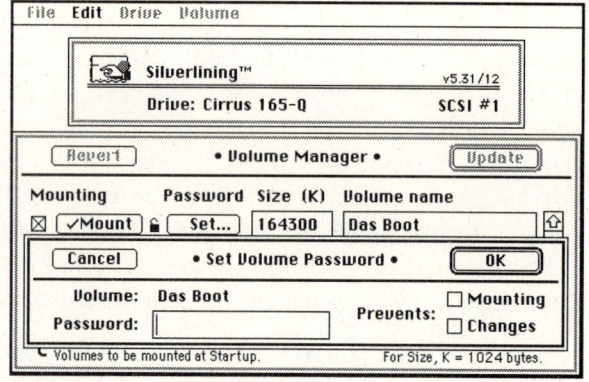

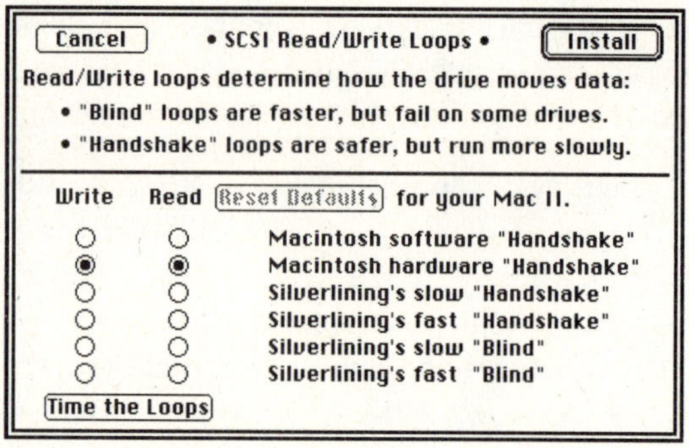

Figure 4.7
Silverlining's analysis of the best method for data transfer, based on timed tests.

Formatting a drive also creates a directory file, and together the formatting lines and directory reduce the real capacity of a disk from its theoretical capacity. For example, a 1M floppy disk contains 800K, a 2M floppy disk contains 1.44M, and a 170M hard drive might contain 158.3M. These numbers depend on the formatting software you use and how often you have written and erased files on the disk.

When you initialize a disk, you *write* all of these formatting lines. You can format a disk, but that is not the same as initialization. Formatting only creates sectors; it does not erase data. This is helpful to know when you are trying to erase confidential information. Some software actually "shreds" data on a disk to make it unreadable.

The Macintosh File System

A *file* is a collection of information written or read sequentially from a disk. A program can read and write data anywhere within a file, and some programs can read and write into the files that describe another program (they are programmers' tools). If a file fits within a sector, it is written there. If there is not enough room for the file to fit, the remaining parts of the file are written to additional sectors. A file can be only as big as the total additional free space on a volume.

Files that are separated on a disk are called *fragmented* files. Reading fragmented files is slower than reading files located in sequential sectors in the same physical location because your disk head has to do additional seeks to find the data. Many utilities on the market can defragment your volumes, including Disk Express II, SUM, Norton Utilities' Speed Disk, and others (including shareware utilities). Disk Express II also prioritizes files so commonly used files are located closer together for faster access.

A Mac file has an unusual construction. It is composed of two parts called *forks* (see figure 4.8). There is a *data fork* and a *resource fork*. You can think of the resource fork as a library of objects that a program organizes in some way. If the file is an application itself, the instructions on what to do with the objects in the resource fork are self-contained, in either the resource fork or the data fork. The data fork is an area of a file that is sequentially stored data.

Chapter 4
How the Macintosh Works

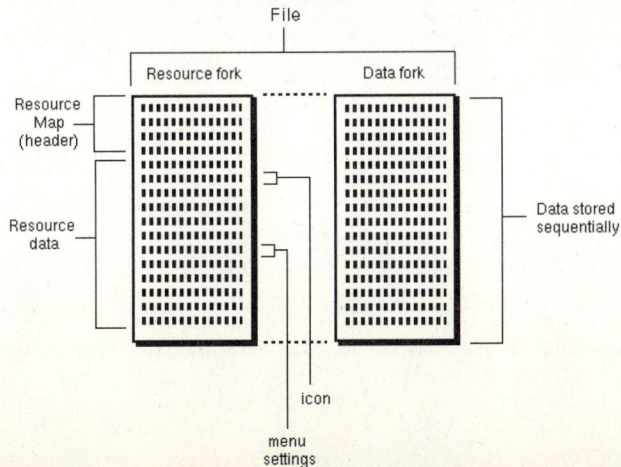

Figure 4.8
Icon and menu settings are resource objects stored randomly and mapped by the header in the resource fork.

111

Part I
Macintosh, the Computer

Separating a file into two forks makes programming easier. The Resource Manager handles programming calls to the resource fork, and the information in the data fork is handled by the File Manager. A data fork can contain anything. For sequential data, use the data fork.

Text, graphics, or code can be a resource. The main attribute of a resource is that it does not change, so for a program, menus, fonts, icons, and the program codes are resources. Reusable items can be stored as resources, and data can be written in a resource in a haphazard way.

Either or both forks of a file can be empty. A number of hex editors enable you to go into a file and change it at the bit level (see figure 4.9).

Desktop File

The Mac keeps track of files in a directory that lists where the file begins, in what additional sectors the file may be found (if any), and where the file ends. Additional information called *attributes* also is maintained about files. One such attribute describes which icon is used to represent the file. Whenever you alter a file in any way—move it, change it, rename it, and so on—your Mac updates the desktop file. Every disk and volume contains a desktop file, and normally this file is invisible to you to prevent it from being altered accidentally.

You can think of the desktop file as a volume's table of contents, although this is a loose definition. In System 6 and before, the file is a single listing, and this system begins to break down at about 2,000 files per disk. With System 6, performance slows noticeably as your Mac searches the desktop file to locate information or to make changes.

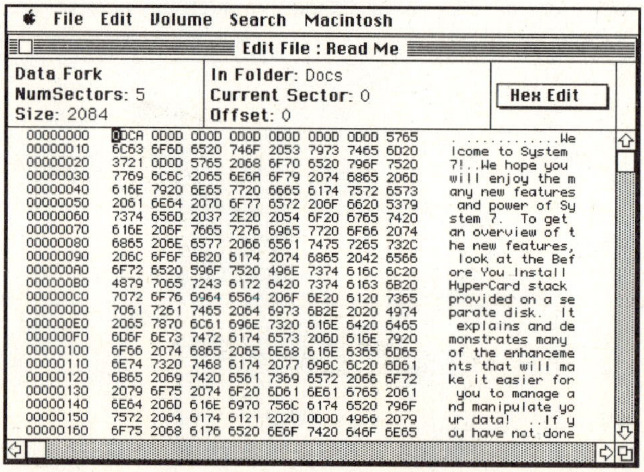

Figure 4.9

Symantec Tools (part of Symantec Utilities) enables you to open the data fork of a file and edit it.

Chapter 4
How the Macintosh Works

Note: To improve file server performance on a network on which a large hard drive can contain many files, Apple created an INIT called the desktop Manager. It creates a database system of files. When added to your System folder, this INIT improves the performance in System 6. For a while, Apple freely distributed the desktop Manager on the online services, but discontinued distributing this INIT to encourage users to upgrade to newer system software versions.

A similar database file system is included in System 7, which cancels the need for desktop Manager. Three files—desktop, desktop DB, and desktop DF—work together in this system. These files are normally invisible on your desktop, however, some utilities will show these files in standard dialog boxes. The improvement of file management is one of System 7's nicer enhancements. When you load System 7 or boot up from a System 7 disk, all your mounted volumes have their desktop files upgraded to this system of three invisible files. Don't worry; your file information is protected.

WARNING! There are times when the desktop file database can be corrupted; for example, when you have a system crash. Your Mac is not able to update changes, and the desktop may not reflect reality, meaning what you see may or may not actually be the same as what's on the disk. Often you can cure this problem simply by restarting your Mac. However, sometimes your Mac's odd behavior requires that you reconstruct (rebuild) the desktop file. Some "troubling" examples include:

▼ Missing file icons and poor file performance. To see new System 7 icons when you replace your applications, you normally have to rebuild the desktop file.

▼ A general document or application icon replaces a file icon.

▼ A document cannot be launched by double-clicking on it; you get a message that says The File "XXX" could not be opened/printed (the application is busy or missing).

▼ Mysterious system crashes.

▼ Programs that cannot remember their preferences after every reboot.

▼ When you insert a disk or mount a volume, you get an alert box message which states that the disk needs minor repairs and asks whether it should perform them. (When you click OK, the desktop file is rebuilt.)

Part I

Macintosh, the Computer

Viruses can cause some of these problems, particularly viruses such as nVir that modify the desktop files. Check first for viruses. You should rebuild your desktop file regularly. Some programs such as Disk Express II do this automatically.

To rebuild your desktop file manually:

1. Reboot and hold down both the Command and Option keys until the disk begins to mount the desktop.

   A dialog box asks whether you want to rebuild the desktop (see figure 4.10).

2. Click the OK button.

3. If you have multiple disks or other volumes on your system, it rebuilds these one at a time when it is done with the Start-up volume.

4. You are returned to your desktop.

Figure 4.10
The Rebuild desktop alert box warns that you will lose information.

Rebuilding your desktop file erases any comments in your Get Info dialog box. Rebuilding your desktop file improves your Macintosh Finder's performance, and is a good habit to get into. Rebuild your desktop every few weeks.

File Attributes

The desktop file stores important information about all your files. In addition to their names and physical locations, details include the *file creator, file type, file format*, and a set of *file attributes*. The file creator is a four-letter code that identifies the program and any files it created or can open. Creator codes are registered by Apple, so no two applications can have the same creator. A program or document's icon is set by the creator code. When you

Before it shipped, it was rumored that System 7 would eliminate this problem. It doesn't. Doesn't much matter—I don't know anyone who uses Get Info comments.

Bob LeVitus

Chapter 4
How the Macintosh Works

double-click a file to open it, the creator code determines which program opens. You can view attributes with Symantec Tools, as shown in figure 4.11.

The second four-letter code used to identify a file is the file type, which identifies a file's format. A file format is a specification that identifies how the data in a file should be read. There are many file formats; some are general formats, called *interchange formats*, which can be read by many programs. TEXT, TIFF, and SYLK (Microsoft's SYmbolic LinK) are interchange formats. Others are specific formats written by one (or more) particular programs. These are called *native formats*. Microsoft Word's WDBN and MacWrite II's MW2S are examples of native formats.

Note: Most programs read a variety of file formats. Claris' XTND technology is a set of extensions you can add to the Claris folder (in your System folder). This set of external commands enables you to open and translate a file created in a foreign format directly from a standard file box. Most programs also enable you to save a file in several formats, a significant selling feature. Aldus PageMaker and Adobe Photoshop are particularly good at converting graphics files, and are worth having just for their capability to convert file types.

Note: The four-letter file type for the Macintosh is directly related to the three-letter extension used to identify IBM PC files. The file XXX.DOC on the PC can be translated directly to a Macintosh TEXT file. The process is called *extension mapping* and can be done automatically with extensions such as DOS Mounter and Access PC. (See chapter 25, "Macintosh and PC Coexistence," for more information.)

Your Macintosh file system attaches 13 file attributes to each file. These fulfill a variety of useful functions. Because the Finder uses them to display and work with files, these attributes often are called Finder flags. However, all Macintosh programs actually use these attributes to work with files. The Mac automatically maintains file attributes, but there are many utilities that enable you to change the file attributes and perform a number of useful system modifications and repairs. Among these are Symantec Tools (part of Symantec Utilities), DiskTop, DiskTool, FileMaster, SetFileKey, FKey, and FileStar (see figure 4.12).

Figure 4.11

Symantec Tools identifies basic file attributes for the Read Me text file that comes with System 7.

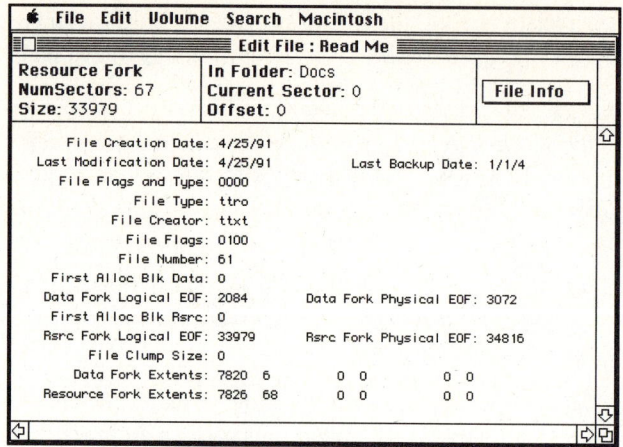

Figure 4.12

DiskTools II can examine a file's Finder flags (attributes) and enable you to change them.

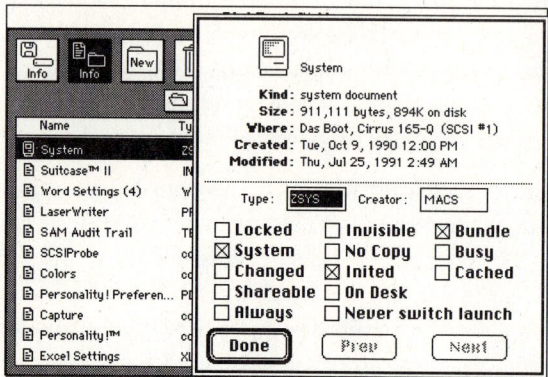

The following list describes all the file attributes:

▼ Invisible: This attribute determines whether or not a file or folder appears on the desktop. The desktop file itself is always invisible, as are other files their creators do not want modified or deleted.

▼ System: Used to indicate files which are part of the system software, these files show the Macintosh icon.

▼ Locked: When on, this attribute prevents you from putting a file in the Trash or deleting it. It also prevents you from modifying the file. You can set this attribute from within the Get Info dialog box. A template, for example, is a locked file.

▼ Bundle: Any file with the bundle attribute on requires you to update the file in the desktop file. Applications always have the bundle bit on.

If an application is acting erratically, sometimes changing the bundle bit can eliminate the problem. Some utilities such as Norton Utilities examine bundle bits and reset them.

▼ Busy: Applications lock a file by marking it "busy" when the file is currently in use to prevent you from deleting an open file. Some applications do not unlock a previously used file until the application quits.

▼ Changed: This attribute indicates that a file has been modified. Backup utilities use Changed to do incremental backups.

▼ No Copy: When set on, this attribute prevents a file from being copied. It disappeared after System 5.

▼ Inited: This Finder sets this attribute when it has read a file's information into the desktop file. Inited indicates that the *BNDL* resource has been read (refer to table 4.1). Inited files normally cannot be deleted.

▼ Cached: This attribute indicates a file's potential to be cached.

▼ Sharable: This attribute allows applications to be launched simultaneously on more than one machine.

▼ Always Switch Launch (or Never Switch Launch): This attribute launches an application and changes the start-up System folder to the System on the same volume as the application.

▼ On Desk: In System 5, the On Desk attribute indicates that the file is on the desktop.

Resources

Resources are objects or program segments you can use to build programs, files, events, and interface structures on the Mac. Just about anything you can think of can be a resource: fonts, FKeys, sounds, menus, dialog boxes, and icons. If a developer intends to make a piece of programming instruction reusable, the programming instruction also may be designated as a resource. This type of object construction makes programming modular. It is a great aid in creating development and debugging programs and, through the use of some simple changes, enables you to customize programs for foreign markets. Also, when used in System files, resources can be shared by all programs running on the Mac, making programming easier and reducing the memory required.

Just as files are flagged with two four-letter descriptions, objects described as resources are flagged with a four-letter description called the *resource type*. Even programming code can be considered a resource and is given the name *CODE*. Apple reserves the use of all resources with only lowercase letters; all other resources can be defined by a program's developer.

You can identify several types of resources: pictorial resources such as cursors (CURS), fonts (FONT), icons (ICON), and patterns (PAT) you can edit with bit editors, and resources you edit in templates. When you open a template editor, a dialog box appears, showing you assignments in fields you can modify. The menu assignments that programs make, such as Cut, Copy, and Paste in the Edit menu, are examples of template resources. Templates are defined as part of a resource editor. Programmers can add their own templates to easily program modifications for special program features.

Lastly, many resources are described by programming code that requires you to use a hexadecimal editor to modify them. You may write templates for this third kind of resource. A description of the most commonly used resource types is shown in table 4.1.

Table 4.1 A partial listing of Macintosh resource types

Type	Explanation
ALRT	Alert dialog box
BNDL	Bundle resource (files and Finder icons)
CDEF	Control definition function
CNTL	Control template
CODE	Programming code
DITL	Items for dialog or alert box
DLOG	Dialog box
DRVR	Desk accessory or driver
DSAT	System error table
FKEY	FKey resource
FOND	Font family information
FONT	Font information
FREF	File reference
FRSV	Font list for system use
FWID	Font width tables
ICN#	Icon lists
ICON	Icons

Table 4.1 continued

Type	Explanation
INIT	INIT resources
INTL	International resource
MBAR	Menu bar resource
MENU	Menu items
NFNT	Font family information
PACK	Package, system software segment
PAT*	QuickDraw pattern
PAT#	Pattern list
PDEF	Printing resource
PICT	PICT format graphic
PREC	Print record
SERD	RAM serial driver
SIZE	Memory requirements
STR*	Dialog box strings
STR#	Dialog box strings
WDEF	Window definition resource
WIND	Window dialog boxes
actb	Alert color table
cctb	Control color table
cicn	Color icon
clut	Color lookup table
crsr	Cursor color table
dctb	Dialog color table
mbdf	Menu bar color table
mctb	Menu color table
pllt	Color palette resource
scrn	Screen configuration
snd*	Sound resource
wctb	Window color table

*Includes a space as the fourth character.

Note: Knowing about resources results in practical, real world benefits. By opening and modifying a program's menu resource, you can alter keyboard shortcut keystrokes or a program's appearance. For example, if you are responsible for the management of a database system and do not want the files copied, you can remove the Save or Save As command from an application's File menu. Other templates enable you to reassign memory, changing the maximum number of windows a program can open. These changes are in addition to modifying icons, altering dialog boxes, and many special effects.

Resource Editors

There are several good programs that enable you to get into a program's resources and hack around. For years now, Apple has been distributing the ResEdit program as freeware (Version 2 is more fully developed than previous versions). Until recently, ResEdit was not well documented by Apple, except in developer literature. Although you could find several online tutorial files such as HMG ResEdit Primer v. 6.0 and others, most users approached ResEdit like an advanced video game: shoot first and ask questions later. There are several books on the market to help you learn about ResEdit, including introductions for beginners (*The ResEdit All-Night Diner,* by Dave Ciskowski and published by Hayden Books, and *Zen and the Art of Resource Editing,* a BMUG book by Derrick Schneider and published by Peachpit) and advanced references (*ResEdit Complete,* by Peter Alley and Carolyn Strange and published by Addison-Wesley).

Note: One of the best ways to get to know a program is to open all its templates in ResEdit and look around. Because changes in resources can be fatal to a program's operation, be sure to work on a copy of the program before you use it regularly. Some people find that working with resources (resource hacking) is so much fun that they become interested in full-fledged programming. More than a few Macintosh programming "wizards" started this way and were never seen in daylight again.

The CPU

The Central Processing Unit (CPU), also known as the *motherboard,* is the main part of the computer that contains the *microprocessor chips* that do the actual computing. Macintosh computers use the MC68000 series of microprocessors built by the Motorola Corporation. All models prior to the Mac II used the 68000, the Mac II (now discontinued) used the more advanced 68020 chip, and the Mac SE 30 (also discontinued) and all other

Chapter 4
How the Macintosh Works

subsequent Macintoshes use the 68030 chip (the exceptions are the Mac Classic and the Macintosh Portable, which use a 68000, and the Mac LC, which uses a 68020). The recently released Quadra 700, 800, 900 and 950 Macs use the 68040, as do the Centris 600 and 630. The rule of thumb is, the larger the number, the faster the chip processes information. (See chapter 4, "Macintosh Hardware: A Technical Look," for more information.)

A Closer Look A CPU's internal performance often is referred to as its clock speed or clock rate. Speeds are measured by the frequency with which the CPU fetches new instructions and are measured in *megahertz (MHz)*. A cycle of three operations—*fetch, decode,* and *execute*—is called the *instruction cycle*. A 10 MHz machine cycles every 100 billionth of a second or every 100 nanoseconds; a 50 MHz machine is five times faster. The Mac Plus, SE, and Classic use a clock speed of 8 MHz; the II, IIx, IIcx, and LC use a 16 MHz chip; the IIsi uses a 20 MHz chip; the IIci uses a 25 MHz chip; and the IIfx uses a 40 MHz chip. The Quadras use chips up to 40 MHz as of this writing. Some 50 MHz chips have been produced but are currently available only in third-party add-in accelerator boards.

A more practical measure of speed is *throughput*, or the number of instructions passing through the microprocessor per unit time. This commonly is measured in *millions of instructions per second (MIPS)*. An SE runs approximately 1 MIPS; a II runs 4 MIPS; and the Mac IIfx runs approximately 16 MIPS. Mainframe or supercomputers can run at 100 MIPS or more.

Note If you want to improve an older Macintosh's performance, several options are available to you. For many of the modular Macs such as the II series, Apple offers a motherboard swap upgrade. You can turn a II into either a IIx or a IIfx. Additionally, many third-party vendors sell add-on accelerator boards with newer or faster chips. It is common to add an 030 chip to an SE to turn it into an SE/30. Be sure a third-party accelerator board is fully compatible with your software before you put down your money.

Coprocessors

The Macintosh enables you to incorporate specialized microprocessors called *coprocessors* to take the load off your computer's CPU. Several different coprocessors are available. You can purchase a *math coprocessor* (for all but the 68000) to do *floating point calculations* or arithmetic. These are calculations that handle long string decimal portions such as 3.3333... or 3.1415... Motorola 68882 math coprocessors are available for the Mac IIsi and LC, and the Mac II ships with a 68881 math coprocessor.

Part I
Macintosh, the Computer

The Mac IIfx comes with several coprocessors on board, including one that aids in input and output. *Input/Output processors (IOP)* manage data transfers coming through the serial or parallel ports. The IIfx also has a *SCSI/DMA (Direct Memory Access)* controller for faster communication between the SCSI port and RAM. Input/Output (I/O) is a performance bottleneck, and this additional horsepower greatly increases read/write operations from peripheral devices.

Video display also greatly benefits from using coprocessors. Video requires that substantial data be stored in memory (buffered) before being brought to the screen. Many video cards such as the Apple 8*24GC ship with a coprocessor chip that does graphics calculations. There are two basic kinds of video coprocessors: one that does vector calculation (draw, for CAD work) and another that does raster calculation (paint or bit map, for imaging or visualization).

Sound files are also large and benefit from coprocessor acceleration and management. A *digital signal processor (DSP)* chip such as the Motorola 56001 often is used on add-in expansion boards that create CD-quality sound. The NuBus DigiDesign Audiomedia board for Mac IIs is one example.

You can never be too rich or too thin. Or have too much RAM or hard disk space.

Bob LeVitus

Memory: RAM, ROM, and Storage

Random Access Memory (RAM) management is the key to dramatically improving the performance of your Macintosh. It is also the Achilles' heel of small computers. RAM's function is to store all the software you use in a temporary workspace, first the system software and then any program you choose to load.

WARNING! It is important to realize that you can lose anything in RAM if the power goes out or if you experience a programming error or conflict. Random Access Memory is volatile and will disappear unless saved to a disk or other storage device. You do not "own" data you see on the screen or any in RAM, only the data you save to your disk. Never go a long time without saving your work.

Chapter 4
How the Macintosh Works

RAM often is referred to as *DRAM*, or *dynamic RAM*, indicating that the semiconductor transistors in the microchip need to be supplied with current (a refresh signal) to retain their electrical state. Chips that do not require refresh are called *static RAM* and are useful in situations in which power consumption is a problem, such as the Mac Portable (not PowerBook). Static RAM is more expensive, so it is used less often. Semiconductor memory is fast; access times are rated in the 70 to 120 nanosecond range (10^8 reads/sec). Compare this to hard drive access times of 10 to 30 milliseconds (10^2 reads/sec) and to floppy disk drives with access times of 100 to 200 milliseconds (10 reads/sec).

Note: You can learn a lot about your Macintosh by choosing the About This Macintosh command on the Apple menu in System 7, or the About The Finder command when in MultiFinder in System 6 or earlier. You learn which Mac you have, which System and Finder you are using, how much memory (RAM) is installed in your computer, and which programs use how much memory. You also learn which is the largest contiguous block of free memory, the essential information in deciding which programs you may launch. The About This Macintosh dialog box is shown in figure 4.13.

A Closer Look: If you hold down the Option key and pull down the Apple menu in System 7, the About This Macintosh command turns into the About The Finder command. Choose it and you are rewarded with the original dialog box that appeared in the 128K Mac's Finder in 1984-85 and the names of the programmers for System 7. It was not possible to capture a screen shot to illustrate it here, so you have to try it on your own.

The Mac uses the entire amount of RAM in your computer as a single stack. It assigns addresses to small blocks of memory and uses different addresses for special purposes. Although the details of these assignments change slightly from one Mac model to another, the overall pattern does not. Memory is described as either low or high, and important system functions are loaded into either end of the stack. Your Mac dynamically assigns programs to a portion of memory called the stack, which is found at the bottom of assigned high memory, or the application heap, which is found at the top of assigned low memory. The stack and application heap grow toward each other, consuming free space until they conflict—at which point you get an Out of Memory message.

Figure 4.13

The About This Macintosh dialog box from System 7 displays vital information about your Mac's RAM and how it is used.

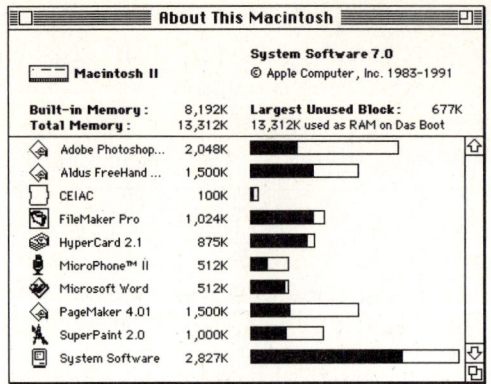

Setting Memory Allocation

It would be nice if system software had enough intelligence to set different applications' memory allotments automatically. Unfortunately, this is not currently the case. You can improve your Macintosh's performance by knowing how to adjust memory allocations to suit your own needs.

To change a program's memory allocation, open the Get Info dialog box (see figure 4.14), and enter a numerical value in the Memory section's Current Size text box. The suggested size is the memory allocation at which the developer feels the program runs best. There are several reasons for changing the current memory size:

▼ You can improve program performance by allowing more of the program's code to reside in RAM, thus requiring less swapping to and from disk.

▼ Sometimes programs refuse to open additional windows or generally misbehave.

▼ You have a particularly large file to manage: for example, a color image.

▼ You want to work with more files than normal.

▼ You are running out of memory space.

You can adjust the amount of memory allocated to a particular program by doing the following:

1. In the Finder, click once on the program icon to select it. (You even may select the Finder for this treatment.)

2. Choose the Get Info command on the File menu.

3. In the text box, type in a larger number than suggested to run the program.

4. Click the close box in the window to dismiss the Get Info dialog box.

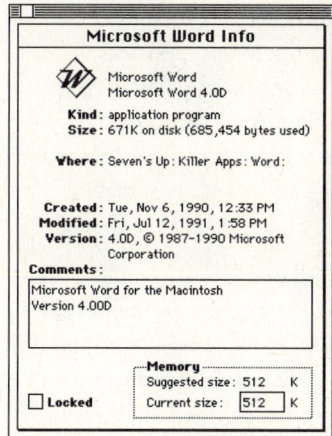

Chapter 4
How the Macintosh Works

Figure 4.14
Changing the Memory allocation in the Get Info dialog box presents several possibilities.

When you relaunch the program after adjusting the memory allocation, it allocates additional RAM. The Finder also can benefit from this treatment. If you are having Finder problems in System 6, try adjusting its memory allocation from 160K to 250K. To adjust Finder memory in System 7, you must boot from another disk. You cannot reset a disk's Finder memory allocation while it is a start-up disk.

If you are low on memory, set the memory allocation below what the program's developer recommends. If you do not set the allocation too low, you sometimes can still operate the program. Beware: starving a program for memory can lead to unpredictable results and often spectacular system crashes. System 7 now automatically gives you a dialog box whenever there is nearly enough memory to open a program, asking whether you would like to use the memory available. This eliminates the need to change the memory allocation in the Get Info dialog box.

Although your Macintosh uses all of its RAM as a single stack, it is not intelligent about how it assigns programs to use blocks of memory. It is easy to have a situation of fragmented memory where there is plenty of free RAM which is not useable because it is in smaller separate blocks. To free up memory, quit programs in the reverse order that they were opened. You also can refresh your memory allocation assignments by rebooting your Macintosh.

If you have an application that "unexpectedly quits," try allocating more RAM. That'll fix it most of the time.

Bob LeVitus

Part I
Macintosh, the Computer

The System 7 Tune Up, currently shipping as part of System 7 with new Macs or available from your Apple dealer, makes various improvements to the memory management under System 7. For low RAM Macs (less than 4M), this is a big improvement. For instance, say you launch an application without enough RAM, and you have another application running but inactive (no open windows). Rather than simply telling you that you do not have enough memory, the "Tuned Up" system now tells you that memory is low, your other application is not in use, and asks if you want to quit it to be able to open the new application. Another Tune Up feature frees up memory by not loading the AppleTalk manager into memory if you have turned off AppleTalk in the Chooser. Numerous other memory management features make this a valuable upgrade for Mac users with 2 and 2.5M machines running System 7. This "Tune-Up" is part of System 7.1.

The *System heap* is a third memory segment, different from the *application heap* and the *stack*. The System heap is memory where important system functions are loaded in memory. Its size is also important; you can see the overall size of the System heap when you view the System's performance in the About This Macintosh dialog box. There should be enough extra free memory (the white space in the bar) so the System file can accommodate additional program function requests. Ideally, free space should be about a third as large as the used System allocation. This is a particular problem in System 6 but is less of a problem in System 7 due to better memory management.

CE Software distributes a very useful CDEV called HeapTool that enables you to adjust the System memory allocation. HeapTool works with both System 6 and System 7. To reset memory, you increase the allocation until it is satisfactory. Changes require rebooting to take effect. Using the Compact button eliminates fragmentation, whereas using the Purge button removes unused resources. You can see the effect of purging the heap in figure 4.15.

Figure 4.15
HeapTool resets the size of the System heap and recovers fragmented memory.

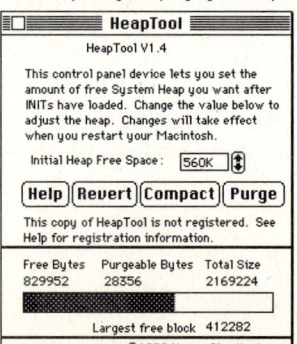

Installing RAM

RAM is installed in a Macintosh by adding *memory chips*. These memory chips come packaged on a small circuit board loaded with chips called *Single Inline Memory Modules*, or *SIMMs*. The amount of memory that you can install is limited by your Macintosh model and the density of the memory chips. For example, 1M SIMMs contain eight megabit DRAM microchips because there are eight bits in a byte. Similarly, 4M SIMMs use eight four-megabit DRAM chips.

Macs have banks of slots where SIMMs can be placed. For example, a Mac Plus or SE has four slots; the Mac II's have eight. Depending on which Mac you have, only certain possible combinations of memory may be allowed. In a Mac II, for example, you must put the same kinds of chips in Bank A's four slots and the same chips (or none) in Bank B. So by using 256K and 1M SIMMs, you can have 1, 2, 4, 5, or 8M of memory in your Macintosh. Other models have different requirements. (See chapter 4, "Macintosh Hardware: A Technical Look," for more information.)

The most recent Macintosh computers use a different system to determine the amount of installed RAM. Models such as the Quadra 950 read memory banks one slot at a time, enabling you to have any configuration of memory you wish.

The main question to ask when buying SIMMs is, "What is the speed rating?" The speed rating is usually coded directly on the chips and ranges from 70 to 120 nanoseconds. A number such as 12 for 120 nanoseconds or 7 for 70 nanoseconds is added at the end of the chip's code name to indicate the speed. Speed is important because some Mac CPUs can outrun a chip that is too slow. The Mac IIfx, for example, requires chips rated at 70 nanoseconds, which are normally what is sold these days.

Prices vary depending on where you buy SIMMs. Apple dealerships may charge up to $250 for four 1M SIMMs. Sometimes an installation fee of $30 or $40 also is added. If you look in the back of different Macintosh magazines, you can find a number of advertisements for memory vendors. Most of the companies that have been around awhile are reliable. They supply a Torx wrench tool to open your Mac's case and very clear instructions for adding memory to each model. No other special tools are required, and after you access the bank of sockets, installation is easy.

When opening your Mac, be sure you are grounded and isolated from either receiving an electric shock or shorting out a component by transferring static charge. If you don't install your SIMMs correctly, you will get a fatal hardware error (three tones).

Chapter 4
How the Macintosh Works

Don't panic! Open up your Macintosh and reseat the SIMMs you just installed.

RAM Cache and RAM Disks

If you have enough available memory, you can improve your computer's performance measurably by configuring RAM as a primary storage device. One technique, the *RAM cache*, loads only the most recently used code or data and provides from 15 to 50 percent speed enhancement, depending on the size of the cache. The truly memory rich can load the system and applications entirely into memory and see speed enhancements up to 200 to 300 percent.

The RAM Cache

A RAM cache (also called a disk cache) is a part of memory reserved to store the most recently read code or data from a disk. Retrieving information from RAM is faster than reading from disk. To set the cache in System 6.0.x, use the arrows in the RAM cache section of the General Control Panel DA. You can turn the cache on or off by clicking the On or Off radio buttons. In System 7, the cache is always on and reserves a minimum of 32K of cache for every megabyte of installed RAM. You can increase this amount by opening the Memory control panel and using the arrows in the Cache Size section (see figures 4.16 and 4.17). (When your computer is incapable of virtual memory or 32-bit addressing, either or both of those sections do not show.) You must restart your Mac before the changes take effect.

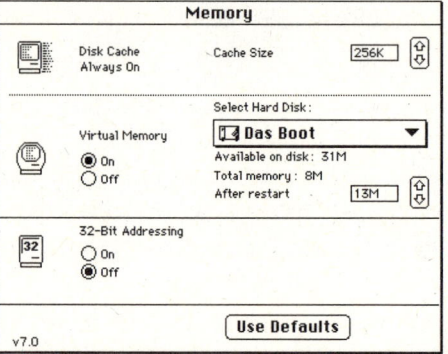

Figure 4.16

Setting the disk cache in the Memory control panel.

Using a RAM cache is a good idea, particularly in situations in which you perform a repetitive task. You see a performance improvement of up to almost 25 percent of the Mac's RAM. The first 256K allotment makes the most dramatic difference. In certain circumstances, large disk caches are quite valuable. On a Mac IIsi with the color (or gray) value set to four and higher, you should set the Disk Cache to 768K. The video and cache then are placed into the memory on the motherboard, and the system and applications go into RAM located on the SIMMs. This results in a substantial performance gain. A similar situation exists in a Mac IIci with 5, 9, or 17M of RAM installed. To get the boost on a IIci, make sure the 256K SIMMs are in the four sockets closest to the disk drive. Other IIci memory configurations require much larger disk caches and are impractical.

Chapter 4
How the Macintosh Works

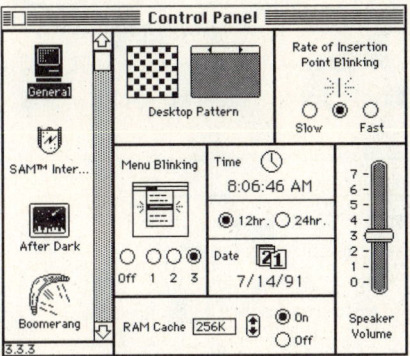

Figure 4.17
Using the General Control Panel to set the RAM cache.

The IIci has an add-in slot that enables you to install a cache memory board. This upgrade is very popular and can make a IIci nearly 20 percent faster and competitive with a IIfx. (A IIfx contains a cache built into its processor.) Also, you can install an Orchid Technology MacSprint II into a Mac II; it is a 32K cache that boosts speed by about 22 to 30 percent. Many accelerator boards also ship with built-in caches.

The RAM Disk

A RAM disk is a partition in RAM configured as though it were a disk drive. It is best used to run a single application at high speed. If your RAM disk is large enough, you also can copy your system files to it for even more performance gain. A RAM disk shows up as a mounted volume (icon) on your desktop. When you buy large memory upgrades (for example, an expansion board filled with memory), vendors often supply a RAM disk utility to enable you to fully utilize the upgrades. Connectix's Maxima is one application that can access a disk of up to 120M.

WARNING! Because a RAM disk is volatile memory, you never should store documents on it. A power outage, a slight electrical fluctuation, a system error, or a crash can destroy the RAM disk's contents. Most utilities now offer an autosave feature that copies the RAM disk's contents to a file on your hard disk. You should turn on this feature because it protects you from losing your work.

To create a RAM disk, you need a utility program. There are several in the public domain, including AppDisk, RamDisk+, and RamStart. AppDisk's current version is System 7–compatible. All are easy to configure. For example, with AppDisk, you open the program's Get Info dialog box, enter the desired application size, and close the dialog box. Then you launch the program. AppDisk creates a *swap file* to save the partition's contents automatically at regular intervals and saves contents on quitting, if you want (see figure 4.18). RamDisk+ provides a similar feature. RamStart is used for large RAM partitions of 16M or more. If you want to load your system onto your RAM disk, copy or install it. To make your RAM disk the start-up volume, be sure you do not have another system on your hard drive.

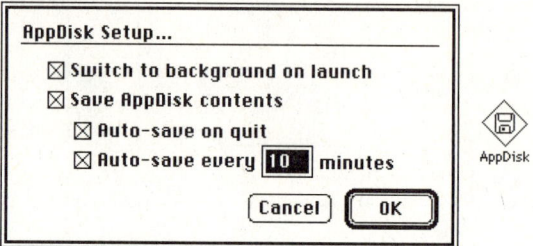

Figure 4.18
The AppDisk Configure dialog box offers several autosave features.

RAM Disks are particularly important when using PowerBooks. Not only do they increase speed, but they also limit disk input/output(I/O). In some situations you can improve battery lifetime up to 25% by using a RAM Disk on a PowerBook. Apple includes a RAM Disk utility as part of its new Memory control panel.

A RAM disk's speed enhancement is often extraordinary. You experience speed increases of 200 percent when you start an application from a RAM disk compared to a floppy disk. If you start an application when its system is on the RAM disk, you experience a more than 600 percent increase in speed compared to using a floppy system. Indeed, using a RAM disk may be the only practical way to use a Mac without a hard disk drive. Speed increases are significant even compared to hard drives.

Virtual Memory

Virtual memory is a portion of your hard disk that you define as an extension of your computer's RAM. This new feature of System 7 works only on Macs with 68030 or above processors.

When you turn on virtual memory, anything that can be written to RAM overflows to your hard disk, if necessary, and anything written to the virtual memory file can be retrieved to RAM when required. The most active code and data is retained in RAM. By using this technique, you can substitute inexpensive and readily available disk storage space for semiconductor memory.

Virtual memory's major drawbacks are the performance penalty you suffer when you must do disk read/writes and the loss of disk space. The process of transferring blocks of memory to a swap file is called *paging*; pages are normally 64K blocks. It is not a good idea to use more than 3:1 virtual to real memory because it creates too much page swapping. If you find your disk access light is flashing constantly , you may want to lower the amount of virtual memory.

WARNING! Applications that require you to transfer large amounts of data (such as video, animation, or games) suffer noticeable performance degradation with virtual memory turned on. The jerkiness may make these programs unusable.

Note Only a Macintosh with a 68030 and above processor (the SE/30, IIx, IIcx, IIci, IIsi, and IIfx, Classic II, Quadras, and so on) can use virtual memory. The paged memory management unit (PMMU) part of the 030 chip is responsible for managing the data transfer. You can retrofit a Mac II with a special PMMU chip for this purpose, and you also can buy an accelerator for an LC that incorporates this functionality. If your Mac cannot use virtual memory, the Virtual Memory section of the Memory control panel does not appear. The CPUs in the Mac Plus, Classic, SE, Portable and PowerBook 100 do not support virtual memory; however, by using accelerator cards with upgraded CPUs, you may be able to install virtual memory into these machines.

When virtual memory is on, you see an entry for Total Memory and the size and location of the swap file used as RAM in the About This Macintosh dialog box. An entry in the Memory control panel also tells you the size and location of the swap file. A Mac using 24-bit addressing can have up to 14M of virtual memory (depending on hard disk space), one less megabyte for every expansion card that is installed.

32-Bit Addressing

In theory, a 32-bit microprocessor should be able to address a gigabyte of memory. For this feature to work, your Mac's ROMs and the programs you are running must support it. System 7 adds new support for 32-bit

Chapter 4
How the Macintosh Works

addressing. Early software used only 24-bit addressing, and major applications currently are being upgraded. Using 32-bit addressing, a Mac can have 128M of real RAM available and use an additional 1 gigabyte of virtual memory.

Most new versions of programs are now compatible with 32-bit addressing. This is one of the criteria for a System 7–friendly application. However, many compatible programs have been written according to the 32-bit clean programming specifications Apple began circulating in 1987. If a program is not compatible, your system warns you, suggests you turn off the option, and then reboots your machine.

WARNING! Some programs do not behave this way; you may get a system crash or errant behavior. Proceed with caution. Only turn the option on in situations in which you have more than 8M of RAM or if you want to use more than 16M of virtual memory. Check with the publisher of the program to make sure that it is "32-bit" clean.

If your machine supports 32-bit addressing, this appears in the Memory control panel where it can be turned on and off. You must reboot before changes take effect.

Note Connectix pioneered the use of virtual memory in Macintosh system software by selling a product called Virtual nearly two years before System 7 shipped. It has the same requirements and benefits as Apple's virtual memory. Maxima, a new Connectix product, enables Macs to use 14M of memory for applications. If your Mac does not support 32-bit addressing, Connectix also sold a product called MODE 32 that may enable you to expand your addressable memory. In 1991, Apple purchased Mode 32 and distributed it freely to users. More recent system software incorporates Mode 32 functionality as part of the operating system.

Buses

A computer, like a program, is useful only if you can get data in and out of it. As previously explained, computers use *buses* (not the school bus kind) to accomplish this task. A bus is a collection of wires that forms a data path. The number of wires going in one direction is called the bus width—the wider the bus, the bigger the bytes that can be transferred. Bigger bytes give faster throughput, result in better performance, and make more advanced computing and computer languages practical. There is a bus structure internal to your CPU and an external bus consisting of wires. Three types of information flow along your computer's bus: *data (I/O)*, *addressing information*, and *timing signals*.

Just as CPUs are rated for their internal bus widths, the I/O buses they connect to are rated for their width, their speed, and whether they are serial or parallel. The 32-bit bus is the current performance standard. When you examine the performance of CPUs versus buses, you find microprocessors are blindingly fast and buses are relatively slow. Bus performance is a critical performance bottleneck and will be the subject of important new advances in new computer architectures.

Apple Desktop Bus

The Apple Desktop Bus (ADB) is a slow, 4,500 bit/second serial bus used for input devices such as keyboards, mice, trackballs, graphics tablets, and MIDI devices. The ADB first was introduced in the Mac SE and was part of the System Enhancement package (hence the name, SE). Most Macs have two ADB ports (the Classic, LC, and IIsi have only one) that require special four-pin adapters to connect to them. Earlier Macs, such as the Plus, use a direct keyboard connection that limits their use and excludes the Apple Extended Keyboard II.

> **Note:** Datadesk's Switchboard provides Plus users with a way to attach an extended keyboard.

ADB devices can be connected in tandem, one to another, because devices usually are built with two ADB connections. This process is called *daisy chaining*. You can put up to 16 devices in a chain, but Apple recommends you use no more than three. A shareware control panel called ADBProbe tells you where and what is connected to your ADB input ports. You can, for example, give computer instructions to a pupil on one attached keyboard while you work on another. Alternatively, if you have two ports, you can attach your mouse to one and your keyboard to the other. There is no functional difference to your Mac.

Part of the ADB is a low power connection, so you do not need a power supply for other devices. The TelePort fax/modem plugs into the ADB chain. You can turn on a Mac using the power button at the upper right on an extended keyboard. Or if you have a model without a power switch, add

Chapter 4
How the Macintosh Works

Sophisticated Circuits' PowerKey or Practical Solutions' Strip Switch to a Classic, SE, SE/30, and LC for this function. They also come with additional power outlets.

WARNING! The ADB chip easily can be damaged by electrical charges. Always ground yourself before using ADB devices, and never plug new devices into your Mac while the Mac is on. It is rare to damage the ADB by making new connections with the power on, but your Mac often has trouble recognizing devices. Damaging the ADB chip in the CPU requires an expensive motherboard replacement. Also, take care not to reconnect ADB plugs too often; they are rated for only a few hundred connections and can become unreliable. If you have trouble with a device, check to see that its ADB connections are well-seated.

SCSI

Whereas ADB is slow, the Small Computer Systems Interface (SCSI) parallel bus is fast, with maximum transfer rates in the several megs/minute range. Hard drives, image scanners, CD-ROM drives, some high-performance printers (imagesetters), and tape backup units are among the devices that can be attached to a SCSI chain. Devices are connected to your Mac with a 25-pin female DB-25 connector, and every Mac since the Plus ships with one on the outside in the back of the case. Many SCSI devices use 50-pin connectors (the actual SCSI standard) requiring a 25/50 hybrid cable. Every Mac since the SE has a 50-pin SCSI connector inside to attach an internal hard drive. The PowerBook series introduces a new type of square SCSI connector.

You can daisy-chain up to seven devices on a SCSI chain, and all is well as long as you assign each device a unique address between 0 and 6. Address 7 is reserved for your Macintosh; address 0 is normally given to an internal hard drive. Addresses are assigned by toggling a hardware switch or knob. Some devices enable you to set the address through a software setting.

Note It is a good idea to buy only a SCSI device whose address settings are readily accessible. Address numbers also assign a device's priority setting, so a hard drive with a higher number should boot up first. Faster hard drives sometimes violate this principle.

SCSI devices require termination so the Mac can sense where the chain begins and ends. Termination involves adding a resistor to a device so signals are absorbed and not reflected back into the chain. There is a simple rule to follow regarding termination: always terminate the first device and the last device in a chain. Internal drives normally are sold self-terminated. Other devices may ship with detachable external SCSI terminators (you can buy these separately) or have built-in termination.

WARNING! Avoid hard drives that require you to open the case to remove or insert the terminating resistor because you will not know whether they are properly terminated. Never use more than two terminators, because they can damage your Mac. (See chapter 4, "Macintosh Hardware: A Technical Look," for more information.) Creating SCSI chains can be troublesome. SCSI cables are notoriously failure-prone, and subject to length limitations. Sometimes you can get SCSI chains to work by rearranging device order; other times, it seems that SCSI chains are affected by the phase of the moon or your current kharma.

Some utilities are available to work with SCSI devices. One kind, exemplified by the shareware program InUse and Norton Utilities' DiskLight, puts a light or flashing icon in your menu bar whenever there is disk access (see figure 4.19). A similar feature is built into Silverlining. This feature is useful when your hard drive does not have an access light or is out of sight.

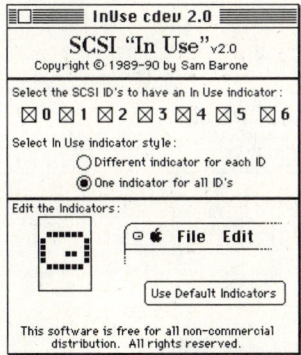

Figure 4.19
InUse puts a flashing disk icon or SCSI number on your menu bar when there is disk access.

SCSI detection and mounting programs are another utility class; the shareware programs SCSIProbe and SCSITools provide this function (see figure 4.20). An FKey called Mount 'Em and QuicKeys' Mounty Extension also provide SCSI disk mounting at a keystroke. Lastly, if you want to do full SCSI chain and device performance analysis, check out the full-featured shareware program SCSI Evaluator, as shown in figure 4.21. (See chapter 22, "Hard Disk Management," for more information.) These utilities are *de rigeur* for use of SCSI chains.

A new SCSI specification based on the SCSI-2 standard is beginning to appear in some of Apple's more powerful Macintosh computers. SCSI-2 has higher transfer rates, better data validity, improved bus mastering with a dedicated processor, and other improvements. It shows greatly improved I/O throughput, and is desirable for use with technology such as graphics, multimedia, sound, video, and other applications where large amounts of data are transferred.

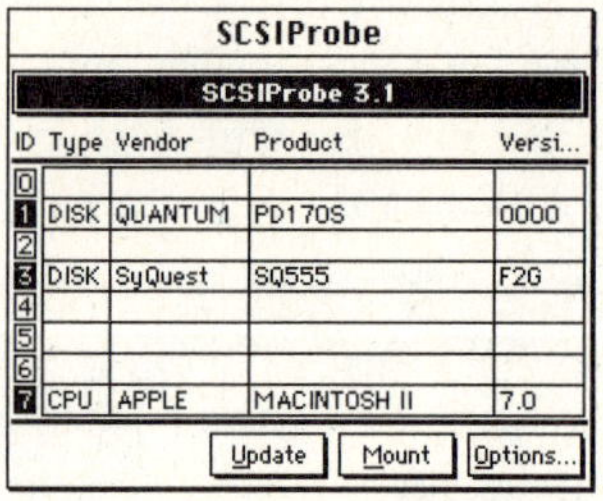

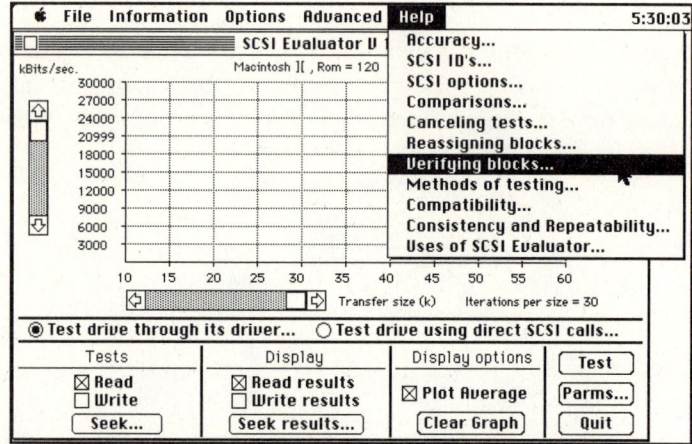

Figure 4.20
SCSIProbe checks your SCSI chain and mounts disks.

Figure 4.21
SCSI Evaluator performs diagnostic tests of your SCSI chain and your hard drive.

NuBus and Other Slots

NuBus is a high-speed (several megs/second) self-configuring bus developed by Texas Instruments and MIT and standardized in mid-1985. It is a circuit board with a 96-pin connector. Each board has a configuration ROM chip that communicates with a Slot Manager that automatically turns on the board properly in the Mac. You do not have to set hardware switches. Slots are designated by letters (A–F) and can accommodate a large number of add-in cards.

Among the vast array of NuBus add-in cards are

▼ Video cards: Apple's 8-bit and 24-bit color video cards are two examples, but there are many manufacturers who supply them. A large screen or color monitor from a vendor often is sold with a compatible or accompanying card.

Recently, Apple began to package video functionality directly on the motherboard. This solution frees up the one required NuBus slot, making it available for other functions.

▼ Memory cards: Large memory upgrades ship on NuBus cards. NuBus' ultra-high speed makes this practical.

▼ Accelerator cards: These cards can be coprocessors for graphics, I/O bus masters (SCSI), or CPU replacements and upgrades. Some Intel 80286 and 80386 coprocessors (from AST and Orange Micro) allow a Mac II to have an IBM AT or 386 computer running inside them. They show up as a mountable volume on your desktop.

▼ Sound processing cards: Digital signal processing requires a hardware solution that NuBus cards address.

▼ Instrument support or data acquisition: Macs can control and process information from complicated equipment such as imagesetters, scanners, and laboratory test equipment. NuBus provides the necessary memory, coprocessor, and interface circuitry to complete the task.

▼ Video equipment: Video capture boards, image processing, and video editing boards are NuBus solutions.

This list is a small sampling of the add-in NuBus boards that are available; there are many more categories.

What if your Mac does not have a NuBus slot? Depending on your model, you still may have a few options. The SE, SE/30, IIsi, and LC have a single expansion slot. The SE's slot can accept accelerators and video cards. The SE/30, IIsi, and LC 030 machines have an 030 Direct Slot, which can accept any type of add-in board. The Apple NuBus Slot adaptor card, which creates a NuBus slot and ships with the 68882 math coprocessor chip, is a notable board for the IIsi. Other direct slot upgrades for the LC are the color video upgrade and the Apple II emulator card that enables an LC to run a vast library of Apple II software.

Chapter 4

How the Macintosh Works

Summary

An operating system is like an orchestra conductor: it manages the hardware (musicians) and software (music) to ensure that they are working together correctly. The Macintosh uses an operating system composed of modules, or a set of routines called managers, to provide a consistent look and feel. Apple also specifies a set of rules called the *Apple Interface Guidelines* that determines how a program can look. The Macintosh is an event-driven system: it monitors your action until it detects input from you, and then it acts. No action ever happens unless you specify it.

Memory determines how many programs you can use at once and how much data you can work with at any one time. The Macintosh enables you to use many different configurations and types of memory. Managing memory is a practiced art. RAM can be configured to save last or commonly used data in a cache, and using a cache can speed up your work. Other enhancements include using a RAM disk or a part of RAM that functions like a hard drive. Additionally, you can create a virtual memory file on your hard drive that works like a RAM extension. If your Mac allows it, you also can use 32-bit addressing to access up to 128M of RAM and 1 gigabyte of virtual memory.

Chapter 5: Macintosh Hardware

This chapter takes an in-depth look at the Macintosh computer in its various hardware versions. If you are not into serious technical information and terminology, this chapter is optional. (Remember, the title of this book is asterisked with "and some things you didn't know you wanted to know!")

In This Chapter

- ▼ Motorola 68000 series processors' architecture
- ▼ Technical descriptions of each Macintosh model
- ▼ Expansion and upgrade capabilities
- ▼ Mac peripherals

Part I
Macintosh, the Computer

WARNING! Apple is introducing new Mac models at a dizzying rate. Many of the Macs listed in this chapter are no longer in production. Check the end of the chapter for a list of production models current at the time of printing.

CPUs

The central processing unit (CPU) is the heart of the Macintosh (or any other computer). The CPU can perform many operations ranging from the simple to the complex. Individual operations are called *instructions,* and any Mac program is merely a sequence of these instructions.

A Closer Look Originally, the single-chip CPUs used in personal computers were called *microprocessors* to distinguish them from mainframe and minicomputers' multi-component CPUs. However, this term has fallen out of fashionable use (along with its cousin *microcomputer*), and most people these days simply refer to them simply as "processors" or "CPUs."

The CPU's operation is regulated by a *system clock,* typically a quartz timing crystal similar to the one used in an electronic watch. Whereas most quartz watch crystals oscillate at 32,768 pulses per second (32 kiloHertz), the slowest Mac has a system clock of 8 *million* cycles per second, or 8 megahertz (abbreviated as 8MHz). The internal operation of the processor is tied to this frequency: individual CPU instructions take a specific number of clock cycles to execute.

The CPU's performance also is tied directly to the clock frequency. For example, it takes only two clock cycles to move 16 bits of data from one internal register, whereas a "divide" instruction takes more than 100 clock cycles. All else being equal (which is rarely the case), a Mac running with a 16MHz clock is twice as fast at a given task as one running an 8MHz system clock. Many third-party manufacturers take advantage of this by offering faster CPUs on boards that can be installed in existing Macs to increase their performance.

But higher clock speeds bring their own problems: CPUs running under faster clocks generate more heat and require larger power supplies and faster memory to keep up with them. This makes the computer larger and more expensive.

Chapter 5
Macintosh Hardware

Communicating with the Hardware

Processors communicate with the rest of the computer through a variety of connections. The most important are the *address lines* and the *data lines*. These lines connect the processor to the computer's memory.

A Closer Look: Some processors—such as the Intel chips commonly used in other PCs—have special I/O ports. All devices such as keyboard and disk drives communicate and are controlled through these ports. The 68000 series is "memory mapped": there are no special I/O ports, and all devices are connected so they appear to be standard memory. For example, a keyboard might be connected to address $C000, and any character typed on the keyboard simply would be the data at that address.

Before any data can be read or written, the address of the data in memory must be specified. This is the function of the address lines. Each address line can be set to either 1 or 0, so a processor with four address lines can specify 16 memory locations from 0000 (0) to 1111 (15).

Setting the address lines to a specific address is called *asserting the address*. Similarly, setting the data lines to a specific value is called *asserting the data*.

The processor's number of address lines determines the maximum amount of memory it can use. The 68000, for example, has 24 address lines, enabling it to access 2 to the 24th power bytes of memory, or 16M.

The Motorola 68000 Family

All Macs to date have used one or another of the Motorola 680x0 series of processors. (Because the part numbers of the common 68000 family processors differ by only one digit—68000, 68010, 68020, 68030, 68040 it is common to write "680x0" when speaking of something that is common to all these processors.) The original member of the family, the 68000, was introduced in 1978 and is used today in the Mac Classic; a special, low-power version is used in the PowerBook 100. Later Macs use the 68020 and 68030 processors, and the new Macintosh Quadras use the advanced 68040 processor.

All 68000 family processors have 32-bit-wide internal *registers*. The 68000, however, has only 16 data lines to connect it to memory, so two accesses to memory are required to read or write a register's contents.

The 68020, 68030, and 68040 processors are very similar internally to the 68000 but have a full 32 data lines, so a register's contents may be read from or written to memory in a single operation. This feature makes these processors almost twice as fast as the 68000 at the same clock speed. For example, the original 68020-based Macintosh II is almost four times the speed of the 68000-based Mac Plus, although the Mac II runs at only twice the clock speed (16MHz versus 8MHz). The faster clock accounts for a doubling of performance; the extra data lines account for the remainder. The 68040s have another advantage: internal operations run at twice the system clock speed (a separate *processor clock* signal is provided), so that a 25MHz 68040 (such as is used in the Centris 650) actually processes instructions at 50MHz.

When you hear people speak of 8-bit computers, 16-bit computers, and 32-bit computers, they are referring to the size of the processor's internal registers. The Apple IIE, for example, uses a 6502 processor with 8-bit wide registers, so it is an 8-bit computer; the newer Apple IIGS computer, which uses a 65816 processor, is a 16-bit computer. By this definition, all Macs are 32-bit machines. However, purists insist the number of data lines match the width of the internal registers: using this criteria, only the 68020 and higher processors are *true* 32-bit processors. It is a philosophical issue that never has been settled and probably never will be.

Whereas the 68000 has 24 address lines—enough to specify 16,777,216 (2 to the 24th power) different memory locations, or 16M—the 68020/030/040 processors have 32 address lines, enabling them to address 4 gigabytes of memory. Architectural limits restrict most current Macs to 128M of physical memory and 1 gigabyte of virtual memory. The Quadra 900 can be expanded to 256M.

The 68020/030/040 processors feature other improvements as well:

▼ Some CPU instructions are more efficient (they execute in fewer clock cycles).

▼ New CPU instructions have been added.

▼ They offer on-chip cache memory for data (68020) and instructions (68030 and 68040).

▼ They have a built-in memory management unit (68030 and 68040) and math processor (68040).

Mac Memory Architecture

The 68000 family treats all available memory as one linear, contiguous chunk. A Mac with, say, 8M of memory has all 8M seamlessly available.

This is in sharp contrast to the Intel 80x6 series processors used in the PC world, which typically treat memory as an array of 64K*segments*. This is an architectural holdover from the original 8080 processor, which was the basis for most CP/M systems a dominant operating system until DOS's arrival with the original IBM PC in early 1981 (in its MS-DOS generic and PC-DOS IBM-specific flavors). The 8080 could access a maximum of 64K of memory, and many of the first programs for the PC were simply "ports" of existing CP/M programs.

The Mac is free from such PC limits. Its constraint is an upper limit on the total amount of usable RAM: Macs based on the 68000 can use a maximum of 4M (except for the Portable, which can go to 9M, and the Powerbook 100, which can go to 8M); Macs without "32-bit clean" ROMs can use a maximum of 8M (this 8M limitation can be bypassed with MODE32, a free utility available from Apple), and Macs with "32-bit clean" ROMs can use a maximum of 128 or 256M.

Coprocessors

Two types of *coprocessors* add capabilities to the 680x0 CPUs. The first type is the *math coprocessor,* which provides very fast execution of certain mathematical operations.

Through the 68030, the 680x0 family offered only simple integer math capabilities; floating-point math and transcendental functions (such as logarithms, sines, and so forth) had to be written as programs. Motorola's math coprocessor chips implemented these functions as processor instructions; the math chips' closely coupled design meant plugging one in was just like getting new instructions in the original processor. Not only were the math chips' functions much faster than the same functions written as programs, but the new instructions were very easy for programmers to use. (The best hardware engineers always strive to make things easy for programmers.)

The original math chip was the 68881; it since has been supplanted by the 68882, an improved version that offers increased performance. The 68882 is a pin-compatible replacement for the 68881. Although older Mac II computers with the 68881 can be upgraded to the 68882 simply by plugging one in, the 68882 still costs several hundred dollars, and the performance improvement for most programs is imperceptible.

The second type of coprocessor is the 68851 *paged memory management unit,* or PMMU. It enables you to use memory in a more versatile fashion. For example, under the Mac system software's control, PMMU can make two non-continuous areas of memory appear to be one large, contiguous area. It also makes implementing virtual memory using unused hard disk space to simulate additional RAM easier.

Chapter 5
Macintosh Hardware

Part I

Macintosh, the Computer

The 68881/68882 chips can be used with any 68000 family processor except the 68040, which has a built-in subset of the 68882 functions. The 68851 PMMU can be used only with the 68020; the 68030 and 68040 chips have most of the 68851 functions built in.

A Closer Look — Two other members of the 68000 family, the 68008 and the 68010, have never been used in a Macintosh computer. The 68008 is a 68000 with only eight data lines, and the 68010 is a slightly enhanced 68000. Table 5.1 categorizes the 68000 processor family.

Table 5.1 68000 Processor family

Processor	68000	68020	68030	68040
Address Lines	24	32	32	32
Data Lines	16	32	32	32
Max. RAM	16M	4G	4G	4G
Math Processor	68881	68881/882	68881/882	built in
Memory Manage.	No	68851	built in	built in
Cache	No	256 bytes, instruction only	256 bytes, instruction & data	4K bytes, instruction & data
Max Clock Speed	16MHz	16MHz	50MHz	40MHz

Macintosh Models

Mac models fall into three categories: compact Macs such as the Mac Classic; modular Macs, such as the Mac LC; and portable Macs, originally represented by the Mac Portable and currently the domain of the PowerBooks.

Compact Macs are "all-in-one" machines ranging from the original Mac 128 to the current Color Classic. These Macs are small computers with integrated video displays. They're easily portable but limited in power and expandability.

Modular Macs range from the Mac LC to the Quadra 950. These machines do not incorporate a video display, which must be purchased separately. All modular Macs have some sort of slot or slots for internal expansion.

Portable Macs run on batteries and are designed to be easily carried from place to place.

Chapter 5
Macintosh Hardware

 The *Performa* series Macs are re-labeled versions of other Mac models. Performas come with a special version of the Mac system software designed for the non-business user, and are sold through mass merchandisers like Sears rather than traditional computer stores. With the current exception of the Performa 600, Performas are physically identical to the Mac model they're based on; the only difference is the "Performa" name on the front, the version of the system software included, and the way in which they're sold. Macs that have Performa equivalents will be noted.

This section describes each Macintosh model in the order of its introduction, with notes on the special features of each machine and its potential for upgrades and expansion. Most of the Macs listed are no longer in production; check the list at the end of this section for current production models.

Lisa and Mac XL

The Lisa predated the Mac by a year, and although it was not known as a Mac originally, it fits into the Mac family line. Lisas came in two flavors: the original Lisa and the later Lisa 2/5 and Lisa 2/10.

Introduced in 1983, the original Lisa came with 1M of memory (the first consumer computer to be shipped with that much memory as standard), a 5MHz 68000 processor, an external "ProFile" 5M hard disk drive, and two strange, dual-headed 5 1/4-inch 800K diskette drives.

Due to a number of factors—not the least of which was its $10,000 retail price—the Lisa never was very popular and sold poorly despite an impressive introduction and ground-breaking software that, in some respects, has never been equaled.

Apple introduced the Lisa 2 series shortly after the Macintosh was introduced in January 1984. The Lisa 2/5 is the original Lisa with its twin 800K, 5 1/4-inch floppies replaced by a single 400K, 3 1/2-inch diskette drive. The Lisa 2/10 uses an internal Apple-manufactured 10M hard drive (known as the "Widget") in place of the external ProFile. Apple offered a free upgrade kit to make original Lisas into Lisa 2/5s.

There are a few other differences between the 2/5 and the 2/10: the 2/5 has a parallel port on the back panel to connect the external hard disk; the 2/10 lacks this port. The 2/10 also lacks the internal batteries of the 2/5, so it loses the time, date, and some other information whenever it is unplugged.

Part I

Macintosh, the Computer

The Lisa 2 can run either special Lisa software (the last version of which was the "Lisa 7/7 Office System") or software that allows it to emulate a Mac and run most Mac software. The Lisa with Mac emulation software was marketed as the Macintosh XL. Some Mac XLs are equipped with a modification to the video circuitry that changes the rectangular Lisa screen pixels to the Mac's square pixels. Without this modification, the screen images appear vertically stretched—circles appear as tall ovals—when running Macintosh software.

Apple stopped manufacturing and supporting the Lisa in 1986. Today, Sun Systems Remarketing of Salt Lake City, Utah, (801) 752-7631, provides support for the Lisa/Mac XL. Sun provides several expansion and upgrade options for Lisa owners, including 800K floppy disk upgrades, Macworks Plus Mac emulation software, SCSI (Small Computer Systems Interface) hard disk interfaces, and more.

The Lisa was a *tour de force* of industrial design: it could be almost completely disassembled with no tools at all! Thumbscrews secured the back cover, which, when removed, exposed a slide-out chassis containing the four circuit boards that composed the Lisa's circuitry: a CPU board, an I/O board, and two 512K memory cards.

The original Lisa's 800K, 5 1/4-inch diskette drives used a proprietary disk with twin openings in the disk jacket for the Lisa's strange, double-headed drives. A free upgrade replaced these two drives with a single 400K, 3 1/2-inch drive and a new front panel.

Three proprietary slots that used expensive ZIF (zero insertion force) connectors provided expansion on the Lisa. Apple produced a dual port parallel card for attaching additional hard disks.

RAM speed: 150ns

Maximum RAM: 2M (two 1M memory cards)

Compact Macs

Mac 128

The original Macintosh was introduced on January 24, 1984. It came with 128K of internal memory, an 8 MHz 68000 processor, and a single 400K diskette drive. An external 400K diskette drive was available as an option.

The original Macintosh vision saw all Macs as identical, allowing programmers to produce software without worrying about different machine configurations. The original Macintosh deliberately was designed to be

Chapter 5
Macintosh Hardware

non-expandable: there was no provision for adding more memory, a hard disk, or a larger display.

Third-party manufacturers considered this a challenge, and they made hard disk and memory upgrades available within a few months of the Mac's introduction. Hard disks were connected through the Mac's serial ports; memory boards were soldered in or connected to the processor via a "clip" device, which was ingenious in concept but unreliable in the field (it tended to slip off if the Mac was moved around).

Because the original Mac was designed specifically to be non-expandable, official Apple upgrades were limited to a 400K external diskette drive (and later, an upgrade to the new 128K ROMs and 800K internal disk drives) and a logic board swap to full Mac Plus capability.

Some third parties offer upgrades that include up to 4M of RAM and SCSI ports. However, given the cost of the necessary ROM and drive upgrade and the Mac Classic's current low cost, expanding a pre-Mac Plus rarely is cost effective.

Mac 512

The Mac 512 was introduced in September, 1984. It was identical to the Mac 128, except it replaced the latter's 16 64K memory chips with 16 256K memory chips. Apple offered upgrades for 128K owners in the form of a logic board swap. It has the same expansion options as the original 128K Mac.

Mac Plus

The Mac Plus was introduced in January, 1986, incorporating several new features that became standard parts of the Mac architecture: a SCSI port for connecting high-speed peripherals such as hard disks, 800K diskette drives, and the use of min-DIN 8-pin connectors for the modem and printer ports.

The Mac Plus marked the switch from the DB-9 serial port connectors to the mini-DIN 8 connectors. The new connectors have one fewer pin than the old connectors; the pin dropped was the one that supplied a small amount of 5 volt current. Several Mac accessories had been developed to use this current, and thus wouldn't work on the Plus. But adapter cables that stole current from the mouse port quickly appeared, and some manufacturers simply switched to external power supplies.

One of the most important Mac Plus features was its new ROM, which at 128K bytes doubled the size of the original Mac ROMs. The new ROMs

Part I

Macintosh, the Computer

incorporated support for 800K diskette drives, SCSI, windows with "zoom boxes," and many other features. The Mac Plus ROM defines the base Mac feature set today. As of this writing, Apple's latest System 7 software supports the Mac Plus (with at least 2M of memory) as the minimal Mac system.

The Mac Plus was the first Mac to officially support any sort of expansion. Its memory, rather than being soldered directly to the logic board, was in the form of small plug-in boards called Single In-line Memory Modules, or SIMMs.

The Plus had sockets for four SIMMs, and Apple delivered it with these filled with 256K SIMMs for a total of 1M of RAM. The maximum RAM a Mac Plus can accommodate is 4M, achieved with four 1M SIMMs.

Some early Mac Plus computers had a bug in the SCSI disk routines in their ROMs, which led to problems with some hard disks. New ROMs that fixed the problem were available as a free upgrade.

The Mac Plus is the Mac that has survived the longest: it was in production for almost five years, from January 1986 until late 1990.

RAM speed: 150ns

Maximum RAM: 4M (4 1M SIMMs)

Mac 512Ke

Introduced in April 1986, the 512Ke was simply a Mac 512 with the new 128K ROMs and an 800K internal diskette drive from the Mac Plus. It replaced the 512K Mac but was discontinued less than a year later. It had the same expansion features as the original 128K and 512K Macs.

 All of the first-generations Macs (128K through Plus) are prone to power supply failures.

Mac SE

The Mac SE was introduced on March 2, 1987, along with the Macintosh II (described below, in the section "Modular Macs"). The Mac 512Ke was dropped at the same time, leaving the Mac lineup at three: Plus, SE, and II.

At this time, Apple abandoned the familiar beige color for its computers, which it had used since the introduction of the Apple][in 1977, and switched to the current platinum color.

The SE replaced the traditional Mac "phone cord" keyboard interface and separate mouse port with the Apple Desktop Bus (ADB), a low-speed serial

Chapter 5
Macintosh Hardware

port designed to interface with multiple peripherals such as keyboards, mice, graphics tablets, and trackballs. ADB has been a source of compatibility problems among third-party hardware developers: it is common for one manufacturer's pointing device not to work with another manufacturer's keyboard. With the cancellation of the Plus in the fall of 1990, ADB is now standard across the entire Mac line.

The SE is similar to the Plus; its major new features are space for either two internal diskette drives or a diskette drive and a hard drive, and a processor direct expansion slot. Performance is slightly faster (about 15 percent) than the Plus, due to changes in the video circuitry. The SE appealed to those who liked the size of the Plus but wanted more expansion capability.

Starting in early 1990, all Mac SEs were equipped with the SuperDrive, the 1.44M diskette drive first introduced on the Mac IIx. SuperDrive-equipped SEs can be identified by the FDHD (floppy disk, high density) logo on the front of the case. Older Mac SEs can be upgraded to the SuperDrive.

The Mac SE included the first expansion slot in a compact Mac case. It is a simple bus-type slot like the one used in the Apple][computers or the ISA-type PCs that consists of the address, data, and some control lines from the processor. Apple calls this architecture a *processor-direct slot*, or PDS. The PDS slot makes enhancements such as an accelerator card or external monitor card more reliable and much easier to install than with the slotless Mac Plus.

The Mac SE has a connector for an external diskette drive. It is the only Mac that supports three diskette drives (two internal and one external).

Early SEs included a vertical "squirrel cage" fan that both was noisy and caused screen interference. A quieter, non-interfering "muffin" type fan was available from Apple (as well as some third parties) as an upgrade.

The SE has a soldered-in lithium battery on the logic board. When this battery dies, the SE's control panel does not retain its settings—which include the time and date, mouse speed, and other information—when the computer is turned off. An Apple dealer must perform the replacement of this battery.

FDHD drives are available as upgrades for earlier SEs. The SE was discontinued with the introduction of the Mac Classic in late 1990. Apple offered upgrades from the SE to the SE/30 (this upgrade is no longer available).

RAM speed: 150ns

Maximum RAM: 4M (4 1M SIMMs)

Mac SE/30

Introduced in January 1989, the SE/30 is a 16MHz 68030-based machine housed in the compact Mac SE-style case. It has eight SIMM sockets rather than four, and its internal video emulates a display card in a NuBus slot for compatibility with the Mac II line. A "processor-direct" slot, provided for expansion, was unique to the SE/30. (SE-30 cards can be used in a Mac IIsi with optional "slot adapter.") Although the built-in monitor displays only black and white, the SE/30 has color QuickDraw built in and can display color with the addition of an external monitor and interface card.

Known as "Jade" while in development at Apple, the SE/30 occupied a unique niche as a high-performance compact Mac. The relatively tiny black and white screen meant the processor never had to manipulate much graphics data, reinforcing the perception of high performance with very fast screen updates. Production of the SE/30 was halted in late 1991.

> **Note:** Although Apple's promotional literature for the SE/30 claims it can support up to 128M of RAM, only 8M of it can be effectively used because the SE/30 does not have the 32-bit clean ROMs required to address more memory. This limitation can be overcome with the "MODE32" INIT Apple licensed from Connectix, which patches out parts of the ROM and enables the SE/30, as well as the II, IIx, and IIcx, to operate as though they have 32-bit clean ROMs.

The SE/30 was the first Mac with internal video designed with separate video RAM, so the processor never has to share access to memory with the video circuitry.

RAM speed: 120ns

Max. RAM: 128M (8 16M SIMMs)

Mac Classic

The Classic replaced the Mac Plus and Mac SE models in October 1990. It's basically a Mac SE without the internal slot. Like its predecessors, it used an 8MHz 68000 processor. It could be configured with one internal diskette drive or a diskette drive and a hard disk.

To keep costs down, the Classic didn't have SIMM sockets; it came with 1M of soldered-in RAM, and additional RAM was added with a small plug-in card that contained two SIMM sockets and 1M of soldered-in RAM. As with earlier models, the maximum amount of memory the Classic can use is 4M.

Software control of screen brightness was seen on this Mac for the first time since the Lisa. Expansion options were limited to additional RAM and larger internal hard disks, although only special, low-powered disk drives could be used.

> **Note:** One interesting and unique feature of the Classic is its built-in ROM disk. If you hold down command-option-X-O at boot time, the Classic will boot from a ROM disk configured with a minimal version of System 6.0.3. This is very handy should you ever find yourself unable to boot from your hard disk.

RAM speed: 150ns

Maximum RAM: 4M (1M soldered in, 3M on expansion board)

Mac Classic II

Essentially the Classic II is a Mac LC logic board in a compact Mac case. Introduced in October 1991, this Mac is functionally identical to the LC. The limited space inside the Classic case precludes the use of the LC's expansion slot. Like the LC, the Classic II has two SIMM sockets for memory expansion, and 2M of soldered-in RAM. The Classic II is otherwise identical to the Classic. For details, see the information on the Mac LC in the section, "Modular Macs," below.

The Mac Classic II is also sold as the Performa 200.

RAM speed: 120ns

Maximum RAM: 10M (2M soldered in, 2 4M SIMMs)

Color Classic

The Color Classic debuted in February 1993. It is based on the LCII logic board, which is similar to the LC, except that it has 4M of soldered-in RAM and uses a 68030 processor instead of the LC's 68020.

In a case slightly larger than previous compact Macs, the Color Classic incorporates a 10" Sony Trinitron picture tube with a desktop size of 512 by 384 pixels. The internal video circuitry can display up to 16,384 colors with additional video RAM; the standard complement of VRAM allows 256 colors to display.

The PDS slot in the Color Classic can accept any board that would fit in an LCII, including the Apple IIe emulation card.

Chapter 5
Macintosh Hardware

Unique features of the Color Classic include:

▼ Integrated microphone for voice recording

▼ Screen brightness and sound volume controls via pushbuttons on the front of the case.

▼ A "pop out" logic board that can be easily removed from the back of the case with no tools and without unplugging any cables.

▼ An automatic screen saver that blanks the display (actually cutting power to the screen) after a user-definable time.

Other Color Classic features, performance, and limitations are the same as those of the LCII.

RAM speed: 120ns

Maximum RAM: 10M (4M soldered in, 2 4M SIMMs, 2M ignored)

Modular Macs

Modular Macs are designed to be expandable. Some, such as the LC series, offer rather limited memory and expansion options; others have almost unlimited potential. The first modular Mac, the Mac II, was designed specifically to address complaints about the non-expandability and closed architecture of the original Macs. The first prototype was called simply, "Open Macintosh."

Although the original Macs were designed to be non-expandable, market forces and third-party cleverness often found a way. Two of the most significant items were Levco's "Monster Mac" upgrade, which equipped an original 128, 512, or 512Ke with a whopping (at the time) 2M of RAM, and General Computer Corporations' "HyperDrive" internal 10M hard drive.

Since the compact Macs had no internal expansion slots, both products used "clips" that fit around the 68000 processor and tapped directly into its connections. While clever, the clips didn't work very well in the field; if the Mac were moved, the clip tended to slip off. The Mac was perceived as a limited, "toy" computer that offered a cute interface but little else: no expandability, no color, and no software. (Who'd write for such a limited machine? Despite Apple's evangelizing there was little software available.)

The modular Macs solved these problems with their array of slots and sockets for memory and peripherals.

Chapter 5
Macintosh Hardware

Mac II

Introduced on March 2, 1987, along with the Mac SE, the Mac II was a completely new machine and the first Mac to be based on a processor other than the 68000. The Mac II uses a 68020 processor running at 16MHz, providing roughly four times the performance of a Plus. The 68881 math processor was included as standard equipment.

The II introduced several new hardware features, including:

- ▼ NuBus slots for expansion
- ▼ True 32-bit hardware architecture
- ▼ Color QuickDraw
- ▼ The ADB for connecting keyboards and mice

Expansion possibilities for the Mac II—or any of the NuBus Macs—are almost limitless. Its 8 SIMM sockets can hold up to 128M of RAM (with the SuperDrive upgrade). The Mac II's six-slot case can accommodate a full range of NuBus cards, as well as a full-height 5 1/4-inch internal hard disk (currently available in 2 gigabyte capacities) and two floppy drives. The power supply is robust enough to handle almost anything you throw at it—a distinct break from traditional Mac power supplies!

Several manufacturers offer accelerators that boost the Mac II's performance by a factor of three or more. Apple upgrades include the SuperDrive 1.44M diskette drive and a logic board swap to the 40MHz, 68030-based Mac IIfx.

There have been three different ROM revisions for the Mac II. The original Revision A version had a bug that prevented use of any NuBus card with more than 1M of internal memory, so a free ROM replacement (Revision B) was made available. The third set of ROMs (Revision C) comes with the SuperDrive upgrade and is necessary for SuperDrive operation. You also need this third set of ROMs if you use more than 8M of memory: a bug in earlier ROMs causes the Mac II to fail if SIMMs larger than 1M are installed in Bank A.

You can tell which ROMs are in a Mac II by looking at the part numbers: the ROMs are the four large chips just to the left of the SIMM sockets, and their part numbers end with "A," "B," or "C." For example, 342-0105A is an "A" ROM, and 342-0105C is a "C" ROM.

 A very few of the original Mac II logic boards have defective PMMU sockets. This defect prevents a 68851 PMMU chip (optional) from operating correctly. Free logic board replacements were mandated at the time but may no longer be available.

The Mac II contains two lithium batteries that are soldered to the logic board. If these batteries die, the computer cannot be turned on, since the batteries supply power to the circuit that senses the "Power On" key on the Mac II keyboard. An Apple dealer must perform battery replacement.

RAM speed: 120ns

Maximum RAM: 68M (Revision A or B ROMs), 128M (Revision C ROMs), 4 1M SIMMs and 4 16M SIMMs or 8 16M SIMMs.

Mac IIx

The 68020 processor offered dramatic performance improvements over the 68000, but its reign as the top Mac processor was a short one: In October 1989, 18 months after introduction of the Mac II, the IIx debuted. It replaced the II's 68020 with a 68030 and sported a 1.44M SuperDrive floppy instead of the Mac II's 800K drive.

The IIx is approximately 15 percent faster than a Mac II since the latter includes provisions for a separate memory management unit (the 68851 PPMMU discussed in the "Processor" section above), which makes it slightly slower. Technically, the Mac II runs with two wait states for each memory access, whereas the IIx runs with only one. The 68030 incorporates an integral memory management unit that eliminates the need for the extra wait state. ("Wait states" are discussed later in this chapter.) The IIx was also the first Mac to include the now-standard FDHD or "SuperDrive," a diskette drive that can read and write DOS 720K and 1.44M diskettes, as well as read and write a new 1.44M Macintosh format. All Macs introduced after the IIx include the SuperDrive as standard equipment.

A IIx upgrade was available for Mac II owners, but was never very popular due to its high price and small performance increase.

The IIx was the first Mac to have its ROMs on a SIMM, as well as the first Mac to have the SuperDrive as standard equipment.

RAM speed:120ns

Maximum RAM: 128M (8 16M SIMMs)

Mac IIcx

Introduced in March, 1989, the Mac IIcx is basically a Mac IIx in a smaller case with three NuBus slots rather than six. It also has room for only a single internal diskette drive (although a connector was provided for an external diskette drive) and a 3-1/2 inch hard drive rather than the 5 1/4-inch hard drive that could fit in a II or IIx. The IIcx was the first Mac designed to operate either flat or on its side—removable rubber feet can be installed on the bottom or side of the machine, as appropriate.

The "three-slotters" reintroduced good industrial design to the Mac world. Like the Lisa but unlike previous Macs, most components are plug-in and can be removed without using tools. A single screw secures the plastic bracket that supports the diskette and hard disk drives.

The IIcx was the first Mac to have socketed lithium batteries that could be easily replaced by the user.

The IIcx was a very popular computer and quickly became the biggest seller in the Mac II line until it was discontinued, along with the IIx, in the fall of 1990.

RAM speed: 120ns

Maximum RAM: 128M (8 16M SIMMs)

The Mac IIci

The Mac IIci was the first Mac positioned specifically as a high-performance computer. Announced in September 1989, it is similar to the Mac IIcx but sports a 25MHz (as opposed to a 16MHz) 68030 processor and includes provision for a cache card to further improve performance. Its other main feature is built-in video circuitry that drives a standard Apple 13-inch monitor or Apple Portrait Display without an interface card, freeing the otherwise required NuBus slot.

The IIci's internal video allocates a buffer from the memory in the first four SIMM sockets (Bank A). Programs running in this part of memory are slowed because the video circuitry takes control of the memory from the CPU to generate the video image. Depending on the size of the screen and number of colors it is set to display, this slowdown can range from 5 percent to slightly more than 45 percent.

The IIci was the first Mac that did not have to have the largest SIMMs in Bank A. For example, a 5M IIci could have four 256K SIMMs in Bank A, and four

Chapter 5
Macintosh Hardware

1M SIMMs in Bank B, but the opposite configuration would work as well and is in fact more common; putting most of the available RAM in Bank B minimizes the chance that some program code or data ends up in Bank A.

> **Note:** One of the best ways to improve overall IIci performance is to use a separate video card to drive the monitor, just like on a IIcx. The internal video circuitry will not be used unless a monitor is plugged into it. If you use the internal video circuitry, you will realize the best performance by running in black and white mode. A twin-monitor system, with a color monitor connected to a separate video card and a black and white monitor connected to the internal video, was a popular setup with this machine inside Apple.

The IIci has a slot designed for a cache memory card to use. Even though the IIci uses fast, 80ns memory, the 25MHz processor must insert three wait states for each access to main memory. A typical IIci cache card supplies 32K to 128K of very fast RAM that can be accessed with no wait states to act as a buffer between the processor and main RAM. Some companies offer cards for the cache slot that are both cache cards and accelerators with fast 40 or 50MHz processors. Since late 1991, Apple has included a cache card with the IIci as standard equipment.

The IIci was the first Mac with "32-bit clean" ROMs. It can accept up to 128M of internal RAM using 16M SIMMs. (Note that System 7 or higher is required to effectively use more than 8M of RAM.) The IIci also was the first Mac to have "32-bit QuickDraw" (which is unrelated to 32-bit cleanliness, although many people confuse the terms) built into the ROM, which seemed to cause compatibility problems with quite a few programs when the IIci first was introduced. Because of this, the IIci gained an undeserved reputation as a quirky, incompatible machine. By now, all programs are compatible with 32 bit QuickDraw and IIcis are in high demand in the used Mac market. The IIci can be upgraded to a Quadra 700 with a logic board swap.

RAM speed: 80ns

Maximum RAM: 128M (8 16M SIMMs)

Maximum internal video: 256 colors at 640 by 480 pixels; 16 grays at 640 by 870 pixels (Apple portrait display)

The IIfx

The Mac IIfx was introduced in March 1990 and was Apple's most powerful computer until the introduction of Quadra series in late 1991. It has a 40MHz 68030, 32K of cache RAM, and special serial port processors consisting of

6502 CPUs (the same CPU used in the Apple][series of computer) with their own RAM and ROM. The IIfx also uses a special memory architecture with 64 pin SIMMs that allows higher performance—although it does mean that memory for the IIfx is unique and cannot be used in other Macs.

Occupying the same six-slot case as the original Mac II and IIx, the IIfx also has an interesting refinement to its power supply: a thermostatically controlled fan whose speed and noise vary with the temperature inside the case.

The IIfx SCSI circuitry introduced DMA to the Mac line. SCSI DMA (Direct Memory Access) can dramatically improve hard disk I/O performance because it can transfer data directly between the IIfx memory and a hard disk without the processor's intervention. Unfortunately, its throughput advantages currently can be realized only by Apple's version of UNIX, A/UX.

The serial ports of the IIfx are actually individual 6502 processors (like the one used in the Apple IIE), complete with their own RAM buffers and ROM drivers. They are not completely compatible with some software written for earlier Macs that address the serial ports directly (MIDI programs are the main offenders). Apple has a "IIfx Serial Switch" CDEV that allows most such software to work.

In addition to its six NuBus slots, the IIfx also has its own PDS slot for high-speed peripherals.

RAM speed: 80ns, special fx-only SIMMs required

Max. RAM: 128M (8 16M SIMMs)

Mac LC

November 1990 saw the introduction of the Mac LC. The LC was designed to be a low-cost color Mac, better suited for homes and schools than the more expensive NuBus color machines. It has a small, "pizza box" case with room for one diskette drive and one low-power 3 1/2-inch hard drive. A 16MHZ 68020 processor provides the power, although it's limited by its 16 bit memory bus (described below).

The LC has 2M of soldered-in RAM and two SIMM sockets. The maximum amount of RAM an LC can have is 10M, achieved with two 4M SIMMs installed. This limit is designed into the memory controller and cannot be overridden.

The LC was the first Mac to have separate dual-ported video RAM for its internal video circuitry. Unlike the Mac IIci and IIsi video setups, where the processor must wait for the video circuitry to relinquish control of RAM, the

Chapter 5
Macintosh Hardware

LC's video RAM can be accessed simultaneously by the processor and the video circuitry (hence the "dual ported" designation). This means the processor need never wait for the video circuitry.

As delivered, the LC supports 256 colors on the 12-inch Apple color monitor's 512 by 384 screen, or 16 colors on the Apple 13- or 14-inch monitor's 640 by 480 screen (the 13- or 14-inch monitors, with 640 by 480 pixel "desktops," are the largest the LC's internal video can support). Replacing the standard 256K VRAM SIMM with an optional 512K VRAM SIMM boosts this to 32,768 colors on the 12-inch monitor and 256 colors on the 13 and 14-inch monitors.

The LC uses the "dynamic bus sizing" feature of the Motorola processors: the same 68020 processor used in the older Mac II with a 32-bit memory bus is used in the LC with a 16-bit memory bus. This makes the LC somewhat slower than the Mac II, even though both run at 16MHz, because the LC must perform two memory accesses to the Mac II's one memory access.

The LC was the first Mac to dispense with the "programmer's switch," a small two-button switch generally provided as a snap-in piece on other Macs. This switch enables programmers to drop into their debuggers or reboot the machine (pressing the switch shorted either the NMI-nonmaskable interrupt or reset lines of the processor). The programmer's switch functions are provided by keyboard commands on these machines. For example, holding the Shift, Command, and Power-on keys forces the computer to reboot. The Option Command Power-on combination drops into the debugger but works only with debuggers that are "aware" of these new machines.

The LC includes sound digitizing capability and a microphone, as well as a single small processor-direct expansion slot. The LC also features a small connector that allows add-in boards to address the VRAM directly.

RAM speed: 120ns

Maximum RAM: 10M (2M soldered in, 2 4M SIMMs)

Maximum internal video: 256 colors at 640 by 480; 32,768 colors at 512 by 384.

Mac IIsi

The IIsi was introduced in October 1990. It has a 20MHz 68030 processor and one internal slot that can accept either an SE/30-style processor-direct slot card or a Mac II-style NuBus card. A "slot adapter" which, curiously, includes a 68882 math coprocessor is required for either type of card. Some third-party slot adapters include other hardware, such as a fast RAM cache.

Chapter 5
Macintosh Hardware

The standard memory configuration is 1M of soldered-in RAM and four SIMM slots. Maximum memory is 65M, achieved with four 16M SIMMs installed. Like the LC, the IIsi has internal video circuitry that can drive the 12-inch or 13-inch color displays or the Apple Portrait Display. Unlike the LC, the IIsi does not use separate video RAM and encounters performance problems similar to the IIci when internal video is used, although the memory design minimizes the problem relative to the IIci.

The IIsi includes sound digitizing hardware and a microphone.

The IIsi is designed to use only special low-power, low-profile hard disks. There is enough room in the case to use a standard size 3.5 inch hard disk, and the power supply is generally up to the task. However, if a full-length NuBus card is installed, it extends over the top of the area the hard disk occupies. The low-profile drives are small enough to allow this; full-sized 3 1/2-inch drives are not.

A Closer Look One common problem users encounter with the IIsi is periodic loss of sound from the internal speaker. The speaker is a snap-in module, and two metal "fingers" touch contact pads on the logic board when the speaker is installed. The contact is light and any slight corrosion or dirt will interrupt power to the speaker. Solutions include soldering the speaker in (drastic), occasional cleaning of the contacts on the speaker and logic board (a standard pencil eraser works well), and using external speakers plugged into the IIsi sound output.

RAM speed: 100ns

Maximum RAM: 69M (1M soldered in, 4 16M SIMMs)

Quadra 700

The Macintosh Quadras are Apple's high end machines. They offer excellent performance and advanced features such as fast internal video circuitry and on-board EtherNet networking capability.

Introduced in October 1991, the Quadra 700 is the "entry level" Quadra. It is packaged in a IIcx/ci-sized case, and in fact, the Quadra 700 logic board is available as an upgrade to the cx and ci. It comes with 4M of soldered-in RAM. Ten SIMM sockets are provided: four for processor RAM and six for video RAM. The supplied VRAM is sufficient to support up to a 16-inch color display at eight bits per pixel (256 colors). Adding 6 256K VRAM SIMMs (the 512K VRAM SIMMs used in the LC and LCII will not work) expands the VRAM to 2M and allows full 24-bit color on up to a 16" monitor. The separate VRAM means that the 700's performance does not suffer when its internal video is used. In fact, the internal video is almost as fast as Apple's 8•24GC accelerated graphics card.

One of Quadra's extra, useful features is support for a bootable, PMMU-protected RAM disk that survives crashes (though not the machine's being turned off).

The 700 has only two NuBus slots; its high-speed video and integrated EtherNet support compensate for the missing slot relative to the Mac IIcx/ci. A separate 20MHz clock signal is available on the NuBus connectors for cards that can use it. A PDS slot is included but is placed so that its use blocks one of the NuBus slots. Like other recently introduced Macs, the 700 comes with microphone and external speaker ports and has sound digitizing capability.

With 4M SIMMs, 20M of total processor RAM is available. 16M SIMMs can be used, but the location of the SIMM sockets under the disk drive bracket, as well as their very close spacing, means most "composite" 16M SIMMs (those made using 32 4 megabit chips rather than 8 16 megabit chips) are physically too large and will not fit. Using thin, low-profile 16M SIMMs gives 68M of memory. Like the IIci, the Quadra 700 requires 80ns RAM.

Like the cx and ci, the 700 can accommodate a 3 1/2-inch hard drive. The 700's fast SCSI port can sustain about 3.5M/second of data transfer, which only today's fastest drives can equal.

RAM speed: 80ns

Maximum RAM: 68M (4M soldered in, 4 16M SIMMs)

Maximum internal video: 256 colors at 1152 by 870 pixels

Quadra 900

Introduced at the same time as the Quadra 700, the Quadra 900 uses the same 25MHz 68040 processor as the 700, but offers much greater expandability.

The 900's extra expandability comes primarily from its larger "form factor": i.e., it is housed in a large vertical case designed to stand on the floor next to a desk. The 900 has no soldered-in RAM but comes with 8 of its 16 SIMM sockets filled with 1M SIMMs for a total of 8M. 256M of RAM is possible with all 16 sockets filled with (low profile) 16M SIMMs.

The standard complement of VRAM is 1M, which allows 16 bit color on up to a 16" monitor. The 4 VRAM SIMM sockets accept 256K SIMMs to expand video memory to 2M.

Chapter 5
Macintosh Hardware

Internally, the Quadra 900 has room for four half-height, 5 1/4-inch storage devices. One bay is occupied by the floppy drive, leaving three bays open on a base system with no hard disk. Five NuBus slots are provided; the extra space in the 900's case allows the use of oversized cards that are 2" taller than standard NuBus cards. External connectors—ADB, serial, EtherTalk, SCSI, and sound I/O—are the same as those on the 700. A PDS socket like the 700's blocks one NuBus slot if used. A 300 watt power supply, the largest ever installed in a Macintosh, provides ample power for all internal expansion.

The 900 is the first Mac to offer two independent SCSI ports. Each can sustain about 3.6M/second, which allows the 900 to realize very high disk drive performance by using a "drive array": two drives (one connected to each SCSI port) that are accessed simultaneously. This does require special disk driver software and matched drives to achieve optimum performance. Such "drive arrays" are offered by Micronet Technology of Irvine, California, (714) 837-6033 and FWB of San Francisco (415) 474-8055. Only one SCSI port is available from outside the machine, however. The 900 can be upgraded to the faster Quadra 950 with a logic board swap.

A Closer Look It is possible to install a CD-ROM drive in the Quadra 900 (and 950). One unique feature of these Macs is a connector on the logic board for the audio-out signals of such a device, allowing CD-ROM audio to be played through the Mac's internal speaker, as well as providing the capability to digitize CD-ROM output.

RAM speed: 80ns

Maximum RAM: 256M (16 16M SIMMs)

Maximum internal video: 256 colors at 1152 by 870 pixels

Quadra 950

The Quadra 950 is identical to the Quadra 900 with the following exceptions:

▼ Clock speed of 33MHz instead of 25MHz

▼ I/O bus speed of 25MHz instead of 16MHz

▼ Support for 16 bit video modes

RAM speed: 80ns

Maximum RAM: 256M (16 16M SIMMs)

Maximum internal video: 32,768 colors at 1152 by 870 pixel

Mac LCII

The LCII was an incremental revision to the Mac LC, and replaced it in March 1992. The 68020 processor was upgraded to a 68030 processor, and 4M of soldered-in RAM is standard as opposed to the 2M of the LC. The LCII does not include the second internal floppy connector the LC does. Performance and expansion are identical to the Mac LC.

The LCII can be upgraded to the LCIII. This consists of replacing the entire computer, including the logic board and complete case, with the exception of the power supply and disk drives.

The 4M of soldered-in RAM combined with the 10M memory limit assures that LCII owners can't achieve the maximum 10M of RAM without installing 2 4M SIMMs—achieving a total of 12M of internal RAM, of which only 10M may be used.

The LCII is sold in various configurations as the Performa 400, the Performa 405, and the Performa 430.

RAM speed: 120ns

Maximum RAM: 10M (4M soldered in, 2 4M SIMMs, 2M ignored)

Maximum internal video: 256 colors at 640 by 480; 32,768 colors at 512 by 384

Mac IIvx

The IIvx was introduced in October 1992, replacing the aging Mac IIci. Although its processor is faster—a 68030 running at 32Mhz, as opposed to the IIci's 25MHz—its memory bus runs at half that speed, slowing overall performance to roughly IIci levels. The IIvx internal video, though, uses separate video RAM and thus does not impose the performance penalty that the IIci's internal video does.

The IIvx was the first Mac to use a metal case. Expansion capability is good: a 3 1/2-inch hard drive, a SuperDrive floppy, and a half-height 5 1/4-inch device all are accommodated in a case slightly larger than the IIci case, along with 4 SIMM sockets, 3 NuBus slots, and a PDS slot. 4M of soldered-in RAM is standard, as is 32K of cache RAM and 512K of video RAM. Video RAM can be expanded to 1M, allowing 16 bit color on 13- and 14-inch color monitors. Curiously, the IIvx does not support 16-inch monitors. A 68882 math processor is standard.

Although it uses the same 120 pin connectors as the IIci PDS slot, the IIvx slot is electrically different and IIci cards should not be used—damage to the card or the computer could result. Cache control signals are not present, so a normal cache card cannot be used. This is not a significant drawback, however, due to the standard 32K cache built into the machine. Officially, the PDS slot is known as an "accelerator slot" and is provided for third party accelerators.

A version of the IIvx without the 32K cache and 68882 math processor is sold as the Performa 600. While the computers are otherwise identical an important consideration is that the IIvx can be upgraded to the Centris 650, while the Performa 600 cannot.

In Europe, a 16MHz version of the IIvx is sold as the IIvi. This version lacks the math processor and cache RAM of the IIvx but is otherwise identical.

RAM speed: 80ns

Maximum RAM: 68M (4M soldered in, 4 16M SIMMs)

Maximum internal video: 32,768 colors at 640 by 480

Mac LCIII

The LCIII was introduced in early 1993 and is the first high performance member of the LC family. Incorporating a 25MHz 68030 processor and a 32 bit memory bus, the LCIII provides performance that is equal or superior to that of the Mac IIci.

The LCIII improves on the previous LC series computers in several aspects:

- ▼ Higher memory capacity: 36M as opposed to 10M
- ▼ Superior performance—roughly 2.5-3 times the speed of the LC/LCII
- ▼ Internal video supports more monitors
- ▼ A socket for an optional 68882 FPU chip is provided on the logic board
- ▼ PDS slot accepts both old LC/LCII style cards and new LCIII specific cards

The LCIII is slightly larger than the previous LC series machines and uses a very similar case. 4M of soldered-in RAM is standard; a single memory socket

Chapter 5
Macintosh Hardware

accepts the 72-pin, 32 bit wide SIMMs used in the newer Macs. SIMMs are available in 4, 8, 16, and 32 capacities—but since there's only one SIMM socket, any installed memory must be replaced when upgrading.

The LCIII's video capabilities are upgraded as well. 512K of video RAM is standard, and a socket for adding a 256K VRAM SIMM is supplied. The internal video supports up to 16" monitors (at 832 by 624 pixels) at 256 colors. With the additional 256K VRAM, 16 bit color (32,768 colors) is supported on 14-inch and smaller displays making the LCIII an ideal low-cost QuickTime platform. The LCIII also supports standard VGA color monitors commonly used in the PC world. Sound digitizing circuitry and a microphone is included.

An interesting enhancement was made to the LCIII video capabilities: 16 bit color can be achieved on the standard system by switching to a 640 by 400 pixel display in the "Monitors" control panel. This ability is unique to the LCIII.

The LCIII is also sold as the Performa 450.

RAM speed: 80ns, 72 pin SIMM

Maximum RAM: 36M (4M soldered in, one 32M SIMM)

Maximum internal video: 256 colors at 832 by 624

Centris 610

Introduced in February 1993, along with the Centris 650 and Quadra 800, the Centris 610 is Apple's attempt to move the 68040 processor down to the consumer level. Actually, the 610 uses a 68LC040 processor the 68040 without the integrated math processor. And even though it runs at 20MHz, the Centris 610 is faster at most tasks than the Mac IIfx due to the advanced architecture of the '040.

Housed in a wide, thin metal case similar in proportion but somewhat larger than the LC series, the 610 offers room for the same three internal storage devices as a IIvx (3 1/2-inch floppy, 3 1/2-inch hard drive, and 5 1/4-inch, half height drive). 4M of RAM is standard, and two SIMM sockets are provided. The 610 is optionally available with built-in EtherNet support.

Like the Quadra 800, the 610 uses 32 bit wide, 72 pin SIMMs. Its two SIMM sockets allow for a maximum of 64M of additional RAM to be added. Although its 68LC040 processor does not include a PMMU, it can be replaced (at some expense) with a standard 68040.

 Like many Macs, the Centris 610 sports a separate power socket on the back, generally used to power a monitor. The 610 is unique in that this socket is not switched—it's always on, so that turning the 610 off does not turn the monitor off.

RAM speed: 80ns

Maximum RAM: 68M (4M soldered in, 2 32M SIMMs)

Maximum internal video: 256 colors at 1152 by 870

Centris 650

The Centris 650 represents the best "bang for the buck" ratio in the Macintosh line today. Housed in the same metal case as the IIvx, it's available in two models: the low end model has a 68LC040 processor, 4M of soldered-in RAM, and no EtherNet; the high end model uses a 68040, and has 8M of soldered-in RAM and on-board EtherNet. Both models run at 25MHz.

The Centris 650 memory controller brings a new capability to the Mac line: interleaved memory accesses. Although common for years in the PC worlds, interleaving was previously unknown in Macintoshes. When two adjacent SIMMs are the same size, the memory controller accesses them in sequence, effectively reducing the latency between asserting an address and reading or writing the data. This can result in performance improvements of up to 15%. This means the 650 is somewhat faster than the 700—it also has the improved QuickDraw routines used in the Quadra 800 for faster video display and manipulation—and is the real heir to this position in the Mac lineup.

It has the same three NuBus slots and 4 SIMM sockets of the vx, although the SIMMs used are the newer 72 pin versions.

RAM speed: 80ns

Maximum RAM: 132M or 136M (4 or 8M soldered in RAM, 4 32M SIMMs)

Quadra 800

Announced with the new Centris computers, the 800 replaced the popular Quadra 700 as the low end Quadra. The 800 comes in above the 700 in capability (the 700's place in the lineup is occupied by the new Centris 650), but below the 900/950 in expansion capability.

At the time of this writing, the Quadra 800 is the fastest Macintosh available. Along with the Centris 610 and 650, it uses an interleaved memory

Chapter 5
Macintosh Hardware

architecture that reduces the effective access time when adjacent SIMMs are the same size, as well as improvements to QuickDraw that use 68040-only instructions to speed the display and manipulation of information in the internal video circuitry.

The Quadra 800 (as well as the LCIII, and Centris 610 and 650) uses a new, 72 pin SIMM design for memory. See the "Memory" section below for a complete explanation.

Three NuBus slots and one PDS slot are provided. Bays for one half-height, 5 1/4-inch drive (typically a CD-ROM), one 1-inch high 3 1/2-inch drive, and one full height 3 1/2-inch drive are provided. SCSI cables and power connectors for all positions are included. Unlike other Macs that use metal brackets to secure drives, the Quadra 800 requires its drives to be mounted on plastic "sleds" that snap into place. When ordered with the CD-ROM drive, the 800 comes with a special CD-ROM from which it can boot if necessary. This is a useful capability when the hard drive crashes!

Unlike the other Quadras, the 800 is limited to a maximum of 1M of VRAM, allowing 16 bit color on a 16-inch monitor, or 256 colors on a two-page monitor.

RAM speed: 60ns

Maximum RAM: 136M (8M soldered in, 4 32M SIMMs)

Max. internal video: 256 colors at 1152 by 870 pixels

Portable Macs

Although the original Mac 128 and its descendants in the "compact Macs" line are eminently portable, with their small size and built-in handles, demand for a truly portable— i.e. a battery-powered—Mac was strong. There were several technical obstacles to such a machine in the late 1980s: the lack of low-power versions of the Motorola 68000 family processors and support chips; the lack of small, low power hard drives (while many laptop PCs could be used effectively without a hard drive, by 1989 a Mac pretty much had to have one), the need for an integrated pointing device, and a flat-panel display with sufficient clarity and resolution to effectively present the Mac's detailed graphics.

Work on the original Mac Portable began in 1986 with the search for a suitable liquid crystal display. Laptop PCs at the time typically used "CGA" resolution displays of 640 by 200 pixels. Since these machines spent most of their time in "text mode," the limited quality of these displays wasn't much of

Chapter 5
Macintosh Hardware

a problem. But the Mac needs to display finely detailed graphics and a lot of single-pixel wide lines, and this simply couldn't be handled well by the LCDs available at the time. Those were "passive matrix" displays, whose pixels were electrically scanned in rows and columns to generate a display. A side effect of this scanning is ghosting and shadowing of adjacent pixels, which would blur the details of many Mac graphics.

A Japanese company called Hosiden came to the rescue with a new "active matrix" liquid crystal panel. This panel used a separate electronic switch on each pixel, allowing them to be turned on and off individually without affecting surrounding pixels. Although much more expensive than passive matrix displays, it made the display quality associated with Macs possible. The very high level of contrast made possible by this display also eliminated the need for a power-hungry backlight in most situations. This was the crowning technical achievement of the original Mac Portable.

> **Note:** A word about X-rays: Many Portable and PowerBook owners are nervous about putting their computers through airport X-ray machines. Despite anecdotal tales to the contrary, X-rays do not affect magnetic media or electronics in any way. Some people claim that the electric motors in the X-ray machine's conveyor belt damages the media, but if you place your computer very near the entrance of the unit (rather than at the beginning of the conveyor belt) you should be okay.

The Portable

The Mac Portable was introduced in September, 1989. It contained a 16MHz low-power version of the 68000 processor and 1M of RAM on board. Although large and heavy (17 pounds) compared to other portable computers, it boasted complete Mac compatibility, unrivaled battery life (typically 8 to 10 hours), and the first commercial use of aforementioned screen technology: active matrix LCD.

Unlike other LCDs, the Portable's display is visible in almost any light level and responds fast enough to prevent "ghosting" effects when the mouse pointer or an image is moved rapidly onscreen. Responding to customer demand, Apple introduced a backlit screen as an upgrade in spring 1991. The backlit screen is easier to see in low-light situations but much harder to see in very bright light (outdoors), and it reduces battery life by about 50 percent.

The Portable's power consumption was so low that a power switch wasn't deemed necessary. The computer will maintain the contents of memory for almost two weeks with a fully charged battery.

The non-backlit Portables use expensive "static" memory; the newer backlit screen models use cheaper "pseudostatic" RAM. When ordering a memory upgrade, make sure you specify the Portable model you have! The Portable is expandable to a maximum of 9M of RAM. Portable memory typically is much more expensive than memory for other Macs. An upgrade to the backlit screen is available for older Portables.

There are three expansion slots in the Portable: a dedicated slot for an internal modem, a slot for memory, and a PDS slot for other expansion. The very limited power available to the PDS slot means few peripherals are available for it, although some companies offer memory cards that occupy this slot.

Production of the Mac Portable was halted in late 1991, with the introduction of the new PowerBook portables.

RAM speed: 120ns

Maximum RAM: 9M

PowerBook 100

The PowerBook 100, along with the 140 and 170, heralded the introduction of new portable Macintoshes built with state-of-the-art technology and design.

Introduced in October 1991, the PowerBooks were much smaller and lighter than the original Mac Portable, and won design awards for their cleverly integrated trackballs. The PowerBook design moves the keyboard up near the screen hinge and places the trackball below it, where it can easily be reached with the thumbs. Space on either side of the trackball serves as a palm rest. This was the first, and so far the best, integration of a pointing device into a portable computer.

Although the expansion capability of the PowerBooks is limited compared to most desktop Macs, they feature a complete complement of external ports: modem, printer, and ADB ports are included, as well as ports for an external floppy (on the 100 only) and SCSI disks. The latter two ports use unique "HDI" connectors due to the limited space on the back of the PowerBook cases. Internal expansion is limited to memory cards and internal modems.

The PowerBook 100 was built for Apple by Sony and is a functional duplicate of the original Mac Portable, albeit about 12 pounds lighter and with a passive matrix display. The standard configuration used a 16MHz 68000

Chapter 5
Macintosh Hardware

processor, 2M of RAM, and a 20M hard drive. Sony kept the size and weight of the 100 down by moving the diskette drive outside of the main case and making it an option. However, users of desktop Macs generally didn't need the floppy, since the 100 can be attached to a desktop Mac as though it were a hard drive, using a special SCSI cable.

RAM for the 100, as for all PowerBooks, is comprised of surface mount chips on a small card that plugs into a special connector on the PowerBook main logic board. The PowerBook 100, 140, and 170 can all use the same RAM cards.

Despite a loyal following of those who wanted the smallest and lightest Macintosh, the PB100 never sold in the quantities that the 140 and 170 did. In late 1992 Apple remaindered thousands of the machines to office supply stores which sold them for anywhere from $600 to $800. Demand was very high at this price and the supply was essentially used up in about six weeks.

Like the original Mac Portable, the PowerBook 100 uses a lead acid battery instead of the more common nickel-cadmium battery. It's also the only PowerBook to offer a backup power source—three lithium batteries—sufficient to maintain the contents of RAM during a battery swap.

WARNING! Some PowerBook AC adapters have a defect in the insulation between the inner and outer contacts in the tip of the cord that plugs into the computer. This can cause a short that blows a small fuse on the PowerBook logic board. The result is that the PowerBook will only run when connected to the AC adapter, and not from the battery. If your PowerBook displays this problem, call 800-SOS-APPL for service.

Maximum RAM: 8M

PowerBook 140 and 170

The 140 and 170 are slightly larger and about 1.5 pounds heavier than the 100 due to their inclusion of an internal diskette drive.

The 140 and 170 are identical except for the 170's faster processor (25MHz as opposed to 16MHz) and active matrix screen. Both machines use 68030 processors. Unlike the PowerBook 100, they cannot be connected to desktop Macs via the SCSI port.

Max. RAM: 8M

PowerBook 145

The PowerBook 145 replaced the PowerBook 140 in August 1992. It's essentially a PowerBook 170 with the cheaper passive-matrix screen. All other specifications are those of the 170.

Max. RAM: 8M

PowerBook 160 and 180

The PowerBook 160 and 180 were introduced in October, 1992, along with the new PowerBook Duos. The 160 and 180 add a number of new features, as follows:

▼ Maximum memory is expanded from 8 to 14 megabytes

▼ A "SCSI disk mode" like that of the PowerBook 100

▼ Gray scale LCDs that can display 16 shades of gray

▼ The ability to connect external monitors

The 160 uses a 25MHz 68030 processor and a passive matrix display capable of displaying 16 gray scales. The PowerBook 180 uses a 33MHz 68030 processor, adds a 68882 math processor, and has an active matrix gray scale display. Both machines can be run at 16MHz to save power.

A standard DB-15 connector is provided for an external monitor. The 160 and 180 can display 256 colors and all Apple displays up to the 16" color monitor. The Apple Portrait Monitor is supported at 16 shades of gray. The internal video can be run in either "mirroring" mode, where the display on the external monitor duplicates the 640 by 400 pixel display of the LCD, or "dual" mode, where the external display is independent. The mirroring mode is useful during presentations, allowing the presenter to see the same image as the audience.

The mirroring mode works by patching QuickDraw to duplicate any QuickDraw operations on the external display. For performance reasons, some games and other programs that bypass QuickDraw will not work on mirrored displays.

PowerBook Duo 210 and 230

The Duos are built to fill a dual role (hence the name) as both desktop and portable computers. They're the smallest, lightest Macs yet—a mere 4.25 pounds in weight and 1.3" thick. The Duo designers achieved these size and weight goals by a combination of exotic design techniques such as a magnesium subframe, and the elimination of an internal diskette drive and all ports or interfaces other than a single serial port and 152 pin expansion connector.

The single difference between the 210 and the 230 is the system clock speed: 25MHz for the 210 and 33MHz for the 230. Both computers use 16 gray scale, passive matrix displays.

To connect SCSI disks, diskette drives, an external monitor, or ADB devices, a "dock" of some sort is needed. Apple provides three such docks: a simple Duo Floppy Adapter for connecting a diskette drive; the more complex Duo Minidock that provides serial, ADB, floppy, SCSI, and external monitor connectors; and the Duo Dock, a IIci-sized box containing two NuBus slots, all the connectors of the Minidock, sockets for additional video RAM and a 68882 math processor, a diskette drive, and room for an internal hard disk. The Duo fits completely inside the Duo Dock; Apple's "PowerLatch" technology uses a motorized mechanism to guide the PowerBook in and make the connection between the dock and the Duo's expansion connector. The Duo Dock makes the Duo a completely functional desktop system and even charges the computer's battery!

The Duos comes with 4M of soldered-in memory. The current maximum memory is 24M, but 32M is theoretically possible according to Apple documents. However, space constraints inside the Duo case mean that special manufacturing techniques would have to be used to keep the necessary 28M memory card inside Apple's size specifications.

At the time of their introduction, the Duos were the only Macs whose warranty was not (technically) voided if the user installed memory themselves.

PowerBook 165c

The first color PowerBook was introduced in February 1993. The PowerBook 165c is a PowerBook 180 with a passive matrix color display capable of 256 simultaneous colors. The battery has slightly more capacity than the 160/180 battery to support the extra-bright backlight needed for the color display. The 165c weighs 0.2 pounds more than the 160/180.

Unlike other PowerBooks, the 165c's internal video memory is comprised of normal DRAM, rather than special video RAM (VRAM). This means that display operations such as scrolling will be somewhat slower on the 165c than on the 180.

All other 165c specifications are identical to the PowerBook 180.

Chapter 5
Macintosh Hardware

PowerBook Expansion: Modems

All PowerBooks contain a second expansion slot specifically designed for an internal modem. Apple's offering (included as standard in the 170 but only when sold in the United States) is a 2400 baud data/9600 baud fax modem. This modem is not entirely compatible with the Hayes standard command and register sets, and in general has not been well-received. Several companies offer internal modems that probably are superior for most uses.

The PowerBook Duos are a special case: their limited interior space doesn't have enough room for a conventional internal modem. The only current option is Apple's "Express Modem", a tiny circuit board consisting of only the "data pump" portion of a normal modem. The functions normally performed by the rest of a modem's circuitry—protocol management, data compression, command parsing, and so forth—are handled by the Duo's processor. This allows the modems to be small and inexpensive for their capabilities (9600 baud data and fax) but their performance lags behind that of true 9600 baud modems.

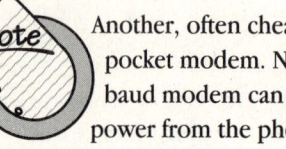

Another, often cheaper solution is to use a line-powered external pocket modem. Not only are these less expensive (a typical 2400 baud modem can be had for about $100) but because they get power from the phone line (when the phone is off the hook), the PowerBook's battery life is not affected.

In Production

At the time of this writing, the following model Macintoshes were being produced:

- ▼ Compact: Classic II, Color Classic
- ▼ Modular: LCII, LCIII, IIvx, Centris 610, Centris 650, Quadra 800, Quadra 950
- ▼ PowerBook: 145, 160, 165C, 180, Duo 210, Duo 230
- ▼ Performa: 200, 405, 415, 430, 450, 600

Mac Internal Video

All modular Macs (and some PowerBooks) currently produced have internal video circuitry that can drive a variety of monitors. This section details the video capabilities of these machines.

Internal Video Hardware

Video data is stored in RAM, just like programs and program data. However, Macs have used two different types of RAM for this purpose: the compact Macs (with the exception of the SE/30, Classic II, and Color Classic), as well as the Mac IIci and Mac IIsi, all used a portion of their main program memory for a video buffer.

Since the video circuitry must scan the video memory 60 times per second to generate the video signal for the monitor, the processor's access to this part of memory is interrupted 60 times per second. This can have a profound effect on the performance of program code that is sharing the same area of memory. Depending on the length of the interrupts (black and white, 1 bit per pixel displays take the least time; 256 color displays take the most), the performance impact can range from minor (15%) to major (45%). One of the best speed secrets for machines like the IIci and IIsi is to simply add a separate video card and not use the internal video circuitry!

Happily, Apple appears headed away from this scheme (though it's resurrected in the PowerBook 165C). Newer Macs use separate video RAM, or VRAM, to store the video image. The difference between VRAM and processor RAM is that VRAM is "dual ported," that is, it can be written to and read from at the same time—so a program can continuously update the contents of VRAM without having to worry about whether the video circuitry is reading it to generate the image.

Macs come with a "Monitors" control panel that allows the user to change the number of colors displayed. The minimum is one bit per pixel, which allows two "colors": black and white. Depending on the model of Mac and the amount of video memory, other choices are 4 colors (2 bits per pixel), 16 colors (4 bits/pixel), 256 colors (8 bits/pixel), "thousands" of colors (actually, 32,768 colors, or 16 bits/pixel), and "millions" of colors (16,777,216 colors, or 24 bits per pixel).

The 16 and 24 bit per pixel modes are different from the other modes. At 8 bits and fewer per pixel, display colors are mapped from a CLUT, or "color lookup table." A CLUT for an 8 bit per pixel display has 256 entries; each entry is 24 bits long and describes the red, green, and blue components of the color at that position. Programs can change the contents of the CLUT so that any 256 colors from a palette of 16,777,216 can be displayed. Some programs use "color table animation," modifying the CLUT on the fly to animate the colors on the display.

At 16 bits per pixel and higher, CLUTs are not used. Rather, each pixel on the screen has a direct color value. In 16 bit mode, the red, green, and blue

Chapter 5
Macintosh Hardware

components have 5 bits each, and the remaining bit is an "alpha channel," which can be used for different purposes depending on the program (most programs ignore it). 24 bit color actually uses 32 bits per pixel, with 8 bits reserved for the alpha channel.

Note that the size of the "desktop," or displayed area, will vary with different monitors. The Mac determines the size of the connected monitor by looking at a set of "sense pins" in the video cable. Sense pin configurations are given later in this section.

The next section describes the video capabilities and monitor sizes supported by each model Macintosh.

Macintosh LC, LCII, Classic II, and Color Classic

The LC style internal video was the first implementation of separate VRAM on the Mac. These machines come with 256K of video RAM standard, and the single 256K SIMM can be replaced with a 512K SIMM. VRAM must be 100ns or faster.

Table 5.2 Monitor characteristics for Mac LC, LCII, Classic II, and Color Classic

Monitor	Desktop Size (in pixels) Colors with 512K VRAM	Colors with 256K VRAM	
12" color	512 x 384	256	32,768
12" mono, 13", 14" color	640 x 480	16	256
VGA	640 x 480	16	256

Note: The Color Classic uses an internal color monitor at 512 x 384.

If the optional Apple IIe emulator card is installed, an Apple II mode of 560 by 384 pixels with 16 colors is supported.

The LC was the first Mac to directly support a standard, non-multisynchronous VGA monitor.

Macintosh IIvx

The IIvx comes with 512K of VRAM, expandable to 1M. Two VRAM SIMM sockets are provided; they must both be used and have the same size VRAM SIMM. There are only two possible configurations: the standard pair of 256K devices or the optional two 512K devices.

The IIvx supports the same monitors, as do the LC series machines, but can display 16 bit color at 640 by 480 pixels.

Table 5.3 Macintosh IIvx Monitor Characteristics

Monitor	Colors with Desktop Size	Colors with 512K VRAM	1M VRAM
12" color	512 x 384	32,768	32,768
12" mono, 13", 14" color	640 x 480	256	32,768
VGA	640 x 480	256	32,768

Quadra 700 and Quadra 900

The Quadra 700 comes with 512K of soldered-in VRAM; the 900 comes with 1M. Six VRAM SIMM sockets are provided in the 700; 4 are provided in the 900. Only 256K devices can be used; the 512K VRAMs used in the LC and IIvx computers will not work.

Note that only the 512K, 1M, and 2M VRAM configurations are supported! You could not, for example, add four 256K SIMMs to the 700, since this would result in 1.5M of VRAM. 100ns devices are required.

The Quadras support a wide array of external monitors, as shown in Table 5.4 below.

Table 5.4 Quadra 700 and 900 Monitor Characteristics

Monitor	Desktop Size	Colors with 512K VRAM	Colors with 1M VRAM	Colors with 1M VRAM
12" color	512 x 384	256	millions	millions
12" mono, 13", 14" color	640 x 480	256[1]	256	millions
VGA	640 x 480	256	256	millions
Super VGA	800 x 600	256	256	millions
15" portrait	640 x 870	256[1]	256	256
16" color	832 by 624	256	256	millions
19"-21" color	1152 x 870	16	16	256

[1]Monochrome monitors are limited to 256 grays.

Chapter 5
Macintosh Hardware

Quadra 950

The 950 internal video is similar to the 700/900. It requires faster VRAM (80ns) due to its faster I/O bus, and a new RAMDAC (digital to analog converter) supports 16 bits per pixel, even on the largest monitors (with 2M VRAM).

Table 5.5 Quadra 950 Monitor Characteristics

Monitor	Desktop Size	Colors with 512K VRAM	Colors with 1M VRAM	Colors with 2M VRAM
12" color	512 x 384	256	millions	millions
12" mono, 13", 14" color	640 x 480	256[1]	32,768	millions
VGA	640 x 480	256	32,768	millions
Super VGA	800 x 600	256	32,768	millions
15" portrait	640 x 870	256[1]	256	256
16" color	832 by 624	256	32,768	millions
19"-21" color	1024 x 768	16	256	32,768
19"-21" color	1152 x 870	16	256	32,768

[1]Monochrome monitors are limited to 256 grays.

Centris 610 and 650, and Quadra 800

These computers are similar to the Quadra 950 except that they are limited to 1M of VRAM and don't support 24 bits per pixel at any video size.

Table 5.6 Centris 610 and 650 and Quadra 800 Monitor Characteristics

Monitor	Desktop Size	Colors with 512K VRAM	Colors with 1M VRAM
12" color	512 x 384	32,768	32,768
12" mono, 13", 14" color	640 x 480	256[1]	32,768
VGA	640 x 480	256	32,768
Super VGA	800 x 600	256	32,768

Monitor	Desktop Size	Colors with 512K VRAM	Colors with 1M VRAM
15" portrait	640 x 870	16[1]	256
16" color	832 by 624	256	32,768
19"-21" color	1024 x 768	16	256
19"-21" color	1152 x 870	16	256

[1]Monochrome monitors are limited to 256 grays.

Monitor Connections

The external video connector on all Macs so equipped is a standard DB-15S socket. The pin assignments are shown above, in table 5.2. These pin assignments apply to all Macs with internal video, but the use of the sense lines will vary from model to model.

Table 5.7 Video pin assignments

Pin	Signal	Description
1	RED.GND	Red Video Ground
2	RED.VID	Red Video
3	CYSNC~	Composite Sync
4	MON.ID1	Monitor ID, Bit 1 (SENSE0)
5	GRN.VID	Green Video
6	GRN.GND	Green Video Ground
7	MON.ID2	Monitor ID, Bit 2 (SENSE1)
8	nc	no connection)
9	BLU.VID	Blue Video
10	MON.ID3	Monitor ID, Bit 3 (SENSE2)
11	C&VSYNC.GND	CSYNC & VSYNC Ground
12	VSYNC~	Vertical Sync
13	BLU.GND	Blue Video Ground
14	HSYNC.GND	HSYNC Ground
15	HSYNC~	Horizontal Sync
Shell	CHASSIS.GND	Chassis Ground

Chapter 5
Macintosh Hardware

Part I
Macintosh, the Computer

A Closer Look — The internal video configures itself for the type and resolution of the display attached by checking the "sense pins" connected to ground (the C&VSYNC.GND on pin 11) on the 15-pin video cable. The primary sense pins—pins 4, 7, and 10—can specify seven different display types (see tables 4.3 and 4.4, above).

The extended sense codes are used if none of pins 4, 7, or 10 are grounded. Extended sense codes are implemented by wiring pairs of these pins together, rather than wiring them to ground.

Table 5.8 Sense codes

Display	Sense Pins (x=grounded)			Pixels, XY
	10	7	4	
12" mono, 13" color	0	0	X	640 x 480
NTSC (overscan)	0	X	0	640 x 480
NTSC (underscan)	0	X	X	512 x 384
21" mono	X	0	0	1152 x 870
12" color	X	0	X	512 x 384
Portrait	X	X	0	640 x 870
21" color	X	X	X	640 x 480
Extended sense codes	0	0	0	N.A.

Table 5.9 Extended sense codes

Display	Sense Pins			Pixels, X–Y
	4-10	7-10	4-7	
No external display	0	0	0	N.A.
PAL option 2	0	0	1[1]	640 x 480
PAL option 1	1	1	1[2]	640 x 480
VGA	0	1	1	640 x 480
Super VGA	0	1	1[3]	800 x 600
16" color	1	0	0	832 x 624

[1]This sense code requires that a diode be installed between pins 10 and 7, with the anode toward pin 7.

[2]24 bits per pixel is not supported. The Quadra video cannot output PAL video directly; an RGB to PAL converter must be used.

[3]SVGA must be enabled in software. After connecting the VGA monitor, open the "Monitors" control panel, click on the Options button, select "Super VGA" from the resulting dialog, and then reboot to enable SVGA.

Macintosh Video Cards

Apple has produced several NuBus video cards. Any of these cards can be used in any NuBus-capable Mac except the Centris 610 (due to space limitations). These cards are:

▼ The original Mac video card introduced with the Mac II. Known simply as the "Apple Macintosh Video Card," it's colloquially referred to as the "Toby card," after Toby Farrand, the Apple employee who designed it.

Toby cards came with enough memory to display 16 colors at 640 by 480 pixels; adding additional VRAM allowed them to display 256 colors. Later cards came with the maximum memory as standard. The Toby card supports the 12" monochrome and 13" and 14" color monitors; 640 by 480 pixels is the only display supported. Toby cards ignore sense pin settings.

▼ The Macintosh 1 Bit Video Card. Like the name says—1 bit per pixel, period. The only size supported is 640 by 480 pixels. This card was introduced solely as a low cost display option.

▼ The Macintosh Display Card 8•24 . This versatile card can display up to 24 bits per pixel at 640 by 480 resolution. Earlier versions were delivered with only enough VRAM for a 256 color display and were referred to as "4*8 cards." Current versions ship with the full complement of VRAM.

The 8•24 card supports all Apple monitors; however, earlier versions of the card will require a ROM upgrade to support the 16" monitor. This card responds to the sense codes described above.

▼ The 8•24GC card. This was an interesting accelerated display card that used an AMD 29000 RISC processor to run a special version of Quick-Draw. It offered 24 bit video on 640 by 480 pixel displays and 8 bit video on larger displays. Revision B of the card offers 16 bit video as well. A ROM upgrade is required for earlier cards to support the 16-inch monitor. The GC responds to the sense codes described above.

The performance of the 8•24GC exceeds even the built-in video of the Quadras, but ironically the acceleration software can't be used on 68040 based Macs; the 8•24GC will work in a Quadra, but only as an unaccelerated video card.

The Portrait Display and now-discontinued Two Page Monochrome display originally shipped with special video cards that only worked with these monitors.

Chapter 5
Macintosh Hardware

Part I
Macintosh, the Computer

Macintosh Hardware Overview Chart

Computer	Processor	Max. RAM	Slots	Video	Keyboard/ Mouse	Diskette
Mac 128	8Mhz 68000	4M[1]	NA	internal mono	standard	400K
Mac 512K(E)	8MHz 68000	4M[3]	NA	internal mono	standard	400K/800K
Plus	8MHz 68000	4M	NA	internal mono	standard	800K
SE	8MHz 68000	4M	1 PDS	internal mono	standard	800K[2]
Classic	8MHz 68000	4M	1 (RAM only)	internal mono	ADB	1.44M
Classic II	16MHZ 68030	10M	1 PDS	internal mono	ADB	1.44M
LC	16MHz 68020	10M	1 PDS	internal color	ADB	1.44M
LCII	16MHz 68030	10M	1 PDS	internal color	ADB	1.44M
LCIII	25MHz 68030	36M	1 PDS	internal color	ADB	1.44M
SE/30	16MHz 68030	128M[3]	1 PDS	internal color	ADB	1.44M
II	16MHz 68030	128M[4]	6 NuBus	req'd video card	ADB	800K[5]
IIx	16MHz 68030	128M	6 NuBus	req'd video card	ADB	1.44M
IIcx	16MHz 68030	128M	3 NuBus	req'd video card	ADB	1.44M
IIvx	32MHz 68030					
IIsi	20MHz 68030	17M	1 PDS or 1 NuBus[6]	internal color	ADB	1.44M
IIci	25MHz 68030	128M	3 NuBus	internal color	ADB	1.44M
IIfx	40MHz 68030	128M	6 NuBus	req'd video card	ADB	1.44M

Chapter 5
Macintosh Hardware

Computer	Processor	Max. RAM	Slots	Video	Keyboard/ Mouse	Diskette
Portable	16MHz 68C000	9M	1 RAM, 1 modem, 1 PDS	internal mono	built in; ADB port included	1.44M
PowerBook 100	16MHz 68C00	8M	1 RAM, 1 modem	internal mono	built in; ADB port included	1.44M
PowerBook 140	16MHz 68030	8M	1 RAM, 1 modem	internal mono	built in; ADB port included	1.44M
PowerBook 145	25MHz 68030	14M	1 RAM, 1 modem	internal mono	built in; ADB port included	1.44M
PowerBook 160	25MHz 68030	14M	1 RAM, 1 modem	internal gray	built in; ADB port included	1.44M
PowerBook 165C	32MHz 68030	14M	1 RAM, 1 modem	internal color	built in; ADB port included	1.44M
PowerBook 170	25MHz 68030	8M	1 RAM, 1 modem	internal mono	built in; ADB port included	1.44M
PowerBook 180	32MHz 68030	14M	1 RAM, 1 modem	internal gray	built in; ADB port included	1.44M
Centris 610	20MHz 68LC040	132M	1 PDS	internal color	ADB	1.44M
Centris 650	25MHZ 68040[6]	136M	3 NuBus, 1 PDS	internal color	ADB	1.44M
Quadra 700	25MHz 68040	68M[8]	2 NuBus, 1 PDS	internal color	ADB	1.44M
Quadra 800	33MHz 68040	136M	3 NuBus, 1 PDS	internal color	ADB	1.44M
Quadra 900	25MHz 68040	256M	5 NuBus, 1 PDS	internal color	ADB	1.44M
Quadra 950	33MHz 68040	256M	5 NuBus, 1 PDS	internal color	ADB	1.44M

See notes on next page.

[1] With upgrade to Plus or third-party expansion.

[2] Later SEs have Superdrives and can be identified by the "FDHD" legend on the front. Upgrade is available for earlier SEs.

[3] Achieved with 16M SIMMs.

[4] Revision "C" ROMs required for more than 68M. Revision "C" ROMs only available w/ SuperDrive upgrade.

[5] Upgrade to 1.44M available.

[6] PDS or NuBus slot depending on which adapter card is chosen. There currently are no cards for the IIsi "native" slot.

[7] Also available with 68LC040 processor.

[8] Requires special low-profile 16M SIMMs.

Memory

Memory is one of the least understood aspects of the Macintosh but it is actually rather simple. With the exception of the Classic, Portable, and PowerBooks, all Macs use SIMM memory. SIMM is an acronym for **s**ingle **i**nline **m**emory **m**odule, an increasingly common method of packaging memory for consumer computers. They are standardized to the point that some Macs can use the same SIMMs IBM PCs use!

A SIMM consists of two or more memory chips mounted on a small, plug-in circuit board. Macs from the Mac Plus up through the Mac IIvx use a 30 pin SIMM; newer Macs use a 72 pin SIMM. The two types of SIMM are not interchangeable.

How Memory Works

The Mac's processor contains a small amount of memory in the form of registers. Data from external memory must be read into these registers for operations to be performed on it; results are written back out to external memory. (Processors in the 68000 family also have from 256 bytes to 4K of built-in cache memory; it is ignored for the purposes of this discussion.)

Before data can be read from memory, the processor must specify which part of memory—the address—the data is to be gotten from. This address is asserted by putting it, in binary form, on the address lines of the processor (as mentioned earlier when discussing the Motorola 68000 CPU family). External *address decoding* circuitry takes this address and decides which chips it refers to.

Chapter 5
Macintosh Hardware

When the address is asserted, it takes the memory chips a certain amount of time to fetch the data and return it on the *data lines*. The time is the chip's speed: for example, a chip rated at 120 nanoseconds (billionths of a second) is guaranteed by the manufacturer to have valid data on the data lines 120 nanoseconds, at most, after a valid address is asserted.

One more signal, a *read/write* signal, determines whether data is read from or written to the memory chip.

RAM and ROM

There are two basic types of computer memory: RAM and ROM. RAM is the memory programs use to run in and store their data. RAM is an acronym for Random Access Memory, which simply means that any part of the memory can be accessed directly. This term is a holdover from the old days of computing, when non-random access memory (like the tape drives seen in old science fiction movies) played a more prominent role than it does today.

All Macs also have some ROM (Read Only Memory) that can be read from but not written to or changed. This ROM contains items such as the instructions the Mac needs to start up, as well as the Mac's toolbox of standard functions, such as the code that creates windows and menus on the screen. (Parts of the ROM can be "patched out" and replaced by RAM routines; this often is done to fix bugs or add new features to the system software.) Replacement ROMs are available for the Mac Plus, the original Mac II and the Mac SE.

Memory Speed and Wait States

Faster memory is more expensive than slower memory, and few computers these days are built with memory fast enough to keep up with the processor. In general, after asserting an address, the processor waits one or more ticks of the system clock before the data is ready. In this instance, each tick of the system clock is called a *wait state*. Wait states are wasted time: most processors cannot do anything while waiting for data to be read or written.

The original Mac II, for example, ran with 120ns memory and inserted two wait states for each memory access. The Mac IIci uses 80ns memory but runs at a faster clock speed (25MHz), so it uses three wait states! Note, however, that a wait state on the IIci is shorter than a wait state on the Mac II because the IIci's clock is faster.

You might think a wait state or three would make little difference to the computer's performance. After all, each wait state on a Mac II is only one sixteen-millionth of a second! But a Mac II accesses memory hundreds of thousands of times per second, generating enough wait states to have a noticeable effect. The Mac IIx is about 15 percent faster than the Mac II because it runs with only one wait state as compared to the Mac II's two wait states.

Wait states are "hard wired" into each Mac, so there is no advantage to using memory that is faster than necessary. A Mac II runs fine with 80ns RAM, but it will not be any faster than it would be with 120ns RAM. Improvements in memory manufacture mean that faster RAM is the norm: these days, for example, just about any 1M SIMM is 80ns or faster.

Caching

A *cache* (pronounced "cash") is simply a small amount of fast storage that acts as a buffer to slower storage. It is a very general principle: for example, all Macs come with the capability to set aside some RAM as a disk cache that keeps copies of often-accessed disk information. This cache is set in the General section of the control panel.

Caching works because it is statistically likely that if an area of the disk recently was accessed, it probably will be accessed again in the near future. By keeping copies of this data, the data can be made available instantly if it is needed again, rather than being reread from the disk.

The same principle can be applied to RAM. Because the faster Mac II–class computers all run with one or more wait states, using a small amount of fast RAM, which can be accessed with no wait states, as a buffer between the processor and main memory can improve performance. A well-designed cache can achieve a "hit rate" of more than 90 percent, which is almost as good as having the entire Mac filled with this fast memory.

Apple doesn't use caches consistently. The IIci, IIfx, and IIvx all had 32K of cache standard (on the IIci the cache was in the form of a plug-in card and was only included on models built in the last year of production, although it could be added to earlier models). The Quadras can use a cache card in their PDS slots but Apple doesn't offer one, leaving this niche for companies such as Daystar Digital of Flowery Branch, Georgia to fill.

Memory Packaging

Macs have used five different packages for memory. The original compact Macs—the Mac 128 and Mac 512/512Ke—used soldered-in DIP (dual inline pin) memory chips. Current Macs use one of two types of SIMMs, sometimes in combination with soldered-in surface mount chips. The Portable uses

Chapter 5
Macintosh Hardware

surface mount memory mounted on plug-in boards designed for the Portable's special memory expansion slot. The PowerBooks use special memory boards unique to these models.

Note that a SIMM is just a way of combining several separate DIP or surface mount memory chips onto a small plug-in board. Most SIMMs use *surface mount* chips, which are chips whose connectors are soldered directly to the surface of the PC board rather than protruding through holes in the PC board as DIPs do. Surface mount chips offer space advantages: they are smaller than DIPs, and surface mount design enables you to use components on both sides of a circuit board, effectively doubling the board's area. For this reason, surface mount components were first used in portable computers where space is at a premium; but most desktop computers now use them as well. Some newer 8 bit SIMMs are comprised of two 4 bit wide memory chips, instead of 8 1 bit wide chips. Due to some subtle timing differences, these newer designs cannot be used in older Macs (the II, IIx, SE/30, and IIcx).

Expanding memory on the Mac 128 and 512 requires an add-in board because no provision for expansion was built in. Adding memory to most newer Macs is a matter of snapping in SIMMs, or, with the PowerBooks, plugging in a memory card.

The Classic is a special case—it comes with 1M of RAM and expansion is via a small plug-in board with another 1M of soldered-in memory and two additional SIMM sockets.

Mac memory is arranged in *banks*, a bank being 16 bits wide for the 68000-based Macs and 32 bits wide for 68020, 68030, and 68040 based Macs. On newer Macs, the first bank of memory (bank "A") is the soldered-in RAM that comes with the machine.

Until recently, Macs have used standard 8 bit wide SIMMs. Two or four of these SIMMs constituted a bank, and thus memory in these Macs must be added, removed, or replaced in groups of two or four. However, the new Macs introduced in February 1993— the LCIII, Centris, and Quadra 800 models—use a new, 32 bit wide SIMM. Each of these SIMMs, which sport 72 pins instead of the 30 used previously, is a bank in itself, so for these models memory can be added, removed, or replaced one SIMM at a time.

Interleaving

Interleaved access is a technique for reducing the latency between consecutive RAM accesses. Adjacent banks of RAM are treated as a single, large area, with accesses to consecutive words of memory being split across the two banks. This technique is used in the Centris 650 and Quadra 800 and can improve overall performance by 10 to 15%. The memory controller used in these machines supports interleaved access only if adjacent SIMMs are of the same size.

32-Bit Cleanliness

There is a lot of confusion over exactly what *32-bit cleanliness* means. Many people confuse it with 32-bit QuickDraw, which is not even remotely related except in name.

As described earlier, the 68000 used in the original Mac had only 24 address lines, even though it had 32-bit internal registers. So when an address was specified, only the lower three bytes of a register needed to be used to hold the complete address. The upper byte was used to store status information about certain memory structures.

Twenty-four bits is enough to address 16M of memory; before the Mac IIci, only the lower 8M of this space was available for RAM. On a six-slot Mac II or IIx, the remaining 8M is split among the NuBus slots (1M per slot), ROM space (512K), and various I/O ports. This six-slot memory architecture is common across the Mac II product line, even on Macs that have only three slots, or, in the SE/30's case, no NuBus slots.

To make more memory readily available, Apple made extensive changes to the Mac ROMs and introduced the Mac IIci with 32-bit clean ROMs. This means all 32 bits are available to specify an address, which extends the addressing range of the Mac OS from 16M to 4 gigabytes (an increase of 256 times). The flags previously kept in an address' upper eight bits were moved to separate data structures.

In the course of writing Mac programs, it is often necessary to modify the status information, or flags, kept in the upper byte of a 24 bit address. Although routines are provided in the Mac ROM to do this, it is much faster to do it directly in the program. Many programmers did just that, twiddling the upper eight bits of an address directly. But in a 32-bit environment, these bits are now part of the address proper rather than flags, so programs that do this generally crash. Programs that do not directly modify this information are said to be 32-bit clean.

Note that this is a problem only for Macs running System 7 with 32-bit addressing turned on in the Memory control panel. If you do not have more than 8M of RAM in your Mac, whichever Mac it is, there is little reason to have this turned on.

Note: If your Mac II–class computer does not have 32-bit clean ROMs (that is, if it is a Mac II, IIx, IIcx, or SE/30), you still can make it 32-bit clean with Connectix' MODE32, which now is distributed free by Apple. Macs running MODE32 are functionally equivalent to Macs with 32-bit clean ROMs. In early 1993, Apple introduced a separate "32 bit enabler" that purports to provide the same function as the Connectix product; reports from the field indicate that the first release is very unstable.

Memory: Who Uses What

The original 128 and 512K Macs were not designed for expansion. Memory on these models can be increased only by using third-party products.

All 68000-based Macs except the Portable and PowerBook 100 are limited to 4M of memory (the Portable can go to 9M; the PB100 to 8M). This is an architectural limit in the ROMs and is not remediable.

When the original Mac II was designed, standards for SIMMs larger than 1M did not exist. As a result, the II, IIx, SE/30, and IIcx cannot use standard 4M or 16M SIMMs. Special SIMMs with additional circuitry must be used. Keep this in mind if you order large SIMMs for these machines.

The Mac II imposes an additional limitation: a design deficiency in its original ROMs means that it cannot even boot if 4M or larger SIMMs are installed in Bank A. The revision C ROMs—the ones included with the "SuperDrive" upgrade—fix this problem. (Note that you need Connectix' MODE32 software to make use of more than 8M in a Mac II.)

The IIfx uses a special type of RAM that offers increased write performance. The 64 pin SIMMs it uses are unique to this model.

The introduction of the 72 pin, 32 bit wide SIMMs on newer Macs means that there are four types of SIMMs in the 4M and larger class. These are:

▼ The special SIMMs for the II, IIx, SE/30, and IIcx.

▼ The special SIMMs for the Mac IIfx.

▼ Normal 30 pin SIMMs for other Macs.

▼ 72 pin SIMMs for the LCIII, Centris, and Quadra 800.

Memory Problems

Memory failures are very rare; in most cases, the problem is poor electrical contact between a memory chip and the computer. Sometimes a SIMM board is manufactured slightly too thick or too thin and does not make good contact with its socket. In other cases, the contacts on the SIMM or the socket can be contaminated with dirt or oil and cause problems.

 Memory contacts can be cleaned with any electrical contact cleaner marked "zero residue." Tuner cleaner should not be used, because it contains a lubricating oil.

Hard Disks

Until a few years ago, hard disks were too expensive for most people. These days, they are virtually mandatory for any significant work on a Mac. The current Mac operating system, System 7, does not even fit on a single floppy disk!

The first hard disk designed specifically for a home computer was a 10M drive made by Corvus Systems. It was the size of a shoe box, used twin 8-inch diameter platters, weighed about 25 pounds, and cost $5,350. These days, a 10M hard drive is not considered adequate even for a notebook computer, and 20M drives are on the way out.

Hard drives are available in three major form factors. One form is 5 1/4-inch drives which, although they were known as "Mini Winnies" when first introduced, now are considered large and clunky. (Mini Winnie refers to a Winchester. IBM invented the technology used in current hard drives and introduced it in its "Model 3030" drive. The model number matched that of the popular Winchester 30-30 carbine, and the nickname stuck.) The other two forms are 3 1/2-inch drives and 2 1/2-inch drives. Currently, 1 1/8-inch drives are being developed but are not yet commercially available. The 5 1/4-inch drives come in full-height (about 4 inches) and half-height configurations. The 3 1/2-inch drives primarily come in standard, 1-inch-high, and low-profile (about 3/4-inch) configurations, but many different heights are available.

 Hewlett-Packard markets their miniscule "Kitty Hawk" 1.3-inch hard disk in 20 and 40M versions. Currently it's sold only to OEMs who include it in palmtop and note pad computers.

The largest capacity currently available in a 5 1/4-inch drive is about 2 gigabytes; 3 1/2-inch drives are also available in this size. The 2 1/2-inch drives currently max out at 212M.

How Data Is Stored

Hard disks are composed of one or more rigid platters. Like floppy disks, these platters are divided into a number of concentric *tracks,* and each track is divided into a number of *sectors.* One sector is the smallest amount of data the disk mechanism can read or write at one time. If only part of a sector is needed, the entire sector is read, a portion of its data modified, and the entire sector written back to the disk.

Hard disks have one read/write head for each platter surface, so a single platter disk has two heads, whereas a disk with four platters has eight heads. All the disk heads move in unison—they all are attached to the same actuator—so when one head is over, say, track 435, all the other heads are over the same track on their respective platters. The collection of tracks that can be read or written without moving the heads is called a *cylinder.*

When data is read from or written to a sector on the disk, the heads must *seek* the correct track, then wait for the disks' rotation to bring the proper sector along.

Hard Drive Connectivity

All current Mac hard drives connect via the SCSI port. The Mac 128 and Mac 512 can use the original Apple HD-20 drive, which connects to the external floppy port, as well as some third-party drives that connect to one of the serial ports. None of these older drives is still manufactured.

Even internal hard drives connect to the SCSI port. There is no performance difference between internal and external drive connections; in fact, the Mac cannot tell whether a given drive is internal or external.

A SCSI device may be either a *block device,* which means it is a random access storage device and can read or write blocks of information, or a *non-block device,* which means it cannot. Hard disks and CD-ROMs, for example, are block devices; most tape drives, SCSI printers, and scanners are non-block devices. The distinction is important: block devices can appear on the desktop, but non-block devices cannot. It is possible, however, to write special driver software that can make some non-block devices, such as tape drives, appear to operate as block devices.

There can be up to eight devices on any given SCSI bus. Each device must have a unique ID number in the zero to seven range. The Mac is permanently set to device number seven, leaving zero through six assignable for other devices.

Chapter 5
Macintosh Hardware

Part I

Macintosh, the Computer

The Boot Sequence

When a Mac boots, it looks for bootable devices in the following sequence:

1. Floppies always have precedence. The Mac tries to boot from a floppy if one is available.

2. If no floppies are available, the Mac scans the SCSI bus for block devices, starting at ID 6 and working down to ID 0. If a block device is present but not "ready" (such as a hard disk that is still spinning up to speed), the Mac skips it and continues the scan.

3. If no bootable devices are found on the SCSI bus, the Mac displays the blinking question mark in a floppy icon on the screen.

Hard Drive Performance

The base performance of a hard drive is defined by two parameters: the average access time of the drive and the maximum data transfer rate.

A disproportionate amount of attention is paid to the *average access time* of a drive, which is the average time it takes to move the read/write heads from one track of a drive to another. Although this is important, so many other factors come into play that it is rarely the most significant factor.

The *transfer rate* is simply the number of megabytes per second the drive can read or write. Some drives quote a *sustained transfer rate* and a *burst transfer rate*. The sustained transfer rate is the most important.

How a drive is designed can have a dramatic effect on its performance. Basically, any design strategy that maximizes the amount of data that can be read or written without moving the heads increases performance. So increasing the data density, the number of platters, or the physical size of the platters increases the drive's performance by allowing more data to be stored on a track/cylinder, thus reducing the amount of head motion necessary.

Other ways of increasing drive performance include increasing the rotational speed from the standard 3600 RPM to 4400 RPM, 5600RPM, or higher and incorporating a RAM cache on the drive controller board. So-called "fast spindle" drives such as the Maxtor MXT series can sustain a transfer rate of 3.5 megabytes per second or more.

Performance

Drive performance also is affected by the performance of the Mac to which it connects. Because the Mac's CPU must mediate all data transferred through the SCSI port, the faster the Mac is, the more data can be transferred.

Chapter 5
Macintosh Hardware

For example, a Mac Classic can transfer less than a megabyte of data per second—about 650K, actually—through its SCSI port, so hooking up a fast hard drive that can transfer 2M of data per second does not result in a significantly increased performance. However, many Macs—especially 68030-based models—often are delivered with drives that are slower than the SCSI ports on the computers, and in these cases, a higher performance drive can significantly increase performance.

Driver software—the control program that enables the Mac to communicate with the hard drive—also can make a noticeable difference. Apple's HD SC Setup program includes drivers for all Apple hard disks; third-party drives come with their own drivers. Several companies, such as LaCie, FWB, and Casablanca Works, supply high-performance SCSI drivers that can be used with almost any drive. Often, these drivers can provide performance improvements for third-party drives.

How data is organized on the drive can affect the Mac's performance. Recall that each track is divided into areas called sectors. The arrangement of the sectors on a given track (which is determined when the drive is formatted) is called its *interleave* or *interleave factor*. A track with sequentially numbered sections has a 1:1 interleave. Macs based on the 68020 and high processors generally format their hard drives with a 1:1 interleave; however, the 68000-based Macs run with a 1:2 or 1:3 interleave, where the next logical sector is two or three sectors beyond the previous physical sector. This is because the smaller Macs cannot finish reading the data the drive delivers on one sector before the next physical sector rotates under the drive's read/write head.

A Closer Look The interleave factor is set at the time the drive is formatted. Virtually all Mac hard drive utilities set the correct interleave factor automatically for the Mac that is running them. However, if you move a drive from one type of Mac to another, you may need to reformat for best performance. Note that you do not have to reformat the drive; for example, a drive that is used on both a Mac IIci and a Mac SE can be switched between the computers with no problem, unless it is the drive the computers boot from. If so, you must ensure the system software on the drive is compatible with both models, although performance is optimum for only one of the machines.

Some hard drives contain small built-in buffers that can hold one or more tracks of data. These drives typically always format with 1:1 interleave because they can hold the data read from the disk platters in the buffer until the Mac is ready for it.

Part I
Macintosh, the Computer

Peripherals and Expansion

The various Mac models differ in how much you can expand them. The original Macs deliberately were designed to be non-expandable, and some Macs, such as the current Mac Classic, still are designed that way.

All current Macs have, at a minimum, the following connections to the outside world: two serial ports, a SCSI port, and an ADB port. These constitute a common base for peripherals. Some Macs have built-in slots for extra expansion; currently, there are NuBus slots and several different processor-direct or PD slots. PD slots generally are ways to connect directly to the processor's data, address, and control lines. NuBus slots are more complex and allow more sophisticated interaction between the computer and its peripherals. However, these advantages are rarely realized in real-world use, and PDS slots provide superior performance.

The Serial Ports

All Macs have two serial ports controlled by a Zilog Z8530 Serial Communications Controller (SCC) or equivalent. The Mac's two serial ports are actually RS-422 ports, not the more common RS-232 ports. The difference is that RS-232 signal levels are defined and measured with respect to ground, whereas RS-422 signal levels are defined with respect to an inverted copy of the signal. The RS-422 signals are less subject to interference and degradation than are RS-232 signals. For most purposes, however, this difference does not matter, and you can connect almost any RS-232 device to the Mac with the proper cable.

The maximum normal speed of either port is 57,600 baud when the port is running in normal, interrupt-driven (synchronous) mode. In asynchronous mode, with external clocking, the speed can be much higher.

The ports are labeled as printer and modem ports in Mac documentation. For most purposes, the ports are equivalent: you could hook a modem to the printer port and a printer to the modem port and use them with no problem.

Only the printer port can be used for LocalTalk. (Although this formerly was called "AppleTalk," Apple has redefined the older term to refer to a set of networking protocols. LocalTalk is the term for the built-in, low-speed implementation of the AppleTalk protocols in all Macs.) This is a restriction of the LocalTalk software built into each Mac.

Chapter 5
Macintosh Hardware

LocalTalk runs at 230.4K baud. However, the printer port can be clocked externally to run at a higher speed, so the speed limit of the port actually is defined by how fast the Mac's processor can read or write data to the port. In the case of the 68000-based Macs, this works out to about 750K bits/second. Several companies offer faster LocalTalk implementations that use connectors containing a crystal and timing circuitry to drive the printer port at this speed.

There are some potential problems with very high-speed serial I/O. Because the processor must mediate every byte transferred to or from a disk, data coming in on a serial port might be missed during disk I/O. The ".SONY" driver built into all Macs contains code to periodically check the modem port (but not the printer port) for data while writing to a diskette, making the modem port more suitable for high-speed telecommunications (this was admittedly more of a consideration when Macs with hard disks were not common). The modem port also is wired to generate a higher priority interrupt than the printer port.

When Two Is Not Enough

In some cases, two serial ports just are not enough. There are two solutions to this problem:

▼ A serial port switch box, which enables you to connect more than one device to a port

▼ A serial port card that adds more serial ports to Macs with NuBus slots

The switch box is the best solution for most users, but there is a catch: the box must be connected to the Mac with a special *straight-through* cable. Standard Mac practice calls for the transmit data and receive data signals to be switched between the Mac and a serial device. If a switch box is used and connected to the Mac with a standard serial cable, the signals are switched twice: once between the Mac and the switch box and once between the switch box and whatever devices are connected to it. As a result, the devices do not work! Generally, a straight-through cable—one that does not switch the signals—is available wherever the switch box is obtained.

 There is no danger to the hardware when changing the settings on a switch box while the Mac is turned on, although doing so at the wrong time—such as in the middle of receiving data from a modem—obviously can cause some problems.

Adding more serial ports is more complex. Although a card with additional ports is available for NuBus Macs, the standard Mac system software does not "know" about anything other than the two built-in ports. Apple developed

the Communications Toolbox software to enable programs to be written that run with any available serial port, but very little software is written to this standard. The incorporation of the Communications Toolbox into System 7 should mean such programs will become more common in the future.

Companies that have worked on solutions to the two-serial-port problem include GDT Softworks, whose Jetlink Express package of printer drivers enables you to use almost any Hewlett-Packard laser or inkjet printer with a serial port card, and Global Village, whose TelePort modem connects via the ADB port rather than the serial port.

The ADB Port

With the introduction of the Mac II and SE in early 1987, Apple introduced what became the standard method for connecting keyboards, mice, and other human interaction peripherals (such as graphics tablets) to the Mac.

ADB stands for Apple Desktop Bus. It is a low-speed serial line (about 11,000 bits per second) with a protocol for handling multiple devices. Although the ADB routines were designed to support up to 16 devices, Apple recommends you connect no more than three at any one time, due to limitations in the hardware that could cause unreliable operation.

Each ADB device has a unique address, which is defined at boot time. General classes of devices have default addresses: for example, all pointing devices default to the same address. If more than one of the same device type is detected, a unique address is assigned for the extra device(s). This is one reason not to unplug or plug in ADB devices with the power on; the device address drops back to its default and the Mac can get confused if the device previously had a different address.

WARNING! Another reason not to connect or disconnect ADB devices with the power on is physical: on some Macs, it is possible the ADB connector's flexing on the logic board as a cable is inserted or removed can short the ADB power to ground. This blows a fuse on the logic board, rendering ADB useless. On Mac II, IIx, and SE computers, this requires an expensive logic board swap to fix. Newer Macs use self-resetting thermal ADB fuses that reset after a minute or two with no power. It is still not a good idea to test this, though!

Several interesting peripherals are available for the ADB port. Keyboards are optional when you buy most Macs, so you can choose a third-party keyboard if you want. *Extended* keyboards with arrays of function and cursor keys that generally duplicate a common PC keyboard layout are useful if you use macro programs: you can assign often-performed key and mouse sequences to be performed with a keystroke!

Alternative pointing devices abound: several manufacturers offer mice and trackballs as well as other, more esoteric devices such as touch screens, cordless mice, and pen-shaped mice. One company, Global Village, even offers a modem that connects as an ADB device.

WARNING! Unfortunately, ADB can be a source of compatibility problems, especially with third-party products. It is not uncommon for one manufacturer's trackball, for example, not to work when another manufacturer's keyboard is connected. Nothing can be done to fix this (short of hardware or firmware changes to the affected devices), so you always should check to make sure the devices you choose work together.

The SCSI Port

The SCSI port is basically a standardized high-speed parallel bus that supports up to eight devices, one of which is the Mac itself. Although it is primarily used for connecting hard disks, it also can be used to connect other devices. It cannot, however, be used to drive normal parallel devices such as the parallel printers popular in the DOS world; it can be used only with SCSI devices.

The two most common non-disk SCSI devices are printers and scanners. SCSI printers can be much faster than printers connected to the printer port, because data can be transferred much faster over the SCSI bus than through the printer port.

Note This does not mean a SCSI printer is faster in all circumstances, though. SCSI printers are rather simple beasts that simply print bitmaps sent over the SCSI connection. A Postscript printer, although hobbled by a slower serial connection, often has to deal with much less data: text can be sent as simple ASCII (after the appropriate font is defined or uploaded to the printer); one byte per character is all you need to send because the Postscript interpreter in the printer generates the appropriate bits to print. A SCSI printer must deal with tens or even hundreds of bytes to define a single character.

Typically, SCSI printers can beat serial port printers on complex graphics, although some high-end graphics programs require Postscript.

Chapter 5
Macintosh Hardware

Apple implements most of the SCSI-1 standard. A new standard, SCSI-2, is emerging, which allows improved performance. It is implemented in three stages: Stage 1 includes additional SCSI commands, some of which can improve performance. Stage II allows much faster data transfer rates for short bursts, up to 10M per second. Stage III is the full SCSI-2 implementation and requires different hardware to implement. Some companies offer high-performance SCSI cards that implement portions of the SCSI-2 standard.

SCSI Problems

SCSI problems are probably the most common Mac problems; most hard disk troubles can be traced to a problem with the SCSI setup. Although theoretically it is standardized, there is enough variance between devices, cables, and Macs to keep Mac users scratching their heads for years to come.

The original SCSI specification calls for 50 conductors between devices: 25 carrying data and control signals, each with its own ground. Apple chose to use a 25-conductor implementation with a common ground; some think this is the cause of the Mac SCSI's almost traditional flakiness. (See chapter 28, "Troubleshooting," for more information on SCSI problems and solutions.)

Slots

There are two types of slots: NuBus slots and *processor direct slots* (PDS). NuBus Macs include the Mac II and Quadra series machines, and IIsi when equipped with the NuBus card adapter. PDS Macs include the SE, SE/30, Portable, IIfx (it has NuBus and PD slots), LC, and IIsi (when equipped with the PDS card adapter). Most newer Macs include both processor direct and NuBus slots.

> **Note:** Some of the compact Macs, such as the Plus and the Classic, have no expansion slots. This has not deterred the aftermarket, which offers accelerators, external monitors adapters, and more for these machines. These accessories typically connect via a spring-loaded clip that fits over the processor and has prongs that contact each pin on it. These do work but are prone to problems caused by their less-than-secure connection, especially if the Mac is moved around. Although some people never have problems, many people do. You should get a slotted Mac if you think you might want such expansion in the future or consider trading up to a slotted Mac if you have a non-slotted one now.

NuBus defines the hardware protocol for communicating with peripherals. It was developed by Texas Instruments and licensed to a number of vendors, including Apple and NeXT. However, its benefits remain largely theoretical—so far, nobody has introduced a NuBus card that can do something a PDS card cannot. This situation parallels the one in the PC world, in which IBM's Micro Channel architecture, introduced approximately the same time Apple introduced its NuBus Macs, has failed to produce any peripherals with compelling advantages over their ISA (industry standard architecture) cousins. The NuBus' troubles may be because Apple did not implement the NuBus block transfer capability on the Mac's logic board, which would have allowed increased performance.

Each processor-direct slot is unique to a particular Mac model, and PD cards designed for one do not work in another. The single exception is the Mac IIsi, whose PDS slot adapter allows it to use the same PDS cards as an SE/30. As a consequence, there is a much wider selection of NuBus cards than PDS cards because manufacturers are reluctant to produce several different varieties of the same card, each with different form factors and power requirements.

NuBus cards accessories are typically those that are not suited for serial, SCSI, or ADB connection. Examples include:

▼ Display cards to drive monitors

▼ Accelerators that need direct access to the Mac hardware

▼ SCSI accelerator cards that implement faster SCSI transfers than the Mac's built-in port

▼ Video digitizers

▼ EtherTalk high-speed network adapters

Power-supply limitations are the only limitations that normally affect NuBus cards. Under Apple's guidelines, no NuBus card should use more than approximately 15 watts of power; however, many cards (including Apple's own 8•24GC card) exceed this specification.

The six-slot Macs have power supplies robust enough to handle almost any combination of NuBus cards and hard disks; the three-slot Macs and the single-slot IIsi do not. In some cases, using power-hungry cards such as accelerated 24-bit display cards can cause the total power usage of the Mac to exceed the nominal output of the power supply. If you are unsure of your situation, check with the card's manufacturer.

Monitors

The Mac world is fortunate: there is only one graphics standard and it is defined by QuickDraw. Even the way a given pattern of data in RAM corresponds to a video image is standardized, so most Mac programs work on any monitor you are likely to hook up to your Mac.

Monitors for the Mac II Class

Mac II–class computers are designed from the ground up for multiple monitors; the only limitation is the number of slots and the internal video connection, if present. Each connected monitor may be any size. No extra software is required for a monitor's basic use—just plug in the card, connect the display, and go.

The original Mac II monitor card could display up to 256 colors (eight bits per pixel). This was the standard for several years because it was the maximum defined by the Color QuickDraw software introduced with the Mac II. The introduction of 32-bit QuickDraw raised the ante to 24 bits per pixel, which is enough to define more than 16 million colors for photo-realistic images. Although it is called 32-bit QuickDraw, only the lower 24 bits are used. The upper 8 bits are called the alpha channel, and Apple has not formally defined their effects. The down side of 24-bit color is that because it is three times as much information to manipulate as 8-bit color, the operation of the display is much slower.

Some monitor/display card systems offer enhanced capabilities, such as:

▼ Hardware pan and zoom, which enable you to magnify any portion of the screen and to use the screen as a window onto a larger virtual desktop that scrolls when the mouse reaches one edge.

▼ Multiple resolutions: 36 dots per inch for close ups, down to 150 dots per inch to fit a large document on the screen.

▼ Accelerated display cards, which use on-board processors to accomplish much of the drawing tasks that the Mac's processor otherwise would have to handle. Apple's own entry in the field, the 8•24GC card, is unique: its AMD 29000 processor runs an entirely new version of QuickDraw that replaces the one built into the Mac, so all connected displays are accelerated to some extent.

68000-Based Macs

Although 68000-based Macs are not designed to use anything but the displays they come with, the aftermarket offers several solutions. The first company to offer an external monitor for any Mac was Radius, which was founded by some of the people involved in the development of the original Mac.

Chapter 5
Macintosh Hardware

Because 68000-based Macs do not have Color QuickDraw, additional monitors are always black and white, one-bit-per-pixel systems. The exception to this rule is to use ScuzzyGraph, a piece of hardware that connects through the Mac's SCSI port and allows the original QuickDraw specification of eight colors to be supported. QuickDraw's design makes it easy to expand the size of the desktop that it operates on, so compatibility is rarely a problem with 68000-based systems.

Summary

The Macintosh is a unique computer that has redefined the look and feel of all computers. Using the Motorola 68000 series of processors, every Mac model from the Lisa to the Quadra and PowerBooks have a common interface. The Macintosh makes unique use of RAM, ROM, and memory in general. Installing memory is simple and enhances the performance of the Mac in individual ways unique to each model. Peripheral devices can be installed and can communicate with the CPU through NuBus expansion cards, SCSI ports, serial ports, ADB ports, and other methods.

Chapter 6: Printing from Your Macintosh

Remember the paperless-office prediction that was so prevalent in the early 1980s? Judging by the importance of printed output in today's business world, that prediction was way off base.

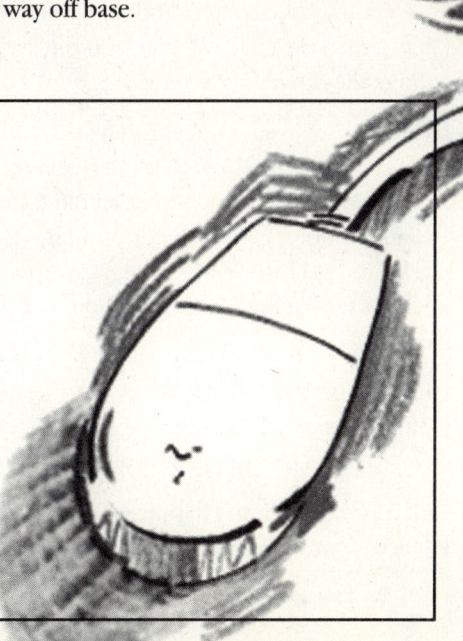

In This Chapter

- ▼ History of printers
- ▼ Types of printers and how they work
- ▼ Page description languages
- ▼ Printer drivers and printer engines
- ▼ What to look for and when to buy

Part I
Macintosh, the Computer

Apple's Macintosh computer played a major role in erasing that prediction by introducing LaserWriter's high-end printing capabilities to the office environment in January 1985.

Introduction

Before Apple introduced the LaserWriter, high-quality desktop printing typically meant grainy or jagged-edge output for graphics, and better-looking but slow-to-print output for text. At the time, *dot-matrix printers* were the standard tool for desktop printing. Dot-matrix printers create characters or graphics from a series of square *pixels* or *dots*. A series of pins located in the print head placed the dots on the page by passing over the paper and pressing through a ribbon or spraying ink to create an image of a dot. Dot-matrix printers have maximum resolutions of about 200 dots per inch (*dpi*) and speeds that can print between 50 characters per second (*cps*) for near-letter quality and 350 cps for *draft,* or low resolution, output.

Daisywheel printers have actual characters (like those on a manual typewriter) raised at the end of small pins that fan out in a circle, resembling the petals of a daisy (hence the name). As a character is printed, the daisywheel spins to the correct character and the pin impresses the character onto the page through pressure. These printers can print attractive business letters at resolutions approaching 700 dpi. (The more dpi, the smaller the dot, so the less jagged the edges of your printout are. Compare this 700 dpi to the 200 dpi of the dot-matrix printer.)

Unfortunately, daisywheel printers are noisy from the impact of the wheel on the paper and too slow to avoid smearing the characters, so more often than not, using a typewriter—even an old-fashioned manual—was preferable. Neither printer is suitable for printing quality graphics or for printing both graphics and text on the same page. You either went to an outside typesetting service for better resolution or did without. There were no other options.

It was this situation that led industry "experts" to forecast the "electronic office" where data would be exchanged electronically and paper printing would be an occasional or avoidable chore.

Of course, this hasn't happened. One reason is that running a fully electronic office is more involved than experts initially estimated, especially because

Chapter 6
Printing from Your Macintosh

there is a large variety of computer operating systems available rather than one standard system. Then, when the first desktop laser printer was introduced, people began to question whether they needed an electronic office at all.

Apple's LaserWriter revolutionized the printing industry for many reasons. Its cost was significantly more than that of its nearest rivals, but it was overwhelmingly superior in terms of quality, speed, convenience, and flexibility. Fast, elegant performance made LaserWriter the choice of many businesses and helped fuel the desktop publishing revolution.

This revolution probably was essential to the continued popularity of the Mac. Previously, the Mac was little more than an attractive paperweight—nice to look at but without the software to make it usable. Then Apple introduced LaserWriter, Aldus introduced PageMaker, and *device-independent* desktop publishing was born. The combination of LaserWriter, PostScript page description language, Aldus' PageMaker, and WYSIWYG display made the Mac a must-have machine for graphic artists.

The laser printer is still the most popular type of printer with its speed, high-quality output, flexible paper handling, and superior connectivity options, although Apple's various LaserWriters have much competition in both price and quality. Dot-matrix printers have made a mild resurgence in the PC market, due to the incorporation of outline fonts (See chapter 9, "Fonts and Typography," for more information about outline fonts). But their place in the Macintosh market as the low-end, workhorse printer is past. The sun has long since gone down on daisywheel technology, and this product joins the dinosaurs in history. In place of these vanishing breeds, new technologies such as *inkjet* and *thermal wax transfer* have gained acceptance in the low-end/personal and color markets, where laser printers are not yet affordable.

The goals of this chapter are to give you enough background to understand and evaluate developments in the printer industry, and to provide tips and advice to help you fully exploit the printer you now use. The first section, "Printing: An Overview," explains the jargon concerning page description languages and fonts, and gives you a feel for how printers work. The next section, "What to Look for in a Printer," discusses some important criteria you should consider if you want to buy a printer. Finally, "Printers: Users and Manufacturers" looks at some of the best performers from several printing manufacturers and identifies how different printers fill your specific needs.

Part I
Macintosh,
the Computer

Printing: An Overview

As printers become more powerful, the number of terms and concepts you need to know to exploit the new capabilities increases. With three different imaging and font management system standards, four separate printing engine technologies, and countless statistics and descriptive terms, Macintosh printing can seem very complicated.

This section paints a broad picture of the printing process, describing what happens between the time you select Print from the File menu and your page comes out of the printer. This section also briefly defines terminology and describes existing technologies.

The Printing Process

The sequence of events for printing on the Mac is, like everything else on the Mac, a straightforward and intuitive process, as shown in figure 6.1.

1. Select the output device through the Chooser desk accessory. (This is usually done only once, not every time you print.)

2. Before beginning work on a new document, go to the **File** menu and select **Page Setup**, and define the size and shape of the page to print (8 1/2 x 11 Tall or 8 1/2 x 14 Wide, and so on).

3. Work on the document until you want to print it.

4. From the **File** menu, select **Print**, and click the **OK** button in the **Print** dialog box to begin printing. This dialog box usually gives you other choices as well, such as printing a range of pages in a multi-page document, changing the percentage of original size, manual or automatic feed, and so on.

5. The application sends an electronically coded copy of the document to the *printer driver* (software that tells the printer how to print) for the selected printer.

6. The printer driver converts the document's graphical images and text to coded commands in the appropriate *page description language (PDL)*. (With QuickDraw, converting the document to printer commands takes place on the Mac. With PostScript, the major conversions take place in the printer.)

7. The printer driver sends the PDL command file to a *raster image processor (RIP)*.

8. The RIP uses the PDL commands file to generate a bit-map rendering of the page to print.
9. The RIP sends the bit-map to the printer's print engine, and moments later, the printed page appears.

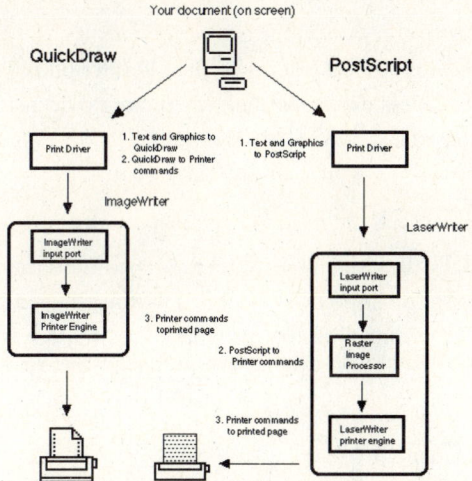

Figure 6.1
From screen to printer, there are three main steps.

A Closer Look The printer driver is a resource driver (RDEV) that is placed in your Extension folder within the System folder. You select an RDEV in the Chooser file, and it translates the graphics and text in your document to a sequence of commands the printer can understand. The grammar and syntax of these commands is called a page description language, referred to as PDL.

Page Description Languages

Page description languages for the Mac include PostScript and PostScript clones, TrueImage (a PostScript clone with special font capabilities), and QuickDraw. Each PDL has commands called *primitives* that display fonts on the screen, draw lines, fill graphical outlines, and perform many other functions. QuickDraw is the Mac's native imaging system and is mainly used to display onscreen images. QuickDraw is also used to print with low-end/personal printers. PostScript and TrueImage are for higher level printers and typeset-quality imagesetters.

Postscript

PostScript, invented by Adobe Systems, Inc., is the industry standard because it is used on the widest range of output devices. It appears on everything from laser and wax printers to high-end imagesetters. However, PostScript printers are usually expensive since manufacturers must pay licensing fees to use the language, and PostScript requires an interpreter to be built into the printer. PostScript also needs an RIP to operate.

QuickDraw

QuickDraw has fewer graphical primitives than PostScript, but printers that use it are significantly less expensive since there are no licensing fees to pay, no need for an interpreter, and no RIP is required.

TrueImage

TrueImage, originally developed by another company and purchased by Microsoft, is a PostScript clone PDL. As of this writing, there are only three manufacturers of TrueImage printing products: LaserMaster, Microtek, and NewGen.

PostScript Clones

Other PostScript clone PDLs are on the market, but there is no guarantee that a clone is 100 percent PostScript compatible, even though most advertise that they are. Clones are PostScript-like languages that have been recreated by reverse-engineering, a process similar to copying expensive perfumes or making generic drugs. Cloning PostScript avoids the high royalty fees Adobe charges and results in less expensive printing devices.

Acceptance of PostScript clones is growing. Most printer companies now use clones on at least one of their model lines. Clones offer similar speed performance and, in most cases, output is virtually indistinguishable from the genuine article. However, they are a copy and not the original, so if you rely on precise graphic element positioning and long-term reliability, you probably want to use PostScript.

Note: If you get a clone printer, make sure it is fully compatible with Adobe's fonts, known as Type 1 and Type 3. One way to test its compatibility is to print some Type 1 fonts at odd sizes ranging from 5 to 17 points on both the clone printer and a PostScript printer. Compare the outputs with a magnifying glass: They should be exactly the same.

The price of PostScript printers and licenses have dropped considerably over the past couple of years. Today, there's little reason not to pay the small difference in price between true PostScript and a PostScript clone.

Chapter 6
Printing from Your Macintosh

Note: The most popular page description language is not PostScript or QuickDraw, but Hewlett-Packard's Page Composition Language (PCL) for its PC-compatible LaserJet series. There are several versions of PCL; PCL 3, PCL 4, and PCL 5 are the latest as of this writing. PCL is primarily a text-composition language with few graphics capabilities. However, the text it produces is very attractive, and there are hundreds of fonts available on special LaserJet ROM cartridges. In addition, PCL 5-compatible printers use Hewlett-Packard's patented *Resolution Enhancement Technology (RET)* to smooth curves and lines and improve apparent resolution beyond the normal LaserJet's 300 dpi (or, in the case of the LaserJet 4M, 600 dpi). (For more about image enhancing techniques, see the section, "Resolution," later in this chapter.)

Comparing PDLs: PostScript, TrueImage, and QuickDraw

QuickDraw printers are distinguished from PostScript/clone and printers in three ways: detailed high-resolution image handling, font handling, and special capabilities. QuickDraw takes a back seat to PostScript in each area.

- ▼ QuickDraw is optimized for the Macintosh screen's 72 dpi resolution, while PostScript and TrueImage (PS/TI) are designed to work on anything from 72 dpi monitors (Display PostScript) to imagesetters at resolutions of over 4,000 dpi. This means that character spacing and general image manipulation are more precise in PS/TI.

- ▼ PS/TI has built-in outline font handling functions; QuickDraw can only use bit-mapped fonts (although utilities exist to give QuickDraw outline font capability, as detailed in chapter 8).

- ▼ PS/TI has special features such as text rotation, curve smoothing, printing text on a line, and continuous grayscale printing that QuickDraw does not have. Again, there are low-cost utilities that add the text manipulation functions to QuickDraw.

TrueImage gives results that are comparable to PostScript for detailed image handling. One advantage to TrueImage is that PostScript does not handle Apple's TrueType fonts very well, while TrueImage can handle both TrueType and hinted Type 1 and 3 fonts. (See chapter 8, "Fonts and Typography," for more information.)

In mid-1991, Adobe introduced an upgrade to PostScript called PostScript Level 2. The new version is a major enhancement, offering quicker imaging, more efficient use of memory (so you need less printer RAM), built-in file compression, improved screening, and better color handling (see the section, "Color Printing," later in this chapter). As of this writing, no PostScript clone, including TrueImage, is Level 2-compatible.

Printers as Computers

All PostScript and PostScript clone printers (including TrueImage) have their own microprocessors and usually one or more megabytes of RAM, as well as an interpreter in ROM. This computing power generates a bit-mapped description of the page from the commands sent by the printer driver. The microprocessor, RAM, and ROM are usually housed on one board, called the *print controller*. In desktop publishing, the combination of microprocessor, RAM, and PostScript interpreter is called the raster image processor, or RIP.

Apple's PostScript LaserWriter series uses the same Motorola 680x0 series of microprocessors used in the Macs themselves; other printer companies are moving to *reduced instruction set computing* (RISC) microprocessors for more speed. The microprocessor's speed and the amount of RAM in the printer has a significant effect on printing performance (see the sections, "Resolution" and "Printer Speed," later in this chapter).

Usually, you can upgrade the controller with more RAM, a better microprocessor, or a later version of PostScript in ROM for better performance. Xante's Accel-A-Writer controller upgrades for LaserWriters offer a number of performance improvements, including resolutions up to 1200 by 300 dpi and SCSI hard disk font storage for LaserWriters that did not previously have that capability. LaserMaster, a Minnesota-based company, also offers controller upgrades for the LaserWriter II series. Their controllers are NuBus cards which fit into the slots of your Mac II so you do not need to take apart your printer. LaserMaster controllers improve resolution up to 800 by 800 dpi, and supplement the LaserWriters' ROM font library with an additional 100 Type 1 typefaces.

The ability to add upgrade boards to printers dramatically improves the useful lifetime of a laser printer. It can also allow you to improve a printer's quality to allow its use in more demanding applications. Usually manufacturers only create add-in boards for very popular printers like the Apple LaserWriter or HP LaserJet series. This is one good reason to buy a printer from one of these two manufacturers.

Printers with microprocessors and RISC generally cost much more. Genuine PostScript printers also have Adobe's licensing fee (usually around $250) factored into their price. However, the microprocessors and RIPs free up your computer so you can continue with additional work during printing.

Printer Drivers

Printer drivers are primarily involved in converting your documents' contents into a form the printer can understand. When you use drivers that support printers which are not native to your computer (for example, the Hewlett-Packard PCL-based LaserJet series), the driver *emulates* the foreign system. The original ImageWriter used a Toshiba engine and had a driver that emulated the Epson FX-80. Printer driver files, also known as RDEVs, go into your System folder in System 6 and the Extensions folder in System 7. Whenever you call up the Chooser or issue a Page Setup or Print command from an application, you use the printer drivers.

WARNING! When you select a printer with the Chooser, the system software uses the driver to configure the page view settings in the active application. These settings affect the page's rectangular size (or print area), font sizes, and graphic image placement, among other things. Because page view settings vary for different printers, it is crucial to start your work sessions by creating a page setup that conforms to the selected output device. Otherwise, you may be surprised at the printed results. (See figures 6.2 and 6.3. Notice the relative locations of the "Printing: An Overview" section heading, and compare the line breaks and number of paragraphs per page.)

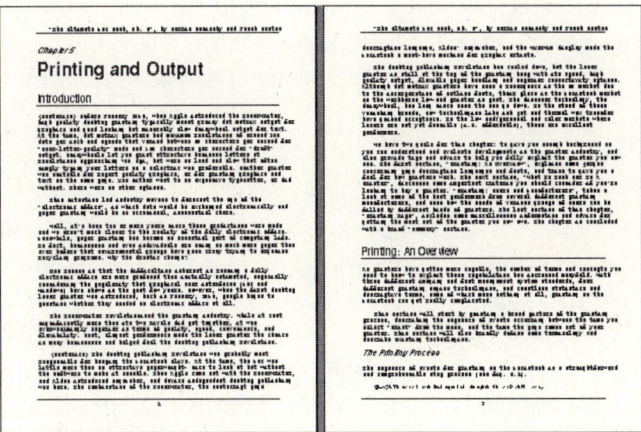

Chapter 6
Printing from Your Macintosh

Figure 6.2
Microsoft Word's Print Preview function when ImageWriter is selected in the Chooser.

If you plan to have a typesetting service print the document, get a copy of the driver file used for the typesetting machine and install it on your Mac. This way, you will have precise control of your final product's appearance. (This is the goal behind the Mac's WYSIWYG display philosophy.)

Issuing a Print command puts the printer driver to work. Its main job is to convert the contents of your document into commands your printer's PDL—whether QuickDraw, PostScript, or TrueImage—can understand. Depending

Part I

Macintosh, the Computer

Figure 6.3
The same document with LaserWriter selected as the output device.

on the application and the settings in the Page Setup dialog boxes (see the section, "Dialog Box Options," later in this chapter), the driver may also perform a number of other tasks.

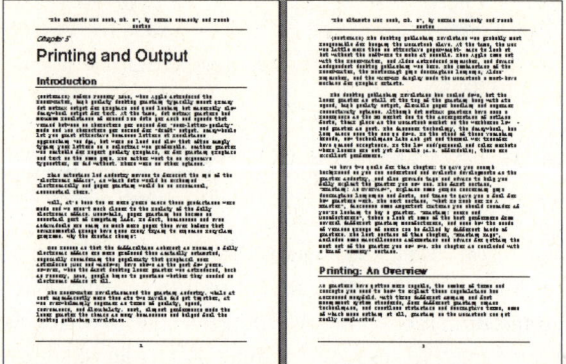

Although different printers may use the same PDL, they cannot all use the same printer drivers. The actual mechanism printers use to put dots on the page (a printer engine) differs from printer to printer (see the section, "Printing Engines," later in this chapter), so its capabilities and limitations differ also. The drivers must also deviate to describe these variations of capabilities exactly. For example, a laser engine's limitations keep it from printing a page rectangle as large as dot-matrix printers such as the ImageWriter can. On the other hand, a laser's superior resolution and speed make the ImageWriter's Draft-Faster-Best output ratings unnecessary.

Note: The Mac comes with printer drivers for Apple's PostScript-based LaserWriters as well as the QuickDraw-based ImageWriter, Personal LaserWriters, and StyleWriter. The drivers are updated with each new version of system software. The drivers' version numbers appear in the top right corner of the Page Setup dialog box. It is important to keep your drivers up-to-date with your system software. (You can sometimes update ahead; using System 7 drivers with System 6 is recommended. System 6.0.8 installation gives you the System 7 drivers, or you can use the System 7 printing installation disk to install them on your 6.0.5 or later system.)

If you are on a network, it is crucial for all users to have the same driver files. This is critical for pre-System 7 (LaserWriter 5.2 or 6.0) printer drivers *only*. System 7 drivers of various versions should not have conflicts with each other. Each time you use a different driver file to access a printer, even if it is only a different version of the same driver, you must restart the printer. This uses valuable time and forces you to re-select the printer through the Chooser each time.

Emulation

With all the PDL standards available now (PostScript, QuickDraw, TrueImage, PCL, plotter standards, and dozens of older protocols such as Diablo 630 for daisywheels and Epson LQ for dot matrix), there are bound to be some communication difficulties. Specifically, when you have an application that requires a printer type that you do not have a driver for, you are out of luck.

Some graphical applications, such as Adobe Illustrator, automatically assume you are printing on a PostScript printer, so the documents it creates consist of PostScript code. If you do not have a PostScript laser printer (or if you want to proof on a non-PostScript device), you must use a program that converts PostScript to the equivalent combination of QuickDraw or other non-PostScript PDL commands.

> **Note** The most popular program for converting to non-PostScript PDL commands is Custom Applications' Freedom of Press. This program enables you to print PostScript documents on QuickDraw printers such as ImageWriter or Personal LaserWriter LS to PCL printers, thermal printers, and film recorders (used for imaging slides). It even comes with outline fonts to substitute for PostScript fonts. Freedom of Press runs quickly and is the best solution for printing PostScript files if you do not have access to a PostScript printer, since it can access so many different printers.

Printing Engines

Printers are frequently classified according to what kind of printing mechanism, or engine, they have. There are five major kinds of engines used by desktop printers today: dot-matrix, laser, LED, ink/bubblejet, and thermal wax transfer.

Dot-matrix

Dot-matrix technology is decades old, which translates to centuries in computer-years. Although supplanted in quality, speed, and flexibility by lasers and inkjets, dot-matrix printers still have their place. Because the print device is an impact type, dot-matrix is the only printer you can use with multi-copy carbon-based or carbonless forms. It also offers the lowest cost per page of any printing technology. For these reasons, do not be surprised to see old ImageWriters and Epsons (a popular dot-matrix printer for PCs) around for at least another decade.

Chapter 6
Printing from Your Macintosh

Part I
Macintosh, the Computer

A Closer Look Dot-matrix printers work by striking a ribbon with print pins or wires (one pin makes one dot), and transferring the ink on the ribbon to the paper underneath (see figure 6.4). The pins are closely spaced, offering resolutions up to 216 dpi. Printing speeds vary from around 30 cps for near-letter quality output to over 300 cps (about one page per minute) on some models for draft quality output.

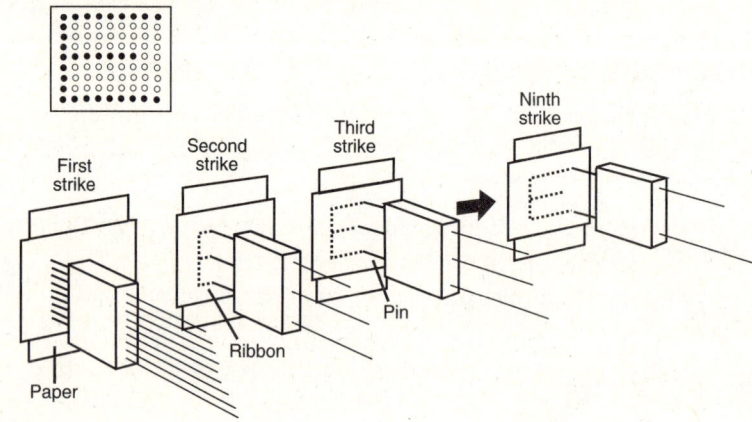

Figure 6.4
Dot-matrix printers use pins on a print head to strike an ink ribbon and impress the image dot by dot on the page.

Note Due to their direct impact printing method, dot-matrix printers are quite loud; many people buy long cables so they can place their dot-matrix printers in closets or unused rooms. Several companies make dot-matrix printer mufflers; Kensington makes one of the best for the ImageWriter called, appropriately enough, The Printer Muffler. There has been a tendency to redesign impact print heads so that the pins are mounted on springs, and the impact is softened. This lessens the noise somewhat.

Apple's ImageWriter is the best-selling dot-matrix printer for the Mac. However, there are several excellent third-party dot-matrix printers available. Only GCC's WriteImpact can directly interface with the Mac; to connect your Mac to printers from companies like Toshiba, Epson, Okidata, NEC, and Seikosha (the watch company), you will need to get the right driver software and a compatible cable (see the section, "Printer Drivers," above). Fortunately, this is easy; several companies supply drivers and cables that connect your Mac to nearly every dot-matrix printer ever made. A third-party printer and driver/cable package can give you access to better quality than you get from the ImageWriter for less money.

Chapter 6
Printing from Your Macintosh

Note: Dot-matrix printers only use QuickDraw and need the Mac to generate the bit-mapped images. You can significantly improve text output on dot-matrix printers by using Adobe Type Manager (ATM) or TrueType fonts. (See chapter 8, "Fonts and Typography," for more information.) Apple's ImageWriter II is also color-capable, but rather than using Apple's driver software, you might consider using Microspot's MacPalette II driver. It uses proprietary technology to give you inkjet-quality color on any ImageWriter II with a color ribbon.

For cables and third-party printer driver software, GDT Softworks offers The PrintLink Collection dot-matrix printer driver software, JetLink Express for HP LaserJet and DeskJet drivers, and Mac Daisy Link for daisywheel printers. Orange Micro's Grappler 9-pin interface is the best-selling serial to parallel interface for third-party 9-pin printers. The Grappler interface automatically emulates ImageWriter II. (See the section, "Emulation," above.)

Note: The only maintenance you should have with dot-matrix printers is replacing the ribbon cartridges when they run dry and occasionally refeeding the paper. Ribbons are inexpensive—even color ones cost less than $20 and when re-inked can last for thousands of pages.

You can use a product called MacInker, sold by Computer Friends (Portland, OR), to re-ink printer ribbons. You can re-ink ribbons up to 50 times (or until they start to fray), and they print just as well or better after each renewal. Using MacInker to ink new ribbons before you use them improves their print quality. MacInker also re-inks color ribbons, which saves a great deal of money, since re-color inks cost about $5. After 50 re-inkings of a color ribbon, for example, MacInker could save you almost $500.

Laser and LED

A Closer Look: Laser printer engines work by using laser light to electrically create an image of the page on the outside of a rotating tube called a *drum*. The laser causes the etched parts of the drum to become electrically charged. Oppositely charged toner particles are applied to the rotating drum, adhering to the laser-charged sections. The drum is then heated while paper is simultaneously pressed against it. The combination of high heat and pressure fuses the toner to the page (see figure 6.5).

Figure 6.5

Laser printers use laser light to write the image on a rotating tube.

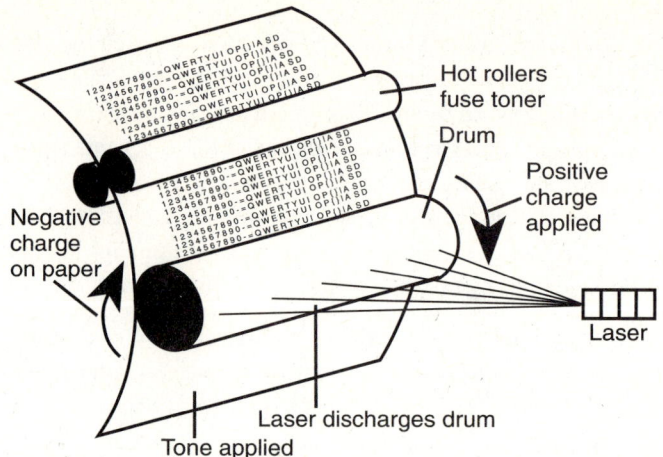

Laser printers are quiet and extremely fast; some can print up to 135 pages per minute (ppm)—although 8 ppm is the most common rate—at sound levels far below dot-matrix printers. Resolution is at least 300 dpi, and some desktop lasers can print up to 1200 dpi. Typeset-quality imagesetting machines start at 1270 dpi and currently go to 3250 dpi. Distinguishing between 1200 dpi and higher resolutions is difficult, especially with text, but the difference dramatically improves grayscale images. Laser printers that print 1200 dpi are now about one-third the price of 2500 dpi imagesetters, rapidly bringing professional-level publishing capabilities within the price range of individual users.

A Closer Look LED printers work similarly to lasers, but instead of laser light, LED printers use light-emitting diodes to create an image on a rotating drum. Laser and LED technology are used in copiers, and there is virtually no qualitative difference between 300 dpi output from either method. However, there are currently no LED printers on the market that offer greater than 300 dpi resolution.

Most LED printer engines are made by Okidata. Canon has several laser engine models: Canon's CX engine was used in the original LaserWriters; the SX engine is used in the LaserWriter II series, and the LX engine is used in the Personal LaserWriter LS. A new Canon engine used in the Apple LaserWriter Pro 600 and 630, and in the HP LaserJet 4M, enables a print resolution of 600 dpi.

A Closer Look Kyocera has introduced a new 300 dpi laser printer called the Ecosys printer that is notable in many regards. This printer uses a SiO_2 imaging drum, and refillable toner with small ceramic particles that refreshes the imaging drum. The net result of this technology is that the print engine has a very long lifetime, and the per page cost is reduced to about 1.5¢ to 2¢ per page.

Chapter 6
Printing from
Your Macintosh

Laser printers that use the PostScript PDL have their own microprocessors and memory, and are powerful computers in their own right. (See the section, "Printers as Computers," above.) In the early days of laser printing, all printers used PostScript; however, today there is a large market for "personal" laser printers which use QuickDraw and do not have expensive CPUs and RAM. These QuickDraw laser and LED printers use the Mac to translate text and graphics commands to a bit-mapped image. If you have a slow Mac, you may have to wait awhile for it to process a 300 dpi image for a QuickDraw laser printer.

The most popular PostScript laser printers for the Mac are the Apple LaserWriter series, although other models from Texas Instruments, QMS, GCC, and Qume offer equal or better performance for less money. Hewlett-Packard makes the top-selling non-PostScript laser printers. To use one on a Mac, you need an interface product such as GDT Softworks' JetLink Express. If you are using both Macintosh and MS DOS computers in a mixed office environment, you may want to investigate the LaserWriter Pro 630 or the LaserWriter 4M which will accept input from either type of computer. The Mac-only personal laser market is intensely competitive, with Apple's Personal LaserWriter series and the GCC PLP II series playing the dominant roles. (For a more complete review of the laser printing market, see the section, "Printers: Users and Manufacturers," later in this chapter.)

Laser printers require little maintenance. After every few thousand pages, you have to replace the toner and possibly the drum. In printers with Canon engines, this is a one-step process; in others, the drum and toner are in separate modules, making them less convenient to replace. Toner and drum cartridges for Canon-based printers generally run $85-$100, but you can get old ones recharged for about $65.

WARNING! Recharging cartridges is a good idea, but quality can vary from company to company. A badly recharged toner cartridge could ruin your laser printer and void the manufacturer's warranty. To get a reputable recharge, ask print shops and copier supply stores in your area if they recharge toner cartridges and, if not, where they purchase their recharged cartridges. Many mail-order recharging services advertise in the back of Mac magazines, but there is no way to check their quality. One good such company is Laser Recharge (located in Swampscott, MA, Tel. 617-451-0033).

A Closer Look Drums in recharged Canon toner cartridges have to be resurfaced every third or fourth refill. A good recharging company should do this for you at an extra charge; be sure to ask when you call for estimates. Some drums are now being finished with an emerald-like surface that is durable and long-lasting. New

Part I
Macintosh, the Computer

emerald cartridges are more expensive ($120-$135), but are worth the cost in the long run since they provide higher-quality, blacker images than many new cartridges.

Note: Would you like to make a T-shirt? Use your laser printer to do it! A company called Easy Transfer Cartridges makes laser printer cartridges using the special dyes used in T-shirt transfer sheets for printers with Canon engines. You can make a transfer graphic, print it on plain paper or special coated laser printer paper, and then transfer it to a poly/cotton T-shirt with a household iron. It takes less than an hour, start to finish.

If you use a program such as Aldus Freehand that does four-color separations, you can make full-color transfers by running the same sheet through your laser printer four times. (Of course, this method requires four different laser cartridges.)

Inkjet and Bubblejet

A Closer Look: Inkjet and bubblejet printers have only recently become flexible and reliable enough to earn respect in the computer market. In an inkjet printer, ink is sprayed through tiny nozzles directly onto a page (see figure 6.6). In a bubblejet, ink at the tip of a nozzle is heated, making it bubble. When this bubble bursts, its ink sprays onto the page. Both technologies are whisper-quiet and offer reasonably fast printing speeds.

Figure 6.6
The inkjet printer head has dozens of tiny nozzles that force ink onto the page.

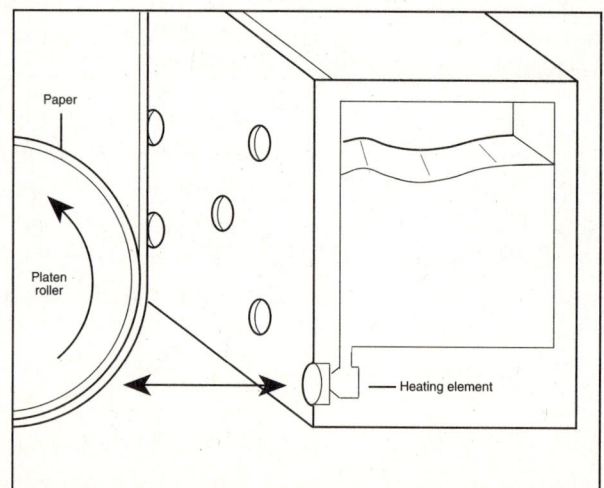

Chapter 6
Printing from Your Macintosh

Inkjet and bubblejet printer resolutions are normally close to laser quality. For example, HP's DeskWriter prints at 300 dpi, while Apple's StyleWriter II reaches 360 dpi. Two portable inkjets, Kodak's Diconix and GCC's Write-Move, use more compact mechanisms and print only at 192 dpi. Bubblejet output is slightly superior to pure inkjet at similar resolutions because the heated ink dries more quickly and is less susceptible to bleeding or smearing.

Bleeding and smearing has hindered inkjets for a long time. While older inkjets printed at a laser-like 300 dpi, their output tended to be fuzzier than a laser. Also, many required a special, coated paper and couldn't print to plain paper at all.

Inkjets today are far more flexible—many can even print on transparencies. Output, while still somewhat fuzzy, has improved greatly as well. Inkjets are inexpensive compared to lasers—cost per page is slightly more, but initial investment is significantly less—and can even be used for good, inexpensive color printing. The new HP DeskWriter C gives notable color output for under $1,000, and an improved model comes with an additional black cartridge to improve the lifetime of the color cartridge.

There are no inkjet printers that use PostScript. (However, see the section "Printer Drivers," above, for information about PostScript emulation.) All models require the Mac to generate the bit-mapped image for printing. While 300 dpi QuickDraw laser output is slow, printing a document with several graphics from a Mac Classic to a StyleWriter inkjet is perhaps even slower. Apple recently released new drivers for the StyleWriter to speed this, and the newer model StyleWriter II is somewhat better in this regard. The StyleWriter II also does grayscale printing.

Apple's StyleWriter II competes primarily with HP's DeskWriter in quality and price for black and white output. There are also two inexpensive, good-quality portable inkjets, one from Kodak (Diconix M150) and one from GCC (WriteMove). For color, the Tektronix ColorQuick, Sharp Color Inkjet, and HP DeskWriter C offer reasonable quality for less money than thermal technology. And perhaps the best color output for your money this side of film printing can be had with the $50,000 Iris true-color, continuous-tone inkjet printer. You must see Iris pages to believe them; they give very accurate color.

Ink cartridge refills for inkjet and bubblejet printers are available at quite a bargain. Third-party sources usually charge 40 to 50 percent less for refills than Apple or HP charge for new cartridges, and the inks are generally higher quality. Ink refills are not as easily found as laser recharging services; however, you can expect them to become more readily available as inkjets' popularity increases.

The future of inkjet printers is perceived to be quite bright, and it is anticipated that inkjets will replace dot-matrix printers, and become the low-cost color printer of choice.

Thermal Transfer

Thermal transfer is a general term encompassing several specific color technologies, including wax printing and dye sublimation. The major difference between the technologies is the kind of print medium used. Lower-end printers use opaque waxes and crayon-like inks, while higher-end printers use transparent inks and dyes that allow for true, continuous-tone printing.

Thermal transfer printers work by touching a heated pin to an inked or waxed ribbon, causing drops to fall at precise locations on the page (see figure 6.7). For black and white printing, this technology offers quiet performance at resolutions up to 300 dpi, much like inkjets. However, thermal transfer is more appropriate than inkjet technology for color printing because there is no bleeding or smearing with wax printers. Low-cost, good-quality color applications are a thermal printer's specialty.

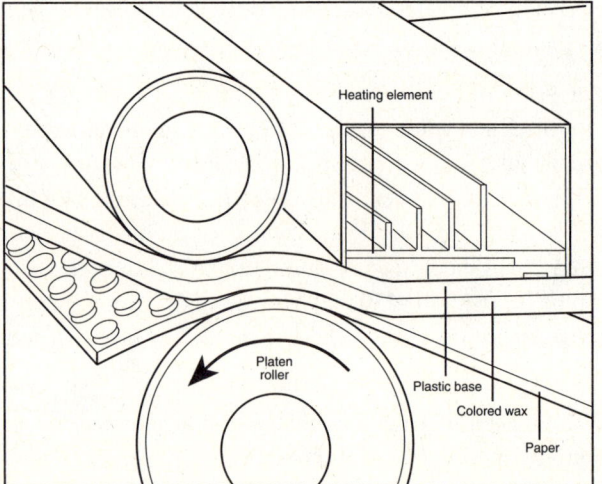

Figure 6.7
Most low-end thermal transfer printers for the Mac use a wax ribbon as their print medium.

Color thermal transfer printers make multiple passes over the page, one pass for each color. Usually, the printers have four wax ribbons: three for the primary printing colors (cyan, magenta, and yellow) and one for black. The multiple-pass system creates slow printing times; you will be lucky to print a half page per minute in actual work situations.

Color thermal transfer printers cannot vary the intensity of their dots. They rely on *dithering*, spacing dots closely in groups with no two dots overprinting, to make color blends. Printed pages look terrific from about three feet away because the eye blends the dots together, and the colors seem rich and true. When you step closer, you can see, for instance, the individual yellow and cyan dots that create green from a distance. This technique reduces a printer's resolution anywhere from 4 to 25 times, depending on the desired color.

Thermal transfer printers may or may not use PostScript, but all have their own microprocessors and RAM since processing a page of color graphics requires up to four times the resources as processing the same page in black and white. Notable color thermal transfer printers include the Tektronix Phaser series, NEC Colormate, CalComp ColorMasters, Océ OcéColor, Seiko ColorPoint, and QMS ColorScript. (For more information about color printing, see the section "What to Look for in a Printer," later in this chapter.)

Dialog Box Options

You will see several different dialog boxes when you print with your Mac. The Chooser offers one when you select a destination printer (see figure 6.8); the others appear with the Page Setup and Print commands from your application. This section explains some of the options in these dialog boxes.

Chapter 6
Printing from
Your Macintosh

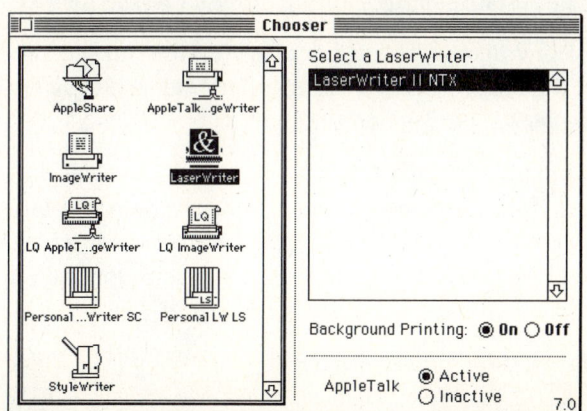

Figure 6.8
The System 7 Chooser dialog box enables you to select an output device.

Part I
Macintosh, the Computer

▼ "Background printing" on the Chooser dialog box is a synonym for *print spooling* using the PrintMonitor software provided with Apple's system. This process is described in more detail later in this chapter. Essentially, instead of sending all the document information to the printer at once, effectively locking up your Mac until the printer completes its job, the driver keeps the data in the background and sends it to the printer in small chunks. You can keep working while the printer is processing.

▼ Figure 6.9 shows the LaserWriter Page Setup options. Checking the Font Substitution box gives the LaserWriter driver permission to substitute its own 300 dpi built-in outline fonts for the lower-quality 72 dpi bit-mapped "city" fonts in your document (see chapter 8, "Fonts and Typography," for more information).

Figure 6.9
The PostScript LaserWriter Page Setup dialog box, as customized by Microsoft Word.

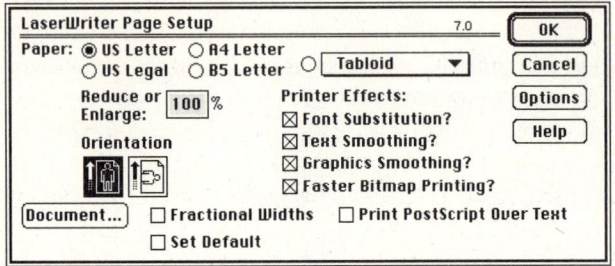

▼ LaserWriters have special functions that automatically smooth jagged curves in text and graphics. Checking the Text and Graphics Smoothing boxes in figure 6.9 nearly always improves a document's appearance, although it increases print time. These functions are not available for some PostScript printer brands; however, most applications that generate PostScript images will automatically do this for you.

▼ If the Faster Bitmap Printing box in figure 6.8 is checked, the printer driver will pre-process bit-mapped images and send them directly to the printer for faster performance.

▼ Every printer driver allows for some degree of automatic document scaling. All printer drivers can reduce: ImageWriters and QuickDraw LaserWriters to 50 percent, StyleWriters to 20 percent, and PostScript LaserWriters to 25 percent. However, only PostScript LaserWriters can enlarge—up to 400 percent (see figure 6.9).

▼ Use the Precision Bitmap Alignment (available on LaserWriter and other lasers' Page Setup Options) box shown in figure 6.10 when you want the printed copy to exactly match the screen image. It reduces the page rectangle area by four percent, lowering the effective resolution of the LaserWriter to 288 dpi. The 300 dpi LaserWriter uses the same number of pixels to print the 96 percent page as a (hypothetical) 288 dpi printer would use to print a 100 percent page. With the Precision Bitmap Alignment option checked, the printed page becomes an exact WYSIWYG representation of the Mac's screen, at precisely four times the resolution.

More recent LaserWriter printers allow you to enhance the number of gray levels at 300 dpi, or switch to 600 dpi printing.

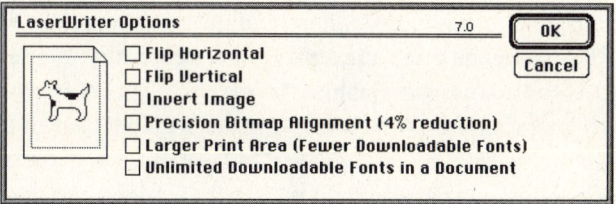

Figure 6.10

The option box from the LaserWriter Page Setup dialog box offers additional image-enhancing functions.

▼ The Larger Print Area option in figure 6.9 tells the LaserWriter to use more RAM for storing the bit-map rendering of the page and less for processing fonts.

▼ The Unlimited Downloadable Fonts box (see figure 6.9) enables you to print documents with more fonts than your printer's RAM can normally handle, since it moves fonts back and forth from your computer to RAM as it needs them. You can use Unlimited Downloadable Fonts with the Larger Print Area option. However, if your document switches fonts often, you can wait hours to get your printout. Your best choice may be to buy more RAM for your printer.

▼ ImageWriters print 72 horizontal dots per inch and 80 vertical dots per inch in the Faster mode (see figure 6.11), resulting in a slight image distortion. Selecting the Tall Adjusted box in Page Setup Options (see figure 6.12) tells the ImageWriter to print at 72 dpi vertically as well as horizontally. Tall Adjusted also allows background printing on the ImageWriter.

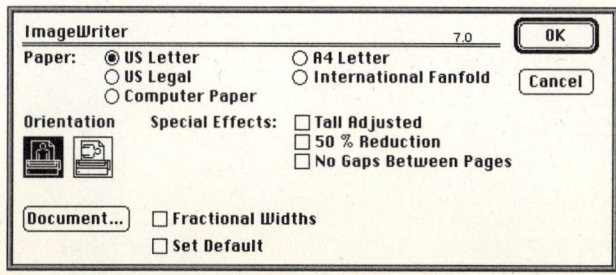

Figure 6.11

The ImageWriter Page Setup dialog box.

Figure 6.12

The ImageWriter Print dialog box.

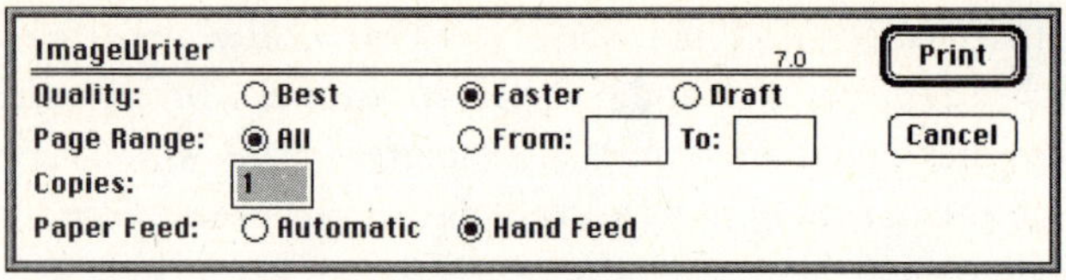

- ▼ Database listings or programming code printouts from an ImageWriter should be continuous, without forced page breaks and top and bottom margins. The No Gap Between Pages option accomplishes this (see figure 6.11).

- ▼ The ImageWriter has three built-in print quality settings (see figure 6.10B). Draft mode prints the text of your document in 10 point Monaco and ignores any graphics you may have. It also inserts spaces between words to keep line breaks and the document length the same. Draft mode speed is rated at 250 cps, but you can only get 200 cps, or approximately one page per minute (see the sections, "Printer Speed" and "Resolution," later in this chapter). Faster mode offers 72 (horizontal) by 80 (vertical) dpi resolution at approximately 70 cps. (Remember, selecting Tall Adjusted in the dialog box makes the Faster mode print at 72 by 72 dpi.) Best mode prints at 144 by 160 dpi at approximately 35 cps.

- ▼ Choosing the Color/Grayscale button (see figure 6.13) tells the print driver to generate a "deep" image. If you have a printer that can print true grayscale, a continuous-tone image is generated (see the section, "Color Printing," later in this chapter). If your printer does not have these capabilities, gray or colored areas are handled by dithering.

Figure 6.13

Choosing the **Color/Grayscale** radio button enables you to print color and continuous-tone images.

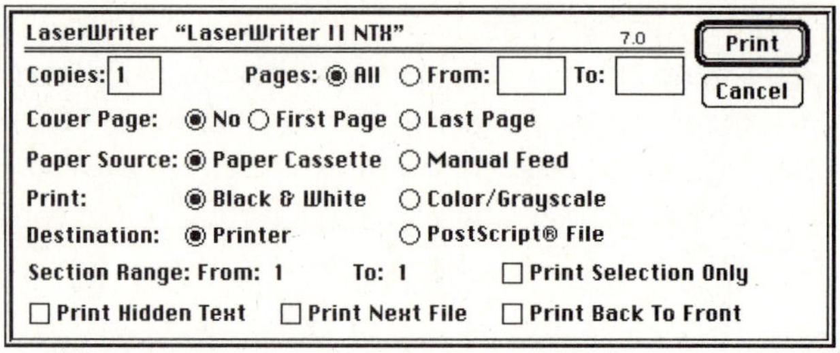

- ▼ Selecting the **PostScript File** button, available only on System 7, creates a file with the contents of your document described in the PostScript PDL (see figure 6.13).

▼ Checking the **Print Back to Front** box, also available only when using System 7, tells the LaserWriter to print the pages in reverse order so that the stack of printouts will have the pages ordered correctly. On the LaserWriter IIs, the pages leave the printer upside down, automatically ordering the pages correctly.

Chapter 6
Printing from
Your Macintosh

Note If you need the high-quality printing capabilities of a service bureau but cannot get to one, you can modem a PostScript file with the contents of your document in PostScript code. You do not need to learn PostScript to do this; the new LaserWriter printer driver for System 7 has a button that enables you to select automatic PostScript file output, and it writes a printable PostScript file to disk.

Note Some applications customize the Print dialog box to allow this option for System 6 printer drivers. To create a PostScript file in System 6, press and hold the letter "F" key immediately after clicking the **Print** button on the **Print** dialog box. If you press the F key in time, the **Creating PostScript File** dialog box appears, enabling you to name the PostScript version of your document.

The benefit of using a PostScript disk file is that all code about that file is contained within the file. A service bureau can send it directly to an image-setter without having to adjust fonts and formatting. Your document will come out exactly as you created it. The disadvantage is that the service bureau cannot change any data in your file.

Print Spoolers

When you print a multi-page document on either a PostScript, TrueImage or QuickDraw printer, you can be stuck waiting for the page processing and actual printing to finish before you can use your Mac again. Most of the time, your Mac is waiting, too. Even when it is preparing a complex graphics document for a QuickDraw-based laser printer, it spends a good portion of the time waiting for the printer.

Instead of waiting, you can use a *print spooler*. Print spoolers capture the information as it is sent to the printer and re-route it to a special file, comparable to wrapping extra thread around a spool until it is needed. The spooler then periodically sends the printer small parts of the file to print.

Apple's System 7 comes with a spooler program called PrintMonitor. (In System 6, PrintMonitor works with a file called Backgrounder which does the actual spooling while under MultiFinder.) PrintMonitor and Backgrounder printing work only on a LaserWriter or StyleWriter. One third-party spooler, Fifth Generation Systems' SuperLaserSpool, uses the LaserQueue DA to enable you to control spooling, even to an ImageWriter printer (see figures 6.14 and 6.15).

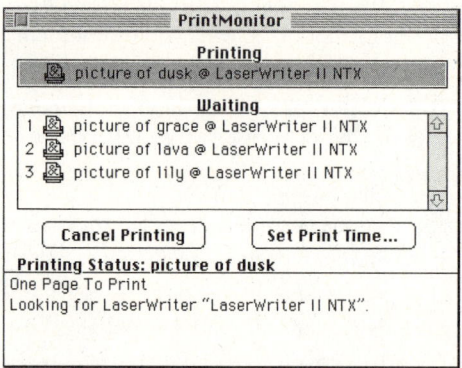

Figure 6.14
Apple's PrintMonitor system software spools files to your laser printer.

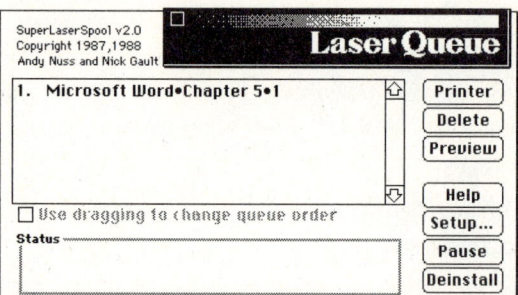

Figure 6.15
SuperLaserSpool's DA gives you more control over spooling activities.

Spoolers increase productivity by letting you get back to work more quickly. However, you may notice a sluggish response time when working on your Mac while a job is printing. The display may seem to fall behind your typing or the cursor may start jumping from place to place when you move the mouse. This behavior occurs only when the spooler is actually sending data to the printer and is temporary.

> **Note** If your Mac has to process the pages before they are printed (for example, if you use a laser printer that is not PostScript-compatible), then you will notice a prolonged system performance slowdown. In this case, your spooler is stealing processing cycles to perform the document processing. If you find you cannot work on such a sluggish system, bring the spooler DA or application to the foreground so it can use all the Mac's processing resources and get the job done more quickly.

A more expensive alternative to spooling is increasing the *print buffer*. A print buffer is a portion of RAM set aside to store data that is coming faster than it can be processed. You can see the effects of a LaserWriter's buffer when you print a long document without a spooler. Notice the first few pages are sent to the printer rather rapidly, and then the sending process slows down. This is because the first few pages are stored in the print buffer. When the buffer fills up, you have to wait for the printer to finish one page before it can accept another.

By adding RAM to your LaserWriter or other PostScript-compatible printer, you automatically increase the size of the print buffer. For non-PostScript printers that cannot have internal RAM upgrades, there are several external products available. Basically, an external buffer is a box containing RAM and two ports: one for input and one for output. Reliable Communications (Cupertino, CA) makes the Universal Print Buffer and the Universal Print Buffer Plus. These products have serial and parallel ports, input and output ports, and 64K to 2M of RAM built in.

Downloading Fonts

PostScript and TrueImage printers that have their own CPUs will always have some outline font definitions, in PostScript and TrueType formats respectively, stored permanently in ROM. This means a font is "built-in;" in type lingo, these are "hard fonts."

Fonts can also be temporarily downloaded to printer RAM by either a manual or an automatic process. If you use a font that the printer does not have in ROM (that is, built-in) but you have in a font file in your System folder, the printer driver automatically sends a copy of the font file to the printer, along with your document data. After your document is printed, all automatically downloaded fonts are purged from the printer's RAM.

You can also manually download fonts before printing by using an application such as CE Software's LaserStatus or Apple's System 7 LaserWriter Font Utility (see figure 6.16) to send copies of the outline font files to the printer. Manually downloaded fonts are pre-processed and ready to use for printing, while automatically downloaded fonts have to be processed concurrently along with the document. Manually downloaded fonts save printing time and cannot be purged, so they stay in the printer's RAM until you either use LaserStatus or LaserWriter Font Utility to clear the printer's RAM or you turn off the printer.

Chapter 6
Printing from
Your Macintosh

Figure 6.16
Apple's LaserWriter Font Utility is hidden away on the System 7 More Tidbits disk.

If you always use a certain group of fonts that your PostScript printer does not have built in, you can save yourself time by manually downloading them at the start of each work session (or whenever you turn on your printer). Some PostScript and TrueImage printers such as the LaserWriter II NTX, IIg, and the LaserWriter Pro 630 also have SCSI ports for attaching hard disks or CD-ROM drives with numerous outline font files. These fonts are automatically accessible and are convenient if you use many different fonts at the same time (see figure 6.17).

Figure 6.17
LaserWriter seeks outline fonts in the sources in this order.

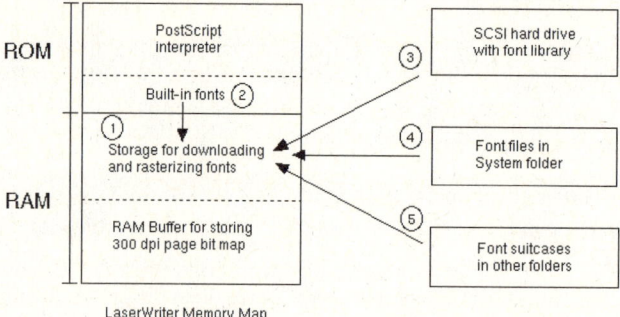

Keep in mind, however, that downloadable and built-in fonts only apply to PostScript or TrueImage printers with their own microprocessors and RAM. With QuickDraw printers, all font processing occurs on the Mac, so this discussion does not apply to them.

Font Handling on QuickDraw Printers

When you print bit-mapped fonts on a low-resolution QuickDraw printer, the driver looks for fonts that are two or three times the size of those used in your documents. In the ImageWriter's 144 dpi Best mode, a 24-point New York font is the equivalent to 12-point New York on the Mac's 72 dpi screen. If the driver cannot find fonts that are the right multiple (that is, if you do not have 24-point New York installed), it looks for the font in double that size multiple

(48-point New York) and then scales it down. For example, if you print 12-point New York font on an ImageWriter, the driver will look first for 24-point New York and then 48-point New York. If it does not find either of these sizes, the driver uses QuickDraw to scale up the original 12-point font, often with undesirable results.

ATM or TrueType uses the font's outline version instead of the bit-mapped version, so scaling is not a problem. Even scaling odd sizes, such as 13-point to 26-point, works well.

Font Handling on PostScript Printers

Printing to a PostScript printer is a little more complicated than to a QuickDraw printer. If you use bit-mapped fonts onscreen and there is a PostScript outline printer version of the font either in the printer's ROM, RAM or System folder, the printer uses the PostScript outline printer font with great results. Because ATM uses PostScript outline printer fonts, the printer automatically downloads any fonts you can display onscreen with ATM.

But, if you use bit-mapped fonts onscreen and there is no PostScript outline version of the font anywhere in your system, the printer does one of two things. If the Font Substitution box in the Page Setup dialog box is checked, then a RAM- or ROM-resident PostScript font is substituted for the bit-mapped font. If the Font Substitution option is not selected, the printer performs a QuickDraw-like scaling of the font with QuickDraw-like results. Later versions of PostScript include code for smoothing the rough edges that result from scaling. If you have a later version of PostScript, the output should be reasonably attractive.

WARNING! Although Apple ships TrueType fonts with System 7, avoid using them with a PostScript printer. When the printer driver identifies TrueType fonts in your document, it downloads the entire TrueType imaging program to the printer's RAM to generate the font images. This process is unsatisfactory because your printer rapidly runs out of memory (four TrueType fonts and the imager take up more RAM than nine PostScript fonts), and you encounter extremely long printing times. For example, on a PostScript printer, documents with TrueType can take 30 minutes to print; the same document with PostScript fonts takes 30 seconds. Unfortunately, this down-loading process occurs even if you have a PostScript version of the TrueType screen font in ROM or in your System folder.

In short, if you have a PostScript printer, you will not want to use TrueType, even if you bought System 7 to get it. The preferred way of working with a PostScript printer is to buy ATM and use PostScript outline fonts.

Chapter 6
Printing from
Your Macintosh

Part I
Macintosh, the Computer

Font Handling on TrueImage Printers

TrueImage printers are more convenient for System 7 users. They are PostScript-compatible, use PostScript outline fonts as easily as PostScript printers can, and handle the TrueType fonts, which PostScript printers cannot do well. If you use bit-mapped fonts, a TrueImage printer looks for either a PostScript or TrueType version in its ROM, RAM, or System folder. If the printer does not find any, it substitutes one of the TrueType fonts it has built into ROM.

What to Look for in a Printer

This section outlines some guidelines and principles you may find useful if you want to buy a printer.

What and When to Buy

Before buying a printer, first determine your needs and printing habits. This helps you narrow the market to only a couple of printers from which to choose. It is more important to narrow by features and your needs than by price, because many similarly priced printers have quite different capabilities. Figure 6.18 gives some printer suggestions.

Figure 6.18
Buying a printer involves deciding what your needs are and then seeing what the market offers.

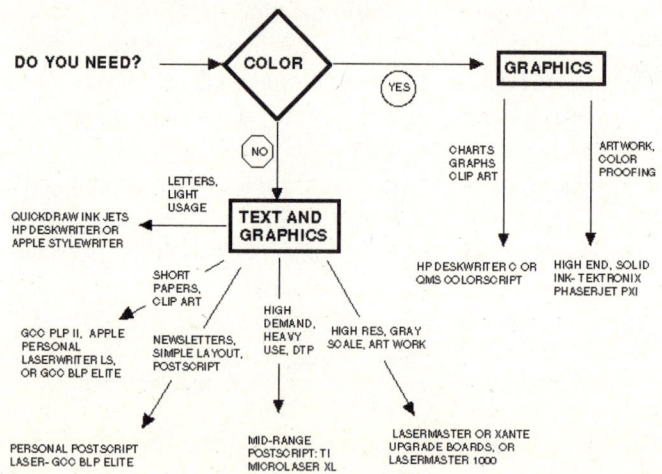

Chapter 6
Printing from Your Macintosh

A Closer Look: Another important guideline: Avoid buying a more expensive and more capable printer than you currently need, thinking you will grow into it. "Thinking-up" is common but misguided. Based on present trends in the printer industry, by the time you need capabilities such as high-powered graphics or color, they will be available in a new product for less money than what you would pay for them now.

PostScript technology worth $4,000 two years ago is available for less than $1,500 today. Color capabilities that sold for $30,000 two years ago can be had for less than $7,500 now. This trend is likely to continue as competition increases and technology advances.

This is not to suggest you should postpone getting something you need right away and wait for a better deal. If you find yourself cursing your present printing situation more than once a day, it is probably time to get a new printer.

Printer Speed

A printer's rated speed is one of the most frequently misunderstood statistics. Speeds are measured in either characters per second (cps) for dot-matrix printers or pages per minute (ppm) for laser, inkjet, and thermal wax transfer printers. These ratings are typically thought to represent the printer's actual performance.

In reality, a printer's speed rating is a raw measure of how fast the engine can produce a page. It is generally true that laser printers with eight ppm engines will print more quickly than those with four ppm engines. However, there are several other factors that can have a greater effect on printing speeds than the engine ppm ratings.

Engine speed ratings are most accurate when you print a simple text document that uses one or two fonts built into the laser printer's ROM. When you print graphics, however, engine ppm ratings are far less important than the printer's microprocessor speed and the amount of RAM it has. If the processor is too slow (some printers use the same underpowered 8 MHz 68000 the Mac Classic uses), you may wait several minutes before the page prints. If you do not have enough RAM, complex pages simply will not print at all.

If you use a laser printer that is not PostScript-compatible, printing speeds are determined by your Mac's CPU speed and the amount of free RAM available when you print. Keep these qualifiers in mind when you shop for a printer.

Speed ratings are not as important for printing technologies such as inkjet and thermal wax transfer. Very often, these products offer laser-like resolution at significantly lower prices, so slower printing speeds are usually accepted as the trade-off for higher image quality.

Speed ratings do not accurately apply to color printers yet, because the speeds at which they operate (often several minutes per page instead of several pages per minute) are not worth advertising. Users generally do not buy a color printer because it is faster than its competitors; they normally buy it because of its functionality.

Resolution

A printer's resolution in dots per inch (dpi) is often taken as the sole measure of image quality. "The higher the resolution, the better the results" is a good rule of thumb, but there are several other factors that affect image quality and help distinguish between 300 dpi laser printers.

For text output that makes the most of your printer's resolution, it is vital to have outline font capabilities and a wide variety of fonts and styles. ATM or TrueType helps ImageWriters obtain results comparable to QuickDraw-based 300 dpi laser printers.

If you print graphics, the quality of your output is affected by several factors in addition to printer resolution. The most obvious is the PDL you use. Detailed graphical output is more attractive with PostScript or TrueImage than QuickDraw.

The particular engine model you use can also affect output quality. Some laser engines print richer, fuller blacks than others. For example, the Canon CX engine in the first LaserWriter was not precise enough to print a large block of pure black without producing bands or streaks of white. It was a 300 dpi, true PostScript printer, but its output would be noticeably inferior next to LaserWriter Pro 630's output.

The kind of paper you use has a big effect on the quality of your printouts. StyleWriter II output tends to bleed on porous, fibrous paper, making printouts from the 360 dpi inkjet fuzzier and less professional-looking than printouts from a 300 dpi laser on plain paper. On its special, coated paper, however, StyleWriter II output is outstanding. The same is true of other kinds of printer engines: Each has a particular paper that gives superior results. (See the section "Paper," later in this chapter, for more information.)

Some printers, including Hewlett-Packard LaserJets, LaserMaster's 800, 1000, and 1200 printers, and Apple's newest LaserWriter IIf, IIg, LaserWriter Pro 600 and 630 models, come with software routines that smooth curves and

Chapter 6
Printing from Your Macintosh

even out jagged lines. HP's Resolution Enhancement Technology (RET) is superior to any other image enhancement technology on the market for text output at 300 dpi. RET improves 300 dpi output's appearance, without the significant slowdown associated with true higher-resolution printing. Apple introduced FinePrint, an RET-like technology, with its new LaserWriter IIf and IIg printers in the fall of 1991. FinePrint helps 300 dpi output look more like 800 dpi.

Different resolutions are appropriate for different jobs. Table 6.1 indicates three categories of printer resolutions, along with the types of printers that deliver these resolutions and some common uses for output.

Table 6.1 Printer resolutions

Resolution	Printer	Usage
192 or lower	Dot-matrix, portable inkjet, color inkjet	Convenient, inexpensive, low-hassle output
300 to 400	Laser, inkjet, color thermal transfer	Medium-quality color and black and white
600 and up	Specialty laser	High-end text and graphics

Keep in mind that 600 dpi has four times the number of dots (and four times the amount of data describing the page) compared with 300 dpi printers. In 1992, Apple introduced the LaserWriter Pro 630 and Hewlett-Packard introduced the LaserJet 4M printers, both of which are 600 dpi printers. The output of both of these printers is far superior to 300 dpi printers, and these printers (both of which cost about $2,100) set a new price/performance milestone. The LaserJet 4M is somewhat superior to the LaserWriter Pro 630 in text quality, and similar or slightly inferior in grayscale image reproduction. When the LaserWriter Pro 630 is placed in its 300 dpi mode, it can print with enhanced grayscale levels. Unfortunately that mode is not available for the 600 dpi mode of the LaserWriter Pro 630. Both of these print models are also notable in that they do emulation switching, connecting to both Macintosh and MS-DOS computers and taking print jobs from either switching automatically to another page description language.

It is amazing to watch the drop in prices for true PostScript printers. If you are on a budget, but still desire a good PostScript printer, models such as the NEC SilentWriter and TI MicroLaser series can satisfy your needs for $1,200 to $1,500. They are great printers for the price, and come highly recommended.

Cost Per Page

The cost per printed page represents the printer's expense more accurately than its price tag. Cost per printed page includes the cost of the printer itself and any accessories you need such as extra paper trays and interfaces. You should also factor in hidden costs such as service contracts, consumable goods (ribbons on dot-matrix printers or toner in laser printers), the actual cost of paper, and productivity index calculations (for example, does the extra money you pay for greater speed pay off in time saved?).

You should count on an active printing life of at least two years in your calculations. If the printer is to receive unusually heavy use, you want to look at its duty cycle specification (maximum number of pages it should print per month) as well as its engine life rating.

Typical costs per page (considering all the previously mentioned factors) for dot-matrix printers are less than one cent; for black and white inkjet, six cents; for laser, three to five cents; for color inkjet, 50 cents; color thermal wax, 50 cents or more; and color solid ink, 15 cents. High-end dye sublimation printers can have costs per page that range anywhere from $1.50 to $5.00 and up.

Talking to Other Computers and Printers

In businesses, schools, and other multi-computer environments, several computers frequently share one printer. Apple PostScript printers are all AppleTalk-compatible, so sharing them among Macintosh computers is easy and straightforward. However, sharing non-PostScript printers among Macs or between Macs and PCs can be more difficult.

Macs expect to talk to printers either over an AppleTalk/LocalTalk network or one-on-one with serial cables or SCSI connectors. (Due to the way SCSI protocols work, SCSI devices cannot be shared by more than one computer.) AppleTalk-compatible printers can be easily shared by any number of Macs (see chapter 25, "Networking").

Note If you need to share a serial device among up to four Macs and do not want the expense and inconvenience of connecting them with AppleTalk/LocalTalk, consider Data Spec's MacSwitch or Computer Friends' AutoSwitch. Both products accept up to four serial inputs, have one serial output port, and queue and switch between inputs automatically.

The best solution to using printers with both Mac and MS-DOS computers is to purchase a printer that connects to both, and switches between each automatically. The LaserJet 4M and LaserWriter Pro 630 described in the previous section are good choices.

On the PC side, printers and computers can use serial or parallel ports for one-on-one connections, or can be networked with EtherNet. The serial ports on Macs and PCs use different protocols, so you need a special cable and driver software combination to use a serial PC printer with your Mac. GDT SoftWorks PrintLink Collection includes a cable and driver software for hundreds of serial printers.

There are several Mac peripherals that provide parallel port capabilities. The simplest is Orange Micro's Grappler 9 pin, a serial-to-parallel converter cable that makes the parallel device act like an ImageWriter. The Grappler LX provides true serial-to-Centronics parallel conversions, as does ConnExperts' Versadapter. Dove's MaraThon Multi-Comm NuBus card adds three serial ports and one Centronics parallel port to your Mac, and its Serial/Parallel card adds one serial port and one Centronics parallel port. And Rose Electronics' Master Switch box is available in a number of configurations with various combinations of serial and parallel ports available for interfacing many compatible devices. Driver software for parallel printers is not necessary because all these products are automatically Centronics-compatible.

If you take a PowerBook on the road, and need a print solution to connect to MS DOS printers, then consider purchasing the Apple PowerBook/DOS Companion package. This software/hardware package includes a cable and MacLinkPlus/PC, Macintosh PC Exchange, Power Print, and MacVGA software. Using this package, you can connect to DOS printer and print your files.

A number of companies provide EtherNet connectivity for the Mac, including Apple, Rascal InterLan, Cabletron Systems, Tri-Data Systems, and Network Resources Corporation. These companies make products that include one or more of the following: a NuBus card, EtherNet cable interfaces, and the 10Base2 cable used to wire EtherNet networks. If you use EtherNet to connect your Mac to a non-Apple printer, you will probably need a driver from GDT SoftWorks to actually talk with the printer.

Hewlett-Packard's LaserJets

LaserJets dominate the PC laser printing industry and outsell all other laser printers by approximately five to one. If you own a Mac, you might not want to buy a LaserJet—there are less expensive, more customized solutions—but because LaserJets are so popular, you may have to connect with one sooner or later.

Chapter 6
Printing from
Your Macintosh

Part I
Macintosh,
the Computer

LaserJets and Macs can communicate through AppleTalk/LocalTalk networks or one-on-one through a serial port. HP provides a LocalTalk upgrade card for its printers; however, you also have to buy an HP PostScript cartridge in order to use AppleTalk/LocalTalk. The LaserJet 4M can connect directly to a LocalTalk network.

If you need to use a LaserJet on an AppleTalk/LocalTalk network, Extended Systems' BridgePort and Pacific Data Products' PacificTalk can help you. They provide LocalTalk-serial and LocalTalk-parallel interfacing, connecting directly to the LocalTalk network and then to the LaserJet through a parallel port. BridgePort has both a parallel and serial port, so you can connect PCs through the serial port and a LaserJet through the parallel port. This is an ideal setup; with BridgePort, your Mac has access to the LaserJet, and PCs have access to any Macintosh printers on the LocalTalk network.

PacificTalk has only one parallel port, so it cannot interface to PCs and LaserJets simultaneously. However, it comes with a LaserJet PostScript cartridge (BridgePort does not). If you need PostScript through the LaserJet, PacificTalk is a good buy (see figure 6.19).

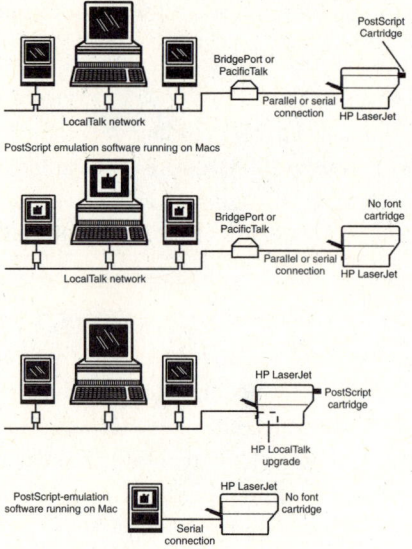

Figure 6.19
There are many ways to connect a Mac to a LaserJet.

As mentioned, Macs and LaserJets can talk directly over a serial port. There are several products designed specifically for one-on-one Mac to LaserJet serial port interfacing. Insight Development Corporation's MacPrint and GDT SoftWorks' JetLink Express provide cables and driver software. Orange Micro's Grappler LX provides a cable but uses the ImageWriter LQ driver. It is somewhat slower, but print quality is about the same.

Chapter 6
Printing from Your Macintosh

You can also make Mac-LaserJet IIP connections with Extended Systems' JetWriter. JetWriter is an add-on board for the LaserJet IIP that connects to the Mac's printer port and operates at LocalTalk speeds (10 times faster than ordinary serial communications). JetWriter comes with MacPrint's cables and driver software; it is more expensive than the simple serial connection products but much faster.

If you need to connect several PCs and Macs to a LaserJet but do not want to get a LocalTalk network, consider one of the new printer-sharing devices. These are either external boxes or LaserJet add-on boards that provide several serial and parallel ports. PCs can connect to the LaserJet through either type of port; Macs need to use the serial ones. You need MacPrint or GDT SoftWorks' JetLink Express to connect your Mac to one of the serial ports.

There are several ways you can print from your Mac to LaserJets. Unfortunately, they are all either slow (due to slow serial protocols) or expensive (the HP PostScript/LocalTalk upgrade costs over $800). Although LaserJets are the answer in the PC world, they are not very compatible to Macs.

Durability

If you need a printer only for personal use, then you do not have to worry about connectivity and durability. Most printers last for years at low to moderate levels of use. Many people are quite happy with their old LaserWriter Pluses, and ImageWriters are legendary for their durability. Inkjets and dot-matrix printers should last a long time, too.

Laser printers used in businesses, however, must be durable. You often see duty cycle and engine life ratings for higher-end laser printers. Duty cycle is the maximum number of pages the printer can be expected to print per month without break down. Most personal laser printers have duty cycles of 5,000 pages a month, while work group and powerhouse office printers can have duty cycles up to 70,000 pages a month.

A Closer Look Engine life ratings measure how many pages the printer's engine can be expected to print without failing (see the section, "Printing Engines," later in this chapter). The duty cycle is the more valuable of the two measurements. If your printer has an engine life rating of 300,000 pages and a duty cycle of 10,000 pages a month, it probably still works fine after 30 months of printing 10,000 pages a month. However, if you print 20,000 pages a month instead, the printer will most likely break down well before page 300,000.

Paper

Printers have become easier to set up, so the variety of paper sizes and types they can print to has expanded enormously. Even inkjet printers can usually accommodate several paper types, including transparencies and extra heavy or light paper.

Most laser printers accept letter (8.5 by 11 inches), legal (8.5 by 14 inches), A4 and B5 letter (European), envelope and other special purpose sizes. Most can also handle transparencies.

Note: Although lasers print well on almost any type of paper, specialty products like Hammermill's Laser Plus and Georgia Pacific's Nekoosa Laser 1000 paper are especially smooth and bright, which significantly improves laser printouts. These specialty papers' grain has been uniquely manufactured so that toner granules do not spread as much when fused to the paper, producing crisp, black images.

Dot-matrix printers work best with tractor-fed paper and labels, although you can also use plain paper with the ImageWriter II (not I) either by manually feeding it through or using an add-on sheet feeder. In either case, the heavier the paper, the more likely it is to jam or misfeed.

Inkjet printers have come a long way but are more difficult to use with certain papers than laser printers. One popular paper brand that HP DeskWriter users like and Apple recommends for StyleWriter is 24-pound Classic Crest in the Solar White color. Paper Direct recently began shipping 28-pound Inkjet Ultra, which is specially coated to allow just the right amount of absorption without smearing or bleeding.

For labels, Avery is the standard source. It offers labels that work well with laser, dot-matrix, and inkjet printers, as well as the new label printers from CoStar and Seiko. (See the section "Printers: Users and Manufacturers," later in this chapter for more information.)

Color Printing

Most people do not know that the original Mac, featuring System 1.0 and 128K of RAM, had eight-color printing capability built into ROM. Not much was done with it, of course; until Mac II was introduced in 1987, the Mac was not considered to be a color machine.

Times have changed. New 32-bit color paint programs for the Mac have set a standard that other platforms (short of dedicated color workstations costing $100,000 or more) have yet to match. And affordable color printing is now a reality, thanks to high-resolution output devices and low-cost inks.

Although true, continuous-tone color output may be beyond your financial reach at this time, there are several levels of good quality color products available from $1,000 inkjets to $7,500 solid ink, plain paper printers. The next two sections briefly review the available technologies under $10,000, while "Printers: Users and Manufacturers" offers product descriptions and recommendations.

Color Inks

Most Macintosh color printing uses inexpensive wax- and crayon-like inks on thermal transfer, inkjet, and dot-matrix printers. These inexpensive inks are opaque, meaning that to make color blends, the printers must use dithering patterns. Dithered output can be grainy and somewhat unattractive up close; however, it is inexpensive and convenient compared to the alternative (see figure 6.20).

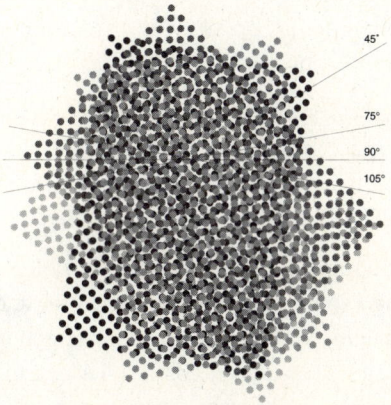

Figure 6.20
Dithered color output uses variable-sized dots placed close together to make color blends.

Using transparent inks for continuous-tone (contone) printing is the alternative. Transparent inks are available for conventional output technologies like thermal transfer and inkjet but are several times more expensive. Output quality approaches color photograph quality. So far, however, the high cost of these inks has prevented the desktop from offering contone printing.

The new solid ink printers provide the best inexpensive color output from a color fidelity standpoint. They use engines similar to thermal transfer engines. Waxy inks are melted by a heated print head and then jetted onto the paper. They rapidly resolidify, avoiding the bleeding and smearing problems of color inkjet output. Printing is fast and the colors are bright, but the biggest advantage of solid ink technology is that you can use it with any type of paper. Other thermal transfer and inkjet printers require expensive, coated paper for good results.

Chapter 6
Printing from Your Macintosh

PostScript Level 2 and Color

Adobe's PostScript 2 solves the *device dependency* problem previously associated with color printing on the Mac. Device dependency means that the same numerically defined color can look completely different depending on which monitor, printer, or plotter you use.

A Closer Look Device dependency evolved from the initial lack of a unified color standard. Although colors can be specified using the Red, Green, Blue (RGB); Hue, Saturation, Brightness (HSB); or Cyan, Magenta, Yellow, Black (CMYK) coordinate systems, the base color definitions (the actual reds, greens, and blues in RGB or the cyans, magentas, and yellows in CMYK are specified by the device's manufacturer. None of the traditional color ordering systems, including the Pantone Matching System (PMS) used since 1963, includes objective definitions for colors that can be used on different output hardware. A new standard called TrueMatch is being pioneered to solve this problem. It will be used as a standard color matching system on everything from printers and monitors to inks, dyes, and even felt-tip markers for artists.

PostScript Level 2 describes colors using the objective, internationally-approved CIE color space specifications, which allows for precise calibrations between the color gamuts of various monitors and printers. PostScript Level 2 allows for true WYSIWYG desktop color processing.

Several vendors, including Apple, have introduced color matching schemes based on the CIE color space. It is anticipated that these new systems will serve as a way of matching what you see on your screen with what appears on a color printed page. The range of colors a device can create (called a color gamut) is unique for each device. These systems allow colors to be mapped to the closest available color, from one device to another.

Printers: Users and Manufacturers

The Macintosh printer market now boasts over 100 different models, from the $249 CoStar LabelWriter to the $25,000 magazine-quality color Kodak XL7700 and beyond. This is an enormous growth from just a few years ago, and the rate seems to be accelerating. New technologies like RISC processors, PostScript Level 2, TrueType and TrueImage, and rapidly improving color printing techniques should continue the market expansion well into next year.

There are now affordable desktop printers for nearly every printing need, including good quality color. This section takes a look at some of the areas that have developed in the printing industry and printers recommended for certain needs.

Portable

There are two nearly identical printers in the portable category: the Kodak Diconix M150 Plus and the GCC WriteMove. Both are three pound, 192 dpi inkjets that can run from batteries as well as AC power, and come with outline fonts for improved text output. Both are excellent performers from respected companies. If you need a light, quiet, portable printer, you will be happy with either of these. The Citizen PN48 is the most portable printer available, weighing in at less than 3 pounds. This impact printer uses a ribbon, gives acceptable print quality, and is the printer to carry if weight is your prime concern.

Low End Dot-matrix

Dot-matrix printers were once the standard for students, casual writers, and for occasional personal use because of their low cost. Dot-matrix printers were at the low end and laser printers at the high end of the market. When Apple introduced its StyleWriter inkjet printer, this market description immediately changed. Inkjet technology gained instant credibility as *the* inexpensive, good quality solution, and dot-matrix technology was relegated to printing labels and multi-part forms, since those require impact printers or tractor-feed devices.

While it is unlikely dot-matrix printers can hold a sizable market share in the Macintosh printer industry much longer, there are still more dot-matrix printers in use than any other kind of technology, including laser.

If you find you need a dot-matrix printer, the most popular Mac model is the ImageWriter II. The ImageWriter with its 9-pin print head and maximum resolution of 144 by 160 dpi has long been surpassed by 24-pin, near-letter quality printers like GCC's Mac-only WriteImpact and the hundreds of PC-compatible, dot-matrix printers from companies such as Epson, Okidata, and NEC. These printers are even less expensive than the ImageWriter.

Chapter 6
Printing from Your Macintosh

Personal QuickDraw Printers

There is a broad range of printers that offer high-quality 200 to 360 dpi output for $1,000 and under. These products are affordable and perform well. Printers in this category include Apple's StyleWriter and Personal LaserWriter LS, GCC's PLP II series, and Hewlett-Packard's DeskWriter.

The inkjet-based StyleWriter II and DeskWriter printers retail at around $400. The StyleWriter offers better resolution, while the DeskWriter is much faster. Both can print to a wide variety of paper, including transparencies, but only the DeskWriter is network-compatible. Either printer is a great choice for beginning Mac users and students.

Further up the price ladder, in the $1,000 range, are Apple's Personal SelectWriter 300 or 310 and GCC's PLP II. These are QuickDraw printers with no upgrade path. The two QuickDraw printers, Apple's Personal LaserWriter NTR, and GCC's PLP IIS are PostScript-upgradeable. The PLP IIS, a faster version of the PLP II, and can be upgraded to a GCC BLP IIS with PostScript for another $1,000.

If you print primarily text documents, a personal laser printer is an excellent choice. If you add TrueType or ATM, text output on these printers is indistinguishable from true PostScript text output. And if you happen to need PostScript later, you can get a copy of CAI's Freedom of Press PostScript emulation software. However, if you know that you want to print PostScript graphics at the start, purchase a PostScript printer instead.

A Closer Look This feature is designed to take advantage of the "thinking up" mind-set—pay more now for a QuickDraw printer so you can have the option of later upgrading to PostScript. This may not be the best move, however, since rapidly changing technology often drops the price of printers. This upgrade path may make sense only if you plan to upgrade in six to 12 months. Even then, it is usually cheaper to buy a printer with PostScript now than it is to pay extra later for the upgrade.

Personal PostScript and TrueImage Printers

Personal laser printers with PostScript or TrueImage compatibility are becoming increasingly affordable. Prices range from the TI microLaser at around $1200, the NEC SilentWriter at $1500, to Apple's Personal LaserWriter NT for about $1,500.

Personal PostScript and TrueImage printers usually have four to six ppm engines, an eight or 16 MHz 68000 CPU, and one to 2M of RAM. Products in this category include Texas Instruments' microLasers 17 and 35, GCC's BLP

Chapter 6
Printing from Your Macintosh

Elite and BLP II, Apple's Personal LaserWriter II NT, HP's LaserJet IIP, Microtek's TrueLaser, and the QMS-PS 410.

The TI microLaser 17 is a small, fast printer that starts at $1,200 for a basic PostScript model with 17 built-in fonts. ROM upgrades to 35 fonts are also available. A dependable performer, the microLaser is ideal for people who need a PostScript laser printer but do not have much desk space.

The QMS-PS 410 has a four ppm engine, but it is probably the fastest printer in this group due to its 16 MHz 68020. (Note that as of this writing, no one has developed a benchmark for the TrueLaser.) With automatic port switching, the QMS is also a versatile printer in a mixed computer networked environment.

WARNING! Although Hewlett-Packard laser printers are the most popular in the world, they do not automatically work with the Mac. There are several connectivity options available on the market (see section, "Talking to Other Computers and Printers," later in this chapter). You should not buy an HP laser printer if you are only going to use it with a Mac; you can get better performance for less money with Mac-specific printers.

If you can afford $2,000 for a laser printer, then your best current choices are the LaserJet 4M and the LaserWriter Pro 630. They give you 600 dpi output, improved grayscale image printing, and automatic emulation switching in packages that have no competitors at their price.

Office and Work Group Printers

The laser printer was quickly adopted for graphics and desktop publishing applications, and high volume text and graphics functions for business were not far behind. There is now a whole fleet of what can be called "workgroup printers"—networkable products with heavy duty cycles, multiple platform compatibility, and convenient paper handling that yield high-speed text and graphics.

There are several levels of functionality in the workgroup printer category. Low-end office printers have standard features, such as PostScript compatibility, eight to 14 ppm engines, plenty of processing power (16 MHz 680x0 or 8 MHz RISC with at least 4M of RAM), 5,000 to 20,000 page per month duty cycles, 200-sheet capacity paper trays, and out-of-box Mac and PC connectivity. High-end office printers have more of the same: PostScript Level 2, 16 to 24 ppm engines, 10 to 20 MHz RISC processors, 4M or more of RAM, and 30,000 or more page per month duty cycles. Most low-end and all high-end products have SCSI ports for accessing fonts stored on a hard disk.

Three to six users can share the lower end printers, while the high-end printers work well for groups of up to 15 users. Product manufacturers in these categories include Apple, Qume, QMS, GCC, Hewlett-Packard, Texas Instruments, DataProducts, LaserMaster, and Kyocera Electronics.

Low-end Office Printers

Preferred products in the low-end office printer category include the QMS-PS 815 MR and 825 MR models, the GCC BLP IIS, the IBM LaserPrinter 6P and 10P, the Apple LaserWriter Pro 600 and 630, the HP LaserJet 4M, the DataProducts LZR-660, and the Texas Instruments microLaser XL series.

The QMS printers use a 20MHz 68020 processor and have the convenient capability of dynamically switching between inputs from three different ports: AppleTalk, RS-232 serial, and Centronics parallel. The DataProducts printers are fast and the most durable of this group, with 20,000 page per month duty cycles. A DataProduct clone from the direct mail order company Hardware that Fits also gets high marks.

The GCC BLP IIS comes with 2M of RAM, a SCSI port, an eight ppm engine, and a 16 MHz 68000 processor. The TI microLaser XL printers are fast (16 ppm, 68020 processors) and small, and are excellent performers.

The Apple's LaserWriter Pros are eight ppm, 68030-based printers with PostScript 2, Hewlett-Packard LaserJet IIP emulation, and automatic AppleTalk/serial port-switching capabilities. They feature FinePrint and PhotoGrade, both of which increase the quality of printed documents. FinePrint is an enhanced PDL similar to Hewlett-Packard's RET, and gives output near 800 dpi by smoothing the edges of objects and text. PhotoGrade is a new grayscale imaging technology that increases the number of grays to 67 and the line screen to 106. The previously discussed LaserJet 4M, which uses the same engine as the LaserWriter Pro, has similar features, and is also a good choice for a small office. If you need 600 dpi printing, then either of these two printers, or the IBM LaserPrinter 10P, is a good choice.

High-end Office Printers

Preferred products in the high-end office printer category include the QMS-PS 2000 and PS 2200, the TI microLaser XL Turbo, the DataProducts LZR2455, the LaserMaster 400XL and 1200, and the Kyocera F-1800A, 3000A, and F-3010. If you are willing to configure them so that they connect to Macintosh computers, then the Compaq PageMarq 15 and 20, and the LaserJet IIsi are excellent choices.

Each printer offers high-end performance. The fastest engines belong to the DataProducts printers (24 ppm) and the QMS-PS 2210 (22 ppm). The QMS-PS 2000 ($16,000) also has a 70,000 page per month duty cycle and a 25 MHz RISC processor. Like the QMS-PS 815 MR, the TI microLaser and QMS-PS 2000 and 2200 include automatic port-switching capabilities. The TI has a 16 ppm engine, a 16MHz Weitek RISC processor, and the smallest footprint (16 inches by 16.5 inches) of any printer in this category. At $5,200, its price-to-performance ratio is unmatched.

The LaserMaster 400XL ($10,000) offers fast performance at 400 by 400 dpi, while the 1200 model ($15,000) can print both 400 by 400 dpi and 1200 by 1200 dpi. The 1200 model's printing speeds in 400 by 400 dpi mode approach 20 ppm, and it can also print 11 by 17-inch tabloid-sized pages. The Unity printer, new from LaserMaster, offers excellent 1000 dpi output, is highly configurable, and is highly recommended.

> **Note** The DataProducts 24 ppm printer, priced at $15,000, may be fast, but it does not compare to two industrial-strength printers from Kodak and Xerox. At 92 ppm, Kodak's Lionheart is probably more speed than you would ever need. It features 300 dpi resolution, a 1,000,000 page per month duty cycle, a 2,500 sheet feeder bin, and PostScript, PCL, and Epson dot-matrix PDL emulation modes. It is a bargain at only $200,000.

For $20,000 more, you can get the Xerox DocuTech, a 600 dpi printer that can whip through 135 pages per minute. The DocuTech includes a high-speed copier/scanner, folds and staples printed or copied pages, and supports PostScript Level 2 and PCL page description languages.

High-Resolution Printers

High-resolution printing is a much sought-after feature in the desktop publishing industry. The standard laser resolution, 300 dpi, is good for amateur newsletter publishing and for proofing but not producing camera-ready copy for professional-quality publications. For good quality output, you need at least 600 dpi—the higher, the better. Professional-level typesetting systems start at 1270 dpi and frequently use 2500 dpi, but the more dots per inch, the higher the cost per page.

There are now two companies that make controller board upgrades for the PostScript-compatible LaserWriter II series. These boards produce high-quality, camera-ready output from your desktop printer. The Xante Accel-A-Writer is a LaserWriter II controller board upgrade that gives 1200 by

Chapter 6
Printing from
Your Macintosh

300 dpi, or 360,000 dots per square inch. This is equivalent to 600 by 600 dpi and is sufficient for medium-grade newsletters and reports. The Xante board also uses a high-speed RISC processor, so it improves the LaserWriter's speed as it increases the resolution.

The LaserMaster 800 board is even better. This board plugs into one of your Mac II's NuBus slots (so you do not have to take your printer apart) and increases LaserWriter's output to 800 by 800 dpi. If you already own a LaserWriter but need higher resolution, one of these boards should do the job nicely. LaserMaster (Eden Prairie, MN) has gained an international reputation for their high resolution laser printers.

If you are in the market for a new printer, there are several high-resolution products available. NewGen has a high-resolution laser printer line offering TrueImage compatibility, RISC processors, and resolutions up to 1200 by 600 dpi. The TurboPS/600T and 1200T also come with NewGen's proprietary Image Enhancement Technology (IET) which works similarly to HP's RET and Apple's FinePrint, improving apparent resolution by smoothing curves and lines. And like QMS' printers, the TurboPS models handle port switching automatically and transparently. The NewGen printers start at about $14,000.

LaserMaster has several high-resolution printer models in addition to its upgrade board. Like NewGen's printers, LaserMaster's 1000 and 1200 are both TrueImage-compatible, have fast RISC processors, and offer excellent resolutions. The 1000 has two modes: 400 by 400 dpi and 1000 by 1000 dpi. The 1200 model can reach 1200 by 1200 dpi (on 11 by 17-inch paper). This resolution is nearly indistinguishable from actual typeset. LaserMaster has also customized TrueImage with its own image enhancing algorithms that, like NewGen's IET, improve the apparent resolution of text and graphics. The LaserMaster 1000 retails for $7,000, while the 1200 costs approximately $15,000. LaserMaster's recently released Unity printer is designed for fast 1000 dpi output in mixed computer network environments.

Personal and Business Color

Inexpensive thermal and inkjet technology has taken some giant steps forward in the past few years. There are now three levels of inexpensive color output. The high-end, solid ink printers offer PostScript Level 2 support; 300 dpi resolutions; excellent, bright colors; and plain paper output capabilities. The mid-range thermal wax transfer printers offer PostScript compatibility, speedy internal processors, 300 dpi resolution, and good color ranges. Inkjet color printers are at the low-end, offering sub-300 dpi resolutions, bright but limited colors, and no built-in processors.

The Tektronix PhaserJet PXI and the DataProducts Jolt PS are the first PostScript Level 2 solid ink printers. Newer models from Textronix called the Phaser IIsd and Phaser III PXi (both $9,995) are highly regarded. The best color printers available for less than $10,000, these printers are fast (up to two ppm), with bright colors and high-resolutions. In addition, they can print to any type of paper, and because the solid inks are less expensive, cost per page is about one-half to one-third that of thermal transfer technology. They are notable for the fidelity of the colors they print vs. other color printer types.

The introduction of solid ink printers should reduce other thermal printers' costs significantly. You may see prices for PostScript-compatible models such as the CalComp ColorMasters, the Tektronix Phaser II series, the QMS ColorScript, the Seiko ColorPoint, and the NEC Colormate drop from $4,000 to $7,000 to around $3,000 over time. Although these printers offer good quality prints with wide color ranges, there is simply no reason, other than price, to get a thermal wax printer instead of a solid ink printer.

For good quality color printing, consider buying an inkjet printer. Hewlett-Packard's PaintJet XL300 ($3,495), Canon's Color BubbleJet BJC-800 ($2,795), or the Apple Color Printer ($1,800) which is based on the Canon printer are good choices moderate price range. For even cheaper color output, consider the Hewlett-Packard DeskWriter C ($1,099).

There are two big differences between inkjets and thermal transfer printers: Inkjets still do not have the precise dot control thermal technology offers, and they do not have their own microprocessors to speed printing times. However, inkjet technology has great potential; the Iris inkjet is probably the best color output device this side of 35mm slide printers.

Color inkjets offer 80 percent of thermal printers' performance for about half the price. If you are on a tight budget and do not need PostScript, a color inkjet is a very good choice.

High-end Color

The high-end color printer market is characterized by high-resolution, true color output that rivals color photography. Conventional thermal transfer, laser, and inkjet engines are used in the high-end color printers on the market now; the expense usually derives from the high-quality inks and dyes.

Color thermal transfer (also known as dye sublimation) printers use transparent dyes which are vaporized and then changed back to a solid (sublimated) onto the page. Dye sublimation technology generates true

Chapter 6
Printing from
Your Macintosh

Part I
Macintosh, the Computer

colors (not dithered) at continuous tones. Kodak, Mitsubishi, and DuPont have dye sublimation printers available for the Mac. The output of these printers gives photographic-like reproduction, but suffers from a somewhat limited color range (gamut).

Color lasers work like black and white lasers but make several passes over the page, laying one color of toner each time. Although color lasers can vary dot sizes and toner intensity, the powdery toner is opaque. Color laser technology has to rely on dithering to achieve the appearance of true color. Output is excellent but slightly more grainy than dye sublimation's. There are only a few color laser printers on the market: Colorocs offers a plain paper, color laser printer for around $30,000, while Canon's combination copier/PostScript printer, the CLC, costs closer to $50,000. Many service bureaus use CLCs to do low cost ($1 to $2 per page) short run color reproductions.

High-end, color inkjets use transparent inks to achieve true color output with continuous tones. The Iris inkjet printer has incredible resolution and vivid colors. If you can sacrifice some color fidelity, then the DuPont 4CAST thermal printer is even better. Its output looks like a photograph.

Each of these printers costs more than $25,000, far beyond the means of the ordinary consumer. Don't worry, though—any moderately sized print shop should have a high-end color printer. When you go to a print shop, expect to pay a high fee per page since these printers require special inks, toners, and dyes that are expensive. Costs for these printers should drop significantly in the next few years, however, as mass producing the inks becomes more viable.

Label and Envelope Printers

The printers listed earlier are primarily for full 8 1/2 by 11-inch (or larger) pages. They can handle labels and envelopes with expensive add-on sheet feeders, but this is usually a tricky proposition. If you print many labels or business-sized envelopes, you might consider one of these specialty products:

▼ CoStar and Seiko currently offer label printers that use small, medium resolution (150 dpi) thermal transfer engines, so you can print multiple fonts and styles, and uncomplicated graphics such as company logos and clip art. These printers are a bit expensive ($250) considering they have only one use, but they are fast and will save some wear and tear on your regular printer.

▼ CoStar also offers a printer called the AddressWriter that prints addresses and simple graphics on number 10 envelopes, postcards, and labels. The AddressWriter has an AppleTalk option and is compatible with System 7 and TrueType. At $595, it is more than twice the price of dedicated label printers, and $100 more than Apple's label-capable StyleWriter. You save time by not sticking the printed labels on the envelopes, but that probably does not justify the price unless you do many bulk mailings.

Plotters

If you work in architecture or with CAD programs, you probably use a plotter. CalComp, Mitsubishi, and Hewlett-Packard make Mac drivers for their own plotters. To find drivers for other plotter products, you can contact MicroSpot (who manufactures the ImageWriter color printing driver). MicroSpot has drivers for nearly every plotter on the market, including products from Roland, Graphtec, and Houston Instrument. Whichever plotter you buy, make sure it supports the Hewlett-Packard Graphic Language (HPGL) plotter language standard.

Fax Modems

Why mention modems in the printing section? If you spend much time printing reports and shipping them overnight, you should consider getting a fax modem. Faxing is perhaps the only technique faster than overnight delivery, and paper fax machines are now the standard for sending copies of short documents.

Fax modems let you connect to paper fax machines (or other fax modems) and transmit a picture of each document page. Like a regular fax machine, you are not sending the actual text. When you receive a file over a fax modem, you view it in a graphics program, not a word processing program. Resolution of the document image is around 200 by 200 dpi.

A good send/receive fax modem is Dove's DoveFAX+ (see figure 6.21), although there are numerous send-only products. Its software is notably better than others on the market. Fax modems usually operate at 9600 bps in fax mode and 2400 bps or better in modem mode. Fax modems typically let you set up a queue of documents to send in the middle of the night when telephone rates are low. They are a good solution when you do not have to send the actual document file.

Chapter 6
Printing from Your Macintosh

Figure 6.21

The DoveFAX+ software has a friendly user interface and is the most full-featured of the fax modem packages.

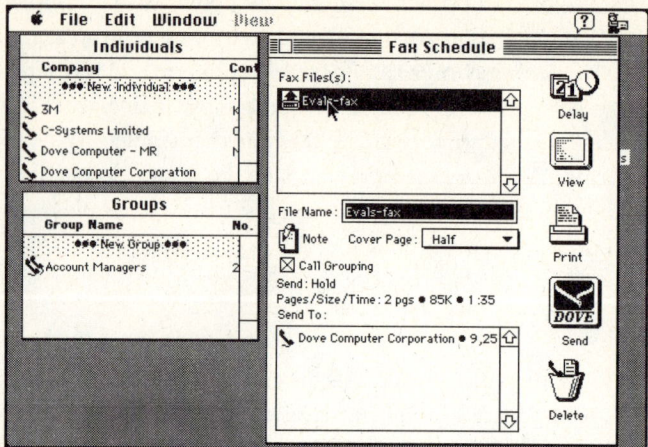

A new generation of PostScript fax devices that will make digital documents as beautiful as the printed page will most likely be introduced in the future.

Summary

The Macintosh printing industry is undergoing a rapid expansion. There are more high-quality products for more types of users than at any previous time in the Mac's history. Several key developments—PostScript 2, TrueImage and TrueType, FinePrint and PhotoGrade, solid ink technology, and RISC-based printer controllers—combined with ordinary evolution in the industry should continue to increase performance standards. The market is getting tougher and more competitive for manufacturers, which means consumers' options are improving, and prices are decreasing.

However, these trends make choosing a printer more complicated. To decide on a printer, you should first determine which features you need and how you will use the printer. Different uses include light- to heavy-duty text, text and simple graphics, more complicated graphics requiring PostScript and a RISC processor, and color output. Additional features include connectivity, real world speed and resolution performance, durability, paper printing options, and more.

Part II
What Put the Mac in Business

In This Part

Chapter 7: Graphics

Chapter 8: Desktop Publishing Programs

Interlude: Cool PageMaker Stuff

Chapter 9: Fonts and Typography

Chapter 10: Graphic Arts Support

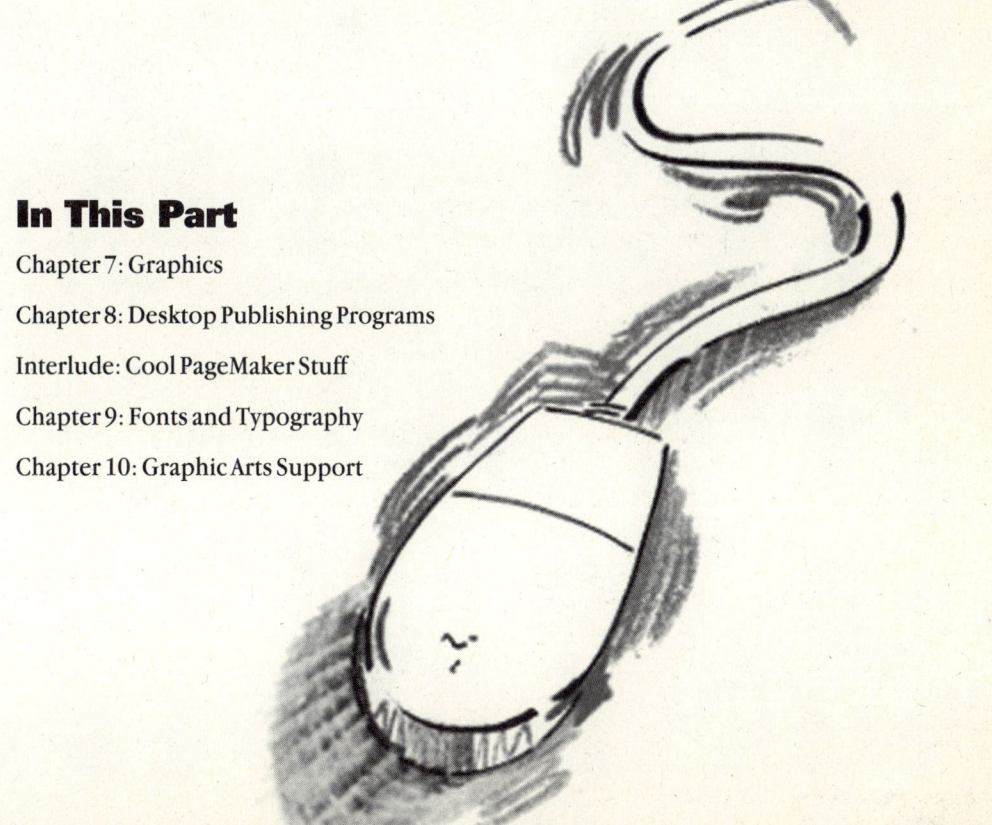

Chapter 7: Drawing and Painting on the Macintosh

The Macintosh computer has many features which make it an excellent tool for creating pictures. This chapter examines different methods of creating and manipulating images with the Mac, and describes how to obtain the best results when printing your works of art.

In This Chapter

- ▼ Painting with a mouse
- ▼ Grayscales and color
- ▼ Retouching and image processing
- ▼ Color printing
- ▼ Object-oriented drawing
- ▼ The art of illustration

Part II
What Put the Mac in Business

Bitmapped Images and Paint Programs

When you look at a Macintosh screen, what do you see? Words, perhaps? A spreadsheet? The desktop? Tetris blocks falling faster than you can rearrange them? Perhaps, but not really. What you are actually seeing are pixels. *Pixel* is jargon that stands for *pic*ture *el*ements. On any of the compact Mac screens, you see 342 rows with 512 pixels per row, or a total of 175,104 individual bits of information. A larger screen, such as a full-page monitor, may be showing you more than a million pixels!

Each pixel is represented in the Mac's video memory as one bit of information. (There is more than one bit per pixel on a color monitor, as you'll learn later.) These bits of information combine to make a *bitmap:* quite literally, a map that shows which bits are "off" or "on," black or white, at any given instant. As you move the pointer across the desktop, the bitmap changes accordingly. Whenever you draw a line or type a letter, you change the screen's bitmap.

Bitmaps are generated for the screen and for some types of printers by a program called QuickDraw, which is part of the Mac's built-in Toolbox and is programmed into the ROM. (See chapter 29, "Programming," for more information on the Mac's Toolbox.) Many printers use QuickDraw to create their printed images; the exception is PostScript printers, which includes most laser printers. Letters and pictures are printed on an ImageWriter at the same 72 dots per inch resolution the Mac screen uses. (Dots per inch, commonly abbreviated as *dpi,* is the standard way to describe the resolution of an image. More dots per inch means a sharper image; 72 dpi is the normal Mac screen resolution, while 300 dpi is common for laser printers. Imagesetters, at 2540 dpi, provide the best resolution commonly available.) Laser printers can print bitmapped images too. Many of the current generation of paint programs can produce images at a higher resolution. DeskPaint, for example, gives you a 300 dpi image that can be printed on a standard laser printer.

MacPaint

Chapter 7
Drawing and Painting on the Macintosh

When the two Steves (Jobs and Wozniak, Apple's founders) unveiled the first 128K Macintosh, much of the excitement it generated was because you actually could take the mouse and draw with it. MacPaint was a major breakthrough in computer technology. It meant the computer no longer was limited to number crunching or to being a "smart typewriter." The Mac became a tool for artists as much as for accountants and authors.

The original MacPaint was not an especially powerful or versatile program by today's standards, but the basic elements were in place. It had Brush, Spray Can, Pencil, and Straight Line tools, and it could create and fill shapes and enter text characters. The cut, copy, and paste capabilities MacPaint shared with MacWrite were augmented by a lasso and drag function to reposition things on the page.

People who had never considered themselves artists had lots of fun using the brick patterns, checkerboards, and stripes to draw houses, stacks of blocks, and other interesting designs. Actual artists were, initially, a bit more skeptical. How could a computer replace a brush, or a pen and ink? Soon, however, they too began to recognize the possibilities. Bitmapped art can convey a real sense of texture and depth. Much of the "computer art" seen today originated as bitmapped graphics, and a good deal of it could have been done with nothing more complicated than the original MacPaint program.

The illustration shown in figure 7.1 was produced almost entirely with the Spray Can and Eraser tools. The Pencil was used only to draw the cat's whiskers.

As figure 7.2 shows, a magnified (fatbits) view reveals that the cat is composed entirely of little squares. These are pixels, and for each pixel on the screen there is a bit of code (a zero or a one, in fact) telling the Mac whether the pixel should be black or white. All these bits of code together make up the bitmap. Bitmapped art's chief advantage is its flexibility. The artist can do finely detailed work and, in a magnified view, can change individual pixels as needed.

Figure 7.1
This cat was created in the original 1983 MacPaint program, Version 0.95.

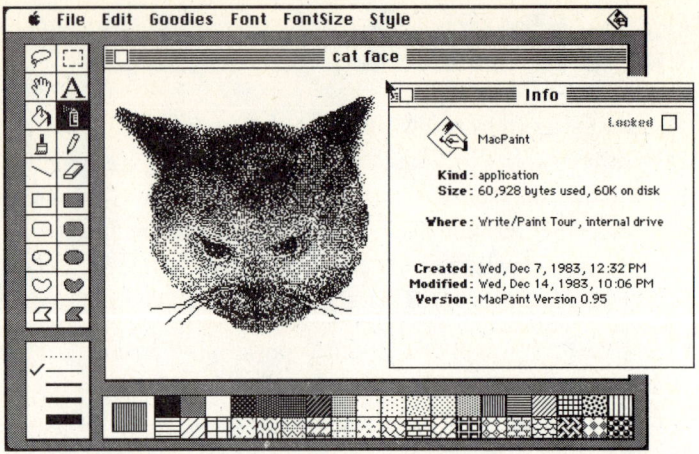

Figure 7.2
A close-up look at pixels reveals their flexibility in creating detailed art.

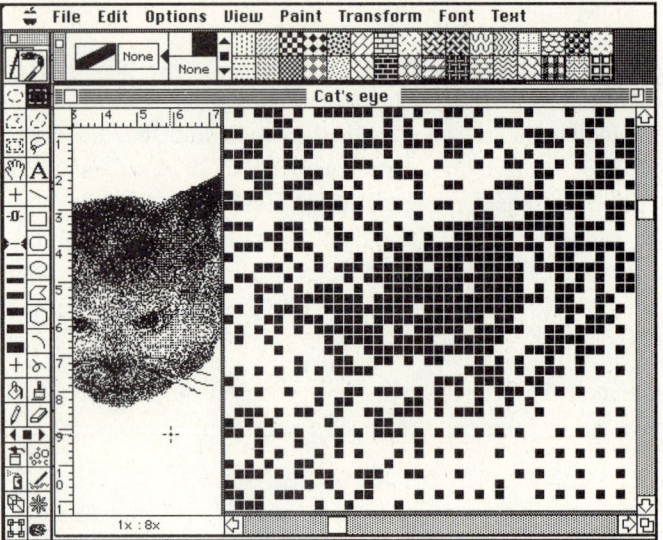

MacPaint was an instant hit. As soon as other people began creating Mac software, other paint programs appeared, with various improvements. Ashton-Tate's FullPaint offered multiple windows, entire screen views of documents, and some new tools that enabled users to skew and distort images, and create a sort of perspective view of things. Today, there are several dozen paint programs. Most are in color as well as black and white; some have added drawing or animation capabilities. Some graphics programs are desk accessories, available while you are working in any other application. No matter which paint program you use, the basics are much the same.

Painting with a Mouse

Chapter 7
Drawing and Painting on the Macintosh

If this section title gives you visions of dipping small rodents into pots of color, stop! The Humane Society frowns on that particular kind of mouse painting. (So do the mice.) Painting with a computer mouse is fun, and there is no mess to clean up afterward. Paint programs create images with a pencil, paintbrush, and a spray-painting device, just as artists do with the "real world" versions of these tools. The pencil draws or erases a single pixel line. Figure 7.3 shows a drawing done with just a pencil. The line is the same weight throughout.

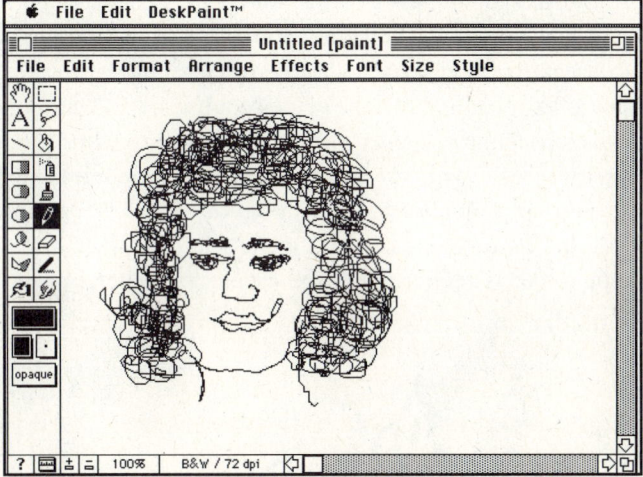

Figure 7.3
Pencil drawings can be quite precise or just freeform scribbles.

To draw, hold the mouse button down as you drag a line to where you want it. To erase, simply click the mouse button on a black dot. The "hot spot" at the end of the pencil turns white to erase, as you hold the mouse button and drag. To go quickly into a magnified view of your work, in most paint programs you simply double-click on the pencil icon. (SuperPaint, however, wants you to hold the Command key as you click the pencil.)

 If you plan to create a lot of art with a paint program, you may find the regular Mac mouse is a less-than-ideal drawing tool. Many prefer the greater precision of an optical mouse such as Mouse Systems' Little Mouse, which is smaller and lighter than a

standard Macintosh mouse and needs only a 6- x 8-inch mouse pad. Appoint's MousePenPro is another good choice. It handles like a ball-point pen.

Perhaps the ultimate painting and drawing tool, however, is the combination of a Wacom tablet and a pressure-sensitive, cordless stylus. It truly handles like a real pen or brush. You press lightly to draw a fine line. As pressure increases, the line thickens, as you would expect if you were using a real drawing pen or brush. The stylus tool comes in two models with your choice of firm or soft tips; the softer tip gives the stylus a more brush-like feeling.

Painting Tools

Unlike pencils, paint brushes come in different shapes. Figure 7.4 shows a selection of lines drawn with paintbrushes and an assortment of brushes. To change paintbrushes, double-click on the brush icon, and a dialog box something like the one shown in figure 7.5 (which is from MacPaint II) appears. Select any existing shape for your brush from those provided. Some paint programs let you edit the shape of the paintbrush too. Simply click on the individual dots of the magnified view to create a custom brush, and then click **OK** after you set a shape you like. SuperPaint lets you select anything on the screen to use as a paint brush. Open the custom brush box and point to whatever you wish to use. Studio/1 has a menu selection which turns the last object you put on the screen (a filled box, a squiggle, a letter, or a word) into a brush.

Figure 7.4

Change the paintbrush to get a different effect.

If your paint program lets you edit the shape of the brush, you can use it to create custom "rubber stamps." Either draw or copy the design you want from elsewhere, and then, rather than dragging the brush across the page, click and move it to the next place you want a stamp. Figure 7.5 shows the general effect, along with a close-up of the paintbrush used to make it. We "borrowed" the star shape from the bottom set of icons by clicking in the **Edit** box, holding the mouse button, and moving the pointer to the area we wanted to copy.

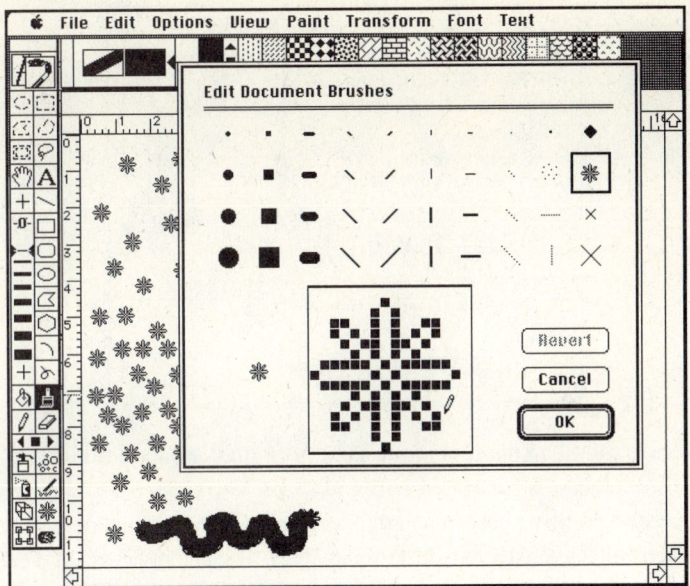

Figure 7.5
The black line at the bottom of the screen resulted from dragging the star brush.

One of the first MacPaint tools was the Spray Can. Many people used it for computerized graffiti against the brick wall pattern that is thoughtfully included. With patience and frequent changes of paint pattern, the Spray Can could be used for fairly intricate art. As noted earlier, the cat in figure 7.1 was drawn almost entirely with the Spray Can. However, as other graphics programs came along, many included airbrushes or other variable paint sprayers rather than, or in addition to, the humble spray can. (Perhaps it was out of concern for the Mac's ozone layer?) In any event, the result was a vastly more controllable tool.

Figure 7.6 shows SuperPaint's Airbrush tool. To access the dialog boxes for any of these tools, double-click their icons. You can gain even more control over the quantity of pixels being "sprayed" by painting with a pattern rather than straight black or a plain color. Use a pattern that is mostly white to spray just a few random dots on the screen. A checkerboard pattern gives you half as many pixels as a solid black pattern.

Some programs, including PixelPaint and DeskPaint, have a tool called Charcoal. It looks and functions a lot like a spray can or airbrush, with one notable exception. If you hold a spray can or airbrush in the same place, it continues to "spray" pixels, just as a real one would continue to spray paint, leaving a dark spot. (Anyone who has attempted to apply an even coat of paint from an aerosol can is all too familiar with this effect.)

Figure 7.6

Adjust the flow for as few or as many splatters as you want.

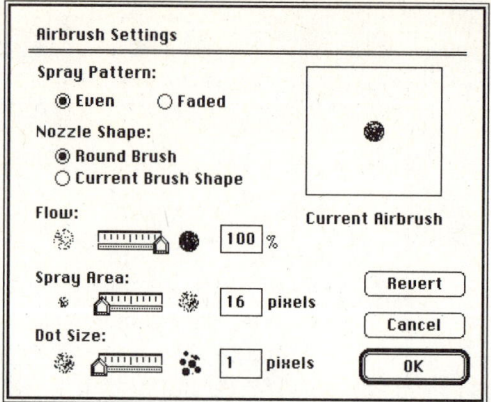

If you leave the Charcoal tool in the same spot on the paper, nothing happens. It places its pattern of dots and stops. The Charcoal tool gives much more precise control and can be adjusted for a relatively fine line or a general "smudged" effect. Charcoal is fun to play with. The girl in figure 7.7 was drawn with DeskPaint's Charcoal tool. To erase Charcoal's effect without leaving white blotches, simply change the paint color from black to white.

Figure 7.7

Charcoal sketches on the Mac won't get your fingers dirty.

Other paint tools draw straight lines and shapes, with or without pattern fills, or let you enter text. Paint programs have limited text capacity. You can change the size, font, style, justification, and line spacing of text you enter, as long as the insertion point still is blinking. However, doing this changes *all* the text. If you want a single word in bold or in a different font, or want to change sizes part way through a line of text, press **Enter** before the word you want to change. This freezes all the previously entered text. Make the change, type whatever you want in the new style, then press **Enter** again to freeze it; change back to the previous style if you need to, and finish the sentence.

Cutting, copying, and pasting work in graphics programs in much the same way they work in other applications, but you will find some special tools for selecting areas to be cut, copied, or dragged around on the page. The Marquee tools are so named because they flash like a theater sign when activated. Double-clicking a Marquee selects the entire screen.

The Lasso looks like a Western lariat and does rope tricks that cowboys never dreamed of. In most paint programs, double-clicking on the Lasso selects whatever is on the screen, without selecting the white space around it. Holding the Option key down while you drag a lassoed image gives you a duplicate. Holding down the Command and Option keys while you drag gives you multiple copies, and adding the Shift key (sometimes called the *three-fingered drag*) keeps the copies in line and evenly spaced. You can set the spacing distance by changing the line width. Figure 7.8 shows some of these effects in MacPaint. Note that lassoed selections, unlike marquee selections, are transparent. To get overlapped images that do not show through, use the Marquee.

Chapter 7
Drawing and Painting on the Macintosh

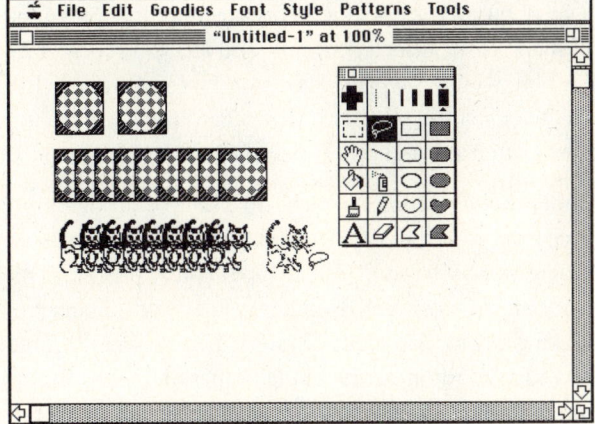

Figure 7.8
Multiple images are easy.

The more powerful and more expensive programs have additional tools. Along with the Charcoal and Airbrush tools previously mentioned, you may find icons that resemble a drop of water, a pointing finger (not to be confused with the grabber hand), a rubber stamp, and a piece of chalk.

The Water Drop simulates the effect of dripping water onto a watercolor painting. It is used to soften the edges of a solid color region and to blend

Part II
What Put the Mac in Business

them into the adjacent color or background. Water Drop shapes are adjustable and customizable in the same way that brush shapes are. The Pointing Finger is similar to Water Drop in effect, but more dramatic. It is the computer equivalent of running your finger through wet paint to smear it. The finger paints in the color that is under the pointer when you start dragging it, and it smears that color into adjacent colors as you drag the mouse. Figure 7.9 shows the effect of a Water Drop and a Pointing Finger on a line.

Figure 7.9
The water "melts" the line into the background; the finger smudges it.

Chalk is similar to Charcoal but denser. It paints textured colors onto your artwork, much like stroking a piece of soft chalk over a textured paper or canvas. If you draw with Chalk over an existing color, some of the previous color shows through. Both Charcoal and Chalk can be assigned to any color you like, and paint programs that feature these tools generally have a range of sizes, shapes, and "hardness" of charcoal or pastel.

The Rubber Stamp tool is best used for manipulating photo images or repeating a small but perfect section of background. It copies a small area—the size and shape of the selected stamp—and lets you repeat it as much as you like anywhere within the page. PixelPaint Professional also lets you use transparent rubber stamps, which let the background show through, and apply diffused, patterned, and other special effects to your stamps.

The Eyedropper tool electronically picks up a sample of whatever color of gray you place it on. When you click on another part of the page, it releases that color where you have put it. The dropper is very precise. It picks up only the color of the single pixel directly under its tip. Eyedroppers are especially useful for picking a color in a blended range. You also may be able to apply special effects such as automatic blending or masking to the Eyedropper, or use the dropper to install a color on the palette, depending on the program.

WARNING! You cannot **Undo** changes made with Eyedroppers! Be very sure you have the color you want and are placing it in the right spot.

Adding Grayscales and Colors

Chapter 7
Drawing and Painting on the Macintosh

In the beginning, black and white art was exciting enough. As technology brought us Macs with more memory and faster CPUs, grayscales and colors became a possibility. To accomplish this, the authors of graphics programs had to redefine the pixel. Rather than one bit per pixel representing either a black or white dot, programmers went first to a 2-bit pixel, which let them use four colors or four shades of gray, then to an 8-bit pixel, and finally to a 32-bit pixel.

You rarely see 2-bit color on a Mac (maybe because of the name?), but you see a lot of 4-bit color. Four bits of memory per pixel lets you display 16 colors, adequate for many games and color screen displays, although not spectacular for color painting. A color Mac with an 8-bit video board and color monitor can display 256 colors. With the addition of 32-bit QuickDraw, you can assign a different color to each of the approximately 750,000 pixels on a standard Mac II monitor and define nearly 16.8 million different colors. Incidentally, 8-bit color can use any of those 16 million colors. It just cannot show you more than 256 of them at one time.

Of course, such programs still are limited by hardware. A black and white Mac is still a black and white Mac. And it takes a lot more memory to handle all those colors. PixelPaint Professional, which is a full-color, full-grayscale paint program, cannot run on anything less than an SE/30 and requires a *minimum* of 5M of RAM. (On a 5M Mac, you cannot use PixelPaint Professional with MultiFinder, and you'll need to strip extra fonts and extensions from your system.) But if you have the right hardware and software, programs at this level can perform extremely high-quality color art and photographic work on the screen. Today, a great many books, magazines, and even "coffee table" art books are produced with a Mac.

A Closer Look 32-bit QuickDraw is really misnamed; it should have been called Enhanced QuickDraw. It improves color function for all Macs, including older models with 4-bit or 8-bit color boards. Color Paint and Draw programs require it. It is included free with System 6.05 and greater, or can be uploaded from user group and online bulletin boards for use with older Macs (it is incorporated into the ROM on current Mac models).

261

Paint programs that work only in black and white save images in the Paint format with no problems. Bitmapped black and white images are small enough to handle. However, when you get into 8-bit color, the bitmap files become larger, which requires more RAM. An 8-bit color screen has a bitmap of 175K. A bitmap of a 24-bit color screen is just over 1M in size; at least 4M of RAM is required to display such an image.

The other problem you encounter with bitmapped images is that they are *resolution dependent*. What looks acceptable on the screen at 72 dots per inch looks rather lumpy when you print it on your laser printer. Even though the printer can handle 300 dots per inch, MacPaint can send it only a 72 dpi image. If you were to take your MacPaint picture and print it on a super high-quality, professional imagesetter at 2,540 dpi, it would not look any better than it does on the ordinary laser printer or the ImageWriter you bought back in 1985 with your Mac 128K! The image is stored at 72 dpi, and there is no way for the printer to fill in the gaps. You can work with bitmapped images that have higher resolutions, but the image is still resolution dependent, and your RAM requirements will increase significantly.

A Higher Resolution

Fortunately for everyone who dislikes the bumpiness of 72-dpi bitmapped graphics, there are other ways to represent bitmapped graphics. The most basic Macintosh graphics file format is the PICT format. A PICT file is a series of QuickDraw commands, so it can represent anything QuickDraw can draw. With the advent of the PICT2 format (an updated version of the original PICT standard), PICT files can represent color and grayscale bitmaps in higher resolutions than the original 72-dpi limitation. PICT files can contain more than just bitmaps—they also can represent object-oriented graphics—but they are a common format for bitmapped graphics.

Another bitmap file format is the TIFF format. *TIFF* stands for *Tagged Image File Format*. TIFF images can vary in the number of grays or colors they include, in the size of the image, and in their resolution. TIFF is used by many painting and image processing programs and most scanners.

The only trouble with all these variables is that as different vendors introduced their TIFF-based scanners and applications, they added their own variations to the TIFF format, making it a somewhat nonstandard standard. Nevertheless, it is a good choice for high-quality images.

Monochrome TIFF, like Paint, stores one bit per pixel, and images are, as the name says, monochrome, or one color—black on white. Grayscale TIFF typically uses eight bits per pixel, enabling you to render objects in 256 different shades of gray. Color TIFF uses 24 bits and handles 16 million colors. Figure 7.10 shows a grayscale TIFF, produced from a home video camera and the ComputerEyes digitizer.

Chapter 7
Drawing and Painting on the Macintosh

Figure 7.10

Josh and Danny in a TIFF rather than a tiff.

Shades of Gray

If you have a color monitor, you also have a grayscale monitor. To make it perform as one, you need only to go to the Control Panel and click on the Monitors icon. You see a dialog box like the one in figure 7.11. Choose the appropriate range of grays. If you have a 4-bit color card, you will be able to see 16 grays, and if you have an 8-bit card or a Mac with a built-in video card, you can see 256. You need a 24-bit card to see all 16 million colors or grays.

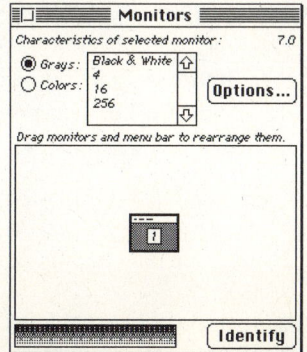

Figure 7.11

Use the Monitor CDEV to adjust your screen for grayscale viewing.

263

Part II
What Put the Mac in Business

> **Note:** Why would you want to change your monitor from colors to grays? Obviously, if you are editing a grayscale TIFF, you need to see it. Some applications run better with the color turned off or with the screen set for 16 colors rather than 256. If you capture screen shots (as we did for this book), you need to remember a strange fact about the color light blue. As anyone who has worked in graphic arts knows, light blue does not photograph. If you use a blue pencil to mark your paste-up, the camera does not see the marks. Black-and-white screen shot programs do not see it either. When you look at the image, the light blues (and other light colors) are missing.

Grayscales are not especially relevant to most Mac applications. You can use spreadsheets, play games, and process words without ever thinking about a grayscale, and you can create some beautiful bitmapped black and white graphics without it, too. Grayscales come into play when you get into more advanced graphics and DTP functions, such as using a scanner.

Scanners come in both black and white and color models. When you have a digitized image recorded on the Mac, the job is not over—it has just begun. Most of the time, scanned images need to be retouched, just as "real world" photos generally need retouching. You may find a shadow or highlight that draws attention away from the subject, or a badly planned background that needs to be replaced or subdued, or perhaps you simply want to make your blue-eyed blond model into an auburn-haired lass with emerald eyes. The Mac is a perfect tool for this kind of image manipulation, because it can change individual pixels one at a time or can shift the tonal range of a photo with just a couple of mouse clicks. You even can custom design a grayscale to increase or decrease contrast—in the whole picture or in just a small area.

Image processing programs work with huge files, so you need lots of RAM and ample hard disk storage. A 5- x 7-inch image scanned with a high enough resolution to be reproduced at 133 lines per inch on an imagesetter takes up about 1.35M of disk space. With that much information to deal with, some operations are very slow—and the rest even slower. Digital Darkroom from Silicon Beach is a very popular image processor. Figure 7.12 shows Digital Darkroom's work area and tool bar. The current version accepts color photos as well, or lets you colorize a black and white image.

Adobe Photoshop is the industry standard for photo manipulation. It handles color as well as black and white and lets you paint directly on your scanned images, color correct them, or merge two or more images. Photoshop can

> Yeah, right. Buying Photoshop for black and white work is like buying a Porsche and only using first gear.
>
>
> Bob LeVitus

open and work with Adobe Illustrator EPS images, although it is less friendly toward Aldus FreeHand's EPS files (both programs and EPS are discussed later in this chapter). Photoshop is about twice as versatile as Digital Darkroom and about twice the price. The tool kit includes a Magic Wand, as well as brushes, an airbrush, rubber stamps, and more. Figure 7.13 shows the Photoshop desktop.

Chapter 7
Drawing and Painting on the Macintosh

Figure 7.12
There are many ways to alter an image.

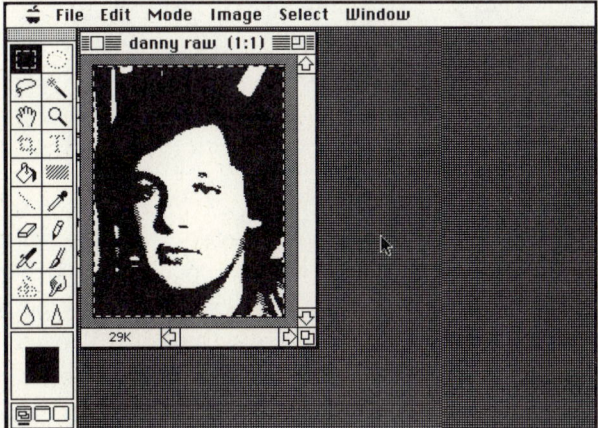

Figure 7.13
Photoshop works in black and white as well as color.

You can use Photoshop's tools to create original art based on your imported images. Posterize a photo and shift the colors, and it becomes an entirely new graphic. Flop it, distort it—the possibilities are endless. Photoshop handles color separations and supports not only Pantone but also the Focaltone and Trumatch process-color-matching systems.

Part II
What Put the Mac in Business

Developed for personal computers and commercial imagesetters, the Trumatch system has 2,000 predictable colors in 1 percent increments at 150 lines per inch. Photoshop 2.5 includes all the tools you need for color separations and color pre-press proofing. Do you need it? Not for ordinary graphics, but if you are seriously involved in color graphics, DTP, or scanned images, it is a necessity.

Choosing a Paint Program

Choosing which paint program to buy can be a difficult task, due to the sheer number of programs available. This section will provide you with an overview of the field, and will point out the defining features of each application.

Black and White Paint Programs

Which black and white paint program should you use with your Macintosh? If you want an easy-to-learn and reasonably versatile painting program, the popular choices are MacPaint II, SuperPaint, and Studio/1. Each has something to recommend it.

MacPaint II

MacPaint II is the easiest to learn (and, incidentally, was developed by David Ramsey, one of the contributing authors of this book). It runs well on any Mac (except the original 128K Mac) and uses a relatively small chunk of disk space. Because its original version served as the model for all other programs, learning to use MacPaint's tools and tricks is good basic training for any of the more advanced programs.

SuperPaint

SuperPaint is the personal choice of many Mac users for an all-around graphics program. In many ways, it is really two programs in one. Because it has both a paint and a draw layer, it provides the benefits of both kinds of graphics and can print images that combine both paint and draw. In the paint layer, you can add many types of plug-in tools that create interesting effects such as bubbles, footprints, and snowflakes on the screen.

By having both Paint and PICT functions within the same program, you can take advantage of the smooth, resizable lines and shapes that draw programs create. You can copy back and forth between layers or use the Autotrace feature to create a PICT outline of a paint image. Figure 7.14 shows the result of autotracing a very complex bitmapped image. Although it is not an exact copy, as it would be if we'd started with a simpler subject, it is potentially useful.

Chapter 7
Drawing and Painting on the Macintosh

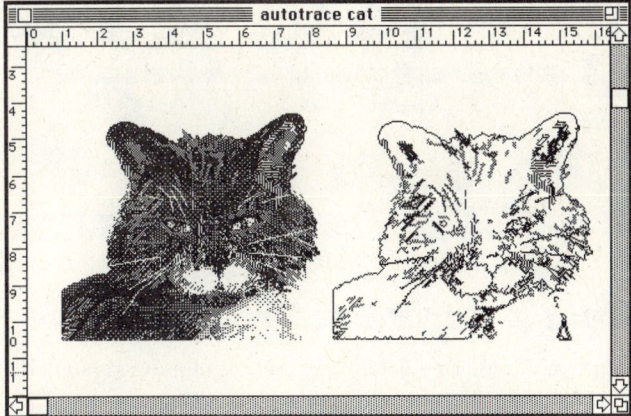

Figure 7.14
Autotracing can produce interesting results.

Studio/1

If you have a black and white Mac and are feeling sorry for yourself because your friends with their LCs and IIs are having fun with color, Studio/1 just might make you feel better. It is a strictly black and white application with a terrific gimmick. In addition to being a fully featured paint program, it can create and record complex animations with sound, and then let you place them into your HyperCard stacks using XCMD functions (additions to the HyperCard scripting language).

Figure 7.15 shows one frame from an animation sequence that Studio/1 provides as a demo. You also can play back art as a desktop presentation "slide show." The program comes with good documentation and tutorials. As a paint program, it has many good features, including gradient fills and a Bézier tool like the ones in draw programs. It is a bit more complicated to learn, but if the notion of animated HyperStacks or black and white desktop presentations intrigues you, Studio/1 is the way to get started.

Figure 7.15

This scene cycles through 20 frames as the balls roll down the assembly line. You even can add sound!

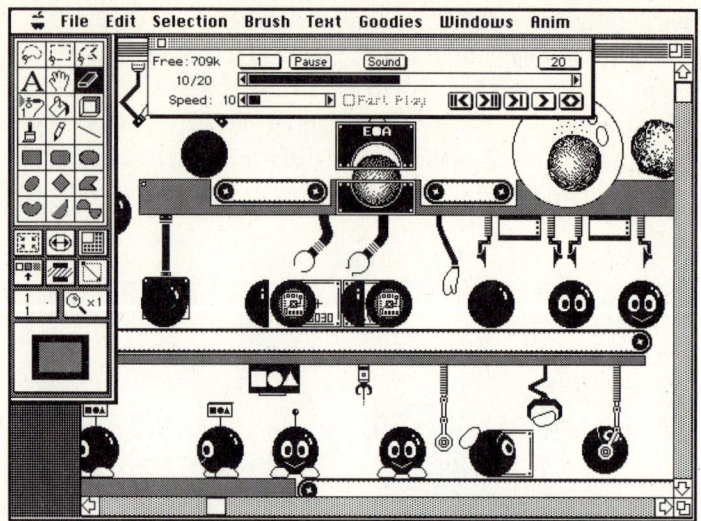

Low Cost Color Paint Programs

There is simply no question—painting in color is more interesting than painting in black and white, whether you use a computer or a brush. Color can get expensive, though. Some of the color paint applications are priced in the $400–500 range. What do you get for this kind of money? Not much more than you can get for much less. Fancier packages have a few more tools, can do more tricks, and save images in more formats. They are more powerful and more versatile, and the prices certainly reflect this.

On the low end of color painting, there are Easy Color Paint, Expert Color Paint, and Color MacCheese. You can buy any of them for about a tenth of the price of PixelPaint Professional. These programs are so simple to learn you might never need to open the manual. Color MacCheese, from Delta Tao, doesn't pretend to be a professional tool. It's not high-resolution, but if you want to get started right away and output to an ImageWriter II or other low-end color printer, you'll have fun with it. Easy Color Paint, from MECC, and Softsync's Expert Color Paint are similar. Expert Color Paint gives you full 32-bit color, while Easy Color Paint is limited to 8-bit (256 colors).

KidPix, from Brøderbund (see figure 7.16), deserves at least a passing mention in the graphics department. Although it was intended for the younger set, like a box of Crayolas, it's capable of some rather remarkable results in the hands of a talented user. In addition to printing in 256 colors, it automatically translates color pictures into appropriately gray patterns on a laser printer. And it's fun.

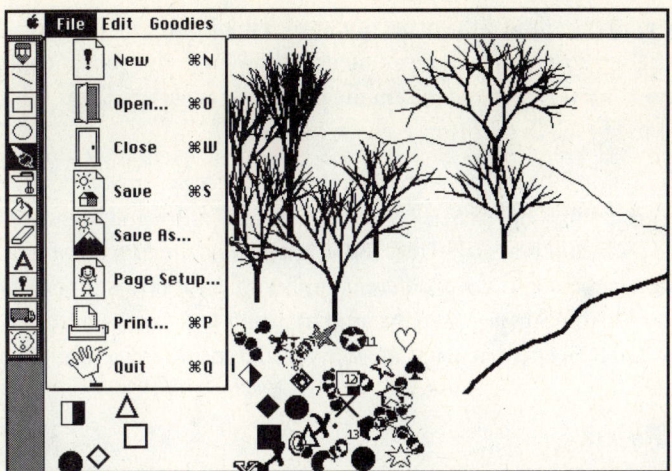

Figure 7.16
KidPix is fine for non-readers, too.

These programs are an inexpensive way to get started with color painting. If you are a professional artist intent on using your Mac as an art tool, it is doubtful any of them will satisfy you. On the other hand, they are well beyond the paint-by-numbers stage and certainly can keep most of us happy.

Canvas

Moving up the price scale, Deneba's Canvas does essentially what SuperPaint does. It integrates object-oriented graphics with bitmap graphics, so you can paint and draw in the same document. Canvas is designed for illustrators, designers, artists, architects, and engineers. Autotracing converts bitmap images into objects. Multipoint Bézier curves and smooth polygons can be joined, split, opened, or closed, and points can be added or deleted at will. Unlimited layers can be viewed, printed, or saved together or individually. QuickDraw-based Canvas even can place, although not edit, PostScript files and also supports Macintosh PICT, TIFF, Paint, and Draw formats, and PC-compatible CGM metafiles.

Studio/8

Studio/8 is the 8-bit color big brother of Studio/1. It has many of the same tools as the black and white version. As its name suggests, Studio/8 supports up to 256 colors per document and now supports the 747-color Pantone Matching System. Because Studio/8 cannot produce color separations, this feature is essentially useless, except as an approximation of what you see when you use Aldus PrePrint. Studio/8 has several useful features for working with scanned images, in color as well as black and white. Colored filters enable you to boost the percentage of red, green, or blue in a painting, as if the picture were viewed through a tinted window. You also can adjust the saturation in a painting or transform the hues. Ever wondered how Whistler's Mother would look in red? Now you can find out.

Studio/8 Version 2.0 supports more graphic formats than any other 8-bit painting program. It opens MacPaint, PICT, and TIFF files and saves in PICT as well as color and grayscale TIFF. (PICT is a generic file format for graphics, which can be opened in many different applications.) It now supports LZW, one of the file compression systems used by StuffIt and CompactPro, to shrink large TIFFs into a manageable size without losing any information.

DeskPaint

DeskPaint is nearly as versatile as the "serious" painting programs mentioned earlier, and it sits in your Apple menu waiting for you to open it from any other application. You can get creative whenever you get the urge, even though you may be in the middle of a spreadsheet or downloading a long file. It has a good selection of tools, including Charcoal and the "smudgy finger." It comes with its twin brother, DeskDraw, which is mentioned in the next section, and is now bundled with DeskWrite, as well.

DeskPaint can print posters and billboards by tiling pages and can scale selections from 1 percent to 3999 percent! It runs happily under MultiFinder or System 7. When it runs low on memory, it simply tells you it cannot undo. Figure 7.17 shows the DeskPaint layout.

Figure 7.17
DeskPaint is a very handy DA.

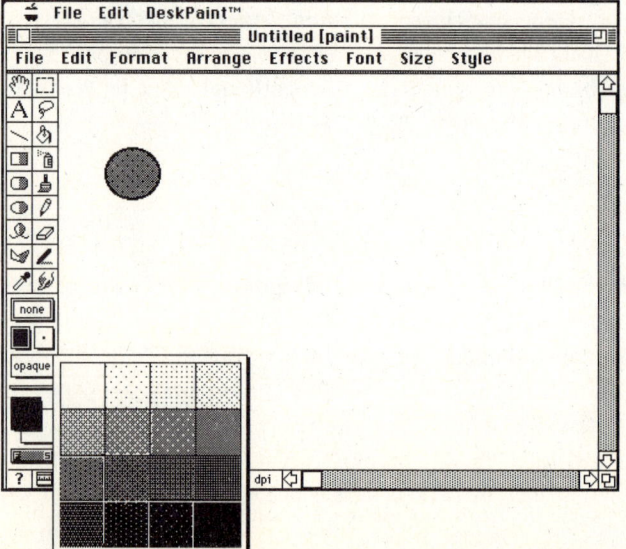

Professional Painters

PixelPaint Professional, Fractal Design Painter, and Studio/32 are among the truly professional paint programs. They provide top-of-the line features—at top-of-the-line prices.

Photoshop

Adobe Photoshop is often thought of as an application for editing scanned photographs—a digital darkroom of sorts. However, it's also a very sophisticated paint program, with paintbrush, air brush, paint bucket, and other standard paint tools. Photoshop also has sets of filters that are used to apply special effects to images; one filter gives images a crystallized appearance, while another creates an effect similar to embossed paper. You can also add filters that weren't available with the original application.

Studio/32

If Studio/8 is the big brother of Studio/1, then Studio/32 is their daddy. It has, of course, all the features of Studio/8 and supports 1-, 4-, 8-, 16-, and 32-bit color, and it reads and writes in all the various graphics formats. Studio/32 includes a scanner utility and the Pantone Matching System. It also includes three-dimensional perspective and even comes with a color screen shot grabber!

PixelPaint Professional

PixelPaint Professional reads MacPaint, PICT, PICT 2, or EPS files. Drawings or scanned images can be manipulated by other graphics processing tools and then imported into PixelPaint Pro for further refinement and colorizing, á la Ted Turner. The program includes many standard palettes to create distinctive moods, such as pastel hues for a landscape or bright primary colors for a chart. The full range of Macintosh colors is accessible by defining color palettes of up to 256 colors at a time. When printing, PixelPaint describes each screen pixel as a PostScript object, taking into account color and grayscale values.

Fractal Design Painter

Fractal Design Painter comes in a one gallon paint can, and works with scanned art or original images to achieve a "painterly" feel. It imitates the behavior of "real" media such as chalk, oils, felt-tipped pens, and watercolors. You can control the simulated textures of canvas and paper surfaces, as well

Chapter 7
Drawing and Painting on the Macintosh

Part II

What Put the Mac in Business

as the brushmarks and degree of transparency. It's most effectively used with the Wacom pressure-sensitive tablet, but will accept mouse input. Many of the effects are incredibly realistic, and the program is a lot of fun to use, although it runs fairly slowly.

Figure 7.18
Painter has the look, if not the smell, of real paint. (It's better in color, of course.)

There is one serious drawback to all of these programs. They are memory hogs. Painter needs 2.5M of RAM and PixelPaint demands 4M of RAM to itself, or else will refuse to open. Studio/32 is as bad or worse. It can open in the available memory, but it creates a disk buffer when it does. This means your document is disk-based. It takes longer to draw and erase, and only a portion of the document can be shown in the work area.

Print It!

Of course, for most of us, color painting is just something to have fun with on the screen. The works of art we create exist only on the disk. Home or small office color laser printers are financially out of range for the average person, but service bureaus usually have them and can run color prints from your files. You also can print to an ImageWriter II or an ImageWriter LQ with a color ribbon, or to a color inkjet printer such as the Tektronix, Kodak Diconix Color 4, or the HP DeskWriter 550C, which support Color QuickDraw. These printers generally have a printing resolution of 216 or 300 dpi, so they are nearly laser quality. The images are more than adequate for color proofing before you go on to a more expensive four-color process.

When you work with a color PostScript printer, the Mac generates color PostScript commands that are sent to the printer to produce the image. *Color PostScript* is quite different from standard black and white PostScript. Color PostScript images usually will not print as black and white images. The results are unpredictable and probably not what you want. Other PostScript options apply when you are printing color, so you still can specify a positive or negative, emulsion up or down, and printed with or without crop marks.

To work with any of these printers, all you need to do is select **Print** and proceed exactly as though you were printing an ordinary black and white page. Individual paint programs vary somewhat, so you may need to specify "color image" or "print color" to get the right output. For the best print quality, make sure the dpi setting matches or is an even multiple of the printer's resolution. Table 7.1 shows typical printer resolutions for some common printers.

Table 7.1 Optimum printer resolutions

Printer	Optimum Resolutions (dpi)
LaserWriter, HP DeskWriter	75; 150; 300
ImageWriter	72; 144
ImageWriter LQ	108; 216
HP PaintJet	94; 188
Imagesetter (Linotronic)	635; 1270; 2540

From Screen to Paper

All printed material is composed of either text or art. Bitmapped images, which you create in MacPaint or a similar program, are considered line art even though they might have patterns or areas of solid black. Scanned images and pictures you create in a more sophisticated paint program can be either line art or *continuous tone,* which means they have a range of grays forming a continuum from black to white. Black-and-white photographs you take with a camera are also continuous tone images.

When you try to print a continuous tone picture either on your laser printer or on a printing press, you run into problems. You have black ink and white paper, and no shades of gray. How can you translate those gray tones into

Chapter 7
Drawing and Painting on the Macintosh

something printable with only black ink? The traditional way is to use a *screen* over the image. (It is called that because the first ones were actually made of metal mesh, although today, printers prefer to use a plastic sheet with dots printed on it.) The screen converts light grays to tiny black dots on a white background and dark grays to tiny white dots on a black background. From a normal reading distance, you can't see the dots, just the shades of gray. When the continuous tone image has been screened, the resulting image is called a *halftone*. Figure 7.19 shows a close-up view of a scanned image converted to a halftone.

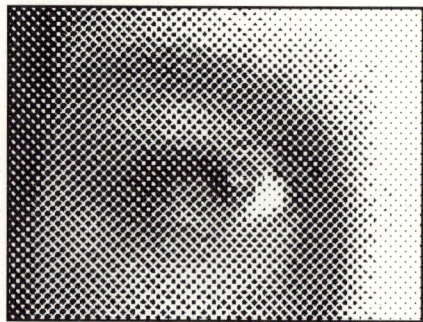

Figure 7.19
Ordinarily, you would not notice the dots.

Halftones can be produced electronically too. Programs such as Digital Darkroom and Adobe Photoshop can generate halftones from grayscale photos and art. The size of the screen, whether "real" or electronic, determines the quality of the halftone. The bigger the dots, the worse it looks. The coarsest screen in general use is 65 lines per inch. Newspapers generally use an 85 line screen, and magazines use a 120 line screen. The finest screen you normally encounter is 150 lines per inch. Image processing programs let you define the size of the screen and the angle it is set at. In general, a 45-degree angle gives good results for a monochromatic screen on a 300 dpi laser printer.

Looking at these numbers, you might think that there is a difference between screen dots and the dots your printer creates. You'd be right. Lines per inch, which refers to halftone resolution, is different from dots per inch. Lines per inch, or lpi, counts the actual number of halftone cells per inch. Printer dots combine to form the cells that determine halftone resolution.

The Real Truth About Color

Frankly, 16 million colors is a bit unrealistic. The Mac can describe all of them, but the human eye can see visible differences in only about a third that many. What the monitor gives you to look at is another matter entirely, and when you want to print it, the story becomes even stranger.

RGB

Remember when you got your first box of paints? There were eight little blobs of water color in the box. You quickly learned that mixing red and yellow gave you orange, blue and yellow made green, and so forth. The people who invented color TV must have gotten a very different box of paints, because on your television set or computer monitor, the three primary colors are red, green, and blue. When you mix red and green here, you get yellow!

No matter how many colors you show on the screen, they are all made of tiny pixels of red, green, and blue. Anything else you see is an optical illusion. Your eye blurs the colors together and convinces you to see lime green, bubble gum pink, and mauve. Each dot of red, green, or blue can be displayed in any of 256 different intensities. Zero equals black, or color off. You see white when all three colors are on fully. When the various intensities of each of the three colors combine, you get 256^3 or 16,777,216 different colors.

CMYK

However, the bottom line is not what you can see on the screen, but what actually reaches the paper. And what does, alas, is never quite what you saw or wanted. Printers, as kids, must have gotten an even more interesting paint box. Instead of plain old red and blue, their paint boxes probably held magenta, a dazzling hot pink, and cyan, a vivid turquoise shade.

The printer's ink palette, like the computer screen, is limited. Cyan, magenta, yellow, and black are what the printer must mix to reproduce our lime green, bubble gum pink, and mauve piece of art. And unlike the computer screen with 256 different intensities, printers are stuck using solid colors. So instead, they vary the number and size of the dots on the page to create more or less color intensity by printing halftones in each of the four ink colors. As with the image on the monitor, your eye fills in the gaps on the printed page and convinces your brain you are seeing a full spectrum.

HSV or HSB

Some artists like to define colors in yet another way. The third system you encounter is called variously HSV or HSB, which stands for *Hue, Saturation,* and *Value* or *Hue, Saturation,* and *Brightness*. Hue is the specific color red

Chapter 7
Drawing and Painting on the Macintosh

Part II
What Put the Mac in Business

or blue. Saturation defines the difference between the color and white. The lower the saturation, the closer the color is to being pure white. Saturation is measured in percent. Value and brightness are used interchangeably to indicate the difference between the color and black. The more black there is in the color, the lower the brightness. When the brightness or value is zero percent, the color is pure black. When the value is 100 percent, there is no black at all. It is as bright as possible. Apple's Color Picker CDEV shows you the HSB and RBG color models, along with the color wheel. (If this book were in color, it would be shown here, too. A color wheel in black and white just does not work.)

Higher Levels of Color Matching

Of course, with systems this complex, much can go wrong. Say you are designing an ad for a company that makes spaghetti sauce. It wants a nice red tomato on the label, like the one in figure 7.20. (OK, *imagine* a nice red!) How you define tomato red may have nothing to do with how the company defines tomato red and even less to do with what the printer thinks of as tomato red.

Figure 7.20
The tomato is red, the background is yellow, the letters are green.

Chapter 7

Drawing and Painting on the Macintosh

If you go to a grocery store and examine a bushel of ripe tomatoes, you probably would discover that no two are exactly the same color. If you, the client, and the printer were to agree on a single tomato as an example of the color, and then looked at it under natural sunlight, incandescent light, and fluorescent light, you would see three different shades of red again. And if you photographed the tomato, the kind of light you use has a big influence. So would the age and strength of the film developer, the temperature in the processing machine, and a dozen other factors over which you have no control whatsoever. When you scan the photo into your Mac, you add another set of variables relating to the adjustment of the color scanner. You could simply draw a red tomato in a color paint program, but you still have to settle on a shade of red and communicate it to the printer.

Pantone Matching System

Fortunately, there *is* a way to be consistent. Nearly 30 years ago, a system for consistent color matching was developed. It is called *Pantone*, and today *PMS*, the *Pantone Matching System*, is the standard for translating colors from one medium to another. Pantone has moved into the world of electronic media and permitted Aldus, Adobe, Quark, Radius, and other software and hardware manufacturers to incorporate Pantone color technology into their products.

The result: you can access the same PMS colors from your Mac that your printer uses. You even can show a printed PMS sample to your clients and know that the tomato red they see and approve is the same one that appears on their labels. Pantone does not offer all 16 million colors, but the 700 or so that most Paint programs can match are sufficient for most purposes. As figure 7.21 shows, Pantone colors are identified by number, so when you specify PMS Red 186 CV, you get the same shade of ripe tomato every time.

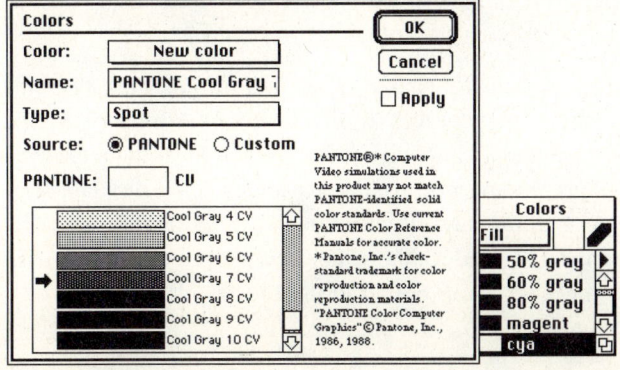

Figure 7.21

Pantone colors come in all shades, including warm and cool grays.

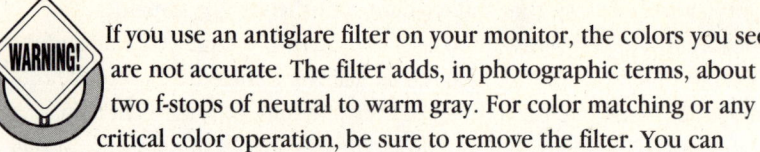 If you use an antiglare filter on your monitor, the colors you see are not accurate. The filter adds, in photographic terms, about two f-stops of neutral to warm gray. For color matching or any critical color operation, be sure to remove the filter. You can check your monitor's color calibration against the monitor adjustment cards provided with many color graphics programs. Aldus FreeHand, for instance, supplies a printed card with cyan, magenta, and yellow samples, plus blends of all three colors. Simply hold the card against the monitor and adjust the color on the screen to match the printed samples by clicking the appropriate shades on the color wheel.

Separation Anxiety and How to Cure It

When you print to a color printer, you do not need to worry about color separations. This process happens within the printer. If you send your work to a professional print shop, however, you may need to supply color separations yourself. The color separation process is the most accurate method of duplicating a color image. Color separation software is included in the high-end graphics programs such as PixelPaint Professional and Aldus FreeHand. Aldus Pre-Print is a stand-alone program that does the same thing for PageMaker 4 and other graphics programs which don't do their own separations. PageMaker 5 has built-in color separation.

In most programs, you merely select the **Print Separations** option to create separate halftones of the four layers the printer needs to make the four color plates for offset lithography printing. The layers, of course, are Cyan, Magenta, Yellow, and blacK. (*K* stands for *black* to avoid confusion with *blue*.) They are printed as halftones, so you need to specify which screen resolution to use. If you print to a LaserWriter or other 300 dpi printer, use 50 or 65 lines per inch. Use a higher setting, at least 150 lpi, if you print to a CompuGraphic or Linotronic at 2,540 dpi. (Obviously, using one of these high-resolution printers gives much better results.)

The screen is the same for all four colors, but the angle must be different for each, within a range of zero to 180 degrees plus or minus. For color separations, you need to use different angles on the different screens to avoid producing moiré patterns. (Moirés are those oil-slick effects you notice when you look through two layers of porch screening. Two or more layers of halftone screen can produce the same effect.) If you are not sure which angle to specify, check with your printer or use the default settings.

A Closer Look Although some experts maintain that Level 1 PostScript imagesetters are not capable of generating the precise screen angles necessary to avoid producing a moiré effect on a fine screen, others are doing it successfully. There are several shareware programs that adjust the angle or change the offset of the screen so the dots print between each other as they should for best results. By screening cyan and magenta at a 45 degree angle and offsetting by a half line, it is possible to arrive at the dot pattern shown in figure 7.22, which does not produce a moiré.

Chapter 7
Drawing and Painting on the Macintosh

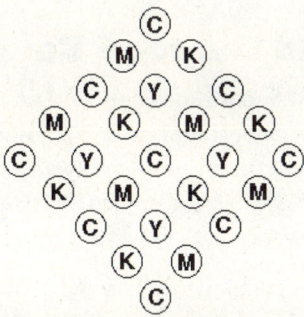

Figure 7.22
The combinations of colored dots make up halftone cells.

Always specify crop marks and registration marks when you prepare color separations by selecting **With Marks** in the PostScript **Options** dialog box. The registration mark looks like a set of crosshairs within a circle. When the separations are printed on transparent film, registration marks are easily aligned. Without accurate registration marks, separations are useless. Figure 7.23 shows part of a set of separations with a register mark in place.

Figure 7.23
Each of these would be on a separate page or piece of film.

Part II
What Put the Mac in Business

WARNING! Preparing and printing perfect color separations takes a great deal of knowledge and skill. Even though programs such as PixelPaint Professional can produce excellent separations, only those who are thoroughly familiar with the four-color process and separation controls should prepare artwork for printing. Even then, it is recommended you work very closely with your printer to ensure the materials you provide produce the printed results you want. For best results, rely on photomechanical, electrophotographic, or press proofs for color matching before you go to press.

Spot Color and Duotone Color

You also can use the **Print Separations** option to prepare spot color separations and duotones. Spot color is used when something less than full color is needed. The second color is produced with a single colored ink, generally specified as a PMS color, rather than by mixing CMYK inks. It is a less expensive printing process that can be very effective.

To produce a spot color separation, begin by defining a color as spot color in your artwork. Figure 7.24 shows how spot color is assigned in Aldus FreeHand. When you print, choose Print Separations, as shown in figure 7.25. Be sure to specify registration marks. The Mac sends the appropriate information to the laser printer to produce one page for black, and one for each spot color you have used, with registration marks placed in the margins. You do not need a color printer to print separations. When you send your artwork to the printing company, it takes your black and white separations and prints them with the appropriately colored inks to produce the result you saw on the screen.

Figure 7.24
Choose your color and place it where you want it.

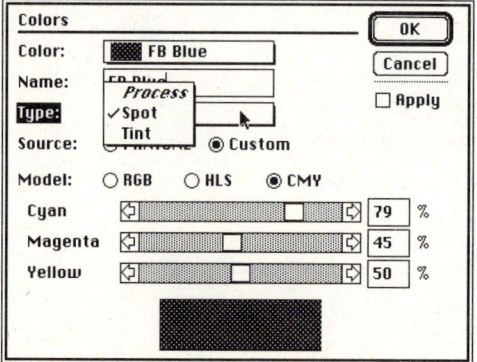

280

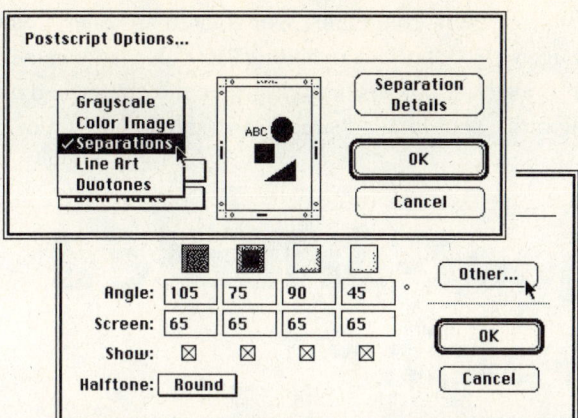

Figure 7.25
These dialog boxes enable you to set separation options.

Duotones can produce interesting effects in a document. A duotone consists of two separate halftone negatives, with changes to the angle of the screen. When printed on an offset press, one negative usually is reserved for black and the other for a color, generally a color related to the subject of the photo or art, or the same color you used as spot color accents elsewhere in the piece. If, for instance, you have a picture of a tree, you can add green to the leaves while using black for the tree trunk.

Cheap Color

If you like to use color but do not have access to a color printer or even a color Mac, here are some quick and easy ways to add color to a document. The first is to use colored papers. Many stationery stores and computer stores have preprinted papers with gradient tones in nice colors and papers with border designs or holiday art. These can perk up a drab document. Some types of laser printers accept toner cartridges in different colors. Red, green, brown, and blue toners are generally available from office supply dealers.

You would be surprised at how good a page can look when it is hand-colored with felt tip pens or even crayons. Line art adapts particularly well to this. You also can create quick duotones with a few strokes of color over a black and white halftone.

If you want colors that stand out, Letraset's ColorTag is a great solution. You can add a color to your type, a photo, drawing, or other graphic. The Color-Tag kit consists of a flat pad to work on, a set of colored foils, and a heating device about the size of an electric razor, with a stand. ColorTag works with laser-printed and photocopied documents. Place the foil over the area to be colored and stroke it with the heater. The color fuses with the black toner, giving you colored letters, colored lines, or colored halftones. ColorTag comes in a huge variety of colors, including PMS colors and metallics. It is great for certificates, dummy ads or packages, report covers, and one-of-a-kind greeting cards. Your local art supply store should have ColorTag.

Object-oriented Graphics

As you have learned, paintings are done bit by bit—literally. Draw programs see things more objectively. Instead of regarding a circle as an arrangement of dots, a draw program looks at it as the outline of an object, which can be described mathematically. Shapes, straight lines, and curves each are considered a separate object, and each has a mathematical formula that precisely defines it. Because number-crunching is done easily on computers, it is a simple matter to change an object's position or size. The computer merely adds or subtracts the necessary numbers and redraws the shape. The computer can also take advantage of printers with better resolution than the Macintosh screen. The computer calculates the best pattern of dots to represent the object, whether at 72 dpi (as on the monitor), 300 dpi (as with a laser printer), or whatever resolution is available.

Draw programs use the same QuickDraw routines that create the Mac's screen display. Most save graphics as PICT files (remember, PICT files can represent objects as well as bitmapped graphics) and also can save them as EPS files. The current format, PICT2, even allows for full 32-bit color. (PICTs can be either bitmapped or object-oriented, depending on which program creates them.) Also, because draw programs are not limited to the MacPaint file's format of 72 dpi resolution (except in terms of screen display), a circle printed on a 300 dpi laser printer is as round and smooth as 300 dpi can make it; the same circle printed on an imagesetter at 2,540 dpi is even smoother. This precision makes it possible to use the computer not only for drafting and mechanical drawing but also for EPS illustration programs such as Adobe Illustrator and Aldus FreeHand. The EPS, or Encapsulated PostScript format, combines PostScript code, which tells the laser printer how to handle an image, and PICT files, which tell the Mac's QuickDraw routines how to display it. EPS files take up a good deal of disk space because they contain so much information.

 It's important to note that the EPS format is by no means a standard. Different programs create slightly different EPS files, and so different programs will display the same EPS file in different ways. In short, you won't always get the same thing.

Draw (Not Paint) By Numbers

When you draw a square in a paint program, the only way to make it larger or smaller is to erase and redraw. Because the Mac has to set a one in place of a zero for each pixel you paint, it has to change the pixels individually. When you draw a square in a draw program, you actually are choosing a shape with four right angles, identifying the location of its upper-left corner, and defining the length of its diagonal. If you change the length of the diagonal, the Mac quickly does some geometry and lengthens the sides of the square accordingly. The computer does the work, so you never have to think about the numbers.

When MacDraw was first introduced in 1985, it shipped along with MacPaint and MacWrite at no charge as a tool for the new 512K "Fat Mac." MacDraw was intended for engineers and architects and was supposed to help secure the Mac's niche in office and industry situations. The program had a great many limitations, some of which remain. For instance, there was (and still is) no eraser. If you make a mistake, you must delete the object you are working on and redraw it. However, the groundwork was laid, not only for other draw programs—including highly specialized CAD and drafting programs and even three-dimensional imaging—but for a use MacDraw's creators probably did not consider. Because it is possible to paste text and graphics from the Clipboard or Scrapbook into MacDraw, some people began to use it to design posters or lay out newsletters. MacDraw could not handle type larger than 48 points and could create only one page at a time. It was not exactly desktop publishing, but it was a beginning.

The Toolbox

MacDraw is fairly primitive by today's standards. Its toolbox has basic drawing tools, shapes, and a text insertion tool. The menu offers custom rulers and a grid to which drawn objects align. The **Cut**, **Copy**, and **Paste**

Chapter 7
Drawing and Painting on the Macintosh

commands work as they do in other applications but with an important difference. Draw programs paste objects in layers. Because draw programs define objects individually rather than as part of a page, hidden layers are still there and can be recalled at any time. Draw programs enable you to paste or draw one box on top of another, and then, with a menu command, send the front layer to the back or bring the back layer to the front. Although you cannot erase, you can use white shapes as an "electronic white-out" to eliminate unwanted lines. Group or ungroup objects by selecting them and using the appropriate command. A graphic in a draw program is made of many separate objects. They can be reassembled in any order, resized singly or in groups, and copied or removed. It is as though each object were on a separate sheet of cellophane, all stacked together on a computerized drafting board.

When new draw programs after MacDraw were introduced, they included MacDraw's tools plus a few others. The second generation of draw programs includes two that have become very popular: Canvas and Silicon Beach's SuperPaint, now published by Aldus. Their outstanding feature is the capability to combine draw and paint in a single application. You can work with bitmapped graphics and objects in different layers of the same document and then print them as one layer. It is as though you had a transparent sketch pad sandwiched with your transparent drafting board. SuperPaint lets you cut and paste between layers and turn a bitmapped drawing into an object that then can be treated more or less like any other. You also can autotrace bitmapped images to convert them into outlines that can be scaled without the problems attendant to enlarging bitmaps.

"Handling" Graphics

After a line or shape is drawn, you may need to move it or change its size or shape. This is done by dragging its handles. Draw programs assign *handles* to the objects they create. When an object is selected, its handles are visible. To resize or stretch a shape or a line, simply click on a handle and drag it to a new position. Figure 7.26 shows handles on various objects. To select more than one object at a time, hold the Shift key as you click or press the Command-A key combination to select all objects (in most programs).

Text entries also have handles. Current draw programs enable you to change the shape of the text block by dragging its handles, and to edit within the text block as though you were using a word processor. You can change fonts, styles, and sizes within the block, and fill the background with a color or pattern. MacDraw Pro, the latest version of MacDraw, even includes a 100,000-word dictionary to check spelling! Figure 7.27 shows how DeskDraw handles text.

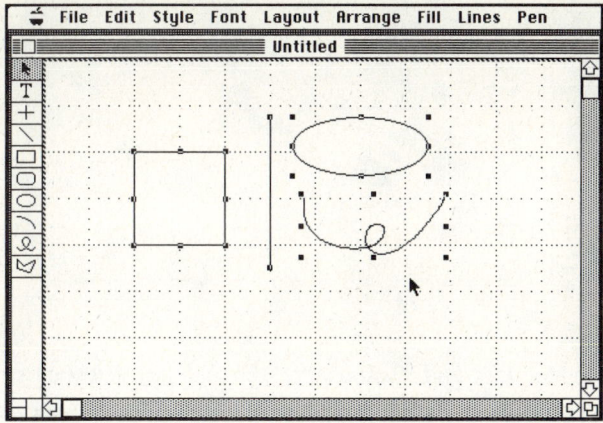

Figure 7.26
The little black boxes around the objects are handles.

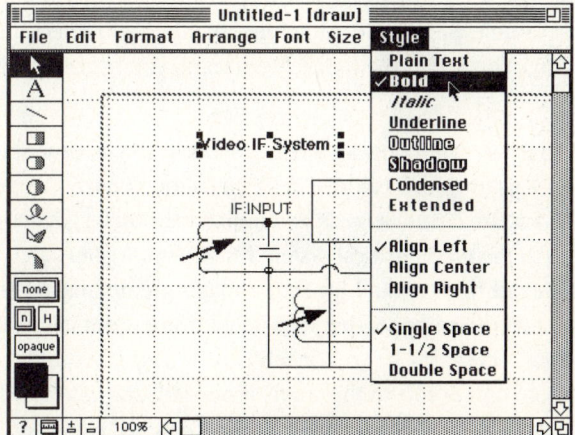

Figure 7.27
Entering captions and callouts on a drawing is as simple as typing them.

Draw programs generally contain two polygon tools for creating irregular filled shapes. One looks like a squashed box. The other, a straight-line polygon, lets you create shapes with more (or fewer) than three sides; figure 7.28 shows examples. To use the straight-line polygon tool, just click from one point to the next. Intersect with the first point, or double-click at the end point to join the ends.

Figure 7.28
These polygons were created in DeskDraw.

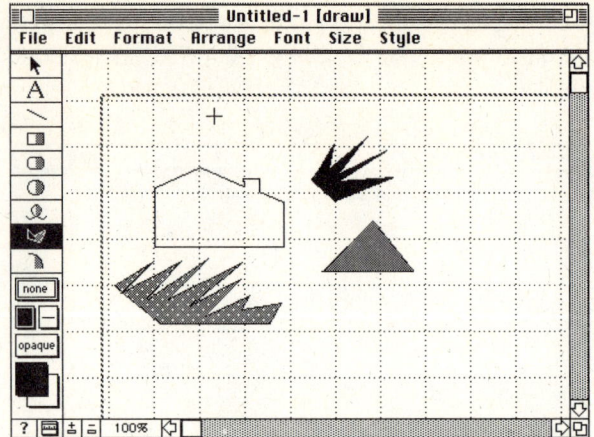

> **Note:** In MacDraw and MacDraw Pro, the tools you select have an annoying habit of turning back into the pointer as soon as you use them once. To retain the tool so you can draw additional lines, boxes, or whatever without returning to the tool palette each time, just double-click the tool icon the first time you select it instead of single-clicking. This keeps the tool selected until you return to the palette again.

It is not hard to understand how a square or a circle can be described in mathematical terms. But how can you define a fishhook curve, a boomerang, or the shapes in figure 7.30? Pierre Bézier apparently knew. Bézier's name has been given to the mathematical system for generating lines that display non-uniform curvature. Freehand, or Bézier, paths are defined by control points and can assume complex shapes. The path smoothes itself out after you draw it. Some programs let you define exactly how smooth the curve becomes. You can add points to the curve, if needed, and reshape the line if it gets too smooth or does something you do not intend. Figure 7.29 shows how a Bézier curve looks while being drawn and after it smoothes itself.

Figure 7.29
Bézier curves are non-uniform, as opposed to arcs, which are segments of an ellipsis.

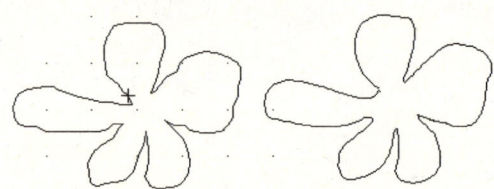

If the Bézier Curve tool does not give you the shape you want, you can edit it. The **Edit** menu in most draw programs contains options that enable you to reshape the curve by making the control points along the line visible. Place the pointer on a control point and drag until it is where you want it. If there are too many control points, select the one that is in the way and delete it. The line smoothes between the remaining points. Figure 7.30 shows control points being used to reshape a curve in IDD's MacDraft.

Chapter 7
Drawing and Painting on the Macintosh

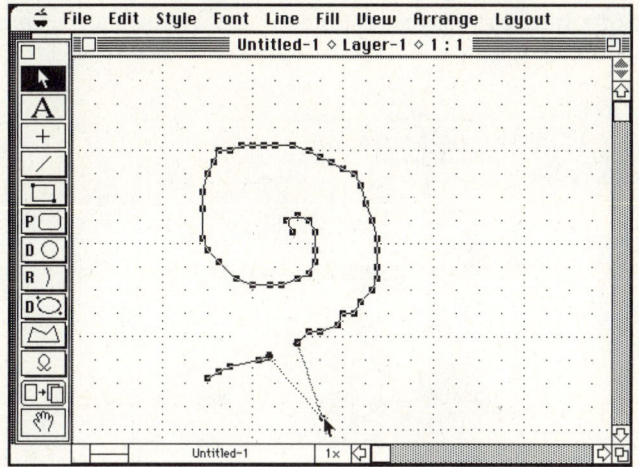

Figure 7.30
In MacDraft, a handle is placed anywhere the line changes direction slightly.

To draw a simple curve, use the straight-line polygon tool to make a square-cornered approximation of what you want. Then, select **Smooth** from the **Edit** menu and the line transforms into a smooth curve. If it needs further editing, select Reshape and reposition the points as needed.

Filling Shapes and Closed Paths

Creating filled shapes, freeform and otherwise, is as simple as drawing them. Select the filled shape from the tool palette, and select the fill pattern from the fill palette. If you've already created the shape, click on the shape to select it, and select the fill pattern. Most draw programs have basic patterns as well as colors. IntelliDraw lets you fill with gray scales, gradients, or colors, but not patterns.

Part II
What Put the Mac in Business

The range of available patterns depends on your draw program's limits. MacDraw originally did not let you edit its palette of patterns. (Neither did DeskDraw.) MacDraw II does enable you to edit the patterns through a dialog box, as does SuperPaint. Figure 7.31 shows how SuperPaint patterns are edited. Most of the draw programs on the market today handle color as well. MacDraw II can even produce 4-color separations. The current version of MacDraw Pro supports QuickTime and the Pantone color matching system, and comes with a HyperCard driver for automated slideshow presentations. IntelliDraw animates from within the program, creating "flipbooks" of drawings.

Figure 7.31
SuperPaint lets you edit its patterns.

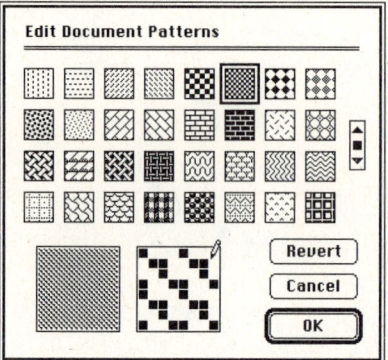

MacDraw Pro's pattern and color capabilities are amazing. The program's electronic palettes can hold thousands of colors, and you can organize them into logically grouped color schemes and create special-purpose palettes for specific jobs. The number of palettes and colors available is limited only by the hardware and available memory. MacDraw Pro also includes special shading patterns, called *gradients,* which are used to produce highlights and to give your graphics a three-dimensional effect. Gradients can be combinations of black and a color, or of two or three colors.

Figure 7.32 shows how a gradient is customized. **Gradients** are selected from the gradient palette. When the palette is "torn off" from the menu bar, its own menu bar can be seen. (Clicking the small box next to the close box on the palette's menu bar hides or reveals the menus.) MacDraw Pro offers three different types of gradient: circular, directional, and shape burst. Select one of these and click the **Edit** button to get the box shown in figure 7.33. As you change the focus of the shape or the direction of the flare, you see the result in the adjacent box. When the gradient suits your needs, click OK.

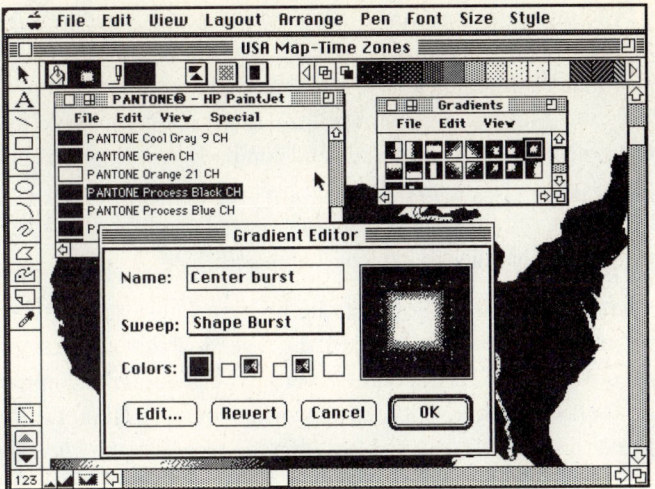

Figure 7.32
Select the gradient shading for any object, or create your own.

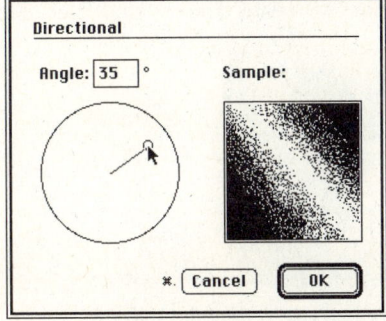

Figure 7.33
MacDraw Pro lets you customize a gradient.

A Closer Look When you work with MacDraw Pro on a color monitor, you may notice the desktop colors change as you open and close the application. This is because, by default, the program uses the Claris 168 color palette rather than the system's 256 Quick-Draw colors to reduce the amount of memory needed. As long as the additional memory is available, you can open the Apple color palette, the Pantone palette, 16-color palette, or 100-gray palette instead. The color shift, although annoying, is temporary.

Tricks with Type

Draw programs can create some interesting effects with type. One is to distort it. You can use your draw program to create stretched, squeezed, and

Part II
What Put the Mac in Business

warped headlines, which are handy for attention-getting headlines. There are several ways to accomplish this. SuperPaint lets you type in a block of text and then rotate it, stretch it, and generally distort it as much as you want. It looks fairly awful on the screen but prints exactly as it is supposed to. If you have Microsoft Word, you can stretch and compress words for headlines by typing them "normally" in MacDraw and pasting them as PICT images in a Word document. After the image is a Word graphic, hold the Shift key and drag the graphic's handles to stretch or compress it.

Reverse type doesn't mean the letters are backward. Instead, the type is white against a black or colored background, the reverse of the black letters on white paper we usually see. Creating reverse type is simple. In SuperPaint, draw the filled shape over which the type will be reversed. Enter the words in a type box and select white or a color. Drag the type over the filled shape. Place black or gray type behind white for a drop shadow effect.

Type can also be flipped, stretched and distorted. Figure 7.34 shows some examples of what you can do with type in SuperPaint.

Figure 7.34
Torturing the type with SuperPaint can be fun.

If you need to copy text from a draw document into another application, how you select it determines what you can do with it. Selecting it with the pointer tool gives you a text block as a PICT file, which can be placed, stretched, scaled, and so on, but not edited. If you select text with the text cursor, you can paste it as text, edit it, change fonts, and handle it exactly as though you had typed it directly into the word processor. In SuperPaint, if you paste text from the draw layer into the paint layer, it becomes part of the bitmap. It cannot be edited. Similarly, if you paste a block of text from the Paint layer into the draw layer, the text simply is treated as a pattern of pixels, as if you had pasted in a block of plaid. It will not become editable text.

Dimensions and Grids

Precision drawings made in a draw program can be very precise. Draw programs include rulers that usually can be set to centimeters, millimeters, and even points and picas as well as inches. Figure 7.35 shows the ruler box from IDD's MacDraft. This program offers a choice of English or metric units and lets you assign scales. Draw programs also have the capability to place a grid of dots on the page to aid you in placing elements more accurately. The **Snap to Grid** feature is a big help in aligning graphics. Once **Snap to Grid** is activated, everything is "magnetically" drawn to the closest grid line.

Chapter 7
Drawing and Painting on the Macintosh

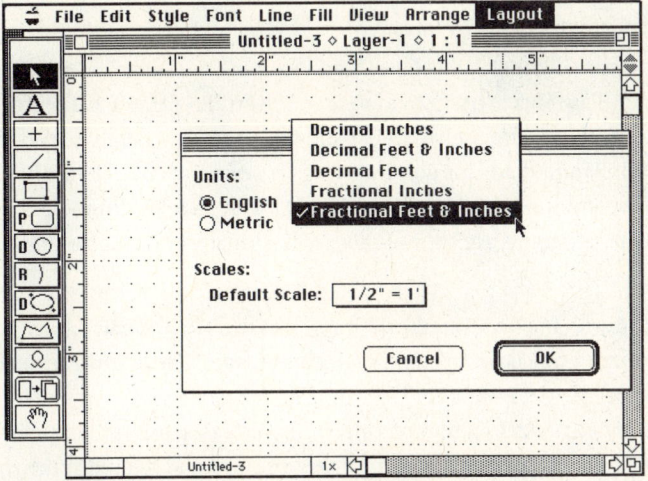

Figure 7.35
MacDraft's Ruler box.

Higher Level Graphics—The Art of Illustration

The draw programs covered in the first part of this chapter address the technical aspects of drawing. Drawing also can be a fine art, even on a computer. Two "professional" illustration programs are the industry standards: Adobe Illustrator and Aldus FreeHand. Chances are excellent you will encounter one or both of them in a design studio, advertising agency, desktop publishing service, or anywhere else high-quality graphics are needed. The two programs are competing for the same market, but because they have somewhat different features, some users buy both. Illustrator offers greater precision in its freehand drawing tools, whereas FreeHand provides more of a WYSIWYG interface and has context-sensitive onscreen help, which Illustrator lacks (and needs).

> **Note:** It used to be true that Illustrator could not handle type very well, which is surprising because Adobe is *the* name in type. Version 3.2 of Illustrator solved the type problems. (Illustrator is now on version 5.0.) You now can create and manipulate type directly in the drawing area, and can even convert Type 1 PostScript fonts into Bézier curves to modify individual letters. Illustrator also includes Adobe Type Manager.

It is not surprising that Aldus FreeHand bears many similarities to Aldus PageMaker. PageMaker users tend to lean toward FreeHand as their graphics program of choice, precisely because the interface is so familiar. You may notice Help Wanted ads for graphic designers often specify: "Must be familiar with Quark and Illustrator" or "Experienced with PageMaker and FreeHand." Both sets of programs are thoroughly professional standards for graphic design.

Both Illustrator and FreeHand save images in the EPS format, which can be imported into page layout programs such as QuarkXPress and PageMaker or printed directly to a PostScript laser printer, imagesetter, or other PostScript imaging device (such as a film recorder). If your laser printer happens to use QuickDraw instead of PostScript, or if you print to an inkjet, dot matrix, or color thermal printer, you still can work with EPS files in FreeHand and/or Illustrator if you use Freedom of Press Light. This program, from Color Age, is a printer utility that converts Mac-generated PostScript codes into information that common non-PostScript printers can use. It supports ATM and PostScript Type 1 fonts, and includes 17 outline fonts. A professional version, Freedom of Press 3.0.1, supports 50 different printers and film recorders.

Special Tools

Both FreeHand and Illustrator have many of the same tools as MacDraw and similar programs. They also have blend tools that let you blend shapes and colors, as well as autotrace tools much like SuperPaint's to draw an outline of a graphic. Figure 7.36 shows the tool palettes from both applications. Most of the tools are virtually identical, as you would expect. FreeHand has additional palettes for colors, layers, and styles, which may be opened, resized, and relocated to a convenient spot on your work area. Illustrator has additional tools that pop out from the palette when you press the mouse button. Illustrator defines styles (which in this case refers to line weights, fills, and colors) from a dialog box rather than from a palette.

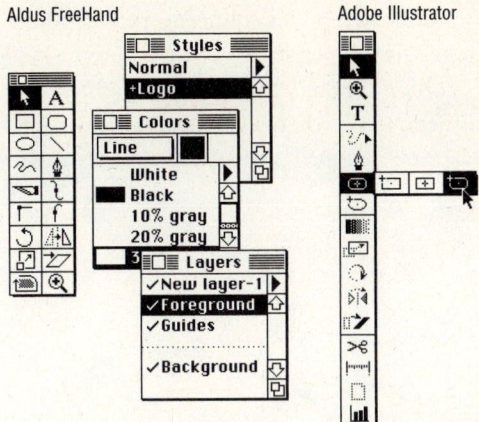

Figure 7.36

FreeHand and Illustrator have similar tools of the trade.

It is as simple to draw shapes in FreeHand as it is in MacDraw or MacPaint. Select the appropriate shape from the tool palette and drag. Illustrator's tool palette has a pop-out shape menu, as shown in figure 7.36. When you select the shape with the small cross in the upper-left corner, you can draw the shape on the screen, as with FreeHand. If you select the other type of shape (minus the cross) you bring up a dialog box like the one shown in figure 7.37. Enter the exact size of the shape you want to draw in the box, and click **OK** to place it on the screen. You can define the size of a line or shape as precisely in FreeHand, but you first must draw an approximation of it and then open the **Element Info...** dialog box under the **Elements** menu to enter exact dimensions for the shape.

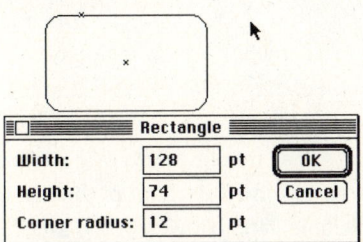

Figure 7.37

It is easy to define a rectangle in Adobe Illustrator.

The freehand drawing tools in both programs give you a great deal of flexibility. Aldus FreeHand lets you choose among five different tools to create your drawings. The Freehand tool draws a line as you drag the mouse. The other tools draw lines a bit differently. Click the tool to place points, and the program draws the line to connect the points. The type of point you place determines the shape of the path.

Use the Corner tool to place corner points and the Curve tool to place curve points. A curve point creates a smoothly curving line to the next point. A corner point sends a straight line between itself and another point (which may be a corner or a connector). Corner points create a definite change in

Part II
What Put the Mac in Business

Figure 7.38
Each FreeHand tool defines the line next to it on the palette.

direction. The Connector tool places connector points, which smoothly connect straight paths and curved paths. If you connect a straight line to a curved line with a corner, they meet at a sharp angle. The Pen tool places both curve and corners. Use it when you must place both kinds of points to save time switching tools. Figure 7.38 shows the points and the tools that make them.

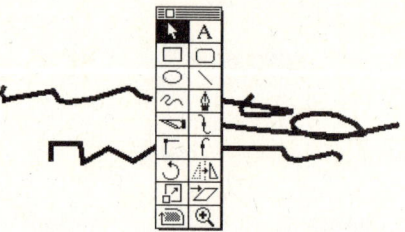

You can tell which kind of point you have selected by its shape. Curve points are represented by small circles, corner points by squares, and connector points look like triangles. The first and last points on the path are endpoints. To extend a path, select an endpoint and place additional points as needed. To close a path (making a solid outline), place the last endpoint over the first. If you close a path, you can begin another path immediately, but if you draw an open path, you must deselect the endpoint before you can start another path.

Objects, as discussed earlier, have handles. Points also have handles but of a slightly different kind. Point handles are clover-shaped and are used to control the curve of the path segments traveling into and out of the point. Handles retract into the point when a path segment is straight and extend as it curves. To change a curve, drag on one of the handles; both handles move. (Corner and connector point handles move independently of each other.) The line that extends from one handle to the other through the control point is called a *lever*. Levers determine the extent of the curve. It is as though the curve is made of very flexible wire, with a stiff rod attached at the curve point. Moving the lever causes the curve to flex. Figure 7.39 shows how a curve can be reshaped by using the handles. If you drag the handle at position A to position B, the thin line shows the new path for the curve. When you release the mouse button, the curve snaps to the new path.

Note: Seeing the levers helps you visualize how the path moves when you move a handle. Levers are visible when **Display Curve Levers** is checked in the **Preferences** dialog box. If you are doing very detailed work, the levers may get in the way. Uncheck the box to hide them. Levers and points do not print in your illustration, even if they are visible when you select **Print**.

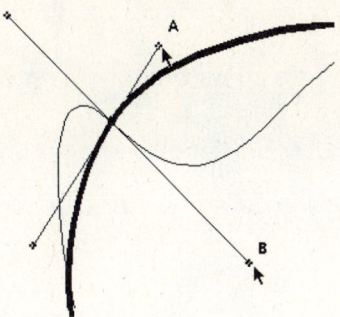

Figure 7.39
The relocated levers are superimposed over their previous position in FreeHand.

Type Styling

One of the reasons many users have preferred FreeHand over Illustrator was its capability to set type along a curved or freeform path. Now that Adobe has added this feature to Illustrator, the two programs have about the same type styling capabilities. Both let you place a line of type along any line or shape you draw. Custom kerning is available in either program.

In either program, you begin by creating the shape to which you want to align the type. Figure 7.40 shows a freehand path, to which you will align the words of your headline. When you click the Text tool, you get a text entry box. Type the word or phrase to be aligned, and press the Command-T key combination to open the **Text Attributes** box. Change the font, size, and style as needed, and add a color if you want. When you close the **Text Attribute** box, the line of type appears on the screen with the desired attributes.

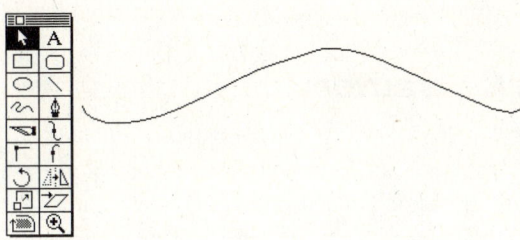

Figure 7.40
Start by drawing the path and typing the words.

Select the type and the line to which it will be aligned, as shown in figure 7.41. Press the Command-J key combination, or select **Join** from the menu. The text positions itself along the line with the first letter at the start of the line. The line becomes invisible, as figure 7.42 shows. If you need to adjust the curve of the line, select the line of text. You see the handles of the invisible baseline and can shift it as needed. Figure 7.43 shows the finished headline.

Figure 7.41

Select the type and path to be joined.

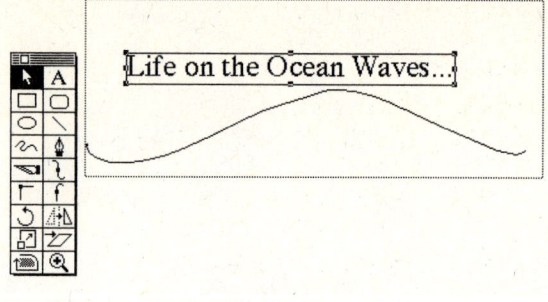

Figure 7.42

Use the handles to smooth the curve as needed.

Figure 7.43

The finished headline with a graphic added looks great!

 In FreeHand, you easily can shift between any other tool and the pointer by pressing the Command key. Whichever tool is active turns into the pointer while you hold the Command key.

Colorful Characters

Both Illustrator and FreeHand are capable of beautiful color work, with airbrushed effects, blends, and patterns in 16 million colors. In both programs, colors are defined in dialog boxes. You may either enter specific percentages of cyan, magenta, yellow, and black, if you know them, or move the sliders back and forth until you see a color you like. When you create custom colors for a project, give them distinctive and easily recognizable names, such as the example shown in figure 7.44 from a FreeHand palette. Some artists like to set up their palette before they start designing. Others prefer to design the shapes and then mix the colors.

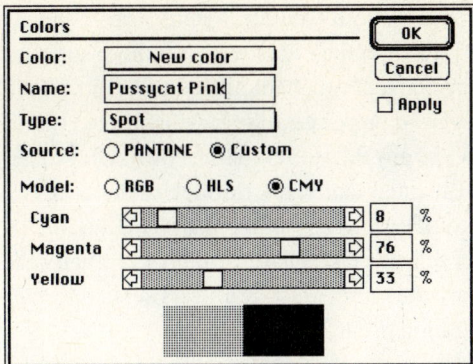

Figure 7.44
You can add custom colors in FreeHand.

If you must do color separations, Illustrator is a good choice. It comes with built-in capabilities for spot color and four-color separations. Figure 7.45 shows how Illustrator prepares a three-color separation. The Adobe package also includes Adobe Type Manager, a must for good-looking type on the screen and on non-PostScript printers. FreeHand 3.1 also does four-color separations from within the program, a nice improvement over previous versions which required a separate color separation program such as Aldus PrePrint.

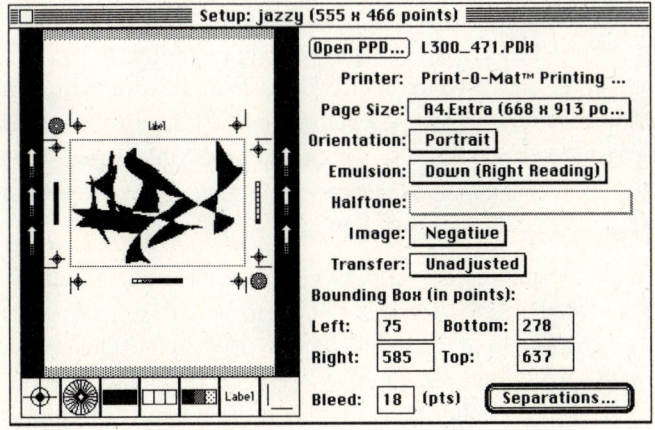

Figure 7.45
Adobe Separator prepares a color separation for the Linotronic.

Which Illustration Program Should You Buy?

Illustrator and FreeHand's features and capabilities are about the same. Many computer artists feel that the Adobe program is a bit more difficult to use.

In their current versions, both are fully System 7-savvy, including Publish and Subscribe and 32-bit addressing. Illustrator has more sophisticated text-editing tools. FreeHand lets you manipulate drawings in layers. Illustrator is more precise, FreeHand more versatile. FreeHand can read Illustrator files, but Illustrator ignores any files other than its own. Of course, you have to be willing to read the manuals and work through the tutorials with either program if you expect to learn to use all the possible tools and techniques. FreeHand is easier to learn if you have worked with PageMaker at all; many of its commands are the same. Illustrator users seem to prefer QuarkXPress as a desktop publishing program.

Summary

The Mac's capability to create graphics makes it an exciting tool for professional and amateur artists of all ages. MacPaint introduced the concepts of the pixel as a painting medium and the mouse as a graphic arts tool. Increasingly sophisticated and complex hardware and software have enabled artists to work with more than 16 million colors and to create breathtakingly beautiful images on the screen and on paper. Graphic arts professionals use the Mac for color separations, image enhancement, and a host of other tasks that used to require a darkroom. Color printing can be accomplished in a variety of ways, from four-color process to spot color, to colored ImageWriter ribbons. The Mac cannot make you into another Picasso or DaVinci if you have no talent to start with, but it can provide virtually all the graphics tools you'll ever need. (And it's fun!)

Object-oriented graphics have come a long way since the first MacDraw program appeared in 1985. The past eight years have taken us from being able to snap shapes to a grid to three-dimensional graphics and virtual realities on one hand, and beautifully smooth full-color illustrations in PostScript file format on the other. The Macintosh is now the technical equal of the most highly skilled draftsperson or artist. With this tool, people with talent and skill truly can do wonders. For the rest of us, it gives us the power to transfer creativity to paper easily, quickly, and enjoyably.

Chapter 8
Desktop Publishing Programs

Desktop publishing—a term coined to describe using a computer, a laser printer, and a page-layout program to publish text and graphics together on a page—was virtually invented on the Mac.

In This Chapter

▼ Combining multiple elements

▼ Page processing

▼ Pictures, charts, and more

▼ Headlines and typography

▼ Comparing leading DTP programs

Part II
What Put the Mac in Business

The process of page make-up, design, and output are all dependent on desktop publishing applications and are explored in depth in this chapter.

Desktop Publishing

The inevitable result of designing a computer like the Mac, which can handle everything from business letters and long text files to elaborately drawn and colored artwork, precise graphs, and elegant typography, was that someone would combine all these features. The first Macintosh programs gave a small taste of the possibilities. MacPaint proved you could do reasonable drawings with a mouse and label your creation on the screen. MacWrite enabled you to use different fonts and type styles on the same page, as well as paste a picture in the middle of the text. In fact, the demonstration that helped Apple sell so many of the first 128K Macs featured a drawing of a sneaker set into a page of text.

Desktop—proof that a noun can become an adjective.

Guy Kawasaki

What made desktop publishing, as this new phenomenon was eventually called, both possible and practical was the Mac's What-You-See-Is-What-You-Get or WYSIWYG screen. What you placed or created on the screen—type, picture, borders, screens, and so on—printed exactly as it looked on the screen, right down to the little square blocks that made big type or objects look as if they were built of bricks. These ragged edges were nicknamed "the jaggies." Those who could tolerate the jaggies started using Macs and ImageWriters to produce newsletters, advertisements, business reports, and other publications. The result was a more timely, cost-effective publication, even though the jaggies obviously signaled it had been created on a computer.

Soon, more versatile software was developed and the quality of many efforts improved. But it took a hardware revolution to make desktop publishing a reality—the laser printer which printed 300 dots per inch (dpi) instead of the 72 dpi the Mac screen displayed. This smaller print dot virtually eliminated the jaggies from the naked eye and smoothed the edges of most type and artwork. Apple introduced its first laser printer, the LaserWriter, late in 1985. (See chapter 6, "Printing from Your Macintosh.")

Chapter 8
Desktop Publishing Programs

Also in 1985, Aldus Corporation introduced a software package called PageMaker. Designed by a graphic artist/programmer, it was the first application to maximize the LaserWriter's capabilities. Aldus' president, Paul Brainard, is credited with coining the phrase "desktop publishing."

PageMaker solved a problem the Mac had created for itself. Because the Mac is more than a "smart typewriter," most users wanted to include more than just type, even on their simplest documents. While all Mac programs boasted the ability to mix type and graphics, no one program could handle much more than pasting a picture onto a page. If you wanted, for example, to draw a border around the picture, it had to be done in an art program such as MacDraw, then copied and pasted back into the word processing program. Because early Macs could only run one program at a time, you had to quit and restart both programs several times before this simple action could be completed.

Then, PageMaker came along. PageMaker combined most of these actions into one program, which looked and worked just like a graphic artist's layout table, with onscreen tools that could perform word processing functions; draw lines, boxes and circles; crop images; create columns for type; and more. It could import and export graphics and word processing files from other programs, too. PageMaker set the standard by which all other desktop publishing programs are measured. By June of 1986, PageMaker became one of Macworld magazine's Top 10 Best-Sellers in business software.

> PageMaker—proof that there is a God, and that He or She loves Apple Computer.
>
>
>
> Guy Kawasaki

Making Pages, Then and Now

"In the Beginning was the Word…." And to record the word, it was scribed on clay tablets, traced with ink on papyrus, chiseled in stone, or patiently hand-lettered on sheets of vellum made from baby goats' skins. From the beginnings of history as we know it, there has always been a need for written communication—not just communication between two people but to a wide audience. The Latin roots of the word "publish" are *publicus*, to make public; and *populus*, people.

Part II
What Put the Mac in Business

In the very early days, publishing was a solitary occupation. Scribes prepared their own inks, pens, and brushes, and often made their own paper, or tanned the kid skins themselves. In medieval monasteries, each monk labored over his own pages. With the advent of the printing press and moveable type, publishing became a joint effort. It no longer depended on individuals; it now required experts such as artists, engravers, typesetters, pressmen, and a lot of specialized equipment.

Until desktop publishing arrived on the scene, issuing a simple four-page newsletter took several weeks and more than a half-dozen specialists. Writers, artists, and photographers produced the copy and art, then gave it to the newsletter editor. All copy had to be edited and marked with special proofreader's marks to indicate which size to set the type, and which text to boldface, italicize, and so on. Edited copy was sent to a typesetter. Photos went to a photo-engraver to be screened into a pattern of dots called a halftone that made the photo suitable for printing. Line art was often scaled as a photostat to reduce or enlarge it to the exact size needed. Headlines and body copy were returned separately from the typesetter, produced on long strips of paper called galleys.

Eventually, the entire package of type, photostats and halftones went to a paste-up artist who first marked the size and placement of all these elements in a special non-printing blue pencil on large sheets of white cardboard, and then carefully glued everything in place. The paste-ups went to a printer, who photographed them, made printing plates and printed the newsletter. It was time-consuming, expensive, and frustrating, especially when a misspelled word or a missing comma meant redoing an entire page of type. Color printing required more specialists and even more technology.

When desktop publishing became a reality, you could, in effect, step forward by stepping backward to the days of "do-it-yourself." Using the Mac, a LaserWriter, and desktop publishing software, you could avoid the usual hassles of traditional publishing methods because you were in complete control of virtually every aspect of the publishing process. You did not have to depend on one specialist to set the type, another to glue it down, and a third to spread ink on the printing plate. Your Macintosh could do the entire job easily, and you could create a new publication any time you had something to say!

As a term, "publishing" is not limited to producing magazines and newsletters. The purpose of a desktop publishing program is to assemble pages of any kind by combining elements into a harmonious and printable document. Desktop publishing (DTP) programs allow even a beginner to design good-looking and easy-to-read posters, flyers, or brochures. Businesses can create custom forms for everything from invoices and purchase orders to phone messages and custom fax cover sheets. Figure 8.1 illustrates thumbnails of the typical documents created with DTP programs.

Chapter 8
Desktop Publishing Programs

Figure 8.1
There are many types of publications you can create on a Macintosh.

Pasteless Paste-up

Computerized page makeup looks very similar to traditional publishing results but is quicker, neater, and less complicated. PageMaker uses many "real world" analogies. Figure 8.2 shows PageMaker's desktop, or *pasteboard,* which simulates an artist's large drawing table. You use the pasteboard to store type and graphics until you are ready to use them, just as you would store physical tools at an artist's table. However, computerized items always stay where you put them, even if it takes several months to return to a job.

Figure 8.2
In PageMaker, the desktop is an artist's drawing table.

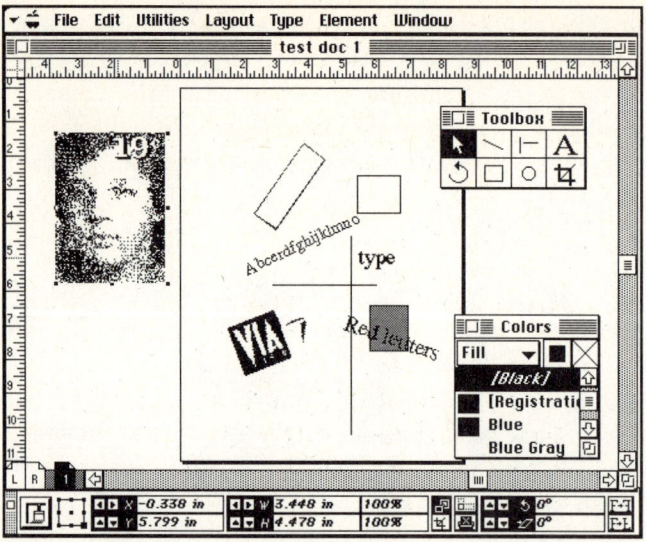

Your page appears in the middle of the screen, with the tools out of the way but still within easy reach. Since this is not a real drawing board, there is a menu bar at the top of the screen with scroll bars, close boxes, zoom boxes, and so forth. There is also a set of rulers to create ruler guides—a process similar to using a T-square and blue pencil to define non-printing guidelines on an actual paste-up.

DTP programs have some type of toolbox, or collection of tools used to modify the document. All have line and shape tools for creating straight or free-form lines, squares, and circles. (Lines and shapes are considered graphics in DTP programs.) Toolboxes always contain a pointer for selecting objects and a text tool for creating or editing type. The circular arrow tool is used for text and graphics rotation. Most programs also include a square with an angled line through it called a cropping tool, after the actual artist's device for cropping and scaling. The cropping tool electronically trims away the edges of imported graphics. Electronic cropping involves changing the size of an invisible frame that surrounds a graphic so only a portion of the picture shows, enabling you to eliminate unwanted parts of it (see figures 8.3 and 8.4). Select the graphic and position the cropping tool over one of its handles. The tool changes to a double-headed arrow when the mouse button is pressed. If you continue to hold down the mouse button, the invisible frame temporarily becomes a black line. Move it in or out as desired, and the picture is cropped accordingly. Should you decide to restore a section, use the cropping tool to expand the invisible frame, and that section reappears.

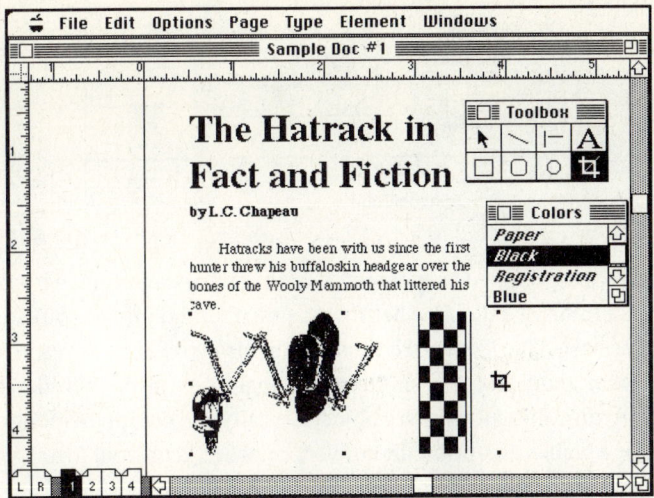

Figure 8.3
Use the cropping tool to cover unwanted parts of a picture.

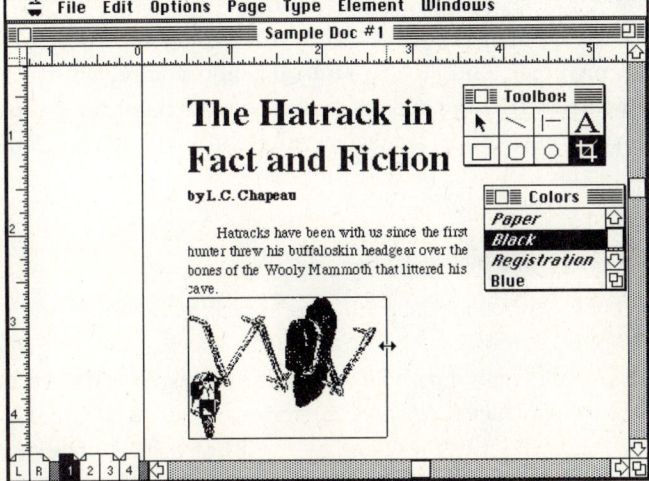

Figure 8.4
Cropping does not change the picture itself.

One program, Ventura Publisher, does not use the cropping tool. Instead, use its Frame tool to size the box appropriately with the handles; you then hold the option key while sliding the picture inside the frame.

Other DTP programs have additional tools to perform functions that PageMaker offers as menu selections. Tool palettes for several popular DTP programs are shown in figure 8.5. Ventura's tools include a table editor and several text placement icons. Personal Press' Links tool allows you to create story chains by linking blocks of text. Simply choose the Link tool from the toolbox, click on the first text block in the chain, and then on the text block you wish to link with it. The Broken Links icon, obviously, unlinks a text block or object from the story chain.

Figure 8.5
Page layout programs have different toolbox configurations.

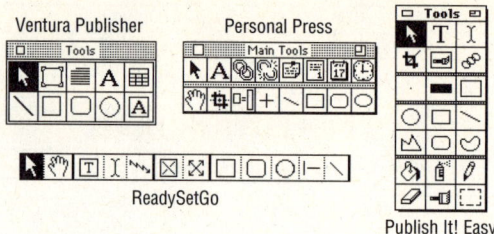

You can also draw linked-text objects such as a line separating two stories in the same column or a block of halftone pattern placed under a pull quote for added emphasis. The icons to the right of the Broken Links represent notes, page number, date, and time stamp. The Equals tool (directly below the Links) lets you automatically size objects equally and give them identical attributes, which is exceptionally convenient when laying out forms.

ReadySetGo (RSG) uses a lightning bolt icon to join text blocks and related graphics. Select the icon and click the elements to link. The two icons to its right are RSG's solution to sizing and placing imported graphics. Draw a box with the Box shaped tool, and fill it with "glue" from the arrows tool. Then, paste your picture. Publish It! Easy's toolkit is more comprehensive than most. It includes a basic set of paint tools so you can create bit-mapped art directly in your publication. Unfortunately, it will not let you touch-up imported pictures.

DTP Terminology

In the 550 or so years since the printing press was created, many terms have been applied to the various parts of a printed page. Some are easy to understand, such as columns, headlines, and by-lines. Others, such as drop caps, gutters, or full bleed, are more mysterious. Figure 8.6 defines some of the terms used to describe the elements on the first page of a newsletter. Figure 8.7 details other commonly encountered terms.

Getting Started

Before you begin working with desktop publishing software, you will need to understand some printing terms. *White space* is the space on the page that contains no text or graphics, including margins, gutters, indents, line spacing, paragraph spacing, and the fringes at the side of ragged-right type.

The term *leading* (which rhymes with sledding) derives from the strips of lead typographers used to separate lines of handset type. Figure 8.8 shows three examples of type: the first leaded normally, the second loosely, and the third tightly. Page layout programs differ in how they customize leading, but all have an automatic leading feature which preassigns the amount of leading, usually at 120 percent of the point size. For example, 10-point type is set on 12 points of leading (120 percent of 10), leaving two points of space between the bottom of a letter and the top of a letter in the following line.

Chapter 8
Desktop Publishing Programs

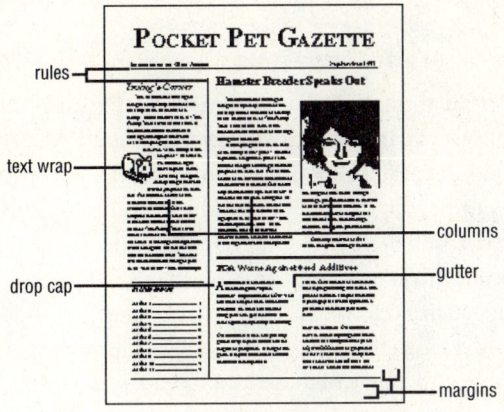

Figure 8.6
Some common newspaper terms used in desktop publishing.

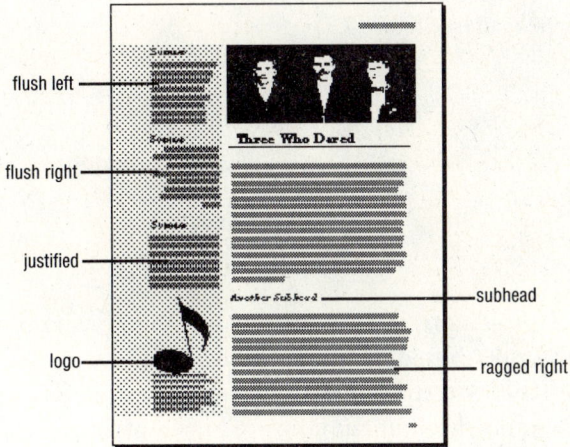

Figure 8.7
These terms generally apply to advertising and printing.

Figure 8.8
The space between lines is called leading.

correct — The Captain often claimed that one of the prettiest sights in the world was the Bourne Bridge just at sunset, as seen from the banks of the Canal.

too much leading — "If you stand in just the right spot," he said, "Late in the summer the sun appears to set directly beneath the center of the bridge."

too little leading — Imagine such a sunset, with a flock of snowy white gulls soaring overhead and an old, but sturdy fishing trawler making its way home with a full load of cod and haddock.

Note: There are thousands of type fonts available for DTP, and since the Mac lets you use so many style variations (bold, condensed, expanded, underlined, and outlined are some of the more common), your end results are almost limitless. You should, however, limit yourself to no more than two fonts per page or your pages become cluttered and distracting. You can still use different sizes and styles of the same font, such as Helvetica Bold 18 for a headline and Helvetica Condensed Italic 12 for a by-line, and not violate the rule. Special character fonts are available, too. Some of these fonts create letters which imitate logs, circus animals, or neon signs. Use these sparingly also, for although a word or two might look fine in a title, body copy set in something hard to read will simply not be read (see figure 8.9).

Figure 8.9
Which font is easier to read?

H is for Horse. "Neigh-h-h-h," says the Horse.

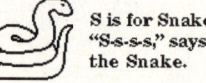
S is for Snake. "S-s-s-s," says the Snake.

To avoid dull, or gray, pages, most desktop publishing programs allow you use subheads, rules, boxed quotes, and similar features to relieve the monotony of endless text. Figure 8.10 illustrates the visual difference. If you have several stories that continue to an inside page of your newsletter, many DTP programs allow you to create different column widths as well as to add variety to the page.

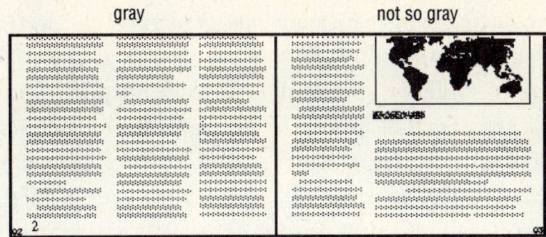

Figure 8.10
DTP can instantly solve a gray problem.

When you have facing pages, such as pages two and three of a four-page newsletter, most DTP programs allow them to be designed as one unit. Many of the programs allow you to view both pages onscreen at the same time.

Setting up the Pages

Depending on the DTP program, you either specify your page set-up before seeing the pasteboard or start out immediately with a blank page. Either way, at some point you must define your publication's page and margins sizes, as well as specify the number of pages and their orientation (tall or wide). Figure 8.11 shows a typical page set-up dialog box. The settings shown are default settings the manufacturer creates, but you can easily change them by typing new numbers into the fields or selecting different settings from the page size and measurements pop-up menus. If you decide to change the margins or use three columns instead of two after you start assembling the pages, you can do so globally (on all pages at once) by re-opening this box and making the changes here.

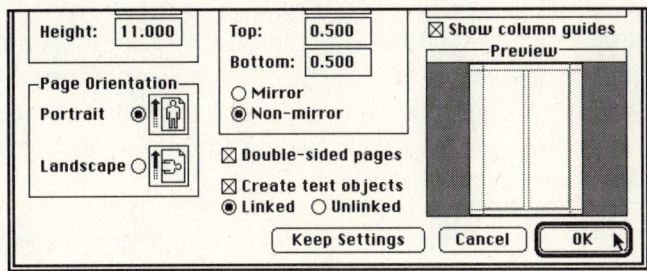

Figure 8.11
Aldus' Personal Press uses a standard dialog to set up pages.

 Each page layout program is slightly different, although most operations are similar. If the operations described here do not work with your software, read and follow the directions in your manual.

Once you decide on the page format, you can place or import the various elements directly into the publication. For most DTP programs, it saves time to create a special folder on your desktop to store the publication's text and graphics files. Any item that appears in the same location on every page of your document should be placed on a master page; left pages are created as copies of the left master page and right pages are copies of the right master. Every page layout program uses some system of icons to represent document pages. Master pages are usually labeled LM, RM or MP. Publish It! Easy provides a typical palette, which the company calls the Page Flipper, as shown in figure 8.12. Other DTP programs may refer to the master pages as base pages, or default pages.

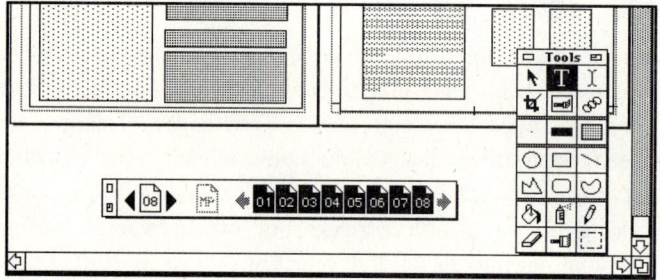

Figure 8.12
Click the arrows to scroll through Publish It! Easy's pages.

Master pages hold items such as page numbers, logos and other repeating graphics, and headers or footers with the name of your publication. They may also contain the formatting for your document and non-printing guidelines. If you are designing a book, for example, you can designate the column width and page number marker on the master page. Then you need only place the text on the first page of the chapter. If you are putting a full-page illustration or chart into a document with many similar pages of text, or placing a full-page ad into a magazine, you may choose to turn off the master page elements on that particular page. Figure 8.13 shows the master pages from a magazine designed in PageMaker.

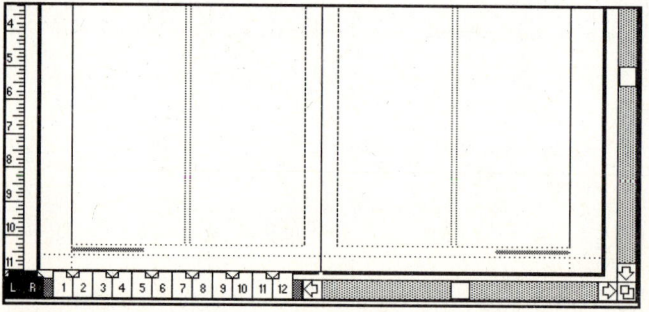

Figure 8.13
PageMaker's master pages include page numbers, column guides, and the magazine's name.

QuarkXPress lets you create as many as 100 different master pages per document. Ventura Publisher lists all of your publication's typography and graphics attributes on a style sheet for the base page. Once the foundation is set, laying out the actual publication is quick and easy.

Importing Graphics

A menu listing known as Place Graphic, Import Graphic, Place, or Import allows you to import graphics. Each program imports differently, but the technique is essentially the same. In some DTP programs, you place a graphics box where you want the picture to appear. In others, it appears with "handles" so you can position the graphic by dragging it to the correct location on the page.

When you select the appropriate menu command, a dialog box similar to the one shown in figure 8.14 opens, and you select the name of the item you wish to place. The program shown here, Personal Press, lets you see a preview of the graphic before you place it. This is convenient when you are selecting clip art and cannot remember the name of the picture you need.

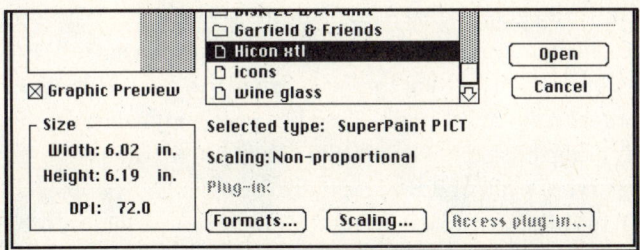

Chapter 8
Desktop Publishing Programs

Figure 8.14
Personal Press gives you a preview of your graphics placement.

After you click on the OK box, the dialog box disappears and either your pointer turns into a graphics placement cursor such as a paintbrush or pencil, or the graphic appears automatically, depending on the program. You can move the graphic, resize it, crop it, and, if your printing method and program allow, add color to it on the screen. To resize a graphic, drag its handles. In some DTP applications, you can precisely resize and/or reposition a graphic or text block by entering the desired measurements in a dialog box (see figure 8.15).

Figure 8.15

To resize an object in Publish It! Easy, enter different numbers in the boxes or drag the object handles.

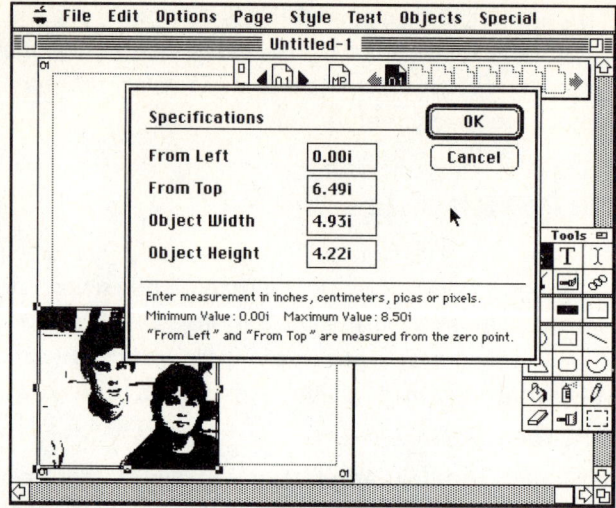

Creating Graphics Within the DTP Program

What do you call a graphic that is not imported—domestic? Whatever you choose to call them, you can create graphics from within most DTP programs, in addition to using graphics created in other programs. Lines and shapes are considered graphics just like photographs and drawings. Creatively using the shapes in the toolbox can sometimes substitute for returning to your paint or draw program to design a logo or other small graphic. It took less than two minutes to draw the universal accessibility logo shown in figure 8.16. The large circle was drawn first and a portion covered with a white square. Then the lines were added, followed by the small black circle.

Figure 8.16

You would not need to open your paint program to draw this symbol.

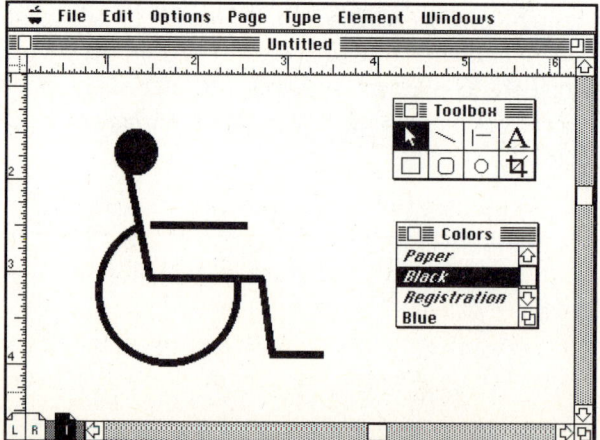

> **Note** The electronic white-out trick used to create figure 8.17 is very handy if you import a piece of clip art and cannot crop out a portion without losing a vital part of the picture. All you have to do is paste a white shape over the area you want to hide. (In programs such as PageMaker, which let you designate a background color other than white, you would choose a paper-colored shape.) Of course, the more objects you add to a page, the larger your file is and the longer it takes to print. It is always faster to delete unwanted elements instead of hiding them, but it is not always possible.

Placing Text

Placing text is similar to placing graphics. For example, in PageMaker, you select the Place… command to open a dialog box. Select the name of the file to import, and click the OK box. When you return to the page, your pointer becomes a text placement icon, which resembles a small piece of type rather than an arrow. Place it where you want the upper left corner of the text block, and click your mouse. Text flows directly into the column without exceeding the column's specified margins. This text flow stops at the bottom of the column where a marker indicates if there is remaining text to place. Click on the marker and repeat the process. Text placed this way is said to be threaded. (Some programs refer to it as chained or linked.) You can add text to an existing thread, or break the thread and start a new one.

PageMaker also offers automatic or semi-automatic placement in addition to the manual technique. Automatic placement of text, which PageMaker calls AutoFlow, is great to use when creating books or manuals where all the pages are the same. As the text flows through a page, it automatically creates as many pages as it needs.

If you use a word processing program which allows you to establish style sheets for your documents, such as Microsoft Word, you can import the formatted text and style sheet into several DTP programs. Style sheets determine the typographical format for the publication. A style sheet includes specific type styles for body text, headlines, subheads, and other styles; a typical style sheet is preset for these elements.

In addition to assigning type attributes, a style sheet can also include paragraph attributes: justification, tabs and indents, leading, paragraph spacing, boxed text, and so forth. Figure 8.17 shows PageMaker's style palette. Style names with asterisks are imported from the word processor file along with the text. These styles were created in Microsoft Word 5.1 and brought into PageMaker 5 along with the text, saving a great deal of layout time.

Chapter 8
Desktop Publishing Programs

Figure 8.17
PageMaker's imported styles are designated with an asterisk.

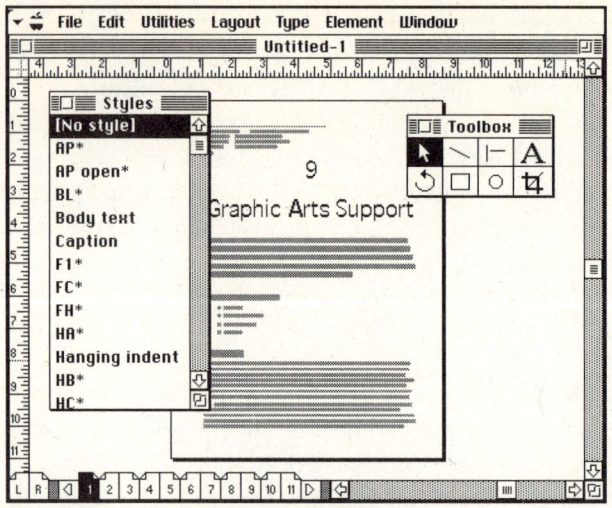

Several DTP programs allow you to import formatted text from older word processors (like WriteNow 2.2) that do not use style sheets, by assigning style-name tags as you create the document in the word processor. Create the appropriate styles in your DTP program using the same names as those used for styles in your word processor. When you import text with style name tags, the matching styles automatically are applied in your DTP program. PageMaker applies tags which are designated with angle brackets (<Style name>). Ventura Publisher only reads tags that are entered with a proceeding "@" symbol and followed by an equal sign (@ TAGNAME =).

You can also reformat text within a DTP application. One of the best features of desktop publishing is the typography control it provides. You can adjust the amount of space between lines and paragraphs, and between words and letters. Adjusting letter and word spacing is called tracking. Adjusting the white space between specific pairs of letters is called kerning. The combination of a DTP program and the Mac's WYSIWYG interface means you can line up type perfectly on the screen, kerning individual letters in your headlines by as much or as little as needed, and the printed result will look truly professional. Figure 8.18 shows kerned letters in Publish It! Easy; figure 8.19 demonstrates PageMaker's kerning capabilities.

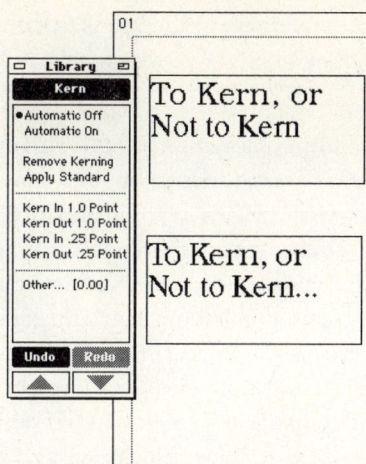

Figure 8.18
Publish It! Easy's letters can be kerned in .01 point increments.

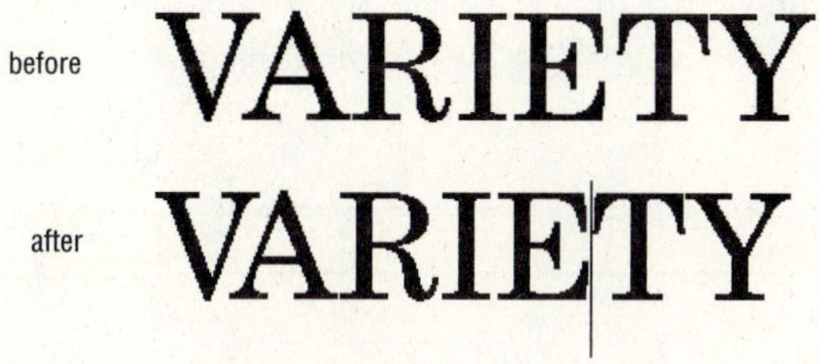

Figure 8.19
PageMaker's letters can be kerned in 1/25th or 1/100th of an em increments.

before VARIETY

after VARIETY

In most DTP programs, kerning is also done automatically by selecting **Pair Kerning** from a menu or dialog box. Kerning information, including which pairs of letters to kern, is included in the type font file. Frequently, though, the amount of kerning the type designer specifies is not quite enough in larger sizes, and many users prefer custom kerning. In some programs, you can change the kerning by as little as .004 inch.

Editing Text

All DTP programs recognize the need to enter new text and edit existing text. You can usually type directly into an existing text box and use standard editing methods such as cutting and pasting, just as you would with a word processor. Generally, if you are working on text which fills more than one linked column, changes made in one column are reflected in the others. When new text is added to the first column, the original lines flow to the second column. Removing text from the first column shortens the last column accordingly. If columns have not been linked, editing changes are not reflected throughout the story, so you may wish to link them for convenience.

PageMaker threads text and graphics automatically. This program uses links to maintain connections between stories and graphics imported into a PageMaker publication and the original text and picture files in the word processor. When you make changes in the original documents, the linked PageMaker versions can, at your option, be automatically updated to reflect those changes. If there is not enough room to add the new text to the column, PageMaker displays a symbol that indicates there is more text to place (Ventura Publisher also offers this feature). If you make changes in a text file and do not want to change the publication version, save the text file with a different name. Figure 8.20 shows PageMaker's Link dialog box. System 7's Publish and Subscribe feature does the same thing for other DTP programs. The advantage to using Links instead of Publish and Subscribe is that linked graphics can be stored outside of your publication, reducing the size of the file.

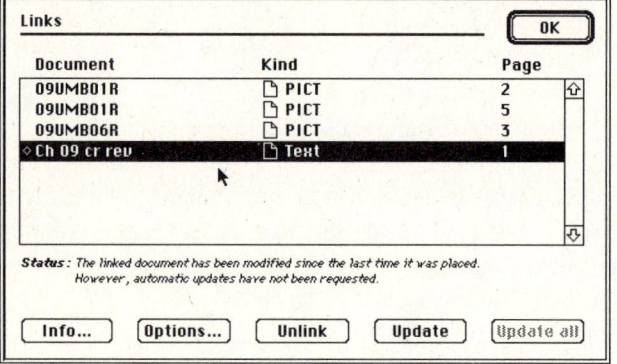

Figure 8.20
PageMaker links stories and graphics with their original sources.

Editing existing text and creating new text is easy in any DTP program. All include word processing features that enable you to write headlines and captions and make changes in imported stories. Many DTP programs include spelling dictionaries, and some even have a thesaurus to make writing easier. Figure 8.21 shows Publish It! Easy's Thesaurus Rex feature. Simply use the text cursor to highlight a word you want to replace, select Thesaurus from the Special menu, and choose a word from the list of synonyms the program supplies for the highlighted word.

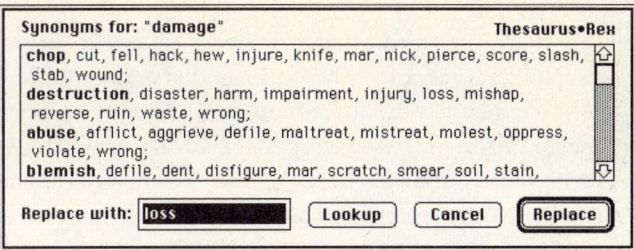

Figure 8.21
Thesauruses can help you find the perfect word.

Spelling checkers are a necessity for most DTP users because they often catch typing errors as well as misspellings. Some DTP programs check spelling in individual stories, while others check the entire publication. (If you have the latter, it may be faster to electronically check the spelling after you create each story in your word processing program. Use your DTP spelling checker to perform a final check before printing the publication.) Spelling checkers generally include a user dictionary that lets you add special words and jargon. In some programs, if you accept a word which the spelling checker considers misspelled, the word is automatically added to the user dictionary. In other programs, you must command the spelling dictionary to add the new word. Figure 8.22 shows Personal Press' spelling checker. Unlike other programs, PageMaker stories can only be spelling checked in the Story Editor window, not on the page view.

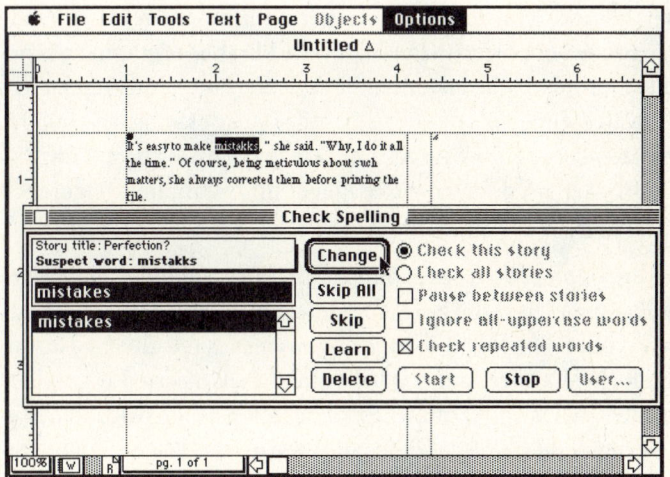

Figure 8.22
The spelling checker catches many mistakes which are often overlooked.

WARNING! There are some errors that a spelling checker will not catch. A spelling checker can only check whether or not your word is in the dictionary; it cannot tell you if you chose the correct word in the first place. For example, spelling checkers would accept the sentence "I grew old two soon and smart to late." You need a grammar checker such as Que Software's RightWriter to spot word-choice errors and grammar errors in your word processor files. To date, no DTP program includes a grammar checker, but current versions of most grammar checkers will check most DTP publications.

Working with Templates

A template is a predesigned publication. When you open a template, you actually open its copy; the original remains unchanged and can always be used again. Templates offer two benefits: They assure consistency in publications, and they save a great deal of time and effort in designing pages. When you use templates for publications which you revise or re-publish frequently, you avoid re-inventing the wheel each time, and spend more time focusing on the publication's contents.

You do not have to be a designer yourself to create great printed pieces. Most DTP programs include an assortment of predesigned templates for nearly any type of publication you desire. You may find still more templates included in clip-art packages or posted in the shareware libraries of graphic arts or publishing forums on the major online services. You can also create your own templates, either by modifying existing ones or saving your publication as a template through the Save As... option in the dialog box. With System 7, you can also save any document or page set-up as stationery. Figure 8.23 shows several ways to create a template.

You may encounter two types of templates, the placeholder and the grid. Placeholder templates which are commercially prepared (such as those which came with your DTP program), have dummy text called greeking inserted in the text blocks as a filler, and may have gray panels inserted as graphics placeholders. When you create a new publication from a placeholder template, highlight the placeholder and then use the Place... command (or its equivalent) from the menu to substitute your own text and graphics in that spot.

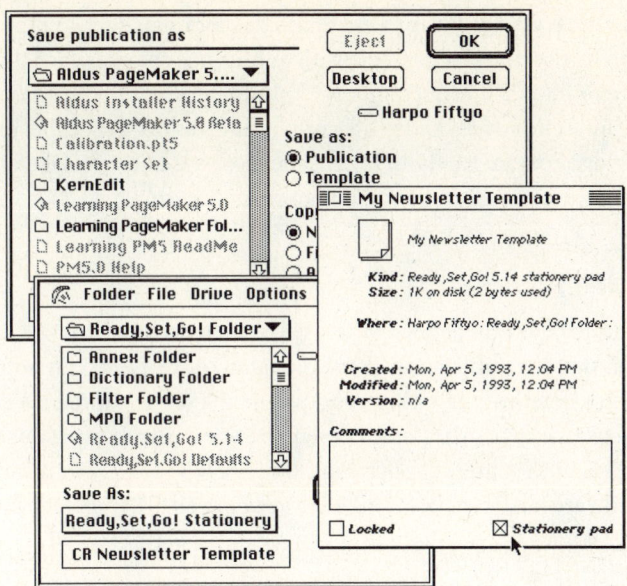

Figure 8.23
There are various ways to save your current publication design as a template.

Grid templates do not contain dummy text; they are simply layout grids on master pages to form a base for your own designs. Grid templates typically have ruler and column guides, page size, orientation, and a measurement system already assigned. They do not have style sheets attached, as placeholder templates do, because there is no text. Figure 8.24 shows samples of various DTP program templates in thumbnail form.

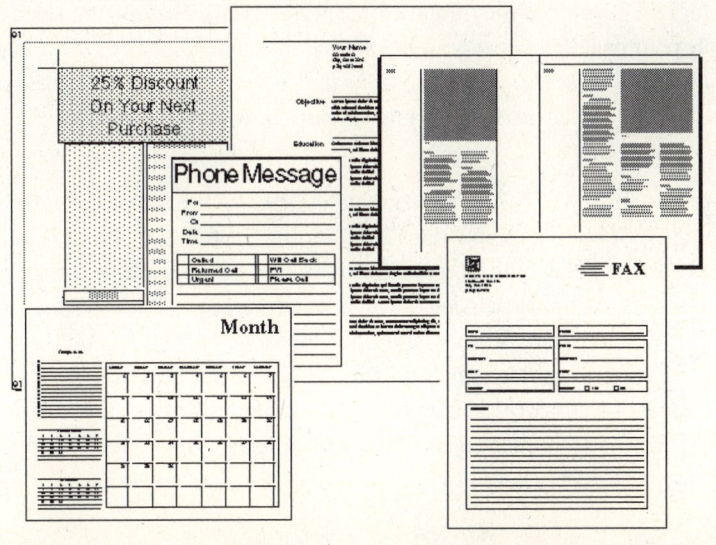

Figure 8.24
There are many templates available to make designing a publication a simple process.

Part II
What Put the Mac in Business

It makes a great deal of sense to use templates for items such as business cards which are created repeatedly with only minor changes each time. If you set up a template with your company logo and information, it is easy to add names of new employees and print cards as often as needed. Label templates let you design custom labels for precut sheets of self-adhesive labels. (See chapter 9, "Graphic Arts Support," for more information.)

Printing

After creating beautiful pages on the screen, what do you do next? Obviously, it depends on your publication's purpose. Many documents can simply be printed on a laser printer, either your own or at a service bureau. A laser-printed master copy can be photocopied, or inexpensively reproduced with adequate results for most applications. If only a few copies of a color publication are needed, a color inkjet printer like the HP550C can give you acceptable copies.

When better quality is needed, the next step is from the typical laser printer's 300 dpi resolution to the 1270 or 2540 dpi imagesetter output. Imagesetters are high-end laser printers that print on photographic paper, and they can be found at service bureaus and commercial printers. You can also use imagesetters to produce film negatives used to make metal plates for high quality printing and publishing jobs. When you use an imagesetter, you need to supply the printer with a list of all the fonts used, as well as the name and version number of your DTP program. You also need to include copies of any graphics files linked to the publication, such as TIFF files. You may need to supply your pages as a PostScript file if the fonts are unusual, or the typographic design is especially complicated. Always supply a laser-printed copy of the publication, so the service bureau knows the type of output to expect.

You can use the laser printer to produce separations for two-color "spot" printing. Spot-color page masters do not require color laser printers since they produce one black master for each spot color. Each master contains only the elements to print in that color. The printer photographs each spot-color master onto a separate printing plate and runs it with the colored ink you chose. Be sure to include registration marks on both the black and color pages. Imagesetters provide finer resolution for halftones, tints, and duotones, because an imagesetter uses the same process to produce spot-color separations as a laser does.

Chapter 8
Desktop Publishing Programs

Full color (more appropriately known as four-color) printing demands color-separated film negatives. You need to use either a separate color-separation program (such as Aldus PrePress) or Quark or PageMaker 5's built-in color separation functions. Color separations tend to be tricky, and most graphic arts professionals prefer to have a specialist do the separations.

Comparing Page Layout Programs

A glance through one software dealer's catalog reveals eight separate DTP programs, with prices ranging from about $100 (discounted) to over five times that price. How do you know which one to buy? It's somewhat like choosing a car. You wouldn't pick a Mercedes to haul your child's soccer team to the game, nor would you enter the family station wagon in the Indianapolis 500. You have to match the vehicle to the purpose—and the same principle holds with DTP programs

Usually the simplest programs to learn are also the least expensive; Ready, Set, Go! and Publish It! Easy are good examples in this category. Each offers enough flexibility to satisfy most casual page-processing needs. If you use desktop publishing to produce your club or local organization's newsletter, create simple business forms and posters, or send custom greeting cards to your friends, either program is sufficient.

A program such as Ventura Publisher is more difficult to master, and its powerful handling of tables and mathematical equations is probably unnecessary for casual users. On the other hand, if you need to produce a magazine, book, or a daily or weekly newspaper, you need PageMaker's flexibility and easily updated source materials. Your choice of program is also going to depend on how much memory you have available. A program like QuarkXPress or PageMaker 5 requires a lot of memory, in fact if you have 5M or less, you may not be able to open it at all. The following programs are listed in order by approximate cost.

Publish It! Easy

Publish It! Easy has been dubbed the Swiss army knife of DTP programs because it contains a paint program, a word processor with a built-in spelling dictionary, and a 240,000-word thesaurus. It includes many of the features of its big brother, Publish It! (which is not reviewed here), and adds a few extras. Multiple levels of Undo commands let you experiment and remove up to five levels of changes. Easy's thumbnail views are editable, so you can design entire pages and multiple-page spreads... if you have good eyesight!

After you create a set of pages in Publish It! Easy, you can use the pages as an onscreen slide show for a desktop presentation, and print audience handouts from the same source. It even has a built-in database and mail merge function so you can edit, search, and sort files as well as create customized form letters without leaving the program. Easy's handling of grayscale images is remarkable. You have full control over contrast and brightness through an easy-to-use dialog box with built-in help.

However, you cannot manage long documents in this program, because Easy is limited to 100 pages per publication; nor can you use style sheets or non-standard page sizes. Easy is also limited to eight colors (including black and white). Spot-color overlays are possible, but difficult to produce compared to other programs. Despite these limitations, Easy is a good choice for the casual user. It runs well on the Macintosh Classic, Plus, and LC (as well as the more powerful Macs), and uses only one megabyte of memory. It is System 7 friendly, too.

ReadySetGo

ReadySetGo originally came from Letraset, a well-known name in graphic arts; the Letraset people pioneered rub-down lettering and graphics for paste-up nearly 40 years ago. RSG's current release, 5.14, has added full color and grayscale. It handles word processing functions well—its spelling dictionary is one of the best among DTP programs. RSG offers global search and replace—a standard word processing feature—and adds global font, style, and size changes so it can search and replace on type specifications as well as words. Automatic or manual hyphenation and kerning give you excellent control over justified type and headlines. Page capacity is unlimited, so you can typeset your novel as well as your business cards.

Personal Press

Since Aldus acquired Silicon Beach Software, Personal Press has been re-issued under the Aldus Personal Press banner. It is a powerful program with enough features to satisfy many professional users' needs. Its AutoCreate feature allows even beginners to produce professionally designed newsletters, calendars, business letterheads, forms, birthday cards, and award certificates by simply replacing placeholders with their own text and graphics. Personal Press also lets you freely rotate both text and graphics in any direction either manually or by entering a specific number of degrees in the dialog box.

Instead of storing items in the pasteboard as other DTP programs do, Personal Press offers its Workbook feature. Text and images placed in the workbook but not pasted into a publication are stored as Workbook pages with the publication.

Another of Personal Press' unique features is its ability to preview and precrop a graphic before you place it in the document. To frequent users of clip art files, this feature alone may be worth the price of the program. It also has built-in dictionary and thesaurus functions and supports 256-color graphics on a Mac SE/30 or Mac II. You can assign spot colors on a black and white Mac, but you cannot preview them. The grayscale and image controls, while not as versatile as those in a darkroom program, enable you to adjust brightness and contrast, and change values to create interesting special effects. The advanced halftone option produces fine detail and an expanded tonal range on both non-PostScript laser printers and ImageWriter. Of course, it does a good job of printing standard halftones on PostScript printers and imagesetters, too. As with ReadySetGo!, your document length is limited only by the available memory.

Ventura Publisher

A product of the Xerox Corporation, Ventura Publisher was first developed for the IBM PC; it was released for the Mac in 1990. Because it started as an IBM program, Ventura does not "think" the same way Mac standards PageMaker and QuarkXPress do. More text-based than Mac object-oriented programs, Ventura relies on style sheets and tags for virtually all its formatting. Text and graphics are not imported into Ventura but are "hot-linked" to it. Unlike PageMaker, which copies files, checks the copy against the original, and asks if you want to update, Ventura automatically changes the original. If you import a text file into Ventura and save the publication, you have completely altered the original document. All of your formatting disappears, replaced with Ventura's codes and tags.

Ventura is complicated, and because it was not originally designed for a Mac, it is hard to learn. Unfortunately, the manuals are not much help; they are technically oriented and poorly indexed. For example, there are no index entries for PostScript, filters, grayscale, TIFF, or even import or export. The documentation also includes two separate sets of technical notes, both titled "Read Me First."

Ventura does feature a built-in table editor which is easily accessed from the tool palette. PageMaker offers a table editor as a separate program which comes with the package, and has a somewhat complicated system for importing a table into a publication. Ventura's table set-up is similar to PageMaker's, but once you create a table in Ventura, you do not have to save the table and then import it into the publication.

Many scientists and mathematicians (and their publishers) prefer Ventura because it has a built-in equation editor. No other DTP program handles complicated mathematical formulas as easily. However, Ventura's equation editor is far from simple. Its language is completely different from that of Excel and other well-known spreadsheet programs. Once mastered, though, you can create dazzling arrays of numbers and symbols.

PageMaker

As noted earlier, PageMaker was the first DTP application. It remains far and away the most popular, having captured over 75 percent of the DTP market. The reasons are many. PageMaker closely simulates the "real world" paste-up analogy and Mac interface concepts. You place text in blocks on the page exactly as if you had cut them from a galley of type. You can also maneuver graphics and pictures on the page. When you draw a box around a picture, the box stays in place if you move the picture. Objects are arranged and resized using the mouse, and you can place objects anywhere, including the pasteboard. Column guides and margins guide rather than limit you.

You can edit text in PageMaker in either the page view or the story editor. However, you can use the spelling checker only in the story editor. PageMaker does not include a thesaurus, but it does include some of the best predesigned templates available anywhere. The corporate report and catalog templates do credit to any upscale business. With PageMaker, you have the option to update files placed into PageMaker publications, as previously noted. This feature is especially handy for publications such as price lists which must be frequently updated. It accepts text from all types of word processors, including non-Macintosh computers. PageMaker can also open and work on PC PageMaker files.

PageMaker outdoes every other DTP program in its ability to generate indexes and tables of contents. This feature makes it the program of choice for many book, catalog, and manual publishers. (This book, incidentally, was produced with PageMaker.) It keeps a list of chapters or individual publications in a book, and assembles and prints them in order, numbering pages to 9,999. A single publication can have up to 999 pages.

Version 5.0 of PageMaker, released in August 1993, addressed many users' complaints. One of the major improvements is the capability to produce 4-color separations from within PageMaker. (Previously, documents had to be exported to another application—Aldus PrePrint—to create separations.) Aldus also added text rotation, multiple open document, and faster printing capabilities.

PageMaker's tools and menus are easy to use, and an excellent system of help screens is always available. If you are serious about desktop publishing, this is an application worth considering.

QuarkXPress

PageMaker and QuarkXPress are twins in many ways. Both allow you to work on a pasteboard and drag temporarily unwanted items to the side. Quark, however, does not consider the pasteboard to be a drawing table top as PageMaker does. When you change pages in PageMaker, items on the pasteboard remain there. Quark's pasteboard more closely resembles large sheets of paper to flip. As you flip pages, the items stay with their associated page. To get around this possible drawback, Quark has added a Library file that lets you store up to 2,000 elements, then drag or cut and paste them into your publication at any time. Unlike PageMaker, Quark requires you to create boxes for all elements before you place them.

Quark boasts powerful type-handling features, including the ability to create automatic drop caps of any size by specifying which characters to drop and the number of lines to drop them. Text within its own text box can be justified vertically or horizontally by adding or deleting space between paragraphs to make the lines fit the box. Although Quark has a good spelling checker, editing can be awkward since you cannot scroll through a document. Quark lacks the indexing and table of contents generation features that PageMaker offers but atones for that with improved graphics capabilities. Quark can also produce full-color separations easily. If you do a great deal of full-color work (i.e. magazine rather than book publishing), choose Quark. If you like to design pages as you go, PageMaker is the more flexible choice.

Summary

Desktop publishing uses a page layout program to combine elements from other applications into a single or multi-page document. By combining text from your word processor, charts and graphs from a database or spreadsheet, and graphics from draw or paint programs, you can assemble anything from a one-page flyer to a thousand-page book. Page layout programs enable you to design master pages and import data into them in large sections, or treat an individual page as an electronic scratch pad, moving elements and experimenting with different type styles and arrangements.

Desktop publishing saves time and money, is highly effective, and gives you control of the process. It is available to everyone who has access to a Mac and the appropriate applications. You do not even need to own a laser printer to take advantage of DTP since you can send your finished files to a service bureau for high-quality imagesetting.

Now there is no technical reason why your newsletter cannot look every bit as professional as the magazines at the newsstand or the books on your coffee table. Many businesses have turned to in-house DTP as a way of producing the documents they need, from letterheads and forms to annual reports and advertising materials. There are DTP applications to handle any task, from the simplest to the most complex.

Interlude 8
Cool PageMaker Stuff

Now that you know a little bit about desktop publishing, some specific advice might come in handy. Here are some tips for PageMaker—just about the most widely used page layout program. This section won't tell you how to use PageMaker; it will explain

In This Interlude:
▼ Master Pages
▼ Placing
▼ Styles
▼ Buried Treasures

Make that "almost anything." It depends on how acrobatic you are.

Christian Boyce

some of PageMaker's more interesting features. Even if you don't use PageMaker, this chapter will give you an idea of some of the useful features of page layout programs—features that are often forgotten. If you do use PageMaker, this chapter will explain some features that you shouldn't do without!

PageMaker

Aldus' PageMaker is a desktop publishing program. It enables you to assemble complex pages using other documents as components. In effect, PageMaker is an electronic pasteboard; anything possible on a real pasteboard is possible on PageMaker's electronic one.

PageMaker hasn't changed much since its introduction in 1985. The interface (a pasteboard with a document on it, eight simple tools, and a full-page view), fortunately, hasn't been "improved" at all; Aldus has left well enough alone. Figure 8.25 shows the famous interface.

Figure 8.25

The PageMaker interface.

 The tips mentioned in this interlude are based on PageMaker 4.2, however, PageMaker 5.0 was released in August, 1993. Most of these tips should apply to PageMaker 5.0 as well, but there will be some differences, too. Many of these tips are not applicable to versions of PageMaker earlier than 4.2; in particular, many of these features were not available until version 4.0.

PageMaker lets you combine things created in other programs into better-looking, more professional-looking documents. You can combine text from Word and charts from Excel, for example, to create good-looking documents like figure 8.26. Naturally you can include elements from other programs if you want to.

Note: PageMaker uses a technique called *greeking* to speed itself up. Rather than draw every character on the screen, PageMaker "greeks" small text sizes, representing slow-to-display characters with fast-to-display gray bars. Many of the illustrations in this chapter include greeked text.

You control the "greeking threshold" from the **Preferences** dialog box, accessed from the **Edit** menu. Figure 8.27 shows a document with greeked text; figure 8.28 shows the same document, without the greeking. The greeked text displayed about twice as fast as the non-greekedtext in this document.

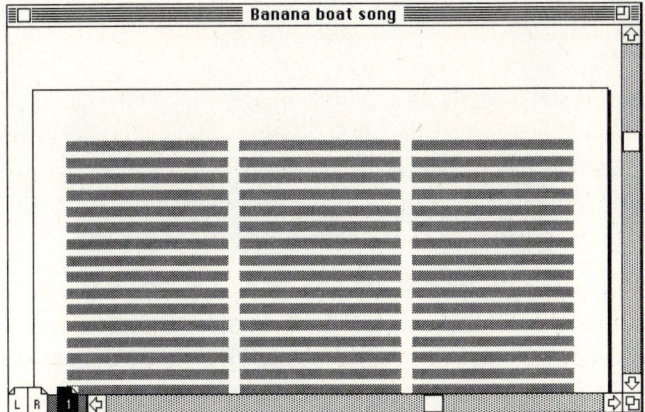

PageMaker is useful even when you use it wrong; that's how good a program it is. Used right, though, PageMaker helps you make gorgeous documents and it helps you make them in a hurry. Three cool PageMaker features—Master Pages, Placing, and Styles help you do things right.

Interlude 8
Cool PageMaker Stuff

Figure 8.26
A good-looking document.

Figure 8.27
Greeked text.

I'm using PageMaker 4.2, but nearly everything I do in this chapter looks and works the same way in PageMaker 4.0 (and 3.0, for that matter). I'll let you know if something is wildly different in the older versions.

Christian Boyce

Part II
What Put the
Mac in Business

Master Pages

A house built on a weak foundation is a bad idea—ask Harry Belafonte. Master pages are the foundation of PageMaker documents; the stronger your master pages, the better your PageMaker documents.

Figure 8.28
Non-greeked text.

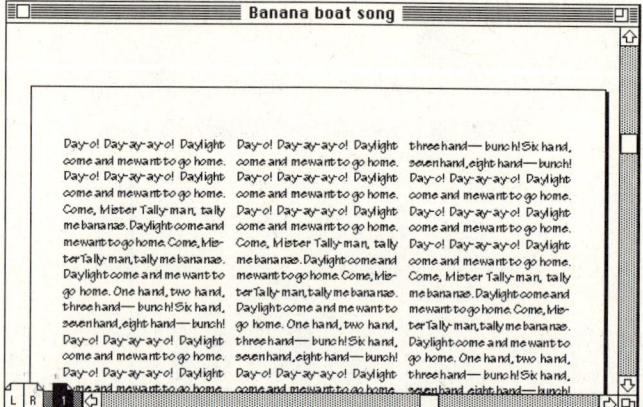

Master pages provide structure for PageMaker pages. Master pages sit underneath your "real" pages; they hold pictures and text you want on every page, and guidelines for columns. Think of master pages as stationery with column guides and you won't be off by much.

 You don't have to use master pages at all. However, if you're planning a multi-page document, plan on using master pages. You'll save time and you'll make a better document.

PageMaker lets you define left-hand master pages differently than right-hand ones. Books and magazines often use left- and right-hand master pages that are near-mirror images of each other; figure 8.29 shows how a master page might look for a left-hand page, and figure 8.30 shows its near-mirror image right-hand page. Figure 8.31 shows both, with greeked text.

The master pages in figures 8.29, 8.30, and 8.31 include column guides and static text, two common master page elements. With these masters in place, every left-hand page begins life with a narrow left-hand column, a wide right-hand column, "The Macintosh Handbook for Beautiful People" left-justified across the top, and "Chapter 1" in the left margin. Every right-hand page starts out with a narrow right-hand column, a wide left-hand column, "The Macintosh Handbook for Beautiful People" right-justified across the top, and "Chapter 1" in the right margin.

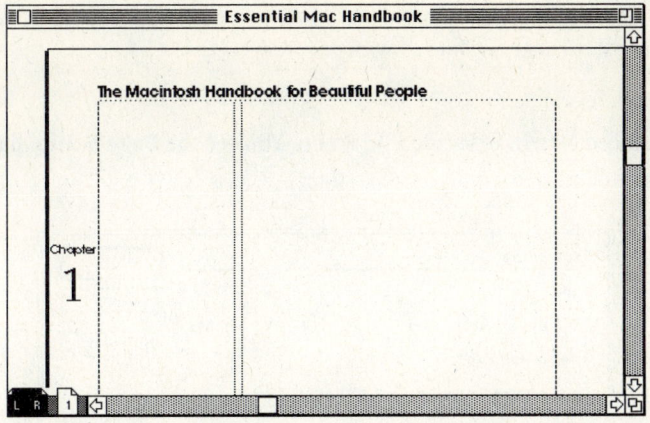

Figure 8.29
Left-hand master page.

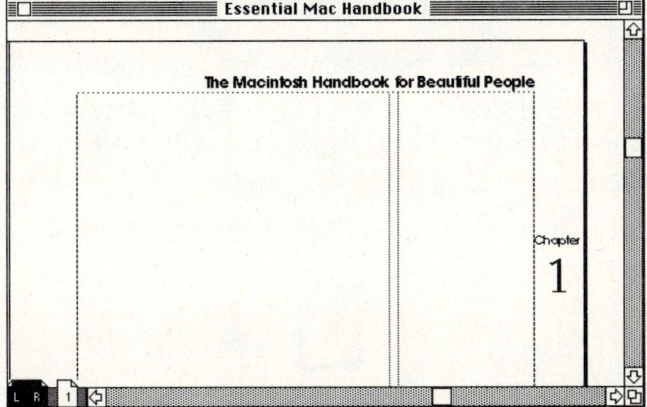

Figure 8.30
Near-mirror image right-hand master page.

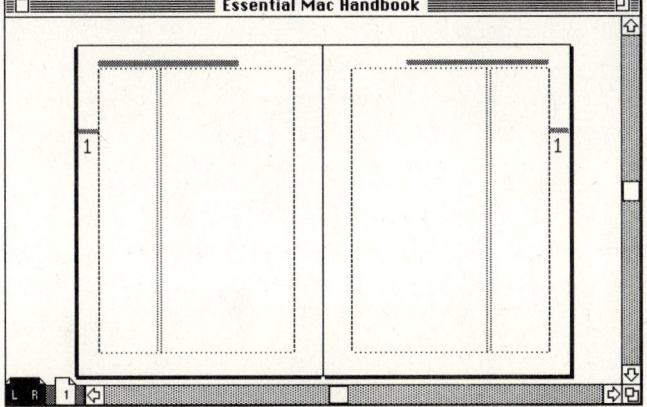

Figure 8.31
Left- and right-hand master pages.

Setting up a master page is easy. You'll make a three-column master page, with some static text, in the following exercise.

1. Start PageMaker.
2. Choose **New...** from the **File** menu. You see the **Page Setup** dialog box of figure 8.32.

Figure 8.32
Page Setup dialog box.

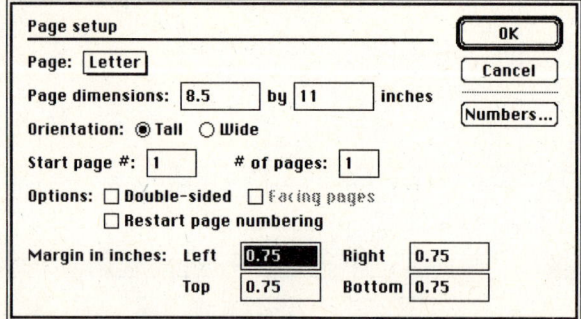

3. Choose the options shown in figure 8.32. You're making a single-sided document with three-quarter inch margins all the way around.
4. Click **OK**.
5. Click on the master page icon. Figure 8.33 shows the master page icon.

Figure 8.33
Master page icon.

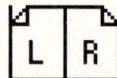

> **Note:** Had you chosen **Double sided** and **Facing Pages** in the **Page Setup** dialog box, you'd have the option to set up left- and right-hand master pages. In that case, the master page icon would look like figure 8.34.

Figure 8.34
Double master page icon.

6. You'll set up the columns first. Choose **Column guides...** from the **Options** menu. Figure 8.35 shows the **Column guides** dialog box.

Figure 8.35
Column guides dialog box.

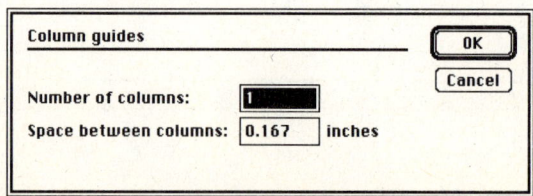

7. Ask for **3** columns and click **OK**.

That's all there is to setting up columns. Your screen looks like figure 8.36.

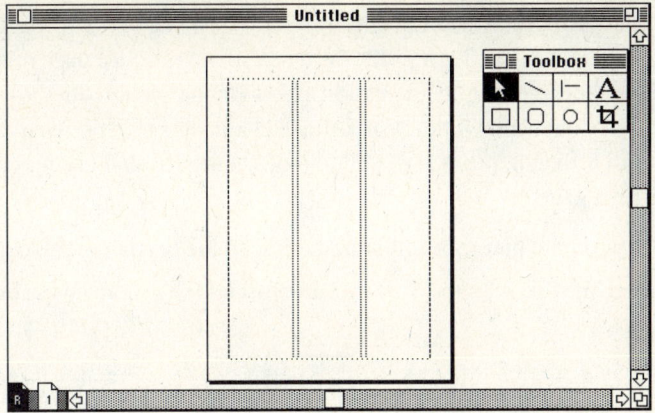

Figure 8.36

Master page with three columns.

PageMaker assumes you want each column to be the same width. You can change the width of any column by dragging the column's guide on the master page.

Now add some static text.

1. Select the Text tool.

A Closer Look You can choose tools from the keyboard if your keyboard has function keys. Shift-F1 selects the Pointer tool, Shift-F2 selects the Line tool, Shift-F3 selects the Perpendicular line tool, and Shift-F4 selects the Text tool. Shift-F5, Shift-F6, Shift-F7, and Shift-F8 select the Box tool, the Rounded-corner box too, the Oval tool, and the Cropping tool, respectively.

2. Click anywhere on the pasteboard.
3. Type a couple of words (how about `Annual Report`?) If the text is too small to see, zoom in by choosing **Actual size** from the **Page** menu. You may need to scroll around a bit to find your place after zooming.
4. Select the Pointer tool and drag the text to the top of the page.
5. Save your work (call it `Practice`).

Your screen looks something like figure 8.37. If you zoomed in, your screen looks like figure 8.38.

That's about it for master pages, except for one thing: page numbers. The next example shows how to add automatic page numbers to master pages. Yup, they're automatic, and nope, you'd never figure this one out by looking at the menus.

1. Select the Text tool.

Part II
What Put the Mac in Business

2. Click anywhere on the pasteboard.
3. Press and hold the Command and Option keys while typing P.

A Closer Look The text reads "RM" which means this page is the Right Master. The text will automatically read "1" on page 1, "2" on page 2, and so on. Typing "RM" yourself won't produce page numbers; only the magic Command-Option-P combination does it. Think of Command-Option-P as a single character (which is what it really is). You can format it, put it in the middle of a sentence, and use it as often as you like on a page.

4. Select the Pointer tool and drag the text to the bottom of the page.
5. Select the text with the Text tool and format the text any way you want.

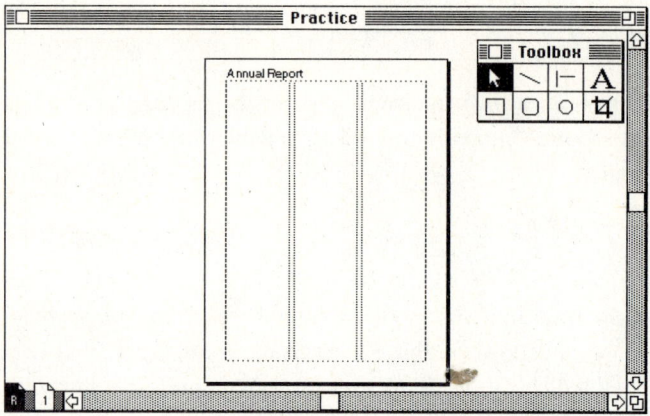

Figure 8.37
Master page with column guides and text.

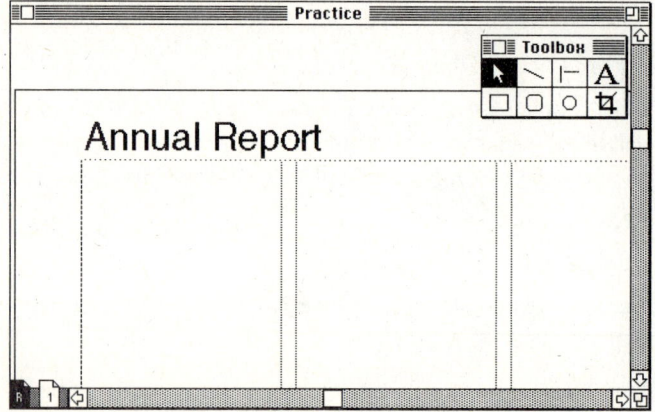

Figure 8.38
Master page with column guides and text (zoomed).

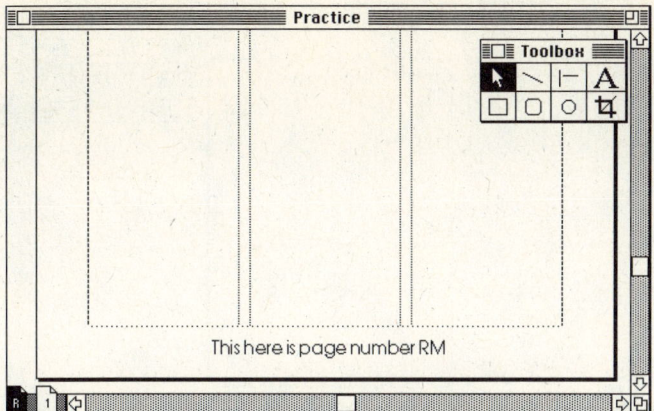

Figure 8.39

One way to format a page number.

You don't have to number pages with Arabic numerals if you don't want to. PageMaker gives you several numbering choices; figure 8.40 shows the **Page numbering** dialog box and its options. You access the Page numbering dialog box by clicking the **Numbers**… button in the **Page setup** dialog box.

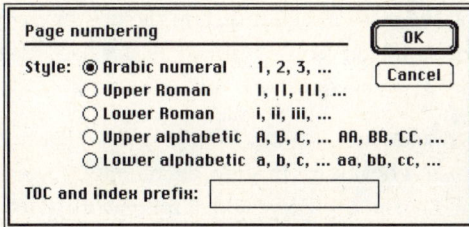

Figure 8.40

Page numbering dialog box.

You can add graphics (logos, lines, whatever) to your master page the same way you added text: create a graphic and drag it to position. I won't put you through an example, but you ought to try it on your own.

You've created a master page with three columns, some text across the top, and an automatic page number. Now you'll use the master page as a starting point for some "real" pages.

1. Click on the **Page 1** icon (it's to the right of the master page icon).
2. Choose **Fit in window** from the **Page** menu.

Your screen looks like figure 8.41.

Figure 8.41
New page, with master items showing.

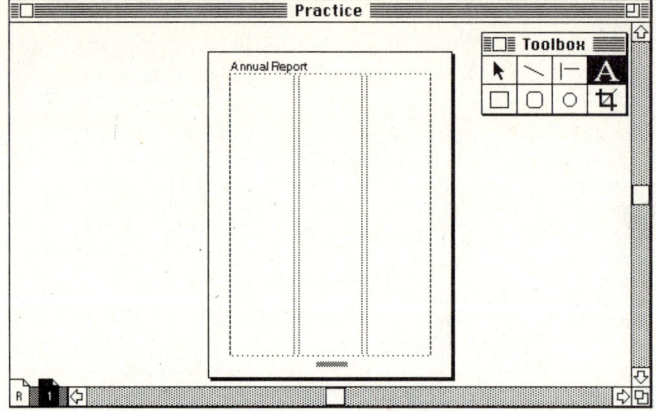

Master pages exist in their own layer, underneath the "real" page layer. The layers don't mix; it's as if there's a piece of glass between them. You can't touch master page items while in the page layer, and vice versa (try it). You can change the column guides on a given page, but that doesn't change the master settings; you'll affect only the guides of the page you're on. If you really want to change items on the master page, switch to the master page layer by clicking the master page icon. You can adjust master pages any time; you don't have to do it before creating "real" pages.

Every page in this document starts out like figure 8.41. Setting up a master page gives every page a headstart. In short documents, master pages give you frameworks to build upon, and keeping that framework in its own layer keeps you from lousing it up while "improving" things. In long documents, master pages give your document consistency and they save you heaps of time. It's great to know that every page you add to a document will have the right number of columns, the right text at the top, the page number in the right place (and in the right font), and so on. It's also great to know that you can change the way "Annual Report" looks on every page simply by changing the master.

Convinced that the master page concept is the key to wealth and a flat stomach? Good. Now you'll learn how to override master page settings for those special occasions when you really have to do it.

Your Practice document is just one page long. Let's add a couple of pages before continuing.

1. Choose **Insert pages...** from the **Page** menu. You see the **Insert pages** dialog box of figure 8.42.

2. Ask for 3 pages (after the current page) and click **OK**.

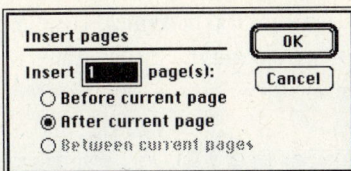

Figure 8.42
Insert pages dialog box.

Your screen looks like figure 8.43. Click on the numbered page icons to see if your new pages include the master page settings. They'd better.

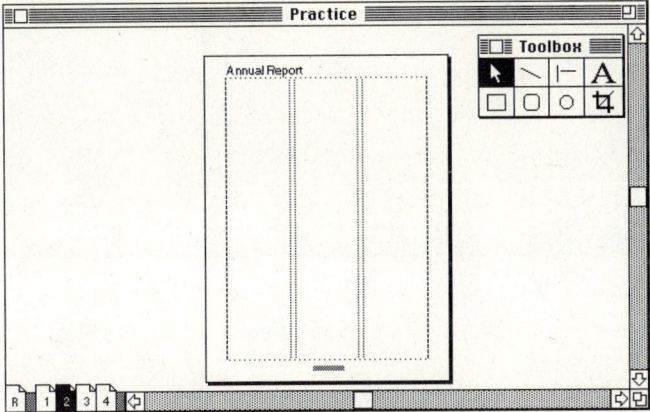

Figure 8.43
Four page document.

If this were a real annual report, you'd want the first page (the cover) to look different from the other pages (you don't usually put page numbers on covers, and you'd want the cover to look different altogether). This isn't a problem. It's easy to override master page settings, as you'll soon see.

1. Go to the first page (click on the Page 1 icon).
2. Choose **Column guides...** from the **Options** menu.
3. Ask for 1 column and say **OK**.
4. Uncheck **Display master items** from the **Page** menu.

Your screen looks like figure 8.44. The first page is a one-column blank piece of paper. Flip through the other pages and convince yourself that what you did on page 1 didn't affect pages 2, 3, or 4. See? Turning off the master page items on page 1 doesn't turn them off for the whole document.

You can do anything you want with the cover; figure 8.45 shows one example.

When you check **Display master items** PageMaker displays all the master items. When you uncheck **Display master items**, PageMaker hides all the master items. You can't tell PageMaker to show some of the master page

If I were King, you'd select "Show master page items under this page" and "Hide master page items under this page" instead of checking and unchecking "Display master items." I hope someone on the Page-Maker team reads this.

Christian Boyce

items and hide the rest, which is too bad since sometimes that's exactly what you want to do. You can get around the problem two ways (but I only recommend one of them).

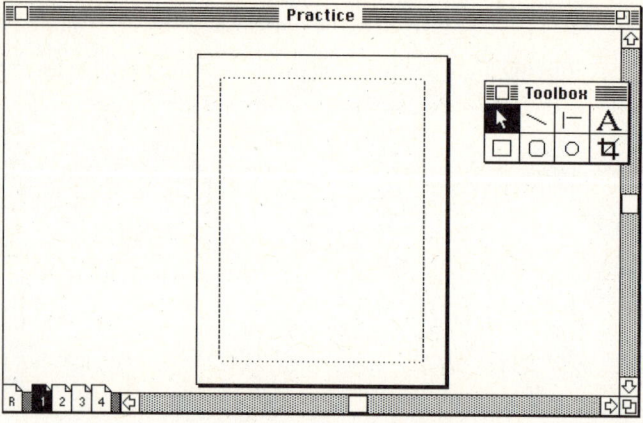

Figure 8.44

Blank first page, no master items.

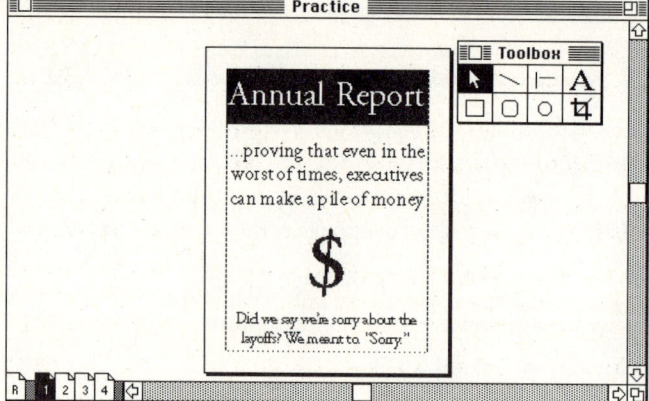

Figure 8.45

Annual report cover.

The obvious way to hide a master item is to cover it with a white box. It's a simple matter of drawing a box, making it white, and dragging it into place. This is the "White-Out" method.

1. Choose the Box tool.

PageMaker calls the Box tool the "square corner tool." Nobody else does.

2. Draw a box big enough to cover up the page number. Figure 8.46 shows a box about the right size.

3. Select the box if it isn't already selected.

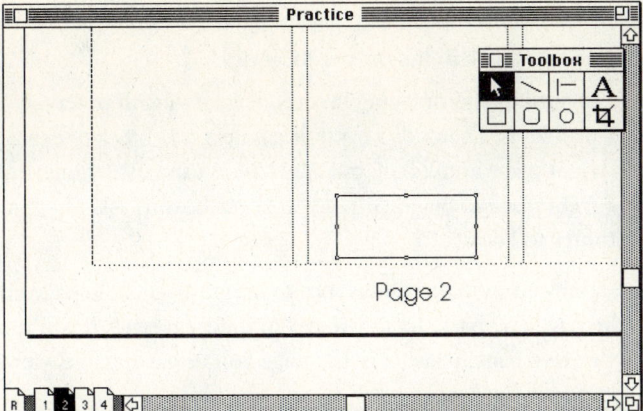

Figure 8.46
A box about the right size.

4. Fill the box with "Paper".

A box filled with "Paper" is not the same as a box filled with "None." "Paper" is opaque. "None" is transparent.

5. Drag the box over the page number.
6. Give the box a line of "None".

Just like that, you've hidden the page number. And just like that, you've done a Bad Thing.

The White-Out method leads to documents that are harder to edit and harder to print. They're harder to edit because invisible boxes are easy to forget. They're harder to print because your printer has to figure out how to print the invisible box *and* how to print the master page item before figuring out that the former covers the latter. This needlessly clogs your printer's memory and may in fact keep the page from printing. Take my advice and avoid the White-Out method, no matter what.

The right way to include a subset of master page items involves copying the items from the master page itself and pasting them onto the page you're working on. Uncheck **Display master items** and there you are. Let's try it.

1. Delete the white box you made in the previous example.
2. Click on the master page icon.
3. Select the **Annual Report** text block.
4. Copy it.
5. Switch back to page 2.
6. Uncheck **Display master items**. The master page items disappear (for this page only).

7. Paste the text block.

8. Drag the text block to the proper location.

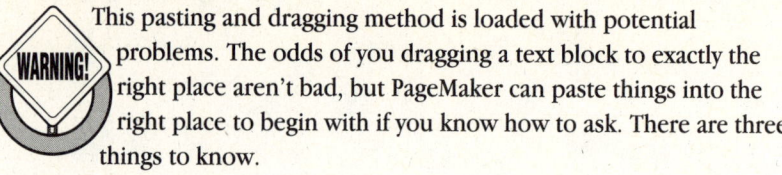 This pasting and dragging method is loaded with potential problems. The odds of you dragging a text block to exactly the right place aren't bad, but PageMaker can paste things into the right place to begin with if you know how to ask. There are three things to know.

First, PageMaker cannot paste things into the right place if the page you copy from and the page you paste to are viewed at different sizes. If you're copying from an Actual size page, make sure the page you're pasting to is viewed in Actual size before you paste.

Second, PageMaker wants you to see what you've pasted, so it won't paste off the screen if it can help it. If you copy something from the bottom of a master page, and you want it to be pasted to the bottom of a real page, be sure the bottom of the real page is showing before you paste.

Third, PageMaker only pastes into the right place if you hold the Option key while you paste. It doesn't matter whether you paste using the mouse and the menu or using Command-V: hold the Option key down before you paste and PageMaker will paste the item in exactly the right place.

That's it. You know everything there is to know about master pages. You know about creating columns, and adding text, and adding graphics, and adding automatic page numbers. You know how to override the master completely, and you know how to override the master partially.

Laying out each page individually (but identically) is silly. Use master pages to give your documents structure and you'll produce consistent documents quickly. Of course, master pages are just the foundation. You still need to build the rest of your document. The next section, Placing, will help you do that.

Placing

You can create a document entirely within PageMaker, but that's doing it the hard way. Typing in PageMaker is slow, and PageMaker doesn't have the features most word processors have. For example, you can't open more than one document at a time with PageMaker, and there's no text ruler to help you lay things out. PageMaker doesn't compare well with graphics programs either; you can't rotate graphics with PageMaker, and PageMaker's tools are very basic. Do your typing with a word processor, and do your graphics with a graphics program. Then use PageMaker to bring it all together.

You bring things into PageMaker by placing them. Placing offers substantially more control than copying and pasting, and it's faster (you don't have to leave PageMaker to do it). PageMaker's **Place**… command lets you import text documents, graphics documents, and the Scrapbook. You'll learn about placing text first.

You'll need a couple of pages of text for the next exercise. Do what I did: start your word processor, type a couple of sentences, copy them all, click at the end of the document, and paste, paste, paste. The typical word processor lets you paste as many times as you want from a single Copy; check it out. Save your word processing document with a good name (I used "Stuff to place"), then come back to your Practice PageMaker document.

Placing Text

Assuming you've created a couple of pages of text in a word processor, and assuming that you've opened your Practice PageMaker document, let's move ahead with that Annual Report. Start by bringing in the text.

1. Choose **Place**… from the **File** menu. You get the **Place** dialog box of figure 8.47.

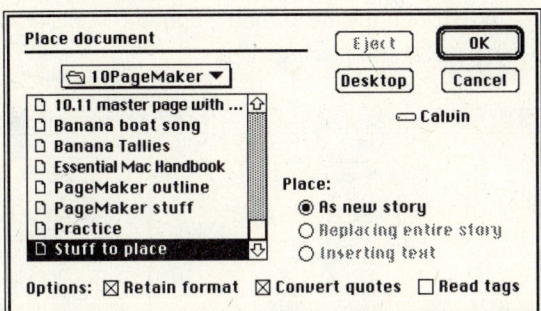

2. Select your text file (the one you made with your word processor) and click **OK**. Your cursor looks like figure 8.48. Text is "loaded" on the cursor and PageMaker is ready for you to place it somewhere, like maybe page 2.

Interlude 8
Cool PageMaker Stuff

Figure 8.47
Place dialog box.

 PageMaker calls the text file a "story."

Figure 8.48
Loaded cursor, ready to autoflow.

3. Click on the page 2 icon.
4. Choose **Fit in window** from the **Page** menu. It's not critical that you see the entire page, but it's more fun when you do.
5. Turn on the **Autoflow** option (put a check next to it) in the **Options** menu. There's no easier way to pour text into columns. The **Autoflow** option tells PageMaker to fill each column with text, adding pages as necessary.

The cursor looks like a piece of a page with text on it when Autoflow is turned off. PageMaker uses several different cursors to tell you what's going on.

6. Click in the upper left-hand corner of the first column and watch the fun!
7. Save your document.

If your text document didn't fit in a single column, PageMaker automatically flowed it into the second column, and the third, and so on. If your PageMaker document wasn't long enough to hold all the text, PageMaker added pages to make room. It's the Autoflow option that makes this happen. Figure 8.49 shows page 2 after placing the text.

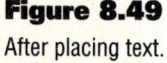

Figure 8.49
After placing text.

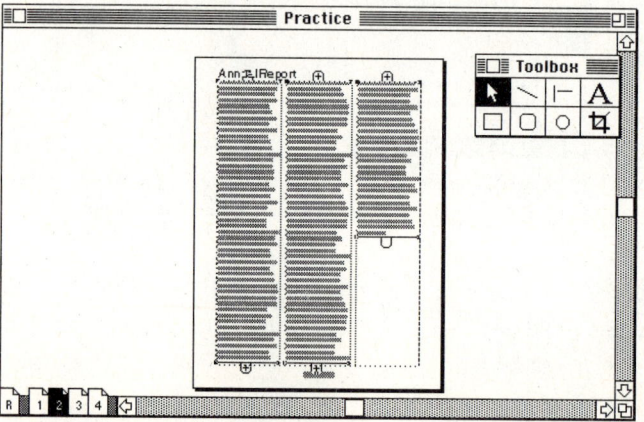

The columns ("text blocks," in the jargon) are connected. Add some text to the first column (type a couple of lines) and PageMaker squishes things around, through the second column and into the third. You simply have to try this. Once you've seen it, you'll believe it. If your screen looks like figure 8.25 and you type ten new lines in the first column, your third column will grow by (guess!) ten lines. The columns stay connected unless you work at disconnecting them. Nine times out of ten you'll want to keep them connected.

Sometimes you'll want to start a story on one page and finish it several pages later. Magazines and newspapers do this to us all the time. PageMaker lets you do this too; all you have to do is turn Autoflow off.

First get rid of the story you just placed. It was just practice, anyway. As usual, there's a boring way and an unbelievably cool way to delete all that text. I'll skip the boring way.

Remember, the text blocks you placed are connected to each other. You can take advantage of this to speed up deleting the whole story.

1. Select the text tool.
2. Click in any part of the story.
3. Choose **Select all** from the **Edit** menu. Every part of the story is selected, not just the part in the block where the cursor is.
4. Press Delete.
5. Save your document.

Now place again, but this time be sure Autoflow is not checked. You know the steps, but I'll provide them (briefly) below.

1. **Place...** (**File** menu).
2. Choose your file, click **OK**. Your cursor looks like Figure 8.50.

3. Click in the upper left-hand corner of the first column of page 2.

   Text fills the first column and stops. Continue this story on page 4, and let it flow automatically from that point.

4. Click the triangle at the bottom of the first column (you may need to click on the column first; it depends on what you've been up to between steps 3 and 4).

   The triangle indicates more story yet to place. Clicking the triangle loads your cursor with what's left of the story.

Interlude 8
Cool PageMaker Stuff

PageMaker calls this "Manual flow." Hmm.

Christian Boyce

Figure 8.50
Loaded cursor, ready to flow manually.

Part II
What Put the Mac in Business

 Holding the Command key changes the cursor from Manual Flow to Autoflow. Try it. It's perfectly OK to start placing text manually and switch to Autoflow mid-stream, so do it if you want to.

5. Click on the page 4 icon.
6. Choose **Fit in window**.
7. Hold the Command key and click in the first column of page 4.

   The rest of the story is placed.

Being able to start a story on one page and finish it a few (or many) pages later is useful. However, this "click on the triangle at the end of the first column" business is awkward. It would be nice to simply click where you want the story to start and to click again where you wanted it to continue. Guess what? You can do that. The technique, a cross between Autoflow and Manual Flow, is called "Semi-autoflow." Another good name!

There's no semi-autoflow option in the menus, but don't let that stop you. Just hold the Shift key while placing; your cursor stays loaded until all the text is placed. Figure 8.51 shows the semi-autoflow cursor.

Figure 8.51
Loaded cursor, ready to flow semi-automatically.

As before, ditch the stuff you've already placed and start fresh. If you haven't saved since placing, you can choose **Revert** from the **File** menu to go back to the last version saved. You can also click in the text with the Text tool, choose **Select all**, and press Delete. Do it any way you want. Just get back to blank pages for every page from 2 on.

Now let's place the story for the last time (I promise).

1. **Place…**.
2. Choose your story; click **OK**.
3. Hold Shift (note cursor) and click in the upper left-hand corner of the first column on page 2. The cursor stays loaded!

   If you let go of the Shift key, the cursor changes to the Autoflow cursor if Autoflow is checked, and the Manual Flow cursor if Autoflow isn't checked. You can change the cursor back to the Semi-autoflow by pressing and holding the Shift key at any time.

4. Move to page 4.
5. Click in the top left-hand corner of the first column on page 4.

If there's more text to place, the cursor stays loaded. When the story's completely placed, the cursor changes to the Pointer tool. If you have lots of text yet to place, changing to Autoflow will help you get it done.

6. Place the remainder of the text any way you wish (autoflow, semi-autoflow, or manual flow).

You now know enough to place text with the best of them. You know about autoflowing, manual flowing, and semi-autoflowing. You also know you can switch between the different placing methods on the fly (that's what the Shift key and Command key let you do).

Placing Graphics

Onward and upward. Let's learn to place pictures.

You'll need a picture to work with. Use a drawing program to create a picture and save it. It doesn't matter what you create; make anything. PageMaker can place graphics saved in many popular formats, including Paint, PICT, TIFF, and EPS; if your drawing program can save in one of these formats, you're all set.

If you don't have a drawing program, don't worry; you can make a graphic using the Mac's built-in screen capture (Command-Shift-3). Pressing Command-Shift-3 on a System 7 Mac gives you an audible click and a document called "Picture 1" on your hard disk. Pressing Command-Shift-3 on a System 6 Mac produces a document called "Screen0" on your hard disk. I'll use a document created with Command-Shift-3 in the example that follows.

Since you already know how to place text, placing graphics will be easy. The fun begins after the graphic is in place.

1. Choose **Place...** from the **File** menu.
2. Select your picture and click **OK**.

    Your cursor is loaded with the picture. Different kinds of pictures get different kinds of cursors. Figure 8.52 shows a cursor loaded with a PICT (the kind of picture you get when you do Command-Shift-3 in System 7).

3. Go to page 2.
4. Click anywhere in the document. Your screen looks something like figure 8.53 if you used a graphic obtained via Command-Shift-3.

Interlude 8
Cool PageMaker Stuff

Figure 8.52
Cursor loaded with a PICT graphic

Part II

What Put the Mac in Business

There are only a couple of things to do to a graphic in PageMaker. You can stretch it or shrink it by dragging handles with the Pointer tool; you can crop it (eliminating the undesirable parts of the picture); you can adjust the contrast and brightness of a picture (not with all pictures, and not with all Macs), and you can make text wrap around it. Of these, cropping and wrapping text are by far the more interesting.

You crop pictures with the Cropping tool. That's the one in the lower right-hand corner of the Toolbox, the tool that no one seems to know about. Let's crop the picture you placed.

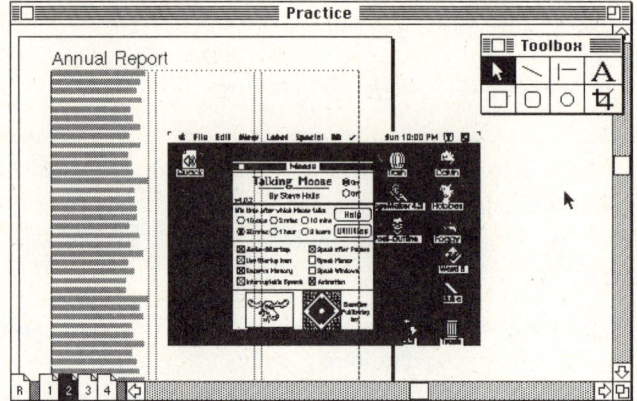

Figure 8.53
After placing the graphic.

1. Select the Cropping tool.
2. Click on the graphic. The graphic shows handles, indicating it's been selected.
3. Put the cursor over one of the handles.
4. Press the mouse button and drag the handle toward the center of the picture. The picture starts to disappear. That's the whole point. Figure 8.54 shows the PICT being cropped.

Figure 8.54
Cropping a picture.

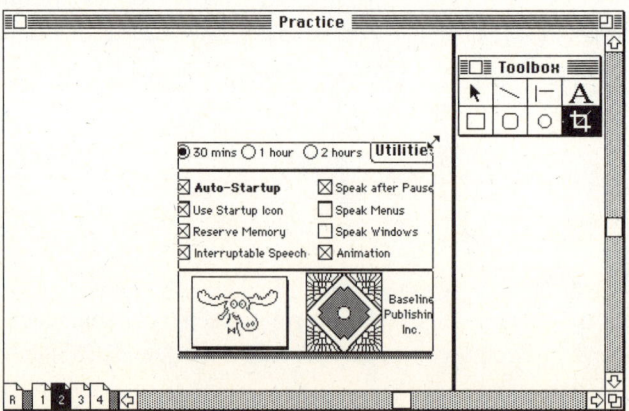

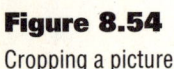

5. Use the Cropping tool on other handles until you've cropped everything you want to crop. Figure 8.55 shows the PICT of Figure 8.53 after final cropping.

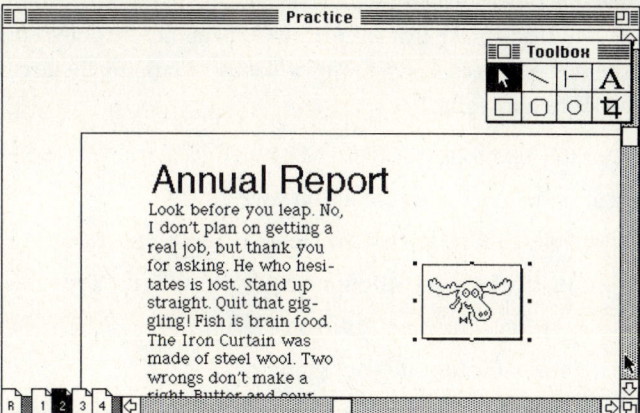

Interlude 8
Cool PageMaker Stuff

Figure 8.55
After final cropping.

Sometimes you know in advance just how big a picture can be. You might have a certain space for the picture to fit in, and you need to fit your picture into that space. You can crop the picture to fit the space, then move the picture around inside the space to see what looks best in that space. You do this using the Cropping tool, except you don't click on a handle. Instead, you click right on the picture. The cursor becomes a hand, and if you hold the mouse button down you can drag the picture around within the frame you cropped to. Figure 8.56 shows the picture of figure 8.55 moved around inside the frame.

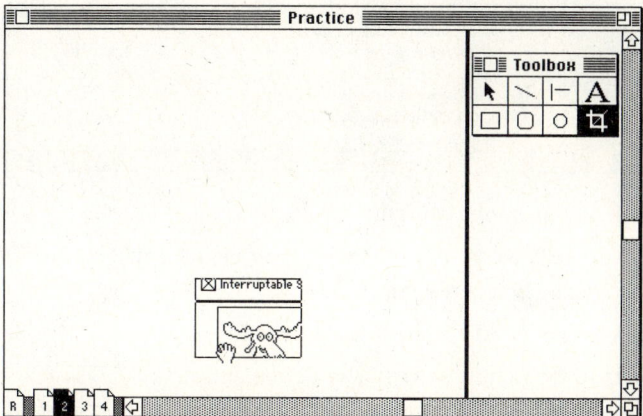

Figure 8.56
Moving around with the Cropping tool.

Part II
What Put the Mac in Business

You can "uncrop" a picture if you want to: just pull on a handle with the Cropping tool. Remember, cropping doesn't erase a picture; it just covers it up. Your picture is always there, underneath the cropping.

There's only one other interesting thing to do with pictures placed into PageMaker, and that's make text wrap around them. Before doing so, let's spiffy up the text on pages 2 and 4. This will make wrapping the text around the graphic more noticeable.

1. Choose the Text tool.
2. Click anywhere in the text block on page 2.
3. Choose **Select all** from the **Edit** menu.
4. Choose **Justify** from the **Alignment** submenu (in the **Type** menu).
5. Choose any font you like and any smallish size.

Now make the text wrap around your graphic.

1. Drag your graphic into the column of text on page 2 (use the Pointer tool). Your screen looks something like figure 8.57. Note that the text is covered by the graphic; there's no wrapping going on here.

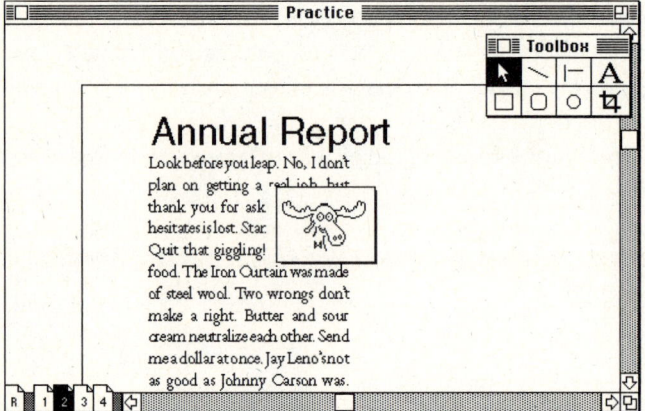

Figure 8.57
Graphic covering text.

2. Click on the graphic with the Pointer tool.
3. Choose **Text wrap...** from the **Element** menu. You'll see the Text Wrap dialog box (see Figure 8.58).
4. Click on the middle **Wrap** option.
5. Click on the rightmost Text flow option and click **OK**. The text wraps around your graphic. Your screen looks something like figure 8.59.

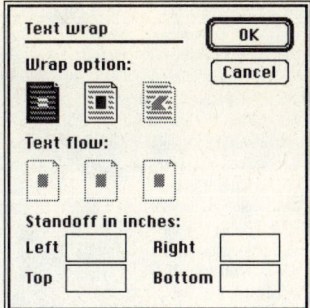

Figure 8.58
Text wrap dialog box.

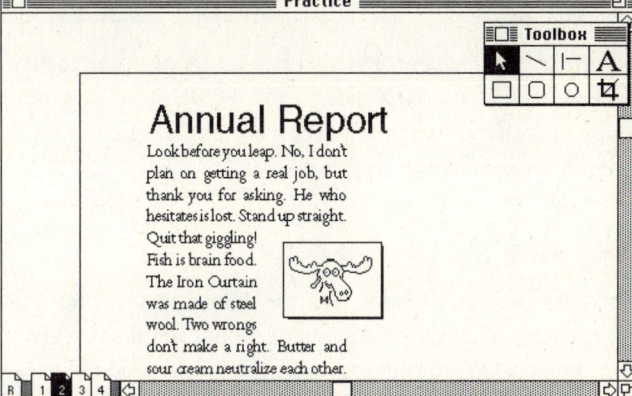

Figure 8.59
Wrapped text.

If you move the graphic, the text will wrap around it in the new location. Try moving the graphic and see for yourself.

 PageMaker doesn't wrap text around your graphic's outline. Rather, it wraps text around a bounding rectangle that completely encloses your picture. PageMaker indicates the bounding rectangle as dotted lines with handles at the corners.

You can adjust the bounding rectangle by dragging its handles. You can add handles by clicking on the boundary's dotted outline. It's too bad that PageMaker can't wrap text around a curve automatically, but at least you can do it yourself. It's not hard to do a custom wrap job; add handles as needed and drag them around. Figure 8.60 shows a custom wrap job.

You know just about everything about placing graphics, cropping them, and wrapping text around them. You also know a lot about placing text. Ninety percent of the things you place will be either graphics or text, so you're in pretty good shape.

Figure 8.60

Custom wrap job.

What about the last ten percent? I'm glad you asked. As usual, the coolest stuff is the least known, and even though you'll only use it every so often, knowing how to do it lets you do things hardly anyone else can. I'm talking about—drum roll—placing the Scrapbook.

Placing the Scrapbook

Placing the Scrapbook? Yup. And it's not the same as copying from the Scrapbook and pasting into your document. Not at all the same. Try copying and pasting after working through this example if you need to prove it to yourself.

1. Make a new PageMaker document.
2. Choose the Text tool, click in the document, and type Spandex.
3. Choose the Pointer tool.
4. Click on the **Spandex** text block.
5. **Cut** it.
6. Open the **Scrapbook** and move to its first page.
7. Paste the text block into the **Scrapbook**.
8. Close the **Scrapbook**.
9. Choose **Place...** from the **File** menu.

You're going to place the **Scrapbook** file. It's in the **System** folder; you'll need to dig around for it.

10. Select the **Scrapbook** file and click **OK**.

Sometimes the Scrapbook doesn't show what you paste into it. Don't worry. If you pasted, your stuff is in there.

Christian Boyce

Your cursor will be loaded with the entire contents of the Scrapbook. Figure 8.61 shows the cursor, loaded with the Scrapbook file. The number on the cursor indicates the number of pages in the Scrapbook.

11. Click once. Your screen looks like figure 8.62. Notice the graphics-style handles around the text. Notice also that your cursor remains loaded with the rest of the Scrapbook.

You could continue to place Scrapbook pages if you wanted to. I don't want you to do that now, so you'll need to unload the cursor.

12. Choose the Pointer tool. The cursor is unloaded.

Now grab a handle and stretch the Spandex. If you used a PostScript font, and if you're using Adobe Type Manager, the text stays smooth no matter what you do to it. If you're not using ATM, you'll still get smooth text when you print so long as the font you used is built into your printer. Figure 8.63 shows some of the ways you could distort the Spandex. No doubt you've seen this effect in real life.

 Placing the Scrapbook converts text to a graphic. That's why this stretching works. It's a very cool feature, and one that nobody seems to know. Nobody except us.

Interlude 8
Cool PageMaker Stuff

Figure 8.61
Cursor loaded with the **Scrapbook**.

Figure 8.62
After placing text from the **Scrapbook**.

You won't see a number higher than 99 on the cursor, no matter what. I have 117 pictures in my Scrapbook but PageMaker shows a 99 on the cursor anyway. Back home we call this a bug.

Christian Boyce

Figure 8.63

Spandex (one size fits all).

You can use the Scrapbook to help you work with graphics too. When graphics are copied to the Scrapbook, then placed (not pasted!), they become a graphic group. Grouping objects lets you scale them, stretch them, and move them easily. This next example shows you how.

1. Create a new PageMaker document.
2. Use the drawing tools to make a picture using a couple of objects. Figure 8.64 shows a simple picture made from three graphic elements.

Figure 8.64

A simple graphic.

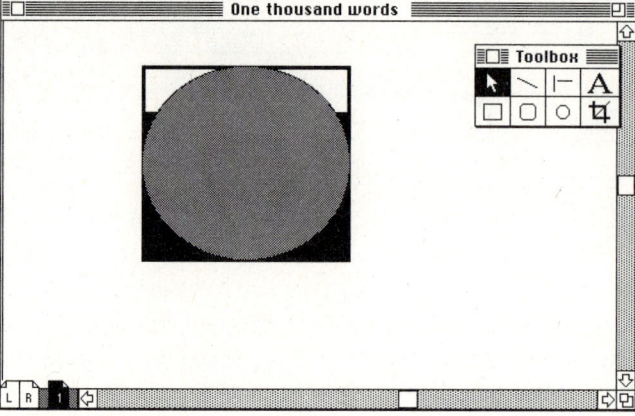

3. Select the entire graphic (**Select All** helps) and **Cut** it.
4. Open the **Scrapbook** and move to its first page.
5. Paste the graphic and close the **Scrapbook**.
6. Place the **Scrapbook** as you did in the previous example.

Figure 8.65 shows several stretched and squashed versions of the same picture.

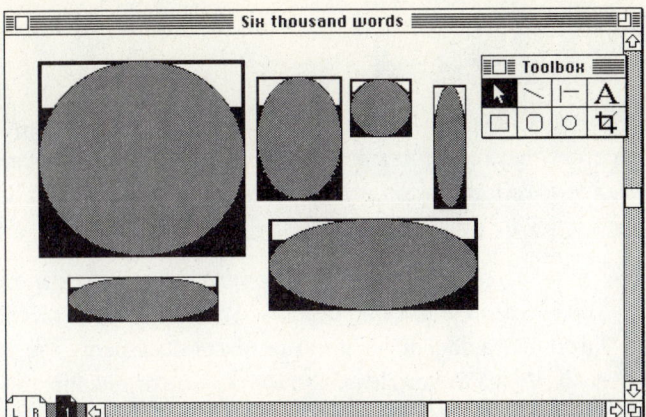

Figure 8.65
Variations on a theme.

You can combine text and graphics into single, stretchable objects via placing the Scrapbook. Figure 8.66 shows what you can do with text, graphics, and the place-the-Scrapbook technique. The upper image was the original; the others were distorted after being placed from the Scrapbook.

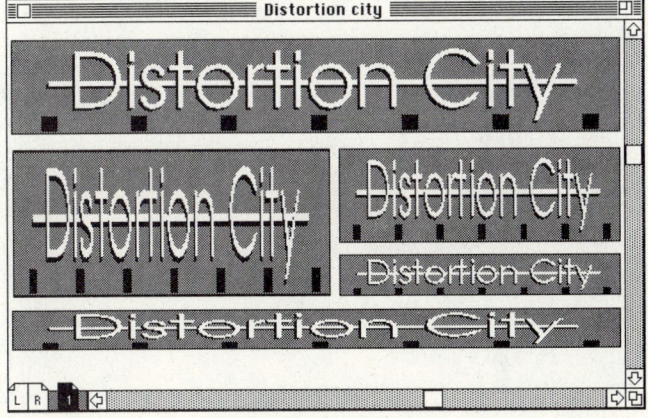

Figure 8.66
Distortion city.

That's all there is to know about placing the Scrapbook. It's a very cool feature, and it lets you do things there's no other way to do. Cool as it is, though, you'll place text much more often. You'll also place text in bigger chunks; it's peanuts to place hundreds of pages of text in one shot, especially if you use Autoflow.

PageMaker's makers aren't dumb. They know you'll use their program to work with lots of text. They know you'll want to experiment, trying this font for headlines and that font for body text, and they know you won't want to take all day doing it. That's why they gave PageMaker a Styles feature. Styles take the work out of reformatting text. As a bonus, they give your documents consistency.

Part II
What Put the
Mac in Business

Styles

PageMaker's Styles are a lot like Word's. They help you format text quickly and consistently, they're one-to-a-paragraph, and they're easy to change. PageMaker's Styles are easier to use, but otherwise Word's Styles and PageMaker's Styles are practically identical.

A Closer Look — Word and PageMaker work very, very well together, and the main reason is that they both use Styles. When you place text from Word documents into PageMaker documents, the Styles come along. You can leave the Styles alone or redefine them as you wish.

Figure 8.67 shows a PageMaker document with two different kinds of paragraphs: headlines and body text. A smart PageMaker user would define styles for these paragraph types, even if he didn't know for sure how the paragraphs should be formatted, because tagging paragraphs with Styles makes for easy reformatting later.

Figure 8.67
Headlines and Body Text.

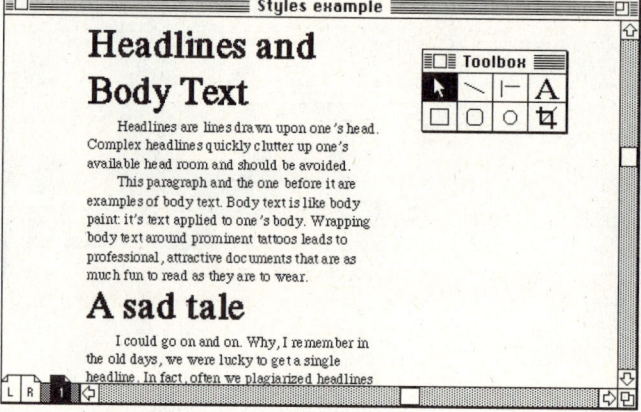

 *Note* — PageMaker automatically provides a headline style, a body text style, and a couple of others for each new document. You can start with those (I did in this example), or define your own.

Figure 8.68 shows the same PageMaker document after a quick redefinition of the Headline and Body Text styles. Figure 8.49 shows another way to format the document. Changing the look of the paragraphs was easy: I just redefined the Headline and Body Text styles. Using Styles makes experimenting with different looks very quick and very easy.

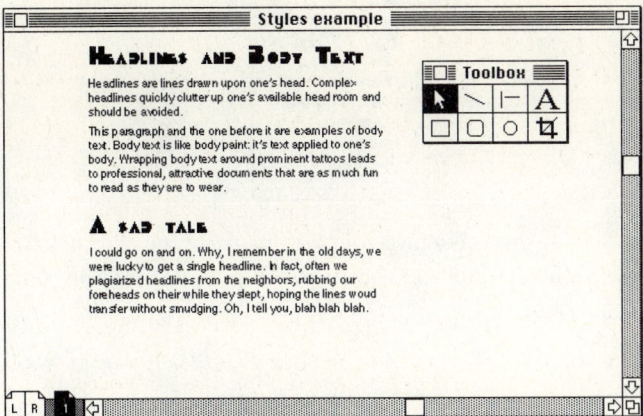

Figure 8.68
Another look.

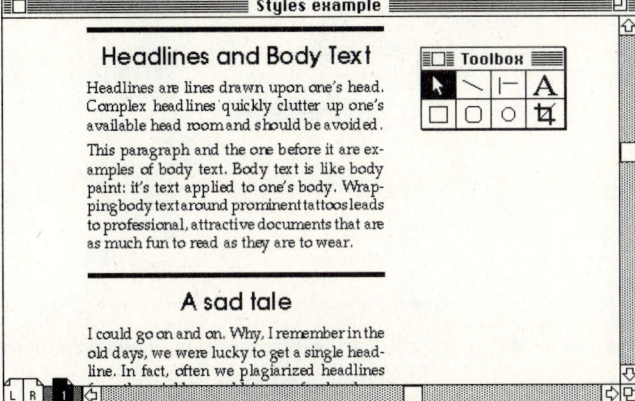

Figure 8.69
Yet another look.

Now you try. You'll need a PageMaker document with a couple of paragraphs for the example, so make one then join us at step 1. You can use the paragraphs in figures 8.67, 8.68, and 8.69 if you experience writer's block.

 Very important: don't format the text at all. Just type it in. You'll format it with Styles.

1. Choose **Style palette** from the **Windows** menu. Figure 8.70 shows the Style palette. I like it a lot.
2. Click in one of your paragraphs with the Text tool.
3. Choose a Style from the **Style** palette. The paragraph changes. Try choosing other Styles to see how they look.
4. Apply Styles to the remaining paragraphs the same way.

Figure 8.70

The Style palette.

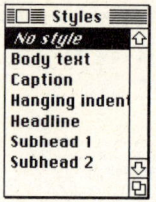

That's it. Applying Styles is a piece of cake, thanks to the Style palette. As usual, there's a harder, dumber way to do things, but there's no room for such nonsense here.

When you want to redefine a Style, the Style palette helps again. You'll redefine one here, and I'll bet you'll think it's easy.

1. Hold the Command key down and click on **Headline** in the **Style** palette. You get the **Edit Style** box of figure 8.71. Nice, huh?

Figure 8.71

Edit Style dialog box.

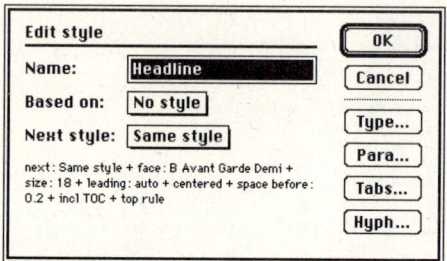

The Style consists of Type (text), Paragraph, Tab, and Hyphenation attributes. The Type and Paragraph attributes are most interesting, so we'll play with them here. Tab and Hyphenation attributes are important, but not so interesting, so I'll let you experiment with them on your own.

2. Click the **Type...** button.

    You get the **Type Specifications** dialog box of figure 8.72. This is the same **Type Specs** dialog box you'd get by choosing **Type specs...** from the **Type** menu.

3. Specify the look you want (font, size, etc.) and click **OK**.

4. Click **OK** again (this time from the **Edit Style** dialog).

Every paragraph with the Headline style changes. It's remarkable. Now you'll change the Body text Style.

1. Command-click on Body text in the Style palette. You get the **Edit Style** dialog box of Figure 8.47.

2. Click the **Type...** button and choose a font, a size, and so on.
3. Click **OK**. You're back at the **Edit Style** dialog box.
4. Click the **Para...** button. You get the **Paragraph Specifications** dialog box of figure 8.73. This is the same **Paragraph Specs** box you'd get by choosing **Paragraph...** from the **Type** menu.
5. Specify the look you want (alignment, indents, spacing between paragraphs, etc.) and click **OK**.
6. Click **OK** again (from the **Edit styles** dialog box).

Every paragraph with the Body text style changes. Naturally you can go back and edit the Body text style's font and size as well.

Styles let you control the way an entire document looks without doing a lot of work. You can experiment like crazy without taking much time. And with Styles, you never have to worry about accidentally formatting one headline one way and another headline another way. Styles give your documents a consistent look. All you have to do is use them.

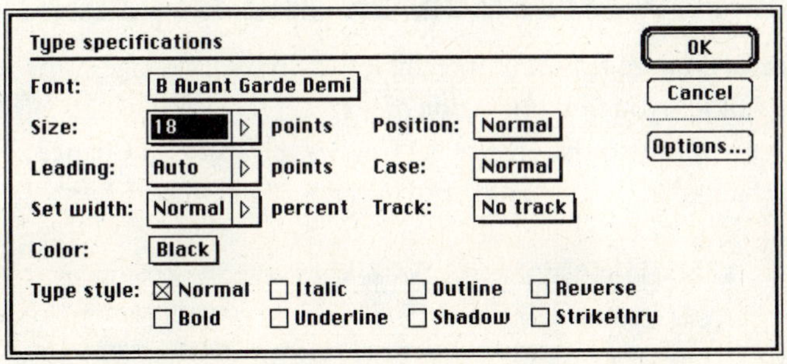

Interlude 8

Cool PageMaker Stuff

Figure 8.72

Type specifications dialog box.

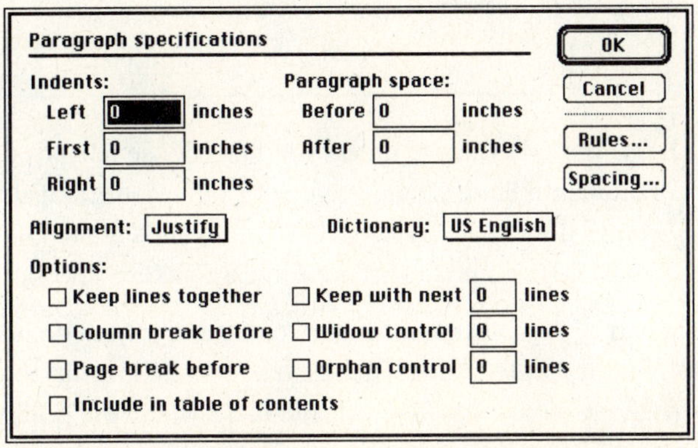

Figure 8.73

Paragraph specifications dialog box.

357

Part II
What Put the
Mac in Business

Buried Treasures

PageMaker's loaded with cool little features that change your life forever. Try these gems; I use them and they save me all kinds of time.

Command-Shift Is Everything

Command-Shift-B makes selected text bold, Command-Shift-U makes it underlined, and Command-Shift-I makes it italicized. Command-Shift-C centers the paragraph the cursor's in, Command-Shift-L left-justifies the paragraph, Command-Shift-R right-justifies it, and Command-Shift-J justifies it on both sides. Command-Shift-> increases the size of selected text and Command-Shift-< decreases the size of text according to the sizes listed in the Type menu. Does this sound a lot like Microsoft Word? You bet. There really are standards.

Super-Powerful Search and Replace

PageMaker's **Change** feature is incredible. The typical Change... (or Search and Replace) lets you find one string of text and replace it with another. PageMaker lets you do that; figure 8.74 shows the standard Change... box, ready to change "straw" to "gold" at the touch of a button.

Figure 8.74
Change dialog box.

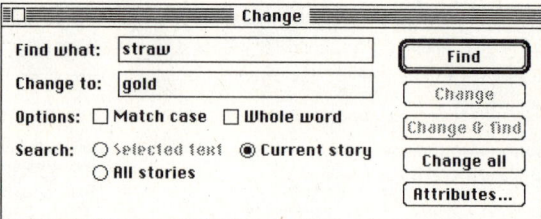

You can't do Change unless you first choose Edit story from the Edit menu. Find, Change, and Spelling become available once you've done that. Look for these commands in the Edit menu. Too bad there's no Story Editor in PageMaker 3 and earlier.

The amazing part of PageMaker's Change... command is buried under the **Attributes**... button in the Change dialog box. Pressing the Attributes... button opens the **Attributes** dialog box, and that's where the power is hidden. Figure 8.75 shows the Attributes dialog box.

358

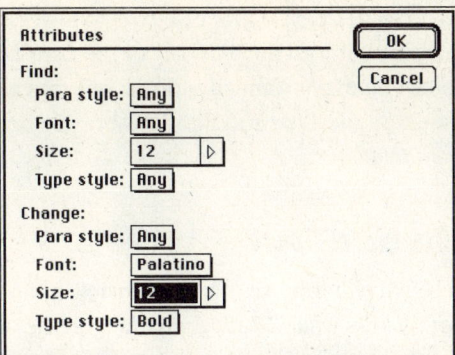

Interlude 8
Cool PageMaker Stuff

You can tell PageMaker to change all 12-point plain instances of "straw" to 12-point Palatino "gold" in one shot and know that other instances of "straw" will not change. For example, 14-point text would not change, nor would bold text. Only the combination of the right words and the right formatting will be affected. This is very handy. You can also use this feature to change all underlined words to bold ones, regardless of what the words are. Play with this one until you really understand it. You'll need it someday.

Change Text from Upper Case to Lower Case and Back

PageMaker's **Type** specs dialog box has a little-known **Case** feature that lets you choose from "Normal" (the way you typed it), "All Caps" (what it sounds like), and "Small Caps" (lower case letters are changed to upper case letters in a smaller point size). With the Case pop-up, you could type "Sweet" and format it three ways (see figure 8.76).

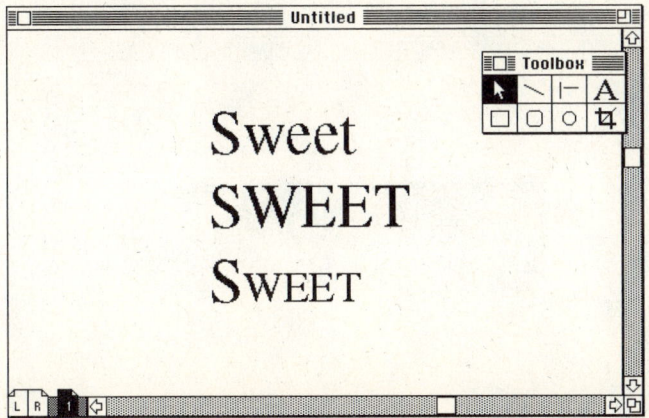

Figure 8.76
Sweet three ways.

Part II
What Put the Mac in Business

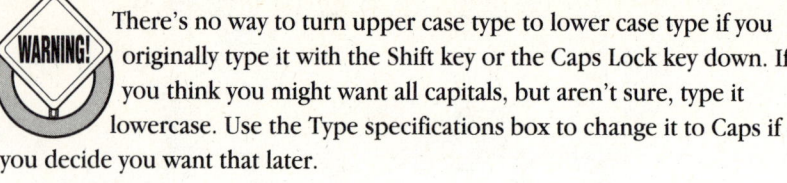 There's no way to turn upper case type to lower case type if you originally type it with the Shift key or the Caps Lock key down. If you think you might want all capitals, but aren't sure, type it lowercase. Use the Type specifications box to change it to Caps if you decide you want that later.

Zooming In and Out

You can switch to "Fit in window" view from Actual Size view by holding the Command and Option keys while clicking anywhere in the window. You can zoom to "Actual size" view from any other view by holding the Command and Option keys and clicking on the part of the document you want to zoom in on. This beats choosing Actual size from the menu because the zoomed-in view is centered around the spot you clicked in.

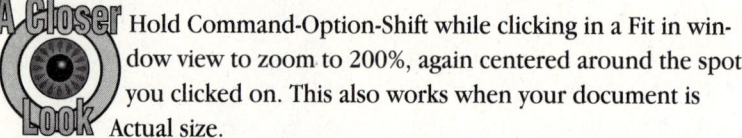 Hold Command-Option-Shift while clicking in a Fit in window view to zoom to 200%, again centered around the spot you clicked on. This also works when your document is Actual size.

Command-Click through the Layers

It happens all the time: you want to click on something, but it's covered up with something else. Figure 8.77 shows an example: a text block of white text completely covers the black rectangle behind. It's impossible to format the black box without selecting it first, but clicking on the box always selects the text block. The solution: hold the Command key down while clicking. The first click selects the topmost item, the next Command-click selects the next item down, and so on.

Figure 8.77
Box behind text.

360

Set Defaults the Way You Want Them

When you make a new document, PageMaker sets it up according to a set of defaults. PageMaker chooses margins, the number of columns, a font and a size for new text blocks, a fill and a line for new graphics, whether or not to display Rulers, and several other options. You can change the default settings very simply. Start PageMaker, but don't open a document. Now go through all the menus, changing things to the setting you want for defaults. When you're finished, you'll have set the defaults. All new documents will reflect your new settings.

Close Multiple Dialog Boxes Quickly

Hold the Option key while clicking OK in a dialog box to close all others associated with it. Figure 8.78 shows a dialog box with several others leading up to it; one click of the OK button, with the Option key held down, closed them all. You can easily get four or five dialogs deep; being able to Option-click to close them all is a real time-saver. You can also Option-click the Cancel button.

Interlude 8
Cool PageMaker Stuff

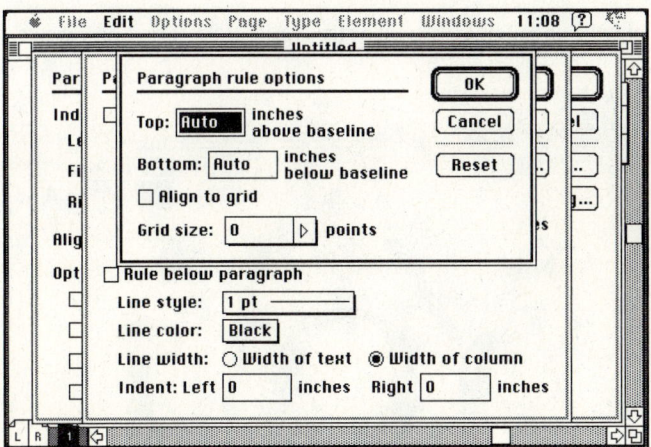

Figure 8.78
Nested dialog boxes.

Kerning: A Little Is Good, a Lot Can Be Fun

Kerning is the process of adjusting the spacing between letters to make text look better. Most small type looks fine (PageMaker takes care of the spacing automatically), but at large sizes, spacing falls apart. Figure 8.79 shows 60-point Palatino text used as part of a headline.

Figure 8.79

Before kerning (viewed at 400%).

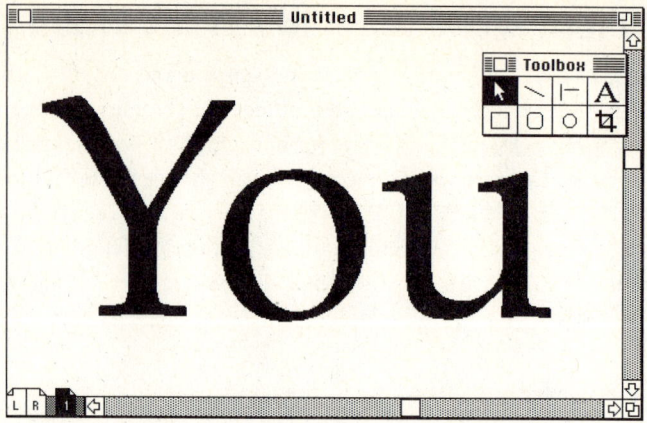

The space between the "Y" and the "o" is too big, and the space between the "o" and the "u" could be smaller as well. It's easy to fix things up. Just click with the Text tool between the letters you want to kern. If you want to bring them closer together, hold the Command key while pressing the Delete key. If you want to spread them apart, hold the Command and Shift keys while pressing Delete. Figure 8.80 shows the result of kerning (I kerned the "Y" and the "o" twice as much as I kerned the "o" and the "u").

You can kern as much as you want to; Figure 8.81 shows an extreme example.

Figure 8.80

After kerning (viewed at 400%).

A Closer Look Ever hear of an *em* space? That's a unit of measure equal in height and width to the point size of the font being used. For example, when you're using 12-point type, an em space is 12 points high and 12 points wide. The amount of tightening (or loosening) you get when you kern is measured in terms of an em:

Command-Delete tightens text by 4% of an em, and Command-Shift-Delete loosens text by the same amount. Clearly, 4% of an em is practically nothing at small point sizes but can be a significant distance at larger sizes. In fact, at large sizes, 4% of an em is so large that kerning becomes a rather coarse and chunky exercise. Fortunately, PageMaker lets you kern in finer increments (1% of an em, to be exact) if you use Option-Delete and Option-Shift-Delete to do it. Some people prefer Command-left arrow for coarse tightening and Command-Shift-left arrow for fine tightening (and Command-right arrow for coarse loosening and Command-Shift-right arrow for fine loosening) but the amounts of kerning are the same: 4% of an em for coarse, and 1% of an em for fine.

Interlude 8
Cool PageMaker Stuff

Figure 8.81
Kern on the cob.

PageMaker lets you kern whole chunks of text at a time: just select some text and kern away. Try this technique (called *range kerning*) when you can't quite get your text to fit in a given space. No one will notice if you kern a paragraph by 1% of an em, but that small amount is often enough to make your text fit where you want it to.

PageMaker's **Track** feature is similar to range kerning, with one important difference: tracked text *automatically* tightens (increasing the amount of kerning) when you increase its point size (and it automatically loosens when you decrease its point size). Big text often needs more kerning than small text does (big text looks looser than small text does); without tracking, you'd need to apply more kerning after making text bigger (and less kerning after making text smaller) if you wanted the text to look right. Tracking can save you boodles of time by *automatically* adjusting letter spacing as you experiment with different font sizes.

Note: Tracking is a character attribute, not a paragraph one; this means you have to select the text you want to track, just as you do when range kerning. After selecting your text, choose a tracking setting from the Track pop-out menu (in the Type menu). Try the different tracking settings (and change the point size of the text once you've tracked it) to see how tracking works.

Selection Secrets

You can select a word by double-clicking it with the Text tool. You can select a whole paragraph by triple-clicking it with the Text tool. Triple-clicking a text block with the Pointer tool opens the Story editor.

Nudge Text Blocks and Graphics with Cursor Keys

You can nudge items up, down, left, and right using the cursor keys on your keyboard. This really helps line things up.

In Conclusion

PageMaker gives you a single facility for bringing together different kinds of documents, and that's pretty impressive. Learn PageMaker once and you'll be able to bring in text from Word, charts from Excel, and just about any kind of document created with any application. That's a powerful thing.

PageMaker's one heck of a program. Master pages, Placing, and Styles are the features that make it so special. When you use these features, your documents come together quickly, letting you experiment more with the fun stuff (like wrapping text around graphics, placing the Scrapbook, and changing looks by redefining Styles). Those features are there for you; go out and use them.

PageMaker epitomizes the Mac ideal of letting you integrate vastly different kinds of information into attractive, informative documents. Of course, you need to know how to create vastly different kinds of information to begin with, and that's where the Macintosh and its software shine.

One thing that all those documents share is fonts. If you don't understand how fonts work, you will have trouble no matter what application you use. The next chapter will help to clear things up just a bit.

Chapter 9: Fonts and Typography

Since the invention of moveable type, nothing has changed the way people put ink on paper the way the Macintosh and desktop publishing have. Fonts and type are a big part of creating any printed document, and how they work on a Macintosh is a highly technical process. Fonts are a source of both delight and dismay on the Mac: The wide array of available fonts is wonderful, but the different formats and conventions are confusing.

In This Chapter

▼ Type's makeup

▼ What a font is

▼ Screen and printer fonts

▼ Font formats

▼ Problems with fonts

Part II
What Put the Mac in Business

Typographical Terms

When you talk about typography, at the most basic level you're talking about the shapes of letters. Designers are employed to create letter designs, which are influenced by both fashion and function. Given a basic design, several different variations are often created—bold, italic, condensed, and so forth. The collection of all the related variations is called a *type family*. The Garamond family contains Garamond Regular, Garamond Condensed (used for this text), Garamond Italic, Garamond Bold, Garamond Bold Italic... the list goes on and on. Each of these variations is a *typeface*. Thus, a type family is made of several different typefaces. Different type families have different members—not every family has a bold or an italic, for instance. (Some typefaces even stand alone, as it were, with no other members of the family.)

Each typeface can be used in different sizes, measured in *points*. Each particular size of a typeface, such as 10 point Garamond Condensed, is called a *font* (as typographers use the term). Thus, each type family has one or more typefaces, and each typeface can be represented in different sizes, called fonts. A point on the Macintosh is exactly 1/72 of an inch. Originally, the point measured the height of the piece of type, when type was actually cast in metal. On the Macintosh, there is no physical piece of type, so point size is an arbitrary measurement. Essentially, the point size measures the vertical space taken up by the font. Because different typefaces have different proportions, different typefaces can seem relatively larger or smaller at the same point size.

The neat and orderly naming convention—type family, typeface, and font—was thrown into confusion by the advent of the Macintosh. The problem is that on the Macintosh, *font* refers to a specific electronic file used to describe a typeface. Originally, each different size of a typeface used a different electronic file, so using the term "font" made some sense. However, the advent of PostScript fonts (and, later, TrueType fonts) meant that one file was used to display a typeface at many different sizes. Those files are still called fonts, though, which is different from the way typographers use the term. The issue is further complicated because Macintosh programs can calculate different type styles based upon the basic font. Most word processors, for instance, have Bold and Italic styles. Thus, one Macintosh "font" actually can represent almost a whole type family! The upshot is this: generally, a Macintosh font is an electronic file used to represent a specific typeface.

Chapter 9
Fonts and Typography

On a computer, a font not only contains all the required information on each character, symbol, and so on, but also gives instructions to the computer on how to draw each item. Usually a computer font contains a mathematical equation outlining each character as part of its instructions, and the computer can create and adjust every character in the font to exact size. The computer uses those same instructions to create the font characters on both the Mac's screen and any printing device you use.

The Makeup of Typography

Although the technology of creating type has changed dramatically over the centuries (see chapter 6, "Printing from Your Macintosh"), the alphabet and its characters' forms have changed very little from the marks in clay tablets, soot on parchment, or pen to paper scribbling. All typefaces, as different as they are, share certain characteristics and parts (see figure 9.1).

The most fundamental difference between typefaces is *serif* and *sans-serif*. As figure 9.1 explains, a serif is a little extension, or *foot,* that many typefaces have as part of their design. The body text in this book is a serif typeface. A sans-serif typeface has no "feet" or extensions and is used in this book for subheads and figure captions.

All other parts of type were designed centuries ago as the printed page evolved and newer techniques for setting the type appeared. Most of the terms used in typography came from the days when type was cast in metal.

How Fonts and Type Work

One of the new terms introduced by desktop publishing is WYSIWYG, or what-you-see-is-what-you-get, meaning that what you see onscreen is the same as what prints. Ironically, the last place you will have true WYSIWYG is with Macintosh fonts and type!

Figure 9.1

All type shares certain aspects.

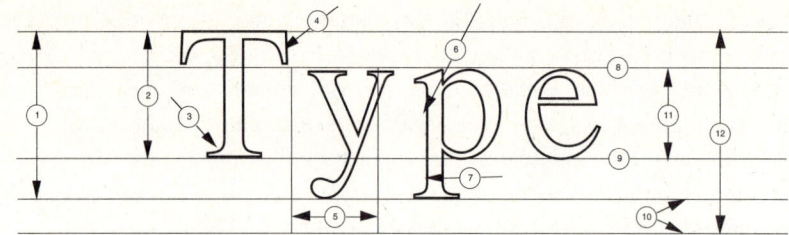

① Point size: The actual measure of type from the top of the *ascender* to the bottom of the *descender*. Typographers and printer use a special measurement system with 72 points to an inch. The type in this figure is 127 points, 36 point type is about one-half inch tall.

② Cap Height: The measure of height from the *baseline* to the top of a capital letter.

③ Serif: A small outstroke from the type. Fonts are classified either as *Serif* or *Sans-Serif* (meaning without serifs). This small finishing stroke adds to the design of different typefaces, and makes small type easier to read by drawing the eye from one character to another through the serifs.

④ Ascender: The portion of any character that extends above the *mean line*. This is usually a capital letter, part of a tall lowercase letter, or the highest part of a curved character (such as an O or S).

⑤ Set Width: The portion of total white space a letter occupies in width. Space is added before or after a letter to keep letters from touching, and this space is included in the Set Width of a letter.

⑥ Counter: The area enclosed within a character, such as the holes in the p or e in this figure.

⑦ Descender: The portion of a lowercase letter that falls below a baseline.

⑧ Mean Line: An imaginary line that runs horizontally along the top of the lowercase letters to define the *x-height*.

⑨ Base Line: An imaginary line that runs horizontally along the base of every letter and on which every letter aligns. *Descenders* fall below this line.

⑩ Shoulder: The fixed space below a font's *descenders*, set by the leading, that assures *descenders* from one line won't touch the *ascenders* of the next line

⑪ x-height: This refers to the height of lowercase letters that do not have *ascenders* or *descenders*. A lowercase x almost always stays within the letter height, thus the name.

⑫ Leading: Pronounced *Ledding*. A term used by typographers to describe the measurement from the top of the *ascender* to the bottom of the *descender* plus the height of the *shoulder*.

Bitmapped Fonts

The first type of Macintosh fonts were *bitmapped* fonts. Each letter was drawn as a pattern of pixels, so a different version of the letter had to be drawn for each size. Bitmapped fonts were created for the 72 dpi (dot-per-inch) resolution of the Macintosh screen, and for a specific point size—10-point, 12-point, and so on. (Apple created a series of typefaces in standard sizes, such as 10, 12, 18, and 24 point, and named them after cities such as Geneva, Monaco, and Chicago. These typefaces are still used for much of the text you see onscreen.) If you don't have the file for the size you need, the Macintosh will change the size of the dots—with mixed results. If you want a 48-point font but all you have is a 12-point version, the Macintosh will take the 12-point version and make the dots sixteen times bigger (four times taller and four times wider). This can make some pretty ugly letters! A diagonal or curved pattern of square pixels has rough, jagged edges; making the squares larger makes the edges that much more jagged. There is no way to improve the appearance of bitmapped fonts—in this case, what you see is what you get.

There was an exception to the WYSIWIG rule, however. The first Macintosh printer, the ImageWriter, is able to print at 144 dpi—twice as good as the 72 dpi screen. When you print at the "faster" quality setting, the ImageWriter just prints the 72 dpi image you see onscreen, ignoring its own superior capabilities. But when you print at the "best" quality setting, the ImageWriter takes advantage of the improved resolution. It does this by using the font file of twice the point size of the font you defined. For instance, if you select 12-point New York, the ImageWriter will use 24-point New York. It doesn't make the letters bigger, it just uses the increased detail of the 24-point letters to print better-looking text. The printed text looks twice as good as the text seen onscreen. (Of course, if the 24-point New York font isn't installed on the Macintosh, the ImageWriter has to use the default 72 dpi letters.) This minor exception to the WYSIWIG rule was a harbinger of things to come.

PostScript Fonts

Apple started the desktop publishing revolution with the introduction of the LaserWriter in January 1985. The LaserWriter prints at 300 dpi—over four times more dots per inch than the screen resolution, and just more than double the resolution of the ImageWriter. Although this may not seem dramatic, the results certainly were. The LaserWriter dots are over 4 times smaller than the ImageWriter dots. The smaller dots enable the printer to deliver near-typeset quality type with smoother, less jagged edges (see figure 9.2).

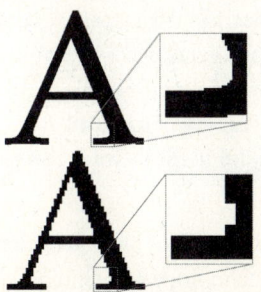

Chapter 9
Fonts and Typography

LaserWriter—A device that jams when you're in a hurry.

Guy Kawasaki

Figure 9.2
The letter *A* is rougher at 72 dpi than at 300 dpi.

Part II
What Put the Mac in Business

The advent of the laser printer changed type technology, too. With the original LaserWriter came a new font technology—*PostScript* fonts. PostScript, created by Adobe, is a *page description* language—a programming language used to describe the appearance of documents. Apple licensed PostScript for the LaserWriter, so that the Macintosh could take advantage of the LaserWriter's 300 dpi resolution. The Macintosh doesn't have to know what resolution the printer prints at; PostScript takes care of the details. This means that when you print on a LaserWriter, at 300 dpi, the letters are as crisp as 300 dpi can make them. If you change to a laser printer that prints at 600 dpi (or even an imagesetter, which prints at the 2540 dpi used for this book), PostScript automatically takes advantage of the improvement in resolution.

This can't be done, however, with the old bitmap fonts. PostScript can print the bitmapped letters, but it will print them at 72 dpi. PostScript doesn't know what the bitmapped letters are supposed to look like. Furthermore, PostScript doesn't know how to change the size of the letters; just as the Macintosh does, it will make the dots sixteen times bigger to make the letter four times bigger. There's no point in having a thousand-dollar, 300 dpi laser printer if it doesn't print any better than your $300 ImageWriter!

To avoid these problems, PostScript fonts describe the *outline* of each letter. The outline is described with mathematical equations, so PostScript can calculate the best pattern of dots to use for the letter no matter what resolution the printer uses—and no matter what size the letter is. So you can print a letter at 12 points, or at 72 points, or at 47 points—at any size—and it will look as good as the printer can print it. You can print type of any size you desire.

However, this advance came at the expense of WYSIWYG. Although PostScript is used for the majority of today's printers, the Macintosh uses a different language, called *QuickDraw,* to tell the monitor what to display. This means that the Macintosh can't use the PostScript font to display anything onscreen—it still needs a bitmapped version of the typeface. The bitmapped version has the problems described above, so you can end up with some very jagged letters onscreen. But because the printer still uses the PostScript font, the printed result will still look fine. What you see is *not* what you get. (Adobe's ATM software helps to solve this problem; it's discussed later in this chapter.)

There are two different PostScript font types: PostScript Type 1 and PostScript Type 3. (Type 2 technology was eliminated before it reached the market.) Type 1 is the standard Adobe font format, which has thousands of typefaces. Type 1 fonts may include *hints* for improving the typeface's appearance at low resolutions or small sizes. (A hint tells the imaging software to turn on or off extra pixels to improve legibility and attractiveness. This is discussed in detail later in this chapter.) Type 3 fonts are usually what Adobe calls "user-defined," or custom fonts you create with special software.

Creating Better Quality Screen Fonts

Printing from your Mac in higher resolutions is no sweat, as long as you are satisfied with seeing poorly-scaled type onscreen. Remember, PostScript fonts need a separate, bitmapped font to display text onscreen. The bitmapped font has the same resolution problems that the original bitmapped fonts did: if you don't have a file for the point size you want to use, the Macintosh will scale another point size to the correct size, usually with poor results. Few Mac users are satisfied with that!

Adobe took a unique approach to this problem and used their page description language, PostScript, to display type on the Macintosh screen. Appropriately enough, they called this *Display PostScript.* Even though this technology still uses bitmaps, the bitmapped fonts are created from an original outline of the character, just as with a PostScript laser printer. This new development means the computer draws a new bitmap font to scale at whatever size you specify, broadening the choices over the limited, hand-rendered sizes. Almost any size imaginable is now available to Mac users at better, more readable views, even though the Mac screen still displays only at 72 dpi.

Adobe packaged Display PostScript for the Mac (and later IBM compatibles) as Adobe Type Manager (ATM). ATM enhances screen images to the point where WYSIWYG is almost true. Figures 9.3 and 9.4 show screen type on a Mac with and without ATM, respectively.

Chapter 9
Fonts and Typography

Figure 9.3
Notice the letters are jagged and stair-stepped.

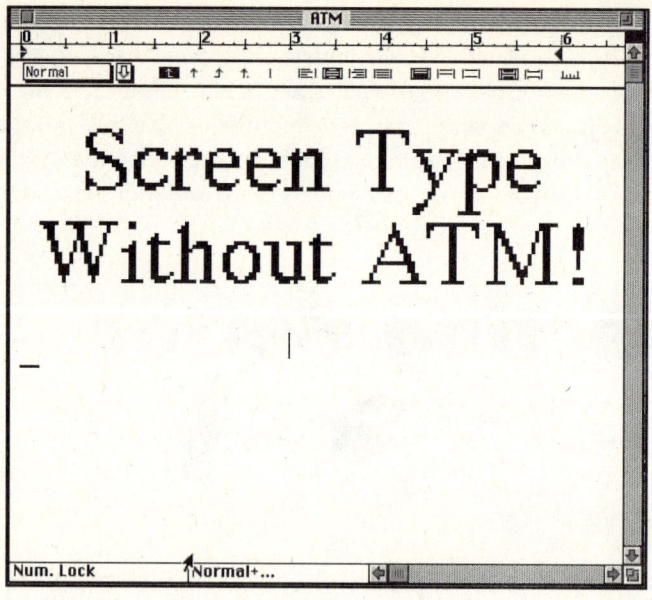

Figure 9.4
Although not completely smooth, this type is more readable, and closer to the look of the actual typeface.

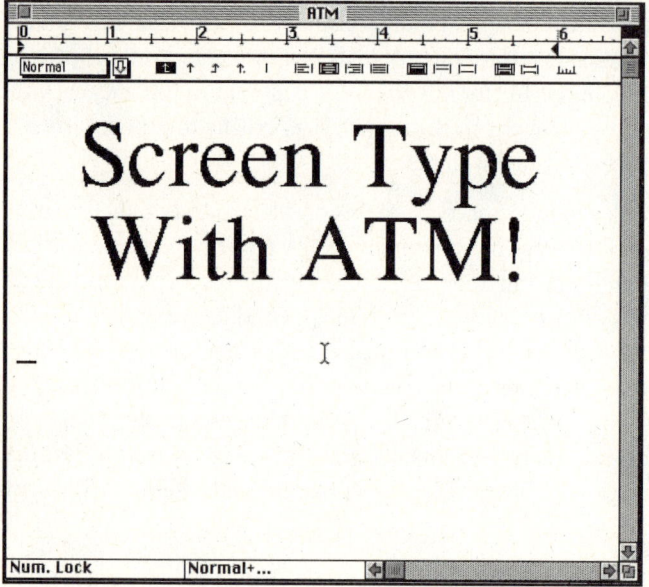

ATM also improves the ImageWriter's output when it prints Type 1 fonts because each letter is generated from an outline rather than a bitmap. With ATM, the ImageWriter can actually take advantage of its 144 dpi resolution with PostScript fonts by using ATM's outline-generated typefaces.

Introduced in 1993, SuperATM is a program from Adobe which performs all the tasks of the original ATM while adding a new feature: creating a screen

Chapter 9
Fonts and Typography

font even if the printer font is not available. The purpose of this program is to solve—onscreen, at least—the problems many Mac users face when trading files with other users. Normally, if a typeface used on one Mac is not available on the other Mac, the Mac substitutes another font (usually Courier) and uses the substitute font's width and spacing measurements. The result of the substitute type is that you lose the look of the original document onscreen. SuperATM re-creates the look and measurements of the original typeface by substituting the closest available typeface and using the spacing, width, and size of the original font. With SuperATM, you can see just about what the person who created the document intended. The letter shapes won't be quite the same—after all, you are using a different font—but at least the lines and pages will be of exactly the same size and length. If you use SuperATM, regular ATM is not necessary. SuperATM is only worth the additional cost (about $100 more than ATM) if you are trading files with many different users.

A Closer Look Adobe has continued to extend type technology with two advances. *Multiple master* fonts are to typefaces what PostScript fonts were to font sizes. PostScript gave users the capability to scale type to any size; Multiple master fonts give users the capability to scale type, not in size but in appearance.

Adobe used multiple master fonts in its *Acrobat* technology. Acrobat gives users the capability to trade digital documents without regard to what fonts the user has. Acrobat goes SuperATM one better: not only does it preserve the arrangements of the letters, it also attempts to preserve the shapes of the letters. It does this through multiple master technology, by scaling two generic fonts (Serif and Sans, included with the Acrobat software) to emulate the appearance of the original fonts used to create the document.

TrueType's Arrival (Or, Font Wars II: The Sequel)

In 1989, Apple announced a new font technology called *TrueType* to accompany the upcoming System 7. Many experts were stunned by the announcement; most wondered why Apple chose to reinvent Adobe's "wheel" and use outline fonts to create bitmap faces for screen display.

Part II
What Put the Mac in Business

Another definition for PostScript: the royalty stream from Apple to Adobe.

Guy Kawasaki

A Closer Look

One compelling reason for Apple's move was that ATM worked only with Adobe's Type 1 PostScript fonts. PostScript fonts use secret "hints" within their programming code to draw a character requested at various sizes. For years, Adobe jealously guarded these hints, which kept PostScript's price high because companies could not create competing fonts that were 100 percent compatible with PostScript printers. PostScript requires a separate "hint" interpreter to print the font, and Adobe's royalties from Apple alone accounted for most of Adobe's income. Apple sought to break Adobe's lock on the industry, free font technology for other manufacturers and software companies, and hopefully lower the price of high-quality Mac-compatible printers.

As mentioned, PostScript Type 1 fonts used to be closed—that is, they were coded in an encrypted format so nobody outside of Adobe knew how to design a Type 1 font. Reverse-engineering by rival firms eventually cracked Adobe's basic codes for creating the master outline of a font, but the "hint" mechanisms remained inaccessible.

One of Apple's advertised advantages for TrueType is that it is an open font format, so anybody can design a TrueType font. Immediately before TrueType was released with System 7, Adobe countered by publishing the secrets to opening the Type 1 format. This had two effects: Type 1 fonts flooded the market, enhancing PostScript's appeal as the standard imaging language; and PostScript clone makers could be sure their clone printer description languages (PDLs) worked with Type 1 fonts, hints and all.

TrueType is part of a new PDL called *TrueImage,* which was developed jointly by Apple and Microsoft (Microsoft bought a small company with the TrueImage technology and Apple signed a co-development contract). Interestingly, TrueType's release has not been followed up with a TrueImage printer as of this writing. This is strange because the express purpose of the new font format, in conjunction with the TrueImage PDL, is to allow Apple and Microsoft to provide customers with a single-vendor operating system-display-printing solution. Although TrueImage has the support of Microsoft, an industry leader with a reputation for working on something until it gets it right, Apple's role with TrueImage soon may be limited to TrueType.

PostScript fonts require both a screen font and a printer font, whereas TrueType creates both the screen fonts and the printer fonts from the same master outline font. Both companies defend their reasons for the difference. TrueType has now been around for over two years, and both font formats seem to be flourishing. PostScript is firmly entrenched as the font format of choice for serious printing, due to its acceptance in virtually every printing situation. TrueType fonts, on the other hand, are widely used for screen and low- to mid-range printing, due to their simplicity (one file for both screen and printer use). If one format is going to gain supremacy, it's certainly not clear which format it will be.

Dumb Fonts Versus Smart Fonts

TrueType fonts, like PostScript fonts, consist of mathematical outlines that describe the curves and lines of a character's letter form. When you use a certain typeface and size—10 point Helvetica, for example—your Mac's System Font Manager looks for that font in that size. If a hand-drawn bitmap font in that size is present, the Font Manager hands it to your application to display on the screen.

If no bitmaps are available for the size you want, TrueType passes its outline information to the Font Manager. The Font Manager puts the information into its *rasterizer,* which is essentially a three-part program. The rasterizer has a scaler that resizes the font outline to the requested size, a hint interpreter that carries out the special instructions contained in the hints to create the best possible letter at the monitor's resolution, and a scan converter that turns the hinted outline into a bitmap.

Because all the information on TrueType's resolutions at various sizes is built directly into the outline, TrueType fonts are dubbed *smart* fonts. By implication, this makes PostScript fonts, which contain only simple hints to define the letter form, *dumb* fonts. PostScript requires a separate interpreter to decide how best to render letter forms at various resolutions. This interpreter is either permanently built into a printer's ROM or is part of ATM.

Rather than being insulted at the "dumb versus smart" implications, Adobe proudly boasts the logic of its technology. Adobe sees hardware and software as continually evolving and prefers to keep fonts "dumb," describing only the outline and its hints. When new technology comes along, the interpreter is updated, not the font.

Apple has taken a completely different approach, putting the instructions on how to render a font within the font itself—the so-called "smart" font. The computer takes all responsibility for rendering (rasterizing) the letter forms. When rasterizing is complete, the computer sends a bitmap page to a simple inexpensive printer. Thus with smart fonts the computer needs to be more powerful to take the load off the printer.

Chapter 9
Fonts and Typography

TrueType and PostScript Advantages

Currently, there is no overall advantage either for TrueType or PostScript onscreen or in printed quality. PostScript requires that you purchase a separate program, Adobe Type Manager, for onscreen quality, whereas TrueType is free with System 7. On the other hand, far more typefaces are available with PostScript—an advantage that may disappear when TrueType fonts begin to take up more printer memory than PostScript fonts because the printer must download a TrueType rasterizer each time a TrueType font is printed. PostScript takes up more storage memory because both screen and printer fonts must be present for ATM to work.

WARNING! It is not a good idea to mix TrueType and PostScript fonts if you have a PostScript printer. TrueType must download its own interpreter to the printer's memory each time it prints; PostScript fonts do not. If you are using PostScript, TrueType fonts needlessly fill your printer's memory with information the PostScript fonts do not need (see chapter 5, "Printing From Your Macintosh"). However, most of Apple's recent LaserWriters (and many third-party printers) include both TrueType and PostScript fonts in their ROMs, so the printer's memory is less of an issue with newer printers, as long as you stick with fonts included on the printer's ROMs.

Problems with Fonts

In the course of working with fonts you may come across conflicting font ID numbers as well as problems with font listings.

Font ID Numbers and Conflicts

In versions before System 6, the Macintosh could not recognize more than 128 fonts (actually 256, but Apple reserved the first 128 for its own use). Each font received a number when it was programmed. However, this soon caused problems. Only one of 128 numbers could be given to any typeface, but soon thousands of fonts were available for Macintosh. Obviously, some fonts were going to be assigned the same ID number. Conflicts arose on systems using large numbers of fonts when a screen font called for a certain

Chapter 9
Fonts and Typography

number font but found a different font. The Mac sometimes printed the other typeface with the same number, rather than the typeface shown on the screen.

 One way to avoid font ID number conflicts is to keep fonts from different manufacturers in different folders on your Mac. By separating different manufacturers' fonts, you minimize the chances for confusion. Special font utilities such as Font/DA Juggler and Suitcase also offer renumbering systems to resolve conflicts.

Renumbering fonts can cause problems if you send your type to a service bureau. A renumbered font might print in a different font altogether because it does not match the service bureau's font of that number. This can be confusing and expensive.

With System 6.0, Apple introduced a new font resource called NFNT, which stands for New Font Numbering System. NFNT supports up to 16,000 ID numbers. Recently, Apple increased the number of available numbers to 32,768, which should eliminate font ID number conflicts—at least for a while!

Apple currently urges software developers to write their programs to recognize typeface names rather than numbers, which will further help avoid conflicts. PageMaker, QuarkXPress, Adobe Illustrator, Aldus FreeHand, and many other applications are adopting this new way to recognize fonts, but most software still relies on the number ID system.

Font Listings

Other problems include the Mac's font usage and how typefaces are listed for use. Each typeface from a family—regular, bold, italic, and bold italic—requires a separate font file. Apple's system originally ignored the other fonts, listing only the regular typeface and giving you boxes to choose bold, italic, and so on. Unfortunately, some applications using this method merely make a typeface "fatter" to make it bold, rather than actually using a bold font for printed output.

This typeface manipulation practice creates poor results; just making the strokes wider can fill in the spaces in letters, for instance. As more type families were introduced, each family had a separate typeface for each style. Unfortunately, the Mac's type menu became so crowded with all the choices (usually at least four per type family) that it could take quite a while to scroll through the available fonts. Adobe solved this problem by introducing Type Reunion, a program that unites an entire type family under one menu selection and pops up a submenu listing each separate but related typeface available—regular, bold, italic, bold italic, condensed and so on (see chapter 10, "Graphic Arts Support," for more information).

> **Note:** How do you discover what a typeface looks like without printing it first? System 7 enables you to double-click on any bitmapped or TrueType font to see a sample of it. Eastgate's Fontina goes a step further and enables you to see the font and size of your choice in your type menu. Fontina also creates a multi-column type menu to eliminate scrolling.

Finding Special Characters

Unlike typewriters, the Macintosh offers special typeface characters once available only from typesetters, such as accent marks (such as é and ö), ligatures (two or more connected characters such as Æ or Œ), dingbats (decorative characters), and other special symbols. Some fonts even offer characters from other alphabets. The Key Caps desk accessory was added to the Macintosh operating system to help you find these characters. Special characters are accessed through combinations of the Shift and Option keys; Key Caps enables you display the characters as they are arranged on your keyboard.

To use Key Caps, move to the **Apple** menu and select **Key Caps**. When it opens, a new menu—titled **Key Caps**—is added to the menu bar. Use this menu to display a list of all typefaces loaded into your Mac. Choose the typeface whose characters you want to display; this is important because not all fonts have the same characters in the same keyboard location (see figure 9.5).

Figure 9.5

The Key Caps desk accessory displays the special typeface characters available.

The typeface is displayed on the regular keyboard in lower case, unless you have your Caps Lock key down. Try holding down the Shift key, then the Option key, and finally the Shift and Option keys together. Typing a letter or character on the keyboard or clicking on the keyboard in the Key Caps window while pressing these keys displays the available special characters in the text bar.

If you highlight these characters in the text bar with your mouse and then select **Cut** or **Copy** from the **Edit** menu, the characters are copied into your computer's clipboard. Return to your document, then choose **Paste** from the **Edit** menu to add the character to your document.

The problem with this is that many applications will convert the text you paste to the font already used in the document, which doesn't help you when you're trying to add a Greek letter to your math homework! For that reason, it usually is best to use Key Caps to figure out what font and key combination you need, and then close KeyCaps to return to your document. Change to the correct typeface and type the correct key combinations. This works much faster than trying copy and paste, especially if the pasting doesn't work anyway.

> **WARNING!** Be sure to close **Key Caps** when you finish with it. Otherwise, Key Caps constantly displays characters in the background and slows your Mac to a snail's pace while it processes the different keystrokes.

> **Note** Creating an accented character, such as the é in the word resumé, is relatively easy on a Mac, although it is a two-step process. First, hold down the Option key and type the letter "e" (or whatever key represents the accent mark you want). The screen stays blank, but if you type the letter "e" next (without the Option key), it appears with the accent. Similarly, to get a tilde (~) over a letter n, press Option-n and then type an "n."

The Future of Font Technology

Digital typography faces many challenges that will be dealt with successfully in the future. One large problem is that type has been considered technology, not necessarily art. Recent innovations promise to take many of the artistic possibilities of type from the realm of programming and return them to you.

Adobe's *multiple masters* font technology is an example of this type of innovation. Multiple masters fonts provide you with at least two outline masters to define a letter form. If both a light and an extra bold version of a font are provided, you can select any weight variation in between those two extremes. Some fonts include width variations too; This enables you to make medium, demibold, or variations of those weights in expanded, condensed, or other combinations.

Graphics artists and designers long have known that type for small text sizes such as 6 or 12 point needs to be designed differently than type used at larger display sizes. When type was cast in metal, the adjustments could be made by hand, including shaving away the sides of character slugs to tweak the space between letters. Digital typefaces allow for spacing variations, but scaling letters from small to large size means the letters themselves merely fatten up as they increase in height.

TrueType has built the capability for designers to program in these subtle variations of weight changes and preserve letter form strokes during scaling into its technology. Adobe's multiple masters fonts enable you to make specific changes in particular masters to preserve not only letter form weight variations during scaling but also changes in x height, shoulders, serifs, and so on. Masters in the smaller sizes can incorporate "ink traps" and other subtle nuances lost in the transfer from metal to digital type. (Ink traps were actually small indentions in corners of letters where part of the letter form was missing. When the ink was smashed onto the paper during printing, ink spread into the missing area instead of rounding the edges of the letter's corners. Only observable under magnification, this small variation contributed greatly to creating sharp, crisp letters at small sizes. If digital letters were to have ink traps under current technology, they would be dramatically apparent and aesthetically unappealing when scaled to larger sizes.)

Summary

Thousands of fonts exist for the Macintosh, and that number grows daily as libraries from old type foundries are digitized. Thanks to software's flexibility, new typefaces are being invented as well. Knowing type and font technology on the Mac can only enhance your efficiency. The future promises to bring more aesthetically pleasing typefaces, along with new technologies that will make type design more accessible to users.

Chapter 10: Graphic Arts Support

What usually separates pros from novices in any given field is that newcomers have yet to master "tricks of the trade." Many of the Macintosh's tricks make life as easy for the computer artist as for the artist on a real-world drawing board. This chapter examines some of the support programs that can save experienced users time and effort and help novices get professional results.

In This Chapter

▼ Clip art

▼ Page templates

▼ Backgrounds

▼ Utilities

Part II
What Put the Mac in Business

Clip Art

Before the Macintosh, artists often subscribed to clip art services. These companies periodically sent out large magazines full of cartoon figures, line art, holiday and seasonal scenes, and other graphics to be photostated, copied, or actually clipped off the page (hence the name clip art) and used in whatever the artist was working on at the moment. Clip art was adequate for many projects. It was fast and inexpensive, and it did not require any artistic ability. You just cut around the edges of the picture, slapped some rubber cement on the back, and pasted it in.

As Mac artists honed their graphics arts skills, they realized the need for "electronic clip art." Today, you can find electronic clip art in every possible format from MacPaint to Encapsulated PostScript (EPS). Because clip art is intended to be copied, there is no problem using it in your company newsletter or a client's advertisement. In fact, generally the only thing you are not allowed to do with a clip art image is resell it as part of another clip art library. What you should do with any clip art images you decide to use, however, is modify them in some way, especially if you use one as a logo or in some highly visible location such as a menu cover or an ad. You can add color, flip the image, ungroup the drawings' individual elements and rearrange them, or combine several images into a new one. If you use unmodified clip art, you are almost certain to see "your" piece of clip art used somewhere else by someone who bought the same clip art disk you did. Figure 10.1 shows several possible uses for the same piece of clip art.

Figure 10.1
Clip art can be used in many different ways.

Chapter 10
Graphic Arts Support

A look through a current software catalog shows at least 10 different publishers and dozens of disks of art files. In fact, many collections even are available on CD-ROM. You also can find huge collections of drawn or scanned art in user group and online services' libraries. These are generally free for the cost of the disk or the download time. Some, of course, are shareware, meaning you pay a small fee directly to the creator rather than to the software publishers. Figure 10.2 shows a montage of typical bitmapped images from DublClick's WetPaint series, combined in SuperPaint.

Figure 10.2
Clip art images are combined in SuperPaint.

Although most bitmapped art comes in standard 72 dpi PAINT (original MacPaint) format, at least one company offers high-resolution 300 dpi images. Metro ImageBase features 14 different art disks scanned as TIFF images usable in PageMaker, QuarkXPress, ReadySetGo, Ventura Publisher, Cricket Paint, and WordPerfect. Although priced beyond reach of the casual user, these disks are a worthwhile investment for design shops, ad agencies, or serious desktop publishers. There are separate libraries for items such as food, weekend sports, business graphics, holiday and seasonal symbols, and even Art Deco and Art Nouveau. You can find special-purpose libraries too, such as medical illustrations, tools and hardware, and cartoon characters. Any photo or drawing can be scanned into a TIFF image. Figure 10.3 shows an illustration from the medical art library.

Most desktop publishing programs and graphics programs such as SuperPaint, Canvas, and MacDraw accept PICT format images like those from the DrawArt collection. DrawArt's high-resolution libraries include sports and leisure, business and education, and a set of borders and graphic designs. Figure 10.4 shows a typical PICT image. This particular image was downloaded from America Online's graphics library.

Figure 10.3

This image was scanned from a medical art library.

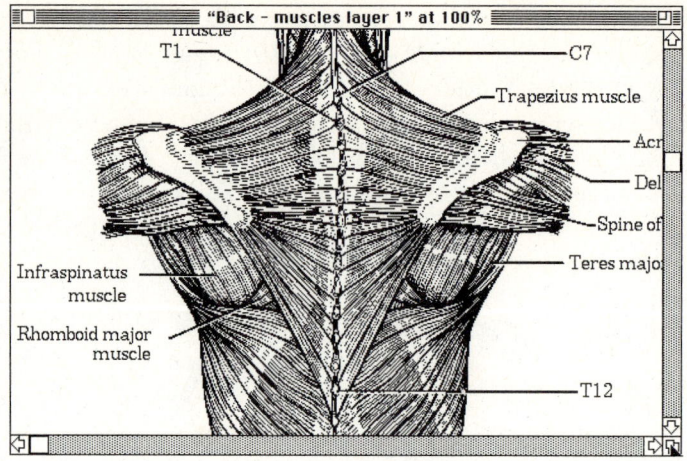

Figure 10.4

There is clip art for almost anything you can imagine.

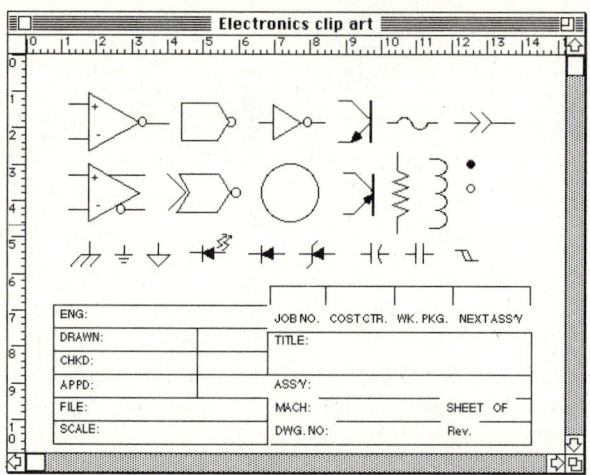

EPS images have some remarkable features, not the least of which is their ability to reproduce well on any PostScript output device, ranging from a home or office laser printer at 300 dpi to a magazine-quality imagesetter at 2,540 dpi. The image's quality depends, obviously, on which printer is used. A 300 dpi printer produces a picture quality that resembles a newspaper photo. A magazine-quality printer, operating at 1,270 or 2,540 dpi, produces smoother, higher quality picture tones from the same piece of art because it has smaller dots with which to work. EPS images can be resized to any dimensions you want, without the annoying "jaggies" that bitmapped images present. Even though EPS images may appear low quality on a 72 dpi screen, they do print properly. They also can be rotated and distorted without losing their "readability." Figure 10.5 shows some clip art from the Images With Impact! series by 3G Graphics.

Chapter 10
Graphic Arts Support

Figure 10.5
PostScript clip art will not look as good onscreen as it does on the printed page.

EPS art's chief disadvantage is that it takes longer to draw an image onscreen, and files are much larger than for bitmapped images. EPS art also tends to cost more because it is more complex and takes longer to create. You can avoid the expense by scanning a picture into your Mac with a scanner and then editing the scanned images with your favorite paint program. Adobe Streamline enables you to take a bitmapped image and convert it to an EPS image, smoothing (or streamlining) all the rough edges. You then can manipulate the EPS file you just created as if it were any commercially produced image. If you use much art and like the flexibility of EPS files, Streamline may be a good investment.

Page Templates

A template is a master layout. Templates are time-savers when you are working with many pages that maintain the same format. You can create templates for virtually any kind of page you might produce, from a page of address labels to a newsletter or corporate brochure.

Placeholder templates usually contain repeating headlines and graphics elements, as well as generic text, or *placeholders*, in the correct type styles and fonts. Rather than placeholders, these templates could contain a style sheet to let you assign type styles as you pour text into the publication from your word processor.

Grid templates are a more general-purpose page setup system that specify settings such as page size, measurement systems, ruler guides, column guides, and margin settings. Grid templates often are used to set up labels, business cards, or similar items.

> **Note** When you save a publication in a graphics or desktop publishing program such as Aldus SuperPaint or PageMaker, or in a word processor like Microsoft Word, you have the option of saving your document in a special template format called a *stationery pad*. When you open a document that is saved as a stationery pad, the application opens an untitled window with the elements from the template. The original document is unchanged.

System 7 lets you create stationery pads from the document's Get Info window. On the Mac's desktop, simply click on a document to select it, go to the **File** menu, and select **Get Info**. Click on the box marked **Stationery Pad** at the lower-right of the window, and close the **Get Info** window. The document's icon now has changed to what looks like two gray pages (see figure 10.6) rather than its usual icon. Many programs support the System 7 stationery pad feature; they have their own stationery icon. Documents created with programs that do not support this feature will use the generic icon shown in figure 10.6 if you change the document to a stationery pad through the **Get Info** window. Other programs use their own unique method for creating templates; you're better off using the method that the program prefers.

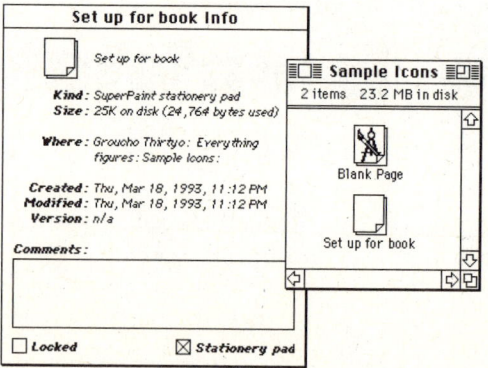

Figure 10.6
Stationery pads have multi-page icons.

Most DTP programs come with a ready-made selection of templates. (Timeworks' Publish It! Easy prefers to call its templates Sample Layouts, but the intent is the same.) Using these professionally designed pages can help you create better looking publications if you are not artistically inclined, and they also can serve as a springboard for your own page design ideas. PageMaker's template collection includes letterheads, envelopes, newsletters, price lists, business cards, and more. Figure 10.7 shows a few samples in thumbnail form.

Chapter 10
Graphic Arts Support

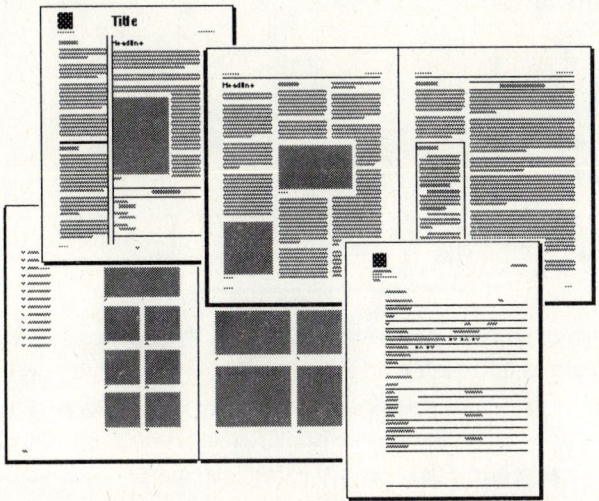

Figure 10.7
PageMaker's template collections cover almost everything you need.

Templates are particularly suited to creating business forms. The tedious chore of designing a workable format for such items as invoices and purchase orders already is done for you. In fact, the business form templates that PageMaker, Publish It! Easy, and similar programs provide have proven so popular there is now at least one commercially available library of clip art business forms. All you need to do is add your company logo and address block to DrawArt's library of PICT-format business forms.

Postcraft has created sets of professionally-designed templates for ReadySetGO!, PageMaker, and QuarkXPress. The package includes 219 different layouts for brochures, newsletters, business reply cards, and stationery, in color and black and white. All you need to do is drop in your own text and graphics. The camera-ready art includes crop and registration marks, and fold/score lines as needed.

Avery's MacLabelPro program has a very specific set of templates for Avery's line of blank labels. It can be used with both ImageWriters and laser printers,

Part II
What Put the Mac in Business

and it has a separate template for each size and style of label, including shipping labels, name tags, rotary file cards, cassette and disk labels, and more. Figure 10.8 shows a selection of Avery label templates.

Figure 10.8
Avery labels come in all sizes and shapes.

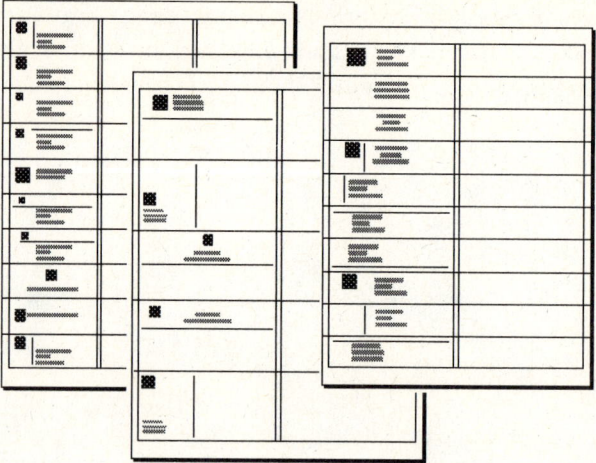

The mail merge function, supported by popular word processors and databases such as Microsoft Works and Word, also lets you import logos or other graphics from your own library or from the clip art library supplied. In addition, its drawing tools let you create original art directly on the label. Although not as versatile as other programs, mail merge works well and cheaply.

Background Patterns and Textures

In the area of graphics and desktop publishing, having the right background is a big help. If your personal background includes a degree in graphic arts, that will help, but the type of background you really need is the pattern or texture you might use behind a block of text or as part of a graphic.

For many years, drawing-board artists have used rub-down patterns or hand-drawn shading and textures for backgrounds. Computer artists have to make do with a limited selection of patterns and textures that come in paint and draw programs. Most of these applications let you create your own patterns pixel by pixel, but usually limit you to working within an 8-pixel by 8-pixel square. DublClick's WetPaint clip art series includes a selection of different 8- by 8-pixel patterns, one set of which is shown in Figure 10.9, and a Pattern Mover that lets you install them in MacPaint.

Chapter 10
Graphic Arts Support

Figure 10.9
Each set of WetPaint files has a different pattern palette.

Adobe has solved the patterns and textures problem by creating five sets of patterns in EPS format, offered as Adobe's Pattern and Texture library. You can choose the right background for virtually anything you create. In addition to basic graphics patterns of dots, lines, and gradient shading, there are many architectural patterns, including a dozen different ways of laying brick. There are standard U.S. Geodetic Survey cartographic and lithologic patterns for various types of rock in cross-section and surface mapping. Another feature you may consider is "wallpaper" patterns: 144 different designs ranging from quilts, geometric patterns, and Art Deco designs to morning glories and tulips.

Is your artwork taken for granite? It could be, if you use Artbeats Marble and Granite textures. These come in CD-ROM format, in a two disk set with 140 high-resolution TIFF images for pre-press plus 120 multi-media backgrounds. They're ideal for rendering and surface mapping, as well as for using as a background for slides or DTP layouts. Artbeats also publishes a library of full-page images, including both abstract designs and common advertising and DTP images.

Figure 10.10
A few of the more than 350 patterns in Adobe's Pattern and Texture library.

Utilities

When you deal with a service bureau, you need to verify that the fonts you use in your publication are available to the service bureau's printer and that there is no problem with font ID conflicts (see chapter 9, "Fonts and Typography," for more information about font ID conflicts). The best way to accomplish this is to use a font usage reporter, such as CheckList, to keep a list of the fonts you have used.

Many service bureaus have one or more of these programs and run them automatically when you bring a disk for printing, but you may find it helpful to have your own copy, particularly if you like to use unusual display fonts or you tend to mix many type styles in your publications. Looking at a long list of faces can be a valuable learning experience. CheckList is available as shareware from most user groups and online services. In addition to telling you exactly which fonts are in use, CheckList checks links and lists the entries in a PageMaker style sheet, complete with examples. Figure 10.11 shows CheckList in action.

Figure 10.11
CheckList creates a list of the fonts you used in a publication.

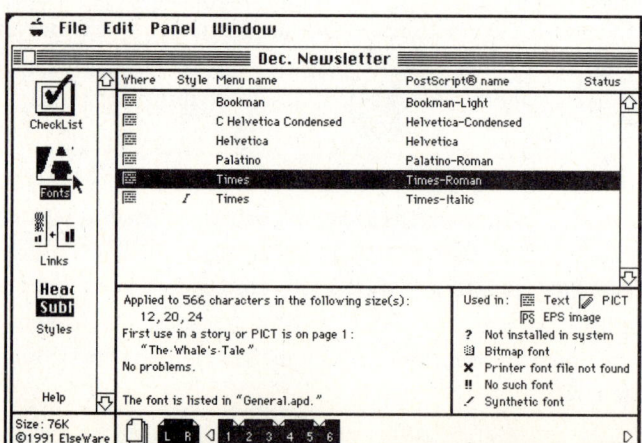

File Finders

When several clip art files are installed on a hard disk, it is often difficult to find the right one. If you know the name of the page you want, a utility like Fast Find locates it, but names are sometimes hard to remember and not always sufficiently descriptive. (Was that Art Deco border on Borders 3 or Borders 5?) Some users keep a printout of their clip art collections in a notebook for quick browsing. Others use the indexes that usually come with all commercial art files. Serious graphic artists and DTP users are beginning to use a file management program such as Mariah or NowScrapbook to keep track of what is where.

Mariah is a multimedia organizer that keeps graphics, sounds, and even text and animation files grouped in collections for easy retrieval. Each collection can hold as many as 32,000 items, and you can open several of these huge files simultaneously, assuming you have a hard disk the size of Cleveland and plenty of RAM. Mariah locates a file by name, type (PICT file, sound resource, and so on), or keyword. Finding a specific file in one of Mariah's huge collections is surprisingly quick. It takes less than three seconds to find a keyword in a 100M collection. When you place a file into a Mariah collection, you can assign it as many keywords as you like by typing them into the keyword box, as shown in figure 10.12. As long as you remember just one of the possible keywords for the graphics you want to locate, you can call the correct file up quickly and easily.

Chapter 10
Graphic Arts Support

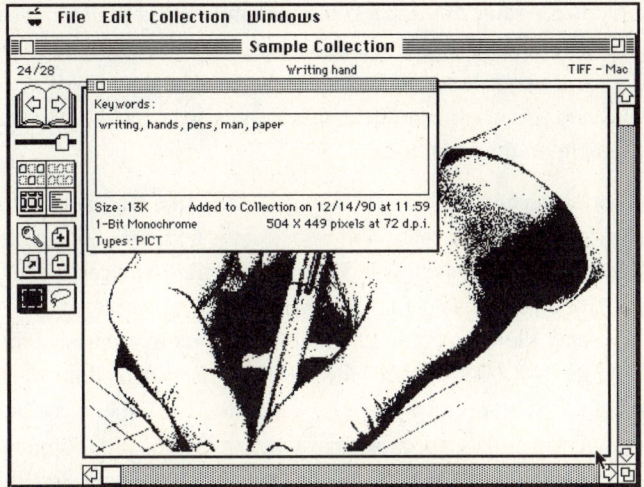

Figure 10.12
Mariah's keyword search lets you assign several words to a graphic.

If you are not sure exactly what you are looking for, you simply can browse through either thumbnail or full-size, full-color versions of your files. Mariah

Part II
What Put the Mac in Business

displays eight thumbnails at a time and provides information about whichever one you select. You can keep project notes together with the graphics. You also can save up to 10 seconds of sound per file and play it back by clicking the Play Sound button. Figure 10.13 shows a page of Mariah's thumbnails.

Figure 10.13

Mariah's thumbnail views of your graphics files help you find what you need.

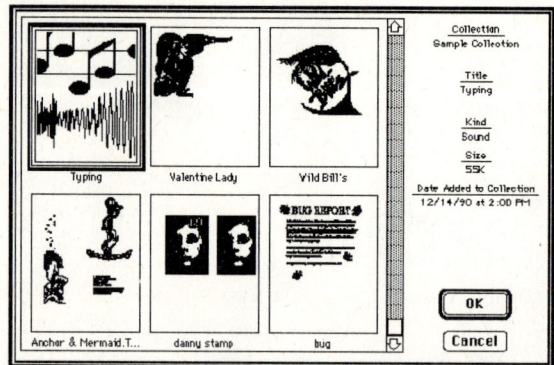

After you find the item you are searching for, you can export it in several ways. Obviously, you can export it in whatever format it is currently in. A paint document can be exported as a paint document, but it also can be converted to a PICT or TIFF file simply by exporting it as one. You even can export some types of files to an IBM-compatible format to share art with IBM users.

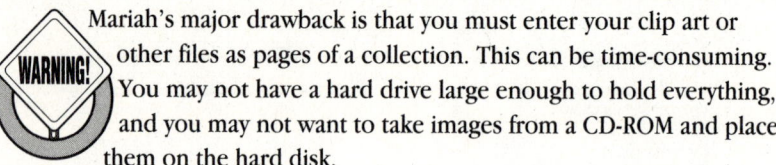

Mariah's major drawback is that you must enter your clip art or other files as pages of a collection. This can be time-consuming. You may not have a hard drive large enough to hold everything, and you may not want to take images from a CD-ROM and place them on the hard disk.

Now Scrapbook is part of the Now Utility package. Like Mariah, it catalogs images in most graphics formats, and also accepts text, AIFF sound files, System 7 sound files, and even QuickTime movie files. You can create different scrapbooks for particular projects and open them from the scrapbook menu. View the contents of the scrapbook in thumbnail format as shown in figure 10.14, or in detail view. Use the Clipboard editor to change text in a scrapbook item, or to touch up a graphic. The clipboard editor includes familiar graphics selection marquees, the lasso, and cropping tools, as well as text entry tools. You can print directly from the Now Scrapbook, too, or print a catalog of your scrapbook files. If you have the QuickTime extension installed, you can use the scrapbook to view the first frame of any QuickTime movie, play the whole movie, or export it to another application.

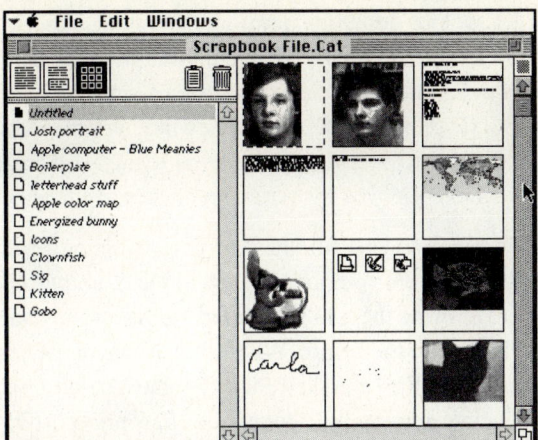

Figure 10.14
If you can't remember the name of an item, use the thumbnail view to find it.

Font Managers

A great many management utilities are available for type. Some let you customize an existing font; others let you apply various special effects to it or adjust its path. Some work not with the characters themselves, but to reorganize fonts by their names or to restructure the type menus.

Brøderbund's TypeStyler is an easy-to-learn program that lets you bend, twist, and rotate type to create special effects for headlines, ads, logos, and whatever other uses you can invent. TypeStyler includes 35 different effects, including arched, skewed, fisheye, and 35-letter styles (inline, outline, filled, and so forth). You can apply these effects to any of the 10 supplied fonts or your own PostScript fonts, which the program converts to its SmoothFont format. You can print directly from TypeStyler or save your creation as an EPS, Paint, PICT, or Adobe Illustrator file and paste it into another document.

Creating Your Own Fonts

Before there were laser printers, you could design your own bit-mapped fonts, one pixel at a time. The results were often quite good, although it was a time-consuming process, and it was necessary to draw a complete character set for every point size you wanted to use. When PostScript and the laser printer were introduced, the process changed. Fonts were described mathematically, rather than by pixels. TrueType has changed the process still more, but it is still possible to create your own fonts or modify existing ones, using Altsys' Fontographer.

Part II
What Put the Mac in Business

Fontographer is a tool for designing new fonts or editing existing ones. It can also convert PICT images to editable PostScript outlines. The main program window displays the entire font, with each letter or symbol in a little box. Clicking on one of these boxes opens another window, which lets you edit a large version of the character. You can start from scratch and create an entire font or modify characters as you wish from an existing alphabet.

The tools are familiar to anyone who has used a drawing program. Fontographer characters are composed of straight lines and Bézier curves, just as if you were drawing them in FreeHand, Illustrator, or some other Draw program. You place the control points exactly where you want them. It is possible to automatically scale, skew, flip, or rotate an entire set of characters by the same amount by entering the appropriate settings in a dialog box. The program also creates bitmapped versions of your fonts for screen display.

Note: Letraset's FontStudio 2.0 and Fontographer 3.5 now let you create or modify TrueType fonts for System 7. With FontStudio, you can make a font from scratch; import Illustrator or EPS graphics; auto-trace a PICT, TIFF, or Paint template; or import a PostScript Type 1, Type 3, or LetraFont, as well as TrueType fonts. Tear-off tool palettes and multiple windows make the job easier. FontStudio even lets you create and store a working library of strokes, serifs, and other letter parts. FontStudio can import fonts from Adobe, Bitstream, LetraStudio Display Type (LetraFonts), Image Club Hot Type, Monotype, Fontographer, Ikarus M, Olduvai, URW, The Font Company, Casady & Greene, CompuGraphic, Emigre Graphics, and Treacyfaces.

If you are already comfortable with a graphics program such as Aldus FreeHand or Adobe Illustrator and do not wish to invest the time or money for a program such as FontStudio or Fontographer, there is another possibility. Metamorphosis Pro, from Altsys, is a conversion utility that turns any PostScript font into an editable outline format you can work with in FreeHand or Illustrator. You can use your graphics program to add color and texture to letters or stretch, flip, distort, or do whatever you like to them. Then you can reconvert them to Type 1 or 3 PostScript or TrueType, and they are compatible with Adobe Type Manager. Metamorphosis also works with Fontographer, enabling you to take advantage of Fontographer's bag of tricks on custom-made fonts.

A Closer Look If you have PostScript fonts formatted for an IBM PC or another non-Mac computer, you can use Metamorphosis to convert them for Mac use. The manual omits this information, but here is how to do it: Download the fonts to the laser printer from the PC, then switch the printer to Macintosh mode. Next, use Apple's LaserWriter font utility to get the official name of the font as the printer sees it. (Be sure to get capitalization, spaces, and so on correct.) In Fontographer, open a new, empty font file with exactly the same name as the printer font; then generate a screen font file for the dummy font. Switch to Metamorphosis, open the dummy screen font, and start the conversion.

Font Menu Managers

If you are "into" type the way some people are "into" collecting stamps, it will not take long before your type menus become unmanageable. Service bureaus, computer typesetting services, designers, and serious desktop publishers may have several hundred fonts available (and very crowded menus)—but some handy utilities can help.

Even if you have only a few dozen fonts, you can spend what seems like ages scrolling down the menu from Aardvark to Zapf. If you do not have a great memory for typefaces, you also can spend a great deal of time trying to remember the difference between Helvetica Bold and Helvetica Black. Some type publishers, including Adobe, put letters in front of the type names, which further confuses the menu. For example, VAG Rounded Bold's true name is B VAG Rounded Bold. (The B stands, redundantly, for bold.) The Mac lists everything alphabetically, so you find B VAG Rounded Bold between Avant Garde and Bookman, not in front of Windsor, where it belongs. If you have several bold faces installed, they all are listed as B whatevers if they are from a company using this naming convention. If not, they are with the rest of their font families.

Several applications handle type for you. Suitcase and Font/DA Juggler let you store your spare fonts (and DAs) in suitcase files to open when you need them. Suitcase also lets you display type names in their own fonts when you pull down the menu, providing a quick and easy catalog if you cannot remember the difference between Bodoni and Bookman. Figure 10.15 shows how this feature works. Simply press the Option key as you open the **Font** menu in any application. It takes a little longer to display the menu this way because the computer draws each font in its own typeface, but it is often worth the extra time.

Chapter 10
Graphic Arts
Support

Figure 10.15
Use Suitcase to display familiar names with faces attached.

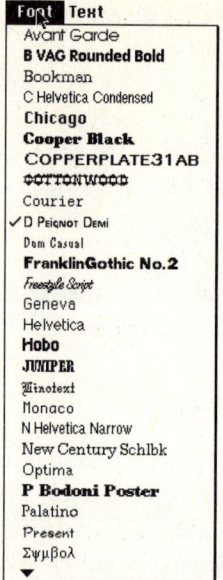

Fontina lists all available styles of a type family together, and it displays all active fonts at once in your choice of type size from 6 to 12 points, narrowing the columns, truncating the names, and displaying as many columns as necessary to fit all the font names onscreen. You never have to scroll a type menu again, but you soon could regret having hundreds of fonts installed. As you drag your pointer down the lists, Fontina displays the full name of the font at the top of the list, in its font, so you can see what you are getting.

Adobe TypeReunion solves Adobe's font-naming convention problem by setting up hierarchical menus. When you select **Helvetica**, for example, an arrow points to a submenu. The submenu lists the styles presently available, with the lightest weight on top and the heaviest at the bottom. Figure 10.16 shows the **Font** menu with TypeReunion installed. The selected font family is underlined, and the weight in use is checked on the submenu.

Figure 10.16
Adobe Type Reunion reunites font families.

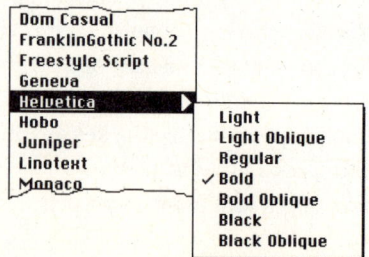

Putting the Best Face Forward

As mentioned in chapter 9, "Fonts and Typography," Adobe's new SuperATM solves yet another type of type problem, one faced by many Mac users when they trade files with other users. If you import a file that uses a font you don't have, SuperATM lets you maintain the look and formatting of the original document by substituting the closest available typeface to the original. The package also includes ATM and Adobe Type Reunion, plus the Adobe CD-ROM with 1,350 typefaces to buy as you go.

Summary

Whatever aspect of graphics or DTP you are involved in, there are utilities to make your job quicker and easier. You can use clip art, predesigned templates, and utilities to find art files or other documents quickly. There are also tools to make onscreen fonts look better or let you create your own fonts. All serve to enhance your Mac's performance.

Part III: Mainstream Mac Applications

In This Part

Chapter 11: Word Processors

Interlude: Cool Word Stuff

Chapter 12: Spreadsheets

Interlude: Cool Excel Stuff

Chapter 13: Databases

Interlude: Cool FileMaker Stuff

Chapter 14: Integrated Programs

Chapter 15: Games for Fun!

Chapter 16: Education on the Mac

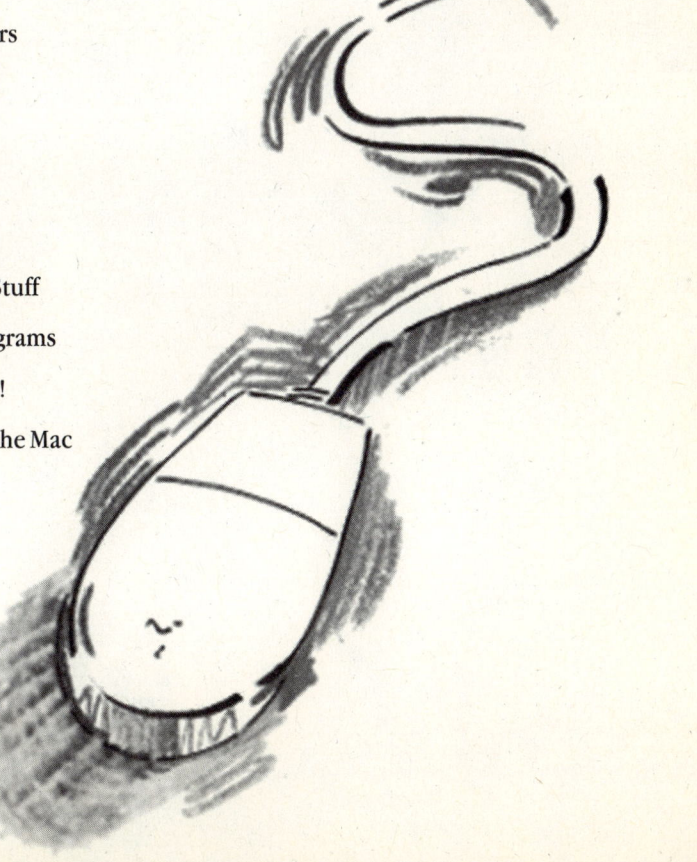

Chapter 11: Word Processors

This chapter discusses word processing programs on the Macintosh computer. All of these programs offers features that, by themselves, are enough to make it worth your while to purchase a Mac. With the transition to System 7, word processors are changing to take advantage of the new operating system. This chapter describes some of the new programs that recently have appeared and the developments you can expect to see.

In This Chapter

- ▼ Word processing versus paper processing
- ▼ Features
- ▼ Text formatting
- ▼ Graphics
- ▼ Searching and changing
- ▼ Importing and exporting
- ▼ Product evaluations

Part III
Mainstream
Mac Applications

Word Processing Versus Paper Processing

Few people can write even a short letter without a typographical or spelling error, improper punctuation, or poor use of grammar. The power of computerized word processing power means errors never need appear in the final product. Whether the project is a one-page memo, a 20-page report, or a 1,000-page computer book (like this one), organizing, writing, and editing are easier with a word processor.

> **Note:** In addition to saving the time and frustration of typing and retyping, computers actually can improve your writing. If you do not know how to spell, one of several excellent spelling checkers can catch your errors—sometimes even as you type them! If you grope for that perfect word, simply open a 1.4 million-word thesaurus while typing. If the word you need is not there, it probably does not exist. If you are not good at organizing your writing, purchase one of the many excellent, easy-to-use outliners and idea processors. Even grammar editors and style editors are available that are almost (but not quite) good enough to replace human editors.

Typical Features

Word processors have come a long way in the years since MacWrite 1.0 was given away with the Macintosh 128K. At one time WYSIWYG and mouse-based text selection was big news; now style sheets, macros, separate editing/drawing layers, and closed-file Global Replace searches have taken center stage. Many of the distinctive features that set apart word processing programs are discussed in this chapter.

Everyone who uses a word processor should know how to use the following features, because they add to your efficiency and enjoyment:

▼ **Searching and Changing:** This standard feature enables you to search and change text and styles.

▼ **Layout and Formatting:** These features give you the power to control how your documents appear onscreen and on paper. Word processors use special codes or symbols that enable you to see every character entered: spaces, tabs, returns, paragraphs, sections, and so on.

▼ **Mail Merging:** This feature enables you to generate any number of personalized documents by combining a word processing document and database information.

▼ **Style Sheets:** Style sheets are preset formats, sometimes called tags, that save keystrokes when you create formats. For instance, one item on a style sheet might contain a command for headline text or body text. With just one or two keystrokes, you can change the styles to your preset format. Many page layout programs can import style sheets. Always try to use a page layout program that enables you to import your word processor styles.

▼ **Outlining:** This feature organizes your document to resemble the outlines you did in high school English classes. An outliner usually collapses your document to main headings so you can rearrange major ideas, categorize headline and body text, and easily view the top-level structure of your document.

▼ **Tables:** This feature enables you to build illustrative tables with or without column and grid lines. Comparative reviews and feature lists are two common uses for tables.

▼ **Graphics:** The Macintosh always has integrated text and graphics easily. Today, several word processors have built-in powerful, full-color, object-oriented drawing functions.

▼ **Macros:** This feature enables you to combine several steps into one easily. Similar in concept to style sheets, macros control actions, enabling you to substitute one keystroke or mouse click for several repetitive actions.

▼ **Importing and Exporting:** All word processors use different formats to store styles and other document data. It is important to be able to read (import) and write (export) formats to and from other word processors and platforms.

Text Editing Features

When you track the time it takes to work on a long document, less than half of it is spent typing. More time is used in selecting, moving, and deleting text—in other words, editing. For this reason, it is important that your word

Part III

Mainstream
Mac Applications

processor has powerful, easy-to-use editing features. Early versions of stand-alone word processing computers set the standard for keyboard-based, onscreen editing. Early Macintosh word processors ignored that standard and made you use a mouse to move the insertion point between characters before you could edit. Today, most Macintosh word processors offer all standard keyboard editing commands—and then some.

 Having a wealth of keyboard editing commands is important when you are writing because your hands do not have to stray from the keyboard, and you can maintain a good typing rhythm. When you are editing, however, use the mouse. It is better for quickly moving and scanning through text.

Additional editing keys and the improved layout of extended, 101-key keyboards are usually worth the extra expense. In addition to providing dedicated numeric keypads and cursor keys, these keyboards have *Reverse Delete*, *Home*, *End*, *Page Up* and *Page Down* keys. These commands enable the typist to view different parts of the document without moving the actual insertion point. When you are looking at one part of a document and the insertion point is at another, press the spacebar (or any other key) to return to the page with the insertion point. This capability is a primitive *marking* feature.

Advanced editing features include noncontiguous text selecting; marking; glossaries; multiple undos; multiple clipboards; annotation; and spell, style, and grammar checking.

Noncontiguous text selecting means you can have separate blocks of text from different places in your document selected at the same time. This feature is helpful for editors or technical writers who need to work with text throughout a document. Marking features enable you to set and name *bookmarks* or *placeholders* at different locations in the document. You quickly can jump to these locations merely by pressing a command key and typing the name of the location. Glossaries enable you to make lists of frequently used words or phrases and use command key shortcuts to insert them into the text instead of typing them every time.

Multiple undos are particularly useful to programmers who can work backward through an involved editing session. At this time, only Nisus offers this feature, leaving the rest to the Mac standard of undoing only the last action performed (see the section, "Nisus," later in this chapter).

Chapter 11
Word Processors

One way to partially get around the limited undo features of most word processors is to create an extra file for major text deletions. Instead of deleting the text permanently, cut and paste it into this extra file.

Multiple clipboards are almost as useful as multiple undos. With this feature, you can have one clipboard for cutting and pasting, and use the others for frequently used text—that is, a simple glossary. Utilities that provide multiple clipboard functionality include Mainstay's ClickPaste and Olduvai's MultiClip.

Spelling checkers and thesauruses are standard for word processors. Grammar and style checkers are somewhat less common. They can help your writing by flagging incorrect syntax or improper phrasing, but they will not help with the organization or flow of your writing, which is usually more important.

Layout and Formatting

The Mac and page-layout software such as PageMaker combined to launch the desktop publishing revolution several years ago, but the layout and formatting features of present-day word processors rival even the best of the original DTP software.

The Mac's graphically based word processors are strong because document layout and formatting are designed on the screen. Rather than type obscure codes to format a document, straightforward commands determine the text's characteristics, such as font styles (bold, italic, underline, and so on) and size. The Mac's WYSIWYG interface also enables you to determine the document's text layout by centering, justifying, putting it in columns, and so on. Like any tool, this one is both good and bad. The combination of powerful features and easy access has led to both well-designed and poorly designed documents.

The aim of this section is not to teach document design techniques but to define terms and show how formatting and layout tools fit together. There are four basic levels of formatting control: characters, paragraphs, sections of documents, and entire documents.

At the lowest level is *character formatting*, which includes font styles such as bold and italic. Building upon the original seven font styles of MacWrite 1.0 (bold, italic, shadow, outline, underline, superscript, and subscript), many word processors have added strikeout, double underline, word underline, boxed, small caps, and multiple levels of superscript and subscript.

Part III
Mainstream Mac Applications

A Closer Look In general, it is better to avoid styles and character formatting functions than to overuse them. Sometimes the job requires many different styles or multiple uses of the same style, but most of the time, using too many styles distracts your audience and hides your message. In most cases, content is more important than appearance.

The next level of formatting includes commands for controlling paragraph margins and line spacing. These functions usually are grouped on a ruler or are accessible through a menu (see figure 11.1). Generally, you want to adjust the spacing between the last line of one paragraph and the first line of the next, and between section heads or headlines and body text. Rulers also give you control over indentation, tab stops for first lines of body text, and tab stops for each line of numbered or bulleted lists.

Figure 11.1
Microsoft Word's ruler enables you to easily control a document's format.

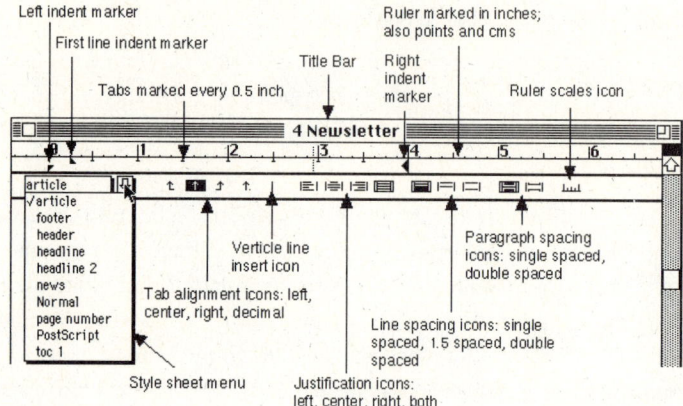

Document formatting controls include headers, footers, tabs, and margins. Usually, you set defaults for the entire document before you begin to work and then adjust the values for different sections of text. For instance, you can have separate headers and footers for different pages, whereas tabs and margins are specific to certain paragraphs.

A Closer Look Many word processors allow you to show formatting characters like spaces, end of paragraph or section markers, page breaks and the like. Learning to write documents with these formatting marks showing can give you important clues to why your document appears the way it does. In Word the command that shows it is called **Show Paragraph Marks** on the **View** menu, and in MacWrite it's called **Show Invisibles**. Whatever this command is called, learn to understand and work with these markers showing.

Style Sheets

Style sheets record frequently used formatting and layout styles. For example, if you create a document that has numerous section headings, manually changing a line of body text with 11-point New York Condensed with a 1/4-inch paragraph indent to a section heading with 18-point Helvetica Bold with no indent certainly would involve a lot of time and mouse work. Creating a style sheet that records a name and format for each style (for example, BodyText or SectionHead) allows you to simply select the corresponding name from a menu. The program automatically applies the recorded format to the selected text (see figure 11.2).

Chapter 11
Word Processors

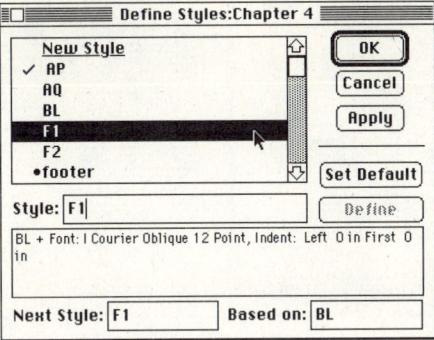

Figure 11.2
Microsoft Word's **Define Styles** dialog box enables you to rapidly format paragraphs.

A recorded style also helps you quickly change the entire document's formatting. For example, if you decide to change the body text from 11-point New York to 12-point Bookman, style sheets automatically convert all body text in the document to the new definition. You avoid manually selecting the body text in each section and changing it yourself.

 Using style sheets can be a tremendous time saver! It is a good idea to create standard style sheets that you can import into new documents.

A template or *stationery* file contains a style sheet and preset formatting (for example, margins, and indentations). Many secretaries set up these files for form letters so they only have to type in a closing. System 7 enables you to turn most documents into stationery files on the desktop, although most word processors allow their creation within the program itself.

Page Preview

Page Preview shows how your printed document will look. Pages in the page preview mode are reduced so that you can see how your page immediately strikes the eye before the reader concentrates on the actual text (see figure

Part III

Mainstream Mac Applications

11.3). Because this view may prompt you to make minor formatting adjustments, the capability to edit in page preview mode is valuable. Instead of switching between views, you immediately can see how your changes affect the printed copy.

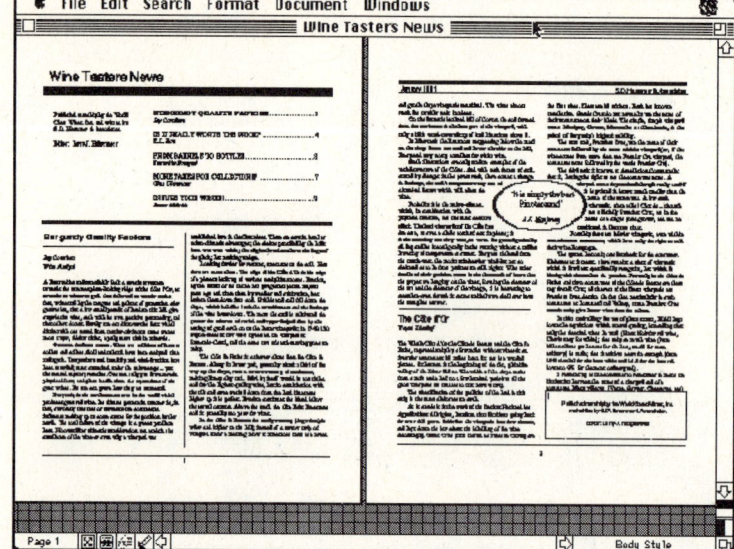

Figure 11.3

Taste's WYSIWYG page preview feature is similar to full-scale page layout programs' display.

WARNING! For the page preview to be accurate, the right printer must be selected through the Chooser. This automatically sets default margins and page sizes. The differences between the ImageWriter page, the LaserWriter page, and the StyleWriter page are small but noticeable and dramatically can affect the final number of pages in a document, page breaks, and so on. Formatting a document for the wrong printer happens often and wastes a lot of time.

Index and Table-of-Contents Generation

In longer documents, you may need to begin with a table of contents and conclude with an index. Both are easy to create—and can be automated—in some word processors.

Most word processors have you select text to be included in the index with an **Insert Index Entry** command, and then select the **Generate Index** command to create the index automatically. Each selected entry in the document has its own entry in the index, along with a list of pages where the selection appears. Generating a table of contents is similar. You select section headers with an **Insert TOC Entry** command, and these selections automatically are listed with page numbers when you generate the table of contents.

A Closer Look It is sometimes hard to remember what already has been indexed or selected for the contents listing with this method, so WordPerfect has introduced an index- and contents-generating feature that uses a concordance (a file with a list of words) to keep track of which words and topics have been selected. Other programs probably will offer this feature in the future as well.

Organizing

Word processors today offer many different aids for organizing information. These include cross-referencing, outlining, and tables.

Cross-referencing ensures that multiple references to a figure or block of text on a page remain consistent at print time. If you refer the reader to other specific sections of your document (for example, "see page 12") and that page number or other reference changes, cross-referencing automatically updates the text. You save time and avoid the embarrassment should you overlook a reference in the text and mislead your readers.

The outliner, an automated version of the technique your teachers taught you in high school writing classes, is another time-saver (see figure 11.4). Only Microsoft Word has a built-in outliner, although the best application outliner is MORE from Symantec and the best desk accessory (DA) outliner is Acta from Symmetry Software. Both should have System 7-compatible versions available at the time of this printing.

Tables are an excellent way to present summary numerical data such as sales records, lab results, and budget statements. Tables are also a good format to describe items or objects with similar features. Microsoft Word is the only package to offer true table generation. You can imitate table generation in other packages by using columns or tabs and drawing lines, but you do not get the convenience of having cells automatically resized to fit the text, and you cannot individually manipulate text from individual cells. The new version of MacWrite Pro should offer table generation similar to Microsoft Word's.

Figure 11.4

Microsoft Word's outlining mode enables you to view your document at different levels of abstraction.

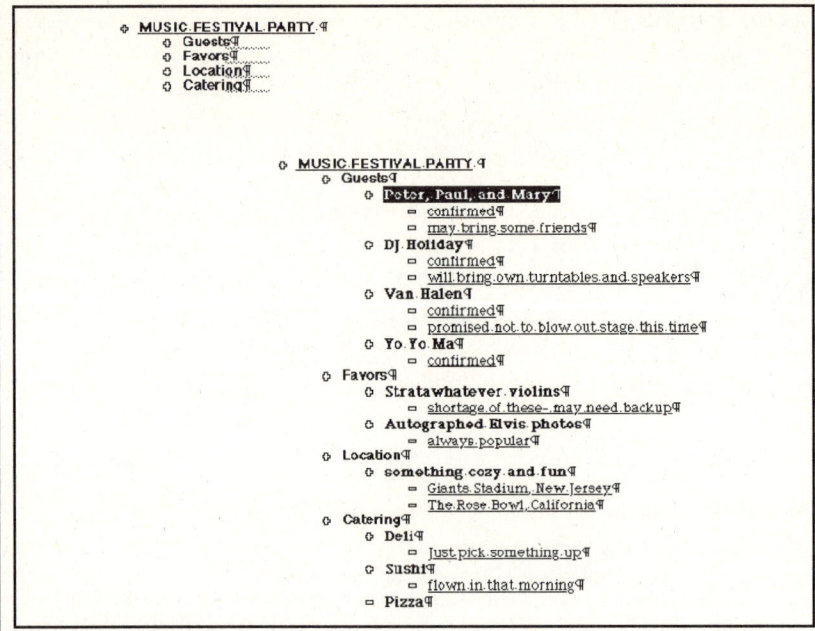

Graphics

There are two levels of graphics control. The first level enables you to directly insert graphics such as clip art, charts, and so on into a word processor document with limited cropping or framing capabilities. Every word processor has this feature.

The second level allows direct graphics editing using full object-oriented tool palettes. Programs such as Nisus, Taste, and WordPerfect offer this second-level capability. With these programs, you can wrap text around irregular objects, paste text inside objects, and precisely place graphics anywhere on a page (see figure 11.5).

Figure 11.5

In the future, documents will incorporate many different kinds of information.

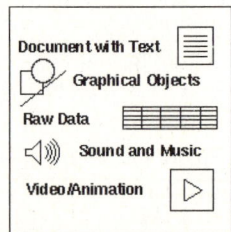

However, unless you absolutely need these graphics capabilities, do not buy a word processor just because it does graphics. It can be difficult to create graphics well, and the word processors that handle them typically are slower and take up more memory.

 High-end word processing programs that have object-oriented graphics capabilities work similarly to many of the higher-end desktop publishing page layout packages. Documents are broken into layers: a text layer and one or more graphics layers. You write text and set margins on the text layer, and make circles, lines, arrows, and so forth on the graphics layer. As you may have guessed, this is not always easy. Although running text around variably shaped objects sounds great, do not expect to sit down at the computer and say, "I want this paragraph to flow around this piece of clip art" and have it effortlessly happen. Unless you are willing to commit a fair amount of time to learn the mechanics of the process, do not buy a word processor with these capabilities.

Searching and Changing

There are at least three distinct levels of flexibility for searching and replacing text. The least flexible programs enable you to look for exact text in any open file. The next level permits wildcard searches that enable you to search for a template of characters (for instance, every word that begins with the letter 'a' and ends with the letter 'd').

The third flexibility level provides the most searching power. Global Regular Expression Parser (GREP) enables you to specify extremely precise descriptions rather than just a template of characters. For example, GREP can search for words with two consecutive vowels that appear at the end of sentences in files that were last edited between two and six months ago. GREP functions are found in Nisus (see figure 11.6), as well as some DAs such as Microlytic's Gofer and On Technologies' On Location.

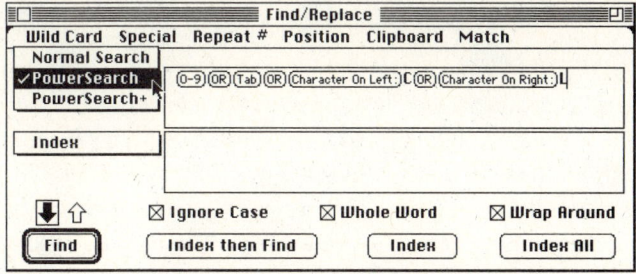

Figure 11.6

Nisus offers three levels of menu-driven searching power.

Style-based searches are independent of text-based searches. These functions enable you to search for a particular font, text size, or display style, and change those characteristics without affecting the actual text. This is especially useful when changing display styles in programs that do not offer true style sheets.

It is unlikely you will need GREP unless you are a technical writer, full-time author, lawyer, or other word processing power-user, but wildcard text and style-based searching is usually essential for people who work with documents of any length or complexity.

Importing and Exporting

In an ideal world, there would be one file format, and every word processor would create files that could be read by any other word processor. However, our world is less than ideal, and we must rely on translators. Translators are utilities that convert documents to different file formats.

A document file contains not only text but font and style information, margins, and countless other variables and formatting information. Interestingly (and possibly infuriatingly), most word processors save the same information but do it in completely different ways.

All computers can save text data in the American Standard Code for Information Interchange (ASCII) format. This originally was designed as a 7-bit code allowing 128 standard characters. The Macintosh has a standard 128 character scheme that its programs use, so ASCII text successfully can be transferred to the Mac without change. ASCII later was revised to an 8-bit code called extended ASCII that allows for an additional 128 characters. This extended ASCII set is used to indicate formatting and styles, among other things. Because these extended ASCII symbols have no standard, they must be translated from program to program to preserve all of your formatting.

The hands-down winner for file translation is Claris' XTND technology. XTND is the resource name for a series of file format translators that can read and write virtually every word processing (and graphics) format available for Macs as well as MS-DOS/Windows computers. For word processors, XTND is used in Claris' MacWrite Pro, and licensed by DeltaPoint's Taste and WordPerfect Corp.'s WordPerfect.

WordPerfect 2.1 is also a good file translator because it exists for so many platforms. For work on both PCs and Macs, Word is also a good choice. Sharing fully formatted files between Macs, PCs, DEC Vaxes, Data General minicomputers, and so on is easy. Called *cross platform compatibility*, this is crucially important for corporations with many different types of computers. Without cross-platform compatibility, you can share text with other word processors, but you may lose formatting.

Apple has created a translation manager called EasyOpen—currently available to developers for stand-alone application utilities that translate one word processing format into another. Eventually, Apple plans to ship EasyOpen with the Macintosh Operating System to make translations both seamless and consistent—replacing the alert box with one presenting several translation options. Two notable products are Systems Compatibility Corp.'s Software Bridge Macintosh, and Dataviz's MacLinkPlus/Translators (which uses EasyOpen). The actual MacLinkPlus translators are compatible with Claris' XTND resources, so you can access powerful import and export capabilities directly from an XTND-compatible word processor.

Mail Merge

Mail merge is used by companies and individuals who need to send out personalized form letters to many clients. Personalization usually means filling in a "Dear _____," blank with each client's name, and including other client-specific information in the body (see figure 11.7).

A Closer Look The merge occurs between a word processing document (the letter) and another text file or document containing personalized information that is separated (delimited) by tabs or commas. Each block of information is called a field. The text file usually is generated by a database, although most word processors can merge with one of their own documents.

Double carats usually are used in the form letter to identify field locations: A "«" signals the field beginning and "»" signals the field ending. The first line of our example would appear as "Dear «Name»,." The double carats also surround merge commands such as If, Then, Else, and Next, which allow flexible control over a document's appearance. In a merge document, "«IF Company="" THEN NEXT»" means: "Print information from the next field here if the company field is blank."

A Closer Look Mail merge usually is useful only when you send personalized letters to large groups of individuals. Setting up a merge document with the proper formatting commands actually could take longer than typing one letter and manually making the changes for a small group. Experience dictates which way is faster for you.

Figure 11.7
Mail merge enables you to create personalized letters from your word processor.

```
«FIELDS FIRSTNAME,LASTNAME,ADDRESS,CITYSTATEZIP,GIFT,USES,DATE»

                                                        «DATE»

«FIRSTNAME» «LASTNAME»
«ADDRESS»
«CITYSTATEZIP»



Dear «FIRSTNAME»,

    I want to thank you for attending my party, and also for the lovely
«GIFT». I am sure I'll enjoy many «USES». Thank you for your consideration and
generosity.



                                                        Sincerely,


                                                        Mike Jones
```

+

"Chrissy", "Strizzi", "1734 Amhearst Ave.", "Leamington, Maine, 01167", "library collection", "hours of delightful reading", "July 28, 1991"

"Brian", "Perutz","87 Ovington Road", "Portsmouth, Maine, 02345", "breadmaker", "loaves of delicious bread for years to come", "August 4, 1991"

"Sunny","Worden", "123 Main Street", "Oldtown, Maine, 01234", "wine glasses", "hours of pleasant consumption from them", "July 21, 1991"

=

Personalized Thank You Letters

Macros

A macro is a single command on a keyboard or menu option that automatically executes several commands. Macros are useful when several actions are performed repeatedly in the same sequence. For example, in many word processors, the date stamping command is located in a menu,

Chapter 11
Word Processors

and no keyboard shortcut is available. Each time you want to insert the date in a letter, you have to:

1. Take your hand from the keyboard and reach for the mouse.
2. Click on the menu bar at the location of the **Date Stamping** menu.
3. Drag the mouse to pull down the menu.
4. Highlight the **Date Stamping** command.
5. Release the mouse and bring your hand back to the keyboard.

With macros, you can record this entire series of steps and assign it to a key combination. (Macro recorders are capable of recording key presses and mouse clicks, but not mouse movements). Once exclusively the domain of utilities like CE Software's QuicKeys, Affinity Microsystems' Tempo II Plus, and Apple's MacroMaker, many word processing programs now have built-in macro functions.

With System 7 and word processors that support AppleScript, you will not only have capabilities similar to macros, but will be able to write scripts that perform long and complex tasks unattended.

An Evaluation of Word Processors

More than ever before, Macintosh word processing applications are characterized by power, speed, and flexibility. After all major publishers upgrade their software for System 7, the products will have more similar features across the board than at any time in Macintosh's history.

The following product descriptions should help you decide which word processor is best for you.

Microsoft Word

As one of the very first Macintosh word processors, Microsoft Word is well-established. It is far and away the market leader, with more than 60 percent of the word processing market. The latest version at this writing, 5.1, is compatible with System 7.

Microsoft products are always excellent performers, and Microsoft Word is no exception. Rich and full-featured, version 5.1 is also reasonably fast—much faster than 4.0. Microsoft Word has a long list of features. This is the original application to use style sheets, and they are easy to make and use. The find and replace feature has been improved so that it now searches for formatting.

Part III

Mainstream Mac Applications

The built-in outliner is not as easy to use (see figure 11.8) as others you might encounter, but is entirely satisfactory. It does not read section headings as outline headings, nor body text as outline body text. The arrow keys move blocks of text up and down the outline rather than within the block. Still, an outline option is a feature many other programs do not offer.

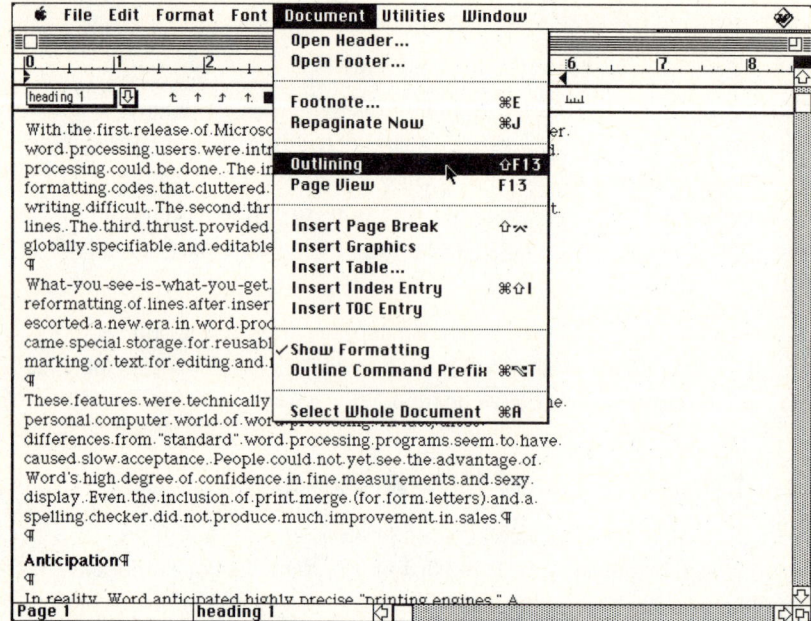

Figure 11.8

Microsoft Word offers sophisticated document formatting features.

Microsoft Word has a very useful context-sensitive help system. After you press Command-?, the pointer changes to a question mark. You merely click the question mark on a menu command or the screen, and the **Help** menu about that item appears. The table feature is excellent. Microsoft Word also can do multiple column layouts and mail merges, and can automatically generate tables of contents and indexes. It even offers links to Microsoft Mail and Excel.

The keyboard editing commands are powerful and fully alterable. You can customize Microsoft Word's shortcuts to mimic any other word processor's keyboard commands.

On the down side, Microsoft Word's spelling checker and counting features are slow. It does not provide cross-referencing or book marking. But users tend to complain most about its "feel." To new users, the menus are complex and poorly laid out, and some editing environment variables are not saved between uses. This aside, it is a powerful, flexible, and professional-level product, and it is the all-time best-selling word processor for the Mac.

You may have heard about compatibility problems with Microsoft products, especially earlier versions of Excel and Microsoft Word. This is because Microsoft products sometimes violate Apple's recommended developer guidelines. Microsoft has developed a high-level applications language of its own, and its software designers use this to build applications for both Macintosh and MS-DOS/Windows computers. The applications language source code then is compiled into 80x86 (for MS-DOS/Windows) and 680x0 (for Macintosh). Low-level operating system standards for MS-DOS machines are much less stringent than for the Mac, and Microsoft optimizes their language to take advantage of the low-level shortcuts permissible on MS-DOS/Windows machines. Unfortunately, the Mac was not designed to allow applications with similar low-level shortcuts, so there are occasional incompatibilities. Microsoft Word 5.1 is quite stable, however.

Nisus

Nisus Professional, complete with sound annotation capabilities, is a professional-level word processor with many outstanding features and few true flaws (see figure 11.9). It is the choice of many power users, but is not a mainstream popular choice.

Chapter 11
Word Processors

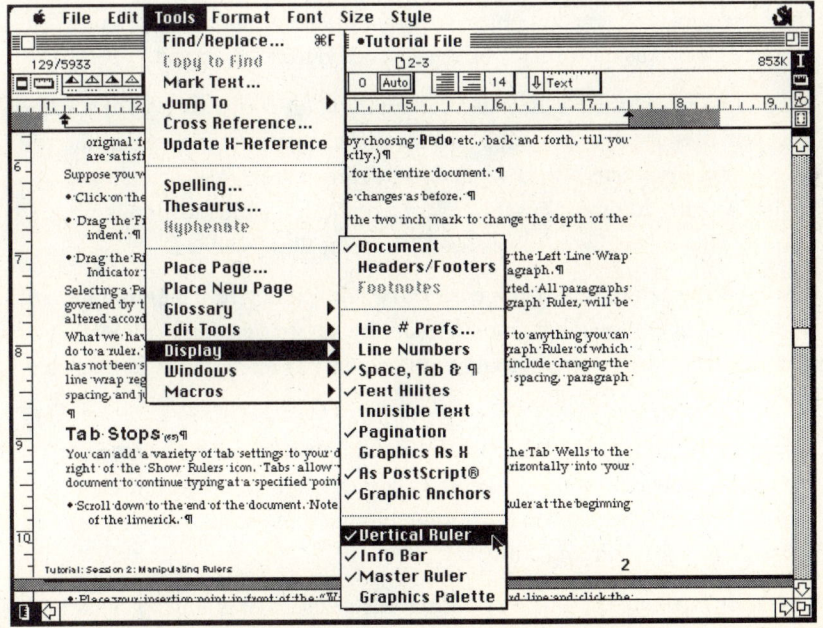

Figure 11.9
Nisus has well-designed but complicated menus.

The program requires 700K of memory and 1.5M of disk space, so you cannot run it on anything less than a machine with 2M of RAM and a hard drive. It is

Part III
Mainstream Mac Applications

crucial to have plenty of RAM when using Nisus because it keeps files in RAM rather than swapping them to disk as other major word processors do. Nisus is the fastest performer with large documents, but only if you have at least 4M of RAM. Nisus can read several word processing formats, and Claris' XTND technology will be incorporated in Nisus Professional.

For pure editing, searching, replacing, and macro customization, Nisus is the best product on the market. It has a fully user-configurable command key set, text and layout styles, vertical and horizontal rulers, noncontiguous and vertical selection of text, cross-references, a 1.4 million-word thesaurus, and an unlimited number of undos.

For searching, Nisus has unmatched GREP capabilities—you can search for words, styles, fonts, and phrases in any combination (even if you are not exactly sure what you are looking for) in any open or closed file. Nisus' GREP works even with files imported from other word processors.

Nisus' macro ability is matched only by WordPerfect's in power and flexibility. Several macro packages, including an appointment calendar and an outlining system, come with Nisus.

Graphics handling is terrific. Nisus offers two drawing layers: one above the text layer and one below. Its toolbox has object-oriented shape tools, a freehand tool, and text and object rotation functions, and the toolbox enables you to display opaque or transparent graphics over text.

Nisus does have its flaws. Because the outlining functions are part of a macro package, they are not integrated and are not as comfortable to use as the rest of the program. Nisus also lacks a table-creating feature. You can imitate tables by using columns, but the lack of a dedicated table function is a big shortcoming to anyone who has used Microsoft Word's tables.

The menu structure is also immense and complex; different menus appear with different Option, Shift, and Shift-Option keystroke combinations. Although the layout is well thought out and easy to learn, this is nevertheless Nisus' biggest shortcoming.

Nisus is a full-featured word processor that tops other word processors in terms of features, power, and speed. However, many of the features are virtually inaccessible, so you must want and need to use all those features before it is worth learning Nisus.

Nisus has introduced a smaller product, Nisus Lite, that is aimed primarily at PowerBook owners. This product, loaded entirely in RAM, conserves battery power while giving the user a strong feature set.

WordPerfect

When WordPerfect 1.0 was introduced for the Mac, it was a slow, MS-DOS-like word processor merely pretending to be a Macintosh application. This best-selling character-based word processor just did not work well in the Mac's graphical interface. The only good feature of the original WordPerfect was its file compatibility with many different platforms.

WordPerfect's 2.1 version is so much better that it is one of the best Macintosh applications around. System 7–friendly, with a vastly improved interface, more high-end features, good online help, and a powerful search and replace, this is a strong entry in the power-user's word processing market.

WordPerfect has integrated drawing tools that save you from switching between the word processor and the draw application. Full-color, object-oriented graphics tools are supported; however, you cannot wrap text around irregularly shaped graphics.

In addition to its multiplatform file import capabilities, WordPerfect comes with an XTND filter so you can use any of the Claris-compatible translators to speak to a range of file formats on both PCs and Macs.

WordPerfect has terrific high-end features such as style sheets, powerful column controls, a page preview mode with editing capabilities, table of contents and multilevel index generation, DTP layout features (see figure 11.10), and a macro editor that is better than Nisus'. It comes with a table maker, but you easily can use the column features for this purpose.

Chapter 11
Word Processors

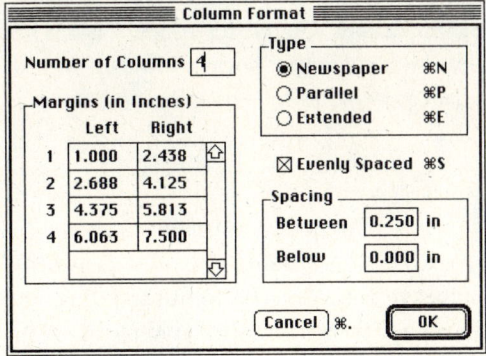

Figure 11.10
WordPerfect has powerful and intuitive column control features.

The spelling checker and thesaurus are respectable, and the online help system is good. On the down side, WordPerfect is slow, and the formatting controls use codes that are difficult to get accustomed to. It also does not have any outlining functions.

419

Part III

Mainstream Mac Applications

WordPerfect is a powerful, high-end word processor with more features but less speed than Microsoft Word or Nisus, its major competitors.

Taste

Taste is DeltaPoint's first entry into the word processing market. It offers mid-range word processing features and an excellent interface. Taste has drawing capabilities, and its graphics tools are superb. It has full-color control, object-oriented drawing, and the ability to wrap text around, in, over, or under pictures. A mini-database gives Taste address-book management features with convenient mail merge (see figure 11.11.)

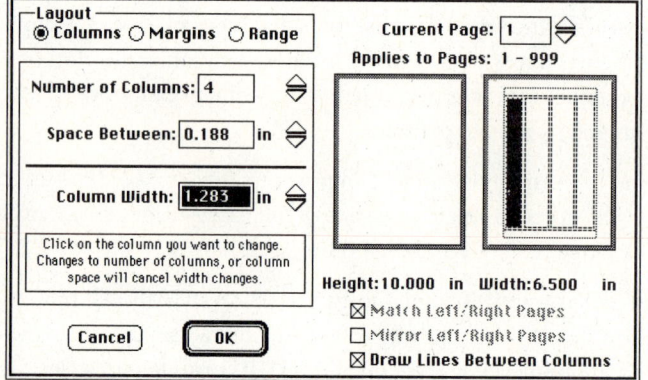

Figure 11.11

Taste's Layout dialog box provides precise control over columns and margins.

Taste offers style sheets and has special links to DeltaGraph (which DeltaPoint also publishes), one of the best-selling Macintosh charting applications. It also incorporates Claris' XTND technology for easy file transfers between applications. On the down side, Taste is somewhat slow, and the initial release was somewhat buggy. However, with all these features, Taste is a real bargain at $99 (and sometimes less).

WriteNow

WriteNow 1.0 was released for both the Macintosh and the NeXT computers in October 1986 as part of a cooperative agreement between T/Maker and Steve Jobs, one of the creators of the Macintosh and the founder of NeXT. (Originally, WriteNow was being developed at Apple at the same time as MacWrite; when Apple decided to bundle MacWrite with the Mac, it sold WriteNow to T/Maker.) Since its introduction, it has won several awards for speed and ease of use.

Chapter 11
Word Processors

WriteNow has had two significant upgrades—2.0 and 2.2—and will be upgraded again to support System 7 features as well as offer better column generation, character and paragraph style sheets, online help, print preview, and direct compatibility with other Mac word processors.

WriteNow is a small, fast, introductory-level word processor, with the smallest memory requirements of any major Macintosh word processor. It takes just 400K for the application, and it can run off of one floppy disk. For letter writing, short papers, and manuscripts, it is a top performer.

Its flaws include minimal keyboard editing commands, no online help, no sophisticated finds, and poor column handling. WriteNow also does not have any advanced features such as endnotes, cross-references, outlining, table of contents and index generation, graphics primitives, or style sheets (although paragraph formats can be copied through rulers).

On the plus side, the spelling checker is superb, the thesaurus is excellent, and WriteNow comes with one of the best grammar checkers on the market: Grammatik Mac. WriteNow also is blindingly fast and can handle an unlimited number of files with multiple headers and footers. Files are displayed automatically in WYSIWYG , so you do not need to preview your pages before printing. It also has mail merge functions and easy time and date stamping.

Altogether, WriteNow is a terrific choice for students, beginning Mac users, and anyone who needs speed and not a lot of power in a small memory configuration. WriteNow is another very good choice for a PowerBook because it is small and RAM based.

MacWrite

The introduction of MacWrite II several years ago marked the first major upgrade to this original Macintosh word processor. The basic word processing standard for most of Mac's history, MacWrite now has some marvelous higher-level features. Its upgrade to MacWrite Pro moves MacWrite even higher on the performance and features ladder, leaving WriteNow and perhaps the next version of Taste as the only fully System 7–friendly basic word processors.

However, the merge functions are top-notch (see figure 11.12). Plus, MacWrite has superior keyboard editing commands and can handle columns. MacWrite also offers footnotes and endnotes, has time and date stamping, and substitutes rulers in place of style sheets, much like WriteNow. Its adequate searching capabilities allow wildcards.

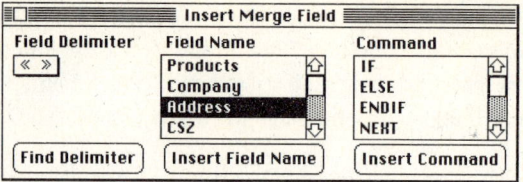

Figure 11.12
MacWrite's merge capabilities are conveniently menu-driven and very flexible.

Despite competition from WriteNow, MacWrite has been the basic word processing standard for the Macintosh since its introduction. New Pro-level features such as tables, precise placement of graphics, and better columns will up the ante.

The long awaited MacWrite Pro appeared in Spring 1993, narrowing the gap between MacWrite and Microsoft Word. It features improved graphics handling, formatting and layout.

Microsoft Works

Because of its unique status as an "integrated" software application, Microsoft Works often is listed on the best-seller lists for different categories at the same time. As a word processor, it is the best seller, second only to Microsoft Word.

For many years, Microsoft Works was the only software package to integrate word processing, spreadsheets, databases, and other functions into one application. Other software companies finally have caught up, however, and new integrated packages from Symantec, Claris, and WordPerfect have been introduced or are expected.

There are advantages and disadvantages to using integrated software. Microsoft Works' word processing module is a version of Microsoft Word 1.0. It is basic, but you may be able to live with it if you need the other modules or if you simply like the "integratedness" (See chapter 13, "Integrated Programs," for more information.) Works 3.0 improves this module slightly, but doesn't add many more new features.

Other integrated software products that compete with Microsoft Works include Symantec's GreatWorks, WordPerfect Works (formally Beagle Brothers Works), and ClarisWorks. ClarisWorks is a notable competitor. It takes a somewhat different (and superior) approach from other module integrated products by enabling you to include graphics, spreadsheets, and charts with your text—also known as compound documents—without requiring you to open and close your document.

The Evolution of Word Processors

As the Macintosh word processing market expanded, users found numerous and varied uses for the more powerful products.

Users who simply write letters or short papers, rarely using word processors for anything other than simple text processing, need primary features: speed, affordability, easy formatting, a spelling checker, and perhaps a grammar checker. These users have a few choices. Letter-writing desk accessories (DAs), such as Working Software's QuickLetter and Power Up Software's Letter Writer Plus, offer speed and convenience along with simple mail merge features.

Applications such as WriteNow, Nisus Lite, and Taste are one step up on the features ladder. WriteNow and Nisus Lite are fast and are good choices for a PowerBook. Taste has superb graphics features as well as links with DeltaGraph for people who occasionally need charts and graphs.

Users who need only to jot down notes occasionally are best suited by a text editor DA. Programmers also like text editors because they usually offer line-based editing, do not use complicated formatting characters that compilers trip over, and do not take up much RAM. Notable products in this category include Baseline Publishing's Vantage and the shareware products MiniWriter and McSink (a shareware version of Vantage; see figure 11.13), available on electronic bulletin board services (BBSs). Vantage is particularly notable for the range of special features it offers to programmers.

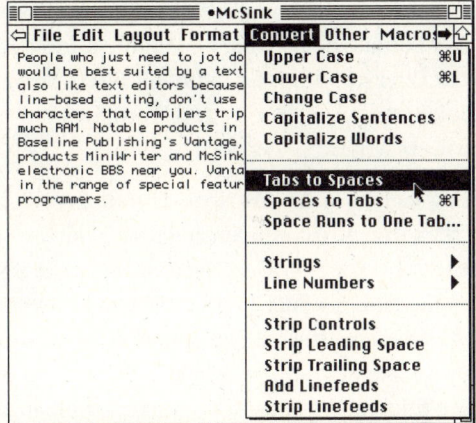

Figure 11.13

McSink is an unusually powerful text editing DA, with a wide range of conversion commands that programmers and BBS devotees find useful.

Business users are a varied group. Their needs range from simple mail merging to proposal preparation, reports, heavy correspondence, and

Chapter 11
Word Processors

desktop publishing. MacWrite is the best at merges, although Taste is great if you can use its built-in database features.

For more involved manuscripts, all of the high-end programs—Nisus, Microsoft Word, MacWrite Pro, and WordPerfect—work very well. For people who are comfortable with a market leader and do not need much graphics capability, Microsoft Word is the best choice. If Microsoft Word seems too complex, MacWrite Pro is better thought out and simpler than Microsoft Word. For inventive users who like to design macros and need formatting and drawing functions, Nisus and WordPerfect are the best choices.

Technical writers, lawyers, and others who edit long, tightly formatted documents need features such as automatic index and table-of-contents generation, easy footnotes and endnotes, outlining, cross-referencing, glossaries, wildcard find and replace in closed files, and style sheets. Unfortunately, no one package supplies all of these. Nisus comes close, offering speed and lots of automated features; Microsoft Word has tables and integrated outlining, although it is not as fast; and WordPerfect has superior formatting control and style sheets, also at the expense of speed. The best option is to get the word processor you are most comfortable using and that best meets your needs, then supplement it with available utilities. (See the section, "Digging Deep: The Expert User's Guide," later in this chapter.)

Word Processing with System 7

System 7 has greatly influenced Macintosh word processing. Although features such as Balloon Help have very little effect (most complex programs already have excellent online help systems), other features such as multitasking and the Inter Application Communications (IAC) tools—Publish and Subscribe, AppleEvents, AppleScript, and WorldScript—have significantly changed how Mac users write.

Full-time multitaking (actually best described as context switching) enables you to have more than one program open at a time, which could be the beginning of the end for text editor DAs. In earlier systems, if you were working with an application, you used Apple's Notepad DA or one of its more sophisticated successors such as MiniWriter or McSink to jot quick notes. Special-purpose text editing DAs—letter writers, label makers, envelope printing utilities, and so on—may remain on the market because they are convenient, especially for users with less powerful Macs, but many users always keep a word processor open in the background under System 7.

IAC is System 7's most promising new feature. It has two components: Publish and Subscribe, and AppleScript. With Publish and Subscribe, you can establish a one-way link between data in a spreadsheet program and a table in your word processing program, for example (see figure 11.14). When both applications are open and you update the spreadsheet (the publisher), the table in the word processor (the subscriber) automatically is updated. If you update the publisher data while one or more subscribing documents are closed, the documents are updated the next time you open them.

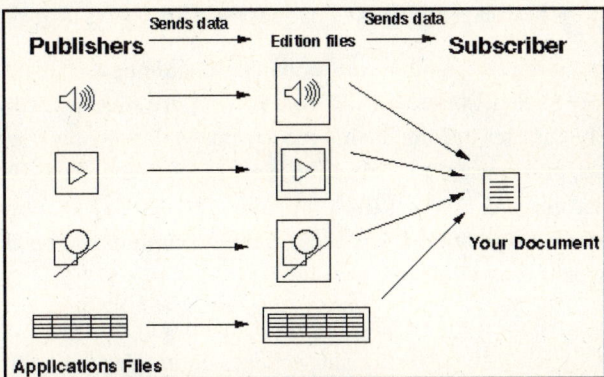

The Publish and Subscribe feature is good for business users and desktop publishing professionals, both of whom frequently use multiple versions of several files and have trouble keeping each up-to-date.

AppleEvents, on the other hand, enables applications to "talk" to one another, exchanging data, editing information, and controlling processes. System 7 requires certain AppleEvents (open, close, save, print...) in application programs. AppleEvents allows small applications, DAs, and extensions to provide advanced services from spelling and grammar checking to on-the-fly file compression. AppleEvents can be used to call an anti-virus program to check incoming files for viruses or a program called Norton Utilities to repair slightly damaged files, as well as by a word processor to have a spreadsheet or symbolic algebra solver perform calculations on data within a document's table.

AppleScript is an extremely useful programming tool based on the manipulation of AppleEvents. You can write scripts to perform tasks similar to macros; however, AppleScript enables you to transfer and manipulate data between applications and is most powerful for automating tasks.

WorldScript is the solution for multinational organizations and people producing documents in multiple languages. Prior to WorldScript, producing

Part III
Mainstream Mac Applications

documents in multiple languages required you to have a separate system file for each language—using loads of memory and inviting crashes. WorldScript has put an end to that, enabling single documents to contain multiple languages, including vertical and right to left scripts.

In short, System 7 consolidated the Mac software market by allowing products to support more features while further automating and simplifying document management.

Digging Deep: The Expert User's Guide

This section examines the numerous utilities and add-ons available for those who need everything. Some, like CD-ROM players, are still somewhat expensive, but as they become mainstream, prices will probably drop. Nevertheless, power users who must have an encyclopedia, the complete works of Shakespeare, dictionaries, a thesaurus, Bartlett's Quotations, and other power tools and reference guides on their computer will be glad to know such features are available now.

To a professional user, the word processor is often only one piece of a multitiered system. The professional user relies on his Mac to handle all the steps in document preparation, such as note-taking, outlining, and reference compiling, each of which may involve a separate utility.

The best outliner as an application is MORE 4.0, from Symantec. MORE 4.0 is System 7–compatible. It began small but has added many features over time. MORE 4.0 is a powerful application that is now more of a presentation package than just an outliner.

If you want a readily accessible dedicated outliner but do not want to use Microsoft Word's outliner, consider Symmetry Corp.'s Acta Advantage. If you are organized but are having trouble getting those ideas flowing, check out Visionary Software's Synchronicity, Fisher Idea Systems' IdeaFisher, or Mindlink Software's MindLink. Ceres Software's Inspiration will help you both generate and organize ideas. With the exception of Synchronicity, all these products are rather expensive, so try them before you buy.

Each of the word processors previously mentioned is suitable for a certain writing and editing niche. Of course, no single application provides all the features you may need, much less in a speedy and easy-to-use package. And even though all these products are continually upgraded, it is unlikely that one will emerge as a true winner.

When editing and exchanging documents, it is helpful to post notes or leave voice messages. The introduction of a microphone with the newer Macs demonstrates Apple's belief that sound integration will be an important new computer communication. MacWrite Pro, Microsoft Word 5.1, and Nisus Professional will have these built-in capabilities. Deneba Software's Comment and Praxitel's Read My Lips are DAs that provide Post-It-type notes and sound annotation functions, respectively, to any application. Movie and video annotation utilities that use QuickTime have also become widely available.

Need a grammar/style checker? Reference Software's Grammatik Mac, LifeTree Software's Correct Grammar, Que Software's RightWriter, and Sensible Software's Sensible Grammar all work well. Most users report that they will help your writing either a lot or not at all. If your writing is semantically good but syntactically poor (perhaps English is not your native language), grammar/style checkers can help. Grammatik Mac seems to have the best overall combination of interactivity and customizable features, although Correct Grammar gets high marks for its user interface (see figure 11.15). This software category continues to improve dramatically over time.

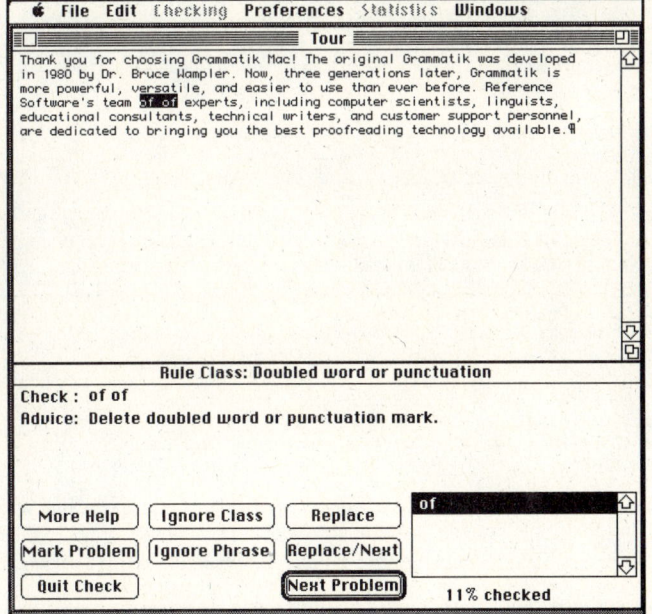

Figure 11.15
Grammatik Mac checks many kinds of grammar and style errors and enables you to interactively make changes as it checks.

Every word processing program can check spelling. Some do it better than others: WriteNow is exceptionally good, Microsoft Word is borderline usable. If you need a quality spelling checker DA, consider Baseline Publishing's

Thunder or the Working Software's SpellsWell/LookUp combination. Both can check spelling as you type, beeping if you misspell a word or type one that is not in the dictionary, a feature some people swear by but many swear at, because it beeps at almost every proper name.

Most word processors also come with a thesaurus. The standard thesaurus DA is Microlytics' WordFinder. Deneba Software, which also publishes BigThesaurus, claims that WordFinder contains more than one million entries. An electronic thesaurus is fast and accurate and is a good investment.

DocuComp from Advanced Software is a very useful product for some groups of users. The program compares two documents and shows the differences by highlighting moved and altered text (see figure 11.16). It then generates a summary report of document changes (see figure 11.17). DocuComp is the best of its kind and is helpful for writing teams needing version control and for individuals who need to quickly see where changes have been made in old documents.

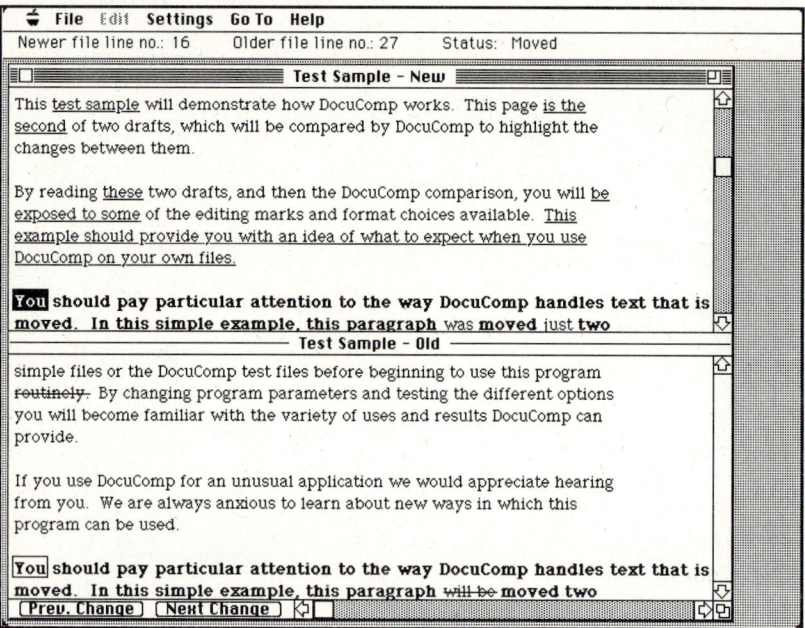

Figure 11.16
DocuComp offers sophisticated version control.

Foreign language dictionaries are available (true translators are still a few years off). Also available are resume guides, such as Bootware Software's ResumeWriter and A Lasting Impression's RésumExpert, and bibliography and foot/endnote assistants, such Personal Bibliographic Software's Pro-Cite for the Macintosh.

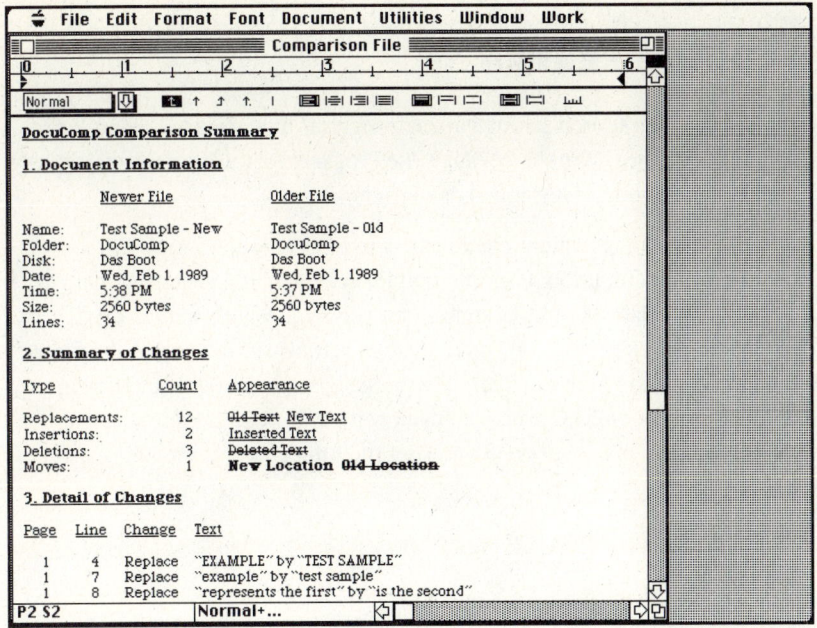

Figure 11.17
Summary reports.

 For a comprehensive list of available Mac software, consult the Macintosh Product Registry, published quarterly by Redgate Communications (800-262-3012).

Keep in mind that many writing resources and reference guides now are available online in the form of CD-ROM disks, offering just about every reference guide a writer could ever need from encyclopedias and Bartlett's Quotations to true dictionaries. Including a list of available disks here is impractical because more are being released every day, and it appears that it is just a matter of time before CD-ROM drives (or another optical equivalent) are considered standard desktop computer equipment, and systems like the Mac IIvx, the Centris line, and Performa 600's that ship with CD-ROM drives becomes the norm. CD-ROM disks and third party drives are available from every major mail-order house.

Writing in a word processor with a library of books instantly accessible will improve your style and content. Products similar to Microsoft's Word and Bookshelf will become standard word processor fare over the next couple of years.

Summary

The Mac features several strong writing programs including Microsoft Word, WordPerfect, Nisus, WriteNow, MacWrite Pro, and Taste. All of these programs are good for certain types of users.

A good writing environment makes heavy use of automated tools. All the word processors mentioned in this chapter offer spelling checkers; many offer other specialized utilities such as word count, search, and so on. Writing continues to develop, and even better tools are coming in the future. Grammar checkers now can analyze writing styles and make your writing even smoother. CD-ROM brings many new tools with high informational content online, which will greatly impact the future.

Interlude 11: Cool Word Stuff

To give you a hint of what word processors are capable of, here are a few hints and tips for Microsoft Word—the word processor that dominates Macintosh word processing. Whether it's the best word processor or not isn't the issue. What's important is, zillions of people use Word everyday—but most of them don't take advantage of the cool things Word can do. I think that's sad.

In This Interlude

▼ Styles

▼ Tables

▼ Print Merge

▼ Buried Treasures

Part III
Mainstream Mac Applications

Word Super Features

The Microsoft Word 5 User's Guide is 829 pages; if it takes Microsoft that long to explain its own program, Word must be a beast. You probably already knew that.

Christian Boyce

Word's not the easiest program to use. It's as complex as anything; even its options have options. For plain typing, Word is definitely overkill. Word suffers from illogically arranged menus and a non-standard interface; simpler word processors are often nicer to use.

Even so, there are good reasons to use Microsoft Word, including three super features that make Word worth the trouble. These features (Styles, Tables, and Print Merge) are waiting for you to exploit them. And exploit them you should. This chapter describes Styles, Tables, and Print Merge, explaining what they do and how you can use them.

Note I'm using Word 5.0. Word 4 looks different than Word 5 (different dialog boxes and different menus), but it works almost exactly the same way. Word 5.1 adds, among other things, a button bar much like Excel. We'll note any important differences between the different versions.

Styles: Ya Gotta Have Some

Styles help you create consistently formatted documents. Consistently formatted documents make you look stable, and they suggest that you know what you're doing. Inconsistent formatting makes documents harder to follow, sometimes to the point that your reader stops reading. Word's Styles feature makes consistent formatting easy.

Styles store font, size, alignment, line spacing, paragraph spacing, tab stops and a couple of other kinds of information. You can define a Style that's 18-point Helvetica, centered and bold, another that's 12-point Times, left justified and plain, and another that's 12-point Helvetica, italicized and indented an inch on both sides (see figure 11.18). Without Styles, formatting figure 11.18 requires several trips to the menus. With Styles, it only takes three.

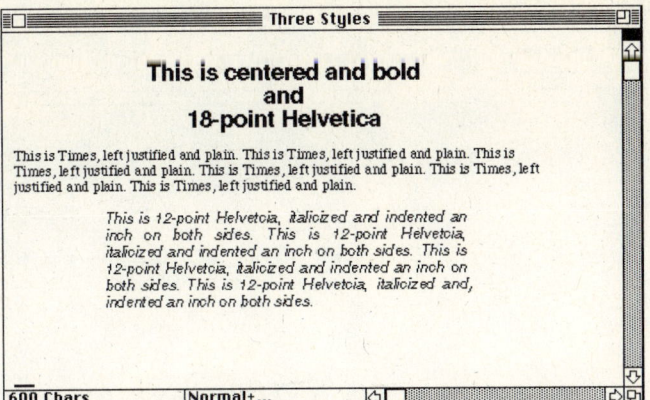

Figure 11.18
Three Styles.

Used properly, styles make reformatting easy, too. If you've ever had a boss tell you "Great, but can you change all the headings to Helvetica, and make them bigger?" you know what a rotten job reformatting is. Scrolling through your document, selecting each heading as it shows up, changing the font to Helvetica, choosing a bigger size, and scrolling to the next heading is a major, major drag. Figure 11.19 shows the reformatting in progress.

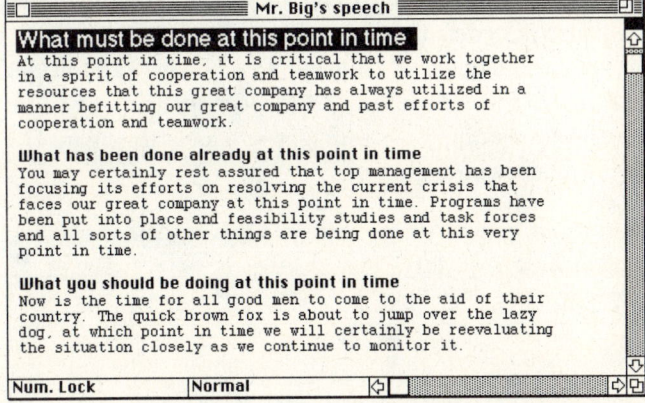

Figure 11.19
Reformatting in progress.

When you've finished, you'll have to check your work, this time scrolling even more slowly because you don't want Mr. Big to find a mistake. Then, when you're sure the document is perfect, the boss takes one look and says, "Maybe the headings should be smaller, but bold." You go outside and scream. Should have used Styles—you'd be done already.

Open a new Word document. Show the **Ribbon** and the **Ruler** (controls are under the **View** menu) if they're not showing. Figure 11.20 shows the document, the Ribbon, and the Ruler.

Figure 11.20

Untitled Word 5 document.

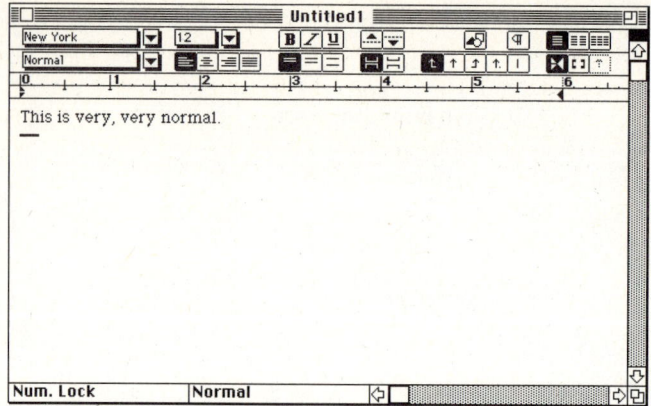

 Word 4 doesn't have a Ribbon, so don't go crazy looking for one. Word 4 doesn't have a **View** menu either; the **Show Ruler** command is under the **Format** menu in Word 4.

The word **Normal** on the left end of the Ruler tells you that the next thing you type will use the Normal Style. And what is the Normal Style? It's the font, size, alignment, line spacing, paragraph spacing, and tab stops that Word gives your text by default. If your documents always begin with 12-point New York type, aligned left, single spaced, you have a good idea of what your Normal Style is. Type the Mr. Big speech of figure 11.19, but don't worry about the formatting. Type it straight, so it looks like figure 11.21. Now format the document with Styles.

Figure 11.21

Speech for Mr. Big.

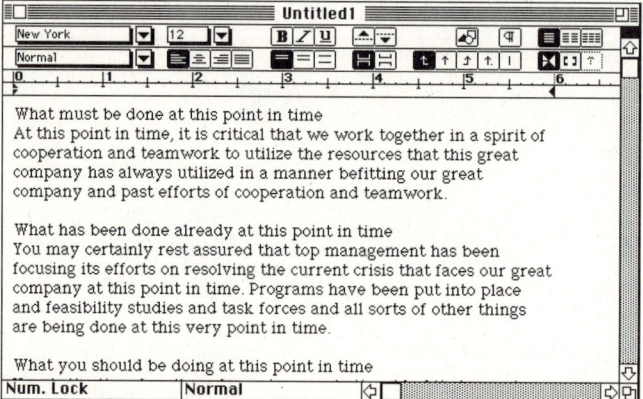

1. Select the first heading ("What must be done at this point in time").
2. Change the font to Helvetica and the size to 18 point.

3. Choose **Style...** from the **Format** menu. Choosing **Style...** produces the Style dialog box (see figure 11.22). The current formatting (Normal + Font: Helvetica 18 Point) is reflected in the box.
4. Name the style Big Headings (just type it in).
5. Click Define.
6. Click OK.

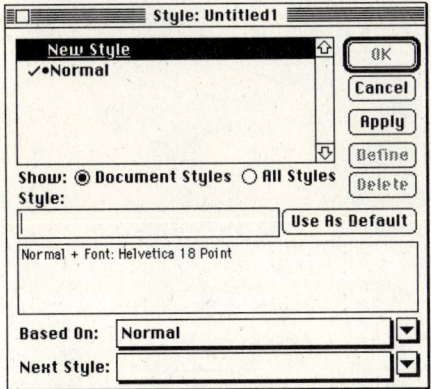

Interlude 11
Cool Word Stuff

Figure 11.22
The **Style** dialog box.

Look at the Ruler. At the far left end is a box with the words "Big Headings" showing. That box is the Style box. You use the downward-pointing triangle next to it to quickly apply (and redefine) Styles. Here's how.

1. Click anywhere in the second heading ("What has been done already...").
2. Click on the triangle next to the **Style** box and hold the mouse button down.
3. Select **Big Headings** from the list under the triangle.

Pretty cool, eh? Format the last heading ("What you should be doing...") the same way and report back here. Figure 11.23 shows how things should look when you're done.

 Every paragraph gets one Style. That means you don't have to select every bit of text in a paragraph before applying a Style to it. The Style will format the entire paragraph the cursor's in, whether you've selected anything or not.

Now for the really cool part. Change the headings to 12-point Helvetica, bold.

1. Select the text of the first heading.
2. Change the size to 12-point.

Part III

Mainstream Mac Applications

3. Make it **Bold**.
4. Choose **Big Headings** from the triangle next to the Ruler's Style box. Figure 11.24 shows the resulting dialog box.
5. Click the button saying Redefine the style based on selection?
6. Click OK.

Figure 11.23
After applying **Big Headings** Style.

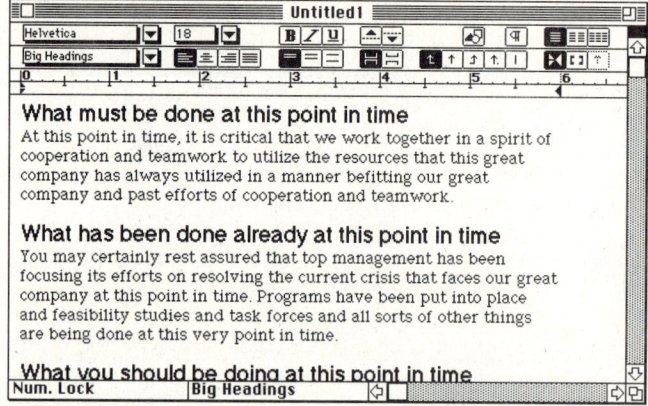

Figure 11.24
Reapply, or **Redefine**? That is the question.

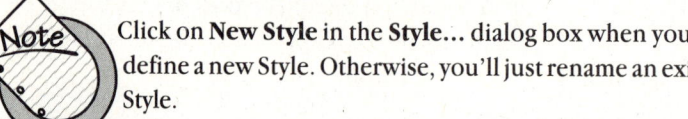

The other headings change to match the first one! With three headings, you save a little time. With a whole document of headings, you save hours and hours.

The key to using Styles is realizing you can redefine them anytime you want. Define their names in advance, even if you don't know how they should look. For example, if you know your document's going to include different kinds of paragraphs (body text, quotations, section titles, and so on), use the Styles... dialog box to define Styles for them. Just get the names defined; don't worry about the formatting (see figure 11.25).

> Click on **New Style** in the **Style...** dialog box when you want to define a new Style. Otherwise, you'll just rename an existing Style.

Apply the Styles as you go, choosing from the list in the Ruler; when you've finished typing your document, format one paragraph of each kind and redefine their Styles "based on the selection." When you fix up one body text paragraph, and redefine the body text Style based on that paragraph, every body text paragraph will change. When you fix up one quotation paragraph and redefine the quotation Style "based on the selection," every quotation paragraph changes. So it goes with the rest of the Styles, giving you quick, consistent formatting, all the way through your document. It's cool.

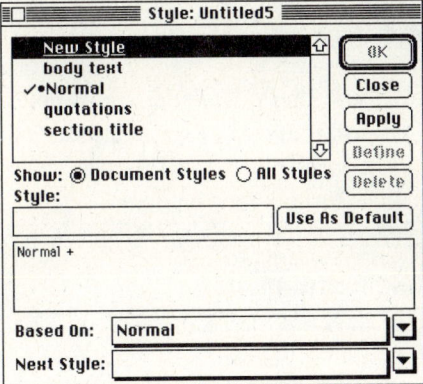

Interlude 11
Cool Word Stuff

Figure 11.25
Defining Styles in advance.

 Each document has its own list of Styles, called a **Style Sheet**. Often you'll want the same Styles available every time you use Word. Can it be done? Of course.

The trick is to click the **Use as Default** button when defining the Style. This places the Style in the Default Style Sheet, making it available to every new document. (Use the **Set Default** button in Word 4.)

Styles make Word worth using. They save you time and make life easier. With Styles, you don't need yellow sticky notes ("Headlines are 18-point Helvetica bold" and "Quotations are Times, italicized and indented one inch both sides") to remind you how to format. Just define your Styles (once) and choose them from the Ruler.

There are other ways to define Styles and other ways to apply them. You can define a Style by opening the **Styles…** dialog box and choosing a font, size, and alignment from the Ruler or the menus. You can apply a style by typing Command-Shift-S, then the Style's name, and then Enter. The Word 5 User's Guide devotes 26 pages to Styles, starting on page 170.

Part III
Mainstream Mac Applications

Tables: Best Invention Since Chairs

Boy oh boy, do I like Tables! They're powerful, and flexible and I use them all the time. Tables let me (and you) create documents like figure 11.26 in a jiffy. Word 4, however, cannot create the white-on-black first row of figure 11.26.

Figure 11.26
A Super Table created in Word 5.

Making a Table is easy: choose **Table...** from the **Insert** menu. This produces the **Insert Table** dialog box (see figure 11.27).

Figure 11.27
The **Insert Table** dialog box.

 Word 4 doesn't have an **Insert** menu. Choose **Insert Table...** from the **Document** menu.

Tell Word how many columns you need in your Table, and click OK. Don't worry about how many rows you need. The rows take care of themselves.

When you insert a Table, it looks like figure 11.28. If you can't see your Table's outline, you need to adjust Word's **Preferences**.

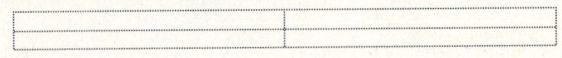

1. Choose **Preferences...** from the **Tools** menu.
2. Click on the **View** icon in the **Preferences** dialog box (see figure 11.29).
3. Check the **Table Gridlines** check box.
4. Close the **Preferences** dialog box.

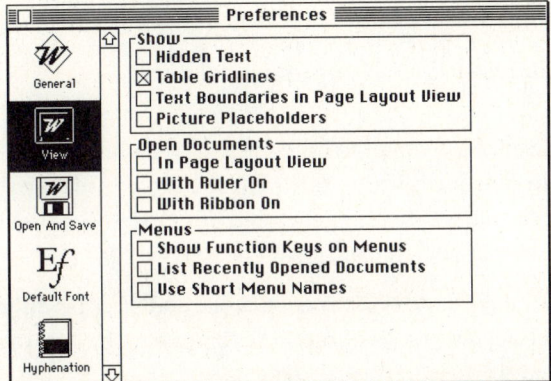

 Word 4 does not have a **Tools** menu. Choose **Preferences...** from the **Edit** menu.

Each box in a Table is called a cell. You can move from cell to cell via the cursor keys (up, down, left, and right arrows) or via the mouse (just click in the proper cell). Those ways work, but it's better to use the Tab key. Here's why.

When you tab through the cells, the cursor moves from left to right across a row. If you press the Tab key at the end of a row, the cursor jumps down to the first cell of the next row. If the cursor is in the last cell of the last row, and you press the Tab key again (here comes the cool part), Word automatically creates a new row and the cursor jumps to the new row's first cell.

Interlude 11
Cool Word Stuff

Figure 11.28
New Table, with gridlines showing.

Figure 11.29
The **Preferences** dialog box.

Part III
Mainstream Mac Applications

It's easy to get a rhythm going: type, then tab, then type, then tab, and so on. You don't have to worry about running out of rows; Word will make more for you. Just be sure to use the Tab key.

Here's how you can make a Table like the one found in figure 11.26.

1. Type **Super Bowl, 1980 to 1984** and Return.
2. Choose **Table...** from the **Format** menu.
3. Tell Word you want 4 columns (the number of rows doesn't matter).
4. Click **OK**.
5. Type **Year** in the first cell, then press the Tab key.
6. Type **Winner** in the second cell, then press the Tab key.
7. Type **Loser** in the third cell, then press the Tab key.
8. Type **Stadium** in the fourth cell, then press the Tab key. Pressing the Tab key after typing "Stadium" takes the cursor to the first cell in the second row.
9. Fill in the rest of the Table by typing and tabbing.

As usual, there are many ways to select the entire Table. You can click in the first cell and drag to the last cell. Clicking in the first cell, holding the Shift key, and clicking in the last cell also works. The best way: hold the Option key while double-clicking anywhere in the Table.

Christian Boyce

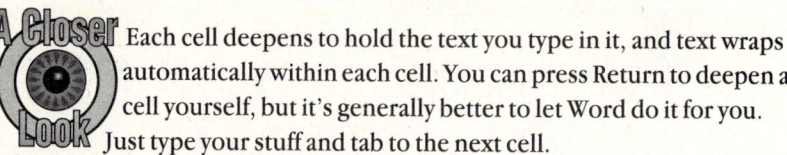 Each cell deepens to hold the text you type in it, and text wraps automatically within each cell. You can press Return to deepen a cell yourself, but it's generally better to let Word do it for you. Just type your stuff and tab to the next cell.

The Return key doesn't do you any good at the end of a row, either. In case you're wondering, it won't take you to the first cell of the next row. Use the Tab key instead. Type, tab, type, tab, type.

Figure 11.30 shows the Table with all the information but before formatting. Clearly, it needs work.

Figure 11.30
Super Table before formatting.

Super Bowl, 1980 to 1984			
Year	Winner	Loser	Stadium
1980	Pittsburgh Steelers, 35	Los Angeles Rams, 19	Rose Bowl
1981	Oakland Raiders, 27	Philadelphia Eagles, 10	Superdome
1982	San Francisco 49ers, 26	Cincinnati Bengals, 21	Silverdome
1983	Washington Redskins, 27	Miami Dolphins, 17	Rose Bowl
1984	Los Angeles Raiders, 38	Washington Redskins, 9	Tampa Stadium

440

The column widths are all wrong. You can change column widths several ways, but it's easiest with the Ruler.

1. Select the entire Table.
2. Show the Ruler (**View** menu, or **Format** menu in Word 4)
3. Click the button at the far right of the Ruler. Your screen should look like figure 11.31.

   Word calls this button **Table Scale**.
4. Drag the markers on the Ruler (they look like the **Table Scale** button) to change the column widths.

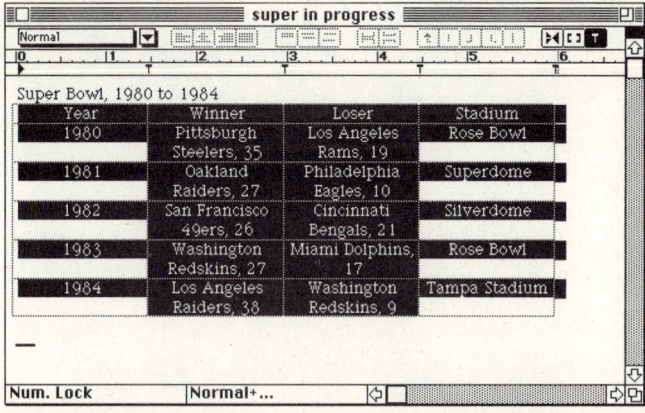

Figure 11.31
Table before column adjustments.

Figure 11.32 shows the Table after adjusting the column widths.

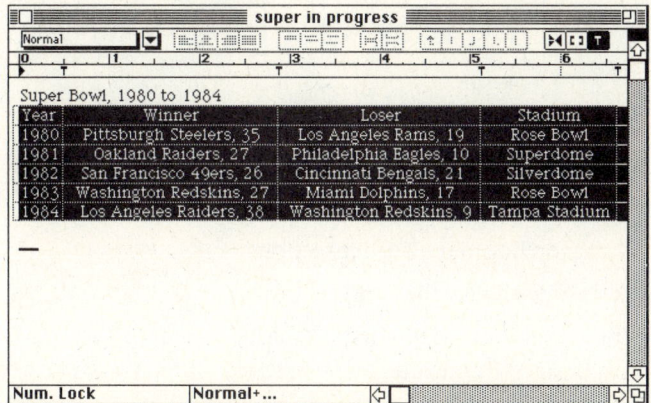

Figure 11.32
Table after column adjustments.

Putting borders on cells is a bit of work, but it's worth it.

1. Select the entire table.
2. Choose **Border...** from the **Format** menu. Figure 11.33 shows the

Interlude 11
Cool Word Stuff

441

Part III
Mainstream Mac Applications

Border dialog box. The Border dialog box has four parts. One of them, **Border** (great name), represents your Table and its cells. You use the **Border** section of the **Border** dialog box to indicate which border you're trying to format.

Figure 11.33
The **Border** dialog box.

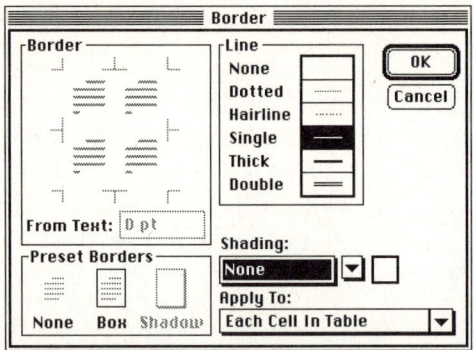

3. Click in the center of the Border section. You've just defined the borders between cells as thin lines. You can change the line thickness by clicking on a different line in the **Line** section of the **Border** dialog box. Figure 11.34 shows the **Border** dialog and the thin line selection for the borders between cells.

Figure 11.34
Border dialog with thin inter-cell borders selected.

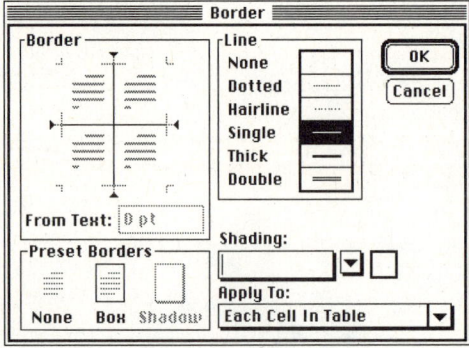

4. Click the top line in the **Border** section.
5. Click the thick line in the **Line** section.
6. Define borders for the rest of the Table perimeter by clicking on the left, right, and bottom lines in the **Border** section. Figure 11.35 shows the **Border** dialog box with all Table borders defined.

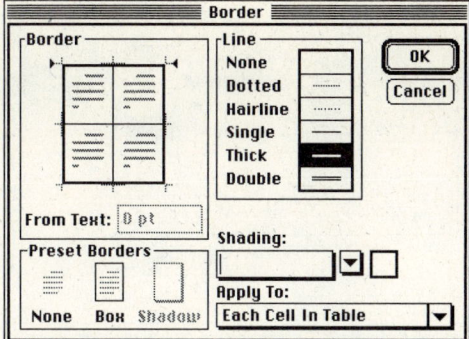

Figure 11.35
Border dialog with all borders defined.

7. Click **OK**. Your Table should look like figure 11.36.

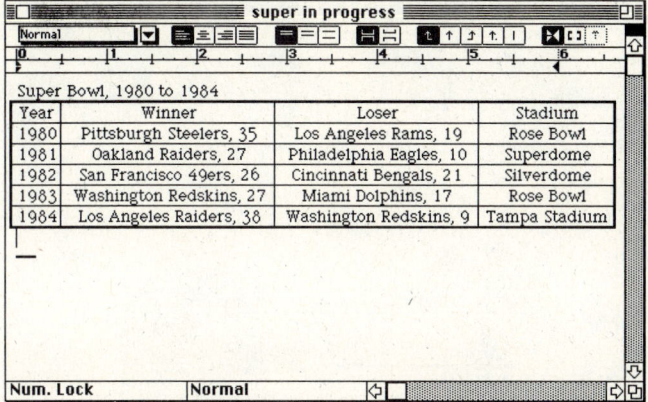

Figure 11.36
Table with borders.

You're almost done! Invert the Table's first row and you're through. That's easier than it looks, especially now that you've been through the Border dialog.

 Word 4 cannot shade cells. It can give them borders, but it cannot shade them.

1. Select the first row of the table by dragging from left to right.
2. Choose **Border...** from the **Format** menu.
3. Choose **100%** from the Shading pop-up menu. Figure 11.37 shows how the dialog box should look.
4. Click **OK**.

Figure 11.37

Applying shading to a Table.

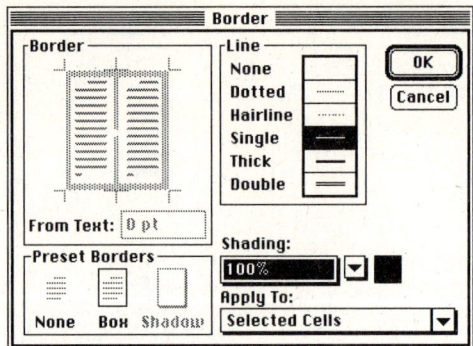

Hey! The text all disappeared! No, it didn't. The text is black, and the cell is black, so you just can't see the text. The text is there, and you'd see it if it weren't black. Make sure the Table's first row is selected, then:

1. Choose **Character...** from the **Format** menu.
2. Choose **White** from the **Color** pop-up.
3. Make any other choices (font, size, underline).
4. Click **OK**.

Figure 11.38 shows the **Character** dialog and the choices I made.

Figure 11.38

The **Character** dialog box.

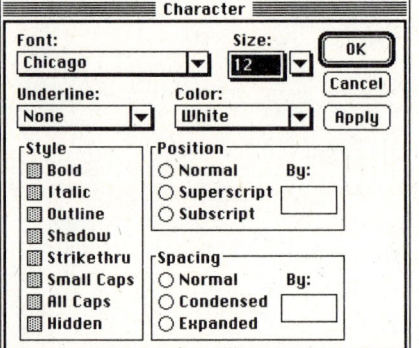

That's it! You're done.

Actually, not quite. You might want to align some of the cells (like the ones with the Winners and Losers) to the left. That's no problem. Word treats Table cells like paragraphs: you can align them any way you want.

5. Select from "Pittsburgh Steelers, 35" to "Washington Redskins, 9" by dragging through the cells.

6. Click the **Align Left** button on the Ruler.

The cells align to the left without affecting the others. Now your Table's all set. Figure 11.39 shows the finished Table.

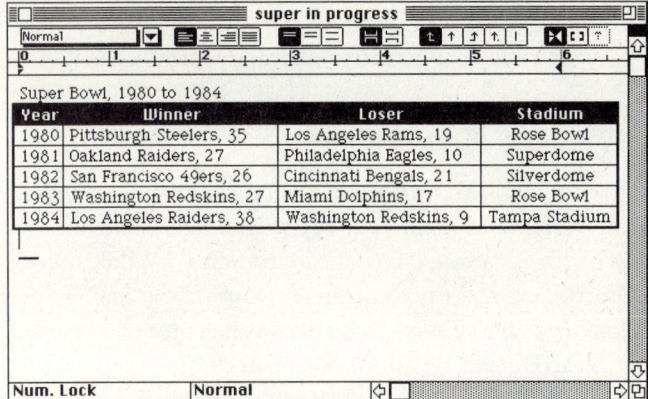

Interlude 11
Cool Word Stuff

Figure 11.39
Finished Table.

You can do more with a Table than show Super Bowl information in tabular form. Using Tables, you can place pictures next to text (yup, you can paste a picture into a table cell) and arrange paragraphs side by side (résumés are easier if you make a Table with a narrow column on the left for dates and a wide column on the right for everything else). Complicated formatting, such as making a headline span two columns, is easy with tables: make a two-column table for your text, and type the headline above the table.

Print Merge: Better Junk Mail, and More

If there's anything I hate more than junk mail, it's lousy junk mail. You know the kind: your name's in it five times, and it's always your whole name, never just your first. These letters usually refer to your hometown as well, something along the lines of "Imagine, Christian D. Boyce, you would be the talk of Beverly Hills, CA 90212 if you won our sweepstakes." This sort of mass mailing is really mass garbage. What a waste of everyone's time.

The phrase "do a Print Merge" means "create a form letter with Microsoft Word, then create a data document with Word (or with some other program that can save the file in a compatible format), then combine the letter and the data document using Word's **Print Merge…** command, inserting the data from the data document into the form letter at the appropriate places."

Christian Boyce
Figure 11.40
A main document.

You can use Word's **Print Merge** feature to do your own mass mailing. If you do it right, no one's going to make fun of your form letter. In fact, no one's going to know it's a form letter. As long as you do it right.

You can use Print Merge to do more than make junk mail. You can make mailing labels, name tags, invitations—you name it. It's much easier to do a Print Merge than to edit, format, and save several individual documents.

Print Merge Basics

Every Print Merge involves two documents. One, the main document, is a generic version of the documents you're trying to make. Lines like "Imagine, Christian D. Boyce…" become "Imagine, «First Name» «Middle Initial» «Last Name»…" but otherwise the main document looks like a "real" letter. You format the main document as you want the finished products (the merged letters) to appear. Figure 11.40 shows a main document.

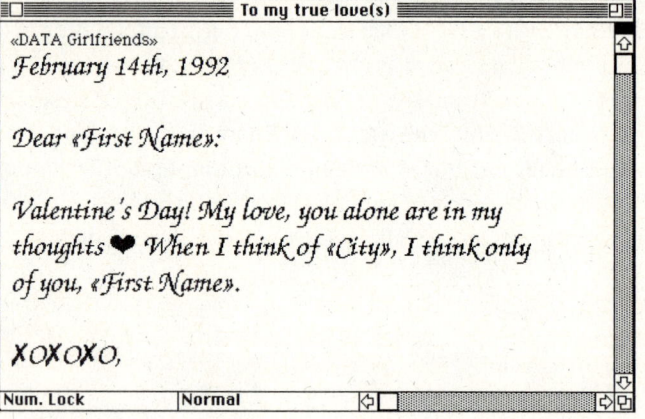

The main document is customized with information stored in the data document. In the case of the "Imagine…" letter, the data document holds name and address information. Data documents are organized into columns and rows: each kind of information (first name, middle initial, last name, city) gets its own column, and every set of information (a set being the information for one person) gets its own row. Data document formatting does not affect the finished product.

 Wait a minute! Columns and rows? Sounds like a Table! I highly recommend you use a Table to make your data document easier to handle.

Figure 11.41 shows a data document using a Table.

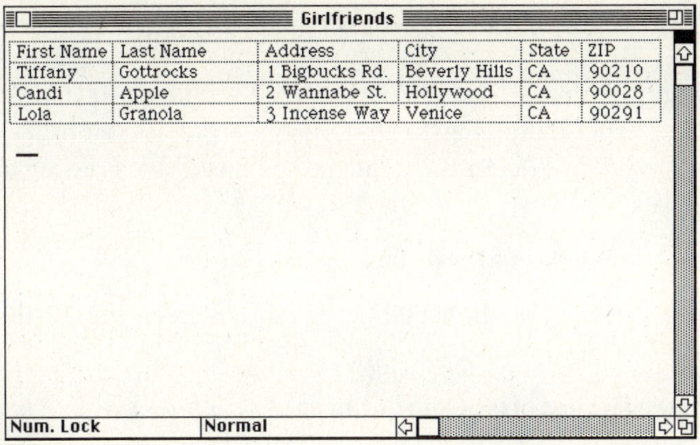

Figure 11.41

A data document.

> **A Closer Look** You don't need to use all the data in a data document. The main document of figure 11.40 uses only two of the columns of information (First Name and City). That's OK. Note also that the main document uses the "First Name" information twice. That's also OK.

When you merge, the main document and the data document combine to create a third document. This third document is generally larger than the main and the data documents combined (a one page main document and ten lines of data lead to a ten page third document). Often, the third document is printed immediately. A better technique saves the third document for further review and editing. Either way, the main and data documents remain separate after the merge.

Print Merge Specifics

You know what to do: make a main document, make a data document, and merge them. Now you need to know how. Fortunately, there isn't much to know.

Look at the first line in the main document in figure 11.40. At merge time, "«DATA Girlfriends»" tells Word to use the names and addresses from a file named "Girlfriends." The "«DATA Girlfriends»" line won't print; if you leave the DATA line alone on the first line of your main document, your merged letters will start on line two.

447

Part III
Mainstream Mac Applications

 The DATA line must be the first item typed in a main document. If a space, or a Return, or anything else is inserted before the DATA line the merge will certainly fail.

The strange little marks "«" and "»" are, in Word's words, "print merge characters." Type « by holding the Option key and pressing the backslash key (\). Type » by holding the Shift key and the Option key and pressing the backslash key.

You could use QuicKeys to make typing « and » easier.

Most merges go wrong at the beginning. It's absolutely critical that the DATA line be typed correctly, which means:

▼ It's the first line of the main document.

▼ There's an opening "«".

▼ The word after "DATA" is the exact name of the data document.

▼ There's a closing "»".

That's not so much to ask. Let's set up a main document.

1. Open a new document.
2. Type `«DATA Names»` .
3. Save your work (any name will do).

Now set up the data document.

4. Choose **New** from the **File** menu (but leave the main document open).
5. Choose **Table...** from the **Insert** menu.
6. Tell Word you want six columns.
7. Click **OK**.
8. Save your work as `Names` (this is important!).

Saving your work as "Names" is important because your main document will look for a data document called "Names" (you set this up in the main document's DATA line). If Word can't find a document called "Names," the merge will fail.

Fill in the Table so it looks like figure 11.42. Don't worry about having enough room to type. Word will wrap the text within the cells, adding space where necessary. Don't forget to save your work.

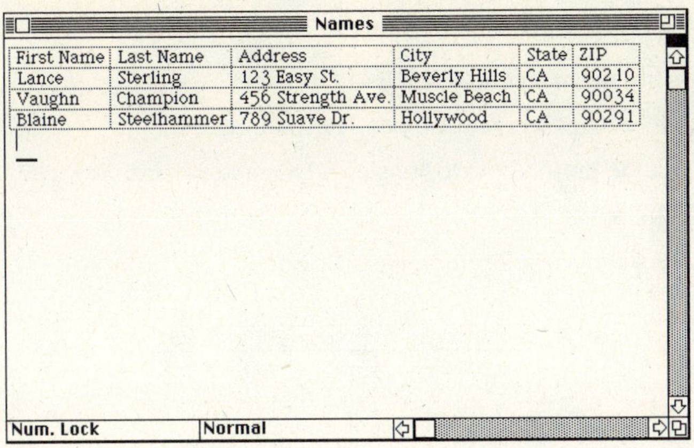

Figure 11.42

Data document called "Names".

A Closer Look The first row in the data document's Table must contain labels for the data. The labels are called "field names" (the columns are called "fields"). You use field names in your main documents to refer to the columns of data, so give the fields names that make sense.

Switch back to your main document. Make it look like figure 11.43. Don't forget to save. Notice that «`first name`» «`last name`» is right next to the DATA line; this starts the merged letters at the top of the page instead of on line two. Also notice that each field name matches a field name in the data document. If, in your main document, you use a field name not found in your data document, the merge will fail.

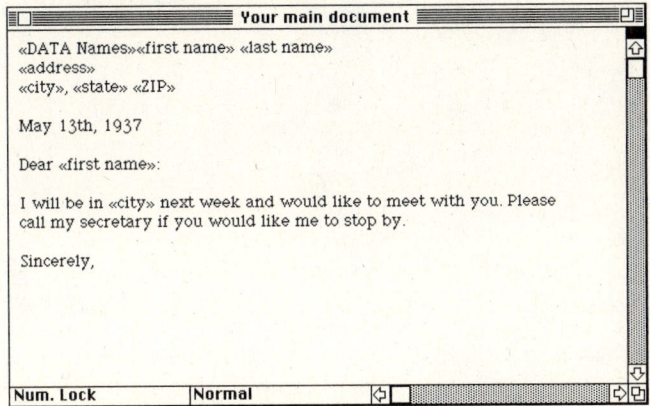

Figure 11.43

Your main document.

Part III

Mainstream Mac Applications

You're ready to merge.

1. Be sure the main document is in the front.
2. Choose **Print Merge...** from the **File** menu.
3. Click the button next to **Merge and Save Results in New File**.
4. Click **OK**.

Figure 11.44 shows the **Print Merge** dialog box.

Figure 11.44
Print Merge dialog box.

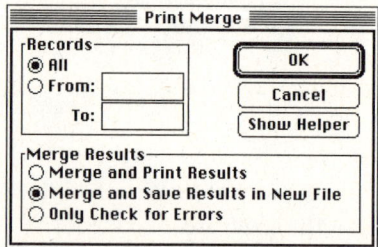

If you've done things right, a new document appears. Figure 11.45 shows part of the document I hope you get. Scroll through this new document and see how the names from the data document were pumped into the main document. If you like it, you can print it. If you don't like it, you can edit it. You could just throw it away and work on improving the main document, the data document, or both and try the merge again.

Figure 11.45
The merged document.

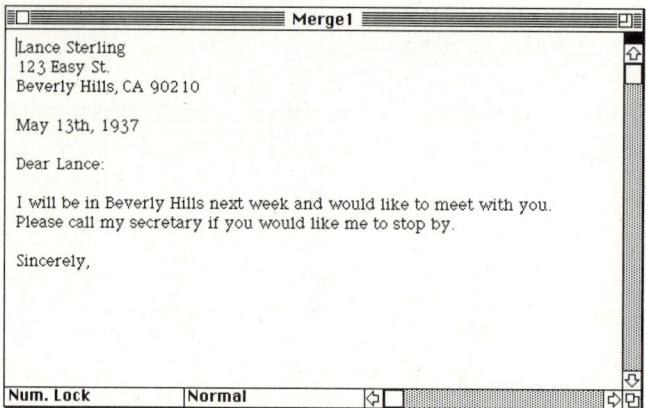

That's all there is to it (though you might want to practice some more, possibly by making a more complicated main document).

Things That Can Go Wrong

Many merges go wrong in the DATA statement. These merges never start because Word can't find their data documents. Typing the DATA line correctly is critical, and don't forget the funny marks around it.

Sometimes Word can't find the data document even though you typed the DATA line perfectly. Solve this problem by opening the data document yourself before you merge (but be sure the main document is in front when you choose Print Merge…). Another way to solve the missing data problem is to store the data document in the same folder as the main document.

A lot of merges get started, then fail. Main document references to field names that don't exist in the data document are the chief sources of this sort of failure. Simply be careful that the field names you use in your main document are listed in the data document. And use those special merge characters to surround field names in the main document.

Sometimes people forget to make the first line of a data document contain the field names. That will ruin things, all right.

It takes Microsoft 73 pages to explain "Print Merge" in the *User's Guide*. You found the right one, baby. Uh-huh.

Christian Boyce

In Closing

Styles, Tables, and Print Merge give you the power to make complicated documents you'd have problems making other ways. Styles speed up repetitive formatting and increase consistency within and between documents. Tables help you create rows and columns, side by side paragraphs, and pictures next to text. Print Merge helps you make many documents that are slightly (or not-so-slightly) different without a lot of work. Look for chances to use these features to simplify, speed up, or improve the work you do.

Buried Treasures

You'd do well to explore Word, clicking all over the place and digging for buried treasure. Here are some jewels to look for.

Word's Print Merge feature has always been awkward. Word 5 includes the "Print Merge Helper" which supposedly makes things easier. I don't think the Print Merge Helper helps at all; you still need a main document and a data document, and you still need those wacky "«" and "»" characters around everything. Print Merge Helper shields you from some of the workings of Print Merge, and Microsoft thinks that's good. I think it's bad, since it keeps you from understanding what is really going on.

Christian Boyce

451

Command-Shift Is Everything

Command-Shift-B makes selected text bold, Command-Shift-U makes it underlined, and Command-Shift-I makes it italicized. Command-Shift-C centers the paragraph the cursor's in; Command-Shift-L left-justifies the paragraph, Command-Shift-R right-justifies it, and Command-Shift-J justifies it on both sides.

Customize Menus with Commands

Choose **Commands...** from the **Tools** menu and experiment with the dialog box that appears. Figure 11.46 shows the **Commands** dialog box with the command **White** about to be added to the **Format** menu. Putting White in the Format menu saves a trip to the Character dialog box when you want to reverse type.

Commands... is under the **Edit** menu in Word 4.

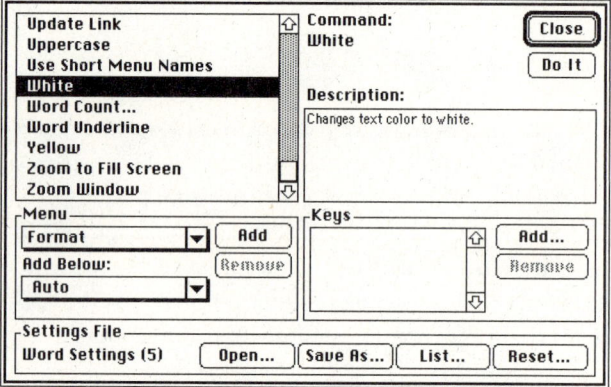

Figure 11.46
The **Commands** dialog box.

Commands... lets you add and delete menu items. If you're not going to use the **Index** and **Table of Contents** features, for example, take them out of the menus so they don't clutter things up. Removing items from menus does not remove them from the program; you can always come back to the Commands dialog box and add the items.

Use the Apply Button

Many dialog boxes have **Apply** buttons. Apply buttons let you try the setting you've chosen without closing the dialog box. You can change a setting, click Apply, change another setting, click Apply again, and so on. Figure 11.47 shows the Apply button in the Character dialog box.

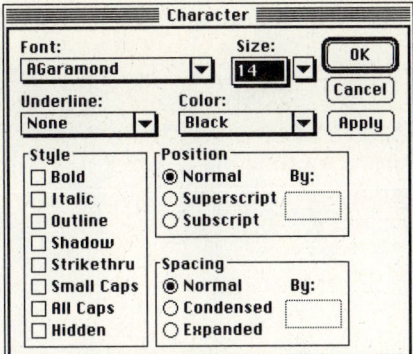

Figure 11.47
The **Apply** button in the **Character** dialog box.

Adjust Margins in the Print Preview Mode

Sometimes you want a document to fit on one page but it goes just slightly over. You could shrink it in the Page Setup dialog box, but shrinking might make the text too small. Smaller margins are your only way out; you can change them graphically in the Print Preview mode. Figure 11.48 shows a document two lines away from fitting on one page.

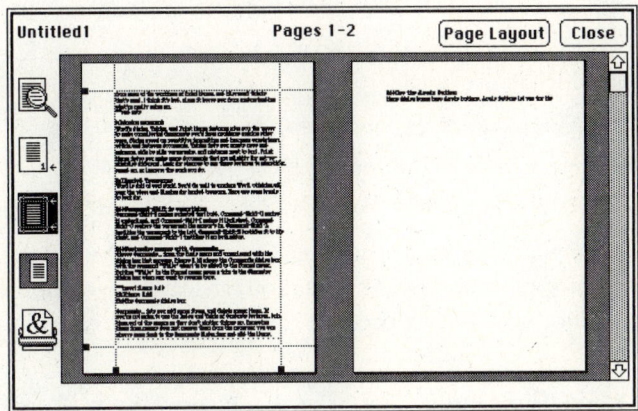

Figure 11.48
Print Preview before adjusting margins.

1. Choose **Print Preview...** from the **File** menu.
2. Click on the margins button (middle button on the left hand side of screen).
3. Drag the margins around by the square black knobs. Absolutely nothing happens. Do not be alarmed.
4. Click in the gray area surrounding the pages.
5. Continue to adjust margins and click in the gray area until your document fits on one page.

Figure 11.49
Print Preview after adjusting margins.

Figure 11.32 shows the document in figure 11.49 now fitting on one page.

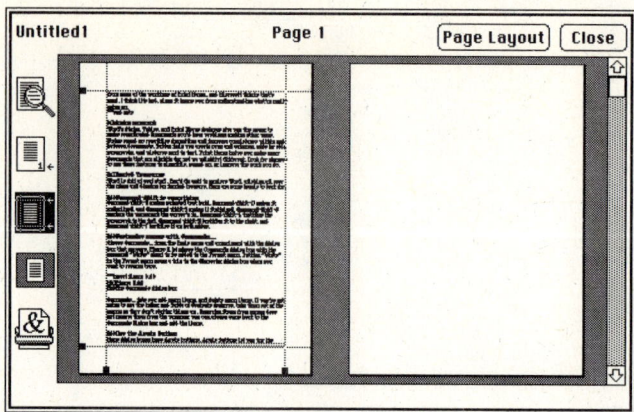

Open a Second Window to View Another Part of a Document

If you're lucky enough to have a two-screen Mac, this is the tip for you. It lets you view one document in two (or more) windows. In a long document, keeping your introductory paragraph on the screen could keep you from straying from your topic.

1. Open a document normally.
2. Choose **Open...** from the **File** menu.
3. Select the file that's already open.
4. Click the **Open** button.

The contents of the windows are the same. Changing one changes the other. But the windows scroll independently, so you can leave one window open to your introduction while you work on the conclusion.

Split the Screen to View Another Part of a Document

Here's the poor man's way of seeing two parts of a document. It's done on a single screen. Simply grab the black bar at the top of the vertical scroll bar and drag it down. Figure 11.50 shows a split screen. Note the double sets of scroll bars; each pane scrolls individually.

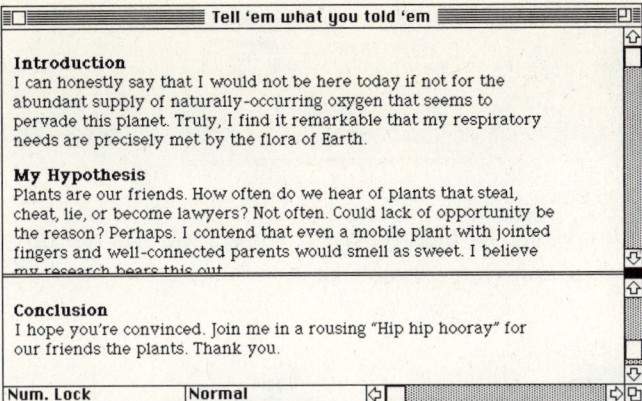

Figure 11.50

Split screen.

Select Text Like a Pro

Like all Mac programs, you can't format text if it isn't selected. Here are my favorite text-selection secrets.

▼ Double-click anywhere in a word to select the whole word.

▼ Hold the Command key down and click anywhere in a sentence to select a whole sentence.

▼ Triple-click anywhere in a paragraph to select the whole paragraph.

▼ Hold the Command key down and click in the selection bar (the white space between the first character on a line and the edge of the screen) to select the whole document.

Recover Brilliantly After Typing a Paragraph with the Caps Lock Down

Ever type a paragraph, or more, not realizing you'd done it with the Caps Lock down? Word 5's **Change Case...** command (in the **Format** menu) lets you fix things up without retyping them. Figure 11.51 shows the **Change Case** dialog box.

 Word 4 does not include this feature.

Figure 11.51
Change Case dialog box.

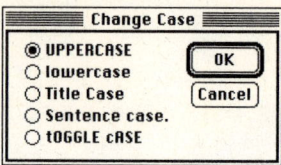

Select some text, choose **Change Case…**, and tell Word what to do. It's that easy (though an Apply button would improve things).

In Conclusion

Word's a cool program, especially when you get to know it. The more you know, the more you can do (and the easier it gets). Eventually, though, you're going to want to do something that Word can't do, no matter how well you know the program. One thing that word processors don't do well is deal with numbers, as in columns and columns of numbers. That skill is in the realm of the spreadsheets, covered in the next chapter.

Chapter 12
Spreadsheets

This chapter discusses spreadsheet programs on the Macintosh computer. Spreadsheets are the workhorse programs for most businesses, but they take on dramatic new capabilities with the Mac because of its outstanding graphics handling. Spreadsheets enable you to visualize data, chart and display the data in different formats, and easily try many "what-if" scenarios.

In This Chapter

▼ Spreadsheet features

▼ Graphing and charting

▼ Macro and scripting capabilities

▼ Spreadsheets as databases

▼ Spreadsheets as presentation tools

▼ Product evaluations

Part III
Mainstream Mac Applications

Spreadsheets and Computers

The word processor may be the single most popular applications package for personal computers, but the spreadsheet has single-handedly sold more computers than all other applications combined. VisiCalc, which was introduced in 1980 for the Apple II series of computers, is the program that caught the business community's eye and opened its wallets.

Big data storage computers already had been in place for 25 years, but the spreadsheet put the personal computer on business executives' and managers' desks. By removing the errors and sheer monotony associated with working with calculators and paper worksheets, spreadsheets enabled everyone with a computer to do forecasting and what-if analysis more quickly and conveniently than ever before. Lotus 1-2-3 was, and is, the MS-DOS spreadsheet standard. It single-handedly made Lotus the number one desktop software developer almost immediately after 1-2-3's introduction (although Microsoft has since taken over this title).

The original Macintosh computer was not suited to running spreadsheets. The Mac's first two spreadsheet programs, MultiPlan from Microsoft and Jazz from Lotus, showed promise of integrating the Mac's graphical user interface with a worksheet. Unfortunately, they were hampered by the small screen, tiny memory capacities, and slow performance of the early Macs. For more than a year after its introduction, the Mac was no match for MS-DOS computers in the spreadsheet arena. Then in 1985, Microsoft bought Excel from a private developer and quickly became the Lotus of the Macintosh world.

Presently, Microsoft Excel is dominating the Macintosh spreadsheet market. Microsoft further solidified its position early in 1991 with the introduction of a powerful new version, Excel 3.0. Just a few months before Excel 3.0's introduction, Ashton-Tate introduced Full Impact 2.0, a solid product that could have benefited greatly from an earlier release date. Claris' Resolve (a rewrite of Informix's Wingz spreadsheet) and (at long last!) Lotus' 1-2-3/Mac followed on the heels of Excel 3.0's introduction. Version 4.0 of Excel appeared in mid–1992.

These new spreadsheet products promise to exploit the Mac's operating system advantages as never before: point-and-click access to functions,

Chapter 12
Spreadsheets

bit-mapped screen and color QuickDraw, and IAC protocols. Now full-color charts and graphs can easily be displayed in two or three dimensions side by side with the source data. IAC tools provide "hot links" to word processors, databases, and presentation programs—functions the application may not support explicitly.

The introduction of System 7 along with several new, niche-oriented Macintosh models like the LC line will help to reopen a market that has been dominated by Excel. Instead of aiming at long-time Excel users, the new spreadsheets address the large and growing number of new Mac owners and new System 7 users.

Spreadsheet Features

Part of the spreadsheet's popularity is due to its attractive simplicity. Contrary to the long list of word processing features that need explaining and justification, the list of spreadsheet components is relatively short and self-explanatory.

Spreadsheets are worthwhile tools because they enable you to visualize data, but they are valuable only if the arrangement of the numbers means something to you. In some applications, graphing data is more important than any other feature.

All of these powerful features come at a price. Pay close attention to the overall appearance and "feel" of any spreadsheet you are thinking about purchasing. Ultimately, your satisfaction is determined by that comfort.

The Worksheet Itself

All spreadsheets show a *matrix* (rows and columns) of cells. This matrix is called a *worksheet* and is similar to the real-world printed worksheet that an accountant uses. Each cell is a like a container; it can hold a number, text (called a label), or a formula that performs a calculation. The rows are referred to by numbers (from one to the maximum worksheet limit), and the columns are referred to with letters (A to Z, AA to AZ, BA to BZ, and so on).

Spreadsheets that offer cell "linking" functions are called 3-D spreadsheets.

Part III
Mainstream Mac Applications

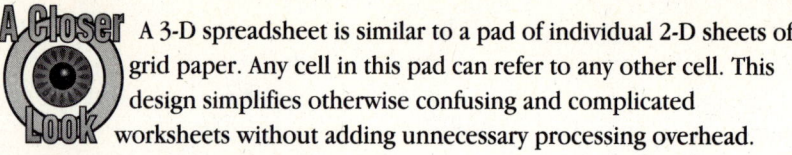 A 3-D spreadsheet is similar to a pad of individual 2-D sheets of grid paper. Any cell in this pad can refer to any other cell. This design simplifies otherwise confusing and complicated worksheets without adding unnecessary processing overhead.

Built-in Functions

If the worksheet is the body of the spreadsheet application, the heart is the spreadsheet's collection of built-in functions. These include formulas from many disciplines. You simply type a formula into a cell, substitute variables with numbers, and receive an answer calculated to an arbitrary level of precision.

Every spreadsheet should include at least the following basic functions:

- ▼ Arithmetic functions: includes addition, subtraction, multiplication, division, and summation over a range

- ▼ Algebraic functions: includes exponents, trigonometric functions, round-offs, and matrix manipulation

- ▼ Logical functions

- ▼ Date and Time functions: includes date and time arithmetic, conditional dates, and absolute dates

- ▼ Statistical functions

- ▼ Financial functions: includes interest and principle calculations, rates of return, and net present value

- ▼ Text functions: includes fixing number of decimal places, matching text strings, truncation, search, and substitution

In addition, spreadsheets can offer functions related to databases and special indexing (lookup) functions. Most spreadsheets ship with more than 100 functions; some can have as many as 250. Good spreadsheets have tools to help you remember what all these functions do. Some enter the function in the right format directly into your worksheet. And a well-designed spreadsheet should have an excellent online help facility included.

The phrase "arbitrary level of precision" simply means that spreadsheets can maintain any degree of accuracy in their floating point calculations for at least nine digits after the decimal place (like a hand-held calculator), and sometimes up to 17 digits. Accuracy is usually not a problem when performing calculations, per se; it is when you need to display the numbers on a less accurate template.

WARNING! Rounding off to two digits after summing a large set of numbers occasionally can cause penny errors.

Chapter 12
Spreadsheets

Note A spreadsheet's speed usually is measured by how quickly it can perform a certain group of calculations a certain number of times. Adding a math coprocessor (chip numbers 68881 or 68882 for users with 68030 or earlier machines; the 68040 has a math coprocessor built in) dramatically improves spreadsheet calculation performance. Adding a math coprocessor to a Mac IIsi increases that machine's performance in numerical calculations by orders of magnitude, especially if the calculations are with floating-point numbers.

Note Look for spreadsheets that do minimal or smart recalculation. This is a network of cell dependencies stored in RAM so that when you change the data in one cell, only the dependent cells that reference it in a calculation are recalculated. (This is why Excel needs so much memory.) Most spreadsheets offer this feature. On large worksheets, minimal recalculation can save minutes of calculation time.

Graphing and Charting Capabilities

Spreadsheets not only put computers on the desks of business executives, but they influenced those same people to buy monitors with graphics capabilities. In addition to pioneering the concept of what-if analysis, spreadsheets also ushered in the era of business graphics. You easily can manipulate raw data to generate various possible scenarios, then display the results of your calculations in any number of flat and 3-D charts and graphs, often in brilliant colors. Spreadsheets that can chart and graph are considered to be second generation spreadsheets.

Although the spreadsheets themselves now have impressive charting capabilities, they cannot compare to the best stand-alone charting package, DeltaGraph Pro. This package, from DeltaPoint, produces more sophisticated graphs that were only previously possible in advanced math programs such as Wolfram Research's Mathematica.

KaleidaGraph is another high-quality charting program. KaleidaGraph is more geared toward mathematical and statistical analysis, and it provides its own 2-D spreadsheet for entering and analyzing data.

Macro and Scripting Capabilities

Macros and scripts are similar; both allow several actions to be condensed into one. However, you record your actions to create macros and you create scripts by writing them in a special scripting language. Many spreadsheets include macro and scripting capabilities that enable you to automate and speed up repetitive calculation tasks.

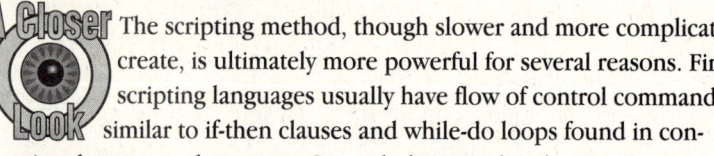 The scripting method, though slower and more complicated to create, is ultimately more powerful for several reasons. First, scripting languages usually have flow of control commands, similar to if-then clauses and while-do loops found in conventional computer languages. Second, the completed script is executed more quickly than a played-back series of commands. Third, in the case of the Wingz spreadsheet, the application's core functions are written in the scripting language; end-users can modify them by writing in the scripting language. Claris' Resolve spreadsheet uses the Wingz engine and shares its HyperScript scripting language, so any Wingz add-on scripts are immediately available to new Resolve users.

Spreadsheets with scripting capabilities offer flexible and fast feature expansion; you actually can make the spreadsheet change to fit your needs, rather than the opposite.

Ready-made macros for Excel and Works and scripts for Wingz and Resolve are available from a variety of sources, notably Heizer Software. (See the section, "Spreadsheets for the Macintosh," later in this chapter.)

The Spreadsheet As a Database

Microsoft Excel is one of the best-selling database applications for Macintosh. But isn't Excel a spreadsheet program?

Yes, but the spreadsheet's rows-and-columns structure lends itself to a database's records and fields structure too. And it is convenient to store and analyze your data on a spreadsheet instead of using a different application for each. Excel and other spreadsheets offer standard database functions such as sorting, indexing, and finding.

One advantage in using a spreadsheet as a database is simple accessibility. Database programs require you to understand terms such as records, fields, keys, and indexes before you can use them. You do not immediately start entering your mailing list in a database; instead, you have to design the database structure, name the fields, and sometimes even design the layout. Who wants to do all that for a simple telephone list?

Also, sometimes you need to perform calculations on data you need to keep in a database-like system. Because databases frequently are short on calculation power, a spreadsheet is a logical choice when functions and number crunching prowess is desired.

The disadvantage to using a spreadsheet rather than a database application itself is that databases are much faster and more flexible in manipulating the manner in which data is stored and retrieved. Get a database if you need to store lots of data, or if you need to find or organize the data quickly.

The Spreadsheet As a Presentation Tool

Charts and graphs usually are supplemented with text boxes, labels, and other enhancements. Graphing modules of spreadsheets and dedicated graphing programs offer object-oriented drawing and text tools to enhance charts with arrows, callouts, labels, titles, or whatever you need. With these capabilities, spreadsheets and graphing programs enable you to quickly and easily generate presentation-quality charts that can be printed, imported to more sophisticated graphics programs, or even transferred to 35mm slides.

Spreadsheets for the Macintosh

Microsoft Excel

Excel currently dominates the Mac spreadsheet industry with a 90+ percent market share, thousands of add-on templates and macros, and its own user groups. The latest version, 4.0, is System 7–savvy with powerful features and a terrific new interface. A similarly well-reviewed version of Excel (4.0) runs on Windows for MS-DOS computers, giving Microsoft cross-platform compatibility, which is important in many large companies.

The most noticeable feature change in Excel is the tool bar found between the menu bar and the worksheet (see figure 12.1). Commonly used spreadsheet functions are available here as push-button icons. The tool bar is powerful, useful, and distinctly Mac-like.

Part III
Mainstream Mac Applications

Other improved functions include an editable Print Preview, a goal-seek function to enable you to work backward from goals to input data (for instance, directly calculating sales levels to maintain a profit margin of four percent with variable monthly costs), hot links with open or closed worksheets (for 3-D worksheet capabilities), and a separate Solver module to find solutions for multivariable models.

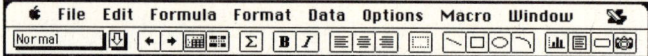

Figure 12.1
The tool bar, located between the menu bar and the worksheet window, offers push button icons and makes Excel much easier to use.

Although charting capabilities have been improved—24 new full-color 3-D charts have been added (see figure 12.2)—Excel still lags behind other dedicated graphing packages. If you use Excel but need professional-quality charts and presentation graphics, you will want to get DeltaPoint's DeltaGraph or Synergy Software's KaleidaGraph.

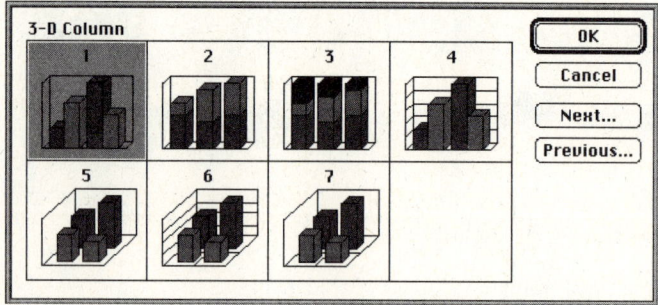

Figure 12.2
Excel 3.0 offers four palettes of 3-D charts and seven palettes of 2-D charts. You move between palettes with the Next and Previous buttons. 3-D palettes available include area, pie, bar, and line.

Excel brings word processor-like style sheets and outlining to spreadsheets. Style sheets simplify the worksheet formatting process, making it easier to create presentation-quality tables of data to accompany the charts (see chapter 10, "Word Processors"). Outlining allows different worksheet levels from summary too detailed to be independently displayed. Complex worksheets easily collapse onscreen so that only summary numbers are visible. There are also tools for simultaneously combining text, worksheet data, and charts onscreen, something you cannot do as easily with dedicated charting programs.

Chapter 12
Spreadsheets

Excel's macro functions are improved, although they still do not beat Resolve's and Wingz's HyperScript language. However, Excel has a huge library of inexpensive, high-quality templates and macro packages available (see the "Resources" section later in this chapter). Whatever you can do for yourself with the other products, Excel can do with one of these add-on packages.

> **Note:** Excel is a disk and memory hog. Memory issues aside, Excel is a powerful, easy-to-use integrated worksheet and presentation tool. Other spreadsheets will be hard-pressed to steal Excel users away, especially because Excel is the first with complete System 7 friendliness.

For more information about Excel, contact Microsoft Corp., One Microsoft Way, Redmond, Washington 98052-6399; (206) 882-8080.

Microsoft Works

The second Macintosh spreadsheet in popularity is probably Microsoft Works' spreadsheet module, one of five modules in this integrated program (see chapter 14, "Integrated Programs," for more information). All of Heizer Software's templates available for Excel also are available for Works. Works 3.0 did little to improve the spreadsheet module.

The Works spreadsheet is fairly functional. It offers basic formulas, the flexibility of a large worksheet area, and some standard charts. Charts are updated automatically when worksheet data is changed, a feature similar on the surface to System 7's Publish and Subscribe.

As with Works' other modules, the spreadsheet will not win any performance awards. But, as with Excel, many add-on packages are available that dramatically improve Works' value both as a spreadsheet and as an integrated package. For some users, the latter may be the best reason for choosing Works.

For more information about Microsoft Works, contact Microsoft Corp., One Microsoft Way, Redmond, Washington 98052-6399; (206) 882-8080.

Wingz

Informix's Wingz was introduced to the market in 1989 after an intense marketing campaign that included Leonard Nimoy leading users on a spreadsheet spaceship journey at Macworld Expos, and Informix giving away impressive carry-bags and jackets, a first in the software world.

Part III

Mainstream
Mac Applications

Figure 12.3

Informix's Wingz was an innovator: Notice the function bar on the left and that the chart and the worksheet data are on the same page. The Show Notes/GO BACK/HOME SHEET text boxes are actually buttons that trigger scripts, more like HyperCard than a spreadsheet.

Wingz was clearly the best of the available spreadsheets at the time. It impressed reviewers with its speed, its scripting language, and the superb quality of its graphs and charts (see figure 12.3). Unfortunately, the program did not attract users in large numbers. Over time Excel was able to catch up.

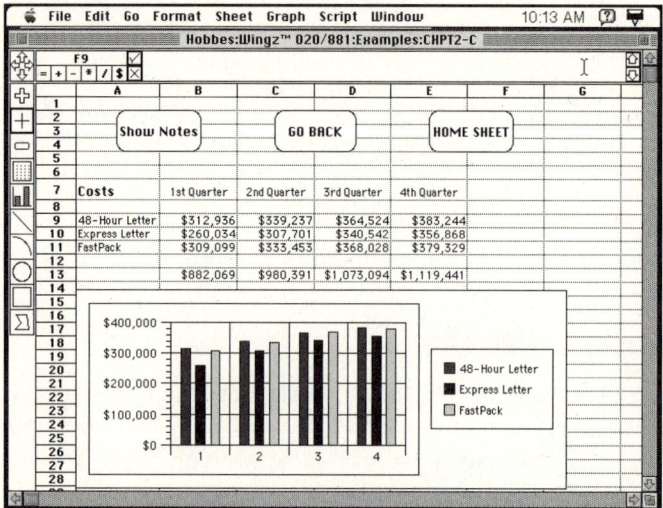

One of Wingz's remarkable features is the HyperScript scripting language. It is a true procedural programming language resembling Pascal. The entire application is written in it, so you conceivably can change how Wingz works and seamlessly integrate new features. Claris has licensed this scripting technology for Resolve, but as yet, Wingz and HyperScript have no competitors for flexibility and expressiveness.

Wingz offers a function list similar to Excel's, and its once-dazzling calculating speed has been matched by Excel. Wingz cannot do background calculations under MultiFinder, so if you need to recalculate a large worksheet, you are forced to wait in Wingz instead of working on something else.

The full-color, 3-D charts and graphs Wingz produces are still outstanding, and the presentation tools (text and drawing functions) are very good. Wingz has integrated database functions also.

Wingz is System 7–compatible. At this writing, Informix has not offered plans for further System 7 integration. For those interested in cross-platform compatibility, Wingz versions are available for Windows and OS/2.

For more information about Wingz, contact Informix Software, Inc., 4100 Bohannon Drive, Menlo Park, California 94025; (800) 331-1763 or (415) 322-4100.

Resolve 1.0

Claris waited until System 7's release to unveil its powerful new spreadsheet, Resolve 1.0. Resolve offers full System 7 friendliness, more built-in functions than any other spreadsheet, sophisticated 3-D color charts, HyperScript capabilities licensed from Wingz, online help, object-oriented drawing tools, and worksheets integrated with charts and drawing objects.

Since System 7's release, Claris has promoted its products in tandem. In late 1991, Claris began offering free copies of Resolve to anyone buying two other Claris applications. Claris boasts about "sophisticated links between its products that go beyond standard Apple events" in its promotions; Claris applications "blend" to form a "hybrid" application with capabilities unattainable with other publishers' software.

For more information about Resolve, contact Claris Corp., 5201 Patrick Henry Drive, P.O. Box 58168, Santa Clara, California 95052; (408) 727-8227 (customer relations), (800) 544-8554 (U.S. upgrades), or (800) 334-3535 (U.S. dealers).

Lotus 1-2-3/Mac

Surprisingly, this is not Lotus' first entry into the Macintosh software market. Several years ago, Lotus introduced the Mac's first integrated package, Jazz, an ill-conceived and poorly implemented product that failed to gain many followers. It was based on Symphony for MS-DOS computers, another ill-fated product that never was very successful. The product Lotus should have developed, rather than Jazz—a Mac equivalent of 1-2-3—was subsequently introduced by Microsoft in Excel. Excel immediately dominated the Mac spreadsheet market, just as 1-2-3 did on PCs.

Six years later, it seems Lotus finally has succeeded in the Mac market. Although it only allows for spreadsheet sizes of 8192 rows by 256 columns, 1-2-3/Mac has true 3-D spreadsheet capability as well as unique functions such as tear-off menus and floating palettes.

1-2-3/Mac's Backsolver feature is similar to Excel 3.0's Goal Seeking function, which enables you to choose the outputs and have the program find the right inputs. The program also has some presentation capabilities: a drawing layer and a variety of 3-D chart types.

1-2-3/Mac offers macro capabilities that are fully compatible with the thousands of macros from MS-DOS versions of 1-2-3. 1-2-3/Mac also can read and write Excel 2.2 files and macros. The MS-DOS 1-2-3 macro library is the

Chapter 12
Spreadsheets

largest available for any spreadsheet; when combined with the capability to use Excel 2.2's huge macro library, it gives Lotus a major functionality advantage.

1-2-3/Mac and Resolve are not marketed to steal Excel users but to make inroads with new Macintosh users. With more Macs being sold today than ever before, the opportunities are ripe for these capable, powerful products. Lotus 1-2-3 is a well designed product with a good design that utilizes the Macintosh design philosophy well.

For more information about 1-2-3/Mac, contact Lotus Development Corporation, 55 Cambridge Parkway, Cambridge, Massachusetts 02142; (800) 343-5414 or (617) 577-8500.

MacCalc

MacCalc from Bravo Technologies is a straightforward calculating powerhouse with no graphing, charting, or presentation capabilities. MacCalc provides a worksheet area of 125 columns by 999 rows and minimal recalculation technology. If you are interested only in number crunching and do not want to pay extra for the more powerful, graphically oriented products, MacCalc is a great choice.

For more information about MacCalc, contact Bravo Technologies, Inc., P.O. Box 10078, Berkeley, California 94709; (415) 841-8552.

Designing a Spreadsheet

Choosing the right spreadsheet is only half the battle. Creating a useful, efficient spreadsheet that you and your associates can use productively is an art you can master with these guidelines:

First, get to know your spreadsheet. Play with the tutorial files, look through the HyperCard help stack, read the documentation—do whatever you can to learn the product as well as possible before you start working with it. The "learn-as-you-go" attitude fostered by other Macintosh software products only causes hours of frustrating trial-and-error and worksheet redesign time with spreadsheets.

Chapter 12
Spreadsheets

When you are comfortable enough with your knowledge of the spreadsheet's functions and behavior to begin building a worksheet, plan your design on paper. It is important to do this in words because there are no good symbolic design tools for spreadsheets in the way that outliners, flow charts, and idea formatters exist to help you plan your work with word processors.

Note: Identify the worksheet's purpose with a one-sentence objective. Make your important outputs—whether numbers or graphs—and the necessary inputs explicit. This objective should consider the potential destiny of the worksheet. Is it an in-house financial statement that needs to be printed on a variety of printers, and be read and understood by many different people? Or is it a personal worksheet that is printed only for your purposes? If possible, write your objective directly on the spreadsheet to remind yourself and inform others of its purpose.

After you define your spreadsheet's inputs, outputs, and goals, work backward to determine what formulas and calculations you will need. Distinguish between inputs, calculations, assumptions, and outputs as much as possible. Assumptions are like variables: you assume rent will go up by a certain amount or that inflation will remain at a certain level. Not making your assumptions explicit causes spreadsheets which misbehave, often several months or years after you created them. Make sure your steps at this level are recorded on paper as well for future reference.

Now you are ready to start building the worksheet. Physically separate the sections you distinguished by establishing a corner of the worksheet for variables and assumptions (best choice: the first few rows). Then build your rows and columns, keeping necessary formulas as simple as possible. It is better to have a sum of a single column than to be summing cells from all over the worksheet.

Seek to maximize modularity and simplicity. For example, if you have two similar formulas that can be consolidated by adding an extra variable, do so and write down what the extra variable means. Put the variable in its own cell so it is always visible and explicit.

Never use constants in formulas because their meaning can be lost over time. Instead, give constants their own cells and name them if possible. Frequently, constants represent assumptions, and assumptions always change.

Name important cells whenever possible. This helps with more complex calculations. This is also crucial if you use linked worksheets. Very often, if worksheets are linked by absolute cell location, moving the data in those cells cancels that link. But if links depend on a name, they are preserved no matter where the cells go.

Also, try to install second checks on calculations for important output data. No matter how simple the calculation is, errors may creep in nevertheless. If there are two ways to independently arrive at a critical number, use both and display the results in adjacent cells so you immediately know if something goes wrong.

Finally, remember that the best worksheets are easy to use for everyone—not just yourself. Use comments and helpful annotations whenever necessary, and avoid personal shorthand descriptions. A good worksheet is self-explanatory.

Note After the worksheet is built, check it manually with a set of sample data. It is helpful to put 1's in all input cells so you can use simple, mental arithmetic to check calculations quickly.

Make sure the outputs you need are easily visible, the raw data inputs are set apart from the formulas and calculations, and the spreadsheet is simple and clear overall. You want to eliminate as many potential problems as possible before you start actually using the worksheet.

If you have to troubleshoot an active worksheet, check to see whether round-off errors and mistaken order-of-operations are the culprits. If you find a more insidious error, fix it and check the results of previous sets of input data. You do not want one element to throw off the others.

These are just a few guidelines for designing effective worksheets. Entire books are available on this subject and might be worth consulting if you desire more in-depth help.

Spreadsheet Engines and Front-ends

The *engine* is the calculation machine that forms the core of any spreadsheet. Give the engine data and it pumps out the numbers. In word processors, the word wrap, scrolling, and keyboard functions form an engine of sorts. In databases, the searching and indexing functions are commonly referred to as the engine.

The *front-end* comprises everything else. In spreadsheets, the grid, menus, dialog boxes, and anything that is part of the interface between the user and the engine forms the front-end. Labels and other display features are front-end. Raw data is considered front-end when it is simply displayed on the screen and as part of the engine when it is used in calculations. Calculated values are also front-end, whereas formulas are considered part of the engine.

This distinction is behind most of the worksheet design functions outlined earlier. Isolating engine functions from front-end functions is always a good strategy for spreadsheet design. Similar distinctions of front-ends versus engines are applied to database products.

Using Spreadsheets with System 7

Under System 7, applications needing quick numerical calculations can send a *background request* to a spreadsheet engine through an AppleEvent (even over a network). The engine transparently performs the calculation and returns the answers to the calling application, without the user's knowledge.

With System 7, spreadsheets, graphing programs, and word processors can be linked as *publishers* and *subscribers*, always operating on one common, up-to-date set of data. For instance, a single change to a spreadsheet cell automatically results in changes to a table in the word processing document and changes to a chart in the graphing program. The new chart then automatically is sent to the word processor, where it is displayed side by side with the updated tabular data.

With file sharing, users on the network who have read-only access to the word processing document instantly can see both the new table data and the new chart. They do not even have to be running System 7; the file-sharing drivers also work with System 6.

Chapter 12
Spreadsheets

Part III
Mainstream
Mac Applications

The Future of Spreadsheets: Lotus Improv

Late in 1990, Lotus introduced a new kind of spreadsheet that it hoped would revolutionize computing as much as 1-2-3 did. The spreadsheet, called Improv, currently is available for the NeXT computers, and as of 1993 for Windows as well.

The spreadsheet model currently in use is an old one. Typically, relationships in a complex spreadsheet are as intricate as tossed spaghetti. If you change overall relationships or concepts, your worksheet is useless. In Improv, however, you define relationships based on labels. What you see displayed depends on the view of the relationships you desire. Change your model and underlying assumptions, and Improv gives you another view.

Improv embodies a new computing paradigm with roots dating back to HyperCard. HyperCard was, and is, terrific not just because of what it does, but what it represents. HyperCard was the first computing tool to give users the power to build their own applications without first learning a programming language.

Improv gives users this same power to build application-like structures that crunch and manipulate numbers, and display the results. Instead of presenting rows and columns pre-identified with numbers and letters, and forcing users to label them in the actual worksheet, Improv has users name the rows and columns (which Improv synonymously calls items) first. Items can be bunched into categories and categories into groups, allowing users several levels of abstraction. And at each level, many data manipulation and display functions are accessible.

Although it sounds complicated, using Improv is quite simple. Existing spreadsheets' rows and columns may be suitable for dealing with numbers over time, but the more modular Improv labels are great for dealing with general types of numerical data.

Improv, though still a young product, has not sold NeXT computers at the same rate 1-2-3 sold IBM PCs in the early '80s. If you get the opportunity to test Improv, do so. Improv has garnered some impressive reviews, but is difficult for long time spreadsheet users to come to terms with. It is a breakthrough product that will change how not only future spreadsheets but also word processors and databases work with information. Improv will probably make its way onto the Macintosh over the next year, but even if it doesn't, it will affect the construction of spreadsheets to come.

Resources

The add-on market for spreadsheets (notably Excel and Works) is enormous. With commercially available templates, you can use your spreadsheet to manage your department's budget, calculate your taxes, or keep score for the company softball team.

Although spreadsheet templates are available from many sources, one of the best is Heizer Software (Pleasant Hill, California, (800) 888-7667). Heizer manages the Excellent Exchange, a clearinghouse for Excel users looking for particular programs. Excellent Exchange publishes a catalog, and many of the products also have demo versions available at very low prices.

Spreadsheet templates and macros also are available from most user group BBSs. Online information services such as CompuServe and America Online have conferences dedicated to spreadsheets and are a good place to look for resources.

 Although many small software brokers advertise Excel templates, shop with caution. Heizer is the only broker we know of that is serious about quality control. Other brokers may be cheaper, but there is often no guarantee that their software will work properly.

Summary

Spreadsheets are great tools for working with numbers and visualizing the results. The Macintosh spreadsheet market is dominated by Excel. Other major products are Resolve, the long-awaited Lotus 1-2-3/Mac, and Wingz.

Good spreadsheet design can save you hours of nightmares when the time comes to change your underlying assumptions and your worksheet's construction. Spreadsheets can be used as databases, and they have a vigorous aftermarket of pre-designed templates that can automate your taxes, track a balance sheet, and perform many other tasks.

Interlude 12: Cool Excel Stuff

I remember seeing Excel 1.0 in 1985 and being absolutely knocked out. Excel was *clearly* the best spreadsheet program available for *any* computer, not that the competition was so stiff. Practically the whole world was using Lotus 1-2-3 on IBM PCs when Excel came out, but Lotus was hardly a wonderful product. It beat working with numbers by hand, but it wasn't any fun. Great sales doesn't equal great products in my book. And, this *is* my book. (Well, my chapter, anyway.)

In This Chapter

▼ Styles

▼ Charting

▼ Buried Treasures

Part III
Mainstream Mac Applications

Numbers for the Rest of Us

Another thing I find off-putting is the screen I see each time Excel starts up. Figure 12.1 shows the Excel 3.0 startup screen. I'd rather they bragged about the program instead of their lawyers.

Christian Boyce

Excel transformed spreadsheets from something for computer jockeys into something for the rest of us. With Excel, anyone who could point a mouse could monkey with the numbers and turn them into pie charts. Even 1-2-3 gurus knew a good thing when they saw it, though most of them wouldn't admit it. A lot of Macs were bought just to run Excel, though.

Excel has evolved a bit, but they got a lot right the first time. Excel 2.2 added tons of formatting capabilities lacking in the original (would you believe the original Excel let you use exactly *one* font in a spreadsheet?), but Excel 2.2 still *looked* like Excel and still *acted* like Excel. The current version (4.0) is long on features but short on looks. Microsoft wanted Excel to look and feel the same whether you used a Mac or a PC with Windows, and they accomplished their goal. In doing so, Microsoft gave Excel a peculiarly non-Mac feel, which I find off-putting.

Figure 12.1
"Thou shalt not steal," Microsoft style.

Excel is still a great spreadsheet, even though its interface makes me want to spit. Two very cool features—Styles and Charting—help me put up with Excel's cosmetic shortcomings; I think they'll do the same for you.

Excel lets you format your spreadsheets beyond a Lotus 1-2-3er's wildest dreams, and with Styles you can do it in a hurry. Excel's Styles—like Word's Styles—let you apply complex formatting quickly and consistently. They're a "change your life" kind of feature. Figure 12.2 shows some Excel spreadsheets formatted excessively, but quickly, with Styles.

Excel lets you make better-than-decent charts, turning your numbers into pictures that are easily understood. (Not to say that you can't turn numbers into charts that *aren't* easily understood. Excel lets you make rotten charts as easily as great ones.) Excel's Charting features help you make charts in a hurry, and you can format them to death. Figure 12.3 shows a screenful of charts, all made with Excel, and all formatted with ease.

Interlude 12
Cool Excel Stuff

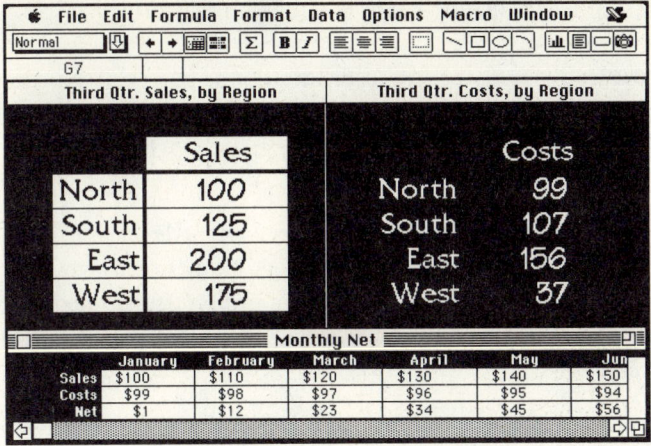

Figure 12.2
Spreadsheets formatted with Styles.

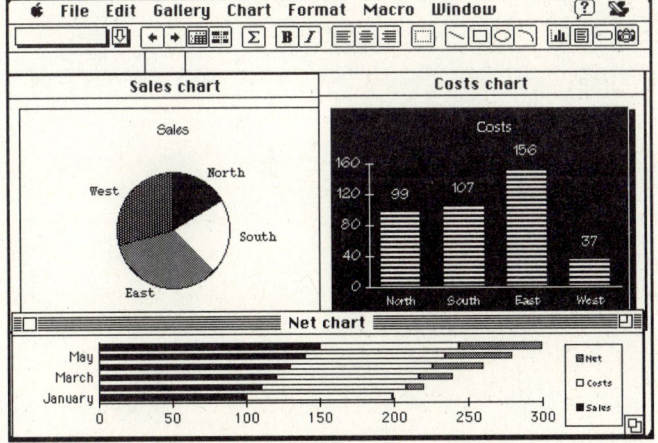

Figure 12.3
Charts created and formatted with Excel.

Styles and Charting make Excel much more worth using. This chapter shows you how to take advantage of these features to make your own Excel work easier and more fun. Work through the examples from beginning to end; you'll use the same spreadsheets to learn Styles and Charting.

> This chapter was written with Excel 3.0 in mind. The current version is 4.0, so you might notice some differences, but the basics are the same.

Part III
Mainstream Mac Applications

Styles: So Fashionable

Excel 3.0 introduced Styles to spreadsheets. With Styles, you can change a cell's font, size, and alignment all at once. You can also use Styles to shade cells and apply borders to them. Excel's Styles are a lot like Word's Styles, except Word's are nicer to use.

> **Note:** You can apply "protection" to cells via Styles as well, but that just keeps you from changing things. I want to show you how you can *do* things, not how you can stop yourself from doing things. If you really want to know about protection, check the Excel User's Guide.

Open up a new spreadsheet (Excel calls it a Worksheet, but no one else does). You'll use it to explore the Style feature, and when you're done with this section, you'll use it again to learn about charts. Your screen should look like figure 12.4.

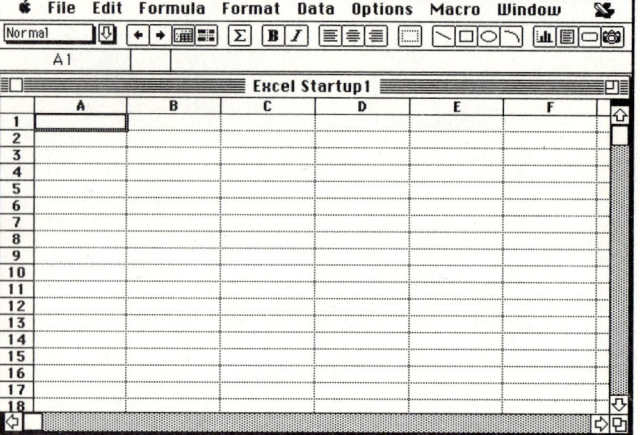

Figure 12.4
New spreadsheet.

If your screen doesn't look like figure 12.4, check the settings in the **Workspace** dialog box. (You get to the Workspace dialog box by choosing **Workspace** from the **Options** menu.) Figure 12.5 shows the Workspace dialog box and the options that lead to figure 12.4.

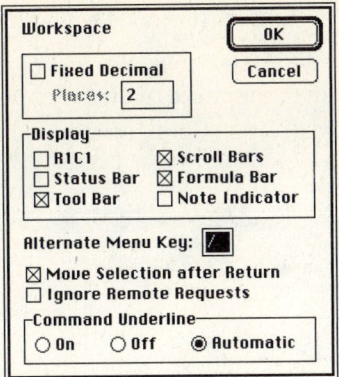

Figure 12.5
Workspace dialog box.

Your First Style

Making a Style is easy. First you format some cells; then you store the formatting as a Style. This example teaches you the basics.

1. Enter the data shown in figure 12.6 (it doesn't matter where you start, just make your spreadsheet look like figure 12.6).

   Figure 12.6
   Sales data.

2. Save the spreadsheet as **Sales**.
3. Select the cell with the word "Sales" in it (click on it).
4. Choose **Styles** from the **Format** menu.

   Excel gives you the **Style** dialog box shown in figure 12.7. Clicking the down arrow shows all the Styles defined for the Sales spreadsheet. New spreadsheets get the Normal style (plain Geneva 10 point), Currency, Percent, and Comma (this one puts commas into long numbers, so "1000000" looks like "1,000,000").

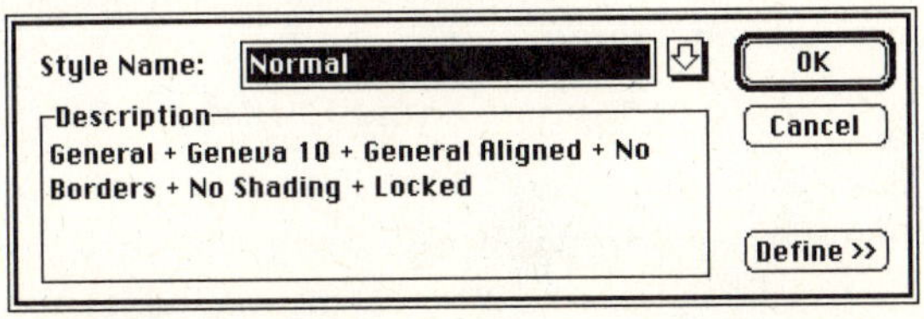

Figure 12.7
Style dialog box.

Figure 12.8
Ready for defining.

Figure 12.9
The Font box, after choosing a font and size.

5. Click the **Define>>** button (very non-standard button!).

   Figure 12.8 shows the **Style** dialog box, ready for you to start defining a new Style (or redefining an old one). The buttons at the bottom of the dialog box lead to various formatting options.

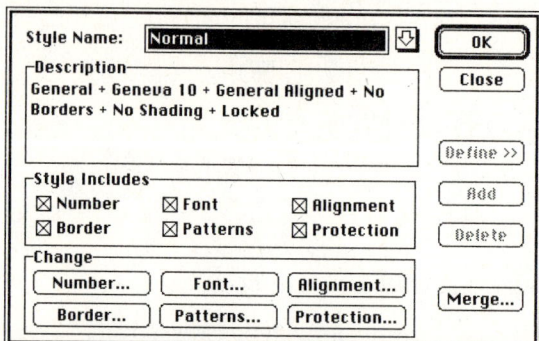

6. Start defining your new Style by clicking the **Font** button. Figure 12.9 shows the **Font** dialog box.

   This is the same dialog box you get by choosing **Font** from the **Format** menu.

7. Change the font to Chicago, 12 point.

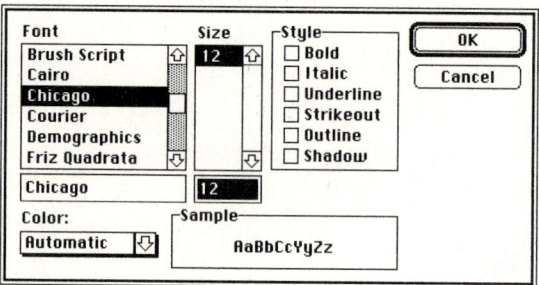

8. Click **OK**. You've chosen a font. Now choose an alignment (left, right, center, whatever).

9. Click the **Alignment** button.

10. Click the **Right aligned** option. Figure 12.10 shows the **Alignment** dialog box.

    Note: This is the same dialog box you get by choosing **Alignment** from the **Format** menu. That **Wrap Text** option does neat things; try it when you need to type a paragraph in a single cell.

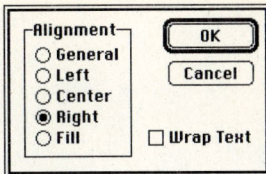

Figure 12.10

The Alignment box, after choosing Right aligned.

11. Click **OK**.

You've just about done it. Give your new Style a name and you're through.

12. Type `Headings` in the **Style Name** box.
13. Click **OK**.

Figure 12.11 shows the spreadsheet, with the formatting applied to one cell. So far, you haven't done anything great with a Style (you've defined one, but you haven't used it). Now apply it to the other cells with words in them.

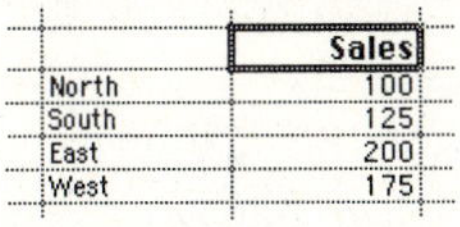

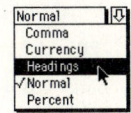

Figure 12.11

Formatting applied to one cell.

1. Select the cells with North, South, East, and West in them. Just click in the North cell and drag to the West cell.
2. Click on the down arrow next to the Style box on the Toolbar. Figure 12.12 shows the down arrow and the Style box.

Click on the down arrow, not on the Style box itself.

Figure 12.12

Choosing a Style from the Style box.

3. Choose **Headings**.

Figure 12.13 shows the spreadsheet after applying the Headings Style. Sure beats working. Try entering some other words in your Sales sheet and applying your Headings Style to them. Change them back to Normal by applying the Normal Style, then back again to Headings. Is this easy, or what?

You can make more complicated Styles if you want to. Your Headings Style includes font and alignment information, but there are four other formatting areas (as indicated by the buttons in figure 12.8). Try making a Style that fills a cell with black. I'll give you hints with the steps below (you should know what you're doing by now).

1. **Styles** from **Format** menu.
2. **Define>>**.
3. **Patterns** button.
4. Choose solid black from the Pattern list.

This is the same dialog box you get by choosing **Patterns** from the **Format** menu.

5. **OK**.
6. Name it `Black`.
7. **OK**.

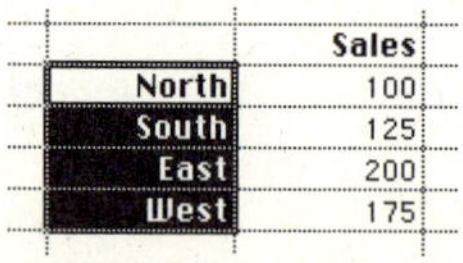

Figure 12.13
After applying the Headings Style.

Try applying your new Black Style to cells in the spreadsheet. If you make a mistake, apply the Normal Style to start over. Figure 12.14 shows a few cells with the Black Style applied.

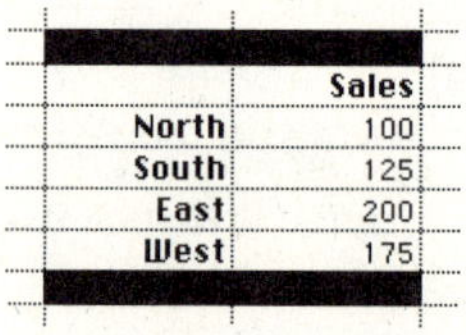

Figure 12.14
Using the Black Style.

One other important Style option involves number formatting. Number formats tell Excel how you want numbers to look; for example, the number "2" could be formatted as "2.0," "$2.00," "200%," and so on. It all depends on the number format. Excel includes a generous variety of number formats; it also lets you define your own formats.

Note: Defining your own formats is pretty powerful stuff. You can define a format that puts the word "July" into a cell when you type "7/27/62" in the cell next to it. You can define a format that makes even numbers read "Even" and odd numbers read "Odd." Or "Uneven," if that's the way you like it. You can define a format that makes positive numbers green, negative numbers red, and zeros invisible. I like defining number formats.

Let's experiment with Number formats before defining another Style.

1. Select the numbers in your Sales spreadsheet.
2. Choose **Number** from the **Format** menu. Figure 12.15 shows the Number format dialog box.

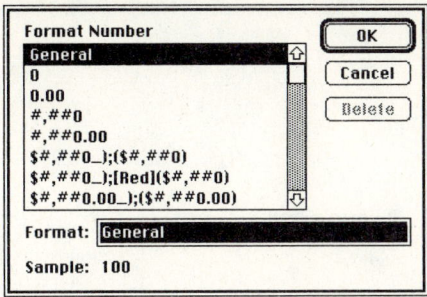

3. Choose **0.00** from the list of formats. (Notice the sample at the bottom of the **Number** dialog box.)
4. Click **OK**.

Your spreadsheet looks like figure 12.16. Choosing a new number format didn't change the *values* of the numbers in your spreadsheet, but it sure made them *look* different. Experiment by applying other number formats to the numbers in the Sales spreadsheet.

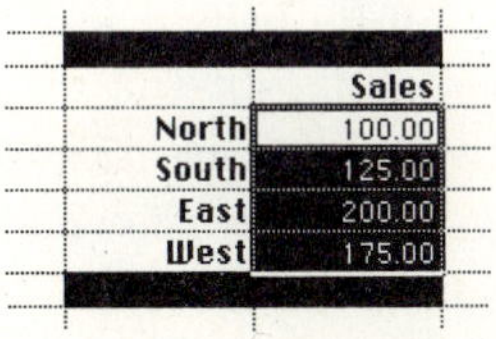

Simple number formats have only one part. All numbers—positives, negatives, and zeros—are formatted exactly the same way. If you want to format positive numbers one way and negative numbers another, you have to use a number format with two parts. Separate the parts with a semicolon.

Figure 12.17 shows two columns of numbers; the column on the left is formatted with the "0.00" format, and the column on the right is formatted with a custom "0.00;(0.00)" format. It's important to note that the numbers in both columns are the same and were entered the same way.

Type the numbers of figure 12.17 and format the left hand column with the "0.00" format as you did in the previous example. Don't type over your Sales numbers (type somewhere, *anywhere*, else).

Interlude 12
Cool Excel Stuff

Figure 12.15
Number formats dialog box.

Figure 12.16
After applying the "0.00" format.

Part III
Mainstream Mac Applications

Figure 12.17
One-part and two-part formatting.

Figure 12.18
Making a custom format.

Create the custom number format "0.00;(0.00)" following these steps.

1. Select the cells you want to format (the column on the right).
2. Choose **Number** from the **Format** menu.
3. Type `0.00;(0.00)`. The format looks like Figure 12.18.

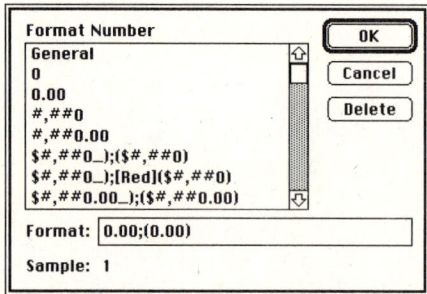

4. Click **OK**.

The column on the left looks good; all the numbers line up. The parentheses around the negative numbers in the column on the right cause alignment problems. Fortunately, this is easy to fix. The trick involves an *invisible parenthesis* at the end of positive numbers. The invisible parenthesis isn't seen (no kidding), but it takes up space. This makes the negative numbers (with their visible right parentheses) and the positive numbers (with their *invisible* right parentheses) line up.

1. Choose **Number** from the **Format** menu.
2. Scroll to the bottom of the list.

   You won't need to scroll if the column on the right in figure 12.18 is still selected.

3. Choose your **0.00;(0.00)** format from the list.
4. Make the format look like `0.00_);(0.00)`.

   The underline and right parenthesis combine to create an invisible right parenthesis. The underline means "make the next character invisible, but make it take up space."

5. Click **OK**.

Your screen looks like figure 12.19. Everything's aligned.

1.00	1.00
-2.00	(2.00)
3.00	3.00
-4.00	(4.00)

Figure 12.19
Properly aligned numbers.

Excel lets you use *words* in number formats. You can change those sales figures in your spreadsheet to read "100 cases" and so on instead of "100.00" by making another custom format.

1. Select the sales figures (just the cells with the numbers).
2. Choose **Number** from the **Format** menu.
3. Type **0 "cases"** (the word "cases" is in quotes). The dialog box looks like figure 12.20.

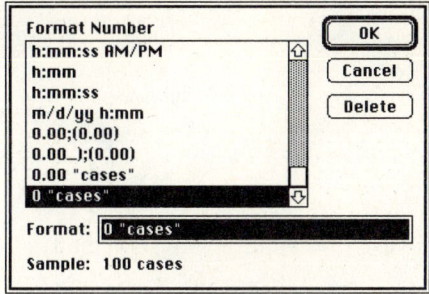

Figure 12.20
Number format with words.

4. Click **OK**. Your Sales spreadsheet looks like figure 12.21.

	Sales
North	100 cases
South	125 cases
East	200 cases
West	175 cases

Figure 12.21
Formatted Sales figures.

A Closer Look Why not just type "100 cases" when you enter the numbers in the first place? Two reasons: one, it's easier to type just the numbers; two, you can't do math with the numbers unless they are typed in purely as numbers. Type in "100" and let Excel format it to "100 cases" and the number's still useable in a formula. Type "100 cases" yourself and Excel won't let you work with it. Try it and see.

Now you know how to define a custom number format. Make one more Style, containing your new "cases" number format, and you'll be a Style-making whiz.

1. Select the sales figures (the numbers with the word "cases" after them).
2. Choose **Style** from the **Format** menu.

Excel's User Guide spends 9 pages covering Number Formats, starting with page 178. It's dull reading, but it's worth glancing at. At least you'll know it's there.

Christian Boyce

Part III
Mainstream
Mac Applications

3. Click the **Define>>** button.
4. Click the **Number** button.
5. Choose your "cases" format.
6. Click **OK**.
7. Name the new Style **Cases**. Your screen looks like figure 12.22.

Figure 12.22
Defining a Style.

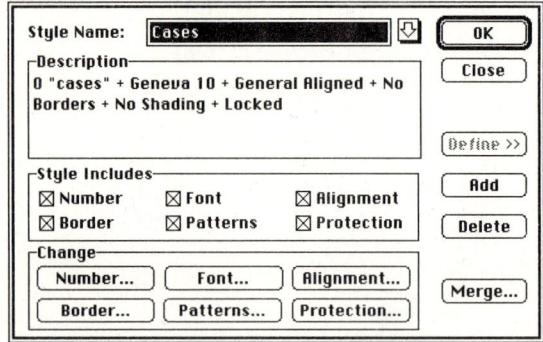

8. Click **OK**.

Your new "Cases" style is now in the Style box on the Toolbar. Try typing some numbers anywhere on your spreadsheet (except where the sales figures are) and applying the "Cases" Style to them.

A Closer Look The Styles you define for the Sales spreadsheet are available only within that spreadsheet. Unlike Microsoft Word, Excel does not let you define universal or default Styles. You can get around this by defining a bunch of Styles in a blank spreadsheet and saving the spreadsheet as a template; when you want those Styles available in a new document, double-click the document. You'll get a copy of the template, and the copy will have all the Styles in it.

When you redefine a Style, every cell formatted with that Style is updated. Everything you learned about redefining Styles in Word works in Excel. You can probably guess how to do it. Work through this example just to be sure.

1. Select the cell holding "Sales" (note it's formatted with the "Headings" Style).
2. Click the left-justification button on the Toolbar.

   The cell with "Sales" becomes left-justified. Now redefine the Style, so all the cells formatted with "Headings" become left-justified.

3. Click on the down arrow next to the Style box on the Toolbar.
4. Choose **Headings**. Figure 12.23 shows the resulting dialog box.

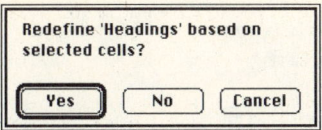

Figure 12.23
Redefining a Style.

5. Click **Yes**.

Figure 12.24 shows the Sales spreadsheet after redefining the "Headings" Style.

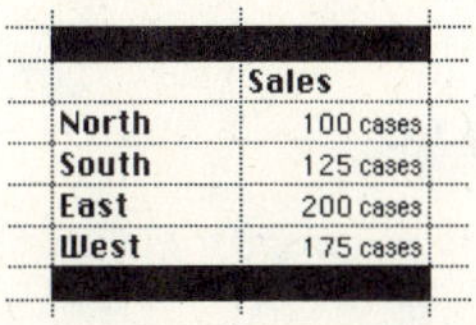

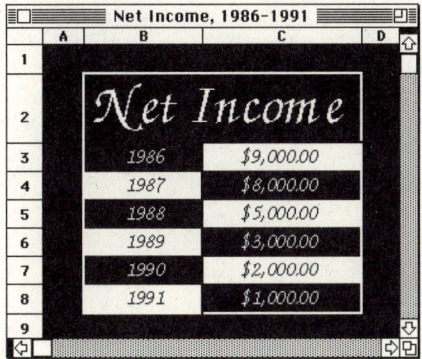

Figure 12.24
After redefining "Headings" Style.

> **Note:** You could do more than change justification before redefining the Headings Style. You could change the font, the size, the shading, and so on and still redefine the Style by selecting Headings under that down arrow.

You now know more about Styles than almost anyone. Styles help you quickly make nicely-formatted spreadsheets, and they keep the formatting consistent. Good formatting isn't going to change bad numbers, but it can make them more pleasant to read. Figure 12.25 shows a nicely formatted bit of bad news.

Figure 12.25
Bad news.

Styles can help you present your numbers more clearly, but sometimes that's still not clear enough. Sometimes you need a picture. Luckily for you, Excel lets you turn your numbers into charts. The next section, Charting, shows you how to make charts and format them.

Part III
Mainstream
Mac Applications

Charting: It's Such Sweet Sorrow

Actually, the only sorry thing about charting is how much better an Excel chart looks compared to your best-effort spreadsheet. Other than that, charting is fun, fun, fun.

Making a Chart

Excel gives you two ways to turn spreadsheet numbers into charts. One way, the so-called "old way," saves the chart as its own document, separate from the spreadsheet. The other way, the so-called "new way," saves the chart as part of the spreadsheet. Either chart-making method is easy as pie.

Open your Sales spreadsheet. (You'll need it for the examples in this section.) The first example teaches you how to make charts the old way. The second teaches you to make them the new way. Knowing how to make charts the old way will help you appreciate the new way more.

 Change the black cells to empty, normal cells by applying the Normal Style to them. You'll have a hard time knowing which cells are selected for charting if you leave them black, because black cells look selected even when they aren't.

1. Select the Sales information. Figure 12.26 shows how the selection should look.

Figure 12.26
Selecting data for charting.

	Sales
North	100 cases
South	125 cases
East	200 cases
West	175 cases

2. Choose **New** from the **File** menu. Figure 12.27 shows the resulting dialog box.

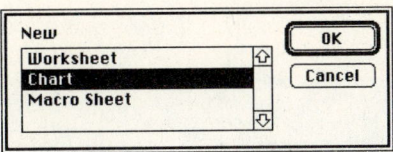

Figure 12.27
Making a new chart.

3. Click **Chart**.
4. Click **OK**. Figure 12.28 shows the chart Excel makes for you automatically.

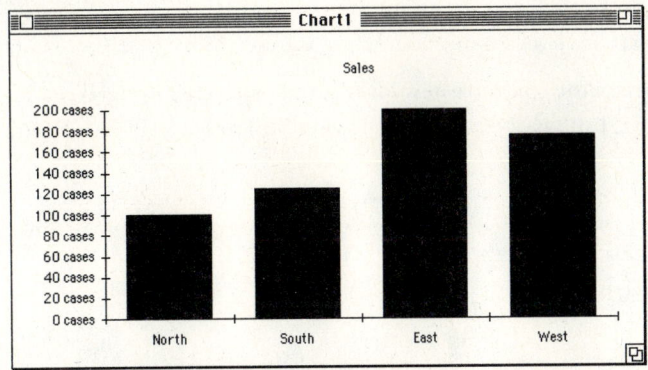

Figure 12.28
Default chart.

5. Save the chart as `Old way chart`.

That's it. Making a chart the old way is easy. Making a chart the new way is even easier. Choose "Sales" from the Window menu to bring the Sales spreadsheet to the front.

1. Select the Sales information as before.
2. Click the Chart button on the Toolbar. Figure 12.29 shows the Chart button.

Figure 12.29
The Chart button.

3. Specify a size and location for the chart by dragging a rectangle.

Figure 12.30 shows the chart, on top of the spreadsheet's cells.

489

Figure 12.30

Chart on top of spreadsheet.

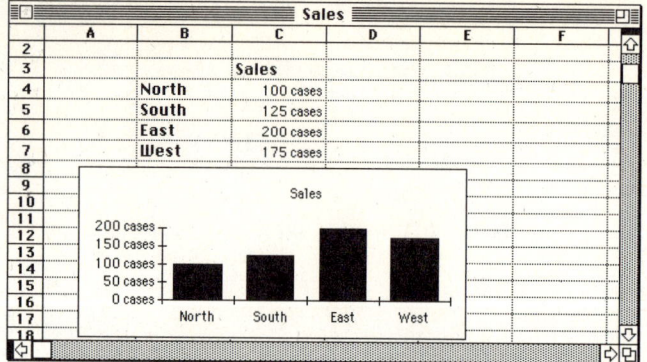

You can drag the chart to a new location and stretch it in any direction. Figure 12.31 shows the chart repositioned and resized.

Figure 12.31

Repositioned and resized chart on spreadsheet.

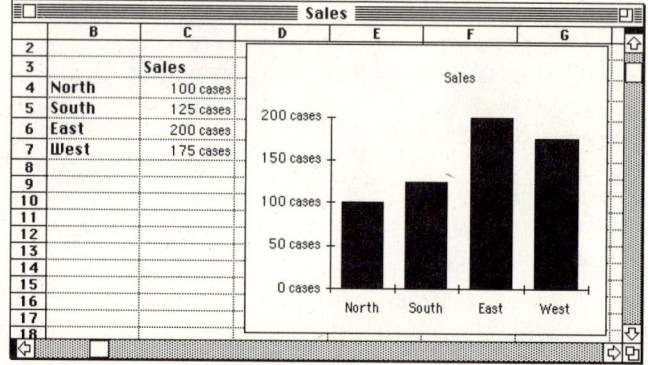

Either way, it's easy to make a chart. Of course, you might want a different kind of chart. If you do, no problem: Excel's got plenty to choose from, and changing chart types is easy.

1. Choose the **Old way chart** from the **Window** menu.
2. Choose **Pie** from the **Gallery** menu.

Figure 12.32 shows the **Gallery** menu. Each menu item leads to several variations. Figure 12.33 shows the various Pie charts.

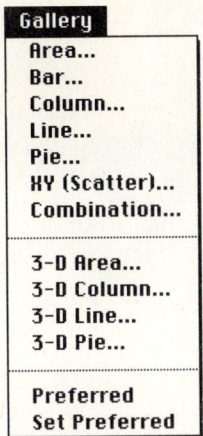

Figure 12.32
Gallery menu for charts.

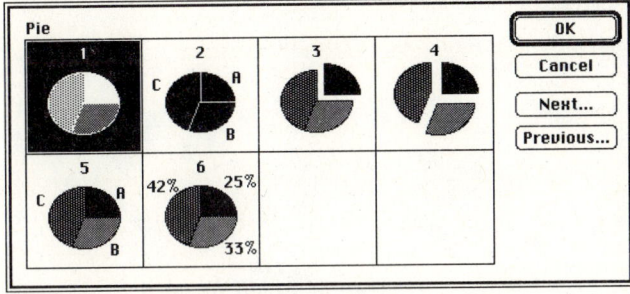

Figure 12.33
Six kinds of Pie.

3. Click on Pie number 6.
4. Click **OK**. Your screen looks like figure 12.34.

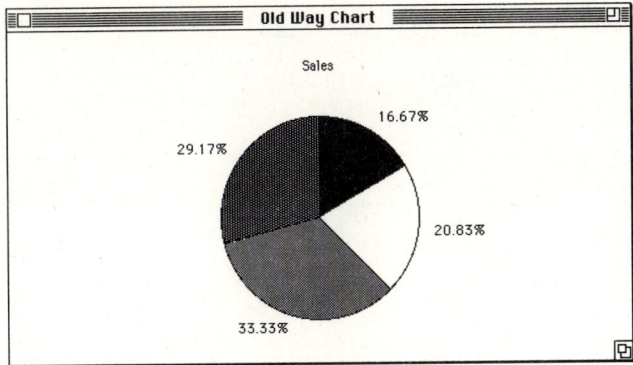

Figure 12.34
Pie chart.

5. Add a legend by choosing **Add Legend** from the **Chart** menu. Your screen looks like figure 12.35.

Figure 12.35
Pie chart with legend.

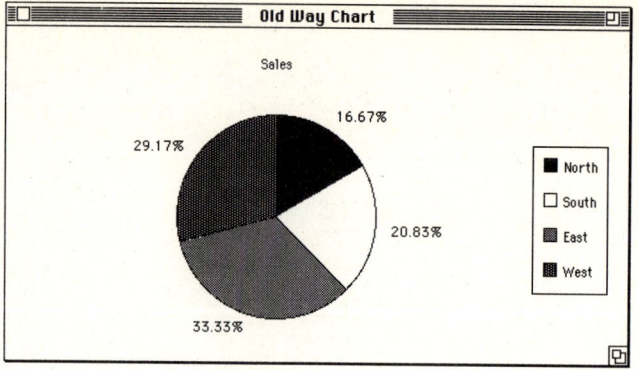

You can also make 3-D charts with Excel, including 3-D pies.

1. Choose **3-D Pie** from the **Gallery** menu.
2. Click on 3-D Pie number 6.
3. Click **OK**. Your screen looks like figure 12.36.

Figure 12.36
3-D pie chart.

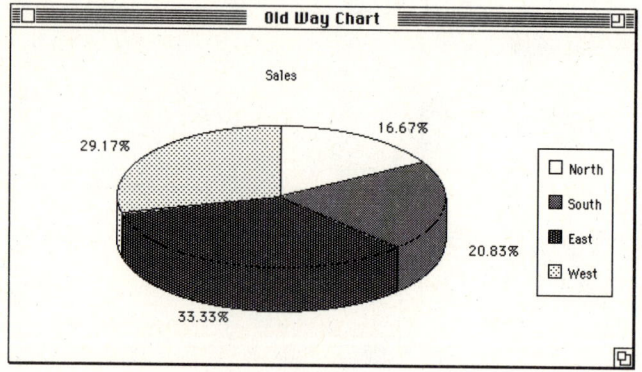

Some of Excel's "3-D" charts are merely 2-D charts with depth. The 3-D pie is one of them. Adding depth to a pie chart distorts it; you're better off using the 2-D. This is a public service announcement.

Christian Boyce

4. Choose **Bar** from the **Gallery** menu.
5. Click on Bar chart number 7.
6. Click **OK**.

You don't need a legend for this kind of chart; delete the legend by choosing **Delete Legend** from the **Chart** menu. Your screen looks like figure 12.37.

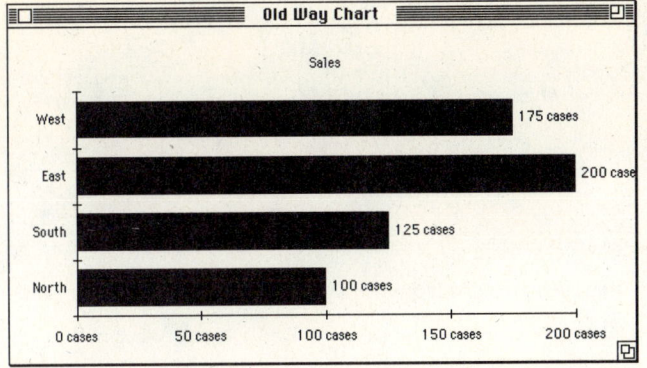

Figure 12.37
Bar chart without legend.

Formatting a Chart

Excel lets you format charts almost any way you want to. You can change patterns, fonts, and lines, add text and arrows, and change the scale of the axes. None of this is hard to do, although Excel's catacomb of dialog boxes makes formatting less straightforward than it ought to be. Figure 12.38 shows a particularly busy formatting dialog box, with buttons leading to several more options.

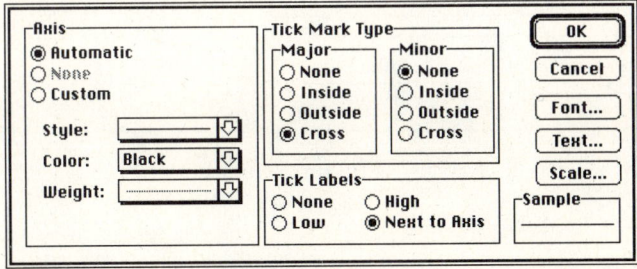

Figure 12.38
Particularly busy dialog box.

There are two ways to do chart formatting: the boring, from-the-menus way, and the cool, double-click-what-you-want-to-format way. You should use the double-click way.

When you double-click a chart element, Excel pops up the appropriate formatting dialog box. You make your choices and click OK—couldn't be simpler. Try formatting your bar chart following the steps below.

1. Double-click any bar. You see the dialog box of figure 12.39.

Figure 12.39

Border and Area dialog box.

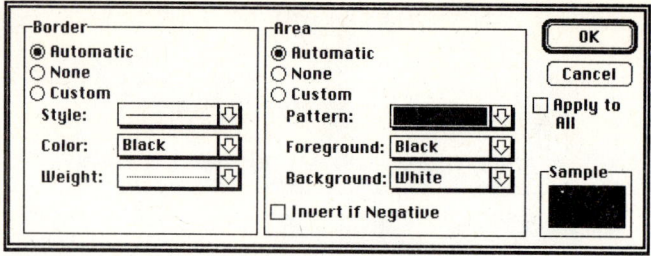

1. Choose a line weight from the pop-up menu in the **Border** section.
2. Choose a pattern from the pop-up menu in the **Area** section.
3. Click **OK**.

Your chart looks like figure 12.40.

Figure 12.40

After changing borders and areas.

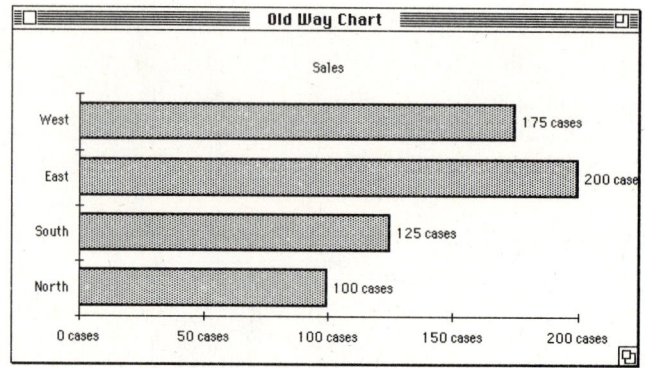

You easily can change the chart's title and font.

1. Click (once) on the title.
2. Type a new title (perhaps `Third Quarter Sales, by Region`).
3. Press the Enter key.
4. Double-click the title.
5. Click the **Font** button in the resulting dialog box. Figure 12.41 shows the **Font** dialog box.
6. Choose a font and a size.
7. Click **OK**.

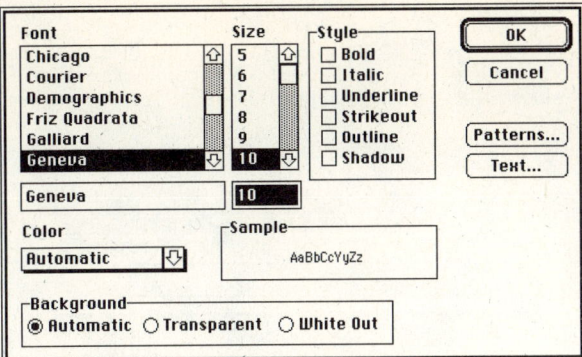

Figure 12.41
Font dialog box.

Your chart looks like figure 12.42

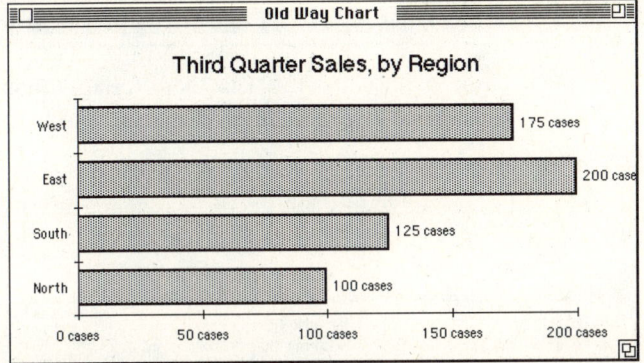

Figure 12.42
After formatting the title.

Excel's far from perfect. Sometimes it does things wrong. This next example shows Excel doing something wrong. Then it shows how you can fix it.

You can apply a trendy shadow to your chart in a couple of steps.

1. Double-click any blank space in the chart. You get the Border and Area dialog box shown in figure 12.43.

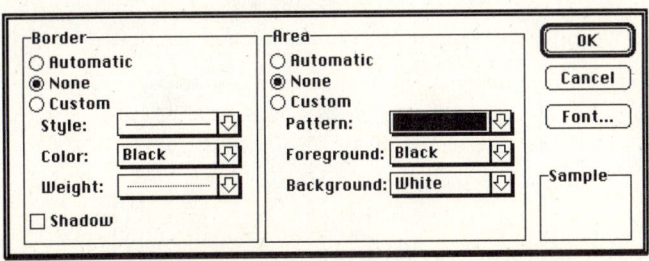

Don't you hate the perfect, white-washed examples in most computer books? I call them "Ozzie and Harriet" examples. Seems like they're chosen more for the authors' convenience than for the education of the readers. I don't like it.

Christian Boyce

Figure 12.43
Border and Area dialog box for entire chart.

Part III
Mainstream Mac Applications

Figure 12.44
Shadowed chart, with problem.

This overlap problem is not so bad on larger screens. If your chart looks OK, read along anyway. You might find something interesting.

Christian Boyce

Figure 12.45
Axis dialog box.

Figure 12.46
Scale dialog box.

2. Check the **Shadow** box.
3. Click **OK**.

Figure 12.44 shows the shadowed chart.

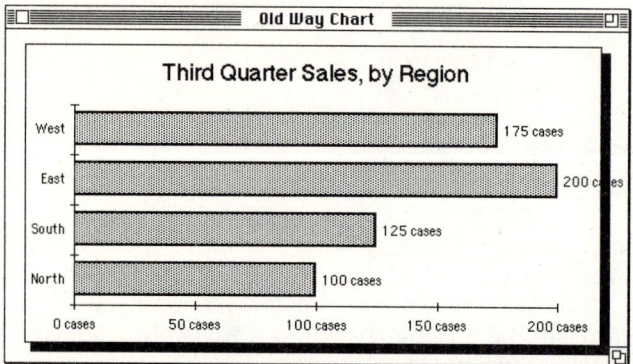

Problem! The word "cases" at the end of the "East" bar overlaps the shadow! This is Excel's fault, but it's *your* problem. There are a couple of ways to fix it, but this one's the best.

1. Double-click the horizontal axis. You get the Axis dialog box of figure 12.45.

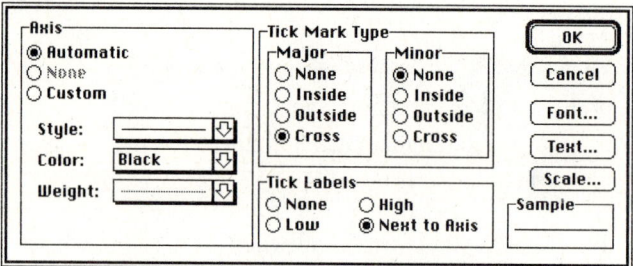

2. Click the **Scale** button. You get the dialog box of figure 12.46.

3. Make the scale dialog box look like figure 12.46.

   You want to extend the axis a bit to the right, past that "200 cases." It's very important to uncheck the box next to **Minimum**; if you don't, Excel will automatically compute a new minimum value for the axis, and it won't be zero. Try it both ways and see.

4. Click **OK**.

The problem's solved. Your chart looks like figure 12.47.

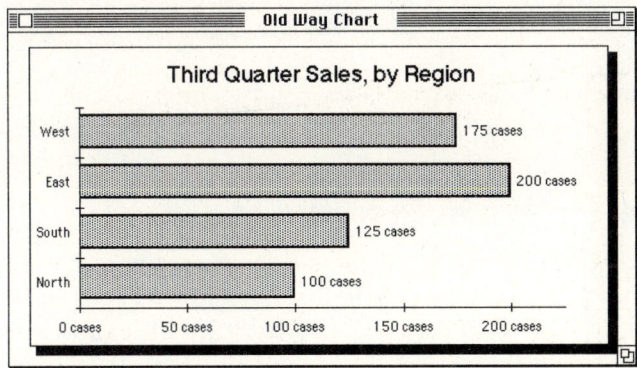

Figure 12.47
The finished chart.

You can call attention to part of your chart by pointing to it with an arrow. Adding an arrow is easy: choose **Add Arrow** from the **Chart** menu. Move it into place by dragging its handles. Add a little text ("Wow!"), and you've got the chart of figure 12.48.

1. Click in any blank area.

2. Type Wow!

3. Press the Enter key. The text ("Wow!") appears in the center of the screen.

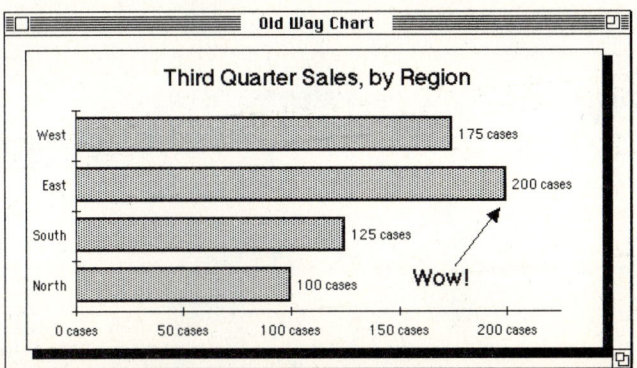

Interlude 12
Cool Excel Stuff

Figure 12.48
Wow!

4. Double-click the text and choose a font and size.
5. Drag the text to position.

You know how to make a chart, and you know how to format it. You also know that Excel's not perfect and that sometimes you have to push the right buttons to make Excel behave.

Buried Treasures

Excel's an unbelievably deep program. I find new stuff in Excel (new to me, anyway) all the time. Here are some of my all-time favorite hints and ideas.

Store Styles in Templates

Make a template (a normal spreadsheet, saved as a Template) holding all your favorite Styles, and save it in the Excel Startup Folder in System 7's Preferences folder. When you choose New… from the File menu, your template will be in the list, and when you click on it, you'll get a copy of the template to do new work in. The copy will have all the Styles of the original template. This is very handy, since Excel does not let you create universal Styles. This is an Excel 3.0 exclusive (no Styles in 2.2).

Make a Default Worksheet

If you make a template called "Excel Startup" and put it in the System Folder, Excel will open a copy of it each time you start Excel. You can store Styles in the Excel Startup template so they're always available in new spreadsheets. Excel 2.2 doesn't have templates, but you can lock a document in the Finder and accomplish the same thing.

Command-Shift Is Everything

Command-Shift-B makes a cell bold, Command-Shift-U makes it underlined, and Command-Shift-I makes it italicized. Same as in Word.

Make Borders the Cool Way

Select the cells you want borders on. Hold the Command and Option keys down while pressing the down arrow (to border the bottoms), the up arrow (to border the tops), the left arrow (to border the left sides), or the right arrow (to border the right sides).

Insert Rows and Columns Jiffy-Quick

Hold the Option key and click on a row heading (at the far left end of the row) to insert a row above the row you clicked. Hold the Option key and click a column heading (at the top of a column) to insert a column to the left of the column you clicked.

Make Columns the Right Width, Automatically

Normally, you drag the right edge of a column heading to resize a column (you have to grab the edge in the column's heading). You can make Excel automatically resize a column so it's wide enough to show everything in every column by double-clicking the right edge of the column heading.

Use Keyboard to Do Mouse Stuff

You can use the keyboard to click buttons in dialog boxes. Usually, typing the first letter of a button clicks the button. You can check and uncheck check boxes by holding the Command key and typing the first letter of the name next to the box.

Split the Screen to See Other Parts of Your Document

You can split the screen vertically (like in Word) by dragging the black bar above the vertical scroll bar. You can split the screen horizontally by dragging the black bar to the left of the horizontal scroll bar. Splitting the screen lets you see your headings as you scroll through a long document. Figure 12.49 shows a split screen. The headings (row 1) stay put while the rest of the document scrolls underneath them.

Interlude 12
Cool Excel Stuff

	A	B	C	D	E	F
1	Date	Check Number	To whom	Description	Amount	Balance
10	5/29/92	109	Apple Computer	Mac hardware	$1,000.00	$29,000.00
11	5/29/92	110	Apple Computer	Mac hardware	$1,500.00	$27,500.00
12	5/29/92	111	Apple Computer	Mac hardware	$2,000.00	$25,500.00
13	5/30/92	112	Apple Computer	Mac hardware	$1,000.00	$24,500.00
14	5/30/92	113	Apple Computer	Mac hardware	$1,500.00	$23,000.00
15	5/31/92	114	Apple Computer	Mac hardware	$3,000.00	$20,000.00
16	6/1/92	115	Apple Computer	Mac hardware	$1,000.00	$19,000.00
17	6/1/92	116	Apple Computer	Mac hardware	$1,000.00	$18,000.00
18	6/1/92	117	Apple Computer	Mac hardware	$2,000.00	$16,000.00
19	6/1/92	118	Apple Computer	Mac hardware	$3,000.00	$13,000.00
20	6/1/92	119	Apple Computer	Mac hardware	$1,500.00	$11,500.00
21	6/1/92	120	Apple Computer	Mac hardware	$2,500.00	$9,000.00
22	6/1/92	121	Apple Computer	Mac hardware	$3,500.00	$5,500.00
23	6/1/92	122	Apple Computer	Mac hardware	$1,500.00	$4,000.00
24	6/1/92	123	Apple Computer	Mac hardware	$2,000.00	$2,000.00
25	6/1/92	124	Apple Computer	Mac hardware	$2,500.00	($500.00)

Figure 12.49
Split screen.

Part III
Mainstream Mac Applications

Use the Text Box Tool to Hold a Lot of Text

You can type as much as you want, and position what you type anywhere on a spreadsheet, if you know how to use the Text Box tool. Click the Text Box tool (third from the right on the Toolbar) and drag a box to hold your text. Then type. You can resize the box later by dragging its handles. This doesn't work in version 2.2 (no Text Box tool).

Use Repeat to Do the Same Thing Again

It happens all the time: you format a cell one way, then realize you need to format a second cell the same way. Click on the second cell and look in the Edit menu. Odds are good you'll see something like "Repeat Font" or "Repeat Patterns" or "Repeat Number" (Number Formatting, it means). Of course, if you remember to put everything in a Style, you won't have to worry about repeating things, but no one remembers to put *everything* in a Style. I sure don't.

Use Fill Down and Fill Right to Save Time

Suppose you have two columns of numbers, and you want a third column to be the difference between the first two. Specifying the formula is easy, but you don't want to define the formula by hand for every row. You don't have to. Define the formula once, and press the Enter key. Select all the cells you want to apply the formula to, *including the cell you've already defined*. Figure 12.50 shows how the selection should look. Choose Fill Down from the Edit menu and watch the fun. You can use Fill Right similarly. Special bonus tip: Fill Down and Fill Right become Fill Up and Fill Left when you hold the Shift key before making your move to the menu.

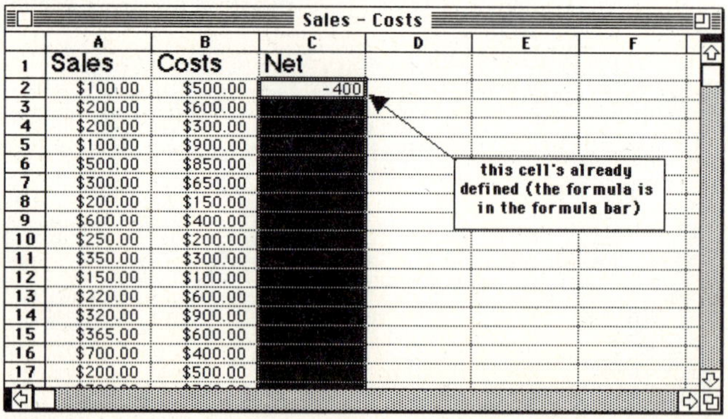

Figure 12.50
Fill Down.

AutoFill

Ever make a spreadsheet with the names of the months across the top? Ever wish you could get out of typing those month names? I sure have. With Excel 4.0, you type "January" and Excel does the rest. Automatically. It's staggering.

Excel will type the days of the week if you start it off with "Monday." Actually, you can start it off with any day you want, and you can even abbreviate; if you type "Fri" Excel can fill in "Sat," "Sun," "Mon," etc.

If you type "Monday" in one cell and "Wednesday "in the next, Excel's smart enough to skip "Thursday" and put "Friday" in the third cell. Type "1980" in one cell and "1990" in the next and Excel can fill in "2000," "2010," and so on for as far as you want to go. Let's see it in action.

1. Open a new Excel spreadsheet.
2. Click in any cell and type **January**.
3. Press the Enter key.

See the small black handle at the lower right hand corner of the cell? That's the new Fill Handle. Figure 12.62 shows the Fill Handle.

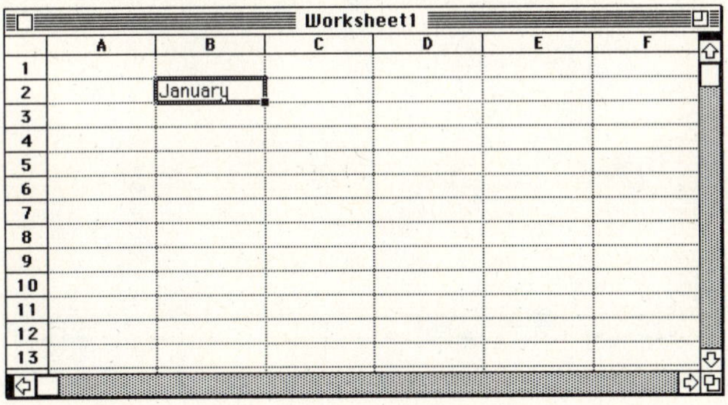

Interlude 12
Cool Excel Stuff

Figure 12.52
Excel's Fill Handle.

4. Move your cursor over the Fill Handle. Your cursor changes to a solid black plus sign.
5. Click on the Fill Handle and drag it across a few columns.

Excel fills in the cells with the names of the months. Truly amazing. Figure 12.51 shows the results.

Figure 12.51
AutoFill in action.

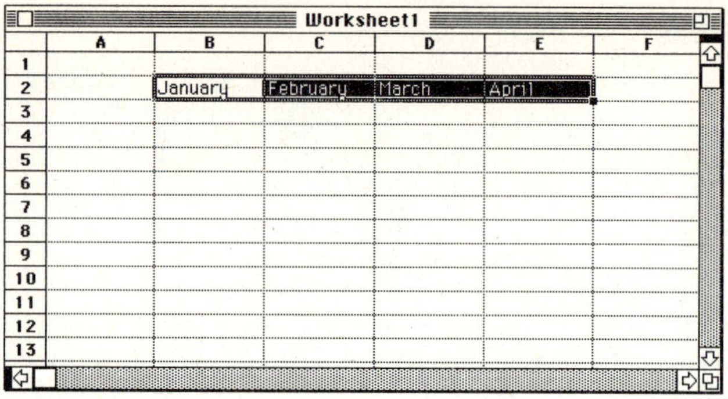

AutoFilling is even more amazing when it recognizes a pattern and continues it for you. The following example shows you how.

1. Type **5** in a cell.
2. Type **10** in the next cell down.
3. Drag through both cells to select them. Your screen looks like Figure 12.52.

Figure 12.52
Five and Ten.

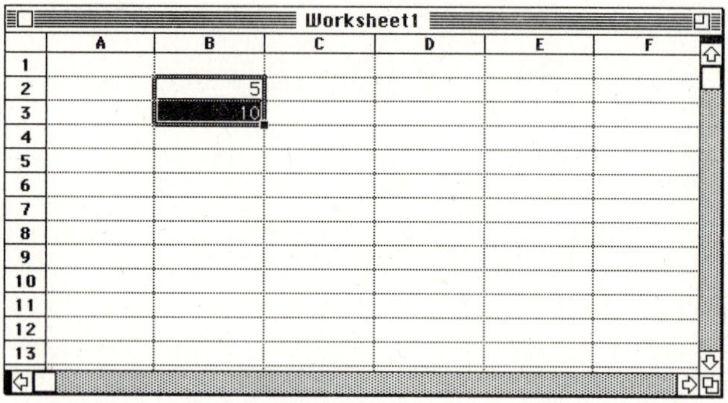

4. Click on the Fill Handle and drag it down a few cells.

Excel fills in the cells with "15," "20," and so on. Figure 12.53 shows how it looks.

Figure 12.53
Five, Ten, Fifteen, Twenty.

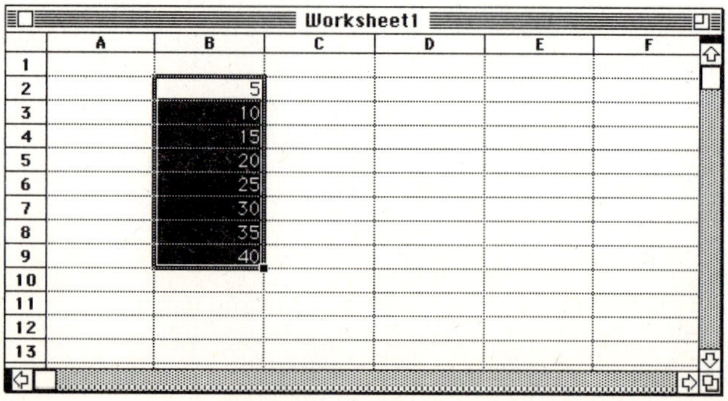

Excel knows enough to fill cells with "2nd," "3rd," and "4th" when you start with "1st." It doesn't know enough to fill in the rest of the reindeer when you start with "Dancer" and "Prancer," and it doesn't know enough to fill in "Dinner" when you give it "Breakfast" and "Lunch," but what it does do is impressive. AutoFilling could be improved, but it's a very welcome feature as it is.

Another welcome feature, Drag and Drop spreadsheet rearranging, is so obvious you'll wonder why Excel wasn't like this from the start. The next section tells you all about it.

Drag and Drop Spreadsheet Rearranging

Moving cells around on an Excel spreadsheet is a one-step operation (it takes two—a Cut and a Paste—in older versions). You simply select some cells and drag them to a new location. The only tricky part is you have to grab the cells by their bounding rectangle. Here's how to do it.

1. Make a spreadsheet that looks like figure 12.54.

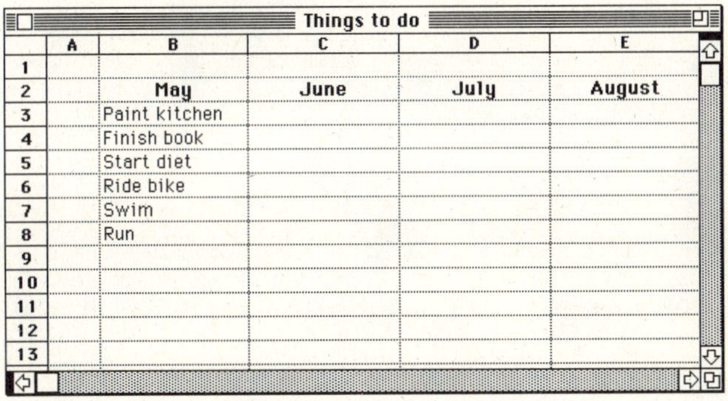

2. Select the cells by dragging through them.
3. Click on the rectangle bounding the cells and drag them to a new location.

A Closer Look The cells stay put, but a copy of their bounding rectangle follows your cursor, showing you where the cells will go. Figure 12.55 shows a bounding rectangle on the move.

Watch the cursor. It changes to an arrow when you've got it over the bounding rectangle.

Interlude 12
Cool Excel Stuff

Figure 12.54
Sample Excel spreadsheet.

Figure 12.55

Rectangle on the move.

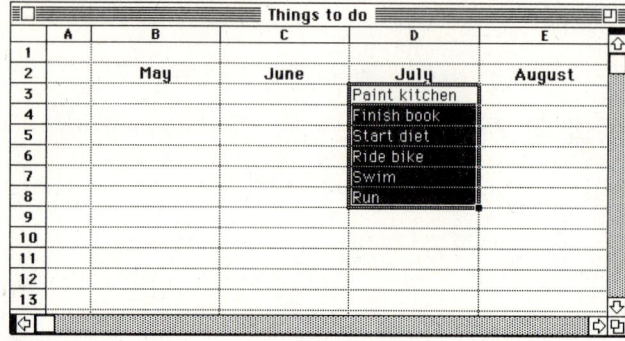

4. Let go of the mouse button when the cells are in the right place.

Figure 12.56 shows the sample spreadsheet, rearranged using the new Drag and Drop feature.

Figure 12.56

Rearranged sample Excel spreadsheet.

Hold the Option key while dragging cells to move a *copy* of them to a new location.

 Dragging and dropping is a very useful new feature. A third new feature, Zooming, lets you zoom in and out to any magnification, letting you fit more (or less, depending) of your spreadsheet on your screen at once.

Zooming In and Out

Excel lets you zoom out (and in) to *any* scale you wish, and it lets you work in these zoomed views as you would when viewing a spreadsheet normally. You can zoom out to see the big picture whenever you want, and zoom back in to a more comfortable magnification whenever you want as well. It's a very handy feature.

> **Note** You can't quite zoom to any scale you wish. You can't make it smaller than 10% nor larger than 400% of actual size. Any smaller, and you couldn't make sense of your spreadsheet; any larger, and you'd have trouble getting even one cell on your screen. I don't think Excel's restrictions in this area will be troublesome.

Figure 12.57 shows a spreadsheet that doesn't quite fit on the screen when viewed at 100%. Figure 12.58 shows the same spreadsheet, viewed at 90%. Switching between views is easy, as you'll see in the next example.

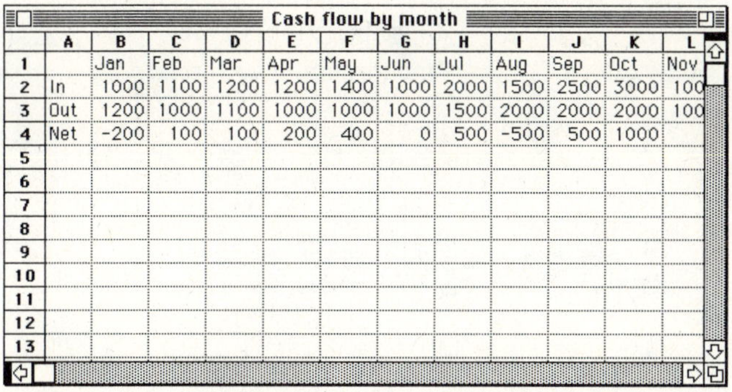

Interlude 12
Cool Excel Stuff

Figure 12.57
Can't fit at 100%.

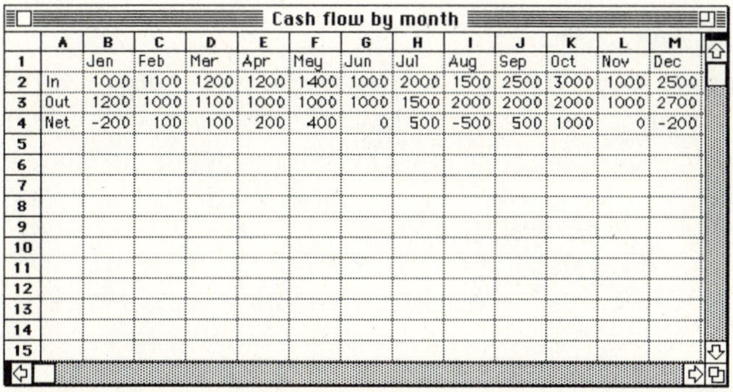

Figure 12.58
Fits great at 90%.

1. Choose **Zoom** from the **Window** menu. Figure 12.59 shows the resulting dialog box.
2. Choose a magnification and click **OK**.

Clicking **Fit Selection** fills your screen with the current selection, and clicking **Custom** lets you type in your own zooming percentage. Whichever zooming percentage you choose, you'll find every Excel command available for your use. In practice, you'll probably zoom out while constructing spreadsheets and zoom in while using them.

Figure 12.59
Zooming dialog box.

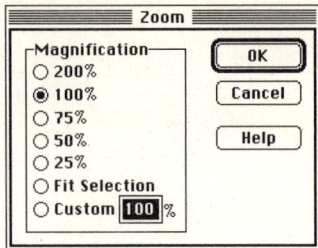

AutoFill, Drag and Drop, and Zooming are Excel's hottest new features. They make creating Excel spreadsheets easier than ever. Many of Excel's other features aren't really new but are significantly better than they were in previous incarnations. Toolbars and formatting are greatly improved in Excel; I describe them in the next section.

In Conclusion

Excel is King of the Spreadsheets no matter which version you use. Each revision's offered either more formatting options or made it easier to use them; the Microsoft gang seems to be catching on to the idea that it's not just what you say, it's how you say it.

One thing people often want to do is manage databases of customers, supplies, art pieces, video cassettes, baseball cards—practically anything. Excel can do some of these things—it includes many powerful tools to do so—but there are programs specifically designed to handle databases. Surprisingly, they're called databases, and they're covered in the next chapter.

Chapter 13
Databases

Exactly what is a database? A database is an organized collection of information (*data*) that is stored in a certain location (*base*), then accessed, modified, updated, manipulated, and retrieved in a useful format. A computerized database also needs to be fast and easy-to-use in creating reports from the stored information.

Introduction

Who might want to store data in a database and access it quickly? Businesses are obvious users, but almost anyone who occasionally or regularly needs to store information that must be *retrieved* (accessed and used),

---

In This Chapter

▼ What a database could look like

▼ How a database works

▼ Types of databases

▼ What a database can do

▼ How to select a database

▼ Developing a database

▼ A review of databases

Part III
Mainstream Mac Applications

reorganized (manipulated), or changed or updated will benefit from using a database.

How can a database assist these users? New Mac owners often maintain a household inventory, keep automobile or large appliance maintenance and repair records, and even enter the ever-lengthening address list for their annual Christmas letter (as well as the letter itself) in order to generate address labels. With most Mac database programs, this same Christmas letter (and the address labels) also can be embellished with Christmas graphics such as a Santa face or a sprig of holly.

This now-enthusiastic Mac user also could develop a list of all published articles and reviews on Mac products, technology, and ideology. This list can be sorted alphabetically in descending order (A through Z) or ascending order (Z through A), by subject matter, by publication name, in chronological order of publication date, and so on for instant reference. After the database is sorted, the final list can be displayed or printed, showing any or all of the fields the user might find useful. Can you imagine how many hours a die-hard Mac user who usually digs through stacks of computer magazines and books looking for that certain "important" article could save? One Mac owner who developed this type of Mac-related reference library swears it saves more than $30 a month on information service rates (to say nothing of time and fingernails).

Small business owners use databases to track and control inventory as well as accounts. The database's report-generating capabilities automatically produce precise, accurate, perfectly calculated statements each month. Add to the database word processing capabilities that produce all types of general correspondence, and the possibilities are endless!

In today's business environment, in which every edge counts, large companies commonly spend millions of dollars for Mac computer systems based solely on user-friendly Mac database products. Some of the more exotic applications have appeared in the science, entertainment, and media industries. These include digitizing, a process that turns scanned images such as photographs into computer-generated data for reconstruction in another format (such as a personnel identification system); simulation, computer-created graphics so real it is almost impossible to distinguish them from a photograph; and multimedia presentations, which combine sound and movement with dissemination of information.

What Does a Database Look Like?

Chapter 13
Databases

Human beings have been using databases since the cave days. Man first etched a crude circle onto the wall of a cave to represent the passing of the full moon. At the end of the following month, he added a second circle. Finally, he added animal symbols to keep track of herd movements during these moon phases on the same cave wall. A database (the cave wall) is a collection of files (the moon pictures are one file, the animal symbols the next); a file is a collection of records (each moon picture and animal symbol is a record); a record is a collection of individual parts called *fields* (the eyes on an animal symbol).

Mac users have a considerable head start over their PC counterparts in visualizing a database structure because they already are familiar with the Mac's hierarchical file system. (See chapter 3, "Exploring the Macintosh System," for more information.) A database is also a hierarchical structure; that is, a database is a collection of files; a file is a collection of records; a record is a collection of fields.

Files

A file is an organized collection of related information (data) maintained in a precise format (record). A file is composed of one or more records. A database file acts like a manila folder that contains copies of a customer's monthly invoices in a paper filing system. Each invoice is a record in the customer's file. Information in a file is determined solely by the end user's needs.

Records

A record contains several precise units of information just as all the items of information on one invoice—product ordered, date of shipment, unit cost—are contained in a customer's file. A single record contains many individual pieces (fields) of information. The record's scope is determined by the end user's needs.

Fields

A field is the smallest increment of information within a file and may include one or more words or symbols. For example, a Name field in a record can be designed to hold one or two words: first name, last name, or both. A field that requires a Yes or No response could be designed to accept only one symbol, either a "Y" or an "N." As with the file and the record, the field's scope is determined by the end user's needs.

Subfiles/Subrecords

Certain categories of information need to be refined to a further degree through subfiles. A subfile is actually a valid and complete file accessed by selecting a particular field in a file's record. When you select the field, the subfile is displayed onscreen, listing additional information or selections. The subfile contains subrecords, and the subrecords contain additional fields.

Subfiles and subrecords in a database structure can be misleading to new users. To get you off on the right foot, consider this hypothetical database situation:

An office supply store keeps a database of customers in its office computer. It stores individual records that contain the name, address, and telephone number for each customer/company, and the same information on any applicable branch offices.

In each of our fictitious office supply company's database records, the company name constitutes one field, the street name and number constitute a second field, the city is a third field, and the state and ZIP code are fields four and five. There is also a sixth field to store information concerning any branch offices.

When the operator selects the Branch Offices field in a customer's record, the database displays a subfile containing a record for each company branch office, complete with addresses and phone numbers. This collection of fields is a subrecord.

A single database may consist of many files. This office supply company also has many other files, including a Vendors file and an Inventory file in its database, in addition to the Customers file.

Input and Output Layouts

In an electronic database, information enters the system through a file input layout. An input layout is designed to hold as many specific elements (fields) of information pertaining to a particular subject as the databases' creator deems necessary. Each file must have at least one layout (the input layout) so that data can be entered into the system. However, each file can have as many layouts for as many purposes as desired—particularly if they are output layouts.

Output layouts enable to the user to view data stored in the system. Different output layouts are designed to present the data in different ways and in different configurations by arranging specific fields. Some common output layouts are mailing labels, invoices, and purchase orders. Each layout uses some or all of the fields in different positions or locations, providing different output.

How Does a Database Work?

There are two types of database structures: the *relational*, or *multifile*, and the *nonrelational*, or *flat file*. Both work on the same file, record, and field hierarchical concept.

Flat File Database Structure

A flat file database may hold many databases in one, but each database is restricted to only one file containing records and, ultimately, fields. With both types of databases, associated layouts, documents, reports, and so on are developed by selecting and combining a group of specific fields from those contained in the original or parent file structure. The similarity ends here, however. With a flat file, information from one database may be accessed from a second database, but it is not a true relationship. Instead, it performs a lookup operation—going to the second database, finding the information, copying it, and finally pasting it into the first database.

Chapter 13
Databases

For example, assume that your company uses a database to compile a catalog. Assume also that the basic output layout for each article featured in that catalog ordinarily consists of a description field (to describe the article), a graphic field (to hold a picture of the article), an item number field (to identify the article in inventory), and a unit price field. Certain items also might require a color field or a size field. These same records and fields also exist in the company's Inventory database. If you are using a flat file database, you can have the database fill the unit price field in the Catalog database with the contents of the unit price field in the Inventory database.

Although a lookup, copy, and paste relationship between an item number in the Inventory file and the same item number in the Catalog file eliminates entering the same information twice, the database essentially is duplicating the information. After the lookup, copy, and paste action is performed, the relationship between the two files ends. Any change in the information from the parent file (Inventory file in this case), such as a price increase, leaves the price field in the Catalog file unchanged unless the lookup, copy, and paste action is performed again after the modification.

Relational Database Structure

A relational database (also known as a multifile database) can contain many databases, just as a flat file database can. But within a relational database, each database may contain dozens of individual files, which each contain hundreds of records themselves. A relational database supports automatic access to data between records within the same file, between one or more files in the same database, and between databases within the same system. Relationships are *one-to-many* (one file to many files) or *many-to-one* (many files to one file) or both.

A one-to-many relational capability allows one file to access and display information in related fields from many files. For example, our fictitious office supply store has an Inventory file in addition to its Customers and Vendors files in the Customers database. The Inventory file contains one record for each inventory item the store carries. One of the fields included on each Inventory record is the name, address, and phone number of the vendor that supplies the item (the Vendor Name field).

Because each vendor's name, address, and phone number already is contained in the Vendors file in the database, you can establish a relationship to automatically display the correct data in the Vendor Name field of the Inventory Item file. Each time you use the information in the Vendor Name field of the Inventory file, the system retrieves the corresponding information from the Vendors file. As each individual record in the Inventory file is displayed, the associated information is automatically loaded from the Vendors file and displayed in the Vendor Name field of that particular inventory record, so any changes in the Vendors file are automatically reflected in the Inventory file. All relationships use a live (and therefore the most current) data source.

In this relationship, the Vendors file is the "one" file (a single record is accessed at a time), and the Inventory file is the "many" file because it accesses many different records in the Vendors file.

It would be a many-to-one relationship if the Vendor Name field in the Inventory Item file displayed a list of many vendors who supplied the respective item. Selecting the Vendor Name field in the Inventory file would produce a list of all associated vendors based on a relationship with the Name field in the Vendors file. Establishing these relationships usually does not require actual programming. However, each database program accomplishes this differently. Figure 13.1 provides a view of two relationships as established in a fictitious office supply company database, in 4th Dimension, a relational database by ACIUS.

Chapter 13
Databases

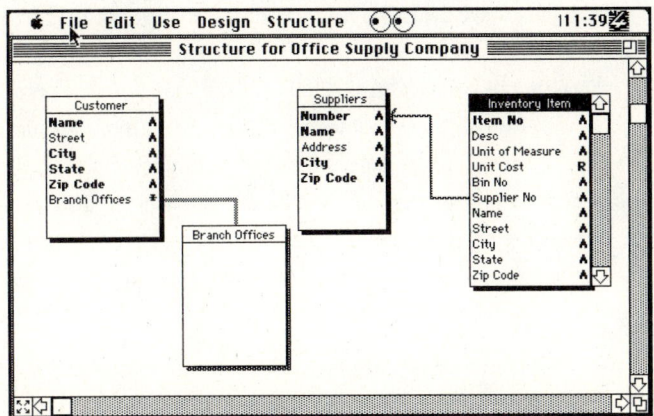

Figure 13.1
A relational database structure (4th Dimension).

Part III
Mainstream Mac Applications

Building a Database

Buying or receiving a database is like acquiring a gigantic electronic Lego set. When you open the box, all you have are possibilities. The final results depend on you, the user. After initially installing a program into your Mac, the possibilities are limited only by the sophistication of your particular software program, your hard disk's capacity (the bigger the better), your personal skills (which you can develop), and your imagination (which develops with experience). Users who are not totally familiar with the dynamics of a database usually are amazed at the power and versatility of the features available to them as they become database designers.

Designing a database in a large corporation is normally a joint project between the systems analyst who performs the data flow analysis (that is, determines what the database needs to do) and the designer/developer who actually programs the design features into the database. In the not-too-distant past, analysts and developers started with the hardware and literally built the program starting with the computer's operating system. It is no wonder, then, that the ordinary computer user found it difficult to create a database if he did not have a programmer's knowledge. A glimpse at any software distributor's shelves today tells you that databases now are sold in shrink-wrapped packages, ready to install and design with little or no instruction.

Prepackaged databases are available for virtually every level of user from the Mac novice to the vastly experienced, highly paid programmer working for the largest international corporation. Databases range from basic commercial programs that must be completely developed to suit the user's requirements to database packages that come pre-configured for a specific use. These autonomous databases can be expanded by various hardware and software components to instigate a seamless interchange of data between different platforms (operating systems), including mainframes and minicomputers.

There are also powerful, sophisticated database packages available that require some, little, or no programming which also can extend an individual's capabilities by integrating modules or smaller add-on software programs into the database. These modules offer vast flexibility by providing

Chapter 13
Databases

spreadsheet capabilities that perform advanced financial or accounting analysis and forecasting; word processing capabilities that enable you to create letters and forms, and merge into it a list of names, addresses, and salutations; and even elaborate cross-referencing merge applications that move selected paragraphs and clauses from one document to a predetermined location in a series of other documents (such as agreements or contracts).

Modules also can provide graphics capabilities. Logos, engineering and architectural drawings, and graphics files such as PICT, paint, and TIFF files (see chapter 7, "Graphics," for more information) are imported into layouts or directly into records and files to be categorized as data in a database. Some integrated modules also provide multimedia capability for presentations featuring movement and sound. Databases can read files from (import) and write files to (export) other operating systems and formats. They may be networked and integrated into multiuser environments (that is, many computers or terminals using one data source) or multisystem environments (different operating systems working together: DOS, UNIX, OS/2, VAX, and so on). These databases usually provide access controls to ensure the security and integrity of the stored data.

A database software program usually requires an add-on multiuser or server module to interface (act as an interpreter or a crossing guard) between these different terminals and platforms. Some programs come with multiuser and server capabilities included in the original package; others have the interface software available at extra cost. Many database packages provide ways for you to customize the application to some degree, such as adding specialized commands to the menu bars. 4th Dimension, a relational database from ACIUS, also has its own unique, natural programming language to provide an additional customizing tool for the nonprogrammer database developer. For more extensive development, most support one or more of the traditional programming languages, such as Basic, C, or Pascal. (See chapter 29, "Programming," for more information.)

Whether you are working with a relational or a nonrelational database, the first step in development is planning. Many developers like to use a flowchart for this purpose, whereas others prefer to make a simple list detailing what to put in the files and records, as well as notes about the desired relational aspects. Both methods work.

Files are the first item to develop. You create them by making and naming the file and then adding fields to the file structure. How you create these files and fields depends on the particular database. With most databases, though, field types, attributes, formats, and filters (which ensure data integrity) can be assigned to the fields when you create them, or even later.

Field Types

When developing a field, you must assign it a field type. Field types further categorize the data and control the size of the field (number of characters allowed). The most common field types are alphanumeric (alphabetical characters and numbers that are treated as text), and real numbers that must hold decimal points. The system cannot perform a numeric calculation on an alphanumeric type field, but it can perform many types of calculations on a real number field. Available field types differ with various programs.

Field Attributes

Field attributes put conditions on specific fields at the data entry level. Many attributes can be assigned depending on the database package. For instance, if the assigned field attribute is "mandatory," the database does not accept the record if the field is empty. "Indexed" gives a field a special identification tag which contains a value that the system uses in a sort function—a ZIP code, for example. "Can't Modify" allows a field to display data, but the user cannot change that data.

Formats

Field entry formats structure the entered data. For example, you can assign a format to a field to ensure that dates within that field are displayed consistently; MM/DD/YYYY creates a date that appears in that format: 11/21/1998. Assigning an XXX-XX-XXXX format yields a Social Security number. In these two instances, you need only enter the numerals and they automatically will be displayed and printed in the assigned format.

Filters

A field entry filter evaluates each character as it is typed into the field. For example, you want to place a filter on a field that requires data in a precise format, such as a customer number composed of four numbers preceded by two letters of the alphabet (SM4954). If the pattern (two letters, four numbers) is broken in any way, the system refuses to display or accept the erroneous input.

Neither formats nor filters have any effect on how the values are stored in the system.

Procedures and Scripts

Two additional, important factors also combine to enhance the database's seemingly self-governing properties. These factors are procedures and scripts, which you enter into the database design. Neither actually is written in most instances, although both could be. Usually, they are "built" by concatenation, or combining a selection of key words, terms, and routines (commands and functions) from a list the system provides (see figure 13.2).

Chapter 13
Databases

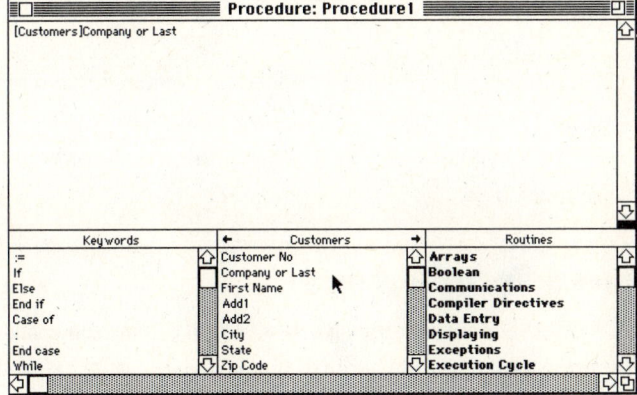

Figure 13.2
A Procedure dialog screen from 4th Dimension.

Procedures

A procedure is a powerful instruction or set of instructions that the database calls up and executes when a certain condition is present. A global procedure influences the entire database, perhaps capitalizing on all instances in which a certain word occurs in the database, for example. A layout procedure affects specific layouts in the database. A file procedure is directly associated to a specific file.

For instance, you could create a global procedure to ensure the word "Macintosh" is always displayed or printed in the same way. Every time the word is incorrectly entered into the database, the system ignores the actual entry and displays the word according to the procedure.

A layout procedure can be created to ensure that a layout with many columns always is displayed or printed in 9-point text. Layout procedures always are executed before each associated layout is displayed or printed.

A file procedure can be created to ensure that all company names in a database's Company file are displayed or printed in uppercase letters only. A file procedure is executed when any layout for the file is loaded for data entry.

Scripts

A script is a short set of instructions that you create. A script exerts a specific set of actions on a field or an object in a layout. Although a procedure can have a much broader effect, a script affects only the field or other object in the layout to which it is attached. A script can be included as part of a procedure.

For example, a script can be written to perform sequential numbering of an Invoice Number field, automatic entry in a Date field, or the mathematical calculations such as a subtotal or a total in a monthly invoice or household budget in a numeric field.

Database Terminology

Database terminology derives from a small core of standardized terms that are readily understood if used in general; that is, file, record, field, subfile. Yet many of these words are unique to specific software programs and can be confusing to a novice user. For example, Double Helix refers to a file as a "collection." Regardless of any given software program's terminology or onscreen characteristics, remember: You still are dealing with the basic hierarchical concept.

Selecting a Database—Requirement Versus Desire

What is feature and what is frill? It is difficult to isolate "requirement" from "desire" when you are not sure exactly what the average database should include. *Referential integrity* and *data validation* are two important considerations for any user.

Referential Integrity

Referential integrity means that any time data is modified in the database—at least in the parent file—all associated forms, layouts, reports, and so on are automatically updated to reflect the change. Databases possess varying degrees of this feature, so the broader the degree, the better. The best-case scenario is to have data modification in any file automatically reflect throughout the database.

Data Validation

Data validation is done in a number of ways and at various times in the database's development. The best place to activate a data validation feature is at the source of data entry, of course. That is accomplished through field types, attributes, formats, and filters. It is also helpful to have syntax validation that checks each line of code, procedure, and script as it is written and immediately rejects any improperly written entries.

Some databases can sort a file of records into any order a field (other than a picture field) specifies, at the rate of 1,000 records per 0.01 minutes. There are databases that can import records from other operating systems, programs, and formats at the rate of 1,000 records in less than a minute. Through relational links, some databases can construct a report, display the company logo on that report, include text and numerical data that relates to several separate departments, divide the data into individual sections, and perform complicated financial calculations using interest accrual rates, amortization charts, overriding royalty percentages, and so on—all in less than a minute.

A database can be developed to produce stand-alone applications called *runtimes*. Runtimes are a series of scripts, procedures, and functions controlled by customized menus or keyboard commands and designed for specialized handling of selected data. Many of these applications are packaged in elaborate graphic interfaces and sold separately. There is a healthy commercial market for runtime products for popular database programs.

Reviews and Demo Packages

Selecting the best database for your needs requires more than pointing and clicking. Most software companies have test kits or demos of their database products available for the asking, and trade magazines are full of product reviews. Past issues of trade magazines can be found at the library under "Articles in Print."

According to the current reviews, it seems the three most important considerations when selecting a database are speed, speed, and speed. Wrong. Speed may be a top essential for some users, but this priority differs with individual users.

For example, according to a hypothetical review, SpeedoBASE is the fastest thing on a footprint. But is speed the most important requirement in your particular application? How complicated is the interface? If it takes 14 dialog boxes and the construction of 12 separate lines of procedure or script to execute a Sort command, how much time did you lose just getting to the point of execution? Speed is a relative requirement.

Chapter 13
Databases

According to another hypothetical review, ExcelloBASE does everything you think you need. It has acceptable speed and is reasonably priced. Unfortunately, you need a personal crash course in computer science to understand the program's terminology. What is your level of experience with advanced computer terminology? Easily associated terminology can be very important to the novice and intermediate user. How long before you master this terminology and the program? What is your ultimate frustration level?

Then there is ObscuroBASE, which has been hypothetically reviewed as reasonably fast with relatively intuitive terminology. Reviewers claim this program does everything you will ever need! However, after 14 attempts, you still cannot get past the first few pages of the demo tutorial, so you call ObscuroBASE's Technical Support number for help. A tech rep explains, "What that really means is…" In other words, the documentation is not written as clearly as it could be and is presumptuous and incomplete. You cannot rely on manuals to provide adequate instruction for your level of expertise. If the demo tutorial is not clearly documented, can you imagine how obscure the actual program's User's Guide is?

Whether you are reasonably familiar with databases in general, have been a Mac user since the days of the Lisa, are a small-business owner who has just joined the Mac legions, or are responsible for making a corporate decision for a company database, all of these scenarios are important when deciding which database to purchase. One or two individual features of a specific software program should not constitute a deciding factor; the overall picture is the key. To get the overall picture, get the demo.

Make a Checklist

If you are unable to run a demo test in privacy for any reason, go to the showroom of a reputable software dealer. But first, make a checklist of your priorities in order of importance, as best as you can. Never shop for a database on an empty checklist. Databases can be exciting when you see them in full flight for the first time. You are apt to find yourself shouting, "I could track, organize, and document the entire insect population of the Amazon rain forest, with relational subfiles and photos identifying the development stages of each species!" But is documenting bugs in the Amazon your main reason for buying this database? Probably not.

Also consider how long your database will be in service. A database is a considerable investment not only in terms of dollars spent but also in time spent. You will invest time becoming proficient with the program, developing the applications, and inputting and maintaining your data. A database is a costly and permanent investment, especially in the business environment. Can this database grow with your needs? Does the manufacturer have a history of timely upgrades offered at reasonable cost? Is the manufacturer responsive to keeping up with state-of-the-art technology, as well as user input?

Refine Your Requirements

The following are the factors that three categories of users typically consider. Of course, there are overlaps, and these considerations are not comprehensive.

Personal User

A personal user generally is concerned with price. A higher price usually means more power and features, but not always.

What kind of information will you store—address lists? If you plan to use those lists to do a mass mailing at some point, look for a program that supports (or can be extended to support) word processing, mail merge, and so on. Databases are not designed to include true word processing capabilities (text formatting), although word processing capabilities can be integrated into some of them. If you plan to store graphics (forms, flyers, or drawing files), you need a program that supports graphics created in a bitmapped, paint, PICT, or TIFF drawing format. If you need to store picture fields, you also need scanner hardware to enter the picture into the system.

Capacity restrictions—maximum size of files in a database, records in a file, fields in a record, and so on—usually are not a requirement for a personal user, but hardware requirements are. Check the RAM (most require at least 1M), floppy disk, and hard disk requirement specifications. These requirements usually are indicated on the package and certainly in a demo package.

Chapter 13
Databases

Small-Business User

Most small-business users have the same concerns as a personal user. In addition, the maximum file, record, and field size or capacity restraints are particularly important to the small-business user, as are spreadsheet capabilities. He also requires simple documentation, ease of use after training, and technical support availability.

The database's upgrade or conversion history should be one of the greatest considerations, particularly ease of upgrade conversion and total compatibility with existing files and programs. The cost of the upgrade versions is also important. If the database you choose grows in capacity, capability, power, and sophistication at a reasonable cost, and can parallel the needs of an expanding business, that can mean dollars and peace of mind.

Corporate User

All of a personal user's and small business' concerns affect the corporate user. Some of the most important questions a corporate buyer must consider are: How will the database be used—multiuser, multisystem? What are the compatibility or connectivity restraints, and is it compatible with any existing software programs and records, or hardware? How difficult is it to integrate into an existing system that contains years of historic data? (In some cases, this conversion could bring needed operations, such as receiving and billing functions, to a grinding halt.)

What are the maximum capacity restraints—maximum files allowable in the database, maximum records in each file, fields in each record, and subfile and subrecord characteristics? And most important: How difficult is it to generate reports with this program, and how many relationships can this program support? How many relationships per file? How are the relationships established? Does the program support referential integrity? Indexed fields make sorting and searching a much faster operation, so how many indexed fields are possible in one file, document, or format? Are there sufficient file types, attributes, filters, and formats to provide data validation protection at the entry process?

Be sure to consider the ease of learning and the ease of use after training. Training and retraining personnel can become costly.

Mac Database Programs Review

The following overviews of selected database management systems for the Mac have been compiled to provide you with sufficient information to become a more knowledgeable prospective user. This is by no means a complete list of databases available for the Macintosh nor a complete list of every feature.

Double Helix 3.5

Double Helix (Helix) is an amiable, object-oriented relational database management system. All facets of the program are managed by manipulating a collection of icons called "tiles." The structure's elements can be viewed by name, icon, or type. "Visual" programming is done in the Abacus window by selecting from a graphic list of more than 100 programming tiles designed to perform various data manipulations.

A file—Double Helix calls it a collection—is built in the Collection window and is literally a group of various shaped icons, with each icon representing some element of the file: an index is represented by a stack of index cards, a field is represented by a document symbol, and the layout structure resembles a T-square on a document symbol (see figure 13.3). The Abacus is the only icon that seems misrepresented; in light of the magic it performs, it should have been depicted by a genie's lamp.

Helix supports alpha, text, numerical, date, logical, and picture field types. Pictures and graphics are treated as a data type; buttons and check boxes also are supported. An unlimited number of windows can be opened at one time, making moving between files convenient. Data verification controls prevent many types of data entry errors before they occur, and a backup log protects against loss of data in the event of power outages or system failure.

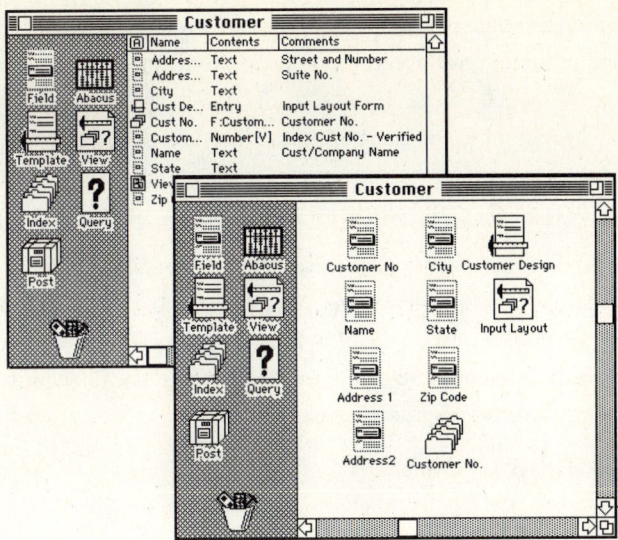

Figure 13.3
Double Helix Collection enables you to view screens by name or icon.

The **Sequence** tile on the **Collection** window palette provides a way to develop a macro that more readily negotiates the program dialog boxes.

Relationships are established through the Abacus and a list of more than 100 **Calculation** tiles that perform many types of operations: math, financial, and text manipulation, to name a few. A relationship is established by linking two or more **Calculation** tiles, with each tile representing two elements of what is traditionally a string of code. The principle is simple, but the implementation becomes more involved depending on the number of calculation tiles required in the relationship. The Abacus creates reports by linking Calculation tiles, so developing a report can become complicated because of the necessity to connect a large number of tiles.

Double Helix 3.5 supports DEC/VAX computers with Helix VMX. The Access icon on the Collection window palette allows a Helix application to include a table from a host computer—an RMS file on a Digital VAX minicomputer, for example. When used in conjunction with supported database servers, the Access icon provides a direct connection between a Double Helix application and data stored in other computers and databases. Helix runs flawlessly under MultiFinder. Helix can import/export ASCII text, SYLK and DIF formats, and although it does not take advantage of all System 7 features, it is fully compatible with System 7.

Part III
Mainstream Mac Applications

Double Helix's multiuser capabilities support referential integrity. The Double Helix Client/Server application (available since 1986) is included in the package. No special file server hardware or software is required beyond the provided program. Helix also supports multithreaded data entry (one user conducting a search does not interrupt a second user who may be performing data entry) and a password-like security system.

The ability to customize applications using the point-and-click method is one of a developer's major considerations. No programming language is required. Developing a Double Helix application is actually very simple. You begin application development by selecting the User icon in the Collection window, where Custom menus are created.

The Double Helix 3.5 documentation is excellent. It consists of eight manuals. The User's Guide and Reference Manual are each approximately two inches thick and packed with illustrations, comprehensive instruction, and useful appendixes. They are extremely well-formatted with a two-inch scholar's margin on each page for the user's notes, and so on. If it isn't covered here, you probably don't need it!

Odesta provides the TechConnect technical support program. Helix also includes an online help feature that generates a "Why?" option whenever the program rejects an action.

Double Helix always has had the reputation of being the friendliest and easiest relational database to learn. It also may be one of the fastest. Users who feel comfortable in a graphics-oriented environment and want or need to develop their own applications quickly and easily will appreciate Double Helix.

For free demo information, contact Odesta Corporation, 4084 Commercial Avenue, Northbrook, Illinois 60062; (800) 323-5423, ext. 234.

4th Dimension 3.0

4th Dimension (4D) operates in three distinctive environments. The structure of the database—its files, layouts, documents, and forms—is developed and designed in the Design environment. A file actually is built in Design's structure editor. Because of the program's graphical interface, the developing database's structure, including all files, fields, field types, subfiles, and relational links, may be viewed in the Structure Editor screen at any time.

Chapter 13
Databases

4D supports 10 field types, six attributes (one of which is a choice list), and dozens of data entry controls in the form of field filters and formats that set associated lists, excluded lists, minimum/maximum values, default values, and so on. All associated documents and layouts are listed for convenient reference with the parent file in the Layout dialog box.

Input/Output Layout screens are developed by selecting fields from the master file. You can generate layouts by selecting from eight different templates or build them from scratch through a "custom" selection in the **New Layout** dialog screen. 4D supports multipage layouts (see figure 13.4).

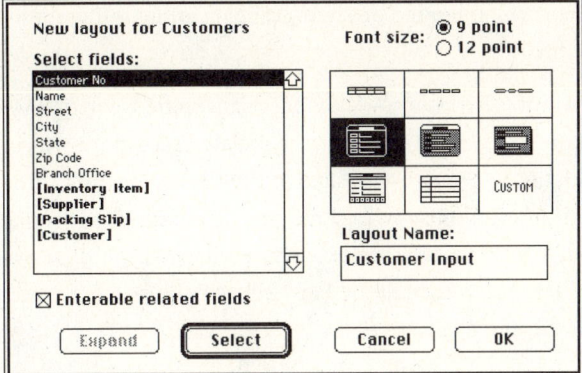

Figure 13.4
The New Layout dialog screen from 4th Dimension.

Customizing the "generated" layout's appearance is a matter of selecting and dragging existing fields, creating new fields, and placing active and graphic objects on the layouts with the tools palette. The graphics capabilities of the design environment are pretty much unlimited, supporting automatic buttons such as accept, cancel, delete, record, check boxes, pop-up menus, and scrollable areas, as well as thermometers, rulers, dials, several types of graphs, and picture fields. 4D supports a very extensive development environment for graphics capabilities, data verification, and integrity controls, together with point-and-click script/procedure building protocols.

Data entry, file maintenance, modification, sort, and search actions all are encompassed in the User environment, which is primarily menu-driven. Data modifications can be made in the list format (output) or the input format and are reflected throughout associated documents/layouts, reports, and so on. 4D performs comparison operators, sequential and indexed searches, and simple and compound searches (searching on more than one factor). **Search** Menu items include **Search by Layout**, **Search by Formula**, and **Search**

527

Part III
Mainstream Mac Applications

and Modify. 4D also performs wildcard searches. Sorts can be performed on up to 30 different fields and formulas on both primary and secondary sort levels. The third 4D environment is Runtime, which is exclusive to the development and customization of stand-alone applications.

The **Report** Menu/Quick Report editor easily generates comprehensive reports. All graphics capabilities, as well as header and footer, justified text, and so on, extend to the Quick Report editor. The Report editor supports fields from multiple files, automatic summary calculations (totals, subtotal, min/max actual count), and user-definable formulas. Labels are simple to create with the Label editor's standard and high-speed serial printing. Label templates are included in the program. Label printing is literally a point-and-click operation.

4D supports both automatic and manual relations between files—you maintain control of whether 4D loads the related record/records into memory. Relationships are established in the structure editor through a point- and-click dialog box; no programming is required. 4D supports simultaneous data entry into multiple related files, as well as searches, sorts, reports, and labels across multiple files. Relationships are removed simply by dragging on the linking arrow.

Note: 4D supports XCMDs/XFCNs as well as C, Pascal, Fortran, and Assembly languages, and it can import/export SYLK, DIF, WKS, and text file formats. However, because 4D uses the Mac ROMs and system files to their limits, certain INITS, DAs, or a combination can cause some runtime applications to report system errors. Tech support readily supplies advice. 4D also supports monochrome and color monitors, all Mac-compatible printers, and 256 colors.

Although traditional programming languages such as Pascal, C, Fortran, and Assembly are fully supported, the program has its own 4th Dimension language, which is extremely powerful and much more flexible than the traditional ones. This natural language uses everyday vocabulary, grammar, and syntax. Ironically, like the Mac itself, the language originally was thought to be too simple to compete with C and Pascal; however, this "no pain, no gain" mentality is fading fast among 4D developers. The 4D language now is recognized as a very powerful development language for building stand-alone commercial applications.

Chapter 13
Databases

The 4D language's flexibility, together with nearly 300 built-in commands and an interactive symbolic debugger (which catches syntax/code mistakes while making a trial run of the procedure), makes 4D an exciting development environment for both nonprogrammers and seasoned developers alike. A welcome feature of the package is 4D Tools, which is designed to recover data if your database is damaged. 4D detects damage to a database via a Checksum feature.

Through 4D's External Kit, the program's open architecture enables the developer to add a plethora of capabilities through external routines. The exact number of procedures and functions you can add is virtually unlimited. 4D has been the pioneer and pacesetter in this area since 1986.

4D's documentation is presented in seven manuals. It is well-planned, well-organized, well-indexed, and clearly written. The manuals provide hundreds of illustrations and screen captures, and even the Language Reference. Technical support is free, with the exception of a special developer's technical support club (Club 4D), which charges an initial fee and reduced renewal rates annually.

ACIUS has developed a series of modules designed to further extend 4D's capabilities: 4D Write (a word processor), 4D Draw (technical illustration, mechanical engineering, architectural design), Graph 3D (3-dimensional graphs), 4D Calc (spreadsheets), 4D Compiler, and 4D Mover (enables the designer to select and combine different parts of existing databases).

4D's clean, synergistic nature is perhaps attributable to the fact that 4th Dimension is the product of a single mind, Laurent Ribardiere, ACI; Paris, France. For a free 4D demo, contact ACIUS, Inc., 10351 Bubb Road, Cupertino, California 95014; (408) 253-DEMO.

FILE FORCE

FILE FORCE is actually a personal/small-business version of the more extensive, heavy-duty 4th Dimension. 4D's concept, terminology, flexibility, design features, scripts/procedure, and multiuser capabilities are all present. FILE FORCE supports automatic file relations, data validation, sorts, searches, and reports; imports data; and has password protection, multiple page design capability, automatic buttons, and more. FILE FORCE is restricted only by the developer's programming capability—it has no Runtime environment and fewer built-in commands—and database file capacity (it supports 10 separate files). FILE FORCE is not restricted in design, flexibility, or power.

One of FILE FORCE's particularly useful features to assist the beginning user/developer is a library of 16 database templates including Contacts, Expenses, Invoices, Mailing List, Product Catalog, Purchase Orders, Recipes, and Video Library, to name a few. The templates can be used as originally designed or modified to your specifications. These templates are fully functional examples of various kinds of databases, and they not only are convenient but also provide a comprehensive education on the subject of databases in general.

FILE FORCE is a more compact version of 4th Dimension designed for the user who needs less database/file capacity but wants the same speed and dynamics as the high-end user. (FILE FORCE actually may be slightly faster than 4D). FILE FORCE database files are totally compatible with 4D, and the program may be upgraded to 4th Dimension at any time by sending ACIUS the difference in price between FILE FORCE and 4th Dimension.

For free 4D and FILE FORCE demos, contact ACIUS, Inc., 10351 Bubb Road, Cupertino, California 95014; (408) 253-DEMO.

FileMaker Pro

FileMaker Pro (FileMaker) supports a text-oriented environment. It is easy to learn, and it seems to anticipate your every move. FileMaker Pro provides a generous supply of point-and-click options at almost every turn.

Here, you structure a file in the **Define Fields** dialog screen (see figure 13.5); the program supports seven different field types, including Calculation and Summary. The **Options** dialog box provides attributes designed to minimize erroneous data entry depending on the field type selected: unique, not empty (mandatory entry), auto-enter date, auto-enter serial number, and so on. The basic input layout automatically is generated from a menu selection, but it can be customized. Graphics options are easy to manage, and FileMaker supports buttons, check boxes, pop-up lists, and menus. Design aids such as automatic alignment, rulers, grids, and a magnetic T-squares are nice surprises. A zoom-in option and move, fill, rectangle, and circle drawing tools are some of the tools provided on the report/layout palette.

Chapter 13
Databases

Linked scripts (built by point-and-click action) are an important feature in FileMaker and may be used very effectively to minimize keystrokes. Calculations and simple strings of code are developed through the keyboard. The **Calculations** Dialog box (Calculation field) provides an interesting selection of formula components, including a calculator. FileMaker supports automatic indexing and a data lookup function. Mail merge and a 100,000-word dictionary are nice features; data is entered into predesigned forms (tab-delimited format) equipped with a convenient record review feature (previous record/next record).

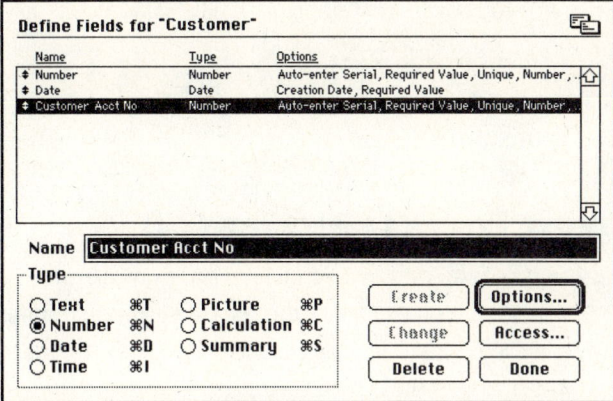

Figure 13.5
FileMaker Pro's Define Fields dialog screen.

Columnar reports and labels are created in a generic form. Both are easy to create and modify to a limited degree. More elaborate reports require field rearrangement (dragging), graphics placement, and considerable data manipulation to include related information. Although FileMaker is considered a flat file, its lookup, copy, and paste feature coupled with the large number of screens that can be open at one time make it very functional and provide a quick, convenient method of relating data (including picture fields) when the underlying associations have been well-defined. Defining the relationship also is easy.

FileMaker Pro incorporates the Claris XTND architecture and is compatible with the large library of Claris-developed Mac programs. FileMaker reads/writes tab-delineated, WKS, SYLK, DBF, DIF, comma-separated, and Basic formats, and runs flawlessly under MultiFinder. FileMaker supports color monitors (81 colors) and all Apple printers.

FileMaker Pro is "network ready" and includes file server capability (with or without special hardware or software). Network Access Overview, automatic record locking/release, and password-protection features provide a large measure of data security. FileMaker provides extensive graphics support; it can import graphics based on PICT, TIFF, encapsulated PostScript (EPSF), and bitmapped formats.

Documentation consists of four manuals. These manuals are attractive, well-written, and generously illustrated. FileMaker Pro provides free technical support and has an online help feature in the program.

FileMaker Pro is a lively program that is enjoyable to use, with good graphics capabilities. The program offers good compatibility and good connectivity. The convenient dialog boxes are well-planned. FileMaker Pro is easy to learn and easy to use.

For free demo information, contact Claris, Box 58168, Santa Clara, California 95052-8168; (800) 3CLARIS.

Microsoft FoxBASE+/Mac 2.01

Originally created by Fox Software and now owned by Microsoft, FoxBASE+/Mac is a functional blend of the Mac and DOS environments. The terminology, code, and syntax are unmistakably dBASE; the interface is essentially Mac. Because of the dBASE language compatibility and powerful language extension properties of FoxBASE+/Mac, dBASE programs/applications designed and developed for the PC can be run on a Macintosh computer without changing a line of source code.

FoxBASE+/Mac opens in the View window. This is a nonprocedural graphic interface and is the program's control element. Working environments can be launched and relationships between files can be established in the View window. Each new file/database is initiated in the View window and developed through a New File Dialog screen that encompasses field names, field types, and sizes.

General file maintenance—modifying, editing, deleting, and so on—can be done in the Browse window as well as the Record menu. You can access the complete complement of associated documents, indexes, screens (layout designs), and format files for any specific database file (folder) only after the appropriate parent database file is defined as the default folder in the Default Definition screen. A different default folder can be defined for each open work area, and all 10 work areas can be open at one time. Theoretically, you

Chapter 13
Databases

can work and move between 10 different database files (folders) simultaneously. Fields may be relocated and resized using a graphics hand device called the Pusher and a Field Resizer tool in the Browse window environment.

The View window's **Setup** button accesses a series of dialog screens that rearrange fields, add field filters and field formats, and so forth through the Expression Builder. The Expression Builder is a tireless workhorse that assists in almost every facet of maintenance and design in some capacity. It is structured around a scrollable list of field names, values, and variables, with four **Type** menus. Each **Type** menu activates a pull-down collection of functions and operators to build strings of code or calculations, which ultimately are displayed in and executed from the Command window. Indexes are built with the Expression Builder.

WARNING! Although FoxBASE+/Mac supports a number of associated indexes for any given database (parent file), when the parent file is modified, only seven indexes can be updated at one time. All seven must be selected in the View window at the time the parent file is updated. Indexes that are not present in the View window when the parent file is modified must be brought into the View window and modified separately through the Reindex feature. This index updating protocol might prove to be considerably inconvenient to the user who needs numerous indexes.

Code also may be typed directly into the Command window. The Command window is a small scrollable window displayed in a section of the screen that records every line of code executed from the opening of a particular work session, whether it is generated by icon selection or Expression Builder, or typed from the keyboard. Novice users who are not accustomed to using code find this feature very helpful.

Labels and relational reports containing calculated and picture fields are relatively easy to design. Simple forms and layouts (format files) with multiple fonts, styles, sizes, colors, picture fields, and graphics, as well as buttons, check boxes, pop-up menus, and scrollable text areas also are not difficult to create.

Input layouts and form designs, however, are generated to code and preserved for access by a feature called FoxGen. Because each change to a format file requires returning to the generator, changes on the fly are not possible.

Part III
Mainstream Mac Applications

FoxBASE+/Mac supports a one-to-many relational concept, and only one relationship may exist between any two files at one time. However, you can set a relationship from one of the related files to a third file. Relationships are set on a record number or on a specific field in an indexed file by a dialog screen.

FoxBASE+/Mac supports most XCMDs/XFCNs written in C or Pascal (as well as some other languages). HyperCard XCMDs and XFCNs can be accessed directly from within the FoxBASE+/Mac program. A total of 16 external XCMDs/XFCNs can be loaded at one time. The dBASE language is fully supported, of course, and the program runs well under MultiFinder. FoxBASE+/Mac does not support import/export of SYLK, DIF, or WKS file formats in Copy and Append. SDF and delimited options are supported.

FoxBASE+/Mac supports color as well as monochrome monitors and all ImageWriter and LaserWriter printers. It is totally compatible with the new System 7, although it does not support many of System 7's advanced features. (However, a new FoxPro/Mac product currently in development is being designed to take full advantage of these advanced features.) FoxBASE+/Mac Multi-User is a separate version of the FoxBASE+/Mac that includes all the requirements necessary in a multiuser environment.

Design capability in the graphics area is somewhat restricted; you must have programming ability if you want to use this area. FoxBASE+/Mac includes an integrated compiler and various debugging and tracing options. Another feature that developers welcome is the automatic backup of program files whenever they are in flux. This feature protects the your present code while modifications are in progress. An unlimited royalty-free runtime program for compiled code is required for user applications when the user does not have a copy of FoxBASE+/Mac installed.

Manuals are well-organized and well-written for easy reference. Special attention has been given to the Tutorial, which includes expanded explanations and numerous illustrations in each of the 10 lessons and six additional sections. According to Dr. Howard Moskowitz at Fox Software, technical support for Fox products always will be free.

FoxBASE+/Mac is a very fast, very responsive, mature database that requires considerable familiarity with programming protocols and the dBASE language. If you have not worked with a database in a PC environment or have little or no association with programming terminology and concepts, you may find FoxBASE+/Mac somewhat overwhelming and complex. (However, the On-line Help feature is a considerable plus in this regard.) The applications templates are also a good feature for a nonprogrammer.

On the other hand, a PC user with some programming and dBASE experience who has longed for the Macintosh operating system's flexibility will revel in FoxBASE+/Mac's power, speed, and compatibility. Its ease and the enhanced graphics capabilities of the Mac interface are added bonuses.

Contact Microsoft, One Microsoft Way, Redmond, WA 98052, (206) 882-8080.

Omnis 7 Plus

Omnis 7 has a comprehensive programming language, intuitive terminology, considerable graphics capabilities, and a comfortable Mac interface. You easily can create new files around a file format listing of 255 numbered fields per file (document). Each field can be assigned a name, but data is tied to the field number and not the field name. A file format is developed into a generic window format (layout) using the **Design** menu/**Window Format** dialog box, an effective and time-saving feature.

For the user/designer who wants to enhance the layout beyond the basic concept, buttons, scroll lists, check boxes, and tools palettes are available. Because this graphics design environment requires working with three different elements onscreen at one time—the developing layout, the tools palette, and the Field Attribute window—it takes a little practice to keep everything visible and under control. The program is very forgiving, however, and you easily can manipulate the windows and tools with no ill effects until the task is accomplished. Clicking on the pointer tool brings everything back to square one.

Although there is no graphic representation of the database/file/field structure per se, the Data Dictionary concept is very prevalent in Omnis 7. A printed recap of each file/format's identifying field numbers, field types, field names, and field attributes, as well as a list of attribute codes, is readily available. Data easily is entered into the designed format (tab delimiter).

> **WARNING!** You must take care to ensure a consistent data entry format in indexed fields. The search (locate) record feature is sensitive to upper- and lowercase letters. An abbreviation (for example, UPS as opposed to United Parcel Service) in an indexed field with a normal format of "uppercase first letter, lowercase remaining

Chapter 13
Databases

Part III
Mainstream Mac Applications

letters" can confuse the search. Although the record is accepted at the time of entry, the misformatted record is not located during the search, and the next closest match is selected. It therefore is important to establish a mandatory format (Upper Case Only selection) in the **Field Attributes** dialog box for indexed character fields before entering data. Each file/format supports 12 separate indexed fields, each of which is set using a check box.

The report feature is effective and flexible, supporting picture fields, calculated fields, and automatic find fields, subtotal sections. You need only a minimum of experience to design a simple report, but more elaborate reports containing related calculations and such require more experience with the program.

Omnis 7 establishes relationships through an optimized relational join (Omnis Connection). In the Omnis Connection principle, you set links on a unique Record Sequencing Number field (RSN) rather than on an optionally selected key field (as with a relational join). Omnis 7 creates and assigns this RSN value each time a parent record is entered into the system. The RSN is never reused, even when the respective parent record is deleted. Connections are established in a procedural manner rather than graphical. The parent file must be located before the child (related file) is updated, however. Otherwise, an empty RSN number is created. This principal allows one relation per record (one-to-one or one-to-many). The connection may be established either in Omnis Express in the initial application generation or by a **Set Connections** dialog box when the file is defined.

Omnis 7 is totally compatible with Microsoft Windows and HyperCard XCMDs. Import/export capabilities include formats such as DIF, DBF, SYLK, dBASE, Lotus WKS, delimited (commas), delimited (tabs), picture fields, one field per line, text files, and the Omnis data transfer format. Omnis 7 applications can be shared with Omnis' DOS, IBM PS/2, and OS/2 versions. Omnis 7 supports color and monochrome monitors and all Mac-compatible printers. Omnis 7 1.2 supports Standard Query Language (SQL) and provides optional support for CL/1 or Oracle as well as all leading AFP servers for the Macintosh, including TOPS, 3Com, Novell, and AppleShare across AppleTalk and EtherNet networks. There is also a record-locking feature to ensure data security. An extra fee is charged for each multiuser node required.

Simple procedure/script building is a matter of pointing and clicking, which eliminates the possibility of typos. Omnis displays an Error screen whenever

Chapter 13
Databases

you enter an erroneous syntactical line of code to eliminate a lot of debugging time. No other debugging or trace features are available. Omnis 7 Express is a unique feature which uses an external routine to speedily develop a basic application that supports one-to-one or one-to-many relationships. Express includes a collection of Data Entry screens and reports generated by selecting and combining various features, procedures, scripts, and graphic elements (buttons, check boxes, and so on). These considerations and the full support for graphics data and color combine to create a comprehensive developer environment.

Three convenient loose-leaf binders and a pocket reference guide compose Omnis 7's documentation. These manuals contain a considerable amount of very useful information, but the documentation is very weak. It is poorly edited, organized, and indexed. It loses its credibility almost immediately. Not uncommonly, an important step in a series of instructions is omitted, or an outlined step is impossible to execute (for example, you are told to click **OK** on a screen with no **OK** button). Pages are miscollated throughout, especially in the Getting Started Tutorial, which is very frustrating. The feeling "There is a decent program under here somewhere" is essentially the only thing that sustains you in the early stages of working with the program.

The included Glossary is very good, and its explanations are well-expanded. Omnis 7 also has a good online help feature. Technical support is provided free for 90 days. After that, the technical support subscription service is provided based on several different support program levels. These programs range from approximately $100 for the basic support program to several thousand dollars for a corporate support program. Members at all program levels are entitled to a free copy of all respective program updates. Bulletin board tech support also is available on CompuServe.

Omnis 7 traces its ancestry back to the PC (Omnis 2, 1984), and it has come a long way in terms of a friendly Mac interface. The average nonprogramming Mac user probably will find the program manageable in the generic form, especially Omnis Express' assistance. Any degree of development or custom design, however, almost certainly requires some dedicated perseverance or some familiarity with database concepts, as well as programming languages and experience.

For a free demo, contact Blyth Software Inc., 1065 E. Hillsdale Boulevard, Suite 300, Foster City, California 94404; (800) 346-6647.

Summary

Database programs allow information (data) to be stored, then accessed, modified, updated, manipulated, and retrieved. Database programs store information in files, and break those files down into records holding specific units of information in different fields. Databases are either flat file or relational in structure. Routine tasks can be automated with scripts, and scripts can be configured to run with the click of an onscreen button.

Many of the top Macintosh database systems are reviewed in this chapter. Although several of the programs presently are in revision or recently have released new versions, the reviews here provide a valid reference point for the future.

Interlude 13: Cool FileMaker Stuff

Claris FileMaker Pro ("FileMaker" in the jargon) is a database management program with powerful features and a reasonable interface. I'd make a few changes if I were King, but all in all, FileMaker is

In This Interlude
▼ Automatic Data Entry
▼ Scripting
▼ Sharing Files
▼ Buried Treasures

Part III
Mainstream Mac Applications

FileMaker helps you manage databases. You'd be completely correct to call FileMaker a database management program. You'd also be completely alone, because nobody calls database management programs "database management programs." Instead, the world calls them "databases," as in "FileMaker's a great database." The world's wrong, but what can ya do?

Christian Boyce

the right choice for managing many databases. Invoices, inventories, invertebrates: all could be managed in FileMaker databases. This interlude explains how to use three of FileMaker's powerful features—automatic data entry, Scripts, and networking—to make your FileMaker work more productive and fun.

Database Management

Database management has its own language. Learn a couple of words and wow 'em at work tomorrow. I'll use a collection of invoices to illustrate the terms.

The collection of invoices is called a database. Each invoice is called a record. Each piece of information on an invoice (invoice number, invoice date, customer name, total due) is called a field. All databases can be described in these terms.

Database management isn't something that sounds exciting or even endurable to most people. But keeping track of stuff, and slicing and dicing the stuff to produce reports like "Third Quarter Sales by Region," actually can be fun. Data entry is the dull part. Data manipulation is not dull. Find someone else to type in the data and you're all set. If you're stuck with typing your own data, cheer up: FileMaker can input data for you.

Slicing and dicing the information is supposed to be fun but sometimes it isn't. It's especially not fun when you can't remember how to do something when you really need it done. When you can't remember how to make a report (do I sort by invoice number or by date?), FileMaker can remember how for you. FileMaker's Scripts feature remembers all kinds of stuff, including which records to select, how to sort them, and how to present them. You should use Scripts even if you've got a memory like a steel trap, because Scripts are fast and easy. Plus, they don't rust.

It looks like you've got things covered: FileMaker's going to input the data, and Scripts are going to remember how to make reports. How could life possibly improve?

What if you didn't have to do all the work? Wouldn't life be better then? You bet it would. FileMaker has a built-in networking feature; it even works with System 6. You can put that kid down the hall to work fixing up your data.

Interlude 13
Cool FileMaker Stuff

These three key FileMaker features (automatic data entry, Scripts, and networking) were in the program when you bought it. If you're not using them, you're probably working too hard.

There's nothing like learning by doing, so do. You'll remember this stuff better if you've tried it with your own hands. You'll need a database to practice on; you'll make one in the next section.

This chapter covers the latest version of FileMaker, the so-called FileMaker Pro. FileMaker II, the previous version, looks a little different but operates very similarly. I'll let you know when a FileMaker Pro feature discussed here is either very different looking or unavailable in FileMaker II.

Making the Practice Database

Remember, databases are made of *records*, and records are made of *fields*. When you want to make a new database, you need to describe the fields. "Describing" can be as basic as simply naming the fields (Net Profit, Gross Sales, Costs) and as complex as defining relationships between fields (Net Profit = Gross Sales - Costs). In FileMaker, this describing step is known as Defining Fields.

When you double-click FileMaker you get a dialog box asking you to either work on an existing database or make a new one. You'll make a new one now, for holding names and addresses.

1. Double-click the **FileMaker** icon. You see the dialog box shown in figure 13.6.
2. Click **New** (you want to make a new database).
3. Name the new database `Names and addresses` (figure 13.7).
4. Click **OK**. You're ready to start defining fields. Figure 13.8 shows the **Define Fields** dialog box.
5. Define the **First Name** field by typing `First Name`.
6. Click the **Create** button.
7. Define the **Last Name** field by typing `Last Name`.
8. Click the **Create** button.
9. Continue typing field names and clicking **Create** until you've created all the fields shown in figure 13.9.

Figure 13.6
After double-clicking **FileMaker**.

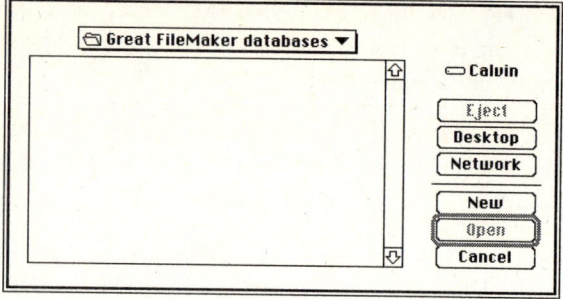

Figure 13.7
Naming the new database.

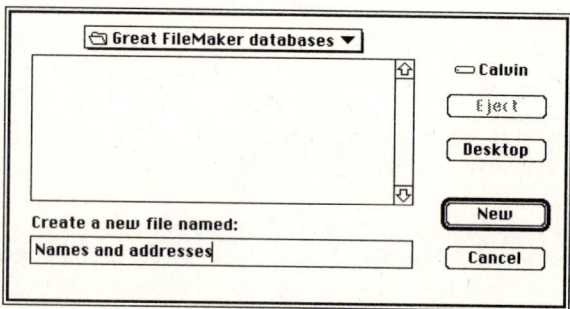

Figure 13.8
Define Fields dialog box.

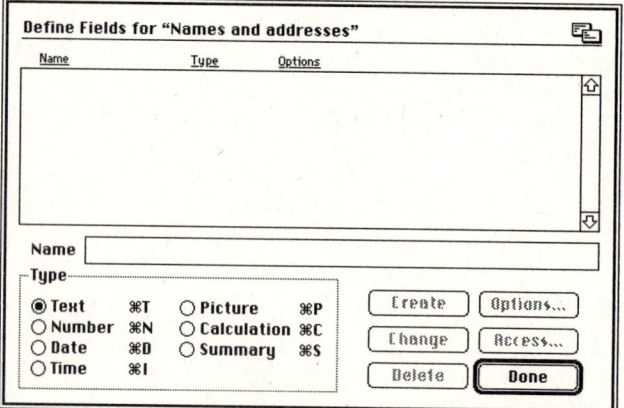

FileMaker provides different kinds of fields for holding different kinds of data. The radio buttons at the bottom of the **Define Fields** dialog box (figure 13.9) let you assign a field type to each field. The **ID Number** field will hold numbers and the **Entry Date** field will hold dates; change the field type for each field to reflect this.

1. Click on the **ID Number** field in the **Define Fields** box.
2. Click on the radio button next to the word **Number**.
3. Click the **Change** button.

4. Click on the **Entry Date** field in the **Define Fields** box.
5. Click on the radio button next to the word **Date**.
6. Click the **Change** button.
7. Click the **Done** button.

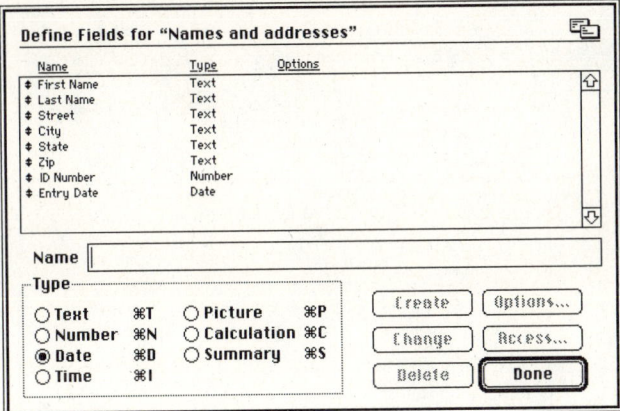

Interlude 13
Cool FileMaker Stuff

Figure 13.9
The fields, all defined.

Although you won't need them here, **Calculation** fields can be very useful. Calculation fields are computed based on data in other fields; you set up a formula and let FileMaker do the rest. FileMaker can do all sorts of calculations, from basic math (Sales Tax = Subtotal x Tax Rate) to logical operations (if Customer Type is "Preferred" then Discount = 15%; otherwise, Discount = 2%). Let FileMaker do all the calculations it can for you.

 FileMaker II's **Exit** button does what FileMaker Pro's **Done** button does.

 Don't format ZIP code fields as numbers. Rather, format them as text. Number fields drop leading zeros because, numerically, leading zeros are meaningless. In a ZIP code, however, a leading zero is important.

Your screen looks like a big bunch of nothing. That's because there are no records in your database yet. FileMaker doesn't show you anything until you've got at least one record. Add a new record by choosing **New Record** from the **Edit** menu.

 FileMaker II automatically creates the first record. If you're using FileMaker II, you don't have to choose New Record to see figure 13.10. Gee, you're using the old version and already you're one step ahead!

543

Part III
Mainstream Mac Applications

Your screen looks like figure 13.10.

You'll look like a rookie if you pull down the Edit menu and choose New Record every time you want to make a new record. The pros use Command-N.

Figure 13.10
New database for names and addresses.

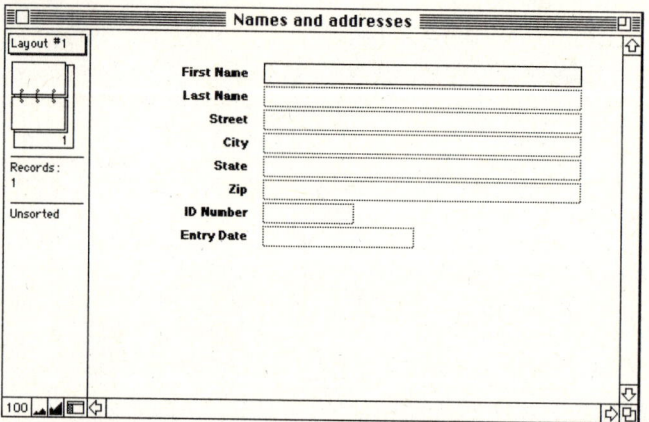

Use your own name and address to fill in the first record in the database. Give yourself ID Number 1000. Use today's date for the Entry Date. The rest I assume you know.

Figure 13.11
A filled-in record.

If by some miracle you and I are the same person your screen will look exactly like figure 13.11.

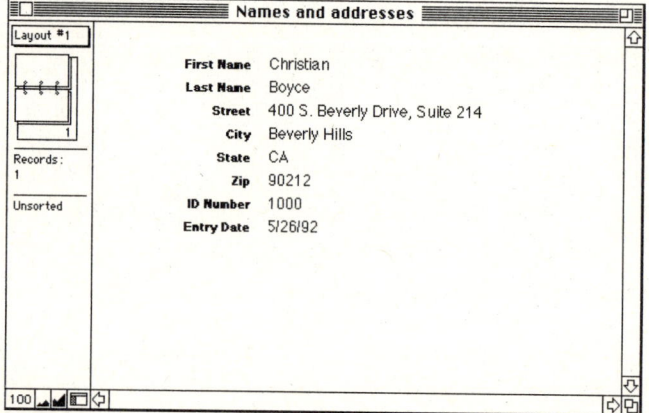

Don't worry about saving your work. FileMaker saves everything automatically.

Press the Tab key to move to the next field. Press Shift and Tab to move to the previous field. You can move to a field by clicking in it with the mouse, but that's a slow way to work.

You'll use your new database in the next section. You might want to make a copy of it (the database, not the next section) before going further, just in case. As I said, FileMaker saves everything automatically. Even mistakes.

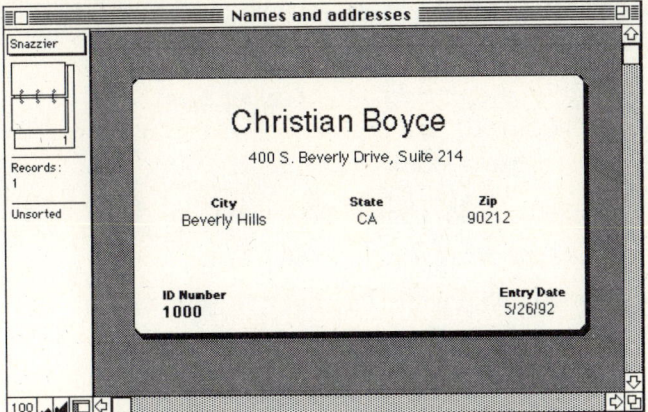

Interlude 13
Cool FileMaker Stuff

Figure 13.12
Nicer layout, but no better functionally.

Automatic Data Entry: Sure Beats Typing

I don't especially like typing, so I'm constantly looking for ways to avoid it. I found two ways in FileMaker. One technique, "Auto-enter values," fills fields in new records with default values. The other technique, "Lookup files," fills fields with data copied from another database when certain conditions are met.

Auto-Enter Values

When you make a new record, FileMaker can enter the date, the time, a serial number, standard data... all sorts of stuff. FileMaker can enter the date and time that you change records, too. If you're sharing a FileMaker file over a network, FileMaker can enter the name of the person responsible for creating or modifying each record. That's a lot of help from one little feature.

FileMaker lets you arrange fields on the screen any way, or ways, you want. You could switch to the **Layout** mode (**Select** menu) and create something like figure 13.12. If you want to, go ahead. However, you'll learn concepts just fine using the default layout that FileMaker made.

Christian Boyce

Part III
Mainstream
Mac Applications

FileMaker doesn't always follow the rules. In the Auto-enter area, the check boxes behave like radio buttons. That is, you can only have one checked at a time. You're supposed to be able to choose any or all of the options offered by check boxes, but FileMaker decided to do things differently. I don't like it.

Christian Boyce

 FileMaker II can automatically enter serial numbers, the date, and standard data in new records. It cannot do the other goodies mentioned above.

Let's start automating data entry for the "Names and addresses" database. Start by defining default data for the State field. Most people I know live in California, so telling FileMaker to automatically put "CA" into the State field for new records makes sense for me.

You'll be in and out of the **Select** menu a million times before you're through with this chapter. Take a minute to learn the Command key shortcuts shown in figure 13.13.

1. Choose **Define Fields** from the **Select** menu.
2. Select the **State** field name (click on it).
3. Press the **Options...** button. Figure 13.14 shows the resulting **Entry Options** dialog box. The "Auto-enter" area is in the upper left-hand part of the box. I've already typed "CA" and checked the proper box to automatically have "CA" entered in the **State** field of new records. If you want to use a different state that's OK with me.
4. Check the **data** box and type in what you want entered in the State field for all new records.

You can type right over automatically-entered data if you want to. If the Auto-entered value is wrong, just type in the right value.

5. Click **OK**.

Figure 13.13
The **Select** menu and Command key shortcuts.

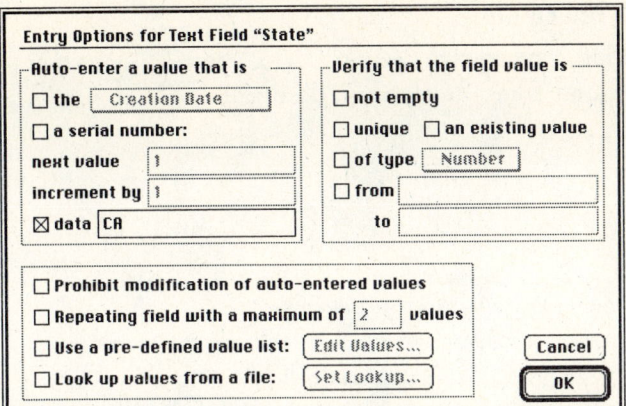

Figure 13.14
Entry Options for Text Field **State**.

You're finished setting up the **State** field. Now set up the **ID Number** field so it automatically numbers the records.

1. Select the **ID Number** field name.
2. Click the **Options...** button.
3. Check the box next to **a serial number**.
4. Type **1001** for the next value (your own information is number 1000). Figure 13.15 shows the **Entry Options** box and the settings for the **ID Number** field.
5. Click **OK**.

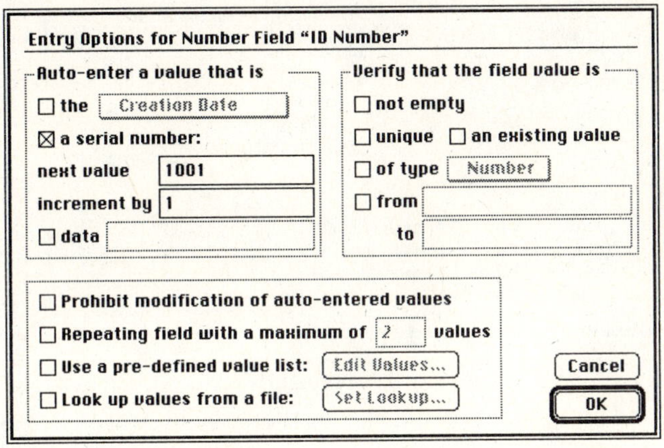

Figure 13.15
Entry Options for **ID Number** field.

Finally, make the Entry Date field automatically put each new record's creation date into the Entry Date field.

1. Select the **Entry Date** field name.

Part III

Mainstream Mac Applications

2. Click the **Options...** button.
3. Check the box next to **Creation Date.** Figure 13.16 shows the **Entry Options** settings for the **Entry Date** field.
4. Click **OK**.

Figure 13.17 shows the **Define Fields** dialog box with the entry options.

5. Click **Done.**

Figure 13.16

Entry Options for **Entry Date** field.

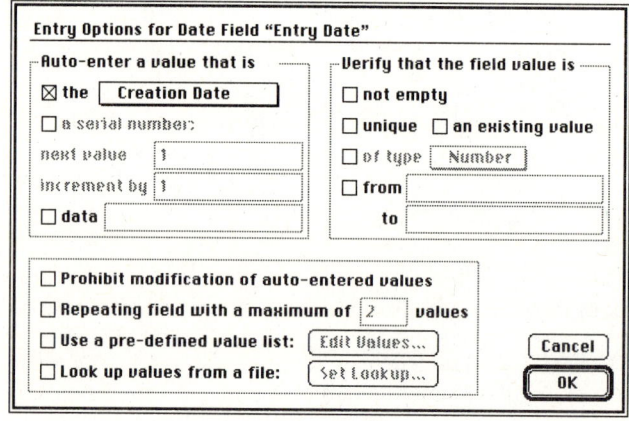

Figure 13.17

Define Fields box with entry options.

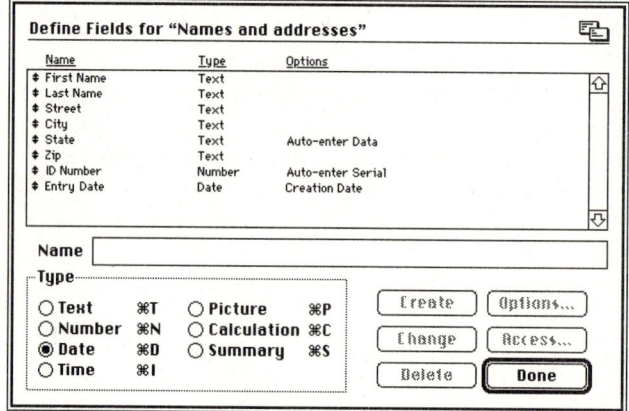

Play with the pop-up menu next to the box you just checked. The pop-up has some interesting options.

Christian Boyce

Next time you make a new record (Command-N, right?), the State, ID Number, and Entry Date fields will automatically fill in. You can type over automatically-entered data, or tab right through it. Create and fill in a handful of records now. You'll use them in the next example.

Auto-entering works for new records only. It does not affect records that were created before the auto-entering was set up. You can change existing records using the **Replace...** and **Relookup** commands, discussed later in this chapter.

548

Lookup Files

Suppose the people in your "Names and addresses" database were your employees, and suppose you used FileMaker to write their paychecks every week. Wouldn't it be great if your paycheck database and your "Names and addresses" database were connected? Typing an employee's ID Number in the paycheck database could trigger FileMaker to fill in the employee's name on his check. It could fill in the paycheck's amount if your "Names and addresses" database held salary information.

FileMaker's **Lookup** feature makes it happen. When you type an ID Number in your paycheck database, FileMaker checks the number against ID Numbers in the "Names and addresses" database. Record by record it goes, looking for an ID Number that matches what you typed. When FileMaker finds a match, it stops.

> **Note:** FileMaker calls the database it looks things up in "a lookup file." "Names and addresses" is the lookup file here.

What happens next depends on what you've asked for. If you want part of the matching record's information copied to your paycheck database, FileMaker will do that. If you want all of the matching record's information copied to your paycheck database, FileMaker will do that. Automatically. Lookup files mean never having to say you're sorry about typing something twice.

> **A Closer Look:** Keeping the paychecks in their own database might seem like a waste. Why not add fields for **Paycheck Date** and **Paycheck Amount** to the "Names and addresses" database and write checks from there? You'd simply duplicate a record (an employee's information) when you wanted to write a check. Sounds easy.

It is easy. But duplicate records make your database big. Big equals slow. Whether you're sorting, or searching, or entering data, big (slow) databases are a drag to work with. They're also a drag to store. Hard disks fill up, and when yours does, you'll wish you hadn't stored the same information over and over and over. In real life you'd enhance your "Names and addresses" database with fields for phone numbers, salaries, birthdays, names of spouses, names of children, and favorite Mac book author—nice things to know about employees but totally unnecessary for writing paychecks. And totally wasteful to duplicate.

Make a Paycheck database to practice on, like so:

1. Open the **Names and addresses** database if it isn't open already.
2. Choose **New...** from the **File** menu.

Interlude 13
Cool FileMaker Stuff

Part III

Mainstream
Mac Applications

Figure 13.18

Field list for Paychecks database.

3. Name your new database **Paychecks** (that's the name I'll use).
4. Create the fields shown in figure 13.18.
5. Leave the **Define Fields** dialog box on your screen.

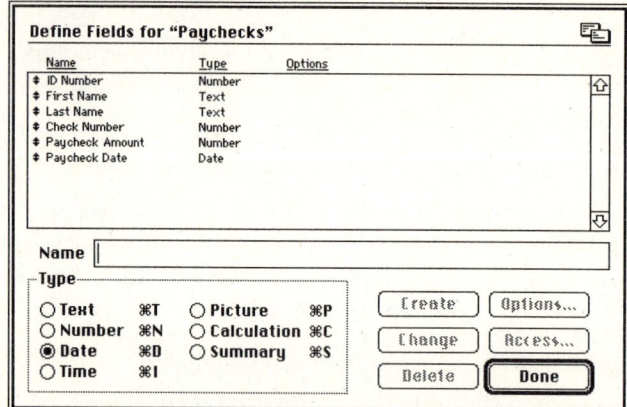

You should assign field types as shown in figure 13.18. If you need to change a field's type (Who, me? Make a mistake?), click on a field, click on the type button (Text, Number, Date, and so on), and click on the **Change** button. You did it before, when you made the "Names and addresses" database. It's still easy.

You can use the auto-enter options to automatically fill in the Check Number field (mine starts at 101) and the Paycheck Date (mine inputs the creation date). You know how to do this, right? Review the creation of the "Names and addresses" database if you can't remember the specifics.

Now define the lookups. Your goal: automatic first and last name data entry based on matching ID Numbers. You type an ID Number, FileMaker fills in the name.

1. Click on **First Name**.
2. Click the **Options...** button. The **Entry Options** dialog box opens (figure 13.19).
3. Check the box for **Look up values from a file.** FileMaker immediately opens a dialog box (figure 13.20). Though FileMaker doesn't tell you, it wants you to use this box to choose a lookup file. You'll use the "Names and addresses" database. If "Names and addresses" isn't listed in the dialog box, you'll have to climb around and find it.

A Closer Look When you're defining lookups, it helps if the lookup file is in the same folder as the one you're doing the defining for. Once you've set things up, don't move either file into another folder or you'll break the links between the databases. You can always re-create the links, but why put yourself through it?

4. When you've found the **Names and addresses** file, click on it.
5. Click **Open**.
6. Use the pop-up menus to specify the lookup procedure.

FileMaker II uses scrolling lists instead of pop-ups. Figure 13.22 shows the FileMaker II **Lookup** dialog box.

7. Click **OK**.
8. Click **OK** again (different dialog box).
9. Click **Done**.

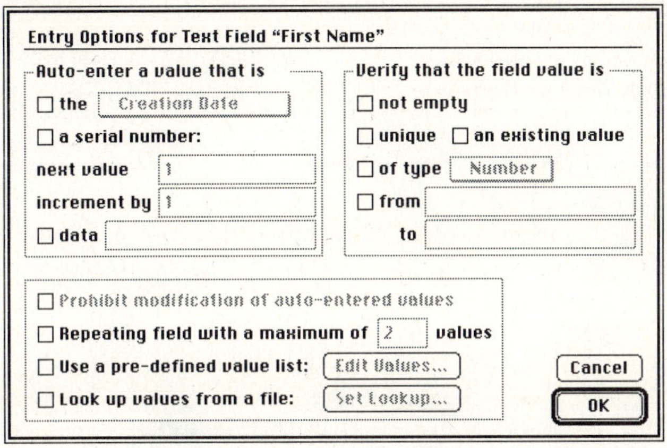

Interlude 13
Cool FileMaker Stuff

Figure 13.19
Entry Options for First Name.

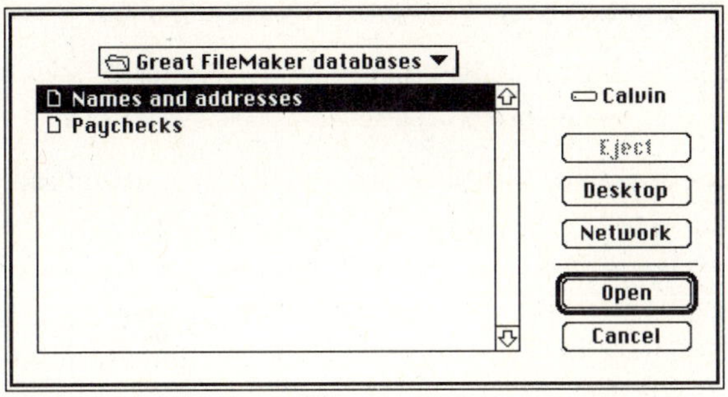

Figure 13.20
Choosing a lookup file.

Now try typing an ID Number you're sure exists in the "Names and addresses" database. Did it work? Yes? Great. You should be able to set up the lookup for the Last Name field without any help.

Part III
Mainstream Mac Applications

> **Note:** If you typed an ID Number into the Paychecks database and nothing happened, fear not. You've got to let FileMaker know you're through typing the number. Best way: press the Tab key to move to another field. That should do it.

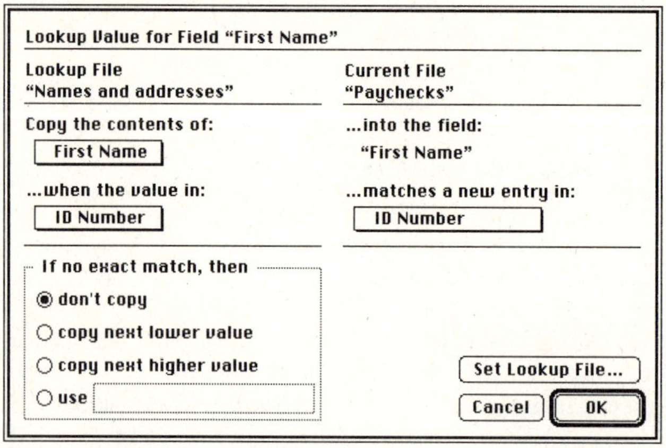

Figure 13.21

Lookup dialog box.

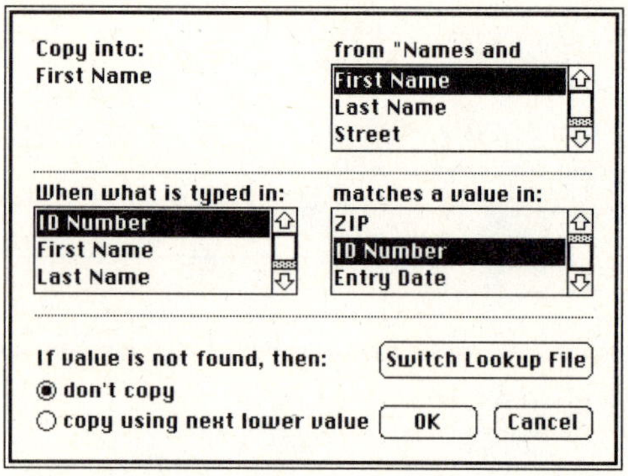

Figure 13.22

FileMaker II **Lookup** dialog box.

Figure 13.21 shows the Lookup dialog box and the proper settings, which mean, roughly, "Check each ID Number typed in the Paychecks database, and if it matches one in the 'Names and addresses' database, copy the info in the First Name field of the 'Names and addresses' database and paste it into the First Name field in the Paychecks database." The picture says it better.

Christian Boyce

Pretty impressive, isn't it? Make a new record (Command-N) to see your other Entry Options at work, and try different ID Numbers just to see the names change. Practice using the Lookup feature (hint: play with the Lookup dialog box) until you feel confident with it. And look for chances to use Lookups in your own databases. With Lookups, you'll spend less time entering data and more time having fun. Bonus: Lookups don't make typos.

A Closer Look Suppose your Paycheck database looked up salaries from your employee file ("Names and addresses"). Suppose you gave an employee a raise. New paychecks will reflect the new salary. What about the old paychecks? Will they change too, now that the Lookup file's changed?

No, they won't. Old records retain their old information. If you re-entered the ID Number in an old record, FileMaker would redo the lookup, returning the new information. If you wanted to update a bunch of records at once, you could: find the records you want to update, click in the ID Number field, and select Relookup from the File menu.

A pretty layout won't help you learn the Lookup feature. However, you would certainly need a good-looking layout for printing checks. Figure 13.23 shows a nicer Paycheck database layout.

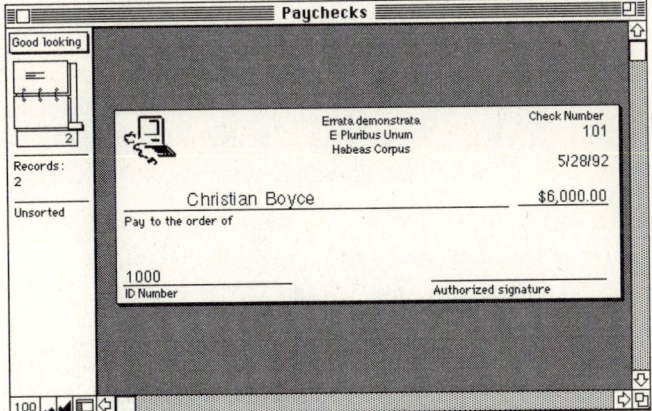

Automatic data entry saves you time, and it's fun to boot. Another benefit of automatic data entry is increased data quality and consistency. In the "Names and addresses" database, automatic data entry keeps you from typing "VA" or "Ca" when you really want "CA." Less work, and better data... it's a good life.

It gets better. Data manipulation can be automated too, and like automatic data entry, automatic data manipulation saves you time and is fun. The next section, Scripts, describes how to automate the searching, sorting, and presenting operations that are the heart and soul of data manipulation.

Scripts: Sure Beats Forgetting

Suppose your "Names and addresses" file holds hundreds of records, and suppose you'd added a field describing each person as a business contact or a friend. Suppose you send monthly letters to business contacts and yearly letters to friends. And suppose you want to use FileMaker to print envelopes for the letters.

Printing the envelopes takes a lot of setting up. You need to find the right records, change to your envelope-printing layout, and change the **Page Setup** so the printing goes sideways (envelopes feed sideways through

Interlude 13
Cool FileMaker Stuff

Figure 13.23
Nicer paycheck layout, no improvement functionally.

Don't print mailing labels when you need to send a bunch of letters. Print right on the envelopes and look classy and cool.

Christian Boyce

Part III
Mainstream Mac Applications

LaserWriters) before you're ready to print. You might also want to sort the records you're about to print (it makes finding the right envelope easier later on).

You'd do all those steps every month for the business contacts. You'd do the same steps every year for friends. In between times you'd use the database in other ways, switching layouts as needed, adding records and information, and so on, guaranteeing that things won't be as you left them last month. No way around it: you can't print the envelopes without going through the steps each month. It's a bit of a drag.

You can use a Script to perform the monthly envelope job, and another to perform the yearly envelope job. Triggering a Script is as easy as choosing it from a menu: all those steps, with one deft move! Scripts remember everything, including which layout to use, whether to print sideways or not, which records to find, and how to sort them. Set a Script in motion and let FileMaker do the rest.

You need to modify your "Names and addresses" file before moving on. You'll use the modifications as you learn about Scripts. First, add a field to your "Names and addresses" database and call it "Group." Put "Friend" into the Group field for some of the records and "Business" into the Group field for the others.

Use the Replace command to quickly fill in the Group field.

1. Type **Friend** in the **Group** field for one record.
2. Click in the **Group** field.
3. Choose **Replace...** from the **Edit** menu. You get the dialog box shown in figure 13.24.
4. Click the **Replace** button.

It's more of a drag to do things wrong. If you've ever wasted time and paper printing an incorrect report (Aargh! I forgot to sort!), you know what I mean. The more complicated things get, the more chances for you to blow it.

Christian Boyce

Figure 13.24
Ready to **Replace**....

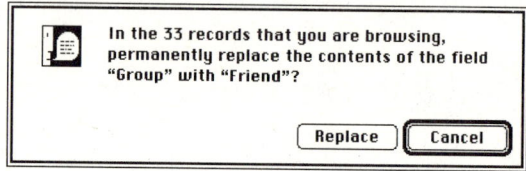

Now every record's Group field holds "Friend." Flip through the records and change a few to "Business."

The Replace command is hot. You can use it to change all instances of "CA" to "California" if you want to. Three easy steps: find the records you want to change, type the right information into one record, and choose **Replace**. Nothing to it. Just be sure you're working with the right bunch of records.

You don't want to change the information in every State field to "California," do you? Of course not. So find the "CA" records first. Then proceed with the replacing.

You are almost ready to make a Script. Make a new layout for printing envelopes and you're all set.

1. Choose **Layout** from the **Select** menu.
2. Choose **New Layout...** from the **Edit** menu. Figure 13.25 shows the dialog box for choosing a layout type.
3. Click the **Blank** button.
4. Name the layout **Envelopes**.
5. Click **OK**.

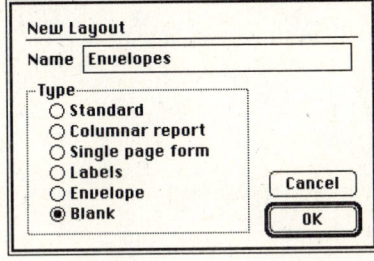

Figure 13.26 shows your new layout. It needs fields. They don't call it "Blank" for nothing.

Those perpendicular lines on Figure 13.26 are "T-Squares." They can help you align things in your layouts. You can turn them on and off whenever you want by pressing Command-T. I'll turn mine off for the rest of this example.

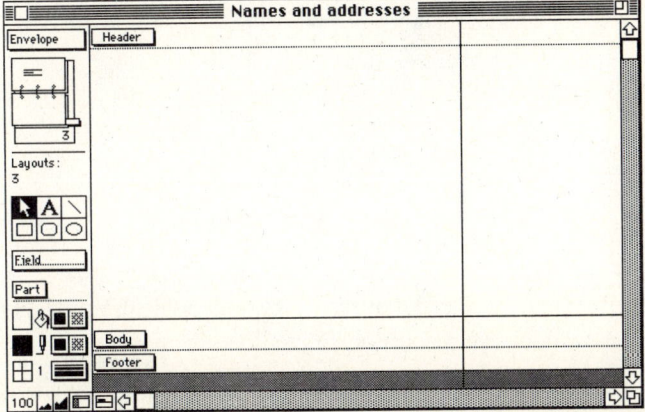

Interlude 13
Cool FileMaker Stuff

Figure 13.25
Choosing a layout type.

Figure 13.26
New blank layout.

555

Part III
Mainstream Mac Applications

You might have noticed the **Envelope** button in figure 13.25. I noticed it too. However, since clicking the Envelope button does not lead to a perfect envelope, and since starting from scratch gives you more flexibility, I have you choose a blank layout. Besides, it's good practice.

Christian Boyce

Figure 13.27
New Field list.

Now add some fields.

1. Click on the button marked **Fields** and drag it onto the white part of the layout. The **New Field** list appears. Figure 13.27 shows the **New Field** list.

2. Choose the **First Name** field (don't include a field label).

3. Stretch the field (so it's long enough to display a long first name) by dragging one of the field's black handles. Figure 13.28 shows the layout with the stretched **First Name** field.

4. Drag the rest of the fields onto the layout following the same procedure.

5. Drag the fields around until your layout looks like figure 13.29. You need to specify sideways printing; otherwise your envelopes will look silly.

6. Choose **Page Setup** from the **File** menu.

7. Choose the sideways printing option and click **OK**. It's probably important that the printing hits the envelope… and it won't unless you position it yourself.

8. Click and drag the Header handle down a good 3 or 4 inches.

The proper Header size depends on how your printer feeds envelopes. There's nothing to do but experiment. If the printing is too high on the envelope, push it down by enlarging the Header. You can change the Header anytime.

9. Zoom out by clicking on the "small mountains" button at the bottom of the window. Figure 13.30 shows the zoomed-out layout.

There is no "small mountains" button in FileMaker II, and zooming is possible only in the **Preview** mode.

You may as well add the finishing touch: fields that slide over to remove blank space. This sliding feature only affects printing and the **Preview** mode. Use the **Preview** mode (**Select** menu) now to see how bad things are. Figure 13.31 shows the terrible spacing you get when you don't use the sliding feature.

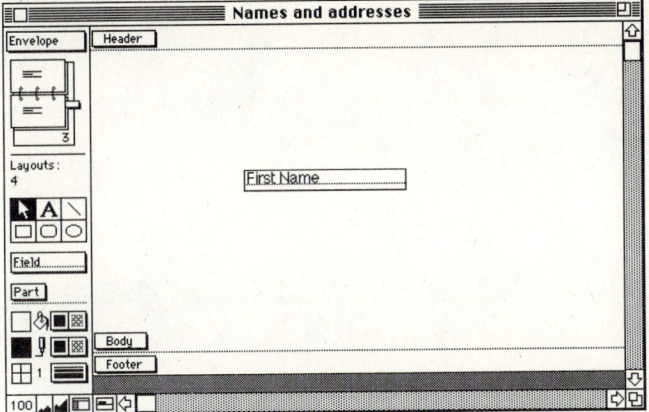

Figure 13.28
Stretched **First Name** field.

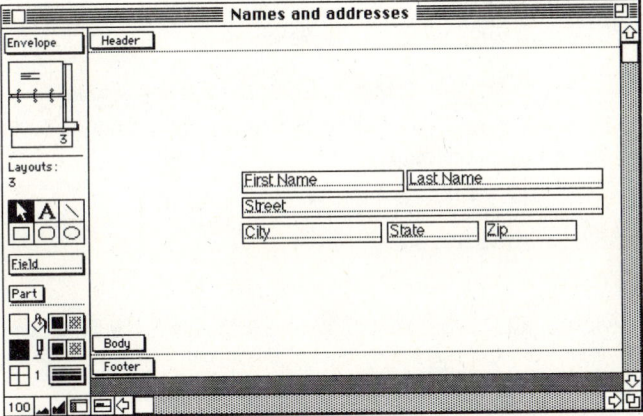

Figure 13.29
Finished Envelope layout.

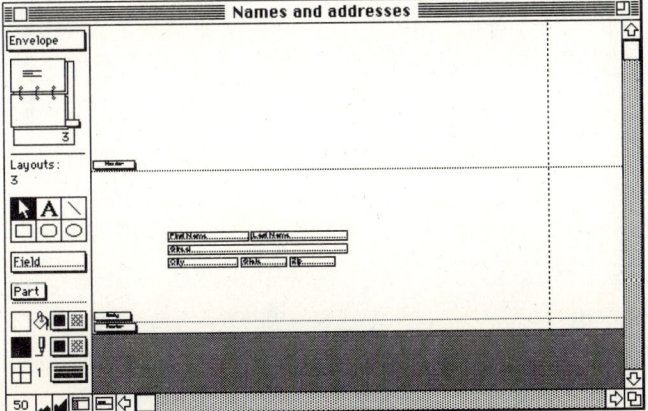

Figure 13.30
Zoomed-out layout.

Figure 13.31

Terrible spacing (no sliding).

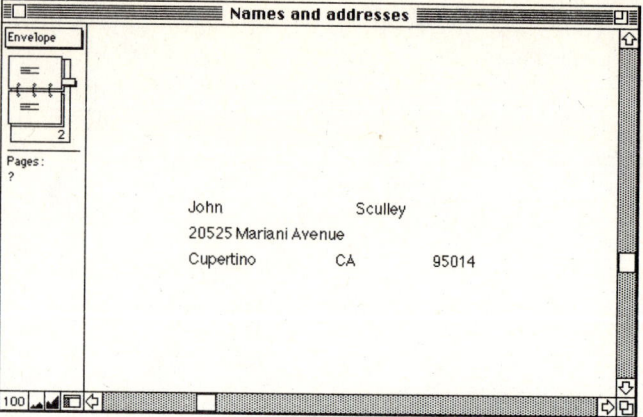

 **Preview** is in the **File** menu in FileMaker II. Check the **Reduced** box in FileMaker II to zoom out while in the **Preview** mode. Uncheck it to go back to full size.

1. Switch back to the **Layout** mode (**Select** menu).
2. Select everything (try **Select All** in the **Edit** menu).
3. Choose **Slide Objects...** from the **Arrange** menu. Figure 13.32 shows the **Slide Objects** dialog box.

Slide Objects... is under the **Gadgets** menu in FileMaker II.

4. Check the **Sliding left** box.
5. Click **OK**.

Try the **Preview** again. Looks better! Figure 13.33 shows the improved spacing.

Figure 13.32

Slide Objects dialog box.

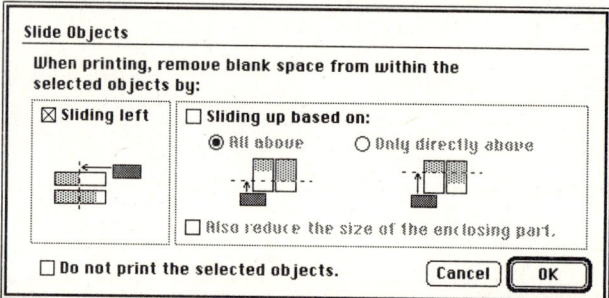

Your envelope layout's more or less complete. Let's move on to doing that monthly envelope job. To begin, you need to find just the Business people. FileMaker's good at that.

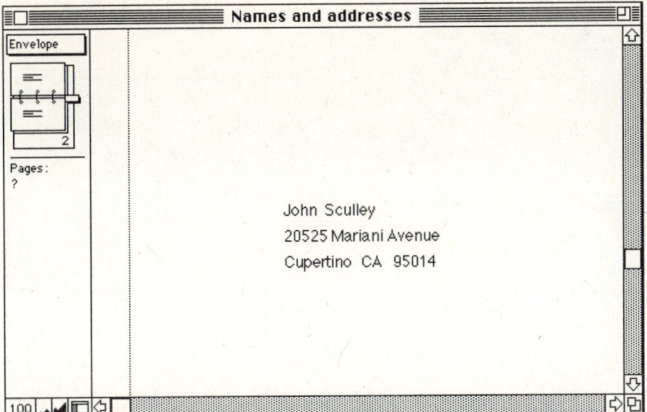

Figure 13.33
Improved spacing via **Sliding Objects**.

6. Choose **Find** from the **Select** menu (or press Command-F). If you're still looking at the Envelope layout, switch to the default layout (Layout #1) using the pop-out menu at the top left of the screen. Figure 13.34 shows the pop-out menu in action.

> **Note:** FileMaker II doesn't have this pop-out. You change layouts in FileMaker II by going to the **Layout** mode and clicking the pages in the book until you find the layout you want. Switch back to **Find** when you're done. Layout switching is handled better by FileMaker Pro's pop-out menu.

7. Type **Business** in the **Group** field. Your screen should look like figure 13.35.
8. Press the **Find** button (or hit Enter on the keyboard).

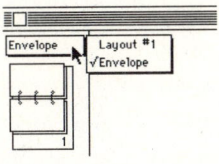

Figure 13.34
Layout pop-out menu.

FileMaker finds the Business people and shows just those records. Flip through them to convince yourself that the Find operation worked.

The records need sorting. You can sort them any way you want; sorting by Last Name seems sensible.

1. Choose **Sort...** from the **Select** menu (or press Command-S). You get the **Sort...** dialog box of figure 13.36.
2. Click on the **Last Name** field.
3. Click the **Move** button.
4. Click the **Sort** button.

Figure 13.35
Finding Business people.

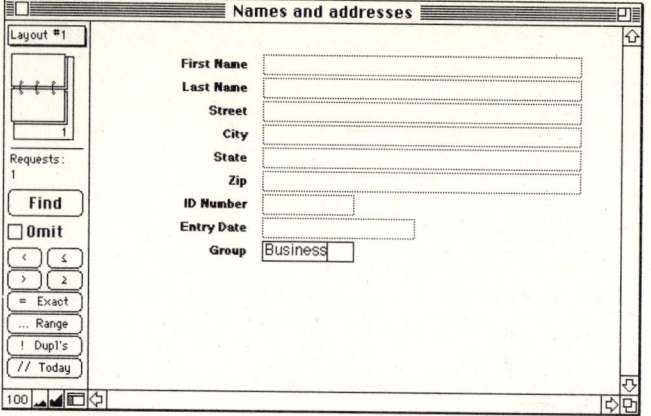

Figure 13.36
Sort... dialog box.

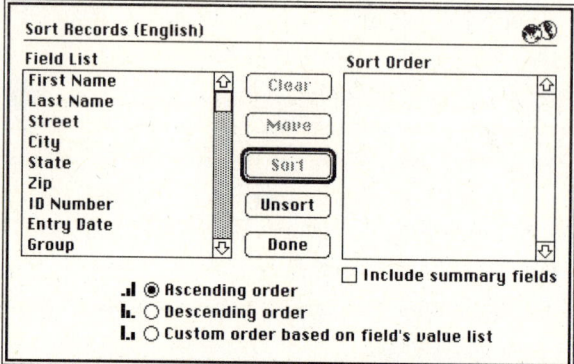

Presto! The records are sorted alphabetically by Last Name. Flip through them and see.

You have the right records (just the Business contacts) and you've sorted them alphabetically. You need to switch to the Envelope layout before printing, and you ought to check the **Page Setup** too. Use the pop-out menu to change layouts, and be sure Page Setup specifies sideways printing.

> Note: Remember, if you're using FileMaker II, you have to switch to the Layout mode to change layouts. When you know what you're doing you can switch layouts with Scripts, but you don't know what you're doing yet.

Now you've done everything: found the right records, sorted them the right way, switched to the right layout, and chosen the right Page Setup options. Lots of work, and you probably don't want to do it again. No problem: make a Script and let FileMaker do the work next time.

Note: Each FileMaker database gets its own set of Scripts. New databases don't have any Scripts at all.

Making a Script is almost as easy as using one. FileMaker watches you work and remembers what you asked for the last time you did a Find, how you sorted the last time you did a Sort, and which options you chose last time you changed the Page Setup. You say "Yo! FileMaker! Write down what I did and store it in a menu!" and the Script is made. Actually, speech recognition is a couple of years away. (Maybe they'll include it in FileMaker UltraMegaPro or some such.) For now, you have to check a few boxes in the **Script Definition** dialog box. Still, it's pretty simple.

1. Chose **Define Scripts…** from the **Scripts** menu. FileMaker wants you to name the Script before you create it (see figure 13.37). Better do it.
2. Give the new Script a name.
3. Click **Create**. You get the **Script Definition** dialog box of figure 13.38.

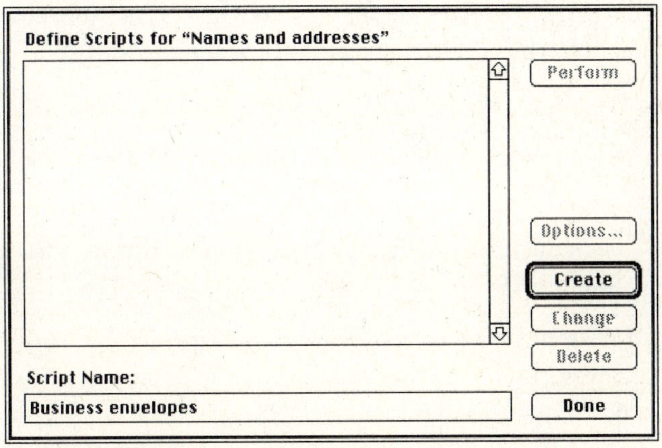

Interlude 13
Cool FileMaker Stuff

Figure 13.37
Naming a Script in advance.

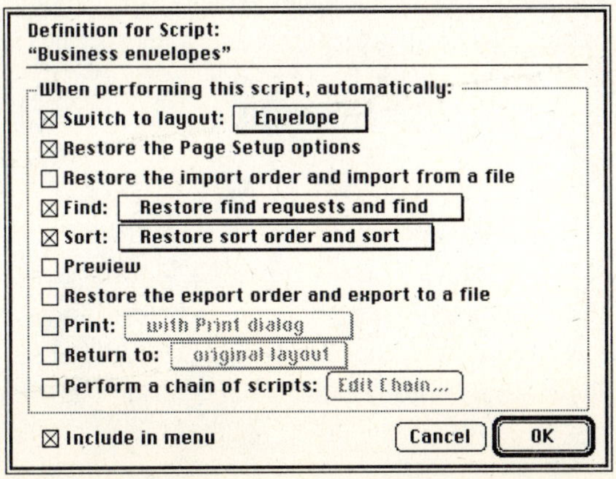

Figure 13.38
Script Definition dialog box.

Part III
Mainstream Mac Applications

"*Restore find requests and find*" means "Remember what I asked for last time, and do the same thing automatically when I run this Script. Restore the sort order and sort" means "Remember how I sorted last time, and do the same thing automatically when I run this Script."

Christian Boyce

You could also make a Script to switch you back to the original layout, Layout #1.

Christian Boyce

It's a little different in FileMaker II:

4. Choose **Scripts…** from the **Custom** menu.
5. Click **New**.
6. Name the Script while in the **Script Definition** dialog box.

Read figure 13.38, the **Script Definition** dialog box, from the top. First, you want the Script to switch to the Envelope layout, so check that box. (You can make the Script switch to a different layout using the pop-up menu.)

> **Note:** FileMaker II does not have a pop-up menu for layouts. You must switch to the desired layout yourself before creating the Script.

You want the Script to use the Page Setup options you chose, so check that box too. You're not importing any data, so don't check that box. You do want the Script to remember what to find, so check that box (and be sure the pop-up menu says "Restore find requests and find").

You want the Script to remember how you sorted, so check that box (and be sure the pop-up menu says **Restore the sort order and sort**).

Everything else should be unchecked, except **Include in menu**.

When you've got the Script defined, click **OK**, then click **Done**. You're finished!

> **Note:** FileMaker II doesn't have a **Done** button. Instead, it has an **Exit** button. Click it.

Rearrange your database before testing the Script. Find all the records, sort them by something other than the Last Name field, switch to a different layout, and change the Page Setup settings. Louse things up so your Script has something to do. Now choose your Script from the Custom menu (it's there because you checked "Include in menu"). FileMaker finds the Business contacts, sorts them by Last Name, switches to the Envelope layout, and changes the Page Setup to sideways. The Script does everything, every time, exactly right, and it does it fast.

> **Note:** Make Scripts that do nothing but switch layouts for you.

You know enough now to make a Script for the yearly "Friends" envelope project. You won't use the Script in any examples here, but it's good practice just the same. As before, find a bunch of records ("Friends"), sort them, choose a layout, and set the Page Setup options. Do all that, then choose Define Scripts…. That's all there is to it.

Scripts can do more than what you've asked yours to do here. They can print automatically, export data automatically, take in data automatically, and more. You can even string Scripts together; you can tell one Script to run another when it's done. These are interesting features, worth exploring, and you now know enough to do that.

FileMaker assigns "Command-1" to the first Script you make, "Command-2" to the second, and so on; you can trigger your Scripts without leaving the keyboard. That's terrific, but you won't know the shortcuts if you don't know the Scripts exist in the first place. Most people have zero experience with Scripts; they don't know to look in the **Scripts** menu, let alone try Command key shortcuts. If people like that will use your database, you'll need to find a way to get them to use your Scripts. The best way to do it? Put the Scripts right out in the open instead of hiding them under a menu.

> **Note:** FileMaker's Button feature lets you trigger a Script by clicking on a button. It's literally 1, 2, 3: (1) Make a Script, (2) Draw an object, and (3) Tell FileMaker to run the Script when you click on the object. Let's do it.

Buttons are a FileMaker Pro exclusive. Sorry.

You draw and define buttons in the Layout mode. Get there.

1. Choose **Layout** from the **Select** menu.
2. Switch to **Layout #1** (the one FileMaker made by itself).
3. Click the oval tool (bottom right-hand tool in the palette).
4. Click and drag an oval (this will be your button).

Your screen looks like Figure 13.39.

Interlude 13
Cool FileMaker Stuff

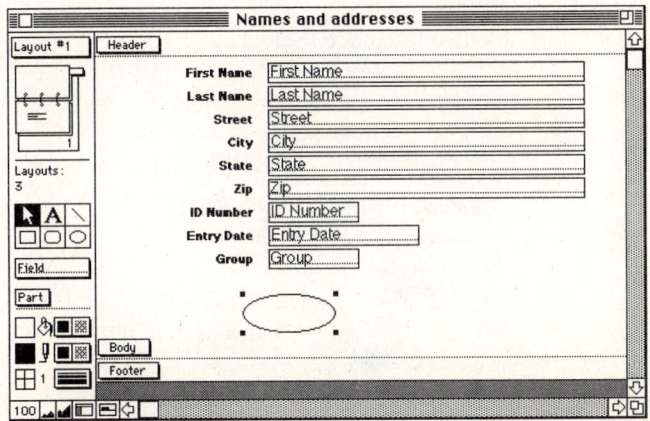

Figure 13.39
Making a button.

You can format the oval any way you want. Experiment with the **Paint Bucket** (for filling in the oval), the **Pen** (for choosing a line pattern) and the **Line Width** pop-up (for choosing a line width). You can put the oval anywhere you want. Figure 13.40 shows my finished oval.

Figure 13.40
My finished oval.

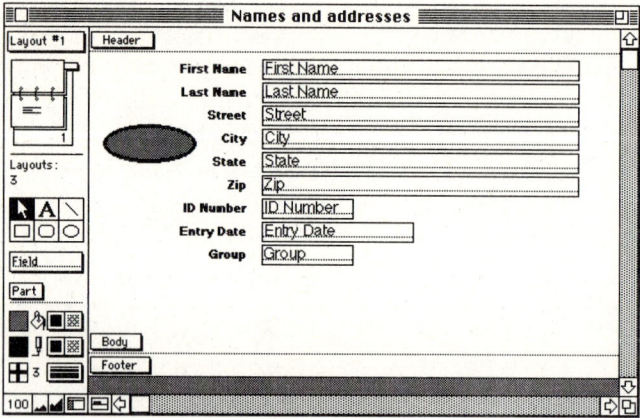

It's not a button until you define it as one. Right now, that oval's just an oval.

You've got a Script, and you've drawn an object. Tell FileMaker to run the Script when you click on the object and you're done.

1. Click on your oval to select it (you see black handles around it).
2. Choose **Define Button...** from the **Scripts** menu. Figure 13.41 shows the resulting **Define Button** dialog box.
3. Check the **Perform a script** box.
4. Choose a Script to perform from the pop-up menu.
5. Click **OK**.
6. Switch back to the **Browse** mode (**Select** menu).

Figure 13.41
Define Button dialog box.

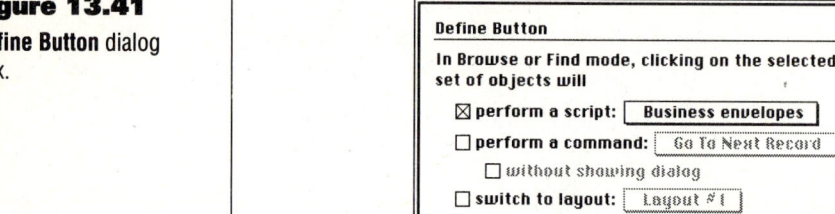

564

Try your button. Neater than neat: it highlights and everything. Not only that, but it works!

You can make buttons as snazzy as you wish. Figure 13.42 shows buttons for the Business Envelope and Friendly Envelope scripts. The buttons were created in FileMaker using the rectangle, line, and text tools. The elements of each button were grouped together (**Group** command in the **Arrange** menu), and the grouped set of elements were turned into buttons.

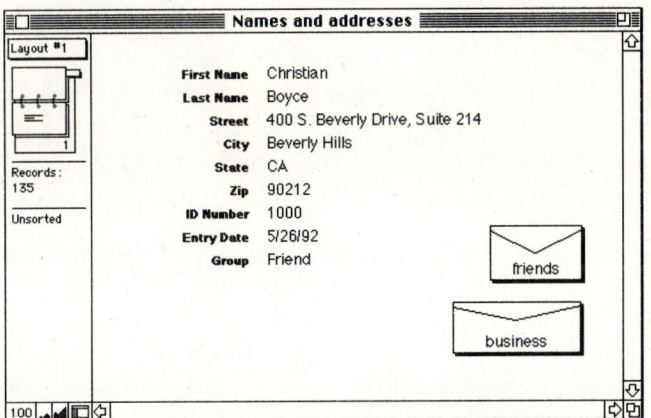

Interlude 13
Cool FileMaker Stuff

Figure 13.42
Snazzy buttons.

Note that buttons don't have to trigger Scripts. They can perform commands, or simply switch layouts. Experiment: draw objects all over the place and define them as buttons. The more buttons you make, the better you'll understand how they work. And don't worry: if you want to delete a button, it's as easy as switching to the Layout mode, selecting the button, and hitting Delete.

FileMaker's Scripts do for data manipulation what auto-entered data and Lookup files do for data entry: they speed up your work, make it more fun, and keep you from making mistakes. Sometimes, though, that just isn't enough. Maybe you can't do everything yourself, or maybe you don't want to, never mind how fast, how fun, or how error-free FileMaker's making everything. What you need is someone else, someone who'll do part of the work for you. This chapter's final section describes FileMaker's networking feature and how it can help others help you.

Part III
Mainstream
Mac Applications

Sharing Files over a Network: Sure Beats Walking

Technically, your Macs have to be on an AppleTalk network to use FileMaker's networking feature. Most Apple LaserWriters have AppleTalk built in, and all Macs do, so if you're using a LaserWriter connected to other Macs, the odds are very good that you're on an AppleTalk network.

Christian Boyce

It's a little-known fact that FileMaker databases can be used by more than one person at a time. It's an even lesser-known fact that you don't need a file server, or even System 7's File Sharing, to use a FileMaker database stored on someone else's Mac. FileMaker's networking feature runs over the same wires that connect Macs to printers, so if your Mac and another Mac share a printer, the networking hardware's in place.

Why should you care about sharing a database with someone else? For starters, sharing a database means sharing the work. With two people working, the work gets done faster. But couldn't you just copy the database, putting one copy on each person's Mac? Sure you could. But multiple copies of the database lead to big problems. If you add a record to the copy on your Mac, and someone else deletes a record from the copy on his Mac, and someone else changes a record in the copy on her Mac, you've got three versions of the database and none of them are right. Sharing a database means you all use the same copy.

Sharing databases is convenient, too. If it's your database, you won't have people standing in your office, asking you to look something up for them. FileMaker lets them look things up for themselves, from their own offices, without bothering you. Likewise, you can look things up in their databases from your office without bothering them. All in all, it's as convenient as can be.

FileMaker provides the networking software, not that you'll ever notice it; the networking software's built into FileMaker itself, so there's nothing to install. Accessing FileMaker databases on other Macs is only a step or two away.

 Actually, if you use a Mac Plus, there is something to install, and there are a couple of places to find it. You need an Apple system file called "AppleTalk" to supplement the AppleTalk built into your machine. Without this file, the networking will not work.

Look for AppleTalk on your original FileMaker disks; if you can't find it there, it's on the original System 6 disks from Apple. Drag the AppleTalk file to your System Folder and restart to install it.

This is only a problem on the Mac Plus, but it's so befuddling to do everything right and not get the network to work that I thought I ought to tell you.

In this real-life example, two Macs (Big Mac and Little Richard) share a "Names and addresses" database. The database is stored on Little Richard's hard disk. This turns out to be important.

Big Mac is an SE/30 running System 7. Little Richard is a Mac Plus running System 6. This turns out to be unimportant.

The networking cable is a modular phone wire. Each Mac has a PhoneNET connector. This turns out to be unimportant too. (What's important is that the things are connected. You could use Apple's own AppleTalk connectors or one of the PhoneNET imitations and the network would work just as well.)

Here's how it's done. The owner of Little Richard opens up his hard disk, finds his "Names and addresses" database, and double-clicks away. The database opens, and the owner gets to work. As far as Little Richard's owner is concerned, there's nothing special going on.

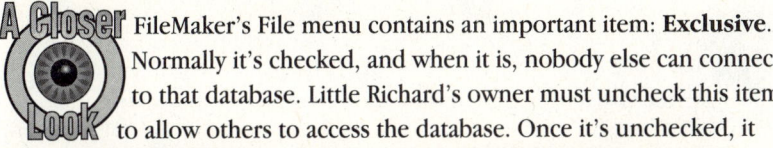FileMaker's File menu contains an important item: **Exclusive**. Normally it's checked, and when it is, nobody else can connect to that database. Little Richard's owner must uncheck this item to allow others to access the database. Once it's unchecked, it stays unchecked, until Little Richard's owner decides to check it again.

Later (this is important), the owner of Big Mac wants to use the "Names and addresses" database. "Names and addresses" is not on Big Mac's hard disk! This, too, is important; there is a single copy of the database, and it's on Little Richard's hard disk.

Big Mac's hard disk does have a copy of FileMaker, which is absolutely essential to this operation. Big Mac's owner double-clicks his FileMaker icon, which leads to a dialog box. You've seen this box before, when you started FileMaker for the first time at the beginning of this chapter. Rather than click **New** to create a new database, Big Mac's owner clicks the **Network** button. The dialog box is shown in figure 13.43 so you can see the Network button.

Clicking the **Network** button tells FileMaker to look for FileMaker databases being used by other Macs on the network. FileMaker presents Big Mac's owner with a list of all FileMaker files open on the network, as shown in figure 13.44. (The list also shows a diamond after each file name, then the file's owner.)

Interlude 13
Cool FileMaker Stuff

If you have two Macs connected, and both have FileMaker on them, great. You can work through this example with me. If not, that's OK. Someday you'll need this stuff, and you'll know how it works even if you haven't tried it before.

Christian Boyce

FileMaker includes extensive password controls; you control who sees what in your databases. That's obviously important, but it's dull as anything and we're focusing on the cool stuff here. FileMaker's manual contains eleven pages of password information; that should be enough.

Christian Boyce

Figure 13.43

Network button in dialog box.

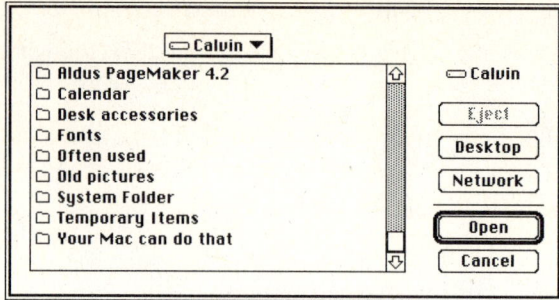

Figure 13.44

Network Access dialog box.

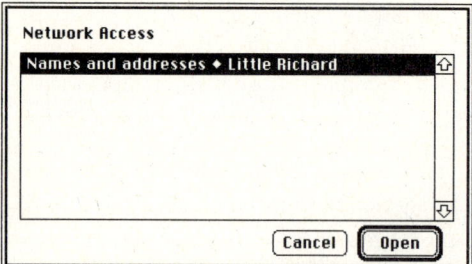

The list does not contain a list of all FileMaker files on Little Richard's hard disk. It only shows the one that is open.

Big Mac's owner clicks on the only file in the list ("Names and addresses"), clicks Open, and "Names and addresses" opens on his screen. It looks like any other FileMaker database, and it acts like any other FileMaker database, except everything is stored on another Mac's disk (in this case, Little Richard's).

If either user adds or deletes records, the other knows it immediately, since the total number of records is always shown on the screen. Big Mac adds a record and Little Richard knows about it. Little Richard deletes a record and Big Mac knows about it.

Other than that, either user can do just about anything he wants to without bothering the other. Big Mac's owner can sort by ZIP code while Little Richard's owner can sort by Last Name. One can look at all the records while the other looks at just a few.

The only trouble comes when Little Richard's owner, who originally opened the database, wants to close the database. In FileMaker's language, Little Richard is the host machine and cannot close the database while others (guests) are connected. When Little Richard's owner tries to close the "Names and addresses" file, he gets the dialog box in figure 13.45.

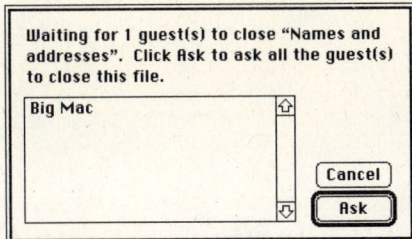

Figure 13.45

Trying to close the database while someone is connected.

Pressing the **Ask** button sends a message to Big Mac, as seen in figure 13.46, and makes Big Mac beep. Little Richard cannot quit FileMaker until Big Mac closes "Names and addresses." This can be annoying. However, it's a small price to pay for sharing a file so effortlessly, and since you can't do anything about it anyway, don't spend time worrying about it. You might spend a moment discussing "network courtesy" with your fellow FileMaker users, though.

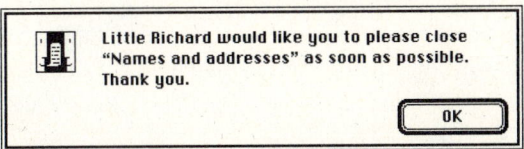

Figure 13.46

Being asked to close a shared file.

Sharing FileMaker databases over a network is almost too good to be true. I say "almost" because it does have limitations. The biggest limitation is you can't use someone else's database unless that person's using it as well—FileMaker lets you connect only to files already opened by their owners. Another limitation involves closing files accessed by others over the network. If you want to quit FileMaker and others are using your file, you've got to hope they respond to your request to close it.

A third limitation is FileMaker only shares FileMaker files. System 7's built-in file sharing lets you share anything you want with anyone you want, and there's no restrictions about who opens what first. However, you'll still have trouble closing a FileMaker database if others connect to it after you opened it.

Limitations and all, FileMaker's networking feature saves you time and headaches. You don't spend time copying files to floppies and walking them down the hall, and you don't have the heartaches of trying to figure out whose file is the "right" one. FileMaker lets your co-workers work on your file, from their Macs. It's a wonderful feature.

Automatic data entry, Scripts, and networking combine to make managing a database as easy as it can be. The data enters itself, the Scripts make the reports, and the kid down the hall does everything else (from his Mac). If it got any easier they wouldn't need you at work at all.

Part III
Mainstream Mac Applications

Buried Treasures

FileMaker's full of quirky shortcuts you'd never figure out for yourself. Here are my favorites.

Flip through Records from the Keyboard

Command-Tab moves you to the next record. Command-Shift-Tab moves you to the previous record.

 Use QuicKeys to make your keyboard's Page Down and Page Up keys do Command-Tab and Command-Shift-Tab. You'll use them all the time.

Change Defaults for Field Formats

FileMaker has a mind of its own when it comes to formatting fields in the Layout mode. Format one field perfectly, then hold the Command key while clicking on that field. When you drag new fields into the layout they'll look like the "perfect" field.

Double-Click to Make Tools Stick

It rhymes! It's true, too: in the Layout mode, it's frustrating that FileMaker automatically selects the pointer tool as soon as you've done anything with another tool. If you want to draw five lines, for example, you'll have to select the line tool five times because every time you've finished one line, FileMaker selects the pointer tool. Double-clicking the line tool keeps it selected until you choose another tool. This works for every tool.

Choose a Default Layout

You can tell FileMaker which layout to use when it first opens a database. In the Layout mode, choose **Layout Options…** from the **Layout** menu, and check the appropriate box in the **Layout Options** dialog box. You can name the layout while you're there. Figure 13.47 shows the **Layout Options** dialog box.

Enter the Current Date Jiffy-Quick

Command-hyphen is the same as typing the date yourself.

570

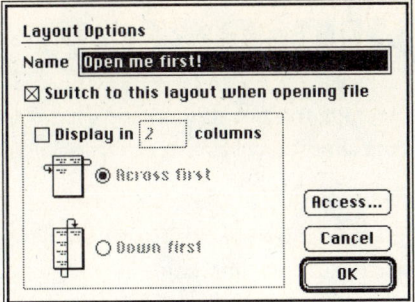

Figure 13.47
Layout Options dialog box.

Do Calculations with Text

FileMaker lets you combine text fields to create other text fields. Figure 13.48 shows the dialog box and the formula used to combine three fields (City, State, and ZIP code) into one perfectly-arranged field. If you've ever struggled trying to get a label or envelope to look good, calculations with text will change your life. (FileMaker's manuals cover this in detail.)

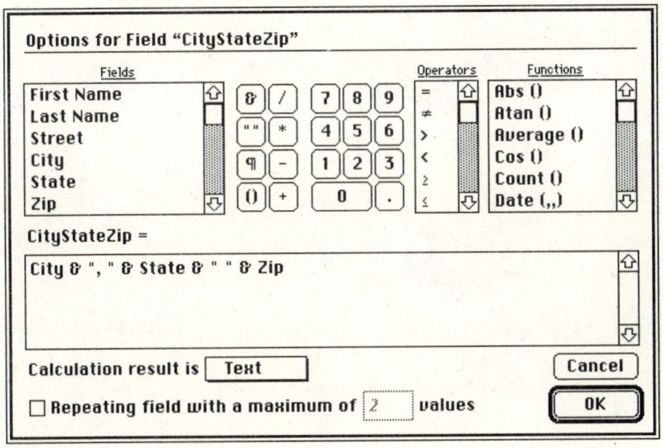

Figure 13.48
Calculation with words.

Add Page Numbers to Layouts

Typing ## with the text tool in the layout mode adds page numbers (determined during printing). You can put the page number anywhere on the layout.

Add the Date to Layouts

Typing // with the text tool in the layout mode adds the current date to a layout. This is not the same as typing the date into a field (you can change the data in a field, and use the data to sort by, or to find by). You can put the date anywhere on the layout.

Part III
Mainstream
Mac Applications

In Conclusion

FileMaker's great at keeping track of stuff. That's what it's meant for. You can slice and dice your data almost anyway you can think of and print it out a million ways.

Sometimes one program can do the work of a whole slew of other applications—and be smaller and simpler, to boot. The next chapter covers those programs that combine several functions into one package: Integrated Programs.

Chapter 14: Integrated Applications

Integrated software is the name given to applications that have more than one built-in software package. The best-selling integrated application for the Mac is Microsoft Works, which combines a word processor, a spreadsheet with graphing, a database, a drawing module, and a communications module in one software program. ClarisWorks has also proved very popular, and breaks new ground through its use of a compound document feature. Integrated software such

In This Chapter

▼ What integrated software is and does

▼ When to use it—and when not to

▼ Product evaluation

▼ When you outgrow the modules

▼ The future of integrated software

Part III
Mainstream Mac Applications

Integrated software—software that David Duke won't use.

Guy Kawasaki

as this is popular with owners of less powerful Macs (1M RAM or less) and with those who need all the different features but cannot pay $200–400 each for five or more separate programs.

Why Use Integrated Software?

Integrated software is targeted to those who need many different functions but are not power users and do not have deep pockets. Integrated packages also appeal to businesspeople who do not have time to learn a more powerful and complex software package. Integrated software also makes sense for users who want to avoid compatibility problems between different programs.

There are countless new ways different software products can have compatibility problems. Problems arise when you use software from different vendors that do not run correctly with each other. Integrated software can circumvent this problem, because instead of running more than one application at a time, you need to run only one.

Note: Integrated software is a good choice for users whose machines do not have much RAM. With integrated software, you do not worry about having enough memory to run Finder with more than one program, hoping "just this once" your Mac will not crash while switching between programs and lose all the data. Although memory is coming down in price, a major RAM upgrade still is not cheap, especially since most users have to pay $50 an hour or more to a dealer to install memory.

Note: PowerBooks are also an ideal application for integrated software. Normally, PowerBooks have limited RAM, and require energy conservation techniques. Integrated software lets you have the convenience of four or five different software applications in the size of a single application.

When Not to Use Integrated Software

Chapter 14
Integrated Applications

When are integrated packages a bad choice? When real power is needed in any particular function, you should look for a stand-alone package that offers a full range of features. After all, if several modules fit into the same space normally occupied by one full-featured application, it only makes sense that some features in the integrated software have to be left out or scaled down.

Product Evaluation

Three new integrated packages entered the marketplace in 1992 to challenge Microsoft Works' dominance in this product area. Symantec offers GreatWorks, Claris offers ClarisWorks, and Beagle Bros. (authors of the world's first integrated package, AppleWorks for the Apple II) introduced BeagleWorks. Late in 1992, WordPerfect purchased BeagleWorks and repackaged the product as WordPerfect Works. The following section describes some of the capabilities of each package so you can compare them.

Microsoft Works

Many users wonder why Microsoft Works sells so well, especially because Works' modules cannot be mistaken for powerhouses when it comes to features, and its interface is not the most attractive of the software packages on the market. However, Works itself is so highly functional that Microsoft proudly advertises it as the "Swiss Army Knife" of software. It serves hundreds of thousands of everyday users well and is ranked as one of the largest selling Macintosh packages of all time!

The word processing module, a boiled-down version of the first version of Microsoft Word, is a good, basic word processor. It leaves out some common word processor features such as Find or Change; allows no special font styles; limits you to only basic formatting commands; allows only one-line

Part III
Mainstream Mac Applications

headers and footers; has limited columns; offers no tables; allows only basic merging with the database module; and has a small spelling checker/dictionary with no thesaurus. Still, it is a far better program than the original MacWrite 1.0 that shipped with the first Macs, and it is effective for such tasks as writing letters.

Works has a drawing module that allows separate and distinct editing of drawings and imported art. Edited drawings then can be transferred into the word processing module. Microsoft has enhanced this drawing module to the point where it is a mini page-layout program that enables you to create and link columns of text and flow type around arcs and lines.

The spreadsheet module offers a range of basic formulas and the capability to make useful charts. It contains 64 built-in functions to analyze statistics, develop forecasts, and manage finances. You can choose from pie, bar, line, and combination charts, and enhance the charts in the drawing module.

The communications module offers many kinds of features for calling bulletin boards or other inter-computer communications via modem. It enables you to transfer information to or from another computer or access online information services while working in another module.

Works' database module is not designed to do much more than maintain address lists, but it does that very well. The database can store up to 60 fields of information in each record, and it enables you to view the data in either forms or lists. All five modules work together, and you can work on up to 14 files at one time (see figure 14.1).

Figure 14.1
All the Works modules are open simultaneously, offering a degree of integration that other applications probably will not achieve for some time.

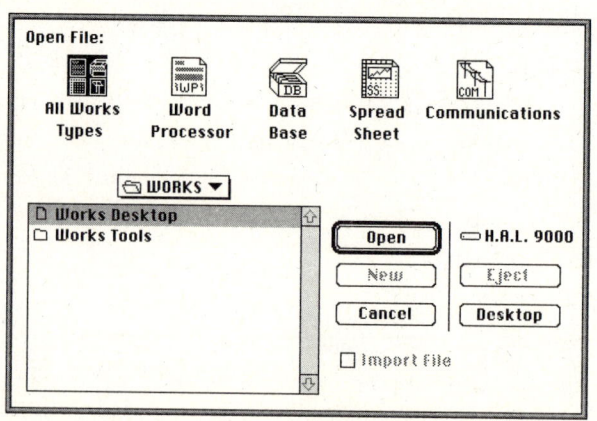

Chapter 14
Integrated Applications

Note: One advantage of a product with a long life span is that support service networks build up around that product, greatly increasing its usefulness. Works enjoys such a network, with user groups, template clearinghouses, dedicated online forums, and so forth. For example, WorksXchange is a template clearinghouse for Microsoft Works run by Heizer Software. It was founded to assist users in finding the exact add-on products they need for Works. Works is also popular with many educational institutions, and several companies sells Works templates aimed at the elementary school market. Such outstanding support services are a major reason Works continues to sell so well. Another is the enormous library of add-on products that has developed over the years.

Works 3.0 shipped in late 1992, several months after Claris released ClarisWorks. While Works 3.0 improved numerous small features of the product, it did not change the overall concept. ClarisWorks stole considerable market share from Microsoft Works, so that now the two products run neck and neck in the marketplace. Expect a major upgrade of Works to appear soon to try to recapture some of its lost market share.

For more information about Microsoft Works, contact Microsoft Corp., One Microsoft Way, Redmond, Washington 98052-6399; (206) 882-8080.

Symantec GreatWorks

GreatWorks is the first new integrated software product to be introduced in several years. It features eight modules: word processing, spreadsheet, database, charting, painting, drawing, outlining, and communications. One of the outstanding features of this program is that all menu commands, tools, and other common features of the different modules work alike. This is dramatically different than Microsoft Works, in which each module is virtually a separate program with its own unique commands and tools (see figure 14.2).

GreatWorks' word processing module offers a full-function word processor with a 100,000-word spelling checker, custom dictionaries, a 660,000-word thesaurus, multiple columns, and five units of measurement. Documents from other word processors are easily imported using XTND translators licensed from Claris (see figure 14.3).

Figure 14.2

You can access GreatWorks' modules easily by clicking on the button of the module you want.

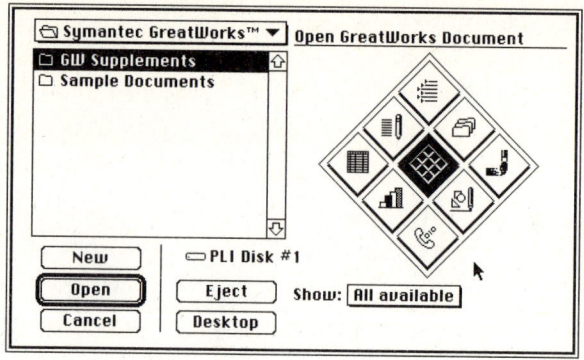

Figure 14.3

Word processing in GreatWorks has a familiar interface and is learned easily.

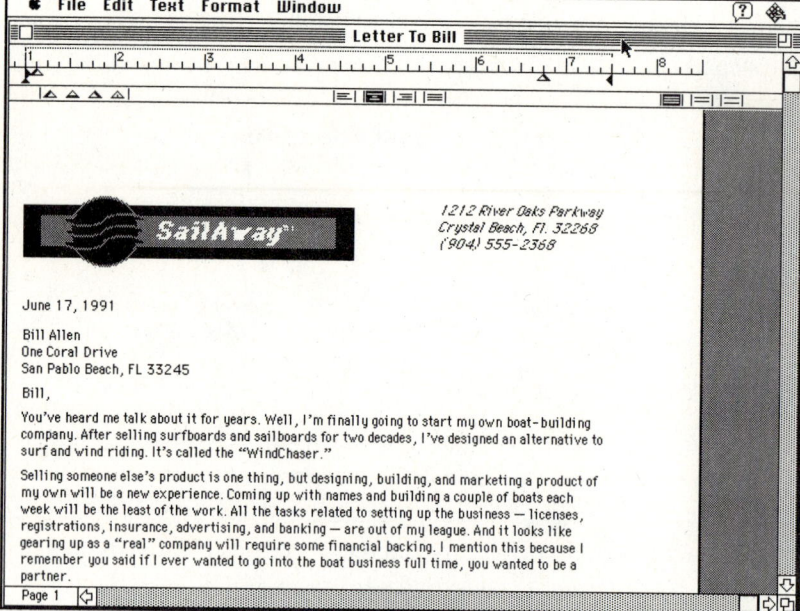

The drawing module produces both object-oriented MacDraw art and the crude but sometimes more flexible MacPaint-type objects (see figure 14.4). Although GreatWorks is not fully System 7 compatible at this writing, users like the interface and compare it favorably to Microsoft Works. GreatWorks got off to an early lead in the new market simply because it was out before the other new products.

For more information about GreatWorks, contact Symantec Corporation, 10201 Torre Avenue, Cupertino, California 95014; (800) 441-7234 or in California (800) 626-8847.

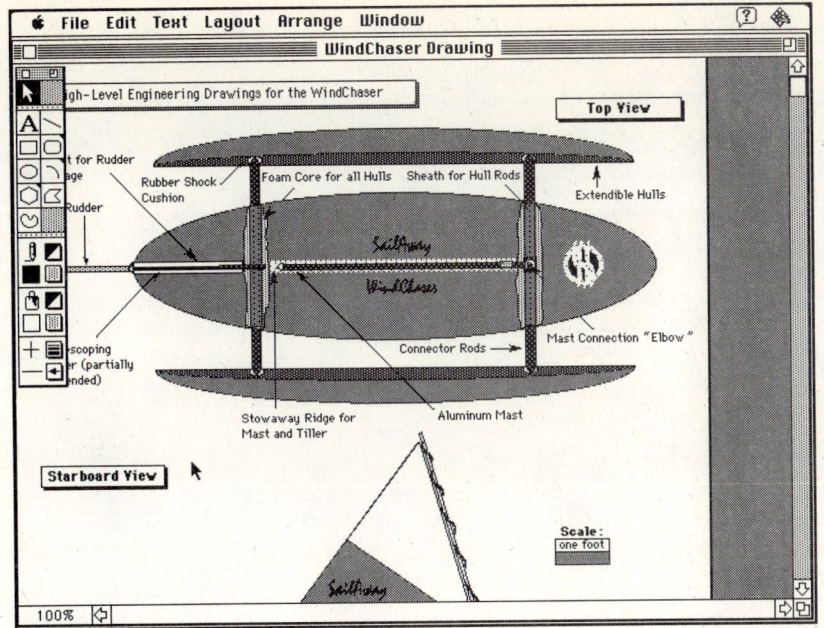

Figure 14.4
GreatWorks' drawing module can create simple or complex works of art.

ClarisWorks

ClarisWorks has five modules, or environments, as Claris prefers to call them. ClarisWorks offers a word processor, a spreadsheet with 3-D charting, a database, communications, and object-oriented drawing capabilities. A spelling checker, 660,000-word thesaurus, and macro-maker are accessible from within each module (see figure 14.5).

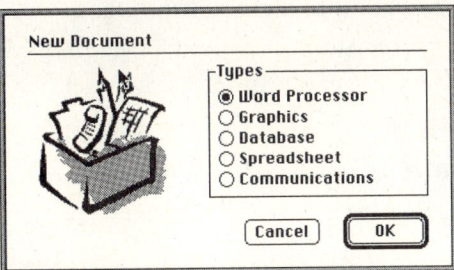

Figure 14.5
ClarisWorks opens its "environment" from this dialog box.

Unlike Microsoft Works and Symantec's GreatWorks, ClarisWorks has a single palette incorporating tools from all the modules that is accessible in every kind of document. You work on a single page and merely change the tools as a new capability is needed on the page. This enables you to easily insert a spreadsheet element into a word processing document and incorporate 3-D

Part III

Mainstream Mac Applications

charts into database documents. Menus are context-sensitive: for example, when you are editing a drawing in a word processing document, the menu bar is automatically redrawn with drawing menus rather than word processing menus. When you return to the word processing mode, the menus automatically change back to word processing. Your view of the page never changes when the modules change; only the menus change. (See figures 13.6 and 13.7.)

Figure 14.6

When you double-click on the bar chart, the chart module instantly appears in ClarisWorks.

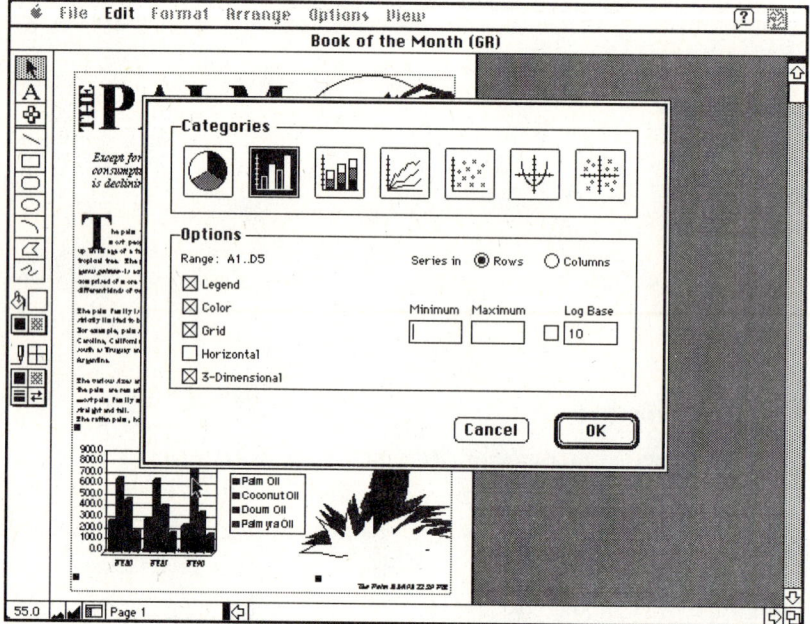

ClarisWorks also has the capability to view the page in WYSIWYG form in customizable views from 3 to 3,200 percent. Upgrading files from ClarisWorks to other Claris products—MacWrite, MacDraw, FileMaker, or Resolve—is virtually seamless.

Version 2.0 of ClarisWorks appeared in early 1993. ClarisWorks has had considerable success at the expense of Microsoft Works.

For more information on ClarisWorks, contact Claris Corp., 5201 Patrick Henry Drive, P.O. Box 58168, Santa Clara, California 95052; (408) 727-8227 (customer relations), (800) 544-8554 (U.S. upgrades), or (800) 334-3535 (U.S. dealers).

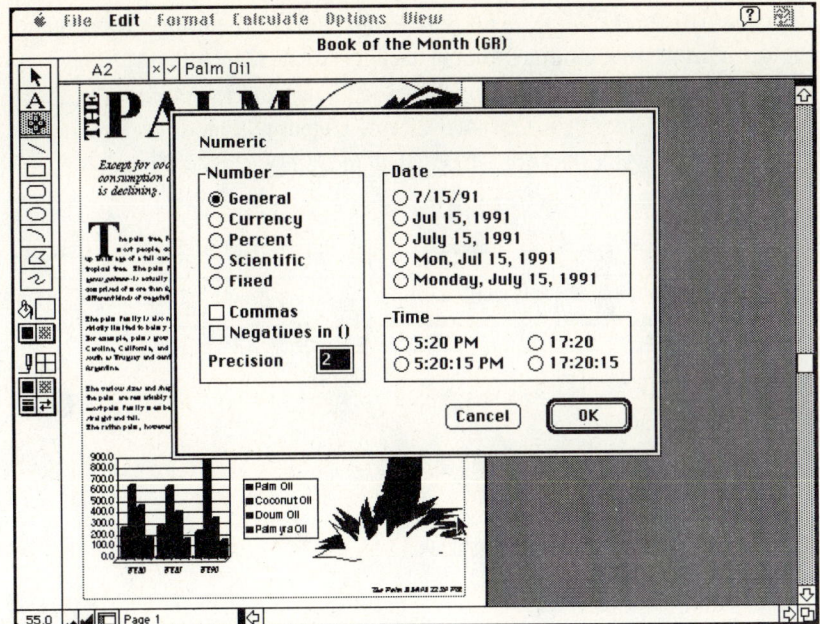

Figure 14.7
Double-clicking on any part of a ClarisWorks document accesses the proper module; only the menus change, not the view.

WordPerfect Works

WordPerfect Works (formally BeagleWorks) offers a standard word processor, spreadsheet, database, draw, paint, communications, graph, macro, spelling checker, and thesaurus modules. These modules are very similar to Microsoft Works—different programs with individual menus and tools. Also like Microsoft Works, you must copy information from one module and paste into another module in WordPerfect Works (see figure 14.8).

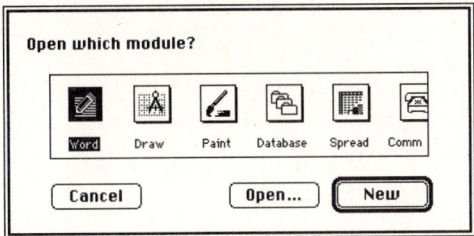

Figure 14.8
You can open any of six modules from the WordPerfect Works dialog box when selecting a new document.

However, the difference between the two programs appears quickly. WordPerfect Works allows a process called *in-context editing*, in which changes are made by double-clicking on the part to edit, and the menus

Part III

Mainstream Mac Applications

change to whatever module is needed; that is, if you are editing a drawing in the word processing module, double-clicking changes the menus to the drawing module's. Similar to ClarisWorks' context-sensitive menus, this feature is not as smooth as ClarisWorks' one-page-for-all-modules interface but is a workable solution not offered at all in GreatWorks or Microsoft Works (see figures 14.9 and 14.10).

Figure 14.9

GreatWorks' word processing module boasts desktop publishing capabilities; all features are accessed through the toolbar just above the window's title bar.

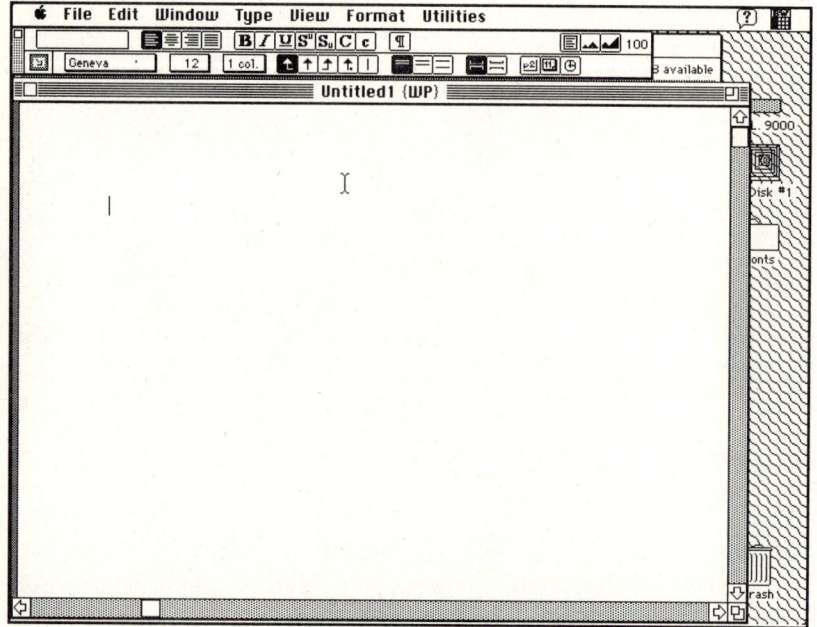

The word processor module also boasts page-layout capabilities. You can lay out multiple-column pages and run text around irregular-shaped objects. The drawing module supports various formats including object-oriented and paint. Importing files created by other programs is also easy with licensing Claris' XTND translators.

WordPerfect Works supports IAC and Balloon Help and provides two-way hot links between its own modules. However, System 7's Publish and Subscribe feature is only one-way for WordPerfect Works at this time.

For more information about WordPerfect Works, contact WordPerfect Corporation, 1555 N. Technology Way, Orem, Utah 84057; (801) 225-5000 or 800-451-5151.

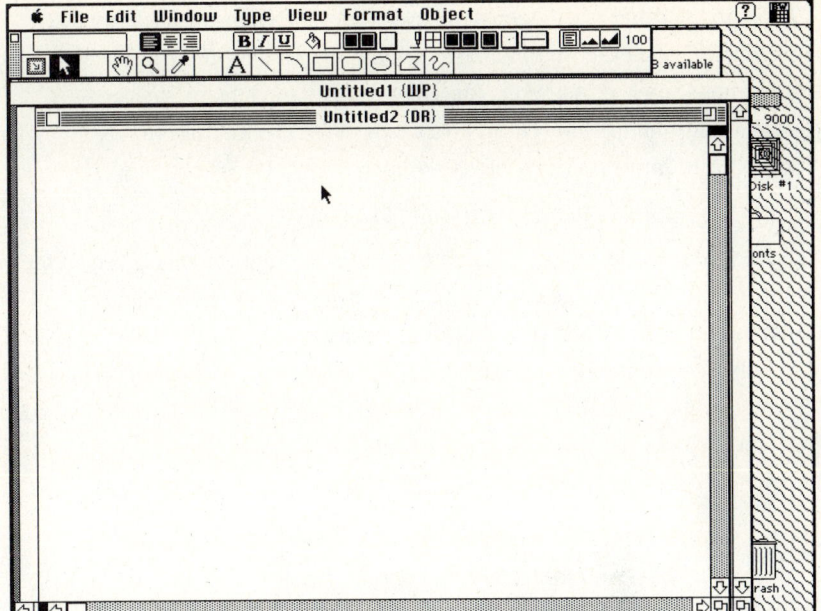

Figure 14.10
Only the tools in the tool bar change when you switch to another module.

What Happens When You Outgrow the Modules?

One of the disadvantages of integrated software is that when you outgrow one module, you outgrow the whole package. Without a clear upgrade migration path, you can become stuck!

Microsoft Works is a good example; there are no easy conversions to other Microsoft products. Data from the word processor and spreadsheet documents can be imported to Word or Excel, but only characters are imported, not formatting. In addition, Word and Excel do not operate at all like corresponding Works modules. Microsoft does not sell a stand-alone communications or database package.

Part III
Mainstream Mac Applications

Claris, on the other hand, seems to have planned for this upward mobility. Individual modules in ClarisWorks resemble their big-brother/big-sister applications, such as MacWrite, MacDraw, and so on. File formats are automatically compatible, because of Claris' XTND technology that is incorporated into every new Claris product.

GreatWorks and WordPerfect Works have less obvious upgrade paths. Symantec doesn't sell any mainstream, stand-alone applications in any of the integrated module categories (Symantec sells SAM, SUM, MORE, and language compilers). WordPerfect sells an outstanding word processor (WordPerfect, of course), but their Works product was not written by Beagle Brothers to be compatible with WordPerfect. In this regard, ClarisWorks and Microsoft Works are at a distinct advantage.

System 7 features such as Publish and Subscribe and Interapplication Communication allow you to achieve a significant amount of interaction between programs from different publishers. I believe this will eventually relegate integrated software packages to use only by new users or those with fairly limited needs. This is not, of course, an insignificant market. But don't buy into integrated software just to get two programs that talk comfortably with one another. Soon, they all will.

Dan Shafer

The Future of Integrated Software

A current trend toward higher degrees of integration in the Macintosh software industry is strongly developing. This integration is accomplished either explicitly in the form of better multimodule applications or implicitly, with a software publisher creating individual software packages that work well together. Claris in particular has used the latter type of integration for all its new products.

WordPerfect Works goes a step further. It supports two-way hot links (where, for example, editing a drawing in a word processing document changes the drawing in the drawing document, and vice versa), allowing for multiple-element editing in a single document.

Summary

Integrated software serves a distinct market, usually new users, users with modest means or needs, machines with low memory, and other special situations—anyone who needs performance without buying more powerful software or hardware to get it. Many users never outgrow an integrated package. Microsoft Works has dominated this market for quite some time, but now faces stiff competition from ClarisWorks, as well as entries such as GreatWorks and the repackaged BeagleWorks, now known as WordPerfect Works. Integrated packages are proving to be a powerful way to link documents and other information.

Chapter 14
Integrated Applications

Too often, integrated software is viewed as something you buy only if you just bought your Macintosh last week or if your finances are so poor that you can't afford anything better. This may have been true at one time, but not anymore. Today's integrated programs have features you couldn't get even in high-end dedicated programs a few years ago.

By the way, in my view, there is no contest as to which integrated package is the best. Get ClarisWorks 2.0. No other package comes close to matching it.

Ted Landau

Chapter 15: Macintosh Games

In other chapters you looked at the Mac's serious functions: databases, accounting, and so forth. But computers and their owners need not be serious all the time. Somewhere inside each of us a child asks, "Can I go out and play now?" The Mac's ability to change itself from a productivity tool into a willing and skillful playmate changes the way you work and play.

In This Chapter

▼ A brief history of computer gaming

▼ Categories of games and how to play them

▼ Software for adults

▼ Toys for the Mac

Part III
Mainstream Mac Applications

Playing games with the Mac also gives you another way to interact with the machine. For the beginner, gaming is a good way to get started in computing. It helps teach the mechanics of Mac use, and the games themselves can be powerful teaching tools.

A Brief History of Computer Gaming

The first computer game came from the Massachusetts Institute of Technology (MIT). To program early computers, including MIT's, you had to punch holes in cards and feed these cards to the computer. The information usually involved strings of numbers that had to be multiplied, divided, or raised to the umpteenth power. The computer did whatever computation was required and printed the numbers. There was not much to see except a teletype machine spitting out reams of paper.

One day, a student decided to hook up an oscilloscope to MIT's computer and watch the images it made on the screen as the computer calculated numbers. The student quickly realized that a blip of light on the screen could be made to move in a particular direction by punching cards for a specific string of numbers. Many midnight computer sessions and the collective efforts of a half-dozen determined programmers later, the game Spacewars was born. Players could tell the computer to "fire" missiles at an alien spaceship. Because both the missiles and alien spacecraft looked like little blips of green light, Spacewars required almost as much imagination to play as it had taken to create it. Still, the computer *screen* or *monitor* had been born; now you could type something on a keyboard and see the results immediately.

Students migrating west from Cambridge to Berkeley brought word of this new use for computers, and eager Berkeley students went to work to create their own game—but on a higher level. Their result was a game called Adventure. Instead of chasing blobs of light, you worked your way through a text scenario which began, "You are standing at the end of a road before a small brick building. Around you is a forest. A small stream flows out of the building and down a gully...."

Chapter 15

Macintosh Games

To complete your adventure, you had to find your way through a cave, pick up treasure, and slay monsters by typing one- or two-word commands such as `go east`, `take keys`, or `fight snake`. The computer recognized only about 50 commands, so if you typed `go right` rather than `go east`, the computer answered: "I do not recognize that." The game was intriguing, and many players spent days figuratively crawling through the underground caverns of its Tolkien-esque landscape.

Note: If you want to experience Adventure, it is still available. Many user groups have it as shareware, and you also can play it on Delphi and CompuServe.

With the advent of computer screens that could show lines and words as well as dots of light, another type of game came along. Hunt the Wumpus was, in some ways, a cross between Adventure and Spacewars. You had to find your way through a maze of rooms firing arrows at the dreaded wumpus, a creature that allegedly smelled so bad you could find it from three rooms away. One of Wumpus' remarkable aspects was that its mazes gave you a sense of being in a 3-D world. Although the objective was to find and shoot the wumpus, this game was less of a shoot 'em up and more of a puzzle. Figure 15.1 shows a screen from a wumpus hunt.

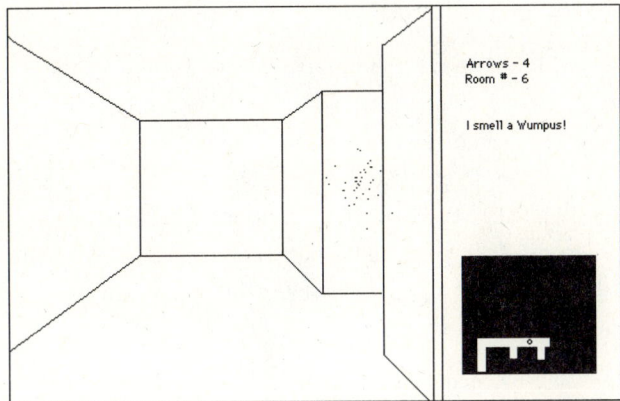

Figure 15.1
Hunt the Wumpus: Do you smell a wumpus?

While people who had access to computers were discovering games like Adventure, Hunt the Wumpus, and Spacewars, others were sitting in their living rooms playing the first actual *video game*. Pong brought onscreen gaming into homes. The game included a box with a small preprogrammed microprocessor. It hooked to your television set and included two "paddle"

589

Part III
Mainstream Mac Applications

controllers, similar to a Mac mouse but with a knob on top. Players twisted the knobs to hit a bouncing blob of light that represented a Ping-Pong ball. The goal was to hit the ball into a position from which your opponent could not hit it back. Pong represented a milestone in many areas; it was the first electronic game, it was the first to simulate an actual game rather than an imaginary one, and it was the first to use a microprocessor. Figure 15.2 shows an artist's rendition of a Pong game in progress.

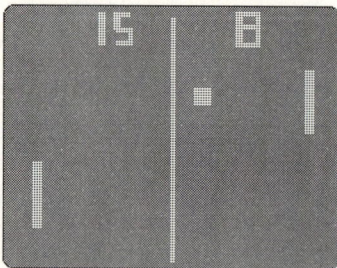

Figure 15.2
Pong was a milestone in the game world.

Pong's success led companies like Atari to realize that there was a serious market for fun. In response, Atari brought out a new video game machine featuring small removable cartridges containing microprocessors. By using different cartridges, you could play new games such as Space Invaders or PacMan. Many Ataris found their way under Christmas trees as this phenomenon swept the country.

Meanwhile, smaller, personal computers were beginning to appear, and their owners wanted to play games as well as balance the checkbook and write letters. As soon as a game appeared on one computer, it quickly was translated to work on others. When the first Macs were introduced, Mac games followed quickly. Today, literally thousands of games are available, either commercially from game publishers such as Sierra Online, Inline Design, Brøderbund, and Maxis, or as shareware sent by the game's creator to an online service or user group.

Because many Mac users tend to be creative, "right-brained" people, they are likely to have many games available at all times. It was probably a Mac user who invented the concept of the "Boss" key, a quick command that hides your game when somebody who should not see you playing comes into the room. Figure 15.3 shows Pipe Dream's Boss key screen.

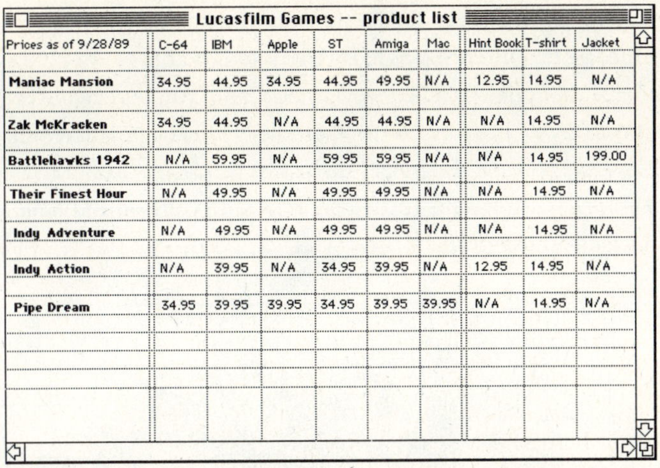

Prices as of 9/28/89	C-64	IBM	Apple	ST	Amiga	Mac	Hint Book	T-shirt	Jacket
Maniac Mansion	34.95	44.95	34.95	44.95	49.95	N/A	12.95	14.95	N/A
Zak McKracken	34.95	44.95	N/A	44.95	44.95	N/A	N/A	14.95	N/A
Battlehawks 1942	N/A	59.95	N/A	59.95	59.95	N/A	N/A	14.95	199.00
Their Finest Hour	N/A	49.95	N/A	49.95	49.95	N/A	N/A	14.95	N/A
Indy Adventure	N/A	49.95	N/A	49.95	49.95	N/A	N/A	14.95	N/A
Indy Action	N/A	39.95	N/A	34.95	39.95	N/A	12.95	14.95	N/A
Pipe Dream	34.95	39.95	39.95	34.95	39.95	39.95	N/A	14.95	N/A

Figure 15.3

Pipe Dream's Boss key screen lets you hide your game from the boss.

The Name of the Game

These four early computer games—Spacewars, Adventure, Wumpus, and Pong—seem hopelessly out-of-date to most computer users now, but they are the archetypes of most of today's popular games. Current Mac games can be divided into four basic categories: *battle*, *adventure*, *puzzle*, and *simulation*.

Battle

The battle category includes the full range of fighting games from Space Invaders and similar zap 'em, nuke 'em, and shoot 'ems to battle scenarios like Patton Strikes Back. (Of course, some of the simulation games also could be classified as battles, such as Bulleye's Fokker Triplane.) Many interesting battle scenarios also are available in shareware or freeware form. In fact, Space Invaders still is available in a shareware version for nostalgia buffs and those too young to remember playing it at the arcade. Check your online service or user group game listings.

Patton Strikes Back, subtitled Battle of the Bulge, is probably the best of the current crop of battle games, both in terms of its graphic implementation and

Part III
Mainstream Mac Applications

historical accuracy. Based on the events of December 16–28, 1944, the game retraces the last major German offensive of World War II. It can be played from either the German or Allied viewpoint. Could you outmaneuver Patton's Third Army and win a victory for the Third Reich? Could you have mustered your troops and crushed the Panzer divisions even faster than the Allied forces? Figure 15.4 shows the battlefield map, with German and American forces engaged at several spots.

Figure 15.4
The symbols represent Allied and German forces.

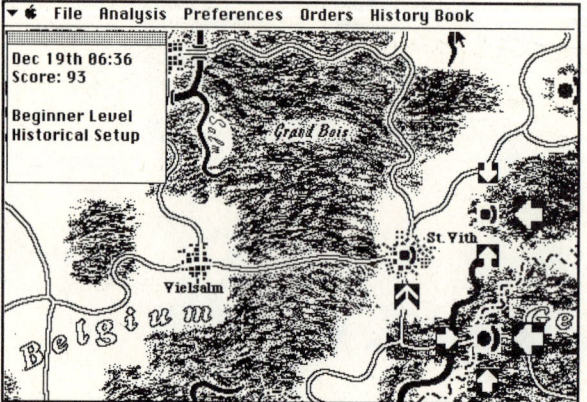

Strategic Conquest, from Delta Tao Software, and RoboSport, from Maxis, are the state of the art in battle simulations. Strategic Conquest is a somewhat different type of battle simulator. Your goal is to capture the world. So, alas, is your opponent's. You must explore and dominate your unknown and dangerous world with armies, fighter planes, bombers, naval support, and all the trappings of conventional warfare. Winning, just as in a real war, requires strategy as well as firepower. You can play against the Mac or, via a network, against another player. Figure 15.5 shows the screen from a game of Strategic Conquest.

RoboSport can also be played through a modem or over an AppleTalk network. This game is actually a set of five different games within the basic scenario. From two to four teams of robots battle each other in games called Survival, Capture the Flag, Treasure Hunt, Hostage, and Baseball. Either you or the Mac can program the robots. Programming is relatively easy; to move the robots, aim, or fire, just point and click. After the first robot skirmish is programmed, the computer generates a "movie replay" of the action. Figure 15.6 shows a scene from Treasure Hunt. After you watch the movie of the first turn, go to the next and program another robot encounter. The game is complicated, but the manual is well-written and easy-to-follow.

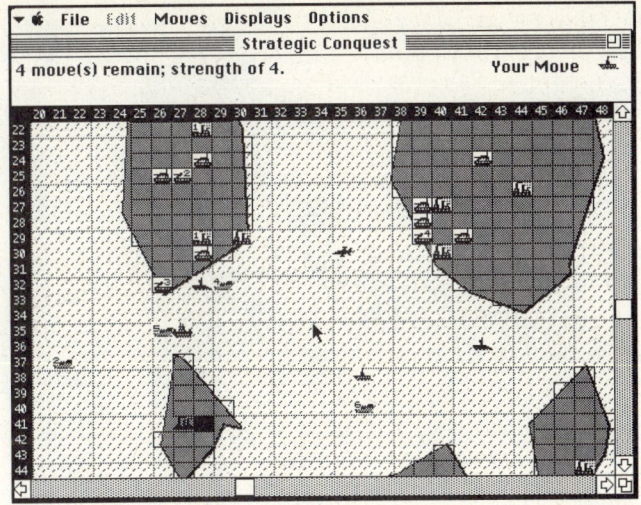

Chapter 15
Macintosh Games

Figure 15.5
Strategic Conquest: Early in the game, create lots of armies and fighter planes. Later on, build bombers and battleships.

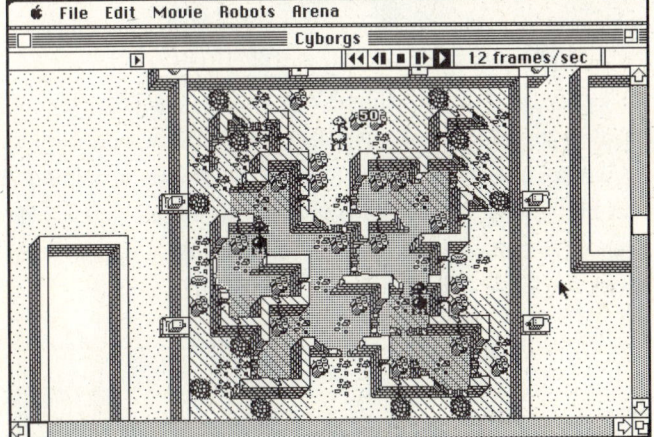

Figure 15.6
You score points in Treasure Hunt by finding the "gold coins" before the other side does.

Dark Castle and Beyond Dark Castle deserve a mention in any battle games listing. Although they have been around since the early days of the Mac, they are compatible with everything from the 512 through the Mac II series. (You will have to play in black and white, though.) Aldus/Silicon Beach still publishes these two best-sellers. Both have similar plots. You must guide Prince Duncan through the castle of the Dark Knight. Along the way, you pick up weapons and potions, and fight off the bats, rats, and other evils along the

Part III

Mainstream Mac Applications

way that would prevent the young hero from engaging in the final battle with the wicked knight. In Beyond Dark Castle, you also must locate and collect five magic orbs to enter the Dark Knight's chambers for the final battle. Figure 15.7 shows a map of the castle.

Figure 15.7

Beyond Dark Castle's orbs are in the catacombs, in the east and west towers, in the guard house in the swamp, and at the edge of the Black Forest.

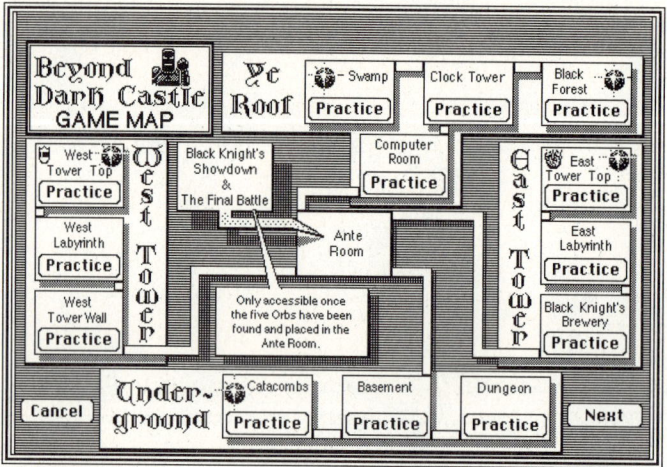

Adventure

Like the original Adventure, which was written for a much larger computer, early Mac adventure games were text-based. Perhaps the most popular of all was Hitchhiker's Guide to the Galaxy. Figure 15.8 shows its opening screen. The game is available in Activision's Lost Treasures of Infocom set, along with the Zork series, Planetfall, and over a dozen other text games. Lost Treasures II includes eleven more adventures in text form.

Figure 15.8

There's an aspirin in the pocket of the dressing gown. Taking it will help.

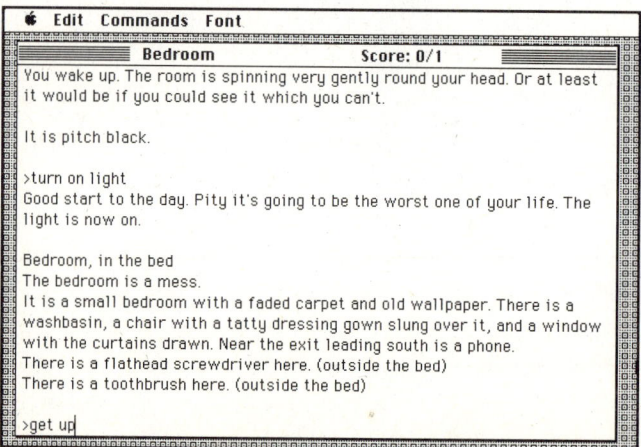

Chapter 15
Macintosh Games

As Hitchhiker Arthur Dent, you must try to save Earth from bulldozers. (It seems the HyperSpace Bypass is to begin construction soon.) Accompanied by your friend, Ford Prefect, you hitch a ride on what turns out to be a Vogon Construction ship. Your journey takes you to plenty of strange places, many of which have tools, bits of fluff, and strange hardware devices like the Sub-Atomic plotter. You must collect all of these items and store them in the "thing your aunt gave you," which is actually a very large shopping bag.

You need to use these collected gadgets (plus a cup of Advanced Tea Substitute) on board the space yacht Heart of Gold to program Eddie, the ship's computer. After you meet the Bugblatter Beast of Traal and bring back the Nutrimat interface, you can get a cup of Real Tea. Eventually, you have the right tool for Marvin the Paranoid Android to repair the broken hatch and let you, Ford, Trillian, and Zaphod Beeblbrox enjoy the pleasures of planet Magrathea. Bulldozers? Earth? Oh well, it was only a minor planet.

Note: Gather all the "fluff" you can. You eventually plant it in the flowerpot you find in the whale's belly. When you eat the fruit from the plant it grows, you dream of the tool Marvin needs to repair the hatch. (The tool varies from game to game.) Consult the Guide about fluff.

More recent adventure games make use of the Mac's capability to combine text with graphics. Sierra Online is known for their carefully crafted adventure games, with elaborate graphics and sound. Quest games are available in several different modes. Track criminals in Police Quest I & II, chase through space in the four games of Space Quest series, and return to the days of knighthood in King's Quest. Be sure to keep the maps and books that come with the games; otherwise, you will be lost. Hint books also are available if you get completely stuck, or you can call Sierra Customer Service at (209) 683-6858 for a prerecorded message that might tell you what you need to know to continue.

Other current adventure games have interesting graphics, especially those on CD-ROM, which take full advantage of the Mac's sound and QuickTime capabilities. ICOM's Sherlock Holmes disks feature over ninety minutes of live action video with elaborately costumed actors and realistic sets. There are now three CDs in the series, each with three adventures. You will interview suspects, look for clues in the newspaper, and bring the guilty party to justice. The Journeyman Project is another fantastic CD-ROM game

Part III
Mainstream Mac Applications

Figure 15.9
You need to replenish your oxygen supply.

with a combination of animation and real actors, plus terrific music. Explore photo-realistic 3-D worlds as you visit the future, and follow a branching storyline. Figure 15.9 illustrates the game's interface.

WARNING! Some games are not suitable for children. Parents, especially those with younger children, are advised to take a good look at the content of the games kids play. If you object to violence, some of the shooting games may be inappropriate. Others are "adults only" due to their subject matter; Sierra's Leisure Suit Larry series is a case in point. It is a graphic adventure, like the previously mentioned quests. This series, however, involves young ladies of dubious virtue, and the graphics are literally *graphic*. Playmate and Virtual Valerie are other commercial games not intended for children. And watch out for adult shareware and adult picture files on some of the online services.

If you want to create your own adventure games, World Builder, from Aldus/Silicon Beach, is an easy way to do so. World Builder lets you design games with the typical Mac look and feel. World Builder games can stand alone; that is, you will not need a copy of World Builder itself to run a game, and there is no restriction on distributing programs you create with it. They can be sold commercially, as Silicon Beach has done with its own World Builder game,

Enchanted Scepters, or game makers can distribute World Builder creations as shareware or freeware. Figure 15.10 shows an interesting World Builder game called the Purpose of Silence. The game creation system allows for graphics editing, sound selection, and animation. The programming language is simple but can do amazing things on a Mac screen. However, as of this writing, it hasn't been upgraded for System 7, and according to Aldus, probably won't be.

Chapter 15
Macintosh Games

Figure 15.10
The Purpose of Silence is one of many shareware World Builder games available.

Puzzles

Although Wumpus was the first computer maze game, the first Mac maze shipped with the original 128K Mac as part of the Mac Guided Tour. "Amazing" taught the new Mac owner how to guide a mouse around the screen, but more important, it proved that a computer could do more than crunch numbers. The game is still available and still challenging, especially at the higher skill levels. Amazing, shown in figure 15.11, runs on any Mac through the SE, but not on the Mac II, and not, alas, with System 7. There are also some clever shareware mazes, including a version of Hunt the Wumpus.

From the beginning, the people at Apple have realized that Mac users like to play. This is why, along with the more functional desk accessories like the notepad and scrapbook, Apple includes Puzzle. (The number puzzle is exactly like the little plastic ones small children enjoy.) Puzzles are a great desk accessory; you can play with them while you wait for a phone call or take a quick break between chapters of your novel.

597

Figure 15.11

Amazing is as difficult today as it was yesterday.

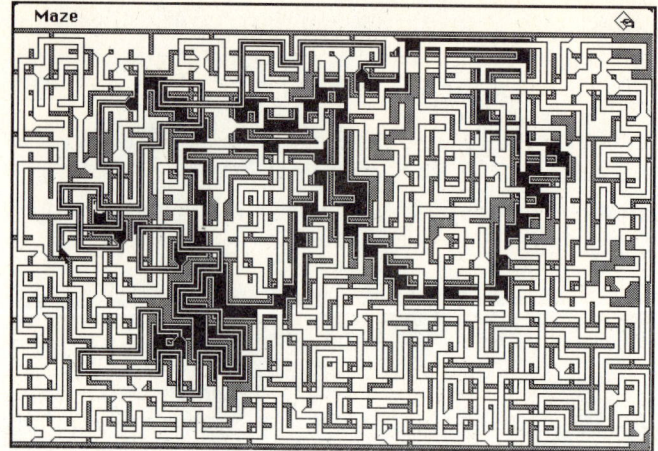

System 7 users can do tricks with the puzzle. If you don't like the picture that's in it, select a different one (in PICT format) and paste it in. It will automatically scale itself to fit.

If there were a prize for the puzzle that has sparked the most imitations, it would go to Tetris. This popular game was developed by two Russian computer enthusiasts, Alexey Pazhitnov and Vadim Gerasimov. The principle is simple. Blocks appear at the top of the screen, and you move them from side to side and rotate them before letting them fall to the bottom of the screen. The object of the game is to complete rows of blocks, which then disappear. Completing a certain number of rows advances the player to a higher level where blocks fall faster. Figure 15.12 shows a Tetris game in progress. The original Tetris also includes a desk accessory (DA) version, perfect for those frustrating times when you are on hold.

Figure 15.12

Tetris: Use the keyboard to move the blocks and flip them before they land.

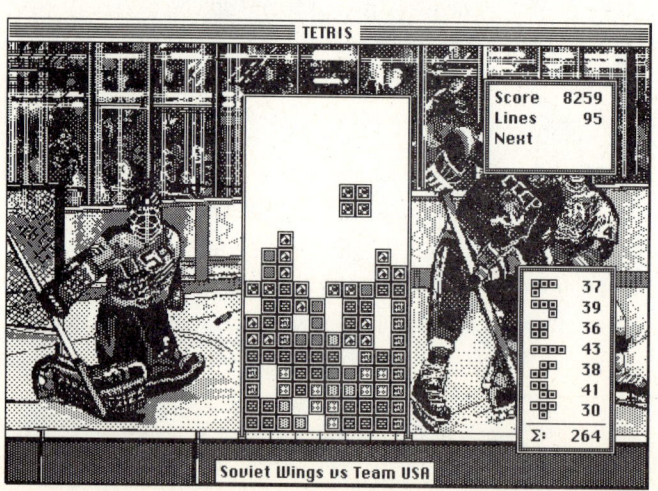

This Russian revolution in computer games continues with four more in the Tris series: Welltris, which takes the concept into a third dimension; Faces, in which you must drop the blocks to form stacks of chins, lips, noses, and so on, in the right order to make faces (see figure 15.13); WordTris, which has you drop letter tiles to spell words; and finally SuperTetris, an improved, full color version of the original, with pictures of the Russian National Circus. All of Spectrum's Tetris games feature beautifully detailed graphics and Russian music.

Chapter 15
Macintosh Games

Figure 15.13
Faces: When the next block falls, the little girl's face will be complete.

Tetris has spawned many shareware imitations, too. The best of the bunch, Jewelbox, is now a commercial game published by Varcon Systems. It deserves special praise, not only for its nice graphics and music, but also for its packaging. Instead of the shelf-hogging cardboard boxes most games come packed in, Jewelbox (like Varcon's other games) comes in a re-useable suede bag.

Tesserae, from Inline Design, is a different kind of block puzzle. The goal is to clear the board of mosaic tiles. To do so, you must flip tiles according to their color or pattern. Tesserae is more beautiful and much easier to play on a color Mac. If you are playing on a black and white monitor, you must mentally combine the symbols—a cross in a circle or a square—which is more difficult than thinking, "Blue and yellow make green." Because the tiles are drawn at random, the puzzle is different every time you play. Figure 15.14 shows a typical Tesserae game.

599

Figure 15.14

Tesserae: Click the tiles and they flip over adjacent ones.

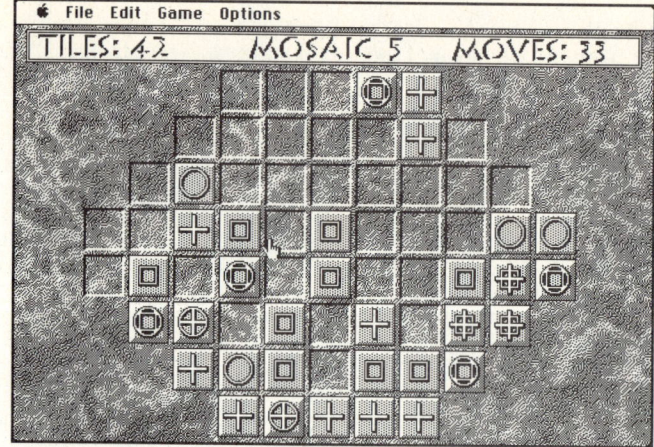

Inline has a number of other popular games in the puzzle category. Darwin's Dilemma features exquisite graphics and an interesting concept. You slide icons around on the screen so that matching icons collide. When they do, they merge and evolve into new icons. Darwin's Dilemma does not teach much about evolution, but it does train you to plan ahead. There are 24 levels of evolution, progressing from amoeba-like blobs to sharks, penguins, trees, unicorns, and the unknown. With version 2.0, you can design your own critters and determine their evolutionary structures. Figure 15.15 shows a game in progress at level 4.

Figure 15.15

Darwin's Dilemma: TeleSwaps let you exchange places with any of the icons.

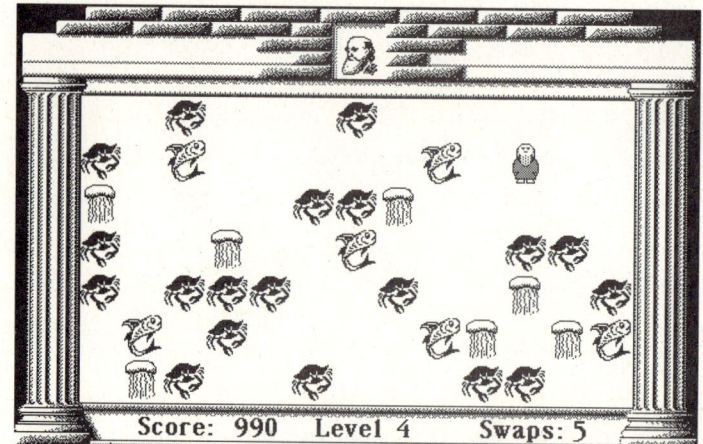

The icons are placed differently each time you begin a game. If you are stuck on a particular level, start over and work your way back up—it may give you an easier placement the next time around. You cannot get past levels 10 and 20 without using several TeleSwaps.

Cliff Johnson may be well-known to many puzzle fans as the creator of Fool's Errand, a fascinating and difficult series of puzzles strung together by a narrative based loosely on real-life tarot cards. Johnson's latest puzzle is 3 in 3, also published by Inline Design. With clever animation, beautiful color (on Mac IIs), and interesting sound effects, 3 in 3 is a tremendous amount of fun. Puzzles range from fairly simple to nearly impossible, with many simply requiring persistence. Figure 15.16 shows one of the easier puzzles.

Chapter 15
Macintosh Games

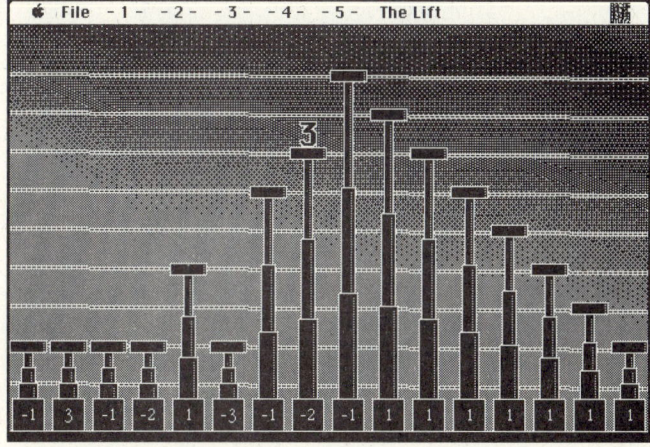

Figure 15.16
3 in 3: The 3 can jump to the next platform only if it is at the same level.

Inline is also the American publisher of several games imported from Europe. Cogito is a Rubik's Cube-like puzzle in which you must move pieces back into a square. Each level has increasingly complex movement patterns. In The Tinies, another European import, the Tinies are little creatures in a space ship. You must direct them back into their sleep pods, otherwise they'll invade Earth. S.C.OUT has you clearing the moon of alien entities, which apparently have taken over an abandoned moon base.

Aqua Blooper Piper, from Casady & Greene, turns you into a plumber. You must join two ends of pipe using pieces that appear on a conveyor belt, while racing against time. At each level, more pieces of pipe are required, and time becomes more critical. A scene from the game is shown in figure 15.17.

Figure 15.17
Aqua Blooper Piper: If the pieces fall off the conveyor belt, you're in trouble.

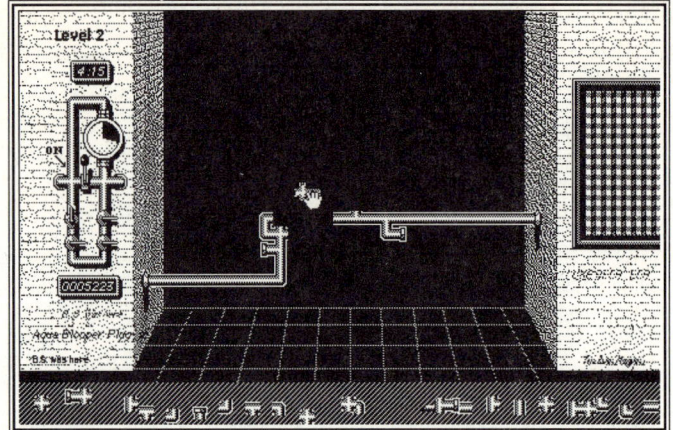

Pipe Dream, from Lucasfilm Games, is also a plumbing race. You must assemble a set of pipes before the "flooz" starts to flow through them. There is a small DA version as well as the full sized game. Pipe Dream also comes with an antitheft device: a 7-inch diameter cardboard wheel you must use to find the secret code to enter before starting a game.

> **Note:** Whenever you open a game package, be sure to save the booklets and other devices that come in it (except for the registration card, which you should mail as soon as possible). These devices and guidebooks are frequently your key to opening and playing the game. If you play many games, you may need a bookshelf for the manuals and a box for the secret decoders, pocket pagers, and other devices or implements.

> **A Closer Look:** Why are these items necessary? Computer game publishers are in the business to make money. As a result, they use various copy-protection schemes to prevent people from "borrowing" the games from friends or coworkers.

Early games did not let you make a backup of a disk or mount the game on your hard drive. Irate game players protested this shortcoming, of course. Today, an increasing number of games ask you to type in information or a code that you find in the manual or on some included decoder before the game will open. While copy protection may be a nuisance, it is unavoidable if the software companies are to remain in business. The first thing you should do when you bring home a new game (or any other piece of software) is to make a backup copy of the disks. This is recommended even if you plan

Chapter 15
Macintosh Games

to install the program on a hard disk. If you have not made a backup or if you use one of the few copy-protected games, there is a chance you could accidentally damage the disk. In this case, you need to check the manual for the game publisher's policy. Most replace defective disks at no charge within the first 90 days. Others do so for a small fee. You need to be able to prove you own the game legitimately, so mail the registration card the day you purchase the game.

Simulations

Remember Walter Mitty, the James Thurber character who imagined himself starring in all sorts of strange situations? Computer simulations bring out the Walter Mitty in everyone. Simulations are programs that let your computer pretend to be something it is not: a Ferrari, a Sopwith Camel, a chess board, or a golf course; or they let you pretend to be something you are not: an Olympic skier, a surgeon, a football coach, or Creator of the Universe.

There are simulated versions of nearly any sport you can name from baseball to billiards. Pong, of course, has the distinction of being the first simulation. The current batch of simulations includes auto racing, flying, and football. The following simulations are a few favorites:

'Vette puts you behind the wheel of a high-powered race car as you thunder through the streets of San Francisco. Scenery, traffic, and pedestrians whiz by, and the driving illusion is quite realistic—if you can imagine steering a car with a mouse and an obscure set of key commands. 'Vette is notable for its scenery. You will recognize many familiar landmarks; Golden Gate Bridge, Coit Tower, the Transamerica building, cable cars, and even street performers add to the fun. Figure 15.18 shows the view from the corner of Grant Avenue, just past the entrance to Chinatown.

MacSki, from XOR, is a clever simulation of downhill racing. You can lay out your own slalom course or use one of the 20 provided and then work on shaving hundredths of a second off your time, just like the real racers do. This game's advantages are many. You do not risk broken bones, unless the mouse gets out of control. You don't need to worry about frostbite. Best of all, you do not need to fit into a spandex ski suit. When you find yourself tensing your hips and shoulders as you steer through a gate, you will agree the illusion is quite good.

Part III
Mainstream Mac Applications

Brøderbund's Playmaker Football lets you design your own plays and is more of a coaching simulation than a game simulation. Its fans give it rave reviews. Figure 15.19 shows the coach's chalkboard as the user sets up a play.

Figure 15.18
'Vette: Chinatown from behind the wheel of your Corvette.

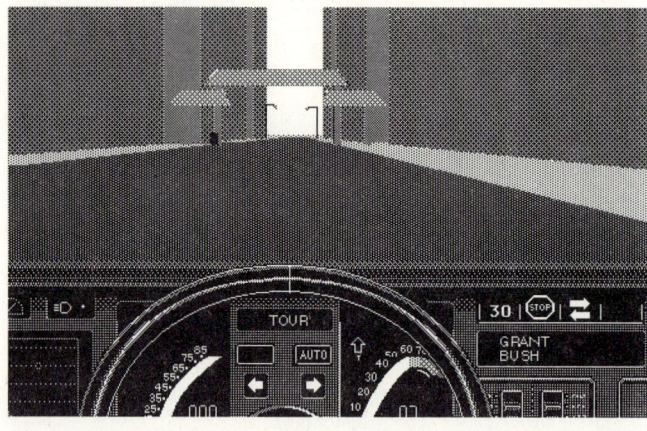

Figure 15.19
Playmaker Football: Will they sack the quarterback?

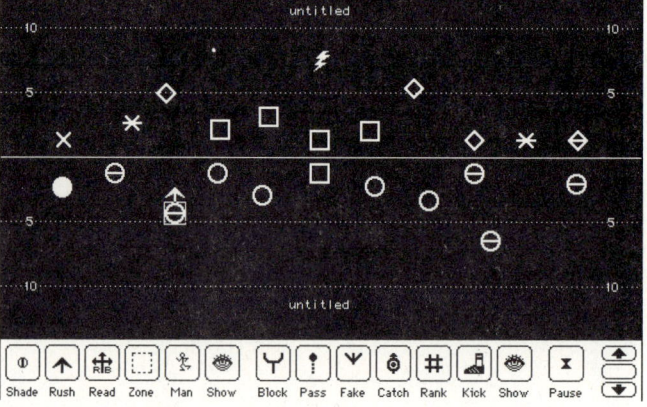

Flight simulators have been around for several years. Microsoft introduced the first Macintosh Flight Simulator in 1986. You could fly either a Cessna 182 or a Learjet 25G. The current version features four different aircraft, 125 airports, and even includes flying lessons as a convenience for novice pilots.

Some pilots say the simulated P-51 Mustang, from Bulleye Software, handles like the real thing. In this simulation, you strafe ground targets and dogfight with Messerschmidt 109s. You can view the action from any of 13 different camera positions, from the control tower, or from other aircraft. You also can bail out, if necessary, and watch the countryside under your parachute as you drift down. Figure 15.20 shows the view from the cockpit as you head toward Paris.

Chapter 15
Macintosh Games

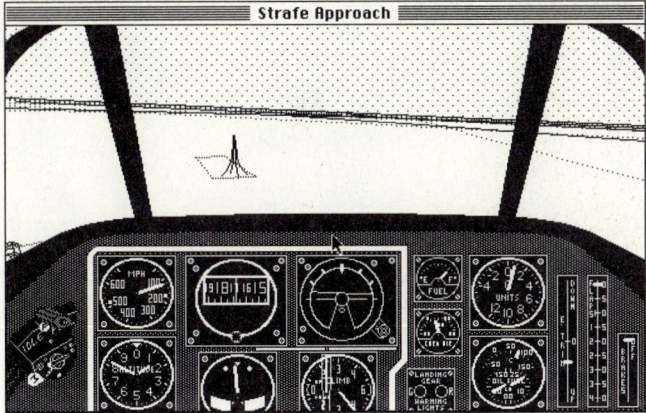

Figure 15.20
Be careful! Don't shoot the Eiffel Tower.

If you're not ready for solo flight, there's always Casady & Greene's Glider. Instead of jets or propeller aircraft, Glider's planes are the paper variety. Fly them through the rooms of a (rather strange) house, catching updrafts from the heating registers, and avoiding obstacles.

Simulations also can be a matter of life and death. Fortunately for the squeamish, Software Toolworks has released its remarkably vivid medical simulation, Life and Death, in black and white. In this simulation, there is an epidemic of appendicitis at Toolworks General Hospital. Scrub up, put on the gloves, pick up the scalpel, and test your skills on patients with stomachaches (Don't forget the anesthetic!). If you are not a smooth operator, you are sent back to medical school for a refresher course. Doctors who complete the appendectomy advance to the upper level of the game, dealing with a ruptured aneurysm. The symptoms and procedures are medically correct, and the art is detailed and accurate (see figure 15.21).

Surgeon 3: The Brain requires even more surgical skill. This game, like Life and Death, was written by a noted surgeon and oncologist. Symptoms and graphics are so real that the product includes a warning not to use the game for diagnosis! Using the latest in medical technology, including CAT scans and MRI, you must diagnose and treat various neurological problems. Some require surgery; others do not. If your treatment is wrong, watch out for the malpractice lawyers!

Figure 15.21

Life and Death lets you test your operating skills in far more detail than the children's game with a similar name.

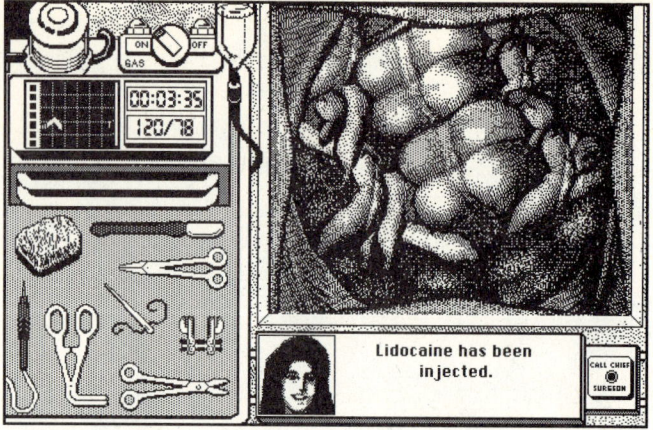

Classifying Moriarty's Revenge is difficult. You could call it a puzzle or a simulation. The object is to decipher clues about the location and appearance of a criminal. You and other players, as members of the Scotland Yard Irregulars, travel around the world pursuing arch villains, bribing informants, and issuing bulletins based on your discoveries. Figure 15.22 shows the scene on your arrival in Toronto. You can visit any of the indicated locations, question witnesses, and attempt to bribe Louie the Lip for information.

Figure 15.22

Moriarty's Revenge: Detective Brainless' travels take him all over the world.

Moriarty's Revenge has more than 1,000 clues and digital sound effects, and increasing levels of difficulty. To help you in your pursuit of Moriarty and his henchpersons, publisher Mysterium Tremendum packs a Pocket World Atlas with the game. Of the several geography-based games on the market, this is the most difficult. Adults will enjoy it, but children and teens may find it frustrating.

The "Sim" series, from Maxis, offers simulations of a different sort. In SimCity, you, as mayor, either build a city from scratch or work with one of the predesigned scenarios. The goal is to keep the citizens (Sims) happy by supplying them with roads, housing, industry, and police and fire protection. Of course, this takes money, so you can adjust the tax rate as necessary. When the taxes get too high, the Sims complain. If enough of them are unhappy, they move out and leave you presiding over a ghost town.

Chapter 15
Macintosh Games

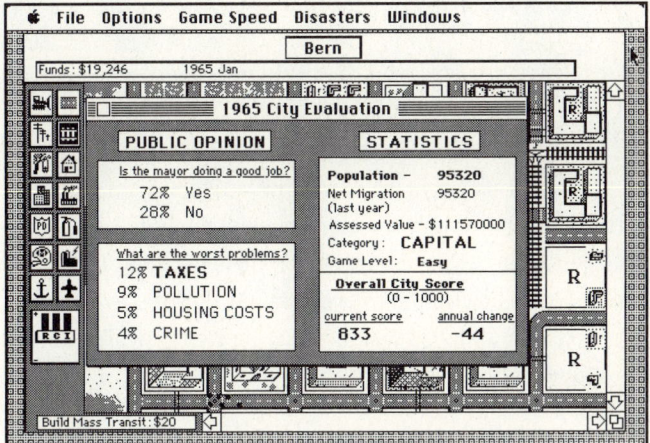

Figure 15.23
SimCity: It's time to lower the taxes.

SimEarth lets you experiment with different paths of evolution. What would the world be like if it were "peopled" by a race of smart squid? What would life be like if the oceans covered 95 percent of the planet? Through a series of procedures, you design a world to your own specifications and then let nature take its course. In SimEarth, you create continents; model them for altitude, terrain, and climate; equip them with *biomes* (ecological environments such as forests and swamps); and then place whatever life forms you like.

Of course, some species will not prosper in some biomes. For example, water-based life-forms will die in the desert. The SimEarth manual gives you a good overview of natural history so you know what effect your actions might have. Evolution occurs when conditions are favorable. Figure 15.24 shows a screen of a planet in poor shape.

Figure 15.24

SimEarth: This planet needs help.

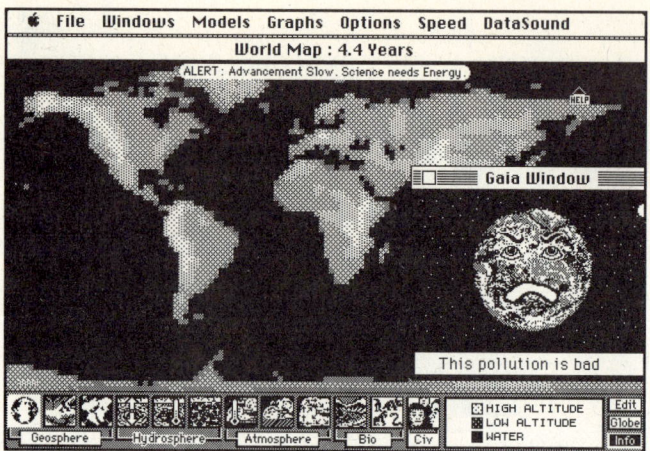

In SimAnt, you are in charge of an ant colony, attempting to take over a suburban backyard and reach your ultimate goal: the house with its ample food supply. In the process, you must manipulate the composition of your anthill (populated by black ants) to overcome obstacles posed by rival red ants, a hungry spider, and, the most devastating enemy of all, human feet. The game designers used a Pulitzer Prize-winning book on ant behavior by two Harvard biologists as a basis for the scenario, making the game educational as well as fun.

SimLife, the newest in the Sim series, lets you experiment with evolution. Design a world and populate it with creatures and plants you create. Change the climate and see what happens to the population. Turn a fruit eater into a grass eater and find out what happens. Add carnivores and watch the population drop. See what happens when a link in the food chain is broken. SimLife is a game, if you choose to make it one. Try to "win" the scenarios by overcoming negative forces to populate the world. Figure 15.25 shows an expanding world. SimLife is also an experimental tool to study the interrelation of species and their environment. As such, it can teach valuable lessons about the need to preserve our ecosystem.

Popular card and board games are also available as computer simulations. You can play go, chess, billiards, card games, or try your luck at casino gambling. BattleChess, from Interplay, is an interesting variation on an old favorite. Instead of moving from square to square as pawns and nobles should, the pieces in this chess game stop and engage in battle, complete with sound effects. Playing BattleChess is a great way to get children

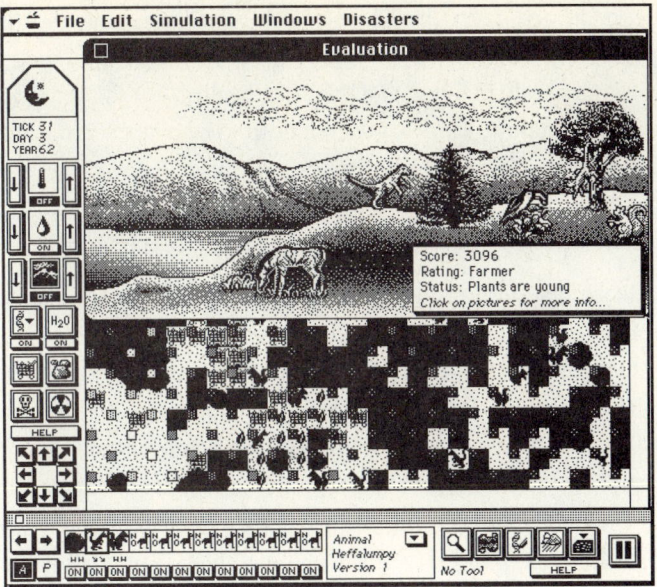

Figure 15.25
SimLife: The plants are growing, the animals reproducing... All's going well.

interested in learning the moves and rules of the game. If you are a serious player, however, you may find yourself switching from the 3-D board, shown in Figure 15.26, to a more traditional point of view. BattleChess is also available on CD-ROM in full color and with even more animation.

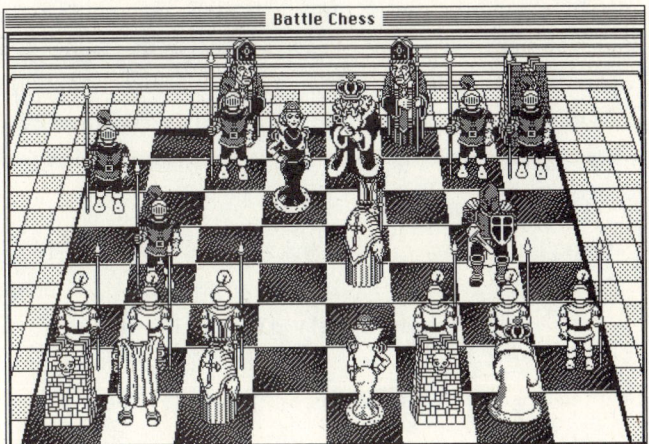

Figure 15.26
BattleChess: These chess pieces come to life on your screen.

Interplay also publishes CheckMate, a more serious chess game that is ranked almost as high as a (human) international master and about twice as strong as an average human player, making it a truly formidable opponent at its higher levels.

Both CheckMate and BattleChess have built-in telecommunications that enable you to play against an opponent by modem. You simply enter your opponent's telephone number, and the game begins after the Mac connects with the other computer (which does not need to be a Mac). You can also play by joining two Macs with a null modem or ImageWriter cable. When play has begun, both players see the moves on the board at the same time, and they can send brief text messages through the **Send Text** option.

Other great simulations include A-Train, a Mac train set that goes far beyond your old Lionel or American Flyer model railroad, and makes you a cross between Casey Jones and John D. Rockefeller. After you develop profitable train routes and schedules for your passengers and freight, go on to become a railroad tycoon. Invest your profits in factories, hotels, shopping centers, and resorts. Play the stock market, and become a billionaire. Pluma's Capitalist Pig is similar in that you're CEO of a company trying to stay in business. Will your company become a multinational corporation, or will tax audits, scandals, or poor business decisions send you into bankruptcy?

WARNING! Can playing games be hazardous? The answer, occasionally, is yes. Some games, particularly arcade-style "twitch" games, are extremely addictive. Players tend to remain frozen in the same position for many minutes at a time, staring intently at the screen and making only small twitching motions with the mouse or typing the same three or four keys repetitively. This leads to stiffness in the hand and wrist and may cause carpal tunnel syndrome, a painful nerve irritation in the wrist. (It also tends to wear out the keyboard.) Watching the action intently can cause eye strain, especially for those who get so involved that they forget to blink.

WARNING! If you find that your eyes or wrists bother you after playing for a while, take frequent breaks. Change position. Place the mouse far back on the table or desktop so your forearm is fully supported. Look away from the screen. Consider investing in an ergonomic mouse or a wrist rest for your keyboard.

Shareware

The games described so far all have been commercial ventures and are relatively expensive (generally in the $25–$50 range), but many low-cost games are available. Some are completely free.

Chapter 15
Macintosh Games

Shareware is a tradition that goes back to the beginning of computing when not many programs were available. Each new piece of software was eagerly shared with anyone who had a computer that could use it. As more computers were built and more people began to use the free software, its authors realized they could earn back some of the time and money it cost them to create and distribute their programs by asking for a few dollars in shareware fees. A typical shareware fee for a game ranges from $5 to $20.

Some shareware games are new concepts. Others are adaptations of existing games, of games from other formats such as Poker and Monopoly, or arcade games such as PacMan, Columns, or Gauntlet. Most shareware creators know they are more likely to collect if the fees are reasonable, and of course, if the game (or other application) is considered worthy of its price. Many are. In fact, a number of shareware games have gone on to find commercial publishers. For example, Diamonds and Jewelbox, both published by Varcon, were originally shareware, as was Inline Design's popular Darwin's Dilemma.

Game publishers look at the bulletin boards regularly. If you design a game for your friends and dream of seeing it on the shelves in your local computer store, releasing it as shareware is a good way to start. Be sure to place a copyright notice on the game to protect yourself, and be sure that your game is not a copy of anyone else's copyrighted material.

WARNING! Bulletin boards, user groups, and online services such as CompuServe and America Online are some of your best sources for shareware games. However, games also may carry computer viruses. Protect yourself by scanning everything you download with a virus detection program such as John Norstad's Disinfectant, which is available as freeware from user groups and online services.

Commercial shareware disks or CD-ROMs are another possible game source. Many companies sell disk libraries of games and other shareware programs. You typically pay about $5 per disk or $30 per CD, but are also responsible for paying the shareware fees to the authors of any programs you actually use.

Note The rule for Shareware: If you use it, pay for it. Remember, if no one pays shareware fees, soon there will be no more shareware.

National Home and School Mac User Group (The GAMER Project)

The National Home & School Mac User Group (NHSMUG), also known as the GAMER Project, is a nonprofit corporation and Apple registered user group with members in more than 20 countries. The group serves the needs of educators, game enthusiasts, and parents introducing their children to computers.

Members of the NHSMUG are mailed 6 issues of the organization's bimonthly disk-based publication, *Home & School Mac*, which features approximately 125 pages of articles and reviews covering educational, game, and children's software. A collection of the best recently released shareware is bundled with each issue.

Members may also access The MacCommonWealth BBS, an information service featuring an easy to use graphic user interface. A library of more than 12,000 files containing virtually every type of Mac program is available for transfer via modem.

> **Note:** For a sample issue of *Home & School Mac*, a membership application, and additional information about their BBS, send $1.00 to: NHSMUG, P. O. Box 640641, Kenner, LA 70064. Membership dues are $18/yr. for US or Canadian residents, $21/yr. for residents of all other countries.

Gaming as a Tool

Educators, psychologists, and physical therapists have found new uses for computer games. Games provide good therapy for many physical and mental disabilities. Because playing to win is part of human nature, games are a great motivational tool. Dyslexia and related spelling difficulties often are helped by playing a computerized version of Hangman or Wheel of Fortune. The game Concentration improves memory, and any of the adventure games can be good practice for those who have difficulties with problem solving.

Sports games are particularly effective for those who need retraining after a stroke or brain injury. These games seem to trigger forgotten words or actions. For example, after a serious automobile accident, one golfer could not remember his wife's or his best friend's names. While still in the hospital, he was introduced to a computer golf simulation. When he set up a scorecard for a group of four players, he automatically entered the names he thought he had forgotten.

Both adults and children often have trouble with eye-to-hand coordination. The traditional therapy for this problem involved watching the end of a pencil as it waved back and forth. It was boring, and most patients did not stick with the therapy long enough to show any improvement. Some therapists now use arcade-style twitch games and simply urge their patients to try for high scores. In many cases, the results have been dramatic.

MacSilliness

There has to be a category for fun things that aren't games, don't teach you anything, and aren't going to change your life. This is the catch-all category for things such as screen savers which fill your screen with a squadron of flying toasters, DAs that create a meltdown, tricks you can play on unsuspecting friends, and our old friend, the Moose.

Talking Moose

In Canada, winter nights can be cold and lonely. It must have been on just such a night that Moose author Steve Hall created this wild critter. The Talking Moose first appeared as shareware back in the mid 1980s. It quickly became one of the best-known and most-beloved applications. Periodically, a little animated moose head appeared in the corner of the screen, spouting such phrases as "I bet other Mac users have more fun than you do." Talking Moose used a phonetic speech translator called MacinTalk and had a built-in vocabulary of dozens of phrases, plus the capability to enable you to insert your own phrases. (See chapter 16, "Sound, Music, and Speech," for an explanation of MacinTalk.) Unfortunately, when System 5 was introduced, the Moose proved incompatible.

Under Baseline Publishing's supervision, careful breeding has produced a new, hardier Moose, able to handle all current Mac systems, including System 7. Figure 15.27 shows the Moose's control panel. You can adjust him to babble almost nonstop or to pop in as shown and surprise you after a long stretch of silence.

Chapter 15
Macintosh Games

Figure 15.27

"Turn on the modem. I want to make a long distance moose call."

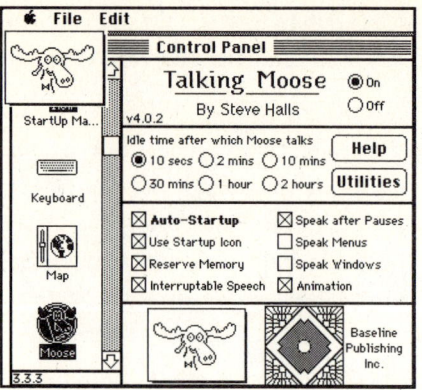

Flying Toasters?

Flying toasters, tropical fish, a little man endlessly cutting the lawn: all these and more are part of Berkeley Systems' screen-saver programs, After Dark and More After Dark. Screen savers are programs that turn themselves on when nothing else is happening to protect your screen from burn-in.

A computer screen is much like a television screen. A chemical phosphor is sprayed on the flat glass at the front end of the tube. When a beam of electrons hits the phosphor, it releases energy. The phosphor glows, creating the image you see. Over-use can exhaust the phosphor, leaving dark spots (called burn-ins or ghosts). You have probably seen these ghosts at a bank's automated teller machine, where the opening message screen may be on for 23 out of 24 hours. The message is so badly burned in you can read it even through the other messages.

Screen savers work by either dimming the screen or keeping something in motion on it so that different bits of phosphor are on at different times. Figure 15.28 shows After Dark's control panel and famous flying toasters. You can tell the screen saver how long to wait for input before taking over.

Insanity

Have you ever gotten really angry at your Mac? Patrick Bertinelli and John Fitzpatrick did. They created a handy CDEV called Insanity. When you hit the correct combination of keys your cursor turns into a "gunsight," so you can blast the screen with your choice of weapons. Choose from a 20 gauge shotgun, BB gun, Uzi, 9mm Glock, or other standard weapon. Show your

Mac what you really think of it by letting loose with the back end of a cow, or a flying seagull. Figure 15.29 shows what happens. There are appropriate sound effects, too. To clean up the mess and get back to work, just hit return.

Chapter 15
Macintosh Games

Figure 15.28
After Dark offers everything from flying toasters to a can of worms.

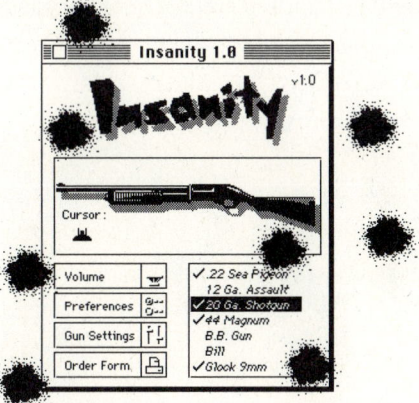

Figure 15.29
"Go ahead. Mac my day..."

More Neat Toys

Other neat Mac toys let you change the Mac's environment. Turn your desktop into a "wall," or a larger, more interesting pattern. Wallpaper, from Thought I Could software, includes hundreds of desktop patterns, plus an editor that enables you to make your own, in up to 128 x 128 pixel squares, and in 256 colors.

615

How about a sound environment? Zounds, by Digital Eclipse, creates fantasy "sound sculptures" which play in the background as you work. Enjoy bird songs, rain on the roof, life on the farm, or any of the dozen included modules, and customize them as you wish.

A look at the software catalog or dealer's shelf will probably reveal more new toys. Mac owners will enjoy.

Summary

The Mac is an ideal game partner — always willing to play and never bored. Mac games may not be as flashy as the Nintendo variety, but you will find many different sports, simulations, puzzles, adventures, and arcade action games to keep you busy. You can find games and toys of all types through your local user group, your online service's libraries, and your dealer's shelf.

No one can say the Mac never cheats—there are a few games in which it probably does. But unlike human players, it does not sulk when it loses and will not gloat when it wins. What else could you want?

Chapter 16: Education on the Mac

As adults have discovered to their delight (and occasional chagrin), children take to computers like ducks to a pond. Children as young as age two can use a mouse, have a wonderful time, and learn the alphabet, numbers, and other concepts in the process. The younger ones, obviously, need some supervision. But as long as the child understands that playing with the keyboard or mouse makes something interesting happen on the screen, he is old enough to begin—after a

In This Chapter

▼ Using games as learning tools

▼ Preschool-to college-level software

▼ Educational software for adults

Part III
Specialized Mac Applications

quick lesson about not eating the mouse or throwing the keyboard at the screen, of course!

Toys That Teach

There are educational and fun programs for children of all ages. Think of them as toys that teach. These programs are not games because they do not keep score. It is not whether you win or lose, as the saying goes, but how you play the game.

The best activities for younger users combine sound and pictures in interesting ways and combine education with fun. The Playroom from Brøderbund has a lot of interesting toys. Figure 16.1 shows the Main screen. Most of the objects in the picture do something when the child clicks on them. For example, the clock shows what Pepper Mouse is doing at various times of day: Clicking on a specific hour reveals Pepper playing in the park, sleeping, or eating his dinner.

Figure 16.1
Brøderbund's Playroom is very well equipped.

One of the important factors in choosing software for younger users is to look for programs that do not insist on following rigid rules. There are no wrong answers in the Playroom. All the Playroom activities encourage creativity and exploration in addition to teaching reading and math skills. Two more fun programs from Brøderbund for preschoolers are McGee and Katie's Farm. Both follow a format similar to the Playroom. Clicking on an object in these programs initiates an activity or an animation.

Brøderbund has taken this concept a step further with its Living Books series on CD-ROM. Lively animation, clever sound effects, cheerful music, and talking characters add to the fun. In Arthur's Teacher Trouble, by Marc Brown, Arthur Aardvark and his classmates prepare for the all-school spelling bee with the help of the infamous Mr. Ratburn, the strictest third grade teacher in school. In Mercer Mayer's delightful Just Grandma and Me, Little Critter and Grandma take a trip to the beach, where they fly a kite, eat hot dogs, and go swimming (see figure 16.2). Clicking on objects in the pictures brings up cute animated sequences with accompanying sounds. This story can be seen and read to the child in English, Japanese, or Spanish. Living Books are good for many hours of fun and learning, and each comes with a printed copy of the book as well, for times when grown-ups monopolize the Mac.

Chapter 16
Education on the Mac

Figure 16.2
Grandma and Little Critter have an exciting day at the beach.

Can You Picture This?

KidPix doesn't fit into a category. It's not a game. It's not "educational." It's fun. KidPix is a simple but astonishingly powerful graphics program aimed at kids of all ages. It even includes a "Small Kid" mode, which hides menu bars and disk icons so your three year-old artist can't accidentally trash your financial records.

Part III
Specialized Mac Applications

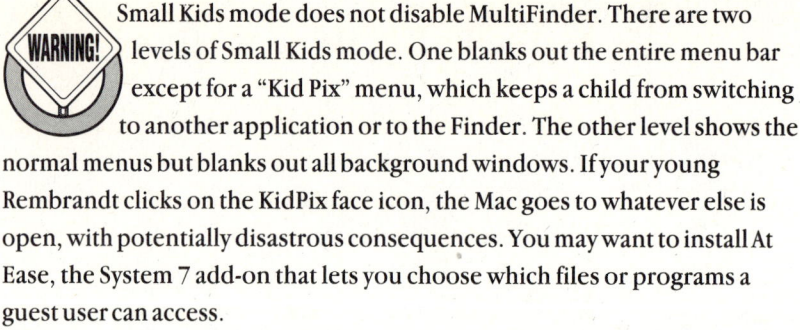

Small Kids mode does not disable MultiFinder. There are two levels of Small Kids mode. One blanks out the entire menu bar except for a "Kid Pix" menu, which keeps a child from switching to another application or to the Finder. The other level shows the normal menus but blanks out all background windows. If your young Rembrandt clicks on the KidPix face icon, the Mac goes to whatever else is open, with potentially disastrous consequences. You may want to install At Ease, the System 7 add-on that lets you choose which files or programs a guest user can access.

KidPix includes tools you probably wish were present in other graphics programs. The pencil is not merely a pencil; it is a variable-width pencil in shades ranging from pale gray to black with 256 colors in between. The rectangle tool works like the one in MacPaint, except you can draw rectangles without black lines around them by simply pressing the Option key. The "wacky brush" has several options from drippy paint and leaky pens to northern lights, swirls, and kaleidoscopes you must see to believe. The drawing in figure 16.3 was created with the tree brush, which generates trees wherever you click. The rest of the scene was drawn in gray pencil. There are various rubber stamps, hidden pictures to discover, and many ways to erase. (One favorite is the firecracker, which erases the entire picture!)

Figure 16.3
KidPix's gray pencil created the snow effect.

KidPix also comes with a dazzling array of sound effects. Whenever you select a tool, you hear its distinctive sound. The pencil scratches, and the Undo key says, "Oh, no!" You also can turn off the sound from the Goodies menu if

Chapter 16
Education on the Mac

you want. If you have a Mac IIsi or a Mac LC, you can take advantage of the computer's built-in microphone, or you can use MacroMind's MacRecorder to record music, special sound effects, a story, or a poem to go with your picture. (See chapter 16, "Sound, Music, and Speech," for more information on MacRecorder.) On color Macs, KidPix runs in full color. You even can print color art on a black and white printer. KidPix automatically translates colors into appropriate grays.

KidPix also opens and works with files created in other graphics programs. You import art through the scrapbook or by opening any file saved in the PICT format. MacDraw and SuperPaint use the PICT format as do many clip art files and digitized photos. (See chapter 6, "Graphics on a Macintosh," for more information.) On a black and white Mac, KidPix is not as colorful but just as much fun.

KidArt and KidPix Companion are two add-ons that increase the fun and learning value of KidPix. KidArt contains sets of backgrounds and additional rubber stamps, on any of (to date) seven different topics, including monsters, sports, and world maps. KidPix Companion includes another 112 rubber stamps, plus an electronic coloring book, more hidden pictures, and "Draw Me's"—recorded voices suggesting ideas for drawings. KidPix Companion also has a "SlideShow" function which lets you play back a series of drawings as a presentation, complete with a narration you record (on appropriate Mac systems) and funny sound and visual effects.

Teaching Tools for Early Grades

With the right software, the Mac is a perfect teacher. It is always ready to go to work and does not mind going over the same problem a dozen times. Finding the right software can take some time, however. Educators and psychologists have done extensive research into learning styles. The bottom line is simple: Some people learn best by seeing, some by hearing, and some by doing. The right software for Josh, who is a visual (seeing) learner, might be the wrong software for his brother Dan, who learns acoustically (hearing), and totally inappropriate for their friend Jennifer, who learns kinesthetically (doing). How do you know your child's learning style? The younger the child, the harder it is to tell. That is why the best software for the younger grades and preschoolers combines aspects of all three.

Two programs that have impressed the experts are Talking Reader Rabbit and Talking Math Rabbit, both from the Learning Company. Both programs are aimed at ages three to seven. Each program includes a selection of different learning games with digitized sounds and clever animation. Reader Rabbit uses about 200 three-letter words and can be used by nonreaders as well as beginning readers. Math Rabbit can be customized to suit various ages from preschool to first grade and beyond. These programs are also available in a special classroom edition, with multiple disks, a teacher's guide suggesting additional activities, blackline masters, and more. Figures 16.4 and 16.5 show activities from Reader Rabbit and Math Rabbit.

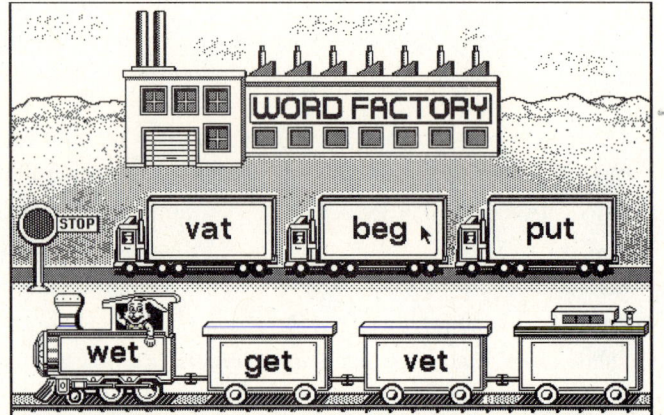

Figure 16.4
Reader Rabbit: Match the short "e" sound.

Math Rabbit contains one odd and inconvenient feature that can cause problems for the uninitiated. When you type two-digit answers to arithmetic problems, you must enter the ones digit before the tens digit. If the answer were 23, you would type 3 and then 2.

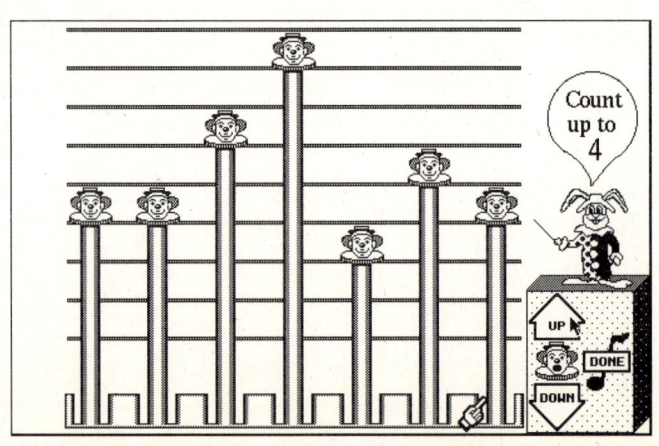

Figure 16.5
Math Rabbit: Each clown sings a different note.

Toucan Press and the Toucan series of story books let kids create their own books, using clip art backgrounds and characters, and typing in the words themselves. Topics range from Dinosaur Days, shown in figure 16.6, to Dracula, Fairy Tales, and Monsters and Make Believe. The word processor included has limited typestyles, but is easy enough for even a beginning writer to master. They can print out their stories, in color or black and white.

Chapter 16
Education on the Mac

Figure 16.6
Dinosaur Days: Choose pictures from menu lists and paste them into the scene.

"By the Time I Get to Phonics"

MECC's Word Munchers game is clever. You move the Muncher on the screen to eat words that match the vowel sound displayed at the top of the grid, as shown in figure 16.7. There are also Muncher-eating Troggles to avoid. The game keeps a running score and an honor roll. This program is intended for use in grades one through five and can be customized to make the matches easier or more difficult. It also speaks a vowel sound if you are confused.

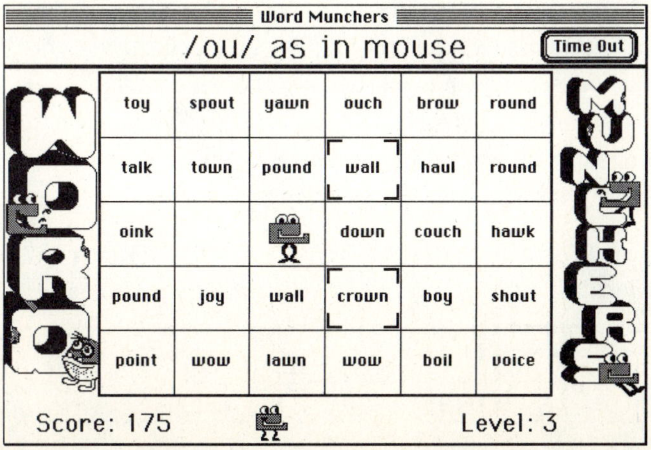

Figure 16.7
Word Munchers combines learning and video games.

623

Part III
Specialized Mac Applications

Math for All Ages

Davidson's Math Blaster Plus is the world's best-selling math program. It is actually fun, and because it is designed for ages 6 to 12, your kids are not going to outgrow it right away. In the four different games, you can define the type of problem to be solved. Clever animations and rewards such as printable certificates for attaining good scores provide a satisfying way to interest children in doing number drills. The Trash Zapper game is shown in figure 16.8. You (or your child) earn missiles by solving problems correctly. There is also a subtle antilittering message in this game. Periodically, the math stops and a selection of space trash floats past the window. You must fire missiles at the trash. You earn a point for each piece you destroy. This program also tracks scores and levels for various players, and you can add more math problems or different kinds of problems to challenge students who have mastered the ones included with the games.

Figure 16.8
A level-one problem in Math Blaster Plus is for younger players.

Davidson's Math Blaster Mystery is designed for slightly older students, ages 10 and up. It teaches more serious math in a more serious way. You must solve word problems step by step, develop a strategy for solving puzzles, decipher codes, and find numbers by reasoning. As with Math Blaster Plus, you can add more problems, keep a record of scores, and print certificates with the name and score. This program is well-conceived and one that could improve anyone's math skills (see figure 16.9).

The Learning Company's Outnumbered! is also fun. The Master of Mischief has invaded the local TV station. You must find out which room he is hiding in by moving through the station and solving various math problems to earn clues. You also must avoid getting zapped by the Live Wire electrical cord;

however, you must zap Telly the Robot to get a set of drill questions. Correct answers give you more pieces of the secret code. The program is designed to provide practice in both number facts and problem-solving skills. The math problems include some that depend on chart or graph interpretation, and others that need analysis. The problems increase in difficulty as your score increases. You also can customize the game to provide only certain types of problems. Sound effects, clever graphics, and familiar classical music themes add to the fun. Figure 16.10 shows a scene from the game.

Chapter 16
Education on the Mac

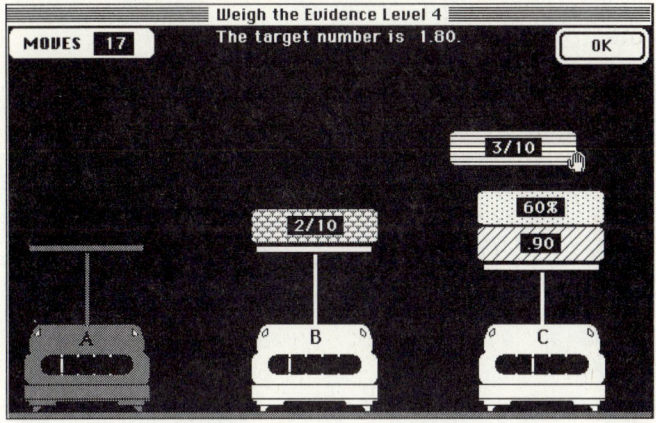

Figure 16.9
Math Blaster Mystery: Move the weights around until you reach the correct total.

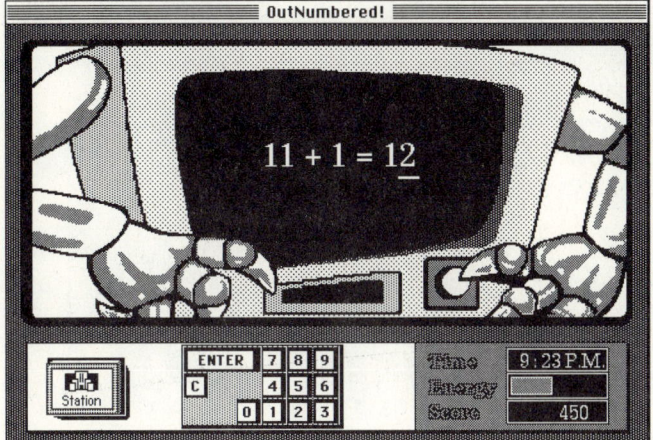

Figure 16.10
Outnumbered!: Telly the Robot drills you in math facts.

Number Munchers, from MECC, drills you in finding multiples, factors, prime numbers, equalities, and inequalities. Its arcade format turns a set of number facts into a fast-paced game, similar to Word Munchers. Password-protected management options enable you to set an appropriate player level or to define certain ranges of numbers and kinds of problems. This program is

Part III
Specialized Mac Applications

intended for grades three through eight and above. You must move around the number grid, munching the right numbers and avoiding the Troggles, who intend to devour the Muncher.

Davidson's Alge-Blaster Plus is a real challenge. There are four learning activities, plus a game that requires graphing slopes and coordinates. If you are not mathematically inclined, you might have trouble with this one. The upper levels are quite difficult. This program would be an excellent review for high school students or the junior high math geniuses. For this age, the print certificate feature probably is unnecessary.

Music Lessons

Adventures in Musicland won't turn your child into another Heifitz or Billy Joel, but it will provide some basic ear training along with a good deal of fun. The package contains four games, with illustrations from the Sir John Tenniel versions of Alice in Wonderland. Most of the games feature sounds that must be matched, so it helps develop a sense of pitch and a memory for sounds. Each game has several different levels of play, making Adventures in Musicland challenging for all ages. The Sound Concentration and Melody Matchup (featuring your choice of trumpeters, bell ringers, or singing cats) games are especially fun (see figure 16.11).

Figure 16.11

Adventures in Musicland: The cats sing notes and the mouse must follow them to win points.

Author, Author

There are various programs to help children (and adults) write better. Probably the best tool for the writer of any age is a simple word processor, such as WriteNow, with a spelling checker. If you have a story in mind, a word processor might be all you need. If not, there are programs that help stir the creative juices. The Once Upon a Time series from Compu-Teach features a total of nine different backgrounds and an assortment of people, animals, and scenery. You assemble a scene and write about it, creating illustrated picture books. The program runs and prints in color if hardware allows. If not, a package of colored pencils is included. Figure 16.12 shows the opening of a story using the Medieval Times backdrop. Although you cannot add your own pictures, you can flip and change the sizes of the pictures provided. You also can use the cast of characters from a different setting. Perhaps the Princess could receive a visit from a spaceman.

The Writing Center, a new program from The Learning Company, is astounding. Use it for reports, letters, and desktop publishing; it includes a library of about 200 different clip art pictures. It is a large program, however, taking up 3200K of hard disk space. Unfortunately, it is impossible to run this program from floppy disks. You can wrap text around your pictures, set several columns per page, and change type sizes and fonts as much as you like, just as you can with an adult program such as PageMaker. The Writing Center, however, is intended for kids. The manual, although long, is written simply and is easy to understand. There are also convenient help messages

Chapter 16
Education on the Mac

Figure 16.12
Once Upon a Time: You decide what happens to the princess and her dog.

Part III
Specialized Mac Applications

Figure 16.13
The Writing Center offers desktop publishing for the younger set.

on a pull-down menu. There is even a library of templates, including a memo form, an award certificate, and so on. Figure 16.13 shows part of a sample document.

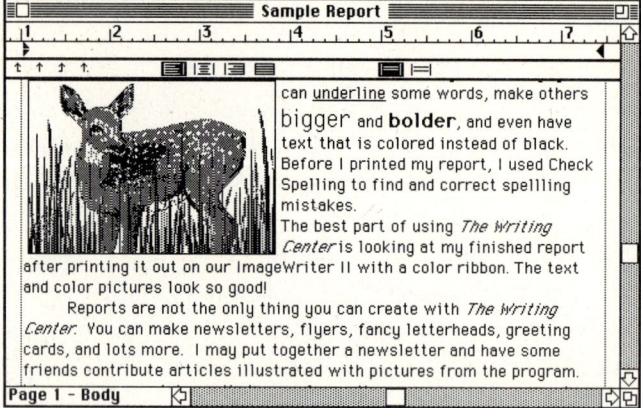

Unlike other desktop publishing templates, the templates in The Writing Center can be changed and destroyed. To prevent this, select each template from the desktop and choose Get Info from the File menu (or type Command-I). When the Get Info dialog box appears for the template, click on the Locked box to put an X in it. The template is now locked so you cannot save a changed version of the template under the same name.

Going Places

Geography is a subject kids used to hate. Of course, that was before Carmen Sandiego. Brøderbund's Carmen Sandiego series is among the all-time best-selling software. There are now six in the series. Carmen has visited Europe, U.S.A., and the world, and even has time-traveled in Where in Time is Carmen Sandiego? The addition of a PBS program has made her into a TV star, too.

The game's plot is simple. Carmen or one of her V.I.L.E. henchpersons has stolen a national treasure. You must track the thief and identify him or her by various clues. Some of the clues require a knowledge of the country to which the thief is heading: "She said she wanted to see the Louvre." Others give clues to identity as well: "The thief had brown hair and changed his money to bahts." Obviously, the historical games require you to identify moments and figures in history. Each of the games also includes an atlas, a world almanac, a guide to the U.S.A., or a desk encyclopedia. Figure 16.14 shows a scene from Where in the World is Carmen Sandiego?

When you visit a country, the screen shows a typical scene from that location and provides a few facts about it. Unfortunately, the facts do not change from one game to the next, so you learn only a little about any one country or state. There is a tendency to ignore these facts when the criminal is close at hand. Nevertheless, Carmen is both good fun and a good introduction to history and geography. True Carmen fans even can purchase watches, shirts, posters, and other artifacts with their heroine's name and face.

Chapter 16
Education on the Mac

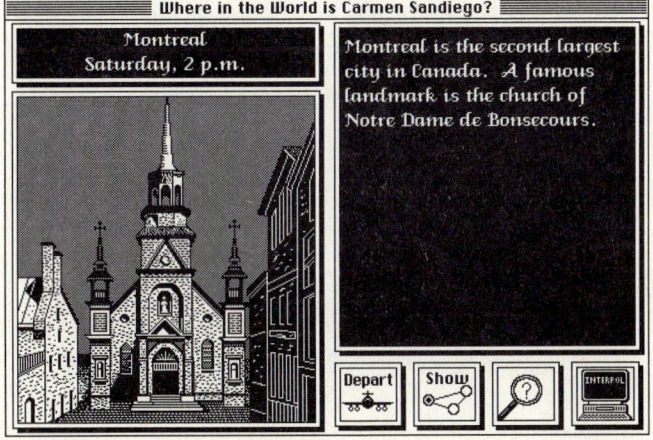

Figure 16.14
Where in the World is Carmen Sandiego? is extremely popular with children.

The Carmen series' success has inspired several other geography games. Compu-Teach's See the U.S.A. has two similar geography games plus a separate quiz disk. The assignment is simple. You need to get from point A to point B by typing the names of the states or state capitals you pass through along the way. There is no scoring method and no competition, so this program is not exactly a game but an activity. The quiz disk contains 60 different 10-question quizzes on everything from state birds to the hometowns of various sports figures. Simply click on the appropriate state to answer the questions. Again, there is no way to keep score. However, there is a question editor that lets you create more quizzes. Perhaps the younger family members would enjoy a quiz with questions such as "Grandma lives in which state?"

Part III
Specialized Mac Applications

Inline Design's Swamp Gas Visits the USA, and Swamp Gas Visits Europe, allow up to four players to compete in a race against time. Disguised as visiting aliens in little U.F.O.s, you and the other players must locate and visit all the places listed on your "mission." Each of you has a different list, but all should require a similar number of moves. The game can accommodate different age levels by asking for cities and landmarks as well as state or country names. During the course of the game, you occasionally are given a Close Encounter quiz question, which you must answer correctly to continue. The questions relate to wherever your spaceship is located. You earn additional points if you answer correctly.

The amount of time remaining appears on the clock at the lower-right corner of the screen. At the end of the game, you can relax by playing a video game in the Alien Arcade on the U.F.O.'s mother ship. The animation is cute, the games are fun, and even grownups who play Swamp Gas may learn some geography facts. Figure 16.15 shows an alien spaceship heading for Luxembourg. The European version includes the current (Spring 1993) names of countries in the former U.S.S.R.

Figure 16.15
Swamp Gas: Click the squares on the map to move along the flight path.

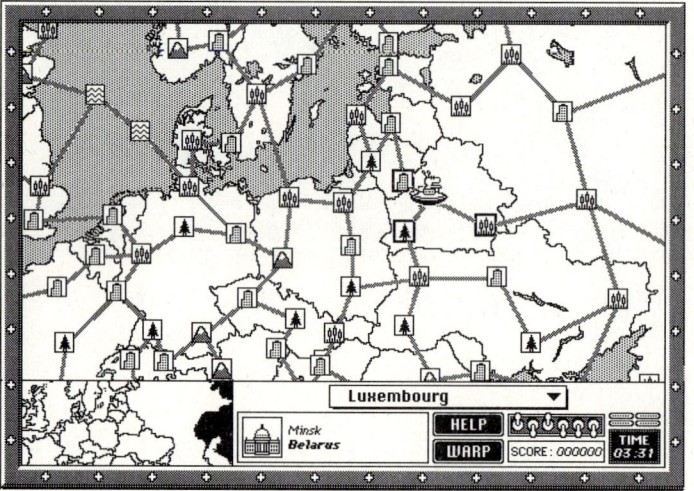

Even if you never have heard of the Oregon Trail game, chances are excellent that your child has played it in school. This computer simulation of a cross-country wagon train trip in 1848 has been around for several years. It was written in 1975 for the MECC Time Share System, a computerized educational network in Minnesota, and then adapted in 1981 for the Apple II computer. It is used in thousands of classrooms throughout the country to give kids in the middle grades a sense of what it was really like to be pioneers.

The hardships the travelers face include broken arms and legs, exhaustion, starvation, snake bites, and broken wagon axles. Each party seems to lose at least one member. You track the travelers' progress on the map and check the guidebook to find out details about landmarks they pass. Figure 16.16 shows a scene midway through the trip.

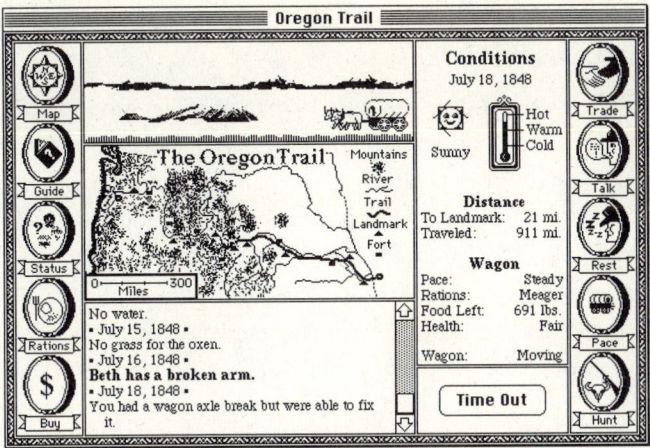

Chapter 16
Education on the Mac

Figure 16.16
Oregon Trail: Players experience pioneer life traveling along the Oregon Trail.

Clicking the icons around the edges of the screen lets you change the travel pace or the amount of food that has been eaten, or to check on your party's health and supply status. You can buy food at settlements along the way, or you can go hunting. The hunt is like an arcade shoot 'em-up. You fire at passing animals and occasionally hit one. The game also teaches an important lesson about conservation. Too much hunting in one place wipes out the animal population.

> **Note** Save your ammunition. The most you can carry back from a hunt is 200 pounds of meat.

The game ends either when disaster strikes and you die along the trail or when you successfully reach the Willamette Valley and join the list of legends who traveled the Oregon Trail and survived. This program may not be as flashy as some, but it is beautifully done and combines real education with fascinating play.

Note: If you own a Mac LC, you also can take advantage of the wealth of educational software available for the Apple IIe or IIc. Because the Apple II is the most popular computer for classroom use, there are hundreds of programs written for it—everything from flash card drills to the economics of a lemonade stand to a layer-by-layer dissection of a frog. By installing the Apple II emulator card in the LC, you can use Apple IIc and Apple IIe programs. Anything written specifically for the Apple IIGS, however, is *not* compatible (many IIGS programs run on a IIe or have IIe versions available).

Go, Go, LOGO

LOGO has been around since the early 1970s and at first was intended to be a simplified programming language for those without an extensive math background. Seymour Papert, an MIT professor, was among the first to suggest that LOGO could teach programming concepts to children. The LOGO language is very powerful and is derived from LISP, the language of artificial intelligence. It is similar in structure to C and Pascal. LOGO lets you define procedures and combine them into programs. For example, LOGO can move a turtle, either a robotic device that crawls on the floor or a cursor on the screen, in patterns you define with commands from the keyboard. The results are immediate and gratifying. Debugging a program is simple because the individual procedures are easy to understand.

Kids enjoy LOGO and, in the process of programming the turtle, learn how to break down an action into steps, write appropriate directions for each step, evaluate the result, and make any necessary changes to reach the goal. There is even a version called LegoLOGO, which you use to build models of objects out of little plastic blocks, attach motors and gears, and program them on the computer. It is available for classroom use on the Apple II and (with the adaptor card) on the Mac LC.

LOGO for the Mac first appeared on the shelves in 1984 but never became very popular, perhaps because relatively few Mac owners are seriously interested in programming. It still is available from the publisher, Terrapin Software, in Portland, Maine.

For High School and Beyond

Chapter 16
Education on the Mac

The educational software we have reviewed so far is definitely "kid stuff." But that doesn't mean you should pack up the computer when your children reach high school age. Aside from the homework help a word processor provides, there are many commercial and shareware programs that can make studying easier and lead to better grades and better understanding of the subject.

Learning Languages on the Mac

Languages are a natural choice for computer learning. A look at a software catalog shows programs to teach everything from Chinese to Hebrew. Penton's VocabuLearn/ce is a combination of interactive HyperCard stacks and audio cassettes in seven different languages, with three levels of each. Although the program does not teach you how to order a croissant and a cup of coffee in Paris or to find the bus stop in Buenos Aires, it does provide an excellent vocabulary review, especially with the cassette playing in the background. Figure 16.17 shows a typical card from the Penton's Level 1 French. Each level includes more than 1,500 useful words and phrases, and you can add your own and create review lists of specific words for test preparation or practice. The cassettes offer a total of three hours of digitally edited sounds. Penton also includes a copy of HyperCard 2.0 with each program. (See chapter 17, "HyperCard and SuperCard," for more information.)

Hyperglot, another language program requiring HyperCard, needs a CD-ROM drive for some of its courses. Others are available on disk. (See chapter 18, "MultiMedia and CD-ROM," for more information.) Their Word Torture vocabulary series runs on disk, and is available in French, Italian, Russian, German, Spanish, and Japanese. The famous Berlitz languages courses also are available on CD-ROM, in your choice of French, Spanish, German, or Italian.

Figure 16.17
VocabuLearn/ce means the Mac can parle français.

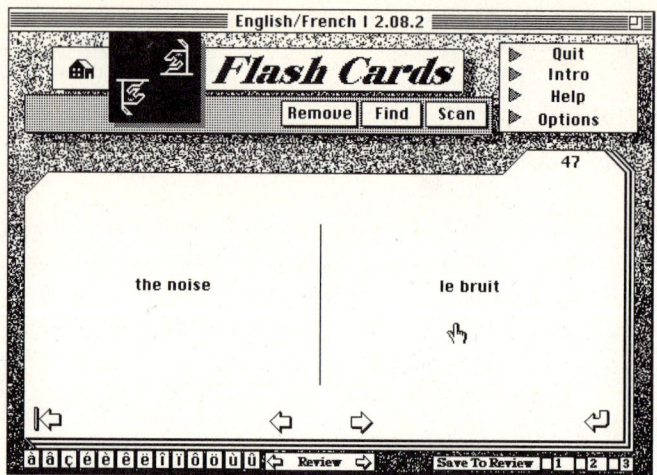

Physics 101

Knowledge Revolution is one software company that lives up to its name. Its Interactive Physics program has revolutionized the way physics is taught. Your computer screen shows what appears to be a standard drawing program. You create circles, squares, rectangles, and free-form polygons and adjust their mass, size, velocity, friction, and elasticity. You also can add dampers, springs, ropes, and constant forces, each fully adjustable.

In just a few seconds, you can set up a basic physics experiment using these tools. For example, if a pendulum swings on your screen, you can draw another pendulum to swing into it, a stack of blocks for the pendulum to knock over, or practically anything else you want to draw. You even can transport your experiment to another planet by adjusting gravity and air resistance. These experiments are not "canned"; instead, they are fully interactive. You simply set up a situation and see what happens. Then change it and see what the differences are!

Figure 16.18 shows Interactive Physics at work. This experiment demonstrates what happens to a passenger not wearing a seat belt when the car hits a solid wall. The program has been set to track and redraw the figure every 32 frames. The initial impact jolts the figure upward. The car rebounds slightly in the next frame, and the victim continues upward, his arm now flung skyward and his head snapped back. Gravity pulls him back down again, and he jackknifes over the edge of the windshield.

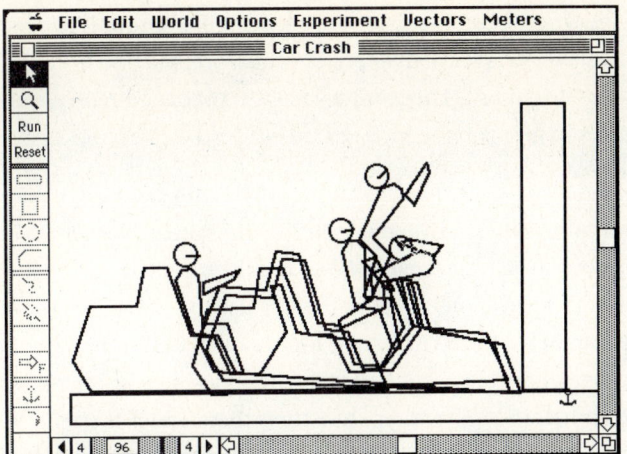

Figure 16.18
Each Interactive Physics experiment is fully interactive.

Of course, the possibilities with this program are endless. It also features numerical readouts and graphing capabilities for 16 different physical properties. The current version also can create QuickTime movies of interactions, so you can import them to other programs. This product is intended for high school or college use, and is even suitable for professional engineers and scientists.

Fun Physics, from the same company, is described as "a Newtonian Erector Set." Essentially, it's a somewhat limited, and much less expensive version of Interactive Physics, more suitable for the science-minded youngster.

Other science programs worth noting include Eco-Adventures. There are two separate adventures: one takes place in a rainforest, the other in an ocean. Visit endangered species and learn about the ecology of the regions. Another worthwhile science program, Voyager II, puts a planetarium in your Mac. View the sky from anywhere in the Solar System, at any time from thousands of nights ago to thousands of nights in the future.

"Testing, 1, 2..."

One of the major events in a teen-ager's life is taking the SAT and similar pre-college tests. The better the score, the better the chance you will be admitted to your school of choice and, in many cases, the better the chance you will receive a scholarship. Because so much depends on good test scores, many parents spend hundreds of dollars on test preparation classes. But does coaching really help? If you ask the people who administer these tests, they say test preparation schools are unnecessary. If you ask the preparation

Part III
Specialized Mac Applications

schools, they practically guarantee your score will improve if you follow their methods. The truth is you can improve your score, but you need not go to special schools to do so. There are several test preparation programs that run on the Mac and give you the tools you need to do well on the SAT or any similar test.

Test preparation can be divided into two distinct areas: the verbal and math skills you need to answer the questions and the test-taking skills you need to recognize which questions to answer and which to ignore. Davidson's Personal Trainer for the SAT comes with a book of exams that use actual questions from previous tests. You begin by taking an assessment test in both math and verbal skills. The computer scores these and lists strengths and areas that need improvement. It also gives scaled scores for math and verbal sections. After these scores are identified, the program determines a training plan, and you begin practicing math and verbal areas that have caused trouble. When you give a wrong answer, the program explains the error, so you can try again. Right answers produce a happy "ta-da" sound. Figure 16.19 shows a screen from the algebra review.

Figure 16.19
Personal Trainer for the SAT helps you improve your weakest academic areas.

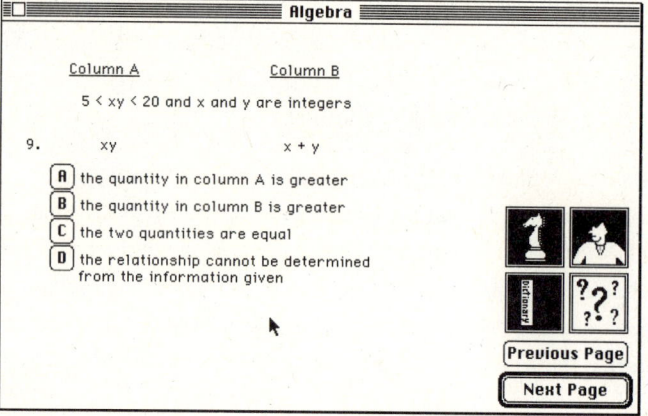

You can check your scores against the average SAT scores required at more than 250 American colleges and universities. The Personal Trainer helps build confidence, as well as vocabulary and math skills. It cannot turn a poor student into a genius overnight, but it is certainly good for scoring some additional points on the test.

Typing

Three or four typing tutor programs are on the market. Mavis Beacon Teaches Typing, from Software Toolworks, is probably the most versatile. It teaches both the standard "Qwerty" keyboard, and the faster Dvorak system. More important for computer users, it lets you set the program to accept a single space after a period, instead of the two spaces traditionally used on typewritten documents. It also lets you enable word wrap and the delete key. The typing lessons are augmented by an arcade game, in which you must correctly type sentences appearing on the screen to keep your race car from being overtaken by another. The program can be customized for typists of all ages.

Chapter 16
Education on the Mac

Figure 16.20
Mavis Beacon Teaches Typing: Clever stories help hold the student's interest.

Adult Education?

If you look through catalogs for adult education courses, you will find a category for self-improvement among cooking classes, language lessons, and aerobic dance instruction. Now, an Oregon company called Visionary Software has brought self-improvement to the computer. These programs may change your life in strange and wondrous ways.

Synchronicity

Imagine a man who makes decisions very simply. He flips a coin and then does a quick mental inventory to see whether he is happy with the result or

Part III
Specialized Mac Applications

Synchronicity is ridiculous! It has no more power than the horoscope published in the daily newspaper (which is to say it has no power at all). It may be amusing to use this program, but to categorize it as "educational" elevates it to a level it does not deserve.

Ted Landau

Figure 16.21
Synchronicity's responses aren't always easy to interpret.

wants to flip it again. His theory is that he knows his decision, at least on some deeper level, but he needs an external event to bring the choice from an unconscious to a conscious level. This person will enjoy Synchronicity.

Synchronicity is a word coined by psychologist Carl Jung to explain the pattern of how things "tend to go together." Jung postulated that events and people coincide in space and time by something more than chance. He suggested related events are interdependent not only with themselves but also with the subjective mental and emotional states of the observer(s). The phenomenon of "meaningful chance," which Jung spent nearly 30 years studying, is directly related to the I Ching, or Book of Changes, a 4,000 year-old mathematically based divination system.

When you open Synchronicity, you are transported to an Oriental garden. After a pleasant and relaxing break, you are invited to enter your question or to focus on it mentally. You are asked to type some keystrokes when you feel the timing is right. This is where meaningful chance enters into the equation. Your timing transforms into a symbol, one of a possible 64 "main" hexagrams from the I Ching. (There are actually 266,144 different reflections possible within the framework.) The hexagram's meaning is explained, as shown in figure 16.21, but it is up to you to interpret it in light of your question or situation. Answers may be saved or printed, and you may ask again when an answer seems unclear.

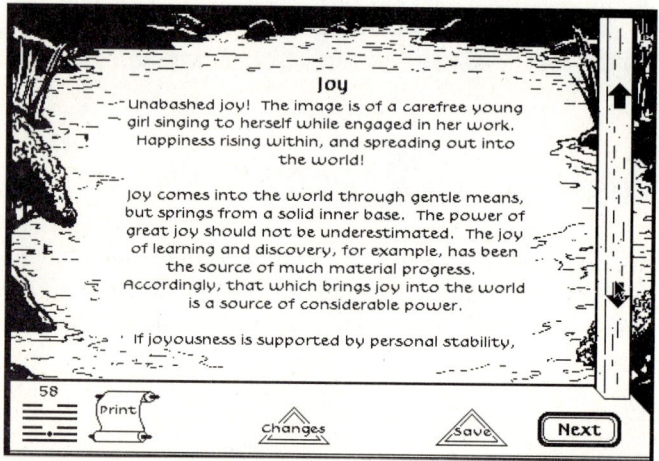

Synchronicity is powerful. If you ask a foolish question, you can expect a foolish answer. If you ask sincerely, you may be surprised and delighted at what you learn.

LifeGuard

Why can't you take a break when you feel like it? You can, but like most people, you probably do not. Psychologists recently coined a term for the "overwork" ethic most people seem to be suffering: existential anhedonism, which is a way to say you have forgotten how to kick off your shoes and relax. A third of the readers in a recent Macworld poll had health problems related to computing: eye and neck strain, wrist problems including carpal tunnel syndrome, backaches, and so on.

LifeGuard reminds you to take a break. You decide how long you want the break to be and how much work time you allow between breaks. It also proposes exercises you can do during these breaks to relieve strain on your arms, neck, wrists, and elsewhere, and it suggests ways to make your work setup more ergonomically suited to your body's demands. Figure 16.22 shows a wrist exercise from the LifeGuard DA. The program has been recommended by occupational health experts as one way to prevent computer hypnosis and its allied problems. But will taking five minutes to stretch slow you down? Experts claim it actually makes you more efficient and productive rather than less productive.

Chapter 16
Education on the Mac

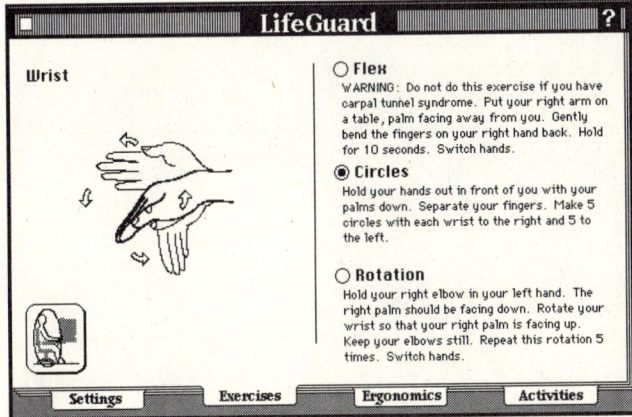

Figure 16.22
When you need a break, LifeGuard makes sure you take one.

MindSet

Do you have a habit you would like to break? Stress to unload? Relationships to strengthen? MindSet helps you reprogram yourself by programming your computer to give you a self-directing, self-supporting message. They are not completely subliminal; the messages flash on the menu bar, so you see them if you watch. However, you probably will not notice them consciously, but you supposedly absorb them unconsciously and find yourself becoming more positive, calmer, more confident, and better able to cope.

Use the message files that come with the program to select specific messages to flash, or write your own. You also can set the frequency and duration of messages and a separate file of quotations, which stays up longer and is meant to be read and enjoyed. Quotation files range from inspirational to downright silly. For example, one menu bar message reads: Oregon, n: Eighty billion gallons of water with no place to go on Saturday night. You can, of course, add new quotes. Figure 16.23 shows some of the possible messages. Does this program actually work? There is every reason to believe it does. If you ever bought anything because you heard a radio commercial or saw an ad for it, you have experienced some of the power of this kind of programming.

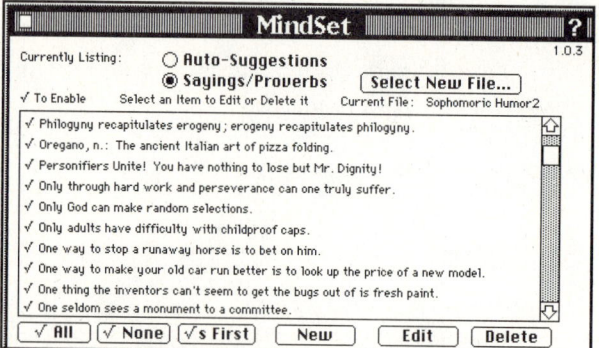

Figure 16.23
MindSet provides a moment of inner reflection or silliness, depending on your choice.

Summary

If going to school were as much fun as learning with the Mac, kids would demand an end to summer vacations. More and more Macs are entering classrooms from preschools on up. The Mac's graphic interface is easy for prereaders to master. Its ability to combine sounds, graphics, and text enhances learning at every level, even once you are out of school. Most of all, the computer is a patient teacher, and one that lets each student move along at an appropriate pace.

Part IV: Specialized Mac Applications

In This Part

Chapter 17: Sound, Music, and Speech

Chapter 18: HyperCard and SuperCard

Chapter 19: Multimedia and CD/ROM

Chapter 20: Macs and the Differently Abled

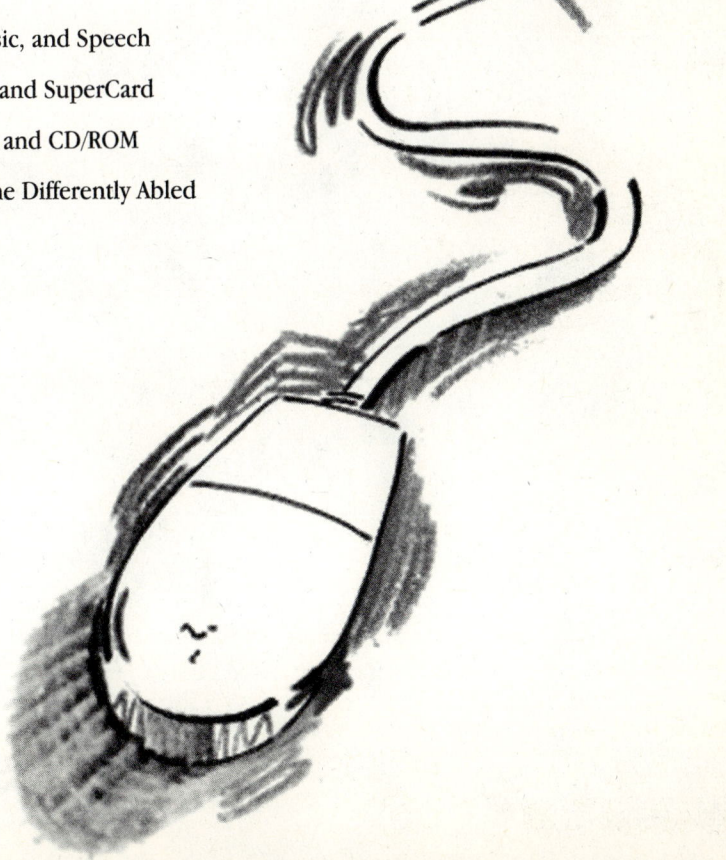

Chapter 17
Sound, Music, and Speech

Turn on the radio, and the hit song you're hearing probably owes a lot to a Mac. Watch a movie, and notice the music under the car chase: a Mac probably helped write that, too. Chances are, another

In This Chapter

▼ Teaching your Mac to talk

▼ Recording and editing sound in a Mac

▼ Getting the most sound on your hard disk

▼ Special effects for presentations and fun

▼ Using your Mac as a voice mail center

Part IV
Specialized Mac Applications

Mac made sure the music climaxed just as the crook's car hit the wall. And a different one might even have created the crash sound itself.

"Mac"ing Beautiful Music

Professional musicians connect their Macs to tens of thousands of dollars worth of digital audio hardware, but you can use any Mac's built-in audio to add sounds to a presentation or to make your computer talk. With a few low-cost gadgets you can turn a Mac into a digital recorder or a complete music workstation.

It's an axiom of modern technology that costs decrease while power increases. This holds true for musical equipment as well as Macintoshes. The home music and sound packages you can get in a computer store today cost only a few hundred dollars, but they're more capable than the best professional systems of a few years ago. Many composers now create their songs on floppy disk, carry the disks and a few favorite synthesizers into a studio, add a few live musicians, and mix their hits.

Most television and film scores—and a surprising amount of dialogue and sound effects—are created in *post-production*: after the cameras are turned off, and usually after the pictures are edited together. Once a scene is edited and polished, music is written to match its mood and pacing. Sounds such as footsteps, clothes rustles, and even some on-camera dialogue replace less-than-ideal location recordings. This is nothing new—*Automatic Dialog Replacement* (ADR) and *Foley*, a system of effects re-recording, were developed in Hollywood decades ago—but modern computers have made these operations standard practice even on low-budget corporate films.

Jukebox Versus Player Piano

Mac music and sound software can be divided into two categories: programs that actually record and manipulate the sound themselves, and those that store and manipulate commands to control other devices. It can be appropriate to use both—sometimes at the same time—depending on what you want to accomplish.

Most music software doesn't make music at all. Sequencers store information about how a synthesizer was played: which keys and pedals are pressed, and

Chapter 17
Sound, Music, and Speech

how hard (if you don't play keyboards, you can use controllers that work like guitars, reed instruments, or drum sets). You can correct mistakes or experiment with the arrangement, and then play everything back to a synthesizer. The notes are stored on MIDI files, which work like player-piano rolls: data represents notes in a song rather than the actual sounds. MIDI is discussed in detail later in this chapter.

Digitizing or *sampling* programs are also used in music, but more commonly in business presentations, hypertext, and film sound design. Programs such as SoundEdit Pro actually record the sound waves on the computer, transforming the Mac into a digital recorder, and then manipulate the sound files with recording studio tricks ranging from echo to pitch-shifting. HyperCard stacks, QuickTime movies, and even games can then become "jukeboxes," playing back the files on command.

The difference between sequencing and sampling is like the difference between MacWrite and MacPaint, the two prototypical Mac programs. *Sequencers* are music word processors that record keystrokes, move groups of them around, and then send them to an output device. *Samplers* are audio painting programs that let you bend and manipulate a sound to the limits of your imagination and ability.

Some software does both. Programs such as Opcode Systems' Studio Vision and OSC's Deck/Metro combination can control both MIDI instruments and a compact disc-quality recording module. Even HyperCard can record and edit an individual sound, or play back simple musical melodies with existing sounds. Playlist editors, like Opcode's Audioshop or the audio module in Adobe Premiere, bridge the gap by letting you play (and to a lesser extent, edit) sequences made up of pieces of audio files on disk or CD-ROM.

Sampled files are usually much larger than sequenced files, just as paint files are usually larger than word-processor ones. The word "Quiet" in 72-point type needs only a few bytes in MacWrite, but a few kilobytes in MacPaint. Similarly, a sixty second digital recording of a song would eat about 10M of disk space, but an equivalent sequence of notes fits in a 4K sequencer file.

Sound Concepts about Recording

The basic Mac digitizers—MacroMind's MacRecorder and newer Macs' built-in recording functions—are nearly foolproof; you can create a usable recording with little or no training. Add a touch of audio knowledge and you can record and edit efficiently, manipulate and refine the sounds quickly, fit them into the smallest possible files, and make sure they are understandable when you play them back. The concepts are not overly technical; if you remember some high school physics, you probably can be recording great sounds in a few minutes!

The Pressure Pitch

All sound is simply variations of air pressure, alternately pushing and pulling your eardrum. If the alternations are quick, you hear a high pitch; if they're slow, you hear a low pitch. Graphing the alterations produces the familiar "sound wave" as shown in figure 17.1. Each push-pull cycle represented in this graph is 1/440th of a second away from the next. Therefore, this particular sound has a *frequency* of 440 *Hertz*, or *440Hz*.

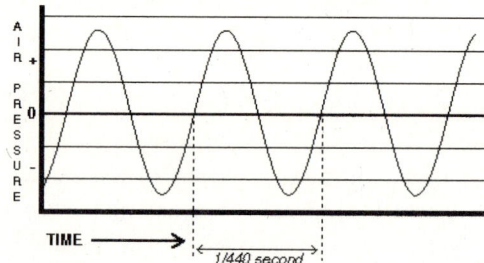

Figure 17.1

The vertical axis describes the pressure, and the horizontal axis shows the variations over time.

This particular frequency, 440Mz, is the A below middle C on a piano; it also happens to be the tuning note an oboe sounds at the beginning of a symphony concert. But even if the piano and oboe are both playing this A (440Hz), nobody mistakes the two instruments. This is because two other factors are involved in creating the sound: *waveform* and *envelope*.

Understanding Waves

Figure 17.1 shows a particularly pure tone, a *sine wave* (so-called because the waves follow a geometric sine function). A sound this pure never occurs in nature: in fact, only electronic test instruments and a few synthesizers can create it. Real-world sounds, like a piano note, can be thought of as many overlaid sine waves, each at its own frequency. The whole mixture repeats at the *fundamental*, or basic frequency. Figure 17.2 shows the same A played on a good piano. Each of the small waves riding on the basic wave is a *harmonic* and has a precise mathematical relationship to the fundamental.

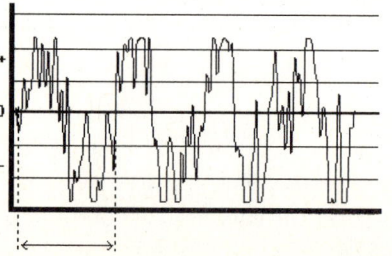

Figure 17.2

A piano plays that same 440Hz sound.

Different combinations of harmonics give sounds qualities we call rich, harsh, bright, and other adjectives. You can experiment with them using Garry Galbreath's public-domain program, Wave Maker, shown in figure 17.3. By moving the sliders in the upper left corner of the window, you can vary harmonics and change the texture of the sound coming out of your Mac's speaker.

Chapter 17
Sound, Music, and Speech

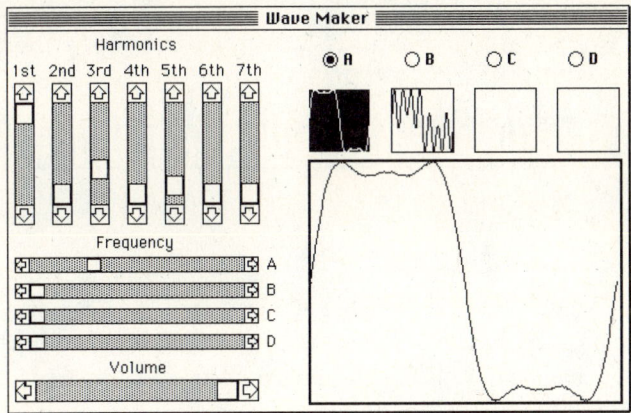

Figure 17.3
Adding harmonics in Wave Maker for a square wave, a particularly rich sound.

A Closer Look Harmonics are named based on the ratio of their frequency to the fundamental. The *second harmonic* is twice the fundamental (or one octave higher). The *third harmonic* is three times higher (a fifth above the octave). The fourth is four times higher (two octaves), and so on. (The *fifth harmonic* is a major third above the octave, so adding the first five harmonics creates a major chord. Music is firmly based in physics.) The fundamental sometimes is called the "first" harmonic because it has a ratio of 1:1 with itself.

A Closer Look The InstrumentMaker in Great Wave's low-cost ConcertWare package lets you adjust any of the first 20 harmonics for very complex waves (see figure 17.4). Click on a harmonic bar in the upper left area of the window, and move the slider control to adjust the ratio of that harmonic. Press Command-C to compute a new wave based on the harmonics you set and display it in the lower right of the window. You can hear the wave at different pitches by clicking the piano keys at the bottom.

Figure 17.4

Creating an oboe in ConcertWare's InstrumentMaker.

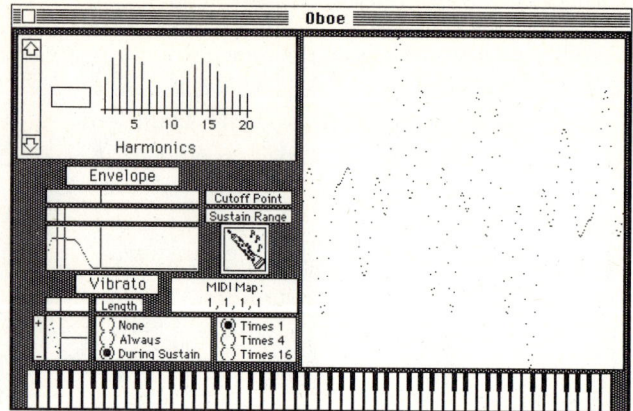

> **Note**
> With ConcertWare, you also can "play" the bottom row of alphabetic keys on your Mac keyboard. The C is a musical C, the V next is a musical D, the B is an E, and so forth. The middle row of keys is equivalent to a piano's black keys, which create sharp and flat notes. Option and Shift take the sound up or down an octave. Other music programs use a similar scheme.

Out of Tune

Some sound waves, such as those from snare drums or spoken words, don't have a pitch. They're still made of alternating positive and negative air pressure, but the alternations don't form a repeating pattern. Instead of having a fundamental frequency, they have a group of fundamentals in a frequency *range*. (The spoken male voice, for example, has a fundamental range between about 100Hz and 600Hz.) Higher harmonics just add "presence" or "brightness." That's why telephones, with a range of only about 3,500Hz, can recognizably carry a friend's voice. If the friend were next to you, you'd hear harmonics up to about 16,000Hz.

> **A Closer Look**
> You can break down all sound waves to their harmonics by a mathematical process, *Fourier analysis*. Even as complex a sound as one produced by an operatic tenor basically is a series of harmonics. A few harmonics in specific frequency ranges, called *formants*, add the sounds we recognize as vowels (which is why your operatic tenor can sing "ooo," "eee," or "aah" on the same note). As few as three formants and a fundamental can synthesize recognizable speech, and scientists at MIT are experimenting with creating the sounds of a full choir and orchestra with just twelve pure tones.

The Envelope, Please

The middle left area of the ConcertWare+'s InstrumentMaker window in figure 17.4 controls the envelope of a sound: how its volume varies over time. If you pluck a violin string pizzacato, the sound is loudest when it starts and then quickly fades. Play the same string legato and the sound gradually builds, stays relatively constant, and then dies when you stop moving the bow. Every sound—musical or not—has an envelope. Many Mac programs enable you to manipulate the envelope by drawing a graph of its volume over time (see figure 17.5).

Chapter 17
Sound, Music, and Speech

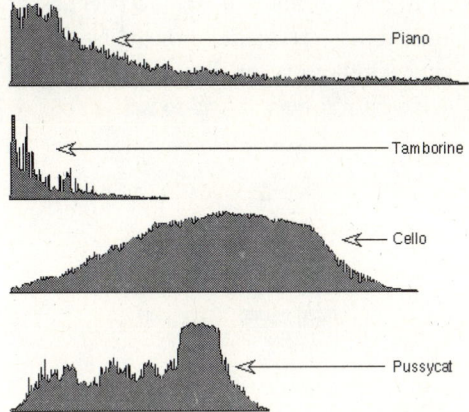

Figure 17.5
An instrument's sound envelope can be graphed, as shown in these examples, to display volume over time.

Recording and Editing in the Mac

There are two main ways to get sound into a Mac: with the digitizing circuits in newer Macs and PowerBooks, or by adding relatively low-cost hardware such as MacroMind's MacRecorder or Articulate Systems' Voice Impact to any Mac. Both work well and are easy to use.

Getting the Best Recording

The key to good recording, on the Mac or in a studio, is getting plenty of the sounds you want and very little of the sounds you don't. Unwanted sounds can come from your Mac's fan or nearby laser printer, but they also can be tiny echoes of your own voice bouncing off nearby walls and furniture. Every room has echoes that detract from intelligibility. The more soft surfaces in

Part IV

Specialized Mac Applications

the room, the less these echoes interfere. That's why radio stations usually pad their walls (not, as you might have thought, to restrain the morning disk jockey).

To get the best voice recording with the fewest echoes and external noises, hold the microphone close to your mouth—no more than three or four inches away. Speak at a normal level, as if you were talking on the phone.

Some noises are a by-product of data compression, or are created by the recording system itself. You'll minimize these noises by recording as loudly as possible, up to the system's maximum. MacRecorder and Voice Impact digitizers have a volume control: adjust it for the highest level that doesn't cause an overload (typical indicators are shown in figure 17.6). New Mac built-in circuits don't have a volume control, so adjust your voice instead.

Figure 17.6
Overload warnings in typical Mac recording programs.

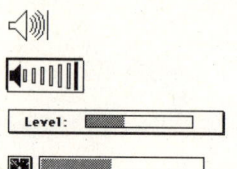

Digital recording circuits in the Mac have a hard time with overloads. Any sound that exceeds the system limit by even a small amount will be badly distorted or crackled. This is the opposite of most home and professional tape recorders, which accept moderate overloads with only slight distortion.

Apple Microphone Tips

The microphone included with newer Macs plugs into the microphone icon jack on the back of the system unit. That part's easy. The hard part is figuring out where to talk: the rubber shock-mounting pad on the back of Apple's microphone looks more official than the little hole where the sound should go in. Figure 17.7 shows the icon and proper side to talk into.

To actually start recording, open the Sound control panel. Make sure a microphone is selected in the bottom of the window, and click **Add...** to get the palette shown on the bottom of figure 17.8. Its buttons work like tape recorder controls. After you've recorded, click **Save** to install the sound in your system and give it a name. If you want the sound to be part of other programs, you can move it with most sound editing programs or with ResEdit. Once you've selected a microphone in this control panel, you also can record by clicking the appropriate button on third-party sound programs like SoundEdit and Audioshop.

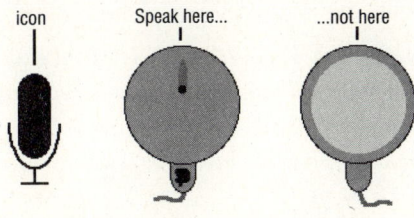

Chapter 17
Sound, Music, and Speech

Figure 17.7
Macintosh input icon and microphone. Speak into the side with the tiny hole, not the side that looks like you should be speaking into it.

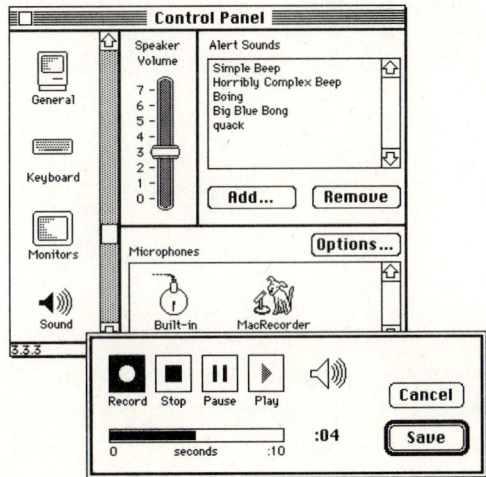

Figure 17.8
Sound control panel and recording palette.

Some tips on recording:

▼ You can re-record as many times as you want until you're happy with the sound.

▼ Start your sound as soon as you click Record. Any pauses will make the sound seem sloppy—it won't start when you want it to. If necessary, use a third-party editing utility to clean up the front of the sound.

▼ HyperCard's Audio Palette lets you record, copy, edit, and move sounds easily. Unfortunately, it is no longer distributed (see chapter 18, "HyperCard and SuperCard").

Part IV
Specialized Mac Applications

▼ Apple gives you a stick-on microphone holder for the side of your monitor. Don't leave the mike in it while you record; it will be too far from the sound source and may pick up vibrations from the computer.

▼ Apple also gives you a little clip to hold the mike on your lapel—exactly the wrong position for your voice, but just right for recording a short, very close friend.

You can connect a CD player, tape recorder, or synthesizer to Apple's microphone input *but only with an adapter cable supplied by Apple*. Make sure the adapter has a microphone icon (see figure 17.9). Plug the small end into the microphone jack and a line-level signal into the RCA jacks on the large end.

Figure 17.9
Adapter for connecting CD players or tape recorders to a Macintosh.

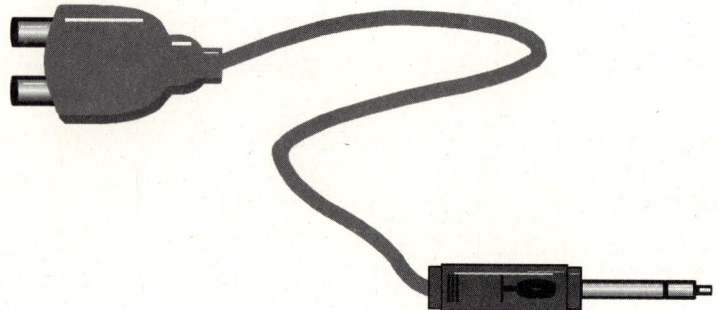

Don't plug anything other than the Apple microphone or Apple's adapter cable into the microphone jack. Apple uses a jack that looks like a standard microphone or headphone connection but is wired very differently. If you plug a third-party mike or hi-fi cable into the jack, you may damage the computer. If you plug a pair of stereo headphones into the jack, you might damage them as well. However, you can make your own safe adapter cable if you're skilled with a soldering iron.

Apple's microphone jack is a three-conductor type; the middle (ring) conductor provides 8 volts to drive an impedance matching circuit. Ordinary two-conductor plugs—found on most microphones—will short out this power supply. And though the tip of the jack is designed for audio, it cannot handle more than a fraction of a normal line or headphone signal (the limit is .004 volt, to be precise).

If you don't have an official Apple adapter, build a circuit like the one shown in figure 16.10 to both isolate the power and reduce the signal level. The resistors are 1/4- or 1/8-watt carbon, and all materials are available from any electronics parts supplier. (Radio Shack's catalog numbers are noted in the figure only because its stores are so ubiquitous.) Use shielded cable to avoid noise and solder neatly; short circuits may damage your equipment.

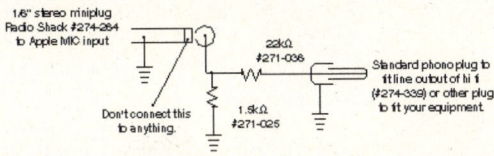

Chapter 17
Sound, Music, and Speech

Figure 16.10
Build this cable to record line-level signals with Apple's microphone input.

MacRecorder and Voice Impact Tips

The MacRecorder box is about the size of a standard Apple mouse, while the Voice Impact Pro box is slightly larger. Both connect to your computer's modem port, using software drivers in your System folder. Each has a microphone at one end, a circuit card in the box, and a volume control along the side (see figure 17.11). Voice Impact Pro also includes advanced circuitry for data compression and filtering. For the best possible sound, adjust level with the microphone's control instead of any volume controls in your software. The Voice Impact disks also include HyperCard sound utilities, something MacRecorder abandoned years ago.

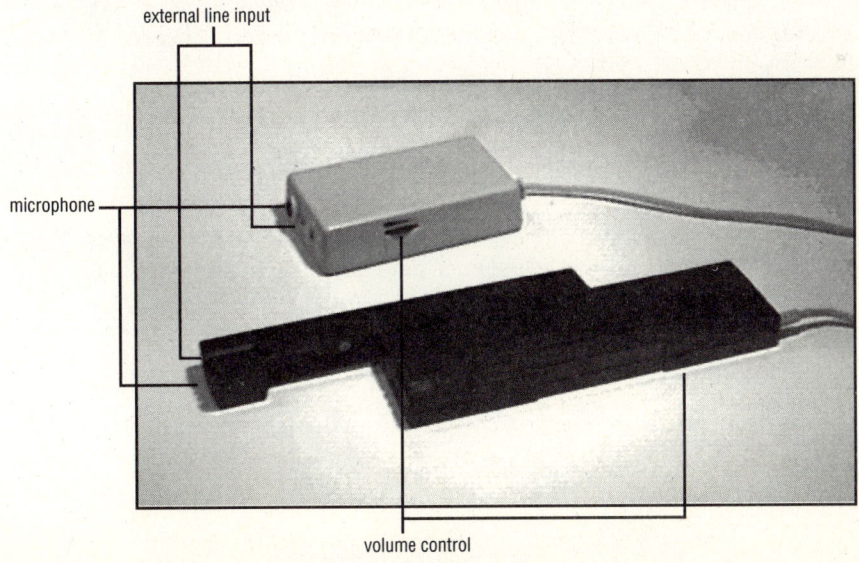

Figure 17.11
MacroMind's MacRecorder (top) and Articulate System's Voice Impact Pro.

Some tips on using these recorders:

▼ MacRecorder and Voice Impact are just the right size to use as a hand-held microphone. When you pick it up, your thumb naturally falls on the volume control.

▼ Voice Impact Pro also works like a hand-held microphone, but you must slide the top forward (as shown in figure 17.11) for it to work.

▼ You can plug directional, tie-tack, or even wireless microphones into MacRecorder's MIC jack. Any microphone designed for home video recorders should work well with MacRecorder.

▼ The LINE jack is directly compatible with home stereos. A "Y" connector lets you pick up both channels.

▼ Record in stereo with two MacRecorders. Connect the second one to the printer port on your Mac and choose **Stereo Recording** in the SoundEdit software.

 Do not connect these units directly to the speaker outputs of a hi-fi or tape player. You likely will get a very noisy recording, and might even damage the circuitry.

Memory and Storage Considerations

You need a lot of disk space for high-quality digital audio. On professional systems, gigabyte disks are common. Three factors—*sampling rate*, *compression*, and *running time*—control how much memory is needed.

Frequency Range, Sampling Rate, and Memory

Digitized sounds are merely files of numbers, representing graphs similar to the one shown in figure 17.1. The height, or *amplitude*, of the wave is measured in thousands of *sample* points along the time axis. The precision of the amplitude is determined by the number of bits used: usually 8 bits on Macs, or 16 bits on professional systems and home CDs. The closeness of the sample points—how many of them there are per second—is the *sampling rate*. With enough bits in a sample, close enough together, you get good quality sound. With less data, the sound ranges from that of voice mail systems to talking greeting cards.

Chapter 17
Sound, Music, and Speech

A Closer Look: If the sound is too high-pitched for the sampling rate, the numbers become ambiguous. One set of samples can represent more than one frequency. This generates *aliases*, false frequencies that are numerically correct but do not sound good. The Nyquest Theorem shows mathematically that incoming frequencies must be limited to less than half the sampling rate. To record a full range of sounds, you need a very high sampling rate. Commercial CD players, for example, use a sampling rate of 44.1kHz to faithfully carry sounds up to 20kHz.

Higher sampling rates also mean more numbers to be manipulated and stored. The fastest a Mac can sample, without special circuits, is 22kHz, to accurately record sounds up to 10kHz. Most recording programs let you set lower rates for an efficient compromise between sound quality and data quantity (though Apple's Sound control panel does not, unless you're using a third-party driver.) Figure 17.12 illustrates some common choices.

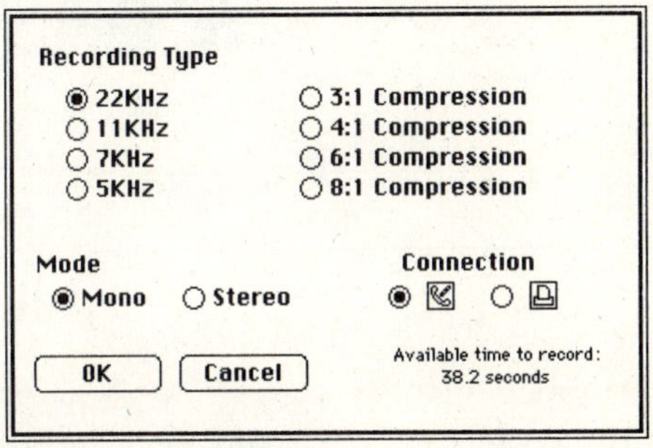

Figure 17.12
Common sampling rates.

Compression and Memory

You can also save data by reducing the number of bits per sample. Brute-force reductions usually sound harsh and noisy, but *compression schemes* use psycho-acoustic tricks to fool the ear into thinking a sound is more complete. This is different from the data compression provided by utilities like Stuffit or Disk Doubler. Compressed audio is never uncompressed: it's stored and played back in reduced form. With the right algorithm, sounds can be compressed to as few as 2 bits per sample and still sound fairly good.

Describing compression is difficult. Different schemes are optimized for speech or music, and some listeners are more sensitive to compression than others. Generally, 8-bit sounds are relatively natural-sounding, and highly compressed ones seem electronic. However, they may be perfectly suitable for your purposes. Compression is expressed as a ratio, usually between 3:1 and 8:1, representing approximately how much disk space the process saves.

Part IV

Specialized Mac Applications

Setting Compression

MacroMind's SoundEdit Pro offers the most complete range of storage options, with the command **Sound Format**. The dialog box (shown in figure 17.13) lets you set sample rate and compression, and shows you the relative memory required for each combination. The MACE options listed in the pull-down menu are Apple's standard algorithms. Articulate Systems' programs let you select MACE ratios in a **Quality** menu, when recording from the Sound CDEV or Voice Record DA. If you're using Apple's built-in microphone, you're out of luck: you cannot set anything without third-part software or HyperCard's Audio Help stack (see chapter 17, "HyperCard and SuperCard").

Figure 17.13
Setting recording options in SoundEdit Pro.

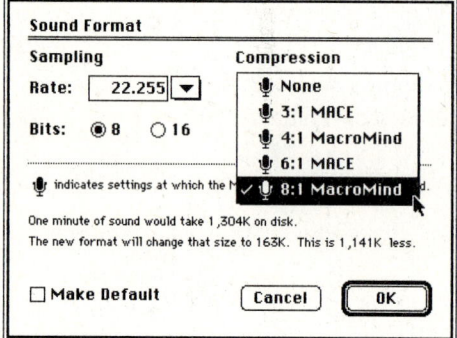

Some tips on compressing audio:

▼ Consider where a sound will be played before you compress. Mac speakers in a noisy office are much more forgiving than hi-fi speakers in an auditorium.

▼ Early Macs (512, Plus, and SE) cannot play MACE-compressed sounds with standard software. They can, however, play MacroMind compression.

▼ Each time you compress a sound, it gets noisier. Don't compress anything until you are sure you're happy with it.

▼ You can only compress sounds sampled at 22 kHz; consequently, for some sounds it is more memory-efficient to record at a different rate uncompressed.

▼ SoundEdit stores the compression ratio with a sound's window. If you paste or record a sound into a window, it gets compressed. To hear the effects of different ratios on the same sound, record it uncompressed and then paste it into differently-compressed windows.

Predicting Memory Needs

If you multiply the sampling rate by the length of the sound and then divide it by the compression ratio, you'll find out how many bytes of disk space a sound needs. Or, you can use table 17.1. You also can use some tricks to save storage space. Most of these techniques require editing (see the section, "Editing and Controlling Sound," later in this chapter), so you will need to save the sound uncompressed, use the trick, and then compress the sound.

▼ Cut any space between the start of a recording and the start of a sound. This also makes your presentation more professional.

▼ Eliminate pauses. Telephone companies estimate one-third of all conversations are actually silence; they fit additional calls on the line during pauses.

▼ Try to break down the sound into commonly used sections that you can play back together. Again, take a tip from the phone company: Rather than record a separate operator's message for every possible situation, it records phrases that fit together. If you edit carefully, the result won't sound too much like an audio "ransom note."

▼ Use time compression, a favorite trick of advertising studios (see the section "Modifying Sounds," later in this chapter).

Table 17.1. Memory requirements for sampled sounds

Sampling Rate or Compression	Kilobytes for a 10-Second Message	Time per Megabyte
22kHz	220K	45 seconds
11kHz	10K	1.5 minutes
7kHz	70K	2.25 minutes
5kHz	50K	3 minutes
3:1	70K	2.25 minutes
4:1	55K	3 minutes
6:1	38K	4.5 minutes
8:1	27.5K	6 minutes

Part IV
Specialized Mac Applications

Creating Sounds Without a Microphone

SoundEdit Pro has three commands in its **Effects** menu—**Noise**, **Tone Generator** and **FM Synthesis**—that create electronic sounds of precise length. (It also has a **Silence** command, which creates exactly what you'd expect.) **Tone Generator** creates constant pitches of a few selected waveforms. **FM Synthesis** makes siren-like pitches at low modulations and deviations, and complex synthesizer-like waveforms at higher ones. **Noise** creates a non-pitched sound in which all frequencies are represented equally. It is similar to steam escaping, or—if you have a good imagination—a snare drum. But add a few effects (see following section), and it can be a lot of other sounds.

Editing and Controlling Sound

Editing sound on the Macintosh is much like editing words. Start an editing program, open a sound file, or record a sound, and you'll see a graphic representation of the sound—something similar to the figures that started this chapter, but a lot more complex. Figure 17.14 shows the display in Garrick McFarlane's elegant shareware Sample Editor, available from online services.

Figure 17.14
Editing sound in the shareware program, Sample Editor.

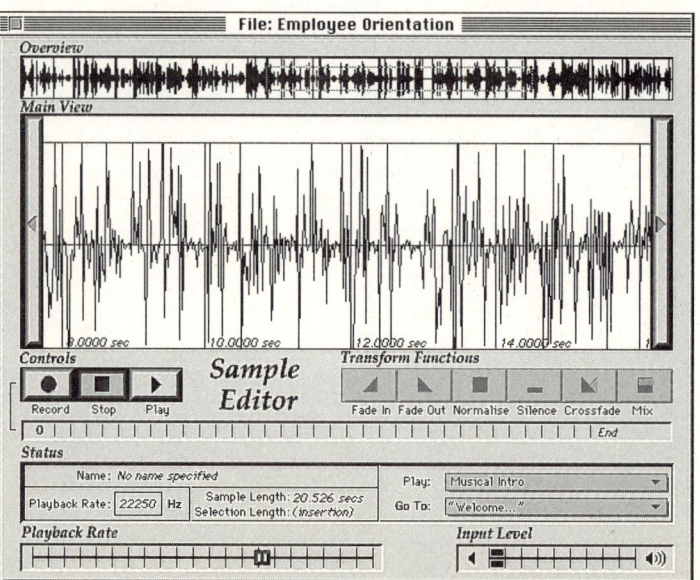

If the entire sound fits in the main window, editing is easy: drag the mouse over part of the sound, and Cut or Copy. All programs also let you check your selection by pressing **Play** (if nothing is selected, they'll play the entire sound). You can make the selection larger or smaller by shift-clicking, just as you would in MacWrite. Then click somewhere else to set an insertion point, and then select **Paste**.

If the sound is longer than the window can display, you can scroll elsewhere. Most programs have a scrollbar along the bottom of the window. Sample Editor and HyperCard's Audio Palette have you drag across an overview of the entire sound to scroll; this also adjusts how much sound fits in the window (see figure 17.15). (Other programs give you a zoom control.)

Chapter 17
Sound, Music, and Speech

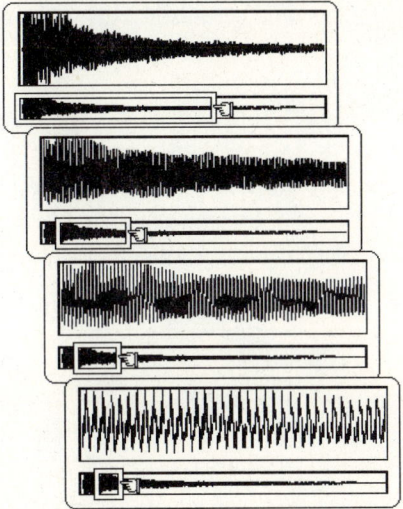

Figure 17.15
The size of the box determines how much of the sample is shown in the larger window.

The best way to learn how to edit is to train your own ear. Record some sounds, edit them, and judge the effect for yourself. You can undo cuts in any sound program, so you're unlikely to make permanent mistakes. Professional sound editors also rely on a few tricks:

▼ Spoken English consists of *phonemes*—sounds the mouth makes—rather than the letters we're used to seeing on a page. Sometimes there's very little relationship between a phoneme and a letter. For example, X is actually two separate phonemes: /k/ followed by /s/. J is a /d/ followed by /zh/ (a phoneme found in the middle of "leisure"). C might be /k/ or /s/, and S is sometimes /s/ and sometimes /z/. Don't try to edit letters: they're simply not there.

Part IV
Specialized Mac Applications

▼ The best place to edit is usually at the start of a loud sound. This way, the ear can ignore the edit. Learn to edit on drumbeats, /t/ or /p/ phonemes, and even coughs.

▼ The small click at the beginning of a sound is only sometimes significant. If you cut the click off a guitar pluck, it won't sound right. If you cut the click off most people's /l/, you do not notice the difference.

▼ Rhythm is as important to speech as it is to music. Sometimes, a small pause between phonemes will make a voice edit sound much better.

 Selecting the sound you want can be tricky, with much shift-clicking and previewing to isolate it. After you refine an edit region, most programs let you label it. Then, whenever you click on the label, the sound automatically is selected and highlighted.

Modifying Sounds

SoundEdit Pro lets you control your sound, offering almost as many special effects as you'll find in a full recording studio. (Audioshop has a much more limited palette.) These effects fall roughly into areas of *pitch*, *waveform*, and *time manipulation*. Figure 17.16 shows SoundEdit's Effects menu and Audioshop's effects buttons.

Figure 17.16
Sound manipulations available in SoundEdit (menu) and Audioshop (buttons).

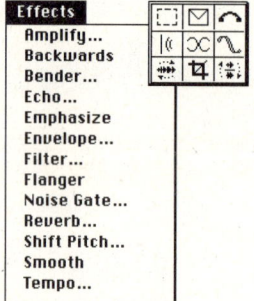

Pitch Effects

If you play back a samples at a different speed than it was recorded at, you change the pitch—just as you do when you play an LP record at 45 RPM. To change pitch in SoundEdit, select **Shift Pitch** in the **Effects** menu. A window similar to figure 17.17 will appear. Click on the appropriate piano note, and the selected sound will be recalculated at the new pitch. You can also adjust the pitch of an entire sound file with SoundEdit's Instrument Pitch…, the Sample Rate adjustment in Audioshop, and with HyperCard commands (see chapter 18, "HyperCard and SuperCard," for more information).

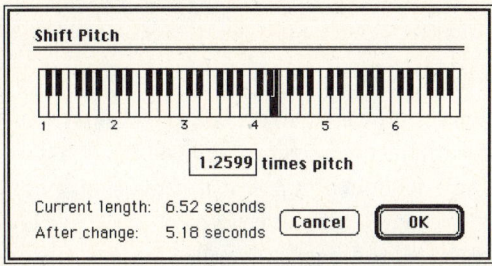

Chapter 17
Sound, Music, and Speech

Figure 17.17
Changing the pitch of a single sound in SoundEdit.

Selecting **Shift Pitch** or changing the sample rate applies a constant and precise pitch effect. You can also apply relative and gradual pitch adjustments, to simulate musical effects or intonation, with the Bender. A window with the selected sound and an overlaid line appears, as in figure 17.18. Move the handles—you can add more by double-clicking, or eliminate them by sliding a handle off the window—to control the bend effect. (The **Envelope** choice in the **Effects** menu lets you vary the volume, instead of the pitch, of a selected sound. But its controls work the same way as the Bender's.)

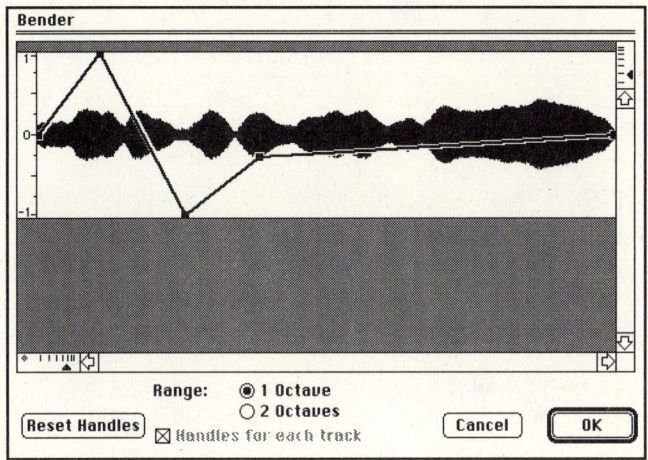

Figure 17.18
This sound will start at its normal pitch, quickly slide up and down, then gradually return to normal.

Part IV
Specialized Mac Applications

A Closer Look In the real world, moving objects often show a *Doppler* effect—that's why a train whistle slides up in pitch as it comes toward you and falls in pitch as it goes away. (The actual sound itself doesn't change, only the way its waves hit your ear.) You can simulate Doppler shifts by dragging one of the end handles.

Waveform Effects

The most common recording-studio effect involves *equalizing*, or varying the relative ratios of harmonics—the same thing you do with the tone controls on a stereo. SoundEdit draws a *graphic equalizer*, similar to those found on car stereos, on the screen. Grab a slider control to raise or lower the volume of that frequency range (as shown in figure 17.19). Or, grab one of the vertical lines between handles, to adjust the frequency range.

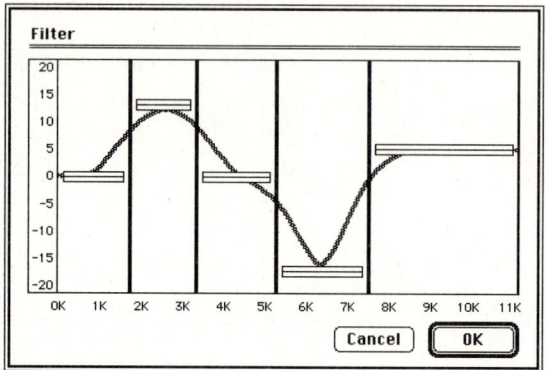

Figure 17.19
SoundEdit's Filter command gives you a graphic equalizer.

Most male voices sound crisper and easier to understand if you raise the 3–4kHz range about two decibels (see figure 17.20).

A Closer Look The **Smooth** and **Emphasize** commands in the **Effects** menu act as very sharp filters, raising or lowering the highest harmonics of a sound without otherwise changing the tonal balance. **Smooth** can eliminate ticks and pops from old recordings or control unwanted *sibilance* (over-emphasized /s/ and /f/ sounds) in a voice. **Emphasize** does what you'd expect, making voices sharper so they cut through noise. Be careful, though: too much emphasis actually decreases sound clarity, by adding distortion.

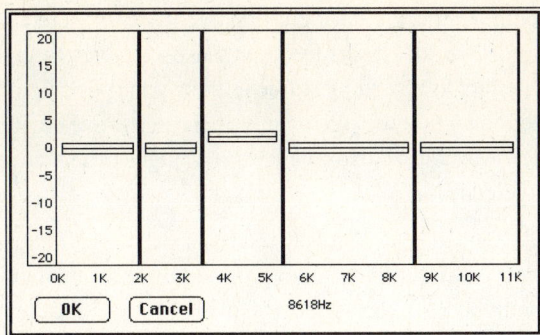

Figure 17.20
This slight adjustment can improve the sound of male voices.

> **Note:** The best way to make a voice "cut through" over music is to equalize the music, not the voice. Lower the 1K to 3K range in the music, and you'll be surprised how much better the voice sounds.

Time Effects

You can add make sounds bigger (or more distant) with **Echo** or **Reverb**. What's the difference? A sound that is repeated more than about a tenth of a second after its original is perceived as an *echo*: the brain assumes the sound is bouncing off a distant object. Repeats that occur sooner aren't heard as echoes but as *reverberation*, a thickening and enhancing of the original sound. Concert halls, for example, are known for reverberations rather than echoes.

> **Note:** Both echo and reverb work within the selected region. But since these may take a long time to die out (just as reverberations can last a few seconds in a concert hall), they can get cut off if the region isn't long enough. If an echo ends abruptly, undo the change and select a longer region. If there's nothing left to select, insert a few seconds of silence.

SoundEdit's longest preprogrammed reverberation is **Outer Space**. This may come as a surprise to those who always thought of space as a soundless, airless, echoless void.

Flanger generates moving echoes close to the original sound. It adds a "whooshing" effect to the selected region and imparts a sense of pitch or movement to sound effects. You often hear a similar effect in pop music.

The **Tempo** command is great for packing twenty seconds of audio into an eighteen-second slot. Advertisers frequently use a similar (though more sophisticated) effect in recording studios. It lets you speed up or slow down a sound without affecting the pitch. Since this can involve creating completely new waveforms, extreme tempo changes can make speech sound unnatural and electronic.

People frequently stretch or speed up individual words within a sentence. You can select them and apply radical tempo changes that might be obtrusive if applied to an entire speech.

Don't forget that **Tempo** slows things down as well as speeding them up. Stretching a word or two can add a more realistic emphasis than you'd get by just increasing the volume.

Mixing Sounds Together

SoundEdit lets you have as many individual tracks as you want in a file, so you can keep voices, music, and sound effects separate while you're editing: simply keep hitting Command-T for each new track you want. The additional tracks will appear in the active window, as shown in figure 17.21. Put the insertion point in a single track, and you can record, play or edit it. You can also click in the patterned parts of a track, to start recording somewhere other than the start of a file. These multitrack files take a lot of memory, and other programs cannot play them, so it's a good idea to mix the tracks together when you're satisfied.

Some tips for mixing sounds with SoundEdit:

▼ Before mixing, click in the gray area between tracks. If you then push **Play**, you'll hear all the tracks in a preview of the mix.

▼ To move a sound so it falls earlier or later in a track, press **Option** while you click on it. This turns the insertion point into a hand, which you can use to slide sounds.

▼ To adjust the relative volume of individual tracks, double-click in the track and use the **Amplify** command. To fade one track into another, use the **Envelope** command on the end of each.

▼ Watch out for volume buildup! If you mix two or three loud sounds, chances are the resultant sound will be louder than the Mac can handle and all you'll get is distortion.

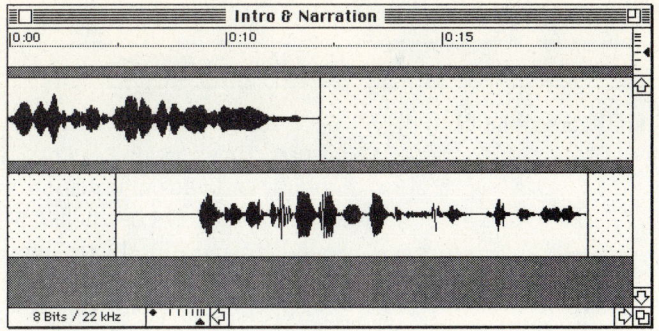

Figure 17.21
Multiple tracks ready for mixing in SoundEdit.

A Closer Look Digital mixing is a complicated process. Every sample of each input has to be added to all other samples occurring at the same time. A second of digital mixing can require hundreds of thousands of calculations. The Mac cannot do all these calculations in real time, so mixing becomes an off-line process. Many mid-priced professional systems also mix off-line for the same reason.

Saving Your Final Version

Saving sounds from the control panel is easy, if limited: sounds can be saved only as System Alerts (they can then be moved with ResEdit). Programs like SoundEdit and Audioshop give you additional options. When you choose **Save As**, you get a standard Mac dialog box with a pulldown menu of file formats (as shown in figure 17.22). Table 17.2 describes the formats; choose one that fits your application.

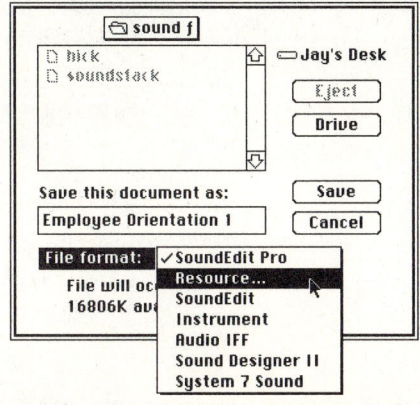

Figure 17.22
File formats in SoundEdit's Save As dialog box.

665

Table 17.2. Sound file formats

Format	Used For
SoundEdit/SoundEdit Pro	These are MacroMind's native file formats. They contain labeling, looping, and pitch information, and SoundEdit also can be opened by SoundCap and SoundWave software. Use this format to save sounds for VideoWorks and MacroMind Director and then import them with the Clip Sounds or Sound-to-Video utilities provided with these applications. SoundEdit Pro lets you save multiple tracks in the same file.
Resource	This format lets you save to the resource fork of any existing file. If you save a sound in HyperCard, you can listen to it with the **Play** command. (See chapter 18, "HyperCard and SuperCard," for more information.) If you save a sound resource to a System 6 system file, you can listen to it with the Sound CDEV and choose it as a system Alert.
Instrument	This is the format used by many Mac music applications, including Jam Session and Studio Sessions. You should record files saved in this format at an 11kHz sample rate.
Audio IFF (Audio Interchange File Format) or stereo sound.	Most musical synthesis programs support this file format. It can use any sample rate, and it provides mono.
Sound Designer II	This format is used by a professional synthesis program.
System 7 Sound	These are standalone files that can be dropped into a System 7 system folder, and then be chosen as Alert sounds.

Professional Sound Editing on the Mac

A few systems can turn a standard Mac into a CD-quality digital recorder. Studer's Dyaxis and DigiDesign's Sound Tools use specialized hardware for CD-quality sampling, and very large hard disks for storage. These programs have screens similar to SoundEdit, but with a lot more windows and options. Otari's PD-464 uses a Mac to control a separate random-access multitrack, playing cues in sync with a videotape.

Mac-based professional sound editing systems have the advantages of a graphic interface and a relatively low-cost control system (though the full systems cost between $15,000 and $200,000). However, many recording engineers complain that the interface also slows them down. Keyboards and mice are relatively alien to tape editing, and engineers are used to *rocking* actual tape reels and moving multiple console faders—both of which need customized hardware. True "reel rocking" requires massive amounts of RAM—as much as a 256M in professional systems.

Voice Mail on the Mac

Some modems can actually record voice mail messages on your Macintosh. Dove Computer's DoveFAX+ combines voice mail, a 2400 bps modem, and fax capabilities in a relatively low-cost integrated system. Prometheus offers two solutions. The base model is comparable to the DoveFax+ in terms of features, price, and size. The Ultima Home Office combines all the features of its Ultima modem (14,400 bps data and 9600 bps fax) with support for voice calls. The hardware digitizes sound from a supplied microphone or directly from the phone line. The voice mail software works like an answering machine, routing incoming messages to private "mailboxes" on the hard disk. You can review calls either at the Mac or remotely.

These modems—and the software that comes with them—can answer and record calls, route custom responses to individual callers, and provide the basis for a voice-driven catalog and ordering system. They run in the background but, unfortunately, tie up much of the system when a call comes in. (Of course, if you're close enough to be doing something else on your Mac, you can probably answer your own phone.)

Chapter 17
Sound, Music, and Speech

Part IV
Specialized Mac Applications

Mac, Phone Home

You might find it handy (or whimsical) to play edited sounds or sound effects while you're on the phone. It's easy with a low-cost, do-it-yourself adapter to connect your Mac directly to the phone lines. The key is using an *isolation transformer*, which keeps the Mac's internal voltages away from the phone system, and a *blocking capacitor*, which stops the phone system from bleeding its voltages through the transformer.

The choice of transformer and connector wiring depends on the kind of Mac and the kind of phone you have. Early Macs (through the SE) had line-level outputs. These require a 1:1 transformer and are not particularly loud on the phone. Newer models work better with a step-up transformer, and can put out more signal than the phone company can handle. The easiest way to choose and wire the parts is to read a 6-page illustrated TeachText document entitled "Mac-2-Phone," written by this author and available from many online services and user groups. Or, send a self-addressed, stamped business envelope to Jay Rose, care of Hayden Books, for a copy.

Playlist Editors

For a true "jukebox" approach to Macintosh sound, use a *playlist editor*, a program that cannot generate sound or control sound devices, but instead loads and plays sound files from disk and CD-ROM. Playlist editors were invented for multimedia, to provide a relatively foolproof soundtrack for Mac slideshows and QuickTime movies. In fact, the sound module in even a high-end presentation package like Adobe Premiere is basically a playlist editor.

Opcode's Audioshop is a typical playlist editor, with some rudimentary wave editing functions tacked on. When you first start the program, you see a home CD player on your screen (as shown in figure 17.23). Use the **Add** button to open sound files, and then play them with the hi-fi controls. If you click **Playlist**, you'll see more details (see figure 17.24). Grab individual soundfile names and move them up or down the list to put them in sequence.

The advantage of this kind of editing is simplicity. Long presentations can be assembled with only a few mouse clicks, and—not counting the sound files themselves—need only a few thousand bytes to store on disk. If a lot of your audio comes from CD-ROM, this can be very efficient. The disadvantage is a lack of control: playlist editors can start or stop playing in the middle of a file, but not with the kind of precision associated with wave editors. It's difficult, if not impossible, to make smooth transitions from one file to another.

Chapter 17
Sound, Music, and Speech

Figure 17.23
Audioshop looks like a home CD player.

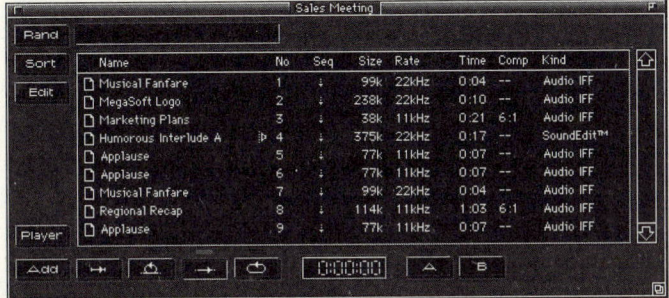

Figure 17.24
Manipulating a playlist in Audioshop.

MIDI and Music Processors

MIDI, the Musical Instrument Digital Interface, is a local area network similar to AppleTalk.

▼ MIDI handles streams of data between musical devices. Rather than sending characters and PostScript instructions to a printer, it sends musical note information to a synthesizer.

▼ MIDI is as standardized as AppleTalk. Just as you can upgrade from a 300-dpi laser printer to a 2400-dpi imagesetter without changing your network, you can switch from a department-store keyboard to the latest high-end synthesizer by simply plugging it in.

669

▼ You also can use MIDI for file transfers, the same way you send files on AppleTalk. But it's not very fast.

It is important to understand that this last operation—sending files of waveform information—is not MIDI's primary function. Most of the time, MIDI data takes a *note on* or *note off* structure: "Synthesizer #1, play middle C pretty loud. Now let go of middle C. Now play the Bflat below it, softly…" The actual musical sounds are generated in the synthesizers.

MIDI is similar to a player-piano roll, in that it tells the instrument which notes to play but not how to manufacture the sounds. Two different instruments can play the same MIDI file with totally different results. Compare this to a tape recording of the piano itself: the recording captures subtleties of sound and style, but is locked to a specific piano's quality.

One of the major differences between a piano roll and a tape recording is the ease of editing. You can completely change a piano roll's C-major chord by covering the E-hole and punching a couple of new ones for an E-flat and a B-flat. No audio editing system can do that, but MIDI sequencers—word processors for musical notes—can; you simply erase the E data and tap in the new notes. Most sequencing software even presents data in a piano-roll style.

A Closer Look The piano roll was so easy to edit that many of its artists used it to develop studio techniques to enhance their performances. Inept pianists would cut their rolls slowly, to simplify difficult passages, and then speed them up on playback to sound flashier. Even George Gershwin would "overdub" his playing, punching the same roll more than once for three-handed chords. Scholars now analyze Gershwin's playing by converting his piano rolls to MIDI files.

The MIDI Studio

You can use your Mac to control synthesizers with only a few plug-in devices. A basic system needs an interface, a couple of cables, and a synthesizer. More complicated systems involve MIDI switchers, processing gear, and dozens of cables and synthesizers. Of course, you also need software, discussed later in this chapter.

MIDI Interfaces

Although a Mac easily can handle MIDI data, it needs an *interface* to match MIDI's electrical specifications. The simplest of these, including Opcode Systems' MIDI Translator, Altech's 1x3, and Apple's own MIDI Interface, are little gray boxes that plug into the modem port (see figure 17.25). Each box has a few MIDI jacks: one for data input and one or more for data output. These interfaces are available from music stores and computer dealers for between $50 and $100. The MIDI plug itself is a standard DIN-5 connector, also found frequently on European hi-fi equipment.

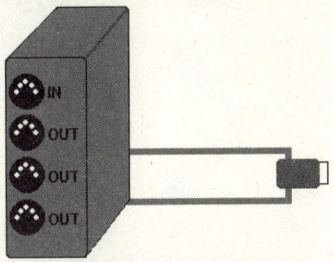

Chapter 17
Sound, Music, and Speech

Figure 17.25
A typical interface connects synthesizers to your Mac.

Most synthesizers have three MIDI jacks on the back, as shown in figure 17.26. There are separate connections for IN, OUT, and THRU. (Department-store keyboards often have only the first two.) MIDI is one-directional: the messages flow from an OUT jack on one device to the IN jack on another. Play your keyboard, and note-on messages go out the OUT jack. Plug a cable with a note-on message into the IN jack, and you'll hear a sound. (Most instruments also have "local control" settings, so you can play them from their own keyboards without cables.) If there is a THRU jack, it simply passes the IN signal along. Effects devices such as echo and equalizers frequently have similar jacks.

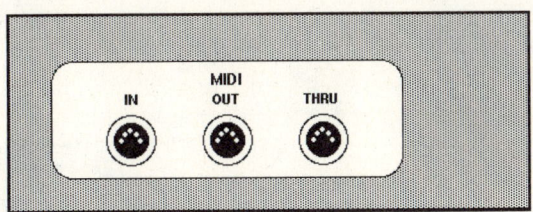

Figure 17.26
MIDI connections on a synthesizer.

MIDI Cables

You don't need anything special to connect MIDI: just a simple cable with plugs on each end. You can make your own cables with Radio Shack #274-003 plugs and shielded 2-conductor wire (connect pins 4, 5, and the shield). But premade cables are so inexpensive—from $2 to $6 at music stores, depending on length—that you may as well buy them. "Oxygen-Free," "Super-Data-Quality," or "Mondo-Hypo-RocknRoll" cables are a waste of money: MIDI doesn't need special handling. Extra rugged cables, however, might be desirable for road use.

Part IV
Specialized Mac Applications

 MIDI cables usually come in decorator colors at no extra charge. It's a good idea to establish a standard for your studio (red for master keyboard out, blue for synthesizer in, green for effects in, and so on) to make reconnecting things simpler.

MIDI Setup

Connecting a basic MIDI studio is simple (see figure 17.27). Use the following steps to set up your MIDI:

1. If you have more than one keyboard or synthesizer, decide which is the *master* for sending data to the Mac's software. Run a cable from this synthesizer's OUT to the interface's IN.

2. Run a cable from an interface's OUT to the master keyboard's IN. Repeat for each additional synthesizer.

3. If you run out of interface OUT jacks, run a cable from each synthesizer's THRU to additional synthesizer IN jacks.

4. Run hi-fi cables from a single synthesizer to your amp, or from multiple synthesizers to a mixer and then an amp. Turn everything on and play each keyboard in turn. If you do not hear anything, fix the audio problems before you try to use MIDI. (Some excellent audio books are available from Sams, a division of Prentice Hall Computer Publishing.)

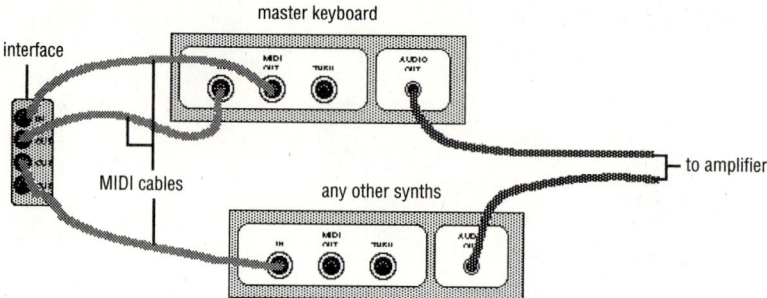

Figure 17.27
Basic MIDI connections are simple.

WARNING! Many synthesizer manufacturers recommend turning off the power before changing MIDI connections. Many musicians ignore this warning, resulting in a healthy repair business for many music stores.

Advanced Setups

As your musical needs and budget grow, you'll want to add more gear: the easiest way is to just keep on looping through the THRU jacks. If you want to synchronize your music to a drum machine, or to an audio or video recorder, you'll need a more sophisticated interface. Drum machines are handled with interfaces that have two inputs: one for the master keyboard, and one for timing. The best way to sync your music to a multitrack audio recorder or to video is with SMPTE code (see the section, "Framed," below). Expect to spend between $250 and $400 for an interface that does everything. If you already have a sophisticated interface with multiple MIDI inputs, you can add SMPTE with Opcode Systems' Timecode Machine for approximately $150.

A Closer Look Many synthesizers process the THRU signal through their internal computers. The data is unchanged, but is slightly delayed. If you connect a series of several synthesizers with the THRU jacks, the last one on the chain will probably be a few sixteenth-notes behind the first one. Avoid these delays by using multiple MIDI outs on the interface, or with PatchBays and through-boxes.

MIDI Patchbays aren't like the plug-and-jack jumbles found in recording studios; instead, they are neat hardware or software switches that let you choose MIDI sources for each connected device. You can route a signal to several synthesizers simultaneously, switching between two or more master keyboards (some people prefer weighted keyboards for their piano lines and a spring keyboard for their brass lines), or temporarily add new equipment without having to rewire everything else. If you've got a sophisticated interface, it probably has Patchbay functions that you can control from a DA. Otherwise, you can get a basic switched Patchbay like the one shown in figure 17.28 for approximately $75. More advanced Patchbays, costing between $125 and $200, add features like transposition, merging two data streams, or routing different notes to different outputs. These data functions are also available separately in MIDI Filters. Filters and through-boxes (which send a signal to several outputs without any delay) cost $75–$100 each.

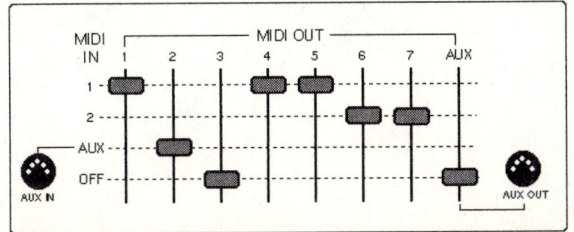

Chapter 17
Sound, Music, and Speech

Figure 17.28

A MIDI PatchBay lets you distribute signals easily.

Part IV
Specialized Mac Applications

Framed

In an ideal world, MIDI programs and tape recorders would run at constant speeds. You could start a song knowing that everything—sequencers, drum machines, multitrack recorders, and videotape—would always stay in step. In the real world, however, we're not so lucky. No two cassette recorders run at the same speed. Carefully-calibrated professional multitracks will play back slightly differently each time you run a tape. Even crystal-locked computers and most DAT recorders don't remain perfectly on-time over the length of a song.

The Society of Motion Picture and Television Engineers (SMPTE) addressed this problem a few years ago when producers started editing sound separately from the picture. The solution was to number each frame of the picture, and use these numbers as a timing guide. SMPTE data is carried on both the video and audio recorders, and constantly counts hours, minutes, seconds, and frames. (After 24 hours, the code is reset to zero.) If the numbers line up, synchronization is guaranteed.

Modern sequencers use this *SMPTE Timecode* to lock the computer to audio tape. Even if you're not working with video, the code guarantees each overdub will stay exactly on the beat. You can add vocals and live players, or modify sequences, and the sounds still come out together.

SMPTE Timecode comes in several forms. Because it's designed for video frames, it can be at 29.97 frames/second (the frame rate of color television) or 30.0 frames/second (the rate for black and white and nonvideo productions). TV program producers sometimes use drop-frame timecode: it runs at 29.97 frames, but jumps a few frames every few minutes to make the slower color TV code agree with a show's actual running length.

Building a sophisticated MIDI studio is simply a question of adding more synthesizers and cables, following the same rules as a basic studio. SMTPE hookup is equally simple: connect the jacks on the interface to the input and output of an audio channel on your multitrack. This may appear to waste a track—after all, you could record another synthesizer where the timecode is—but it really means you can have an almost infinite number of virtual tracks on your sequencer whenever you roll the tape. Additional effects, including MIDI-controlled echoes, equalizers, and mixer automation, are wired just like synthesizers. When you run out of outputs, add a PatchBay. The whole setup can end up looking like figure 17.29.

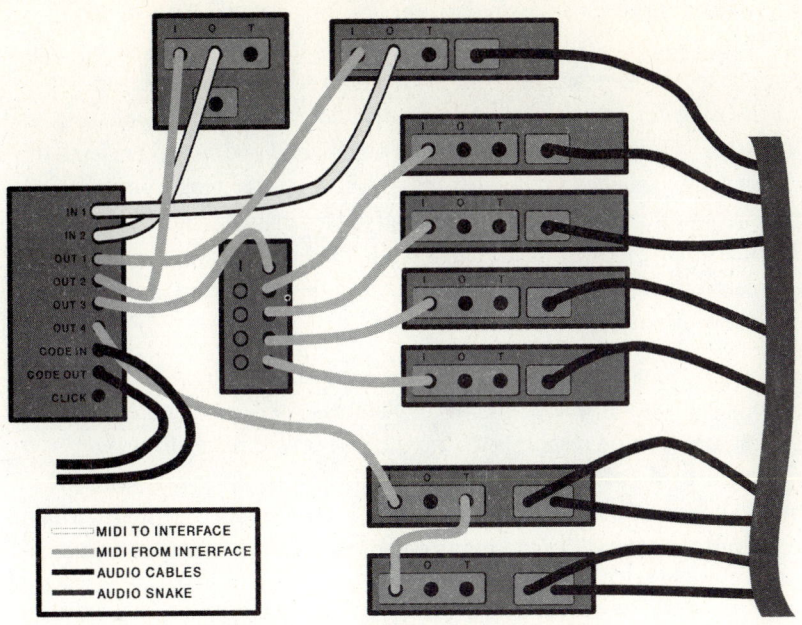

Figure 17.29
A sophisticated MIDI setup is just a matter of adding more synthesizers, cables, and a through-box.

MIDI Messages

Every device on an AppleTalk network has a unique *chooser name* ("Steve's IIsi," "Marketing Department Laser," and so on). The names are attached to messages sent over the network, and each device listens only its own messages. MIDI is less sophisticated, with 16 numbered channels. Each command is preceded by a channel number. Set each synthesizer separately to tell it how to use the channel information:

▼ Omni: The synthesizer plays every note on the network. (Its keyboard sends on a primary channel, chosen from its front panel.) If every synthesizer is set to Omni, they'll all play in unison.

▼ Poly: The synthesizer responds only to notes received on its primary channel. By sending different notes on different channels, you can split a chord among different instruments.

▼ Multi: The synthesizer generates multiple sounds simultaneously. Many can create 16 different waveforms at the same time, one for each channel it receives.

Part IV
Specialized Mac Applications

Every musical instrument manufacturer has agreed to the MIDI standard, allowing for more than just "turn this note on" and "turn that note off" data. Specific messages reflect how quickly the note is pressed or released, whether the key is leaned on while it's held down (*after-touch pressure*), and the status of pitchbenders, modulation wheels, and pedals. Other standard messages are assigned to timing, tuning, and voice changing. Some messages—called *sysex*—have been reserved for manufacturers to control features unique to their instruments. Each MIDI device comes with a standardized implementation chart, usually found at the end of its manual, to explain which messages it handles.

If an instrument follows General MIDI, it's capable of at least 24 simultaneous notes spread over all 16 channels (some channels can be playing chords) and responds in a predictable way to voice-changing messages: by definition, voice 1 is always piano, voice 30 is always heavy-metal guitar, and so on. This way, a General MIDI sequence written with one set of instruments will sound pretty much the same when played on any other General MIDI device. General MIDI Sound Modules—small, keyboard-less boxes that can be connected directly to your Mac or through an interface—are handy both in the music studio and for playing prepackaged *clip music* scores.

Clip Music

The General MIDI specification has made it possible for publishers to release libraries of pre-sequenced music files that can be opened with any sequencer and used with any standard synthesizer. Since files can be edited to match length, mood, or specific hit-points, they're frequently useful for quick multimedia presentations. The sound quality of clip music is, alas, limited by the synthesizers you have on hand: don't expect high production values, unless you already own high-priced production equipment. The CD-ROM, from Prosonus, is typical of the breed; it includes both MIDI and AIFF files of 27 different songs.

Sequencers and MIDI Software

Dozens of excellent MIDI programs are available. Choosing one is a matter of deciding which features you like and how much you are willing to pay (it's also dependent on your dealer's inventory, and which programs your friends or collaborators are using). Generally, however, sequencers fall into two types: personal applications costing about $100, and professional applications which cost much, much more. Discounts and new, remarkably capable low-cost sequencers have blurred this line. New categories of programs for beginners—ranging from ones that help you write and harmonize a song, to a computerized piano teacher—are also usable by professionals.

The following survey, roughly arranged by ascending price and features, represents only a few of the dozens of programs available. Many features introduced by a program at one level are shared by all the programs at higher levels. If you see something you like, great. If not, you've got lots of other choices.

Deluxe Music Construction Set

Deluxe Music Construction Set from Electronic Arts (DMCS) was one of the first music programs developed for the Mac, even before MIDI interfaces were available. Its current version, introduced in 1988, supports MIDI, simple score printing, and voice editing; it sells for about $90. DMCS is organized around a musical staff (see figure 17.30). You enter notes by selecting a time value from the palette on the left and then dropping the note in place on the staff. You also can click the piano keyboard on the bottom of the screen if you prefer. If you play on a connected MIDI keyboard, the program computes the note value and places it on the staff.

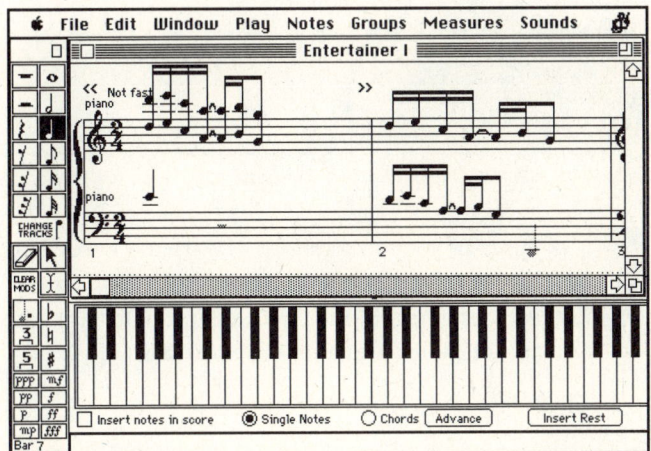

Figure 17.30
Deluxe Music Construction Set uses a musical staff to record and edit notes.

DMCS dialog boxes let you insert time and key signatures, adjust the staff's size or spacing on the page, and add lyrics. The program includes a bitmapped version of Adobe's Sonata font, but you have to purchase the PostScript version—and possibly ATM—for high-quality printing (see chapter 5, "Printing From Your Macintosh," for more information).

Chapter 17
Sound, Music, and Speech

Part IV
Specialized Mac Applications

ConcertWare

Great Wave's ConcertWare is another venerable music program. Its current version (about $100) supports eight-voice MIDI, user-friendly instrument editing, and high-quality laser score printing. ConcertWare is really three linked programs: Music Writer, Music Player, and InstrumentMaker. Music Writer uses the same score-oriented approach as DMCS. It lacks an onscreen keyboard (you enter music directly on the staff or from a MIDI instrument) but adds extensive professional manuscript tools including automatic transposition for non-concert-pitch instruments. You can print orchestral parts with counted rests, and you can print melody lines with chords for guitarists. ConcertWare includes its own high-quality laser font. Figure 17.31 shows its main screen. ConcertWare's InstrumentMaker is discussed earlier in this chapter and pictured in figure 17.4.

Figure 17.31
ConcertWare's main screen is simple and intuitive.

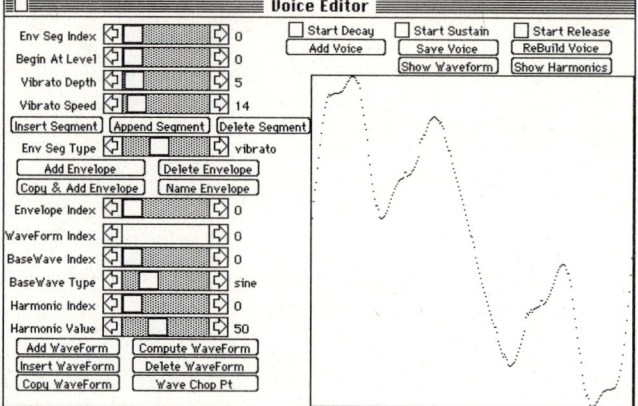

A Closer Look As this book went to press, Great Wave was developing a high-powered (and much more expensive) version, ConcertWare Pro. At least according to press releases, it should have full sequencer features with a similar music-staff interface.

Musicshop

Opcode Systems' Musicshop (approximately $125) bridges the gap between personal and professional systems. It also introduces two graphic approaches used in high-end sequencers. The piano roll, shown on the right side of figure 17.32, can show nuances of timing that would be lost in conventional notation. The continuous data display along the bottom can be switched to show everything from tempo to pitchbend. Either display can be edited by simply redrawing the data.

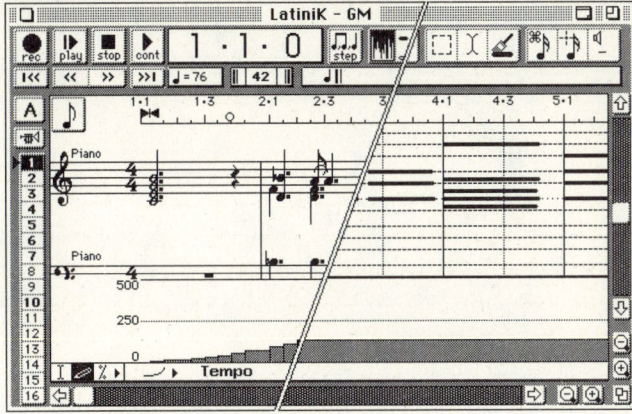

Chapter 17
Sound, Music, and Speech

Figure 17.32
We cut our Mac's screen in half to show both conventional notation and a piano roll display in Musicshop.

Musicshop is a simplified version of Opcode's Vision series, which is discussed later in this chapter. It supports 16 simultaneous tracks—one for each MIDI channel—and also has an on-screen mixer (shown in figure 17.33) to let you control the relative volumes of each track.

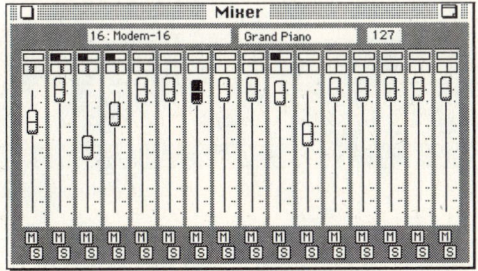

Figure 17.33
Musicshop's on-screen mixer enables you to create a good ensemble sound.

Metro

OSC's Metro is a newly-rewritten version of the popular Beyond sequencer (approximately $200), with more compositional tools than most other sequencers at any price (see figure 17.34). The program is easy to learn, with icons that do a good job of suggesting their function (note the Punch-in icon in the upper right of figure 17.35), and little doors in most windows to bring up more information. Metro is also one of the easiest programs for integrating MIDI-controlled sound effects with pictures: you can place events precisely at SMPTE Timecode frame numbers, or play a sequence a note at a time while inching the picture forward or backward.

Figure 17.34

Some of the powerful composition tools in Metro.

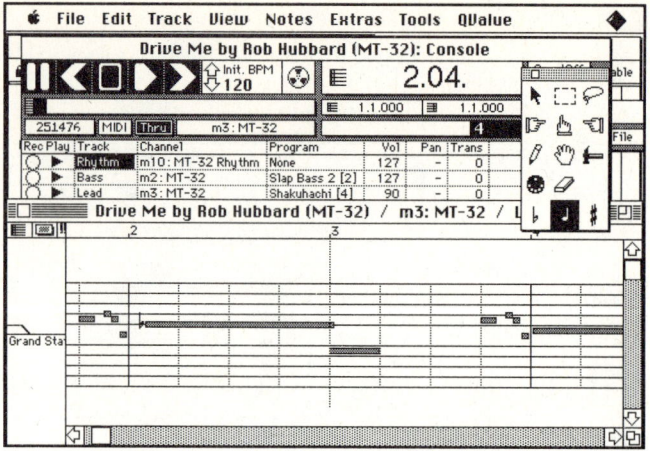

Figure 17.35

Beyond uses many icons to speed learning of its functions.

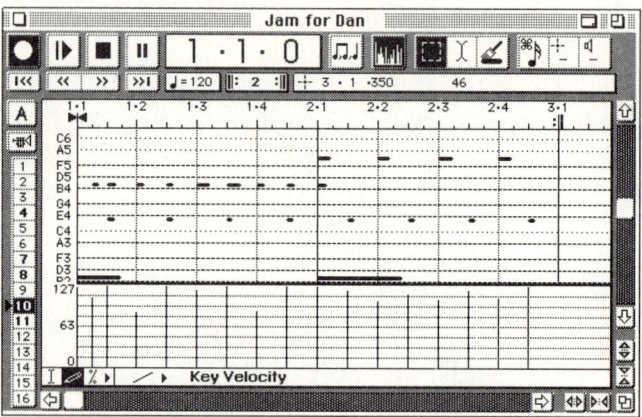

Vision and Studio Vision

Opcode Systems' high-power sequencers, Vision and Studio Vision, include a host of features for the professional, including the ability to experiment with timing and playing styles while a sequence is running. More than 2,500 separate tracks are available simultaneously, and each track can control all 16 MIDI channels. If you want to avoid using your mouse while you compose, you can assign functions to musical notes, sliders, pedals, or other controllers on your keyboard. Despite this power, Vision's screens are a logical extension of other, simpler sequencers (see figure 17.36). However, with all the windows open, you quickly can cover the monitor on a Mac II. Vision sequencing software costs approximately $350.

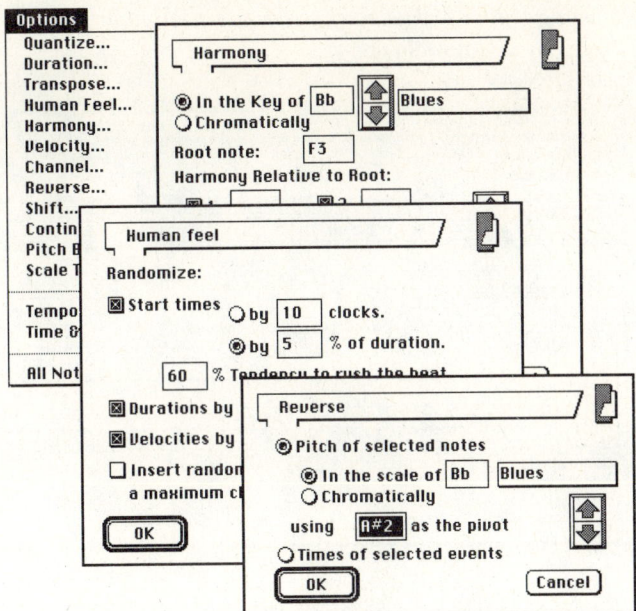

Figure 17.36
Vision allows professional control of up to 2,500 separate tracks simultaneously, along with other features displayed in this figure.

Studio Vision adds full, high-fidelity audio digitizing under sequencer control. It uses DigiDesign add-on hardware, also found in professional Mac-based sound editors. The waves are displayed as part of the sequencer's piano roll. You can record vocals into the computer, move them around, and play them back along with MIDI accompaniment. Be warned, though, a full setup with software, add-on hardware, a 600M or larger hard disk, and a Mac IIfx or Quadra to tie it all together can get very expensive.

Performer

Mark of the Unicorn's Performer (approximately $400) is considered the most powerful sequencer for complex music. It can support up to 512 simultaneous MIDI channels on 32 separate output cables when connected to four of their optional MIDI Time Piece interfaces (about $375 each): a full orchestra at your fingertips. Performer comes full circle, supporting music-staff notational editing as well as graphic editing. But its range of windows and controllers can be intimidating for the casual user (see figure 17.37).

Other Music Software

Sequencers, no matter how sophisticated, are still based on the century-old model of the player piano. But imagine a player piano that can automatically write a song for you, print a complex orchestral score, or even teach you how

Figure 17.37

Sorting all the windows and controllers in Performer is a performance in itself.

to play! It's no surprise that a computer as powerful as the Mac has spawned a wide range of musical programs.

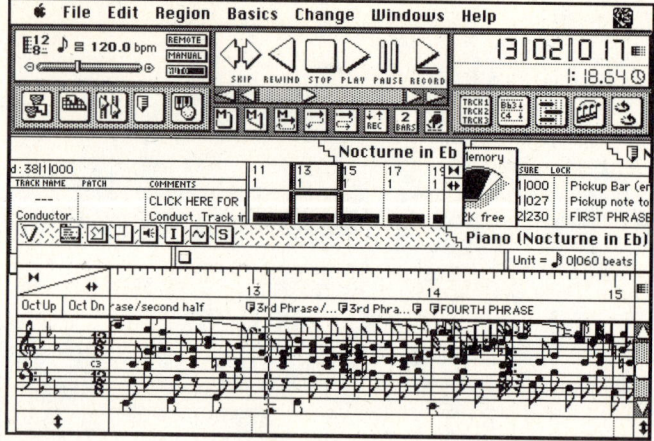

Songworks

If you've got a song in your heart, but no idea of how to set it on paper (or even play it on a keyboard), consider Ars Nova's Songworks. This program lets you enter a melody with a MIDI keyboard or computer keys, figures out a reasonably musical accompaniment, plays it back via MIDI or the Mac's speaker, helps you apply professional arranging tricks, and then prints the whole thing as a leadsheet (melody plus piano or guitar chord symbols, similar to a musician's "Fake Book") with a built-in laser font. For about $70, it may be all a budding composer needs. In fact, you don't need to be a composer at all: if you can type your lyrics and tap the rhythm on your Mac's keyboard, Songworks will do the rest. That's how we generated the song in figure 17.38.

Music Education

Ars Nova's other program, Practica Musica ($70) comes with a 200-page manual that takes you through a first-year college theory and harmony course. Exercises work with melody and rhythm, ear training, score reading, and chord spotting. The book also includes such topics as historic forms and voice leading. You can use Practica Musica with or without MIDI, although non-MIDI users can get stuck when the program asks you to identify sounds beyond the Mac speaker's range. Despite this, it's a worthwhile addition to a nonprofessional musician's arsenal.

Figure 17.38
All we did was write the lyrics and tap the rhythm. Songworks created the melody, harmonized it, and printed the sheet music.

Software Toolworks' Miracle Piano System ($350) tries to teach piano technique with software and a custom synthesizer. Unfortunately, the designers were distracted by videogames. The program eats a hefty five megabytes of disk space, mostly for high-resolution color graphics (see figure 17.39). It would have been better to refine its musical values: Miracle is notoriously inflexible with rhythm and ignores dynamics; and while its games have interesting animation, they're musically inept. (In the example, you have to play a C-major chord to keep the jumpers from crashing. But as soon as you can read music well enough to play the chord quickly, Miracle cannot keep up: the jumpers crash anyway.) The program also includes an eight-track sequencer with no editing capability.

Patch Librarians

Modern synthesizers are capable of almost infinite sound variation, sometimes in very non-intuitive ways. While most instruments can store a few dozen patches, or sound settings, musicians frequently build and trade much larger collections. Since modern synths can transmit patches over MIDI, you can use software to keep track of the sounds. Patch librarians such as

Part IV
Specialized Mac Applications

Opcode's Galaxy let you catalog and switch sounds you've programmed on an instrument. Library editors, like Mark of the Unicorn's Unisyn (figure 17.40), let you also create new sounds on your Mac's screen—usually, with less effort than using the synth's controls. All of these programs have to be configured for specific synthesizers, so make sure the librarian supports the instruments you own.

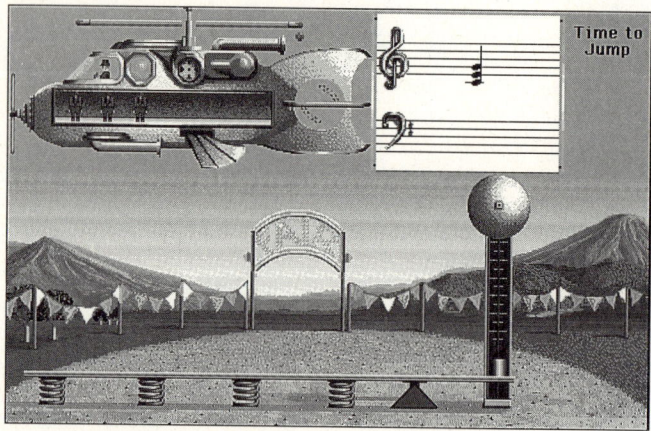

Figure 17.39

Miracle Piano is mostly videogames.

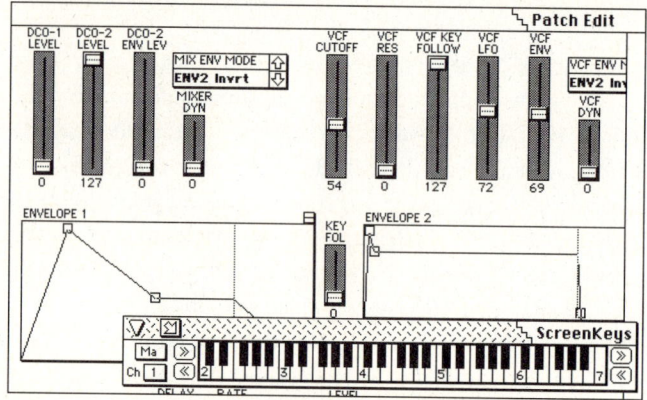

Figure 17.40

A few of Unisyn's many controls and sliders for the Roland JX8P synthesizer.

Software for serious professionals

We started this chapter by describing music from a television car chase, climaxing just as the bad guy hits the wall. A sophisticated composer would probably keep track of the crash (as well as the gunshots and kisses) by entering SMPTE timecode numbers into a scoring or spotting program, such as Opcode's Cue or DigiDesign's Q-Sheet. The programs determine an appropriate tempo and meter to keep these events on downbeats, and pass that information to a sequencer. Then, all the composer has to do is write music that fits these measures.

The Mac can also handle desktop music publishing, with sophisticated score-creation packages like Mark of the Unicorn's Mosaic (approximately $475, including Adobe's Sonata laser font). The programs let you import notes from a sequencer, play them on a MIDI keyboard, or paint them on appropriate staves for everything from a full orchestra to the latest experimental electronic music. Then you can add just about every musical sign, embellishment, and marking from the past few hundred years worth of musical tradition. It's unlikely a composer would use all of Mosaic's palettes (shown in figure 17.41) in the same piece, but it's good to know they're there.

Chapter 17
Sound, Music, and Speech

Figure 17.41
Mosaic's musical markings range from jazz to symphonic.

MIDI Manager and OMS

You can run more than one music application at a time under MultiFinder. But if you do, programming can get very messy as each application tries to take over the serial ports. Apple's MIDI Manager software, bundled with a number of sequencers, is an INIT and DA that handles all internal MIDI routing, even enabling one program to send MIDI to another. MIDI Manager sets itself automatically when you run just one music application. If you want to do more sophisticated routing, you can wire patchcords with your mouse, by using Apple's PatchBay DA.

Part IV
Specialized Mac Applications

Opcode's MIDI System (OMS) improves the process considerably. It lets you control hundreds of MIDI channels, customizing each for the particular instruments in your studio. If you have compatible sequencing or library software (not necessarily Opcode's, since other publishers also support OMS), you can access synths by name or reconfigure sequences automatically when you add new instruments.

Speech and Beyond

The Mac can do more than just play sounds and accompany them on a synthesizer. It also can speak, using a simple public-domain utility.

MacinTalk

In early 1984, Steve Jobs stunned an audience of Apple stockholders and reporters by having a small plastic box announce, "Hello, I am Macintosh. Never trust a computer you cannot lift." The voice was the result of one of the first INITs, MacinTalk.

There was plenty of scurrying behind that announcement. At the last minute, Jobs decided it would be interesting to have Mac speak for itself. But nobody was available to write software to do more than beep, so the MacinTalk project was given to a third-party developer. Unfortunately, Apple's contract didn't require the developer to supply more than a compiled program. The source code—essential if Apple wanted to upgrade or modify MacinTalk—wasn't part of the deal.

MacinTalk was created for the original 128K Mac. It proved so useful that other programmers started linking applications to it, and when Apple introduced the Mac II Sound Manager, it had to emulate part of the 128's logic just to support MacinTalk. Apple warns the utility might not function in future systems, if the company grows tired of imitating 128K Macs.

The easiest and most entertaining way to experience MacinTalk is to install Talking Moose. (for more information, see chapter 14, "Games for Fun!"). MacinTalk also is used by OutSpoken to read menu commands and dialog boxes aloud. (See chapter 19, "Macs and the Differently Abled.")

Chapter 17
Sound, Music, and Speech

MacinTalk synthesizes speech by generating phonemes. It uses nonstandard phonetic transcriptions that look like this: DHIHS IHZ AH SAH5TUL PLAHG FOHR DHAX MAE5KINTAA1SH #. Fortunately, the program also includes a sophisticated editor that can read English and translate it. (English is easier, but phonemes allow more subtle control.) Other MacinTalk messages control speed, intonation, and pitch. Used properly, this 31 kilobyte 1984 program creates completely understandable (if slightly nasal) speech.

A Closer Look You can learn more about MacinTalk and its language with the HyperMacinTalk stack by Dennis C. DeMars. This stack, copyrighted in 1987 and still carried on major bulletin boards, includes a complete description of speech programming and an XCMD to trigger MacinTalk.

Sound and ResEdit

Most Mac hackers have played with ResEdit, a program that teaches you a great deal about your computer. It can also damage your programs, so use it carefully—and only on *copies* of files. ResEdit lets you play and move sound resources, or create new sounds from simple commands. But it's not intuitive: be prepared for an adventure if you set out to learn ResEdit.

Summary

The Macintosh lets you use sound for fun or to communicate important messages. You can record and edit sound on any Mac (even those that don't include built-in microphone circuits), or make the Mac talk with just a few simple shareware utilities. Add a few MIDI devices and the right software, and you can also use your Mac for sophisticated music composition and publishing.

Chapter 18
HyperCard and SuperCard

HyperCard is a little like Steve Allen. The great comedian and talk show pioneer is also a writer/producer, dramatic film actor, author of count-less books, and one of the most prolific songwriters in America. Ask most people what Steve Allen does, and they'll probably leave something out. Ask most people what HyperCard does, and they'll probably leave out half a dozen of its functions.

In This Chapter

▼ How to get the most out of HyperCard

▼ Using simple tricks to make HyperCard more efficient

▼ HyperCard add-ons

Part IV
Specialized Mac Applications

Introduction

HyperCard can be a database, an onscreen animation system, a Finder and desktop organizer, a paint program, a sound editor, a gaming environment, a basis for custom applications, and more. It does these jobs at least as well as any specialized program of a few years ago.

You probably already have a copy of HyperCard. Up until very recently, it was shipped with every new Mac, and was distributed freely by user groups. Even though the full program now sells for approximately $125, it can save you money by eliminating the need for a lot of other applications. One business uses HyperCard to manage payables and receivables, maintain cross-referenced databases, keep a schedule, track new contacts, and generate personalized letters without a word processor. The stacks that make this possible—HyperCard's combination programming and data source—are easy to create, and thousands are available for free or as shareware. Claris Corporation claims there are more than 100,000 people writing stacks, and three million active users. Figure 18.1 shows some stack possibilities.

Figure 18.1
Some of the many faces of HyperCard.

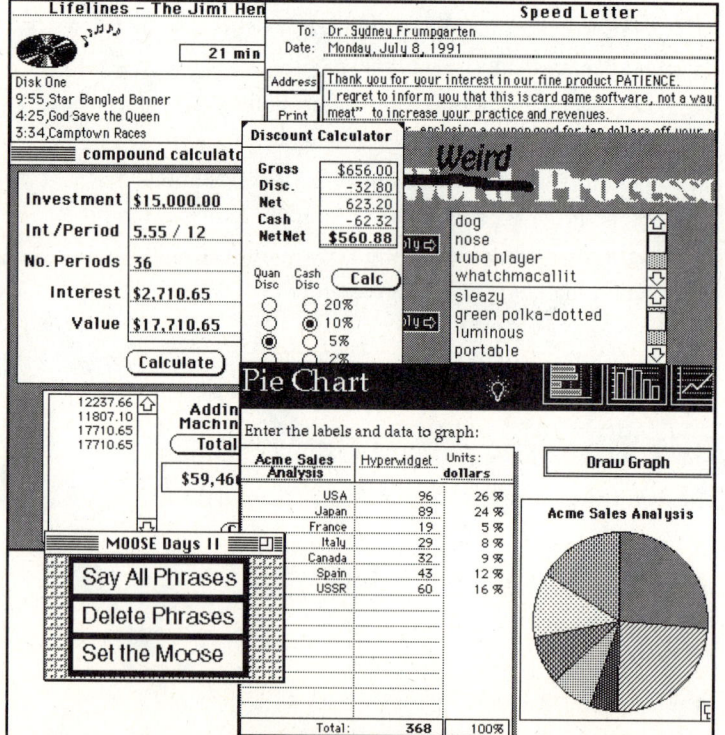

Chapter 18
HyperCard and SuperCard

You can approach HyperCard either as a program or as a programming environment. It's probably best to do both: use it with prepackaged stacks and, at the same time, learn its concepts so you can develop your own solutions to more complicated tasks.

As you read about HyperCard in this chapter, you'll also learn how to program it. The following sections build on each other, presenting bite-sized chunks of information in simple language, and reinforcing your learning with hands-on, interactive examples.

HyperCard is almost MacPaint

MacPaint, shipped with early Macs, was a revolutionary program (see chapter 7, "Graphics"). But according to legend, its author Bill Atkinson was never satisfied with the features. He'd keep writing new things for it to do, but Apple wouldn't include them in a free program. When Atkinson created the original HyperCard, he gave it the power he felt was missing from MacPaint. HyperCard 1.0 had more graphic tools than most versions of MacPaint I, and HyperCard 2.0's painting capabilities almost match MacPaint II's. The programs are by no means equivalent: MacPaint requires less memory, but HyperCard includes database functions, sound, and programmability. Figure 18.2 shows painting tools in MacPaint II and HyperCard. The "line width" and "filled shape" tools are available in HyperCard by double-clicking.

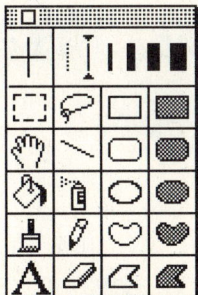 

Figure 18.2
Graphic tools in MacPaint (left) and HyperCard (right).

Part IV
Specialized Mac Applications

HyperCard and Hypertext

Many people confuse HyperCard with *hypertext*, an informational format that links words to other words or graphics. A typical hypertext document shows you a screen of graphics and text. You click on specific words or pictures to see definitions or more information. The more you click, the deeper you get into the subject (the "touch-screen" information kiosks found in airports and hotel lobbies are a simple form of hypertext). HyperCard can be a good *platform*, or programming environment, for hypertext, and is what Apple uses for the Guided Tours and Help files included with new Macs. Figure 18.3 shows Hypertext in HyperCard.

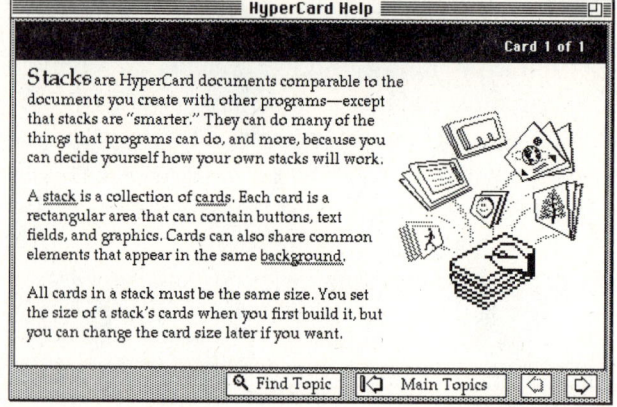

Figure 18.3
Hypertext can create Help files or Guided Tours for Mac applications, as in this HyperCard Help example.

Getting Your Hands on HyperCard

The reason there are so many HyperCard programmers and users is that Apple included the program with every Mac sold until mid-1992. Like the previously-bundled MacPaint and MacWrite, the program demonstrated the Mac's power as no other software could. (Also, Apple's original agreement with Atkinson said that for the first few years, it could give away HyperCard but could not sell it.) MacPaint and MacWrite were eventually withdrawn, revised, and commercially distributed by Claris Corporation. HyperCard followed a similar path, with Claris taking it over in late 1991. Their stripped-down version, HyperCard Player, is still included free with new Macs. The Player lets you do everything except customize or create stacks. (In early 1993, Apple took HyperCard back. They've announced plans for a new version based on AppleScript—Apple's method of letting programs send commands and data directly to one another—but as this book went to press no release date had been set.)

Chapter 18
HyperCard and SuperCard

HyperCard's Interpreter

HyperCard's original simplicity owed much to its *interpreted* nature. Interpreted languages examine English-language commands as you type them, translate them into microprocessor instructions, and immediately execute them. You can demonstrate this "type and respond" feature with the following exercise:

1. Start HyperCard. First, double-click on its icon or select its icon and then pull down the **File** menu to **Open** (or press Command-O). Or open any HyperCard stack.

2. When the program is running, open the Message box, a window that enables you to enter commands directly. Pull down the **Go** menu to **Message** (or press Command-M).

3. In the text window that appears, type: `The Date`. Press Return. Your typing is replaced with the correct date (unless your Mac's clock is wrong).

4. Try typing other commands such as `The Long Date` or `The Abbreviated Date` before pressing Return.

5. Type a mathematical formula using numbers and the following symbols for operators:

    + or –   Addition or subtraction

    * or /   Multiplication or division

    ^ (Shift-6) Exponent

    Do not type an equals sign at the end of the formula; just press Return. Typing `(6 *10^2) / 32` and pressing Return instantly gives you "18.75" in the Message box.

6. Try `The Time`, `The Name of This Stack`, or even `The Random of 100` for more examples.

Part IV
Specialized Mac Applications

Each time you press Return, HyperCard parses, or examines, the English-language instructions you typed. If it can understand them, it turns them into a code the chips can use. If it cannot understand them, it says so.

Compilers

The problem with interpreted languages is speed—or rather, lack of it. While the immediate interpretation makes learning the language and debugging a program easy, it also takes longer than if the instructions were already in machine-usable form. Repetitive tasks—common to most programs—must be interpreted over and over. This can really slow things down.

More powerful languages are compiled. After you write the instructions, they're run through a separate program and translated to CPU-level code that is carried out quickly. Almost every commercial Mac program (including HyperCard itself) is written in a compiled language.

The first versions of HyperCard were only interpretive, so complicated processes took a long time. Starting with version 2.0, HyperCard also included an automatic compiler. If you type a single instruction in the Message box, the system interprets it. But if you create a script, a series of instructions to do a specific task, the system compiles it! Operation is several times faster.

Which version should you run?

HyperCard 1.0 was introduced in the summer of 1987. Over the next three years, it worked its way through various bug fixes and minor enhancements to version 1.2.2. The program was replaced completely in late 1990 by HyperCard 2.0 (which, because of bugs, was immediately supplanted by version 2.0v2). That was the last version distributed for free. The current, commercially-available version is HyperCard 2.1. If you're running anything earlier than 2.0v2, you should switch. The new versions are faster, more powerful, and much more flexible.

Starting with version 2.0, you can also create windows of any size; mix text sizes and styles within fields of text; print more sophisticated lists of the data in a stack (either as reports or directly as mailing labels); display color drawings; record, edit, and play sounds; and customize menus. Version 2.1 added a few extra user shortcuts and script commands, as well as support for System 7's Apple Events. Both 2.0v2 and 2.1 can read early HyperCard stacks without modifying them, or can convert them to take advantage of the newer features.

Chapter 18
HyperCard and
SuperCard

If you have a pre-Summer 1990 Mac, you probably have an early version of HyperCard. Version 2.0 was available from some of the larger user groups, and may still be on their CD-ROMs. Until recently, you could upgrade 2.0 to 2.0v2 by sending a few dollars to Claris. If you did this, it's probably all you need. Don't use version 2.0 without the upgrade: it can crash while you're working.

If you paid full price for 2.0 or 2.0v2 or got it with a new Mac, Claris will upgrade to 2.1 for free. Just give them your serial number. If you're still running version 1.x, they'll upgrade you for $100 with proof of ownership. Most dealers will sell you a whole package, including example stacks, hypertext tutorials, about four inches worth of manuals, and the right to call Claris with technical questions, for approximately $150. If you plan on creating commercial stacks, you should spring for the $350 Developer's Licensing Kit, which also includes some other tools and the right to distribute HyperCard Player royalty-free.

All this will probably change, of course, when Apple releases the next version. Table 18.1 summarizes existing versions and upgrade options.

Table 18.1 HyperCard versions

	1.0 - 1.2.5	2.0	2.0v2	2.1	Player
Ease of Use:	Very easy	Same	Same	Same	Same
Speed:	Interpreted, slow	Compiled, 16x faster	Same	Same	Same
Graphic Tools:	Good	Excellent; includes programmable animation	Same	Adds more powerkeys	Can draw in existing stacks
Text Styling Tools:	Very limited	Good	Same	Same	Same
Image Size:	4.75" x 7.1"	.9" square to 17.8" square	Same	Same	Same
Sound:	Play only	Record and edit with Audio Palette	Same	Audio Palette no longer included	Determined by stack
Print Options:	Very limited	Good, but not perfect	Same	Same	Same

continues

Table 18.1 Continued

	1.0 - 1.2.5	2.0	2.0v2	2.1	Player
Programmability:	Easy	Easier features, with more debugging	Same	Adds even more commands	None
Reliability:	v 1.2.2: very good	Notoriously buggy	Good	Same	Same
Distribution:	No longer available	Free with Macs 8/90-1/91, still on some user group CD-ROMs	Free with some later Macs	Discounted to approximately $150 at dealers. Registered owners can upgrade for free or $100 (see text).	Free with current Macs. Or you can buy Claris for $30.
System 7 Support:	No	Compatible, but not 32-bit clean	Same	32-bit clean, Support Apple Events	Determined by stack

Running HyperCard

HyperCard documents, called *stacks*, aren't like documents created in other applications. A typical word processor or paint file includes only words (or paintings). HyperCard files include not only data but also the controls and interface to let you manipulate that data. That's why HyperCard can have so many different faces.

Well-designed stacks follow familiar Mac point-and-click conventions, so you can work them without knowing anything about the program. Figure 18.4 shows part of one simple stack; most stacks have similar features. The fields (Name, Notes, and so on) are straightforward Mac text-input boxes. You position the mouse over the field, click for an insertion point, and type just as you would with a word processor. You also can cut, copy, and paste (or use the Command-key equivalents). In version 2.0 and later, you can even use Command keys to select different styles of text. For instance, Command-Shift-B changes the selected text to Bold.

Two of the fields in the example, Notes and Expenses, have scroll bars. These work just like scroll bars in other programs. HyperCard's buttons also work like those in other programs, in that you click them to make them work. But what the buttons do might be unpredictable. It's up to the human creating the stack to make the button do something useful.

Chapter 18
HyperCard and SuperCard

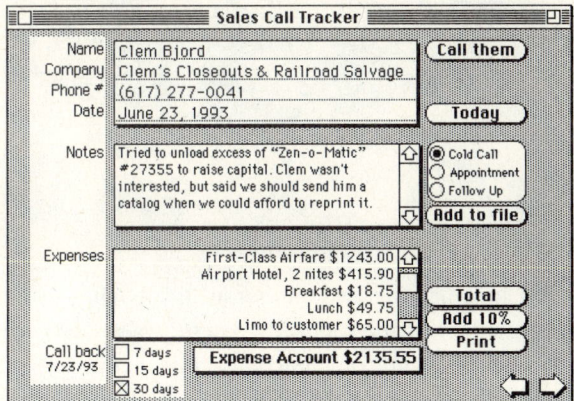

Figure 18.4
Familiar fields and buttons from other programs carry over to HyperCard.

Every stack is made of buttons and fields, no matter what it looks like. Some fields may be locked: the program, instead of the user, inserts the data. (If a field is locked, the cursor will not turn into an I-beam over it.) Similarly, buttons may be hidden, invisible, or otherwise not immediately accessible.

> **Note:** You can see all of a stack's usable buttons—even those that don't have a recognizable button shape—by holding down the Option and Command keys simultaneously. The outline of each button temporarily shows through as a dotted line, as shown in figure 18.5. If you single-click a button while holding down these keys, and have a high enough userLevel (defined in the section, "PowerUsers and userLevels," later in this chapter), you can read and edit the button's script.

Saving Your Data

One major difference between HyperCard and other Mac programs is that Command-S doesn't save your work. If you're an experienced user, you probably press that key combination several times an hour. HyperCard has no separate Save function; instead, it saves data whenever you change cards. (When you're using paint tools, HyperCard's **Keep** and **Revert** functions let you save and undo complicated changes.)

Figure 18.5
The gray dotted boxes show you where the buttons are.

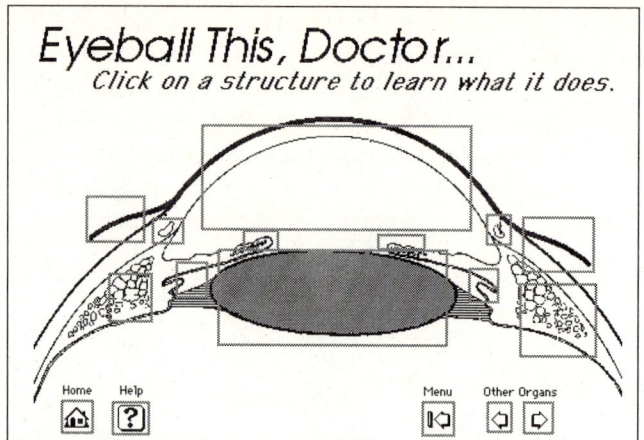

A Closer Look Because the program saves automatically, changes are written permanently to disk. If you're not sure of what you're changing, click **Save a Copy** first. It's on the **File** menu, where **Save as...** normally would appear. This makes a duplicate of the current stack. After you've checked your new version, you can throw the copy in the trash.

PowerUsers and userLevels

Often you don't want inexperienced users messing with a stack's scripts. Sometimes you don't even want them to interfere with the data—an information kiosk, for example, should be read-only to guard against pranksters. HyperCard lets you control user intervention by assigning userLevels. A low-level user is limited to reading data; a high-level user can modify stacks and menus.

Note Many HyperCard words are long and strangely capitalized. You'll see newCard, enterKey, and even mouseDownInPicture. Bill Atkinson probably figured mouseDownInPicture would be easier to remember than something like "mousedip," so he assigned portmanteau words to most functions. Since HyperCard cannot tell the difference between uppercase and lowercase, it treats USERLEVEL, userlevel, and userLevel the same. Programmers usually capitalize individual words in a command to make a script easier to read.

Table 18.2 shows the various userLevels and what they can do. Each level includes the privileges of the levels below it. All five levels are accessible from HyperCard 2.1; HyperCard Player has only the lower three.

Table 18.2 HyperCard userLevels

Level	Name	User Access
1	Browsing	Users can click buttons or move from card to card, but not change any data. Useful for running hypertext.
2	Typing	Ideal for data entry. The user can click and type in any unlocked field. User can also erase unprotected stacks, so be careful.
3	Painting	Can use MacPaint-like tools and keyboard shortcuts. Possibly useful in a child's entertainment stack.
4	Authoring	Can add, delete, lock, or unlock fields. Can create buttons that automatically take the user to other information. Used for creating hypertext.
5	Scripting	Can create any kind of stack, button or field. Can write scripts in a simple but powerful programming language. Can change or delete menu items, open other programs, and wreak general Mac havoc.

Changing the userLevel

Unless a stack has been locked with **Protect Stack** under the **File** menu, you can change the level by opening the Message box (Command-M). Type Set userLevel to, followed by the desired number, in the box. When you hit Return, the level is set. The change is temporary and not saved when you quit HyperCard.

You can also set a default userLevel in Apple's Home stack. Open the stack and select **Last** from the **Go** menu (or press Command-4). You'll see something similar to figure 18.6. Click the userLevel you like. (If you don't see a card similar to the one shown in the figure, you probably don't have

Part IV
Specialized Mac Applications

Figure 18.6
Apple's Preferences card lets you change the userLevel permanently.

Apple's official Home stack. You can still change userLevel in the Message box, or use the technique described in the section, "Your First Script," later in this chapter.)

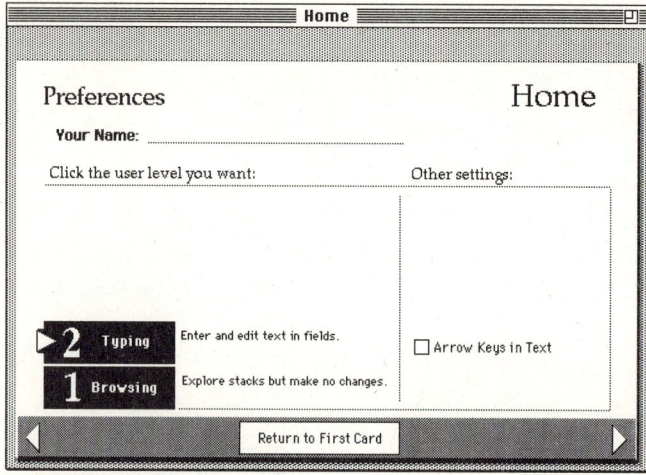

Apple's Magic Word

The Home stack as shipped with HyperCard may not let you choose a userLevel beyond two. If you want a higher level, use a little magic: type magic in the message box, and press Return. The card should change to look similar to figure 18.7. (If you type magic again, the card will change back. But it saves the higher level you set.)

Figure 18.7
Higher levels can be accessed by using a little "magic."

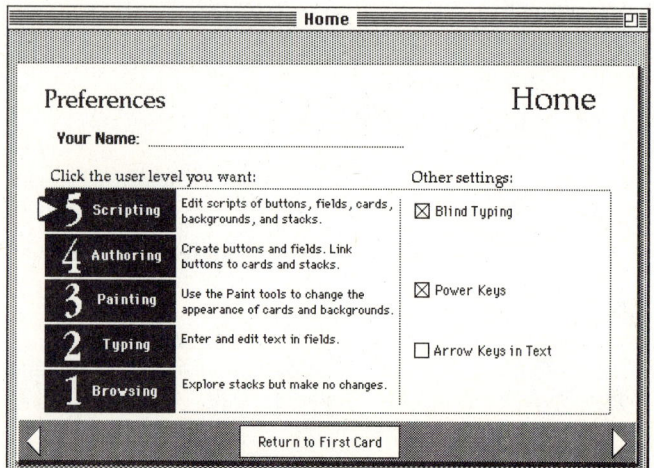

Your First Script

Chapter 18
HyperCard and SuperCard

You can set the userLevel permanently, even if no Preferences card is available, by modifying your Home stack's script. Just follow these five steps (later, you'll learn how scripts work):

1. Open HyperCard by double-clicking its icon. This takes you directly to the Home stack. If HyperCard is already open, select **Home** from the **Go** menu or press Command-H.

2. Press Command-M, and, in the box that appears, type: `Set userLevel to five`. This gives you temporary access.

3. Select **Stack Info** from the **Objects** menu. Click on **Script** in the dialog box that appears.

4. A large text-editing window appears. Place the insertion point after any text that's already there, and press Return to get a new line.

5. Type the following lines exactly as listed:

   ```
   -- patch to raise userLevel
   on openStack
   set userLevel to 5
   end openStack
   ```

6. Press Return and click the **Close** box. When HyperCard asks whether you want to save the script changes, click Yes.

The next time you start HyperCard, this script will execute. If you examine your script by repeating step three, you'll see that HyperCard has indented your typing to make it easier to read. If HyperCard cannot find a stack called "Home" in the first step, it'll ask for one. If there isn't one, open any other stack and use **New Stack...** in the **File** menu to make one—it's a handy thing to have. If you don't have any stacks at all, you cannot open HyperCard.

> **Note:** HyperCard starts with the Home stack unless you launch it by opening another stack from the Finder. The script you just wrote runs only when you open the Home stack (on openCard). If you start by double-clicking a different stack, HyperCard won't execute "your first script" until you select **Go Home**.

701

Part IV
Specialized Mac Applications

Stack Sources

New Macs come with a couple of stacks that discuss using your Mac, but the full program includes two disks of highly useful business and programming stacks. The two easiest to start with are Addresses and Appointments: to use them, just click and type. There's an invisible button in the top corner of the Address card (you can see it by pressing Option-Command). Click on it, and the corner of the card folds down (as shown in figure 18.8). This means the card is marked so you can retrieve it easily when it's time to print.

Figure 18.8
Dog-earing a card by clicking on an invisible button.

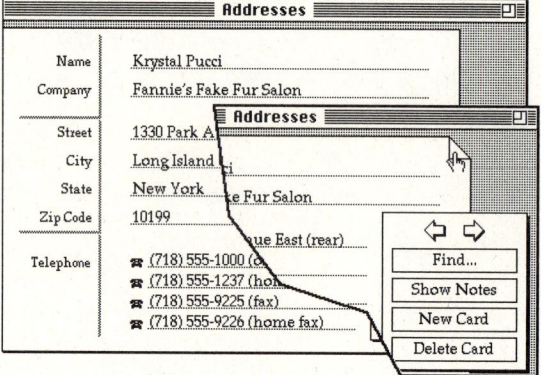

The best source for ready-to-use stacks is other satisfied HyperCard users. Because creating stacks doesn't require specialized computer training, many people write their own. They frequently give away their stacks or ask a small shareware fee. The two giant Mac user groups, BMUG and BCS•Mac, publish large libraries of public-domain stacks on floppy disk and CD-ROM. (See chapter 26, "The Macintosh Community," for more information.) National online services also have large downloadable HyperCard libraries; America Online's is particularly huge, with more than 3,500 stacks.

You probably won't find many HyperCard stacks available commercially. Stacks are so easy to write and customize that there isn't enough exclusivity to generate profits for the large software publishers, except for stacks linked to CD-ROMs. On the other hand, Heizer Software (Pleasant Hill, California; (800) 888-7667) acts as a clearinghouse for low-cost commercial stacks. If you cannot find what you're looking for at a user group or online, try this company. Its catalog is free, and most of the disks it sells cost less than $50.

HyperCard Structure

Chapter 18
HyperCard and SuperCard

The easiest way to get a stack you like is to build it yourself. All you need is a quick understanding of how HyperCard stacks are organized, and how instructions are passed in them.

Stack Organization

As you probably surmised, individual pages of data are *cards*. Cards can hold text fields, buttons, or graphics. Several cards with a related theme are a *stack*. But—and this is one of the reasons HyperCard is so powerful—cards are essentially transparent! Anything common to more than one card can be kept on a *background*, so it doesn't need to be repeated. Buttons, ruled lines, and identifying graphics usually are kept at the background layer, and only specific data and graphics are usually on the card. But you can also put buttons or fields on a single card if only that card uses them. To see the two layers, open any stack and select **Background** from the **Edit** menu (or press Command-B). The menu bar will have striped borders when you're looking at a background layer (see figure 18.9). Some stacks hide the menu bar entirely in their scripts. Press Command-Spacebar to alternately show and hide the menu bar.

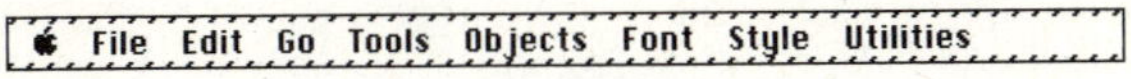

  File   Edit   Go   Tools   Objects   Font   Style   Utilities

Figure 18.9
Striped borders on the menu bar mean you're in the background layer.

A single stack can have one or many backgrounds, and each background can have as few or as many cards as you want. Figure 18.10 shows how background and card layers hold different elements of the Address stack. Figure 18.11 illustrates how multiple backgrounds and cards come together.

Figure 18.10

A single background and card from the Address stack.

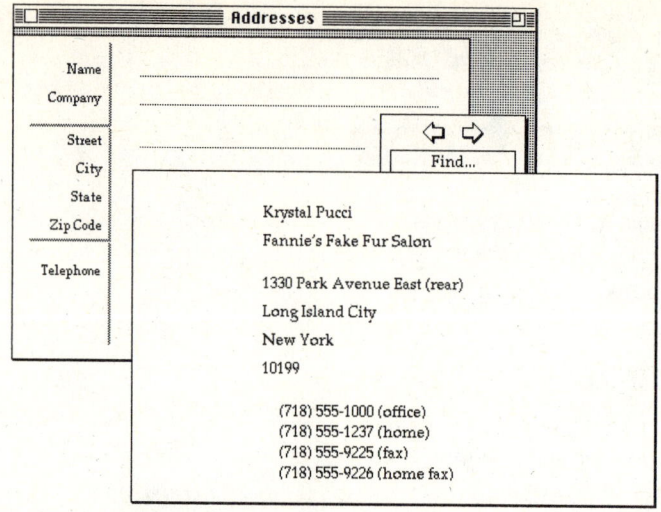

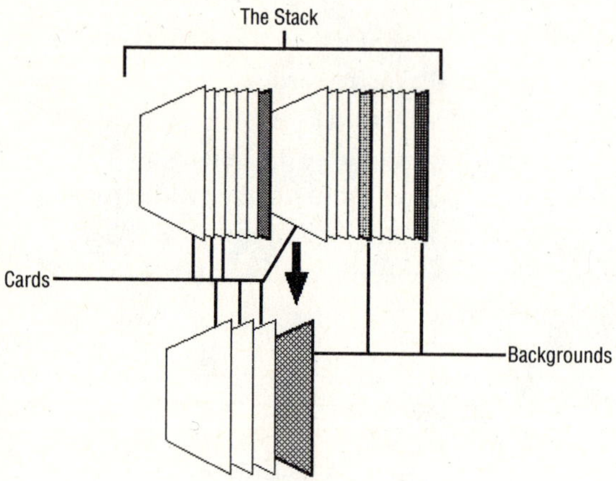

Figure 18.11

A lot of cards and backgrounds can make up a stack.

Objects and Scripts

Fields, buttons, cards, backgrounds, and stacks are all *objects*, elements that can have properties and scripts. (HyperCard graphics cannot have scripts, but you can put invisible buttons over them.) Scripts are activated by *messages*, basic reports of HyperCard activity that bubble upward from the card level, looking for something to trigger. This can be as simple as "the Return key is down" or "the user has pressed the mouse button." Of course, in HyperCard's one-word commands, the actual messages would be returnInField or mouseDown. When you typed magic in the home stack, the word looked for a script to trigger. You can see this script by selecting **Card Info** in the stack's **Objects** menu, while looking at the Home stack's Preferences card. Click on the **Script** button that appears, and you'll see something that essentially says:

```
When you see the word "Magic"
     Show extra userLevels
     or
     If they are already being shown, hide them
That's the end of instructions for the word "Magic."
```

Actual HyperCard scripts aren't much more complicated than this plain-English example. Scripts always start and end with the name of the message that triggers them. They have simple instructions in between, sometimes identical to the two- or three-word message box commands you saw earlier. No matter how long a script is, it still follows this structure. Here's a typical short script, from the **Total Expenses** button of the Sales Call Tracking stack shown in figure 18.4:

```
on mouseUp


  --Get all the items

  put field "Expense List" into ItemList
  put the number of lines in ItemList into TotalLines
  put empty into total

  - - Take each item and strip the "$" so we can add it to total


  repeat with LineNumber = 1 to TotalLines
    get the last word of line LineNumber of ItemList
    delete the first character of it
    add it to total
  end repeat
```

Chapter 18
HyperCard and SuperCard

```
  - - Put the "$" back and show it to the user
  put "$" before total
  put total into field "Expense Total"
    - - Get the user's attention
    beep

end mouseUp
```

It's easy to follow how this script works:

▼ The script's first and last lines name the message that triggers it. In this case, it's triggered when a mouse has been clicked and released within the button's borders.

▼ Lines with "- -" are comments: messages to help human readers understand the script's flow. Comments use little disk space and don't affect the way a script runs, so experienced HyperCard scripters use lots of them. Few experiences are more frustrating than trying to modify an un-commented script you wrote six months ago.

▼ The three indented lines in the middle are a loop that repeats itself for each line of data.

▼ When you save the script, HyperCard adds the indenting, even within the loop and between on mouseUp and end mouseUp. Type your scripts without tabs or initial spaces. You can preview the indentations by pressing the Tab key.

Note: Why make a button active when the mouse is released, instead of when it's pressed? Because users are fickle. If you press a screen button and then change your mind, you can slide off it without activating the button. Most Mac programs (and well-written HyperCard stacks) follow this same convention. Try it yourself: in stacks, word processors, and much of real life, things don't really happen until you let go.

HyperCard Workarounds

Even though HyperCard is a well-thought-out program, it still has some failings. For example, graphics created within the program cannot have scripts because they aren't objects. But you can place an invisible button over

Chapter 18
HyperCard and SuperCard

an area of the graphic (see figure 18.5). You can also create a color or black-and-white graphic in a separate drawing program such as MacDraw or SuperPaint (see chapter 6, "Graphics On a Macintosh," for more information) and import it in PICT format. In this case, you can use the mouseDownInPicture command.

Menus aren't objects either, but if you make custom menus with the **create menu** command (actually two one-word commands), you can then assign menuMessages to each line. Each message then requires a separate script to do the actual work. It isn't elegant, but it works.

SuperCard, a commercial HyperCard clone from Aldus with advanced features for professional programmers, lets you treat anything—even menus and paintings—as an object. You'll learn more about SuperCard later in this chapter.

Moving Through HyperCard

With HyperCard, you can jump instantly from any one card to any other card in any other stack on your disk. There are five ways to move:

- ▼ With the **Open** and **Go** menu commands and their keyboard shortcuts
- ▼ Using the arrow keys on the Mac keyboard
- ▼ With buttons in a stack (or selected words in fields that are programmed to work like buttons)
- ▼ With the Navigator palette
- ▼ Through **Go** commands in scripts and the Message box.

Navigating with Menu Commands

Selecting **Open** in the **File** menu (or pressing Command-O) takes you from one stack directly to the first card of another stack. When you click **Open**, a standard Mac dialog box like the one in figure 18.12 appears. The **Open Stack in New Window** option enables you to have more than one stack onscreen at a time (normally, each stack closes as the next opens). By choosing stack functions and window attributes carefully, you can use this function to simulate dialog boxes and desk accessories (see figure 18.13).

Figure 18.12
Open stack dialog box.

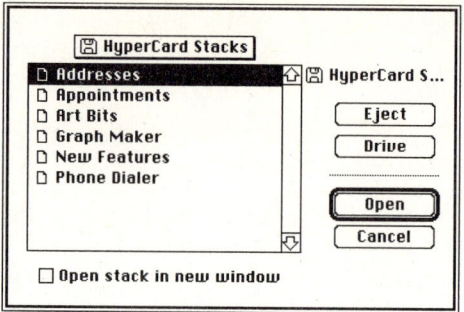

Figure 18.13
Multiple stacks can masquerade as DAs and other Mac features.

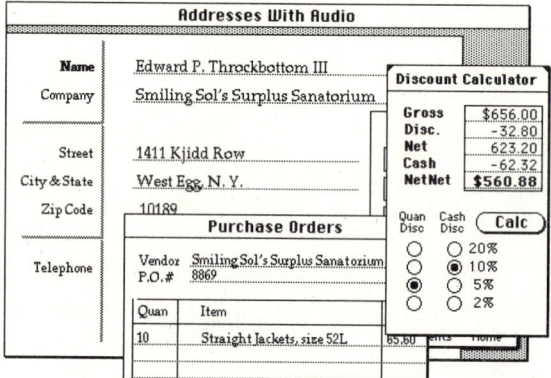

The **Go** menu lets you move easily to different cards in the current stack, the Home stack, or stacks you may have opened recently. This may be the handiest way to get around, since the menu's command keys are easily accessible. Table 18.3 summarizes the menu.

Table 18.3 The Go menu

Command*	Shortcut	Takes You To
Back	Command-~	The last card you had open
Home	Command-H	The first card of the Home stack
Help	Command-?	The Help stack, if HyperCard knows where to find it
Recent	Command-R	Mini-views of the last 42 cards you had open
First	Command-1	The first card of this stack

Command*	Shortcut	Takes You To
Prev	Command-2	The previous or preceding card in this stack
Next	Command-3	The next card in this stack
Last	Command-4	The last card in this stack

***Find**, **Message**, **Scroll**, and **Next Window** also appear in the **Go** menu, but they aren't really navigation commands: they activate other HyperCard functions.

What's the difference between **Back** and **Prev**(ious)? **Back** refers to the cards you've opened as user. If you've been jumping from stack to stack, it still takes you to the last card you had open (if the stack is still in your Mac). **Prev** refers strictly to how cards are placed in the current stack. It takes you to the card immediately in front (or to the left) of the one that is open, even if you never saw that card before. Of course, if you're browsing forward through a stack, one card after another, **Back** and **Prev** will do the same thing.

Recent shows you a thumbnail history of the previous 42 cards you visited, with a box around the current card. Click on any of the tiny cards to go directly to the full-size one it represents. These drawings are small, but if you have several different-looking cards (or are good at guessing), this screen can get you around quickly. Figure 18.14 shows a typical Recent view.

Chapter 18
HyperCard and SuperCard

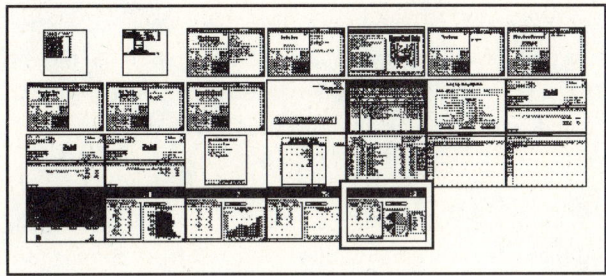

Figure 18.14
The Recent view shows miniature versions of the last 42 cards you had open.

Using the Navigator Palette

Palettes are little windows that can be used to control HyperCard. They usually hover over the current card, but you can drag them with the mouse to anyplace on your screen. The *Navigator palette*, included with HyperCard Version 2.0 and later, has icons that work like **Go menu** commands. You can

Part IV
Specialized Mac Applications

turn the Navigator on by typing `palette Navigator` or just `nav`: you'll see a little box similar to the one shown in figure 18.15. The bottom three buttons let you find text in a stack, open and close the message window, and bring other open stacks to the front.

Figure 18.15
The Navigator palette.

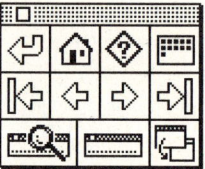

 The Nav command works because of a script in Apple's Home stack. If it doesn't work for you, add this script to your Home stack.

```
on nav
-- Requires XCMD: palette "Navigator"
palette "Navigator"
end nav
```

As you've learned, messages work their way from the current card and stack to the Home stack. Because the "on nav" script is in the Home stack, the **Nav** command works anywhere in HyperCard. The XCMD in the comments refers to an *External Command*, a set of compiled system-level instructions added to HyperCard to enhance existing commands (discussed later in this chapter). The palette XCMD and the Navigator palette itself is included, already installed, with each current copy of HyperCard.

Navigating with Arrow Keys

The Left and Right Arrow keys work like **Prev** and **Next** commands; the Down Arrow works like **Back**, stepping you backward through the Recent window. But the Up Arrow is not like any menu or Navigator command; it takes you to the card opened after the one you're looking at. In other words, if you have looked at cards 2, 4, 9, and 13 in order, then move backward to card 4, the Up Arrow takes you to card 9—the one you opened after card 4. Up Arrow cannot read the future, of course: if you're already at the last card to be opened (card 13 in this example), the key takes you back to the first one.

Chapter 18
HyperCard and
SuperCard

> **Note:** Most word processing programs use the arrow keys to move the insertion point through text. Some users prefer to have arrow keys work that way in HyperCard, so they check **Arrow Keys in Text** on the Preferences card (or type Set textArrows to true in a script or in the Message box). With textArrows set to true, the arrow keys move the insertion point around in a field when you have clicked in a field. When the cursor is outside a field, the arrow keys go back to navigation.

If you find that arrow keys are working word processor-style, press Option-arrow instead. Option forces the arrow key to its navigation function, no matter what.

Navigating with Buttons

Many stacks include buttons that either duplicate the **Go** menu's functions or link to specific cards. Usually these buttons have icons to indicate their function, although it is completely up to the person who created the stack. To make things easy, most stack creators match their icons to the ones Apple has established (see table 18.4). Click on one of the icons, and it probably moves as the table indicates.

Table 18.4 Common HyperCard navigation icons

Typical Icon	Where It Takes You
	First card of stack
	Last card of stack
	Next card in stack
	Prior card in stack
	Back to previous card you opened
	First card of Home stack
	Help card or stack
	"About" card or stack

711

Navigating with the Message Box and Scripts

Note: You can turn almost every **Go** menu choice into a HyperTalk command just by adding the word Go.

▼ If you type `Go Home`, `Go Next`, `Go First`, `Go Last`, or `Go Back` in the Message box you'll get there. You also can add to or card if you want, to make the sentence more readable: `Go to First Card`. You can expand this construction in powerful ways: `Go to Card "Zipcodes" of Stack "Addresses"`, `Go to Card 17 of this stack`, or even `Go to Second Card of first background of this stack`.

▼ You can name cards or backgrounds by typing in the **Objects** menu's appropriate **Info** dialog box.

▼ Named or not, HyperCard assigns each card and background a unique identification number when it's created. You can find this number by checking the **Info** dialog box or by typing `The ID of this Card (or Background or Stack)` in the Message box. Then you can issue commands such as `Go to Card ID 3829` or `Go to the First Card of Background ID 1917`.

▼ Each card also has a unique number relative to its background, but that number changes if you sort or rearrange cards. `Go to Card 17 of this stack` might not always take you the same place.

With the **LinkTo** option described later in this chapter, you also can automatically create buttons with Go to Card ID scripts.

Painting in HyperCard

HyperCard's painting capabilities and MacPaint work almost the same way. If you're familiar with MacPaint, you already know how to use its tools. (If not, see chapter 6, "Graphics On a Macintosh," for more information.) HyperCard also gives you some extensive paint options that are missing from MacPaint and MacPaint II but available in programs like Aldus SuperPaint. And HyperCard can paint on itself: you can write scripts that control the painting tools for automated graphics and animation.

Where the Paint Goes

You can use HyperCard's paint tools on the background layer or the card layer, depending on whether you want the graphic to show on one card or many. Figure 18.16 shows the differences. Effectively, there are four layers: background buttons and fields always cover background paintings, anything on the card layer always covers the background, and card-layer buttons or fields cover card-layer graphics. Figure 18.17 shows how it all fits together.

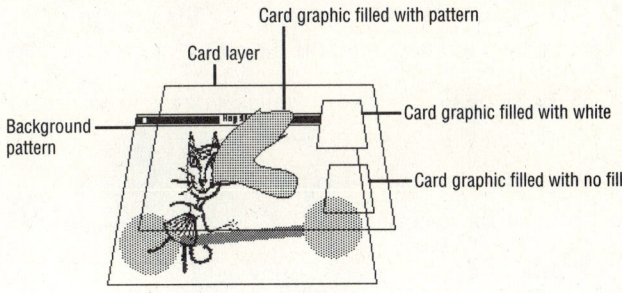

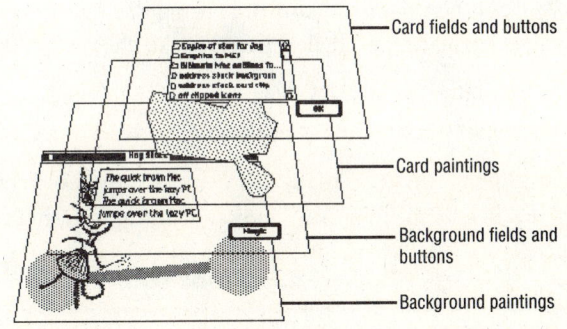

Chapter 18
HyperCard and SuperCard

Figure 18.16
Anything on the card layer covers anything on the background layer.

Figure 18.17
Buttons and fields always cover graphics.

 If you paint a white or black pattern on the card layer, it covers up and effectively erases anything on the background layer while that card is open. If you show or hide an empty text field, you can make the graphics below it appear to turn on or off.

Using Painting Tools and Menus

The paint tools are on a tear-off palette under the **Tools** menu. You can move the palette anywhere on the screen by holding down the mouse button over the word Tools and dragging to the new location. The palette looks like the one shown in figure 18.18 when it's on the menu bar; when you drag it elsewhere the word "tools" disappears from it.

Figure 18.18
The Paint tools are available if you are at userLevel three or higher.

A few of the tools have multiple functions:

▼ Hold the Command key while using the Pencil for a zoomed-in, FatBits view to edit individual pixels.

▼ Hold the Option key while using any tool in FatBits for a Hand tool to move the picture around.

▼ Hold the Shift key while using most of the drawing tools to force regular shapes and lines into exact 15° increments.

▼ Hold the Command key while using the Selection rectangle to force the rectangle to the smallest possible size that will fit the selected image.

▼ Hold the Command key while clicking the Lasso on any part of an image to select the entire image.

Most of the tools in the menu also work as shortcuts to other functions if you double-click them. Table 18.5 summarizes these shortcuts.

Table 18.5 Paint tool shortcuts

Double-click	*Function*
Eraser	Erases all the graphics on the card or background
Lasso	Selects every element
Line tool	Changes the line width
Most polygon tools	Turns Draw Filled on or off
Paint bucket	Brings up the Patterns menu
Paintbrush	Changes brush shape
Regular Polygon	Changes the number of sides
Selection Rectangle	Selects an area the size of the full card or background
Text tool	Changes the font, size, or style

Using the Painting Menus

When you select a paint tool, the menu bar changes to show **Paint**, **Options**, and **Patterns** menus. The **Patterns** menu is identical to the Pattern Selection palette in MacPaint II. The other two, shown in figure 18.19, do some things you might not find in other programs.

Chapter 18
HyperCard and SuperCard

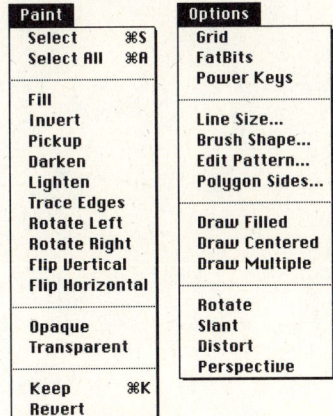

Figure 18.19
The **Paint** and **Options** menus offer advanced features.

HyperCard's **Options** menu is roughly equivalent to MacPaint II's **Goodies** menu. The **PowerKeys** selection (also available on the Preferences card of the Home stack) lets you choose any paint tool with a keyboard shortcut. The **Polygon Sides** selection lets you set the regular Polygon tool to create anything from a triangle to an octagon. You also can select a circle in **Polygon Sides** to make the regular Polygon tool work like the Shift-constrained Circle tool. The **Draw Multiple** selection makes any of the drawing tools repeat while you drag them, as illustrated in figure 18.20.

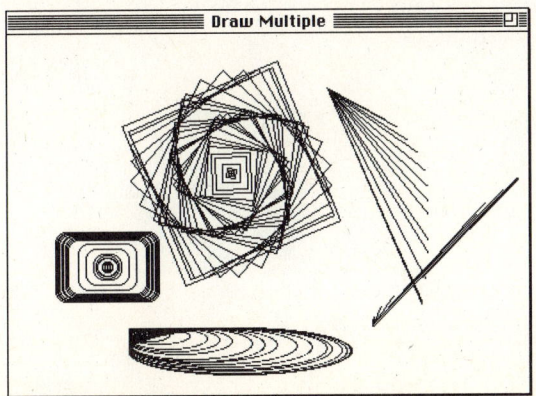

Figure 18.20
Draw Multiple multiplies itself when you drag the tool.

715

Part IV
Specialized Mac Applications

The **Rotate**, **Slant**, **Distort**, and **Perspective** options let you alter any image chosen with the Selection Rectangle. These options put large handles in each of the image's corners. If you move one of the handles, the selection distorts to fit. Figure 18.21 shows its effects.

Figure 18.21
HyperCard's paint effects and an altered waterfowl.

Original   Distorted   Rotated   Perspective

The **Paint** menu is similar to MacPaint II's **Edit** menu, but with some extra functions. **Trace Edges**, **Flip**, and **Rotate** work on any image you choose with the Selection Rectangle or Lasso; in MacPaint these selections affect only objects you select with the Rectangle. **Darken** and **Lighten** add random black or white pixels inside the selection. **Opaque** and **Transparent** control how HyperCard mixes images when moving or pasting. These work like the Option-Command drag options you can set in MacPaint II's **Preferences** menu.

Note: **Pickup** lets you fill any image with pixels from any other area on the card. Select the target image with the Lasso and move it over the desired background. Its outline should continue flashing. Then, without clicking anywhere else, select **Pickup** from the **Paint** menu. Finally, click back inside the target image and move it somewhere else; when you do, a copy of the background comes with it. Figure 18.22 illustrates these steps.

Figure 18.22
Using the Pickup selection.

Keep and **Revert** ask HyperCard to save your drawing as part of the open stack. HyperCard saves text and object changes automatically but not drawing changes. Your graphics aren't saved until you take one of the following actions:

▼ Select **Keep** from the **Paint** menu or press Command-K.

▼ Leave the Graphic mode by selecting the Hand, Button, or Field tools.

▼ Leave the card or stack, or quit HyperCard.

If you're happy with your work but want to try something else, press Command-K. This works like the Snapshot function in MacPaint. **Revert** then undoes all of your recent changes and restores the graphics to the last version you kept. **Undo**, of course, still functions in the usual way; it removes only the last change you made.

Making HyperCard Draw on Itself

Imagine creating hypertext that draws a circle around selected words in a field or an inventory that blacks out missing items. You can control HyperCard's drawing tools with two simple HyperTalk commands: **Choose** and **Drag**. (The commands are simple; getting the drawing to look the way you want may take some experimentation.)

Using Coordinates in Drawing

The key to successful art, whether with oil paints or computers, is knowing where to put the image. HyperCard determines points on the screen with two coordinates. The first number is always the number of horizontal pixels (dots) from the left margin of the active window; the second is the number of vertical pixels from the top. You can guess an approximate location by remembering there are 72 pixels to an inch, so the coordinate "150,75" is approximately two inches in from the left and one inch down. Figure 18.23 shows various coordinate locations.

> **Note:** If you've started up with Apple's Home stack and type xy into the message box, the box turns into a coordinate display when you press Return. It then displays horizontal and vertical coordinates of your mouse, constantly updating as you move the mouse.

When you click in a specific location, the coordinates are no longer updated. You can then copy these coordinates and paste them into a drawing script.

Chapter 18
HyperCard and SuperCard

Figure 18.23

HyperCard uses coordinates to determine a point on the screen.

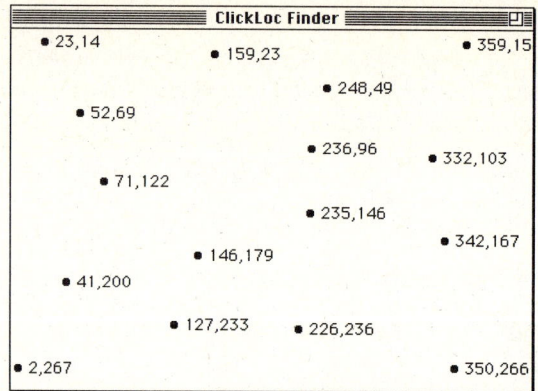

You don't need a map or Apple's home stack to find any point on the screen. HyperCard names the point for you when you use the clickLoc function:

1. Click anywhere on the HyperCard screen.
2. Open the Message box (press Command-M). Don't click in the box; the insertion point will already be flashing there.
3. Type The clickLoc and press Return.
4. The coordinates where you clicked in step one appear in the Message box. You now can copy and paste them into your script.

WARNING! If you click to set the insertion point in step two, that new click becomes the clickLoc—and this procedure just tells you the Message box's coordinates.

Note You also can use clickLoc in scripts. Figure 18.23 was generated by creating a transparent button the size of the full stack's window and then writing a short script. The script also shows the **Choose** command:

```
on mouseUp

    --this script draws coordinates on the screen where you click

    choose text tool

    click at the clickLoc

    type "·" & the clickLoc

    choose browse tool

end mouseUp
```

718

The first line mimics the Text tool icon in the Tools palette. You can choose any other painting tool with a similar command. The second and third lines mimic clicking the mouse and typing a number. The bullet symbol (Option-8 on the Mac keyboard) makes the point easier to identify. The last line mimics clicking the HyperCard Browse tool to give normal mouse response back to the user.

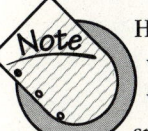

To be precise, the bullet symbols are a few pixels above and to the right of the actual clickLocs, depending on which font you use. When you click with the Paint Text tool, you actually set the baseline and starting point for a line of type. We could have asked HyperCard the textSize, and then subtracted appropriate pixels from the horizontal and added them to the vertical, but that would be a little complicated for this stage in the chapter.

Dragging to Paint

To automatically paint an image after you've chosen a tool, simply tell it to drag from one set of coordinates to another. The effect is exactly the same as if you had held down the mouse button and manually dragged the tool across the screen. You can try it easily:

1. Open the Message box (press Command-M).
2. Choose a Paint tool either by clicking or with a command.
3. Type `Drag from 0,0 to 150,150` and press Return.

You undo this the same way you would if you'd used a mouse.

HyperCard can drag only in straight lines. Dragging at an angle with the oval or rectangle tool creates circles and boxes. If you want to draw complex shapes, you must break them down into small units. You can see this in the following script. It joins random straight lines to create the "Drunkard's Walk," a classic test of computer graphics. The script looks long because we've added so many comments. You could leave them out and it would work exactly the same.

```
on mouseUp

    -- get something to draw with

    choose line tool

    set linesize to 2  -- medium thick line
```

Chapter 18
HyperCard and SuperCard

```
    -- determine the starting points
    put 200 into horizStart
    put 130 into vertStart
    -- and also initialize the endpoints
    put horizStart into horizEnd
    put vertStart into vertEnd


    -- erase any old lines. doMenu is just like clicking a menu choice
    doMenu "Select All"
    doMenu "Clear Picture"


    -- keep the steps from being too close
    set the grid to true


    -- start a loop of fifteen random, connected lines
    repeat 15 times
        -- create someplace to stop. MakeRandom defined below.
        add MakeRandom() to horizEnd
        add MakeRandom() to vertEnd
        -- do it!
        drag from horizStart,vertStart to horizEnd,vertEnd
        -- make the next segment start where this one ended
        put vertEnd into vertStart
        put horizEnd into horizStart
    end repeat
```

```
        - - give control back to the user

    choose browse tool

end mouseUp


Function MakeRandom

    - - function is called by the mouseUp script

    Return (the random of 100) - 50

end MakeRandom
```

We put this script into the **Walk** button, in the card shown in figure 18.24. Each click of the button gave us a different random Walk pattern.

Chapter 18
HyperCard and SuperCard

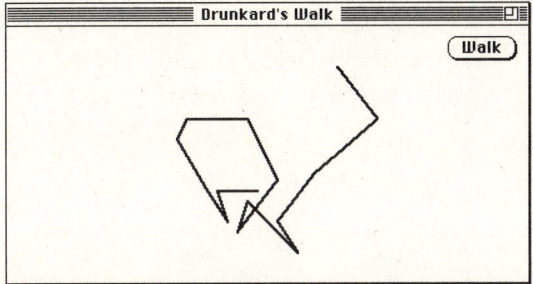

Figure 18.24
A classic "Drunkard's Walk."

> **Note** This listing actually shows two scripts. The "on mouseUp" through "end mouseUp" lines draw the image. The last four lines define a *user function*, a procedure that becomes part of the message hierarchy after it is compiled. If we put those lines in the Home stack script, you could use the function anywhere in HyperCard just by calling for it. In this case, typing the MakeRandom() in the Message Box would show you a random number between -50 and +50.

The () is a dummy argument. All functions use *arguments*, numbers within parentheses that tell the function what to work on. For example, we might define a function to calculate square roots, SqrRt x; if you put "4" in place of "x," it would return "2." MakeRandom doesn't work on an argument, but HyperCard still needs the parentheses to identify it as a function. Hence the

Part IV
Specialized Mac Applications

dummy argument: you could put (4), (3.14), or (Fred) in the parentheses, and the results would be just as random. This script uses one active argument:

```
function biggerNumber yourNumber
    add 10 to yourNumber - - this adds 10 to the argument
    Return yourNumber - - this sends it to whoever called
the function
end biggerNumber
```

Copy this script into your home script. Then, if you type `biggerNumber(100)` in the Message box, you get 110 when you press Return.

Using Options and Effects Not on the Tool Menu

There are two ways to use options and effects that aren't on the Tool Palette, and both appear in the Drunkard's Walk script:

1. Use the **doMenu** command followed by any menu item. You can use this command to do anything that appears in a menu if:

   ▼ You specify the menu item exactly (**Paste** is not the same as **Paste Text**, and **Print Stack** is different from **Print Stack...**)

and

   ▼ The item is available when you ask. (You cannot **doMenu Paste Text** when no text has been copied or cut.) **doMenu** also activates most things on the Apple menu, so you can call desk accessories with it.

2. Set the *property* directly. An object's properties are simply the sum of all the choices you can make through menus or Info boxes. You almost always can make these choices with the command set A to B, where A is the name of the property, and B is either true or false, or a number.

You can see it in these script lines:

```
set linesize to 2
set the grid to true
```

We used the set command because it always works, even if the menu item is missing or has changed state. **DoMenu** causes problems with toggling menu choices: if we had used **doMenu Grid** to turn the grid on in our script, running the script a second time would have turned the grid back off!

Printing from HyperCard

Chapter 18
HyperCard and SuperCard

Early versions of HyperCard had limited printing capabilities. You could print a single card, you could print all the cards with one command, or you could list the contents of a field in "plain-vanilla" Geneva. If you wanted anything more complex, you had to export the data to a word processor or buy a third-party printing utility. But starting with HyperCard 2.0, you can

▼ Print the text from a single field, or the image of a single card;

▼ Print just the cards you've selected (with a set marked command, through a card's **Info** box, or by dog-earing the page in some Apple stacks);

▼ Print groups of cards in various page formats;

▼ Print sophisticated reports, phone lists, and labels in an infinite variety of sizes and styles.

Printing a Single Card or Field

Printing a single, whole card is the easiest. Select **Print Card** from the **File** menu, press Command-P, or type `Print Card` in a script. The card is sent directly to a printer without showing the Mac **Print** dialog box.

Selecting **Print Field** brings up the dialog box shown in figure 18.25. Highlight the field you want to print in the scrolling list. Sample text in the font and style on your card appears in the Contents box. Click **Use Width of Field** to make each line exactly as wide as it is onscreen (useful for formatted lists). Otherwise, text is printed the full width of the page. Either way, all the text in a field is printed, even if the field has scrolled to hide some if it.

723

Figure 18.25

The **Print Field** dialog box, where options are selected for printing.

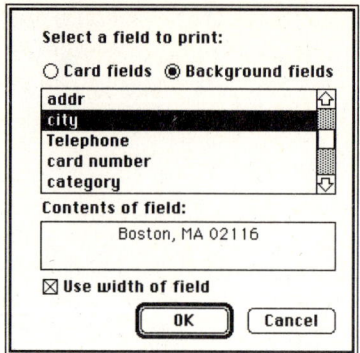

HyperTalk gives you two ways to print a field without a dialog box. The command `Print field "Notes"` works as though you had turned on the **Use Width** selection. `Print (field "Notes")`—the parentheses are important—uses the full width of the page, 10-point Geneva type (Helvetica on laser printers), and left alignment. You can specify other printing styles with commands like `set printTextFont to Times`, `set printTextSize to 12`, `set printTextAlign to center`, and so on.

Printing Groups of Cards

Choosing **Print Stack...** in the **File** menu brings up a dialog box where you can choose which cards to print, the page layout, and a page header. After you choose your options, click **Print** and a standard Mac printing dialog box appears. HyperCard saves **Print Stack...** with the stack, so you don't have to reformat every time you print.

A few things you should know about Print stack:

▼ The large Preview window on the left continually updates itself, using mini-images of the current card. If you click **View Margins** or **View Spacing** in the lower right, you can change those characteristics by dragging the preview images with your mouse. **View Size** is different: it reports the actual size of the **Printed Card Size** you chose. If you try to move an image with this View selected, it will automatically switch to **View Spacing**.

▼ Split-page format leaves a blank area across the middle of the page, so you can fold pages in half easily.

Chapter 18
HyperCard and SuperCard

▼ High-quality printing sends the fields in your cards as text, so a printer can use its built-in fonts. Leaving this option off keeps the screen fonts, which may be illegible if you have reduced the cards.

▼ Text you type in the **Header** box appears at the top of each page. The first four icons in the lower left of the screen add the date, time, stack name, or page number to that box. The arrow icon tabs to the center or right margin of the page. Thus, our example would print something like:

7/2/73   Accounts Payable   p. 4

Note: **Print stack** draws a PICT image of every object the card. If you have several cards, this can take a long time. High-quality text and open areas print faster than patterns and bitmap drawings. Covered fields and buttons slow things considerably—the program has to draw them and then cover them up. If all you want is the text, you can save time by using **Print Report** instead. If you want very fast printing with graphics, consider FormsProgrammer (discussed later in this chapter).

A Closer Look: The scripting commands **print all cards** or **print marked cards** use the options set in the **Print stack** dialog box. These commands bypass the print dialog box, so you can write scripts that automatically print without user intervention. These commands can get very powerful, in structures like **print next marked card**, **print five cards**, or **print card from 0,0 to 150,72** (to print only the specified area). If you want to print multiple cards on a single page, try a script like this:

```
on mouseUp

    open printing

    print card 17 - - this will be the top of the page

    print card "My Page Bottom Card"

    close printing

end mouseUp
```

In this script, open printing treats everything that follows as one print job. Nothing is sent to the printer until you close printing; then HyperCard tries to fit as many cards on a page as it can.

Note: HyperCard even lets you print documents from other programs. A command like

```
print "HD80:memos folder:Vacation request" with "HD80:Word
folder:Microsoft Word"
```

temporarily stops HyperCard, launches Word, prints the memo, quits Word, and restarts HyperCard. This works in System 6 as well as System 7, so it can serve as a limited substitute for Apple Events.

Type the entire command on one line of the script or Message box (it's split here for readability) and specify the file paths exactly; otherwise, HyperCard will give you a dialog box asking you to locate the files. Of course, you also must specify real documents and applications.

Printing Reports of Data

When you print reports, you deal with text only. You can arrange them for custom mailing labels or index cards as easily as for data printouts, and you can save multiple report formats in a stack. **Print Report...** lets you design and save a *template* of how the text will appear, with a dialog box like figure 18.26. Templates are made of *cells*, little boxes that hold selected, formatted data from each card. You can name templates with the **Edit** menu, and call up templates from the **Reports** menu or by typing a command such as `Open report printing with template "Inventory Cards"`.

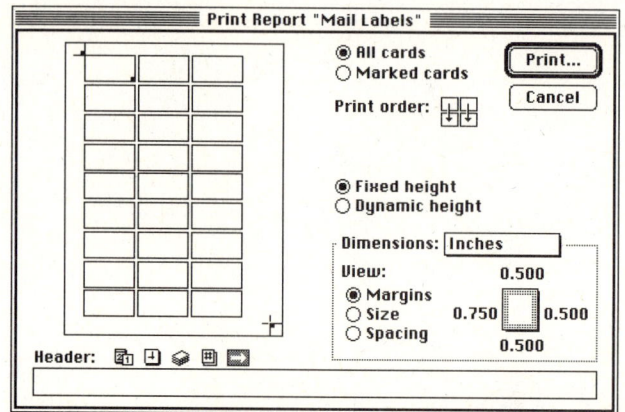

Figure 18.26
The **Print Report** dialog box lets you custom-format a text report.

The **Print Report** dialog box's functions are similar to **Print stack**, with three exceptions:

▼ **View Size** lets you use the handle in the lower-right corner of the first cell in the Preview window to resize the cells to fit your application. You can use any convenient shape, from labels and cards to single-line cells for a phone list.

▼ **Dynamic Height** lets a cell grow to fit the text, useful for data reports. **Fixed Height** cuts off text that doesn't fit the cell, so it won't mess up label formats.

▼ Double-click any cell to edit how data appears in it. A second dialog box, **Report Items**, appears (as shown in figure 18.27).

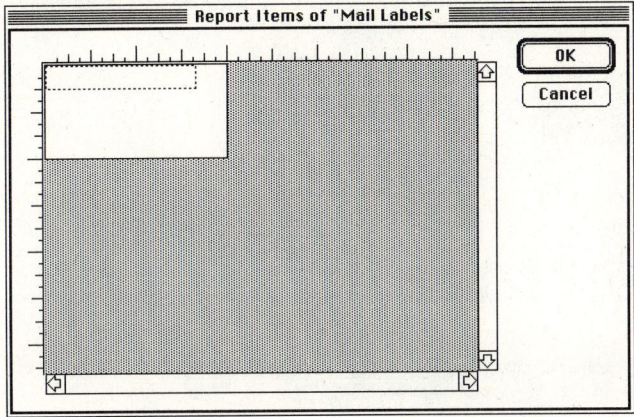

Chapter 18
HyperCard and SuperCard

Figure 18.27
The **Report Items** dialog box lets you arrange data in a cell.

The **Report Items** dialog box lets you create *items* to hold the report's text. Place an item by selecting **New** in the **Items** menu (or by pressing Command-N). This gives you the text box outlined in figure 18.28. You can move or resize the box by dragging. Make a new box for each field you want in the report. Then double-click within each box to specify how and what to print. You'll see a third dialog box, shown in figure 18.28.

▼ Double-click an item in **Background fields**, and its name appears in **Contents of item**.

▼ The **Font**, **Size**, **Style**, and **Line height** areas initially are grayed to indicate that default printText styles will be used. Click the box next to any of these attributes to change the styling.

▼ When you click OK, the **Report Items** dialog box appears again. Sample text now appears, using data from the current card. If the text doesn't fit, you can resize the item.

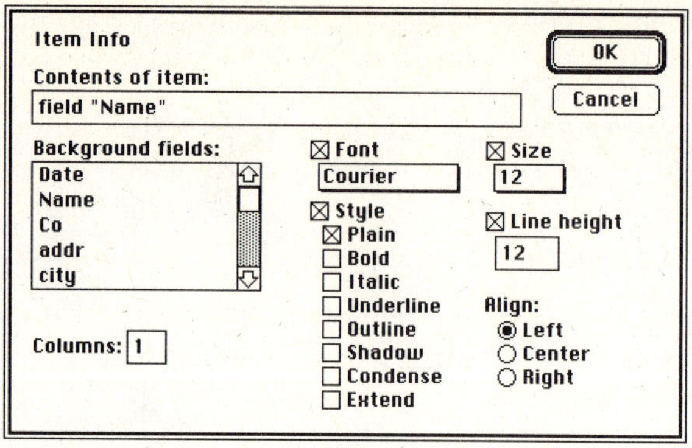

Figure 18.28

Each item has an **Item Info** dialog box to specify its text.

> **Note:** An item can contain any HyperTalk expression that results in text. `Field Name`, `line 2 of field 2`, `Their number is:`, and `field phone` are all valid. You can try expressions in the Message box before you use them, by preceding them with the command `Put`.

Music and Sound in HyperCard

HyperCard can make your Mac a very musical—or noisy—companion. Any Mac can play melodies on command, or load and play sounds from pre-recorded libraries. With a few simple utilities (and add-on hardware for Macs that don't have microphones) you can record and edit voice messages, and play them back under script or button control.

The Mac's sound quality is limited, of course, by its hardware. And you should expect to use a lot of disk space unless you're simply playing melodies: sampled audio files can get very large. (See chapter 16, "Sound, Music, and Speech," for more information.)

Recording and Editing with the Audio Palette

Until very recently, HyperCard came with an "Audio Help" stack. The name was particularly apt: not only did the stack teach you to use sound, it also had the scripts and resources that turned HyperCard into a full-featured audio recorder. The stack added items at the bottom of other stacks' **Edit** menus, including **Audio...** and **Audio Help**. If **Audio Help** is in the same folder as your Home stack when you start up, you'll see commands like those shown in figure 18.30.

Chapter 18
HyperCard and SuperCard

Figure 18.30
Audio edit menu commands may appear at the bottom of your **Edit** menu.

> Even though Audio Help isn't being shipped any more, there's nothing wrong with it. Claris stopped including it because of distribution problems. If you have a copy of Audio Help, you can use it with HyperCard 2.0v2 or 2.1, and under Systems 6 or 7.

Add Audio Memo and **Audio...** both open the palette shown in figure 18.31. The controls on the left work like a tape recorder to let you record or play a sound. If your Mac doesn't support a built-in microphone, the **Rec** button is inactive.

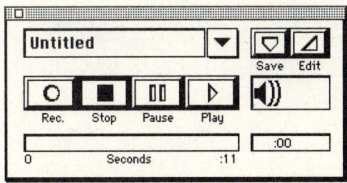

Figure 18.31
The Audio palette in HyperCard.

▼ The pop-up menu lets you choose any sound saved with that stack. Its name then appears in the box to the left, and you can play the sound or replace it by recording over it.

▼ The speaker icon shows you the incoming volume. If "sound wave" lines are not flashing near the speaker, the microphone isn't working.

▼ The Seconds bar shows you how much memory is available. It fills up as you record.

▼ The Length window shows you the length of your recorded sound.

▼ The **Save** button installs the sound in the current stack and creates a button to play the sound.

▼ The **Edit** button expands the palette to the one in figure 18.32.

Figure 18.32

The Audio Editing palette allows changing of sounds in HyperCard.

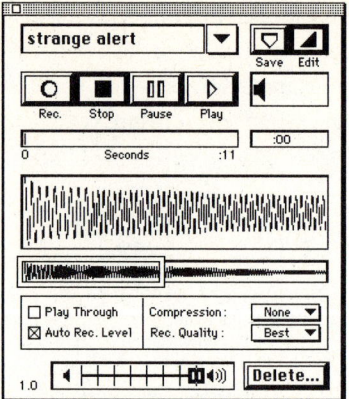

The Audio Editing palette may look confusing, but it's explained in the Audio Help stack. However, the stack ignores one potential problem: compression compatibility.

Compression Pressures...

The **Compression** pop-up menu lets you save sounds in a format that uses less disk space. (This information is covered in the Help stack.) Unfortunately, compression is not friendly to older Macs. A file compressed by the Audio palette may not be playable on these machines. At best, HyperCard warns you that your system cannot handle these files. At worst, you get silence. If you're creating a sound that may need to run on older Macs, don't compress it.

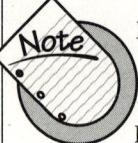 Even if you have the Audio Help stack, you won't see the audio commands unless your Home stack knows to look for it. If audio isn't working properly, you must add these instructions to your Home stack's script:

```
on startUp
    if there is a stack "Audio Help" then
        start using stack "Audio Help"
        send "startSound" to stack "Audio Help"
    end if
    pass startUp
end startUp
```

Chapter 18
HyperCard and SuperCard

If you already have an "on startUp" script, just add the commands to the beginning of your existing script. `Start using` lets the Home stack—and therefore, all of HyperCard—use any of a specified stack's scripts. `Send "startSound"` tells Audio Help to modify HyperCard's menus. `Pass startUp` lets the startUp message continue along the hierarchy.

This script also demonstrates a conditional: the commands if, then, and end if check to see whether a condition is true. If it is, they carry out the commands between them.

Audio Alternatives

As we mentioned, even though Audio Help still works perfectly, it's not being shipped by Claris any more. The same can be said for HyperSound, a collection of sound recording and editing tools that used to be included with MacRecorder but was dropped after MacroMind acquired the product. If you have either of these two stacks, you can use them safely with any current version of HyperCard. If you want a currently-supported product, consider Articulate System's Voice Record or Voice Impact. These two relatively low-cost packages (approximately $60 or $100, depending on whether you need a separate microphone) share software that can add recording commands to existing stacks.

Playing Sounds in HyperCard

Once you install a sound, playing it is easy; just click the button. In most stacks, the button carries the name of the sound or has a small picture of a loudspeaker.

You also can play any sound in a stack with HyperTalk commands. Try these:

1. Open the Message box (press Command-M).
2. Type `Beep` and press Return. If you don't hear anything, make sure the volume is turned up in the control panel.
3. Type `Beep 3`.
4. Type `Play "Boing"`.

The last command plays any sound you name, as long as it's available to HyperCard. You can see a list of sounds in your system file by opening the Sound control panel. You can use the Audio palette, ResEdit, or most sound editing programs to check which sounds are saved with a particular stack. In addition, HyperCard itself includes some built-in sounds: try `Play "flute"` and "harpsichord", as well as telephone dialing tones (dial0 through dial9, plus dialA through dialD and dial* and dial#, for accessing voice mail and other services).

Making Melodies

When you type Play you hear the sound once, exactly as it was recorded. But you also can also play tunes, if you add parameters to the command. HyperCard assumes you know something about standard musical notation:

▼ The letters *A* through *G* specify pitch.

▼ A *#* or *b* following a note sharpens or flattens the note.

▼ The numbers *1* through *7* set the octave, starting on C. *C4* to *b4* is the octave starting at middle C. *B3* is a half-step below middle C.

▼ Following a note with *s*, *e*, *q*, *h*, or *w* sets the rhythm as *sixteenth*, *eighth*, *quarter*, *half*, or *whole* notes. (You can use *t* for a *thirty-second* note or *x* for a *sixty-fourth* if you're in a hurry.)

▼ Adding the word *tempo* and a number before the list sets the tempo in beats per minute.

▼ An *r* adds a rest (okay, that's not standard).

You can use capital or lower-case letters (*Bb* and *bB* both mean "B-flat"). The octave and rhythm value commands all the following notes until you specify new values. Accidentals apply only to a single note at a time. You can set the tempo only once. If you don't specify anything, the melody plays in quarter-notes, tempo 120, at octave 4. To try putting it all together, open the Message box and type:

```
play "harpsichord" tempo 100 c5 c ge f# g g# aq ae re gh
```

Put groups of these commands in a script to play more complicated melodies. Harmony in HyperCard is nearly impossible, unless you're incredibly nimble with arpeggios.

Playing Pictures in HyperCard

Chapter 18
HyperCard and SuperCard

Claris' QuickTime Tool Kit, shipped with HyperCard 2.1, lets you add animation to your stacks. Move this compressed folder to your hard disk and double-click: it expands to a QuickTime Tools stack, and a sample QuickTime movie (a zooming "Claris" logo—what else?—with fanfare). The stack itself includes full instructions and commands for everything from building an animation window to synchronizing playback with other stack actions. You must create the movie itself in a multimedia program, as discussed in the next chapter. Figure 18.33 shows some of the controls available in QuickTime Tool Kit.

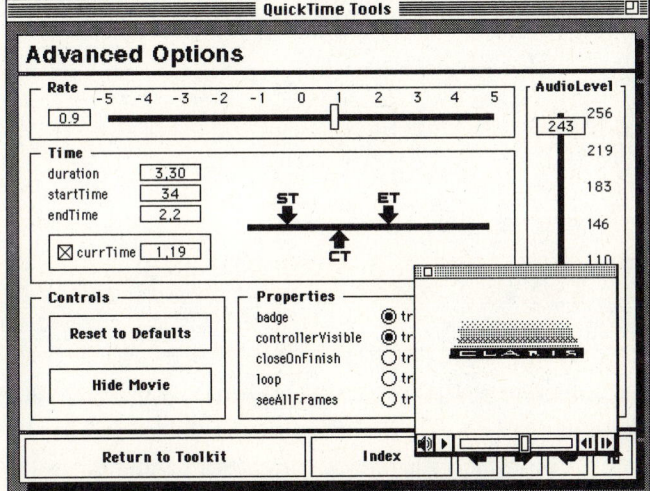

Figure 18.33
Some of the QuickTime Tools controlling a sample QuickTime movie.

Customizing Your Stacks

Even if you're not a power user, you can make HyperCard do what you want. At userLevel four, you can build new stacks and add fields or buttons—all without typing a line of HyperTalk. Add some simple userLevel five

Part IV
Specialized Mac Applications

commands, and you can change menus, import or export data, design palettes, and create stacks that look and feel like commercial programs.

No Programming Allowed

UserLevel four is ideal for creating information stacks without worrying about programming languages. In fact, at this level you cannot even read a stack's script. But you still have a lot of control.

Starting a New Stack

Say you want to create a filing system for your compact discs. You want to be able to search for particular songs or artists, or print a list of your entire music library. You also want a button that takes you directly to the record store listing in your Addresses stack. **Choose New Stack...** in the **File** menu, and you'll see a dialog box like the one shown in figure 18.34.

Figure 18.34
Every new stack starts with a dialog box similar to this one.

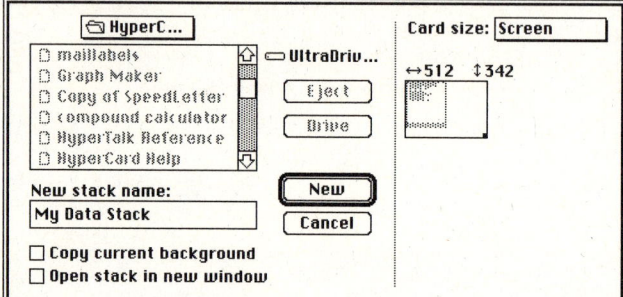

The dialog box works like a standard Mac **Save As...** dialog box. Give your stack a name, and make sure it's in an appropriate folder or disk. **Open stack in new window** lets you see the current stack and this new one at the same time, and is handy for copying data or objects. If you don't check this option, the current stack closes as you start the new one. **Copy Current Background** does exactly what it implies; use it if you want to keep the fields and buttons from your current stack.

The **Card Size** section lets you specify sizes up to a foot and a half square, depending on the amount of memory available (if the card is bigger than your Mac's screen, a scroll palette automatically appears). Every card of a stack must be the same size. Adjust it by selecting a size in the pop-up menu or by dragging the handle on the lower right of the card icon. The size is displayed in pixels, 72 to an inch. If you cannot make a large enough card, you need more memory. Quit HyperCard, open its **Get Info** dialog box on your desktop, and increase the Application memory size.

Creating Fields

First, decide if the new field should be on the card layer (holding only one set of data) or on the background layer (available to a number of cards, and holding either the same or different data on each). For our CD database, we'll need background fields: choose **Background** in the **Edit** menu (or press Command-B) and make sure the menu bar has striped borders. (You can review this with figures 18.9 through 18.11.) **Select New Field** in the **Objects** menu, and an empty field similar to the one in figure 18.35 appears. At the same time, HyperCard automatically selects the Field tool. With this tool, you can relocate the field by dragging, or you can resize it by moving its corners.

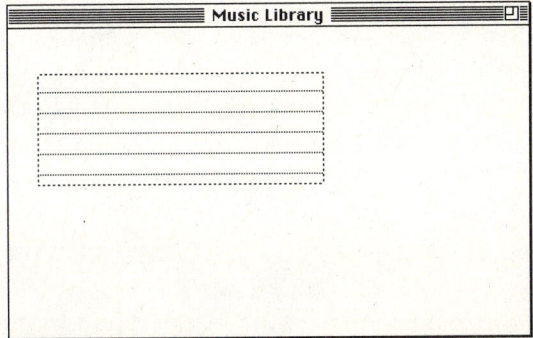

When you're happy with the field's size and location, double-click on it: a dialog box where you can set its properties will appear (see figure 18.36). You don't have to give the field a name, but it's easier to work with if you do. While most of the options are intuitive, a few require explanation. **Auto Tab** makes data entry easier: with this option on, pressing return in this field takes you to the start of the next field. **Shared Text** means the field's data can be seen by every card, and you can only change data when you're in the Background layer. (This is useful for "About…" fields or status reports.) The **Font…** button lets you set a default font, size, and style for this field. You'll still be able to change how individual characters appear when you enter data. The **Script…** button is dimmed until you're at userLevel five.

Chapter 18
HyperCard and SuperCard

Figure 18.35
A New Field appears as a dashed box with lines in it.

Figure 18.36
Double-clicking in a field lets you specify options with this dialog box.

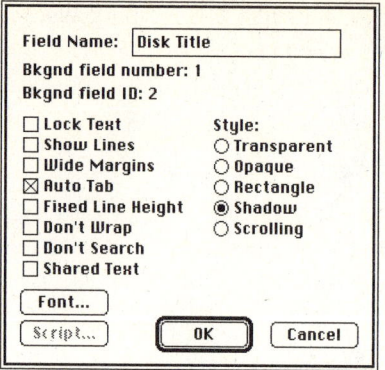

Repeat the process to create other fields on the background. Don't worry if you're not sure how you want to organize things. HyperCard lets you create and modify fields even after a stack is in use. Once the fields are in place, use the Paint tools to add labels and other graphic embellishments. The result may resemble figure 18.37. We added the speckled background by double-clicking the Selection tool (to select the whole background) and then choosing **Darken**. We cannot enter data yet since we're still in the background. But if we use the **Background** command again and select the Browse tool (or press Command-B and then tap Command-Tab once), we can start filling in the blanks. To get new cards for other disks, just select **New Card** in the **Edit** menu (or press Command-N).

Shortcuts:

Command + Tab	Chooses the Browse tool
Command + Tab + Tab	Chooses the Button tool
Command + Tab + Tab + Tab	Chooses the Field tool
Command + Option	Shows buttons
Command + Option + Click	Opens the script of a button
Command + Option +Shift	Shows fields
Command + Option+ Shift+ Click	Opens a field's script
Command + Option + B	Opens the script of the current background
Command + Option + C	Opens the script of the current card
Enter (while editing a script)	Saves changes and closes the script

Not all shortcuts may be available, depending on the userLevel.

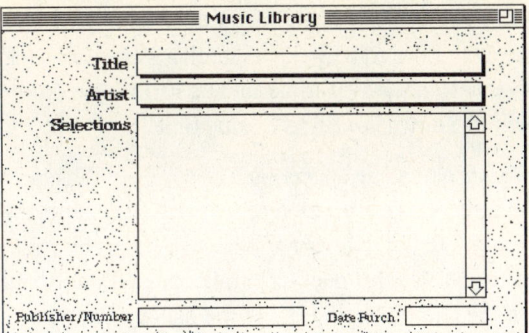

Figure 18.37
These completed fields are ready for use.

Buttons—The Easy Way

Now let's add a button, using a similar procedure. Go to the background, select **New Button**, adjust the size and location, and double-click. You see the **Button info** dialog box, as shown in figure 18.38.

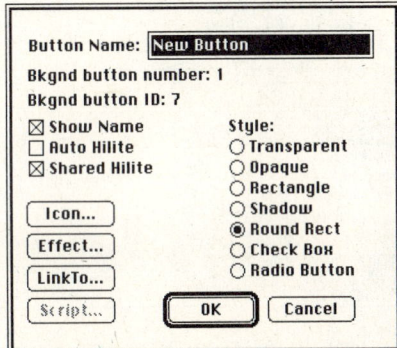

Figure 18.38
Double-click on a new button for the **Button info** dialog box.

▼ You don't have to give the button a name. But if you do, and you click **Show Name**, the name makes it easier for a user to figure out what the button's supposed to do.

▼ **Auto Hilite** makes the button flash when you click it. Macintosh programming guidelines recommend highlighting buttons this way, to confirm the user's choice.

▼ Check **Shared Hilite** if you create the button in userLevel four. With it off, you can use buttons to hold "yes/no" information on individual cards. But this requires scripting with userLevel five.

▼ **Icon...** lets you give the button an icon, for a more Mac-like interface. Click here, then chose one from the immense display of icons that appears. There are more than 180 icon designs built into HyperCard,

Part IV
Specialized Mac Applications

and you can also use any icons currently in your System. But if you don't like any of the choices, pick one that's close and select **Edit**: you'll be able to draw a custom one in a FatBits-like window. You can use **Icon** and **Show Name** at the same time.

▼ **Effect...** adds cinematic effects such as wipes, zooms, or dissolves when the button takes you to another card. Click here, and choose an effect from the dialog box that appears (some of the choices are shown in figure 18.39). The proper HyperTalk command for your effect will appear in the text box at the top of the dialog. When you click on OK, the visual-effect command is inserted into the button's script.

▼ **LinkTo...** makes the button actually do something useful, without your having written one line of HyperTalk. Once you set up a link, the button will take you instantly to any other card—in this stack, or on any mounted disk. If the card then is deleted, the button then does nothing.

Figure 18.39
A few of the many effects you can choose for going from one card to another.

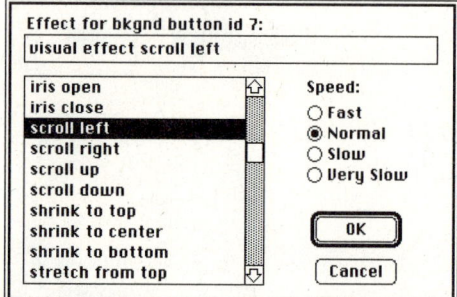

When you click the **LinkTo...** button, HyperCard immediately closes the dialog box and puts a palette on the screen like the floating above the card in figure 18.40. The palette stays there while you go to another card (using menus, arrow keys, or via any other navigation technique). When you get where you want the link to go, click one of the palette's buttons: **This Stack** creates a path to the most recently opened card in the new stack; **This Card** creates one to the specific card that is showing.

That's it! Anytime a user clicks the button on the card you were programming, HyperCard will jump immediately to the new card (using any visual effects you've chosen). You have successfully programmed a button. You can add as many more buttons as you want this way, now or any time the stack is open.

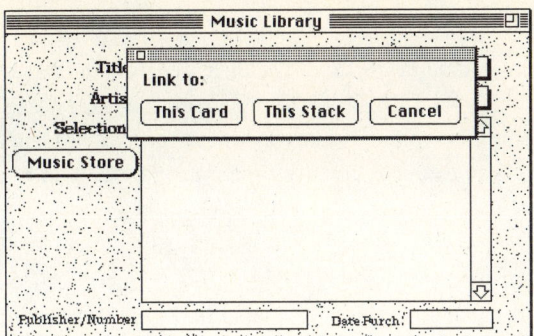

Figure 18.40
Clicking **LinkTo...** gives you this palette, to automatically program a button.

Making HyperCard Do Anything You Want

Throughout this chapter, you learn hints and practice working with HyperTalk. If you set a userLevel of five, you can add scripts from this chapter (or any of your own) to HyperCard objects. The **Script...** button in figure 18.38 will be undimmed, or you can click a similar button in any other object's **Get Info** dialog box. Learning a few shortcuts, and the concept of *containers*, will help you get started. First, consider the following shortcuts:

▼ If the Button tool is active, you can Shift-double-click on a button to open its script immediately. (If the tool isn't active, press Command-Tab twice quickly to select it.)

▼ Pressing Command-Option shows you outlines of every button on the screen. Command-Shift-Option adds outlines of every field. Click once in any of these outlines to open the object's script.

▼ When you open the script of a new button, **on mouseUp** and **end mouseUp** are already there. Just type your commands between them.

▼ When you close the script of a button, a box appears asking if you want to save the changes. Choose **No**, and your new script disappears. You can close a script and save the changes instantly by pressing Enter.

▼ If you try to run a script with a programming error, the HyperCard shows a dialog explaining the problem. It also gives you a **Script** button: click to go directly to the offending line of the script.

▼ The Error window also has a **Debug** button, which activates a powerful programmer's tool. A discussion of this tool would go beyond the scope of this chapter, but the tool itself is perfectly safe. Feel free to experiment.

Part IV
Specialized Mac Applications

Containers

HyperCard stores data in *containers*. Fields are containers that keep data onscreen and automatically save it to disk. You also can establish *variables*, temporary containers that exist only as long as a script or HyperCard is running. Here's an example, a script for a button to tell you how long you've owned a CD:

```
on mouseUp

    -- get the date you bought it, in seconds since Jan 1 1904.
    put background field "Date Purch" into boughtDate
    convert boughtDate to seconds


    -- do the same thing with today's date from the Mac clock
    put the date into todayDate
    convert todayDate to seconds


    -- subtract one from the other, and display
    put (todayDate - boughtDate) into age
    put "Record is " & age & " seconds old." into Message
end mouseUp
```

BoughtDate, **todayDate**, and **age** are all containers. Unlike other programming languages, HyperTalk does not require you to *declare* variables, or indicate whether they hold text or numbers. All you have to do is put something into a container, and it's ready to use. Everything is treated as text until you try to do something mathematical with it.

Convert... to Seconds is a HyperTalk command that takes any standard date format and calculates how many seconds have elapsed since January 1, 1904 (the starting date of the Mac's internal clock). This command is useful for calculating the time between two events, as is done in this example script. If we wanted to display age in days, we could have divided it by 60*60*24—sixty seconds in a minute, sixty minutes in an hour, and twenty-four hours in a day (we can tell HyperCard to divide with the number drawn out that way, as well as by dividing by 86400).

Chapter 18
HyperCard and SuperCard

Even after we converted the containers to seconds, **boughtDate** and **todayDate** still held text—in this case, a string of text like 2784931200. When you try to subtract the containers, HyperCard first checks to see that the subtraction makes sense, then it does the calculation and puts a text string with the answer into the container. If it doesn't recognize the parts of the problem as numbers, it gives you a dialog box explaining the problem.

You name variables in a script as single words without quotation marks surrounding them. But fields are also containers; to use them in a script, identify them by name, number on the background or card, or unique ID number. Depending on where the script is, you may also have to identify it as a background or card field.

You can create **global variables** that hold their contents as long as HyperCard is running and can be accessed by any script. These variables are defined with the word *global*, usually in the first lines of any script that uses them. In the following linked scripts, the global *howManyNew* is advanced each time you make a new entry:

```
on openStack
    - - let's start the counter from zero
    global howManyNew
    put 0 into howManyNew
end openStack


on newCard
    global howManyNew
    add 1 to howManyNew
    - - if you've typed ten new disks, you're working too hard
    if howManyNew > 10 then
        beep
        put "Take a break, then type 'more' to reset." into message
    end if
    pass newCard
end newCard
```

```
on More
    global howManyNew
    - - reset the counter
    put 0 into howManyNew
end More
```

The first script makes sure the global starts out with a number that can be added to. The second script is triggered each time you use the menu command **New Card**, and increments the global. If it thinks you've been working too hard, it reminds you to take a break. The third script resets the global when you type the secret word More. All three would be part of the background's script.

Working on Your Own

There's no way to cover all of HyperTalk in a chapter this size. (Some users frequently consult three or more large references while creating complex stacks.) But this chapter includes enough information to get you started. To learn more about scripting:

- ▼ Use the Message box liberally to run tests. It responds to most HyperTalk commands and functions.

- ▼ Examine scripts other people have written. Ask online or at a user group to see which scripts have been well commented. Make a copy of a stack you like, and try changing some of the scripts.

- ▼ Get a HyperTalk reference manual. The one in the HyperCard Developers' Kit (from Claris) is helpful, and you also can find good ones in bookstores.

- ▼ Above all, experiment. Try different commands and concepts. No command you can issue will damage HyperCard permanently. At the worst, you must restart or get a fresh Home stack from the backup disk.

Most people find HyperTalk easier to learn, faster, and more powerful than the traditional teaching language, BASIC. It also gently forces you to use *object oriented programming* techniques for greater programming efficiency. But the rewards of learning HyperTalk are financial as well as intellectual: once you know how to control your Mac directly, you can use it more productively without having to spend money on commercial software.

Beyond HyperCard

Chapter 18
HyperCard and SuperCard

As strong as the HyperTalk language is, it cannot do everything. Some tasks, such as accessing the Mac's Finder and System-level functions, were deliberately left out for safety reasons. Others, including massive screen and text manipulations, are slow and cumbersome in HyperTalk. Some advanced programmers use more powerful languages to create modules that address these limitations. Others use HyperCard's style and construction in a more powerful third-party application, that picks up where Apple's quits.

Externals

External Commands and External Functions, *XCMD*s and *XFCN*s, are powerful resources you can add to any stack. They're created in programming languages such as C and Pascal, but once in place they become part of HyperTalk. Then you access them like any other HyperCard command or function. The range of externals is mind-boggling. Any function not already in HyperCard—from changing your Chooser name to controlling MIDI instruments—is probably available as an external.

Externals are usually available through bulletin boards and user groups, either free or for small shareware fees. America Online lists 750 downloadable stacks of externals; many with multiple commands or functions. Most of these stacks both demonstrate the external and have a button to install the external on your own stacks. You can also move externals with ResEdit, a powerful (but potentially dangerous in the wrong hands) program available from public-domain sources. Or just keep the demonstration stack on your disk, and add a Start using stack command as we did in the section on Audio Palette.

FormsProgrammer

Printing complex layouts in HyperCard has always been slow. One low-cost commercial software package generates custom printing XCMDs for you. Ohm Software's FormsProgrammer enables you to design printed pages in a separate window, as shown in figure 18.41. You specify the data to be printed with standard HyperTalk expressions. Once the form is designed, name it and FormsProgrammer quickly creates an XCMD to print it, and transfers the XCMD to any stack you specify. If we name the form in our example "printInvoice," typing `printInvoice` in the Message box or a script sends the finished invoice to the printer, using the data from the current

Part IV
Specialized Mac Applications

card, in less than a quarter of the time HyperCard normally takes. Because your computer is effectively frozen while HyperCard prints, this increased speed can make a big difference if you have several pages. FormsProgrammer may be difficult to find at software stores, but you can contact Ohm in Tiverton, Rhode Island, at (401) 253-9354.

Figure 18.41
A sample invoice created in Ohm Software's Forms Programmer.

SuperCard

SuperCard is a third-party workalike for HyperCard, not a mutant teenaged version of Apple's product. Users of the original HyperCard were both excited by the concept and dismayed at its limitations. Silicon Beach Software (now a subsidiary of Aldus) responded with SuperCard, a completely re-engineered application that improves on the Apple original. Many of HyperCard's gaps were filled in with version 2.0, but SuperCard has also kept growing. Its present version, 1.6, offers almost all the graphic capability of Aldus' SuperPaint (see chapter 6, "Graphics On a Macintosh"), as well as System 7 functions, including Apple events and user-defined Balloon Help.

SuperCard Features

In SuperCard, everything is an object. This includes drawings and pop-up menus as well as fields and buttons, so *projects* (roughly equivalent to stacks) easily can look and feel like full-blown Mac applications. In fact, the utilities supplied with the program—and there are many of them—were written in SuperCard using standard scripts. Scripting follows the same conventions as HyperCard (although with many more commands). SuperCard also supports multiple window sizes, something that requires multiple stacks in HyperCard. Figure 18.42 shows a basic SuperCard screen with some of the utility windows open. Figure 18.43 shows some of the additional choices available for text.

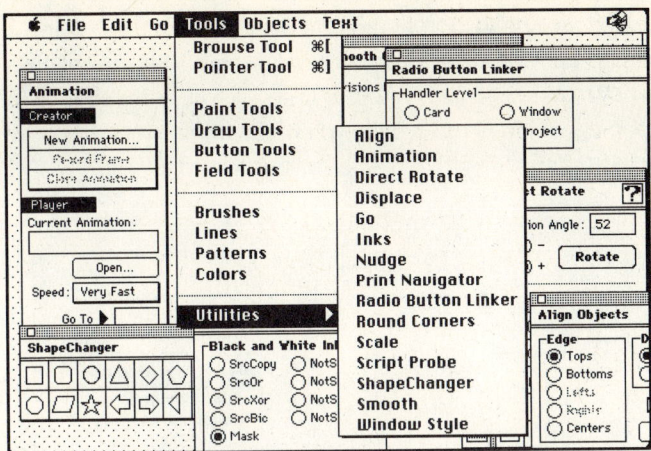

Figure 18.42
A SuperCard screen with several menu options open.

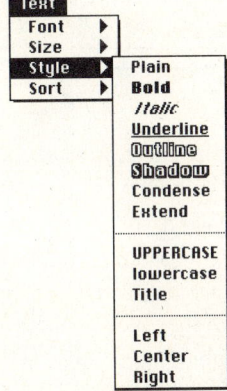

Figure 18.43
SuperCard offers many choices for text.

SuperCard's graphics allow both drawings and paintings, in up to 256 colors at once. The program also can import full-color PICT and TIFF images from other applications and video digitizers. By combining graphic power and object orientation, SuperCard becomes an excellent platform for animation. Special commands have been provided to move objects along editable paths, flash multiple colors onscreen, and play back images at up to 60 frames per second. The program also can import standard PICS animation files.

SuperCard even can create projects that do not use SuperCard. You can design custom applications, tell the program to save them as standalones, and give—or sell—them to Mac owners who do not have SuperCard.

SuperCard Organization

SuperCard is actually two programs (plus a small utility that enables you to easily switch between them). You create objects in the *editor*, and then move the project to the *application* to run. The script editing window includes immense pop-up windows with scrolling lists of available commands. To add a command to the script, just click. It is faster to type in the script window, but the pop-up windows can remind you of the more advanced commands and control structure. Figure 18.44 shows this feature in use.

Figure 18.44
Pop-up windows make writing a script in SuperCard much easier than in HyperCard.

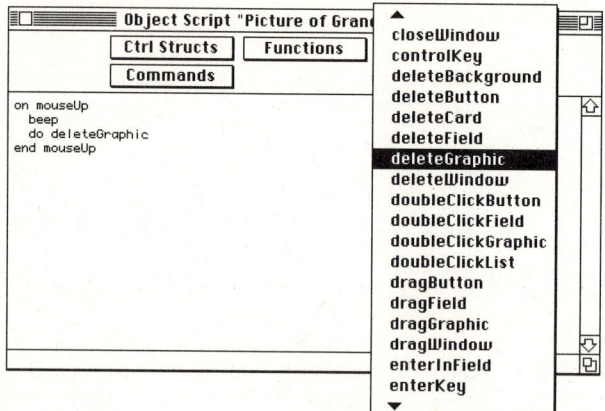

Switching between editor and application slows the development process, so there also is a runtime editor with many of the full editor's capabilities. You can polish scripts without having to move between the two programs repeatedly. But be prepared to spend time anyway. With all the features to choose from, creating useful projects is not as simple as HyperCard's point-and-click links. SuperCard also uses more memory than HyperCard: about 60% more in black and white, and many times more in color.

Summary

HyperCard is a valuable application for any Mac owner. You can use the stacks Apple provides as a database with no modification and without paying for any software. Or, you can teach yourself simple scripting techniques and use it as a basis for all kinds of useful functions. By adding third-party extensions and enhancements, you can use HyperCard to control your whole computing world.

Chapter 19
Multimedia on the Macintosh

What exactly is multimedia? In a nutshell, it is the capability to capture, create, manipulate, and present various media with the computer to communicate and share information with others. This chapter takes a broad approach to the technologies that enable you to create multimedia messages on the Mac.

In This Chapter

▼ An explanation of multimedia

▼ QuickTime

▼ Terminology and definitions

▼ Hypermedia

▼ Hardware needed

▼ Application overview

Part IV
Specialized Mac Applications

What Is Multimedia?

Personal computing has a number of common trends. One is from a command-line interface to a graphical interface. Another is from separate applications to integrated applications like ClarisWorks. For instance, consider desktop publishing, which has reached into many aspects of personal computing. Today's typical Macintosh word processor, spreadsheet, and database share many of the DTP packages' layout and design features. Integrated packages further confuse this crossover issue by mixing spreadsheets, word processors, databases, graphics packages and telecommunications packages into one package, often in one "environment," such as in ClarisWorks (see figure 19.1).

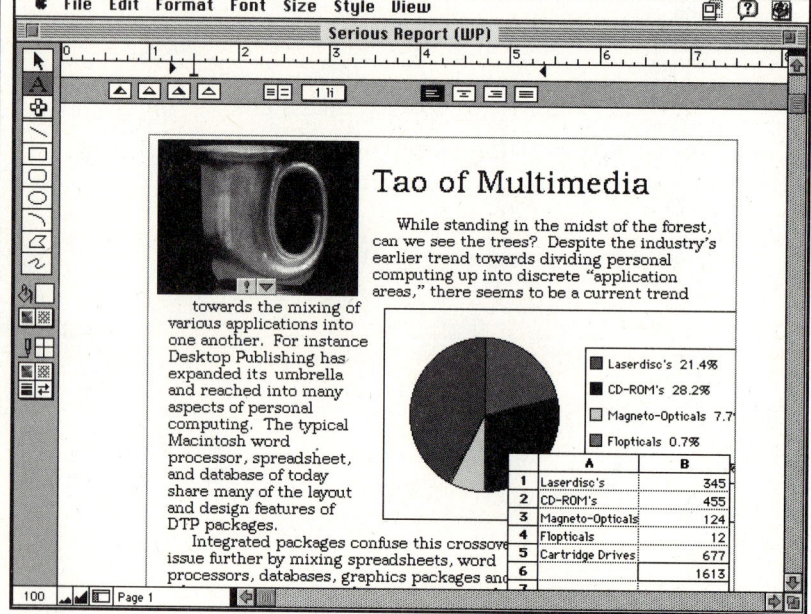

Figure 19.1
ClarisWorks offers multiple tools in one package, evidence of a trend that foreshadows the coming of a multimedia interface and compound documents.

These trends also can be seen in the use of various media in all different aspects of computing. Apple refers to this as "media integration" or as "new media" although the industry as a whole lumps it under the generic term *multimedia*.

Chapter 19
Multimedia on the Macintosh

Multimedia, in the generic sense, is a special set of technologies that allow you to combine text, sound, graphics, animation, high-quality music, and video together into one experience under computer control. But the problem with this description is that it removes these capabilities to a "special" rank—putting beyond the approach of mere mortals.

On the other hand, multimedia on the Macintosh is not just a word, it is a way of life. Mac users expect a seamless, transparent mixing of media through "copy and paste" between graphics packages, word processors, charting packages, and desktop publishing packages. In fact, most users are surprised and dismayed when they cannot copy and paste something between packages. So why shouldn't you be able to copy and paste sounds, animations, digital movies, and other media just as easily? You can on a Mac, and you don't have to be a rocket scientist to do so.

Your Mac is, in a sense, a whole new communications medium. It displays visuals onscreen, plays audible sounds and music from its speakers, plays video in a window on your desktop, controls external devices through its interface ports, and accepts information from you through the keyboard, mouse, touchscreen, microphone, and video camera. Using various interactive tools (such as HyperCard and SuperCard), you can create interactive multimedia applications. These technologies combine on your Macintosh, creating a new medium for communicating—the "multimedia" medium!

Multimedia's origins are conceptually found in the birth of the first illustrated books—the use of pictures and text together on the same page. But more practically, its roots lie with the electronic technologies of television and computers. In the late 1940s, Vannevar Bush, who had been FDR's science advisor during the incredible technological development period spawned by World War II, wrote an article for the *Atlantic Monthly* entitled "As We May Think," in which he described a vision of a future computer repository of information. This vast bank of knowledge would be accessible through a device called a *memex* that you could direct to search and retrieve the information by keywords, leaving relevant linkages between related information and assisting in sifting through the mountains of information that Bush only had a faint notion anyone would be accumulating.

In the late 1960s, this concept was furthered by the computer theorist, Doug Engelbart, through his development work on graphical user interfaces, the combination of multiple media on a computer screen, and the invention and use of kinesthetic devices (the mouse) to directly manipulate objects

Part IV
Specialized Mac Applications

onscreen. Ted Nelson, in his 1974 book *Computer Lib*, coined the terms *hypertext* and *hypermedia* to describe "nonsequential documents" made of text, sounds, and graphical information. The computer would be used to search, retrieve, and interconnect these chunks of information into a "web of information" that would not be viewed linearly, as you normally view a television program, but in a tangential branching fashion. Users would collect their own unique linkages, paths, and interrelated information, share them, and interactively participate in creating a collective understanding of the information.

So, how is this connected to our pursuit of the multimedia basics? The environment these men envisioned is a multimedia environment. It is based on a variety of "transparently" integrated media technologies combined with searching and retrieval tools. These technologies enable "hypermedial" interactive communications between users and between a viewer and information devised by other users. It is an extension of your curiosity, knowledge, and understanding through the use of manipulative tools that enable you to sift through this gritty fabric of information, forming your own webs of understanding. It is the direction of the evolution of the human-computer interface. It can be as simple as a HyperCard stack on a Macintosh Classic, or as complex as an interactive animation using multiple monitors, laser disc, CD-ROM, touchscreen, and stereo speakers. In all cases, the technology of the medium enables the message, and that technology is part of every Macintosh computer.

The newest of these technologies, Digital Video and Image Compression, has been available for several years to those who were willing and able to purchase special add-on equipment to do the compression, storage, and playback. Digital Video is a technology that lets you view video displayed from a file on your hard disk as a full-motion image on your Mac's screen—video in a digital file format. Image Compression is a technology that takes graphic image files and decreases their size from 1/20 to 1/50 of the original size without drastically destroying the files' visual appearance. The trouble with these technologies, until recently, has been that creating and playing back Digital Video requires expensive hardware and often a special processing lab to compress the Digital Video onto a CD-ROM.

But, late in 1991, Apple released an operating system extension called *QuickTime*, which effectively enables people who own color Macs to play back and manipulate digital video and compressed images from a hard disk, a floppy disk, or a CD-ROM without special hardware. QuickTime is an addition to your operating system (see figure 19.2) that enables the Mac to handle dynamic media such as motion video, animation, and sound in a synchronized, true-to-time fashion. It also handles compression and decompression of still images and digital video, and the connections and control of various hardware components that have been added to the Mac, including video capture cards, serially connected tape recorders, and MIDI devices.

Because QuickTime implements this management at the operating system level, developers can write applications that use this "universal" set of tools, rather than creating their own. Developers also can create QuickTime movie editors that rival sophisticated video editing equipment in features and function. This allows integration between tools and free exchange of one tool to another—theoretically, any application works with any video capture board. Neither cares which compression methods were used on the still image or digital video file, and they are capable of "printing to video" despite which kind of tape deck is plugged into the serial port.

As a Macintosh user, you take copy and paste for granted. You do not copy and paste still text and images with skepticism—you expect it to happen flawlessly and transparently (see figure 19.3). With QuickTime, this transparency extends to include dynamic media. You can copy and paste movies, animations, sounds, and other types of time-dependent data from one document to another, across applications, and across your network, just as you do now with still data. QuickTime takes you the next step closer to realizing the multimedia environments Vannevar Bush, Doug Engelbart, and Ted Nelson envisioned.

Chapter 19
Multimedia on the Macintosh

Figure 19.2
The QuickTime extension icon is a small item for such a powerful tool!

Basic Concepts

There are several ways to look at the term multimedia. In one sense, life itself can be described as multimedia. You use all of your senses, selectively paying attention to objects that you see, sounds you hear, the temperature and humidity of the air, and you constantly are filtering out various information and messages amidst a cacophony of sights and sounds. As a communicating being, your world is one large multimedia experience.

Figure 19.3

Macintosh users have grown accustomed to simple tasks such as Copy and Paste between applications, something QuickTime enhances with copy and paste of movies, animation, sounds, and so on.

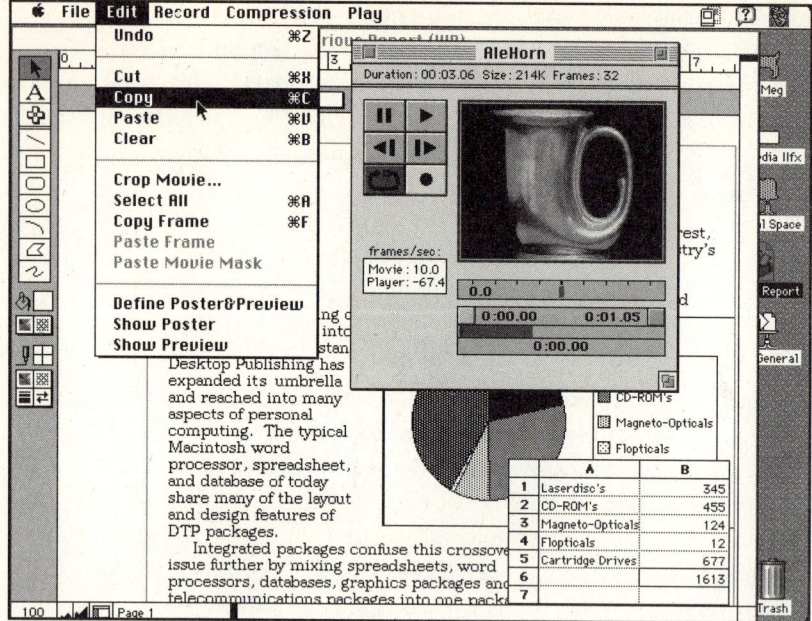

But this chapter is devoted to the subject of multimedia as part of computing, and in particular as a means to communicate messages. A *medium*, or *media*, is any material or technique used to communicate or express a message. Multimedia describes using several media at the same time. It focuses on the many modes that can express a message; in this case, various electronic and computer-based technologies. A single medium in this environment might be simple onscreen text, but multiple media, such as graphics, animation, sound, video, or movies in a window weave a much richer message.

Unfortunately, multimedia as a term has been overused in the computer industry. It seems everyone has jumped on the bandwagon and introduced his own version of a multimedia machine. This is particularly true with various "multimedia PC" standards and the general confusion over whether multimedia is a market, a type of machine, or a specific product.

Recently, Apple has described its multimedia strategy as "media integration" because Apple believes it is important to clarify and distinguish the Macintosh as an integrated media machine without any additions. *Integration* means that graphics, sound, text, animation, and other media can be integrated on this one platform, regardless of the model or configuration. And because every Mac can handle nearly all components of these media, Apple's vision is that all of these media will be integrated into all aspects of personal computing.

Chapter 19
Multimedia on the Macintosh

This chapter uses the term multimedia to describe the *substance* of presentations and instructional applications that include multiple media. This substance is carried on the technological canvas: the computer. Various terms are being used in this regard, *computer-based* and *computer-centered media* among them. They all focus on the notion that the computer's screen, keyboard, mouse, and speaker are the base materials upon which multimedia messages are painted. But this is a canvas unlike any other material used before, because this material can be molded to interact with the user.

Interactivity involves a two-way exchange, both in information and in the pursuit of that information. In a simple sense, this is the difference between being a spectator and a participant, between being a passenger and a pilot. A television program or movie is a linear presentation of information, whereas the computer offers an interactive approach that gives information and options for you to choose and move in that direction. The result is a unique nonlinear presentation of the information, in which information is pursued according to an individual's needs and interests (sometimes called *Interactive Media*). A large base of educational research supports the instructional value of this self-moderated exploration of information, and a computer-based multimedia environment's interactivity promotes this type of learning.

Interactive devices are external media devices (such as a VCR, *laser disc player*, or CD-ROM drive) that can be controlled with a computer to allow real-time nonlinear access to the data stored on their medium. A laser disc player, which can be controlled by a computer to play back different parts of a laser disc, jumping from spot to spot with a very small amount of time between sequences, is an example of an interactive device. A 16 mm movie projector, which does not have a computer interface and only can play a movie back in a linear fashion (fast forwarding and rewinding is not fast enough to be useful for an interactive real-time application) is an example of a *noninteractive* device.

The speed of access is critical. For instance, the typical access time for a laser disc player to move from the first frames to the last frames of a laser disc is several seconds; shorter jumps are made in fractions of seconds. On the other hand, although there are computer-controllable video tape recorders that can act as interactive devices, the access time from beginning to end of the tape can be 10 to 15 minutes, and minor jumps can take 10 to 15 seconds. This makes typical video tape players less acceptable as interactive devices.

Part IV
Specialized Mac Applications

The prefix *hyper* is being used liberally along with multi in a variety of multimedia terms: *hypertext*, *hypermedia*, and *HyperCard* are a few examples. Hyper means "more than the normal, over, or above." In multimedia usage, it means "more than what you already have, an expansion upon current information by way of a link to additional content." For example, *hypertext* in its simplest form is linking additional text to the current paragraph of text you see onscreen (see figure 19.4). You might want more information on a term in an onscreen paragraph you are reading. By clicking on the term, an additional window of information appears to tell you a bit about the history of the term, who coined it, where you might find other sources of information on it, and so on. Simply linking one piece of text to another enables you to move nonlinearly through a hypertextual environment of information, pursuing a specific thread of interest, doubling back to look for parallels, or branching off to look for a related topic.

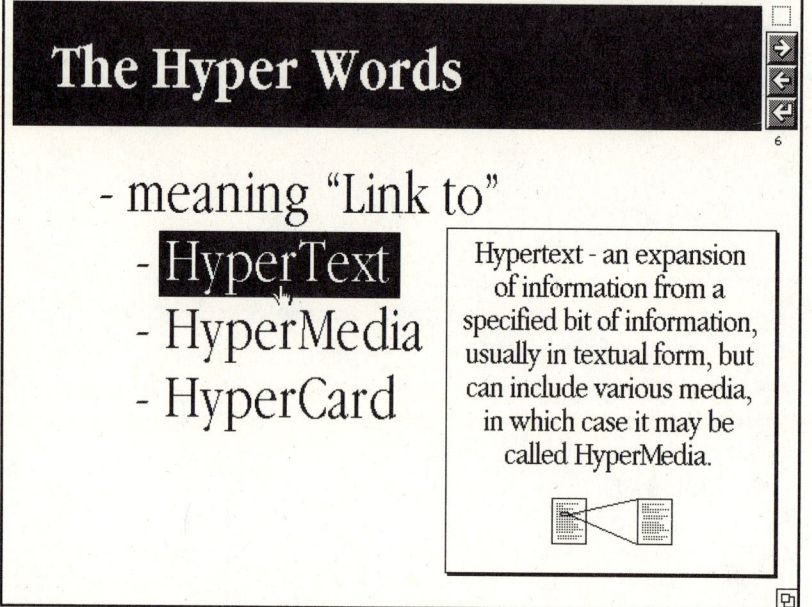

Figure 19.4
Hypertext is the linkage of expanded information to an initial piece of information.

Hypermedia is an expansion on the concept of hypertext, where both onscreen information and the linked content are in multiple media (see figure 19.5). For example, you click on a graphic of a bird and its song plays, or you click on the name of a person and a window pops up with the person's picture, a short biography, and buttons that let you see more information about the person's life and times. This type of multimedia message is available through various multimedia applications outlined in this chapter, including HyperCard.

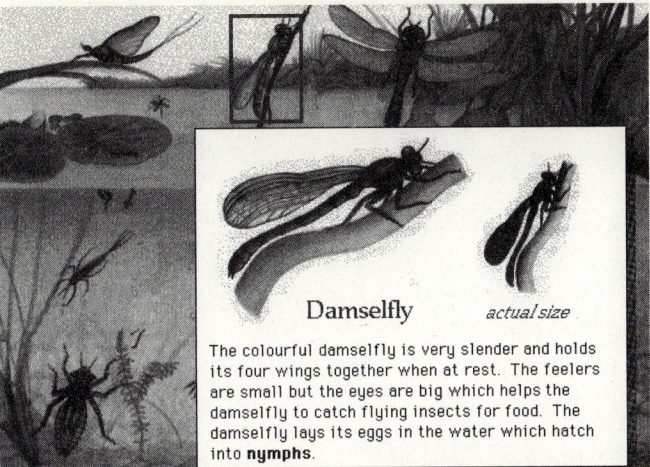

Figure 19.5
Clicking on one of the pictures brings up linked media so further information can be accessed about the subject.

HyperCard is a software package that has shipped in various versions and forms with every Mac sold since late 1987 and can be used to create hypertextual or hypermedial applications. It gets its name because the organizing metaphor of a single screen of information is a card (see figure 19.6). That card can be linked to other cards; a collection of linked cards is called a stack. HyperCard sometimes is described as a general user programming application that can be used to prototype and create various types of programs quickly and easily. It can play various types of animation and sound files created with other multimedia applications, control other external devices such as laser disc players, and create interactive interfaces for use in multimedia.

 The bundeled version of HyperCard that is currently shipped with new Macintoshes is the HyperCard Player, which only enables you to play back stacks. To create your own stacks, you need to purchase the HyperCard Developer's Kit.

The term *video* describes full motion images, typically displayed on a television, video monitor, or computer screen, whose playback source is usually a video camera, video tape player, or laser disc player. Video is a term that is in a state of flux, due to the evolution of various sources of video images, several different digital video formats, and compression/decompression techniques. The term *movie*, or *moovie*, recently arrived in the Macintosh vocabulary: it is used for video (or animation) images that have been digitized and compressed into digital video using Apple's QuickTime architecture and are decompressed and played back on the computer's screen without needing the original video source device.

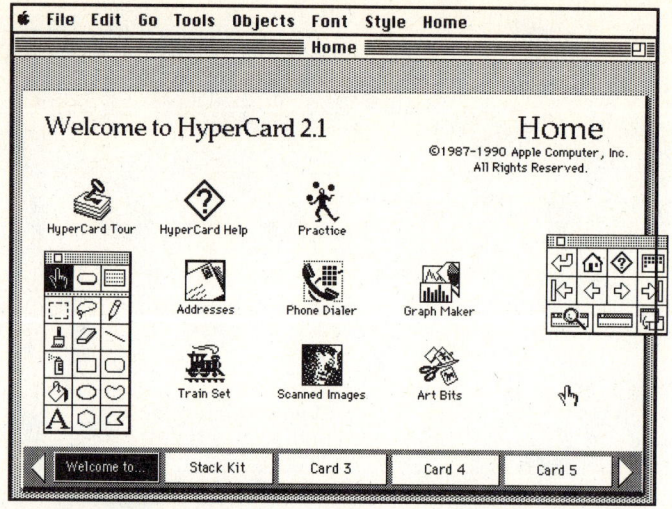

Figure 19.6
HyperCard works as a series of cards in a stack, with buttons and icons to move around. Illustrated is the Home Card.

Multimedia Uses

Given the great scope of computer use today in education, business, and home, this chapter cannot cover all possible uses, but perhaps a few ideas will help. Multimedia can be used in presentations, information access, tutorials, simulations, mediated libraries, and collaborative electronic conferencing. These are not mutually exclusive; many multimedia applications serve several uses at the same time.

Multimedia offers the perfect tool to prepare informative and influential presentations. It is common to see business people and educators using both textual and graphical overhead slides in presentations. But the wave of tomorrow (and today's cutting edge) is to present interactive multimedia instead. Anything that can be created and shown on a Mac screen can be displayed using appropriate projection equipment (for instance, an ElectroHome or a Barco projector or an nView or InFocus overhead projector panel).Presentation programs such as Aldus Persuasion and Macromedia's Director and MediaMaker are the simplest examples.

You also can sit down in front of a Macintosh, perhaps one that is connected to a laser disc player or CD-ROM drive, and interactively investigate a prepared body of multimedia information. Unlike presentations, your role is not that of a passenger riding through a linear series of information; instead you are a pilot deciding which information to pursue, which questions to answer. This is referred to as *interactive information access*, and the ABC News Interactive Series (Martin Luther King, Jr., In the Holy Land, and so on) and the Voyager Expanded Books (such as *Jurassic Park*) and Music Series (CD Companion to Beethoven's 9th and such) are good examples for the Mac.

Using the computer as a tutor through *tutorial* applications is a third common multimedia function. In the 1970s and '80s, education and industry pioneered interactive video applications to instruct students and train employees. Most of these interactive applications took the form of tutorials and included computer interaction, laser disc video, graphics (both from laser disc and computer sources), and various forms of input devices such as touchscreens that made it simple for the viewer to respond to questions. Since the rollout of HyperCard, the vast majority of stacks that educators have developed are tutorials for their students. A tutorial application instructs the user on some information using integrated media and often includes background information, core content, examples, and quizzes or tests with remediation, tracking the user's performance.

Simulations are a fourth multimedia usage. A multimedia engine can simulate various systems or environments, and the user interacts with this application, learning how the various components of the simulated environment interact and what forces are at work in the system. For instance, HyperCard can be used with other system modeling software such as Stella (see figure 19.7) or Labview to create "virtual" machines, on which students or employees learn how to operate scientific or industrial equipment. Or a biological ecosystem may be simulated so students can learn what factors effect population growth of interdependent species.

With the advent of "client-server" connections and solutions for the Mac, a "real" potential for mediated libraries has developed. This new type of integrated media application uses a multimedia "front-end" on the Mac to enable you to explore a vast and rich base of information stored in a database engine, such as a mini- or mainframe, across a network.

Using the Data Access Manager in System 7 (or various other connectivity and query tools), a Mac across the network can query a database residing on a mainframe. The requested data may be multimedia objects, which can be downloaded to the Mac for your perusal. For instance, a library could place its references and collection information, as well as multimedia examples of the items in those holdings, in the database and have network-connected Macs act as windows into those collections.

Chapter 19
Multimedia on the Macintosh

Figure 19.7
Stella can work with other applications, such as HyperCard, to create learning systems.

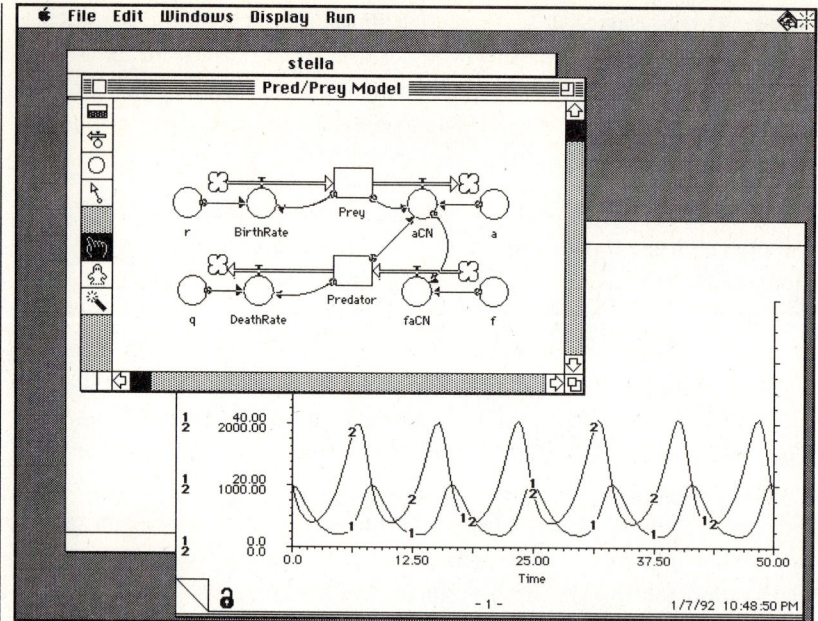

High-speed networks and the new compression technologies offered by QuickTime bring Collaborative Electronic Conferencing within reach. QuickTime movies today can be played across a high-speed network with minimal degradation. As network and telephone system technologies grow, video conferences across networks and phone lines will be possible. For instance, using currently available products that include a video camera, microphone, and video digitizer that captures and compresses the video, you can send full-motion compressed digital video of one or two users across a network or phone lines to another person's Mac, where it is played back on that screen by QuickTime decompression. Along with the collaborative technologies built into System 7—Publish and Subscribe, Apple Events, and the Apple Open Collaboration Environment—this offers another productive multimedia use in work group computing.

Multimedia Engines

A multimedia application is typically experienced as an interaction; you click on buttons, watch or listen to visual and audible information, and explore

Chapter 19
Multimedia on the Macintosh

that information space with navigational tools and maps. The presentation of those images, animations, and other media "chunks" is carried out by the central interactive application—sometimes referred to as a *multimedia engine*. HyperCard, SuperCard, Spinnaker Plus, Macromedia Director, and Authorware are examples of multimedia engines.

You experience the multimedia application's information and interface, while the heart, or controlling part, of the application—its engine—interprets the requests you make and accesses the various media and interactive devices to create the presentation of information. This access sometimes is built into the engine and sometimes is added onto it with an additional *toolkit* available from the engine's publisher or through other third-party sources. Often these multimedia engines are referred to as *authoring* tools or systems because they facilitate creating multimedia presentations in much the same way an author composes a manuscript.

Engine features—the types of media they can display, how they control interactive devices, the style and forms of interactive interfaces they can support—are discussed later in this chapter. But their importance cannot be understated: without their interactive capabilities, a multimedia presentation would be indistinguishable from playing a videotape.

To provide a means to discuss multimedia engines, this chapter configures the following typical "mid-range" multimedia setup, as of the time of this writing:

▼ Macintosh Centris 610 (a single slot Macintosh with a 68040 CPU, built-in CD-ROM, and sound recording capabilities) with 4M to 8M of RAM, an 80M internal hard disk, and a NuBus Adapter

▼ (Optional) RasterOps 24STV video card, a relatively inexpensive 24-bit video display card that can display full-motion video in a window on the Mac's screen; and has the capability of recording QuickTime movies from video

▼ Apple 14-inch RGB monitor

▼ Pioneer 2000 laser disc player connected with a serial cable to the modem port and with an RCA/Phono cable from the player's composite video out port to the composite video in port on the back of the RasterOps 24STV board; (optionally, a monitor for the laser disc player)

▼ Apple CD 300 CD-ROM player connected to the Mac's SCSI port (if the Mac doesn't have a built-in CD-ROM)

▼ Amplified speaker system connected to the RCA plugs on the back of the CD-ROM player or to the audio-out port on the Mac and to the audio-out plugs on the back of the laser disc player

As an example of a multimedia engine in this setup, you could use HyperCard as the multimedia engine, supplemented with a Videodisc toolkit, Audio CD toolkit, QuickTime Tools, and a Macromedia Player toolkit. HyperCard alone enables you to create an interactive information system with sounds, graphics, buttons, and menus on the Mac's screen. But the additional toolkits and components allow control of the two interactive devices, the laser disc player and CD-ROM player, so you can play sections of laser discs and audio CDs interactively. The QuickTime Tools let you record, edit, and play back QuickTime movies using the RasterOps capture board. In addition, you can play back Macromedia Director movies, which also can contain interactive elements, and you can display the played back video from the laser disc player in a window (or full screen) on the Macintosh's monitor through control of the RasterOps video card. All the multimedia engines mentioned earlier can give you similar functionality.

What Is In an Interface?

The introduction of HyperCard in August 1987 spawned more educational and multimedia applications (stacks) than any other event in the Mac's history. But it also spawned a plethora of interactive interfaces with such different looks and feels that you wonder how they all could be created on the same platform with the same application. This is the power, and perhaps the bane, of HyperCard—it can be used to create both beautifully intuitive as well as confoundingly confusing interfaces. As with desktop publishing, a good tool does not necessarily a good product make!

Quite a few books have been written on interface design, so this issue is not handled in great depth here. An interface can make or break an application. The Macintosh software market has seen its fair share of failed applications, driven to extinction because their interfaces were too complex, too confusing, or simply not what users call "Mac-like" or "Mac-intuitive." Interactive interface designers should be aware that their products are measured by the same yardstick. For more information on interface design see Apple's book *HyperCard Stack Design Guidelines,* as well as numerous other interface guidelines books available from Apple.

Clarity and simplicity are the secret ingredients for an interface. To outline these aspects further, here are five simple principles that should be applied to any multimedia interactive interface design:

- ▼ Decide who your users are: Are they Mac-literate? Are they mouse-literate? Are they "interactive-" literate? Depending on their characteristics, design your interface to use their previous knowledge and educate them, perhaps with an optional introduction section, on how to use your application.

- ▼ Clearly define the content: Define what the application's subject matter is and is not, and decide how to present it to your users—clear planning promotes clear structure and presentation.

- ▼ Make your application easy to navigate: Use consistent navigational buttons and tools; keep the application's look consistent so users can distinguish where they are by the appearance as well as the information on the screen.

- ▼ Use an "integrated design" approach: Integrate the various media in your presentation so you give a consistent and coherent message. Integrate your writing, graphical design, and audio design.

- ▼ Test and revise early and often: Test your application and interface on people who are like your intended audience. Watch what they do and where they get confused, and revise where necessary. Test it on colleagues and listen to their reviews. Plan to change your stack several times.

The interface is a product of three things: the creator's talents, the information in the message, and most important, the user's interaction needs.

Multimedia Media Technologies

What you see on the screen, hear through speakers, and interact with through an interface are the essence of the multimedia message. The supporting multimedia engine software simply coordinates these various pieces in an orchestrated composition. Because this chapter has taken an overview approach to the engines and architecture that enable you to create multimedia messages, it takes a similar approach to the actual elements that make up these compositions. The basic elements of the message can be divided into three essential groups: *visuals*, *audibles*, and *interactables*.

Visuals

The visual elements of a multimedia message are those chunks of information that can be viewed either onscreen—the computer's screen or a television monitor—or with some form of projection device. The array of visual elements includes text, simple black and white graphics, color and 3-D graphics, animation, full-motion video images, and QuickTime movies. A number of the multimedia engine applications have built-in graphics creation capabilities, and most also can import graphics created with other graphics applications.

Text

Text in a multimedia application can be presented in two forms: text which can be edited and text which is primarily used for information presentation. Most of the multimedia engines support editing fields or text boxes that use standard Macintosh text editing functions, enabling you to type in text and edit it for use within the application. In instructional applications, this is particularly useful for acquiring personal information on the user, typing in answers to questions, and involving the user in richer forms of interaction.

Presentation of textual information in bullet charts, tables, and outlines is by far the most common visual seen today in education and business. It is said a picture is worth a thousand words, but it is not always predictable which thousand words a person will interpret from that picture. Text is still a critical part of any presentation, especially when communicating concise data. Most multimedia engines support various ways of displaying text (see figure 19.8), both statically and dynamically, and in the various fonts, styles, and sizes you have come to expect on the Mac. Dynamic effects and presentations can include animation of letters, dissolves and zooms to bring text onscreen, color, glittering, and other special effects. Getting text into the application can be done either through simple Copy and Paste or through import from a text file directly into the multimedia engine.

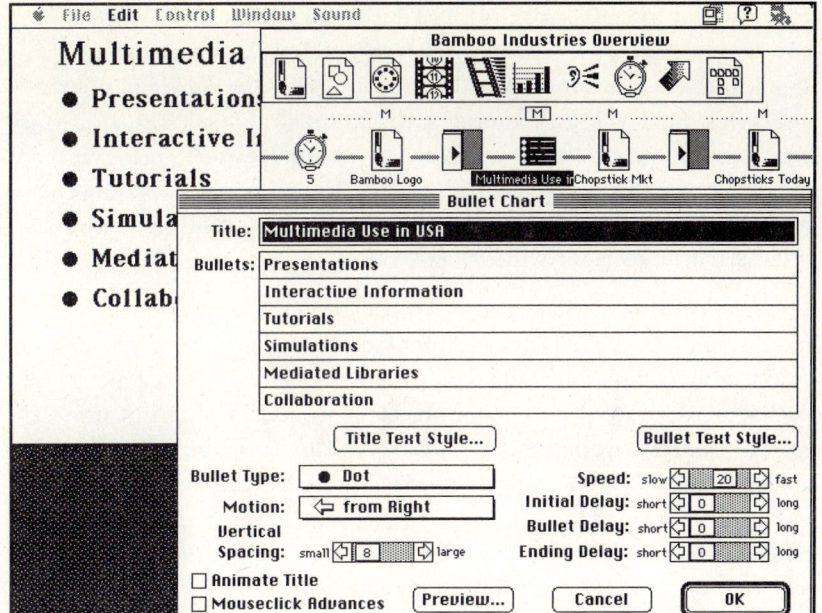

Figure 19.8
Macromedia Director enables you to define text display attributes for a presentation.

Still Images

There are basically two types of graphics file formats for *still images*: "paint," or bitmapped, and "draw," or vector-mapped (see chapter 7, "Graphics," for information). Because of the fixed dpi resolution of bitmapped images, they sometimes are referred to as *resolution-* or *display-device* dependent. For most multimedia uses, this is not a critical issue. However, this file format requires careful consideration when you print the screen images on a higher resolution device such as a 300 dpi laser or color printer, on which the 72 dpi resolution looks large and chunky and shows jagged, diagonal edges.

Simple object-oriented "draw" graphics can be displayed onscreen more rapidly than bitmapped images, but because you have to draw each object one at a time to display it, this format is not always desirable for multimedia uses, especially with very complex images. You can accelerate bitmapped and PICT image drawing for multimedia presentations by drawing into off-screen buffers, by using graphical and QuickDraw accelerators, by compressing the images and using fast decompression algorithms to display them (that is, QuickTime), by using faster hard drives and faster SCSI bus implementations, or by creating a bitmapped PICT2 file of the drawn image.

Part IV
Specialized Mac Applications

These two file formats comprise the majority of what is referred to as simple multimedia graphics. By far, the majority of multimedia images are in a simple graphical file format, usually bitmapped; even the individual objects and "cast members" in animation and overlay applications are either bitmapped or draw graphics. But simple is not an adequate term for the incredible complexity and creativity possible with color paint and draw packages. This chapter has referred briefly to still image compression: this is discussed in more depth in the "Digital Video" section of this chapter.

Three-dimensional graphics (sometimes called 3-D modeling) are seen increasingly in multimedia presentations; they are coming more into their own as an animation and multimedia imaging technology. Typical 3-D packages give you four views of the objects being manipulated: top, front, side, and perspective or camera view, and the tools to create, manipulate, and light the objects. In general, these packages work within three modes or modules: (1) where a stick figure or rough is created with its connected parts, surfaces, and object relationships; (2) where the figure is animated, lit, and the camera position is determined and moved; and (3) where the animated figure is "rendered" into the animation frames that are ultimately used for the multimedia application.

The first takes a minimal amount of time, the second takes a moderate amount of time, and the third can take more hours or even days than you expect, depending on the detail, the complexity, and the image's required color depth. Some packages can combine all three modes in one view in "real time," as long as you work at a low resolution and low color depth. Many of the 3-D applications output to file formats that can be used in other animation packages and multimedia engines (the PICS file format is the most common of these—devised by Macromedia, the PICS file is basically a string of PICT images).

Animation

The use of animated graphics in multimedia presentations is very common—in fact, you could call it one of multimedia's "lowest common denominator" elements. The range of animation methods and packages is wide, but the basics of how animation works are very simple. If you have ever seen a child's "flipbook" toy, you already have grasped the idea. This simple animation form, over hundreds of years old, is a small booklet with a series of figures drawn on each of its pages. You view the figures by holding the binding of the booklet with one hand and rapidly flipping through the pages with the other. The individual figures on the flipping pages appear to the eye to be

Chapter 19
Multimedia on the Macintosh

moving, the result of a phenomenon called *persistence of vision*. Early animators took this basic method a step further and created color film animated cartoons (like the ones you grew up with on Saturday mornings), and today, this flipbook concept is still a basic part of computer-generated animations.

Based on the flipbook example, you might expect animation packages to include the entire screen of information as a single frame of an animation sequence, but this is impractical. To do this effectively with large color images requires considerable horsepower in the Mac, lower color depth onscreen, and compression and decompression technologies (essentially what you are doing when you use QuickTime movies). A single full-screen PICT at 24 bits is roughly 1M in size; running a full-screen animation at anything approximating 15 to 20 frames per second (the approximate rate to create persistence of vision) requires data transfer rates that surpass the capabilities of the Mac's various data transfer buses.

So the majority of animation packages use a method that moves various objects, called *sprites*, across a background that does not change, or changes little. These sprites may be fully animated themselves because they do not use the full screen. For example, a series of sprites could be all the frames of a walking man, with arms and legs swinging, being moved across a background of a city street: the sprite-objects run through their sequence by animating the walking man while they are moved across the stable, unchanging background.

Even with this sprite/background animation method, more complex animations can require such high throughput of graphical data that it can exceed the Mac's capabilities (primarily NuBus and SCSI limitations). This can create a ceiling effect for complex animations: it runs faster if you use fewer elements, but slows if you add more elements. And even under the best conditions, rapid vertical movement onscreen can result in an effect called *tearing*, in which the sprites appear to tear horizontally as they move across the screen: their upper part may seem to move ahead of the lower part, which lags behind by a small distance. Regardless of these limitations, however, animation on the Mac can result in very impressive visuals at a very reasonable price-performance ratio.

There are a number of ways to bring animations into your multimedia presentations. Some of the "general" multimedia engines have either their own built-in animation tools or add-on toolkits for this purpose. For instance, HyperCard can create simple animations by moving buttons around onscreen, changing the icons of the buttons to simulate various sprites of an animated figure. Or the Macromedia Player Toolkit can be used with HyperCard to play Director animations within a HyperCard stack. You also can add an animation module to Authorware, which lets you create animations and use them in your Authorware applications.

Some multimedia engines are primarily animation-based environments. Macromedia's Director, for example, evolved from the premier animation package for the Mac, VideoWorks (when the Mac had only 512K of RAM), to the popular and powerful tool of today (refer to figure 19.8). Its tools and authoring environment still are based on these animation principles and methods, with the addition of interactive scripting capabilities and extensions to control interactive devices.

The animation packages support animation creation in various ways. Macromedia Director has painting tools to create the individual sprites, and specialized tools to move and manipulate those sprites onscreen—in, essentially, a modeless environment. A number of other high-end animation packages work more like the 3-D products mentioned earlier. You use one module or mode of the product to create the objects, another to specify their paths and the movements of the camera, and a third to "render" the frames of the animation. You then can play back these frames with either the original package, a special run-time player, from within one of the multimedia engines with some sort of toolkit, or exported in a format that can be imported into one of the multimedia engines for eventual playback. And as noted in the previous 3-D section, most 3-D applications can create animated sequences that can be imported into the multimedia engines for playback within a multimedia presentation.

Video

With the coming of QuickTime, video elements are very easy to implement on any color-capable Macintosh (68020 or better). Video is discussed in four sections: video concepts, video signal types, video media and devices, and a cluster of issues related to getting video into and out of the Mac.

Video Concepts

Onscreen video that you view on your TV or computer screen is what we'll call *analog video*. Its source may be an analog device, like a VCR or laser disc, or it may be digital, like a QuickTime movie. To understand digital video, we need to look at the basic analog video concepts first.

Chapter 19
Multimedia on the Macintosh

American television video is in an electronic signal format referred to as NTSC (National Television Standards Committee). In this format, the television's screen is painted with electron guns in the back of the tube every 1/30 of a second. The screen is made of 525 horizontal lines, and the guns first paint all the odd lines onscreen, top to bottom (called a field), return to the top of the screen, and then paint all the even lines. This is called an *interlaced* signal. The fields are painted every 1/60 of a second, and it takes two fields (odd and even) to make a full frame, thus the 1/30 of a second "frame rate" interval.

The full-signal screen size is effectively 525 lines high by roughly 620 lines wide (although there are no true horizontal lines in the format), but most displays show only the center 85 percent of this image, allowing the other 15 percent to fall outside of the viewable screen. This larger-than-viewable scan size is referred to as *overscan*. NTSC is a 40-year-old standard established prior to color technologies. The addition of color was an afterthought that has often resulted in poor color balance. Most NTSC video viewing devices (TVs and monitors) are equipped with a hue control to adjust color tones, which rarely are stable from device to device due to this design flaw. (This may be a source of the acronym's other, more comical name: Never Twice the Same Color).

Mac video, on the other hand, is in a very different format. Rather than painting first the odd and then the even lines, the signal paints all the lines top to bottom. This is called *noninterlaced*, or *progressive*, scan. And the screen is painted at a much higher frame rate, between 67 and 82 frames per second, depending on the monitor. (The 13-inch Hi Res RGB monitor displays at 66.67 frames per second and a single horizontal line is painted in 1/35,000 of a second: a 35 KHz horizontal frame rate). Most Macintosh video cards and built-in video circuitry can sense the type of monitor attached to them by the pin configurations in the monitor itself, and they adjust their frame rates and screen sizes accordingly. The higher frame rate gives a crisp, nonflickering image. Because Macintosh video is different from NTSC, however, combining the two types of video is complicated.

Combining NTSC video and Mac video into one signal for viewing is done in essentially two ways. One requires the Mac's video be encoded to NTSC and combined with the NTSC source on an NTSC viewing device, as when using the TrueVision NuVista+ video board. The other takes the NTSC video and converts it to Mac video to be displayed on a normal Mac 13-inch RGB monitor, as with the RasterOps 364 and 24STV and the VideoLogic DVA-4000.

Conversely, dumping that combined video signal to an NTSC device such as an SVHS tape deck is done in two ways. In the NuVista+ scenario, it is simply a matter of plugging the video card into the tape deck because the signal is in an NTSC format. For the RasterOps and VideoLogic boards, you need special conversion hardware to encode the Mac's signal to NTSC. To look at these solutions, you need to understand more about the technology of the signals, their differences, and the devices used as video sources and receivers.

First, you need to know a bit about how your color video monitor works. The back of the video tube in your TV and color monitor contains three electron guns: red, green, and blue. Each gun paints a particular set of phosphor dots on your screen in the interlaced or noninterlaced format. The red gun paints the red phosphor dots, the green gun paints the green dots, and the blue gun paints the blue dots. Your eye combines a set of dots onscreen into a color. The three guns combine their electron beams in a tight stream, painting the screen effectively as a single beam.

When television first was devised more than 60 years ago, no one planned for color in the signal, so the black and white signal held only intensity information for painting various levels of gray on the black and white screen. But with RCA's development of color television in the mid '50s, there was a need to include red, green, and blue (RGB) color information in the television signal without outdating the large installed base of black and white television set owners.

This was done by taking the RGB information and breaking it into two separate signals: its intensity information—*luminance*—and its color information—*chrominance*. The luminance and chrominance information was combined with synchronization and blanking pulses into a single composite signal that could be used by the older black and white sets, but which carried the necessary information for color sets to decode into the RGB components.

Video Signal Types

To simplify this discussion, let's break the different analog video signals you encounter in the multimedia world into essentially four different forms: *RF*, *composite*, *RGB*, and *component video*. The electromagnetic waves that are broadcast through the air carry a host of signal types, such as radio, microwave, cellular phone, and television signals. The coaxial cable that carries cable TV to your set works similarly. These electromagnetic waves carry the NTSC signal for more than 70 channels in a format referred to as Radio Frequency (RF) because the transmission frequencies are in the "radio" frequency region of the spectrum.

Chapter 19
Multimedia on the Macintosh

The potentially broad spectrum of possible frequencies in the signal transmitted through the air or on the cable is divided into a number of individual bands. The video signal for a specific television program has been "modulated" and funneled into each of those bands, so you get 70+ channels delivered to your home. Modern consumer televisions, which have a built-in tuner that essentially "demodulates" the signals carried on any of the air frequencies its antenna captures, also can demodulate the signal from the cable, breaking the RF signal into its individual channels. If you work with RF sources of video with your Macintosh, you need to use a tuner or demodulator box to get the signal from the RF form into a straight composite, RGB, or component form.

The composite video signal is the most common, used primarily with consumer video equipment. Most VCRs, video cameras, laser disc players, and other video components have the capability to input and output a composite signal, which typically is carried on cable that ends in a BNC connector or an RCA or Phono Jack. As mentioned earlier, the composite signal holds all the information for the image's color (called chrominance) and intensity (called luminance) in a single signal. Of the three forms of "straight" video, composite video suffers most from image degradation. This is primarily because the video signal recorded by the red, green, and blue "tubes" in the video camera needs to be converted into the composite form to transmit through a single wire, and then converted back into the red, green, and blue components necessary to display the color image on a television set or monitor. Despite its shortcomings, composite is used universally in the United States in consumer-grade equipment. Most video input-capable cards for the Mac accept composite sources of video.

The third form of video signal is RGB, which stands for red/green/blue. Instead of carrying the video color and intensity information on a single wire, RGB carries these qualities on three wires, which breaks the information for the three color guns in your video tube into separate signals and improves the image quality significantly. There is usually a fourth wire that carries the synchronization pulse signal used to ensure that the different pieces of video equipment are in sync, a process referred to as genlocking. RGB is used extensively in computer monitor and projection technologies and along with a similar YUV (Y-luminance, U-blue minus luminance, V-red minus luminance) method, is a popular format found in professional video production. In these situations, all video signals between equipment components are RGB; they are converted to composite only if the final use is consumer equipment. RGB can support very high-quality multimedia video images.

Component video is the fourth common form of video signal. There are several component video types—the most common in the U.S. outside of broadcast production is called S Video, and it is available with 8mm and Hi8 video equipment. Basically, component video breaks the video signal into its chrominance and luminance information carried on separate wires. This avoids most of video image degradation that occurs in composite equipment and keeps many of the RGB advantages by carrying the color and intensity information on different wires. As a result, Hi8 video approaches the quality of broadcast-quality equipment used by television producers.

Video Media and Devices

The terms *video media* and *video devices* actually refer to the type of material used for recording to and playing back the video signal—typically, videotape, still video, laser disc and compressed digital video media such as CD-ROMs—and the devices which record and play back these media—video tape players, still video cameras, laser disc players, and mass storage devices such as CD-ROMs. Each of these media and device technologies is discussed separately.

There are six basic video tape formats you will encounter in current multimedia situations: VHS, SVHS, 8mm, Hi8 mm, 3/4-inch (predominantly U-Matic) and 1-inch broadcast formats. Roughly speaking, the fidelity and image quality of these various media range from poorest to best: VHS, 8mm, SVHS, Hi8, 3/4- and 1-inch broadcast tape formats. Although the image quality is also dependent on the quality of the camera and playback equipment, this order can be used as a rule of thumb to compare the different formats' overall quality. The quality difference may not show up in the first generation of the signal, but you see a marked degradation of the image if you copy a VHS or 8mm tapes more than once or twice (one or two generations away from the original). This may not be as critical if you intend to digitize the video straight from the source, but you should definitely take it into consideration if you produce your own laser disc or videotape from source material. Starting with the best quality source you can afford greatly enhances the final product.

Chapter 19
Multimedia on the Macintosh

All these tape formats and devices can be sources of multimedia images, but if you intend to use the devices to interactively play back sections of the recorded video, you should consider two things. First, interactive use of videotape is typically slow; fast forwarding or rewinding to the next segment of tape can take several seconds to several minutes, depending on how the tape is produced and in which format it is recorded. This slow response may not be satisfactory if you plan to use it beyond proving a concept that ultimately will be converted to a laser disc or digital compressed video. However, by thoughtfully planning which video sequences are most likely to be accessed at any one point and editing the videotape to optimize for this access, you can use VCRs as interactive devices.

Second, you need to choose equipment that allows for interactive control. Most consumer-grade VHS videotape recorders are incapable of interactive control from a computer. Voyager markets a device called The Box, which can connect to consumer decks that have a remote input socket and can be configured to control them, but access is not frame-accurate. NEC recently introduced its PC-VCR that allows for almost frame-accurate SVHS and VHS tape playback, and a number of other video equipment manufacturers are following its lead. However, the price of such equipment is well above consumer-grade VHS equipment.

Near frame-accurate playback and recording also can be done with 8mm and Hi8 equipment. Sony's 8mm and Hi8 devices include Control-L and Control-S ports and protocols for serial remote control. Sony also recently introduced its Vbox, which handles the connections and communications from the Mac's serial ports to Sony devices using Sony's new VISCA (Video System Control Architecture) machine control codes for synchronized computer control of multiple video peripherals. And there are a number of products for the Mac that allow interactive control of 8mm and Hi8 equipment through their Control L and Control S ports for both playback and printing to video, including Macromedia MediaMaker, and OnTrack.

Most of the good production-quality 3/4-inch decks include computer interface ports for control. If you plan to do much video output recording of your multimedia compositions, especially those requiring time-consuming frame-by-frame renderings of 3-D animations, a U-Matic tape deck controlled with a DiaQuest DA-Animaq card is one of the more popular combinations to use.

A variety of still video cameras has come to market over the past two years. These range from systems that replace the normal film back of a 35mm camera with a still video recording device (the Minolta system) to the

Part IV
Specialized Mac Applications

pocket-sized still video cameras such as the Canon ZapShot, which is approximately 1 x 3 x 4 inches in size with an integrated flash. Typically, these different still video systems use the tiny 2-inch microfloppy disk to record 25 to 50 single images. Most of the systems do not digitize the image within their circuitry but lay down an analog-recorded strip on the magnetic disk, which later is played back and displayed on a monitor or TV, or digitized into a computer.

Still video cameras can be divided into two groups: high-resolution and field cameras. The field cameras record only one field of the video frame; for example, the Canon ZapShot records only the odd lines of a video picture. The circuitry for this is smaller and less expensive than for recording both sets of fields, and the resulting image takes up less room on the micro floppy disk. The overall benefit is a smaller, cheaper camera with the capability to record 50 frames per disk.

The high-resolution cameras record both odd and even fields and can save 25 pictures on a micro floppy disk, with typically a larger camera body. Using a field camera's image at full-screen size results in a poorer image than using a high-resolution camera's image at full screen.

The laser disc player (or video disc player) is a video device that plays back video that has been stored on a plastic or glass laser disc. A laser disc is usually a 12-inch-diameter disc that yields either 30 minutes or a full hour of video per side of the disc, although 8-inch and smaller diameter formats are available for shorter playback uses. The playback unit uses a very narrow laser beam of light to read the video information from a spinning laser disc. Essentially, that information is laid down in a tight spiral on the disc in much the same fashion as older, long-play audio records, on which the audio information was laid down in a spiral of tracks that were read using a diamond-tipped stylus.

When you use a laser disc player, each video frame can be addressed as a discrete unit, so you can effectively use a laser disc in several different ways. For instance, you can use it as a full-motion video source running at the standard 30 frames per second, as a slide library source that contains 30 still images per second of playing time on the disc (that equals 54,000 still images on a half hour disc), or both. Typical educational laser discs, such as the ABC New Interactive disc sets, combine still images and motion sequences on each disc. Laser disc players can be used to interactively play back the still images individually or to play back any portion of the motion sequences, and some players can be controlled by a computer in a multimedia presentation as an interactive device.

Chapter 19
Multimedia on the Macintosh

Lower-cost player units can only play back, but a number of manufacturers use a Write Once Read Many (WORM) method to make models that record video onto a special format laser disc for later playback on the same machines. Typically, these read-and-write players are more expensive than read-only players, and the format they use to write the video to disc cannot be played back with standard laser disc players. Most standard laser disc players can play the two popular laser disc formats: continuous angular velocity (CAV) and continuous linear velocity (CLV). Many commercial movies, educational films, and informational videos are available in the CAV and CLV formats.

CAV-formatted laser discs are spun at a continuous speed: 1,800 rpm, or 30 revolutions per second (you recall there are 30 frames per second in the NTSC video signal). There is one frame of video (both odd and even fields) per revolution of a CAV-formatted disc, whose surface has a distinctive bar that runs straight across the disc from edge to edge through the center. This bar is a visual effect created by the sync pulse and retrace blanking information in each frame of the video. Because this occurs as the video guns retrace from the lower-right corner of the screen to the upper-left corner of the screen in between fields of each frame. The composite of all these sync/blanking pulses creates the visual bar that spans the disk across all the frames. One half of the disc is the odd fields and the other is the even fields of every frame of video on that side of the disc. CAV discs can hold 30 minutes of video on a side—that equals 54,000 frames.

Playing back a CAV disc is as simple as moving the laser disc "stylus" at an even speed across the continuous-speed disc. To quickly move from one frame to another nonsequential frame anywhere on the disc, the player only needs to move the stylus to that frame's location. To play a single frame, the player only needs to move the stylus to that location and hold the stylus stationary. Interactive control of a CAV disc, as a result, is quite simple and can be done with relatively inexpensive laser disc players. The Pioneer 2200, for instance, is priced in the $500 range.

CLV-formatted laser discs are spun so their surfaces move at a constant linear speed relative to the stylus, which naturally changes the spinning speed as it reads from the inner edge to the outer edge of the disc. When the stylus reads from the inner edge, the disc spins faster; when it reads from the outer edge, the disc spins slower, yet the same quantity of "video track inches" moves beneath the laser stylus during both phases. This allows the laser disc to hold more frames in its outer edge than CAV-formatted discs, extending the laser disc's playing time to a full hour of video. These discs sometimes are

Part IV
Specialized Mac Applications

called extended-play or long-play laser discs. There is no regular pattern or visible bars on a CLV disc.

However, it is more complex to play back a CLV disc than a CAV disc, because the player must change the disc's spinning speed as it plays it, as well as move the laser stylus across the disc. Moving from one spot on the disc to another nonsequential spot on the disc requires the player to not only move the laser stylus but also adjust the disc's spinning speed until it comes into sync with the frame rate laid down on the disc. To play a single frame from a CLV disc, the player must be able to locate the frame, bring the speed of the disc into correct sync for playback, and then play just the one frame and read it into a digital frame buffer so that only the one frame can be displayed to the screen.

As a result, interactive playback of a CLV disc requires a much more sophisticated and expensive laser disc player. The Pioneer 8000, which interactively plays back CLV discs with frame accuracy and single-frame capabilities, lists in the neighborhood of $2,500. The Pioneer 2200 (approximately $500) can be used to play CLV disc motion sequences but cannot do single-frame buffering and is not frame-accurate in sequence playback.

To use a laser disc player, or any interactive device for that matter, you need some way for the computer to communicate with the device—usually from the computer's serial port to an RS232-style computer interface port on the device. Not all laser disc players have computer interface ports on them, and you should investigate their capabilities before purchasing one to use as an interactive device. The Pioneer 2000, for instance, does not have a computer interface port, whereas the Pioneer 2200 does at an increased cost of approximately $100.

Several other devices can be used to control laser disc players. Consumer-oriented players typically do not have computer interface ports, but they may have a plug-in remote control unit or a port for a bar code reader. Voyager's The Box can be connected into the laser disc player's remote control port, plugged into the Mac's serial port, and then configured to send the remote control's commands to the player, effectively controlling the player. However, this does not produce the same response as a serial control cable directly linking the Mac to the laser disc player.

A bar code reader is another useful control device, especially for cataloging video sequences on the laser disc. This is a short, wandlike device with a glowing tip that can be wiped across a bar code to execute various laser disc commands, search for spots on the laser disc, and play sequences of video.

Many laser discs are packaged with a set of sheets that contain a catalog listing of the still images and sequences on the disc with a bar code stripe next to each entry, which can be used with the bar code reader to quickly access that spot on the disc.

Video Into and Out of the Mac

The video sources discussed to this point can be viewed in a variety of ways. The least expensive and simplest way is to display them on a second screen—typically a television set or video monitor—attached to the source, and allow the Mac to interactively control the source device with a serial connection. Side-by-side screens can create confusion for the user, who may be caught in the dilemma of which screen to watch at any point in time. But for many budgets and uses, this is often the most practical setup.

Other viewing setups center around bringing the video and Macintosh images onto a single screen: either the Mac's RGB monitor or an NTSC monitor screen. NTSC video is brought into the Mac video environment as still digitized (or grabbed) images, multiple-frame grabbed motion sequences, or full-motion video "streamed" through to the screen from the original video source, using special video display capabilities of some third-party video cards, such as the VideoLogic DVA-4000 or the RasterOps 364 or 24STV. In these cases, you use the Macintosh screen as your display area for both your Mac-created graphics and interface, as well as the video still and motion images from the various video source devices. When combining NTSC and Mac's digital video signal into the NTSC environment, the Mac video is encoded into an analog NTSC format and combined with another NTSC source to be displayed on an NTSC monitor—for instance, by use of the TrueVision NuVista+ board.

Four methods use video as a source of multimedia images and sound on the Mac: single-frame digitizing, frame grabbing (single and multiple frame), video in a window, and Overlay/chromakey.

Digitizers are low-cost, single-frame capture devices that digitize a video image in just over a fraction of a second. Digital Vision's ComputerEyes/Pro is a good example of this type of device. This is an inexpensive NuBus card that accepts either composite or S-Video signals and captures a 24-bit full-color

Chapter 19
Multimedia on the Macintosh

image (black and white images as well) in about six seconds. Due to the slow digitizing speed, you need either a laser disc player or a high-quality VCR to play a good quality still image, or you need to get your subject to stay still for the length of the capture. After the image is captured, it can be manipulated with the software that comes with the card or saved in a PICT or TIFF file format that can be imported into other graphics packages.

Frame grabbing is instantaneous digitizing—typically in 1/30 of a second. Frame-grabber hardware tends to be low- to moderate-cost NuBus cards that allow for composite and S-Video input and include software that enables you to grab the image while viewing a preview of the motion video onscreen (see figure 19.9). Some frame-grabbing cards grab only single frames; others enable you to grab multiple frames at the highest speed the card can support, with the available RAM in the Mac limiting the number of frames. Still images captured by either digitizers or frame grabbers can be used in all the multimedia engine applications.

Figure 19.9
Frame-grabber hardware enables you to capture video images.

Mass Microsystems' QuickImage 24 is a good example of a low-cost frame grabber. This is a NuBus card with composite and S-Video inputs that does not have a Mac video output, so it must be used on Macs that already have a monitor card or built-in video. The frame-grabbing software presents a preview window on the Mac's monitor and displays the video the card is previewing at between 5 and 30 frames per second, depending on the size and color mode of the Mac monitor. When you select the Grab command, the current frame is grabbed instantaneously and displayed in a window. You can save the file in standard PICT format as 24-bit, 8-bit, and grayscale.

Other frame-grabbing cards also enable you to capture multiple frames in a row using QuickTime. The RasterOps 24STV and SuperMac VideoSpigot cards, for example, perform either single image grabs or multiple images in a sequential recording of a QuickTime movie either to your hard disk to the

Chapter 19
Multimedia on the Macintosh

Mac's memory. The larger the size of the image onscreen, the fewer number of total frames can be captured and the fewer frames per second are grabbed. Each of these frames is digitized and compressed and either held in memory or on disk as the others are accumulated. When the stream of grabs is complete, the sequence can be further compressed by QuickTime into a movie for later use in one of the multimedia engine applications.

When full-motion video from an analog video source device is displayed in a window on a Mac monitor, it is referred to as a *video in a window* (see figure 19.10). The RasterOps 24STV video card is a good example of this type of card. The 24STV has composite and S-Video inputs and a Mac video monitor output port, which is attached to a Mac monitor. A video source device is attached to one of the input ports. Using the display and capture utilities that come with the 24STV, you can display full-motion video in a window in the Finder, in any other application, or in the frame grabber application by itself. This window can be sized in real time, as you would size normal Mac windows, by grabbing the lower-right corner of the video window and adjusting its size anywhere from postage stamp size to full screen.

Figure 19.10
Video in a window is the full-motion display of a video on a Macintosh screen.

In addition, RasterOps has included a developer's kit with its cards that contains toolkit stacks and files for the popular multimedia engine applications. Its HyperCard Toolkit Stack, for instance, offers an example that displays full-motion video in a designated rectangle within the HyperCard card window. This capability can also be handled with QuickTime's VDIG Component Manager. Using a HyperCard Videodisc toolkit to control a laser disc player in conjunction with the 24STV toolkit or QuickTime and the 24STV's VDIG component, control of the display of video on the monitor yields a pleasant, single-screen interactive video environment for development of laser disc-based video material for multimedia compositions..

The RasterOps 24STV's video in a window is a good way to display full-motion video onscreen, but if you want to overlay a graphical arrow to point out a feature in the video or overlay text on the video for titling purposes, you need a card that can combine the Mac graphics signal into the digitized video signal onscreen. The RasterOps 24STV is capable of this also, as are the VideoLogic DVA-4000 and TrueVision NuVista+. These boards take two separate approaches to combining the NTSC and Mac images onscreen: one in the Mac video environment and the other in an NTSC environment. In both situations, however, they mix the two signals in a process that is referred to as *overlay*.

Overlay mixes Mac graphics with full-motion video so that one appears to be floating on top of the other. It typically is done by selecting one particular color, called the *key* color, from either the Mac's image or the video image. When the two signals are mixed, the areas of the source containing the key color are replaced by the video from the other source. For instance, say you are working with a picture of a person standing against a green backdrop. If green is chosen as the key color and the Mac's desktop image is mixed with the video image, it will appear as if the person is standing in front of the Mac's desktop. The term *chromakey* is used in broadcast video when a particular color is "keyed" to be transparent.

Television news weathermen use overlay and chromakey to stand in front of a computer-generated weather map, combining both a video and computer source. The video source is the weatherman standing in front of a saturated blue backdrop with a camera pointed at him; the computer-imaged map is the other. Blue is selected as the transparent color, the two signals are combined so the video source is on top of the computer source, and the map is seen through the transparent chromakeyed blue backdrop.

Mixing in the Mac Video Environment Versus NTSC

The VideoLogic DVA-4000 video board set is an example of a product that combines the two signals in a Mac video environment. The 4000 is actually two NuBus cards, placed in a Mac with at least two slots. These two cards are connected across the NuBus as well as with a separate cable. This is needed most likely because of the fast transfer rates necessary to quickly integrate the

Chapter 19
Multimedia on the Macintosh

two types of signals and update the screen at the speed of the Mac monitor. The DVA-4000 mixes the two signals, allowing for some versatile special effects, keyed overlays, and transitions, all viewed on the Macintosh Hi-Res monitor. The advantages: you work in the Macintosh environment, view the presentation from the Mac screen (or from a Mac-video capable display device), and can use the high resolution and color saturation of Mac graphics.

With its concentration on Mac video production uses, TrueVision's NuVista+ does not bring the NTSC signal into the Mac environment at all, but mixes the Mac signal in the NTSC environment. For efficiency's sake in video production, this makes a lot of sense. For instance, to use the RasterOps 24STV for video production, you take analog NTSC video, digitize and mix it with Mac video to display it on the Mac's screen, and then encode it back into analog NTSC to take it to video tape or an NTSC display device. The NuVista+ board, on the other hand, encodes the Mac's video signal into an analog NTSC signal and mixes it into the NTSC video signal, outputting directly to a tape or display device from the board.

The NuVista+ is a NuBus card with an RGB input and an RGB output port. You can purchase a variety of cables to enable composite, RGB, or S-Video signals to be input to the board. Other cables can be used to output the video signal to RGB, composite, or S-Video equipment. The NuVista software allows for single-frame capture, overlay and chromakey in NTSC output mode, and a variety of digital effects, in addition to quickly switching the video signal from Mac video to an interlaced NTSC signal.

> **Note** Note that the NuVista+ does not do video in a window and does not display NTSC video on a Mac monitor. However, given the strengths of its overlaying and transitioning capabilities coupled with the new VideoScript software from TrueVision, it can be a very useful board for creating multimedia presentations. For a flexible NuVista+ setup, plug NuVista+ into a multisync/multiscan monitor (such as an NEC MultiSync 3-D). In this case, you can prepare your Mac graphics in Mac video mode, then switch the output to NTSC mode and perform the overlay or chromakey effects, viewing them on the multisync monitor while perhaps recording to an S-Video or composite VCR.

Another card well worth mentioning is the Radius VideoVision. This card comes with an attachable bar that has various video and audio input and output connectors. It can be used to imput any two video signals to the Mac's screen, for display or QuickTime capture, as well as outputting the Mac's screen directly to NTSC composite on S-video. It also digitizes and blends audio signals in and out. Radius has recently also released its studio product—a daughterboard which is attached to the VideoVision board and gives it the capability to do QuickTime movie captures at full screen size, 20 frames per second—60 fields per second at very high quality.

Outputting Mac Video to NTSC

A different set of issues must be considered when you want to take a standard Mac video signal to NTSC video equipment. Getting the video image from the Mac's monitor to video equipment requires translating the Mac's video information into a signal format and onto the correct number of wires for the external video equipment to understand. If you plan to connect a Macintosh to a multisync device—a Mitsubishi 37-inch monitor, or a Barco or ElectroHome multisync projector, for instance—the signal itself does not need to be changed but the wiring arrangements might. Conversion boxes (sometimes called *covids*) are available to convert the Mac monitor cable's lines to the appropriate cable configurations for these multisync devices. Consult the device's manufacturer if you are unsure of what you need.

Outputting Mac video to NTSC video equipment can be done in several ways. One, as mentioned in the previous NuVista+ section, is to use a video card that is capable of outputting an NTSC signal. Generally, most video overlay cards have the capability to output an NTSC signal, given the appropriate cable. However, you can get NTSC output from a number of cards without paying the high price for the video overlay capabilities: using the EasyVideo 8 from Mass Microsystems, and using an NTSC encoder box with one of the newer Mac video cards (4•8, 8•24, and 8•24GC cards) or the built-in video on the Quadra and Centris models are a few possibilities. Another, more expensive, method of getting an NTSC signal from a Mac signal is to use a conversion box that takes the original Mac video RGB signal and converts it to an NTSC signal. And a final, less technical (and less expensive) alternative is to use a video camera pointed at a Macintosh monitor in a darkened room, synchronizing the Mac video with the camera's scan rate with an Apple utility called VideoSync.

You need only an NTSC encoder box attached to a 4•8, 8•24, or 8•24GC card, or the built-in video on the Quadra and Centris models, to get NTSC out of a Macintosh. These cards (or the built-in video described) can sense the type of monitor they are attached to by the pin configurations in the monitor. When pins four, seven, and 11 are grounded together, these cards are told an interlaced NTSC monitor is attached, and they alter their output signal accordingly. But the output signal is in an RGB format, so to convert it to a composite signal, you must use an RGB-to-composite converter—the ComputerVideo NTSC converter box, which is priced under $400, for example—to encode the RGB signal into the NTSC composite signal. Using such a converter plugged into one of these cards, the Mac outputs the NTSC interlaced signal, and a composite signal is available from a phono plug on the converter. This can be plugged into a large television or monitor, or fed into a VCR.

Taking a straight-up Mac video signal (not the NTSC interlaced signal that the cards mentioned in the previous paragraph can output, but the RGB noninterlaced Mac video signal) to NTSC is more involved because you go from noninterlaced to interlaced, from the 66.67 MHz to the 30 MHz scan rate, and from RGB to composite. The current popular products include the VideoLogic Mediator, a shoebox-sized box that sports impressive features such as a digital readout and automatic flicker reduction of the Mac image, and the Radius VideoVision card which will output 24-bit clicker-free video to NTSC. But these technological marvels come at a steep price—both list at around $2000. If you can get "good enough" with the ComputerVideo's NTSC encoder, it may be unnecessary to pay five times as much for the Mediator's features.

Mac to NTSC Conversion Issues

When you take Mac video signals into the NTSC world, you need to consider several things. First, because you are taking a high-resolution noninterlaced screen image, which has the capability to handle one-pixel height lines, to a video standard which cannot, any narrow horizontal lines appear to vibrate on the NTSC screen. This is because that one-pixel height line is shown only in one field line of the frame being displayed—say a line in the odd field—and the even field's lines around it have no information for it. The net result is a blinking or vibrating visual effect because the odd field paints the line

Chapter 19
Multimedia on the Macintosh

Part IV
Specialized Mac Applications

every 1/60 of a second, and the even field's lines paint no line the other 1/60 of a second of every frame.

To prevent this effect, you can avoid all single-pixel height lines on the screen. Alternatively, you can use a technique called *anti-aliasing* to blend those narrow lines out to neighboring pixels (see figure 19.11). Most of the good graphics packages support anti-aliasing effects and anti-aliased text. Adobe Photoshop has an anti-aliasing filter and can use anti-aliasing techniques on text. VideoQuill is a graphical text creation package that includes a wide variety of dynamic anti-aliased display fonts, specifically intended for video use.

Figure 19.11
Converting Mac video signals to NTSC can result in a bad case of the "jaggies," as in the top figure, unless smoothed out by anti-aliasing, as in the bottom figure.

Another solution for this one-pixel height line problem is included in the newer Macintosh video cards. In addition to supporting NTSC output, the 4•8, 8•24, and 8•24GC Apple video cards can use a built-in technology called *convolution* when they are used in 8-bit mode with the NTSC signal. This technique combines upper and lower rows of pixels in an averaging scheme that effectively eliminates the vibrating one-pixel height lines, at the expense of making the entire screen a bit fuzzy on the NTSC monitor. The VideoLogic Mediator mentioned earlier has a higher price, due partly to its capability to intelligently eliminate flickering lines with anti-aliasing techniques at 24-bit color depth. The Radius VideoVision card uses a 24-bit convolution technology to control flicker.

The second consideration when converting Macintosh video to NTSC is NTSC's inability to display all the colors the Mac is capable of displaying. Deeply saturated reds and blues glow and smear in the NTSC signal if they are not corrected. A number of the good Mac graphics packages, Adobe Photoshop included, enable you to set up with or convert to an *NTSC video palette*, which uses slightly muted colors that are not as saturated as the Mac can produce. These translate to the NTSC video side with much better results.

Digital Video

So far, we have discussed video-annotated multimedia presentations when the video source is an analog device such as a VCR, video camera, or laser disc player. By changing that analog signal into something that can be recorded on your Mac's hard disk, technology converts it into digital video. But there are problems with saving those digital video images onto your Mac.

Grabbing individual frames or multiple frames and converting them into graphics files enables you to save them to your hard drive, where you can manipulate and view the images and strings of images as you would any other computer document or graphics file. However, such files can be rather large—even at 1/4 of a 13-inch RGB Mac screen size, each individual 24-bit frame is approximately 350K. At 30 frames per second, that is easily in the neighborhood of 10M of computer data per second that needs to be recorded to and played from a hard drive. Full-screen images can take upwards of 50 to 60M per second. However, the hard drive mechanisms' throughput and SCSI and NuBus architectures cannot sustain such high data transfer rates in currently available Macs.

The solution is to compress visual information of the frames of the digitally captured video into a smaller size that can be managed by the throughput of data buses on commonly available and affordable Macintoshes. To view the compressed digital video, you decompress it using a similar technology, then play the digital video back onto the screen. This is part of what QuickTime does.

These compression schemes are performed using various mathematical algorithms that look at the detail, contrast, and color information of small sections of the image, and effectively simplify that information while only minimally compromising the quality of the image. These algorithms and schemes are typically asymmetrical—where playback is done in real time, but the recording process itself has to be done under a controlled, slowed-down input. This is due to the complexity or inefficiency of most compression

Chapter 19
Multimedia on the Macintosh

Part IV
Specialized Mac Applications

schemes (DVI, for instance), which prompted the use of special hardware chips and boards to adequately achieve real-time decompressed playback and in some cases, real-time *symmetrical* capture. The basic QuickTime algorithm (Apple Video Compression) is a symmetrical method, where capture is done in real time.

All compression algorithms juggle three variables: the image's size, the number of frames per second, and the image's quality. Given a specific algorithm (the QuickTime 1.0 AVC algorithm, for example), you may be able to get a great image quality and a fast frame rate but only at smaller frame sizes. Or you may be able to get a large frame size with good image quality but at the expense of frame rate. By adding special chips that are streamlined to apply these algorithms to digital video, manufacturers can increase the levels of these three variables and approach symmetrical schemes where both compression and playback can be done in real time. For instance, Radius has implemented the motion JPEG (Joint Photographic Expert Group) compression standard in their studio daughter board that attaches to their VideoVision board, which allows capture and playback of full-screen, 24-bit color images at 30 frames per second from a fast hard disk. Another capture card, the SuperMac VideoSpigot, implements a similar technology that can capture and compress video in a smaller window in real time at very high rates and then convert the compressed digital video to a QuickTime movie, all for under $400.

While competing platforms work on implementing compression at an applications and hardware level, Apple has chosen to incorporate toolbox managers to handle compression technologies within the Macintosh's operating system in the QuickTime extension. Building compression managers into the Mac's architecture means applications that use QuickTime-compressed videos do not have to know how to do compression, only how to call to the QuickTime compression manager. The QuickTime (QT) managers take care of which algorithms to use on a specific image, which hardware is used to capture or play back the images, and how the images are displayed. In effect, any application can play back a QT movie as long as it knows what a movie is. And if not, it can display movies with the help of a control-panel extension called Wild Magic, which lets any application that supports PICT files display and play QT movies. So you can paste a QT movie into your favorite word processor or desktop publishing package.

QuickTime 1.6 ships with several digital video algorithms (Apple Video Compressor, Compact Video, and so forth) that have been optimized for use with the normal Mac 68020, 030, and 040 processors and architectures found

Chapter 19
Multimedia on the Macintosh

in most Macs, and can achieve a compression of 20:1 to 30:1 at playback of 10 to 30 frames per second for a 320 x 240 pixel window—without the addition of other hardware. Maximum real-time capture speeds tend to be slower than maximum playback speeds, due to the greater processor demands during compression, so QuickTime is not strictly symmetrical. Because non-hardware-assisted QuickTime capture depends on the Mac's processor speed, the maximum real-time capture speeds with a capture board, which has no special on-board chip support for compression, varies across Macs. For instance, capturing a 120- x 160-pixel window in real time using a RasterOps 24STV with a IIsi maxs out at roughly six frames per second, with a IIfx at nine frames per second, a Quadra 700 at 17 frames per second, and a Quadra 950 at 24 frames per second.

A number of different compression algorithms are being implemented in the industry: DVI (Digital Video Interactive from Intel/IBM), CD-I (Compact Disc Interactive from Philips), JPEG, AVC, and MPEG (Motion Picture Experts Group) to name a few. DVI and CD-I, based on CD-ROM delivery, are not symmetrical by their very nature. Both require a non-real-time mastering and duplication process that is time-consuming and costly. CD-I is specified with a slower transfer rate for use with less expensive CD-ROM drives, so its 150K per second currently has only recently become fast enough to display full-motion video. DVI is well suited for video from CD-ROM but requires special hardware for playback and capture of high quality video— a proprietary mainframe for costly mastering, averaging $250 per finished minute of video.

JPEG and MPEG are both international standards but are optimized for different uses. JPEG is oriented at still image compression and can be used on multiple frames of digitized video; it is ideal for frame-accurate editing and quick interactive access. A version of JPEG, called motion JPEG, has been built into a number of the full screen, full motion Macintosh capture cards that have recently appeared on the market. MPEG, although still under development by the standards committee, uses a *frame differencing* algorithm that captures the first frame in a specific-length segment of frames and then records only the changes or differences in that frame over the rest of the frames in the sequence. The compressed files are much smaller and often higher quality than JPEG's, so MPEG is ideal for CD-ROM but not so good for quick frame-accurate access. Because QuickTime is a set of managers, you can add different compression/decompression algorithms (called *codecs*) to it to handle these various compression schemes.

Compression algorithms also can be used on still images from video or PICT files from a graphics package. QuickTime and a number of third-party compression schemes work with still images; for instance, both SuperMac and Kodak have software and hardware still image compression schemes. QuickTime 1.6 ships with the JPEG standard for use on still images for compression ratios of roughly 20:1 (a 1M full-screen, 24-bit image is compressed to 50K) at an operating systems level. This means applications such as PageMaker and HyperCard that currently work with PICT files do not have to know about decompression to open a compressed PICT file: the QT compression manager handles it for them.

Audibles

With its built-in speaker and sound chip, the Mac always has had the capability to include sound as a media type for presentations. This sound playback capability, which on most other platforms is limited to a simple system beep, enables you to use rich, diverse sounds to communicate a wide range of information on the Macintosh. Using a sound input device, such as Farallon's MacRecorder, or the built-in sound input capabilities of the newer Macs, you can record and attach sound to multimedia applications and documents, with copy-and-paste ease.

Sound Uses

Sound possibilities in multimedia messages fall into essentially three areas, although these are in no way exclusive: *iconic cues*, *reinforcement*, and *content*. Although described independently here, they often are used in combination, and the lines defining them easily are blurred in application. When adding sound, make sure you do not overburden the user with audible information that competes with visible messages. Integrated sounds should reiterate and reinforce the total message.

Iconic cues are the consistent uses of a sound to warn or indicate something has happened as a result of your action. For example, when you do something the Mac cannot interpret or "does not like," it beeps to indicate a warning. When you click on a button inside a HyperCard stack to go to the next page of information, a page-turning sound may be played, accompanied by a visual effect of the page wiping or scrolling from the right to the left. Different sounds and visual effects can indicate when you go to other areas in the information or use various types of tools, such as a scissors icon and a snipping sound for editing.

Chapter 19
Multimedia on the Macintosh

Reinforcement sounds tell you how you are doing and what type of progress you are making, and they assist in the learning process by acknowledging good work. The sounds can range from minimal indicators—using a short sound that says: "correct" whenever you answer a question correctly—to complex chunks of information, such as a spoken sentence that gives the correct answer and some additional remedial information when you answer a question incorrectly. Reinforcement strongly can affect certain types of learners, especially novice or young learners, but beware of using the same sound continually, especially longer sounds. It is also wise to give the more advanced user a way to turn off audio reinforcement.

When communicating content, sounds can be used as an explanation, in support of the message, or the content of the message itself. In the explanation form, sounds are used in much the same way a person explains something to students—by speaking or reading to them. For example, the digitized sound of a person's voice can say the same textual information being displayed onscreen or describe concepts being displayed graphically with an animation. In a supporting role, sound can be used to create the environmental background sounds or metaphorical cues to help create the full experience of the message—for instance, traffic sounds as background for a message on traffic safety. As direct content, the sound itself is a basic element of the experience or the focus of the learning: for example, using a musical piece such as Beethoven's 9th Symphony in Audio-CD format accompanied by screens of information that give a running commentary on the development of a particular musical theme. Or in a more affective presentation, images may be displayed onscreen while a digitized narration is played back from the Mac and an audio CD is played underneath as background music.

Sound Sources

There are essentially five sources of sound for multimedia purposes: digitized sound played from a sound file or as part of a QuickTime movie on your hard disk or CD-ROM; a synthesized voice using voice synthesis drivers such as MacinTalk and the Mac's sound chip; digitized sound played from an audio CD in the CD-ROM player; sound recorded in the audio tracks of other interactive devices (such as a laser disc player); and sound sources attached to the Macintosh through MIDI (musical instrument digital interface) connections.

Digitized sounds comprise a large part of the lower and middle range of multimedia's use of sound. At this lower and middle range, these sounds can

Part IV
Specialized Mac Applications

be *sampled* using either the built-in microphone on the newer Macs (LC and IIsi) or with inexpensive sampling devices such as Macromedia Paracomp's MacRecorder (see figure 19.12). Sampling turns an analog sound created with a voice or instrument into a digital file that can be edited, stored, and played back on the Macintosh. A sampled digitized sound can be saved as an independent sound file or as a resource inside of a file created by one of the multimedia engines for playback; that is, a sound in a HyperCard stack or Director movie.

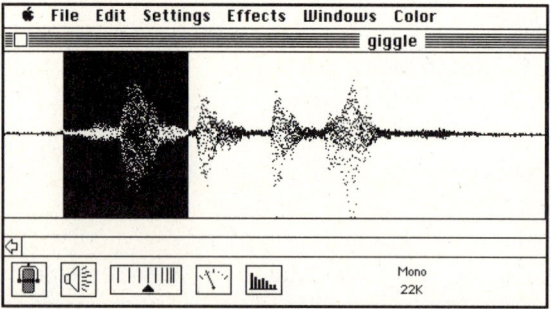

Figure 19.12
Sound takes on a visual effect when edited digitally in SoundEdit, software shipped with Farallon's MacRecorder.

Sampling can be done with most QuickTime capture tools either as sound-only files or at the same time you record a QuickTime movie from video; a sound "track" can be added to a movie later. As a matter of fact, part of QuickTime's technology ties sound data and the digital video data to a timing track so both the video and the sound play back true to time—similar to a multiple-track tape. And like a multiple-track tape, you can go back into a QuickTime movie using an editing application and insert or "dub" in audio over a section of less useful audio, keeping the sound and video accurate in playback and dynamically true to time. QuickTime 1.6 added several new capabilities, including the capability to directly record an audio track into a movie off of an audio CD.

These sound files, resources, and QuickTime sounds can be stored on and played from any of the Macintosh storage media, including CD-ROM, Magneto-optical drives, floppies, and hard disks. However, with sound files (not QuickTime movies), until the new Sound Manager was available, you had to have enough RAM to play the sound on these low-end sound files; the earlier sound manager would load the entire sound into RAM before playing it. System 7's new sound manager alleviates this problem by playing from disk. At the high end, the AudioMedia board from DigiDesign enables you to sample and mix high-fidelity audio, CD-quality digital sound—recorded to and played from your hard drive—without using your Mac's much needed

RAM. Audio played back in a QuickTime movie is also played directly off the storage medium, not from RAM.

Many sound sampling tools take advantage of the Macintosh Audio Compression Expansion (MACE) tools built into the operating system. These tools support the compression and playback of sounds that are algorithmically reduced in size: for instance, to one-sixth or one-third of their original size (see figure 19.13). The amount of compression and the rate at which the sounds are sampled affect the size of the sounds. Both the Mac sound chip and the chip used in Farallon's MacRecorder have a maximum sampling rate of 22 KHz, or 22,000 times per second. These chips also can sample at 11 KHz—which decreases the sound file's size by half—and lower.

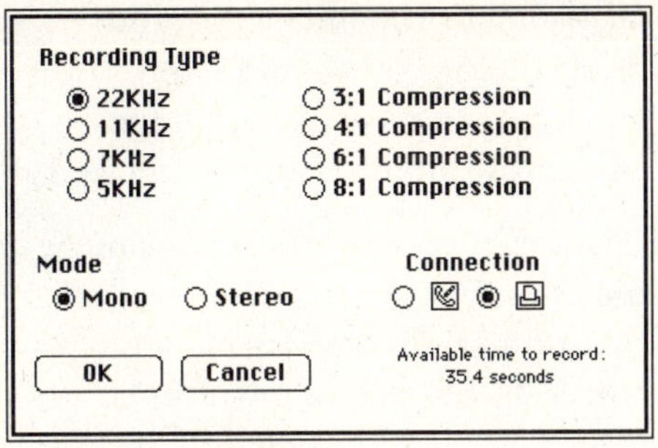

Chapter 19
Multimedia on the Macintosh

Figure 19.13
Sound Compression dialog box in SoundEdit shows various sampling rates and compression levels.

These space-saving technologies do not come without a cost. The greater the amount of compression and the slower the sampling rates, the lower the sound's fidelity and the more muffled the sound. If you want high fidelity and crisp sounds, sample at 22 KHz with no compression. If you are recording only the human voice, sample at 7 KHz and compress at the 6:1 ratio.

Apple is working on a new Speech Manager for high-quality text-to-speech capability, but as of this writing it has not been released. With the current solution—MacinTalk—the Mac's sound chip can be used to produce synthesized voice. This enables you to type words into an application and have the Mac read them back using various phonetic rules to distinguish vowels and consonants, and interpret confusing phonetic sounds such as "ea" in bear and fear, "oo" in wool and moon, and so forth. The audible voice is tinny and mechanical, but once your ear adjusts to the sound, it is quite useful in voicing information.

Early in the Mac's life cycle, Apple developed a system driver called MacinTalk to drive the sound chip for producing voice synthesis. Various applications and toolkits have been developed around this driver, but

Part IV
Specialized Mac Applications

MacinTalk itself never has been released as a supported driver and so is not readily available to the consumer. With its recent release of QuickTime, Apple has made a commitment to developing voice synthesis technologies that will replace and update the original MacinTalk capabilities. Code-named Casper, this capability has been demonstrated publicly a number of times and has just been released (as of August, 1993) in conjunction with Apple's new multimedia Macs, the Centris 660AV and Quadra 840AV.

Multimedia's use of sound played directly from an audio CD, sometimes called *interactive audio*, requires a Macintosh CD-ROM player that supports audio-CD services and a pair of amplified speakers or headphones attached to the playing device. In most cases, the Mac connection is through a SCSI cable, and the multimedia engine controls and plays back certain sections of the audio CD by using a toolkit or built-in facilities that address and control the CD-ROM player. Any audio CD can be used with this type of interactive setup. Examples include using a music CD for background music or a language CD for an interactive tutorial to teach French.

The audio tracks from various interactive media, including laser discs and video tape, are another source of sound. For instance, a laser disc has two audio tracks that can contain stereo sound or entirely different audio information in each track. Interactive control of the laser disc player can turn either one or both of these tracks on and off, and you can play back the laser disc without displaying a picture onscreen, thus allowing audio playback from either or both of the audio tracks. Several interactive video products have been developed with this idea in mind: for instance, ABC News Interactive's In the Holy Land, a laser disc and set of HyperCard stacks, narrates events in English on one laser disk track and in Spanish on the other.

The last sound source for multimedia purposes is devices that use MIDI (musical instrument digital interface) connections. MIDI is a type of communications protocol that enables various electronic instruments, synthesizers, keyboards, playback devices, and the computer to control and talk to each other to create synchronized and complexly orchestrated synthesized music. A MIDI interface device connects a Macintosh to a multitude of electronic instruments and devices through the computer's modem or printer port. The Mac uses a sequencing application to control these devices for synchronized playback of music, effectively turning the Mac into a cross between a tape recorder and a player piano. A number of multimedia engines enable you to play back MIDI documents that originally were recorded with a MIDI setup and sequencer.

Interactables

> **Chapter 19**
> Multimedia on the Macintosh

Interactables are the basic pieces of the multimedia application that often are described as tools. These tools include screen elements, input and output dialog devices, and navigational structures that enable you to move through the information's architecture. They are the result of several forces: the structure of the information to be communicated, the author's talents, and the multimedia engine's interface features and capabilities. Interactive interfaces were discussed earlier in the chapter. This section concentrates on items to consider when crafting the interface with these tools.

It is difficult to pin down interactivity's substance. You could describe it as an array of available tools. Tools are both conceptual and tangible devices that enable you to view and manipulate information. Multimedia engines offer a wealth of interactivity tools that can be used "as is" or molded and augmented to create other tools to suit your needs. Buttons, sounds, check boxes, text fields, beeps, pull-down menus, floating windows and palettes, the keyboard and mouse, dialog boxes, scroll bars, icons, and cursors are but a few of these elements. It is your task to use these tools to create the array your users will employ to move through the structured information you compose.

The interactive application is a two-way street. The user prods the application for a change in direction or for more information, and the application reacts in some way, prodding back by asking questions, feeding information to the user, or moving in a new direction. This interaction is crafted partly by the multimedia engine's features and partly by the author's design and foresight. There are several topics that affect the nature and interactivity of your interface to consider in your design: reactivity, the nature of the dialog, navigational issues, and the use of metaphors and models.

The first of these is the application's *reactivity*, or "smarts." What burden of operation have you put on the user, and how much is taken on by the application itself? How foolproof is the application? You must think through not only these types of interactions—displaying information and choices, questions and answers, and such—but also all likely outcomes of those interactions. This includes accidental and intentional mistakes in data entry and decisions, keeping track of the users' characteristics—feeding them appropriate information for their performance and mastery level—and allowing the tools to be customized for master versus novice users.

The second topic is the *nature of the dialog*—its style and substance. How you display the information and tools depends on and sets the stage for the

Part IV
Specialized Mac Applications

nature of the interaction. In the simplest sense, this means the presentation style—blocky textual boxes that require typed answers and information to proceed or graphical animations supplemented by audio narration and button-driven choices—is influenced by the content itself and, at the same time, influences how the user works with the application. For instance, a tool that allows movement through the information can take many forms. It can indicate through an icon that it moves you linearly to the next card. Or it can indicate that it branches off to an adjacent topic. Through various stylistic indicators, you can let the user know where he is and where he can go.

The third topic to consider is *navigational issues and tools*. The information's structure yields its architecture, but you must give the user navigational tools to determine the lay of that information. These are described as macro and micro navigational tools. Macro navigational tools indicate where the user is in the big picture, how far the user has traveled, and how much territory is left. A button that brings up a map to indicate where the user is in the larger structure is an example of a macro navigational tool. Micro navigational tools indicate which pieces of information are directly available to the user at any point, which related topics are available, how to get help, and how to quit. A list of related topics that takes the user to any specific topic he clicks on is a micro navigational tool.

The fourth consideration is the method in which you establish a larger conceptual understanding of your application through a *user-familiar metaphor or model*. This is particularly important if the user is unfamiliar with an interactive application or never has worked with the new content you are showing them. A library metaphor for a broad information environment, an office metaphor for an executive information system, a map of a wooded area to explore the ecological concepts of that biome, and a graphic of a simple cell for teaching the interrelated nature of cell biology are examples of models and metaphors.

Presentation and Delivery Issues

In an ideal world, everyone has unlimited money and access to all the leading-edge technologies, all the time. But sadly, this is not an ideal world.

Chapter 19
Multimedia on the Macintosh

The choice of platform, drop-in cards, storage devices, interactive devices, and display/delivery methods is always a balance of budget, the affordable level of new technologies, and that technology's rate of obsolescence. This section looks at issues related to making these choices.

Planning Your Platform

You may assume this discussion starts with "which Mac should I buy?" and sometimes it does. However, you can work with all the rudimentary multimedia tools on the breadth of Macintosh platforms. All Macs from the Classic through the Quadra can run most of the popular multimedia engines, can be expanded in memory with additional RAM, can control a video disc player and CD-ROM player, can record and play back sounds, and can create and play back animations with any of a number of the available animation packages;, and all of the 68020 and higher Macs can play back QuickTime movies. The main distinction between the low end and the high end, besides price, is overall performance, color and screen size, and available slots. So if you develop an application on one Mac, you easily can take it to any of the other platforms, as long as you are realistic about the performance differences and your need for color and slots.

The platform and configuration discussion actually should start at an earlier spot in your planning. You should begin with an estimation of what you really need to compose and deliver your multimedia application, particularly if you are starting from scratch, with no previously purchased Macs. This includes how the multimedia application will be delivered, the media you want to include in the message, how much technology you can afford now versus what you can afford to add on as its cost decreases, and the growth you anticipate needing from your configuration. The following questions should help you determine your general needs.

Planning Questions

Is the final delivery situation for your application on slower Macs, black and white Macs, or Macs with less RAM than what you will be authoring on? Will your authoring machine be the same machine you use to deliver the final composition to your end user? Will you deliver across a low-speed or high-speed network? These performance issues should be taken into account up front. If your authoring and delivery environments are different, you need to be aware that your delivery environment may not be able to deliver the performance (speed of animation, quality of audio, and so on) that you observe in your authoring environment.

Part IV
Specialized Mac Applications

Which media will you include in the final composition? Will you include some video from a video source in the final composition? If the media you will use requires special hardware for video or audio capture or playback, you need to choose a Macintosh that enables you to add digitizing hardware to it; that is, you may require a Mac with one or more NuBus slots.

If you are including video, can you include the video as a QuickTime movie rather than as live video from the source? QuickTime movies can be recorded on a Macintosh equipped with a video capture card and then played back on any Macintosh with a 68020 or better CPU chip. This means if you author using a Mac with a RasterOps card, a VideoSpigot, or another capture card, you can record your required video as a QuickTime movie and use the movie playback as your video in the final application. The only restrictions here are that QuickTime movies play at a small size (roughly 320 x 240 pixels) and take up approximately 2M of hard disk or CD-ROM space per minute of running time.

If you are including video, will it be seen on the Mac's screen or on a second monitor? Using a second video monitor with a laser disc player versus running the video on the Mac's screen (through the use of a special video card) embraces two considerations: cost and real estate. First, although a single-screen solution may be more elegant in an aesthetic sense, it is more expensive. The cost of an inexpensive color monitor for a laser disc player is roughly $280, whereas the cost of an inexpensive video card that allows video in a window on the Mac's monitor starts around $900. Second, a single-screen solution has less "real estate" than a two-screen solution; that is, the amount of screen space available to display information. You gain significant real estate by using more than one monitor, enabling you to put video information on the video monitor's screen and supplement it with information on the Mac's monitor. However, two screens may be confusing to your users.

Will you want to use more than one Mac monitor? Because the modular Macs support more than one monitor (up to the number of slots they have, plus one if they have built-in video), you conceivably could take a IIci, IIvx, or Centris 650 and plug up to three video cards into its slots and hang four Mac or multisync monitors off those cards and the built-in video, effectively giving the Mac a monitor space that is two monitors wide (2 x 640 = 1280 pixels wide) by two monitors high. You could have animations and video displayed on one screen, have textual information on another in a HyperCard window, give the user note-taking space in a third, and use a fourth for desktop, disk, and file access. Admittedly, this may take it to an extreme, but the Mac video standard's extensible nature allows for a wide variety of expansion options.

Will you need 32-bit graphics or are 8-bit or black and white graphics enough? The built-in video on most of the modular Macs (LC II with 512K VRAM expansion, IIsi, and IIci) is 8-bit when used with an Apple 14-inch RGB monitor. If you use higher color depth images, you need a video card that supports this: any of Apple's, such as the 8•24 or 8•24 GC cards, or a number of third-party cards. (The RasterOps 24STV, for instance, is a 24-bit card that also allows for video in a window) The IIvx, Centris, and Quadra Macs can have their video RAM expanded, allowing for support of up to 16-bit or 24-bit color depth.

Will you need to render animations that require a lot of horsepower in your CPU? The greater the demand on your Macintosh, the smarter it is to get a high-end authoring station: a Centris 610 or better.

Will the final output of your composition need to be projected using a projection unit, or will it be output to a videotape recorder? Not all projection units are the same. Many earlier models and some lower priced models do not support the Mac video signal. It usually requires a multisync projection device, which is a more expensive item. If you need to output to a projection unit or a videotape recorder that accepts an NTSC signal, and you can live with the lower resolution and artifacts from the interlaced video signal, make sure you choose a video card or Macintosh model that outputs to an NTSC signal, or use a converter that takes the Mac video signal to NTSC.

Configurations, Additions, and Considerations

After you mull through the different performance, color, slots, screens, input(video and audio), interactive devices, and output considerations, you are probably in a better position to decide which Macintosh you should purchase as your multimedia platform. Following are three example configurations. Remember, you can mix and match parts. Specific products are included as examples of the indicated hardware and software.

Low-end Example Configuration

▼ Macintosh Classic, Classic II, Color Classic (4M RAM/80M internal hard disk)

or

Macintosh LC, LC II, or LC III (4M RAM/80M HD) with 12-inch Apple color monitor or 14-inch Apple Basic Color Monitor

Chapter 19
Multimedia on the Macintosh

Part IV
Specialized Mac Applications

Bob LeVitus

Is that it for speakers? Amplified speakers? C'mon. A good pair of speakers makes a big difference in multimedia. Persona's MacSpeakers are a good choice for modest budgets; if you've got the bucks, Altec/Lansing's multimedia speakers with a subwoofer are totally awesome.

- ▼ Laser disc player (Pioneer 2200) with Mac cable and video/audio cables
- ▼ Video monitor (Hitachi or Sony monitors with built-in speakers)
- ▼ Sound input device (built-in microphone or MacRecorder)
- ▼ HyperCard and toolkits (ADDmotion)

Mid-range Example Configuration

- ▼ Macintosh IIsi, IIci, IIvx, or Centris 610 (4M/80M)
- ▼ Macintosh 14-inch RGB monitor
- ▼ Apple CD 300 CD-ROM player
- ▼ Laserdisc player (Pioneer 2200 or better) with Mac cable and video/audio cables
- ▼ Video-in-a-window video/QuickTime capture card (RasterOps 24STV, SuperMac VideoSpigot, or similar card) attached to monitor and laser disc player
- ▼ Amplified speakers attached to laser disc player and CD-ROM player
- ▼ HyperCard, Macromedia Director, Aldus Persuasion, Swivel 3-D, Adobe Photoshop, and so on

Upper-end Example Configuration

- ▼ Macintosh Centris 650 or 660AV or Quadra 700/800/950 or 840AV (20M/160M or greater)
- ▼ Two Macintosh 14-inch RGB monitors (or one 16-inch and one 14-inch)
- ▼ Apple CD 300 CD-ROM player
- ▼ Laser disc player (Pioneer 8000) with Mac cable and video/audio cables
- ▼ Video overlay and/or video-in-a-window video or QuickTime capture card attached to monitor and laser disc player (RasterOps 24STV or MediaTime video cards, RasterOps VideoVision, VideoLogic DVA 4000 card, or TrueVision NuVista+ card) and/or Macintosh 8•24 video card
- ▼ 24-bit color flatbed scanner
- ▼ Sound mixer from CD, laser disc, and Mac
- ▼ Amplified speakers attached to sound mixer
- ▼ AudioMedia card for sound recording

▼ HyperCard, Macromedia Director, MediaMaker, Swivel 3-D, StrataVision, Infini-D, Adobe Photoshop, Virtus Walkthrough, Alias Upfront, Adobe Premier, VideoFusion, Morph, and so on

High-end and Performance-Enhancing Additions

▼ Increase the SCSI bus throughput by adding one of the third-party SCSI-2 NuBus boards (such as the MicroNet NuPort board), which effectively can double the throughput from your hard drives.

▼ Increase the speed of your hard drives by using larger hard drives and hard disk "arrays" that synchronize several hard drives, using all of their heads at the same time and making all appear to be one drive. This increases the sustained throughput of the array.

▼ Add some 4M or 16M SIMMs to increase your RAM, and create a RAM disk to run your files from; this bypasses the SCSI bus bottleneck entirely.

▼ Add processor accelerators. For instance, you can get 68030 40 and 50 MHz accelerators for your Mac that take it to the speed of a IIfx or better, and the newer 68040 accelerators approach or exceed Quadra performance.

▼ Add video acceleration, but be aware that not all acceleration is created equal. Some accelerators speed QuickDraw commands, but if your applications bypass QuickDraw for drawing to the screen, they do not benefit from this acceleration. Test before you buy.

▼ Add alternative input and output devices: mouse alternatives such as trackballs, graphics tablets, joysticks, datagloves, and touchscreens.

▼ Add voice input control through the Casper technology in the Centris 660AV and Quadra 840AV Macintoshes, or through a product such as the Voice Navigator.

Storage Considerations

You have several issues to consider when deciding which storage medium to work with in your authoring and delivery situations. How much space does the medium offer? What is the medium's cost per megabyte? What are the writing and reading speeds? Does the reading speed influence how fast sounds, animations, and movies can be played from the medium? How durable is the medium? How flexible is the medium—is it an old technology that soon will be outmoded? Can you use various formats with the reading device?

Consider the following tips:

▼ Floppy disks are inexpensive but small and slow. For smaller HyperCard stacks with some minimal black and white animation, this is a practical medium for delivery. But when your application gets larger or you start using dynamic data that requires higher transfer rates, look to faster and larger media.

▼ Flopticals, opticals, and magneto-opticals meet many of the criteria for excellent delivery media, except for speed. Transfer rates tend to be slow, making them good for compressed data but not for high-speed animations. Writing throughput tends to be lower than reading throughput. They are particularly suited as secondary storage and backup.

▼ CD-ROM is a read-only medium, so make sure anything you intend to run from CD can function without changing the files—HyperCard is particularly sensitive about this. CD-ROM is more expensive to master—$500 for a single pressed disc, $2,000 to create a master for multiple discs—but the costs per CD are under $2 after you press several hundred, making it an ideal low-cost delivery medium for very large applications (up to 650M). A CD's transfer rates are lower, maxing out around 300K per second on the double-speed drives, so compressed digital movies are a must if you will be using full motion onscreen. New CD makers have just come to the market for attachment directly to the Macintosh for around $3500, where the mastering blank CDs cost $35 each.

▼ Cartridge drives—both the Bernoulli, Syquest, and Ricoh types, as well as the newer magneto-optical cartridge drives—make ideal delivery and distribution media if you can live with the sizes (44 or 88M, or 120M or higher for the magneto-opticals) and slower access speeds and throughput, and if you can count on your users having compatible cartridge drives. Depending on their design, they can be nearly as fast as standard hard drives and work well for development and secondary storage/backup.

▼ Tape drives, particularly the newer DAT drives, can be used for backups and in some cases delivery of material. Their streaming mechanisms can allow for direct playback of long QuickTime movie sequences such as with Optima's TapeDisk utility, which allows a tape in a DAT drive to be mounted directly to the desktop, enabling access files directly off the media. DAT tapes can hold roughly 2G to 8G of information.

▼ Hard drives, particularly very large drives, and hard disk arrays (in which several hard drives are synchronized and treated as one large drive) are ideal for multimedia presentations that include a great deal of CD-quality sound files, colorful graphics, and fast-moving animations that require high-speed throughput of 24-bit graphics to screen. In this case, you are looking for the fastest access, highest sustained transfer rates you can afford. However, this media is not removable, so it must be backed up to some secondary storage media, and it is not easily distributed. Note: If you create a project on hard disk that you intend to take to CD-ROM or optical, be sure you test it on those media to determine your throughput needs.

Tools and Engines

Much of this chapter has been devoted to discussing multimedia technologies' hardware. In this section, the software tools and multimedia engines are organized into a model that follows how a multimedia presentation is created—in a fashion similar to composing music. It is important to note that although multimedia is considered chiefly a presentation media, it is possible to use multiple media integrated into all aspects of computing tasks on the Macintosh: for instance, using digital QuickTime movies as well as still graphics in a word processing document or annotating an E-mail note with a verbal audible comment. However, this chapter does not address the scope of integrated media uses; it focuses on integrated media in presentations and authoring instructional interactive multimedia applications.

Composer's Process Model

Creating multimedia applications and presentations is a bit like the process a composer goes through to create an opera—from inception to composition to performance. The composer outlines a plot and story line, hears inspired musical themes in his head, scripts for the characters and composes the musical themes, picks instruments for the orchestra and visualizes settings for the staging, gathers all the ideas and pieces together and composes a multilined score that defines the performance. Then the characters are cast, the orchestra is picked, the set is created, and the performance is rehearsed; the entire opera culminates in the performance of his visualized composition. Multimedia applications in some respects can be thought of as performances,

Part IV
Specialized Mac Applications

so their development is similar and can be discussed using the compositional model (see figure 19.14).

The term *inspiration* does not mean you have to be spiritually moved to consider creating a multimedia work, but it is a helpful a concept to discuss the visualization and planning phase of the creative process. In this stage, you determine the presentation's goals, outline the content, and use inspiration and visualization to mold the basic ideas and events for the final piece. Various idea outlining, project management, and productivity tools can be useful in this phase. At the very least, you should have an outline of the presentation's contents, a time line of events and transitions, and possibly a story board of sequences when you complete this phase. If it is an interactive application, you also should have a rough map of the branching structure of the work. Don't worry too much about setting your plans in stone at this point, but the firmer you make these plans, the easier it is to focus on its individual sections.

Figure 19.14
Creating multimedia compares to the process a conductor goes through in orchestrating a symphony.

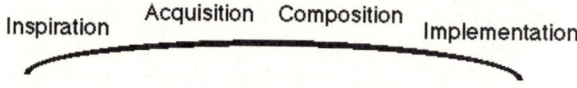

The *acquisition* phase includes gathering and creating the materials and ideas you will use in the work. This includes the visuals, audibles, and interactables discussed earlier in this chapter. Activities here could include gathering the music and sounds from sound libraries or CDs, digitizing sounds with a built-in microphone or sampling device (MacRecorder), scanning black and white or color photographs with a flatbed scanner, grabbing still frames of specific video images, or grabbing QuickTime movie clips of video.

You also should gather interface and interactivity ideas: menu and button designs, navigation and choice array tools, interactive structure ideas, useful scripts, XCMDs, and toolkits. The acquisition tasks usually overlap into the composing tasks, and depending on how you divide the phases of your development, you may acquire and compose each specific section of your application/presentation.

You need to be aware of copyright laws when you gather existing materials. In general, if your material will be sold commercially, you must acquire the rights to use any previously copyrighted material in your composition. This means getting written permission from the copyright holder, typically the

Chapter 19
Multimedia on the Macintosh

material's publisher, to use the material in the way you intend. Copyrighted materials include published pictures and photographs; graphics; sounds; animations including clip art, clip sounds, clip movies, and clip animations; compact discs, record, and taped music; published written materials; video and film; and XCMDs and any special toolkit drivers. If you use copyrighted material for educational purposes, consult your institution's audio-visual copyright use doctrine, typically available from the audio-visual support services in your organization. "One copy, one time, and not the heart of the work," is the general rule of thumb for fair, educational use, but you probably will find many interpretations of this idea. The best choice on your part may be to create your own materials rather than get into the quagmire of using copyrighted materials.

If you cannot find the pieces or cannot find pieces you legally can use, you have to create them yourself, which is the second part of the acquisition phase. A wide variety of tools for creating images, video, sounds, music, and animations abound. Some of the applications for creating multimedia elements include color painting and drawing graphics packages, MIDI and music creation hardware and software, video cameras, recording and editing equipment, and 3-D modeling and animation packages. Many of these tools are used also to manipulate and modify the pieces you have gathered, so the gathering and creating activities overlap each other significantly. A number of multimedia engine tools have creation packages built into them: for instance, Macromedia Director has a good built-in paint package.

The third phase, *composition*, is where you assemble the pieces into a presentation or application. This phase is based on using one (or a number) of the multimedia engine applications mentioned earlier in this chapter. For instance, if you use HyperCard as your engine, you would create the structure of your stack, script the buttons and design the interface, pull in the different multimedia elements, and use the various toolkits to work with the interactive devices to be used in your final presentation or application. Or, if you use Macromedia Director, you would create the animations, pull in the images and sounds, craft the interface, script the buttons and interface, and work with the Director X objects to control the interactive devices. Each engine uses a slightly different set of tools for composing your work, but the overall process is the same: you create the general structure, pull in the different elements you have gathered and created, and craft the presentation of material.

The final *implementation* phase involves the output use or delivery of your composition. For instance, it might be a screen-based one-on-one interactive session, a projection-based presentation for an audience, a linear

Part IV
Specialized Mac Applications

presentation dumped to videotape, or an interactive application used concurrently by many students in a computer lab. Many possibilities are available, and combinations are not uncommon. It is one thing to create the work on your authoring machine and another to implement its delivery, which is most likely in a different environment.

You need to thoroughly explore the system design and the logistical plan for its implementation before you can roll it out to your intended audience for use. This includes considering various pieces of hardware that assist with projection and getting NTSC video out of your Macintosh, software for preparing the images and text for optimized viewing in these output environments, and networking issues such as your network's speed and your server's capabilities to enable multiple users to work through your application simultaneously. You also may be working closely with the people who run the labs or public facilities you will be delivering in. Although it is a final phase, implementation must be planned for, particularly if you are delivering in a multiple user environment—this can change the entire structure of your application.

Composing a multimedia work can be very simple or very complex. It can be undertaken by an individual or by a team. As its complexity increases and as you include more people in the process, it pays to plan out the sections and events in the work, dividing it into logical units so you can budget your time and resources across the span of the development process. The four-phase process outlined here—inspiration, acquisition, composition, and implementation—is by no means the only way this can be done. Each author/composer will develop his own way of working with these different sets of tasks.

A Look at the Engines

As discussed earlier, the core application that manages the display and presentation of images, sounds, and other interactive elements is called the multimedia engine. This includes applications such as HyperCard, SuperCard, Spinnaker Plus, Macromedia Director, and Authorware. They are sometimes referred to as "authoring" tools or engines, because they allow a developer to create instruction in much the same way as an author writes a work of literature.

Authoring Engines: The Continuum

If you look at the various authoring and multimedia engines in a matrix, the horizontal side of the matrix is a continuum from general to specific-authoring engines, and the vertical side is singular-tool engines to multitool-system engines (see figure 19.15). A general engine is one that can be used to create multimedia applications as well as strictly text or graphics applications and various productivity applications: HyperCard, SuperCard, or Spinnaker Plus. Specific-authoring engines are designed to assist in creating instruction and computer-based training: for instance, Authorware, which has specific-answer judging tools built into it that judge true or false, multiple choice, and short answer, gives the needed branching structure for the author as it creates each question array.

Chapter 19
Multimedia on the Macintosh

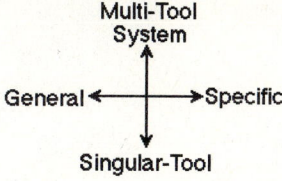

Figure 19.15
This multimedia engine matrix shows the considerations important in choosing a multimedia engine.

In the other dimension of the matrix, singular-tool engines are those that contain one type or set of tools that effectively do one thing or work in one media. Often, these singular tools are incorporated into other engines. For example, Swivel 3-D creates wonderful three-dimensional animations with its own integrated set of tools, and these can be exported into a PICS file to be included in a Macromedia Director movie, but Swivel 3-D cannot control a laser disc player or respond to clicks on buttons. The multitool-system engines are at the other end of this dimension, where an engine contains animation, interactivity, audible, visual, and external device control tools within it. Macromedia Director falls into this category, with its wealth of animation, interactivity, and interface tools.

Different Engines

HyperCard, as a general authoring/multimedia engine, is often referred to as a personal toolkit for building custom applications. It enables you to create interfaces, information environments, and interactive multimedia applications. More HyperCard stack applications have been created since its rollout in October 1987 than all other software on all other platforms combined. The tools are easy for the beginner to learn. You can create simple stacks as a brand-new novice, and as you gain experience, you can create more complex applications. HyperCard can be extended by adding various

Part IV
Specialized Mac Applications

toolkits and external resources, which enable it to control laser disc players and CD-ROM drives, connect to servers across networks, carry on a querying discourse with a complex database, or front-end a terminal session with an IBM mainframe. Due to its flexible set of interface tools, it can be molded into a variety of interfaces, which makes it ideal as a general authoring engine.

Aldus SuperCard and Spinnaker Plus are general authoring engines similar to HyperCard; their scripting and architecture follow the HyperTalk scripting language conventions and HyperCard's inheritance structure. But the tools they use to design applications and the creation and editing environments are different. Both SuperCard and Spinnaker Plus are color environments and contain color editing tools. The use of color does come with a hit in their applications' performance, but this is expected when you start moving large color images around onscreen.

SuperCard is a popular general authoring tool, especially when used on more powerful Macintosh platforms, such as IIci and IIfx. It uses a superset of the HyperTalk scripting language, including commands for multiple windows, draw-object graphics, and irregularly shaped buttons. Its editing environment might take some getting used to if you come from the HyperCard world. You do most of your creating and scripting in a SuperEdit application, whereas you actually run the created application in SuperCard proper, so you have to leave one to go to the other for every test and edit you do in your authoring. SuperCard applications can be saved as stand-alone applications that do not require the authoring engine to run the created work. Many HyperCard XCMDs and XFCNs can be directly translated and used in SuperCard. Aldus has not updated SuperCard in several years, so despite its loyal following, its future is unclear.

Spinnaker Plus has an editing environment similar to HyperCard's; the editing and running are done in one "mode," but the tool array is broader in Plus. It has different kinds of fields and draw-object buttons and includes color editing features. Plus has the capability to run developed applications across platforms, both Mac and IBM-compatible computers. This is not done without some sacrifice because many of the features you take for granted on the Mac cannot be found in the PC world, or are found at a higher cost. The design of an application that will be used on both platforms must gravitate to the lowest common denominator of interface features, often making for a simple or dull and non-Mac-like application. Nevertheless, although it is not the most stable of environments of these three general tools, Plus contains a strong set of tools and is capable of creating powerful multimedia applications.

Chapter 19
Multimedia on the Macintosh

A number of toolkits that can be added to HyperCard are worth mentioning. One, ADDmotion, is a package used inside HyperCard to create color animations. It contains a 24-bit color paint editing package, animation sequencer, and sound editor that enable it to integrate color, sound, and animation into a HyperCard stack. Videodisc and CD-ROM toolkits available from The Voyager Co. and from the Apple Programmers' and Developer's Association (APDA) are additional toolkits you may want to consider. These are sets of extensions that allow the interactive control of a wide variety of laser disc players and CD-ROM drives, attached either via serial cable or through the SCSI bus.

The APDA (Apple Programmers and Developers Association) Catalog is an excellent source of toolkits for HyperCard, including the QuickTime Starter Kit and Developer's Kit, XCMD sets, and connectivity tools. APDA can be contacted at (800) 282-APDA.

FilmMaker, Swivel 3-D, StrataVision, and other 3-D and animation tools have their own price points, strengths, and capabilities. Some create animations that can be played back with "player" applications supplied with the main application, and many output to PICS file formats that can be brought into Macromedia Director for playback or can be converted into a QuickTime movie. They take up only a fraction of the space of the original and are playable from inside the main multimedia engines.

Macromedia Director, along with HyperCard, is one of the most popular multimedia engines. Macromedia Director started out as a black and white animation tool called VideoWorks soon after the Mac was introduced, and it has come a long way since then. It now sports rich animation and interface design tools, a full 32-bit graphics paint package, support for external resources for controlling interactive devices, a scripting environment to create interactive elements and buttons, and a new 3-D modeling environment to perform 3-D animations. Although it is not as "general" an engine as HyperCard, its tools are specifically designed to create multimedia presentations that can include a fair amount of branching and interactivity. It can create stand-alone projectors that do not require the application to be played, and it comes with a HyperCard toolkit for playing Director animations inside a stack.

MediaMaker is another product from Macromedia. It is more of a sequencer for creating multimedia presentations that include Mac audio, Director animations, PICT files, CD audio sound, laser disc video, and other serially controlled video from tape players. In MediaMaker, you gather a collection of different media snippets you eventually will use in your presentation, then

Part IV
Specialized Mac Applications

you assemble them on a time line score called a sequence, with visuals and audibles falling in different tracks. By arranging and manipulating these elements in the tracks, you easily can change the pace and sequence of media events and eventually record the final sequence to a computer-controlled video tape recorder—"printing to video."

Macromedia Authorware is by far the most specifically delineated authoring tool for the Mac on the market today, sporting a wide array of tools to create animated, graphical, interactive, instructional applications. It can be supplemented with modules that can control laser discs and CD audio playback, as well as a number of other interactive devices. In Authorware, you create a map of the information environment's structure that the user potentially can work through. Each icon in this map symbolizes different elements of the experience: for instance, icons can stand for events, screen designs, animations, question or decision points, or resulting actions upon answering a question. Authorware has extensive built-in record-keeping and profile information and offers a broad spectrum of ways to ask questions and judge answers. Its applications can be "compiled" to run with a run-time version of the software, so the authoring tools are not needed to play back and use the instructional multimedia application.

These are just a few of the tools available to create multimedia presentations and applications on the Mac. As QuickTime proliferates in the Mac market, you will see a wide array of applications to create and edit QuickTime movies (such as Adobe Premiere, Diva VideoShop, VideoFusion and CameraMan, to name a few), captured using a variety of cards and capture devices. QuickTime's great impact on the use of media in the near term comes first from the benefits of compressed graphics, animation, and digital video, which enables people to include more visual elements onscreen and in their applications. Second, because QuickTime has been implemented at an operating system level, QuickTime-supported dynamic data types will be available to people in all aspects of computing, not just the multimedia applications.

All Macs with 68020 processors or better can take advantage of these benefits. Examples of its use include the capability to play digital video movies in your word processing documents; to carry around a full-screen, 24-bit color slide presentation with 30 compressed color PICT files and a HyperCard stack on a floppy disk; and manipulate multiple audio tracks for a specific digital movie with English in one track, French in another, and German in another to teach languages or use on a Mac notebook as a travel guide and translator.

Chapter 19
Multimedia on the Macintosh

Summary

The Macintosh's current capabilities to integrate various media into all aspects of personal computing through a simple copy and paste is due to its layered architecture. That architecture allows Apple to insert other data types at a very low level, adding another type of media for use in all applications. This is the case with QuickTime. By adding the QuickTime extension to your system, you effectively give your Mac the capability to display dynamic and compressed media: QuickTime movies and compressed PICT files. And these new media are available across all applications on the Mac, not just on certain ones.

Multimedia on the Macintosh is a much different concept than on other computer platforms because of the Mac's capability to integrate various media across the breadth of personal computing applications. But QuickTime's impact on how you work with the Mac is much broader than just using motion images in what you traditionally think of as still applications.

Some say multimedia is the configuration of a certain type of personal computer. Others talk about it as a set of technologies. The forward perspective views multimedia as the wave of the future, in which computers are integrated into video and display technologies and into communications technologies. This platform's technology allows it to become a tool that enables the media to be the message. The Macintosh has an architecture that enables it to grow into a machine with these capabilities.

Chapter 20: Macs and the Differently Abled

"Our goal has always been to create products that help ordinary people do extraordinary things. And to remember that our products also help extraordinary people to do ordinary things," says John

In This Chapter

▼ The Mac as a level playing field

▼ Different interfaces for different people

▼ Sources for help

Part IV
Specialized Mac Applications

Sculley, Chairman of Apple Computer. Whereas the rest of this book is about extraordinary things the Mac can do, this chapter is about ordinary things the Mac can do, such as turning on lights, playing cards with a friend, making a phone call—things some people take for granted, but tasks that used to be impossible for others. The same Mac that can handle word processing and graphics can handle many of the chores of daily living, with the help of facilitative devices such as infrared switches and a modem. The Mac can make a tremendous difference in the quality of life for many of the estimated 40 million people in the United States who have some form of limitation.

Computers and the Differently Abled

Harnessing a computer's power can mean the difference between just living and earning a living for many individuals with disabilities. *Telecommuting*, working at home rather than in the office, has opened doors for thousands of people who find it difficult or impossible to report to a desk downtown every day. These employees handle skilled jobs ranging from typing and accounting to electronic publishing, art and design, writing, programming, and research.

For some, the computer is a tool for play or for learning. For many, it is a bridge to the outside world. "I may never get out of this room," observed one member of America Online, "but I have friends all over the country, and there is always somebody who wants to chat." Online services have forums and software libraries for all interests. Most services have an area where special-needs users can share information and support, as well as libraries of helpful programs and other resources.

Computers are powerful tools, and they can be equally powerful to all users. The Mac is a level playing field, whether the game is chess or earning a living. But what if your physical limitations mean that you can't see what is on the screen or can't slide the mouse around on the table? Does this mean you can't use a computer? No, but it does mean that you may need to interact with your computer in a different way.

The technical term for the way a computer interacts with another computer or with the person using it is *interface*. The common Macintosh-user

Chapter 20
Macs and the Differently Abled

interface is through a combination of the mouse, keyboard, and screen. You give the computer *input* by using the mouse or keys, and the Mac responds with onscreen (or printed if you desire) *output*. It is a fine system for many people. Others need different kinds of interfaces, either for input or output. What is needed is not just a personal computer but a *personalized* computer, one that accommodates your abilities.

> **A Closer Look**
> A Word About "Words": There have been many debates about what to call people with disabilities. "Handicapped," "disabled," "challenged"—each word has its supporters and naysayers. This text refers to specific conditions, when necessary, such as "blindness" or "quadriplegia," but recognizes that people with limits are people, not diagnoses.

Personalizing the Mac

People are different in different ways. The interface that works for one may be all wrong for someone else. There is no one-size-fits-all solution to personalized computing, just as there is no one perfect hat. The fireman's helmet is as useless to the airline pilot as the Braille-lettered keyboard is to someone with 20/20 vision and no hands. Each solves the wrong problem.

Obviously, the first step in solving the *right* problem is identifying it. Sometimes the problem is obvious, sometimes it is not. And the solution can consist of many pieces or simply can use one of the Mac's existing utilities.

Easy Access

A woman posted a message recently on one of the online service bulletin boards. She had broken her wrist and it was encased in a large fiberglass cast that totally immobilized her left hand. "I can type one-handed," she complained, "but I can't use most of the command key combinations in the word processor. If I try to reach Command, Shift, and P, I'll end up with the other hand in a cast, too." After sympathizing with her plight, another member suggested Sticky Keys, one of several Easy Access utilities that come with all Mac systems. Figure 20.1 shows the Easy Access control panel.

Figure 20.1
Sticky Keys solves typing problems for those who can't reach key combinations.

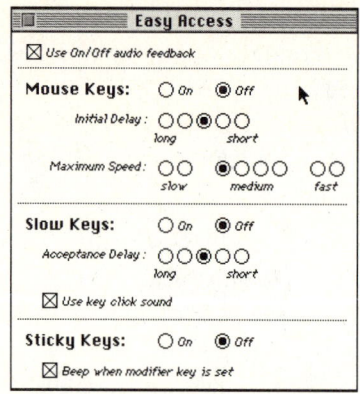

Sticky Keys lets you type key combinations one stroke at a time rather than all at once. This capability is obviously a big help to the one-handed or one-fingered typist. Install Sticky Keys by placing the Easy Access document into your System folder, restarting the Mac, and then tapping the Shift key five times without moving the mouse. The Sticky Keys icon appears at the upper-right corner of the menu bar to show that it is activated. (It looks like a bowl.) When you press one of the modifier keys (Command, Shift, Option, or Control), an arrow points down into the icon. Then, press the second key of the combination. Turn off Sticky Keys by tapping the Shift key five times or by pressing any two modifiers together. The easiest pair to use is Command-Option because they are adjacent; you can press them together with one finger or the equivalent.

Mouse Keys, another Easy Access utility, enables you to substitute the numeric keypad for the mouse. With Mouse Keys turned on, the numeric keypad lets you click, drag, and move the pointer around onscreen with precise control. Mouse Keys also functions with paint programs such as MacPaint, KidPix, and SuperPaint, enabling you to control paint brushes, pencils, and all the drawing tools. It is not fast enough to be used with many arcade games but works well with games in which speed is not a factor.

To activate Mouse Keys after Easy Access has been installed, press Command, Shift, and Clear (at the upper-left corner of the numeric keypad). If necessary, turn on Sticky Keys first. The diagram in figure 20.2 shows the layout of the keypad. The 0 key locks the mouse button for dragging and makes menus drop down from the menu bar. (The decimal point unlocks it again.) The 5 acts as a mouse button. Press once to click or twice to double-click. Pressing any of the directional keys moves the pointer one pixel in that direction. Holding the directional key down moves the pointer rapidly in that direction. If it is too hard to control, change the Control Panel's Mouse Tracking settings to **Very Slow** (see figure 20.3).

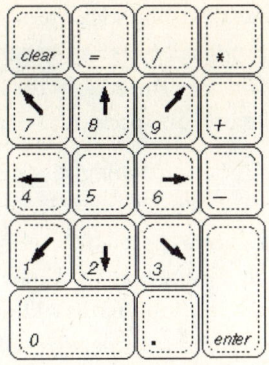

Figure 20.2
The Mouse Keys layout lets you use the numeric pad.

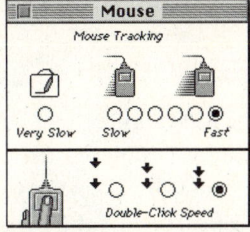

Figure 20.3
You can control the numeric "mouse" speed with the Mouse Tracking settings.

Mouse Keys only works with numeric keypads attached to the keyboard (the Mac Plus, Apple Extended, and Apple Adjustable keyboards). The early separate keypads do not work. It will, however, work with the Kensington PowerPad numeric keypad for the PowerBook.

Typists with wrist problems such as arthritis or carpal tunnel syndrome might appreciate the ergonomic wrist rests available from several companies. These rests are simply strips of dense foam rubber, approximately the same height as the Mac's keyboard. They fit snugly against the bottom of the keyboard and provide a place to rest your wrists while typing. To find out whether this solution is worthy of further investigation, try a rolled dish towel or something similar as a temporary support. If it seems to help, invest in a real wrist rest.

Other Ways to Type

Mouse Keys and Sticky Keys might not be the complete answer if you do not use your fingers for typing. The simplest substitutes for fingers are mouthsticks and headpointers. These are nothing more complicated than rubber-tipped sticks with a rubber grip that you can hold between your teeth or a headset that holds the stick at forehead level. You press keys with the pointer. Typing sticks have been around for many years, helping people use typewriters, adding machines and other keyboard devices.

Part IV
Specialized Mac Applications

Before the advent of Sticky Keys, typing stick users installed *keylatches* to hold down the Shift key for capital letters and symbols. The latch is a simple plastic or metal device that fits over the edge of the keyboard. It may be installed for the Shift, Command, or Option keys or any combination.

For stick users and those who have trouble pressing just one key at a time, a *keyguard* can be useful. This is a sheet of clear Plexiglass with holes drilled in the pattern of the keyboard. It is mounted over the keyboard and guides the stick or finger as it presses the key beneath it. The keyguard, which also can serve as a platform where you rest your hands while typing, makes it almost impossible to press a key or combination accidentally and perhaps erase your work. TASH, Inc. and Prentke-Romich are sources for keylatches and keyguards.

Nonrepeating Keys

One problem some typing stick users encounter is the keys repeating themselves if held down too long. Ordinarily, it is convenient to get a whole string of characters (!!!!!!!!!) with a single keystroke. But it can be annoying if you want only one letter and can't release the key in time. To avoid the problem, select the keyboard icon in the Control Panel and set the delay to **Off**, as shown in figure 20.4, or set the Key Repeat Rate to slow if you want to keep the repeat but make it more controllable.

Figure 20.4
Setting the repeat rate avoids typing likeeee thissss.

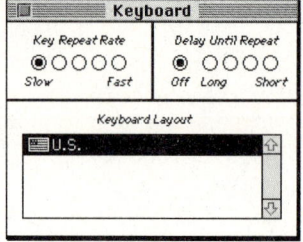

An expanded keyboard is the answer for some users with limited movement. These keyboards come in different configurations but generally are larger and much flatter than a standard Mac keyboard. Many can be customized to cluster frequently used keys together or to replace letters and numbers with pictures or other symbols. Expanded keyboards are easily positioned for use in bed or in a wheelchair. Some people use them for typing with their feet rather than their fingers. Others simply find it easier to use the larger keys an expanded keyboard provides. The Unicorn Adaptive keyboard, like many alternative input devices, requires an interface box between it and the Mac. Ke:nx, from Don Johnston Developmental Equipment, accepts many kinds of inputs, and it plugs into the Apple Desktop Bus.

Chapter 20
Macs and the Differently Abled

The Ke:nx On:Board is an extra-large portable keyboard that works with a Macintosh PowerBook. It gives the user full communications capability anywhere he or she happens to be: outdoors, in a van or bus, at school or work, even in a shopping mall. The PowerBook/On:Board combination fits neatly on a wheelchair tray or slides into a briefcase. The built-in wrist rest gives hand stability. It's easy to use, and comes with a standard (enlarged) Qwerty keyboard, plus four colorful overlays to match special physical, cognitive, or visual needs. Use Macintalk or a built-in digitized speech synthesizer to hear what you type. On:Board is fully custom-configurable with included software. Design your own key layouts, with letters, numbers, or any of the over 500 included icons. On:Board weighs about three pounds, and plugs into the ADB port on any Mac, so it can be used with a desktop Macintosh as well as with a PowerBook.

For true portability, plug a PowerBook Wheelchair Battery Power Adapter into a 12 volt wheelchair battery and plug in the PowerBook for all-day computing power as you roll along.

From extra-large to extra-small, there are keyboards for everyone. Miniature keyboards are a good choice for those with minimal hand movements but good accuracy. The total length of the TASH mini-keyboard is about four inches, so you can place your middle finger in the center of it and touch any key without moving your hand.

KeyLargo is an adaptive membrane keyboard, with 128 squares that can be grouped into keys of any size. It uses a standard 8 1/2 by 14 inch legal size paper overlay, which you can custom print to your own configuration, using KE:nx Create software.

Note: Keyboards do not work well when they are wet or sticky. Dampness, crumbs, spilled drinks, and saliva can interfere with many kinds of keyboards. Expanded keyboards usually come with a plastic covering, and because they are made with flat touch-sensitive keys rather than pressable keys, they tend to have fewer problems. Standard Mac keyboards can be equipped with a thin, flexible, molded-plastic covering to protect them from dust, dirt, and dampness. Visiflex Seels and FlexShields are two brands available at many computer stores.

Children and those who can point a finger but lack control to type frequently use touch screens. The Mac'n Touch screen fits over a regular Macintosh screen and is touch-sensitive. Target areas for touching can be as large as needed. Most important, Mac'n Touch works with all Macintosh computers, including the Mac Portable. It comes with software that includes a special control panel which lets you calibrate the screen and adjust the cursor so it appears above your finger when you touch the screen. Mac 'n Touch, made by MicroTouch Systems, can be used with screen keyboards for word processing or with specialized software.

Switches and Scanners

Mouthsticks and head pointers can be tiring to use, and they require you to have strong neck muscles. People whose motion is more limited may find that the combination of a switch and scanning software is a better solution. Switches can be designed to accept any reliable body movement as input. You can activate the switch with the touch of a finger; by lifting an eyebrow; by pressing with your toe, chin, or head; or by whatever motion is available. Scanning software presents a representation of the keyboard or a line of characters onscreen. A cursor moves across at a comfortable (and adjustable) interval, and you activate the switch to enter the desired character or command. This method is time-consuming. But for people for whom this is the only workable interface, it's nothing short of miraculous.

Morse Code Switches

When Samuel Morse invented his combinations of dots and dashes, he certainly did not realize how useful they would be as a way to talk back to a computer. There are codes for every letter, number, and essential punctuation mark. Morse code is relatively easy to learn and can be "sent" by any combination of two switches: one for "dits" and one for "dahs." The word "code" is "dah-dit-dah-dit, dah-dah-dah, dah-dit-dit, dit". Ham radio operators have been communicating by Morse code for 60 years or more, many using a simple paddle switch that sends dots when pushed in one direction and dashes when pushed in the other. Such a switch, or a combination of two switches, and the Ke:nx interface package of hardware and software allows code input with very limited motion, at speeds up to 15 words a minute.

Differently Abled Mice

For some users, a mouse is a better answer than a keyboard. Many kinds of computer mouse and mouse replacement devices are available. Joysticks, like those used with arcade games or some electric wheelchairs, are often a good choice. You can move them with your chin, teeth, foot, or knee, as well as hand. The LipStick, from McIntyre Computer Systems, is a mouth-operated joystick. Its flexible gooseneck shaft may be positioned to allow movement by any available part of the body. Another type of mouth device, a *switch*, fits inside the mouth, much like an orthodontic retainer. Switches are activated by pressing the tongue against the roof of the mouth. These must be custom fitted and, when in place, are comfortable and do not interfere with normal speech.

A *trackball* looks like an upside-down mouse and functions exactly like one. However, it requires much less arm and hand movement. Trackballs have a freely rotating ball, about the size of a billiard ball, which activates rollers inside its case. Joysticks and trackballs are easier for many people to use because you do not need to move them; you can mount one on a desk or tabletop with double-stick tape if necessary. These devices can be used with an onscreen keyboard like the one shown in figure 20.5. (The keyboard pictured is a public-domain utility called KeyMouse from the University of Utah Computer Center.) To use this keyboard, just position the pointer on the letter and click to type it. The Shift, Caps Lock, Option, and Command keys work exactly as they do on the regular keyboard.

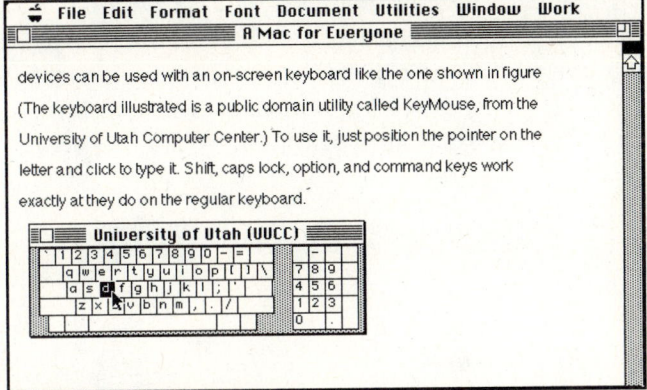

Figure 20.5
KeyMouse offers a typical onscreen keyboard, which combines well with a trackball.

Head-Controlled Mice

The head-controlled mouse is a device that uses your head, rather than a trackball, to press switches and simulate the mouse's movement. Prentke-Romich's HeadMaster and Pointer Systems' Freewheel are two brands of head-controlled mice. HeadMaster's special headset incorporates three position-sensitive switches that correspond to the switches inside a mouse or trackball. You move the pointer around onscreen by tilting forward or to the side. A separate switch or an attached sip-and-puff tube (a switch device activated by blowing and sucking on a plastic straw; the air pressure changes open or close a switch) replaces the mouse button.

FreeWheel is a cordless pointing device that combines a small reflector on the forehead and an optical camera that sits in a box on top of the Mac. The camera tracks light bouncing off the reflector and moves the pointer accordingly. Like using the trackball and joystick, you can use these devices with a screen keyboard or with any Mac software, including paint programs and games.

Part IV
Specialized Mac Applications

Voice Navigator

The ultimate mouse replacement to date is the human voice. Imagine controlling your Mac simply by telling it what you want to do. Articulate Systems' Voice Navigator does exactly that. It claims to recognize any voice, any language, any accent, or any distinguishable, repeatable sound. You do not need to speak clearly to use Voice Navigator, as long as you can make a sound consistently. It recognizes patterns rather than words and responds to only one voice at a time, although it can keep a file of different users and recognize whichever one is using the Mac at the time.

Voice Navigator consists of a small microphone attached to a little black box and the appropriate software. You "train" the system by repeating the commands three times and recording the input, as shown in figure 20.6. After Voice Navigator learns a command, it executes the desired action any time you speak the command in the correct tone of voice. The system works as quickly as you speak and speeds operations by as much as 50 percent over traditional mouse or keyboard input devices.

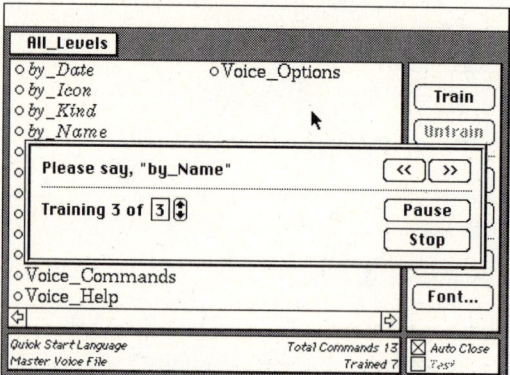

Figure 20.6
You must repeat a command three times with slightly different inflections to teach it to Voice Navigator.

Alternatives to Keyboard Typing

Many shortcuts can make typing easier and quicker for anyone. Not only the differently abled but most computer users use some of these shortcuts every day. Perhaps the simplest is to use *macros*, single or combination keystrokes that represent a frequently used word or phrase. Many of these macros are built into the Mac, and you use them without even thinking. Commands such as Command-S to save or Command-Q to quit are technically macros. Think how convenient it could be to copy a file from one disk to another with a keystroke. Wouldn't life be easier if you could type your name at the bottom of a letter and then add the correct date with one or two keystrokes instead of a dozen? Of course it would, especially if typing is difficult for you.

QuicKeys, from CE Software, is a program that creates and stores macros. It works with virtually any application, and even between applications. It records your actions, mouse clicks as well as key strokes, and lets you assign key strokes to them to make as many sets of macros as you need. QuicKeys can keep sets of macros for different applications as well as a global set to work with the finder and all applications. Figure 20.7 shows the QuicKeys' dialog box with some global macros.

Chapter 20
Macs and the Differently Abled

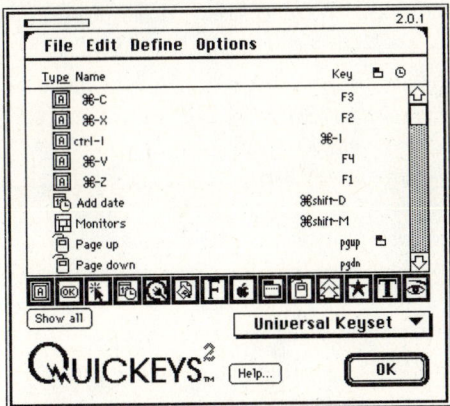

Figure 20.7
QuicKeys' dialog box displays some simple macros and their key assignments.

Predicting More Than the Future

Suppose you could type the first two or three letters of a word, then the Mac guessed your intentions and completed the word for you. That would save a lot of energy, especially if typing a letter means selecting it as the cursor scans a row, tapping it out in Morse code, or pressing a key with a head-pointer. That is why *predictor* programs are useful. As the name suggests, these programs are designed to read the first few letters of a word and supply a list of words that start with these letters. You select the intended word and go on to the next. MacIntyre's WordWriter is a DA that can be accessed with any other software: a word processor, page layout program, or even a game. WordWriter places a small keyboard at the bottom of the screen. You select a letter or two with a mouse or mouse substitute, and WordWriter responds by providing words that might be the intended word. You select the right word, and the others disappear.

Magic Typist, from Tactic Software, comes with a 1,000-word library of common words and the capability to learn any words you want to teach it. To begin, you define a word length the program should watch for—words of more than four letters, for instance. From that point, whenever the Mac sees a combination it recognizes—"univ", for example—it responds with a dialog

Part IV
Specialized Mac Applications

box asking, "Do you mean university?" (see figure 20.8). It also learns and accesses entire paragraphs of *boilerplate*, the repetitive paragraphs used in contracts and other legal documents. Magic Typist even handles text formatting: type the letters *sin*; it automatically types "Sincerely," scrolls down several lines, and adds the writer's name. Magic Typist is an INIT, and you can use it with all kinds of software, as well as for desktop management. It can rename documents, and locate and open files.

Figure 20.8
Magic Typist does most of the work automatically.

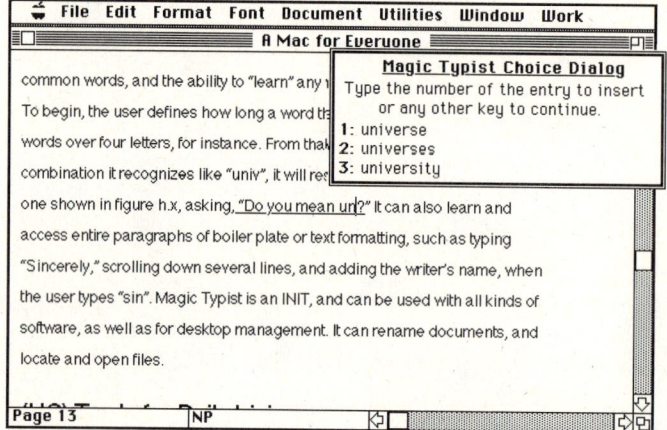

Co:Writer from Don Johnston Developmental Equipment is another excellent word prediction program which works with your word processor or other text entry program. You can even use it with a telecommunications program to send e-mail, or to converse online. It makes predictions logically, based on grammar rules and subject-verb agreement. It comes with three dictionaries—2,000; 10,000; or 40,000 words—making it appropriate for all ages.

Tools for Daily Living

Obviously, computers can make typing a letter or adding a series of numbers easier. But the Mac also can make coffee for you, turn on a light, or even call the police if someone is burglarizing your house.

Chapter 20
Macs and the Differently Abled

Several environmental control devices are available for use with the Macintosh. With X-10, you draw a map of your home using Install icons to represent what you want to control. Appliances, lights, and wall switches are plugged into X-10 control modules, which receive signals from your Mac through the house wiring. You then point and click on the screen icon to control the device you designated. The Mac can control as many as 256 differently coded X-10 modules. A DA lets you access modules while you work in another application. Too warm? Need more light? Turn on the air conditioner or a lamp without moving anything more than whatever you normally use for pointing and clicking. X-10's software and three plug-in modules retails for less than $120 from X-10 (USA), Inc.; 185A Legrand Avenue; Northvale, New Jersey 07647.

The Mac Talks Back

So far you have looked at different ways to send information to the Mac. But information needs to flow in both directions. Normally, the Mac responds to your input by displaying something on its screen. This display might be the words you just typed, the movement of the pointer in response to your mouse motion, the Mac's pawn capturing your queen in a game of chess, and so on. For many Mac users, the screen interface works fine. For others with limited vision or none at all, it is difficult or impossible to use. These users need personalized interfaces that respond differently.

People who have limited vision may be able to see enlarged objects fairly well. Some users find they can handle word processing tasks easily by simply taking advantage of the Mac's different fonts and point sizes. Changing the screen type to 24-point type in a highly readable face like New Century Schoolbook may be all that is needed, as figure 20.9 shows. Just remember to choose a smaller type size for printing.

 Using Macintosh's System 7's TrueType Fonts or Adobe TypeManager helps keep large type readable onscreen.

Figure 20.9
For some with vision difficulties, large print is easier to read.

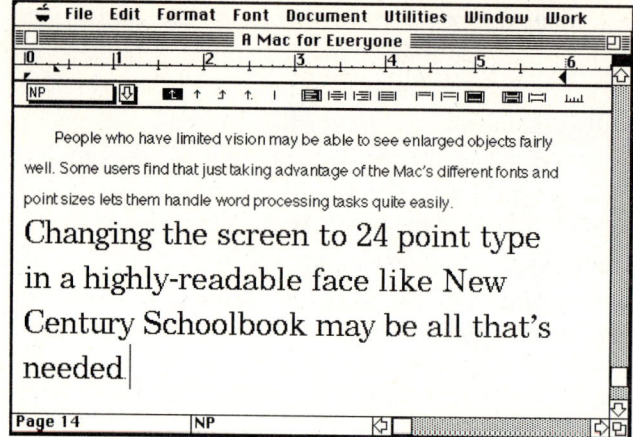

Some people carry magnifying glasses to read printed materials or to help bring fuzzy pictures into better focus. It is awkward trying to hold a magnifying glass up to the screen, especially if you try to type at the same time. One easy-to-use solution is a plastic magnifying lens that fits on top of the regular screen and enlarges the size of the characters. These screens use a *Fresnel lens*, an etched pattern of concentric circles which has a magnifying effect, and which usually incorporate an antiglare coating as well. These screens give about a 30% enlargement, which may be enough to help users with low vision.

Close View

The Macintosh also includes an electronic magnifying glass called Close View with its Easy Access Extension. To install it, simply drag Close View into the System folder and then restart. Turn Close View on and off from the control panel or by pressing Command-Option-O. When Close View is activated, a heavy black box appears onscreen, framing a small area (see figure 20.10). To magnify that area, press Command-Option-X. The result is shown in figure 20.11.

You can use the Close View control panel, as shown in figure 20.12, or the key commands to adjust the magnification from 2 to 16 times normal size. The glare from a large white screen can be overwhelming for people with certain eye problems, so users who are light-sensitive appreciate yet another of Close View's control panel options. Macintosh screens usually give a black image on white. Close View lets you reverse the image to white on black for easier viewing. It works with all applications and on the desktop. Close View also changes color screens to different hues, which some users find disconcerting.

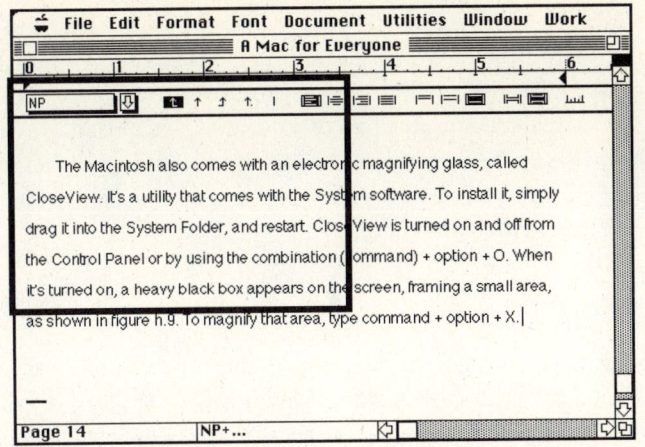

Figure 20.10
The area in the box can be brought to full screen

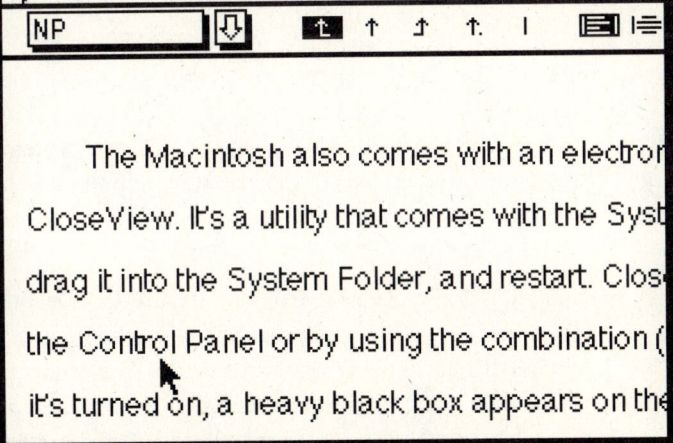

Figure 20.11
Close View's magnified text doubles the original print size.

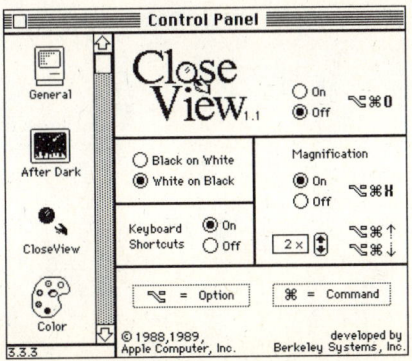

Figure 20.12
Use the Close View control panel to change settings.

Close View can be very helpful, but it may take some time to get accustomed to it. The screen movement corresponding to mouse movements can be annoying. You also may have the tendency to move too far or too fast. Because you actually view only a part of the screen, you must move the pointer up to locate the menu bar. Also, you can't see the whole screen at once. Positioning the cursor between two letters, as you might to correct a typing error, can be difficult.

The Big Picture

Berkeley Systems' inLARGE has many of the same functions as Close View (Berkeley Systems developed the Close View utility for Apple), but inLARGE is a more versatile program. Among the features Berkeley Systems added are a cross-hair cursor, a magnification window, and the capability to scan across a page at a rate of speed you set without having to move the mouse. Usually the magnified area fills the screen, but with inLARGE you can define a smaller magnification window, perhaps a single line of type, and blank out the rest of the screen to reduce distractions. inLarge 2.0 works with all Macs from the 512 and Plus through the PowerBooks and Quadras, and provides 2X to 16X magnification. It also offers black/white inversion with other colors remaining "true" on a color monitor. Also, it can scan a page from right to left or bottom to top as well as conventionally, a convenience in some spreadsheet and graphics applications.

Mac users with limited vision also may find it helpful to use an *enlarging monitor*. These monitors copy the normal 9-inch Macintosh screen on a Plus, SE, or Mac Classic and display its image on a separate, larger monitor. You do not see more of a document, as you do on larger or full-page screens on the Mac II series. Instead, you see the same area, 512 pixels wide by 342 pixels tall, with larger pixels. Figure 20.13 illustrates this effect.

Figure 20.13
Backgammon is more fun when you can see the dice.

People with limited vision generally have little trouble with the Macintosh keyboard. There are raised dots on the D and K keys and on the numeric keypad's 5 to help you locate keys by touch. Large letter stickers and a special label maker that creates Braille letters to place on the keyboard are available from National Braille Press, American Foundation for the Blind, and similar groups. If the problem is simply that the cursor is hard to see, BigCursor, a public-domain utility, is available from many user groups and bulletin boards.

> **Note** Many low vision Mac users have found it helpful to place a colored filter over the screen to increase contrast. Theatrical "gels," used to add color to stage lights, work well. Simply tape them in place. You may need to experiment to see what color (or combination of colors) works best for your eyes.

outSPOKEN

As the first Mac was being designed, Steve Jobs commissioned a piece of software called MacinTalk that could be programmed to give the Mac an understandable, if somewhat tinny, voice. Instead of introducing Macintosh at an early Apple stockholder's meeting, Jobs had Macintosh introduce him (see chapter 16, "Sound, Music, and Speech"). It did not take long before someone realized the differently abled could take advantage of this capability. The result was outSPOKEN.

outSPOKEN enables people who can't read the screen to hear what is on the screen. outSPOKEN has made it possible for blind, visually impaired, dyslexic, and learning disabled people of all ages to use the Mac. It is the first such product to work with a graphic interface and a pixel-based display.

outSPOKEN reads text. It works with any text-based program from word processors to spreadsheets, databases, and even text-based games. outSPOKEN users have access to most of the programs their coworkers or classmates use. It even functions with telecommunications programs to let non-print-reading users access online services such as Delphi and CompuServe for e-mail, daily news and weather, and other interesting and useful activities.

> **WARNING!** outSPOKEN does not work with Prodigy at this writing.

outSPOKEN comes with a printed manual, a manual on cassette tape, and a manual as a text file that can be read using outSPOKEN after you have it installed. A Braille manual and raised-line representations of Mac screens also are available on request. Other manufacturers, including Apple, do not

Chapter 20
Macs and the Differently Abled

Part IV
Specialized Mac Applications

publish Braille or taped manuals but have allowed National Braille Press and American Printing House for the Blind to do so.

Even more important for nonsighted users, outSPOKEN reads menus, file and folder names, and keys on the keyboard to help you find your location. outSPOKEN replaces the mouse with a new set of functions on the numeric keypad. Figure 20.14 shows a partial map of these key functions. You also can modify each key by pressing Command, Shift, or Option. For example, pressing Shift-Top takes you to the bottom of the page. Pressing Command-Top takes you to the Close box. If you need the number keys to enter spreadsheet data, you simply hold down the tilde (~) key while you enter the number. Releasing it restores control of the keypad to outSPOKEN.

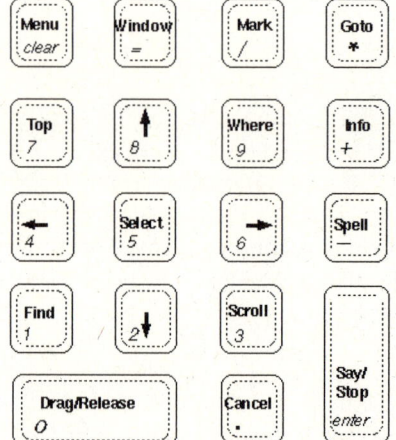

Figure 20.14
outSPOKEN's keypad can type numerals and replace the mouse.

outSPOKEN can read scanned text, so it is possible to use a scanner to import text from a book or magazine into a Mac file and then let the computer read it to you. You can adjust the speed of speaking and the pitch of the Mac's voice. (People with mild hearing loss may find higher pitches easier to understand.)

Write:OutLoud is a talking word processor developed by the Don Johnston Developmental Equipment company. It has the powerful features Mac users expect, like color capability, a built-in spell checker, and an easy-to-use ribbon toolbar. A "print-one" button on the toolbar avoids the print dialog box and gives you a quick copy of your page. Unlike outSPOKEN, the speech program doesn't work with other software, but it's ideal for those who need a little extra help with writing. It supports multi-sensory learning and lets the user configure it to read letter by letter, word by word, or sentence by sentence.

Chapter 20
Macs and the Differently Abled

Tactile Displays

Of course, outSPOKEN assumes that you can hear. People who can neither see nor hear, as well as blind people who use graphics programs, can use a *tactile output device* called Optacon to give an exact tactile image of whatever is onscreen. Berkeley's inTouch software works with Optacon to translate the screen to the sensing device. Optacon has pins that correspond directly to the pixels on the Mac's screen. You feel the raised pins to get a sense of what the screen image looks like. You can use Optacon to read maps, architectural drawings, scanned images, and text. Letters become raised letters on Optacon's touchpad, perfect for those who have learned to read the print alphabet. A similar system, the Braille Display Processor, scans the screen and converts the characters into Braille letters. These programs require patience to learn, but many users become quite skilled with them.

Printing Braille Pages

Several printers can produce Braille pages. Some can print Braille and text characters on the same page, allowing sighted and nonsighted coworkers to share their memos and other output or a teacher to create classroom materials for both sighted and nonsighted students. American Thermoform's Ohtsuki Printer and Enabling Technology's Romeo Brailler work well with the Mac, as does Howtek's PixelMaster, which prints Braille and raised-line drawings on plain paper and works as a conventional inkjet printer.

Communication Disorders and the Mac

Because the Mac is a tool for many types of communications, it can help those who have difficulty with language. There are programs to aid you in developing fluent speech, and some that speak for you. There are programs to teach finger spelling and American Sign Language (ASL). Tony Martin's ASL FingerSpelling Tutor is a HyperCard stack available as freeware from America

Part IV
Specialized Mac Applications

Online and Delphi. It teaches the ASL alphabet, which can be used with standard ASL signs, for proper names and other words that must be spelled for clarity. (In ASL, there are signs for most common words and phrases.)

Figure 20.15 shows a card from this stack. Hearing-impaired users may want to give this program to their hearing friends because it is easy to learn and can improve communication for everyone. An *Amslan font*, also available as shareware, illustrates the ASL finger positions for letters and numbers. It can be used with a keyboard to spell words in ASL.

Figure 20.15
Tony Martin's ASL FingerSpelling Tutor shows you how to form letters of the alphabet.

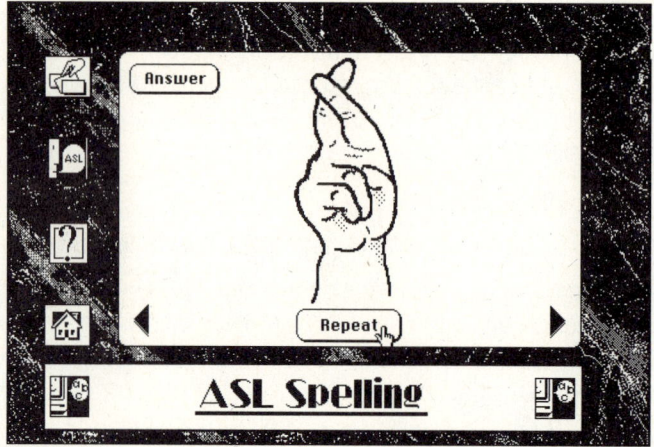

Mac users who can hear are familiar with the boings, chimes, beeps, and other sounds that announce various alert boxes and signal the Mac's protest when you try an invalid action. Deaf and hearing-impaired users simply can adjust the speaker volume to zero in the Mac's Control Panel. This action replaces the sounds with a menu bar flash as an alternative signal. Mac users who share offices or who have light-sleeping roommates have been using this feature for years.

People who are unable to speak often communicate by pointing to pictures or symbols to represent words. Mayer-Johnson's Communication Board Builder is a HyperCard program that creates communication symbol boards. The program includes over 1600 symbols. The user can print customized picture boards in English or Spanish. Boards can be assembled into a book for ease of carrying, or pasted together to make a larger communication board for home or classroom use.

Sources for Help and Ideas

Chapter 20
Macs and the Differently Abled

This chapter has touched on some of the different ways to interact with the Mac and make life easier, more interesting, and more efficient. But new interfaces and methods always are coming along. Technology is not a static process, and as soon as someone needs a new solution, more people are helping to discover it.

Where can you go for more information? Apple's WorldWide Disability Solutions Group is a good place to start. Its Solutions database is available at Apple dealers as well as many schools and rehabilitation facilities. Solutions is a HyperCard stack that lists more than 1,000 adaptive devices and appl-ications and includes lists of disability-related publications, organizations, and networks. You can reach WorldWide Disability Solutions Group at (408) 974-7910, through TDD at (408)974-7911, or by mail at the Office of Special Education and Rehabilitation, Apple Computer, 20525 Mariani Avenue, MS 43-S, Cupertino, California 95014.

The Alliance for Technology Access is a nonprofit group whose mission is "to provide access to computer technology for the disabled." Its network of 45 resource centers nationwide is staffed by volunteers who are specialists in special-needs computing. You can reach them at 1307 Solano Avenue, Albany, California 94706, or call (415) 528-0747 for the center nearest you.

Closing the Gap publishes a comprehensive newsletter for disability technology and conducts conferences and workshops for people who have an interest in this field. Its address is Closing the Gap, P.O. Box 68, Henderson, Minnesota 56044; (612) 248-3294.

The Trace Research and Development Center generally is recognized as the force which ensures that computer technology is available to everyone. Finding personalized solutions for children and adults with limited motion and adapting interfaces for many kinds of special needs are among its special interests. Whatever the problem may be, there is a good chance Trace Research already has solved it. You can call (608) 262-6966 or write Trace Research and Development Center, s-151 Waisman Center, 1500 Highland Avenue, Madison, Wisconsin 53705.

Part IV
Specialized Mac Applications

Local rehabilitation facilities, university computing centers, and your Apple dealer also may have good ideas for you. Ask—and keep asking. If your personalized solution is not already waiting on a shelf, there are many concerned people and groups dedicated to helping you find and apply it.

Summary

Computers truly are for everyone. Max Cleland said it best: "The real disabled people of the future are going to be those who do not have a computer to use." There is a way around your limits, whatever they may be.

Personalizing the Mac can be as easy as installing a magnifying lens over the screen, or as complex as having a dentist fit a micro-switch equipped plate for the roof of your mouth. Mobility as limited as eye-blinking is still enough to enable you to share the power of computing. Lack of vision, hearing, or speech are no barriers when it comes to communicating with a Mac. Technology and human ingenuity have brought computing out of the lab and office, and have made it available to anyone who wants it to work, to play, to learn, and to improve the quality of life. Computers make it possible for all people, regardless of physical or mental limits, to go as far as their ideas can take them.

Part V: Managing Your Mac

In This Part

Chapter 21: Utilities

Chapter 22: Hard Disk Management

Chapter 23: Viruses and System Security

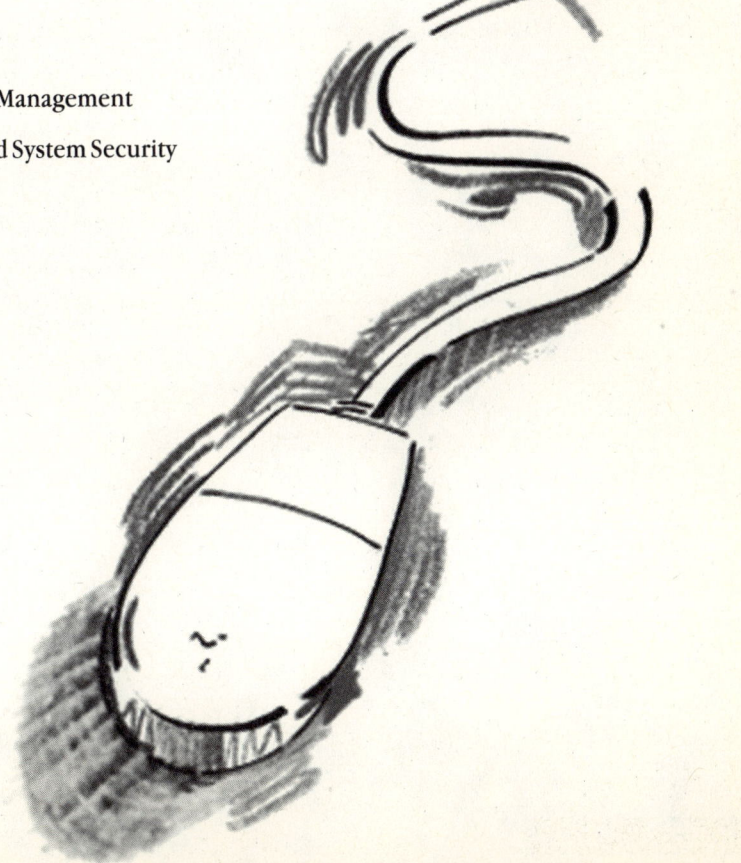

Chapter 21: Utilities

Utilities are the wrenches and screwdrivers of computing—tools that perform specific functions such as searching for a virus or repairing a damaged disk. Because most utilities work on the system level rather than with specific applications, utilities are usually regarded as part of the Mac's operating system, not as separate applications. In fact, most utilities are not programs in the ordinary sense of the word: some are desk accessories; some are extensions (special programs that execute only at start-up, formerly called INITs), and still others are control panels (cdevs), that enable the user to control various aspects of the System.

In This Chapter

▼ Defining a utility

▼ How to build a basic toolbox of utilities

▼ Adding to your toolbox

▼ Utilities for every occasion

▼ Where to find free and shareware utilities

Part V
Managing Your Mac

The Tools of Computing

Regardless of the form a utility takes—program, desk accessory, extension, or control panel—nearly all utilities serve a single purpose. With rare exceptions, a well-conceived utility performs just one function or a set of closely related functions, rather than the more-features-the-merrier attitude found in application programs. In keeping with this philosophy, commercial utility packages are almost always collections of utilities, each of which performs a different function. The one-function-per-utility approach keeps the program as small as possible, allowing it to cohabit with your applications without taking up large amounts of memory. It also means you can selectively install only those utilities you use on a regular basis, saving your hard disk space for more important items.

Literally thousands of utilities are available for the Macintosh. This chapter helps you determine what kinds of utilities you need, but it cannot possibly review every utility written. Even if specific products are mentioned, be sure to check out the marketplace; you may find a utility not mentioned here that is better suited to your needs.

Building a Utility Toolbox

There is no such thing as having too many utilities. Even when two utilities do the same thing, you may find that one performs better in a particular situation. It is wise to start with a basic set of utilities that cover your requirements, then add to your collection as the need arises and your pocketbook permits.

Utilities are the best bargains in computing, with most ranging from free to cheap in price. You can build quite an impressive collection without digging deep holes in your pocket, especially if you take advantage of the huge software libraries maintained by online services and major user groups. Even the commercially distributed products are usually a good bargain.

Chapter 21
Utilities

The problem for most people is not that they have too many utilities, but that they have too few. Many Macintosh users are not as productive as they could be because they do not have or do not use a utility that makes life easier. The following sections give you some guidelines to help you determine what utilities you should put in your toolbox.

WARNING! Beware of compatibility problems! Not all utilities work with all versions of the system software, and some utilities do not work with each other. To avoid conflicts between utilities, never have two utilities that do the same thing active at the same time. To avoid conflicts with the system software, always check the documentation before using any software product for the first time.

The Starter Kit

The following starter kit contains suggested utilities that every Macintosh user should own. Apple's system software includes most of what you need, but there are several others you should add to round out your collection.

Control Panels

Control panels are small programs that are similar to extensions. They load when the Macintosh starts up, like extensions. They also, however, offer a mini-interface that enables you to configure options. In System 6, the Control Panel was a desk accessory that you selected from the Apple menu. Each control panel (called a CDEV) was accessed within the Control Panel desk accessory from a scrolling list. In System 7, the control panels reside in the Control Panels folder inside the System Folder. Selecting **Control Panels** from the **Apple** menu opens a window that contains all the control panels. You double-click on the icon to launch a control panel. The control panel displays an interface to customize its operation.

WARNING! Under System 7, you can have more than one control panel open at the same time, but that does not mean you should. When configuring your system, change only one set of parameters at a time. This way, if something stops working as a result of the change, you have a better idea what you did wrong.

Part V
Managing Your Mac

The control panels Apple supplies perform functions such as setting the key repeat rate on your keyboard, the speed of the mouse cursor, the number of displayed colors for color monitors, the cursor blink rate, the desktop pattern, and so on. Many third-party utility products need to be installed as control panels.

A Clock Utility

You need a clock utility to set the Mac system's internal clock. The Macintosh system software comes with three ways to do so: the Alarm Clock desk accessory (which also has a mildly useful alarm function), the General Controls control panel, and the Date & Time control panel.

 If you never have any reason to use Alarm Clock, check it once in a while anyway to make sure the system clock is set correctly. A slow system clock could indicate the Macintosh's battery is running low and needs to be changed.

Chooser

The Chooser desk accessory comes with the Macintosh system software and configures your connection to various external devices and resources. The Chooser enables you to configure your Macintosh to connect to a specific type of printer, and determines what printer you will use if you're hooked up to more than one (such as over a network). The Chooser is also used to configure your connection to other Macs via AppleShare and System 7 file sharing.

If you have an ImageWriter and want to format a document in LaserWriter format (perhaps before taking it to a desktop publishing service to print), use Chooser to temporarily change the printer type to LaserWriter. Then choose Page Setup from the File menu to format your document's page for the LaserWriter's printing abilities. Create and format your document, save it, then run Chooser again to set the printer type back to ImageWriter. Again, use Page Setup from the File menu to reset your page for the ImageWriter. For this to work, both the LaserWriter and ImageWriter printer drivers must be installed in the System folder. (See chapter 6, "Printing from Your Macintosh," for more information.)

Chapter 21
Utilities

Installer

You need this program to install or reinstall the system software on a hard disk. Installer comes with, and is usually run from, the original Apple system disks (or better yet, from backup copies), so you do not need to install it on the hard drive. Always make sure you have a complete set of system disks so that you can reinstall the system software if necessary.

Font/DA Mover

If you're using System 7, you probably don't need the Font/DA Mover, but if you're using System 6 or earlier, you can't live without it. Font/DA Mover is used with Mac's System 6 (and earlier) to install and remove fonts and desk accessories in the System file. It is easier to use than it first looks. The key things to remember about using Font/DA Mover are:

▼ You can open only three types of files: 1) your Mac's System file; 2) a font or DA "suitcase" file, so-called because of its suitcase icon; or (3) a System 7 font file (if you have the very latest version of the utility, available as a free upgrade from Apple).

▼ You can copy in either direction—that is, from the right window to the left or from the left window to the right. Be sure of what you are attempting to accomplish and read the information displayed under each window.

 Do not perform massive multiple copies with Font/DA Mover. Every version ever written crashes if you try to copy too many items in one session or operation. It is wise to copy different sizes of fonts one at a time, especially in the larger sizes.

With System 7, you no longer need the Font/DA Mover to install fonts and desk accessories in your System file. If you still use a System 6 or earlier version of the operating system and want to copy System 7 fonts or DAs into your older system, you must have a 4.1 or later version of the utility available as an upgrade from Apple or your local dealership. If you are using System 7, your installer disks will include the new Font/DA Mover.

Virus Hunters

No Macintosh is complete without at least one good utility for sniffing out viruses. Even if your Macintosh does not have much contact with disks or software from the outside world, you still occasionally should scan your hard disk for viruses to make sure nothing nasty has slipped in. Disinfectant is a very good utility for detecting viruses, and it is free. It can also install an extension into your System folder, which loads into your Mac's memory at start-up and monitors for virus activity as you work with your Mac. If it detects a virus, it notifies you with a dialog box explaining the situation and suggesting a cure. (See chapter 23, "Viruses and System Security," for more information.)

WARNING! Make sure that you have the latest version of whatever virus utility you use. As new viruses are discovered, new versions of the software are created to combat the viruses. If you don't have the latest version, you won't be protected against the latest viruses—the very viruses you should be most worried about!

Disk Doctors

If you have a hard disk, you should own at least one utility that diagnoses disk problems. The best options in this category are the commercial products. (See chapter 23, "Hard Disk Management," for more information.)

Screen Saver

Screen savers postpone the onset of phosphor burn-in, which makes the burned-in areas dimmer and therefore harder to read. You can tell if a monitor has burn-in by looking at it in bright light when it is turned off—if you can see the shadow of a menu bar across the top, your monitor is already afflicted. You can see this effect in many ATM machines. They display the welcoming message for a vast majority of the time, so eventually you can see the specter of that message as you make your transaction.

There are two commercial products that address this problem, Pyro! and After Dark. Both do a great job and add a little fun at the same time. (After Dark is described at length in chapter 15, "Games for Fun!") If you do not want to spend money on a commercial version, check out the various shareware and freeware offerings. You also can turn down your Mac's brightness knob to blacken the screen when you are not using your computer, or, if you have a Macintosh with a separate monitor, just turn it off.

Expanding the Toolbox

Chapter 21
Utilities

The basic starter kit is enough at first, but later you will want to expand it. In some cases, you may have a specific need for a particular utility; in others, a utility is not really necessary but may make your life easier. The following sections describe utilities that you might want to consider acquiring. This is by no means a complete list—there are simply too many possible categories to cover. Also, we have omitted so-called utilities such as calculators and address books that are actually small applications.

RAM Disks

A RAM *disk* is not really a disk—it is a section of random-access memory (RAM) that your computer uses as if it were a disk. The advantage of using a RAM disk is speed; a computer can access its RAM many times faster than its hard disk and about a zillion times faster (or at least it seems) than a floppy disk. RAM disks are also useful for PowerBook users; RAM takes less battery power to operate than a hard disk, so using a RAM disk can extend your battery life. However, in either case, if the power fails or your lights blink, you lose any data stored in the RAM disk. For this reason, you should always save files to a hard disk, not a RAM disk.

A Closer Look There are two common uses for RAM disks: to speed execution of programs that load pieces of themselves from a disk to memory (before you launch the program, copy it to the RAM disk and launch it from there) and for storing copies of files that a program reads but does not modify, such as HyperCard stacks. Because copying the file from a hard disk into a RAM disk takes some time, it does not make much sense to do this unless you are going to use that data frequently.

Using a RAM disk as a start-up disk on your PowerBook Mac conserves your battery life. To do this, you need at least 6M of RAM; configure your RAM disk for 2M, copy your System folder onto it, use the start-up disk Control Panel to boot from the RAM disk, and restart your PowerBook. Because most disk access on a Mac is done for the System files, your PowerBook does not need to read from the hard drive as much and turns it off. The hard drive takes a lot of your battery's power, so you give yourself a lot more working time from one charge.

The System software supports the creation of RAM disks on PowerBooks and Quadras. The RAM disk is set up through the Memory control panel. You can configure the amount of RAM set aside for the RAM disk. PowerBooks keep the contents of the RAM disk when you put the computer to sleep; the PowerBook 100 even keeps the RAM disk alive when you shut down the computer, though this doesn't work on the other models.

WARNING! Although numerous freeware and shareware RAM disk utilities are available—all of which are basically the same—watch out for compatibility problems with various system software versions and certain Mac models. Also, if your Mac has a relatively small memory, you would be better off using the available memory to run applications rather than trying to use it as a RAM disk. There are some RAM disk utilities that copy their contents back to the hard drive before shutting down; these may be desirable in some cases.

Note: Do not confuse RAM *disk* with RAM *cache*. RAM disk is a section of memory used as if it were a disk drive. RAM cache is an area of memory the operating system uses to optimize access to a physical disk. Using a RAM cache speeds some disk operations, but not as much as using a RAM disk does.

Extension Managers

Extensions (called *INITs* before System 7) are special programs that execute at system start-up, or during the initializing phase. All of those little icons that pop up on the bottom-left corner of your screen (or across the bottom, if you have quite a few) when you boot the Mac are extensions.

A Closer Look: Extensions apply *patches* (software modifications) to the programming code of the Mac's system software, modifying the behavior of a particular system function. For example, extensions that scan for viruses apply a patch to the code that detects a disk insertion. The extension can stop the usual process, check the inserted floppy for viruses, and then allow the normal code routine to

Chapter 21
Utilities

continue. This makes sure that the disk is checked before it can transmit an infection to the Macintosh.

> **WARNING!** One major problem with patching is that two or more extensions may try to patch the same piece of code. If this does not work correctly, you have an *INIT conflict*, which can cause the system or program to lock up or crash. Sometimes, the conflict can be avoided by changing the order in which the Macintosh loads the extensions. They are loaded alphabetically, so adding a space to the beginning of the extension's name will cause it to load earlier in the startup process. If that does not work, the only solution is to remove one of the extensions.

An extension-managing utility can be a tremendous help, especially if you have many extensions. A good extensions manager helps you find conflicts and change the load order, as well as selectively turn extensions on and off. Extensions Manager, a shareware product from Ricardo Bautista, does a good job, and the Now Utilities package includes a System 7 extensions manager. If you ever have a problem, any of these products save you a lot of time tracking it down.

In addition, if you are always running out of memory, it may be because extensions have taken up a lot of your RAM memory. Using an extensions manager to selectively turn on only the ones you need at any given time helps you conserve memory.

MS-DOS Transfer and Translation Utilities

If your Mac is equipped with a SuperDrive or with certain third-party floppy disk drives, your Mac can read and write 3 1/2-inch floppy disks formatted for MS-DOS and Apple II systems. Apple File Exchange, a utility included with your Mac's system software, initializes Apple II and MS-DOS floppies and copies files between Mac and MS-DOS disks (see figure 20.1). DOS Mounter and Access PC go a step further and display the MS-DOS disk as an icon on the Macintosh desktop. They also enable you to copy files between Mac and MS-DOS disks and in many cases, let you double-click on the MS-DOS file icons to launch a Mac application that opens and edits the MS-DOS file.

Figure 20.1

Clicking the Translate button copies all files in the selected folder from the Mac disk to the MS-DOS floppy.

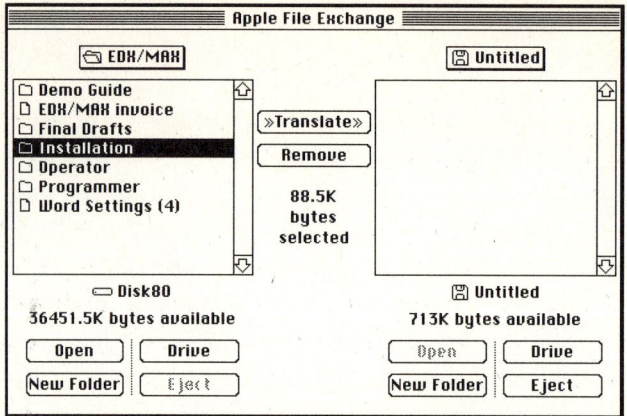

You also can transfer files between a Mac and an MS-DOS system over a cable wire physically linked between a Mac and a PC. MacLink Plus/PC, a commercial product, provides a cable and all the software you need for both ends of the connection. It also works if the systems are connected by modems and telephone lines. The DOS Mounter utility is included in the product.

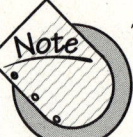 The MacLink Plus/Translators can also be used with Claris's XTND tools to allow MacWrite and other XTND-using applications to open any of the MS-DOS file types the Translators support.

LapLink Mac, too, provides excellent file transfer capability via a communications link and is a little less expensive than MacLink Plus/PC, but not as feature-laden. If the PC does not have a 3 1/2-inch drive, your only real choice is to use a communications link.

Do not format low-density disks as high density and vice versa. If a 3 1/2-inch low-density disk is formatted as a high-density disk, the Mac cannot read it. If a high-density disk has been formatted as a low- density DOS disk, cover the hole in the upper left corner of the disk with tape, and the Mac can then read it.

If you want to translate and copy files without using a communications link, MacLink Plus/Translators contains the same file translators as MacLink Plus/PC and DOS Mounter but without the cable and communications software. It can also be used on a Mac with a SuperDrive to do translations. Another good file translation product is Word for Word, which does not offer as many translators as the other products but does a better job with certain types of files. Apple File Exchange can be used with the Dataviz Translators. But it is slower and more tedious to use than MacLink Plus. If you have many files to transfer, your best bet is to get a Mac with a SuperDrive and use DOS Mounter or Access PC along with either the MacLink Plus translation utility or an application that can do the translations for you, such as MacWrite for word processing documents.

Resource Managers and Editors

In the Macintosh world, *resources* are pieces of code and data that the Mac uses to perform various functions. Fonts, windows, menus, dialog boxes, and sounds usually are stored as resources, as are code segments that make up a program. Mac's System file contains a great many resources, which both the system and application programs use.

With minor exceptions, you can get by without ever needing to know about resources. Two exceptions are fonts and desk accessories. These resources get moved around often, which is why Apple provides the Font/DA Mover utility on systems up to 6.0.7 (remember, Font/DA Mover is not required with System 7). Most Macintosh users manage quite happily with Font/DA Mover and have no need for any other resource management utilities.

ResEdit

If you want to do more than just move fonts and desk accessories, there are quite a few utilities to help you manage and edit resources, ranging from freeware utilities that handle just one type of resource to commercial packages that offer a variety of functions. ResEdit, Apple's general-purpose resource editor, installs, removes, and edits any kind of resource, but the editing functions for some types of resources (fonts, for example) are so primitive that if you plan to do any serious work, you should get a special-purpose program.

ResEdit is a utility Apple supplies through user groups, bulletin boards, and Apple's Programmers and Developers Association (APDA). ResEdit is sometimes the best and easiest way to handle certain situations. For example, if an application stores its menus as resources in the application file, ResEdit enables you to change those menus and the command-key assignments for

Chapter 21
Utilities

individual items. You also can use ResEdit to install fonts in applications and document files that Font/DA Mover will not. This is handy when you need a font for only a specific application or document and do not want to install it in the System file.

> **Note:** Make sure you have the most recent version of ResEdit. Unless you understand the concept of Macintosh resources fairly well, you probably also need some form of instruction; there are several books available that can help. For a gentle introduction to resource editing, check out the *ResEdit All-Night Diner,* by Dave Ciskowski and published by Hayden Books, or *Zen and the Art of Resource Editing,* by BMUG and published by Peachpit Press. For more in-depth coverage, look for *ResEdit Complete,* by Peter Alley and Carolyn Strange, and published by Addison-Wesley. The *ResEdit Reference,* Apple's official ResEdit guide, also published by Addison-Wesley, is geared toward programmers and as such is not very useful for the casual user.

> **WARNING!** Always make a backup of a file before editing its resources. ResEdit is a powerful program that is potentially dangerous for novice users. It is capable of altering virtually every file, resource, and function of your Mac. Using ResEdit on your operating system is like performing brain surgery on yourself. One misplaced or changed function could prove very frustrating and time consuming to solve, and perhaps require you to reinstall the system software or reformat your disk.

Master Juggler and SuitCase

Master Juggler, a commercial product, allows your programs to access fonts, desk accessories, and sounds without storing them in the System file. The product is generally easier to use than ResEdit or Font/DA Mover. It is handy for installing and removing various resources and for resolving resource number conflicts, which often occur when you are installing freeware fonts. SuitCase II, another commercial product, offers similar features. These products are especially handy for System 6 or earlier users, as they enable you to overcome the limited number of desk accessories (15) you can install on the system.

> **Note:** With System 7, desk accessories are no longer installed in the System file, so there is no limit (other than your hard disk's storage capacity) on how many you can use.

Chapter 21
Utilities

Printer Utilities

Most printer utilities are designed to either speed your printing or to enable you to use non-Apple printers. It is often hard to distinguish between a "printer" and a "font" utility, so be sure to check out font utilities when you are looking for a solution to a printing problem.

A Closer Look A *print spooler* utility enables you to keep working on your Mac while printing is in progress. The print spooler intercepts the output from the **Print** command and saves it in a temporary disk file. The spooler then returns control of the system to your applications program. Meanwhile, the spooler prints as much as it can from the spool file before another application resumes processing. This sounds wonderful, but in practice, it can slow down the system to the point where trying to do anything while the spooler is running can be more frustrating than simply waiting for the print operation to complete. The real advantage of print spoolers—at least the better ones—is that you can start another print job while one is already active. You can queue up a whole series of print jobs and then leave for a meeting or lunch.

The Macintosh system software comes with a print spooler called Print Monitor, which works with laser printers and StyleWriters. It is adequate for most purposes; however, Fifth Generation Systems' SuperSpool and SuperLaserSpool are even more versatile. SuperSpool works only with ImageWriters; SuperLaserSpool supports almost any kind of bit-mapped or PostScript printer, with the exception of a very few third-party devices.

Utilities that enable you to use non-Apple printers can be money-savers. JetLink Express is designed for use with Canon and Hewlett Packard jet or laser printers (and compatibles) that have an RS-232 serial interface, but it also works with some models that have a Centronics parallel interface if you purchase a serial-to-parallel converter. JetLink Express comes with all necessary printer drivers, fonts, and cables to get you in business. MacPrint also provides the necessary software and cabling to connect your Mac to an HP jet or laser printer. It is not quite as feature-laden as JetLink Express, but the manual is easier to understand.

Note Many non-Apple printers such as the Qume ScripTen do work with Apple's laser-printer drivers, so be sure to check the documentation before deciding whether you need any additional software to support the device.

Freedom of Press and its scaled-down version, Freedom of Press Light, enable you to print PostScript files on a range of non-PostScript printers. The other utilities do not handle PostScript (you would need Adobe Type Manager). However, Freedom of Press does not include cables, so allow for that expense in your purchase price.

> **A Closer Look** No matter which utilities you use, printing to a non-Apple-compatible printer might never produce acceptable results. A conversion process always must be performed on the output image, and the conversion process on third-party printers may not work correctly, especially if you are printing complicated graphics.

Font Utilities

In addition to Font/DA Mover, which is more of a resource manager than a font utility, it is handy to have one good font editor to make minor changes to bit-mapped fonts. A number of these are available as freeware and shareware. (ResEdit also has some font-editing capability.) The commercial products that support PostScript and TrueType fonts editing are either too expensive for casual users or lack enough features to make them worth the bother. With the hundreds of fonts available for the Macintosh, it generally makes more sense to buy the ones you need than to spend hours creating your own.

Adobe Type Manager (ATM) is a utility that enables you to use PostScript fonts with non-PostScript devices such as CRT displays and certain kinds of printers. ATM enables you to create crisp-looking output in any font size, within the devices' limitations. Even if you have a PostScript printer, ATM can greatly improve the readability of text displayed on a monitor, which is much easier on your eyes.

Adobe Type Align, which requires ATM to run, enables you to rotate, stretch, distort, and otherwise manipulate text in ways that application programs do not normally support. For the occasional user, Adobe Type Align is handy when creating posters, brochures, and similar materials in which unusual font effects might help catch the reader's attention. Graphics artists and desktop publishers are the most common users for this utility.

The Metamorphosis utility converts PostScript fonts to TrueType format for System 7 (and 6.0.7 and above) users. Such utilities have only recently appeared, and no doubt more are on the way, so try before you buy. If you have a PostScript printer, however, you should continue to use PostScript fonts and ATM to make them look good onscreen, rather than mix TrueType and PostScript fonts. The only reason to convert a PostScript font to TrueType is that you have a PostScript font and a non-PostScript printer. Even then, you might be better off using ATM—converting a font between formats does not always produce the best results. (See chapter 8, "Fonts and Typography," for more information.)

Keyboard Utilities

Most keyboard utilities are designed to make your life easier by enabling you to assign *macros* to key combinations. A macro performs a sequence of keystrokes and mouse actions with just one keystroke. (See chapter 20, "Macs and the Differently Abled," for more information.) Probably the best-known macro utility is CE Software's QuicKeys. QuicKeys enables you to record and play back sequences of mouse clicks, menu selections, typing, and so forth; it can save you a lot of time if you perform repetitive tasks. QuicKeys also provides shortcuts for such tasks as selecting printers, switching the number of colors on your monitor, launching control panels, and other basic tasks through a group of associated extensions.

MacroMaker, included with Macintosh System 6, is not compatible with System 7; AutoMac, shipped with some Microsoft products, isn't System 7–compatible either.

Keyboard macro utilities sound great in theory, but they do not always work right with some applications. If you are getting garbled text, or if the application crashes mysteriously or does not respond correctly to keyboard input, see whether turning off the macro utility solves the problem.

Key Caps, a desk accessory included with the Mac system software, enables you to examine the characters that each key displays in a given font. This is handy when you cannot remember, for example, that the copyright symbol (©) is Option G in most fonts. Key Caps is even handier when you want to examine special fonts like Symbol or Zapf Dingbats to see whether they contain characters you might want to use.

Chapter 21
Utilities

Part V
Managing Your Mac

> **Note:** Easy Access, a control panel included with the Mac system software, is intended for people who have trouble manipulating a mouse or who cannot hold down two keys at the same time. (See chapter 20, "Macs and the Differently Abled," for more information.) Easy Access also can be a life-saver when you have a dead or malfunctioning mouse. The "mouse keys" function enables you to move the mouse pointer with the keys on your numeric keypad. It is somewhat difficult to get used to, but it is better than nothing when your mouse dies at 2 a.m. and the boss expects you to turn in that report first thing in the morning.

AppleScript

AppleScript is a scripting language designed to work with Macintosh programs. More than a macro utility, AppleScript enables you to write programs to control the operation of your Macintosh. Its potential is astounding: BMUG used AppleScript to automate the layout of their 300-page catalog of disks! AppleScript depends on the support of individual applications, and as of August 1993, many applications don't support AppleScript yet. However, as more and more applications add AppleScript support, the power of this tool will continue to grow. For an introduction to AppleScript, read BMUG's book *The Tao of AppleScript,* by Derrick Schneider with Tim Holmes and Hans Hansen, and published by Hayden Books. The book includes the AppleScript extension and Apple's Script Editor—everything you need to get started.

Disk Utilities

As mentioned earlier, your basic toolbox should include a disk diagnosis utility to help track down hard-disk problems. Other utilities are available to make incremental backups of your hard disk, partition a hard disk for easier management, and defragment files and disks. (See chapter 22, "Hard Disk Management," for more information.)

Odds and Ends

Many utilities do not fit into specific categories but are worth mentioning. MyDiskLabeler, from Williams & Macias, lets you design and print custom disk labels on either ImageWriter or laser printers. It even supports color. Solutions International's SuperGlue enables you to print almost any file to a disk rather than to a printer.

Chapter 21
Utilities

SuperGlue is also extremely handy for cutting and pasting between otherwise incompatible applications. Boomerang, a popular shareware utility, enables you to navigate more quickly through **Open** and **Save** dialogs by displaying a list of the files and folders you most recently accessed.

Utility Packages and Libraries

Surprisingly, there are very few general-purpose utility packages on the market. Most packages focus on hard disk management or security (these are covered in the respective chapters). The notable exception is Now Software's Now Utilities, which does just about everything except disk management. Now Utilities includes an improved alarm clock, menu managers, an auto-saver to save files automatically to a disk, a basic security package, an extensions manager, and Super Boomerang, a fancier version of the original Boomerang utility.

Major user groups (BMUG, BCS, and so on) and online services such as CompuServe and America Online operate the biggest and best libraries. These libraries contain hundreds of freeware and shareware utilities available at little or no cost. The major libraries usually have the same utilities selection, so if you already belong to BMUG, for example, there is no need to join BCS just to get more utilities.

Hear, hear for Now Utilities. Quickeys 2 and Now Utilities are the two utility packages I'd be lost without. If you haven't already, buy both today. You won't be sorry.

Bob LeVitus

Summary

Utilities are the tools of computing—you use them to perform functions which are not specific to any particular application. Utilities may be programs, desk accessories, extensions, or control panels.

A good utility is usually small in size and, therefore, requires few system resources. It typically performs only one function or a small set of closely related functions. It is best to start with a basic toolbox of utilities and add to it as the occasion arises. After all, you never can have too many!

Chapter 22: Hard Disk Management

Hard disks and closets have a lot in common. Both take some effort to keep neat and tidy. Both quickly can fill up with useless clutter, depriving you of space when you need it. And trying to find something—even if you keep things neat, tidy, and clutter-free—can be frustrating and time-consuming. Just as you may have to look in every box in a closet to find what you are searching for, you may at times find yourself hunting through every folder on your disk drive. The larger the disk, the worse these problems are.

In This Chapter

- ▼ Why managing a hard disk is important
- ▼ General principles for managing a hard disk
- ▼ Tips for organizing a hard disk
- ▼ Partitioning: what it is and whether to do it
- ▼ How to make backups easier
- ▼ Tuning your disk

Part V
Managing Your Mac

Managing a Disk

Hard disks offer a few challenges that closets do not. If a closet is destroyed by fire, you can replace most of the contents by purchasing new items. But if a hard disk is damaged, the data on it may be lost forever. Hard disks also can suffer performance problems that slow down your entire system.

For these reasons, you need to manage your hard disk. When people talk about *hard disk management*, they usually are referring to three basics:

▼ Organizing the disk's contents in a useful and efficient manner

▼ Making backups and taking other measures to avert disasters

▼ "Tuning" the disk for optimum performance

These activities are more closely related than you might think. Hard disk management consists of 90 percent organization. A well-organized disk takes less time to back up and requires less performance tuning. A well-organized disk can save you hours of time you otherwise might waste searching for lost files and identifying "mystery file" contents, to say nothing of re-creating work that unintentionally is deleted.

General Principles

Although entire books have been written on hard disk management, there really is not that much to it. Managing your hard disk properly requires no special knowledge, just common sense and good habits. Database programs on huge mainframe computers with hundreds of hard disks have genuine management problems. In comparison, the relatively small drive on your Mac offers no major challenges. Even the latest "monster" drives with 600-plus-megabyte capacity are easy to care for if you follow a few simple guidelines:

▼ Keep things "cleaned up" as you go along. If you save a file by the wrong name or into the wrong folder, stop immediately and fix the problem—change the name or move the file into the right folder. If you wait, you will forget. This cleanup eliminates one of the two major sources of disk drive clutter.

▼ Delete files as soon as you know they no longer are needed. The longer you wait, the harder it is to remember what the file contains and whether it is important. Deleting files as you go eliminates the other major cause of disk drive clutter.

Chapter 22
Hard Disk Management

- ▼ Never delete a file or folder that has not been backed up, just in case you ever might find you need it.

- ▼ Never delete a folder without discovering what is in it first. Do not trust the name of the folder alone to tell you what it contains—it is easy to drag something accidentally into the wrong folder and not realize you have done so.

- ▼ Use meaningful names for files and folders. A name like "1992 Budget First Draft" makes a lot more sense to you six months down the road than does "92Bud1."

- ▼ Organize your files and folders so that *you* can find things. No system of organization is perfect, but any system is better than none.

- ▼ When organizing your disk, think about your backup requirements. You may be able to drastically reduce the time it takes to do a backup if you keep documents and applications in separate folders.

- ▼ Get in the habit of doing backups regularly. At the very least, make a backup copy of an important file as soon as you are done creating it.

If you follow these basic principles, you will have few problems with your hard disk, other than those caused by mechanical failures or acts of nature. The secret to success is to get into the habit of caring for your hard drive daily. It is always easy to wait until later, but waiting until you forget where everything is and what it is called is precisely what causes all the trouble.

Organizing a Hard Disk

As mentioned earlier, hard disk management is largely a matter of getting items organized properly. There are no hard and fast rules for disk organization, but you should consider the following tips when trying to devise the scheme that works for you:

- ▼ It is easier and faster to back up a few folders than to back up a whole disk. Try to organize your files and folders so items that need to be backed up are kept separate from items that do not. You only have to back up newly created files or files you have altered since the previous backup.

▼ It generally is better to have a wide folder "tree" than a deep one (see figure 22.1). This cuts down on the number of folders you have to open to reach your destination.
It also reduces the chance of files getting buried in folders within folders within folders.

▼ If an application has auxiliary files, put the application and all its accessories in their own dedicated folder.

▼ If an application requires you to install certain files in certain folders, do it, even if that setup does not match your scheme. Forcing an application to organize things your way usually causes more trouble than it is worth.

▼ Check your System folder occasionally for stray files. Some applications leave temporary files in the System folder and never bother to remove them (Microsoft Word is notorious for this).

▼ Take advantage of System 7 aliases to find items easier. If a file or program has to be buried in your folder tree because of an application requirement, make an alias for it and put the alias in a more accessible folder.

 Do not use the information box of the **Get Info** command to make notes about a file or program. This information is erased when you rebuild the desktop. Instead, create a Read Me! file and put in the same folder.

The most important rule is to arrange items so you understand how the system works and feel comfortable with it. If you find yourself frequently digging through folders to find files, you have not yet developed your optimum organization system and need to rethink your strategy.

Organization Utilities

Many utilities—far too many to mention here—make it easier for you to organize your disk and find things on it. DiskQuick is a handy "librarian" that shines when it comes to keeping track of what is on your floppies. The same functions are useful for keeping track of what is where on your hard disk. CanOpener and OnLocation both are designed to search for files by their names or contents and to perform related functions such as renaming a file or folder. Either is better than Apple's Find File desk accessory, which only can search for files by name and has no other capabilities. There are also *file launchers* such as On Cue, which enable you to create a list of commonly used files and applications: you open the file or application by selecting it from the list, rather than returning to the Finder and double-clicking the icon.

System 7's **Find** function, which replaces the Apple menu's Find File on older systems, works only when you are on your Mac's desktop, which is always available (as in MultiFinder with System 6). Some of the previously mentioned utilities enable you to perform their searching and disk management functions without leaving the program and toggling to the desktop.

Chapter 22
Hard Disk Management

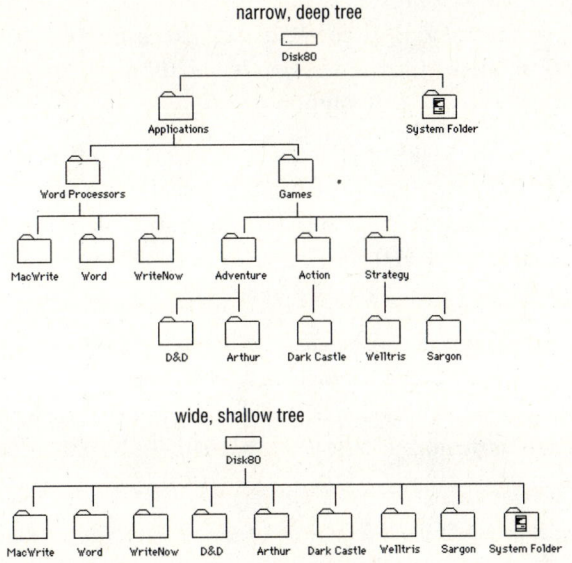

Figure 22.1
Shallow trees are easier to navigate and are less likely to conceal misplaced files.

Partitioning a Large Disk

Technically speaking, *partitioning* a hard disk means dividing it into segments called *partitions*. The computer treats each as though it were a separate disk device. In the Macintosh world, the term *partitioning* has been adulterated to also mean dividing a disk partition into *volumes*. These volumes then are incorrectly referred to as "partitions." A volume is a disk area whose contents (files and folders) are listed in a directory. The volume is represented on the desktop by a disk icon. In a losing effort to keep terms straight, some Mac users refer to true partitions as *hard partitions* and to volumes as *soft partitions*. To further complicate matters, the term "partition" also refers to the memory that MultiFinder or the System 7 Process Manager allocates to an application.

Part V
Managing Your Mac

Confused? Don't worry. The real question is whether you should partition a disk drive, regardless of whether the partitions are real or make-believe. The answer: The Macintosh operating system does not support partitioning, so that alone is a good reason not to do it!

Partitioning a Mac disk requires running special software that tricks the Mac's system into accepting what is otherwise an unnatural situation. This software makes disk access noticeably slower, so unless there is an absolutely good reason to partition a hard drive, do not do it. Some situations, however, may necessitate partitioning a drive:

▼ If the manufacturer recommends or requires it. Larger disks often need to be partitioned to work correctly. In these cases, the disk's documentation should provide the details, and the disk usually comes with the necessary software to support partitioning.

▼ If you are using a backup system that can handle only entire volumes, as opposed to enabling you to select individual files or folders. In this case, you might want to create a separate partition to contain only those items that need to be backed up daily. This way you do not have to back up the entire drive every time.

▼ If you need to make sure an application always has a certain minimum amount of space available. By setting aside a partition with that exact amount of space for the application to use, you ensure that other applications do not steal the space when they fill up their own partitions.

▼ If the number of files in a volume becomes too large for Finder to handle, or so large it takes extreme amounts of time to open a file.

In most other situations, partitioning does not do anything for you that cannot be done just as easily by better organizing your folders. Because of the added overhead and general problems of supporting multiple partitions on a Macintosh disk, you should avoid doing partitioning unless you have a good reason.

 If you want to partition a disk for security reasons, you would do better to use a "locked folder" program. Products like FolderBolt and DiskLock enable you to password-protect individual folders.

Disk partitioning software is available in disk utility packages such as SUM II and MacTools Deluxe. It is also available in stand-alone products like MultiDisk.

Chapter 22
Hard Disk Management

> **WARNING!** If you partition a disk to make backups easier, be aware that many utilities which support "soft" partitioning put hidden files in the main ("parent") volume's directory. These hidden files are the volume directories for partitions ("children") other than the parent. If you do not have a backup of the parent volume, you may not be able to restore a child volume. Because of this, you should include the parent volume with those that are backed up.

Backups

Maintaining an up-to-date backup of the data on your hard drive is crucial. If something happens to that drive and you do not have a current backup, you will regret it. Hard drives do not fail very often, but sooner or later, something always breaks.

People do not make backups as often as they should because they do not want to spend the time. The secret to minimizing this time requirement is to minimize the amount of data to back up each session. You only need to back up what you have changed since your previous session, which is usually very little. You do not need to back up application programs and the System folder if you save your original master copies and keep them in a safe place.

> **Note** Where you store your backups is as important as making them in the first place. You should store your backups in a separate part of the house or office, away from the computer's location, to cut down the potential of loss from fire. The ideal solution is to maintain two backups and keep one off-site, but this is not always practical for most people. Putting your data in a fire-proof safe is a good idea, but keep in mind that safes usually are designed to protect only paper, which can withstand much higher temperatures than magnetic media. Also, if you experience a fire, it may be several days before the safe can be opened (they have to cool before you can open them without damaging the contents). If you need to get back into business right away, you should look at other storage options.

You do not necessarily need a backup utility to maintain a proper set of backups. If you have master copies of all your application programs and system software, and if you have very little to back up each day, you probably can get by with just dragging appropriate files or folders onto a floppy disk. If your backup requirements are more complicated, use any number of utility programs for this purpose. The right solution depends mostly on how much data you need to back up each day, what kind of equipment you have or are willing to buy, and how much money you want to spend.

Incremental Versus Volume Backups

If you want to back up an entire disk (or volume, if your disk is partitioned), there are two approaches. One method is simply to back up the entire disk every day, which is usually not practical unless you are using a tape or cartridge drive as the backup device (backing up to floppies takes forever and requires a large number of floppies). The second approach is to make *incremental* backups by starting with a *master backup* of the entire hard disk. After you create the master backup, the backup utility copies only files that were changed since your previous backup. Almost all backup utilities designed to work with floppy disks can perform incremental backups.

Better utilities also enable you to back up one folder (and all its contents) rather than an entire disk. This can significantly reduce the number of floppies required to create the master backup, and it prevents the utility from making incremental copies of application programs that have made insignificant changes to themselves, such as user option changes.

> **Note** The larger your disk and the busier it is, the more it makes sense to use a cartridge drive as your backup device rather than floppies. The money you spend for floppies, as well as the cost of the time you waste, goes a long way toward purchasing a cartridge system.

Permanent Backups

You generally assume that the medium where you store backups will be reused, usually to make a newer backup. When the backup medium is reused, you lose any files that were copied to it and then deleted from the hard disk.

Because of this, you need to maintain a separate set of permanent backups in addition to your rotating set. For most people, just copying the files to a floppy is good enough. If a file is too big to fit on a floppy, you can compress it with a program such as Stuffit Deluxe or Compactor. If it is still too large, you can segment it using Stuffit Deluxe or Compactor. You also can get a backup utility that handles large files, or copy the file to a tape or cartridge device.

Like your rotating backups, permanent backups should be stored someplace other than where the computer is located. Creating two copies and keeping one off-site is best.

Backup Utilities

A number of good backup utilities are available, including freeware and shareware. Some of the commercial entries include SUM II, which contains a useful but limited incremental backup utility; MacTools Deluxe, whose backup utility is smarter than SUM's; and Retrospect, which is far more powerful and flexible than either of the first two. The network version, Retrospect Remote, enables you to centralize this task from one Macintosh on your network and make backups automatically; network users do not have to remember to do it before they go home at night. There are many other backup programs, so if the products mentioned here do not meet your needs, check out the marketplace.

Other utilities are not strictly backup utilities but fall in the same general category. Stuffit Deluxe (the commercial version of the older Stuffit shareware program) compresses files and enables you to segment and later recombine them into larger single files that can be decompressed when needed. This is handy when you put a large file on a floppy or send it over the telephone line. You also can view compressed files without decompressing them first. The Copy II Mac program overrides the copy protection on most products so you can make backup copies (this is legal, as long as the copies are strictly for your own use). As a bonus, it contains MacTools, a set of disk diagnosis and repair utilities.

 With so many choices available, it is better to design your backup plan and then find the utility that fits it, rather than buying a utility and changing how you work so you can use it.

Tuning a Disk

Tuning, or optimizing, a hard disk means arranging data on it in a way that optimizes the disk's performance. It minimizes the time needed to read data from or write data to the disk. The idea is to reduce the time it takes for the read/write head to find the area of the disk to access. This is done in two ways: (1) by reducing the *seek* time, which is a function of how many tracks the head has to cross to get to the right one, and (2) by reducing the

Part V
Managing Your Mac

Figure 22.2
Reducing the seek time and the rotational delay in your hard disk reduces the time it takes for the read/write head to find the area of the disk to access.

rotational delay, which is a function of how far the disk has to rotate to bring the desired track section beneath the read/write head. (See figure 22.2.)

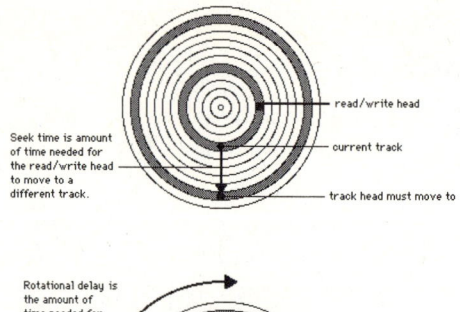

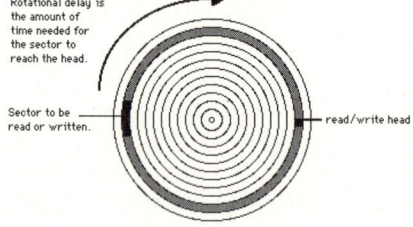

The whole subject of disk tuning tends to get overblown, especially by people who sell disk-tuning (optimizing) software. For the vast majority of users, the time and trouble it takes to tune a disk simply is not worth it. Today's disk drives are so fast that the improvements in disk access times are barely noticeable, if at all. In addition, disk-tuning software does not always work correctly—sometimes it corrupts the volume directory, making some or all of the data on the disk inaccessible. Even if the software functions properly, you still might wind up with a corrupted disk if the power should fail or the lights blink while you run a disk-optimizing program.

In some situations, though, it is important to make a disk run as fast as possible. A network disk server, such as an AppleShare server, is one example. When a large amount of disk activity is taking place, even minor performance improvements can be very noticeable. The more a disk is used, or the more crowded it is with data, the more it benefits from optimizing.

There are three basic steps you can take to optimize a hard disk: (1) change its *interleave ratio*, (2) *defragment* the files stored on it, and (3) change the locations where the files are stored on disk.

Adjusting the Interleave Ratio

A hard disk's interleave ratio is the number of sectors that pass under the read/write head before the next-higher-numbered sector on a track reaches the head (see figure 22.3). Disks read or write consecutively numbered sectors, which are not necessarily physically adjacent sectors. The correct interleave factor for your hard disk is a function of how fast the disk rotates and how fast your Mac is. In general, the slower the disk rotates, the lower the interleave factor can be, but the slower the Macintosh is, the higher the interleave factor must be to compensate. If the disk rotates too fast, the Mac is not ready to read or write the next sector by the time it reaches the head. As a result, the Mac has to wait until that sector rotates back around to reach the head again. An incorrect interleave ratio can cause significant rotational delays.

Chapter 22
Hard Disk Management

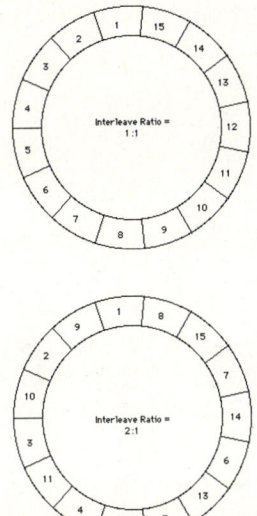

Figure 22.3
A hard disk's interleave ratio refers to the number of sectors that pass under the read/write head before the next-higher-numbered sector appears.

As a rule, you should not mess with a disk's interleave factor, set when the disk is initialized. Be sure, however, that if the initialization command asks you which type of Macintosh you are running on, you give the correct answer. The initialization software then correctly sets the interleave factor.

> **Note:** If you acquire a disk that has been used on a different Macintosh, you should reinitialize it to be sure the interleave factor is set correctly for your Mac. Also, if you plan to use this disk on several different Mac models, consider which you will use it on most, and initialize the disk for that model.

> **Note:** If you use an accelerator board in your Macintosh, you may have to lie about the kind of Macintosh you are using when running the initialization software. For example, if you have a Mac SE with a 68030 accelerator, you should tell the initialization software it is an SE/30. Otherwise, the interleave ratio won't take advantage of the performance capabilities of your machine.

861

Part V
Managing Your Mac

Defragmenting a Disk

Defragmenting a disk involves making sure the files stored on it are not in pieces (see figure 22.4). There is a lot of misunderstanding about how files are fragmented and the extent to which this affects performance.

Figure 22.4
File fragmentation can affect a hard disk's performance.

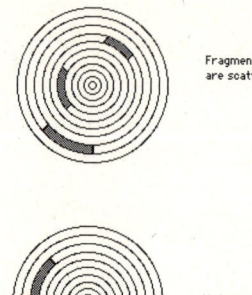

Fragmented file—pieces of the file are scattered throughout the disk.

Unfragmented file—the file is stored as one contiguous segment on disk.

A Closer Look You usually fragment a file by adding to it. When a file is first saved to a disk, the application program tries to write the entire file as one segment across several contiguous disk sectors. The only time a file is fragmented on the initial save is when there is no contiguous set of sectors on your disk large enough to hold the entire file. This is rarely the case, except on extremely crowded drives or on drives on which many files have been added and deleted in a different order over time.

If you later add to the file and save it again, you are likely to wind up with a fragmented file in two sections—the segment allocated the first time you saved the file, plus the new segment allocated to hold the new material. As you continue to add to your file, you end up with additional segments located in open spots all over the hard disk.

When a program tries to read your file, the disk's read/write head has to move from track to track, as well as wait for the correct sectors to rotate beneath the head, to access all of your file's pieces. As you can guess, file fragmentation affects both seek time and rotational delay.

Free (unused) space on a disk also can become fragmented. Any time you delete a file, you leave a "hole" in that space. If this hole is adjacent to an existing hole, the two combine to form one continuous free space segment, and no fragmentation occurs. But if there is no adjacent free space, the deleted file's space results in a new free space fragment. Eventually, even though you have enough free space on disk to hold a new file, it is possible that no single segment is big enough to hold the entire file, so the file, too, becomes fragmented.

But is fragmentation a significant problem? Not necessarily. The fact is, when you open a file, most programs try to read the entire file into memory. If they cannot, they attempt to keep the portions you are working on instead. In either case, you are working on data located in memory, not on disk. Any present file fragmentation only slows down the initial file read and any of your subsequent saves. Unless the file is enormous, you probably do not notice much slowdown.

Note: You often can defragment a file by copying it and deleting the original. Moving it into a different folder is not good enough, as this does not actually make a copy of the file—it only changes the directory entries. Copy the file either by using the Duplicate command in the Finder's File menu or by holding down the Option key while dragging the file into a different folder.

File fragmentation is much more likely to be a problem when a program does not load the file contents into memory. This tends to be the case with database programs and other programs designed to work with large amounts of data. For example, if you have a customer database that is indexed by account number, you may wind up with the account number index in one fragment and the customer record in another fragment. The read/write head must read the index first to find out where to locate the customer record, then move to another part of the disk to read the actual record. File fragmentation also can slow down any program that copies files, including backup utilities and the Finder.

WARNING! Should you defragment your disk files? Maybe not. Defragmenting a disk is a time-consuming and potentially dangerous procedure. Defragmentation utilities work with the disk volume directory's internal control blocks. Therefore, any number of events—a bug in the program, an error in the directory, a lack of available memory on the Mac, a power surge, and so on—might cause a destroyed or fatally altered volume directory and lost files. If you do decide to defragment the disk, make sure you back up everything first. Chances are, however, all the trouble and bother (it can take a few hours to do a very large disk) will not justify the small performance gains. Very crowded disks, disks which have been in use for a long time, and disks containing large database-type files, including

Chapter 22
Hard Disk Management

HyperCard stacks, are the most likely exceptions. Network servers also may benefit from disk defragmentation. In these cases, you may want to try running a defragmenting utility to see whether defragmenting will make a difference.

There is no way to completely avoid fragmentation, but you can take steps to minimize it. Your best defense against excessive fragmentation is to keep your disk clean of old files and always make sure a good chunk of free space is available. If you have two hard disks, put stable, permanent files like applications on one disk and volatile, temporary files on the other to keep at least one of the disks from becoming fragmented.

WARNING! Before running a defragmentation program, run a disk diagnosis utility to check for corrupted or damaged files and directories. If any are found, fix them with the diagnostic utility before starting the defragmentation process. This reduces the chance of a corrupted disk causing the defragmentation utility to crash and possibly making things worse.

Changing a File's Location

Changing a file's location on a disk can improve disk performance by reducing seek times. The idea is to arrange the files in a most-accessed to least-accessed order. This concentrates movements of the read/write head in a narrower range of tracks.

To move files, you need a disk optimization product that adjusts file placement as well as performs defragmentation. DiskExpress II, from ALSoft, is the notable entry in this market. It monitors file access activity and tries to arrange the file locations on disks to accommodate how you work. Most utilities simply defragment files and free space, although squeezing out the free space "holes" and allocating all files contiguously puts the files closer together and thus reduces read/write head movement and seek times. DiskExpress II goes a step further by trying to improve the file's position as much as possible.

Moving files does not make a big difference either, however; it has the same drawback as disk defragmentation. It depends on whether you access the file on disk or copy it into memory when it is opened. Because the latter is usually the case, improving file placement is likely to help only on large database-type files.

Other Ways to Tune a Disk

You can use a few other tricks to improve disk performance, although the results are not likely to be noticeable, let alone dramatic:

▼ Rebuild the Desktop file: This may improve the internal organization of the Desktop file enough to speed things a little when you open files. Rebuild the Desktop file on your start-up disk by holding down the Command and Option keys as you reboot the Mac. For other disks, hold down the Command and Option keys as you insert the disk.

▼ Clean up the disk: The more files a disk has, the longer it takes the Mac to find the one you want to open. Also, the more crowded your disk, the more fragmentation problems you have and the greater the territory the read/write head has to cover.

▼ Turn on the RAM cache: Use the Control Panel to turn on the RAM cache (it is always on in System 7). This helps applications that do many disk reads.

As a rule, the larger the RAM cache, the more it helps, but if you are using System 6 or older, do not make the cache larger than 256K. If it is too large, the algorithm used to manage the cache actually reduces disk performance instead of enhancing it.

▼ Turn off the RAM cache: If you have RAM cache on, try turning it off or making it smaller. Backup programs in particular are likely to run faster if RAM cache is disabled.

▼ Partition the disk: Although partitioning software usually slows down operations, if you have a very large number of files, partitioning a disk could make the processing faster.

▼ Check for viruses: Some viruses are known to impede disk access. (See chapter 23, "Viruses and System Security," for more information.) The Scores and WDEF viruses in particular are likely to cause problems.

Finally, you might consider getting a faster disk or a faster Mac. You can do only so much to make a system run faster. After all, you can tune a Ford Escort all you want, but you never will get it to go as fast as an Indy 500 race car!

Part V
Managing Your Mac

Disk Management Utilities

We already have mentioned several utilities that help organize and back up your hard disk. The products listed next are packages containing several utilities (some of which may not have anything to do with disks). You also may want to look into security software to help protect your hard disk. (See chapter 23, "Viruses and System Security," for more information.)

▼ SUM II (Symantec Utilities for Macintosh): Contains diagnosis and repair utilities, a backup program, an optimizer, a partitioning utility with password and encryption support, a disk editor, a utility for making fast copies of floppy disks, and a file encryption utility.

▼ Norton Utilities for the Macintosh: Contains diagnosis and repair utilities, an optimizer, a file finder, a utility to customize the appearance of icons on the desktop, a key finder to determine which key sequence is needed to type a special character, and a disk monitor to track disk activity.

▼ 911 Utilities: Contains the Virex antivirus program, a utility to recover lost and deleted files, a program to recover sectors the disk has marked as bad, a utility that rebuilds the Desktop file without erasing the Get Info information, and a few other miscellaneous utilities.

▼ MacTools Deluxe: Contains diagnostic and repair utilities, programs to recover deleted files and initialized disks, an application launcher, a file finder, disk partitioning software, a better backup utility than most, an optimizer, a file editor, and a floppy disk duplicator.

▼ Hard Disk Toolkit: Contains diagnostic, repair, recovery, and security utilities for SCSI devices (all hard disks except the old Apple HD20 are SCSI devices; floppy drives are not). This is one of the few products that does true "hard" partitioning as opposed to "soft" partitioning.

▼ Silver Lining: Similar to Hard Disk Toolkit.

As always, check online services and users groups for other utilities. In general though, hard disk management is one area in which the commercial products almost always outshine free and shareware ones.

Summary

Managing your hard disk properly improves your productivity by reducing the time you spend searching for files and making backups. The key to managing your hard disk is to keep it organized. Your hard disk is easier to keep organized if you clean it up and fix mistakes as you work, rather than putting off the work to some unspecified future date.

Get in the habit of making backups regularly. Try to store your backup copies in a location separate from the computer. To reduce the amount of time needed to make backups, organize your disk so files that do not need to be backed up are kept separate from those that do. And always make a separate permanent backup of important files before you delete them.

Partitioning a disk means dividing it into separate volumes; the Macintosh treats each as a separate disk. Partition a disk only if you have a good reason to do so. Tuning a hard disk also may improve performance, depending on the circumstances.

Defragmenting a disk means reorganizing files so that each file occupies a contiguous segment of disk rather than a number of segments scattered throughout the disk. However, this procedure may not be as beneficial as you have been led to believe, and it can be a dangerous operation.

Chapter 23
Viruses and System Security

In 1949, John von Neumann presented a paper entitled "Theory and Organization of Complicated Automata" in which he introduced his theory that computer programs could reproduce and

In This Chapter

▼ What is a virus

▼ Protection from viruses

▼ Eradicating a virus

▼ Types of viruses

▼ Virus-detecting programs

multiply. As is usual in history, von Neumann's colleagues largely dismissed his theory—actually understandable because the first electronic computer would not be invented for seven more years! Still, von Neumann was the first to foresee a problem with computers now known as "computer viruses."

Introduction

Computer viruses are not biological. They are software programs maliciously, unethically, and immorally created by someone for the sole purpose of disrupting or destroying legal computer software or operation. Viruses are real, they are dangerous, and along with other destructive programs such as worms and Trojan Horses, they pose a serious threat to computer users everywhere, not just Macintosh computers.

What Is a Virus

A computer *virus* is not a "flu bug." It is a piece of destructive software programmed to specifically attach itself to, or "infect," other applications or files, then reproduce or cause other damage. After you run an infected application, the virus quickly spreads to your system files and other software. Viruses spread from one Macintosh to another through sharing and distributing infected software or disks.

Worms and Trojan Horses

Recently, the news media has labeled all forms of destructive software, including "worms" and "Trojan horses," as viruses. Viruses are completely different and should not be confused with worms and Trojan horses.

A *worm* is an application that reproduces and spreads itself, but does not attach itself to other applications. A worm's sole purpose is usually to reproduce itself until it fills up the computer's operating or storage memory and shuts the computer down. Unlike a virus, a worm stands by itself and does not require a host program to survive and replicate. Worms usually

Chapter 23
Viruses and System Security

spread over a network of computers rather than through program sharing. Probably the best known example of a worm is the one that infected the Internet, a huge national computer network, in the fall of 1988 and disabled thousands of government and university computers in a single day.

A *Trojan horse*, on the other hand, is a program designed to look like it is doing something useful, but that instead does something destructive behind the scenes. The best known example of a Trojan horse is the Sexy Ladies or Chippendales HyperCard stack, which secretly erases a Mac's hard disk while someone looks at the nude pictures on the screen. Trojan horses do not replicate, and they require someone to actually run them for their insidious destruction to occur.

Types of Viruses

Viruses can be *malicious* or *nonmalicious*. Nonmalicious viruses usually are programmed merely to replicate themselves unceasingly. These benign viruses may simply cause your Mac to beep or display a message on your screen but do not intentionally try to do any damage. Malicious viruses, on the other hand, deliberately attempt to damage something in addition to replicating themselves. There are several viruses in the IBM PC world that intentionally delete files or destroy the contents of hard drives, and are designed to pass themselves on to other systems and do the same there.

To date, Mac users are graciously blessed, because most known Macintosh viruses have been nonmalicious. However, even nonmalicious viruses almost always cause inadvertent damage—and more malicious viruses have appeared recently, too. Most Mac users who experience viral infections report problems with their computer's normal operation until the virus is eradicated. These problems are usually the first clue that a Mac has an infection.

Viruses can occupy both a Mac's memory and disk space, which in itself is enough to cause problems. Viruses also can live in the Mac's operating system and can interfere in unexpected ways with other pieces of the system. Almost all viruses have errors present in the programming code that later cause unexplained system crashes or strange behavior, such as blank menus or see-through windows.

Even though viruses are not biological, the similarities between real-life and computer viruses are dramatic. Both viruses are designed to reproduce themselves, and both require a host to live in. The system that gets infected can face severe damage. And in both cases, it is sometimes possible to remove the infection without damage to the system and vaccinate a system to protect it against infection or re-infection.

However, it is possible to carry this analogy too far. Computers are not living organisms. Biological viruses usually occur naturally; computer viruses always are created by people. It also is not possible to compare the enormous pain and suffering from biological viruses such as HIV, which causes AIDS in humans, to the damage computer viruses cause.

Preventing a Viral Infection

Although viruses can be a problem, there is no need to panic. It takes only a few minutes to effectively protect your Mac against the known viruses, and common sense practices to keep it virus-free.

▼ Install a protection extension (for instance, the Disinfectant INIT or Gatekeeper) on your Mac. Both programs are free and usually found on electronic BBSs or through a local user group. Both programs prevent your system from performing certain computing routines common to virus infections without your permission (some applications run those routines legally and are not viruses). Installing either of these programs can save you hours of time and frustration by heading off a virus before it infects your system. Two commercial packages are worth mentioning: Symantec Antivirus for the Mac (SAM) and Virex.

▼ Whenever you obtain a new piece of software, immediately lock the disk it comes on, make a copy of the program (usually on your hard disk), and use the copy. Never unlock your original disks and it will be impossible for a virus to infect the files on them.

▼ Make periodic backups of your hard drive, usually once a week. If your system becomes infected, you can restore your files and applications from the uninfected backups.

▼ Just before you make any backup, run a virus-detecting program on your hard disk. This ensures that your backups are not infected and your system has not been infected since your last backup.

▼ Check any new software for possible infections before using it. This applies to all software including commercially distributed, shrink-wrapped software, shareware, and freeware.

Virus Prevention on Networks and Other Environments

Any environment where many people share Macs, or operate over a Mac network, is a perfect breeding ground for viruses. People who sell or distribute software also have a responsibility to make certain that their software is free from viral infections. The following recommendations apply to those who operate or use Mac networks, laboratories, bulletin boards, or public domain collections and shareware software:

▼ Install a protection extension such as Disinfectant INIT or Gatekeeper on all start-up disks.

▼ Frequently check all disks to make certain they remain uninfected, and that Disinfectant INIT or Gatekeeper is still installed and active on any start-up disks.

▼ Educate all users in your organization about viruses and how to protect against them.

▼ On AppleShare server disks, try to keep software in write-protected folders. Applications cannot be infected if they are in folders that do not have the "Make Changes" privilege activated by the AppleShare Administrator. On the other hand, if an application is in a writable server folder, any infected Mac on the network that accesses it can spread the infection to the application on the server. If it is a popular application, it quickly infects other Macs on the network that are not protected by Disinfectant INIT or Gatekeeper. This is one way in which viruses spread very rapidly. Because some applications insist on writing to their own file or folder, it is not always possible to put applications in write-protected folders, but this should be done whenever possible.

▼ Check all server disks frequently with a virus-detecting program to make certain they remain uninfected. For best results, you should take the server out of operation, start up the server from your virus-detecting program master disk, and run the virus-detecting program from this disk. This is the only way to guarantee that the virus-detecting program is able to scan all the files on the server disk, including the System and Finder files.

▼ Check all new software with a virus-detecting program before installing it on a server.

▼ Back up your servers frequently. Run a virus-detecting program just before each backup.

▼ Bulletin board operators and other people who maintain and distribute public domain and shareware software have a special responsibility to the Mac community and should carefully test all new software before distributing it. You also, of course, should run a virus-detecting program on all new software you receive.

▼ If you sell software, check master disks for infections before sending them out to be duplicated and distributed.

The Viruses

The following sections describe all known Mac viruses at the time of this writing, thanks to the publishers of Disinfectant.

The Scores Virus

Also known as the Eric, Vult, NASA, and San Jose Flu virus, Scores gets its most common name from the invisible Scores file it creates in a Mac's System folder.

First discovered in the spring of 1988, the Scores virus reportedly was written by a disgruntled programmer. It was designed specifically to attack two applications under development at his former company. The programmer released Scores to the general public in hopes it would attack those programs and cause so many problems that it would undermine or destroy his former company. Fortunately for that company, its two applications never were released to the general public. Unfortunately for the general public, Scores was.

A Closer Look

Scores infects your Mac's System, Note Pad, and Scrapbook files. It also creates two invisible files in your System folder named "Scores" and "Desktop." Although Scores does not intentionally try to do any damage other than spread itself, it does occupy and use up valuable memory and disk space. People have reported problems printing and using MacDraw and Excel. And several program code errors in Scores could cause system crashes or other unexplained behavior in your Mac. Scores does not infect or modify document files, only applications and system files.

Two days after your system becomes infected, Scores begins to spread to every application you run. The infection occurs two to three minutes after you start a program, and the Finder and DA Handler usually become infected, too.

There is an easy way to see whether you have a Scores infection. Open your System folder and check the icons for the Note Pad and Scrapbook files. Under System 6, they should look like the little Macintoshes shown in figure 23.1. If they look like blank sheets of paper with turned-down corners instead (shown in figure 23.2), your software is infected. However, it is still possible to have normal Note Pad and Scrapbook icons in the early stages of a Scores infection. The only sure way to diagnose Scores is to use virus-detecting software.

Chapter 23
Viruses and System Security

Figure 23.1

Normal System file and Finder icons resemble Macs.

Figure 23.2

The System file and Finder icons look like turned-down pages when the Scores virus is present.

875

The nVIR Virus

The nVIR virus reportedly first appeared in Europe in 1987 and in the United States in early 1988. At least one variation of the virus has been written, so there are two basic strains called nVIR A and nVIR B. (A third, malicious version that destroyed files in a Mac's System folder has been reported. This version thankfully appears to be extinct.)

nVIR is a simpler virus than Scores. It infects a Mac's System file but not the Note Pad or Scrapbook files, and it does not create invisible files. One of the viral resources nVIR adds to infected files has the resource type "nVIR," which is how the virus got its name.

A Closer Look When nVIR first infects the System file, a counter is set to 1000. The counter ticks off by one each time the system is started up and by two each time an infected application is run. When the counter reaches zero, nVIR A either beeps or makes your Mac say, "Don't panic" if MacinTalk is installed. nVIR B sometimes beeps but does nothing with MacinTalk.

At first, nVIR A and B only replicate, spreading to other applications immediately. Whenever a new application is run, it becomes infected immediately. Later, it is possible for nVIR A and nVIR B to "mate" and reproduce, resulting in new viruses that combine parts of their parents.

As with Scores, nVIR occupies both memory and disk space. Also like Scores, the Finder and DA Handler become infected, but document files are not infected or modified. Unlike Scores, there is no way to tell that you have an nVIR infection just by looking at your system. You must run viral detection software.

The INIT 29 Virus

The INIT 29 virus first appeared in late 1988. INIT 29 is extremely virulent and spreads rapidly. Unlike Scores and nVIR, you do not have to run an application for it to become infected. Also, unlike Scores and nVIR, INIT 29 can and does infect almost any file, including applications, system files, and document files. Document files are infected, but they are not contagious. The virus can spread only via system and application files.

A Closer Look: INIT 29 has one side effect that reveals its presence. When you try to insert a *locked* floppy disk on an INIT 29-infected system, you get the following alert:

```
The disk "xxxxx" needs minor repairs.

Do you want to repair it?
```

As with Scores and nVIR, INIT 29 does not intentionally try to do any damage other than spread itself. Nevertheless, it can cause problems. In particular, some people have reported problems printing on INIT 29-infected systems. System crashes, problems with MultiFinder, and incompatibilities with start-up documents are other difficulties.

One of the viral resources INIT 29 adds to infect files is the resource type "INIT" and the resource ID 29, after which the virus was named.

The ANTI Virus

There are two known strains of the ANTI virus, both first discovered in France. ANTI A was discovered in February 1989; ANTI B was discovered in September 1990.

A Closer Look: Unlike most other viruses, ANTI does not infect the System file. It only infects applications and files that resemble applications (for example, the Finder). ANTI does not infect document files, so it is less contagious than the INIT 29 virus. But ANTI is more contagious than Scores and nVIR because it is possible for an application to become infected with ANTI even if the application is never run.

Due to a technical programming quirk, ANTI does not spread at all when MultiFinder is turned on. It spreads only when Finder is used.

As with the other viruses, ANTI does not intentionally attempt to do any damage other than spread itself. As with all viruses, however, it still can cause problems. The string "ANTI" appears within the virus, hence its name.

Even though the ANTI B was not discovered until about 19 months after ANTI A, it appears the B strain actually was written before the A strain. ANTI A contains special code that neutralizes any copies of the B strain it encounters. It is possible for an application to be infected by both the neutralized version of the B strain and the A strain at the same time.

Chapter 23
Viruses and System Security

Other than the special A strain code, which looks for and neutralizes the B strain, there are only minor technical differences between the two versions.

The MacMag Virus

The MacMag virus appeared in December 1987. This virus is also known as the Drew, Brandow, Aldus, and Peace virus. It was named after the Montreal offices of *MacMag* magazine, where it originated.

Unlike other viruses, MacMag infects only system files, not applications. It originated as a HyperCard stack named "New Apple Products," which contained some poorly digitized pictures of the then-new Apple scanner. When the stack was run, the virus spread to the currently active System file. When other floppy disks containing system files subsequently were inserted in a floppy disk drive, the virus spread to the system files on the floppies. Although it sounds like a Trojan Horse, MacMag is a virus, infecting files and replicating itself, then spreading.

Because MacMag does not infect applications, it spreads more slowly than other viruses; people share system files much less frequently than they share applications. Even though the virus originated on a HyperCard stack, it does not spread to other stacks.

MacMag was programmed to activate on March 2, 1988, the second anniversary of the Mac II's introduction. The first time the system was started up on March 2, 1988, the virus displayed a message of peace on the screen and then deleted itself from the System file. Since MacMag was programmed to self-destruct, it is unlikely your software is infected with this virus.

The WDEF Virus

The WDEF virus first was discovered in December 1989 in Belgium and at Northwestern University. Since its initial discovery, this virus has become extremely widespread. There are two known strains: WDEF A and WDEF B.

WDEF infects only the invisible Desktop file the Finder uses. With a few exceptions, every Macintosh disk (hard drives and floppies) contains this file. WDEF does not infect applications, document files, or other system files. Unlike other viruses, it is not spread by sharing applications but rather by sharing and distributing disks, usually floppies.

WDEF spreads from disk to disk very rapidly. It is not necessary to run an application for the virus to spread.

The WDEF A and WDEF B strains are very similar. The only significant difference is that WDEF B beeps every time it infects a Desktop file, whereas WDEF A does not beep.

WARNING! Although the virus does not intentionally try to do any damage, WDEF contains programming errors that can cause serious problems. In particular, the virus causes newer Mac models (the IIci, IIfx, Portable, Classic, LC, IIsi, Quadra, and PowerBook) to crash almost immediately after you insert an infected floppy. The virus causes other Macs to crash much more frequently than usual and can damage hard disks. The virus also causes problems with the proper display of font styles, the outline font style in particular. Many other symptoms have been reported, and it appears the errors in the virus can cause almost any kind of problem with your Macintosh's proper functioning.

Although WDEF is a complex and dangerous virus, you can remove a WDEF infection from a disk simply by rebuilding your Mac's Desktop file.

To rebuild the Desktop file on a hard disk, start up your Mac using Finder (not MultiFinder), and hold down the Command and Option keys throughout the start-up process. An alert dialog box appears asking if you truly want to rebuild the Desktop file. Click on the OK button, and WDEF is eliminated when the Desktop appears on your screen.

 **WARNING!** It is safe to rebuild your Mac's Desktop file, but any comments you may have entered in a file's **Get Info** box is erased in the process.

To rebuild the Desktop file on a floppy disk, hold down the Command and Option keys while inserting the disk into a drive. Click on the **OK** button in the alert box.

Even though AppleShare servers do not use the normal Finder Desktop file, many servers have an unused copy of this file. If the AppleShare administrator grants the "Make Changes" privilege to the root directory on the server, then any infected server user can infect the Desktop file on the server. If a server Desktop file becomes infected, performance on the network is very severely degraded. For this reason, administrators should never grant the "Make Changes" privilege on server root directories. It also is recommended you delete the Desktop file if it exists.

The WDEF virus can spread from a TOPS server to a TOPS client if a published volume's Desktop file is infected and the client mounts the infected volume.

WARNING! If you use ResEdit, VirusDetective, or some other software tool to search for WDEF resources, do not be alarmed if you find them in files other than the Finder Desktop files. WDEF resources are a normal part of the Macintosh operating system and not a virus. Only a WDEF resource in a Finder Desktop file is cause for concern.

The ZUC Virus

There are three known strains of the ZUC virus, all discovered in Italy. ZUC A was discovered in March 1990, ZUC B in November 1990, and ZUC C in June 1991. The virus is named after the reported discoverer of the first strain, Don Ernesto Zucchini.

 ZUC infects only applications. It does not infect system files or document files. Applications do not have to be run to become infected.

ZUC A and B were timed to activate on March 2, 1990, or two weeks after an application first became infected, whichever was later. Before that date, these viruses only spread from application to application. After that date, approximately 90 seconds after an infected application is run, the Mac's cursor begins to behave unusually whenever the mouse button is held down. The cursor moves diagonally across the screen, changing direction erratically and bouncing like a billiard ball whenever it reaches any of the four sides of the screen. The cursor stops moving when the mouse button is released.

ZUC C is very similar to ZUC A and ZUC B. The only significant differences are that ZUC C was timed to cause the unusual cursor behavior between 13 and 26 days after an application becomes infected (but not earlier than August 13, 1990), and the cursor begins to behave unusually approximately 67 seconds rather than 90 seconds after an infected application is run.

The ZUC's behavior is similar to that of a desk accessory named Bouncy. The virus and the desk accessory are different and they should not be confused. The desk accessory does not spread and is not a virus. ZUC does spread, and it is a virus.

ZUC has two noticeable side effects. On some Macintoshes, the A and B strains can cause the desktop pattern to change. All three strains also sometimes can cause long delays and an unusually large amount of disk activity when you open infected applications.

> **WARNING!** ZUC can spread over a network from individual Macintoshes to servers and vice versa. Except for the unusual cursor behavior, ZUC does not attempt to do any damage.

The MDEF Virus

There are four known strains of the MDEF virus. All of them were discovered in Ithaca, New York. The MDEF A strain was discovered in May 1990 and sometimes is called the Garfield virus. The MDEF B strain was discovered in August 1990 and sometimes is called the Top Cat virus. The C and D strains were discovered in October 1990 and January 1991, respectively.

Computer security personnel and New York State Police investigators' prompt action identified the author. Reportedly, the author, a juvenile, was released into his parent's custody . The same juvenile was allegedly responsible for writing the CDEF virus, too.

A Closer Look The A, B, and C strains of MDEF infect both applications and the System file. They also can infect document files, other system files, and Finder Desktop files. The Finder and DA Handler usually become infected also. The System file is infected as soon as an infected application is run. Other applications become infected as soon as they are run on an infected system.

The D strain infects only applications, not system or document files. Applications can become infected even if they are never run. An application infected by MDEF D beeps every time it is run.

> **WARNING!** The MDEF A strain has an unfortunate interaction with Vaccine, a popular but older virus-detecting software application. When an infected application is run on a Vaccine-protected system, Vaccine properly notifies you of the attack but blocks only part of the virus's attempt to infect the System file. The virus cannot spread from the System file to applications in this situation, but the System file is damaged and menus no longer work; you cannot pull them down. Menus continue to work only in infected applications. Strangely, they do not work in the Finder

Chapter 23
Viruses and System Security

881

or in uninfected applications. The MDEF B and C strains attempt to bypass some of the popular protection INITs.

 The MDEF C strain contains a serious programming error that can cause crashes and other problems. These problems can permanently delete some files or cause damage to hard disks that may or may not be repairable.

The MDEF viruses are named after the type of resource they use to infect files. MDEF resources are a normal part of the Macintosh system, so you should not become alarmed if you see them with ResEdit or some other tool. The MDEF, WDEF, and CDEF viruses have similar names, but they are completely different and should not be confused with each other.

The CDEF Virus

The CDEF virus first was discovered in Ithaca, New York, in August 1990. The same juvenile who wrote the MDEF virus also admitted to writing the CDEF virus. (See the description of the MDEF virus for details.) CDEF is very similar to the WDEF virus. It infects only the invisible Desktop file the Finder uses. It does not infect applications, document files, or other system files. It spreads from disk to disk very rapidly.

Although the CDEF virus's behavior is similar to WDEF's , it is not a WDEF clone. It is a completely different virus. CDEF does not intentionally try to do damage. It does not appear to cause as many problems as the WDEF virus does. As with all viruses, however, the CDEF virus is still dangerous.

As with the WDEF virus, you can remove a CDEF infection from a disk by rebuilding the Desktop file. (See the section, "The WDEF Virus," earlier in this chapter, for details.)

The CDEF virus is named after the type of resource it uses to infect files. CDEF resources are a normal part of the Macintosh system, so you should not become alarmed if you see them with ResEdit or some other tool. Any CDEF resource in a Finder Desktop file, however, is cause for concern.

The MBDF Virus

The MBDF virus was reportedly discovered in Wales in February 1992. As with many viruses, MBDF was spread through games. The games were named "10 Tile Puzzle" and "Obnoxious Tetris," and were located on several Internet sites. In addition to these two games, a third game named "Tetricycle" or "tetris-rotating" was a Trojan horse which installed the virus. Worldwide infection was swift because of the popularity of these particular sites.

Unlike other viruses, though, the creators of this virus were discovered. Computer systems are becoming much more sophisticated in recording information that leaves a trail for detectives to follow. Following these trails resulted in the arrest of three undergraduate students at Cornell University. They were charged under New York state law with multiple felony counts of first-degree computer tampering in connection with the release of the MBDF virus. At the time of this book's writing, they were awaiting trial.

A Closer Look Like CDEF and WDEF, the MBDF virus is named after the type of resource it uses to infect files. (MBDF resources are a normal part of the Macintosh system, so you should not become alarmed if you see them with ResEdit or some other tool.) The System file is infected as soon as an infected application is run, while other applications become infected as soon as they are run on an infected system.

The MBDF virus is a non-malicious virus, but, unfortunately it can still cause damage. In particular, the virus takes an unusually long time to infect a Mac's System file when it first attacks. More often than not, the delay is so long that people think their Mac is locked up and they restart the Macintosh. Unfortunately, restarting the Mac while the virus is in the process of attacking results in a severely damaged System file which cannot be repaired. When this occurs, the only solution is completely reinstalling the System file from scratch.

The INIT 1984 Virus

The INIT 1984 virus was first discovered in the Netherlands, and then in several locations in the United States in March 1992.

Chapter 23
Viruses and System Security

Part V
Managing Your Mac

WARNING! INIT 1984 is a malicious virus, and is designed to trigger if an infected system is restarted on any Friday the 13th from 1991 on. The virus caused significant damage to the hard drives of several Mac users throughout the world on Friday, March 13, 1992, and many Mac users are currently experiencing problems related to this virus without realizing it. Versions of virus-detecting software written prior to this date are probably not capable of detecting this virus, and the damage is going on unchecked.

A Closer Look INIT 1984 is specifically designed to damage folders and files, with file and folder names usually changed to random 1-8 character strings. Init 1984 also damages files by changing the file creators and file types to random 4 character strings, which changes the icons associated with the files and destroys the relationships between programs and their documents. One symptom associated with an infection is the disappearance of files and folders from the desktop, usually from part of the alphabet to the end. Trying to make a file or folder with the same name usually results in a message "name is already in use," even though the file cannot be seen. Using utilities to make the file visible works only for a few moments. Sometimes, creation and modification dates are changed to Jan. 1, 1904. In addition, the virus deletes files at random.

The virus only infects INITs (also known as startup documents or system extensions), and not the System file, desktop files, control panel files, applications, or document files. The virus spreads from INIT to INIT at startup time. Because INIT files are not shared as frequently as programs, the INIT 1984 virus has not spread as rapidly as most other viruses. The virus spreads and causes damage on every type of Macintosh, and under both System 6 and System 7. On very early model Macintoshes such as the Mac 128K, 512K, and XL, the virus causes a system crash at startup which cannot be recovered from without reinstalling the System file.

The CODE 252 Virus

The CODE 252 virus was first discovered in California in April 1992, and is designed to trigger when an infected application is run or an infected system is started up any time between June 6 and December 31 (inclusive) of any year. Between January 1 and June 5 (inclusive) of any year, the virus simply spreads from applications to System files, and then on to other application files.

Once activated, the following message is displayed on the Mac's screen by the virus:

```
You have a virus.

Ha Ha Ha Ha Ha Ha Ha

Now erasing all disks…

Ha Ha Ha Ha Ha Ha Ha

P.S. Have a nice day

Ha Ha Ha Ha Ha Ha Ha

(Click to continue…)
```

The message is not true; no files or directories are deleted by the virus. In fact, the message *is* the virus. However, upon seeing this message many Mac users immediately turn off their Macintoshes in an attempt to stop any erasure and hopefully save some files. Inadvertently, the power-down usually corrupts the hard drive or System file and the drive must be reformatted, losing everything.

Under any Mac system, the virus infects the System file. Due to errors in the programming code of the virus, it only spreads to new applications under System 6 when not using MultiFinder. The Finder usually also becomes infected. Under System 6 running MultiFinder, the virus infects the System file and the "MultiFinder" file, but does not spread to new applications or the Finder. Under System 7, the virus infects the System file, but it does not spread to new applications. Unfortunately, a particularly bad programming error in the virus causes crashes and/or damaged files under System 7.

The T4 Virus

The T4 virus was discovered in several locations around the world in June 1992 in versions 2.0 and 2.1 of a game called GoMoku. Copies of this game, with the virus encoded within it, were posted to a number of popular bulletin boards and quickly distributed.

One particularly disturbing aspect of this virus is that it has the capacity to masquerade as a popular piece of virus-detecting software. The virus attempts to run-around the real software by displaying the same alerts as real general-purpose suspicious

Chapter 23
Viruses and System Security

activity-monitoring software, such as Gatekeeper or Disinfectant. Your only clue that this is happening is if your system suddenly stops loading INITs and system extensions for no good reason. Such an event is a good indication that you are about to be attacked by the T4 virus. The masquerading virus displays an antivirus program's "alert," telling you it is trying to make a change to a file, and do you want to grant permission to allow the change. Okaying the change automatically bypasses any real virus-detecting software you may have, and T4 begins its attack.

A Closer Look The T4 virus is a malicious virus that causes irreparable damage to applications. The virus spreads to applications and to the Finder, and also attempts to alter the System file. When you use virus-detecting software to repair an infected application, it usually removes the T4 virus from the file but leaves the file damaged, rendering it useless.

The change to the System file results in alterations to the startup code under both Systems 6 and 7. Under System 6 and System 7.0, the change results in INIT files and system extensions not loading. Under System 7.0.1, the change may render the system unbootable, or cause crashes in unpredictable circumstances. This damage to the System file cannot be repaired. If the T4 virus damages your System file, you will have to reinstall it.

There are two known strains of the T4 virus: T4-A (contained in GoMoku 2.0) and T4-B (contained in GoMoku 2.1). The only significant difference between them is the trigger date: the trigger date for T4-A is on or after August 15, 1992, while the trigger date for T4-B is on or after June 26, 1992.

The INIT 17 Virus

The INIT 17 virus was discovered in April, 1993. It Infects both System files and applications. Although not a malicious virus, it can cause crashes, particularly on 68000-based Macintoshes. INIT 17 activates the first time the Mac is restarted after 6:06:06 AM on October 31, 1993. It displays the message "From the depths of Cyberspace."

The INIT-M Virus

INIT-M was also discovered in April, 1993. It, unlike INIT-17, is a malicious virus. It activates on any Friday the 13th. When it activates, it changes file and folder names to random 8-character names; it also randomizes the file creators and types as well, making it almost impossible to determine what application each file belongs to. The virus has other effects, too; it can potentially delete files.

Virus-Detecting Software

There are many free and shareware virus-fighting tools. Most are available from user groups, bulletin boards, and commercial online services. Table 22.1 is a partial list, although many in this list are obsolete or have limited use. These tools are included because so many are still distributed. Disinfectant, Disinfectant INIT, Gatekeeper, Gatekeeper Aid, VirusDetective, and Eradicat'Em are six distinctive exceptions. These tools are actively supported by their authors, have general utility, and are highly recommended by users.

Table 22.1 Virus-detecting software

Program Name	What It Does	Cost	Description
AntiPan 1.5	nVIR repair	Free	Scans disks and removes nVIR infections. Recognizes nVIR clones. Also "inoculates" the system to prevent future infections.
AntiVirus 1.0E	nVIR repair	Free	Scans disks and removes nVIR infections. Also "inoculates" the system to prevent future infections.
Assassin	nVIR repair	Free	Scans disks and removes nVIR infections.
Disinfectant	Virus detection and repair	Free	Undoubtedly the best virus-detection software available.

continues

Table 22.1 Continued

Program Name	What It Does	Cost	Description
			Constantly updated by John Norstad of Northwestern University and a group of international experts. Disinfectant can detect and eradicate more viruses than any other known software. Distributed free over bulletin boards and online services and through user groups, it is updated as soon as any new virus becomes known.
Disinfectant INIT	Virus detection	Free	A Control Panel document (INIT/CDEV) that monitors and blocks suspicious activity characteristic of viruses.
Eradicat'Em 1.0	WDEF and CDEF	Free	A system start-up protection and repair document that protects your system against WDEF and CDEF virus infection and automatically removes any infections it encounters.
Ferret 1.1	Scores detection and repair	Free	Scans disks and removes Scores infections.
Gatekeeper 1.2.1	Virus protection	Free	A Control Panel document (INIT/CDEV) that monitors and blocks suspicious activity characteristic of viruses. This version does not offer WDEF or CDEF virus protection. (See Gatekeeper Aid below.)

Chapter 23
Viruses and System Security

Program Name	What It Does	Cost	Description
Gatekeeper Aid 1.2.1	WDEF and CDEF protection and repair	Free	A system start-up document that protects your system against WDEF and CDEF virus infection and automatically removes any infections it encounters.
Interferon 3.1	Virus detection	Free	Detects both Scores and nVIR but cannot repair infected programs. Interferon was one of the first virus-fighting tools. The author no longer supports Interferon and recommends that you no longer use it. (Woodhead is the author of the commercial virus-detector Virex).
KillScores 1.0	Scores detection and repair	Free	Scans disks and removes Scores infections.
KillVirus	nVIR repair	Free	Also sometimes named "KillnVIR." A system start-up document that repairs your System file and automatically repairs any infected applications when they are run. Adds an "nVIR 10 inhibitor" to your System file, which some of the other virus-detecting software tools improperly report as an nVIR infection. Does not notify you when it finds and repairs infected files.
N.O.M.A.D. 1.0a1	nVIR repair	Free	Scans disks and removes nVIR infections from applications, but not from system files.

continues

Table 22.1 Continued

Program Name	What It Does	Cost	Description
QuickScores	Scores detection	Free	This desk accessory quickly checks to see whether the currently active System file is infected by Scores.
Repair 1.5	nVIR repair	Free	Does not do disk scanning. You must repair each infected application one at a time. Can repair an infected System file. Recognizes clones.
RezSearch 1.0b	Virus detection	Free	Searches a disk for files containing a specific resource or resource type. Configurable. Also can be used for purposes other than virus-detection.
RWatcher 1.0	Virus protection	Free	A system start-up document that protects against Scores and nVIR. Configurable. For non-MPW programmers who do not use Vaccine because of Vaccine's constant complaints about the creation of CODE resources. Has weaker checks than Vaccine's. The author no longer supports RWatcher, recommending that programmers use Disinfectant INIT or Gatekeeper instead.
Vaccination 1.1	nVIR repair	Free	Does not do disk scanning. You must repair each infected application one at a time. Cannot repair an infected System file.

Chapter 23
Viruses and System Security

Program Name	What It Does	Cost	Description
Vaccine 1.0.1	Virus protection	Free	A Control Panel document (INIT/CDEV) that monitors suspicious activity characteristic of viruses. Vaccine was the original Macintosh virus protection tool and is still widely used. It is not supported and is not effective against some of the newer viruses. Author recommends you use Disinfectant INIT or Gatekeeper instead.
Vaxene	Scores detection	Free	Does not do disk scanning; you must check each file one at a time. Cannot repair files. The about box claims the author is also the author of the Scores virus itself.
VCheck 1.3	Virus detection	Free	Takes a "snapshot" of your system and compares it to previous snapshots. Tells you which files have changed.
VirusBlockade II 1.0	Virus detection	Shareware, $30	A Control Panel device. Among many other features, it can be used together with the author's VirusDetective to automatically scan floppies for viruses when they are inserted in a disk drive.
VirusDetective 4.0.4	Virus detection	Shareware, $40	A desk accessory. Cannot repair infected applications, except for WDEF and CDEF. Configurability is one of VirusDetective's strongest

continues

Table 22.1 Continued

Program Name	What It Does	Cost	Description
			features. When a new virus appears, you often can configure VirusDetective to recognize it without waiting for a new version to be released. For example, when the WDEF virus first appeared, VirusDetective was the only virus-fighting tool that could detect it (with proper configuration). Also detects clones.
Virus Encyclopedia	Virus info	Free	This detailed HyperCard stack presents information about Macintosh viruses.
Virus Rx 1.6	Virus detection	Free	Detects Scores, nVIR, INIT 29, ANTI, WDEF, and CDEF. Cannot repair infected applications. Has not been updated to detect more recent viruses.
VirusWarning	nVIR detection	Free	A system start-up document that beeps if and when an nVIR attack occurs but does not prevent the infection.
Warning 1.1	Virus detection	Free	A system start-up document that checks your System file to see whether it is infected by a virus and warns you with a dialog box if it discovers an infection.

Chapter 23
Viruses and System Security

Keeping Up-to-Date on Viruses

There are several ways you can keep abreast of the latest news about Macintosh viruses:

▼ Join a local user group or a larger Mac user group such as BMUG (Berkeley Macintosh User Group) or BCS (Boston Computer Society).

▼ Read Macintosh magazines. In particular, *Macworld* publishes a list of recent viruses every month.

▼ Join a Macintosh electronic bulletin board. Many user groups operate excellent bulletin boards for their members.

▼ Subscribe to a commercial online service such as America Online, CompuServe, or GEnie. Join the Macintosh forums.

▼ Subscribe to the BITNET distribution lists VIRUS-L and INFO-MAC.

▼ Read the USENET news groups called "comp.sys.mac.announce" and "comp.virus."

▼ Read the postings in the AppleLink folder User Groups: User Group Resource Folder, Virus Information.

Summary

Viruses and other types of destructive computer software have become an increasingly serious problem in the computing world. In the Macintosh community, viruses continue to spread rapidly and widely and probably will continue to cause problems for some time.

A virus is a piece of software that attaches itself to other applications or files. Once you run an infected application, the virus quickly spreads to your system files and to other software. Viruses spread from one Mac to another through sharing and distributing infected software or infected disks.

Part VI
Expanding Your Mac's Horizons

In This Part

Chapter 24: Communications and On-line Services

Chapter 25: Networking

Chapter 26: Macintosh and PC Coexistence

Chapter 27: The Macintosh Community

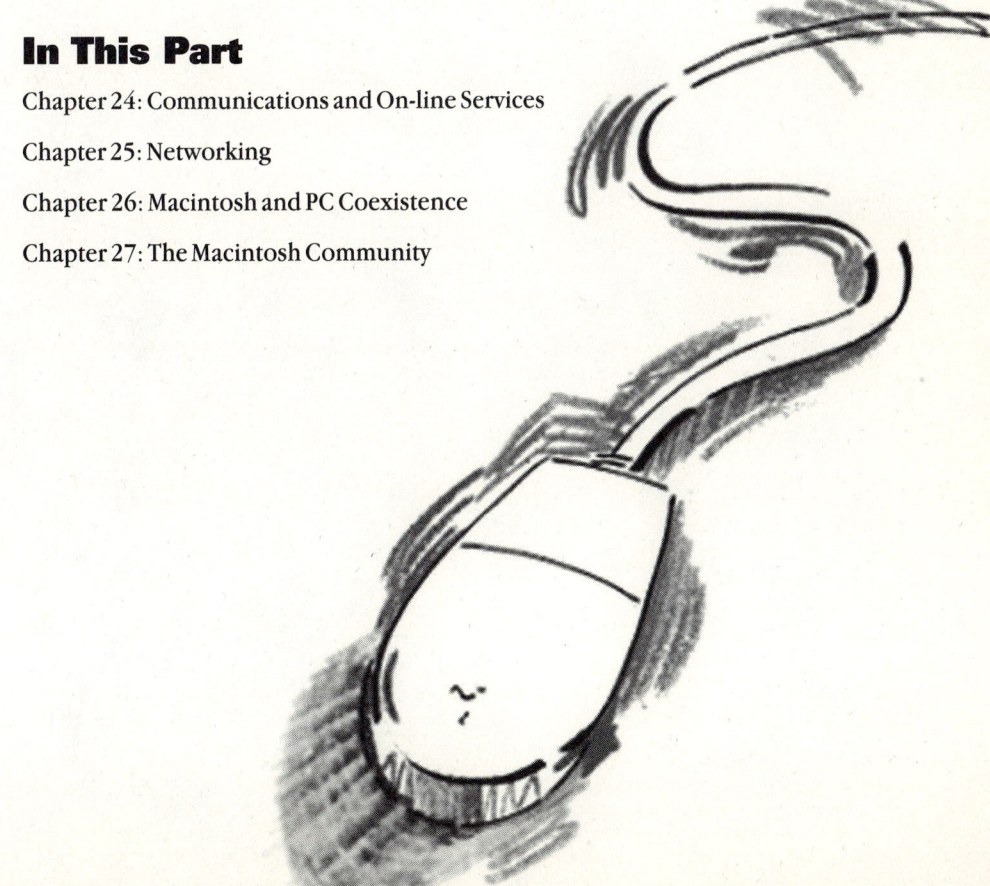

Chapter 24
Communications and Online Services

By itself, the Macintosh is a good productivity tool as well as a great toy for children of all ages. When you add a modem and plug the Mac into phone lines, you increase its usefulness 100 times or more. Now, instead of just

In This Chapter

- ▼ How modems work
- ▼ Using communications programs
- ▼ Choosing the right information services
- ▼ Uploading and downloading
- ▼ Using bulletin board systems

Part VI
Expanding Your Mac's Horizons

talking to itself, the Mac can talk to other computers, letting you share information with people across the world. You can do your banking and shopping online, manage your investments, research encyclopedias and specialized databases, work at home and retrieve needed files from the office, check the latest news and weather, chat with friends, or play a friendly game of poker. The possibilities are practically unlimited.

Modems: Turning Numbers into Noise

The box that makes communications possible is called a modem, which stands for *modulate-dem*odulate. You need one because computers "think" in a digital format; everything that appears on the screen is a combination of ones and zeros. The computer connected to yours thinks in exactly the same way, whether it is your friend's Mac, the office's IBM-compatible, or a switching network that supports information services such as CompuServe or Prodigy.

So why do you need a modem? There is a phone line between your computer and the computer you want to call, and therein lies the problem. When Alexander Graham Bell invented the telephone, he was not thinking in terms of transmitting computer data. He was looking for a way to transmit the human voice. Figure 24.1 shows the mechanics of the phone system.

Figure 24.1
The mechanics of a telephone system designed for transmitting the human voice.

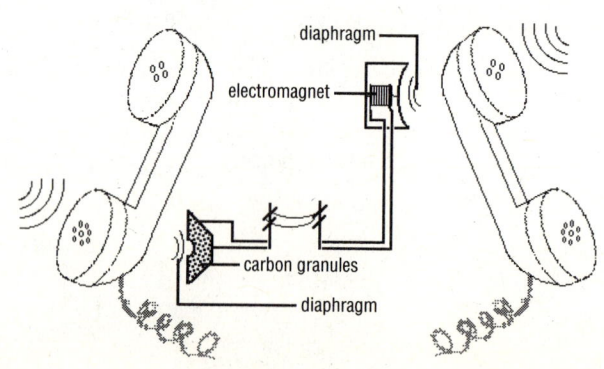

Telephones use a carbon microphone, which essentially is a drum that is filled with carbon granules and then electrified. When you talk into the microphone, a diaphragm (or drumhead) vibrates and compresses the carbon with each vibration. An electric current flows through the microphone. As carbon granules are compressed and released, their ability to resist the current flow fluctuates, and the current varies in strength as you speak. This varying current flows from your phone through the wires to a central telephone exchange, and then to the phone of the person you call. There the current enters a small speaker in the other phone's ear piece and goes into an electromagnet, and the variations cause the speaker diaphragm to vibrate in the same pattern. The listener hears your voice. There are amplifiers and filters in the circuit too, to keep the signal clean and retain all the minute variations in current as the signal is sent down the wire.

Complicated? Yes, but these *analog* signals, which the telephone system uses, are very effective. An analog signal is a kind of a "scribble" of different frequencies and harmonics, which is why on the phone one person sounds different from another. *Digital* signals from computers and other devices work differently. Figure 24.2 shows the difference. Digital signals are either there or they are not—on or off, one or zero. To send the digital signal from your computer to another computer, you must fool the telephone line into thinking the signal is an analog one.

Chapter 24
Communications and Online Services

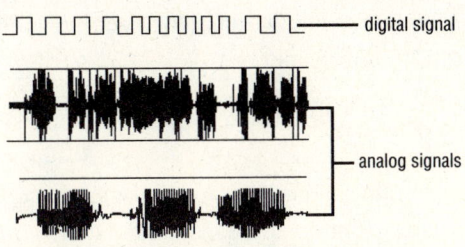

Figure 24.2
Digital and analog signals.

This is where your modem comes in. A modem changes, or modulates, the digital signal by adding voice-like frequencies to it. If you pick up the phone while the computers are talking to each other, you hear a sound resembling a continuous "Shhhhhhh" (some people say it sounds like hard rain falling on a tin roof). This noise is the sound of modulated data flowing back and forth. At the other end of the phone line, the signal passes through another modem and is *demodulated*. All signals except the ones and zeros are stripped away so that the other computer can understand your message.

899

Part VI
Expanding Your
Mac's Horizons

Soon, the way you send and receive information may change. Telephone companies are working on a new system called *Integrated Systems Digital Network*, or ISDN, which uses existing telephone lines to carry digital signals and much more. ISDN enables you to send computer data over a phone line while you talk to someone on the same line. Exactly how this works is far too complicated to explain here, but it is safe to say that ISDN someday will make your modem obsolete. Instead, you will need a *gateway*, which filters and boosts your computer's signal to match the phone company's needs.

Buying a Modem

There are many different kinds of modems on your dealer's shelf. Which one you buy depends on how you plan to use it. Speed is one factor that increases cost. Another is versatility. Many of the current generation of modems can send facsimile signals (faxes), and some can receive them as well. This capability can add to your productivity, if faxing is something you are likely to need. If you want a modem so you can play games online, you can save as much as a hundred dollars or more by not getting a fax/modem.

A Closer Look

What about speed? First, you need to understand what this term means. Speed is expressed in either *baud* or *bits per second* (bps). A bit is a single unit of binary information. Modem speeds refer to the number of bits of information that can be sent from one computer to another in a single second. Modem speeds can range from 300 to 57,600 or higher bps.

Baud rate often is confused with bit rate, but baud rate refers to the data's number of changes in *status* per second as it is sent across the phone line. A signal in a communications line varies in frequencies, voltage levels, and other factors many times per second, and a baud equals one of those changes. Therefore, a 300-baud modem changes status 300 times per second. The baud rate and bit rate are generally the same at low speeds, when the modem is sending one bit per baud. Usually, 300 bps equals 300 baud.

There are ways to send more or less than one bit per baud. Modems that are 1200 bps actually operate at 300 baud and send 4 bits per baud (4 x 300 = 1200 bps). The 2400 bps modems actually use a 600 baud rate to send 4 bits per baud, equaling 2400 bps. When you see modems advertised as 2400 baud or 9600 baud, they are really 2400 bps or 9600 bps. The practical upper

Chapter 24
Communications and Online Services

limit for acceptable phone line transmission appears to be 14,400 bps. At higher speeds, too many errors occur. Ultra-high speed communications require special phone lines or direct computer-to-computer hookups, which are far beyond most users' needs or abilities.

Which speed of modem you need actually depends on what you do with it. Some online services can support 9600 bps communications; most cannot. A 2400 bps modem is fine for talking to a service, and a 1200 bps modem may be adequate if you only call services or bulletin boards that don't charge by the minute. You still may find an old 300 baud modem for sale somewhere. Do not buy it. It's obsolete.

> **Note:** No matter which modem you buy, be sure it is *Hayes-compatible*. Virtually all modems available today use a communication shorthand called *Hayes commands* or *AT commands*, which have become the industry standard for dialing and connection. You need not buy a Hayes brand modem (although Hayes makes very good ones), just one that is compatible with the Hayes command set.

Most modern modems are *direct connect*. They plug into your phone line on one side and your computer on the other. You still may find *acoustic* modems on your dealer's shelf. These devices have a pair of rubber cups on top into which you place the telephone handset—a convenient device if you are at a telephone booth or hotel where you cannot plug in a direct modem. However, acoustic modems are not very reliable, because they are prone to picking up background noise along with the data. The computer cannot determine the difference between the report you try to send to the home office and the loudspeaker announcing the next flight to London.

Fax Modems

The introduction of the facsimile machine makes it possible to transmit printed documents by telephone almost instantly. Today, fax machines are virtually a necessity in most businesses; you even can fax your lunch order to the local deli. Because the fax machine operates in much the same way as a modem, it is logical to combine the two functions in one box, enabling you to send or receive a file as a fax directly from your Mac. There are many advantages to doing so: the recipient gets a much better looking document than one merely "copied" by a traditional fax machine, especially if you use

Part VI
Expanding Your Mac's Horizons

Don't get trapped into buying an internal fax modem if it will be your only such device. If you can't scan data into your computer, you can't fax it; if your data is already on the Mac, you can probably find some non-fax way to get it there. I tell my friends and clients: a fax modem should only be your second system—not your only one.

Dan Shafer

Figure 24.3
Ordering lunch by fax is easy.

TrueType or a Postscript font with ATM; you save the time and paper you would use in making a copy for the traditional fax machine; and confidential files are more likely to stay confidential if no paper copy is involved.

If you are going to use your modem for faxing, you have two options: send only or send/receive. Modems that can receive faxes cost a little more but are much more versatile. Among the features to look for are:

▼ **Background sending:** Enables you to do other work while your fax is sending.

▼ **Scheduled transmissions:** Enables you to set a timer to send the fax whenever you desire. (Send your long-distance faxes when the rates are lower!)

▼ **Group III compatibility:** Most fax machines send and receive at 9600 bps according to a specific set of protocols established by the CCITT, an international communications commission. These are called *Group III modems*, and your fax modem must be Group III–compatible if it is to communicate with others.

Sending a fax to another computer or fax machine is easy. Simply prepare your document and enter the phone number to which you want it sent. Figure 24.3 shows the Global Village Teleport's **Send dialog** box.

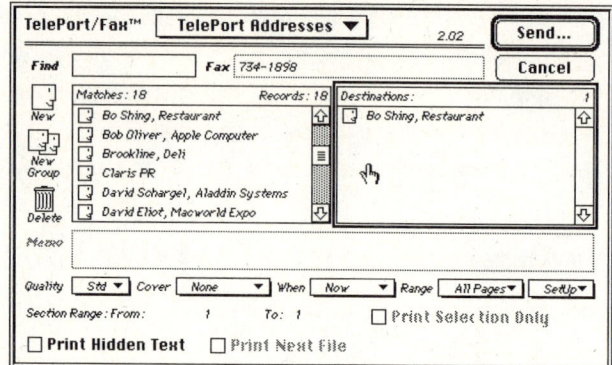

 Some print spoolers may conflict with the fax software. Check the manual to find out whether you need to disable the spooler to send faxes.

Adobe Type Manager's (ATM) current version works well with most fax software and makes the faxes look even better than if they were sent from printed copies. Fax software uses up to 200 dots per inch as an adequate resolution, a perfectly acceptable format for ATM. With ATM installed, the type on your faxed pages is nicely formed from outline masters of the typeface, so the receiver gets a "first generation" original rather than a "second generation" fax copy.

TrueType fonts introduced with System 7 also create outstanding-looking faxes because the type also is generated from original outlines of the typefaces.

Installing the Modem

Some people use their regular telephone line for both voice and modem calls. Others install a second line just for the computer. Either method works, although you may run into problems with others who want to make phone calls while you are online. (You cannot use the phone and the modem on the same line at the same time.) Modems interfere with answering machines, too, because you cannot receive calls while you are sending data. Picking up an extension phone while the computer is online causes noises that generate strange characters on your screen and may disconnect you. If you choose to use one phone line for all purposes, you may want to invest in *privacy switches*. These devices disable all other phones when one is in use and keep others from listening to your calls. They usually cost less than $10 each at electronics stores. You will need a separate switch for each phone you shut off, but adding switches is often less expensive than adding a second phone line.

WARNING! You should make all direct connections to telephone lines through standard plugs and jacks. If you do not have a modular phone (RJ-11 or RJ-14) jack near the computer, have the phone company or an electrician install one, or do it yourself. (After the wire passes through the telephone company interface, you can do anything you want to it in your home or office. However, Federal Communications Commission rules say that if the phone company thinks you are not following their specifications, they can cut off service.)

After you have the correct phone jack, hooking up a modem is simple. The modem has a power cord, a modular phone cord, and a cable to connect to the computer. Be sure the computer and modem are turned off before you

Chapter 24
Communications and Online Services

Part VI

Expanding Your Mac's Horizons

Figure 24.4

There are two types of modem connectors.

start plugging in cables and cords. You could damage your Mac by plugging in the modem while the computer is on. Plug the cable into the modem port, which looks like one of the two connectors shown in figure 24.4.

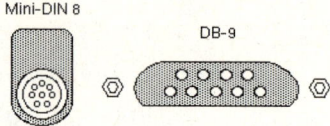

Earlier Macs use the DB-9, an oblong connector. Newer models use the Mini-DIN 8, a rounded one. The modem port is located next to the printer port. It has a telephone icon over it. Theoretically, you can use either port. But it is preferable to hook the modem to the modem port because the Mac gives this port priority when it checks for communications activity. Using the modem port helps keep your communications uninterrupted.

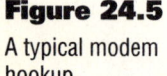 One modem brand, the TelePort from Global Village Communications, does not use the modem port. Instead, it plugs into the Mac's ADB (Apple Desktop Bus), just like your keyboard and mouse on Macs produced since the SE (SE, SE/30, Mac II, Portable, and so on). If you purchase one of these modems, follow the installation instructions that come with it.

Most modems use low voltage and a combination power cord/transformer like the type that comes with cassette recorders or video games. Just plug the cord/transformer into a regular outlet or your computer's filtered power supply. You also may plug a telephone into the phone jack on the back of the modem. Figure 24.5 shows a typical hookup.

Figure 24.5

A typical modem hookup.

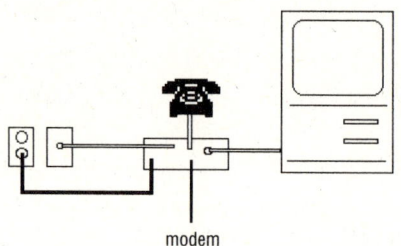

When the cords and cables are plugged in, turn on the computer and the modem. You should see a row of status lights on the front of the modem box. These help you keep track of the action. Table 23.1 shows the codes for the various lights and what they mean.

Table 23.1 Status lights

Code	Represents	What's Happening
MR	Modem Ready	Power is on
SD	Send Data	Transmitting
HS	High Speed	If modem has a choice of 1200/2400
OH	Off Hook	Computer is online
TR	Terminal Ready	Computer is in host mode
RD	Receive Data	Receiving
AA	Auto Answer	Computer in host mode, waiting for call
CD	Carrier Detect	Connecting to another computer
VM	Voice Mode (Only on fax/modems)	Ready to receive voice messages
FM	Fax Mode (Only on fax/modems)	Ready to receive or send fax messages

WARNING! There are many horror stories about lightning striking phone wires and burning out not only the modem, but the Mac connected to it. Be aware of the danger. Surge protectors for phone lines recently have become available in electronics and phone stores.

You probably already have a surge protector for your Mac and for such items as disk drives and printers. If at all possible, plug the modem power cord into it, too. But do not rely on it. If there is a thunderstorm and you get hit, electricity *can* arc across the contacts and do a great deal of damage. If you live in an area where thunderstorms are severe, especially if you are in a high spot or otherwise are likely to get hit, get in the habit of unplugging the system from the outlet when you shut down for any length of time. Unplug the phone connector, too. It is an inexpensive and effective protection.

Chapter 24
Communications and Online Services

Part VI
Expanding Your Mac's Horizons

Communications Programs

Before you place your first modem call, you need something else in addition to the modem and cable. You need a communications program to tell your Mac how to communicate with the modem. Data has to be put into a format the modem can accept, and that another computer can understand. The communications program, sometimes called a terminal program or terminal emulation program, is a set of instructions that tells the Mac how to call another computer and how to send the data.

To the phone company, your modem call is no different than any other phone call. The phone rings and another party answers. So as long as both computers use the same set of data-sending and receiving instructions, they can communicate. If not, it is the same as if they speak two different languages. When you place a modem call, the first thing you hear after the other computer answers is a carrier signal, a sort of two-toned whistle that means "I am answering. Who is calling?" Immediately, both computers begin a process called *handshaking*, verifying that they both speak the same language and use the same *protocols*. Protocols are simply the ground rules that determine how each side acknowledges the other.

Three critical protocol issues must be determined. The first is baud rate. Both computers must handle data at the same speed. When you call a commercial online service, you may find the service uses different telephone numbers for different speeds or possibly a modem that adjusts itself automatically to match whatever speed you use. If you call a friend or your office, you need to confer ahead of time to ensure both modems are set to the same baud rate.

The second issue is to decide how the computers will share the single line between them. The computer calls this sharing *duplex mode*. In theory, if you had two telephone lines and could talk on one and listen on the other simultaneously, you could handle twice as many conversations. Because your mind can manage only one line and one conversation at a time, you talk and then listen, and then you talk again. To your modem, this kind of transmission is called *half duplex*. In full duplex mode, the computer can send and receive, or "talk" and "listen," at the same time.

 If you cannot see what you type, switch to half duplex. If you find that every character you type turns into two characters, making the screen look lliikkee tthhiiss, switch to full duplex.

The third protocol issue concerns data format. This is similar to a grammar that determines the length of the "words" of data sent and how the words are organized. The Mac, and other computers, understand a special set of 8-bit characters known as ASCII.

There is a separate ASCII character for each letter, number, and symbol on the keyboard, plus a few characters for carriage returns, tabs, and other invisible characters. Some of these characters date back to the days of the teletype machine, which newspapers, radio, and TV stations relied on before the advent of the computer and fax machine. There were characters that rolled down the paper an extra line or rang a bell to let the operator know that a big story was coming. You can use the bell character to make your friend's computer "beep." Just press Option G (but try not to do it too often, lest you lose a friend).

When the Mac sends data back and forth to its disk drive or memory, the 8 bits for each character go in parallel. They all arrive at the same time. But when the Mac is sending information to a modem (or to a printer, which thinks in a similar *serial* way), it must send the bits in "single file." To show the computer at the other end of the phone line where one 8-bit "word" ends and the next begins, the communications program adds extra bits, called start or stop bits. Most programs and most of the computers you communicate with use N-8-1. This means no parity (*parity* is a virtually obsolete system of error checking), an 8-bit word, and one stop bit. Figure 24.6 shows a typical Communications Settings dialog box. This example is taken from MicroPhone II, but other programs use a similar system. You simply click on the appropriate settings, and the Mac does the rest of the work.

Chapter 24
Communications and Online Services

Figure 24.6

Click the appropriate button for 2400 bps, N-8-1.

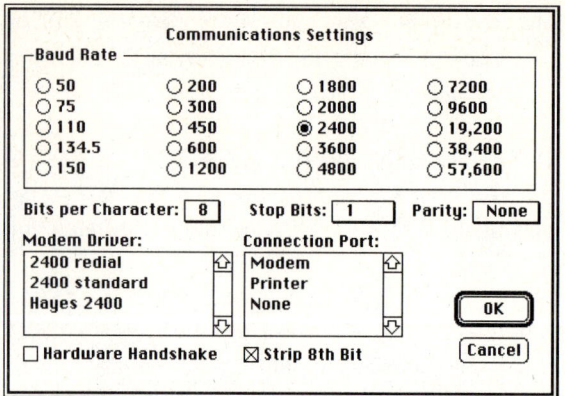

Finding the Right Terminal Program

When you buy a modem, it may come with a terminal program. If not, or if you dislike the one that came with it, you have to go shopping. What you look for depends on what you plan to do with the modem. Some online services, notably Prodigy and America Online, supply their own front-end communications program. Prodigy's program, however, will only call Prodigy. It will not talk to CompuServe or to your neighbor's Mac, any more than you could walk through the doorway of the Prodigy building in White Plains, New York, and expect to find yourself in CompuServe's offices in Columbus, Ohio.

Some terminal programs, such as Microphone II, use icons to point and click on, and dialog boxes to let you know what is happening (see figure 24.7). In this example, the user has placed a call to Delphi, an online service, to see what is happening in the Macintosh forum.

Other terminal programs (White Knight is probably the best known) are text-based. Although there are a few icons, you mainly use menus to select your options and steer yourself through an online session by typing the commands for what you want to do. It is simple and direct. Figure 24.8 shows how White Knight handles the same call placed in the preceding example. Simply type `gr mac`.

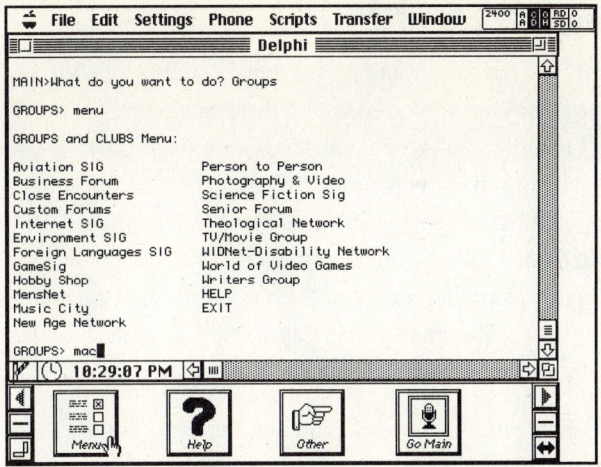

Figure 24.7
You can use Microphone II to call any text-based service or BBS.

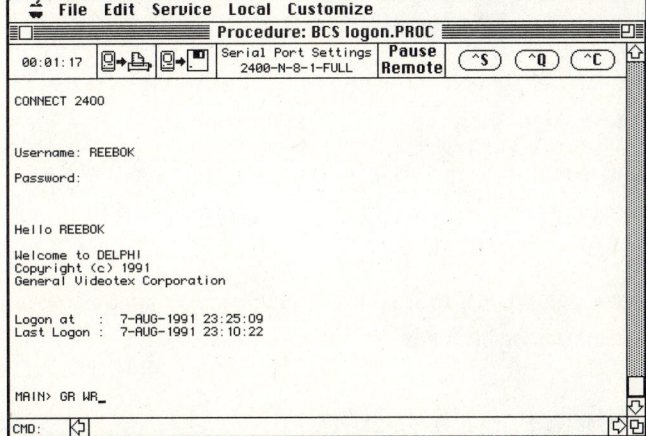

Figure 24.8
White Knight relies on menus and typing to call Delphi.

Other programs also are available. The simplest programs of all are shareware. There are dozens of shareware telecommunication programs. Bill Bond's FreeTerm, available from most of the user groups and BBSs, is one of the best, and as its name suggests, it is free. Although it does not have the special features that White Knight or Microphone have, it works very well and does XMODEM file transfers (see the section, "Downloading and Uploading," later in this chapter). ZTerm is another deservedly popular shareware terminal program.

Placing a Call

WARNING! If you have call waiting, you should disable it before you try to go online. While you are on the modem, the beep signal for incoming calls is enough to confuse the modem and make it hang up. If yours is a tone phone that dials by beeping in different pitches, you need to enter *70 in front of any number you call. If your phone is the old-fashioned rotary kind that makes clicks instead of beeps, you need to add 1170 in front of the number. When call waiting is shut off, your callers hear a busy signal rather than a ring. Call waiting turns itself back on automatically as soon as you hang up.

No matter which terminal program you use, there are four steps in communicating by modem:

1. Select the settings. Tell your computer what protocols to use and how to display whatever it receives.

2. Place the call. Remember to disable call waiting if necessary. Use whatever identification and passwords are needed.

3. Transfer information. This includes reading and sending E-mail (electronic mail), real-time chatting, playing games, transferring files, or whatever you decide to do.

4. Disconnect. When you are through, you need to sign off and tell the modem to hang up the phone and reset itself.

Determining the Settings

To select the modem settings, you need to know what protocol the *host* computer (the one that is receiving the call) uses. If you call a commercial service and are not sure what settings to use, try N-8-1. If you call a friend, you may want to use these settings anyway. They are relatively standard and easy to remember. You also want to set up your own Mac to display the data in the most convenient format. Figure 24.9 shows White Knight's Setup window. Each item has a pop-up menu that lists possible choices.

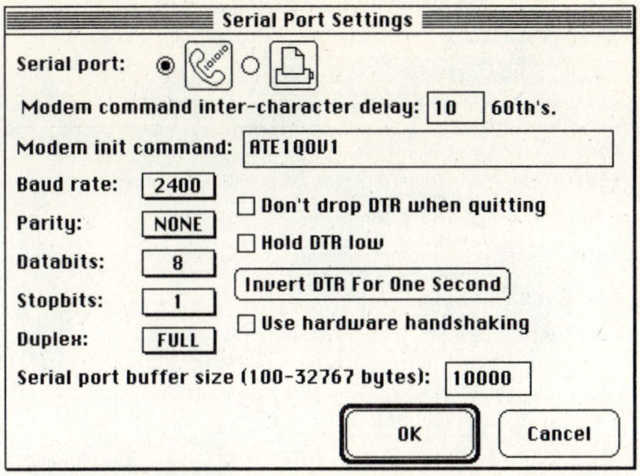

Figure 24.9
Use White Knight's Setup window to set protocols.

After you tell the computer how to send data, you need to tell it how to receive. This is called *terminal emulation* because it teaches the Mac how to emulate a teletype or video terminal. Teletype (TTY) sometimes is referred to as a *dumb terminal*. It is the most basic, and least versatile, mode of telecommunications. The three video terminal (VT) modes—VT 52, VT 100, and VT102—represent three different terminals manufactured by Digital Equipment Corporation (DEC).

DEC's terminals have become the standards for compatibility. If you call an online service, you may be able to use one of the VT modes. (VT100 and VT 102 also are called ANSI-compatible on some systems.) If you can use one, it may enable you to see graphics on some bulletin boards and use the arrow keys to move around the screen. If these features are not important to you or if the service you call does not support VT modes, stick with TTY. If you call another individual computer, always use TTY; it is the lowest common denominator for communicating.

You also can set the number of characters per line. Some programs let you change the font and point size of the display type to make it easier to read. Some even let you add color on the screen if you use a color Mac. Figure 24.10 shows some of Microphone's options.

Figure 24.10
Microphone lets you format the display type for easier reading.

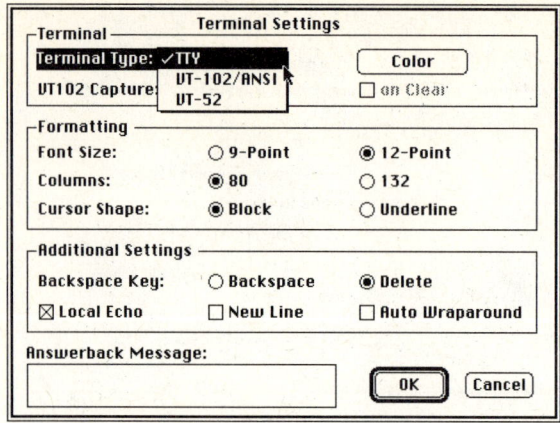

Getting Connected

Earlier in this chapter you read about buying Hayes-compatible modems. The Hayes command set, also called AT commands, is a set of three- and four-letter commands that tell the modem to perform various tasks. AT, which stands for Attention, precedes all other commands. ATDT 5551212 means Attention, Dial using Tones 555-1212. ATDP tells the modem to dial using pulses.

Most modems initialize themselves automatically when you activate them. Initializing restores the modem to its default settings, which is necessary whenever you initiate a call. If you need to reinitialize, the AT command is ATZ. Using this command instead of clicking the power switch saves wear and tear on the modem. ATH means Hang up. There are other AT commands, but these are the ones you are most likely to use; read your manual for more.

If you call a text-based service such as GEnie or Delphi, you will use your terminal program to log in, rather than a front-end program like Prodigy's. The following is a script from a call to GEnie, with comments:

```
AT                    (Attention)
OK                    (OK, Modem is listening)
ATE1Q0V1              (Attention, Echo characters, Return result
                       codes, Answer in words, not numbers)
OK                    (Modem is initialized)
ATDT8683269           (Attention, dial tone 8683269)
```

Chapter 24
Communications and Online Services

```
CONNECT 2400                    (Connected at 2400 bps)
Enter U#                        (Enter user ID #)
XVY61661,****
              ** Thank you for choosing GEnie **
                 The Consumer Information Service
                       from General Electric
                        Copyright (C), 1993
                GEnie Logon at: 18:56 EDT on: 930731
                Last Access at: 14:56 EDT on: 930731
```

You will not need to type all these numbers and command sets each time you go online. Most terminal programs let you set up *procedures* to do the work for you. Enter the settings, the phone number, and your user ID once and then save this data as a procedure to call GEnie. Then, the next time you want to get into the GEnie system, you simply click the GEnie icon and let the Mac place the call for you. White Knight offers this "watch me and learn" feature as well as an elaborate scripting language for procedure writing. Microphone II has a similar system but also comes with prewritten procedures for all the major online services. You need to add only the local access number.

The log-on procedure is even easier if you use the special software provided by services such as America Online. When you first copy the program onto your hard disk or run from the floppy, you enter the numbers to call and the speed. Figure 24.11 shows the **Modem & Network Configurations** dialog box. You reach this box by selecting **Customize** from the **Goto** menu and choosing **Network Setu**p.

After you enter these settings, you can forget about them. You may never need to open the dialog box again, unless you need to use a different access number. To log on, simply click the **Sign On** button on America Online's opening screen, as shown in figure 24.12.

After a few seconds, the modem beeps, and a series of dialog boxes tell you what is happening. Eventually, you need to type in your password. When it is verified, an opening screen message, perhaps listing the day's top news story or a new feature, appears, and a cheerful voice says, "Welcome!" and possibly, "You've got mail!"

Figure 24.11

Select **Customize** from the **Go To** menu and choose **Network Setup** to reach America Online's **Modem & Network Configurations** dialog box.

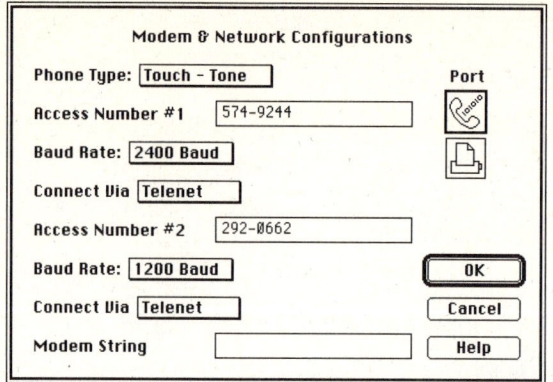

Figure 24.12

Logging into America Online is as simple as clicking a button.

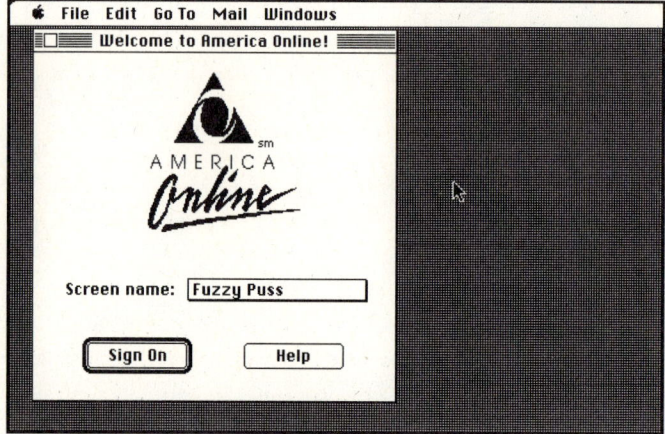

Protect Your Password!

Online services and many bulletin boards require passwords to prevent unauthorized entry. Never reveal your password to anyone. Services like CompuServe and America Online, which charge by the hour, hold you responsible for any online charges incurred. If you let your friend borrow your password to look up something in the online encyclopedia, and he then chats for three hours on the CB Simulator or spends the whole day downloading games, you are responsible.

Services with online shopping malls or airline ticketing use your credit card numbers to make charges to your account. This means that anyone using your password can run up hundreds of dollars in charges for everything from computer books to Mickey Mouse watches to trips to Club Med. Giving away

Chapter 24
Communications and Online Services

your password is more dangerous than giving away your checkbook. The computer does not have to match your signature.

On the other hand, be sure you choose a password you can remember (but not one somebody else could guess). Because of the security issues involved, if you forget your password the service positively will *not* tell you what it is. You have to open a new account.

Online Work and Play

After you go online with most services, there are so many things to do that it is easy to get distracted and forget why you dialed. However, chasing down items can get expensive if you use a service that charges by the hour. White Knight keeps a running total of your online minutes and connect fees so you can stick to your budget. Microphone II is not quite as helpful but does keep track of time for you.

Every service and BBS has an index to its various departments. You may automatically see an index icon when you enter, or you may need to type top to get there. It is a good idea to decide ahead of time what you want to do. Browsing is fun too, but save it for late-night hours when connect charges are lower or for using up any leftover "minimum" connect time. (Many users of Delphi's 20-hours-per month Advantage plan spend most of their hours on the very last day.)

> **Note** If you want to pick up your online mail as economically as possible, don't read it online. Just copy it, using the appropriate system commands, and quit. Then read the mail off-line, compose your answers, and go back online long enough to send your responses (see the section, "Mail," later in this chapter).

Saying Good-bye

Because many services charge by the minute, make sure you actually sign off. Disconnecting appears as a menu item in some programs. Text-based services, such as GEnie, Delphi, and most BBSs, ask you to type Exit or Bye when you want to log off. Sometimes, the system you are logged onto has problems. The screen may appear to freeze completely, or you may get strings of garbage characters for no reason. Generally, this is a sign you have been disconnected, but you cannot be sure. Typing ATH, the command to

Part VI
Expanding Your Mac's Horizons

What's with the emphasis on commercial services? Geez, Prodigy is the online version of a commercial interruption! Telecom and the Internet go together like a Mac and a SCSI drive. The Internet, with, millions of people communicating for next to nothing, thousands of discussions, and free software archives, is the network for all of us. It's the model of an egalitarian Information Age. Get on the net, and when you do, send me some mail. I'll send you my most recent list of cool Internet sites and resources. My address is coyote@well.sf.ca.us.

Mitch Ratcliffe

To get your Mac on the Internet, you need a modem, software, a connection site, and advice. The <u>Internet Starter Kit for Macintosh</u>, by Adam Engst and published by Hayden Books, supplies everything except the modem.
—Editor

hang up the phone, may restore your screen to its normal appearance. If all else fails, turn the modem off and on again to reinitialize it. Doing so will automatically disconnect you.

Choosing a Service

When you choose an online service for your own use, you should consider at least three different factors: cost, ease of use, and features offered. These are the most logical criteria, although you might place different levels of importance on each factor. The cost to use some services can be greater than you think. A sports fan who reads CompuServe's Associated Press Sports Wire is charged a $15 per hour tab over and above the $12.50 per hour for 2400 bps service.

Ease of use is especially important on the high-priced services. Getting lost in library-limbo can be both expensive and frustrating. Most services have essentially the same features, although some charge extra for them. Others may have a less friendly interface to take you into the feature you want. It is often only a guess as to which service best meets your needs. Ask your friends who subscribe to an online service why they chose their service and what they like and dislike about it. Most new modems and communications software packages come with trial offers from one or more of the services.

You may have other reasons for choosing a particular service. Perhaps family or friends in other parts of the country belong to a particular service. You could, as many people do, use the service to pass messages to a child away at college or chat with a far-away friend. When you own the equipment, telecommunication costs much less than a long-distance call to communicate the same information, and you are more likely to leave a daily E-mail message than to call or write a letter that often.

Mail

It is important to consider the telecommunication services' mail possibilities. On virtually any commercial service, you can send electronic mail (E-mail) to anyone else on that same service. CompuServe, Delphi, and America Online also offer interconnections with Internet. Many services, including MCI mail and CompuServe let you send international Telex and TWX messages and faxes. Prodigy sets a limit for the number of mail messages you can send privately to fellow users (30 free per month), although you can pay for extra letters and post as many public announcements as you want (subject to Prodigy's rules).

Delphi's mail options enable you to send faxes and telexes (including MCI Mail) and arrange to translate your message into any of more than 100 foreign languages—for a price, of course. Delphi also offers EasyLink, a public network E-mail service AT&T runs for U.S. and United Kingdom subscribers. GEnie, as of this writing, sends mail only within its own system, but it also lets you upload a file as mail (see the section, "Downloading and Uploading," later in this chapter). America Online and CompuServe let you attach files to your letters by clicking the appropriate icon. Figure 24.13 shows how to send mail on America Online. Additionally, America Online and MCI mail will print your letter and send it as paper mail in a #10 envelope to any U.S. or Canadian postal address for a small fee.

Chapter 24
Communications and Online Services

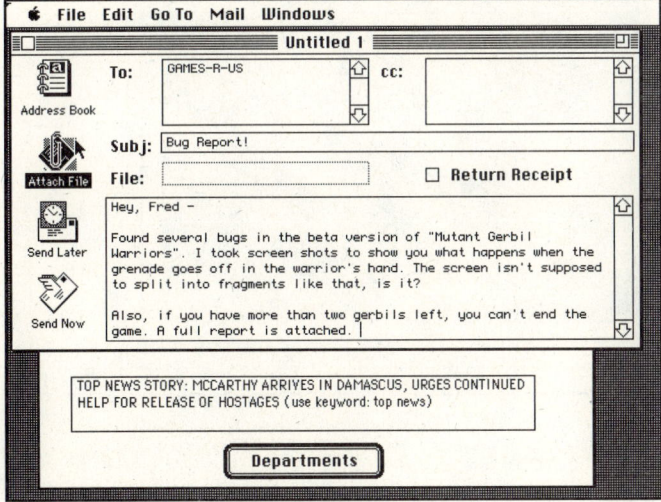

Figure 24.13
America Online enables you to attach a file by clicking the icon and uploading it.

And Now the News...

Every online service offers some version of the latest news and weather. Prodigy writes its own in a journalistic style that appeals to *USA Today* readers. CompuServe offers AP Online as a basic service, with hourly updates plus in-depth reports on national and world news, science, entertainment, sports, business, and more. Executive options give you more news sources, and a clipping service which will watch for and collect stories with keywords you designate, so you can retrieve them to read at your convenience. CompuServe has the most comprehensive weather reports, including aviation and marine forecasts where available.

Delphi gives you a choice of UPI's Newsbriefs capsule summary or in-depth reports from UPI, plus Accu-weather forecasts, financial news, the Reuters news service, Cineman's Movie News and Reviews (also available on some of the other services), and the UPI sports wire. America Online has selected stories from UPI, as well as from *USA Today* and an assortment of financial and technology news services. Prodigy, America Online, and CompuServe all provide weather maps; there are maps for expected daily highs and lows, frontal activity, and predictions for the following day. Figure 24.14 shows a map copied from CompuServe and displayed through CompuServe's Information Manager program.

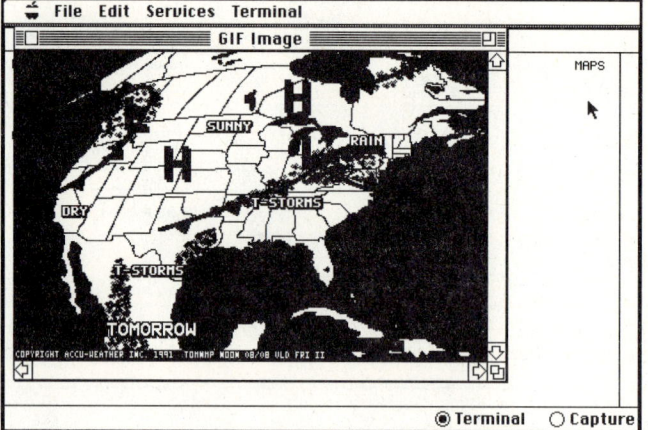

Figure 24.14
This weather map can be viewed online or saved and printed in color.

Going Places?

All the services provide travel information. You can check city and country profiles through MetroLine City Search and WorldLine Country Search or Adventure Atlas. After you choose a destination, you can directly book airline flights, rental cars, and hotel rooms online. If you have enough lead time, the airline tickets are mailed to you. Otherwise, you can pick them up through your local travel agent. If you charge tickets, you need to provide the usual credit card information. Most services also have a forum where travelers can post questions and get answers from others who have been to your destination.

Chapter 24
Communications and Online Services

A Closer Look Prodigy's travel board is exceptionally active. You can get rapid responses from Prodigy members to questions your travel agent may not be able to answer. A helpful Disney employee even posts up-to-the-minute reports on Walt Disney World events and hours.

Most services offer both the *Official Airline Guide* (OAG) and EAASY SABRE. The latter is an American Airlines and Sabre (a Travel Agency Information network) service. You do not need to be a travel agent to use either service. You do, however, need to understand how the flight schedule is arranged. You are asked to enter the following:

▼ Departure city (where you are departing)

▼ Destination (where you are going)

▼ Date of departure

▼ Time of departure (earliest time you are able to leave)

▼ Number of seats needed

You can spell out the names of the cities or use the three-letter airport codes, if you know them. If more than one city has the same name, you are given a list of the possibilities and asked to specify which (that is, Portland, Maine or Portland, Oregon).

Flights are listed by arrival time. If two or more flights arrive at the same time, the one with the shortest flying time is listed first. Figure 24.15 shows a typical flight schedule. (Because the service acts as a gateway to connect you to EAASY SABRE or OAG, the actual listings are the same, no matter where you access them.) The listing also shows the type of aircraft used on the route, the meal service (if any), the number of stops, and the airline's on-time rating. The number indicates the percentage of flights that arrive on time for a particular flight number. A 9, for example, means that flight PA527 arrives on time 90 percent of the time.

To book a flight or get ticket prices, enter the flight's line number. You then must determine which class is which, according to the string of letters: *F*, *Y*, *M*, *B*, *Q*, and so on. Most travelers want the lowest possible fares. EAASY SABRE makes it easy by adding a L.O.W. (Lowest One Way) fare classification.

Figure 24.15

Travelers can choose the most convenient flight through Delphi.

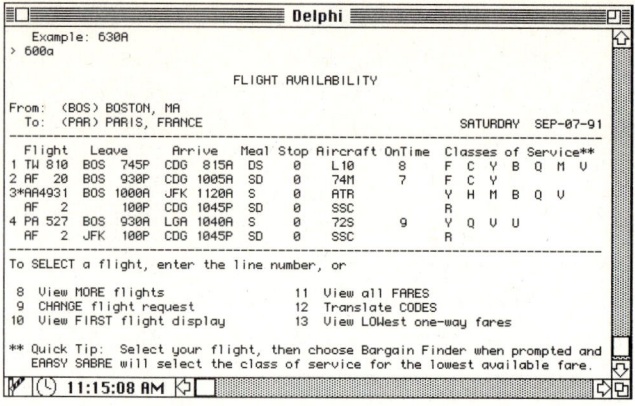

Going Shopping

If you hate crowded stores, electronic shopping might be the perfect solution. You can buy almost anything online from coffee beans to computers. Every service has some form of electronic shopping, but Prodigy's shopping services are probably the most comprehensive. Because Prodigy is jointly owned by IBM and Sears, you can be sure it knows merchandising!

If you go into Prodigy specifically to shop, you will find several stores listed on the Opening Highlights screen, or you can use the Jump command to get to a specific store or into the shopping finder. Once you are there, you see two dozen categories, including apparel, auto, computing, electronics, housewares, and so on, just like an actual department store. Selecting any one category gives you a list of merchants, and selecting a merchant gives you still more lists of things to buy. Figure 24.16 shows your gateway to a Prodigy shopping spree.

Figure 24.16

Click number 7 to begin your shopping spree.

If you read bulletin board messages, you will discover a string of advertisements across the lower third of the screen. When something catches your eye, click your mouse to get more information, and then select Zip from the Jump commands to return to what you were doing. Prodigy's merchants selection includes the Disney store for all sorts of Mickey and Minnie fashions and memorabilia, book stores, florists, gift shops, Sears, J.C. Penney, and Spiegel.

CompuServe's Electronic Mall has something for everyone, with a listing of 100 merchants including Brooks Brothers, Hammacher Schlemmer, computer companies with software and hardware for all kinds of computers, book and record stores, foods for you and your pet, flowers, Godiva chocolates, and catalog shopping with J.C. Penney. GEnie's shopping center includes Sears and JC Penney, too, plus a wide assortment of smaller retailers. Figure 24.17 shows a typical catalog item from the J.C. Penney collection on GEnie. Someday soon, it probably will be able to include a picture of the merchandise as well. (You have to know your size, though. Nobody has invented electronic fitting rooms.)

Chapter 24
Communications and Online Services

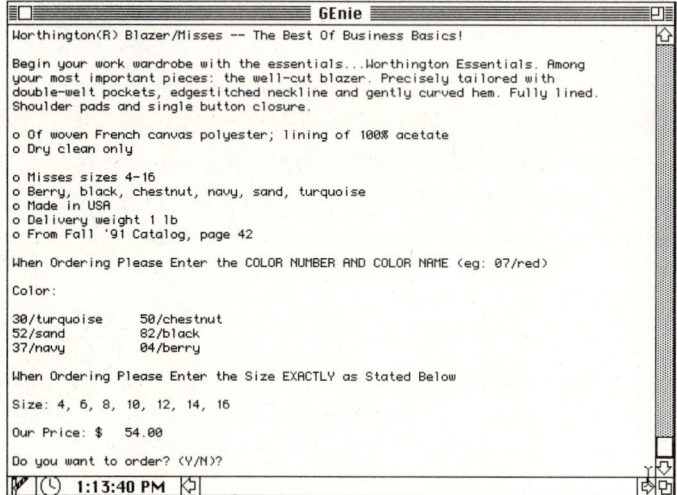

Figure 24.17
Online shopping through GEnie enables you to browse through J.C. Penney.

Comp-u-store, available on Delphi and America Online, offers thousands of computer and general merchandise items at a discount. Because these boards are merely a gateway to the store, the interface becomes somewhat clunky. Still, you can find long lists of brand-name goods at good prices. Delphi's Merchant's Row also includes a gateway to the Boston Computer Exchange, a listing and brokerage service for used Macintosh equipment. Information is updated weekly.

Part VI
Expanding Your
Mac's Horizons

Money, Money...

You can handle many financial services by modem. The serious investor will find Dow Jones News/Retrieval (DJN/R) a worthwhile investment. It includes access to corporate profiles, current and past stock quotes, earnings reports and forecasts, plus online access to the *Wall Street Journal*, *Business Week*, *Forbes*, and the *Washington Post*. Other services provide some, if not all, of this information. GEnie offers access to DJN/R plus the Schwab Discount Brokerage service. After you find out how your stocks are doing, you can buy or sell through Schwab.

Prodigy lets you handle all your banking electronically through any of its member banks. You can borrow money, pay bills, and buy Certificates of Deposit and insurance. Banking online beats standing in line.

Delphi does not support electronic banking but does offer financial information, including commodity prices and money market rates for the top-30 funds. CompuServe has a long list of financial information services and three different brokerage firms but offers no banking. America Online offers stock quotes and business news as well as an investment forum, as well as earnings reports and corporate profiles. All the services have reasonably good reference departments, including the *Grolier Encyclopedia* or *American Academic Encyclopedia*. Delphi now offers the Dictionary of Cultural Literacy, a compendium of useful information on the arts and sciences. CompuServe offers a selection of databases including medical, legal, and even Who's Who. Prodigy, CompuServe and America Online all offer *Consumer Reports*, which can be read online or downloaded.

Forums for All Interests

No matter what your hobby, favorite sport, or other interest, you can find people online who share it. There are forums, or special interest groups, on every possible aspect of computing, of course. There are also forums on genealogy, wine-tasting, scuba, travel, parenting, auto mechanics, pet care, and much more. Every service has some kind of forum system. Members join to share ideas, give and receive information, attend online lectures or conferences, use the forum's private libraries of information and programs, and find friends with similar interests. There is no cost or obligation to join a forum beyond whatever the system charges for connect time.

Chapter 24
Communications and Online Services

On all services except Prodigy, forums have three sections, which you can think of as three different rooms. There is a message room, a library, and a conference area. The message board is precisely that. Consider it a large room lined with bulletin boards and hundreds of messages posted on the walls. Messages follow "threads," meaning there is some logical sequence. Even though a message may be addressed to one person, it is considered public, and anyone is allowed to respond.

Different services handle message boards in different ways. America Online has the easiest system. Here, messages are kept in folders. To start a new thread, you create a folder describing the subject and place your note in it. Others add their messages to the folder, and the reader can read straight through or browse. Figure 24.18 shows one of America Online's message boards.

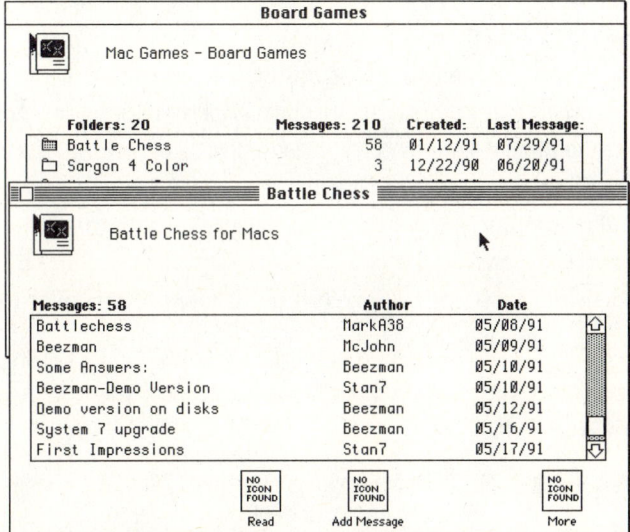

Figure 24.18
Finding a message is easy on America Online.

CompuServe gives you a map right on the message. Click on the map to move to replies or to the next related message. Delphi sequentially numbers messages but lets you type "follow" to jump to the next note on a particular thread. You easily can get lost in GEnie's maze of message boards. If this happens to you, type *P* to return to the previous menu and *top* to return to the opening screen.

Part VI
Expanding Your Mac's Horizons

Prodigy's bulletin boards list messages by topic or let you search by the listed ID number of the member who posted them or the member to whom they are addressed. As previously mentioned, Prodigy does not offer conferences or chat, nor does it presently maintain libraries of useful programs and information as the other services do (at least, not for Mac users. They now offer downloadable software for PCs using DOS or Windows).

Sysops (short for *system op*erators), hosts, managers, or forum leaders host forums. They answer questions for newcomers and provide help with problems. They also keep track of what the forum members add to the library, moderate discussions, sometimes help keep message boards tasteful, and generally watch over the forum.

Censorship?

On most services, your messages appear as soon as you post them. But not on Prodigy. One of the things that sets it apart from other online services is that its sysops review messages before posting and return any message to your mailbox that does not meet their standards. Prodigy's censors are called *Catos*, after the Roman statesman Marcus Porcius Cato, the original censor, whose stated mission as arbiter of Roman manners and morals was to suppress all innovations in thought and behavior. Many disgruntled Prodigy users claim that the present-day Catos do precisely the same thing. These users make these claims on an apparently uncensored section of board called About Prodigy, which may be one of the liveliest areas online.

Can We Talk?

One of the main reasons many people join an online service is to take advantage of real-time conferences. Your keyboard can connect you to old and new friends all over the world. All the major services except Prodigy offer some form of real-time chat. CompuServe calls its service CB Simulator and offers 72 channels—some dedicated to particular interests or lifestyles, some for beginners, and some open to all. Many newcomers find the multiple conversations going on at once the most confusing aspect of group chats that occur on the CB channels. If you can manage to find a small group or think of it as a particularly lively family sitting around the kitchen table interrupting

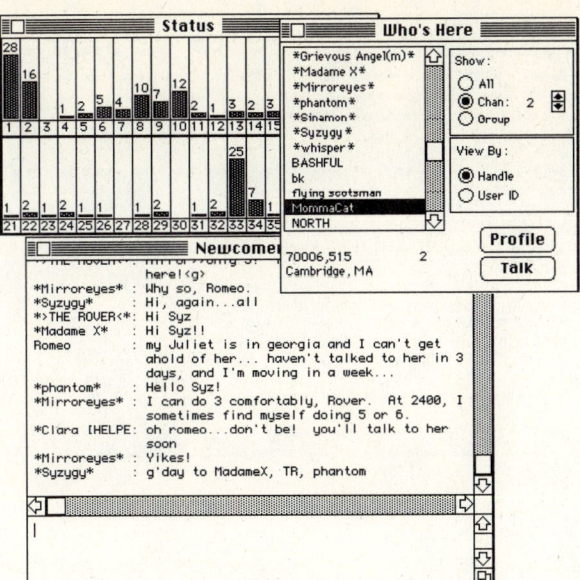

Figure 24.19
Chatting on CompuServe can be confusing at first.

each other, you will catch on to CB Simulator quickly. Figure 24.19 shows a conversation in progress on CompuServe. In the background, you also can see the channel selector and Who's Here screens.

Delphi has a main conference area, as well as conference rooms that are accessible through forums. When you enter Delphi's conference room, typing /*who* gives you a list of conference groups underway. You can join any that the participants have not declared private, or you can page an online friend and start your own group.

There are also "special interest" conference rooms within individual forums. These rooms are available at any time, and many have scheduled conferences at specific hours, sometimes with guest speakers or a moderated discussion on a particular topic. General interest conferences usually are announced on the opening screen, so be sure to look at it when you log on. As an example of the kind of things you are likely to find, one night GEnie hosted a 90-minute conference with writer/comedian/musician Steve Allen. Figure 24.20 shows a short excerpt from that conference. Meanwhile, on Delphi, 40 players gathered for a trivia game, and America Online offered a game of its own as well as several different Macintosh-user conferences. No matter what your interest, there is always something to do or someone to talk to online.

Figure 24.20

GEnie sponsored a conference with Steve Allen for subscribers.

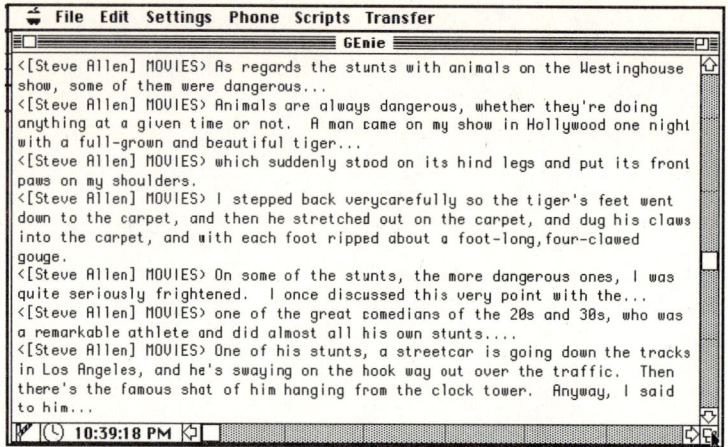

Online Etiquette

The best way to learn how to chat online is to plunge right into a discussion. CompuServe and GEnie set aside chat channels for newcomers, with hosts to answer your questions and help you get started. America Online's Lobby and La Pub areas are particularly attuned to welcoming new members, and you find a friendly group of people on all the services. There are a few things to be aware of, however.

The rules of conference etiquette demand that you ignore spelling mistakes. They are inevitable, anyway. If you discover something totally unreadable, type er... and add whatever you want to say. Do not leave the CAPS LOCK on. It is the equivalent of yelling through a bullhorn and is considered extremely rude. Expect a round of *Hi*, {{{*Hugs*}}}, and so on when anyone enters the group. "Lurking," being present but silent, generally is frowned upon.

Conference Shorthand

One of the most baffling things to a conference newcomer is the abbreviations, slang words, and strange symbols used in chatting. The following list explains the more common ones:

AFK	Away From Keys
BAK	Back At Keys
BRB	Be Right Back
BTW	By The Way
GA	Go Ahead
GMTA	Great Minds Think Alike

Chapter 24
Communications and Online Services

```
Hi, Re-Hi            Hello again
IMHO (or IMO)        In My (Humble) Opinion
LOL                  Laughing Out Loud
OTF (or ROTF)        (Rolling) On the Floor (Laughing)
OTOH                 On the Other Hand
TTFN                 TaTa For Now (CU L8R)
<grin>               Exactly what it says, sometimes written <g>
{{{hugs}}}           The curly brackets represent arms, perhaps?
```

And then there are ASCII graphics, or smileys. (You have to look at most of these sideways.)

```
:-)                  Smiley
B-)                  Smiley wearing glasses
:-(                  Sad
K:-)                 Wearing propeller beanie
=:O                  Surprised
:-P'                 Nyahh, nyahh
{:-)                 Wearing toupee
;-)                  Winkie
[_])                 Beer Mug
@——>—>———            A rose for milady
```

There are dozens more symbols, of course, and new ones are being invented all the time. Probably the most complete list to date is in the Smiley Face DA, available in America Online's Mac Utilities library.

Some services set aside conference rooms for specific groups. "Adult" groups expect privacy but welcome qualified members. There is a fair amount of "hot chat" on some services. Generally speaking, the participants' handles, or screen names, or the title of the group indicates the topic, but it is not wise to let the kids use your account without supervision—computing could be more educational than you intend. Prodigy's bulletin boards, at least, have a G-rating.

Come Play with Me...

Playing games against the computer is fun, but it is even more fun to play games against real, live opponents. All the online services, including Prodigy, have some form of interactive gaming. Prodigy's games include several just for kids and a few for adults. One of the best games on Prodigy is Carmen Sandiego, an online version of Brøderbund's popular geography game.

Part VI
Expanding Your Mac's Horizons

Adults may enjoy Fortuneteller, a computerized tarot reading that has nice graphics, as shown in figure 24.21.

Figure 24.21
Prodigy's Fortuneteller knows what your future holds.

America Online's interactive games take place either in the conference areas or in the Center Stage auditorium. Game topics range from movie trivia to "Let's Make a Deal." The game host chooses participants from the audience, and winners receive free hours of connect time. America Online also has a large roster of play-by-mail games: players send in moves daily or weekly by E-mail, and a games master moderates. Some of these games have extra charges added on to the regular connect fees. Others simply involve a group of people agreeing to play a game such as Monopoly or Diplomacy through bulletin board, E-mail, or real-time conference. The Phantasy Guild is home base for Dungeons and Dragons, Myth and Magic, and similar fantasy role-playing games. Online games occur frequently, and a gaming schedule is posted. There are also forums and game playing aids libraries to download.

GEnie has a list of adventure games as well as brand new multiplayer games. You can access any of them by going to the games section. GEnie also maintains a huge joke library and a bulletin board of current funny stuff for your downloading pleasure. New additions are welcome. A separate "adult" section requires special access privileges for which you must apply in advance and pass a short "exam" with questions on the order of "Do you remember the '60s?"

Trivia games on Delphi are real-time conferences with as many as 40 or more players competing to win a T-shirt or Delphi coffee mug. There are five rounds of questions with multiple-choice answers. The chatter that goes on between questions in Trivia Quest, or TQ, provides much of the fun. Games currently are played three times a week, and a TQ Anytime version allows for practice sessions between the games. Delphi also offers online poker with your choice of five games: straight poker, 5- and 7-card stud, draw poker, and Texas Hold'em. Play against others or against robot players, or enter the Thursday night poker tournament and win prizes. Figure 24.22 shows a poker game in progress.

```
                              Delphi
3 MARKMC sees the 20 and raises 20.
4 Maxi Mum, you can only FOLD, it seems.
4 Maxi Mum>
4 Maxi Mum folds, 2 still in.
>>> Your bet? (Between 20 and 40, Pot 442)
s
2 cat sees it
Next card (7 of 7).
You get [4H], giving AH [JC] 5H 5S [4D] 4C [4H] (Full House - Fours, Fives

2 cat           shows AH 5H 5S 4C (Pair of Fives)
3 MARKMC        shows KS 7H 6S 5D (3-Straight)

2 cat shows the high hand - Open, please.
>>> Your bet? (Between 0 and 20, pot 462)
5
2 cat opens with 5.
3 MARKMC sees the 5 and raises 5.
>>> Your bet? (Between 5 and 25, pot 477)
15
2 cat sees the 5 and raises 10.
3 MARKMC sees the 10 and raises 20.
The pot now has 522.
>>> Your bet? (Between 20 and 40, pot 522)
s
2 cat sees it

   10:58:54 PM
```

Other games include Flipit, an Othello-like game you can play against Max the Vax or a live opponent. Scramble is a game much like Boggle. Players must create as many words as possible from the 16 given letters. The top 10 scores are cleared weekly. Lunar Lander, Adventure, and other games are included on the menu, along with astrological forecasts, Penn & Teller's Comedy forum, the Delphi Yacht Club, and much more.

CompuServe also has a long list of games, including sports simulations, fantasy role-playing adventures, war games, and a list of parlor and trivia games that includes several different trivia quizzes, blackjack, and Hangman. There is even an online IQ test. Because most of these games are text-based, the graphics are limited to charts composed of letters and punctuation. Figure 24.23 shows CompuServe's Hangman. (See chapter 14, "Games for Fun!," for more information.)

Chapter 24
Communications and Online Services

Figure 24.22
Delphi's poker game lets you in on the deal any time.

A long with describing the joys of playing games online (and they are undeniably fun!), I would also caution people about the money it can cost to play them. Some folks become "addicted" to these games and wind up playing a couple hours a night, several days a week. At $5/hr or more, this can quickly add up to hundreds of dollars a month. Beware.

Ted Landau

Figure 24.23
CompuServe's ASCII graphics sets up a game of Hangman.

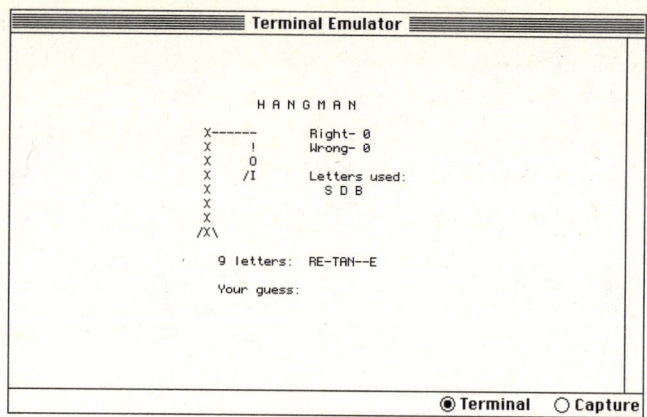

A Trip to the Library

Libraries within the online forums are your best source for games and features such as type fonts, handy utilities, and programs to do everything from keeping a scuba log to installing System 7. Much of this material is *shareware*, which means that you pay the author directly instead of buying it at your local computer store. Programmers may decide to release their work as shareware to avoid the hassles of dealing with commercial publishers or because they are willing to take a chance on your honesty. Some programs are *freeware*, which, as the name implies, are yours for the asking.

Downloading and Uploading

The process of transferring a program from a library into your Mac is called *downloading*. You may encounter several different kinds of downloading protocols, depending on your terminal software and the capabilities of the system you call. Some BBSs and services support all protocols; others restrict you to one or two possibilities.

WARNING! If you simply dump a text file from one computer to another by modem, you invite disaster. Your terminal program undoubtedly has a menu item that says **Send File (text)....** Do not use it unless there is no other way to transfer, you do not need to retain the format, and the file is short. Phone lines are noisier than you think. A pop or click at the wrong moment can turn a whole day's work into trash. For this reason, special error-correcting file transfer protocols were devised to make the job less risky. These protocols are a set of rules for breaking data into manageable blocks, sending the blocks at a given speed, and comparing them at both ends to make sure what arrived is the same as what was sent. As with the handshaking protocols, both sender and receiver must agree on the transfer method. Kermit and XMODEM are still the two most common, and probably most foolproof, methods. They are, in effect, the lowest common denominators of file transfer.

XMODEM can send any Mac file or program, including word processor files, spreadsheets, sounds, pictures, or applications. You find XMODEM just about anywhere you might need to transfer a file. There are actually three types of XMODEM. Classic, the original, is widely supported everywhere. XMODEM-CRC uses an improved error correction system and is also well-supported. XMODEM-1K Blocks is the newest version and is much faster because it extends the size of the blocks of data being sent from 128 bytes to 1024 bytes. It is more efficient unless you have a noisy line; you still would use the 128-byte block size then.

Mainframe-to-microcomputer transfers frequently use Kermit, which is available for all kinds of systems through Columbia University's Kermit Distribution Center. Kermit, however, is slow. New variations using longer packets and sliding windows have helped, but it is not most people's protocol of choice.

YMODEM differs from XMODEM in that it can send a batch of files rather than just one at a time. YMODEM-1K, like its XMODEM counterpart, sends longer blocks. YMODEM-G is a speedy but non-error-correcting protocol. It may whiz through the first 490,000 bytes of a 500,000-byte file and then choke on a dropped bit. If this happens, the transfer fails. And it happens frequently. Do not use YMODEM unless you have a very clean line or an error-correcting MNP modem.

ZMODEM currently is the fastest and best transfer protocol. Use it whenever it is available, and if it is not, ask your online service or favorite BBS to consider supporting it. ZMODEM combines the best features of the other protocols. It can support batch file transmission and has built-in error correction. In addition, if something happens while you use ZMODEM, you can resume the transfer at the point at which it was dropped. You do not have to start over. GEnie and Delphi support ZMODEM transfers, as do many BBSs.

Chapter 24
Communications and Online Services

America Online and CompuServe have their own transfer protocols, both of which are similar to ZMODEM. Batch downloads and resumable transfers are possible with both.

MacBinary

Macintosh files are different from other computer files because they each are divided into two forks or subfiles. The data fork is where the actual data in the file is stored. Items such as icons and dialog boxes are in the resource fork. When you upload a text file of business letters you stored on your office computer, the data fork holds the actual letters, and the resource fork is empty. If, on the other hand, you download an application—a game, perhaps—there is probably screen information in the resource fork and data to make the program operate in the data fork. A separate packet of Finder information also is attached to each file. This is what tells the Mac which icon to use, the name of the program, and so on.

Mac communications software authors agreed on the MacBinary format to handle this resource and data fork information. You can use MacBinary to handle files that originate on a Mac and will be used on a Mac (even though they may be stored on a BBS's PC or a service's mainframe). The receiving computer simply does not recognize the different format and saves the whole file as data. But when the file is sent to another Mac, the second one sees MacBinary and automatically makes whatever accommodations are needed. When you transfer a file for use on a Mac, specify MacBinary in addition to whatever protocol (that is, XMODEM, ZMODEM) you use.

File Transfers

Most people approach their first upload or download with a good deal of nervousness. Even though transferring files might seem complicated, it is really quite simple. On a specialized communications program like America Online's, you simply pick the file you want to copy and click the button to download it, as shown in figure 24.24. You can download a single file immediately, or collect a bunch of files and download them later, using the Download Manager which is part of America Online's updated software package.

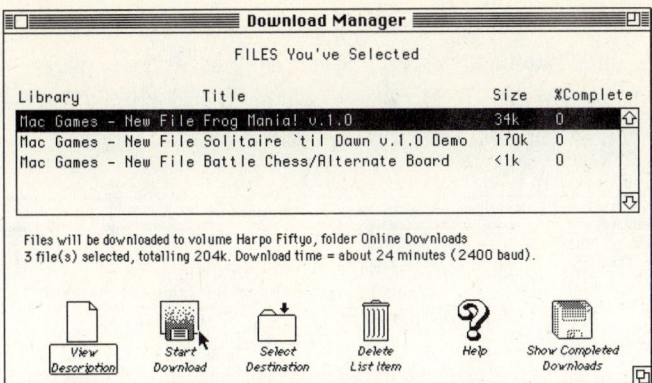

Figure 24.24
Downloading a batch of files is as easy as downloading just one.

The transfer happens almost automatically. You see a standard dialog box asking where you want to save the file and by what title. Then a sort of ruler-shaped graph, like the one in figure 24.25, appears to let you know the status of the transfer. It counts down the number of minutes remaining.

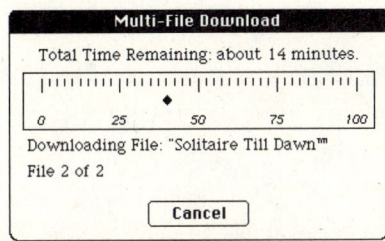

Figure 24.25
The ruler keeps track of the remaining time.

Your computer is not necessarily useless while transfers take place. If you run under MultiFinder or are running System 7, you can leave the transfer and do something else. Working on other tasks does affect the speed of the transfer somewhat, but the convenience of writing a letter or playing a game while downloading may be worth the extra minute or two. If you do not use MultiFinder, your DAs under the Apple menu still are active. You may play with a DA game or use any of your other desk accessories. When the transfer is complete, America Online sends you a spoken message that says "File's done," or if you choose, it will automatically sign off.

Other communications programs are almost equally friendly, and any BBS or online service that has files to download will also welcome your shareware or freeware uploads. Microphone's status box, shown in figure 24.26, changes every few seconds to let you know how many bits are left to transfer and approximately how much more time it should take. This status box also gives you some other potentially useful information, such as the application that created the file and the number of errors in the transmission. (This indicates whether you have a noisy line. Too many errors aborts a transfer.)

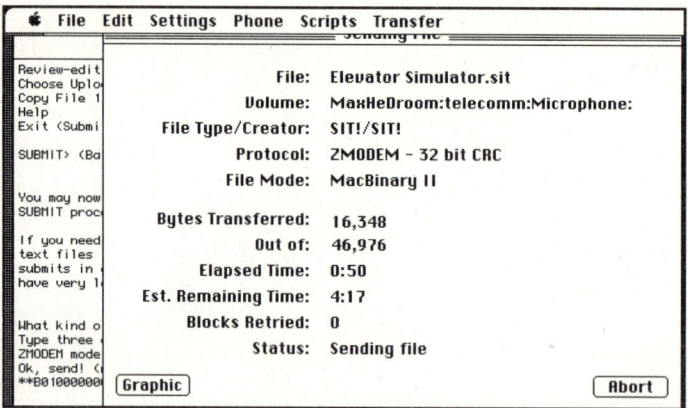

Figure 24.26

You can upload a file with Microphone.

Saving Time with Compacting Programs

If you pay by the minute for uploads and downloads, sending data in the most compact form possible makes sense. For this reason, several different kinds of "compacting" programs have been developed. Raymond Lau's Stuffit first was released as shareware; later, an upgraded version, Stuffit Deluxe, was made available commercially. The current shareware version, Stuffit Lite, is available from user groups, services, and elsewhere, and is excellent.

Another compression utility, called CompactPro, is also very effective, and is widely distributed as shareware. CompactPro can expand files that were compressed with most versions of Stuffit, as well as expanding its own compressed files.

You can tell which compression utility was used by the file extension that usually is added to its name. Any file with an .SIT extension has been compressed by some form of Stuffit. You may find old files that are labeled .PIT; a utility called Packit compressed these. Files with names that end in .CPT have been compressed with CompactPro or its earlier version, Compactor. Files with names that end in .SEA extensions are self-extracting archives created with CompactPro or Stuffit. To open a self-extracting file, just click on it and it opens itself.

A Closer Look When you have financial records or other materials you do not need to refer to but should keep "just in case," use compacting programs to compress data and eliminate "dead" storage on disks. You often can save 50 percent or more of your disk space, enabling you to put 1600K of data on a standard 800K disk.

DiskDoubler is a slightly different kind of compression utility, intended more for disk storage than for compressing files for modem transmission (although there's no reason why it wouldn't work just as well). Most online services and BBS prefer that you use either CompactPro or Stuffit for files that you're uploading to them.

You may become confused when using CompactPro for the first time to decompress a file, unless you follow this step-by-step procedure:

1. Open CompactPro by clicking on its icon. An empty window and the CompactPro menu bar appears.

2. Use the **File** menu and select the **Open** command to locate and open the document to decompress. The window's title bar changes from Untitled to the file's name, and information about that file appears in the window. If there are several files within a folder, they are listed separately and the folder name appears on the title bar. Select the documents to open by clicking on their names. (Select multiple documents by holding the Shift key as you click.)

3. Choose **Extract** from the **Archive** menu, as shown in figure 24.27, or press Command-E. You are asked to designate a destination to save the opened files. When you click the **Extract** button, the file is saved in its decompressed format. A status box, much like the file transfer boxes, tells you how much more of your file is left to extract.

When the decompression is finished, you can throw away the compressed version or keep it as a backup. To compress a file, you essentially reverse the preceding process:

Chapter 24
Communications and Online Services

Figure 24.27
Compressing a file with CompactPro involves a three-step process.

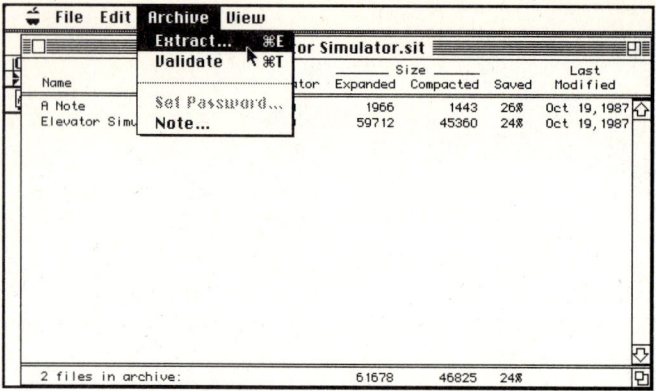

1. Open CompactPro. Rather than use the Open command to select a folder or file, choose **Add** from the **Edit** window to select the desired documents. A dialog box appears. Select as many documents as you want to compress in this file.

2. When the list is complete, choose **Save As...** from the **File** menu. Figure 24.28 shows the default title CompactPro gives to new files. Change it to whatever you like, but for convenience, keep the .CPT extension.

3. Select **Self Extracting** (optional) and tell the Mac where to save the compressed data. Then click the **Save** button. The files are compressed in a matter of minutes or even seconds.

Figure 24.28
Use CompactPro to choose the documents to be compressed as part of this archive.

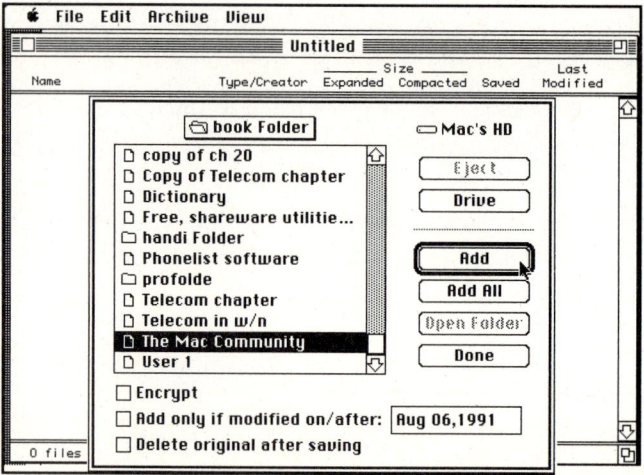

Rating the Services

Now that you have seen what is on the various online services and how to use them, you probably have a better idea which services you would like to try. The following information briefly runs down each of the major online services. Note: Fees for the various services are constantly changing, as are the features offered. Before you sign up for any service, check the prices to find out exactly what's included and whether there are higher "prime time" rates for daytime use.

America Online is the most Mac-like of the services, making it easy to use. Although America Online is also open to PC users, many of its forums and data libraries are specifically dedicated to Mac and Apple II. The service's extensive use of icons and dialog boxes makes it the easiest system to navigate, which is why the startup kit comes with only a disk and a couple of pages of very basic information. America Online enables users to establish up to five user names per account, so each family member can receive his or her own mail. The basic monthly fee includes 5 hours of online time; additional time is reasonable (under $10 an hour).

CompuServe does its best to be user friendly by giving you several connecting choices. In addition to using a straight text-based service, you can buy either or both of CompuServe's custom software sets. CompuServe Information Manager, or CIM, is a semi-graphic interface designed to be easier for Mac users; it is an improvement over text-access. Figure 24.29 shows CIM in use. There is also the CompuServe Navigator, another software package designed to let you plan your CompuServe session off-line, log on, transfer data, and get out again as quickly and economically as possible.

One problem with CompuServe is there is so much to explore. You easily could spend a small fortune discovering the more than 1,400 databases, staggering numbers of forums, catalog items to shop for, and additional services. The monthly fee covers only "basic services," such as shopping, the AP news and weather, and E-mail. Other features—including most forums, CB Simulator, and more in-depth news and reference services—cost extra (some cost a lot extra!). The bottom line is: CompuServe is great if you can afford it. But a couple hours of browsing can be very expensive.

Chapter 24
Communications and Online Services

America Online recently teamed up with the *San Jose Mercury News* to create Mercury Center, a combination newspaper and electronic information service that is a definite precursor of things to come. Check it out! You can get more detail on key stories (like the full text of an important speech) than the newspaper had space for. In a few years, I expect I won't subscribe to a printed newspaper; I'll have an online newspaper with intelligent agents that filter stuff I'm interested in.

Dan Shafer

Figure 24.29

The Information Manager helps make CompuServe manageable.

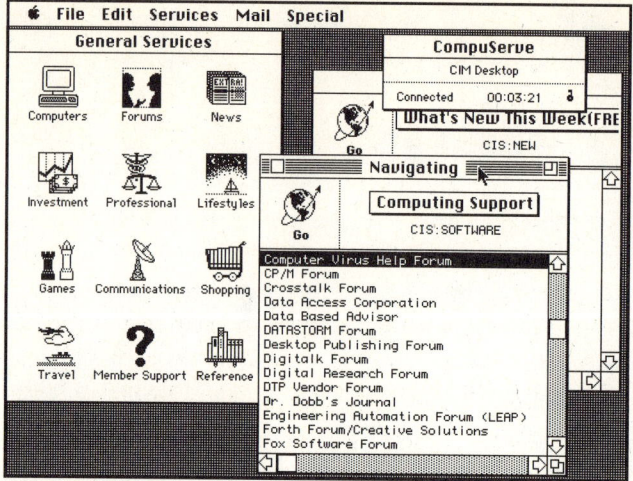

Delphi's services are not quite as limitless, but they are much more affordable. The user-friendliness quotient of this text-based service depends strictly on the friendliness of your own terminal program. When you log on, the menus are easy to understand. Forums, which Delphi calls groups, are all basically in one area. Games are in another. Delphi also allows members to set up their own "custom" forums, for a small additional charge.

Delphi divides its services into basic and premium levels. Basic Delphi service costs $5.95 per month with one free premium hour. After that, the charge is $6.00 per hour, day or night. There is also a second option called the 20/20 Advantage. For $20.00 per month, you get 20 hours of premium services, such as forums and games, and unlimited basic service time for conferences, E-mail, news, and other basics. Financially, Delphi makes good sense.

GEnie, like Delphi, is text-based, and its ease of use depends, in part, on your own software. However, GEnie is not laid out for easy use the way Delphi is. You have to pass through more levels of menus to get to your destination; at a fairly hefty charge per prime-time hour, the costs can mount. And GEnie charges you the full prime-time rate (if you access during those hours) for all of its services, including basic items such as billing information, which other services usually do not charge for. On nights and weekends, basic service has no extra charge, but "value services," which include forums, conferences, libraries, and so on, cost extra.

Chapter 24
Communications and Online Services

If you want low prices, Prodigy is the answer, although it offers a relatively low level of service. It does not have libraries of Mac software. It does not have real-time chats, and your mail is limited to 30 messages per month (more if you pay extra for them). It does have news, sports, weather, games, EAASY SABRE, many bulletin boards, and shopping. Prodigy, unlike some other services, encourages you to share your account with up to five other family members. For the same price, each user can have his or her own ID and mailbox. But that does not mean each member can send 30 messages. The limit applies per account, not per user. Prodigy recently announced a change in its pricing structure, effective July 1993. Only a few Prodigy services will be offered for the basic monthly rate, including shopping, E-mail, and electronic banking. All others, including most bulletin boards, games, and reference services, will be treated as "premium" services with additional fees.

There are a couple of other drawbacks. Prodigy is slow. And, more important for Mac users, the interface is not Mac-friendly. In fact, it works by crippling your Mac and turning it into an imitation PC. You cannot access your menus, your desk accessories, or MultiFinder while Prodigy is running. Some former Prodigy users resigned when they discovered that Prodigy was reading and writing to their hard disks every time they signed on. Part of its program checks your software against its current software and updates yours as often as necessary. This means that the Prodigy system examines the contents of your disk and adds new data to it without your permission, and that makes many Mac users very uneasy.

WARNING! Can Prodigy really read all the files on your hard disk? They say, "No way!" Some users claim, however, that they found pieces of their financial data, legal briefs, and other potentially sensitive material stored on their desktops in a Prodigy file called STAGE.DAT. Prodigy contends the data is unerased material previously stored on that section of disk and is unreadable. It is not impossible that someone could write a program that scans your hard disk for "interesting" items and then copies them while it sends you the weather report. It is unlikely, however, that any reputable company has done so. Prodigy claims to have more than one million subscribers. Logically, it could not store that much data. For this reason alone, you should be skeptical about claims of data snatching. However, if it bothers you, you may want to run Prodigy only from floppy disks.

Ultimately, there is no perfect service. And, to some extent, you get what you pay for. The more expensive a service is, the more features it has. If you want numerous shareware files, unlimited worldwide E-mail, and endless hours of real-time conferences, you would not be happy with Prodigy. If you are new to telecommunications and not sure of what you are doing, GEnie and CompuServe might make you regret buying a modem. Many users are comfortable with Delphi and America Online, although others find them too "computer-ish."

The Internet

The Internet is a worldwide network of computers originally set up to link academic and government research facilities. Composed of millions of members all over the world, the Internet dwarfs all online services. It includes tremendous libraries of files of all kinds, forum threads on thousands of topics from the mundane to the esoteric, and E-mail all over the world. Several online services have established gateways to the Internet, connecting ordinary people to the world of university, government, and industry Internet sites. Navigating the Internet is complicated, but sending mail via Internet is fairly easy. Delphi, America Online, and CompuServe are all connected to the Internet, as of this writing, so you can send mail from one service to another via the Internet. The major drawback to the Internet is its complexity—it is much more difficult to work with than an online service. However, if you can connect to the Internet and become comfortable with it, the wealth of information is staggering. For more information on connecting to the Internet with your Macintosh, see the *Internet Starter Kit for Macintosh*, by Adam Engst, published by Hayden Books.

What About Free Bulletin Board Systems (BBSs)?

Although it is generally true you get what you pay for, there are a great many bulletin boards you can call without paying a cent. You cannot find airline schedules or the current UPI news here, but you may find forums, libraries, games to play, and even conferencing. If you join a Mac user group, you are also a member of its bulletin board. Some, like the Boston Computer Society and BMUG in Berkeley, have very large and active BBSs. (See chapter 27, "The Macintosh Community," for more information.)

Chapter 24
Communications and Online Services

The amateur bulletin boards network, Fidonet, first appeared in 1984. It now has nearly 7,000 separate boards networked together. Fidonet members pass E-mail coast-to-coast free. Many user groups belong to the Fidonet system and may also belong to other noncommercial networks such as AlterNet. You can get a list of BBSs from your user group or from Mac forums on commercial services.

Starting Your Own BBS

Any terminal program can place your Mac in host mode to receive calls one at a time. If you want to become a point on the Fidonet, you need special software. Two programs are recommended to handle Fidonet protocols: Copernicus and Tabby. You can get information on these programs from a local user group or BBS operator. BBS software designed specifically for the Mac is also available. The two most popular programs are TeleFinder and FirstClass.

There are always risks involved in starting a BBS; the main risk is that somebody may send you a virus, either on purpose or by accident, or may decide to see what other mischief can be done to your system. Nevertheless, many people find that bulletin board systems are as fun and rewarding as worldwide amateur ham radio.

Summary

When you add a modem and a telephone line to your computer system, you add a new dimension to your Mac's usefulness. Whether you want to talk to the next desk or the next continent, you can do it as long as you have the necessary hardware and software. The hardware part of the package is called a modem. It modulates the Mac's digital information into analog sounds that can be sent by telephone and demodulates them when it receives them. The software simply tells the modem how to handle the information it is getting and lets you handle the mechanics of communicating with another computer.

Commercial services can bring you everything from the latest news and stock prices to a huge selection of games, and new friends to play them with. You can make travel reservations, shop for everything from computer software

Part VI
Expanding Your Mac's Horizons

and hardware to clothing, candy, and condominiums. Sending mail and sharing files is easy and can increase your productivity, and even improve your social life. Bulletin boards, both commercial and otherwise, enable you to share ideas and information with people from all over the globe, on virtually any topic that interests you. With special software packages, you even can run your own bulletin board and play host to other computer users.

Chapter 25
Networking the Macintosh

Macintosh networking can be a confusing and complex subject. Even networking experts are often baffled by the never-ending array of acronyms, services and products. In this chapter, we'll try to make this involved subject a bit more understandable. We'll start by introducing a common framework that explains the various layers associated with communication and networking.

In This Chapter

▼ Networking fundamentals

▼ Macintosh networking software and hardware

▼ Networking Macs with other computers

▼ Common networking scenarios

Part VI
Expanding Your Mac's Horizons

Networking Fundamentals

All forms of communication can be broken down into four basic elements; the Idea, Expression, Transport and Medium (see figure 25.1).

Figure 25.1
The four fundamental layers of communication

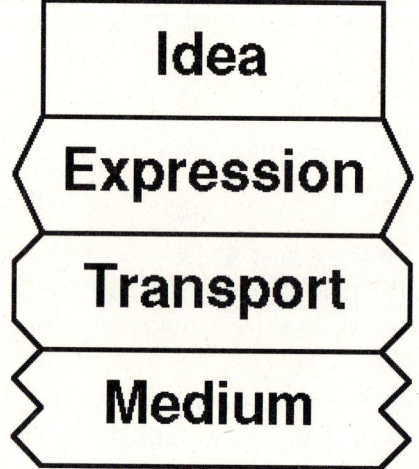

Idea

The idea is the reason, or purpose behind the communication. It's the thought or essence behind the message. It can be as simple as eating breakfast or as complex as a Space Shuttle launch.

Expression

The expression is the external form of the idea. It can take the form of English, French, Braille, ASCII or Morse Code. Of course, for any given idea, there are an infinite number of ways of expression.

Transport

Once the idea has been expressed in an external form, the expressed idea has to be transported from the sender to the receiver. Just as there are many different forms of expression, there are also many different transport mechanisms. I could convey an English-based message about the next Shuttle launch by using a written transport protocol, or with a spoken protocol. The rules for conveying written English are much different than those for spoken English.

Medium

The last step in the process is the communications medium. In other words, what's the physical connection between the sender and receiver? When you deliver a message by speaking, the delivery mechanism is compressed air. I could also write my message and deliver it by hand, mail, fax or Federal Express. Each method has its own benefits and disadvantages, but they all would achieve the desired end result of message delivery.

Matching The Layers

By using separate four-layer diagrams for the sender and the recipient of the message, we can better illustrate the interaction between the two parties (see figure 25.2).

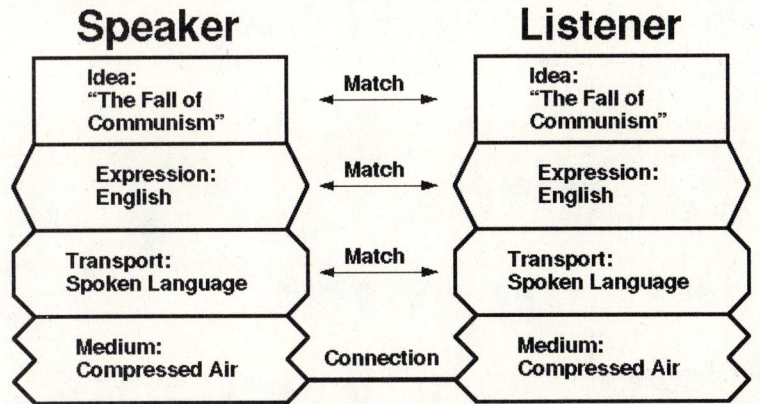

Figure 25.2
Diagramming a simple conversation.

In order for communications to be successful, each corresponding layer of the sender and the recipient must match. We'll start at the bottom and work upward.

The sender's and the recipient's chosen communications medium (Layer 4) is compressed air. We'll assume that both of them can speak and hear to take advantage of the medium.

Since both parties are familiar with the protocol of spoken language, the Transport layer (Layer 3), matches as well. If one of the participants only

Chapter 25
Networking the Macintosh

Part VI
Expanding Your Mac's Horizons

understood the protocol of spoken language and the other only understood the reading of lips, the layers would not match and communication would be unlikely.

Moving up to the Expression layer (Layer 2), both parties understand the English format. Here, as with the other layers, if there was a mismatch where one person understood English and the other only French, the communication process would not occur.

Finally, even at the uppermost Idea layer (Layer 1), there must be a match between the sender and the receiver. They both need to understand the basic idea behind the message.

The beauty of this diagramming technique is that all forms and instances of communications can be diagrammed and analyzed. Each layer of the communication process serves a specific function, but provides us with unlimited choice. We can choose and tailor the method of expression, transport, and medium to best convey our ideas. Each layer is connected to its neighbor, but each layer can also stand independently and can be analyzed and judged on its own merits.

The key tenet of this idea is that when two or more parties are involved, communication can only occur when their corresponding layers match identically. The same can be said for Macintosh networking as well.

Macintosh Networking: Services, Formats, Transports and Media

As with any communication, Macintosh networking can be broken down into four layers (see figure 25.3). We'll use slightly different nomenclature, that's specific to networking, to describe these layers.

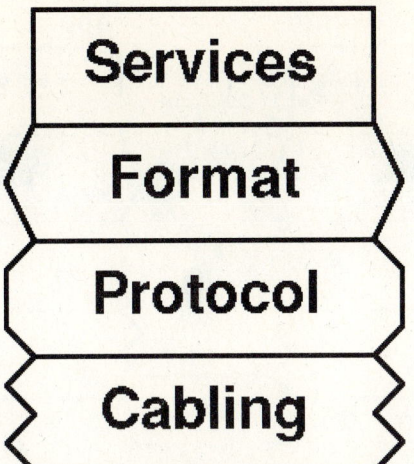

Figure 25.3
The four fundamental layers of computer networking.

Services

Earlier, the first layer represented the idea, or the reason behind the communication. With Macintosh and all computer networking, the purpose or reason behind the communication is to deliver services to the participants. Let's examine those network services that have helped over the past decade to make the Macintosh unique.

AppleShare (AFP)

To many Macintosh users, networking means shared, controlled access to documents. To provide such access, Apple developed a service layer protocol called the Apple Filing Protocol, or AFP. When Apple introduced AFP, Macintosh users were introduced to new concepts such as usernames, passwords, groups, ownership and protection. Apple's first implementation of an AFP server was on Macintosh hardware and they called it AppleShare. AppleShare was easy to use, since the files stored on the server appeared as an extension of the user's local hard disk. So, all the techniques learned in creating and naming folders and files were immediately transferable to the file server environment.

Today, Apple has several AFP implementations, two versions that run under System 7 and a high-performance A/UX version. Figure 25.4 shows a NetPICT diagram of an AFP Server. In this example, the AFP server is running on a Macintosh with an Ethernet card.

Figure 25.4

NetPICT of a Macintosh running AppleShare.

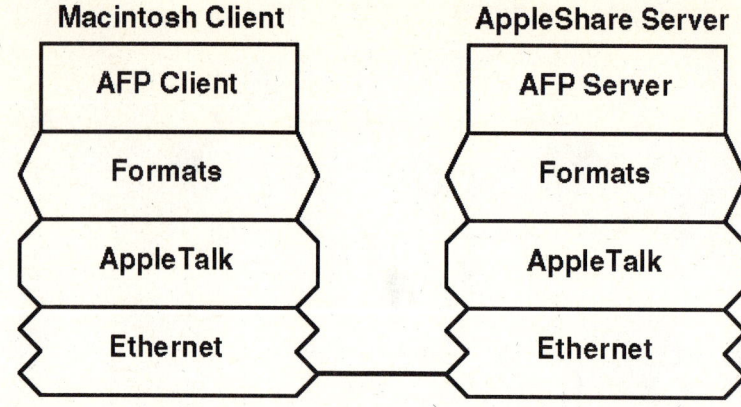

File Sharing

Starting with System 7, Apple expanded the concept of AFP services so that any Macintosh can be both an AFP server and client. This is known as Macintosh FileSharing. Assuming your Macintosh is running System 7, you can grant or deny access to your Macintosh on a user or group (a collection of users) basis. You designate folders on your hard disk that you wish to make available to certain users or groups. Figure 25.5 shows several of the Macintosh dialog boxes, under System 7, that control or monitor FileSharing. With Macintosh FileSharing, there is no dedicated centralized file service. Each participating user acts as a client and a server.

Figure 25.5

With System 7, each Macintosh can be an AFP client or server.

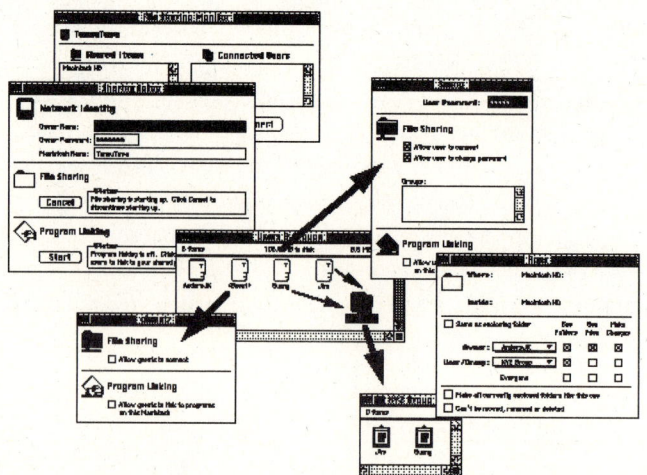

Other AFP Clients and Servers

The AFP service is not limited to the Macintosh. In fact, Apple made sure that AFP was an open standard that could be implemented on other computers.

As shown in figure 25.6, there are AFP servers available for most popular platforms including DEC VAX, IBM PC, UNIX and even dedicated hardware boxes.

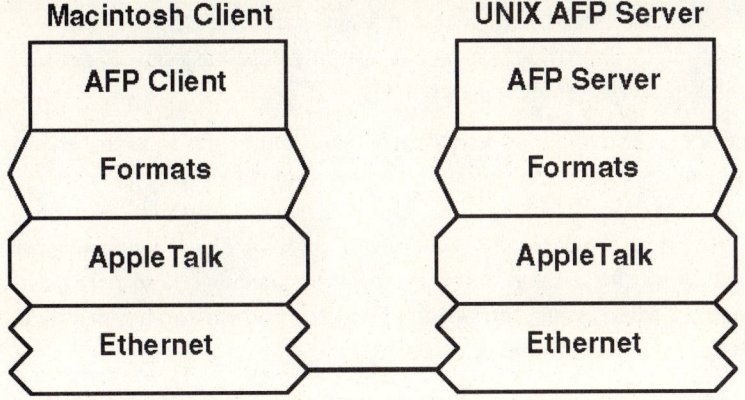

Figure 25.6
AFP Servers aren't limited to Macintosh.

Print Services (PAP)

Perhaps the most common network service is the printing of documents to an Apple network printer. As was the case with AFP, Apple developed a special protocol called the Printer Access Protocol (PAP) to handle the unique and specific requirements of networked laser printing. PAP manages the printing specifics, provides the queuing, downloads fonts when required, and even informs the user if the printer is out of paper or if the paper tray is out of the printer. Figure 25.7 shows the corresponding NetPICT of a LaserWriter. As with AFP, PAP print services aren't limited to the Macintosh. They can also be found on UNIX and VAX/VMS hosts as well. There are numerous products that allow these computers to accept and spool Macintosh print jobs.

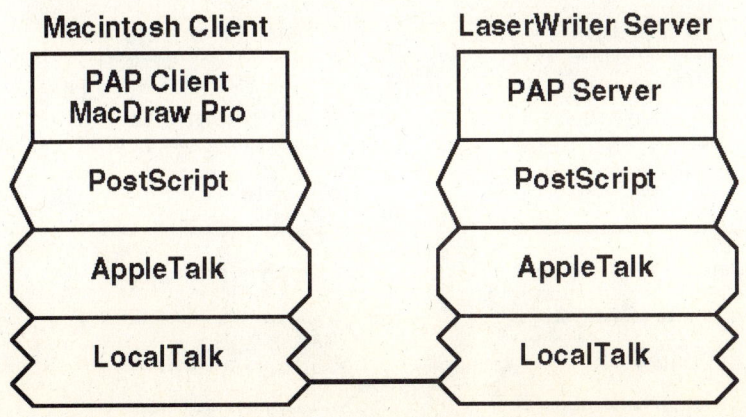

Figure 25.7
NetPICT of an Apple LaserWriter.

Apple Open Collaboration Environment (AOCE)

AOCE is a new set of Apple tools that integrates a wide variety of services necessary for collaborative activities. These services will let the Macintosh manage personal communications, workgroup collaboration and enterprise-wide work flow. An important part of AOCE is the extensible directory services that will provide personal or distributed listings of users, network services and even phone numbers.

Network security is always a concern and AOCE provides tools that ensure private and secure communications. A new AppleTalk protocol, the AppleTalk Secure Data Stream Protocol (ASDSP) encrypts network traffic to prevent "packet snooping." Another AOCE offering, digital signatures, will provide a way for users to "sign" electronic documents. These electronic signatures will be tamperproof and provide users the assurance that their messages and authorizations are secure.

AOCE will lay the foundation for a new generation of shared, cooperative applications. Messages such as voice, fax, mail and even video will be managed through a consistent interface.

Terminal Services

Although terminal emulation is a throwback to an earlier time, there are still a number of application services that require the use of terminals. The Macintosh offers a number of terminal emulators that work with DEC, UNIX, IBM, Prime, Data General and many other hosts. The types of terminals supported include most of Digital's VT-series (such as the VT100, VT220, VT340...), IBM 3270 and 5250 terminals, Tektronix graphics terminals and many others. These emulators are able to connect with direct serial connections (see figure 25.8) or through network connections such as LAT, TCP/IP, DECnet or SNA.

Figure 25.8
In the past, most terminal services were provided over serial transmission lines (RS-232) that used an asynchronous protocol.

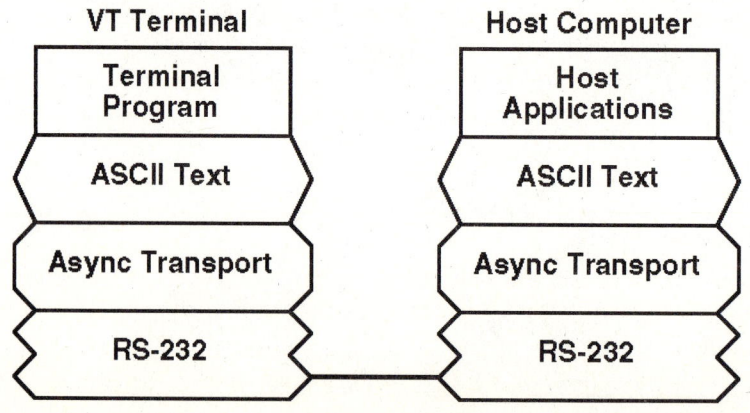

Data Access Language (DAL) and other Database Services

DAL's purpose is to let Macs (and other DAL clients, such as PCs) to uniformly access relational databases. Extending the SQL language, DAL provides a standard that can be used on different computing platforms and different databases (see figure 25.9).

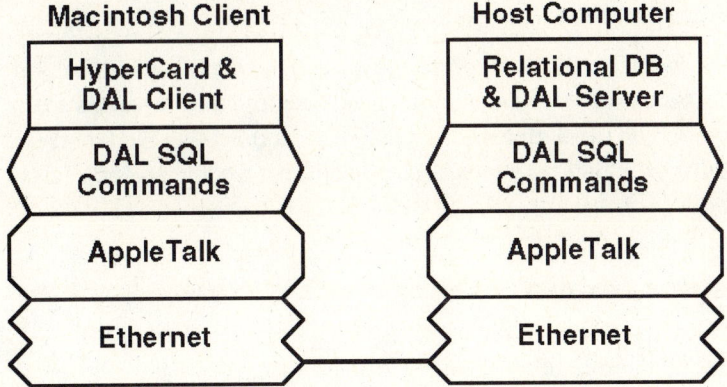

Figure 25.9
NetPICT of a Client/Server DAL relationship.

The DAL software on the client side is implemented as an optional extension for System 7. DAL client applications can be written as Mac applications or as HyperCard stacks. There are also many Mac applications that have DAL client capabilities built-in. Spreadsheets such as Microsoft Excel and Lotus 1-2-3 are DAL-equipped and can be used to access and retrieve data managed by relational databases. Clear Access, from Fairfield Software, is an application that makes it easy to construct ad-hoc database queries with a point and click interface.

DAL servers are currently sold by Apple, DEC, Tandem, Novell and Pacer Software. Apple offers DAL servers for DEC VAX/VMS, IBM mainframes, IBM AS/400 and Macs running A/UX (Apple's version on UNIX). The VAX/VMS version supports DEC's Rdb, Ingres, Oracle, Sybase and Informix. The IBM mainframe version supports IBM's DB2 and SQL/DS databases. Pacer offers a DAL server for HP UNIX computers, DEC Ultrix and Sun's SPARCstation. Tandem has a DAL server for their line of computers and Novell has added DAL support for NetWare's SQL NLM.

Mail Services

Perhaps more than any other Macintosh service, E-mail has the potential for truly transforming an organization. Users can finally quit the annoying game of telephone tag and enhance their communications with their co-workers. E-mail can be used as a communications framework where voice, textual

Part VI
Expanding Your
Mac's Horizons

messages and binary file attachments are sent and tracked over the entire network.

During the past five years, support for Macintosh E-mail has become widespread. As mentioned before, Apple's AOCE initiative is setting the foundation for a new generation of mail applications where various message formats (i.e. mail, fax, voice, video) are integrated and presented to the user within a consistent interface. AOCE is also providing the necessary security and authentication that's required by collaborative applications.

Today, the Macintosh is supported by most of the popular multiplatform E-mail systems. Two of the most popular Macintosh mail programs are Microsoft Mail for Macintosh and CE Software's QuickMail. Both of these products offer client and server components that work in an AppleTalk network environment.

Service Summary

Of course the services listed previously only scratch the surface. The Macintosh offers hundreds of networkable applications such as time management, resource management, backup/archival, and even games that work over an AppleTalk network. Since the Mac was designed at the outset to operate in a networked environment, most of the applications naturally take advantage. Today, with the System 7 features of Publish and Subscribe and AppleEvents, the Macintosh has gone beyond mere client/server applications and uses the AppleTalk network to automatically update shared objects and to let applications directly control and manipulate other application services that are available on the network.

Formats

Humans rely on standard languages to provide effective communications. We have numerous expressive formats to satisfy different situations and cultures. The same is true for computers. There are thousands of computer formats used to represent information. Some of these formats are widely adopted standards while most of them are unique to a specific computer application.

Every document that you have created on your Macintosh is written to the disk in a specific file format. Most formats are unique to the application which created it.

There are also many standard formats such as: PostScript, QuickDraw, PICT, TIFF, GIF, EBCDIC, QuickTime, DXF and IGES. For the most part, these formats are independent of the computer on which they were created. A QuickTime file composed of a unique sequence of ones and zeros can be played on a Macintosh, a PC or a Silicon Graphics workstation. All that is needed is an application that understands the QuickTime format. Establishing a common format for communications is by far the most difficult challenge in computer networking. It's the task that deserves the most thought and effort to solve.

Protocols

Until this point, all we've done was to establish a service and agree on a common descriptive format. No information has been moved across the network. The rules for moving formatted information across the network is the function of the third level.

It's this level where the networking protocols reside. Shortly after introducing the Mac, Apple announced a protocol known as AppleTalk that very elegantly solved the problem of identifying the sender and the recipient, providing reliable error-free transmission and choosing an appropriate route on the network.

While your Mac's primary networking protocol is AppleTalk, it's important to realize that your Macintosh can have several transport protocols loaded at the same time. In addition to the standard AppleTalk protocol, you could install MacTCP from Apple and DECnet for Macintosh from Digital (see figure 25.10). These protocols would let your Macintosh communicate using the native transport protocol of other computers.

Chapter 25
Networking the Macintosh

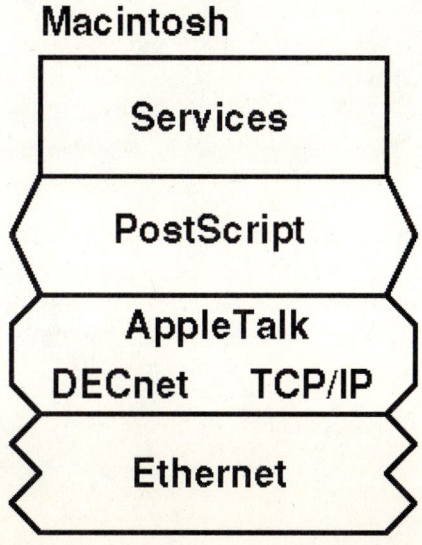

Figure 25.10
Macintosh running multiple protocols.

Part VI
Expanding Your Mac's Horizons

Though it's possible for a Macintosh to run multiple transport protocols, it's important to note that these transports don't always support every Macintosh service. For example, the Chooser only works with AppleTalk transport protocol. The popular UNIX file service, NFS, is only accessible with the TCP/IP transport. There are only a few Macintosh services, such as MacX, that work with multiple transport protocols. Although your Mac can support other networking protocols, it's the AppleTalk protocol that makes it unique.

How does AppleTalk work?

AppleTalk uses three entities to uniquely identify a particular service on a particular node in a specific network. Every networking protocol, such as AppleTalk, DECnet and TCP/IP, has a similar scheme to identify members of their respective network. Essentially, this means every network member, or node, has a unique identification number.

With AppleTalk, this identifying number, or *node number*, is based on an eight-bit number. With eight bits of information, the maximum number of nodes is 2^8 or 256 (see figure 25.11). For small networks, having a limit of 256 nodes is not a problem. In fact, Apple's LocalTalk cabling system permits no more than 32 nodes. This restriction is a physical or electrical limit, not a logical limit of node addresses.

Figure 25.11
AppleTalk Node numbers.

But many networks require more than 256 AppleTalk nodes and another mechanism is needed to support these larger networks. So, Apple developed a concept that permitted groups of nodes, called "networks," to be established and each AppleTalk network would have its own range of 256 potential node IDs.

To create the boundaries between these different AppleTalk networks, Apple developed the specifications for a device known as an AppleTalk router. AppleTalk routers are the glue that connects separate AppleTalk networks into a larger whole known as an Internetwork. AppleTalk routers separate and define the boundaries between AppleTalk networks.

Each AppleTalk network has a unique ID number that is stored inside each router that is connected to that network. In the simplest case of two

AppleTalk networks connected by a single router, the router maintains the AppleTalk network numbers for each of the two networks.

The current AppleTalk specifications provide a 16-bit network number (see figure 25.12). With 16 bits there can be 2^{16} or 65,536 unique AppleTalk networks. And since each network can potentially support 256 nodes, AppleTalk can support a theoretical maximum of 16,777,216 devices!

Chapter 25
Networking the Macintosh

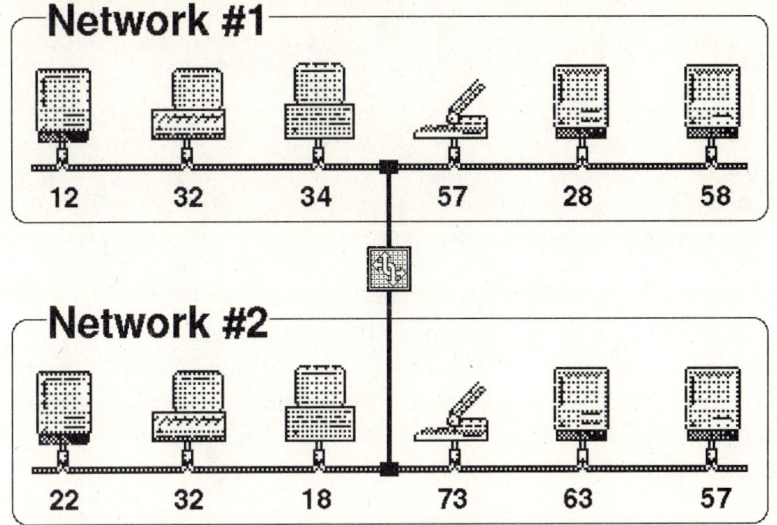

Figure 25.12
AppleTalk Network numbers.

The 16-bit network and 8-bit node number make up only part of a complete AppleTalk logical address. An additional 8 bits is used to define something known as an AppleTalk socket number.

Your Macintosh can handle a number of network chores at one time. At any given instant, your Macintosh could be accessing a file server, printing to a LaserWriter print server or receiving a mail message. To keep these diverse transactions separate and distinct, AppleTalk assigns a unique *socket number* for every logical connection (see figure 25.13). With socket numbers consisting of 8 bit values, there are 256 possible socket numbers that can be used. Socket numbers start at 0 and end at 255. Both of these values are undefined. Half of the socket numbers, from 1 to 127, are reserved for special system use by Apple. The upper half, from 128 to 254, are pooled resources available for general use by applications.

When you print a document, a socket number for that transaction is automatically assigned from the pool. When the job is completed, the number is returned to the pool for subsequent use.

Figure 25.13
AppleTalk Socket numbers.

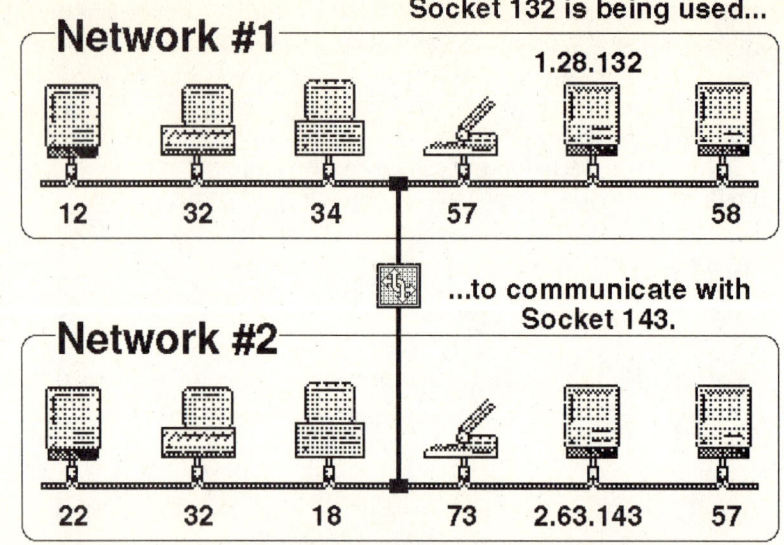

Collectively, these three numbers (network, node and socket,) make up a unique AppleTalk logical address. When a Macintosh and LaserWriter engage in printing transactions, they must use network, node and socket numbers to identify that Macintosh node number 22, located in network 100, is communicating over socket 129 to LaserWriter node 32, in network 101 with socket 130.

The choice of three numbers, a 16 bit network number and an 8 bit node and socket number, are specific to AppleTalk. Other networking protocols such as DECnet and TCP/IP use similar, but different, numbering schemes to logically identify their nodes.

Since Macintosh and other computers can often run multiple networking protocols concurrently, it's often common to have multiple logical addresses on a single computer. For example, one Macintosh that's running AppleTalk, DECnet and TCP/IP concurrently, would have three different logical addresses (see figure 25.14). Its AppleTalk address could be 12.22 (network.node), its DECnet address could be 5.2 (area.node), and its TCP/IP address could be 100.22.128.132.

AppleTalk Phase 1 & 2

In the beginning, when Apple developed EtherTalk, which is nothing more than AppleTalk protocols on Ethernet cabling, they simply carried the original AppleTalk protocol used on LocalTalk networks over to Ethernet.

Phase 1 EtherTalk networks were restricted to a maximum of 254 devices and were inefficient when it came to certain aspects of routing and broadcasting. In 1989, Apple developed AppleTalk Phase 2 to address certain shortcomings that were present in this initial EtherTalk implementation. Phase 2 fixed these problems and provided the first version of TokenTalk, which was Apple's implementation of the AppleTalk protocols on Token Ring networks.

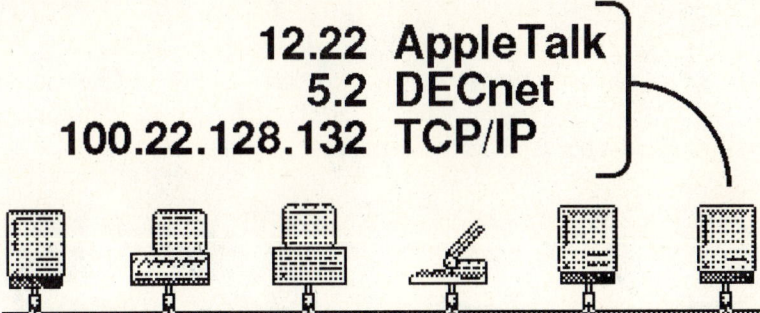

Figure 25.14
Different logical addresses on one Macintosh.

Phase 1 networks can only have a single network number per cable segment. Because AppleTalk only supports 256 potential nodes per network number, each cable segment was therefore limited to 256 devices. Actually, the limit is 254 devices. With Phase 1 networks, node numbers range from 0 to 255. 0 is not used and 255 is reserved for broadcasts heard by all devices.

With LocalTalk, this is hardly a problem. LocalTalk networks have electrical and isolation restrictions that limit the number of nodes to the recommended limit of 32 devices. When Apple introduced the first version of EtherTalk, it too was limited to a single network number and 254 nodes per segment. This was bad news for large organizations that wanted to start populating their corporate Ethernets with Macs.

Phase 1 and 2 Network Number Assignment

Phase 2 broke the 254 node limit by eliminating the restriction of a single network number per cable segment. Instead, the cable, either Ethernet or Token Ring, can be assigned a range of values. In a Phase 2 network, the network numbers range from 0 to 65,534. Zero (0) is undefined and not used. A special range, called the startup range, runs from 65,280 through 65,534. This leaves the numbers 1 through 65,279 for general assignment. By using ranges of network numbers, it's possible to place thousands of AppleTalk nodes on an Ethernet cable.

Let's review the network number assignment rules.

▼ Phase 1 (LocalTalk, and the now extinct first version of EtherTalk) with no routers.

The network number is always 0. In practice the 16 bit zero network number is omitted from the address to conserve space. This is known as a Short DDP address.

▼ Phase 1 with routers.

The network number is a single number between 1 and 65,536 (see figure 25.15). Each network segment, either LocalTalk or the old EtherTalk, must have a single number assigned. No duplicates are permitted.

Figure 25.15
Phase 1 with routers.

▼ Phase 2 (The current version of EtherTalk, TokenTalk) with no routers.

The network numbers fall in a range between 65,280 and 65,534. This is known as the Startup range. There are 254 numbers in this range that are used by AppleTalk nodes as they come onto the network. The choice of a network number, like the node number, is made at random.

One Macintosh could be in network 65,288 and be node 23 and an adjacent Mac could be in network 65,500 and be node 23.

In Phase 2 networks, there is an additional reserved node number, so there can only be 253 nodes per network. This means that for a single, logical segment of Ethernet, there can be 254 networks each having 253 nodes. This multiplies for a total of 64,262 AppleTalk devices per segment. If you need more than this, an AppleTalk router will be required.

▼ Phase 2 with routers.

The network numbers are a range between 1 and 65,279. 0 is not used and 65,280 through 65,534 is reserved for the startup range. Theoretically, you could use the entire range of numbers for a single segment, but this would be wasteful. Instead, it makes sense to assign a modest range of numbers to a cable. This way, growth and expansion can be easily accommodated.

For example, in a large organization, it might make sense to assign ranges to the various divisional locations. Houston can have 1-100, Dallas 101-200 and San Antonio 201-300. Then, local network managers could add routers using network numbers in their pre-assigned range. Since each number can support 253 nodes, Houston could theoretically have (100 times 253) 25,3000 nodes. We'll see later on how Apple's new routing protocol, AURP, extends this concept even further and provides additional flexibility in network number assignment.

The Importance of Dynamic Addressing

Imagine moving into a new house. One of the first things you need to do is to get a new phone. Normally, when you get a new phone, the phone company assigns you a number from their registry of phone numbers. But imagine a phone company that doesn't want to be bothered with the tedious administrative details of assigning unique phone numbers.

This phone company has a system, whereby you simply dial any phone number at random. If someone answers the phone (figure 25.16), you apologize and hang up. If there's no answer, then that number becomes your new phone number.

Figure 25.16

Someone answers the phone...

Part VI
Expanding Your
Mac's Horizons

This imaginary scenario is the mechanism that Apple uses to dynamically assign AppleTalk node addresses. With other protocols, such as DECnet and TCP/IP, the node ID number is determined and assigned by a human. This human usually has a big list or a spreadsheet of node assignments in order to determine which numbers are available for use.

Apple tried to avoid this problem with AppleTalk by implementing a dynamic node addressing scheme. When a LocalTalk-connected Macintosh boots up on a network for the first time, it chooses a node number at random. The Macintosh has no way of knowing whether this random number is already in use by another node, so it sends a special packet, known as an enquiry control packet, to the node in question. If the enquiry reaches its destination, the node responds to the inquiring Mac with an acknowledge control packet. Of course, this means that the number is in use and cannot be used by the new Mac on the network.

Therefore, another random node id and enquiry control packet is generated. If no acknowledge control packet is received, then the new Mac is free to use the number. Once a Macintosh determines a unique node id for itself, it stores the number in non-volatile (kept alive with a battery) memory known as Parameter RAM or PRAM. The Macintosh will use the stored node ID as an educated first guess the next time the machine is booted. This minimizes node ID contention during startup. Generally, a Mac's node number remains with a given Mac, but this is not always the case.

When a Macintosh, or any AppleTalk node, is turned off, it's unable to respond to the enquiry control packets sent out by the other machines. Using the phone example, it's as if the receiver of the message was asleep or out of the house. He would be unable to answer the phone (see figure 25.17). Likewise, if a new Mac is added to the network, the possibility exists that it could randomly guess, and steal, a node id that is locked away in the PRAM of a powered-down Mac. Then, when this Mac is powered on, and it tries to use its stored node ID as its first guess, the other Mac responds with the acknowledgment packet. This causes the original Mac to establish a new node ID. Therefore, it's quite possible for your Mac to be node 44 on Monday and node 32 on Tuesday. With AppleTalk, it's not important that a node number be permanently associated with a given Macintosh. The Mac uses a similar technique when connected to an EtherTalk, TokenTalk or FDDItalk network.

Dynamic addressing is a very important and significant feature of the AppleTalk protocol. As computers get smaller and more commonplace, and as wireless networking catches on, dynamic node addressing will be crucial to their use. It would be ridiculous to have to stop at the front door of a company that has a wireless LAN in place, simply to be assigned a network node id for your Newton personal digital assistant (see figure 25.18). These node numbers don't possess any intrinsic meaning, they're simply unique numbers, and it just so happens that computers do an excellent job of assigning unique numbers.

Chapter 25
Networking the Macintosh

Figure 25.17
Nobody home!

AppleTalk Zones

Zones are simply names assigned to AppleTalk networks. They, along with network numbers, are stored within the AppleTalk routers. In the case of LocalTalk (Phase 1) networks, there can be only one network number and one zone name per network. Imagine the simple internet, figure 25.19, consisting of two LocalTalk networks connected by a router.

Each network has a unique network number: 10 and 20, and each network has a zone name: Left and Right. Here, the zone name, Left, is used to identify the devices in network number 10 and Right is used to identify devices in network number 20.

There's no uniqueness requirement, however, for zone names. It's perfectly fine to have duplicate zone names in order to logically organize services. Therefore, in figure 25.20, networks 10 and 20 could have the same zone name of "CAL."

Figure 25.18
I need a node number?!?

When networks have the same zone name, similar devices are grouped together. So, if there were two LaserWriters in network 10 and three LaserWriters in network number 20, there would be a total of five LaserWriters in the "CAL" zone. Keep in mind, however, that when there's no zones, or only one zone, the Macintosh Chooser does not display the zone list. This is true even when there are multiple networks with the same zone name.

In the case of Ethernet and Token Ring networks (Phase 2), a cable segment can be assigned a range of network numbers and multiple zone names (see figure 25.21). The zone names are not associated with any specific network number.

With Phase 2 networks the zone names are defined for the entire network segment. When a Macintosh, or other AppleTalk node, is added to the cable, it automatically belongs to a special zone called the Default zone.

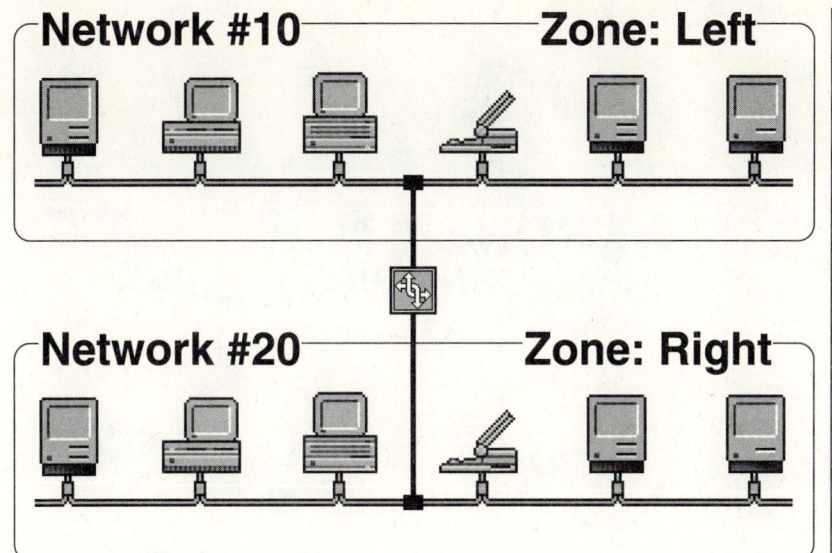

Figure 25.19
Two LocalTalk networks connected with a router. Each network has a unique network number and different zone names.

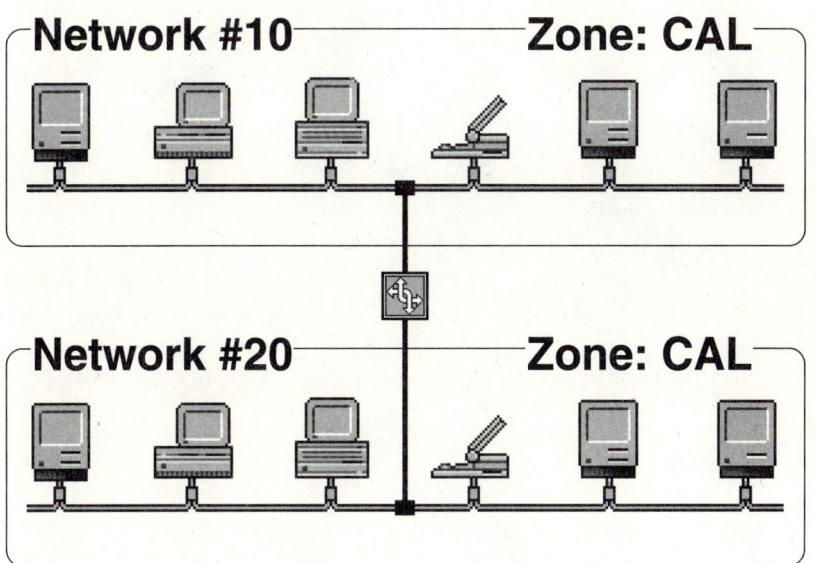

Figure 25.20
In this example, each network still has a unique network number, but the zone names are the same.

The Default zone is a designated zone where AppleTalk nodes appear by default. It's established by choosing a zone from the list of defined zones maintained by the router configuration software. If there are multiple routers on the cable, as in figure 25.22, all routers must agree on the network range, zone list and default zone assignment for the cable. Mismatched net numbers and zone lists are the most frequent causes of AppleTalk network problems.

Figure 25.21
Ethernet and Token Ring AppleTalk networks can use a range of network numbers.

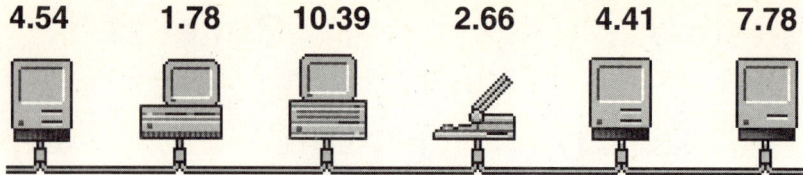

Figure 25.22
All routers on a given segment must agree on the network number range, zones and the default zone.

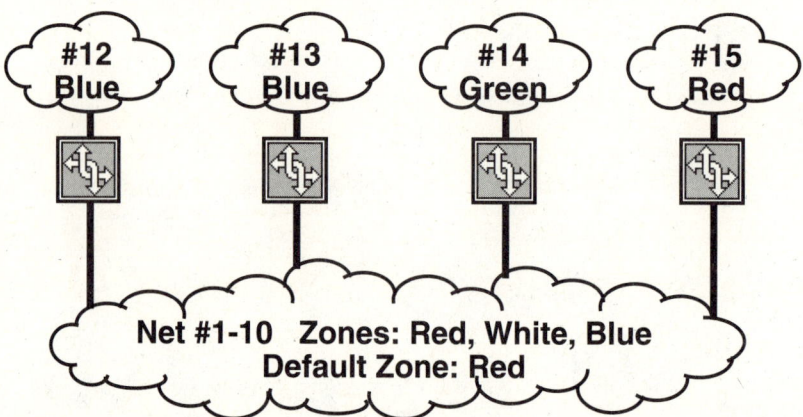

You can change your Mac's default zone assignment by opening the Network control panel and double-clicking on the EtherTalk or TokenTalk icon. A zone list will appear along with a prompt to change the Mac's zone. From then on, your Mac will belong to that zone, until you decide to change it again. If you're unsure which zone your Mac belongs to, simply open the Chooser. The highlighted zone is the zone to which your Macintosh belongs.

Zone names can be up to 32 characters in length. They are case-insensitive. This means that zone "Beavis" is the same as zone "BEAVIS". Zones are much easier to read, however, if the standard sentence case is used. Spaces are significant, so be careful not to type an extra space between words or add an unwanted space at the end of a name. This will appear as another zone in the Chooser.

If you're creating a zoned network, try to establish a meaningful zone naming convention prior to router installation. Remember that network numbers are for the computer's convenience and zone names for the users' convenience. Your zone naming standard should help users find networked printers and file servers and be flexible to support future expansion.

Chapter 25

Networking the Macintosh

How does the Chooser work?

The Chooser is one of the coolest, yet least understood, aspects of the Macintosh. With it, a user can find and select network (and local) services in an easy and consistent manner. The Chooser does many interesting things behind the scenes. First, it dynamically generates a list of available network zones. Then, when you choose a particular service, by clicking on an icon, the Chooser then generates a list of those devices that meet the selection criteria. Finally, once you've selected a particular named service, the Chooser proceeds to discover the AppleTalk address of the chosen service. You see, the names in the Chooser are for your benefit while the network addresses are for the benefit of the Macintosh.

We've discussed how AppleTalk dynamically assigns a node number to a device. This was a wonderful achievement, but Apple had an additional problem to solve. Each AppleTalk device automatically generates a unique node number but initially it's only known by that device. Nodes don't automatically know the node numbers of other devices.

Apple, desiring a plug-and-play environment, decided that a manual creation of a node list was not in keeping with the spirit of Macintosh. An alternative approach was developed to solve the problem of address determination. Let's consider a Mac that needs to print a document to a particular LaserWriter on the network. The Mac doesn't have any idea of the other nodes on the network. Therefore, it must go through a process of discovery to identify the available services. This is done by the AppleTalk protocol known as the Name Binding Protocol, or NBP.

The process is simple. When a user opens the Chooser and clicks on a service icon, such as the LaserWriter icon, the Macintosh first acquires a list of zones from the nearest routers with the AppleTalk Zone Information Protocol (ZIP), it then sends out a NBP Lookup Request packet. Actually, it doesn't simply send it out, it broadcasts, or multicasts, the request to all devices on the cable. This makes sense, since the Mac has no idea who to send the request to anyway. Essentially, the NBP Lookup Request packet contains information on the requested named service.

Of course, when LaserWriters respond to the NBP Lookup Request your Macintosh displays their names in the Chooser. Then, when you select a printer, the Macintosh simply stores in memory the name and network address of the currently selected printer. This is why, for example, when someone moves their PowerBook from the office network to their home network, the office printer will still be chosen. To solve this problem, the LaserWriter must be reselected from the Chooser.

AppleTalk Routing

As mentioned before, big AppleTalk internetworks are created by interconnecting little AppleTalk networks. The devices that are used to connect the networks are called *routers*. AppleTalk routers are an important part of many AppleTalk networks. In addition to providing a mechanism for growth, they also are used to provide traffic isolation and a way to logically group, or organize network services. Next, we'll explore how AppleTalk routers provide these basic tasks.

Routing Tables

As discussed earlier, AppleTalk routers are used to physically and logically connect network segments. Each AppleTalk network that connects to a port on the router is assigned a number, or a range of numbers, that identify that particular network. These AppleTalk network numbers are key to the operation of the router.

AppleTalk routers rely on tables, stored within the router, to forward AppleTalk datagrams from one network to another. The routing tables keep track of all networks by containing an entry for each network number. For each network number on the internet, as shown in Table 25.1, the routing table includes the distance of each network (measured in *hops*, which is the number of routers between the router and the destination network), which port on the router should be used to connect the destination network, and the AppleTalk node ID of the next router.

Table 25.1 Simple Routing Table

Net #	Distance	Port	Next Router #
10	0	1	0
20	0	2	0
30	1	3	12
40	2	3	12

Originally, RTMP, or the Routing Table Maintenance Protocol, was Apple's only protocol to maintain routing tables among the routers of an AppleTalk internet. With RTMP, these routing tables are regularly updated every 10 seconds. This is accomplished by each router exchanging routing tables with the other routers on the network. When a router receives a new routing table, it compares it to the existing table and if a new network has been added, or a network distance has been changed, the router updates its table.

Chapter 25
Networking the Macintosh

RTMP traffic is normally present only between the routers on the internet, but still represents a certain percentage of the total traffic on the network. One of the problems with RTMP is the regular transmission of the routing tables, which occurs even when the network is stable and the network numbers and the routing tables remain unchanged.

To help solve the problem of excessive RTMP traffic, particularly on WANs, Apple has developed a new routing protocol called the Apple Update Routing Protocol, or AURP. It updates the routing tables only when a change has been made to the network. Typically, this means whenever a new network has been added to the internet. AURP is not intended to replace RTMP, which remains a viable protocol for small and medium sized LANs, but rather AURP is seen as a complement to RTMP.

The first product to support AURP is the Apple Internet Router, or AIR. This new product supersedes the AppleTalk Internet Router 2.0. AIR, like its predecessor, runs on a suitably configured Macintosh. AIR fully supports AURP over LAN and WAN connections using a modular approach. AIR also includes support for the industry-standard Simple Network Management Protocol (SNMP) which provides remote network management.

A common configuration is to use the AIR to connect AppleTalk LANs over standard phone lines. For a dial-up connection, Apple recommends a minimum of a pair of V.32/9600 baud modems. Obviously, the faster the modem, the faster and more responsive the AppleTalk connection will be. Since AIR was developed in a modular fashion, additional capabilities can be simply plugged in as needed. Apple offers several optional products including an AppleTalk/X.25 and AppleTalk/IP extension.

The AppleTalk/X.25 Wide Area Extension enables multiple AppleTalk networks to communicate through an X.25 wide area network. One chief advantage of X.25 connections is that, unlike conventional phone lines which are billed solely based on time, regardless of traffic, X.25 uses traffic as a prime determining factor in billing. Considering that most network traffic is not continual and tends to be "bursty," X.25 is very often a cost-effective alternative to traditional dial-up lines.

The other optional AIR module is the AppleTalk/IP Wide Area Extension. It links multiple AppleTalk networks over a TCP/IP network. The AppleTalk/IP extension is supported on Ethernet or Token Ring cabling. As with the X.25 option, the IP option relies on a networking trick known as tunneling. The process of placing one transport protocol inside another is called protocol encapsulation or tunneling. Tunneling AppleTalk inside of another protocol, such as TCP/IP or DECnet, may be necessary or desirable for several reasons.

Part VI

Expanding Your Mac's Horizons

Transport Summary

The Macintosh supports a number of transport protocols. Its native protocol, AppleTalk, provides plug and play connectivity. AppleTalk nodes use dynamic node addressing and name binding to self-configure, which avoids the manual configuration required by other protocols such as DECnet and TCP/IP. Since its inception, Apple has continued to evolve AppleTalk, the most recent changes providing enhanced routing over wide-area networks.

Media

At some point, the networking software, or protocols, must deal with the physical world to send the message. When we speak, it's the air that carries our words. When computers speak, they rely on electromagnetic signals to carry the sequences of ones and zeros. These encode the networking protocols which contain the formatted information which ultimately delivers the service to the user. There are several ways computers can transmit electromagnetic signals, but the most common way is through a cable.

LocalTalk/Phone-type Connectors

LocalTalk, along with the phone-type variants, is one reason for the popularity of Macintosh networking. Its low cost and easy installation has set the standard for desktop networking. Although LocalTalk is rapidly being supplanted by Ethernet, it still offers a viable solution for many Macintosh users.

LocalTalk, shown in figure 25.23, was the first network cabling system available for the Macintosh. Introduced in 1985, along with the LaserWriter printer, LocalTalk was a low-cost plug and play solution in a world of one-thousand dollar Ethernet cards. LocalTalk, and its variants, are still used today, but its popularity is rapidly declining. LocalTalk provides a bandwidth of 230.4 Kbps. Compared to a 9600 bps modem connection, it's pretty quick. Compared to a 10 Mbps Ethernet connection or a 100 Mbps FDDI connection, it's pretty slow.

The LocalTalk cabling system normally connects to a Mac's "Printer" serial port, shown in figure 25.24, and to the appropriate LocalTalk ports of other devices. The "Modem" port is not used for LocalTalk connections unless you intend to run router software on your Mac, such as the Apple Internet Router, to route between two LocalTalk segments.

The heart of LocalTalk is the small connector box which contains a small transformer that electrically isolates the network connection. It has three connections. One side of the box has a length of wire and a connector, either a circular 8-pin, DIN8 connector, or a D-shaped 9 pin, DB9 connector, that is used to connect to the AppleTalk node. The other side of the LocalTalk box has two receptacles that are used to connect the node to the chain of other LocalTalk devices.

Chapter 25
Networking the Macintosh

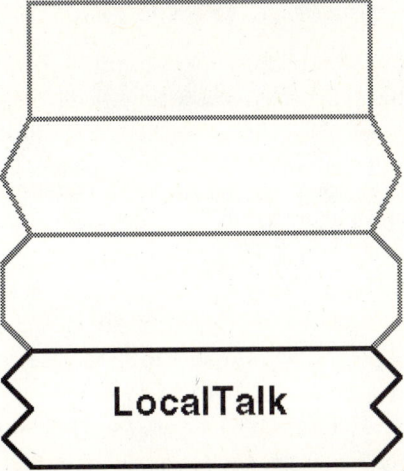

Figure 25.23
LocalTalk resides at the Cabling Layer of the NetPICT.

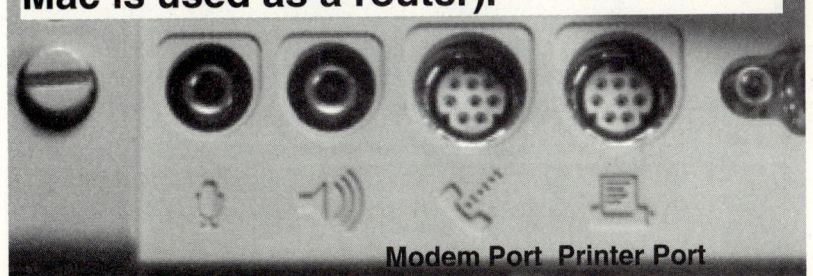

Figure 25.24
Modem and Printer Port.

Part VI
Expanding Your Mac's Horizons

Apple's LocalTalk connectors are rarely used today for several reasons. First, when a LocalTalk network is indicated, it usually makes sense to consider the LocalTalk-compatible phone-type connectors, such as Farallon's PhoneNET, which uses twisted pair telephone type wiring, as an alternative. Another reason is that the LocalTalk connectors do not have a positive locking arrangement—they can be easily pulled out or disrupted. People have been known to wrap electrical tape around the boxes or even Crazy Glue the connectors in place. Perhaps the most important reason for the decline and fall of LocalTalk is that it's rapidly being replaced by Ethernet. The price of an Ethernet connection has dropped dramatically over the past few years so the cost differential is not as great as it was in the past.

LocalTalk does have cable shielding, so in electrically noisy areas, it might be better than the unshielded twisted-pair wiring used by the phone-type connectors. For most small installations, where the anticipated network traffic is modest, you'll want to consider the phone-type devices.

Farallon was the first company to offer a functional replacement for LocalTalk. As shown in figure 25.25, they replaced the DIN8 connectors of LocalTalk with the positive locking RJ-11 connectors found on most telephones. They also replaced the expensive shielded LocalTalk cable with conventional twisted-pair phone wiring. The PhoneNET connectors were, and remain, completely compatible with the LocalTalk Link Access Protocol (LLAP), so switching over to PhoneNET from LocalTalk requires no software changes or special configuration. The success of PhoneNET, and other similar products, was twofold.

Figure 25.25
The Farallon PhoneNET Connector uses telephone-style RJ-11 locking connectors. Courtesy of Farallon Computing.

Small companies were able to create simple, inexpensive LANs in an hour or so by simply going to Radio Shack and buying a spool of phone wire, a box of RJ-11 connectors, and a $15 crimping tool. Large companies soon found that it was possible to integrate the PhoneNET connectors into their existing wiring schemes that were previously used for connecting "dumb" terminals to mainframes and minicomputers over twisted-pair RS-232 wiring.

The PhoneNET connectors also made it possible to move to a star, or radial topology, instead of the daisy chain topology of LocalTalk. PhoneNET currently supports two kinds of stars: passive stars, in which each of the segments is interconnected at a panel or junction block, and active stars, where the segments join at a LocalTalk repeater. Farallon's first repeater was called a StarController.

Since the star topology only requires a single connection at the node, only one RJ-11 receptacle is required. When a PhoneNET connector is used, the extra receptacle is filled with a terminating resistor. Other brands are self-terminating and don't require a separate resistor. Farallon also offers a single-receptacle connector called the StarConnector. This small connector, shown in figure 25.26, plugs directly into the printer port of a Macintosh, and is ideally suited for star networks. StarConnectors are also useful in pairs, where they can be used to connect two devices, a PowerBook and a desktop Mac for example, with a single RJ-11 cable.

Chapter 25
Networking the Macintosh

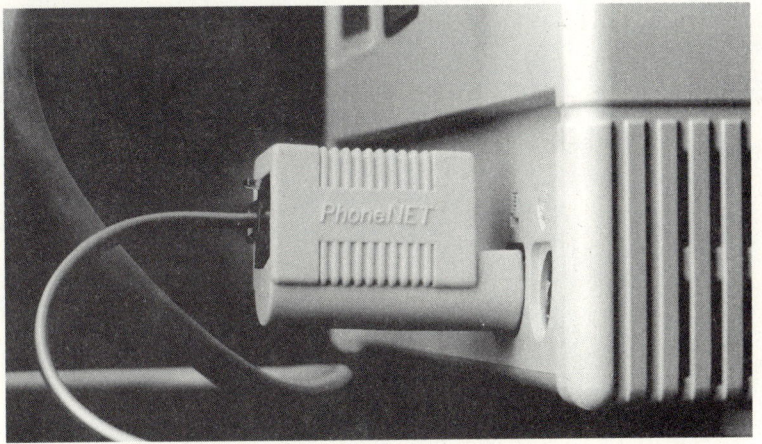

Figure 25.26
The Farallon PhoneNET StarConnector plugs directly into the Printer port. Used in star networks, the device is self-terminating. Courtesy of Farallon Computing.

Today, there are many LocalTalk-compatible products. In addition to Farallon, there are several companies, including Apple, that make the phone-type connectors and products.

Part VI

Expanding Your Mac's Horizons

Ethernet/EtherTalk

At one time, Ethernet was the FDDI of cabling systems. It was expensive, and offered a bandwidth well beyond the requirements of most applications. Paradoxically, today, Ethernet is fast becoming the modern equivalent of RS-232. Nearly all computer systems offer Ethernet connections and with the advent of very-large scale integration, the Ethernet components have been reduced to a single chip implementation. This has driven the cost of Ethernet cards down to less than $200. Fortunately, these price reductions aren't limited to the PC world, as Macintosh Ethernet cards are fast becoming a commodity item.

Even though Apple developed LocalTalk to provide a basic physical connection between devices, they also recognized the need to provide alternative wiring choices to their customers. One of the most popular local-area networks (LANs), diagrammed in figure 25.27, is Ethernet. It was developed with multiprotocol support in mind. A single Ethernet network can support many different protocols at the same time.

Figure 25.27

Ethernet resides at the Cabling Layer of the NetPICT.

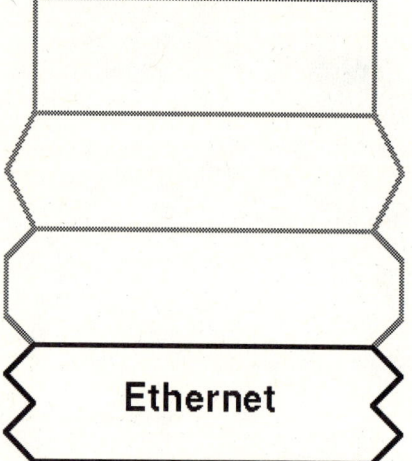

When AppleTalk protocols run over Ethernet cables, Apple calls this EtherTalk. Whereas LocalTalk cables have a bandwidth of 230.4 Kbps, Ethernet has a bandwidth of 10 million bits per second (Mbps). So instead of being limited to 32 nodes, as with LocalTalk, EtherTalk networks can support

Chapter 25
Networking the Macintosh

thousands of devices. Theoretically, with the latest version of AppleTalk (Phase 2), a network can have over 16 million devices. Of course, on a single cable you would run out of room to connect all those devices, but Ethernet cables are often "connected" by network bridges, microwave links, and even satellites to other Ethernet networks to create an "extended" Ethernet LAN. Many large companies have extensive world-wide Ethernet LANs with thousands of computers produced by different companies.

The throughput of an Ethernet network is greater than LocalTalk. Actual transmission rates will depend on many factors, such as network traffic, size of the transmitted file, and performance of the individual Ethernet controller. On average, you can expect a three to five times improvement over a LocalTalk network. Why such a difference? The factors limiting Ethernet throughput are numerous and complex, but the speed of the Macintosh CPU, hard disk, and Ethernet hardware coupled with network configuration, application performance and other network traffic all play a role in Ethernet performance.

All Macs and most LaserWriters come standard with the hardware to support LocalTalk communications. Some Macs, such as the Quadra family, and LaserWriters, such as the LaserWriter IIG and LaserWriter Pro 630, come equipped with built-in Ethernet hardware. For those Macs that don't have Ethernet, connections are made with the addition of a networking card. LocalTalk LaserWriters, such as the LaserWriter IINT, can connect to Ethernet with adapter devices, such as Dayna's EtherPrint device.

Ethernet cards, for those Macs with card slots, are made by Apple and other vendors (see figure 25.28). The cost varies between $150 and $300. Several companies also sell SCSI/Ethernet adapters for those Macs, such as the Classic and the PowerBook family, without card slots. These devices connect to the SCSI port of the Macintosh, just like any other SCSI device, such as a hard disk, and then connect to the Ethernet network.

For both the Ethernet cards or the SCSI/Ethernet devices, EtherTalk software drivers are included. This software provides additional network driver programs that give you the option, through the Control Panel, to select between LocalTalk or EtherTalk. Unless you turn your Mac into a router, the AppleTalk traffic can only go through one port at a time.

There are several variants of Ethernet cabling. Even though the cabling is different, the electrical signaling remains the same. Because of this, all Ethernet cable variations use the same EtherTalk drivers. The only significant difference is the cable type and the connectors.

Figure 25.28

A sampling of Ethernet cards. The two-piece units are for the Macintosh SE and SE/30. The one-piece unit is for any NuBus-equipped Macintosh. Courtesy of Farallon Computing.

▼ **Thickwire 10Base-5**

Thickwire Ethernet, shown in figure 25.29, is a stiff coaxial (one wire inside another wire) cable about 3/8" in diameter and employs a 15-pin D-style connector. The cable is terminated at both ends with special resistive fittings that minimize signal reflections that would otherwise degrade communications. Usually thickwire Ethernet is employed as a central "backbone" running throughout a building, although fiber-optic Ethernet is rapidly replacing thickwire as a backbone media. Thick-wire Ethernet permits a maximum of 200 devices on a 1640 foot segment. Thickwire Ethernet is often referred to as 10Base-5 wiring.

Thickwire connections are established by clamping a device called a transceiver to the cable. Most transceivers are installed by drilling a small hole in the cable with a special tool followed by clamping the transceiver which pierces the cable with sharp contact pins that make electrical contact. This method of connection is sometimes referred to as a "vampire tap." These taps can only be made at regular intervals along the cable. Most cables have indicator markings every 2.5 meters to help position the transceivers.

Adding transceivers to a backbone cable is not difficult, but this is not a cost-effective way to make a single network connection. Usually transceivers are used to connect hubs, or repeaters, which support the connection of multiple devices through a single transceiver connection to the backbone.

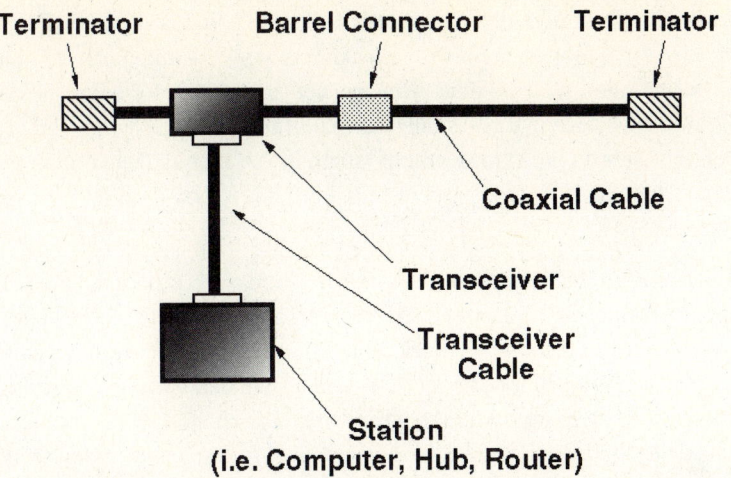

Figure 25.29
Thickwire Ethernet 10Base-5 componentry.

With the 10Base-5 nomenclature, the "10" refers to the bandwidth. All Ethernet implementations have a 10 megabit bandwidth. The term "Base" refers to baseband (as opposed to broadband). Baseband means that the cable only supports a single communications channel. The last value of "5" refers to the maximum length of the cable segment, which for 10Base-5 is 500 meters. There is a specification for broadband Ethernet called 10Broad-36. It runs over a coaxial cable and has a maximum segment length of 3,600 meters.

▼ **Thinwire 10Base-2**

Thinwire Ethernet, shown in figure 25.30, is thinner (about 3/16 inch) and considerably more flexible than the original thickwire. It used to be a popular choice to connect desktop devices and workstations. Today, however, for desktop connections, thinwire is being rapidly replaced by twisted-pair Ethernet.

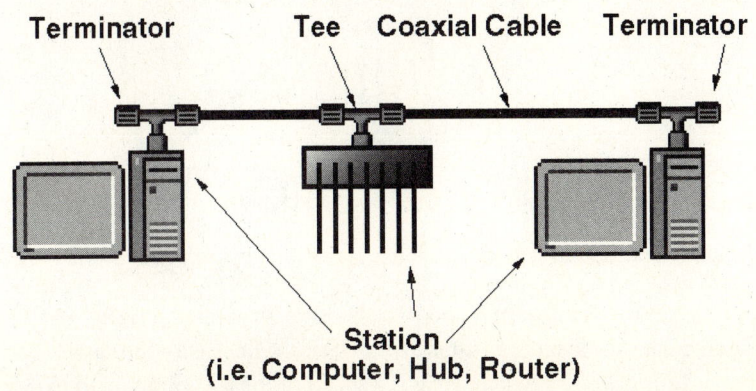

Figure 25.30
Thinwire Ethernet 10Base-2 componentry.

Part VI
Expanding Your Mac's Horizons

Thinwire Ethernet uses BNC (twist and lock) type connections and allows 30 devices per 656 foot segment over a maximum network length of 3281 feet. Thin-wire is often referred to as "Cheapernet" or its more formal name of 10Base-2. This designation is similar to that of thickwire except for the "2," which indicates a maximum segment length of 200 meters (actually, the maximum segment length is 185 meters, but I guess they didn't want to call it 10Base-1.85).

Connections are made with a tee connector, similar to LocalTalk. One branch of the tee connects to the network device, while the other two connections are used to connect to the network. When thinwire is connected in a daisy-chain, the free ends of the last tees must be terminated with special resistive end caps. Adding more devices to a thinwire daisy-chain disrupts the network because the chain must be broken. It is possible to disconnect a device at the attachment point without disrupting the network chain.

Thinwire can also be configured in a star topology using a thinwire Ethernet repeater. Here, each tee at the end of each branch of the star must be terminated. The use of thinwire star topologies is rapidly declining due to the arrival of the newer, more flexible twisted-pair Ethernet.

▼ **Twisted pair 10Base-T**

Lately, another Ethernet variant has started to become popular. Twisted-pair Ethernet, shown in figure 25.31, has been around for several years, but during the past two years it has virtually dominated the desktop. With this system, Ethernet can be implemented on standard unshielded twisted-pair wiring. Thinwire Ethernet requires two pairs of wires that meet certain industry requirements.

Figure 25.31
Twisted-pair Ethernet 10Base-T componentry.

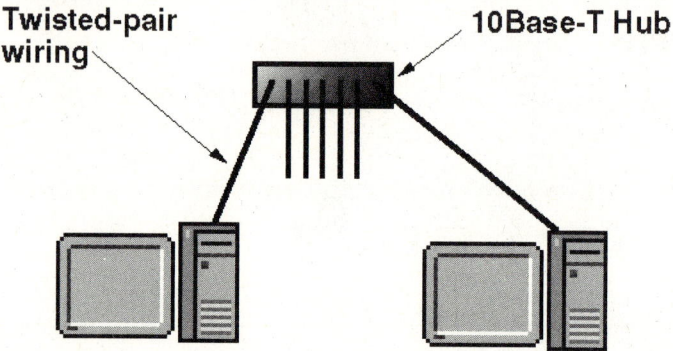

The choice of wire may depend on local building or electrical codes, or the recommendations of suppliers. It's always best to check with the various codes and suppliers for detailed cabling specifications. As mentioned earlier, it's always wise to cable for thinwire Ethernet even if you're planning to use LocalTalk. It also may be prudent to consider the anticipated wiring standards for the newer high-speed cabling systems such as FDDI (Fiber Data Distributed Interface). There is currently work underway to implement FDDI over copper twisted-pair wiring and to develop a 100 Mbps version of Ethernet that runs over four twisted-pairs. Often, if your wiring strategy covers the most stringent wiring scenario, you'll be able to design for future growth and enhancements.

Unlike thickwire or thinwire that can be connected in a bus or daisy-chain, twisted-pair Ethernet requires the use of a hub. These hubs come in a wide variety of prices and configurations with a varying number of ports and extra features. Some hubs offer a modular construction that make it easy to provide additional connections as required.

All the Ethernet card vendors for the Macintosh offer twisted-pair Ethernet versions, with many cards offering multiple connectors (thick, thin and twisted-pair) on one card. Twisted pair Ethernet underwent some changes during its early years and there have been several implementations, but now, the standard is set and is widely known as 10Base-T.

▼ **Apple's Ethernet Cabling System**

Apple announced in January of 1990 a new line of low-cost Ethernet cards. These new cards, one for the Macs with NuBus slots and one for the Macintosh LC, use a separate attachment unit, known as an Apple AUI (attachment unit interface) that attaches to either thick wire, thin wire or twisted pair Ethernet. Resembling LocalTalk connectors, these connectors attach to the Mac or LaserWriter with a new style connector (see figure 25.32). This permits Apple to use these new compact connectors on the motherboards of all their new machines. The appropriate attachment unit, either thick, thin, or twisted-pair, is then connected to the device. This approach offers Apple a single, compact connector for their new products, while still offering the flexibility of three attachment options. Apple has provided the specification for Apple AUI, so these new connectors are also offered by third-party suppliers. These new devices will bring the ease-of-installation and low cost of LocalTalk to Ethernet networks.

Other Cabling Systems

LocalTalk and Ethernet are the most popular cabling choices for the Macintosh, but the Mac also supports a wide range of other industry standard cabling.

Chapter 25
Networking the Macintosh

Part VI
Expanding Your Mac's Horizons

Figure 25.32
Apple's Ethernet cabling system.

▼ **Token Ring**

Token Ring networks (see figure 25.33) operate using a different principal than Ethernet. Ethernet devices listen to the cable before transmitting, whereas Token Ring devices wait their turn till an electronic token comes their way. Because of this fundamental difference, Token Ring networks enjoy certain benefits over Ethernet networks.

First, when it comes to traffic, Token Ring networks are self-limiting. Unlike Ethernet networks that degrade when excessive traffic causes collisions and retransmissions, Token Ring networks simply reach their maximum throughput and then level out. Another advantage of Token Ring is that a node is always guaranteed access to the cable within a finite period of time. Ethernet nodes play a statistical game where access to the cable is not guaranteed. This makes Token Ring networks appealing for time critical, real-time, or process control applications.

Most decisions to select Token Ring technology (other than FDDI) are not made because of its technical advantage, but rather to connect to the IBM environment, where Token Ring is a popular choice. There are currently two implementations of Token Ring, a 4 Mbit and a 16 Mbit.

Figure 25.33
Token Ring NetPICT.

Token Ring cards are more expensive than their Ethernet counterparts. Prices range from $500 to $800 per card. Apple and several third-party vendors offer NuBus Token Ring cards.

▼ FDDI

Likely to succeed Ethernet, FDDI (Fiber Distributed Data Interface) is an ANSI and ISO standard network based on dual fiber optic rings (see figure 25.34). FDDI has a bandwidth of 100 Mbps. This is 10 times the bandwidth of Ethernet. Just as Apple offered EtherTalk and TokenTalk drivers for Ethernet and Token Ring, they have also developed FDDITalk drivers. The Apple drivers currently support AppleTalk Phase 2 and MacTCP. FDDI networks can contain 1000 nodes, no more than 2 kilometers apart, for a total aggregate distance of 100 kilometers.

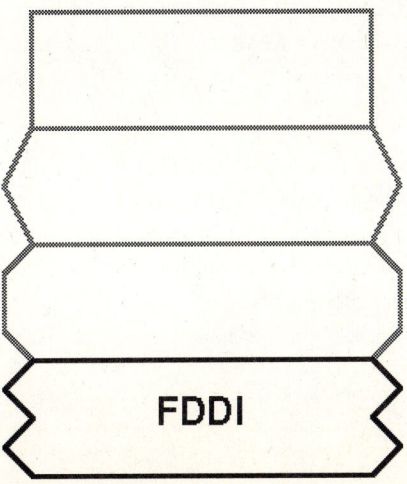

Figure 25.34
FDDI resides at the cabling layer.

Part VI
Expanding Your
Mac's Horizons

FDDI cards, shown in figure 25.35, are still a bit on the expensive side at over a $1000 per card, but just as cost of Ethernet cards dropped several years ago, expect the same to happen to FDDI cards as well. FDDI cards are currently offered by several companies, Codenoll, Cabletron and Impulse Technology being three examples. While FDDI is still rare on the desktop, it's becoming increasingly prevalent as a backbone cabling system.

Figure 25.35
A Macintosh FDDI card.

Although FDDI is gaining in popularity there are other upcoming standards vying for acceptance. A proposed "CDDI" standard would offer the performance of FDDI over less costly copper cabling. HP and AT&T are proposing an upgrade to the Ethernet standard to achieve FDDI performance levels (100 Mbps) over 10Base-T twisted-pair wiring. Instead of two twisted-pairs, this approach requires four twisted-pairs.

▼ **Serial RS-232/422**

Serial communications has only recently become a popular cabling medium for AppleTalk. Starting with Apple's Remote Access Protocol (ARAP), many Macintosh users are using serial connections and modems to dial-in to remote Macintosh computers. ARAP (see figure 25.36) uses data compression and buffering techniques to get the most out of the relatively slow dial-up links.

ARAP uses the client/server model to make the remote connection. A Macintosh running the client portion of Remote Access dials in to a Remote Access server. With Apple's software, the server is a Macintosh. There are other servers from third-party vendors that use dedicated hardware devices. These servers, such as Shiva's LANrover, connect to multiple dial-up lines and also make a network connection to LocalTalk or Ethernet networks.

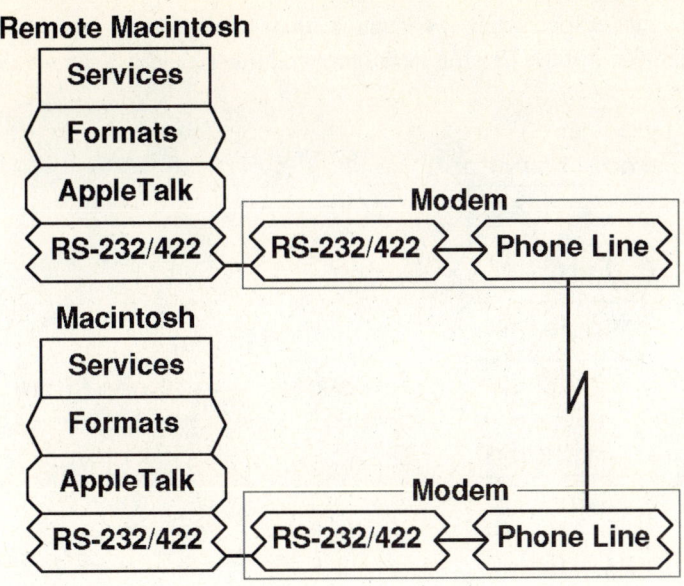

Figure 25.36
AppleTalk Remote Access NePICT.

▼ Wireless

As computers get smaller and smaller, the cabling systems used to connect them also tie them down to the desktop. The solution is to eliminate the cabling. Wireless networks are a recent development. There are several wireless technologies available for the Macintosh.

One option, for a wireless network shown in figure 25.37, is to use Apple's Remote Access with a cellular phone/modem combination. This makes sense for wide-area network connections for a limited number of devices. For LAN connectivity, wireless technology may be useful in locations where conventional wiring is difficult or impossible to run. Motorola, the leader manufacturer of cellular telephones, has a Macintosh product called EMBARC which provides a one-way wireless messaging service to remote Mac users.

There are also options for LAN mediums such as LocalTalk and Ethernet. Starting with LocalTalk, Photonics makes LocalTalk devices, figure 25.38, that use reflected infrared to link a number of nodes. The infrared devices focus their energy at a single point on the ceiling.

Motorola has developed a wireless version of Ethernet called Altair II. These devices use low-power radio waves as a transmission medium. Altair's transmission rate of 5.7 Mbps is somewhat less than Ethernet bandwidth.

Compared to conventional wired networks, these new technologies are still somewhat expensive and are only cost-effective in those cases where wiring is difficult or where rewiring costs would exceed the cost of the wireless components. Expect wireless communications to continue to increase in popularity as Apple's Newton technology and other handheld computers become popular.

Figure 25.37
Cellular modem/ARA NetPICT.

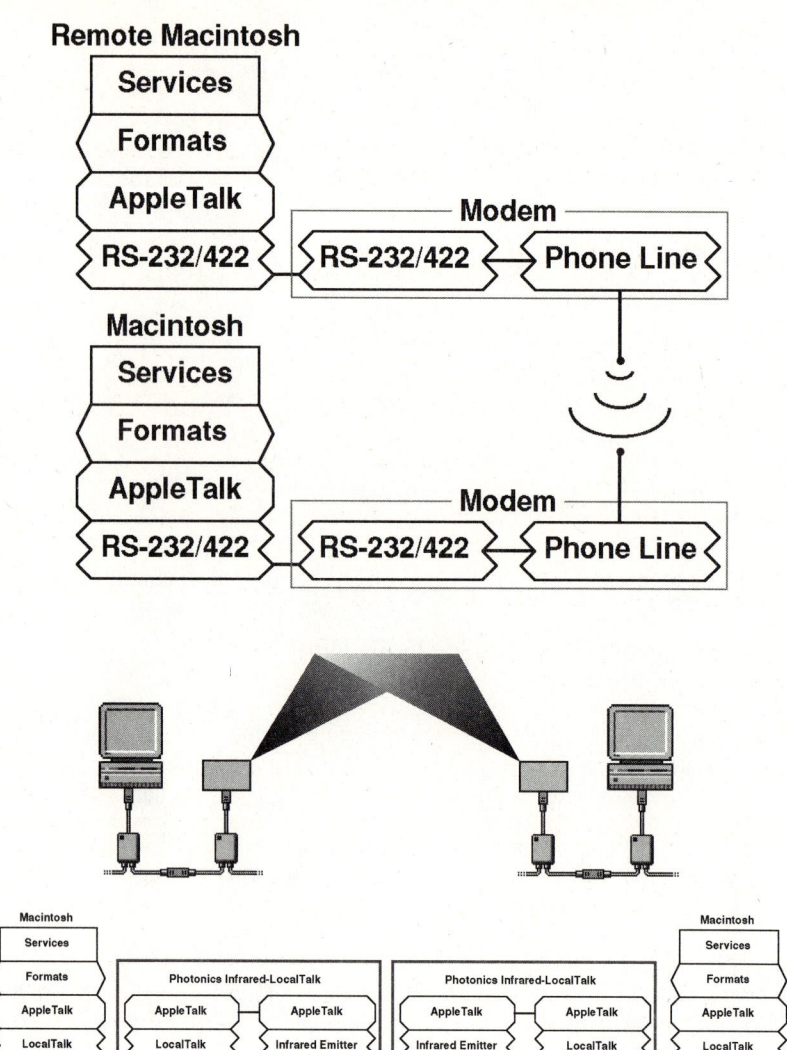

Figure 25.38
Photonics makes a LocalTalk device that uses infrared waves as a connection medium.

Media Summary

The Macintosh, LaserWriter and many other peripherals have a built-in networking capability known as LocalTalk. It is a low-cost cabling system that works over twisted-pair cabling. AppleTalk protocols aren't limited to LocalTalk, they can be sent over Ethernet, Token Ring and most other mediums. While AppleTalk has been extremely popular on LANs, it's only recently begun to be accepted as a viable WAN protocol.

Chapter 25
Networking the Macintosh

Macintosh Networking with Other Computers

Connecting Macs into networks is difficult enough; connecting Macs with other types of computers can be even more confusing! Fortunately, when it comes to multivendor networks, the Macintosh is a team player. It supports a wide variety of network Services, Formats, Transports, and Media. AppleTalk is also fast becoming a de-facto industry standard that is supported on many different computers, from the IBM PC to Digital's VAX minicomputer.

Living in an Intel/DOS world

Macintosh computers and PCs, when connected, form the most common type of multivendor network. Exchanging documents and sharing resources between Macs and PCs is becoming more commonplace as software developers have been increasingly offering separate Macintosh and Windows versions of their applications. With all the attention and focus on these two platforms, it's not surprising that there are so many networking choices available. This section will highlight some of the leading choices for putting your Macintosh computers and PCs on speaking terms.

AppleTalk on the PC

If you have a network where Macs are predominant and there are just a few PCs, then consider turning those PCs into AppleTalk nodes. One way to do this is with Farallon's PhoneNET PC. It equips a DOS or Windows PC with the AppleTalk protocol stack and also provides the equivalent of the Chooser, so that the user is able to select AppleTalk network services, such as AFP file services, System 7 File Sharing and PAP print services. PhoneNET PC works either with a LocalTalk/PhoneNET card (offered by Apple, Dayna, COPS Inc. and also available from Farallon), most common PC Ethernet cards, as well as IBM Token Ring 16/4 cards.

▼ Farallon Timbuktu (PhoneNET PC included with all versions of Timbuktu for Windows)

▼ Microsoft Mail 3.0 and 3.1

▼ QuickMail from CE Software

▼ Lotus cc:Mail

▼ WordPerfect Office

▼ Claris FileMaker Pro 2.0

▼ Blyth Omnis 7 (Can access DAL services)

▼ Microsoft FoxBase+

Novell Solutions

Novell, the networking giant, offers two approaches to Macintosh PC connectivity. First, Novell NetWare servers can be configured as AFP file servers. As shown in figure 25.39, Macs access these services with the AppleTalk transport and PC users access the same server with Novell IPX protocols. Normally, it's not recommended, but it is possible for the two environments to share a common file space. Thus, it is possible to share files between the two environments.

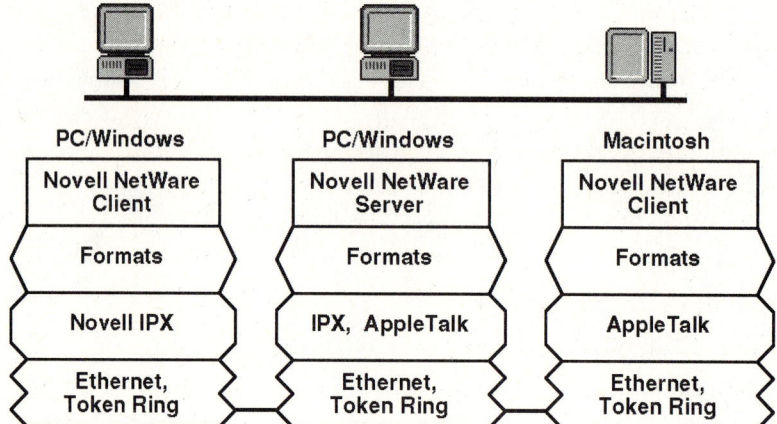

Figure 25.39
Novell's NetWare for Macintosh adds AppleTalk, AFP, and PAP support to PC/Windows computers.

In the past, Novell concentrated on the file service support for the Mac, but has more recently begun to develop another approach, called MacIPX, which as shown in figure 25.40, involves placing Novell's IPX protocol onto the Macintosh. Intended for developers, MacIPX will provide an avenue for cross-platform peer-to-peer communications between applications on the two different platforms. MacIPX should help the Macintosh make inroads into environments where PCs and Novell networks prevail.

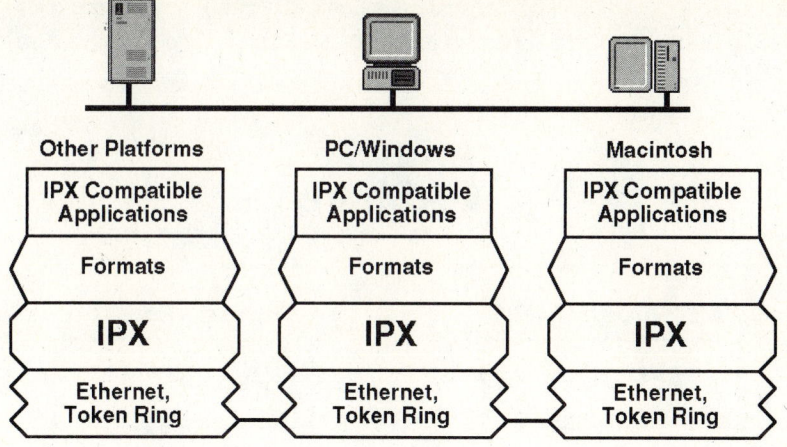

Figure 25.40
Novell's MacIPX should provide the developer community with the tools to develop peer-to-peer IPX applications.

Banyan VINES

Banyan VINES, a popular enterprise-wide networking system, offers client support for Macintosh workstations, allowing them to share resources with DOS, OS/2 and Windows workstations on the same network. VINES supports the AppleTalk filing protocol and the Printer Access Protocol from their Intel/PC-based VINES server. In addition, AppleTalk tunneling through VINES enables disjointed AppleTalk networks to be connected with each other via the VINES network.

The choices of a cabling system for Mac/PC connectivity are as varied as the cabling choices available for the Macintosh. You'll have the choice of LocalTalk, Ethernet, Token Ring and even the popular PC cabling system of ARCNET.

UNIX Connectivity

While not as prevalent as the PC or the Mac, UNIX-based workstations and other UNIX computers are very common, particularly in the engineering and technical environments where Macintosh is also very popular. This section explores the networking options for Macintosh and UNIX computers.

Most of the services in the Macintosh/UNIX world revolve around file access and terminal services. To a Macintosh user, file service means AFP. There are several products that provide this service. Xinet sells K-AShare which

Part VI
Expanding Your Mac's Horizons

implements AFP on a Sun or HP UNIX host (see figure 25.41). So, just like with any other AFP server, the Macintosh user accesses UNIX files through the Chooser. The mounted volumes provide access to the UNIX files as if they were local disk files on the Mac. The Sun or HP running K-AShare could also be set up as an NFS server, so in a sense K-AShare can be thought of an AFP/NFS gateway.

Figure 25.41
Xinet's K-AShare turns a Sun or HP UNIX workstation into an AFP Server.

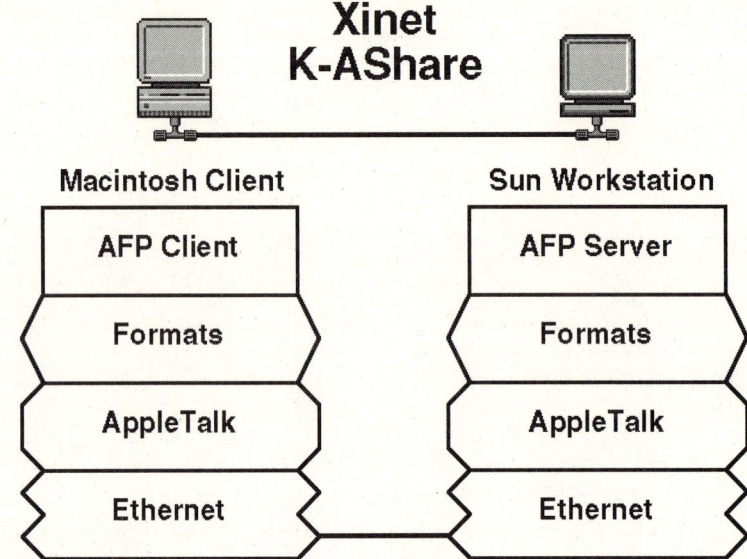

Data Access Language (DAL)

When it comes to databases, DAL services are there to provide access to relational databases on UNIX systems (see figure 25.42). Apple sells a version of DAL for A/UX equipped Macs and Pacer offers a DAL server for HP UNIX computers, DEC Ultrix and Sun's SPARCstation. These services use the AppleTalk transport on each of their respective platforms.

File Services: FTP & NFS

The File Transfer Protocol (FTP) is commonly used in UNIX and TCP/IP networks to move files between nodes (see figure 25.43). FTP provides directory services so a user can get a listing of candidate files on a remote machine. It also provides support for a variety of formats (i.e. ASCII, Binary) and insures security by requiring login IDs and passwords.

Developed by Sun Microsystems, NFS provides additional capabilities not found in FTP. It can be used to transfer files between computers, but it also provides a mechanism for distributed applications that are network-aware. There are several implementations of NFS on the Macintosh, two of the more popular products are NFS/Share from InterCon and Pathway NFS from Wollongong. Both of these products, shown in figure 25.44, work with Apple's MacTCP product and bring NFS services to the desktop of the Macintosh, thus retaining the ease-of-use of the Mac desktop.

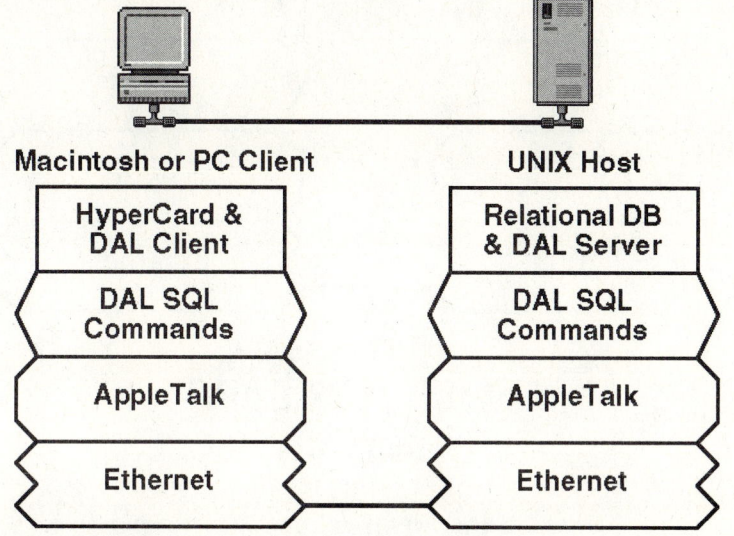

Figure 25.42
Apple and Pacer provide DAL database services on UNIX computers. All UNIX DAL servers use AppleTalk as a transport.

X-Window

The X-Window, also called X or X11, standard evolved from initial work done at the Massachusetts Institute of Technology. It is a client/server windowing environment that is extensible and customizable. DEC's implementation of X, known as DECwindows, is used as their standard windowing environment on their VAX/VMS computers and UNIX-based workstations. Motif is the name of the X implementation created by the Open Software Foundation (OSF).

For all its flexibility, X has yet to really take off. The number of X applications continues to grow, but at a slow pace. The bulk of X applications can be found in the scientific and technical world where UNIX is an established standard. X is also reasonably popular in its DECwindows guise, where Digital continues to migrate its traditionally VT terminal-based applications over to X.

Chapter 25
Networking the Macintosh

Figure 25.43
Terminal emulators, such as VersaTerm-Pro, provide FTP services to MacTCP-equipped Macs.

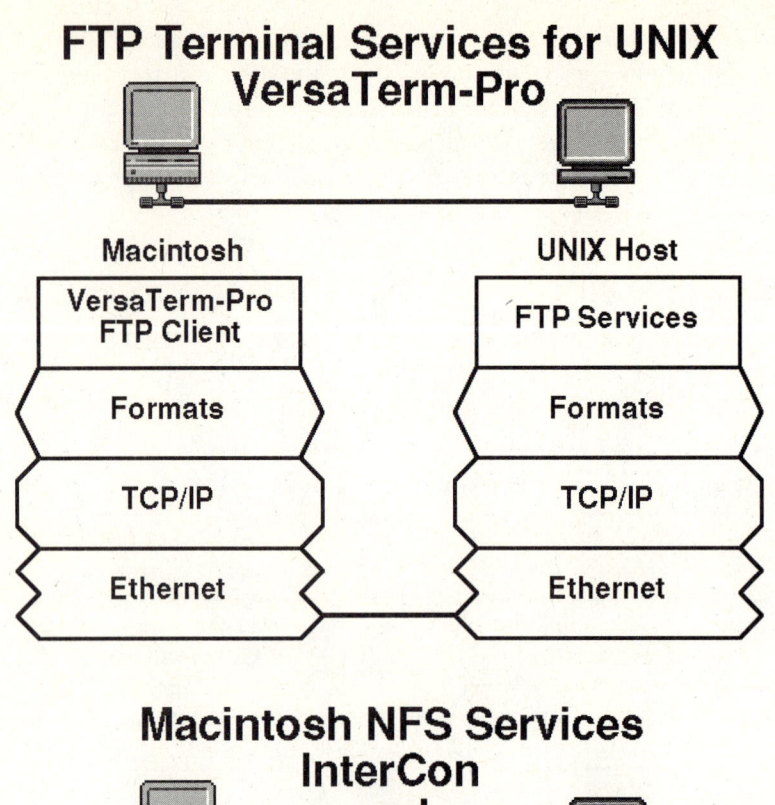

Figure 25.44
InterCon and Wollongong offer NFS services for the Macintosh. They both use the MacTCP transport protocol.

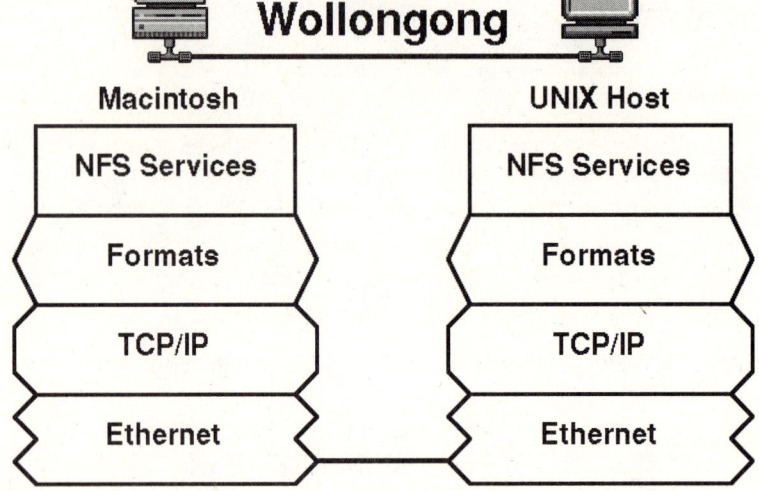

Terminal Services

The most basic of TCP/IP services is the Telnet terminal service. It is a simple protocol that allows a user to remotely connect to a server and appear as a local terminal. There are several popular terminal emulators that offer Telnet and work in concert with MacTCP. NCSA Telnet and VersaTerm-Pro are two examples. With these applications, you'll be able to log onto remote TCP/IP hosts over a dial-up connection or over a network connection such as Ethernet.

The flip side of AppleTalk on UNIX is TCP/IP on the Macintosh. Apple's MacTCP is widely supported by many third-party vendors listed in this chapter. It is the engine that is used by these vendors to create their applications.

If you're familiar with TCP/IP networks, configuring MacTCP is a snap. If you're a Mac person and a TCP novice, be prepared for a different world. TCP/IP nodes can obtain their addresses manually or by a dedicated server. There is a mechanism for dynamically assigning addresses, but unlike AppleTalk, it's somewhat limited.

The Macintosh can connect to UNIX computers at all levels. UNIX computers can speak the AppleTalk protocol and Macs can speak the TCP/IP protocol and most UNIX computers and workstations utilize Ethernet cabling so the integration process is often as simple as installing software.

Digital VAX Connectivity

Before the famous Apple-IBM Alliance, there was the Apple-Digital Alliance. The collaboration between these two companies resulted in an architecture that combines the best of both worlds. The services offered by DEC's PATHWORKS for Macintosh are a combination of products developed by Apple, Digital and third-party vendors. They address the basic requirements of terminal emulation, X-Window (DECwindows) emulation, AFP file services, PAP print services, DEC print services, DAL database services and E-mail.

VAXshare is the name given to AFP file services and PAP print services that run on a VAX. The VAXshare file server, diagrammed in figure 25.45, can be set up to support multiple servers, each potentially with multiple volumes. These volumes can be set up to reference any VMS directory. These directories can contain VMS files, either ASCII or binary, or foreign files, such

Chapter 25
Networking the Macintosh

Part VI
Expanding Your Mac's Horizons

Figure 25.45
DEC's VAXshare file server turns a VAX into an AFP file server. Macintosh users are able to access VAX directories and files.

as those from a PC. This way, Mac users can edit VMS text files with Mac text editors or word processors. They can also exchange binary application files with corresponding VAX or PC applications.

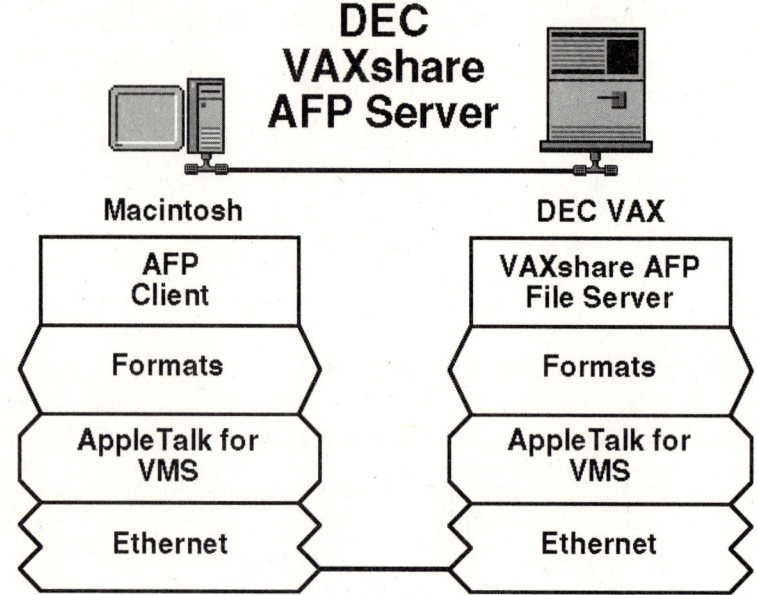

The print services let Mac users spool LaserWriter print jobs to the VAX, print to DEC PostScript printer and let interactive VAX VT terminal users print to Apple LaserWriters through a standard VMS print queue. An example is diagrammed in figure 25.46.

The most common VAX/VMS transport protocol is DECnet. VAX/VMS systems usually come with DECnet, but Macs do not. So part of DEC's PATHWORKS for Macintosh solution is installing DECnet on the Macintosh. DECnet on the Macintosh requires a configuration process that includes the assignment of a DECnet area and node number (similar to an AppleTalk network and node number) and the generation of a list of other DECnet nodes where communication is desired. This explicit address assignment and node listing is contrary to the AppleTalk philosophy of dynamic addressing and name binding with NBP.

Digital redefined computing in the 70's and Apple did the same in the 80's. In the 90's, Apple and Digital both realize that the network is the common battleground for computing services. Digital, with its PATHWORKS for Macintosh product has recognized the importance of the Macintosh. They have successfully integrated two supposedly closed architectures by providing terminal emulation, DECwindows (X-Window), AFP file and print services, database access and two E-mail packages.

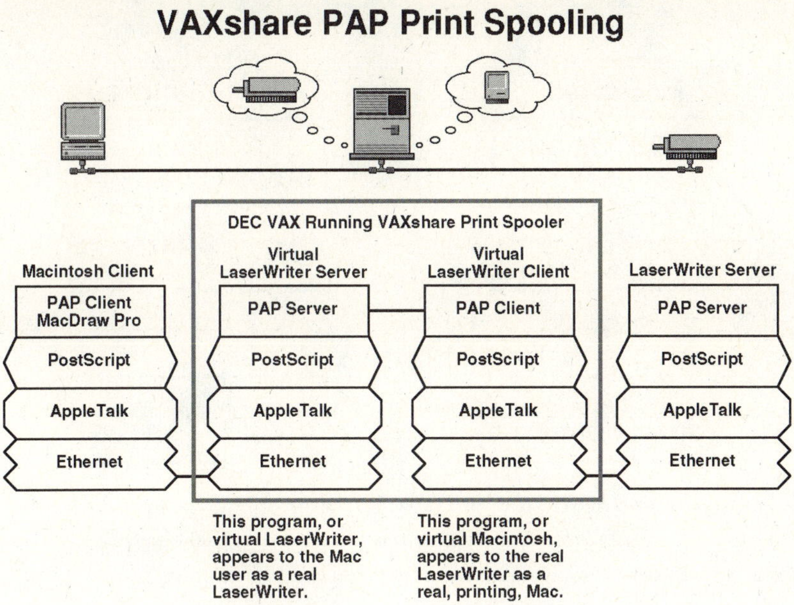

VAXshare PAP Print Spooling

```
Macintosh Client        DEC VAX Running VAXshare Print Spooler      LaserWriter Server
                        Virtual                  Virtual
                        LaserWriter Server       LaserWriter Client
PAP Client              PAP Server               PAP Client          PAP Server
MacDraw Pro
PostScript              PostScript               PostScript          PostScript
AppleTalk               AppleTalk                AppleTalk           AppleTalk
Ethernet                Ethernet                 Ethernet            Ethernet
```

This program, or virtual LaserWriter, appears to the Mac user as a real LaserWriter.

This program, or virtual Macintosh, appears to the real LaserWriter as a real, printing, Mac.

Figure 25.46
One aspect of VAXshare's print services turns a VAX into an PAP print spooler. Macintosh users are able to send print jobs to the VAX. The VAX queues the job and sends to the "real" printer.

IBM Connectivity

Still a large part of the corporate world, IBM's mainframe and minicomputers are an important part of Apple's network strategy. Once again the Macintosh proves its worth as the "universal client" and can readily connect to the Big Blue world. Here are a few examples of Macintosh-to-IBM products.

3270 terminal emulation, as diagrammed in figure 25.47, is the most common type of IBM connectivity. There are a number of 3270 terminal emulators available for the Macintosh. These emulators let a suitably equipped Macintosh to access IBM mainframes. Most Mac emulators add value by adding features such as programmable "hot keys" or a macro capability. Some emulators support keyboard remapping where 3270 keys can be reassigned to the Macintosh keyboard. A common feature in 3270 emulators is the ability to perform IND$FILE file transfers from within the terminal session. Three popular 3270 emulators include Apple's SNA•ps 3270, DCA's IRMA Workstation for Macintosh, ASC's asc3270 and Avatar's MacMainFrame.

Figure 25.47
A Macintosh running a 3270 emulator over a coaxial connection to the host.

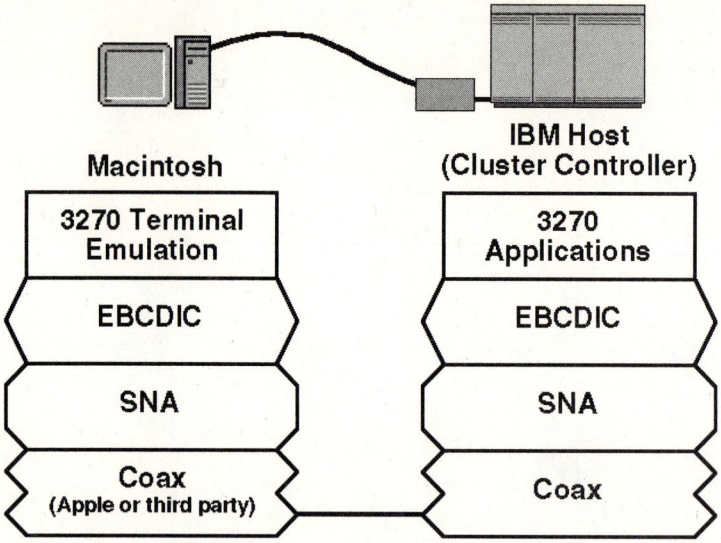

The most common direct connection to an IBM mainframe is made with a coaxial (coax) cable. Traditionally, this has been the method employed by IBM terminals for years. It's also used by Macs and PCs running terminal emulation programs. Since Macs don't come with a coax connection, an expansion card is required. The coax card is usually connected to an intermediate device known as a cluster controller, which is used to connect multiple coax devices to the mainframe. The IBM mainframe world is changing, but is still typified by terminal-type applications. The Macintosh can easily adapt to this environment with numerous terminal emulators and front-ending programs. These products support IBM's cabling (i.e. coax, twinax, Token Ring) and protocols (i.e. SAA, SNA, APPC, APPN). They also support non-traditional cabling and protocols like LocalTalk, Ethernet, TCP/IP and AppleTalk through the use of gateways.

A Sampling of Common Mac Networking Scenarios

Chapter 25
Networking the Macintosh

Let's examine some common networking scenarios. These scenarios will serve several purposes. First, they will expose you to a number of different wiring schemes, along with their benefits and disadvantages. Next, because the scenarios progress from the simplest to the most complex, you'll be able to establish a growth path for your environment.

Scenario 1: Single LocalTalk Network Daisy-Chain Topology

The simplest Macintosh network is the single LocalTalk daisy-chain network. This network has been around since 1985 and in many cases is still an entirely acceptable network architecture. This network is inexpensive. All that is required is the LocalTalk, or phone-type, connectors and necessary wiring. In nearly all cases, the phone-type connectors (Farallon's PhoneNET) are recommended. Since these connectors use the telephone-style RJ-11 jacks, you'll be able to make your own cables by purchasing a spool of twisted-pair phone wire, jacks and a crimping tool. Electronics stores like Radio Shack should have everything you'll need.

The cost of this network is the lowest of any of the other scenarios. Expect to pay $25 for the LocalTalk/phone-type connectors. With the additional cost of the wiring, the total per node connection cost should be well under $50.

With this network design, you'll be able to provide modest bandwidth for any number between two and thirty devices. The maximum distance of the network may vary somewhat, but plan on a maximum of 1000 total feet of wiring. If you need more distance, consider the use of a LocalTalk repeater.

The tradeoffs for this design are the low-cost and ease-of-installation versus the limited bandwidth of LocalTalk. If you plan on using services that demand high bandwidth, then the simple LocalTalk is not for you. These applications include networked databases, demanding AFP services where large files are frequently transferred, and demanding print jobs submitted from a number of users. As a rule of thumb, try to avoid putting more than five networked printers on a single segment of LocalTalk. If you need this many printers to service your users, then a routed scenario or a higher bandwidth cabling system is probably required.

This network scenario is ideal for small offices that deal with smaller documents and have modest print requirements. It also helps if the physical layout of the area to be networked can easily support the daisy-chain topology. If the devices are all located within a single room, then the daisy-chain can simply run around the periphery of the room. On the other hand, if your network nodes are distributed throughout a large building that doesn't provide ready wiring access, then a more structured wiring approach may make more sense.

Scenario 2: Single Ethernet Network Daisy-Chain Topology

If you find the simplicity of Scenario 1 appealing, but you're concerned about the limited bandwidth of LocalTalk, then an Ethernet solution may be just the ticket. In this case, we'll use the thinwire variant of Ethernet known as 10Base-2. Although twisted-pair Ethernet (10Base-T) is getting all the attention in the press, a thinwire daisy-chain is still a valid solution for small network installations in one compact area.

With the thinwire tee connectors, the nodes can simply be connected one after the other. The total cable length is 185 meters, or about 600 feet. Like the LocalTalk example in Scenario 1 changes made to the network will cause a brief disruption of services.

This scenario is ideal for small workgroups that require more bandwidth than LocalTalk. The Ethernet cabling should provide a 3 to 5 times improvement in throughput over the LocalTalk cabling. The number of nodes is still somewhat limited as 30 is the recommended maximum number of devices on a single segment of thinwire.

One difficulty with thinwire is the cabling. Each cable must have the twist-lock BNC connector fittings. You can purchase pre-assembled lengths of these cables, or invest in the bulk fittings and cable and crimp your own. You may need to go to a networking supply house, such as Black Box, to find these components and the proper crimping tools.

The cost of a thinwire network is somewhat more than a LocalTalk network. If your Macs, LaserWriters and other network devices aren't equipped with

Ethernet, then Ethernet cards will be required. Expect to pay $150-$300 per card. Devices that don't offer Ethernet connections, such as PowerBooks or certain LaserWriters, will require special Ethernet devices that connect via the SCSI port or through the LocalTalk port. Add the cost of the cables, and you're likely to spend $200 to $400 per node.

A similar scenario to a single Ethernet network involves the use of FDDI as a cabling medium. Of course, the per node connection cost would be considerably higher. If your network requirements are severe, then this approach should be considered. Perhaps you need to network a number of Quadras in a desktop publishing environment where users are continually transferring 10 MB Photoshop files, or perhaps you need to upgrade a number of CAD users that are continually taxing the network. In these cases, the extra bandwidth and throughput of Ethernet or FDDI may pay for itself in short order.

Scenario 3: Single LocalTalk Network Active Star Topology

A common LocalTalk option is the active star. It uses a multiport LocalTalk repeater to separately feed each segment of the star. Active stars are generally more reliable and easier to maintain than their passive counterparts. Each cable run has a maximum length of 3000 feet. For a twelve port repeater the total cabling distance would be 36,000 feet. Most LocalTalk star repeaters are equipped with management software that can enable or disable ports and perform basic line quality testing.

While it's possible to place forty, or even more, devices on an active star it's important to remember that the entire star is a single AppleTalk network sharing the LocalTalk bandwidth of 230.4 Kbps. So, unless your network demands are modest, it's best to limit the number of nodes to 30 or 40.

The cost of an active LocalTalk star network is more than the passive star since you must factor in the cost of the repeater. Depending on the number of nodes, and the cost of the repeater, this could add a considerable amount to the per node cost.

Scenario 4: Single Ethernet Network Star Topology (10Base-T)

This scenario provides the bandwidth of the thinwire scenario 2, with the flexibility of a star wiring topology. Twisted-pair (10Base-T) Ethernet networks require a repeater hub. These hubs come in many different sizes

Chapter 25
Networking the Macintosh

and prices. There are even low-cost mini-hubs that have anywhere between four and eight ports.

As in the case of the LocalTalk stars, you may be able to use existing building wiring, although 10Base-T wiring requires four pairs of wires that meet certain requirements. If you must create your own wiring, it will be an easy task. As with the RJ-11 connectors used by the phone-type of LocalTalk connectors, 10Base-T Ethernet uses a larger RJ-45 version. You can buy the bulk cable, connectors and proper crimping tools from network supply houses such as Black Box. Consider the use of Level 5 wiring just in case you plan to migrate to a high-speed network such as 100 Mbps Ethernet or CDDI.

This single hub approach makes a lot of sense when you need the extra bandwidth of Ethernet and are planning for future growth. As you add devices and require additional hubs, they can be linked together with an Ethernet backbone. Of course, the cost of hubs add to the per node cost, but that's the price for the additional flexibility.

The length of each twisted-pair segment cannot exceed the 100 meter restriction, so the maximum distance between devices (assuming the hub is centrally located) is 200 meters.

Scenario 5: Single LocalTalk Network Bridged Star Topology

An alternative to the LocalTalk repeater is Tribe's LocalTalk bridge. This device uses packet switching technology to maximize the limited bandwidth of LocalTalk. If the low-cost and easy installation of LocalTalk appeals to you, but you're finding the bandwidth limiting, then Tribe's LocalSwitch may provide a good alternative. It increases the throughput and extends the number of devices that you can place on your LocalTalk segment. According to Tribe, you should be able to put a total of 60 devices on the bridge.

Scenario 6: Multiple LocalTalk Networks Routed Backbone Topology

When you outgrow your single LocalTalk network, or when you have to connect LocalTalk devices to other Ethernet-equipped devices, the easiest way is to link the LocalTalk networks to an Ethernet backbone. Each LocalTalk network will connect to the backbone with a LocalTalk-to-Ethernet AppleTalk router.

With this approach you'll be able to interconnect hundreds of LocalTalk devices. It still makes sense to use some kind of star repeater or bridge in combination with the router. Some vendors (e.g., Farallon) offer combination devices that merge a LocalTalk-Ethernet router with a star repeater.

Scenario 7: Multiple Ethernet Networks Routed Backbone and Star Topology

As the cost of Ethernet connections continue to fall, and as Apple continues to offer built-in Ethernet in more and more models, the trend is clearly away from LocalTalk connections. The direction that most network designers are taking is to use Ethernet to all desktop devices and then to use an Ethernet segment as a connecting backbone. The key component is an Ethernet-to-Ethernet AppleTalk router. These devices are starting to become more prevalent. Cayman, for example, has just released such a router and other companies are likely to follow suit. The router could also be a Macintosh with two Ethernet cards running the Apple Internet Router.

This scenario represents the most flexible and high-performance option for all but the most demanding applications. This scenario also fits in nicely with structured wiring plans, which makes it easy to respond to growth and redistribution of network resources. It also makes it easy to add routers to the network in response to excessive traffic. This approach lends itself well to intelligent hubs and concentrators that work in conjunction, or incorporate, AppleTalk routers. Standalone high-performance multiprotocol routers are also likely candidates, as they provide the necessary performance with a wide range of protocol support. These routers are supplied by several vendors with Cisco and Wellfleet being the popular choices.

Scenario 8: Multiple Ethernet Networks with FDDI Backbone

As the number of routers increase on an Ethernet backbone, its ability to handle the inter-network traffic plus the inter-router traffic can become strained. For these very large networks, the replacement of the Ethernet backbone with an FDDI replacement is becoming more prevalent. For now, the main role of FDDI is likely to be its use as a high-speed backbone medium. Since FDDI LANs can extend over great distances, this scenario is indicated for the very large networks with many attached subnetworks.

Chapter 25
Networking the Macintosh

Scenario 9: Ethernet and FDDI WAN Topology

This scenario adds a high-speed WAN connection. These WAN connections are commonly made with the multiprotocol routers mentioned earlier. As mentioned before, one of AppleTalk's past shortcomings was the regular transmission of routing table updates. These updates tended to be burdensome to AppleTalk WAN links. Today, there are many options to solve this problem.

First, Apple has added the AURP routing protocol, which only sends routing updates when necessary. AURP support is included with Apple's Internet Router, and currently being added to many third-party routers. Another solution for WAN AppleTalk support is through the encapsulation of AppleTalk within another protocol such as TCP/IP. The process of IP encapsulation of AppleTalk has been recently defined and standardized. Lastly, many high-end router developers offer specialized routing protocols that can be applied to the routing of AppleTalk over the WAN.

It is expected that Apple will take additional steps in the near future to enhance AppleTalk's viability over wide-area networks. These include the support of upcoming Point-to-Point Protocol (PPP), which should enhance remote access and routed connections, and the adoption of other popular routing protocols such as Open Shortest Path First (OSPF) which is popular in large IP internets.

Scenario 10: Structured Wiring Example

This last example illustrates a possible wiring scenario that uses a technique sometimes referred to as a structured wiring implementation. In this example, a star topology is used to wire all offices and cubicles with several runs of 10Base-T, or even Level 5, compliant twisted-pair wiring. All wires converge at a master patch panel within a wiring closet. From this patch panel, connections are made to the appropriate wiring devices based on requirements of the connected device.

LocalTalk devices are interconnected to a LocalTalk hub and router. Ethernet devices are connected to an Ethernet hub. While it's not shown in the diagram, the 10Base-T hub could also be connected to an Ethernet-to-Ethernet router. Serially connected devices are patched to a terminal server. What's key about this scheme is that all devices use identical Level 5-compliant wiring. Changes are confined to the wiring closet, where if a LocalTalk Mac Plus is replaced with an Ethernet Quadra, the only required change is to move a patch cord from the LocalTalk hub to the Ethernet hub.

Some integrated hubs merge the different hubs, such as terminal servers, 10Base-T and even LocalTalk, into a single, unified chassis. These devices make the wiring process even easier and less cluttered by eliminating the cross-connects that are now part of the hub's backplane.

Scenario Summary

The development and implementation of an AppleTalk network is not a one time activity. It is an ongoing process that continues to evolve as users are added and technology changes. In this chapter, a number of network scenarios were outlined and discussed. Each successive scenario provided additional complexity, or capabilities, over the previous examples. Collectively, these examples delineate a full range of options for the reader; they also illustrate a clear and progressive growth path from the simplest of LocalTalk networks to the most complex combinations of Ethernet, Token Ring and FDDI cabling.

Conclusion

Hopefully this chapter has given you an understanding of the theories, components and implementation details involved with Macintosh networking. This chapter is largely based on the Hayden book, *LiveWired: A Guide to Networking Macs* by Jim Anders. It provides a more detailed examination of Macintosh networking and also includes a disk that contains a comprehensive library of the four-layer symbols used throughout this chapter.

Chapter 26
Macintosh and PC Coexistence

Macs and PCs are quite different; from the microprocessor to the operating system to the applications software, the two computers are separate and distinct species. In rare cases, software

In This Chapter

▼ Physical connections between Macs and PCs

▼ Moving data between platforms

▼ Translating Mac and PC files

▼ File compression

Part VI
Expanding Your Mac's Horizons

versions for each system (like Microsoft's Word for Macintosh and Word for Windows) may look and feel similar. However, most of the time, programs for one machine bear little resemblance to programs for the other. And yet, communicating and transferring data between the two is surprisingly easy. There are numerous connectivity and translation solutions that are easy to implement and relatively inexpensive.

Introduction

In the 1950s, '60s, and '70s, computer business software was written in COBOL. But when inexpensive, powerful desktop computers came into being in the '80s and '90s, very little of this old code was ported over as part of the new systems. As a result, businesses today employ legions of COBOL programmers whose work is simply to update and maintain 20- or 30-year-old software. These businesses figure, and probably rightly so, that spending $40,000 or more a year on a programmer's salary is better than potentially spending millions to deal with headaches from data conversion nightmares.

When IBM created the PC and implemented DOS as its operating system standard, many businesses thought their data translation troubles were over. Unfortunately, that was not the case as broader implementation of PCs, networks, cross-platform communication, and electronic telecommunication gave more access to, and a greater need for, data sharing. The Macintosh computer, which Apple touted as extremely versatile in communicating and sharing with PCs, lives up to this claim if you use the right software and/or hardware.

Macintosh-PC coexistence has received a great deal of attention from the Mac side, mostly because of the disparity in the numbers of installed machines. About 12 million of the estimated 80 million computers in use worldwide are Macs. Perhaps one or two million more are Apple IIs, CP/M machines, and other desktop dinosaurs. The other 68 or so million, comprising the overwhelming majority of computers in use today, are PC-compatibles. Apple may have dubbed the Mac "the computer for the rest of us," but the fact is Macintosh users are a relatively small group. Don't worry, however; if you need to work alongside PCs, you can find options available to suit nearly every purpose.

Chapter 26
Macintosh and PC Coexistence

A Closer Look: Macintosh-PC coexistence can be summed up in two words: *connectivity* and *translation*. Connectivity covers all the ways Macs and PCs can talk to each other for moving files, sharing resources, and using electronic mail. Translation means converting data from a form that one application can use to a form another application can use. Good translation tools enable you to coordinate different Macintosh and PC application capabilities.

Physical Connections

If you want Macs and PCs to work together, the first thing you have to do is establish a *data bridge*, or a link where the two machines can transfer data. You can do this in a variety of ways from environments where one computer is physically inside the other to environments where the two systems are separated by thousands of miles.

Disk Drives

For occasional file transfers between Macs and PCs in the office, where a network's continuous communication capabilities are not necessary, the floppy disk is the best medium. It is convenient and inexpensive, and using floppies as a data bridge also means you automatically have a backup of the files you transfer.

WARNING! Apple has advertised its FDHD SuperDrive floppy disk drive (shipping in all Mac IIs and SEs since mid 1989, and in all IIcx's, IIci's, and beyond) as capable of reading PC-formatted floppy disks. Although this is true in letter, it is not altogether true in spirit. You can configure SuperDrives to read and mount PC disks, but they do not read or mount automatically. If you insert a PC disk into a SuperDrive, an alert box which says, "This is not a Macintosh disk. Do you want to initialize it?" appears. Initializing the disk destroys the data. You must have a utility called Apple File Exchange (included with Mac system disks) or other similar commercial utilities before the Mac can read the disk as a PC

Part VI
Expanding Your Mac's Horizons

disk and not automatically attempt to initialize it as a Mac disk. (See the section, "Apple File Exchange," later in this chapter for more information.)

A Closer Look If you want to read and mount PC disks from the Finder, use something like Apple's Macintosh PC Exchange, Dayna Communications' DOS Mounter, or Insignia Systems' AccessPC. They all include INITs/Extensions that mount PC disks so that they appear on the desktop (see figure 26.1). After you mount the PC disks, you can navigate through DOS directories as if they were Mac folders, and you may open compatible and translatable PC files with Mac applications that can read them, simply by double-clicking on the file's icon. (A "compatible" file is one created by an application such as WordPerfect and PageMaker that exists on both Macs and PCs. For more about compatibility, see the section "Translation," later in this chapter.)

Figure 26.1
DOS Mounter lets you mount PC disks and then open and read them as if they were Mac disks.

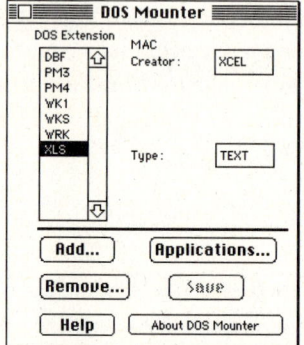

Note You also can use DOS Mounter to mount some kinds of PC-compatible removable hard drive cartridges, a major convenience for quick access to lots of data. If you use a Bernoulli box with both Mac- and PC-formatted cartridges and have another dedicated Mac or PC hard drive, DOS Mounter makes PC-to-Mac file transfers as easy as clicking and dragging. A new version of DOS Mounter will even mount network compatible DOS remote drives and removable drives. To perform the reverse trick of mounting Macintosh disks on MS DOS computers, use a product like Mac-in-DOS from PLI.

Dayna Communications also makes DaynaFile II, a disk drive that comes in both 5 1/4-inch and 3 1/2-inch sizes. The drives can accept DOS floppies and, without additional software, automatically mount them as though they were Macintosh disks. Apple also has an older 5 1/4-inch PC drive that works with

Chapter 26
Macintosh and PC Coexistence

II, IIx, IIcx, and SE/30, but you cannot use it to mount PC disks on the desktop, even with DOS Mounter or AccessPC (which are designed only for the SuperDrive). To access PC files from Apple's 5 1/4-inch drive, you must use Apple File Exchange (see the section "Translation," below).

There are other floppy disk data bridge solutions. Kennect Technologies makes Drive 360 and Drive 1200: 5 1/4-inch disk drives you can use to read, write, and initialize 360K to 1.2M DOS diskettes. These drives require Kennect's companion microprocessor and drive controller, Rapport, which costs $295, bringing the total cost of the drive systems to about $700.

Applied Engineering and Peripheral Land, Inc., both make external 3 1/2-inch SuperDrive clones that are slightly less expensive than Apple's external SuperDrive. Kennect also makes the Drive 2.4, a 3 1/2-inch floppy drive that automatically can mimic the SuperDrive and be configured with Rapport to format 2.4M super high-density disks.

Local Serial Cabling

Using serial cables to connect Macs and PCs lags behind floppies in terms of ease of setup but moves ahead in terms of speed and power. Serial cables offer transfer rates up to 115,200 bits per second, enabling you to transfer more than 800K of data in less than a minute. Serial cables interface between the Mac's printer or modem port and one of the PC's COM (communication) ports.

> **Note:** LapLink also makes a serial port accelerator that can speed Mac-to-Mac file transfers to more than 700 kbps (kilobits per second)—almost 4.5M of data a minute.

> **Note:** Although LapLink can transfer files from a laptop PC to a Mac or PC, many people use LapLink to back up files from one computer to another with a remote network or modem. Having LapLink remotely set up one computer's files from another's is even more useful. LapLink is included in the Mac PowerBook/DOS Companion.

The Macintosh serial ports use mini-DIN 8 connectors, whereas the PC serial ports require either DB9 or DB25 connectors (see figure 26.2). File transfer products such as Traveling Software's LapLink/Mac and Dataviz's MacLinkPlus

Part VI
Expanding Your Mac's Horizons

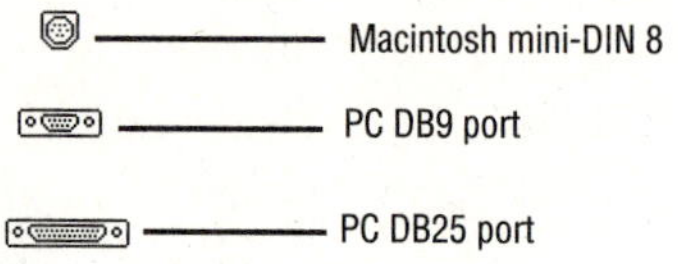

Figure 26.2
Serial port connectors vary by computer.

come with Mac-to-PC cables, and any large office supply store or mail-order firm also has these kinds of connectors.

You may have heard of RS-232C serial port interfaces: these refer both to the

⊙ ──────── Macintosh mini-DIN 8
▭ ──────── PC DB9 port
▭ ──────── PC DB25 port

PC's standard 9-pin DB9 interface or an alternative 25-pin interface called DB25. The Mac's modem and printer serial ports are not standard RS-232C interfaces.

Null Modem Connections

If you do not own a SuperDrive and do not do enough local file transfers to justify LapLink/Mac's price of $149 or MacLinkPlus' $199, you can move files with a *null modem interface* and your standard telecommunications software. Null modem cables are just like serial cables except that some of the pins have been switched to make the telecommunication software think it is talking to a high-speed modem. Null modem cables are available from computer supply stores and mail-order firms. Transfer rates are up to the serial port limit of 115.2 kbps, and all popular telecommunication programs (such as Software Ventures Corporation's MicroPhone and FreeSoft's White Knight on the Mac, and PC-Talk and ProComm on the PC) should make these types of transfers easy.

Use the following step-by-step procedure to initiate null modem or direct modem-to-modem connections. The two computers play host and guest: the guest must call the host, but either one may send files to the other.

1. You and the person operating the host and guest computers must agree in advance on baud rate, number of databits, number of stop bits, and so on (see figure 26.3).

2. At a prearranged time, the host sets his telecommunications software to Auto-Answer.

3. The guest chooses the **Dial** command from her telecommunications program. With a null modem, the telecommunications software automatically configures itself to perform a serial port transfer.

4. When connected, both of you see a message such as "CONNECT 2400" on your monitors.

5. To ensure a reliable connection has been made, each of you should type a few lines of plain text. For example:

    Guest: Hi, Paul. Are you ready to transfer those files?

    Host: Yes, Laura, I'm all set to go.

6. The sender selects the **Send File** or **Upload** command and chooses the appropriate protocol, such as XMODEM. The sender then selects the file.

7. The receiver selects the **Download File** or **Receive File** command, and the transfer is accomplished.

8. The receiver ensures that the transfer went well, and you sign off.

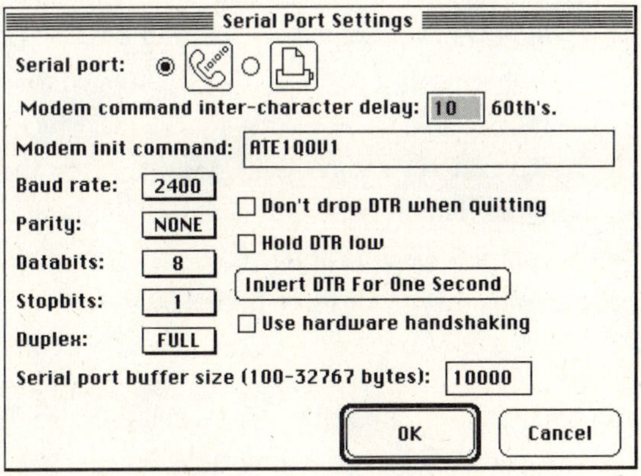

Chapter 26
Macintosh and PC Coexistence

Figure 26.3
Standard communications settings for null or direct modem transfers are 2400 to 155,200 bps, full duplex, 8 databits, 1 stopbit, and no parity error checking.

Modem Transfers

Using modems and telecommunications software, you can perform either direct or indirect file transfers between Macs and PCs. Direct file transfers require both users to be at their computers at the same time so one can call the other and send files directly over the phone lines. This procedure is identical to the null modem transfer procedure.

Part VI
Expanding Your Mac's Horizons

Indirect transfers make use of bulletin board services (BBSs), electronic mail services, or information and database networks. One user calls the service and uploads the file to a place where another user can retrieve it: either in a private electronic mailbox or in a public bulletin board–like directory.

Popular information and database services include CompuServe, America Online, Prodigy, GEnie, and Delphi. (See chapter 24, "Communications and Online Services," for more information.) All of these services provide electronic mail, and all except Delphi enable you to upload files for cross-platform transferring. The uploading and downloading process is relatively easy to follow. If you find you are performing many of the same activities over several sessions, generate a script of your actions. Popular telecommunications software packages such as FreeSoft's White Knight and Software Venture's MicroPhone enable you to save modem settings and record keystrokes and mouse clicks in script files. Then, to run the session again, all you need to do is double-click on the script file.

For readers of this book, there is a special free-trial offer from Delphi, detailed in chapter 23, "Communications and Online Services."

America Online is a heavily Mac-oriented service, and it is also one of the least expensive. A runtime version of the software you need to get onto America Online now is available in GeoWorks for the PC, which enables you to transfer files. Prodigy charges a start-up fee (however, you should be able to find a free or discounted offer for this) and a monthly surcharge, but there are no connect time charges, so uploading and downloading files does not cost a great deal. (See chapter 23 for more information.)

CompuServe is by far the largest information service, with well over a half million subscribers; however, it is also the most expensive and arguably the most difficult for a Mac user. If you are going to spend any time with CompuServe, consider trying Navigator, a graphic utility which makes it easy to generate session scripts that simplify sending and receiving electronic mail, and participate in conferences (see figure 26.4).

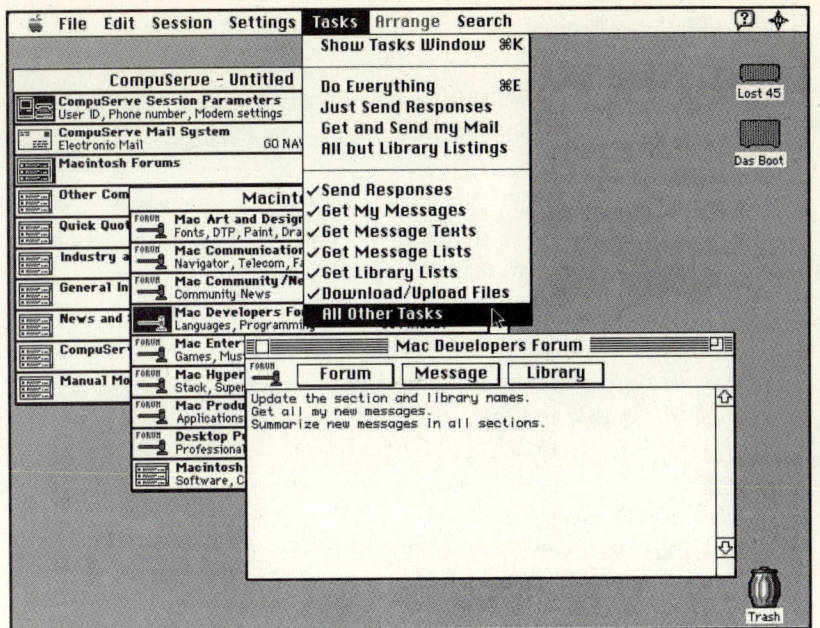

Figure 26.4

Navigator can streamline CompuServe online sessions and reduce connect time charges.

Networking

Networking is covered in-depth in chapter 24, "Networking." Therefore, this section merely outlines and highlights special Mac-to-PC networking features without delving into the process details. If you are unfamiliar with Macintosh and PC networks, read chapter 24 first.

AppleTalk

AppleTalk is the standard Macintosh networking protocol, and every Macintosh from the original 128K model to the latest Quadra 900 tower system has built-in AppleTalk support. The AppleTalk protocols can run over a wide variety of cabling from the unused black and yellow wires in phone cable to thick coaxial cable.

AppleTalk recently has been upgraded; the original implementation was called AppleTalk Phase 1, and the new version is called AppleTalk Phase 2. Phase 2 is faster and more efficient, and it includes support for millions of users on a variety of cabling systems, such as EtherNet and Token-Ring.

Part VI
Expanding Your
Mac's Horizons

Most PCs do not have built-in networking capabilities. However, LocalTalk and EtherNet cards are available for PCs for less than $300 that give them AppleTalk capabilities. (LocalTalk is Apple's name for its inexpensive brand of cabling that AppleTalk networks can use; others are available.)

PhoneNet PC II Network Interface Card (NIC), sold by Farralon, lets you connect PCs via AppleTalk to Macs. You can save files to a Mac, print on Macintosh printers, and perform other network tasks with this system. PhoneNet PC comes bundled with Timbuktu for Windows. With Timbuktu for Windows running on a PC, and Timbuktu running on a Macintosh, you can run applications on either computer and transparently write files to either computer. A very slick proposition.

With the appropriate file sharing software, such as Sitka's MacTOPS and DosTOPS (formerly a single product called TOPS), Apple's AppleShare, System 7, or Novell's NetWare (with AFP support) PCs and Macs can live in harmony on the same network, transferring files, sharing printers, and so on.

The major difference between AppleShare and MacTOPS is that AppleShare is meant to be used on a dedicated Macintosh server on the network, whereas MacTOPS can work either with a server or in a peer-to-peer (computer-to-computer) file sharing system. With a server, AppleShare is the faster of the two in both Mac-only and mixed Mac-PC networks.

System 7's new file sharing capabilities resemble a personal AppleShare server for the Mac System 7 user—a form of peer-to-peer networking. Macintosh file sharing allows any Mac on an AppleTalk network (LocalTalk, EtherNet, or Token-Ring) to share up to 10 local files, folders, or disks to the network. Published resources then appear in the Chooser to every other Macintosh on the network, as well as any PC equipped with an AppleTalk network card and Chooser. They look to the networked machines as though they were AppleShare volumes and support similar file sharing.

Although System 7 file sharing can work only with Macs running System 7, it can be accessed by Macs running System 6 (or 7) as well as PCs using the AppleTalk protocols. For peer-to-peer file sharing that can integrate Macintosh and PC computers (in which both Macs and PCs can share files from their disks), Sitka's MacTOPS and DosTOPS are the best answer. Refer to table 25.1 for a comparison of the networking software available.

Table 25.2 Distributed and server-based networking software available on the Mac

Product	Pros	Cons
AppleShare with server	Fast, secure, stable. Easy integration of AppleTalk-equipped PCs	Dedicated computer highly recommended Impractical for use as peer-to-peer networking.
TOPS	Secure and stable. Easy integration of AppleTalk-equipped PCs. Can switch between server-based and peer-to-peer networking	Not as fast as AppleShare with servers. Cannot take as many users (20 versus 120 for AppleShare).
System 7 file sharing	Convenient. Allows every System 7 Mac in a network to easily share data. Allows System 6 Macs and AppleTalk-equipped PCs to copy to and from shared volumes.	Slower than dedicated AppleShare server. Supports maximum of 10 connected users at one time. Cannot copy files directly from AppleTalk-equipped PCs.

Chapter 26
Macintosh and PC Coexistence

Other Products

Although the LocalTalk network, built into all Macs since the 128K, is relatively cheap, it also is fairly slow. Macs and PCs can use faster, more flexible network standards such as EtherNet and IBM's Token-Ring. Connecting Macs to EtherNet and Token-Ring networks is easy: cards are available from several companies (including Apple, Asante, Dove, Technology Works, 3Com, Shiva, and others) for NuBus-equipped Macs that provide interfaces and external connectors. Several manufacturers also make network connections for the SE/30, the LC, and any Mac with a SCSI port.

 To connect to Token-Ring networks, you can use Apple's TokenTalk NuBus interface card, which supplies the appropriate external connector and a Token-Ring–compatible protocol for use on 4- and 16-megabit Token-Ring networks. This 4/16 card is

1011

one of the first fruits of the Apple-IBM technology exchange agreement signed in 1991, improving Mac-to-Token-Ring connectivity solutions through the use of IBM's 16-megabit chip set.

Connecting Macs to Novell networks is straightforward and easy to understand. Novell's NetWare for Macintosh adds AppleTalk compatibility to PC servers running NetWare, which allows Macs to be *clients* on Novell networks simply by establishing the physical connection with LocalTalk, EtherNet, Token-Ring, or any other cabling NetWare supports. Connecting your Mac to a PC server running NetWare is like connecting to a Mac server running AppleShare or a System 7 Mac with file sharing. NetWare has the distinction of being the most widely sold networking software, and is a good choice for large enterprises.

Using EtherNet- and Token-Ring-equipped PCs in AppleTalk networks is also straightforward as long as their network cards support the AppleTalk Phase 2 protocols.

Miramar's MacLAN Connect software allows AppleTalk-equipped PCs to act as AppleShare-compatible servers for AppleTalk and other networks. This product is useful if you have been using TOPS for cross-platform peer-to-peer networking but now need the improved speed and security server-based networks offer.

Gateways and Routers

You can link PC and Mac networks that may be on EtherNet, Token-Ring, or LocalTalk through routers and gateways. Each network can be divided into multiple zones. In multizone setups, the Chooser displays all the names of available zones connected through the routers and gateways independent of which type of network they are on, as well as all the shared devices in the selected zones. Gateway products range in price but are typically somewhat expensive (usually around $2,000) and are cost effective only if you need to integrate large LocalTalk, Token-Ring, and EtherNet networks. Compatible Systems Corporation (Ether-Route), Cayman Systems (GatorBox), Shiva (FastPath), and Network Resources Corporation (MultiGate) all make gateway products. Apple's AppleTalk Internet Router routes AppleTalk protocols between LocalTalk, EtherNet, and Token-Ring on a Mac equipped with the appropriate networking cards.

There's a PC in My Mac!

There are three Macintosh products that let you work directly with PC applications instead of transferring and translating data files. Argosy's RunPC, Orange Micro's PC plug-in boards, and Insignia Solutions' SoftPC all answer the connectivity issue by giving direct control of a PC to your Mac in three different ways.

RunPC

Argosy's RunPC allows Macs to operate or "run" PC software in a Macintosh window by "taking over" and remotely controlling a PC that is connected through the Mac's serial port, with a modem, or over an AppleTalk network (see figure 26.5). RunPC also can transfer documents between the two platforms and perform file format translation on most word processing files. RunPC supports cutting and pasting text and graphics between Macintosh and PC applications, and it is MultiFinder-compatible. One valuable feature is that PC programs running in a Macintosh window have access to whatever printer you select in the Macintosh Chooser. At this writing, RunPC is not compatible with Microsoft Windows.

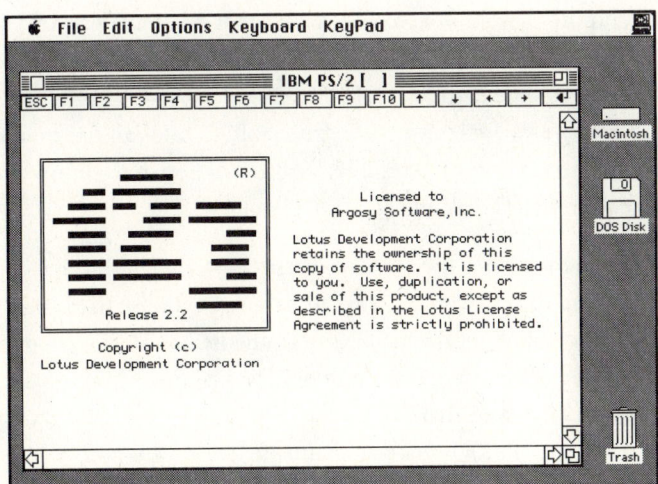

Figure 26.5
RunPC allows your Mac to take over a local or remote PC.

Mac86, Mac286, and Orange386

Mac86, Mac286, and Orange386 from Orange Micro put fully compatible PCs into your Mac through a plug-in NuBus board. As hardware units, the boards allow for true multiprocessing; you can run PC software in one window and

Chapter 26
Macintosh and PC Coexistence

Mac software in another (with MultiFinder) and experience no slowdown in system performance. All three can use Apple's SuperDrive, Apple's 5 1/4-inch floppy, or any of the third-party floppy drives on the market to read PC disks.

Mac86 is an 8086-based coprocessor that provides IBM PC XT performance for the Mac SE. Mac286 is a NuBus board that comes with an 8 MHz 80286 microprocessor and 1M of RAM for a system that puts IBM PC AT performance into your Mac II. Most major DOS programs run acceptably with Mac286.

Orange386 is an 80386SX-based coprocessor that can run Microsoft Windows and Windows-based applications. The Orange386 board also has slots for plugging in two IBM PC AT-style boards of its own, so you can put boards on a board. You need a full five- or six-slot Macintosh II to take advantage of this feature because the piggybacked boards are about three NuBus slots wide. The kinds of PC boards you can use also are limited by the amount of power they draw. Nevertheless, this feature is useful for installing PC video and EtherNet cards.

SoftPC

Insignia Solutions' SoftPC is a software-based IBM PC emulator; you actually can run PC programs on your Macintosh with no special hardware. There is also an add-on module to emulate the PC AT, the software equivalent of Mac286. There are two versions of the basic SoftPC: one can run on 68000-based Macs, whereas the other requires a 68020 or better Macintosh. Both versions require a hard disk and at least 2M of RAM.

When you install SoftPC, it creates a document that acts as a DOS hard drive partition. You can have two of these hard drive documents, and you also can configure any Macintosh directory to act as a PC hard drive partition. SoftPC treats Macintosh directories as "networked" hard drives, so certain functions that could be destructive, such as the DOS Format command, are not allowed.

Double-clicking on a PC application or document icon runs SoftPC but does not open the application. You have to do that manually from DOS. After you open a PC application in a Mac window, you can treat it just like any Macintosh application (see figure 26.6). You can cut and paste between Mac and PC windows, and switch between Mac and PC modes with MultiFinder. Unfortunately, SoftPC cannot emulate expanded memory, so there is a 640K of RAM limit available for PC applications.

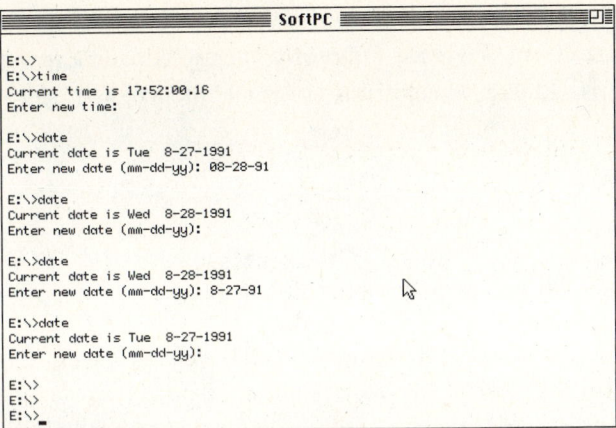

Figure 26.6
SoftPC enables you to run PC applications in a Macintosh window.

SoftPC and the Orange Micro boards are quite similar in function. They both provide a high degree of compatibility with PC software and are MultiFinder-compatible. However, SoftPC for the Classic, SE, Plus, LC, or Portable runs about $199; Mac86 (which is only available for the Classic, SE, and LC with expansion board) costs about $349 for PC-level performance. For AT-level compatibility, SoftPC with the add-on AT module is $500; Mac286 costs $1,400.

Insignia Solutions has released SoftPC for Windows, an emulation of Microsoft Windows running on a Macintosh. The product works fine, but is very slow compared to Windows running on a PC. In order to get acceptable performance you need to be using a Macintosh Quadra computer. The severe hardware requirements of this software make this an unlikely solution for most people.

As hardware-based solutions, the Orange Micro boards are faster and, at times, significantly so. Mac286 runs WordPerfect (PC) up to three times faster than SoftPC's AT version. However, you may find the Orange Micro boards overpriced: one Mac286 board costs two-and-a-half times the cost of a full-scale desktop PC clone. 80386SX-based clones start at less than $900, compared to $2,300 for the Orange386.

These products are primarily designed for people who edit documents that require integrating resources and data from both PC and Mac platforms. If your tasks require cutting and pasting, and cross-platform file transfers are not sufficient, then one of these products is a good choice. If you need Windows, your best option is the Orange386 board. Otherwise, you can buy an inexpensive PC clone and use RunPC. If you just want to run PC programs occasionally, consider buying SoftPC to save money.

Moving Data

File transfers are only one of the functions an integrated Mac-PC environment can provide. Two others include resource sharing and electronic mail. Resources that may be shared between Macs and PCs include printers, individual folders and files, storage devices, telephone and fax modems, and other kinds of serial devices.

PostScript Printers

The introduction of Apple's LaserWriter in 1985 helped launch the first stage of the desktop publishing (DTP) revolution. The LaserWriter's accompanying Adobe's PostScript page description language (PDL) enabled users to generate high-quality printouts combining both text and graphics. (See chapter 5, "Printing From Your Macintosh," for more information.) Many users need access to a PostScript printer for a variety of reasons, but until recently it has been notoriously difficult to connect both Macs and PCs to share a PostScript printer.

Macintosh computers easily can connect to PostScript printers through any AppleTalk network. The hardware part of AppleTalk that is built into every Macintosh is called LocalTalk. Most of Apple's PostScript LaserWriters also have LocalTalk ports. In the past, PCs typically connected to a PostScript printer directly with a serial or parallel connection, meaning only one PC could use the printer.

If you need to share a PostScript printer with Macs and PCs, you must connect the PC to an AppleTalk network, which is done through a hardware addition to the PC, usually a LocalTalk card. As mentioned earlier, several products for PCs can make this connection, including Dayna's DL card series, Farallon's Phone Net, TalkEMAC's SpeedTalk, DayStar Digital's LT200, Sitka's Flashcard, and others. Farallon's PhoneNet PC software has a program called

Chapter 26
Macintosh and PC Coexistence

DA on DOS and one called Choose on Windows that let you select and print to LaserWriters on an AppleTalk network.

After you install the hardware and make the connection, you need to use a PostScript *printer driver*, software installed in the PC that acts as liaison for the PC-printer interface and tells the printer how to work with the files to print. Most graphics and some word processing applications for the PC now ship with PostScript drivers and have installation programs that enable you to designate the AppleTalk PostScript printer as your output device.

Hewlett Packard LaserJets

Although connecting PCs to PostScript printers is important for many businesses, connecting Macs to HP LaserJet printers probably is even more crucial. Although PCs outsell Macs 10 to one, non-PostScript LaserJets outsell all other kinds of laser printers by approximately five to one. It is certainly more common for a business to add a Macintosh to a network of PCs and LaserJets than to add a PC to a network of Macs and LaserWriters.

Fortunately, there are several ways to connect a Mac to a LaserJet. One way is to use Insight Development Corporation's MacPrint or GDT SoftWorks' JetLink Express to connect the two via serial ports. Extended Systems and Pacific Data Products also make hardware interfaces to connect LaserJets to LocalTalk networks. For the older LaserJets (before the III series), you must buy a separate LocalTalk upgrade card and PostScript cartridge from Hewlett-Packard to make this work; newer LaserJets have built-in LocalTalk interface capabilities.

Storage Devices

Most CD-ROMs and hard drives on the Macintosh market are SCSI devices and can be directly connected to any Mac with a SCSI port. Using System 7, that SCSI device can be shared to the rest of the Macs and PCs on the connected AppleTalk network. You can access data on any System 7 user's SCSI drive if that person uses the file sharing and network access techniques discussed earlier. And with AppleShare, any SCSI hard drives or CD-ROM drives connected to the server can be made accessible from networked computers—Macs or PCs.

Part VI
Expanding Your
Mac's Horizons

Peripherals such as tape backup units and other high-capacity storage devices usually are intended to be used on a network for backup purposes but are not necessarily meant to be shared. A network administrator would not appreciate a client user accidentally deleting recent system backups on a shared tape unit. Although mass storage devices may be used to back up and service all members of the network, only the network administrator usually has access to them.

Serial Peripherals

Shiva's NetSerial peripheral interface allows any kind of serial device, from PC-compatible printers to modems, fax modems, and scanners, to connect to a network. NetSerial has a small 8K RAM buffer and can communicate at up to 57.6 kbps. It connects to a LocalTalk network and plugs into the serial devices with a serial cable.

Shiva also makes NetModem, a modem designed to allow any node on the AppleTalk network to directly access it without going through a NetSerial interface. NetModem also allows remote dial-in access so anyone with a Mac or PC and a modem can call in and use the AppleTalk network resources.

Because the Hewlett Packard LaserJets are serial devices, you can use any of the LaserJet connectivity products from Pacific Data Products and Extended Systems to allow access to PC serial devices from a Macintosh computer over an AppleTalk network.

Electronic Mail

Aside from the "paperless office," electronic mail (E-mail) is perhaps the computer revolution's most promoted feature. Proponents envisioned E-mail and voice mail replacing traditional paper-based correspondence in the office. Entire conversations were to take place over the network easily and conveniently; benefits included a complete, dated record of communications, increased speed of transmissions, and minimized data loss. (See chapter 23, "Communications and Online Services," for more information.)

Two kinds of E-mail systems are in use today: internal systems, which use a network and usually connect users in the same company or organization; and external systems, which are like electronic post offices and require a modem to use. Internal systems require E-mail network software such as CE

Software's QuickMail, Microsoft Mail, or 3Com Software's 3+Mail, and they can work with mixed Mac and PC networks.

Perhaps the best dedicated external system is MCI Mail, although many users send E-mail over information and database services like CompuServe. AppleLink is an external mail system that developers and writers in the Macintosh community can access. Recently AppleLink has been offered to the general public at reduced rates to increase the subscriber base. Gateways that connect internal systems to MCI Mail also are available: Solutions, Inc.'s CommGate, Cayman Systems' GatorMail, 3Com, CE Software, and Microsoft.

A Closer Look If you are using an internal E-mail system, you need to designate one Mac on the network as a mail server. You still can use that Mac to run applications as a regular computer, but if you are going to demand this kind of double duty, you should consider investing in a speedy Mac to prevent massive processing slowdowns when mail traffic rises. Otherwise, a dedicated Plus, SE, or Classic with a hard drive should work just fine.

Internal Mail Systems

QuickMail, Microsoft Mail, 3+Mail, and cc:Mail are all complete, powerful, electronic mail systems that run over networks and can be used by both Macs and PCs. CE Software's QuickMail and Microsoft Mail are full-featured products designed to run over any AppleTalk network. 3+Mail and cc:Mail can run over most popular network protocols in addition to AppleTalk. Microsoft Mail has links into Microsoft applications (on both PC and Mac) so that you can check your mail and send a response directly from inside Word (and other Microsoft applications) without exiting. All these products, however, now offer desk accessories or Apple menu item utilities that provide convenient access to mail functions from within any application.

You can use internal systems to send almost any kind of file to anyone on the network instantly, and they also can allow for one-on-one conversations and larger group discussions. Most internal mail systems also automatically can inform you of an urgent message that just arrived. Some also support voice and sound annotation of mail notes if you have a built-in microphone or one of the add-on microphones (such as MacRecorder).

Chapter 26
Macintosh and PC Coexistence

External Services

Both Mac and PC users can access external E-mail services. MCI Mail is a popular service that enables you to send E-mail to members of various information networks, including MCI Mail, CompuServe, and Telex. It also enables you to send E-mail to a particular ZIP code, where the message is printed and delivered by the U.S. Postal Service to a street address you specify. MCI Mail also can send messages to any Group 3 fax machine in the world. (See chapter 23, "Communications and Online Services," for more information.)

Other online services also provide external E-mail features. To decide which one is right for you, you must weigh certain factors: with whom you will communicate most often (sending messages to members of the same service is always less expensive), how often you will use E-mail (some services charge on a per-message basis; others charge for connect time), and when you will use the service (peak versus off-peak hours). One benefit of using other online services is that they provide many more features such as conferences and shopping, in addition to E-mail.

Translation

In many cases, it is not enough to set up a data bridge between a Mac and a PC so that you can copy files. In cases in which the actual file content and formatting matters, you need to preserve your data's integrity as much as possible. Therefore, you need to use file translation utilities. *Translation* is a catch-all term for preserving files' content and format across platforms and across applications on the same platform. This section reviews various procedures and utilities that can make file translation between the Mac and PC platforms a painless, even convenient, process.

Mac and PC Files

There are some fundamental differences between Macintosh and PC files that occasionally handicap the translation process. At first glance, the most obvious one is the difference in name lengths. Macintosh files can have names up to 31 characters long composed of any typable character except a colon (:), including spaces and option characters. PC files can use only eight-character names along with three-character extensions.

A Closer Look The three-character extensions in PC file names generally attempt to describe the file type and application that created it. For instance, a DB3 extension means a dBASE III document; a PM4 extension means a PageMaker 4.0 document. On the Macintosh, files use one four-character field to describe the file type and another to identify the creator application. Normally, these fields are hidden from you; to view and edit them (not recommended), you can use ResEdit (see figure 26.7) or one of the disk management DAs like CE Software's DiskTop.

Chapter 26
Macintosh and PC Coexistence

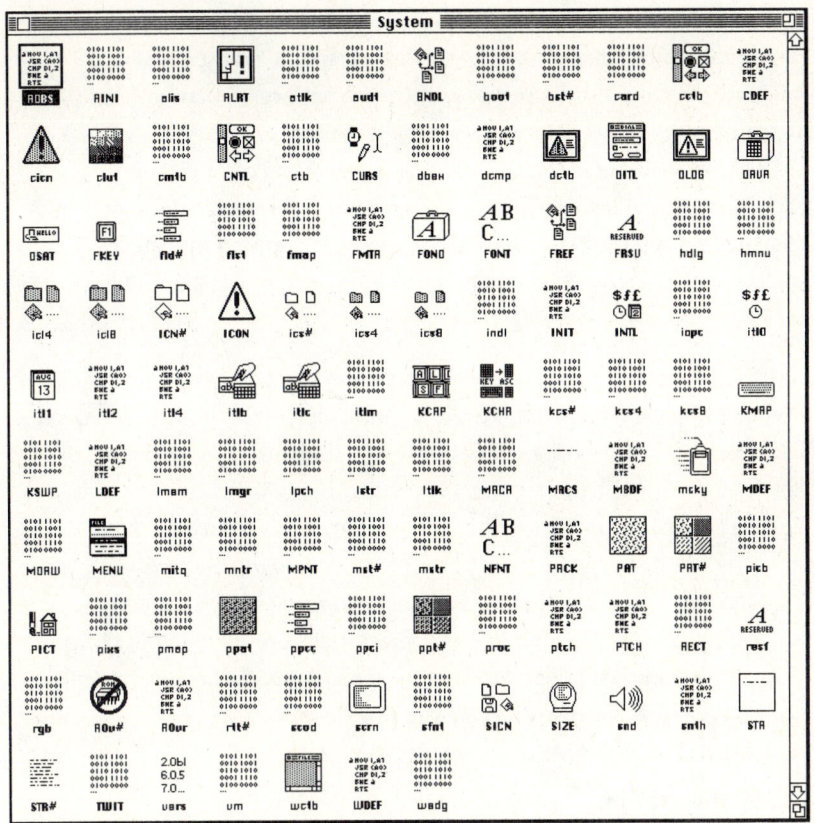

Figure 26.7
ResEdit can display the different kinds of resources in a Macintosh System file.

Another of Macintosh files' distinguishing features is their use of separate resource and data forks—separate sections of a Mac file. Resource forks contain resources—application-specific tools such as menus, icons, and dialog boxes, as well as the application's code, which the application uses to give itself a Mac standard look. Some resources that applications use are located in the system. Typically, only application files contain resource forks.

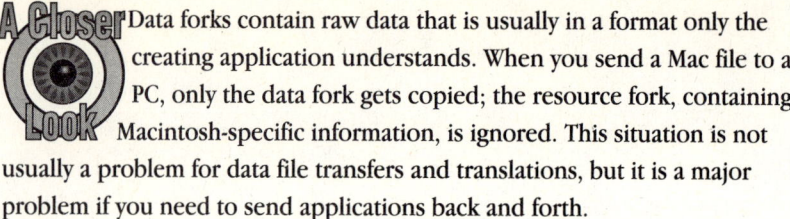Data forks contain raw data that is usually in a format only the creating application understands. When you send a Mac file to a PC, only the data fork gets copied; the resource fork, containing Macintosh-specific information, is ignored. This situation is not usually a problem for data file transfers and translations, but it is a major problem if you need to send applications back and forth.

File Formats

A large portion of Mac and PC files, with all their different extensions, file types, and creator fields, nevertheless may be divided into three major categories of file formats: word processing, graphics, and spreadsheet/database. Effective translations usually can be performed between formats within a category; translations across categories are uncommon but occasionally necessary. The application you are using can perform translations internally, or a translation utility such as MacLinkPlus, LapLink/Mac, or the Macintosh PC Exchange can perform applications externally. The Apple File Exchange has limited functionality, but can use MacLinkPlus translators.

The three major categories of file formats cover text and word processing files, object-oriented and bitmapped graphics files, and files with cell-based data. Most applications work with only one of these categories of data, although some programs, such as PageMaker, ClarisWorks, and Microsoft Works, can manipulate files with several different kinds of data. The files these applications generate are referred to as *compound documents*. Although Mac users have taken mixed-media documents for granted for many years, these documents are becoming increasingly prevalent in the PC world too as applications gain new capabilities. The compound document's role in Mac-PC coexistence is discussed later in this chapter.

Text Formats

A text file format includes a specification for the 128 extended ASCII characters. The format definition is considered native if it is customized for an individual application. Various interchange formats exist as well; these format definitions save some font, style, and related information and have been adopted by more than one application. Applications that can read and write interchange formats can exchange files, losing only some native format features in the process. Text interchange formats to and from the PC world include Document Content Architecture (DCA) and Rich Text Format (RTF).

A Closer Look If you select **All Files** from the **List Files of Type** pop-up menu in Microsoft Word's **Open File** dialog box, you can open any file, no matter what file type it is. This enables you to see the formatting characters that different programs such as Microsoft Excel use (see figure 26.8).

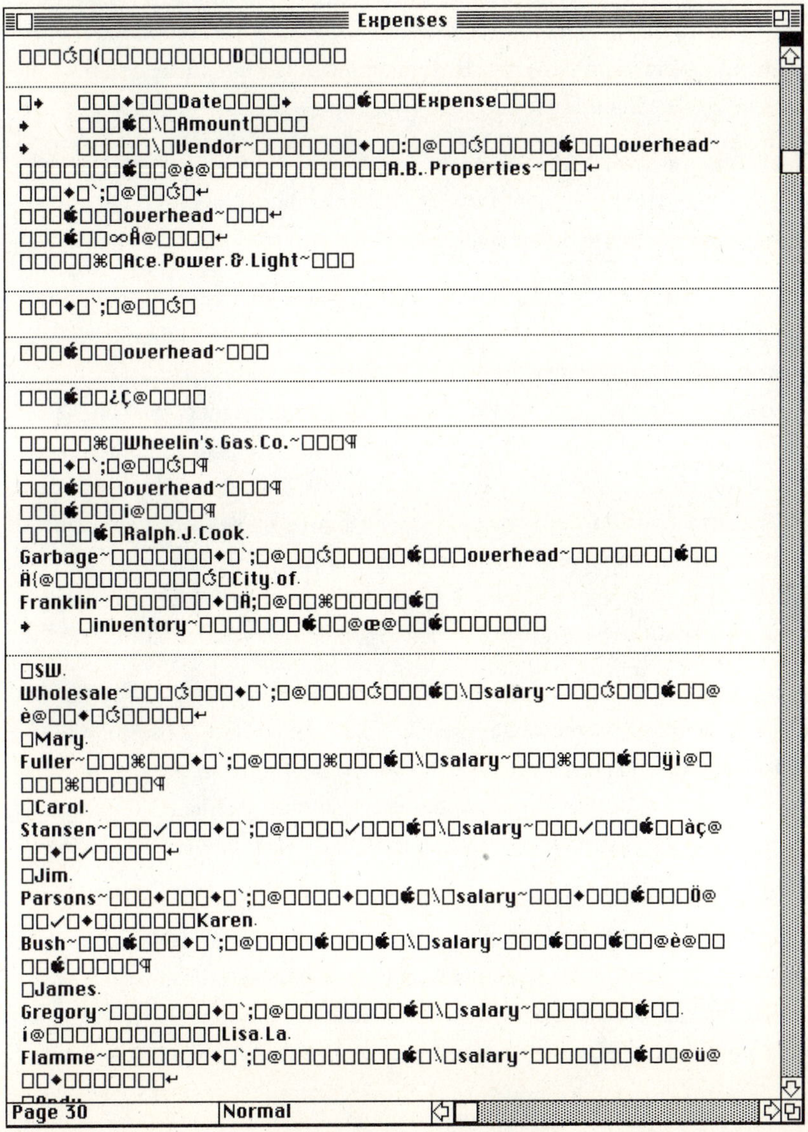

Chapter 26
Macintosh and PC Coexistence

Figure 26.8
Open Any File shows the formatting characters in a Microsoft Excel file.

Part VI
Expanding Your Mac's Horizons

Graphics Formats

Graphical data can be stored in two ways: as a bitmap or as a collection of object definitions. The original MacPaint program saved files as black-and-white, 72-dot-per-inch (dpi) bitmaps (file type PNTG); most newer programs can manipulate both higher resolution bitmaps and object-oriented graphics.

Object-oriented graphics have an advantage because they use mathematical equations to describe standard shapes, and they can be reproduced and manipulated at any resolution and any scale (rotating, flipping, and skewing are standard object manipulation features). However, for complicated pictures, object definitions may be more difficult to manipulate and may take up more space than simple bitmaps.

PNTG is a standard 72 dpi, monochrome, bitmapped format. Tagged Image File Format (TIFF) is another bitmapped format that allows for higher resolutions and up to 32-bit color.

PICT (PICTure) is Macintosh's standard object-oriented image format. PICT files contain lists of screen coordinates and QuickDraw programming statements. Objects can be arranged in layers and can be opaque or transparent. The original PICT definition allowed for eight colors. PICT2 allows for 256 colors, and 32-bit PICT allows for more than 16 million colors. File conversions between different PICT formats work somewhat better than TIFF conversions do. PICT works best with simple shapes, but it also can store complex bitmapped screen areas in data structures called *regions*. Regions generally are used to save text in PICT graphics images because the Macintosh did not have a native, object-oriented text standard until TrueType arrived with System 7.

PICT is the format of the Macintosh Clipboard, and it finds a cousin in the Windows Metafile (WMF) file on Windows. Transferring vector graphics from the PC in either WMF, or in the Computer Graphics Metafile (CGM) format generally leads to successful translations with most competent graphic file translation software.

PostScript is an object-oriented page description language (PDL) that can describe and manipulate text as well as graphical objects. PostScript is far richer in programming options than QuickDraw and can be used to describe nearly every kind of graphic, including shaded, colored, and pattern-filled objects. PostScript is the standard page description language for high-resolution imagesetters.

Two other popular graphics formats are PICS (PICture Sequence) and EPS (Encapsulated PostScript). Both are combination bitmap object-oriented formats. PICS is a Macintosh format used for animated sequences, whereas EPS is the most popular object-oriented image format for PCs.

Cell-Based Data

SYLK (SYmbolic LinK) and DIF (Data Interchange Format) are the two major interchange formats for describing cell-based information used in spreadsheets (rows and columns) and databases (records and fields). Both can store cell values, although cell functions in spreadsheets are lost. SYLK can store font and style information for cell data. Most Macintosh spreadsheets and databases can read and write SYLK files; DIF is common on PCs.

Translation Solutions

One of the easiest and most common translation techniques is called *extension mapping*. As discussed earlier, various types of Macintosh files are distinguished by their four-letter type and creator codes, whereas PC files use a three-letter extension. Extension mapping techniques use a table that lists various PC file extensions, such as PM4 and WPF, along with Macintosh applications' (PageMaker and WordPerfect, respectively) type and creator codes that can open these files.

Extension mapping is appropriate for a small portion of translation scenarios; in other cases, more direct means are necessary. Translation utilities like the ones listed in the following sections try first to match extensions; failing that, they change the source file's content to match the destination application's format.

Apple File Exchange

Apple File Exchange (AFX) is one of the utilities supplied with Apple's Systems 6 and 7. With AFX, you can read and translate MS-DOS, Apple II, and other kinds of files to and from Macintosh formats. AFX solves both parts of the Mac-PC linking problem: it transfers and translates files in one step.

Chapter 26
Macintosh and PC Coexistence

Part VI
Expanding Your Mac's Horizons

Although perhaps not as convenient as the automatic opening and closing capabilities Claris' XTND technology offers, one-step utilities are certainly a viable solution. Other one-step packages include Traveling Software's LapLink/Mac and Dataviz's MacLinkPlus.

The AFX interface resembles the Font/DA Mover in that you can select groups of files in one of two listed locations and perform different procedures on them simply by clicking buttons. AFX supports several popular file formats on the Apple II, PC, and Macintosh platforms; you need a translator package for more obscure translations. Dataviz is one translator manufacturer. When you try to load the translators Dataviz supplies, you have to wait several minutes because AFX adds the translators to the menu.

Apple File Exchange offers an easy way to transfer or translate files from a PC floppy disk (see figure 26.9), provided you have a Mac with a SuperDrive. You also can use AFX to translate PC files that you already have on your hard disk, but the transfer process (getting the file from the PC to your Mac's hard disk) must have been performed already (see the transfer methods mentioned earlier in this chapter).

As supplied, AFX is very limited. By adding the translators in MacLinkPlus PC you can greatly increase its capabilities. Apple sells a product called the Macintosh PC Exchange that uses the LapLink translation filters (see the section below). The PC Exchange offers little or no competitive advantage to either MacLinkPlus PC or LapLink, and currently is not the best choice in this category.

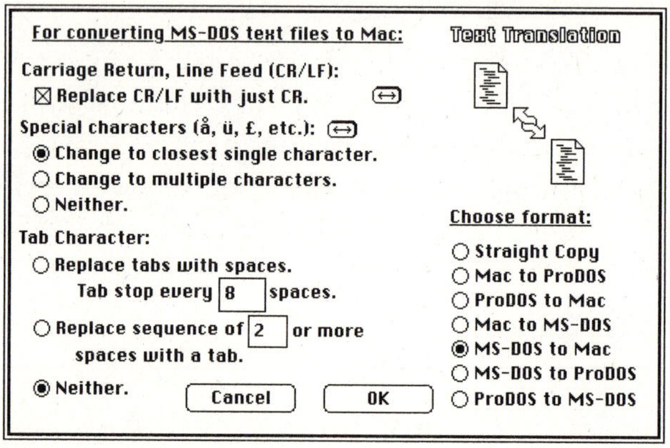

Figure 26.9
Apple File Exchange allows for highly user-regulated text file translations.

Chapter 26
Macintosh and PC Coexistence

To use the Apple File Exchange, follow these steps:

1. Double-click on the Apple File Exchange icon to start the Exchange process.
2. When AFX has finished loading, insert the PC floppy into the SuperDrive (or equivalent). The floppy directory should appear in the scroll box on the right, and **Mac To PC** should appear on the menu bar.
3. Select the file you want to translate, and make sure you have selected the proper translation scheme in the pull-down **Mac To PC** or **PC To Mac** menu. For text file translations, you can configure AFX to strip out unnecessary characters and perform other housecleaning functions on the file by selecting **Text translation** on the menu.
4. If you need to load additional translators, select **Other Translations** from the **Mac To PC** menu. Be prepared to wait for AFX to search your hard disk for translators.
5. Click the **Translate** button.

In just a few seconds, the translation is complete!

LapLink/Mac

Traveling Software's original LapLink product made file transfers and translations between PCs and Radio Shack Model 100 portable computers painless and simple, making LapLink responsible (in part) for Model 100's acceptance as the notebook computer of choice for many desktop PC users.

LapLink/Mac is equally popular. Incorporating cables and software for both Macs and PCs, LapLink/Mac is a complete package for transferring files through serial ports (see figure 26.10). The software also can be used to transfer files over modems, AppleTalk networks, and SCSI connections. LapLink is fast: serial cable communication rates run at more than 115 kbps, and SCSI transfer rates are closer to 10 Mbps (megabits per second)—almost 1.25M of data a second or more than 4 gigabytes per hour. Some word processing file format translators are supplied; however, for extensive file translation capabilities, you should check out Dataviz's MacLinkPlus/PC.

Figure 26.10

When translating files, LapLink/Mac first tries to match extensions and then queries you for a destination format.

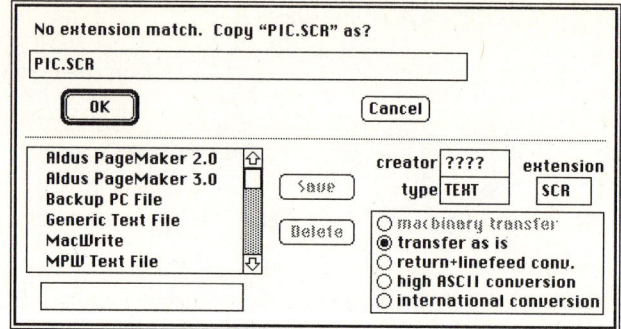

One advantage LapLink/Mac offers over other products is that it supports many transfer paths, and its transfer speed rates are among the fastest in the industry. LapLink/Mac supports background operation, so you can work on something else while your files are transferring. You also can use LapLink to remotely back up and configure computers.

LapLink filters are found in Apple's Macintosh PC Exchange, and in applications such as Microsoft Word 5.1.

MacLinkPlus

Whereas LapLink/Mac specializes in transferring files between local or remote Macs and PCs, Dataviz's MacLinkPlus 7.0 also provides interfaces for transferring files between Mac and Sun or Mac and NeXT computers, either locally through serial cables or remotely through modem. MacLinkPlus also comes with powerful file translation capabilities for word processing, database, spreadsheet, graphics, and other format transfers. If you work with many kinds of files on both Macs and PCs, MacLinkPlus is a must-have. The translators (also available separately) are compatible with Apple File Exchange and the Claris XTND system. Just place the translator files into the correct folder—the AFX folder, or the Claris XTND folder—in your System folder. Then reboot and launch the program.

Like LapLink/Mac, MacLinkPlus comes with Macintosh and PC applications, both of which must be running to transfer files. After you start up, you can select one of four modes to enter: MacLink, Desktop, Terminal, or MacLink Answer. MacLink enables you to connect to a PC over the enclosed serial cable or through modem. Desktop mode enables you to directly translate files you already have either on a floppy disk or accessible through the desktop. Terminal mode enables you to transfer files with another computer that is not running a MacLinkPlus version. Terminal mode simulates a telecommunication program's behavior on your Macintosh, and it requires a telecommunication program on the other computer to transfer files. Finally, MacLink Answer mode allows your Macintosh to receive phone calls either from another computer running MacLinkPlus or with third-party telecommunication software.

MacLinkPlus is probably the most complete file translation utility, although you may prefer LapLink for its wider variety of transfer options. With either of these products, however, you can get files from one computer to the other relatively quickly (see figure 26.11).

Chapter 26
Macintosh and PC Coexistence

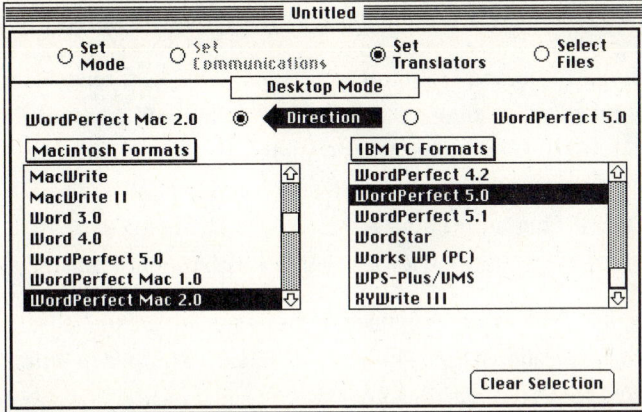

Figure 26.11
MacLinkPlus uses the format Font/DA Mover introduced to help you translate files from PCs to Macs and vice versa.

Using XTND

The file translation mechanisms mentioned in the previous sections all require intermediate steps before you can work with a file on another platform. Although this technique gets the job done, it is not necessarily the most convenient method possible. The Claris XTND system cuts out this intermediate step, allowing compatible applications to do the translations directly. You can save the file in one native format, open another application, and directly read the file as though it were in the new native format—all without any intermediate translation steps. The Dataviz translators are also XTND-compatible.

 XTND-compatible applications for the Mac include all the Claris products, WordPerfect Works, WordPerfect, DeltaPoint's Taste, GreatWorks (the new integrated software package from

Part VI
Expanding Your Mac's Horizons

Symantec), and others. The list is growing rapidly. The technology is inexpensive and convenient (Claris is licensing it), and it represents the future of file translation.

A Closer Look: Applications that are XTND-compatible can use the MacLinkPlus/Translators file from Dataviz to read and write other formats as though they were native. All you need to do is put a copy of the Translators file either in the same folder as your XTND-compatible application or in the Claris folder that resides in your System folder. Then, when you want to open a document, all files in compatible formats appear automatically in the Open menu list. Unfortunately, you cannot double-click on a document in a foreign format and have the XTND-compatible application open; you must open the application first.

With System 7's Drag and Drop feature, you can drag the foreign file to an XTND-equipped application and drop it on that application's icon. The application launches and translates the foreign file using XTND. For example, dropping a PC-Xywrite document onto MacWrite Pro equipped with XTND and the Dataviz translators launches MacWrite and then translates the Xywrite file, opening it in a MacWrite window with proper formatting.

Of course, the changes you can make to the document are limited by your destination application's capabilities. If you open a Word file in WriteNow, you are not able to use Word's automatic indexing function, for example, because WriteNow does not have such a function. But all other formatting capabilities are preserved.

Additional Topics

This section covers file compression and compound documents' roles in Macintosh-PC coexistence. These fields have seen a great deal of development in recent years. File compression techniques that reduce graphics and animation files to reasonable sizes are being improved all the time, bringing true multimedia to Mac and PC owners; and compound documents that integrate different kinds of data—text, graphics, sound, animation—are moving from the science fiction realm right onto your desktop. Both Windows and Macintosh applications are being readied to take advantage of these new technologies.

File Compression

Although transfer rates for some types of file transfers are reaching acceptable speed levels, modem and other indirect transfer methods remain very slow. Most modems can transfer data at 2400 bits per second, or slightly more than 1M an hour. Obviously, compressing files so that more data can be transferred in the same time is advantageous.

Several different compression utilities are available for both Macs and PCs. Most compressed PC files are either in a ZIP (*FILENAME*.ZIP) or an ARC (*FILENAME*.ARC) format. Aladdin Systems' Stuffit Deluxe—the commercial upgrade of the original Stuffit shareware Macintosh file compression utility (now called Stuffit Classic)—and freeware products MacArc and UnZip (available on bulletin boards around the country) can work with ZIP and ARC files. The file compression formats used most on Mac bulletin boards and online services include Stuffit's SIT (*filename*.SIT) and Compact Pro's CPT (*filename*.CPT) files. Both may be decompressed with available PC utilities. Fifth Generation's DiskDoubler (formally from Salient Software) is also widely used on the Macintosh.

Although Mac and PC files usually are segregated on information services like CompuServe and compressed according to different standards, you still can use compressed files with graphics, text, and other forms of data on both computers. After you download and decompress the PC file with Stuffit Deluxe, MacArc, or UnZip, you then can use MacLinkPlus in Desktop mode to convert the file to the Macintosh format you need.

WARNING! Another shareware program, BinHex, converts CompuServe BIN files to Macintosh HEX formats and vice versa. Be aware, however, that Macintosh SEA (Self Extracting Archive) files cannot be used directly on PCs. These files contain Macintosh code that decompresses the files on Macs but does not work on PCs. SEA files are self-contained programs (the equivalent of executable files on the PC) that run and expand the encapsulated compressed file.

Compound Documents

Compound documents can take many forms. Any word processing or desktop publishing file incorporating graphics and text is a compound document, as are all other files that incorporate various types of media.

Chapter 26
Macintosh and PC
Coexistence

Part VI
Expanding Your Mac's Horizons

Applications that include sound with your documents are already here, and the ability to incorporate animated movie and video clip sequences now are appearing. At the present, each application that supports annotation of documents with sound and video handles it independently.

Apple's QuickTime extension to the system software (6.0.7 or later) provides standardized tools for recording, editing, synchronizing, and storing any time-based data (voice, sound, music, video, and animation). (See chapter 18, "MultiMedia and CD/ROM," for more information.) No other major computer company has similar technology, although Microsoft's multimedia extension for Windows roughly parallels some of the features of Apple's QuickTime technology.

Microsoft has specified a standard basic level of PC-compatible computer that you can use, called the MultiMedia Personal Computer, as any 80386 PC with CD-ROM, which some argue is grossly underpowered for the intended use. Eventually there will be file compatibility between PC and Mac, even for multimedia files. Apple is involved in several standards committees to achieve this. The first of these products to work on both platforms is MacroMind's Windows Player accelerator board, which, under Windows, runs MacroMind files created on the Mac. An Apple Windows QuickTime player is scheduled for release sometime in the near future.

DOS and Windows products slowly are gaining sound annotation, but the technology, as yet, is not standardized. In the Mac Operating System, sound is handled in a standard way with the sound manager, and compression is handled with the Mac Audio Compression Expansion (MACE) tools. QuickTime uses this standard manager to seamlessly and transparently incorporate sound into other dynamic media.

Microsoft has been pushing multimedia and CD-ROM for several years but has only recently introduced a compound document file format standard to incorporate with Windows. Many new Macintosh products support annotation (especially sound—many new Macintosh models have built-in microphones), and workgroup productivity applications will use annotative files, but these files will not be entirely PC-compatible because of the platform's' lack of a similar process or standards. Although these new technologies bode well for Mac users, PC applications in this area lag behind the Macintosh by at least a couple of years.

Summary

Chapter 26
Macintosh and PC Coexistence

There always will be competing file format standards. Every software manufacturer boasts that its new product makes data access easier and quicker while keeping file sizes smaller than ever before. Fortunately, manufacturers also are learning that users do not switch to new products if they cannot easily access their old data!

Currently, there are numerous products to link your new computer with your old data—not just across Mac-PC lines but also across Mac-Vax, Mac-minicomputer, Mac-mainframe, and other lines as well. After you establish a link, you can move data simply by copying files back and forth, or translate data with one of the several translation utilities.

For the most part, file translation has required an intermediate utility (such as MacLinkPlus) to explicitly change a particular file's formatting before you can open it in the alternate application. Now, Claris' XTND technology allows for alternative applications to directly access other native file formats, and it is one example of the new trend of increasing application compatibility. This is a welcome and long-overdue transition that should make Mac and PC coexistence in the future far simpler to manage.

Other coexistence benefits such as resource sharing and electronic mail continue to improve with age. The convergence of Macintosh and PC graphical user interface features will lead to standardized procedures that make accessing shared printers and modems, and sending electronic mail, easier and more convenient.

The day is quickly coming when a program or file on disk is loaded on a PC or Mac and your machine makes it operate. One disk, any machine.

Chapter 27: The Macintosh Community

There is a camaraderie among Macintosh users that just does not seem to exist in the PC environment. The Mac's consistent interface encourages people to think in terms of their machine rather

In This Chapter

▼ Sources of information

▼ Macintosh User Groups

▼ Asking for help

▼ Learning more about the Mac

Part VI
Expanding Your
Mac's Horizons

than just one or two favorite programs: we consider ourselves Mac users rather than WordPerfect or PageMaker users.

Sharing Macintosh Resources

In the early days, it made sense for Mac owners to get together and share the information and programs they wrote. Very little was available on the market for the Macintosh. In fact, in the mid '80s, any kind of Mac disk—with or without software—was almost impossible to find. Apple shipped its computers with MacWrite, MacPaint, system files, and *one* blank disk. Dealers were unable to provide much help because they had only limited software or disks to sell, so it made sense for users to band together in support groups, just as prior groups of Apple II and other computer users had.

Sony, which manufactured the 3 1/2-inch drives used in the first Macs, was also the only manufacturer of media for them. Because it was unprepared for the Mac's overwhelming success—as was Apple—Sony was not ready to make enough disks to keep up with demand. For a while there was, quite literally, a worldwide shortage of 3 1/2-inch floppy disks. This shortage drove the price up to as much as $5 per disk—when you could find one. Mac-style floppies were so scarce that dealers rationed them.

Fortunately, the situation has changed, and you now can buy disks and Mac magazines at the corner drugstore. But there is still a need to share information, and user groups are one of many ways to stay informed about new Macintosh developments.

What You Need to Know (and How to Find Out)

Chapter 27
The Macintosh Community

Your Mac is up and running. You mastered the ins and outs of Microsoft Word or 4th Dimension or PageMaker. You even won a game of Mutant Beach. What else could you possibly want or need? For starters, it might be helpful to know whether you are using the latest software versions. Perhaps there are new products that could resolve a specific situation for you. And it certainly would not hurt to get tips on the various programs you do have and to have a source for solutions to any hardware or software problems.

Even though most companies do extensive testing before releasing a program to the general public, a few bugs still can occur. When users discover bugs, they post warnings to other users on bulletin boards and elsewhere. As soon as the company fixes the bug, its solution also is posted. However, when there are several bug fixes involved or when the company adds new features, it generally releases an upgrade. So if the company that developed your spreadsheet fixes some bugs and adds a word processor to it, you need a reliable network to inform you about the new release.

Be a Registered User

The most obvious—and important—way to find out about software upgrades is directly from the manufacturer. Mail the registration card as soon as you are sure you want to keep a program. This way, your name and address are in the manufacturer's database. They can send you information about new versions. Most companies offer free or low-cost upgrades—but only to registered users.

Depending on the company and product, you also can get other special features. Aldus sends a magazine to its registered PageMaker and FreeHand users. Adobe sends its type catalogs. Other publishers may send you demos of new products, often with special reduced prices for registered users. One user was pleasantly surprised when Dove Computer sent a $100 voice-upgrade for her fax modem as a reward for being among the first to buy its original product. (From the company's standpoint, sending free hardware is probably more practical than supporting the early boxes.)

 Shareware also is upgraded. Be sure to pay your shareware fees and become a registered user. Shareware authors even may send you a disk with some of their other creations.

Check Your Mailbox

Another way to keep in touch with new developments is to get on a few good mailing lists. Your name often is added automatically when you send in your registration cards. Software publishers, dealers, and user groups also sell their mailing lists to other Mac-oriented companies; if you request a catalog from a mail-order house, you soon may have one of the busiest mailboxes in town. Some of the contents could be labeled "junk mail," but much of the material includes special offers, discounts, and other useful information.

You also can get information online from user group bulletin boards and commercial services such as GEnie and America Online. (See chapter 23, "Communications and Online Services," for more information.) Members post bug reports and comments on various programs, and software publishers frequently post bug fixes, updated programs, and demonstration versions of new releases. You can download any of them for just the cost of the connect time.

America Online has the most to offer the Mac user in this capacity. There are separate forums, with bulletin boards and software libraries for special interests ranging from business and education to music and sound. America Online's Industry Connection section, shown in figure 27.1, currently has special areas for nearly 100 different software and hardware manufacturers. Each has a variety of choices ranging from product descriptions and direct-support bulletin boards to "wish lists" on which you can post ideas for new products or features. There are conference halls where users can chat with other users and experts from the companies. Many even feature software libraries with downloadable add-on modules, templates, and text files.

America Online has frequent online lectures and question-and-answer sessions with guest experts in virtually all areas of computing. It is also a source for "official information," with a complete library of Apple Macintosh Technical Notes, short downloadable articles in MacWrite format with accurate (and readable) advice about Mac system-level programming and internal hardware.

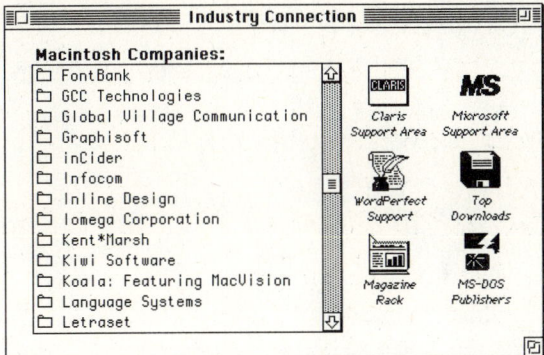

Chapter 27
The Macintosh Community

Figure 27.1
Get help online from companies listed with America Online.

Magazines

Your local newsstand and your favorite online service are two good places to turn for Macintosh information. Both offer great sources of up-to-date news, reviews, and perspectives specially targeted to Mac users' needs and interests.

Hard copy magazines

There are three major Mac magazines: *Macworld*, *MacUser*, and *MacWEEK*. A fourth, *InCider/A+*, targets both Apple II and Mac owners. *MacWEEK*, as the name suggests, appears weekly. The others are published monthly.

Macworld and *MacUser* have much in common. Both contain product reviews, features on Mac-related topics, and tips for users of all kinds of software. Both are slickly produced and include many pages of ads—which is as important as the editorial content to those whose favorite pastime is looking for new applications. *Macworld* is a little thicker and costs a few dollars more per year. Otherwise, there is little difference.

By trying to cover both the Apple II and Mac markets, *InCider/A+* does not really do justice to either. At $3.95 a copy, it is priced the same as the more comprehensive *Macworld* and a dollar more per copy than *MacUser*. It is worthwhile, however, if you own both a Mac and an Apple II.

Part VI
Expanding Your
Mac's Horizons

America Online subscribers get free previews of both *Macworld* and *InCider/A+*. The Computer section features a "magazine rack" with excerpts from the current issues of both magazines, a library of reviews and articles from past issues, and an address book of Macintosh software publishers. Figure 27.2 shows America Online's *Macworld* screen.

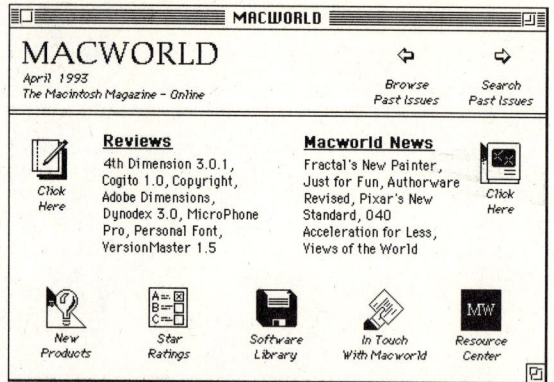

Figure 27.2
America Online is great help when tracking down information from past issues.

MacWEEK features a great deal of current industry news. It is a good way for software developers and computer sales people to stay abreast with the very latest trends and keep a finger on Apple's pulse. It specializes in product reviews, sales and marketing news, and industry gossip. It is also free to qualified parties. The magazine is paid for by its advertisers, so to qualify you have to show the publisher you are a continuing prospect for these advertised products: dealers, manufacturers, and those who are in a business that supports or recommends Macs. You do not need any special qualifications, however, to preview *MacWEEK* online on CompuServe.

Electronic Magazines

Two informative and advertising-free magazines are available at no cost—you simply download them. *Info-Mac Digest* is updated weekly by Bill Lipa and Jon Pugh at Stanford, and many bulletin boards subscribe to it. It is not as much "edited" as "gathered": readers around the country send E-mail, and relevant or interesting postings are combined to form the final publication. You find short articles, reviews, and technical tips, as well as user postings of problems and technical questions that are answered in subsequent issues. *TidBITS* is a weekly electronic magazine edited by Adam and Tonya Engst. It also finds its way to bulletin board systems around the country and often commercial services as well. It consists of longer articles and technical reviews, often related to a single subject per issue, in .ETX format, viewable with TeachText or any word processor (see figure 27.3). *TidBITS* is well worth looking for.

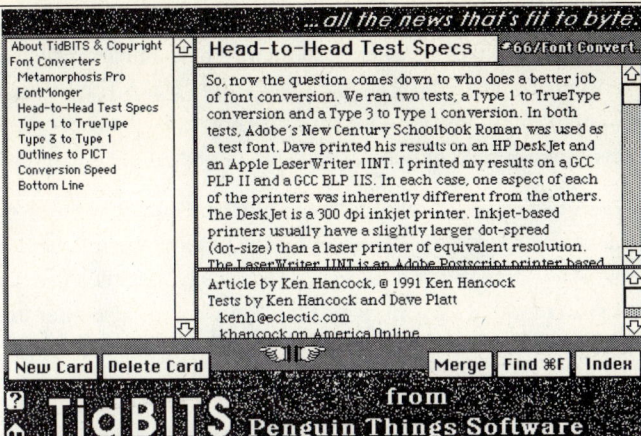

Figure 27.3
TidBITS can be found on many BBSs.

User Groups

Mac users often like to associate with other Mac users, just as people who own particular brands of boats or sports cars form clubs. Macintosh User Groups, or "MUGs" as many call themselves, have sprung up all over the country. They are typically nonprofit, so for tax reasons they must stay independent of Apple or any particular software publisher. But this also makes MUGs a good source for unbiased information. Apple maintains a database of these groups; you can get a list of groups in your area by calling Apple's Customer Service line at (800) 538-9696. Unless you live in a remote area, there is likely to be a group within commuting, or at least telecommuting, distance.

The Megagroups

There are two MUG forerunners, and conveniently, you find one on the East Coast and one on the West. BCS•Mac is the Boston Computer Society's Macintosh User Group. BMUG is based in Berkeley (across the Bay from San Francisco).

BMUG originally was called the Berkeley Macintosh User Group. Because the group met on the University of California campus (in Berkeley) to talk about using the Mac, the name seemed a logical choice. However, the Internal Revenue Service had a different opinion. Even though the group had no organizational or financial ties to Apple, the government considered any single brand or product user group a promotional effort by the company involved. To keep its nonprofit status and stay out of trouble, the group had to adopt its nickname, BMUG, as its legal name. (In a similar story, the New York MUG originally wanted to call itself "Big Apple Mac." The IRS had no complaint, but a certain fast-food hamburger chain was afraid people would confuse it with its specialty sandwich and threatened an expensive lawsuit.)

BMUG has recently started a satellite user group in Boston, with its own full-service bulletin board system. This gives local residents the unique opportunity to log onto the two largest collections of Macintosh advice and files with just a couple of local phone calls. (Both boards also offer limited free access for non-members.)

These groups are not available just to local Boston or Berkeley residents—anyone can join. Even though you might not be within driving distance of their weekly or monthly meetings, the groups still have much to offer you. Over the years, the BCS•Mac's monthly newsletter, *The Active Window*, has grown from a glorified flyer to a 50-page magazine. BMUG sends out a 400-page book of Mac information twice a year, and also publishes *BMAG*, a HyperCard-readable electronic magazine you can download from their bulletin boards.

Local User Groups

Many user groups in other cities have features similar to the larger groups. Expect to get some or all of the following when you pay your dues:

- ▼ A magazine or newsletter
- ▼ Monthly meetings and special events
- ▼ Classes and seminars in various applications
- ▼ Subgroups or *Special Interest Groups* (SIGs)
- ▼ A technical help hot line, staffed by knowledgeable volunteers
- ▼ A bulletin board system (BBS) for members
- ▼ Disk libraries of thousands of public-domain and shareware programs, yours for the cost of duplication (some groups also publish CD-ROM collections)
- ▼ A resource center, with Mac publications, hardware and software information, community activities, and so on

▼ Volunteer opportunities

▼ Discounts on hardware and software from local dealers, up to 40 percent in some cases

These features are all good reasons to join a group. BMUG offers still another, unique reason. As a free service to members, it attempts to recover a crashed hard disk or corrupted data. BMUG offers no guarantees, but it is successful in most cases. Comparable services from commercial recovery specialists cost $100 or more per hour and are not any better. This service is only for BMUG members, but you can join after your disk crashes. Like most Mac groups, membership is an excellent value: a single membership in BMUG is only $40 per year as of this writing.

SIGs

Special Interest Groups, or SIGs, are subgroups within the user groups dedicated to a particular application, such as HyperCard, or toward Mac applications for a particular profession. BCS•Mac has dozens of SIGs, including groups for business, legal, technical, and design applications. BMUG SIGs include music, multimedia, Japanese, and a group dedicated to freedom, privacy, and technology, or "being politically correct with your Mac or PC." The New York MUG has a MacKids SIG for the younger set and an advertising SIG for the Madison Avenue crowd. The Washington (DC) Apple Pi group includes a SIG dedicated to stock market analysis.

When you join a SIG, you meet other Mac owners who share your interests. SIGs are a good place to network if you are looking for a job or freelance work. They are also a fine source for answers, advice, and industry gossip. Here, you can make new friends and share your own talents and skills as a volunteer.

Independent SIGs

Some users with special interests, such as desktop publishers, have formed independent groups that pool information relevant to both Macs and PCs. If you share their interests, you may want to join. The National Association of Desktop Publishers offers members a journal and newsletter, meetings and local user groups, a national directory, discounts on hardware and software, training seminars, telephone support, and much more for an annual fee of $95. There are also corporate user groups, formed by software or hardware companies to support their own products. These groups may have their own bulletin boards, newsletters, and/or may hold conferences on an online service like GEnie, or America Online.

A Macintosh Convention

Imagine what would happen if you put all the members of all Mac user groups in one room and then threw in representatives from all the software publishers, hardware and peripheral manufacturers, services, publications, and used-Mac dealers. Several times each year such an event takes place. It's called Macworld Expo, and it is the largest gathering of Macintosh people and equipment in the world. There's a winter Expo in San Francisco, a summer one in Boston, and others during the year in Europe, the Far East, Australia, New Zealand, Canada, and Mexico. The numbers are staggering: 80,000 attendees, 400 participating companies, and 300,000 square feet of exhibits. There are also seminars on topics such as "QuickTime in Your Future," "Interconnectivity," and "Maximizing Your Macintosh."

Much of what is shown at Macworld Expo is aimed at particular, but diverse, market segments. There are advanced business management applications and high-resolution laser printers for the graphic arts industry elbow-to-elbow with companies that sell novelty mouse pads, "Happy Mac" neckties, and stuffed Macs. Some people attend the show to collect the buttons, T-shirts, hats, and other merchandise that various software and hardware companies hand out. Others come to take advantage of the discounted show prices that exhibiting dealers offer on hardware and programs. Many come to see new program demonstrations and to get their questions answered, although it is often difficult to get a salesperson's undivided attention in such a scene.

Macworld, the magazine, sponsors Macworld, the Expo. For dates, advance tickets (to avoid long lines and to get a discounted admission), and a preview of what to expect, consult *Macworld*.

If you are not able to go to Macworld, you are still in luck. During the year, there are many smaller expositions, conventions, and shows throughout the country, often held by user groups or in conjunction with seminars on a particular field such as desktop publishing. You find many of the same exhibitors at these shows, although there is generally less of a carnival atmosphere.

Of course, you always can go window shopping at your local dealer's store. This is probably the best place to try a new Mac or a new program because most dealers allow you to spend some time with a new machine or a demo version of a new application. Naturally, you have to act and look as though you are serious about buying something. The stores frown on those who treat them like a video arcade.

Stranger in a Strange Land

Travel, whether for business or pleasure, is a major cause of separation anxiety for some Mac users. Fortunately, there is also a Mac community for transients. Airport executive lounges for first-class and business-class passengers sometimes offer computers and modems so you can check E-mail or transfer files. Hotels that cater to business travelers often have a similar arrangement. Executive office centers may include Macintosh systems when you rent space by the week or month, and of course, you can rent just the machine—without the office—in most major cities. If you plan to rent, bring your own software; these Macs have a system installed, but nothing else. It is illegal to rent software. Small, travel-sized hard disks and removable hard disks like the Bernoulli 90 M transportable are very useful for travelers who need to bring files and applications with them.

If none of these solutions seems appropriate, there is yet another easy one. Open the Yellow Pages of the telephone directory to "Desktop Publishing Services" or "Typesetting." You will find a list of service bureaus, many of which rent Mac workstations by the hour for a reasonable fee. Of course, they may also provide fine quality imagesetting, slide imaging, scanning, color printing, and copying. But when you rent time on their Mac, you usually can do whatever you like, as long as you do not damage the computer. You can compose a letter—or a symphony, if you have brought your music software. (The service bureau usually provides word processors, page layout programs, and other standard software to use on their machines.)

 Do not attempt to pirate software from a "public" computer. You are likely to pick up a virus along with the program. Documents created with most programs are probably safe from infections because of the way the Mac handles files, but the applications can,

Chapter 27
The Macintosh Community

Part VI
Expanding Your Mac's Horizons

and often do, contain viruses. (Almost all known viruses work in the resource fork rather than the data fork.) Also, always use a program such as Disinfectant to check disks you bring back to your own computer. (See chapter 22, "Viruses and System Security," for more information.)

When You Need Help

Sooner or later, something does not work as expected or the system crashes. At such a time, cursing and dramatic gesturing, though momentarily satisfying, are not much of a long-term solution. Where can you go for help?

The first and most obvious place is often the most overlooked: the manual. It is an unfortunate compliment to the Mac interface that many users simply start using their software without ever looking at the book. You are doing yourself no favors by ignoring the manuals. It is probably safe to say that every program has a few features that are not intuitive. Furthermore, if something does go wrong and you call for help, the first thing you are told to do is "look in the book."

One thing you will find in the manual is the phone number for the manufacturer's help line. Virtually every software publisher and hardware manufacturer has some type of customer support system. It often is called "technical assistance," "user support," or "customer service," and the call may or may not be toll free. When you call for assistance, you usually can choose to wait on hold or leave your name and number for a return call.

Some software publishers may charge a subscription fee for telephone support beyond the warranty period or for "priority" access or minor upgrades. Others have a 900 number, so charges for technical help appear on your phone bill. However, many companies not only provide free phone help but maintain their own product support bulletin boards or their own areas in CompuServe, GEnie, America Online, or other online services.

You also can get help from your local user group. Each group has a slightly different help system, but all have some kind of telephone support for baffled Mac users. BCS•Mac's monthly magazine lists names and phone numbers of more than 200 volunteer specialists from 13 states for various programs, plus some who will help beginners in all areas. BMUG has a single phone number for help, plus a fax number for written questions. It researches answers and returns calls promptly. Help from user groups is always free. If anyone tries to charge you, notify the group at once. By the same token, do not try to cheat a help service. These people are justified in asking whether you are a legitimate owner of the program and have the original manual. Most software publishers do not help at all unless you are in their database as a registered user. You become one by returning the registration card that comes with the product. Registration is the publisher's best protection against software piracy.

Before you call anyone for answers to your computer problems, make sure you can provide some answers yourself, such as:

▼ The program's name and version number. (You can find this with the **About...** command under the Apple menu or by selecting **Get Info** from the desktop; the name and version number are also are printed on the master disk.) You also need the serial number of your registered copy of the program if you call a software publisher.

▼ What you were doing, as specifically as possible, when you encountered the problem. Write down the exact wording and error code numbers (if any) of any dialog boxes you saw.

▼ What kind of Mac you have, how much RAM is installed, and the type and size of hard disk you have (if any).

▼ Version numbers of the System and Finder you use, and the names of any INITs you have installed.

▼ Whether MultiFinder was in use if you use any version of System 6.0.

After you gather this information and a pen and paper for notes, move the phone next to your Mac, turn on the computer, and make the call. People who answer help lines are prepared to walk you through the program step by step, but that will not help unless you are within reach of the keyboard.

Service bureaus, schools or colleges with computer departments, and dealers are some other possible sources for help. Service bureau personnel are often extremely knowledgeable about desktop publishing, word processing applications, and anything to do with graphics or type. They usually are willing to answer your questions, as long as you do not come in at a very busy time. Colleges and schools may have adult education classes in Mac use. Dealers also are usually very good about helping you solve your problems. As a last resort, after checking with your dealer, you can call Apple's Assistance Center at (800) 776-2333.

Chapter 27
The Macintosh Community

Part VI
Expanding Your
Mac's Horizons

Training

Where can you go to learn more about the Mac? You often can enroll in classes for computer use and specific applications, such as FreeHand or QuarkExpress, at your local high school, college, or adult education center. User groups also sponsor classes, but you can learn much of what you need to know simply by playing around with your computer. This section covers some additional resources you may not have considered.

Audio and Video Instruction

The latest trend in Mac instruction is audio- and videotaped tutorials for some of the more complex applications such as Microsoft Excel, Works, and Word. You find these tapes in mail-order catalogs and possibly on the dealer's shelf. You may find it difficult, however, for a single 90-minute videotape to teach you the tricks and shortcuts you can learn in a class or from reading a good book on the program.

When you work with the tapes, you have to go at the instructor's pace. Audio tapes require you to wear your personal tape player or set up a cassette recorder next to your Mac, a relatively simple operation compared to the videotapes, which assume you have your Mac, hard drive, VCR, and television set all on your desk at once. One nice feature is that you can use the rewind button to go back over a point or step that you missed. And, of course, if the pace is too slow, use the fast-forward button.

Seminars

If you want to learn a particular application or technique, just watch your mailbox. As soon as you become a registered Mac user, you start receiving mailings announcing various Macintosh seminars. Typically, seminar announcements read like this one: "Powerful two-day workshop featuring... unique Speed Learning System." For your money, you often get several hours of lectures and the opportunity to ask questions. During the seminar, you may receive instructions on many different programs.

Software publishers and local dealers typically cooperate to present hands-on seminars. The dealer supplies a meeting room in the store or at a local hotel, and the publisher supplies an expert for the application. The event usually is promoted through the store's mailing list or newspaper ads. There is typically less ground to cover in these seminars, and you follow the instructor step-by-step. These usually cost less to attend, and you can pick up inside information and shortcuts.

Summary

When you bought your Mac, you didn't just buy a computer. You bought into a community of Mac owners. This neighborly feeling prevails throughout the many Mac user groups. When you join a group, you receive newsletters, discounts from local computer stores, help when you need it, seminars, and much more. If you choose not to join a group, you can buy a variety of Mac magazines and get help directly from software publishers. There are seminars and classes of all kinds, including video- and audiotaped lectures. Whatever your question, someone has an answer.

Chapter 27
The Macintosh Community

Part VII

For the More Technically Minded

In This Part

Chapter 28: Troubleshooting

Chapter 29: Programming

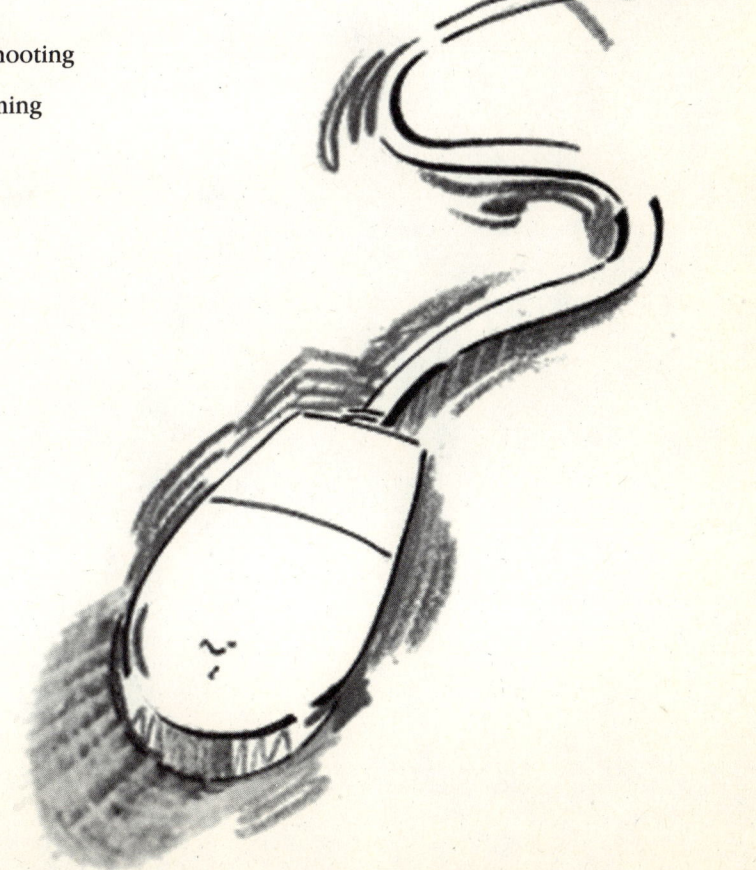

Chapter 28: Troubleshooting

The Mac is a reliable machine, but things still can go wrong. The key to fixing a problem is to diagnose what is causing it—in some cases, it can be quite difficult to figure out whether the problem lies with the hardware or with the software!

In This Chapter

- ▼ Reducing the variables
- ▼ Error codes
- ▼ Sad Mac icon
- ▼ Chords of death
- ▼ Software problems
- ▼ SCSI problems
- ▼ Automated diagnostics

Part VII
For the More
Technically Minded

Hardware Problems

There are two stages to diagnosing a problem on your Mac:

▼ Reduce the variables to a minimum

▼ Change the variables (and collect the data)

Variables are simply things about the Mac's configuration you can change. Often, when a problem first manifests itself, the cause is not obvious. Take, for example, a common problem: the Mac will not boot. If you have some external devices connected to the SCSI port, remove them. If they are not hooked up, they cannot cause problems, and you have reduced a variable. (This example assumes a hardware problem; it could be a software problem instead. We'll discuss how to determine which it might be later in the chapter.)

If your keyboard or mouse seems to be acting up and another Mac is nearby, swap your keyboard or mouse with another one. If the problem still exists, it is something in the Mac; otherwise, the problem probably lies with the keyboard or mouse. This is an example of changing a variable; by switching the suspect component to another Mac, you isolate the problem.

Software problems can be handled in the same way. INITs often cause problems; if your Mac is doing weird things such as crashing when you try to save a MacWrite document, remove all of your INITs (or disable them with an INIT manager). Again, you reduce the number of variables.

This section describes some of the more common hardware problems the Mac can encounter. It does not delve into repairs; for the ambitious, Larry Pina's *Macintosh Repair and Upgrade Secrets* is recommended reading.

The Sad Mac Errors

All Macs perform a quick series of checks when they are powered on. If errors are detected in the hardware, the result is the Sad Mac: a black screen,

Chapter 28
Troubleshooting

a little Mac icon with its eyes X'd out, and a cryptic set of numbers and letters below the icon.

You do not need to worry too much about diagnosis at this point because the Sad Mac error code tells you what is wrong. This section contains a comprehensive list of Sad Mac error codes.

Be warned, though:

- ▼ Sad Mac error codes are not *always* correct: they can indicate an error that either does not exist or is a consequence of another error.

- ▼ Some error codes, especially for the SE and later Macs, are either very obscure or indicate conditions that require a trained technician to correct.

- ▼ Many Sad Mac error codes are for conditions you cannot do anything about.

In the interest of completeness, all error codes are presented here, with official Apple explanations as well as whatever additional information could be provided. Like the codes that appear in the infamous "bomb box," they are often of little use. Occasionally, these errors have an outside cause: if you get a Sad Mac error, try removing any peripherals you have connected, especially on the SCSI port, then power down, wait a minute or so, and power on again. The problem simply may disappear.

Mac 128 Through Mac Plus

Sad Macs on the original Macintosh computers had one row of error codes to indicate what problem the Mac encountered, as shown above in figure 28.1.

On these Macs, error codes are in the XX YYYY form, in which the first two digits indicate the type of error and the last four digits provide additional information (see table 28.1).

Table 28.1 Mac Error Code Explanations

First Two Digits	Type of Failure
01	ROM error
02, 03, 04, 05	RAM error
0F	Software error

1055

Part VII
For the More Technically Minded

ROM Errors

ROM errors are quite rare, and when they occur, it is almost always because there is poor contact between the ROM and its socket. (Some newer Macs have ROMs soldered directly to the logic board. If you get a ROM error at boot time with these Macs, it is time for a trip to the dealer.) Removing the ROMs and spraying their pins and sockets with a zero-residue contact cleaner generally fixes the problem. In some cases, a firm push to reseat the ROMs in their sockets is all that is required.

The last four digits of the error code are undefined for ROM errors and can be ignored.

RAM Errors

If the first two digits of the Sad Mac code are 02 through 05, a RAM error has occurred.

What you can do about RAM errors depends on the Mac you have and how adventurous you are. The Mac 128 and 512 have their RAM soldered in. Fortunately, RAM errors in these machines are rare, but if one occurs, all you can do, more or less, is visit the dealer for a logic board exchange (unless you have experience soldering and desoldering components on multilayer PC boards).

The Mac Plus' SIMM memory is replaceable, and the last four digits of the error code identifies which SIMM failed. To replace a SIMM, open the Mac and remove the logic board. If you never have opened a Mac before, this probably is not the time to start on your own. Be aware: it is quite easy to damage your Mac permanently if you decide to take it apart, so get someone who has done this before, if you can.

When the logic board is in front of you, notice that the upper edge of the board is labeled with the numbers 1 through 13, and the left edge of the board is labeled with the letters A through G. Components on the board are referred to by the intersection of these "board coordinates." For example, the programmer's switch is at A1.

To find where the RAM error occurred, match the last four digits of the error code to table 28.2.

Table 28.2 RAM Error Codes and Where the Errors Occurred

Error Code	Location of Failed Chip
0001	F5
0002	F6
0004	F7
0008	F8
000A	F9
0014	F10
0028	F11
0050	F12
0064	G5
00C8	G6
0190	G7
0320	G8
03E8	G9
07D0	G10
0FA0	G11
1F40	G12

Obviously, you need only to isolate the problem to the SIMM level. If a SIMM in Bank A fails, you can replace it with one from Bank B and see whether the Mac boots normally.

Software Errors

In this example, the hardware checks out but the Mac ran into trouble when it tried to boot. The error codes for software errors at this point, shown in table 28.3, are rarely useful; if your Mac crashes with one of these errors before it finishes booting, your best bet is to boot from the System Tools diskettes, trash the System and Finder files on your hard disk, and run the Installer to build a new system.

Note it is rare to actually get a Sad Mac code with one of these errors—the system almost always makes it far enough into the boot process to display the more familiar "bomb box."

Table 28.3 Software Error Code Explanations

Error Code	Error
0001	Bus error
0002	Address error
0003	Illegal instruction
0004	Divide by zero
0005	Check trap error
0006	Overflow trap error
0007	Privilege violation error
0008	Trace mode error
0009	Line 1010 trap error
000A	Line 1111 trap error
000B	Misc. hardware error
000C	Unimplemented core routine*
000D	Uninstalled interrupt handler
0064	Failed to load System file

*This particular error is often an indication that you are trying to run Mac II–class software on a non-Mac II machine.

Mac SE and Beyond

On these Macs, the Sad Mac codes have been substantially extended and changed to a two-row format.

Viewing these codes as

XXXXYYYY

ZZZZZZZZ,

the first four digits in the first row (XXXX) can be ignored, the second four digits (YYYY) indicate which type of error has occurred, and the bottom row of digits (ZZZZZZZZ) contains additional information on the error.
The Mac SE has a different SIMM layout than the Plus.

Many of these error codes either are obscure or indicate conditions that require a trained technician to correct.

Table 28.4 details the YYYY error codes.

Table 28.4 YYYY Error Code Explanations

Code	Error
0001	ROM failure. Ignore the Z field.
0002	RAM failure. This error code always indicates a problem with Bank B of RAM. Each two digits of the Z field refer to an 8-bit portion of a 32-bit "word" composed of the data from both Bank B SIMMs. The format of the Z field is "AABBCCDD" in which: AA = bits 31-24 BB = bits 23-16 CC = bits 15-8 DD = bits 7-0
0003	The RAM test failed while testing Bank B, after passing the test for code 0002. The Z field indicates which bits failed, as in code 0002.
0004	The RAM test failed while testing Bank A. The Z field indicates which bits failed, as in code 0002.
0005	The RAM external addressing test failed. The Z field indicates a failed address line.
0006	Unable to properly address the VIA1 chip. The Z field is not applicable. This chip controls the ADB port.
0007	Unable to properly address the VIA2 chip (Macintosh II only). This chip controls a variety of functions on a Mac II-class machine, including control of the MMU, NuBus slot interrupts, the power-on switch, and so on. The Z field is not applicable.
0008	Unable to properly access the ADB circuitry. The Z field is not applicable.
0009	Unable to properly access the MMU (Mac II-class machines only). The Z field is not applicable.

continues

Chapter 28
Troubleshooting

Table 28.4 Continued.

Code	Error
000A	Unable to properly access NuBus (NuBus Macs only). The Z field is not applicable.
000B	Unable to properly access the SCSI chip. The Z field is not applicable.
000C	Unable to properly access the IWM or SWIM floppy disk controller chip. The Z field is not applicable.
000D	Unable to properly access the SCC chip. This chip controls the printer and modem ports. The Z field is not applicable.
000E	Failed data bus test. The Z field indicates the bad bit(s), as with error code 002. This may indicate either a bad SIMM or data bus failure.
000F	Reserved for Macintosh compatibility.
FFxx	A 680xx hardware exception occurred during power-on testing.

The xx in the FFxx message indicates the exception detailed in table 28.5.

Table 28.5 FFxx Error Code Explanations

Exception Error Code	Error
0001	Bus error
0002	Address error
0003	Illegal instruction
0004	Divide by zero
0005	Check trap error
0006	Overflow trap error
0007	Privilege violation error
0008	Trace mode error
0009	Line 1010 trap error
000A	Line 1111 trap error
000B	unassigned (should not occur)
000C	CP protocol violation

Chapter 28
Troubleshooting

Exception Error Code	Error
000D	Format exception
000E	Spurious interrupt
000F	Trap 0-15 exception
0010	Interrupt level 1
0011	Interrupt level 2
0012	Interrupt level 3
0013	Interrupt level 4
0014	Interrupt level 5
0015	Interrupt level 6
0016	Interrupt level 7
0017	Math coprocessor error
0018	Math coprocessor inexact result
0019	Math coprocessor divide by zero
001A	Math coprocessor underflow
001B	Math coprocessor operand error
001C	Math coprocessor overflow
001D	Math coprocessor NAN1
001E	MMU configuration error
001F	MMU illegal operation
0020	MMU access level violation

*NAN = "Not a number," a result returned for things like the square root of –1.

The Mac Portable

The Portable has its own set of Sad Mac error codes. Like the Mac II-level codes, these appear in two rows of eight digits. The first four digits of the upper row are test flags, the second four digits are the major error code, and the entire bottom row is the minor error code.

The major error code is broken down further: the first two digits contain the number of any 680x0 exception that may have occurred, whereas the last two digits indicate which test was running at the time. The errors for the last two digits are the "YYYY" error codes for the Mac SE above.

Part VII
For the More
Technically Minded

In practice, only the format of the error codes and the addition of the codes for the Power Manager differentiate the Portable's Sad Mac errors.

Major Error Codes

The major error codes (first two digits) for the Mac Portable are listed in table 28.6.

Table 28.6 Mac Portable Major Error Code Explanations

Error Code	Error
01	ROM failure
02	RAM failure; minor error code indicates which bits failed
05	RAM addressing circuitry failure
06	VIA 1 chip failed (ADB control)
08	Data bus failure (may indicate RAM failure)
0B	Unable to address SCSI controller
0C	Unable to access IWM/SWIM floppy controller
0E	Data bus failure (may indicate RAM failure)
10	Video RAM test failure
11	Video RAM addressing circuitry failure
14	Power Manager communications failure (see minor error code for details)
15	Power Manager self-test failure
16	RAM configuration error (occurred while Mac was figuring out how much RAM it has)

Power Manager Error Codes

The Power Manager error codes are used on the Macintosh PowerBooks and portables. They are listed in table 28.7.

Table 28.7 Power Manager Error Code Explanations

Code	Error
CD38	Initial handshake
CD37	No reply to initial handshake
CD36	No handshake start during send
CD35	No handshake finish during send
CD34	No handshake start during receive
CD33	No handshake end during receive

The new PowerBook 100 uses the same error codes as the now-discontinued Mac Portable.

The Chords of Death

Depending on the type of error they encounter, Mac II-class machines sometimes play a series of musical chords to indicate an error. All these Macs sound one chord at power-on; any notes played after this time indicate an error.

These sounds are not very specific and are hard to describe. Apple has a program called the Diagnostic Sounds Sampler that plays these sounds and explains what they mean, but unfortunately, it never has been released for public distribution.

In any case, if you hear a second chord shortly after the first one, a hardware error has occurred. At least one more sound follows, and it is specific to the error:

- ▼ A short chord indicates a hardware error.
- ▼ A short single tone indicates that a RAM problem was detected in Bank A.
- ▼ A short double-note sequence indicates that a RAM problem was detected in Bank B.

In many cases, the *chords of death* (as Mac aficionados call them) immediately are followed by a Sad Mac whose error codes may provide more information on what has occurred.

Part VII
For the More
Technically Minded

Dead Battery

Macs depend heavily on having a good battery; newer Macs—those that can be turned on by pressing a button on the keyboard—do not even boot if the battery is dead!

All Macs use their batteries to retain system configuration information in a special chip called the *clock/parameter RAM chip*, or simply "PRAM." This is a custom chip made for Apple and is not available as a separate part.

As its name implies, this chip contains both the system clock and a small amount of RAM used to store some system information. The Mac's battery maintains the information in this RAM when the machine is turned off, and if the battery dies, this information is lost or scrambled. Having to reset the time, date, and other parameters, such as the number of times a menu item blinks when it is selected, is an early symptom of a dead or dying battery.

Macs with a physical power switch (the 128, 512, Plus, LC, SE, SE/30, and Classic) can run with a dead battery; Macs that use an electronic power switch (the II, IIx, IIcx, IIci, IIfx, and IIsi) cannot. If the battery on these latter Macs dies, the Mac cannot be started.

Macs through the Plus use a 4.5V battery called the NEDA 1306A. It looks remarkably like a standard AA cell, but it is not; an AA battery does not work. The best place to find the correct battery is at a well-equipped camera store; this battery often is used in photographic equipment too. An Eveready Energizer 523 is a typical example of an NEDA 1306A.

Later Macs use one or two cylindrical lithium batteries with the designation ER3S (1/2 AA). The Mac II, IIx, and SE use a version of the battery with a wire lead on each end so it can be soldered directly to the logic board; newer Macs use a version without the wire leads that fits into a special socket. (You can use the lead version in a socket by cutting off the leads.)

These typically last for several years before needing replacement. The Mac II, IIx, and SE batteries must be replaced by a dealer when they die (two each on the II and IIx; one on the SE). You can replace the socketed batteries that start with the IIcx, but they are not easy to find: you probably still need to find an electronics store or distributor instead.

The Mac Portable uses a standard 9V "transistor radio" battery to maintain PRAM and other items.

Hard Disk SCSI Problems

The SCSI port and the devices users connect to it are probably the single largest source of hardware-related problems for the Mac. SCSI is a high-speed parallel data bus; nothing like it had been in wide use on consumer computers before its introduction on the Mac Plus.

The high speed of SCSI data makes the data more vulnerable to interference and poor transmission/reception than other computer connections, such as serial lines and parallel printer ports. The SCSI specification calls for a 50-line connector, with 25 ground lines and 25 signal lines. Apple's use of a standard DB-25 connector for the SCSI port is a compromise (for space reasons) that makes proper cabling and SCSI device construction more important.

Mac SCSIs can be made to operate reliably; the major issues are termination, cable length, and quality. Before you get involved with this issue, however, you should be reasonably sure your problem is SCSI-related. Always remember the first rule of SCSI: If it works, leave it alone.

SCSI Problem Diagnosis

SCSI problems often are random and flaky, and can look similar to software problems: odd, irreproducible crashes that do not seem to have any relationship to what you are doing at the moment. Other times, the problem is more obvious: you connect your new external hard drive and hear the dreaded chords of death when you turn on your machine.

If you think you have a SCSI problem, you can perform a simple test that almost always verifies a problem exists: simply copy (or duplicate) a 10M chunk of data or files. If you can do this with no errors—such as "File could not be read due to a disk error"—it is unlikely your SCSI setup has problems.

Part VII
For the More Technically Minded

Note: The II Macs Mac IIs—such as the Mac IIci, IIfx, and IIsi—are significantly more sensitive to SCSI problems than earlier Macs.

SCSI Problem Resolution

If your SCSI setup does have problems, try to isolate them. First, remove any external SCSI devices you may have connected to your Mac; then repeat the file duplicating test described earlier (assuming your Mac has an internal hard disk).

Improper termination and, to a lesser extent, cabling problems are the most common causes of SCSI problems.

Termination

Approximately 85 percent of Mac SCSI problems are directly related to improper termination. A *terminator* is simply a resistor pack that, in most circumstances, should exist at either physical end of the SCSI chain. Your Mac, or the hard drive inside it, is at one end of the chain; whatever you hook to the external SCSI port is at the other.

Termination both cleans up the SCSI signals and prevents ringing, which is the reflection of a signal that has reached the end of the SCSI chain. Proper termination is essential for reliable SCSI operation!

You probably have seen terminators for external drives: they are anonymous gray or beige plastic blocks that plug into the unused SCSI connector on the external device. (The block also can be placed between the drive and the cable on the SCSI connector being used.) This is the most common type of terminator, but there are two other types as well: logic board terminators and drive controller board terminators.

The Mac IIfx requires a special terminator for reliable operation. This terminator is easily identified: it is black. It is included with all new IIfx computers and *should* be included with all IIfx upgrades; if you do not have one, get one from your dealer.

Logic board terminators are used inside Macs that have no internal hard drive but do have external SCSI devices. In this case, the terminator is a plastic plug or strip that plugs into the SCSI connector inside the Mac, in the same place you would connect an internal drive if one were used.

Most hard drives also provide for termination directly on the drive's controller board, usually by three small SIP or DIP resistor packs located near the 50-pin cable connector on the drive body.

These termination packs can be in SIP (single inline pin) form, as in the illustration, or in DIP (dual inline pin) form like "normal" chips. In either case, they are almost always either blue, red, or yellow—and easy to spot. Internal hard drives always should be terminated.

In most cases, these drive terminators are socketed and can be removed (a pair of needle-nose pliers works well); however, you may find them soldered in place on older drives. If so, the drive must be located at the end of the SCSI chain. If you have an internal hard drive in your Mac, it must have these terminators on its controller board.

There are only two potential termination problems:

▼ Insufficient termination

▼ Too much termination: for example, an external terminator placed on an older drive equipped with internal terminators on the controller board.

You should inspect your SCSI chain and make sure each end is terminated, and *only* each end is terminated. There are rare exceptions: if the cable length between any two SCSI devices (and remember the Mac counts as a SCSI device!) is greater than 10 feet, termination should be used at the 10-foot point as well as elsewhere. And if the total SCSI cable length is 18 inches or less, termination is generally required only at one end: for example, you do not need to terminate an external drive if the cable is only 12 inches long and the Mac you connect it to has an internal drive as well.

Total SCSI cable length should not be more than 6 meters (approximately 20 feet).

Cabling

The other major SCSI problem involves cabling. Because SCSI is a very high-speed protocol, quality cabling is a must. Cables should be shielded; never use an RS-232-type serial cable even if you have an external SCSI device that uses DB-25 connectors rather than the 50-pin SCSI connectors.

Chapter 28
Troubleshooting

Part VII
For the More Technically Minded

Apple SCSI cables are about the best there are; however, other manufacturers make high-quality cables as well. Inexpensive cables often use only a simple foil shield, which promptly breaks the first time the cable is bent. Braided shielding is much better, but it is not something you easily can check without cutting the cable open, a tactic to which many computer and electronics store owners object.

Sometimes using different brands of cables can cause problems, even if all the cables are high quality. The cables' construction and their electrical characteristics can differ enough to cause reflections and signal degradation. Avoid very short cables (less than 12 inches) and very long cables (greater than 6 feet) if possible.

Some SCSI devices offer only one SCSI connector—hand scanners are a common offender. Using a "Y" connector to allow the SCSI chain to continue off such devices is asking for trouble! Any type of cable extension or splitter can cause problems and should be avoided.

The Reset Line

Line 40 of the SCSI cable is the *Reset* line. The Mac uses this line to reset all attached SCSI devices when it is first turned on. Some older nonblock devices, such as scanners, do not recover well from SCSI resets; such devices can keep the Mac from booting as long as they are connected.

Many SCSI devices respond to the Reset command by entering the "unit attention" mode. This mode is designed to alert the computer that something significant has occurred (reset events are considered significant). However, some early Macs—particularly older versions of the Mac Plus—do not respond correctly to the unit attention condition. After a device has entered this mode, it is up to the host computer to clear it—and these older Macs do not. The result is a drive that often seems to have trouble booting or a drive that does not boot at all.

The solution to this problem is simply to cut line 40. The ribbon cable marks line one with a red (or other color) stripe; line 40 is the 40th line from this position, although it is generally easier to start at the other side of the cable with line 50 and count inward 10 lines. (This is generally done on the ribbon cable inside the affected drive's case.) This prevents the Mac's reset signal from reaching the SCSI device, so the device never enters the unit attention mode. This is kind of a hack but seems to work well. Some manufacturers even cut line 40 on the cabling inside their cabinets.

However, this can cause problems: line 40 must be terminated. If it is cut on the cable leading to the drive, the drive must be terminated with the drive controller terminators described earlier, because external terminators obviously cannot terminate a broken line. If these internal terminators are removed—to allow the drive to be used in the middle of the SCSI chain, for example—the drive generally stops working. You can either restore the terminators and keep the drive at the end of the chain, or replace the internal cabling.

A Final Word on SCSI

In the real world, people have Macs with SCSI peripherals from different vendors, and each device often comes with a cable from the manufacturer. So the potential for trouble and device and cable incompatibilities is significant.

Fortunately, SCSI problems often can be solved simply by rearranging the SCSI chain's components. When you determine that a SCSI problem exists, and that it goes away with all or most external SCSI devices disconnected, experiment with different setups and cable lengths. For instance, you may have some devices that prevent the Mac from booting unless they are turned on when you boot.

It is generally a good idea to run the 10M copy test mentioned at the start of this section whenever you change your SCSI configuration to help prevent any nasty surprises.

SCSI is an inexact discipline at best, and it is possible for a configuration that breaks all the rules to work perfectly. Bearing this in mind, continue to observe the first rule of SCSI: If it works, leave it alone!

Non-SCSI Hard Drive Problems

Problems with the drive mechanism include mechanical problems such as spindle motor failure, or platter *stiction*, and electronic problems with the drive's controller board or SCSI interface.

Chapter 28
Troubleshooting

Part VII
For the More
Technically Minded

Stiction

Stiction, or static friction, once a rare phenomenon, seems to be on the rise. When a hard drive stops, the read/write heads, which were supported on a cushion of air generated by the disk's rotation, actually land on the disk surface. The disk surface is coated with a thin layer of lubricant to prevent damaging the heads as well as the disk surface. It is possible for the heads to become stuck to the disk surface—the effect is similar to two pieces of glass with water between them—to a degree that the starting torque of the spindle motor (the motor that spins the platters) is insufficient to break the contact. Sometimes the problem is caused by heavier lubricant leaking from the spindle motor itself; old Quantum 280 5-1/4 inch hard drives had this problem.

It is generally possible to tell whether a drive is spinning by listening carefully: the drive makes a sound that is distinguishable from the sound caused by the fan that is often present. If the drive is internal, you may have to open the Mac to hear it.

When stiction first appears, you often can overcome it by rapping sharply on the drive casing or rotating the drive quickly about the axis of spin of its platters. Unfortunately, there is no way to permanently cure stiction: the problem generally worsens until the drive does not spin at all. You can use a drive with stiction problems almost indefinitely, though, if you never turn it off. Obviously, you also should keep your backups up-to-date!

Spindle Motor Failure

Spindle motor failure is rare, but when it happens, your drive does not spin at all. It could simply be a severe case of stiction, but the result is the same in either case: a drive that does not work. A major failure of the drive electronics can cause similar symptoms; there is really no way to tell without elaborate test equipment. (Unless, of course, you smell that wonderful odor of burning insulation from your drive!)

This problem can be repaired by replacing the spindle motor. Contact a company that specializes in Mac hard drive repair and recovery. One such company is listed at the end of this section.

Bad Blocks

Some drives come with utilities that comprehensively test the drive and note any portions that cannot store data reliably. Such areas are called *bad blocks*, and although some drives these days have "perfect platters" with no bad blocks, many drives do not. A small number of bad blocks is normal and acceptable; after they are mapped out by the utility—a process known as *sparing*—your drive does not even "see" them and they do not affect the drive's operation. (Most drives come from the factory pretested with bad blocks marked and spared.)

If successive scans reveal changing numbers of bad blocks and blocks that seem to "move" (that is, are good one pass and bad the next, or vice versa), the problem is likely SCSI-related rather than a hardware problem with the drive.

A Word About Head Parking

Parking the heads used to be gospel whenever you moved a drive. Because the heads actually touch the disk surface when the drive is not spinning, the vibrations and shock during transport could cause the heads to bounce against the platter, damaging the magnetic media. For this reason, most drives had a landing zone where no data was stored; "parking" the heads moved them to this zone.

Today, separate parking utilities are not necessary:

▼ All current drives use thin-film metallic media rather than the soft ferrous oxide media of older drives. Metallic media is very hard and is almost immune to physical damage caused by head impact.

▼ All but the very cheapest low-capacity drives auto-park their heads anyway.

Modern hard drives easily can survive the rigors of ordinary transportation, although they should be packed securely if they are checked as luggage.

Drive Repair

One company that specializes in Mac hard drive repair and data recovery is DriveSavers, 30-D Camaron Way, Novato, CA 94949; phone (415) 883-4232, or on CompuServe at 76117,3055.

Part VII
For the More
Technically Minded

Software Problems

Software problems can be even more insidious than hardware problems, but they often are easier to cure. Again, the key is diagnosis: isolating the sequence of actions that causes the problem. In some cases, this is easy ("My Mac crashes during boot."); in others, it may be quite difficult ("My Mac crashes at random whether I am doing anything or not.").

This section discusses the most common software problems on the Mac and how to diagnose and cure them. One particular problem—a Mac that does not boot successfully—is handled in a separate section.

Common Software Problems

The most common software problems are caused by

▼ An INIT conflict;

▼ Older software that simply will not run on newer Mac models or with a newer Macintosh operating system; or

▼ Damaged system or application software.

INIT Conflicts

An INIT is a small, specialized program run automatically when you boot your Mac. After the boot, the INIT code stays in the background, normally not making itself evident unless you use the capabilities it provides.

INITs can exist in four places under System 6:

▼ INIT resources in the System file

▼ INIT resources in a control panel device (CDEV)

▼ INIT resources in a Chooser device (RDEV)

▼ Separate INIT files

Chapter 28
Troubleshooting

Under System 7, INITs also can exist in a special Extensions folder.

INITs, by their nature, commonly perform *trap patching*, hooking into the low-level routines of the Mac's ROM code and toolbox. This is necessary for the INITs' operation: for example, an interactive spelling checker would hook into the keyboard input routines so it can "see" what you are typing, regardless of the application that is running at the time.

INITs can do amazing things, but they are more vulnerable to conflicts and compatibility problems than ordinary application programs. If you are having problems with your system, you might well find that problems with your system vanish after you remove or disable some INITs. Sometimes the conflict occurs only when one INIT loads before or after another INIT.

Unfortunately, it is no longer uncommon to have 10 or more INITs on your machine. Performing comprehensive testing on all the possible combinations of these INITs is almost impossible.

It's a good idea to invest in an INIT manager that enables you to selectively disable INITs without opening the System folder and moving them around. Apple's own "Extentions Manager" is available free from dealers and most online services.

Older Software

It used to be that each new Mac model and each new version of the operating system caused compatibility problems. As Mac system software became more stable and developers gained more experience, this became less of a problem. In fact, the current System 7 is the most stable version of the Mac OS to date.

Compatibility problems still crop up now and then, though, and are fairly easy to spot: a program simply stops working or becomes unusable after you upgrade your system software. For example, saving a document crashes the Mac every time without fail.

WARNING! When you upgrade your system software, always use the Installer. It is found on the System Tools disk (for System 6 versions), and it is always better than simply dragging over the System and Finder files. Many people do not realize that a new system upgrade—even an incremental upgrade such as from 6.0.5 to 6.0.7—consists

Part VII
For the More Technically Minded

of more than a new System and Finder. The Installer installs everything you need, as well as preserves anything you might have installed in your current System file, such as fonts and desk accessories.

Damaged System or Application Software

The System file is open any time the Mac is in use, and so is more vulnerable to corruption than other files. It is not unusual, for example, for the system file to be damaged in a particularly nasty crash. Crashes also can damage to any applications or files that are open at the time.

If an application that has worked correctly in the past suddenly becomes unstable and prone to problems, and you have not changed anything in your hardware or software configuration recently, the application may be damaged.

A Closer Look: A good way to check a suspect application or system file is to open it with ResEdit. File damage is often a case of damaged resources or a damaged resource map; ResEdit spots such damage instantly and alerts you when you try to open the file. If ResEdit indicates the file is damaged, throw the file away!

In some cases, it is not the application itself but an auxiliary file, such as a Preferences file, that is damaged. Many applications do not perform thorough checks on their Preferences files; these simply are assumed to be correct. It is not always obvious when a program has a Preferences file; if you are unsure, check your System folder (and the Preferences folder inside the System folder if you are running System 7). Many programs automatically create Preferences files the first time the programs are run, and update them thereafter. Microsoft Word, for example, creates a file in the System folder called Word Settings. If you suspect an application is damaged, replace both it and any auxiliary files from the original disks.

A damaged System file can wreak widespread havoc. If you think your System file might be damaged, follow this procedure:

1. Start up from the System Tools disk.
2. Throw the System and Finder files on your hard disk into the trash; then select **Empty Trash** from the Finder's **Special** menu.
3. Run the Installer to create a new system.

Simply running the Installer does not guarantee you will fix a damaged System file; you *must* dispose of the old System file to force the Mac to build a completely new one.

Boot Problems

Boot problems are a real pain: it is hard to check things out when you cannot even get your machine to boot! A number of software problems can cause boot failure; most are easily fixed.

The first step is to determine how far along in the boot process the Mac can get, which you can do by carefully watching your Mac as it boots.

The Boot Stages

After the Mac completes its self-test routines, it first attempts to boot from a disk. If one is not present, the Mac scans the SCSI device chain looking for bootable devices. It starts with SCSI ID 6 and works its way down to 0.

After your Mac finds a block SCSI device, it attempts to boot from it. A valid boot device has a set of boot blocks—special software the Mac requires on any bootable disk—recorded on it. When the Mac finds and loads these boot blocks, you see the Smiling Mac icon on your screen.

Next, the Mac looks for a valid System file. This file must be called System (the actual name of the System file is recorded in the boot blocks, and this is what the Mac looks for) and must be located in the special blessed folder on your hard disk. You can tell which folder is blessed because it has a little Mac icon in it to distinguish it from the other folders. (The special icon for the System folder appears only if you run System 6 or later software). If it finds a valid System file, the Mac loads the DSAT resource from the System file and uses the information to show the "Welcome to Macintosh" message. (If you have a separate StartUpScreen file, it is displayed rather than the "Welcome to Macintosh" message.)

Next, the Mac runs any INITs in the System file, then any INITs external to the System file (but still in the System folder). The last step of the boot process is to run the program designated as the start-up program, which is generally the Finder.

Chapter 28
Troubleshooting

Part VII
For the More Technically Minded

If the Mac is unable to find a bootable device, it displays a blinking question mark in a disk icon.

Note: There are several ways this process can be disturbed (we assume there is no hardware problem with the drive):

▼ The drive may not have valid boot blocks.

▼ The drive may not have a valid System file.

▼ There may be a problem with or conflict between INITs.

If you never get the Smiling Mac, you probably have damaged or absent boot blocks; if the Smiling Mac does appear, even for just a second, the boot blocks are probably okay. To write new boot blocks, run the Installer from the System Tools disk, or, alternatively, drag a copy of a System file of the same version as the one you are using from another disk. The Finder automatically writes new boot blocks on a volume when you copy a System file to it.

If you get the Smiling Mac but do not get the "Welcome to Macintosh," message, there are two possible problems. Most likely, the System file is missing or damaged, in which case the solution is to run the Installer or drag over a new System file as before.

Another, less common problem occurs after a crash. The Mac contains a small amount of special memory called *parameter RAM*, or pRAM. It mostly contains items you set in the Control Panel: the mouse speed, the menu item blink rate, and so forth. One of the little-known items it also contains is which partition to boot from on your hard disk! Normally, this is the first partition, but it is possible for a crash to set this to some weird number such as 42.

In this case, the Mac looks for partition 42 on your hard disk, fails to find it, and presents you with the blinking question mark. This particular problem can stymie even Mac experts; the Mac boots fine from disks (after which the hard disk appears on the desktop and is perfectly usable), and other Macs boot from the same hard disk with no problem. And no SCSI problems are found, either!

The solution to this problem is to reset the Parameter RAM (PRAM) with its default values. If you run System 6, hold down the Option, Command, and Shift keys while selecting **Control Panel** from the Apple menu. You are presented with a dialog asking whether you actually want to "zap the PRAM." Click the **OK** button.

If you run System 7 or later, zapping the PRAM requires some manual dexterity. Restart your Mac while holding down the Option, Command, P and R keys at the same time. You are presented with a dialog asking whether you actually want to "zap the PRAM." Click the **OK** button.

First Boot Attempt Fails, Second Works

This problem can be puzzling: your Mac presents you with the blinking question mark, indicating it could not find a bootable disk. Yet when you reboot with the programmer's switch, everything works normally.

This happens because when you turn on a hard drive, it takes some time to spin up to speed. If the Mac checks it before the hard drive is ready, the drive reports it is not ready, the Mac goes to the next device in line, and, failing to find any other boot devices, decides none exists.

If you have an external hard drive, the solution is simple: turn the hard drive on first, wait perhaps 10 seconds, then turn the Mac on. This gives the hard drive time to come up to speed.

If your hard drive is internal, or you do not want to bother with this, set the drive's SCSI ID to 0. The boot code in the Mac ROMs handles this as a special case: if a SCSI block device is detected at SCSI 0, the Mac waits forever, if necessary, for that device to "come ready."

To change the SCSI ID on an internal drive, remove the drive and flip it over to look at the controller board on the bottom. Somewhere on the board, you see a group of pairs of pins; there may be several such groups. Look for one that has pins labeled "A0 A1 A2": these pins are used to set the SCSI address. One or more of the pairs of pins are covered with a small blue or black plastic rectangle (called a *DIP shunt*) that serves to short the two pins together. Remove all these shunts from A0, A1, and A2 to set your drive's SCSI address to 0.

 Some drives from Connors Peripherals label these pins "E1, E2, E3" instead of "A0, A1, A2."

Chapter 28
Troubleshooting

Part VII
For the More
Technically Minded

Automated Diagnostics

Recently, several utilities have become available that can greatly simplify the task of diagnosing various software problems. Since programmatic determination of conflicts (examining the code of various INITs and such to see if it would conflict with other code) is impossible, such products typically work from a database of known problems. By comparing your setup with the database, known conflicts can be identified.

Other products can check your system for a range of hardware problems, or non-conflict types of software problems.

Teknosys Inc.'s product is Help!, a utility that scans your Mac and offers advice on everything from INIT conflicts to current versions of application software. Teknosys Inc. is located at 3923 Coconut Palm Drive, Suite 111, Tampa, FL 33619; phone (813) 620-3494; fax (813) 620-4039. Teknosys offers both stand-alone and network versions of Help!

Polybus Systems Corp. offers Snooper, a product designed to detect hardware problems. Snooper identifies the model Mac it's running on and suggests possible problem areas to check, as well as performing tests of most hardware components, including video RAM and third party accelerators. An options NuBus card is available to check power supply errors if a Mac refuses to boot. Polybus Systems Corp. is located at 150 Westford Road, Tyngsboro, MA 01879; phone (508) 649-7396 or (800) 695-4239; fax (508) 649-7397.

MicroMAT Computer Systems' MacEKG product provides simple hardware diagnostics at boot time, and also keeps a record of machine performance, so users can easily see the performance impact of different INITs, extensions, or system configurations. A digitized voice announces the results. MacEKG can export text files of performance statistics that can be imported into a word processor or spreadsheet. MicroMAT is located at 7075 Redwood Blvd., Building 4, Novato, CA 94947; phone (415) 898-6227; fax (415) 897-3901.

Apple Computer offers both software and hardware diagnostic packages, but they're available only to dealers and other authorized service providers. MacTest Pro performs both hardware and software tests, and allows custom tests to be designed. Detailed test logs are kept for later analysis. For detailed hardware diagnostics, there's the TechStep, a 2 pound handheld device, that connects to every external port on a Mac and can even pinpoint individual failed SIMMs. TechStep is configured for a particular model Mac with plug-in ROM packs.

Summary

Troubleshooting problems on your Macintosh is merely a matter of reducing the variables and collecting data. Eventually, the problems are narrowed to either hardware or software problems. Apple has built many signals into the hardware itself to help diagnose problems. Sad Macs, error codes, and the infamous chords of death all point to where the problem is so you can take proper actions to resolve the situation.

Chapter 29
Programming on the Macintosh

Computer programming is a vast subject that a single chapter cannot expect to cover. Rather than trying to explain everything about how to

In This Chapter
- ▼ The components of a Macintosh program
- ▼ Object-oriented versus procedural programming
- ▼ The Macintosh Toolbox
- ▼ Programming languages used on the Mac

Part VII
For the More Technically Minded

write a Macintosh program, this chapter explains the basic concepts and attempts to answer common questions such as what programming language to use and whether or not to take a class.

But Can I Do It?

One question many beginners ask is "How hard is it to program on a Mac?" Good programming is not something you are likely to learn overnight (after all, there *is* a reason professional computer programmers are paid). On the other hand, most people can learn enough programming in a reasonably short time to be able to write programs for their own use. The results might not be as slick or pretty as they would be if a professional did the work, but that fact does not detract from the program's usefulness. Most shareware gets its start this way.

You may have heard that a Macintosh is a difficult computer to program, and probably these reports have discouraged you from trying it. In reality, the Mac is not much harder to program than other computers—you just have more to learn before you can start. This is because you need to know how to display and manage the various components of the *Macintosh User Interface* (windows, menus, dialog boxes, scroll bars, text, graphics, and so on) that other computers do not support.

On the other hand, getting a Macintosh to display a menu is easier than getting a PC to do so because a Mac has built-in instructions in ROM to draw menus, whereas the PC does not. In other words, it is easier to make a Macintosh act like a Macintosh than it is to make other computers act like a Mac. When looked at from that standpoint, programming a Mac does not seem very tough at all, does it?

In the past, a big reason for the Mac's poor reputation for programming was its almost total lack of good programming tools and useful documentation. That situation has improved dramatically in recent years with the development of *prototypers*, *source-level debuggers*, and *object-oriented programming systems*, and with the publication of Mac programming books and reference manuals. In fact, Macintosh programmers today have access to some of the best software development products available on any computer system of any size. Apple's programming documentation is far more complete, accurate, and understandable than that provided for almost any other computer. The bottom line is that the obstacles which made Macintosh programming difficult in the past have been either removed or reduced to a

With the advent of some new tools in the last year or two, it is definitely possible for Mere Mortals to program full-blown Macintosh applications **without** learning more before you start. In fact, you can easily segué from HyperCard to full Finder-clickable application development quite easily using such tools as WindowScript and Double-XX (both from Heizer Software), with HyperCard, Prograph from TGS Systems, and Serius Workshop from Serius Development. And that doesn't even count the amazing power of system-level scripting tools such as UserLand Software's Frontier and Apple's own AppleScript. We're not in Impossible-Land any more, Toto!

Dan Shafer

manageable level, making the Macintosh just as accessible as other computers for beginning programmers.

Chapter 29
Programming on the Macintosh

Inside a Macintosh Program

A computer program consists of *instructions* and *data*. Instructions tell the computer how to do something, and data provides information the instructions need to carry out requested operations. For example, if you want to display a window on a Mac screen, one way to do it is to execute an instruction called **NewWindow** and supply a list of data indicating the size of the window, where to locate it on the screen, what title to give it, whether it has a zoom box, and so on.

In the Macintosh world, *program* is a generic term for several different types of executable entities, including applications, desk accessories, control panels, INITs, and other system extensions and resources (WDEFs, MDEFs, and so on). The technical differences among these are beyond the scope of this chapter, but the steps in the programming process are much the same regardless of the type being created. The next section applies mainly to application programs, but the concepts apply to the other types as well.

Resources in a Program

In Macintosh programs, instructions and data are contained in *resources* stored in the program file. Typical resources include menus, windows, dialog boxes, controls (scroll bars, buttons, check boxes, and so on), icons, fonts, cursors, and graphics. Table 29.1, which lists the resources that make up Apple's Font/DA Mover utility program, gives you an idea of the kinds of resources in a program file.

Table 29.1 Resources in Font/DA Mover

Type	Quantity	Contents
ALRT	4	Size, position, and appearance of alert windows
CODE	5	Instructions executed by the program
DITL	9	Contents of alert and dialog windows (buttons, text boxes, and so on)

continues

Table 29.1 continued

Resources used by the Finder		
DLOG	5	Size, position, and appearance of dialog windows
STR#	1	Text and messages displayed by the program
BNDL	1	List of file types and their associated desktop icons
DMOV	1	Unique application ID of this program
FREF	3	Used with BNDL resource to determine which icon to display for a particular file type
ICN#	3	Application's desktop icons
vers	2	Information about the current version of the program (version number, bug fixes, and so on)
Resource used by the System		
SIZE	1	Tells the System how much memory the program requires

As programs go, Font/DA Mover has very few resources, and it is missing some you normally would expect to find: MENU resources, which describe the title and items in each menu the program displays, and WIND resources, which define the size, position, and appearance of document windows. Font/DA Mover does not display any menus or document windows, which is why it does not have resources of the corresponding types.

CODE resources contain the instructions the program executes, as well as any data the program uses that is not defined in other resources. Each CODE resource is called a *code segment*. There is always a *main code segment*, which is loaded into memory when the program is started, but there also may be other segments, which are loaded in as needed (see figure 29.1).

There are two reasons to split a program into segments instead of leaving it in one large piece. First, a code segment can be only up to a certain size (32K), and most programs are usually much larger than this. Second, a program does not occupy as much memory if it loads code segments into memory only when they are needed and unloads (purges) them when it is done. For example, almost all programs put their *initialization code* (instructions executed only when a program is started) in a separate segment that is purged from memory when initialization is complete. This frees the space that initialization code occupies so it can be used for other purposes, such as loading additional code segments or storing user documents.

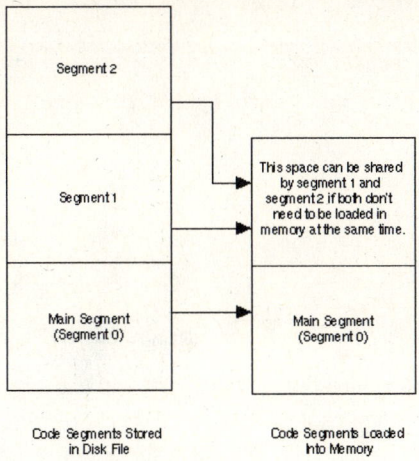

Figure 29.1
By loading code segments into memory only when needed and unloading them when it finishes, a program takes up much less space in memory than it does on disk.

Creating a Macintosh Program

Creating a Macintosh program means building the resources that make up the program and combining them to form a program file. Except for CODE resources, which are explained later, resources usually are created with a *resource editor* such as ResEdit or Resorcerer. You type instructions to tell the resource editor which type of resource you want to create, and the editor asks for the appropriate information so it can build the resource.

If the resource represents something that can be displayed, such as a menu, the resource editor shows you what it looks like so you can make sure you enter all the information correctly. For example, figure 29.2 shows the window that Resorcerer displays when you tell it you want to edit a CURS (mouse cursor) resource. Rather than knowing the internal format of the resource, you can just turn on and off individual pixels in the cursor by clicking on them with the mouse. Resorcerer figures out how to store this information in the CURS resource.

Part VII
For the More Technically Minded

Figure 29.2
Click on the individual pixels in the cursor and mask to turn them on and off; Resorcerer takes care of formatting the resource data.

The box above the **Try Me** button shows how the cursor looks against different backgrounds. Similar capabilities are provided for editing menus, windows, dialog boxes, and other graphical entities. Using a resource editor frees you from knowing the internal format of resources, which is basically indecipherable lists of numbers.

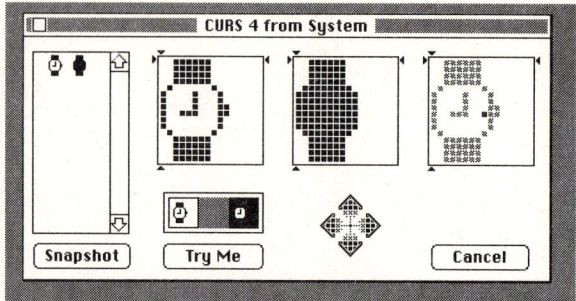

As an alternative to using a resource editor, you can use a *resource compiler* such as Apple's Rez or the obsolete RMaker. To use a resource compiler, use a text editor to create a textual description of the resource; then run the resource compiler to read your description and generate the actual resource. The problem with this approach is that you have to know not only the resources' format, but also the resource description language used to define the resources. As a rule, resource editors are much easier to use than resource compilers to create standard resources, but resource compilers can be quite useful in creating custom resources that your resource editor does not know how to handle.

When you are creating resources for a program, you usually do not put them directly into the program file. Instead, you store them in a temporary resource file and combine them with the CODE resources later to create the finished product. The program file itself usually is deleted and rebuilt many times during the development and testing process, and you do not want to re-create your resources every time you create a new program file.

You often can tell a lot about how other programmers' programs work by poking around in the programs with a resource editor. It is an especially good way to see how other programmers lay out their alert and dialog boxes.

Creating CODE Resources

Resource editors and resource compilers are acceptable for creating almost any sort of resource except CODE resources, which contain the instructions the program executes. To create CODE resources, you need a *text editor*, a *compiler* (or an *assembler*, which is discussed later), and a *linker*. The editor, compiler, and linker can be separate programs, or they may be combined into a single program—it depends on which software development package you use.

The text editor is used to write a *source program*, which contains the instructions the program executes, plus definitions of any data not stored as separate resources. The source program is written in a *programming language* designed specifically for that purpose. If the program is small enough, you can put all source instructions (called *source code*) into a single text file, but it is standard practice to split a large project into several smaller files organized by function: for example, all menu routines in one file, all window routines in another, all printing routines in a third, and so on. And some programming systems require the source code for each segment to be in a separate file if you plan to segment your program.

Compiling the Program

The Macintosh cannot "execute" a source file because instructions written in a programming language are not in a form the Mac can understand. Programming languages are designed to be used by human beings, whereas computers expect programs to be in *machine language*—numerical code that the computer understands.

The source code the programmer writes therefore must be translated to machine language before the computer can execute it. This translation is done by a *compiler*, which examines each instruction in the source program and replaces it with one or more machine-language instructions that carry out the requested operation. The output from the compiler—that is, the machine language instructions—is called *object code*. Exactly where the compiler puts the object code depends on which development system you use. Some compilers put all object code into a master "project file"; others create a separate object file for each source file compiled. As a rule, a compiler can understand only the specific programming language (such as C or Pascal) it was created for, so if you write your program in C, you cannot use a Pascal compiler to translate it, or vice versa.

An *optimizing compiler* tries to produce the fastest possible machine-language object code. When deciding which compiler you should purchase, consider whether it has an optimizer, because normally this is a feature you want to have. When the

Chapter 29
Programming on the Macintosh

Part VII
For the More Technically Minded

optimizer is enabled, the program takes much longer to compile and is more difficult (or even impossible) to debug, but the resulting object code executes more quickly than if compiled without the optimizer.

Building the Program File

Finally, after you write all your source files and compile them into object code, you need a *linker* (sometimes called a *builder*) to create the program file. The linker allocates the program file, converts the object code into CODE resources and stores them in the program file, and then copies in the noncode resources from your temporary resource file. If all goes well (which it probably won't yet—a normal expectation), you can double-click on the program file's icon and run your newly created masterpiece.

However, it is more likely your new baby will crash, and you will have to go back and find the bug, fix the source code, recompile and relink the program, and try again. *Debugging* a program—that is, finding all your goofs—is the most frustrating and time-consuming part of the programming process.

A Closer Look Figure 29.3 shows the general steps in creating a program on the Macintosh. One problem: this figure implies that you write an entire program at once, then compile and link it. In actual practice, programmers start by writing just enough code to create a skeleton program. After compiling, linking, and testing the code to make sure it works, they add more functionality to the program, then compile, link, and test the enhanced version, repeating this cycle until the program is complete. This way, they know that any new bugs that crop up are in the code they just added, rather than in the previously tested portions. This approach tends to reduce greatly the number of aspirin programmers require to debug a large and complicated program!

Assemblers and Interpreters

An *assembler* is a program that translates *assembly language* source code into machine language. Assembly language is actually machine language represented in a form human beings can digest easier. Instead of using numeric codes, as machine language does, assembly language enables you to use names or abbreviations for the various instructions and the data on which they operate. Because assembly language is a symbolic form of machine language, each instruction in an assembly language program translates to exactly one instruction in machine language. In comparison, a single instruction in a compiled language may translate into several machine-language instructions.

Chapter 29
Programming on the Macintosh

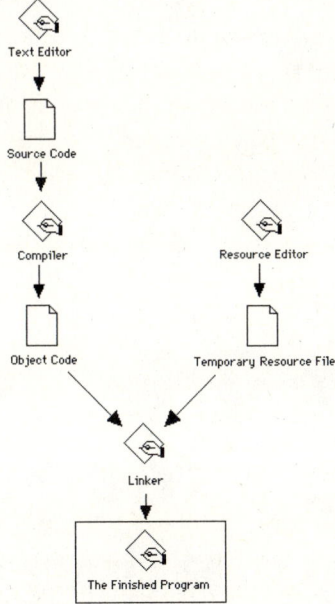

Figure 29.3
Steps in the programming process.

A Closer Look Machine language and assembly language often are referred to as *low-level languages* because they consist only of instructions the computer can understood directly (that is, at the hardware level). In contrast, *high-level* languages contain instructions for which there are no directly corresponding machine-language instructions, so a given instruction in a high-level language may have to be translated into more than one, and possibly many, low-level (that is, machine-language) instructions. Programmers often misuse these terms. For example, they refer to C as a low-level language because it has some features ordinarily associated with assembly language, but in fact C is a high-level language, and most instructions in a C program translate into machine language on a one-to-many basis.

Part VII
For the More Technically Minded

Interpreters

An *interpreter* is a program that "executes" a source file rather than actually translating it into object code. The interpreter reads each instruction in the source program one at a time, examines each to determine which function to perform, and then carries out the requested operation. Using an interpreter saves you the trouble of compiling and linking your program every time you want to test it, but only a handful of languages—notably BASIC and FORTH—are designed to be interpreted, and they are not always the best languages for Mac programming.

The main problem with interpretation is that executing a source program with an interpreter is many times slower than executing a compiled program: the translation is performed while the program is being executed rather than ahead of time, adding a tremendous amount of overhead at run-time. Programmers who use interpreters during the development and testing phase usually compile the final product so it runs faster when the end user executes it.

Object-Oriented Versus Procedural Programming

You will not be a Macintosh programmer long before you start hearing a lot about object-oriented programming. Although object-oriented programming has been around for many years, only recently has it started to enjoy widespread use, and the Macintosh is a major reason. The Macintosh User Interface, with its windows and menus and such, begs to be managed with object-oriented programming techniques rather than with more traditional *procedural* programming methods.

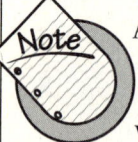
Apple prefers to refer to object-oriented programming as "object programming," perhaps to avoid the unfortunate acronym "OOP." So far, however, few people are heeding Apple's wishes. Whichever term you use, people know what you are talking about.

Chapter 29
Programming on the Macintosh

The difference between object-oriented and procedural programming lies largely in how the program is organized. In procedural programming, a program is made of *procedures* (also called *subprograms*, *routines*, *subroutines*, *paragraphs*, or *functions*) that are *called* (executed) by other procedures. In object programming, the program is organized as objects, each of which contains some data plus the procedures that operate on that data. Instead of calling the desired procedure, you send a message to the object, telling it which of its built-in procedures (also called a method) to execute. Figure 29.4 shows, in general terms, how you might organize a file conversion utility as either procedures or objects.

Remember: In procedural programming, you call a procedure and tell it which data to use; in object-oriented programming, you send a message to an object to tell it which procedure to use.

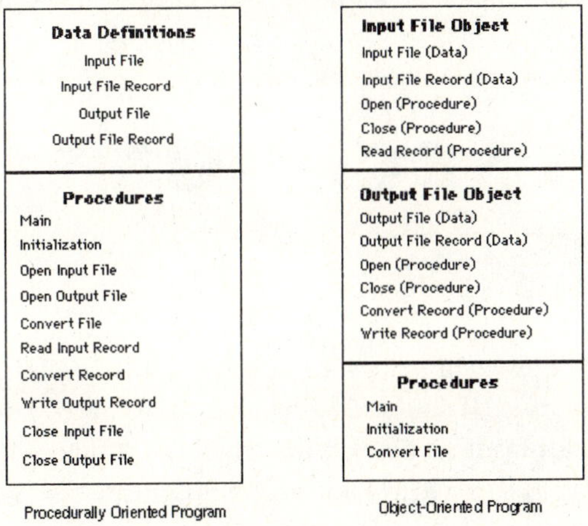

Data Definitions
Input File
Input File Record
Output File
Output File Record

Procedures
Main
Initialization
Open Input File
Open Output File
Convert File
Read Input Record
Convert Record
Write Output Record
Close Input File
Close Output File

Procedurally Oriented Program

Input File Object
Input File (Data)
Input File Record (Data)
Open (Procedure)
Close (Procedure)
Read Record (Procedure)

Output File Object
Output File (Data)
Output File Record (Data)
Open (Procedure)
Close (Procedure)
Convert Record (Procedure)
Write Record (Procedure)

Procedures
Main
Initialization
Convert File

Object-Oriented Program

Figure 29.4
Object programming results in data and the associated procedures being more tightly bound than in procedural programming.

Object-oriented programming works best when you have a well-defined data object, such as a window, and a set of well-defined operations to be performed on it (open, close, move, resize, and so on). It helps you keep your program better organized because the data and the procedures that operate on the data are tied together. Furthermore, after you create a class — a definition of an object and its procedures—you easily can reuse it in other programs, greatly improving your productivity.

Object programming is not so helpful when there is an action to perform but no well-defined data object on which to perform it. For example, a program monitoring a refrigeration unit examines the temperature readings coming from the unit and sounds an alarm if the temperature is too high or too low. In this situation, there is no well-defined object for the "sound alarm"

Part VII
For the More Technically Minded

function to operate on, so it is probably easier to write a procedure that makes the alarm go off than it is to create some made-up data object to represent the alarm and send a message to it.

Most computer languages that support object-oriented programming also support procedural programming, so you can use both approaches in the same program. Because object-oriented techniques are extremely handy for manipulating objects in the Macintosh User Interface, object-oriented programming rapidly is becoming universal in the Macintosh world.

One of the big advantages to using object-oriented programming is you can obtain prewritten libraries of classes (that is, object definitions) to use in your own programs so you do not waste time writing your own. Two of the most popular class libraries are Symantec's Think Class Library and Apple's MacApp. In both cases, you merely add some code and—presto!—you have a working program with menus, windows, and the whole nine yards.

The Macintosh Toolbox

The Macintosh comes equipped with a huge number of useful routines already built into its ROM chip and System file. Collectively, programmers refer to these ready-made routines as the Toolbox—although strictly speaking, the Toolbox (officially known as the User Interface Toolbox) comprises only a portion of the Mac's built-in routines; the rest are supposedly Operating System routines.

In the real world, programmers usually do not bother with such distinctions, and just about everybody uses Toolbox to mean both Toolbox and Operating System functions. Most Toolbox routines are built into the Mac's ROM chip. Some of the less-used ones are stored as resources in the System file and loaded into memory if an application needs to execute them. Also, the System file usually contains numerous *patches* to the ROM routines to fix any bugs that may have slipped into the ROM-based code. These patches are loaded into RAM when the computer is first started up and are executed rather than, or in addition to, the original ROM routines whenever a program calls a patched routine.

Macintosh programs call Toolbox routines to create menus, draw windows, read and write disk files, and handle mouse clicks and keyboard input.

Chapter 29
Programming on the Macintosh

Having a set of standardized routines that all programs call is what makes the user interface consistent across all Macintosh applications—at least, across those applications that play by the rules. Most other computers do not have built-in sets of standardized routines to create the user interface, which results in wide variations among applications in how they interact with the user. The development of software packages such as Microsoft Windows, X Window, and Curses has overcome this problem somewhat, but most such packages do not even begin to provide the kind of functionality the Macintosh Toolbox and Operating System supply.

A Closer Look Many PC programmers mistakenly refer to the Macintosh Toolbox as the *Mac BIOS*. Although the ROM-based portion of the Macintosh Operating System is roughly equivalent to the BIOS on a PC, the PC has nothing to correspond to the Macintosh User Interface Toolbox. To get anything even remotely like the Toolbox on a PC, you have to either use a software package such as Windows or write your own software to create windows, menus, and other graphics. The PC does not even have routines to draw simple shapes such as circles and rectangles, which means a program has to control each individual pixel in the display device to draw something like a box. Mac programmers can just tell the Toolbox to draw a rectangle by supplying the coordinates of the top-left and bottom-right corners.

Programming Languages

Macintosh compilers are available for practically every programming language ever invented. The following sections summarize the ones you are most likely to encounter and are intended to help you decide which programming language (or languages) best meets your needs. This is not a complete list, but anything not mentioned below should be eyed with some suspicion, as it is probably obscure, obsolete, or of limited usefulness.

Macintosh Pascal and Object Pascal

The original Pascal language was developed as a tool to teach students good programming habits. Pascal gained popularity with the boom in microcomputers because it was one of the few languages that could be used

Part VII
For the More Technically Minded

on computers with small memories. Macintosh Pascal is an enhanced version of Pascal, with support for the Macintosh Toolbox. Pascal is the second most popular language for Macintosh programming, after C, and it is the language used in *Inside Macintosh*, Apple's reference library for Macintosh programmers. Object Pascal is Pascal with support added for object-oriented programming.

Pros: Pascal is powerful, easy to learn, easy to use, and well-suited to Macintosh programming. It encourages writing well-organized, readable programs. Mac Pascal is highly standardized across Macintosh implementations but is not portable to other machines. Strict rules make it a good language for beginners because the compiler catches some of the more common errors beginners make. It is similar enough to C that Pascal programmers easily can learn C later. Debugging a Pascal program is usually much easier than debugging a program written in C. Support for object-oriented programming is available with the better compilers.

Cons: Pascal's strict rules sometimes get in your way rather than help you. In particular, it can be very difficult to manipulate large *arrays* (lists and tables) of data in Pascal. Writing a Pascal program often seems like a typing exercise because of many BEGINs and ENDs you have to put in the program. And the true meaning of semicolons in Pascal is sometimes hard for beginners to grasp, leading to some unusual and even entertaining bugs.

Bottom Line: Pascal is an excellent language for beginners but powerful enough for professionals to use. Some programmers may find it too restrictive.

C and C++

The C programming language originally was developed to use with the UNIX operating system but now is available on many computers and operating systems. C++ is C with additional features, called *extensions*, to support object-oriented programming. C is by far the most popular programming language for the Macintosh, and several good C and C++ compilers are available. C has a number of extremely useful features missing from other high-level languages and is better than most at handling large arrays of data.

Pros: C is powerful, flexible, compact, and very well-suited to Macintosh programming. C is highly standardized and will become even more so now that a new official standard finally has been agreed on, although not all compilers have been brought up to the new guidelines yet. Most C compilers

Chapter 29
Programming on the Macintosh

have a built-in assembler, which saves you the cost of purchasing one separately. Although C contains a few hurdles that beginners often find difficult to get over, at least two zillion books have been written about C, making it one of the easiest languages to learn on your own. Also, C programmers are in big demand, which makes learning it a smart career move.

Cons: C can be dense and unreadable, even when well-written. C's unique treatment of arrays takes some getting used to and trips up nearly everyone who is new to C—beginners and experienced programmers alike. The compiler allows certain kinds of mistakes that more restrictive languages would not permit, although a good "lint" utility helps find such bugs. Some compiler manufacturers, notably Symantec (makers of Think C), have been a tad pokey in getting C++ fully implemented in their products, although the situation is getting better and the missing features are not going to ruin your day. Debugging a C program can be painful and frustrating, especially for novices.

Bottom Line: C is the best language for general-purpose Macintosh programming but presents more challenges for beginners than Pascal.

A Closer Look A *lint* program is a utility that examines C source programs and looks for "fuzzy" bits of code (lint) that are perfectly legal as far as the compiler is concerned, but probably not what the programmer intended. For example, the following is a very common mistake in C:

    if(a = b) c++ ;

This means: "Assign the current value of the variable 'b' to the variable 'a,' then check the value of 'a.' If it is not zero, add 1 to the value of 'c.'" The programmer almost certainly meant to write

    if(a == b) c++;

which means, "If 'a' has the same value as 'b,' add 1 to the value of 'c.'" Either construction is legal, so the C compiler does not flag the first as an error, but a good lint utility would issue a warning so the programmer can make sure what is written is what is intended.

Assembly Language

Assembly language is a symbolic representation of machine language in which each assembly language instruction translates into exactly one

C is **not** the best language for general-purpose Macintosh programming. There is no such animal. Too much depends on the programmer's needs, backgrounds, interests, capabilities, etc. The Language Wars don't need a winner.

Dan Shafer

Part VII
For the More Technically Minded

machine-language instruction. It is used mostly when speed is required or when the program needs access to hardware features not available to higher-level languages. Macintosh assembly language is called M680X0 Assembly Language, after the Mac's Motorola 68000-series processors. Programmers often refer to it as "68K assembly language" or by the more generic term ALC, for assembly language code.

Pros: When properly written, assembly language results in much faster and more efficient object code than a compiler can generate. Motorola's 68000-series processors are used in many computers other than the Macintosh, so learning assembly language can expand your career opportunities enormously.

Cons: Assembly language is difficult to learn and use and requires highly technical knowledge of the computer. Assembly language programs are specific to the machine they are written for and cannot be exported to other platforms (this is true of most Mac programs anyway, but with assembly language, you don't have a chance). If you use the instructions unique to the newer Motorola processors, such as the 68030, the code does not run on Macs that use the older 68000 or 68020 processors. It can be almost impossible to find bugs.

Bottom Line: This is for experts and thrill-seekers only.

BASIC

BASIC was developed as a means to teach programming to beginners. Its name is derived from its real nomenclature: Beginner's All-Purpose Symbolic Instruction Code. It became very popular on early microcomputers because a BASIC interpreter takes very little memory. Now that computers have acres of memory, BASIC is falling out of fashion, and some people say, "Good riddance."

H ah! You guys got caught, too, eh? There is **no** serious BASIC for the Mac. Forget it. Delete it. It ain't there.

Dan Shafer

Pros: BASIC is very easy to learn, and beginners can start writing programs almost immediately. It is not a bad choice for the hobbyist who wants to write "quick and dirty" programs for strictly personal use.

Cons: BASIC lends itself to disorganized and unreadable "spaghetti" code. A total lack of industry standards means programs written for one implementation of BASIC almost never run on another, even on the same machine. The language's design is poorly suited for Macintosh programming, although the available implementations do a fair job of alleviating this problem.

Bottom Line: OK for hobbyists, but serious programmers should stick to C or Pascal.

Other Languages

C, Pascal, Assembly, and BASIC together account for nearly all programming done on the Macintosh, but many other compilers also are available. That they even exist suggests they have their place in the scheme of things. The following sections offer brief descriptions of some of the more useful and important ones.

Ada

Ada is the official language of the U.S. Department of Defense for use in applications such as navigational computers and weapons guidance systems. It is very difficult to learn, and there is not much point in using it on the Macintosh unless you are bidding on a government contract that requires it. Ada is one of those languages that tries to implement every imaginable feature a programming language possibly could have. As a result, the compilers are extremely large, expensive, and slow.

APL

APL (A Programming Language) originally was developed as a mathematical notation and later implemented as a programming language. Its specialty is manipulating large multidimensional arrays of data. APL is almost useless for anything else and is impossible for anyone but its initiates to read, a situation that has led some people to dub it "A Private Language." APL is used mostly in universities and research laboratories.

COBOL

COBOL (Common Business Oriented Language) is a very popular language in business data processing shops—banks and insurance companies use it almost exclusively. It has an English-like syntax that makes it very easy to read if the program is properly written (which it usually is not, as nobody wants to do that much typing).

COBOL's major strength is you can format data in almost any way you please using a simple set of symbols; creating printed reports is especially easy. On the minus side, COBOL compilers are big and slow, and on a relatively small machine such as the Macintosh, it can take an hour or two to compile a large COBOL program.

COBOL comes in two basic flavors widely, if inaccurately, referred to as COBOL and COBOL II. The latter, a recent development, adds some features lacking in the original language and eliminates a couple that never should have been there in the first place. If you plan to purchase a COBOL compiler, make sure to get one that handles the type of COBOL you use, because the two kinds are not cross-compatible.

FORTRAN

FORTRAN (Formula Translation) was once *the* language for scientific, mathematical, and engineering applications until C and other languages started elbowing in on its turf. FORTRAN's big plus is that it comes with a huge library of prewritten subroutines that programmers can use rather than writing their own. On the minus side, FORTRAN comes in numerous versions, some of which are barely recognizable as FORTRAN—RATFOR, for example—and some strains lack the basic features expected these days from serious programming languages. The only good reasons to use FORTRAN on the Mac are to run FORTRAN programs imported from other systems, or because you already know it and do not want to learn C. As with COBOL, make sure you get a compiler that handles the FORTRAN version you deal with.

FORTH

FORTH is easily the most perverse language in popular use. It is the only widely used language that is truly extensible—that is, which enables programmers to add their own instructions to the language. This is not necessarily a plus, because other programmers working on the same program cannot decipher a custom instruction's meaning just by looking at it. Like APL, FORTH is totally unreadable to anyone but its initiates. Despite this drawback, FORTH has a wide following and is used in control systems and artificial intelligence research, as well as general-purpose programming.

LISP

LISP (List Processing) originally was developed as a language to manipulate lists of non-numerical data. Until recently, it was used almost exclusively in artificial intelligence applications, such as "expert" systems that help doctors diagnose illnesses, but the development of a newer version, Common LISP, has made it more attractive for general-purpose programming. Some visionaries claim it is the wave of the future in the Macintosh world, but given C's and Pascal's overwhelming popularity, this seems a bit optimistic. Programmers who think C uses too many parentheses will hate LISP, which has been accused of standing for "Lots of Irritating Silly Parentheses."

LOGO

LOGO was developed to teach children about computers and programming. LOGO uses *turtle graphics* to draw pictures—children tell the "turtle" which direction to go and how far to move, and the turtle draws a line as it goes. The language is too restrictive to be useful for serious programming, but educators may be interested in using it as a teaching tool.

Modula and Modula 2

Modula and Modula 2 are Pascal spin-offs designed to write operating systems, although they are also excellent general-purpose programming languages. They never really caught on, but they do have their fans, and Modula implementations are available for most computers. Macintosh Pascal corrects some of the same deficiencies in plain Pascal that Modula does, so the benefits of using Modula on the Mac are dubious unless you are importing Modula programs from another computer.

MUMPS

MUMPS (Massachusetts Utility MultiProgramming System) was developed at Massachusetts General Hospital and is widely used in the health-care field for nearly everything from patient records to expert-systems databases. Despite having some admirable string-handling capabilities and being one of the first object-oriented languages, MUMPS never has made much of a splash in the wider world, perhaps because of its unfortunate name. It interests mostly programmers working on medical applications.

Prolog

Prolog (Programming Logic) is used widely in artificial intelligence applications and is similar to LISP. It is very popular in Europe but only recently has started to gain fans in the United States, where LISP is more widely used. Whether it can compete against the new Common LISP remains to be seen.

Smalltalk

Smalltalk was the first fully object-oriented programming environment. Developed at the Xerox Palo Alto Research Center (PARC), Smalltalk is the system on which many Macintosh User Interface principles were based. It is an interesting language, but Mac programmers probably would do better to stick with object-oriented C or Pascal implementations.

Chapter 29
Programming on the Macintosh

I'm not sure the comment at the end of this paragraph is so accurate any longer. Object Logo from Paradigm Software lets you build stand-alone Mac applications and is fully object-oriented to boot. It may not be industrial-strength, but it's certainly no longer "too restrictive for serious programming."

Dan Shafer

See the comments on Smalltalk on page 1102.

Part VII
For the More Technically Minded

You left out a long-time favorite programming language that has been Mac-only from its earliest days: Prograph. But you put in MUMPS? All three of the MUMPS programmers on the planet probably clapped their hands with joy.

Prograph is a highly visual, fully object-oriented, high end programming language that is accessible to people with experience with things like HyperCard. Yet it has no real walls or limits; the entire Mac Toolbox is accessible from Prograph. It includes a compiler so you can create true stand-alone applications. It is an amazingly productive environment in which to program the Mac. And TGS Systems, the makers of Prograph, have announced a Windows version to be available before the end of 1993. Prograph represents the wave of the future in programming languages.

Dan Shafer

Special-Purpose Languages

The languages mentioned in the previous sections are general-purpose languages that can be used for a variety of programming tasks. Some languages, however, are designed for a specific purpose and cannot be used for anything else. Two such languages are used on just about every Macintosh: HyperTalk and PostScript.

HyperTalk

HyperTalk is used to define various HyperCard stack features: for example, you can write a HyperTalk script to define what should happen when a user clicks on a particular button. If you are new to programming and are interested in creating your own HyperCard stacks, learning HyperTalk is a fairly painless way to become familiar with basic programming concepts. On the other hand, if you do not use HyperCard, don't waste your time. (See chapter 17, "HyperCard and SuperCard," for more information.)

PostScript

PostScript is a *page description language* developed by Adobe Systems. Basically, it is a set of drawing commands that tells a printer or display device how to draw text and graphics. Programmers generally have no need to know PostScript unless they are developing sophisticated word processors, page layout programs, or graphics applications that need to do fancy drawing on a laser printer. The Macintosh Operating System automatically converts a program's drawing commands to PostScript commands when the output device is a PostScript device. (See chapters 5 through 9 for more information on Macintosh PostScript uses.)

Which Language Is Right for You?

Every newcomer to Macintosh programming asks the same question: "Which language should I use?" The glib answer is, "The one that best fits your particular situation," but most people, especially beginners, are not sure what the situation is. So start with either C or Pascal unless you have a good reason to choose something else. C and Pascal are so ideally suited for Macintosh programming (and almost everything else is so poorly suited) that you really cannot go wrong if you purchase a C or Pascal compiler. Keep in mind too that you always can add other programming languages to your repertoire later, if the need arises.

Tools of the Trade

Unlike some personal computers, the Macintosh contains no built-in facilities for programming, so you have to acquire whatever software you need. You also want to obtain a good set of reference manuals and perhaps some how-to books on Macintosh programming.

As for hardware, you do not need the most powerful Mac to get started in programming. A Plus or SE will do, providing it has a hard disk and enough memory to run the compiler you choose. If you work on large projects, however, you probably want something a little faster, such as an SE/30 or a IIci, because compiling a large program can take a long time (perhaps hours) on a slow Mac. Some languages are worse as far as time than others—for example, C is worse than Pascal, COBOL is worse than C, and Ada takes longer than all of them, hands down. Other than having enough memory and disk, you do not need any special hardware, although you may have to add a CD-ROM player if you plan to use Apple's programming products, because these products are now shipping almost exclusively on CDs rather than floppy disks.

Software for Programmers

The collection of editors, compilers, linkers, and other utilities you use to create programs usually is referred to as a *development system*, or *development environment*. You can buy software packages that contain almost everything you need in one box, or you can purchase the components separately and construct your own system. Whichever approach you take, make sure your system includes the following items:

▼ An editor, to enter and edit your source programs

▼ One or more compilers and/or assemblers, to translate your source into machine-language object modules

▼ A linker, to combine object modules into executable programs

▼ A resource editor, to create and modify windows, menus, icons, dialog boxes, and other Macintosh resources

▼ A source-code debugger, to help you find your mistakes

▼ A machine-level debugger (also known as a monitor) to find mistakes the source-level debugger cannot locate

Chapter 29
Programming on the Macintosh

Serius Workshop is a visual programming tool from Serius Development. It lets you build stand-alone Macintosh applications by dragging icons around and connecting them to each other. No real textual programming in the traditional sense. Serius runs on both Mac (where it got its somewhat slow start) and Windows. It is really priced and structured for use in corporate environments where delivery of multiple applications is important and programming talent isn't readily available at the department level. Not recommended for building shareware or commercial shrink-wrap software because of licensing restrictions and fees.

Dan Shafer

Part VII
For the More Technically Minded

This was apparently written by someone who had never programmed in Smalltalk. There is no way that Mac programmers "would do better to stick with object-oriented C or Pascal." Smalltalk is more robust, more productive, and more intuitive than C or Pascal will ever be. Unless you've already mastered C or Pascal, check out Smalltalk. Don't let this advice throw you off; Smalltalk may well be a dominant language in the future. Apple and IBM have both included Smalltalk in their enterprise programming recommendations (Apple's VITAL and IBM's AD/Cycle). They have not done the same for C or Pascal. Or for the **really** ugly C++, either!

Dan Shafer

WARNING: Most compilers sold for the Macintosh are either stand-alone development systems (that is, they come with their own editor, compiler, linker, and so on) or are meant to be used with the Macintosh Programmer's Workshop development system (MPW) from Apple. If you are not using MPW, make sure you do not accidentally buy a compiler that requires it—you cannot use that compiler.

The following sections describe some of the more popular and useful compilers, editors, and utilities available to Macintosh programmers. This list is intended only to give you an idea of what is available; it is not comprehensive. Failure to mention a specific product does not necessarily mean something is wrong with it.

MPW

Macintosh Programmer's Workshop (MPW) is Apple's development system for the Macintosh. On the plus side, MPW is a modular system that enables you to add compilers and other components as you need them (very handy if you use more than one programming language, especially in the same program). MPW also has a powerful scripting language that simplifies managing big projects with many source and object files. On the minus side, MPW is not strict about adhering to the Macintosh User Interface, is more expensive than many competing products, and can be hard to learn. You need a CD-ROM player to install it; Apple is going to stop distributing MPW on floppy disks. MPW is available from Apple through its APDA program. (For more information about this program, see the section, "User Groups and Developer Associations," later in this chapter.)

Think C and Think Pascal

Think C and Think Pascal are excellent stand-alone development systems from Symantec. Both are less expensive and easier to use than MPW but not as flexible or powerful. Despite their name similarities, Think C and Think Pascal are two separate products and do not interact with each other. You cannot, for example, run the Think C compiler from the Think Pascal interface.

Each includes an above-average editor, an integrated compiler/linker, an excellent source-level debugger, and a resource editor (ResEdit). Both support object programming and come with the *Think Class Library*, a complete set of modules to create your own object-oriented applications. There is even a Starter program that contains much of what you need to write your own applications, so you do not have to develop everything from scratch. Think Pascal supports MacApp, Apple's object-programming library, which you can purchase separately.

Although Think C is a great system, Think Pascal has the better editor and debuggers. Think C has one of the fastest C compilers in the known universe. However, Think C does not yet fully implement C++, although Version 5 comes a lot closer than Version 4 did, and you can live with the missing pieces. If you need full C++ compatibility (most people do not) you have to use MPW C++ or another C++ compiler.

ResEdit

ResEdit is Apple's resource editor. It is adequate for most programming projects. Get the latest version (2.1 or later), which is a vast improvement over its predecessor. Despite some annoying bugs, it is not a bad product, and in any case it is free, so who's complaining? ResEdit is shipped with most development systems, including non-Apple products. It also is available from bulletin boards and users' groups. The manual has to be purchased separately.

Resorcerer

Resorcerer (note the spelling: no *u*) is a commercial resource editor that drives circles around ResEdit. If you do a lot of resource editing or need to create and maintain large, complicated resources, Resorcerer can be a real time-saver. Overall, it is easier to use than ResEdit. It is also more expensive ($256), but the price includes the manual and more Read Me files than practically any product on the market.

Rez and DeRez

Rez and DeRez are a resource compiler and decompiler, respectively. They are handy when defining your own resources, but otherwise, ResEdit and Resorcerer are easier to deal with. DeRez is useful for decompiling resources (converting them from object to source format) when you want to look at a resource's internal structure. Both products are included when you purchase MPW or the Think compilers.

MacsBug

MacsBug is Apple's machine-level debugger, and like ResEdit, it is not a bad product considering what you pay for it. You can obtain it from Apple for a modest fee or through user groups and bulletin boards, and it is included

---

With the addition of some new tools from Heizer Software, you can start with a HyperCard stack and create a true stand-alone, Finder-clickable application, complete with color, the full Mac user interface (including pieces not available in HyperCard), and a custom Finder icon. In fact, if you're one of the tens of thousands of people who have become very comfortable with HyperCard but have run into its walls, you should give serious thought to building on that experience rather than tossing it overboard for some new language with which you will have to get comfortable.

Using WindowScript, you can put a true Mac user interface on your old HyperCard applications. Then you can compile those rejuvenated stacks into stand-alone applications using Double-XX. The resulting applications don't need HyperCard to run, are much smaller than a stack combined with HyperCard, and run almost as quickly as applications written in more conventional programming languages.

Dan Shafer

Part VII
For the More Technically Minded

with MPW. Make sure you have the most recent version. If your development system has a good source-code debugger, you will not use a machine-level debugger much, so MacsBug is adequate for most purposes.

TMON and TMON Professional

TMON and TMON Professional are commercial products that provide more sophisticated machine-level debugging than MacsBug. TMON Professional in particular does just about everything you could possibly want a machine-level debugger to do, and then some. If MacsBug is the Ford Escort of debuggers, TMON Professional is the Ferrari. TMON Professional, as the name implies, is really meant for experienced programmers with sophisticated debugging requirements.

Debugger V2 and MacNosy

Debugger V2 and MacNosy are highly sophisticated debugging tools intended for experienced programmers. Debugger is a high-level symbolic debugger with features similar to source-level debuggers. MacNosy is a very slick disassembler that converts machine-language instructions to assembly language (it is especially good for snooping around in the Mac's ROM chip to see how Toolbox routines are written). The other debuggers mentioned also have disassemblers, but MacNosy offers additional capabilities, such as assigning labels to memory locations and saving the disassembled source to disk.

SADE

Symbolic Application Debugging Environment (SADE) is a source-level debugger that works with various MPW compilers and assemblers. It includes a scripting language that enables you to automate repetitive or complicated debugging chores. It requires at least an SE/30 or Mac II with 4M. Order it from APDA.

PopUp Funcs

PopUp Funcs is a nifty patch you add to Think or MPW C and Pascal compilers. It inserts a pop-up menu into the title bar of the window you are currently editing. The pop-up menu displays every function or procedure in the program (if you hold down the Option key, it alphabetizes the list). Just select the function or procedure you want to move to and—poof!—there you are. As simple-minded as this sounds, it can save you many hours over the course of a programming project by eliminating the time you waste scrolling through your source files.

DTS Sample Code

Apple's Developer Technical Support (DTS) Sample Code disks, available through APDA (the Apple Programmers and Developers Association), demonstrate various Macintosh programming techniques in both C and Pascal. Although you do not want to use the code as is (it is not *that* well-written), the examples can save you a lot of time when you are trying to figure out how to do something. A new disk comes out about once a year with improved and added samples. The only problem is that the source code, written for MPW compilers, needs minor massaging before it compiles correctly on other systems.

AppMaker

AppMaker is a *prototyping* tool that writes C or Pascal source code for you. Using simple point-and-click techniques, you set up the menus, windows, dialogs, and alerts your program will use, then tell AppMaker to generate the appropriate source code to manage these entities. The source is compatible with a variety of platforms, including MPW C, MPW Object Pascal, Think C, and Think Pascal. It supports both MacApp and the Think Class Library. The generated code is of surprisingly good quality, considering a computer created it, and is better than some professional programmers write. AppMaker can be a huge time-saver, because much of the effort invested in a programming project goes into writing the user-interface routines.

McCLint

McCLint is a syntax checker for C programs. It helps catch some of the more common C programming errors that the compiler allows, such as typing "if(a=b)" when you mean "if(a==b)." It is compatible with all popular C compilers for the Macintosh, and unlike most shareware lint utilities, it has been designed specifically to analyze Macintosh programs. Many C programmers often manage fine without ever using a lint program, but if you feel you need one, this is certainly a product to strongly consider.

MacApp

MacApp, from Apple, is a class library for object-oriented programming. Like the Think Class Library that comes with Think C and Think Pascal, MacApp provides a basic framework that you can turn into a complete application by

Chapter 29

Programming on the Macintosh

Dave Wilson, who taught most of the MacApp programmers on the planet, has developed an object-oriented framework that does a lot of what MacApp does, but does so a lot more simply. He calls his product QuickApp. It's written in object-oriented C. While not intended as a replacement for MacApp, QuickApp has some interesting design features that make it a useful tool as well as a valuable learning experience.

Dan Shafer

Part VII
For the More Technically Minded

adding a few lines of code. It is more feature-laden than the Think Class Library, but you have to pay for it, whereas the TCL is bundled with the Think products. The original version was written in Pascal, but Apple recently developed a C++ version.

Where to Go Next

By now you should have some idea of what programming is all about and what you need to get started. The next step is to learn how to do it. Your best approach depends on your previous experience, knowledge of computers, and preferred learning style—some people prefer to teach themselves; others would rather take classes. Most programmers eventually do both.

Universities and Colleges

Note

Most universities now offer at least some classes in computer science, although few have courses tailored specifically to Macintosh programming. If you can get into one (demand often exceeds capacity), an introductory college course in programming is often the easiest and least expensive way to learn the basics. Many community colleges, trade schools, and adult-education programs offer introductory classes. But take care: be sure the equipment and software are reasonably up-to-date, as far too many schools are using obsolete systems. At many colleges, the night classes often tend to have better instructors—working programmers who want to pick up spare change rather than college professors with no experience in real-world programming.

Commercial Classes and Seminars

Several companies, including Apple, offer one- or two-week courses in Macintosh programming. These courses are never cheap, and they usually require prior experience with C or Pascal. They are intended for professional programmers whose employers are willing to foot the bill, but they can be a good way to learn a lot in a hurry, if you do not mind overloading your brain cells.

Self-study Programs

There are several products in this category, but a few stand out. Symantec's Just Enough Pascal is a self-teaching program you use with Think Pascal to learn basic Pascal programming. Apple's Macintosh Programming Fundamentals is a massive HyperCard stack (you need a CD-ROM player to use it) that teaches C programming on the Macintosh. It interfaces with Think C to enable you to do lab assignments. Its animation prevents you from nodding off during the dry parts.

Books

You can learn everything you need to know about Macintosh programming by reading books, and a lot of programmers have done exactly that. In addition to *Inside Macintosh* and other technical references, there is a long list of how-to books available for Macintosh programmers. The better books explain things more thoroughly and comprehensively than *Inside Macintosh*, and they sometimes show you clever programming tricks you never would think of on your own. However, beware of out-of-date books still lurking around bookstores.

Magazines

The only major entry in this category, not counting the SPLAsh newsletter, is *MacTutor*. The programming examples it offers are not always useful, but accompanying articles usually do a good job of explaining the concepts. If you do not want to subscribe to the magazine, you can buy the *Best of MacTutor* volume that comes out each year.

User Groups and Developer Associations

User groups and developer associations can be valuable sources of assistance and support when you are learning to program—most programmers are flattered when you ask them for help or advice. Many such organizations also sell products at discounts to members and offer sample code and utilities free or at little cost. A complete list would take too much space—the following are simply the biggest or best known.

APDA

APDA stands for Apple Programmers and Developers Association. For a small annual fee, you get the APDA catalog, a customer number, and the privilege of ordering a few items not available to the world at large. Apple also offers programs for commercial software developers. Call APDA at (800) 282-2732 to place orders or for more information.

Part VII
For the More Technically Minded

SPLAsh

Symantec Programming Languages Association (SPLAsh) is for Think C and Think Pascal users. Membership fees include a subscription to a first-rate quarterly newsletter containing how-to articles and a sample code disk. Contact SPLAsh Resources at 1678 Shattuck Avenue, #302, Berkeley, California 94709.

BMUG and BCS

Berkeley Macintosh User Group (BMUG) claims to be the largest Macintosh user group in the world. It has an extensive disk library of utilities, fonts, games, and other goodies available at basically the cost of shipping and handling. Membership entitles you to free support from the BMUG Help Line. The Boston Computer Society (BCS), BMUG's biggest rival, offers similar products and services. Call (510) 849-9114 for BMUG membership information, and (617) 625-7080 to contact BCS.

Other User Groups

Check other user groups that also may have special meetings for programmers and offer libraries of utilities and other useful software or services. There are more than 1,200 registered Apple user groups in the United States and many more overseas. To find out about the ones in your area, call Apple at (800) 538-9696, ext. 500.

Summary

Programming on the Macintosh is no more difficult than programming on any other computer—it even may be easier. Many utilities and languages, along with user groups and services, are available to help programmers. Programs can be created in object-oriented language or procedural language and use the Macintosh's unique user interface, which includes windows, menus, icons, and scroll bars. Although more knowledge may be required to create a Macintosh program to begin with, tools built into the Mac by Apple help speed the process.

Glossary of Common Macintosh Terms

64K ROM   The original ROM size on the Mac 128 and the 512. See also *Read Only Memory (ROM)*.

128K ROM   ROM size on the Mac Plus, SE, 512K Enhanced, LC, and the Classic. See also *Read Only Memory (ROM)*.

256K ROM   ROM size on the Mac II, IIx, IIcx, IIci, IIfx, IIsi, SE/30, Classic II, Quadra 700 and Quadra 900. See also *Read Only Memory (ROM)*.

Glossary

-A-

About…   The first item on the Apple menu. If you select it while an application is running, it tells you the version number (and frequently how much RAM is available for additional documents). If you click it from the Finder, it tells you the system version number and total RAM.

Accelerator   An expansion board; an accessory that makes the Mac run faster.

Acoustic modem   Early version of a modem using two cups that fit around the earpiece and mouthpiece of a telephone receiver. It is used to convert a computer's signals into sounds that are sent as normal phone signals. See also *Modem*.

Active window   The open window: always the one on top, with a highlighted title bar. Also, a publication of the BCS•Mac group. See also *Boston Computer Society (BCS)*.

ADB   See *Apple Desktop Bus*.

AIFF   Audio Interchange File Format: File standard supported by many digitizing and multimedia applications.

Alarm clock   A desk accessory included with Apple's System software that displays the current time and date. It can be set to sound an alarm tone at a specified time.

Alert box   A box that appears on the screen to give you information or a warning.

Aliasing   Feature of System 7 that allows you to create dummy icons so you can open an application from different folders.

Analog   A signal, usually a telephone signal, that modulates or varies in strength, just like a person's voice or music. See also *Digital, Modem*.

APDA   Apple Programmers and Developers Association.

Apple Desktop Bus (ADB)   The connection for keyboards and mice on the Mac SE and later machines.

Apple HD SC setup   A utility packaged with Apple's System software that is used to initialize and set up a Macintosh hard disk. See also *Initialize; Hard disk; Hard drive; Hard disk drive*.

Apple key   Synonymous with the Command key on Mac keyboards introduced with the new Apple Desktop Bus (ADB) standard. See also *Command key*.

Glossary

Glossary of Common Macintosh Terms

Apple menu The first menu heading in any standard Mac application, identified by the apple symbol. Always contains Desk Accessories; frequently also contains the About… command.

AppleTalk Apple's machine-to-machine networking standard. Commonly used to refer to the network hardware, as well.

Application A software program that creates, manages, or manipulates data. Any software that is not an application is either part of the Mac's operating system or a utility program.

Arrow keys On most Mac keyboards, the four keys with arrows on them. They can be used to position the pointer, scroll down a list, or nudge a graphic. Other computers call them *cursor* keys, but Apple's creator did not like the word "cursor."

Arrow pointer The basic shape the pointer takes—a tool used to select an item on the desktop or in a graphics program.

ASCII (ASK-ee) American Standard Code for Information Interchange: a format with one-byte equivalents for every character and punctuation mark. In ASCII, 67-97-116 spells "cat."

ASCII file A file containing characters that can be read by any computer and by most word processors. Also called a "text file" or "ASCII text."

ASCII graphics Drawings made from standard text characters that can be read by any computer. Often used in telecommunications. See also *Emoticons*.

AT commands See *Hayes command set*.

-B-

Backup A copy of a program or document that can be used in place of the original. To backup is to make an identical copy.

BASIC Beginners All-purpose Symbolic Instruction Code: a programming language largely obsolete on the Mac. HyperTalk and White Knight's scripting language are very similar.

Baud The unit of measurement for data transmission speeds, approximately equal to one bit per second.

BBS Bulletin Board System: a computer system maintained by an individual or computer user group to share messages and software. See also *Online service, CompuServe, Prodigy*.

Glossary

BCS   Boston Computer Society; an active and well-known computer user group based in Boston, Massachusetts. See also *Boston Computer Society, Active window*.

Berkeley Macintosh Users' Group   See *BMUG*.

Beta testing   A program's second-round debugging, as opposed to alpha testing or first-round trials. Beta versions may be posted on BBS as shareware.

Bézier curves (BEHZ-ee-ay)   Mathematically generated lines which can display non-uniform curves (as opposed to uniformly-curved arcs), frequently used in drawing programs.

Binary   The base-2 numbering system, which allows computers to express everything in terms of "on" or "off."

Bit   Binary digit: the smallest possible single unit of information; either "on" or "off," 1 or 0.

Bitmap   Any image described by bits or dots, including the Mac screen and ImageWriter printer output. Paint programs produce bitmapped graphics.

Bitmapped font   A typeface made from dots and designed for use on dot matrix printers and the Mac screen. Also called an ImageWriter font.

Blessed folder   The folder that contains the System file and other files necessary to operate the Macintosh. From System 6.0.1 to 6.0.8, the blessed folder displays a small Mac icon. From System 7 on, any folder with a usable system carries the Mac icon. See also *System folder*.

BMUG   Berkeley Macintosh Users' Group: a well-known Macintosh users' group based in Berkeley, California.

Bomb   Any system malfunction that irrecoverably stops your program. Also, the message or alert box with a picture of a bomb in it, warning you that the system has been brought to its knees. The only cure for most bombs is to reboot.

Boot   To start the computer, loading its operating system and reorganizing its memory. From "bootstrapping," or pulling oneself up by the bootstraps.

Boston Computer Society   See *BCS, Active window*.

Box   1) An enclosed area with a message, such as a dialog box or alert box on the Mac's screen. 2) Any of the various squares that control windows: close boxes, scroll bars, and zoom boxes.

Bridge   An interface between groups of separate networks (called zones). See also *Gateway, Router*.

Glossary

Glossary of Common Macintosh Terms

Buffer A space in the computer's memory for temporary data storage. For instance, a print buffer stores data until the printer is ready.

Bug A problem within a program that causes it to misbehave, crash, or even bomb the system. From early computer terminology, when real bugs used to eat the cloth insulation from the wiring.

Button 1) An outlined area in a dialog box, which you click to choose a command. 2) The switch on top of the mouse, also called the mouse button.

Byte Eight bits of data, representing a decimal number between zero and 255. Bytes frequently stand for individual characters in text.

-C-

Cache A section of Random Access memory or RAM, which temporarily holds data on its way to or from a disk. Because data in RAM is faster to access than data on disks, caches make computer operations go faster.

CAD/CAM (CAD-cam) Computer Aided Design and Manufacturing.

Cancel To stop an activity. Cancel buttons appear in most dialog boxes, enabling you to change your mind before you permanently modify or print a file.

Card 1) HyperCard's equivalent to a database record, usually holding information and graphics about a single subject. It may also contain specially-programmed buttons. 2) Shorthand for printed circuit card. Accelerator cards, modem cards, etc., can be plugged into some Macs to add speed or functions.

CCITT An international communications commission that sets standards for communication signals, particularly modems.

CD-ROM Compact Disk, Read Only Memory: a system for optical storage and retrieval of information.

CDEV (SEA-dehv) Control Panel device, a utility program kept in the System folder and activated through an icon on the Control Panel.

Cell The basic unit of a spreadsheet, containing a number, label, or formula.

Checkbox A button that works as a toggle. When you click it, an *x* appears in the box, and the activity it represents is "on." Clicking again removes the *x* and turns off the option.

Chooser A desk accessory used to select input and output devices, usually printers or network connections.

Glossary

Chooser resources   Files that display an icon in the Chooser window, usually printer drivers or network resources.

Clipboard   Memory devoted to temporary storage of selected text or graphics. The clipboard can hold one item at a time. Its contents disappear when the computer is turned off.

Close box   A small box in the left corner of the title bar. Clicking here closes the document, or removes its window from the screen.

Code   Basic program instructions, in a language the computer can read and understand.

Color wheel   On color Macs, a segmented circle used to select one of several thousand colors. Found in the Color CDEV, and within many programs.

Command   Anything you tell a computer to do. On the Macintosh, commands are generally chosen by clicking on a menu or holding the Command key simultaneously with one or more other keys.

Command key   Sometimes called the Apple key or the Clover key because of the apple and clover symbols imprinted on it. Pressed simultaneously with other keys to issue commands. See also *Apple key*.

Compiler   Utility application that converts human-readable programs into more compact and faster computer-readable ones, which can then be installed in another application. The current version of HyperCard uses compilers.

CompuServe   A commercial online service. See also *BBS, Online service*.

Control key   Generally useless key, put on ADB keyboards as a sop to former IBM users who missed having one. Used primarily in telecommunications with non-Macintosh systems.

Control Panel(s)   A desk accessory that allows you to set the volume of sound, the typing and clicking speed, and other system functions.

CPU   Central Processing Unit: the "brains" of the computer, from the days when computers consisted of more than one refrigerator-sized unit. Sometimes used to refer to the main processing chip; sometimes used to refer to the system unit in modular Macs.

Crash   A condition of total computer failure, usually accompanied by a frozen screen and no response to the mouse or keyboard. A crash generally means the system must be restarted. See also *Bomb, Lockup*.

Glossary
Glossary of Common Macintosh Terms

Cross-platform   Between two different types of computers, such as between Macs and IBM PC compatibles.

CRT   Cathode Ray Tube: a nickname for a computer monitor that displays the images on a screen via phosphor coating on the inside of the tube and energized by cathode rays so the phosphor glows, creating the image. See also *Monitor*.

Cursor   Non-Mac term sometimes applied to the pointer or text insertion point. See also *Arrow keys*.

-D-

DA   See *Desk Accessory*.

Database   A collection of organized information stored as a file; or the program used to create and organize the information.

Debug   The process of finding errors in a program.

Default   An action, command, or specification the computer carries out unless you specify otherwise. Plain type (as opposed to **bold face** or italic) is the default style in most word processors.

Default button   Button designated by a heavy border in a dialog box. The least damaging or suggested action; can be chosen simply by pressing the Return key.

Defragmenting   Reorganizing a hard disk so that each file is in one contiguous space on the disk, rather than being fragmented in many different locations.

Delete key   A key that erases characters from the insertion point in a word processor, or deletes the entire selection in most programs.

Desk Accessory (DA)   Any of a set of small applications or utilities that can be used while another program is open. Listed under the Apple menu.

Desktop   The computer screen with no document windows open; the basic working environment for the Macintosh. Also, a piece of furniture that, when dirty, ruins a mouse.

Desktop bus   See *Apple Desktop Bus (ADB)*.

Dialog box   A box that appears on the screen asking for information or actions from the user.

Digital   A signal, usually a computer type of signal, that does not vary and is either on or off, x or y, 1 or 0. See also *Analog, Modem*.

Glossary

Digitizer A peripheral used to convert images or sound into a form the computer can use. Audio digitizers are called samplers; image digitizers are called scanners.

Dimmed A menu choice or button that is unavailable and therefore grayed-out on the Mac screen.

Directory 1) A list of a disk's contents; may appear as a collection of icons and folders. 2) A critical section of the disk's surface that steers the magnetic heads to data and program instructions.

Dithering In color printing, a process of spacing dots closely in groups with no two dots overprinting, to make color blends. For example, a series of yellow and cyan dots printed close together blend into green from a distance.

DOS Disk Operating System: every computer uses one, but the term generally refers to MS DOS (used on IBM and clone PCs). Macintosh's DOS is usually called the System and Finder.

Dot matrix A printer that uses pins pressed against an inked ribbon to form images on the paper. ImageWriters are dot matrix printers.

Downloadable fonts PostScript or QuickDraw typefaces stored on a disk, which must be downloaded to the printer's memory before the font can be used.

Downloading Retrieving a file from one computer and storing it on another. The opposite of uploading.

DPI Dots per inch: a measure of the resolution of monitors, laser printers, and scanners.

Draft quality High speed, low resolution printing.

Driver Software that tells the computer how to send screen or memory information to an outside device (usually a printer).

-E-

Electronic mail or E-mail Personal messages exchanged via computer on BBS or an online service.

Encapsulated PostScript (EPS) A graphics file format that allows finely detailed pictures to be manipulated by desktop publishing programs.

Expansion Board A circuit board which can be added to a Mac to improve its performance or add to its capabilities.

Extension A System 7 utility which extends the functionality of the system. Known as an INIT or CDEV in earlier systems.

Glossary

Glossary of Common Macintosh Terms

-F-

Fax Shortened form of **Fac**similie; refers to the transmission of an image (usually of a printed page) over telephone lines. Personal computers can send images to fax machines through the use of fax modems.

Field In a database record, the area for a particular piece of data.

File Any collection of data on disk; an application or program.

Finder The basic Macintosh program that creates the desktop and allows you to manage files and disks. Along with the System file, it comprises the Mac's operating system.

Fkey A Mac command accessed by typing Shift, Command, and a number. Has no relationship to the function keys on extended keyboards.

Floppy disk A removable magnetic disk; in the Mac, housed in a plastic shell approximately 3 1/2-inches square. Mac floppies do not flop or flex.

Folder A collection of documents and/or other folders, represented by a folder-shaped icon on the desktop. Roughly equivalent to an MS DOS subdirectory, which is not defined here.

Font A complete set of numbers, letters, and symbols in a particular typeface, style, and size; also the file that contains a bitmap of those characters.

Font/DA mover A utility program used to install and remove fonts and desk accessories from the system.

Font ID conflict A conflict created when two fonts have the same identification number. More common when the Mac Operating System only recognized 128 font numbers, instead of 32, 768 in System 7.

Font usage utility A utility program that catalogues fonts used in a particular document, usually used with a service bureau to avoid font ID number conflicts.

Footprint The physical space the computer occupies on the surface where it sits. Compared to most PCs, the Mac has a small footprint.

Fork Mac files are organized into two forks: the resource fork holds file instructions, and the data fork holds text, graphic, or numerical data.

Format 1) To design pages on a word processor. 2) To initialize a disk, checking its sectors and organizing a directory.

Freeware Copyrighted programs which are available free of charge. See also *Shareware, Public Domain*.

Glossary

-G-

Gateway   1) A future replacement for a modem that will filter and boost a computer's digital signals to communicate over telephone lines using a digital phone line called ISDN. 2) An interface between groups of separate networks (called zones). See also *Integrated Systems Digital Network (ISDN), Analog, Digital, Modem, Router, Bridge.*

Get Info window   The window that appears when you select Get Info from the desktop File menu. It tells you the size of a selected file, when it was most recently modified, and where it is. You can also lock or unlock a file or disk in this window.

Graphic User Interface (GUI)   A program design that enables the user to click icons instead of typing text commands.

Group III–compatible   A set of standards for modems communicating at 9600 bps, usually facsimile, or fax, machines. See also *Fax, CCITT, Modem.*

-H-

Hacker   Person who enjoys computers and programming, sometimes to the exclusion of job, family, eating, or sleeping.

Handshake   A computer-to-computer message saying essentially "Yes, I got that last instruction and am ready for the next."

Hard disk; Hard drive; Hard disk drive   A rigid, usually nonremovable, magnetic disk and its housing and reading mechanism. A hard disk stores more information than a floppy disk, and can be read more quickly.

Hardware   Parts of a computer that have wires and electronics: any part that is not software. See *Software.*

Hayes command set   A standard collection of commands to control modems.

HFS   Hierarchical File System: a method of organizing data on a Mac disk in which folders are active in List boxes as well as on the desktop. See also *MFS.*

Highlighting   Indication that something has been selected, chosen, or is active.

Host   A computer set up to accept modem calls from other computers.

HyperCard   General-purpose database manager and programming environment unique to Macs. Essentially, it enables average users to create their own programs.

Glossary

Glossary of Common Macintosh Terms

HyperTalk HyperCard's supplied programming language, based on simple English-language statements.

Hypertext Any program that enables you to explore information or answer questions by clicking subjects on the screen. Frequently adds graphics, animation, and sound.

-I-

I/O See Input/Output.

I-beam pointer Pointer that indicates where the Mac will modify text; also called the text tool.

Icon A picture symbolizing and linked to a file or command. See also Graphical User Interface.

Imagesetter A high-quality printer that can produce both graphics and type, frequently from PostScript files generated on a Mac.

ImageWriter A line of dot matrix printers made by Apple.

Import To load information created by one program into another.

INIT (in-IT) Initialization program that alters the Mac's working system at start-up, usually for some worthwhile purpose that Apple left out. Print spoolers and screen savers are typical INITs. System 7 calls them Extensions.

INIT conflict A situation where two INITs attempt to patch code to the same resource fork in Mac's System software, resulting in a system lock-up or crash. See also *Crash, Lockup*.

Initialize 1) To reset a program or device to its starting values.
2) To format a disk.

Input/Output Usually refers to the function of reading to or writing from a disk.

Integrated Systems Digital Network (ISDN) A new data transmission standard being developed to carry digital signals over telephone lines without converting them to analog signals, using a modem. See also Analog, Digital, Modem, Gateway.

Interface A connection between two objects. Often, short for "user interface": how a person gives commands to the computer.

Glossary

-J-K-L-

Jaggies Block-like or stair-step effect seen when bitmapped characters are enlarged beyond their original size.

Kerning Closing up the space between two letters for a better appearance.

Key combination Also called keyboard equivalent or key command. A fast way to issue a command without using mouse or menu, by pressing the Command key and another key simultaneously. Key combinations are usually indicated next to the appropriate command in the menu.

Kilobyte (K) 1,024 bytes.

LAN See *Local Area Network*.

Laser font See *Outline font*.

Laser printer A computer printer that creates images from tiny dots of laser-generated light, reproducing them through a process similar to an office copier. The LaserWriter is an Apple laser printer.

Launching Starting an application.

List box Part of a dialog box, with a long list of files to open or commands to execute.

Local Area Network (LAN) A system tying together several computers and one or more printers.

LocalTalk Apple's cabling hardware standard for LAN; now usually included in the term AppleTalk.

Locking Preventing a disk or file from being accidentally changed. A locked disk is sometimes called write-protected.

Lockup A condition of total computer failure, accompanied by a frozen screen showing no response to the mouse or keyboard. A crash generally means the system must be restarted. See also *Crash, Bomb*.

Log on Connecting to a computer network or BBS.

Look and feel The style of a computer or program interface. Because all Mac programs share a similar look and feel, users can switch among them easily.

-M-

MacinTalk Simple but elegant speech-synthesis program created for the first Macintosh, and still usable on most systems.

Glossary

Glossary of Common Macintosh Terms

MacRecorder   Farallon hardware adapter that adds sound input to any Macintosh.

Macro   A command, usually created or editable by the user, that initiates a series of other commands and keystrokes.

Marquee   The flashing rectangle surrounding selected items, usually found in paint programs.

Megabyte (M)   1024 kilobytes; roughly a million bytes.

Memory   The place within the computer where information is electronically stored. Usually refers strictly to RAM, but also includes the Mac's basic operating instructions, programmed in Read Only Memory at the factory.

Menu   A list of commands you can choose by clicking on them with a mouse.

Menu bar   The strip at the top of the Mac screen containing menu titles.

Message box   A box that appears on the screen with information or warnings. Also called an alert box.

MFS   Macintosh File System: an early Macintosh desktop scheme that enabled you to put files into folders. The folders, unfortunately, were not recognized by other programs. Superseded by HFS.

MIDI   Musical Instrument Digital Interface: 1) LAN standard for both connectors and commands that allows musical synthesizers, sequencers, and audio effects devices to talk to one another. 2) Standard file format for exchanging songs between sequencer programs.

MIDI manager   Apple INIT and DA combination that routes MIDI signals among multiple sequencer programs running under MultiFinder.

Modem   **M**odulate/**dem**odulate: Essential telecommunications hardware, which converts digital data to analog or voice-like frequencies that the telephone system can reproduce. See also *Digital, Analog*.

Modifier key   A key that modifies the effect of another key being pressed. Standard modifier keys are the Shift, Option, Command, Caps Lock, and Control keys.

Monitor   The screen on which a computer displays items. Compact Macs have a built-in monitor. Mac IIs use a separate monitor. See also *CRT*.

Mouse   Device for moving any of various pointers on the Mac screen or selecting and dragging objects.

Glossary

MUG **M**acintosh **U**sers **G**roup: User groups that offer help, shareware, BBS, and other services for Mac users. BMUG is probably the best known.

MultiFinder An Apple-supplied INIT that allows several programs to be open at one time, in machines with sufficient memory. Obsolete with the advent of System 7, which performs these functions automatically.

-N-

Navigator 1) Apple-supplied HyperCard palette containing buttons to move from one card to another. 2) Speech-recognition system enabling voice commands.

Network Any collection of computers or peripherals wired together to share resources or information. Local Area Networks generally use high-speed cables within a single building; other networks can use modems or digital telephone connections.

Node Any computer or other device connected to a network.

-O-

Object-oriented A programming technique that allows any screen element or typed phrase to carry program instructions. Macintosh buttons are objects.

Object-oriented graphic A collection of lines and shapes the program treats as a single unit; graphics created in a draw program, as opposed to bitmapped graphics.

OCR **O**ptical **C**haracter **R**ecognition: software, or software/hardware combinations that can recognize bitmaps of individual letters and convert them to ASCII.

Online service A commercial online service accessed by a modem. See also *BBS, CompuServe, Prodigy*.

Outline font A font intended for use on a laser printer or Imagesetter. Rather than made of dots like a bitmapped font, each letter is defined by its outline, which is filled to display the character. Outline fonts can be scaled to any size without losing quality. Frequently described in the PostScript language. Sometimes called a "laser" font.

-P-

Packet The form in which data is sent over a network. Each packet consists of a header, body, and footer.

Glossary
Glossary of Common Macintosh Terms

Paint   A graphics format for bitmapped images, based on the original MacPaint program.

Paint program   A graphics program that generates low resolution (72 dpi) bitmapped graphics, in which each dot can be manipulated separately.

Palette   A small window that can be moved around the Mac screen, with buttons to control program operation. The "tools" selector in most graphics programs is a palette. HyperCard enables you to program custom palettes.

Parking   Locking the head of a disk drive so neither it nor the disk is harmed by vibration. Choosing Shut Down parks the head; many modern hard disks park automatically when the power is turned off.

Paste   To put the contents of the clipboard into a document.

Pasteboard   In page layout programs, the temporary storage and work area outside the boundaries of the page.

Personal Computer (PC)   Properly, any computer designed to be used by one person at a time. In modern usage, it refers specifically to small computers that are compatible with the IBM text-based standard.

Peer-to-peer file sharing   Refers to computers sharing files with each other on a network, computer-to-computer.

Peripheral   Device that was not an original, integral part of the computer. A standard Mac mouse is not a peripheral; a trackball is. Common peripherals include printers, hard drives, and modems.

PICT (Picked)   A standard file format for object-oriented graphics.

Pixel (PICK-sill)   A single dot. The individual units that make bitmapped characters or graphics. Short for **pic**ture **el**ement.

Pointer   The indicator that moves on the screen when you move the mouse.

Pop-up menu   A list of options that stays hidden until you click on it in a dialog box.

Port   Any data-connection jack on a computer or peripheral.

PostScript   Adobe's proprietary page description language, designed to relay instructions about fonts and objects to a printer.

PostScript font   A typeface designed to work with PostScript; an outline font file in the PostScript format.

Glossary

PRAM   Parameter **RAM**: a portion of the Mac's memory used to store time, date, Control Panel settings, and other user-specific information. A small battery keeps the PRAM from losing information when the computer is shut off. See also *Zap the PRAM*.

Print buffer   A hardware device that intercepts a print file and holds it in its own memory until the printer is ready to accept it, freeing the computer for other things.

Print spooler   An INIT that acts like a print buffer but intercepts the print instructions within the system and directs them on hard disk. Usually requires MultiFinder to send the disk file to the printer while another program is running.

Printer driver   A Chooser document that tells the Mac how to translate a file's text and graphics to a form a specific printer can use. Also called a printer resource.

Prodigy   A commercial online service. See also *BBS, Online service*.

Program   A group of instructions that tells a computer how to do something. Also called software. Saying "software programs," however, is like saying an armchair chair or a car automobile. Saying "Application software programs" is just plain silly.

Programmer's switch   A piece of plastic containing small buttons that clips onto the side of some Macs, touching an internal restart switch and a program debugging switch. Others do the same functions with key combinations.

Prompt   A symbol on the screen, usually represented by >, !, or :, indicating that a computer is waiting to be told what to do. Found on mainframes, IBM PCs, and other old-fashioned machines; you may encounter these on telecommunications services.

Protocols   A set of standard procedures controlling how information is exchanged between computers.

Public Domain (PD)   Software which is not copyrighted and can be distributed and used freely. Sometimes incorrectly used to refer to freeware and shareware as well. See also *freeware, shareware*.

-Q-

QuickDraw   Apple's built-in graphics software, and the programming heart of the Macintosh look and feel: Allows programs to draw or print lines and shapes much faster than on other small computers.

QuickDraw printer High-quality (usually laser) printer that uses QuickDraw commands through the SCSI port, rather than PostScript.

Quitting Leaving an application properly, and returning to the Finder or equivalent. Programs usually clean up files and do other housekeeping tasks upon quitting.

-R-

Radio buttons Groups of buttons shaped as small circles. Only one circle in the group can be filled, indicating that option has been selected. Named because they look and work like station-selecting buttons on a car radio.

RAM Random Access Memory: Electronic data storage, much faster than disk storage. Also, unfortunately, volatile; power or program disruptions can destroy the data in RAM. Turning off the computer erases any data in RAM.

RAM cache Area of computer memory devoted to temporary storage of hard-disk data. Lets the Macintosh system manage disk access better and run programs faster. Also ties up memory that could be used for other program purposes.

RDEV (ARE-dehv) Resource driver: a resource that can be accessed through the Mac's Chooser, such as a printer driver.

Read Me A file included on a new software disk, usually including last-minute instructions and program changes that could not be included in the manual. Often, but not necessarily, written in TeachText.

Record (noun) In a database, a set of fields pertaining to one item.

Relational A database manager that can access or change information in one file based on user input to another file.

Resolution The spacing of dots on a page or pixels on a monitor or printer, usually expressed in DPI. A higher resolution indicates finer-quality output: the Mac screen is 72 DPI; ImageWriter "Best" quality is 144 DPI; most laser printers are 300 DPI.

Restart Rebooting from the disk, without actually turning off the power. (Also known as warm start or warm boot.) Restarting loses anything that was not saved.

RIP Raster Image Processor: Used in laser printers to create an image on a page.

RISC Reduced Instruction Set Computer microprocessors: faster, more powerful chips developed by IBM.

Glossary

Glossary of Common Macintosh Terms

Glossary

ROM   Read Only Memory: non-volatile computer memory that holds "hardwired" programs installed at the factory. QuickDraw and most of Mac's file and mouse interpreting routines are stored in ROM.

Router   An interface between groups of separate networks (called zones). See also *Bridge, Gateway*.

-S-

Sampler   A digitizer, specifically one for audio input.

Save   Transfers data from memory to disk.

Save As…   Command that lets you save a document under a different name or in a different location or format.

Scanner   A device to convert images into digital form for use by a graphics program.

Scrapbook   Desk accessory that stores a library of text or graphics material chosen by the user.

Screen font   Bitmapped version of an outline font, used to display the font on the computer screen.

Screen saver   INIT designed to prevent burnout of computer screens by blacking out the screen or putting up a moving pattern after a pre-determined period of inactivity.

Screen shot   A picture of the Macintosh screen, saved as a Paint file (with System 7, as a PICT file) or sent to the printer. Use a separate utility or press Command+Shift+3 to take a screen shot.

Script   A program or routine written by the user within a larger program such as HyperCard or White Knight.

Scroll arrow   The arrows at either end of the scroll bar. Clicking them changes the window's view, or moves a list up or down one line.

Scroll bar   Rectangular bar that appears at right side or bottom of the window if the window isn't large enough to display all the information at once. Allows the user to display different portions of the document.

SCSI (SCUZZ-ee)   Small Computer Systems Interface: a standard for hard disks and other devices that allows very rapid data transfer.

Sequencer   Musical equivalent of a word processor. It allows you to enter parts of a song via MIDI, edit individual notes, and add other effects.

Serial port   Either of the jacks on the back of the Mac labeled for the printer or modem. Serial means data is sent one bit at a time (as opposed to

Glossary

Glossary of Common Macintosh Terms

the parallel SCSI port). The ADB ports are also serial ports but are not commonly referred to as such.

Server   A dedicated computer on a network that "serves" all other devices hooked onto the network

Service bureau   A facility that rents time on a Mac (or other computer) and peripherals. Services vary, but usually include 300 dpi (or better) laser printing, scanning, and imagesetting.

Shareware   Software distributed on the honor system. Users are expected to send in modest shareware fees to compensate the author and support further development. Shareware is not free.

Shift-clicking   Holding the Shift key while clicking the mouse button. Lets you select multiple objects or large amounts of text.

Shut Down   A command on the Special menu in the Finder. It parks hard disk heads, ejects floppies, and prepares the Mac to be turned off. On newer Macs, it even turns off the power.

SIG   A **S**pecial **I**nterest **G**roup within a larger user group or BBS.

SIMM   **S**ingle **I**n-line **M**emory **M**odule: Plug-in RAM chip arrays, used in many Mac models.

Smiley   ASCII graphics used in telecommunications to express an emotion. For example =:-o indicates surprise, :-) indicates a grin, and ;-) indicates a wink.

SMPTE Code   Synchronizing standard that keeps audio and video tape recorders, and musical sequencers running in step with each other.

Stack   The basic HyperCard document, consisting of data (such as documents of other programs) but also frequently including specialized program instructions.

Start-up disk   The disk that contains the System and Finder software the Mac is currently running. Also, any disk which contains System and Finder files and can be used to start up the Mac.

Start-up screen   The screen displayed during the start-up process. Using many paint programs, you can replace the default "Welcome to Macintosh" screen with an image of your choice.

Stationery   A feature of many programs that enables you to create documents with prearranged formatting, such as memos or order forms.

Style   A variation of a font, including **bold**, *italic*, and other typographic features.

Glossary

Submenu   A menu you open by selecting an item on a larger menu. Menu items with submenus are indicated with an arrow next to the item name.

Suitcase   A file that stores fonts or DAs, which is moved into the System file before use.

Sysop   System operator: Manager of a BBS or online service.

System file   The set of instructions that tells the Macintosh how to read and organize disks, how to open and create the Finder, and how to communicate with the user.

System folder   A standard folder on a Macintosh containing the System file and Finder. Depending on the user, it may also contain INITs, CDEVs, RDEVs, outline fonts, and temporary files put there by applications. When it contains the System file and Finder that is currently operating the Mac, it is known as the *blessed folder*.

-T-

TeachText   An application on the System Tools disk that lets you read and print Read Me files.

Tear-off menu   A menu or palette you can move around the screen like a window. Found in HyperCard and some graphics programs.

Text file   An ASCII-only file with no formatting codes or resource fork; can be opened by most word processors.

TIFF   Tagged Image File Format: a standard graphics format for high resolution bitmapped or scanned images.

Title bar   Strip at the top of an open window containing its name. When the window is active, the title bar is highlighted with horizontal stripes and a close box.

Trash   Represented by a Trash Can icon. Lets you discard unwanted files.

Trojan horse   A program that purports to do something useful while it actually does something destructive. See also *virus, worm*.

TrueType   Apple's new font technology that allows complete scaling of a font from one to 32,000 points.

-U-

Undo   A standard Mac command that removes the effect of the last thing you did. You can undo text or graphic changes, but usually not a save. See Chapter 5 for other limitations.

Glossary

Glossary of Common Macintosh Terms

Uploading   Sending a file from one computer to another over a network.

User group   A group of people who share an interest in a specific computer or application and meet to discuss information and rumors about it. Usually nonprofit and independent of the manufacturer; frequently supported by a BBS.

Utilities   Short programs that perform simple support tasks, usually within the Finder or other programs.

-V-

Vaporware   Exciting new computer programs supported by public relations and advertising but not by usable program code. Often the result of well-intentioned marketing types who do not realize the product is not ready to sell; sometime a fraudulent attempt to raise development money. Apple's System 7 was vaporware for several years.

Version number   A way to track changes the publisher makes to software, similar to edition numbers of a book.

Virus   A section of program code that can copy itself to other programs without your consent. Often has destructive effects. See also *Trojan Horse, Worm*.

Volatile   Memory which will lose data if it loses power (such as when the computer is turned off). RAM is volatile memory; ROM is not.

-W-

Wetware   Human beings. That part of a real-world computer system that is not hardware or software; often ignored by program developers and technical writers.

Worm   An application which does nothing but reproduce (duplicate itself), usually until it fills all available RAM or disk space. See also *Trojan Horse, Virus*.

Wristwatch   The shape the pointer assumes when the Mac is doing something that may take a long time. Some programs substitute a Spinning Beachball icon.

-X-Y-Z-

XCMD, XFCN   External **Command** or External **Function**: Short utilities that can be added to HyperCard, MicroPhone, and a few other programs to extend and customize their programming languages.

Glossary

Zap the PRAM Apple's technical term for clearing out the PRAM (Parameter RAM). Done in System 6, by holding down the Option, Command, and Shift keys while selecting the Control Panel from the Apple menu. In System 7 or later, restart while holding down the Option, Command, P, and R keys at the same time. See also *Parameter RAM*.

Zoom box Box to the right of the title bar on most windows, allowing you to shrink and expand the window with a single click. Helpful when you have many layers of open windows.

Index

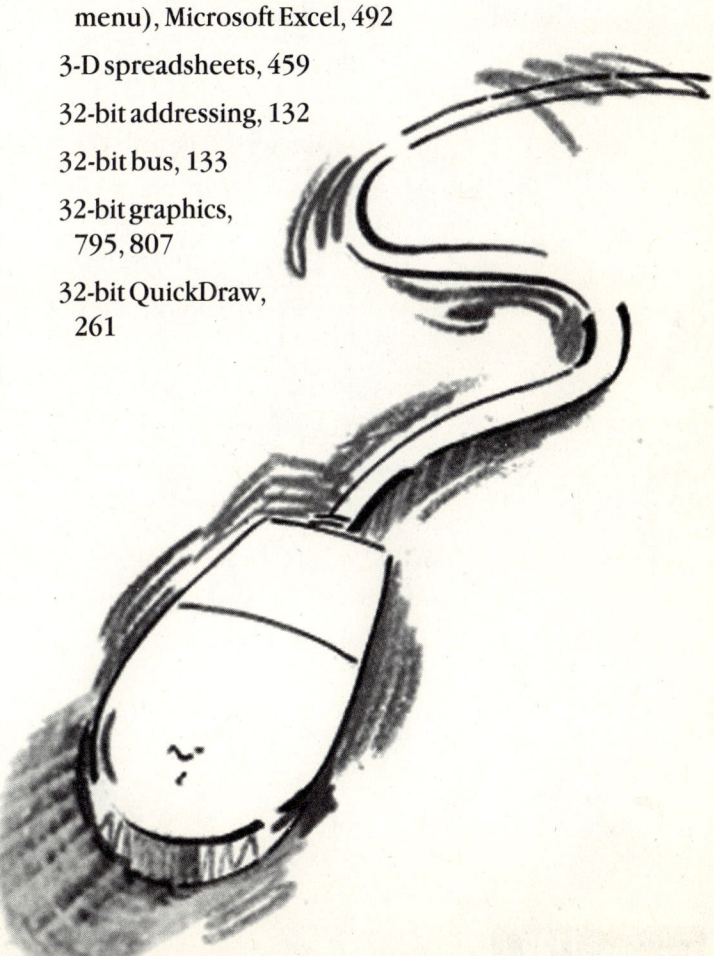

Symbols

030 Direct Slot add-in boards, 137

1 Bit Video Card, 179

10Base-T compliant twisted-pair cable, 998

128K ROM, 1109

16 bit color, Mac LCIII, 164

1x3 MIDI interface (Altech), 670

230.4K baud speed, LocalTalk, 193

24-pound printer paper, 236

256K ROM, 1109

28-pound printer paper, 236

3 in 3 puzzle game (Inline Design), 601

3+Mail (3Com Software), 1019

3-D (three-dimensional) graphics, 764

3-D Pie command (Gallery menu), Microsoft Excel, 492

3-D spreadsheets, 459

32-bit addressing, 132

32-bit bus, 133

32-bit graphics, 795, 807

32-bit QuickDraw, 261

Everything You Wanted to Know About the Mac

32-bit ROM, Mac IIci, 156

32-bit-wide internal registers, 141

3270 terminal emulators, 991

3Com Software, 3+Mail, 1019

3G Graphics, Images With Impact!, 385

4th Dimension (ACIUS), 513, 526-529

56001 digital signal processors (Motorola), 122

640K Barrier, 1109

64K ROM, 1109

68000 processors (Motorola), 141, 198

68020 processors (Motorola), 120, 142, 153, 806

68030 processors (Motorola), 121, 131, 154, 162, 169-170

68040 processors (Motorola), 121, 142, 165

68851 PPMMUs (paged memory management units), 143, 154

68881 math coprocessors (Motorola), 143, 153

68882 math coprocessors (Motorola), 121, 137, 143, 162

68LC040 processors (Motorola), 164-165

8•24GC card (Apple), 179, 197

911 Utilities, 866

A

A Lasting Impression, RésumExpert, 428

A-Train simulation game, 610

A/UX, Apple/Unix operating system, 157

Abacus window, Double Helix 3.5 (Helix), 524

ABC News Interactive Series, 757, 790

About The Finder command (MultiFinder menu), 123

About the Finder command (Apple menu), 30

About This Macintosh command (Apple menu), 123

About This Macintosh dialog box, 123, 126

About... command (Apple menu), 1110

absolute pointing devices, graphics tablets, 73

Accel-A-Writer controllers (Xante), 208

Accelerator, 1110

accented characters, 379

Access PC (Insignia Systems), 115, 1004

ACIUS

    4th Dimension, 513, 526-529

    FILE FORCE, 529-530

Index

acknowledge control packets, AppleTalk node addresses, 960

acoustic modems, 901, 1110

Acrobat multiple master fonts, 373

Acta DA (Symmetry Software), 409

Acta Advantage (Symmetry Software), 426

active arguments in scripts (HyperCard), 722

active matrix LCDs in Mac Portables, 167

active star networking, LocalTalk, 995

active windows, 1110

Activision games, 594

Actual size command (Page menu, PageMaker), 333

Ada programming language, 1097

adapter cables connecting music tools to Mac, 652

adaptive membrane keyboards (KeyLargo), 815

ADB (Apple Desktop Bus), 133-134, 148, 194-195, 904, 1110

ADBProbe, shareware control panel, 133

Add Legend command (Chart menu), Microsoft Excel, 491

add-in cards, NuBus, 136-137

adding date to layout mode with text tool (FileMaker Pro), 571

ADDmotion HyperCard toolkit, 805

address decoding in memory, 182

address lines and processors, 141

Address stacks, HyperCard, 703

addressing data in memory, 141

Adjustable Keyboard (Apple), 76

Adobe Systems

    Display PostScript language, 371

    Illustrator, 291

    multiple master fonts, 379

    Pattern and Texture library, 389

    Photoshop, 115, 264, 271, 782

    PostScript fonts, 369-371, 1100

    PostScript Level 2, 238

    Premiere, 645, 668, 806

    Streamline, 385

    SuperATM, 372

    Type 1/Type 3 fonts, 206

    Type Align utility, 846

    Type Reunion program, 377, 396

ADR (Automatic Dialog Replacement), 644

Everything You Wanted to Know About the Mac

adult-oriented shareware, 596

advanced MIDI setups, 673

Advanced Software, DocuComp, 428

Adventure Atlas, 918

Adventure game, 588

adventure games, 594-597

Adventures in Musicland program, 626

Affinity Microsystems, Tempo II Plus, 415

AFP (Apple Filing Protocol), 947

AFP servers, 947-948

After Dark screen savers, 87, 614, 838

AIFF, 1110

AIR (Apple Internet Router), 967

Airbrush tool, SuperPaint, 257

airbrushes in paint programs, 257

Aladdin Systems, Stuffit Deluxe, 1031

Alarm clock, 1110

Aldus Corporation
   FreeHand, 291
   PageMaker, 115, 203, 301, 328-329
   Personal Press, 322-323
   Persuasion, 756
   PrePress, 321
   SuperCard, 804

Aldus/Silicon Beach games, 593, 596

alert boxes, 77-78, 1110

Alge-Blaster Plus (Davidson), 626

algebraic functions in spreadsheets, 460

algorithms, Apple Video Compression, 784

aliases, 37-41, 1110

Alignment command (Format menu), Microsoft Excel, 480

Alignment dialog box, Microsoft Excel, 480

Alliance for Technology Access, 829

AlSoft MasterJuggler, 81

Altair II wireless Ethernet (Motorola), 981

Altech 1x3 MIDI interface, 670

alternative programming languages, 1097-1099

AlterNet network, 941

Altsys
   Fontographer, 393-395
   Metamorphosis Pro, 394

Amazing maze (Apple), 597

AMD 29000 processors, 198

America Online, 937
   Apple Macintosh Technical Notes, 1039
   Comp-u-store, 921
   E-mail, 917

Index

file transfers, Mac/PC, 1008

graphics library, 383

Industry Connection section, 1038

interactive games, 928

Internet connections, 916

Mac Utilities library, 927

message boards, 923

news service, 918

shareware games, 611

software updates, 1038

weather reports, 918

American Academic Encyclopedia online services, 922

American Thermoform, Ohtsuki Braille Printer, 827

amplitude of sound waves, 654

Amslan fonts, 828

analog, 1110

    electronic signals, 899

    video, 766

animation, multimedia, 764-766

animation in HyperCard, 733

ANTI virus, 877-878

anti-aliasing, 782

AntiPan 1.5 program, 887

Antivirus (Symantec), 872, 887

AOCE (Apple Open Collaboration Environment), 950

AP Online news, CompuServe, 917

APDA (Apple Programmers and Developers Association) catalog, 805, 1107, 1110

APL (A Programming Language), 1097

AppDisk program, 130

Apple

    Close View utility, 822-824

    Developer Technical Support (DTS) Sample Code disk, 1105

    history, 4-15

    LaserWriter printers, 13, 215, 1016

    Macintosh PC Exchange, 1004, 1026

    menu commands

        About the Finder, 30

        About This Macintosh, 123

        About…, 1110

        Calculator, 34

        Control Panels, 33, 835

        Key Caps, 378

        Note Pad, 34

        Scrapbook, 31

    MODE32 utility, 143

    NFNT (New Font Numbering System), 377

    Office of Special Education and Rehabilitation, 829

    PostScript printers, 232

    Puzzle, 597

Everything You Wanted to Know About the Mac

QuickTime, 750, 1032

ResEdit program, 120

Speech Manager, 789

System 7, 1010

TokenTalk NuBus interface card, 1011

TrueType fonts, 373-375

video cards, 179

VideoSync utilities, 780

WorldWide Disability Solutions Group, 829

Apple AUI (attachment unit interface), 977

Apple Events, System 7, 96, 758

Apple File Exchange, 841

   MacLinkPlus translators, 1022, 1025-1027

   reading PC floppy disks, 1003

Apple HD SC setup utility, 1110

Apple II emulator cards, 137, 632

Apple IIe emulator cards, 174

Apple key, 1110

Apple manuals, 26

Apple Menu Items alias icon, 39

Apple Menu Items folder, 79

Apple NuBus Slot adaptor card, 137

Apple Open Collaboration Environment, System 7, 758

Apple Portrait Display, Mac IIci, 155

Apple PowerBook/DOS Companion software, 233

Apple Sound Chips, 92

Apple video cards, 782

Apple Video Compression algorithms, 784

AppleEvents feature, System 7, 425

AppleLink, 1019

AppleScript feature, 97-98, 415, 425, 848

AppleShare, 947, 1010, 1017-1018

AppleTalk, 953-956, 1111

   Mac/PC networking, 1009-1011

   node addresses, 960

   routers, 966-967

AppleTalk Internet Router (Apple), 1012

AppleTalk network cards, 1010

AppleTalk networks, 961-964, 1016

AppleTalk Phase 2, 957-959

AppleTalk routers, 954, 996

AppleTalk Zone Information Protocol (ZIP), 965

AppleTalk/IP Wide Area Extension, 967

AppleTalk/LocalTalk networks, 232

AppleTalk/X.25 Wide Area Extension, 967

Index

application heaps, 123, 126

Application menu, 29, 69

application outliners, MORE (Symantec), 409

applications, 1111

Applied Engineering SuperDrive clone, 1005

Apply button, Microsoft Word, 452

AppMaker development system, 1105

Appoint MousePenPro, 256

Aqua Blooper Piper puzzle game (Casady & Greene), 601

ARAP (Apple Remote Access Protocol), 980

ARC file format (PCs), 1031

Argosy RunPC program, 1013-1016

arguments of script functions (HyperCard), 721

arithmetic functions, spreadsheets, 460

Arrow keys, 1111

Arrow pointer, 1111

arrow tool, 304

arrows, adding to charts, 497-498

Ars Nova Practica Musica/ Songworks programs, 682-683

Artbeats, Marble and Granite textures, 389

Arthur's Teacher Trouble (Marc Brown), 619

Articulate Systems
    Voice Impact, 649, 731
    Voice Navigator, 818
    Voice Record, 731

asc3270 emulators, 991

ASCII (American Standard Code for Information Interchange), 412, 1111
    characters, 907
    data format for modem protocols, 907
    files, 1111
    graphics, 1111

ASDSP (AppleTalk Secure Data Stream Protocol), 950

Ashton-Tate
    Full Impact 2.0 program, 458
    FullPaint program, 254

ASL FingerSpelling Tutor (Tony Martin), 827

Assassin program, 887

assemblers, 1088-1090

Assembly programming language, 1088, 1095-1096

AT commands, modems, 901, 912, 1111

At Ease access-limiting program, 620

Everything You Wanted to Know About the Mac

Atari

  Pong, 5

  video games, 590

Atkinson, Bill, HyperCard program author, 691

ATM (Adobe Type Manager)

  fonts, 213

    font utility, 371, 376, 846

    fax modem compatibility, 902

attributes of files, 112, 116-117

audio compressing, 656-657

Audio CD toolkit, 760

Audio Editing palette, 730

Audio Help stack, HyperCard, 730

Audio Interchange File Format, 93

Audio Palette (HyperCard), 651, 728-731

AudioMedia board (DigiDesign), 788

Audioshop (Opcode), 645, 668

AURP (Apple Update Routing Protocol), 967, 998

authoring tools, multimedia engines, 759, 803-806

Authorware (Macromedia), 759, 766, 803, 806

Auto Enter Values, FileMaker Pro, 545-548

Autofill feature (Microsoft Excel), 501-503

AutoFlow feature, PageMaker, 313

AutoMac utility, 847

automated diagnostic utilities, 1078-1079

automatic data entry in FileMaker Pro, 545-565

automatic kerning, 315

automatic leading features, 307

automatic placement of text, 313

autoscrolling windows, 71

AutoSwitch (Computer Friends), 232

autotrace tools, illustration programs, 292

Avatar MacMainFrame emulator, 991

AVC compression algorithms, 785

average access time of hard disks, 190

Avery MacLabelPro, 387

Axis dialog box, Microsoft Excel, 496

B

backgrounds, 388-389, 703, 713

Backsolver feature, Lotus 1-2-3/Mac, 467

Backspace key, 75

Index

backups, 1111
    hard disks, 853, 857-859
    masters of hard disks, 858
    utilities, 859
    volume, incremental and permanent, 858-859

bad blocks in hard disks, 1071

Balloon Help menu commands, 68-69

banks of memory, 185

Banyan VINES, Mac/PC networks, 985

bar charts, 493-494

bar code readers, 774

Bar command (Gallery menu), Microsoft Excel, 492

Barco projectors, 756

Baseline Publishing
    The Talking Moose, 613
    Vantage, 423

BASIC, 1111

BASIC programming language, 1096

Basics tour, 26

batteries, 1064-1065

battle games, 591-594

BattleChess game (Interplay), 608

baud rate, 900, 906, 1111

Bautista, Ricardo, Extensions Manager freeware, 88, 841
    BBS programs, FirstClass/TeleFinder, 941

BBSs (Bulletin Board Services), 423, 940-941, 1111
    indirect file transfers, 1008
    software updates, 1038
    virus updates, 893
    see also online services

BCS•Mac (Boston Computer Society Macintosh User's Group), 1041-1042

Berkeley Systems
    inLARGE program, 824-825
    inTouch, 827
    screen savers, 614

Bernoulli boxes, Mac/PC formatted cartridges, 1004

Bertinelli, Patrick, Insanity program, 614

Best mode, ImageWriter, 222

beta testing, 1112

Beyond Dark Castle battle game (Aldus/Silicon Beach), 593

Bézier curves, 1112

binary, 1112

BinHex shareware, 1031

bit editors, 118

bitmapped file formats, 763

bitmapped fonts, 368-369, 1112

bitmapped images
    paint programs, 252
    resolution dependent, 262

bitmaps, 252, 1112

Everything You Wanted to Know About the Mac

BITNET VIRUS-L/INFO-MAC distribution lists, 893

bits, 900, 1112

black and white paint programs, 266-267

blend tools in illustration programs, 292

Blessed folder, 1112

blinking question mark disk icon, 1076

block devices, 189

blocking capacitors, 668

blue boxes, 5

Blyth Software, Inc., Omnis 7, 535-537

BMUG Mac user group, 940, 1041-1042, 1108, 1112

bombing, 1112

Bond, Bill, FreeTerm communications program, 909

bookmarks, 404

Boomerang shareware utility, 849

boot blocks, 1075

boot disks, 105

booting, 1054, 1112
    problems, 1075-1077
    sequence for hard disks, 190

bootstrapping, 107

Bootware Software, ResumeWriter, 428

Border dialog box, Microsoft Word, 442

Border... command (Format menu), Microsoft Word, 441, 443

borders on cells in worksheets (Microsoft Excel), 498

Boss key screen, Pipe Dream, 590

Boston Computer Exchange, 921

Box shaped tool, RSG (ReadySetGo), 306

boxed quotes, 308

boxes, 1112

bps (bits per second), modem speeds, 900

Braille Display Processor program, 827

Braille pages, printing, 827

Brainard, Paul, 301

Bravo Technologies, MacCalc, 468

bridged star networking, LocalTalk, 996

BridgePort (Extended Systems), 234

bridges, 1112

Brøderbund
    Carmen Sandiego program series, 628
    games, 590
    Katie's Farm program, 618
    KidPix program, 268
    Living Books program series, 619

Index

McGee program, 618

Playmaker Football simulation game, 604

Playroom program, 618

TypeStyler, 393

Broken Links icon, Personal Press, 305

Brown, Marc, Arthur's Teacher Trouble program, 619

bubblejet printers, 216-218

buffers, 1113

bugs, 1113

building
- databases, 514-518
- program files, 1088
- worksheets, 469-470

built-in equation editor, Ventura Publisher, 324

built-in functions, spreadsheets, 460-461

built-in outlining, Microsoft Word, 409

built-in ROM disk, Mac Classic, 151

Bulleye Software
- Fokker Triplane battle game, 591
- P-51 Mustang flight simulator, 604

burst transfer rate of hard disks, 190

bus width, 132

buses, 132-137

Bush, Dr. Vannevar, memex device, 749

buttons, 1113
- adding to HyperCard stacks, 737-738
- defining in FileMaker Pro, 564
- Scripts in FileMaker Pro, 563

bytes, 1113

C

C/C++ programming language, 1094-1095

cables
- MIDI, 671-672
- SCSI ports, 1067

caching memory, 184, 1113

CAD/CAM (Computer Aided Design/Manufacturing), 1113

Calculation fields, 543

Calculation tiles, Double Helix 3.5 (Helix), 525-526

Calculations dialog box, FileMaker Pro (Claris), 531

Calculator command (Apple menu), 34

CameraMan (Diva), 806

cancelling, 1113

Canon laser printer engines, 214

Canon toner cartridge drums, 215

Everything You Wanted to Know About the Mac

Canon ZapShot, 772

Canvas (Deneba), 269

Capitalist Pig simulation game (Pluma), 610

captions, 316

card layer, HyperCard paint tools, 713

cards, 1113
    HyperCard, 703, 707-712
    serial port, 193-194

Carmen Sandiego program series (Brøderbund), 628

cartographic background patterns, 389

cartridge drives, multimedia storage, 798

Casady & Greene
    Aqua Blooper Piper puzzle game, 601
    Glider flight simulator, 605

Casblanca Works driver programs, 191

Case feature (PageMaker), 359-360

Casper system software, 94

Catos, Prodigy, 924

CAV (continuous angular velocity) laser disc format, 773

CB Simulator, CompuServe, 924

cc:Mail, 1019

CCITT, 1113

CD-ROM drives, 1017-1018, 1113
    clip art files, 383
    multimedia storage, 798
    Prosonus, 676
    Quadra 900, 161
    removing from desktop, 21

CDEF virus, 882

CDEVs (Control Panel devices), 1113

CDI (Compact Disc Interactive, Philips), 785

CE Software
    DiskTop, 1021
    HeapTool, 126
    LaserStatus, 225
    QuicKeys, 415, 819
    QuickMail, 952, 1018

cells, 1113

Centris 610, 164, 176-177

Centris 650, 165, 176-177

Centris 660AV, 94

Ceres Software, Inspiration word processor, 426

CGM files, 1024

Chalk tool in paint programs, 260

Change Case dialog box, Microsoft Word, 455

Change Case... command (Format menu), (Microsoft Word), 455

Change feature (PageMaker), 358-359

Index

channel standards, MIDI, 676

Character command (Format menu), Microsoft Word, 444

character formatting in documents, 405-406

Charcoal tool, DeskPaint/PixelPaint, 257

Chart button, Toolbar, (Microsoft Excel), 489

Chart menu commands (Microsoft Excel)
- Add Legend, 491
- Delete Legend, 492

charting/graphing spreadsheets, 461

charts Microsoft Excel, 488-498

checkboxes, 1113

CheckList font usage reporters, 390

CheckMate game (Interplay), 609

Chooser, 965, 1113
- extensions, 84
- resources, 1114
- selecting printers, 408

Chooser DA, 836

chooser names, MIDI, 675-676

chords of death, 1063

chromakey, 778

chrominance of video, 768

Claris Corporation.
- FileMaker Pro, 530-532
- HyperCard, 693
- HyperCard Player, 693
- MacWrite Pro, 412
- QuickTime Tool Kit, 733
- Resolve 1.0, 458, 467
- XTND, 115, 412, 1029-1030

ClarisWorks, 422, 573, 579-580

class libraries, 1092

Clean Up Window command (Special menu), 72

cleaning up hard disks, 852

Clear Access (Fairfield Software), 951

Clear command (Edit menu), 35

click-dragging items, 59

ClickChange utility, 102

clicking mouse, 19, 22

clickLoc function (HyperCard), 718

ClickPaste (Mainstay), 405

clip art, 382-385
- DrawArt library, 383
- managers, 391-392
- WetPaint (DublClick), 389

clip music, 676

Clipboard, 28-30, 1114

Clipboard editor, 392

clipboards, multiple, 405

Everything You Wanted to Know About the Mac

clock frequency and processor performance, 140

clock speeds, processors, 121

clock utility, 836

clock/parameter RAM chip, 1064

Close box, 1114

close boxes, windows, 71

Close View control panel, 822

Close View utility, 822-824

closed system architecture, 100

closing dialog boxes in PageMaker, 361

Closing the Gap disability technology newsletter, 829

CLV (continuous linear velocity) laser disc format, 773-774

CMYK color scheme, 275

Co:Writer (Don Johnston Developmental Equipment), 820

COBOL programming language, 1097-1098

code, 1114

CODE 252 virus, 884-885

CODE resources, 1084-1087

code segments in resources, 1084

codecs, 785

Cogito puzzle game (Inline Design), 601

Collaborative Electronic Conferencing, 758

Collection window, Double Helix 3.5 (Helix), 524-526

color
  draw programs, 296-297
  schemes, 274-276

Color Age Freedom of Press 3.0.1/Freedom of Press Light, 292

color images, 272-276

color inkjet printers, 245, 248, 320

color inks, 237

color laser printers, 246

Color MacCheese program (Delta Tao), 268

color matching systems, 276-282

color pages, 272-276

Color Picker CDEV, 276

Color Picker dialog box, 46

Color PostScript, 273

color printers, 244-246

color printing, 236-238

color publications, 320

color separations, 278-280, 297

color thermal transfer printers, 219, 245

color video monitors, 768

Color wheel, 1114

color-matching systems, 265

color-separation programs, 321

colored paper in documents, 281-282

Index

ColorFinder program, 60

colors

    paint programs, 261-262

    Pantone Matching System, 238

ColorTag (Letraset), 281

Columbia University, Kermit Distribution Center, 931

Column guides dialog box (PageMaker), 332

Column guides... command, Options menu (PageMaker), 332, 337

columns

    Microsoft Excel, 499

    PageMaker, 333

combining text fields (FileMaker Pro), 571

Command key, 74, 1114

Command window, FoxBASE+/Mac 2.1 (Fox Software), 533

Command-C keys, Copy command, 48

command-clicking, 23, 360

Command-E keys, ejecting floppy disks, 20

Command-hyphen keys, entering current data (FileMaker Pro), 570

Command-P keys, Print command, 49

Command-period keys, Cancel command, 49

Command-Q keys, Quit command, 49

Command-S keys, Save command, 49

Command-Shift key combinations

    Microsoft Excel, 498

    Microsoft Word, 452

    PageMaker, 358

Command-Tab keys, moving through records, 570

Command-V keys, Paste command, 48

Command-X keys, Cut command, 48

Command-Z keys, Undo command, 48

commands, 1114

    Apple menu, 62-63

        About the Finder, 30

        About This Macintosh, 123

        About..., 1110

        Calculator, 34

        Control Panels, 33, 835

        Key Caps, 378

        Note Pad, 34

        Scrapbook, 31

    Application menu, 69

    AT, 1111

    Balloon Help menu, 68-69

    Chart menu, Add/Delete Legend (Microsoft Excel), 492

Everything You Wanted to Know About the Mac

Document menu, Insert Table (Microsoft Word 4), 438

Edit menu, 28-30, 65-66

   Clear, 35

   Commands… (Microsoft Word 4), 452

   Copy, 29, 379

   Create Publisher, 36

   Cut, 379

   Duplicate, 82

   Fill Down/Fill Right (Microsoft Excel), 500

   New Layout (FileMaker Pro), 555

   New Record (FileMaker Pro), 543

   Paste, 29, 379

   Preferences… (Microsoft Word 4), 439

   Preferences (PageMaker), 329

   Repeat (Microsoft Excel), 500

   Replace (FileMaker Pro), 554

   Select All (FileMaker Pro), 558

   "Subscribe To…", 36

File menu, 63-65

   Eject, 20

   Find…, 52

   Get Info, 34, 60, 386

   Make Alias, 38

   New (Microsoft Excel/Word), 448

   New… (FileMaker Pro), 549

   New… (PageMaker), 332

   Open… (Microsoft Word), 454

   Page Setup, 204

   Page Setup (FileMaker Pro), 556

   Print, 204

   Print Merge… (Microsoft Word), 450

   Print Preview… (Microsoft Word), 453

   Quit, 21, 29

   Relookup (FileMaker Pro), 553

   Sharing, 60

Finder menu, 56

Format menu (Microsoft Excel/Word)

   Alignment, 480

   Border…, 441-443

   Change Case…, 455

   Character, 444

   Font, 480

   Number, 483-485

   Patterns, 482

   Show Ruler, 434, 441

   Style, 485

Index

Style..., 435

Styles, 479, 482

Table..., 440

Gallery menu (Microsoft Excel)

 3-D Pie, 492

 Bar, 492

 Pie, 490

Insert menu, Table... (Microsoft Word), 438, 448

Label menu, 66

MultiFinder menu, About The Finder, 123

Options menu, Workspace (Microsoft Excel), 478

Options menu, Column guides... (PageMaker), 332, 337

Page menu (PageMaker)

 Actual size, 333

 Fit in window, 335

 Insert pages..., 336

Select menu (FileMaker Pro)

 Define Fields, 546

 Layout, 555

Special menu, 67-68

 Clean Up Window, 72

 Empty Trash, 57

 Selection, 72

 Set Startup..., 30, 44

 Shut Down, 21, 25, 1127

Tools menu (Microsoft Word)

 Commands..., 452

 Preferences..., 439

View menu, 66

Window menu (Microsoft Excel)

 Old way chart, 490

 Zoom, 505

Commands dialog box, Microsoft Word, 452

Comment (Deneba Software), 427

commercial classes in programming, 1106

commercial stacks from Heizer Software, 702

Communication Board Builder (Mayer-Johnson), 828

communications module, Microsoft Works, 576

communications programs

 America Online, 908

 FreeTerm, 909

 Microphone II, 907

 Prodigy, 908

 White Knight, 908

 ZTerm, 909

Communications Toolbox (Apple), 194

Comp-u-store, America Online/Delphi, 921

compact Macs, 146-152

compacting programs, file transfers, 934

CompactPro compression utility, 934-936

comparisons of desktop publishing programs, 321-325

compatibility problems with software, 1073

compilers, 694, 1087-1088, 1114

component video signals, 770

components of spreadsheets, 459-463

composite video signals, 769

compound documents, 1022, 1031-1032

compressed digital video, 783

compressing

  audio, 655-657

  files, 935-936, 1031

compression algorithms, 783-784

Compression pop-up menu (HyperCard), 730-731

compression utilities

  CompactPro, 934

  DiskDoubler, 935

  Stuffit/Stuffit Deluxe/Stuffit Lite, 934

Compu-Teach

  Once Upon a Time series, 627

  See the U.S.A., 629

CompuServe, 1114

  AP Online news, 917

  CB Simulator, 924

  email, 917

  Electronic Mail, 921

  faxes/messages, 916

  features, 937

  financial information, 922

  interactive games, 929

  Internet connections, 916

  message boards, 923

  Navigator file transfer, 937, 1008

  shareware games, 611

  weather reports, 918

CompuServe Information Manager, 937

Computer Friends

  AutoSwitch, 232

  MacInker, 213

computer games, 588-590

computer interface ports on laser disc players, 774

computer simulation games, 603-610

computer viruses, 870-872

ComputerEyes digitizer, 263

ComputerVideo NTSC converter box, 781

Index

ConcertWare (Great Wave), 647, 678

concordances, word processors, 409

conference areas/rooms

    Delphi, 925

    forums, 923

configuring multimedia systems, 795-797

connectivity of Macs and PCs, 1003

Connectix

    Maxima, 129, 132

    MODE32 software, 187

    Virtual, 132

Connector tool in illustration programs, 294

ConnExperts, Versadapter, 233

Consumer Reports on online services, 922

containers, HyperCard data, 740-742

content, sound used to convey, 787

context-sensitive help, Microsoft Word, 416

continuous tone images, 273-274

Control key, 74, 1114

Control Panels, 85-87, 1114

control panels, 45-48, 822, 835-836

Control Panels command (Apple menu), 33, 835

Control Panels folder (System 7), 45, 79, 835

controlling PCs, 1013-1016

controlling sound, 658-667

conversion boxes, video, 780

convolution, video, 782

coordinates, drawing in HyperCard, 717-719

Copernicus, Fidonet network protocol, 941

coprocessors, 121-122, 137, 143-144

Copy command (Edit menu), 29, 379

Copy II Mac program, 859

copy protection, computer games, 602

copying

    documents, 28-30

    Scrapbook images, 29-34

copyright laws and multimedia, 800

cordless stylus and graphics tablets, 256

Corner tool in illustration programs, 293

corporate users of databases, 523-524

Correct Grammar (LifeTree Software), 427

covids, 780

cps (characters per second), 202

.CPT extensions, CompactPro files, 934

CPUs (Central Processing Units), *see* processors

crashing, 1114

Create (KE:nx), 815

Create Publisher command (Edit menu), 36

creator codes, files, 114

cropping tool, 304

cross-networking with other platforms and Macintosh, 983-992

cross-platforming, 1115

cross-referencing in documents, 409

CRT (Cathode Ray Tube), 1115

Cue scoring program (Opcode), 684

cursors, 56, 1115

Curve tool, illustration programs, 293

custom colors in draw programs, 296

custom fonts, Fontographer (Altsys), 393-395

customizing HyperCard stacks, 733-742

Cut command (Edit menu), 379

cylinders of tracks, hard disks, 189

D

DA Handler program, 91

DA-Animaq card (DiaQuest), 771

daisy chaining
   ADB devices, 133
   networks
      Ethernet, 994-995
      LocalTalk, 993-994
   SCSI devices, 134

daisywheel printers, 202

DAL (Data Access Language) servers, 951, 986

Dark Castle battle game (Aldus/Silicon Beach), 593

Darwin's Dilemma puzzle game (Inline Design), 600

DAs (desk accessories), 40, 90-91, 1115
   Find File (Apple), 854
   WordWriter (MacIntyre), 819

DAT drives, multimedia storage, 798

Data Access Manager, System 7, 757

data bridges, Mac/PC interaction, 1003-1006

data documents, print merge problems, 451

data entry, morse code switches, 816

Index

data entry, automatic in FileMaker Pro, 545-565

data forks, files, 111, 932, 1022

data in programs, 1083

data input, 816

data lines
  and memory, 183
  and processors, 141

Data Spec MacSwitch, 232

database files, 1025

database module, Microsoft Works, 576

database spreadsheets, 462-463

databases, 507-511, 1115
  Auto Enter Values (FileMaker Pro), 545-548
  building, 514-518
  data validation, 519-520
  Double Helix 3.5 (Helix), 524-526
  FileMaker Pro management, 540-541
  flat file, 511-512
  modules, 514-515
  multisystem, 515
  multiuser, 515
  program review, 524-537
  relational, 512-513, 1125
  sharing on networks (FileMaker Pro), 566-569
  test kits, 520-521

Datadesk Switchboard keyboard, 76

Dataviz
  MacLinkPlus, 1005, 1026-1029
  MacLinkPlus/Translators, 413

date and time functions, spreadsheets, 460

Davidson
  Alge-Blaster Plus, 626
  Math Blaster Mystery/Math Blaster Plus programs, 624
  Personal Trainer for the SAT, 636

Dayna Communications
  DaynaFile II floppy disk drives, 1004
  DOS Mounter, 1004
  EtherPrint, 973

Daystar Digital cache cards, 184

DB-15S sockets, external video connectors, 177

DB-25 connectors, SCSI devices, 134

DB-9 connectors, modems, 904

DCA (Document Content Architecture)
  text interchange format, 1023
  IRMA Workstation for Macintosh emulators, 991

DDE (Dynamic Data Exchange), 96

Debugger V2 development system, 1104

debugging programs, 1088, 1115

DEC (Digital Equipment Corp.)
- networking Vax/Macintosh, 989-991
- PATHWORKS for Macintosh, 990
- VT modes, 911

DECnet for Macintosh (Digital), 953

decompressing files with CompactPro, 935

DECwindows (DEC), 987

Default button, 1115

defaults, 1115
- field formats (FileMaker Pro), 570
- PageMaker, 361
- userLevels, 699
- worksheets (Microsoft Excel), 498
- zone assignments on networks, 964

Define Fields command (Select menu), FileMaker Pro, 546

defining
- buttons in FileMaker Pro, 564
- lookups in Lookup feature, FileMaker Pro, 550-551

defragmenting files on hard disks, 860-864, 1115

Delete key, 75, 1115

Delete Legend command, Chart menu, (Microsoft Excel), 492

deleting files from hard disks, 852

Delphi
- Comp-u-store, 921
- conference rooms, 925
- Dictionary of Cultural Literacy, 922
- EasyLink E-mail, 917
- features, 938
- financial information, 922
- interactive games, 929
- Internet connections, 916
- mail options, 917
- Merchant's Row, 921
- message boards, 923
- news service, 918

Delta Tao Software
- Color MacCheese, 268
- Strategic Conquest battle game, 592

DeltaPoint
- DeltaGraph, 420, 464
- DeltaGraph Pro, 461
- Taste, 412

Deluxe Music Construction Set (Electronic Arts), 677

demo packages, databases, 520-521

Index

Deneba Software
- Canvas, 269
- Comment, 427

DeRez development system, 1103

DeskPaint program, 257, 270

DeskPicture (NOW Utilities), 58, 102

Desktop, 18, 45-46, 56-58, 174, 1115
- rebuilding, 114, 865
- reconstructing, 22, 113
- removing
  - Bernoullis, 21
  - CD-ROMs, 21
  - floppy disks, 20
  - SyQuest disks, 21

Desktop bus, 1115

Desktop Manager, 113

Desktop Pattern area, General Controls panel, 45-46

desktop printing, 202-203

desktop publishing, 13, 300-321

desktop publishing programs, 303, 321-325
- Aldus PageMaker, 301, 328-329
- editing text, 315-318
- graphics, 311-313
- importing style sheets, 313
- MacWrite, 300
- master pages, 310
- page set-up, 309-311
- Personal Press, 305, 311
- printing terms, 306-309
- Publish It! Easy, 306
- QuarkXPress, 311
- reformatting text, 314
- RSG (ReadySetGo), 306
- terminology, 306

Developer Technical Support (DTS) Sample Code disk (Apple), 1105

developer's associations, teaching programming, 1107-1108

diagnostic utilities, automated, 1078-1079

Diamonds game (Varcon), 611

DiaQuest DA-Animaq card, 771

dictionaries, foreign language, 428

Dictionary of Cultural Literacy, Delphi, 922

DIF (Data Interchange Format) file interchange formats, 1025

differently abled persons and Macs, 810-811

DigiDesign
- AudioMedia board, 788
- Q-Sheet program, 684
- Sound Tools, 667

Everything You Wanted to Know About the Mac

Digital DECnet for Macintosh program, 953

digital, 1115

Digital Darkroom (Silicon Beach), 264

Digital Eclipse, Zounds, 616

digital electronic signals, 899

digital signal processors, Motorola 56001, 122

digital video, 750, 767, 783-786

Digital VT terminals, 950

digitized sounds, 787

digitized speech synthesizers, 815

digitizers, 263, 775-776, 1116

digitizing programs, 645, 649

dimmed, 1116

DIP (dual inline pin) memory chips, 184

DIP shunts, SCSI addresses, 1077

direct connect modems, 901

Director (Macromedia), 756, 766

directories, 1116

directory files, 110

disabled persons, *see* differently abled persons

Disinfectant program (John Norstad), 611, 872, 887-888

disk doctor utilities, 838

Disk Express II program, 111

Disk First Aid utility, 106

disk icons, 56

disk management utilities, 848, 866

DiskDoubler (Fifth Generation), 1031

DiskDoubler compression utility, 935

DiskLight (Norton Utilities), 135

DiskTool program, 115

DiskTop DA (CE Software), 115, 1021

Display Card 8•24, 179

Display PostScript language, 371

distorted type, 290

dithering, 219, 1116

Diva CameraMan/VideoFusion/ VideoShop programs, 806

DJN/R (Dow Jones News/ Retrieval) financial service, 922

DocuComp (Advanced Software), 428

documents, 23

    character formatting, 405

    color, 281-282

    colored paper, 281-282

    compound, 1031-1032

    copying, 28-30

    cross-referencing, 409

    data, print merge problems, 451

    formatting, 406

    graphics layers, 411

Index

layout tools, rulers, 406

line spacing, 406

Microsoft Word

    Insert Table command (Document menu), 438

    Print Merge feature, 446-447

outlining, 409

PageMaker

    graphics, 345

    pages, 336

    Scrapbook, 350-353

    text, 341-345

paragraph margins, 406

pasting, 28-30

print merging, 447-450

printing, 320-321

printing from other programs in HyperCard, 726

scaling, printer drivers, 220

tables, 409

text layers, 411

viewing with two windows, 454

doMenu command in HyperCard scripts, 722-723

Don Johnston Developmental Equipment

    Co:Writer, 820

    Ke:nx keyboards, 814

    Ke:nx On:Board keyboards, 815

    Write:OutLoud, 826

Doppler effect and sound, 662

DOS (Disk Operating System), 1116

DOS Mounter (Dayna Communications), 115, 842, 1004

DosTOPS program (Sitka), 1010

dot matrix printers, 202, 211-213, 239, 1116

Double Helix 3.5 (Helix), 524-526

double-clicking, 22

    mouse, 20

    selecting tools (FileMaker Pro), 570

    words in PageMaker, 364

Dove Computer

    MaraThon Multi-Comm NuBus card, 233

    DoveFAX+, 247, 667

downloadable fonts, 1116

downloading, 1116

    files, 932-934

    fonts, 225-228

    programs from libraries, 930-932

dpi (dots per inch), 202, 252, 1116

Draft mode, ImageWriter, 222

draft output, printing, 202
Draft quality, 1116
Drag and Drop feature, Microsoft Excel, 503-504
dragging, 22
   mouse, 19
   sounds onto System file, 93
   to paint in HyperCard, 719-722
draw programs, 283-291
   color, 296-297
   graphics handles, 284-287
   illustration, 291-298
   point handles, 294
   type effects, 289-290
DrawArt clip art libraries, 383
drawing
   HyperCard, 717-723
   with mouse, 255-260
drawing module
   GreatWorks (Symantec), 578
   Microsoft Works, 576
drawing programs, MacPaint, 300
Drive 1200 floppy disk drives (Kennect Technologies), 1005
Drive 2.4 floppy disk drives (Kennect Technologies), 1005
drive controller board terminators, 1066

drivers, 193, 1116
DSPs (digital signal processors), 94
dual mode, PowerBook 160/180, 170
dual-ported video RAM, Mac LC, 157
DublClick WetPaint, 383, 389
dummy arguments in scripts (HyperCard), 721
Duo Dock, PowerBook Duos, 171
Duo Floppy Adapter, PowerBook Duos, 171
Duo Minidock, PowerBook Duos, 171
duotones, 280-281
duplex mode protocols, modems, 906
Duplicate command (Edit menu), 82
durability of printers, 235
DVI (Digital Video Interactive, Intel/IBM), 785
Dyaxis (Studer), 667
dynamic addressing, AppleTalk network nodes, 959-961
dynamic bus sizing, Mac LC, 158
dynamic RAM, 123

E

EAASY SABRE online travel service, 919

Eastgate Fontina, 378

Easy Access utilities, 848
- Close View utility, 822
- Mouse Keys (numeric keypad substitution for mouse), 812
- Sticky Keys (special typing needs), 811

Easy Color Paint program (MECC), 268

Easy Transfer Cartridges, t-shirt transfers, 216

EasyLink E-mail, Delphi online service, 917

EasyOpen (Apple), 413

EasyVideo 8 (Mass Microsystems), 780

echoes in sound, 663-664

Eco-Adventures program, 635

Ecosys laser printer (Kyocera), 214

Edit menu commands, 28-30, 65-66
- Clear, 35
- Copy, 29, 379
- Create Publisher, 36
- Cut, 379
- Duplicate, 82

FileMaker Pro program
- New Layout, 555
- New Record, 543
- Replace, 554
- Select All, 558

Microsoft Excel program
- Fill Down, 500
- Fill Right, 500
- Repeat, 500

Microsoft Word 4
- Commands…, 452
- Preferences…, 439

PageMaker program
- Preferences, 329

Paste, 29, 379

Subscribe To…, 36

editing
- sound, 649-667, 728-731
- text
  - desktop publishing programs, 315-318
  - word processors, 403-405

Edition file, 37

editor (SuperCard), 745-746

educational programs, 618-632
- early grades, 621-623
- high school and higher, 633-637

Eject command (File menu), 20

Index

Everything You Wanted to Know About the Mac

ElectroHome projector, 756

Electronic Arts, Deluxe Music Construction Set, 677

electronic clip art, *see* clip art

electronic cropping, 304

electronic halftones, 274

electronic magnifying glasses, 822-824

Electronic Mall, CompuServe, 921

electronic pasteboard, PageMaker, 328

electronic shopping, 920-921

electronic signals, 899

electronic white-out, 313

email, 916-917, 951-952, 1018-1020, 1116

EMBARC (Motorola), 981

emergency startup disks, 106

Empty Trash command (Special menu), 57

emulators, 211

Enabling Technology, Romeo Brailler printer, 827

End key, 75

Engelbart, Douglas
    graphical user interface development, 749
    mouse father, 73

enlarging
    monitors, 824
    screen views for ease of reading, 821-822

enquiry control packets, AppleTalk node addresses, 960

Enter key, 75

envelope of sound, 649

envelope printers, 246-247

environmental control devices, 821

EPS (Encapsulated PostScript), 282, 382, 1116
    files, 1025
    graphics format, 292
    images, 384

equalizing sound, 662-663

equation editor, Ventura Publisher, 324

ER3S lithium batteries, 1064

Eradicat'Em 1.0 program, 888

ergonomics of keyboards, 76

errors
    codes
        explanations, 1055
        for Mac Portables, 1061-1062
        for Mac SEs, 1058
        for programs, 1057-1058
        Power Manager (PowerBooks), 1062-1063
        Sad Mac, 1055
    hardware, 1063
    RAM, 1056-1057
    ROM, 1056

Index

Esc (Escape) key, 75
EtherNet
  cards, PC/AppleTalk compatibility, 972, 1010
  connectivity for Mac, 233
  fiber-optic, 974
  networking, 972-977, 1011
    daisy-chain, 994-995
    FDDI WAN, 998
    multiple FDDI backbone; 997
    multiple routed backbone/star, 997
    star, 995-996
  Thickwire, 974
  Thinwire, 975
  twisted-pair, 976
  wireless, Altair II (Motorola), 981
EtherPrint (Dayna), 973
EtherTalk (Apple), 956-957, 972
etiquette for online services, 926-927
evaluating
  integrated software, 575-582
  word processors, 415-422
Event Manager program, 102
event-driven programming, 103
Eveready Energizer 523 battery, 1064
Excel program (Microsoft), 458

expanded keyboards for limited movement typing, 814
expanding toolbox utilities, 839-849
expansion board, 1116
Expert Color Paint program (SoftSync), 268
exporting files, 412-413
Expression Builder, FoxBASE+/Mac 2.1 (Fox Software), 533
extended keyboards, 75
extended keyboards and ADB, 194
Extended Systems
  BridgePort, 234
  JetWriter, 235
extensions, 1116
  C++ programming language, 1094-1095
  conflicts, 88
  management utilities, 840-841
  mapping, 115
  mapping in file translation, 1025-1030
  start-up order, 87-88
Extensions folder, System 7 folder, 79
Extensions Manager freeware (Ricardo Bautista), 88, 841
extensions managers, Now Utilities, 841

External Commands, *see* XCMDs

external email systems, 1020

External Functions, *see* XFCNs

external hard drives
  rebooting, 1077
  SCSI port problems, 1065
  terminators, 1066-1067

External Kit program, 4th Dimension (ACIUS), 529

external pocket modems, PowerBooks, 172

external ports, PowerBook 100, 168

external systems of email, 1018

external video connectors, 177-178

F

Faces puzzle game (Spectrum), 599

failures in memory, 187-188

Fairfield Software, Clear Access program, 951

Farallon
  MacRecorder, 92, 789, 1121
  PhoneNET LocalTalk connectors, 970
  PhoneNET PC, Mac/PC networks, 983
  PhoneNet PC II Network Interface Card, 1010
  StarController LocalTalk repeater, 971

fast spindle hard drives, 190

Faster mode, ImageWriter, 222

fax modems, 247-248, 901-903

faxes, 916, 1117

FDDI (Fiber Data Distributed Interface)
  cabling systems, 977
  networking, 979-980
    backbone, 997
    WAN, 998

FDHD SuperDrive floppy disk drives, 1003

features of word processors, 402-403

Ferret 1.1 program, 888

fiber-optic Ethernet, 974

Fidonet network, 941

fields, 1117
  Calculation, 543
  databases, 509-510, 541
    attributes, 516
    entry filters, 516-517
    entry formats, 516
    field types, 516, 542-543
  format defaults, (FileMaker Pro), 570
  in stacks, 735-736

Fifth Generation Systems
  DiskDoubler, 1031

Index

Suitcase II program, 81

SuperLaserSpool print spooler, 224, 845

SuperSpool print spooler, 845

file compression, 1031

file extensions, 934

FILE FORCE (ACIUS), 529-530

file format translators, 412-413

file formats, 115, 1022-1025
    ARC (PCs), 1031
    bitmapped, 763
    cross platform compatibility, 412
    graphics, 262, 1024-1025
    Macintosh networking, 952-953
    PICT, 262
    sound, 666
    text, 1022-1023
    TIFF, 262
    vector-mapped, 763
    ZIP (PCs), 1031

file launchers, 854

File Manager, 112

File menu commands, 63-65
    Eject, 20
    FileMaker Pro program
        New…, 549
        Page Setup, 556
        Relookup, 553

    Find…, 52
    Get Info, 34, 60, 386
    Make Alias, 38
    Microsoft Excel program
        New, 448, 488
        Open…, 454
    Microsoft Word program
        Print Merge…, 450
        Print Preview…, 453
    Page Setup, 204
    PageMaker program, New…, 332
    Print, 204
    Quit, 21, 29
    Sharing, 60

file output layouts in databases, 511

file procedures, 517

file servers, VAXshare, 989

File System program, 102

file transfers
    accessing CompuServe with Navigator, 1008
    with floppy disks, 1003-1005
    with modems, 1007-1008

file translation, 1020-1030

file types, 115

file type flags, 80

FileMaker icons, 541

FileMaker Pro (Claris), 530-532, 539-572

automatic data entry, 545-565

databases

    management, 540-541

    sharing on networks, 566-569

  Lookup feature, 549-553

  shortcuts, 570-572

FileMaster program, 115

files, 111-114, 1117

  AppDisk swap, 130

  ASCII, 1111

  attributes, 112, 116-117

  CGM, 1024

  changing location to optimize disks, 864

  clip art, 383

  compressing/decompressing with CompactPro, 935-936

  data forks, 932, 1022

  databases, 509, 1025

  deleting from hard disks, 852

  Desktop, 113, 865

  directory, 110

  downloading, 932-934

  Edition, 37

  EPS, 1025

  exporting, 412-413

  forks, 111

  fragmented, 111, 863

  importing, 412-413

  interchange formats, 115

  Mac/PC differences, 1020-1022

  name extensions (PCs), 1021

  PICS, 1025

  PICT, 1024, 1123

  PNTG, 1024

  PostScript, 320

  printer driver, 209

  problems, spotting with ResEdit program, 1074

  program, 1088

  Read Me, 1125

  resource forks, 1021

  sampled music, 645

  sound, 788

  spreadsheet, 1025

  stationery, 407

  Suitcase, 81-82

  System, 1128

  System 7, 82

  System Enabler, 83-84, 106

  temporary resource, 1086

  text, 313, 1128

  TIFF, 1024

  transferring

    Apple File Exchange, 1025-1027

    serial ports, 1027

Index

translating
   Apple File Exchange, 1025-1027
   Claris XTND system, 1029-1030
uploading, 932-934
WMF, 1024

FileSharing, 948

FileStar program, 115

Fill Down command (Edit menu), Microsoft Excel, 500

Fill Right command (Edit menu), Microsoft Excel, 500

filling shapes, 287-289

FilmMaker, 805

filters
   field entries in databases, 516-517
   MIDI, 673

financial functions, spreadsheets, 460

financial services on online services, 922

Find feature, 52-54

Find File DA, 52, 854

Find... command (File menu), 52

Finder, 27, 1117
   Desktop, 56
   keyboard shortcuts, 50-52
   reading PC floppy disks, 1004
   System 6, 18

Finder flags, 115

Finder menu commands, 56

Finder windows, 70-72

firmware, *see* ROM

FirstClass BBS program, 941

Fisher Idea Systems, IdeaFisher word processor, 426

Fit in window command, Page menu (PageMaker), 335

Fitzpatrick, John, Insanity program, 614

FKey Manager/Mover shareware, 89, 115

Fkeys programs, 89-90, 1117

flanging sound, 663

flat file databases, 511-512

FlexShields keyboard covers, 815

Flight Simulator, 604

flipped type, 290

floating point calculations, 121

floppy disks, 20-21, 1117
   drives
      DaynaFile II (Dayna Communications), 1004
      Drive 1200 (Kennect Technologies), 1005
      SuperDrive 1.44M, 149, 153
   file transfers, 1003-1005
   icons, 20
   removing from desktop, 20
   System Tools, 1076

flopticals and multimedia storage, 798

Focaltone color-matching systems, 265

Fokker Triplane battle game (Bulleye), 591

folders, 23, 1117

Foley effects re-recording, 644

Font command, Format menu (Microsoft Excel), 480

font ID conflicts, 1117

font listings, 377-378

Font Manager program, 102, 375

font managers, 393-396

font resources, 118

font utilities, 377, 390-397, 846-847, 1117

Font/DA Juggler font utility, 377, 395, 837

Font/DA Mover utility, 41, 80, 1083-1084, 1117

Fontina (Eastgate), 378, 396

Fontographer (Altsys), 393-395

fonts, 308, 366-371, 1117
   Adobe
      ATM (Adobe Type Manager), 213
      Sonata laser, 685
      Type 1/Type 3, 206
   Amslan, 828
   changing in charts, 494
   creating original, 393-395
   custom (Fontographer), 393-395
   downloading, 225-228, 1116
   ID numbers, 376-377
   laser, 1120
   multiple master, 373, 379
   outline, 1122
   PostScript, 227, 369-371, 395, 1123
   problems, 376-379
   QuickDraw printers, 226-227
   rasterizers, 375
   resolution, 371-373
   screen, 1126
   styles, 1127
   substitution, 373
   TrueImage printers, 228
   TrueType, 213, 373-375, 1128

Fonts folder, System 7 folder, 79

FontStudio 2.0 (Letraset), 394

Fool's Errand puzzle game (Cliff Johnson), 601

footers, 310, 406

footprint, 1117

foreign language dictionaries, 428

foreign language programs, 633

forks of files, 111, 1117

Format 1/Format 2 sound resources, 93

Index

Format menu commands
  Microsoft Excel
    Alignment, 480
    Font, 480
    Number, 483-485
    Patterns, 482
    Styles, 479, 482, 485
  Microsoft Word
    Border..., 441-443
    Change Case..., 455
    Character, 444
    Show Ruler, 434, 441
    Style..., 435
    Table..., 440
formats, 1117
formatting
  characters, 406
  charts, 493-498
  documents, 406
  storing as Styles, 479-487
  volumes, 109
  word processors, 405-406
FormsProgrammer (Ohm Software), 743-744
FORTH programming language, 1098
FORTRAN programming language, 1098
forums on online services, 922-924

four-color printing, *see* full color printing
Fourier analysis of sound, 648
Fox Software, FoxBASE+/Mac 2.1, 532-535
Fractal Design Painter, 271-272
fragmentation of files, 111, 863
frame differencing algorithms, video, 785
frame grabbing, 776
Freedom of Press 3.0.1 (Color Age), 292
  emulator, 211
  print spooler, 846
Freedom of Press Light (Color Age), 292, 846
FreeHand (Aldus), 291, 297-298
FreeSoft, White Knight on the Mac, 1006-1008
FreeTerm communications program (Bill Bond), 909
freeware, 930, 1117
  ASL FingerSpelling Tutor (Tony Martin), 827
  Extensions Manager (Ricardo Bautista), 88
  MacArc file compression, 1031
  RAM disk utilities, 840
  ResEdit, 120
  System Picker utility, 78
  UnZip file compression, 1031

Freewheel head-controlled mouse (Pointer Systems), 817

frequency of sound, 646-648, 654-655

Fresnel lens, magnifying screen view, 822

front-ends, spreadsheets, 471

FTP (File Transfer Protocol), 986-987

full color printing, 321

Full Impact 2.0 program (Ashton-Tate), 458

FullPaint program (Ashton-Tate), 254

Fun Physics program (Knowledge Revolution), 635

function keys, 75

functioning of AppleTalk, 954-956

FWB driver programs, 191

G

Galaxy patch librarian (Opcode), 683-684

Galbreath, Garry, Wave Maker program, 647

Gallery menu commands, Microsoft Excel, 490-492

GAMER Project, 612

games, 588-590

   adventure, 594-597

   battle, 591-594

   interactive, 927-929

   mathematics, 624

   puzzles, 597-603

   shareware, 610-611

   tools for learning, 612-613

Garamond Bold typeface, 366

Gatekeeper 1.2.1 program, 872, 888

Gatekeeper Aid 1.2.1 program, 889

Gateway, 1118

gateways for networks, 900, 1012

GDT SoftWorks

   JetLink Express, 194, 213, 234, 1017

   PrintLink Collection, 233

General Computer Corporation, HyperDrive hard drive, 152

General Control Panel DA, 128

General Controls panel, 45-46

General MIDI Sound Modules, 676

GEnie, 938

   DJN/R, 922

   electronic shopping, 921

   email, 917

   interactive games, 928

Index

message boards, 923

online service call script, 912

Schwab Discount Brokerage service, 922

software updates, 1038

geography programs, 628-632

Georgia Pacific laser printer paper, 236

Gerasimov, Vadim, Tetris puzzle game, 598

Get Info command (File menu), 34, 60, 386

Get Info window, System 7, 386

Glider flight simulator (Casady & Greene), 605

global procedures, 517

global variables in HyperCard stacks, 741-742

Global Village TelePort modems, 194, 904

glossaries, 404

Go menu, HyperCard, 708

Gofer (Microlytic), 411

gradients, 288

grammar checkers, 318, 405, 421, 427

Grammatik Mac (Reference Software), 421, 427

graphic equalizers, 662

graphics, 410-411
  3-D, 764
  America Online graphics library, 383
  ASCII, 1111
  file formats, 262, 763, 1024-1025
  handles, 284-287
  importing, 311
  in desktop publishing programs, 312-313
  KidPix program, 619-621
  layers in documents, 411
  modules in databases, 515
  object-oriented, 282-283, 411
  PageMaker program
    adding to master pages, 335
    placing in documents, 345
    threading automatically, 316
  resizing, 311
  resolution, 262-266
  SuperCard, 745

graphics tablet (Wacom), 256

graphics terminals (Tektronix), 950

graphing/charting spreadsheets, 461

Grappler 9-pin interface (Orange Micro), 213, 233

1167

Everything You Wanted to Know About the Mac

Grappler LX (Orange Micro), 234

grayscale scanners, 264

grayscale monitors, 263-266

grayscales in paint programs, 261-262

Great Wave ConcertWare/ConcertWare Pro, 647, 678

GreatWorks (Symantec), 422, 577-578

greeking in placeholder templates, 318

greeking text, 329

GREP functions
  Global Regular Expression Parser, 411
  Nisus Professional, 418

grid templates, 319, 386

grids in draw programs, 291

Grolier Encyclopedia, online services, 922

Group III compatibility, fax modems, 902, 1118

GUIs (Graphic User Interfaces), 3, 11, 749, 1118

gutters, 306

H

Hackers, 1118

half duplex protocols, modems, 907

halftone images, 274

halftones, electronic, 274

Hall, Steve, The Talking Moose, 613

Hammermill printer paper, 236

handicapped persons, *see* differently abled persons

handles
  graphics in draw programs, 284-287
  levers/points in draw programs, 294

handshaking, modems, 906

Happy Mac neckties, 1044

Hard Disk Toolkit utilities, 866

hard disks, 20-21, 188, 852, 1118
  arrays, multimedia storage, 799
  backups, 853, 857-859
  bad blocks, 1071
  booting sequence, 190
  burst transfer rate, 190
  cleaning up, 852
  defragmenting files, 862-864
  deleting files, 852
  icons, 20
  interleave factor of tracks, 191, 860-861
  management, 852-853
  master backups, 858
  optimizing, 859-865

Index

organization utilities, 854-855

organizing, 853-857

partitioning, 855-857, 865

rotational delay, 860

sustained transfer rate, 190

tracks, 189

transfer rate, 190

hard drives, 20-21, 188, 1017-1018

   external, 1065, 1077

   fast spindle, 190

   HyperDrive (General Computer Corporation), 152

   internal, 1077

   multimedia storage, 799

   parking heads, 1071

   performance, 190-191

   problems, 1069-1071

   repairing, 1071

   SCSI port connections, 189

   spindle motor failure, 1070

   Widget, Lisa PC, 145

hard partitions on hard disks, 855

hardware, 24, 1118

   errors indicated by short musical chords, 1063

   overview listing, 180-182

   problems, 1054

Hayes command sets, 901, 912, 1118

Hayes-compatible modems, 901

HD SC Setup program (Apple), 191

head-controlled mouse, 817

headers, 310, 406

headlines, 316

headpointers, 813

HeapTool (CE Software), 126

hearing screen information with outSPOKEN program, 825-826

hearing-impaired Mac users, 827-828

Heizer Software

   commercial stacks, 702

   macros/scripts for spreadsheet programs, 462

   spreadsheet templates, 473

Helix VMX Double Helix 3.5 (Helix), 525-526

help, context-sensitive (Microsoft Word), 416

Help key, 75

Help! utility (Teknosys Inc.), 1078

Hewlett Packard

   Kitty Hawk hard drives, 188

   LaserJet printers, 233-235, 1017

   Page Composition Language (PCL) PDL, 207

   RET (Resolution Enhancement Technology), 207

hex editors, 112

Everything You Wanted to Know About the Mac

HFS (Hierarchical File System), 56, 1118

Hi8mm video tape formats, 770

high-level languages, 1089

high-resolution laser printers, 244

high-resolution printers, 243-244

high-resolution video cameras, 772

high-speed video, Quadra 700, 160

highlighting, 1118

history of Apple Computer, 4-15

Hitchhiker's Guide to the Galaxy (Activision), 594

HMG ResEdit Primer v. 6.0, 120

Home & School Mac disk magazine, shareware, 612

Home key, 75

home stacks in scripts, HyperCard, 701

Hosiden active matrix liquid crystal panels, 167

host computers and modem calls, 910

hosts, 1118

Howtek PixelMaster Braille printer, 827

HP550C color inkjet printers, 320

HPGL (Hewlett-Packard Graphic Language) plotter language standard, 247

HSB color scheme, 275

Hunt the Wumpus game, 589

Hunt the Wumpus shareware maze, 597

HyperCard, 690-696, 755, 760, 803, 1118
  animation, 733, 765
  Audio Palette, 651
  compiler, 694
  containers, 740-742
  differences from hypertext, 692
  drawing, 717-723
  Go menu, 708
  interpreter, 693-694
  melodies, 732
  multimedia engines, 759
  Navigator palette (Version 2.0), 709-710
  painting tools, 712-723
  playing sound, 731-732
  printing from, 723-728
  saving stacks, 697-698
  sound, 728-732
  userLevels, 699
  versions, 694-696
  workarounds, 706-707

HyperCard Player (Claris Corp.), 693, 755

HyperCard Toolkit Stack (RasterOps), 777

Index

HyperDrive hard drive (General Computer Corporation), 152

Hyperglot program, 633

hypermedia, 750, 754

HyperScript scripting language, Wingz program, 466

HyperTalk, 1119
   commands, 731
      programming language, 1100

hypertext, 692, 750, 754

I

I-beam cursors, 60

I-beam pointers, 1119

I/O (Input/Output), 1119

I/O buses, 133

IAC (Interapplication Communications), 96-97

IBM Corporation
   3270 terminal emulators, 991
   networking with Macintosh, 991-992
   PC emulators, 1014-1016
   PCs, 10
   terminals, 950

ICOM, Sherlock Holmes adventure game, 595

icon resources, 118

Icon template, 60

iconic cues, sound, 786

icons, 4, 60, 1119
   Apple Menu Items alias, 39
   blinking question mark, 1076
   Broken Links, Personal Press, 305
   changing with ResEdit program, 60
   disk, 56
   FileMaker, 541
   Finder, 56
   floppy disk, 20
   hard disk, 20
   HyperCard navigation, 711
   lightning bolt, RSG (ReadySetGo), 306
   Macintosh computer, MultiFinder, 56
   Map, 33
   Microphone II communications program, 908
   Monitors, 263
   MultiFinder, 44
   navigating stacks, 711
   renaming, 60
   Sad Mac, 84, 1054-1057
   Smiling Mac, 18
   Spinning Beachball, 1129
   System 7, 113
   System folder, 80
   Trash Can, 57, 1128
   volumes, 109

Everything You Wanted to Know About the Mac

ID numbers of fonts, 376-377

IdeaFisher (Fisher Idea Systems), 426

IIfx terminators, 1066

illustration programs, 291-298

Illustrator program (Adobe), 291

image compression, 750

image processing programs, 264

ImageBase (Metro), 383

Images With Impact! (3G Graphics), 385

Imagesetters, 320, 1119

ImageWriter dot-matrix printers (Apple), 212, 221-222, 369, 1119

ImageWriter II dot-matrix printer (Apple), 213

importing, 1119

    files, 412-413

    graphics, 311

    style sheets to desktop publishing programs, 313

    text files, 313

In the Holy Land (ABC News Interactive), 790

in-context editing, WordPerfect Works, 581

InCider/A+ magazine, 1039

incremental backups and volume backups, 858

indents, 306

independent SIGs (Special Interest Groups), 1043-1048

indexes, 408-409

Industry Connection section, America Online, 1038

Info-Mac Digest electronic magazine, 1040

INFO-MAC distribution lists (BITNET), 893

InFocus overhead projector panel, 756

information stacks, userLevel four, 734-738

Informix Wingz, 465-466

infrared mice, 73

INIT 17 virus, 886

INIT 1984 virus, 883-884

INIT 29 virus, 876-877

INIT conflicts, 1072-1073, 1119

INIT conflicts, *see* Extension conflicts

INIT managers, 1073

INIT-M virus, 886-887

initialization codes in programs, 1084

initializing volumes, 109, 1119

INITs (initialization programs), 113, 1119

ink cartridge refills for inkjet printers, 217

inkjet printers, 203, 216-218

inks, color, 237

inks, transparent, 237

Index

inLARGE program (Berkeley Systems), 824-825

Inline Design

    3 in 3/Cogito puzzle games, 601

    Darwin's Dilemma puzzle game, 600

    games, 590

    S.C.OUT puzzle game, 601

    Swamp Gas Visits the USA program, 630

    Tesserae puzzle game, 599

    The Tinies puzzle game, 601

Input/Output processors, 122

Insanity program (Bertinelli/Fitzpatrick), 614-615

Insert menu commands, Table... (Microsoft Word), 438, 448

Insert pages... command, Page menu (PageMaker), 336

Insert Table... command, Document menu (Microsoft Word), 438

Insight Development Corporation, MacPrint, 234, 1017

Insignia Solutions

    SoftPC for Windows, 1015

    SoftPC IBM PC emulator, 1014-1016

Insignia Systems, AccessPC, 1004

Inspiration (Ceres Software), 426

Installer utility, 837

    Minimum System script, 106

    program installation, 1073

installing

    modems, 903-905

    RAM, 127-128

instruction cycles, clock speeds, 121

instructions in Mac programs, 140, 1083

integrated media presentations, 799-802

integrated software, 573-584

integration of media, 752

Intel processors, 6

Inter Application Communications (IAC) tools, 424

interactables, multimedia applications, 791-792

interaction of communication in networking, 945-946

interactive

    audio, 790

    control of videotape recorders, 771

    devices, media, 753

    games, 927-929

    information access, 757

    interfaces, 760-761

Interactive Physics program (Knowledge Revolution), 634

Everything You Wanted to Know About the Mac

interchange formats, files, 115

InterCon NFS/Share, 987

interfaces, 1119

    differently abled persons and Macs, 810

    guidelines, 100-101

    MIDI, 670-671, 790

Interferon 3.1 program, 889

interlaced video signal, 767

interleave factor, hard disk tracks, 191, 860-861

interleaved access in RAM, 185-186

interleaved memory architecture, Quadra 800, 165

internal email systems, 1018-1019

internal hard drives, SCSI IDs, 1077

internal video, 172-182

Internet network, 916, 940

Internetwork, AppleTalk networks, 954

Interplay

    BattleChess game, 608

    CheckMate game, 609

interpreters, 693-694, 1090

inTouch (Berkeley Systems), 827

InUse shareware program, 135

IRMA Workstation for Macintosh emulators (DCA), 991

ISDN (Integrated Systems Digital Network), 900, 1119

isolation transformers, 668

J

jaggies, 300, 384, 1120

Jazz program (Lotus), 458

JetLink Express (GDT SoftWorks), 194, 213, 234-235, 845, 1017

Jewelbox (Varcon Systems), 599, 611

Jobs, Steve, 3, 420

Johnson, Cliff, Fool's Errand puzzle game, 601

Journeyman Project adventure game, 595

joysticks, 816

JPEG compression algorithms, 785

Just Grandma and Me program (Mercer Mayer), 619

K

K-AShare (Xinet), Mac/UNIX networks, 985

KaleidaGraph (Synergy Software), 461, 464

Katie's Farm program (Brøderbund), 618

Index

KE:nx program (Don Johnston Developmental Equipment), 814-815

Kennect Technologies floppy disk drives, 1005

Kensington
- PowerPad numeric keypad, 813
- The Printer Muffler, 212
- trackballs, 73

Kermit Distribution Center, Columbia University, 931

Kermit file transfer, 931

kerning, 1120
- automatic, 315
- text, 314
- type in PageMaker, 361-364

Key Caps command (Apple menu), 378

Key Caps DA, 74

Key Caps desk accessory, 378

Key Caps utility, 847

key combinations, 1120

keyboard, 74-76
- commands in Microsoft Excel, 499
- Datadesk Switchboard, 76
- equivalents for menu items, 61
- Ke:nx (Don Johnston Developmental Equipment), 814
- Ke:nx On:Board (Don Johnston Developmental Equipment), 815
- miniature, 815
- onscreen, 817
- operating Mac, 48-54
- plastic coverings, 815
- problems, 1054
- remapping, 61
- shortcuts, 48-52
- tactile click feel, 76
- Unicorn Adaptive, 814
- utilities, 847-848

keyguards for typing, 814

KeyLargo adaptive membrane keyboards, 815

keylatches for typing, 814

KeyMouse utility (University of Utah Computer Center), 817

KidArt program, 621

KidPix Companion program, 621

KidPix program (Brøderbund), 268, 619-621

KillScores 1.0 program, 889

KillVirus program, 889

kilobytes, 1120

King's Quest adventure games (Sierra Online), 595

Kitty Hawk hard drives (Hewlett-Packard), 188

Everything You Wanted to Know About the Mac

Knowledge Revolution
 Fun Physics program, 635
 Interactive Physics program, 634
Kyocera Ecosys laser printer, 214

L

Label menu commands, 66
label printers, 246-247
label templates, 320, 388
Labview program, 757
LaCie driver programs, 191
LANs (Local Area Networks), Ethernet, 972, 1120
LapLink filters, Macintosh PC Exchange, 1028
LapLink serial port accelerators, 1005
LapLink/Mac (Traveling Software), 842, 1005, 1022, 1026-1028
Larger Print Area option, LaserWriters, 221
laser disc formats, 773-774
laser disc players, 772-774
laser fonts, 1120
Laser Plus printer paper (Hammermill), 236
laser printer engines (Canon), 214

laser printers, 203, 213-216, 300, 1120
 high-resolution, 244
 LaserWriter, 300
 printed images, 252
LaserJet 4M printers, Mac/PC compatibility, 233
LaserJet printers (Hewlett-Packard), 233-235, 1017
LaserMaster controllers, 208
LaserStatus (CE Software), 225
LaserWriter 4M (Apple), 215
LaserWriter Font Utility (System 7), 225
LaserWriter printers (Apple), 203, 1016
LaserWriter Pro 630 (Apple), 215, 233
Lau, Raymond, Stuffit compression utility, 934
launching programs, 1120
layout, word processors, 405-406
Layout command (Select menu), FileMaker Pro, 555
Layout Manager, 98
layout procedures, 517
layouts, defaults (FileMaker Pro), 570
leading, 307
Learning Company
 Outnumbered! program, 624
 Talking Math Rabbit program, 622

Index

Talking Reader Rabbit program, 622

The Writing Center program, 627

LED printer engines (Okidata), 214

LED printers, 214

left-hand master pages (PageMaker), 330

LegoLOGO programming language, 632

Leisure Suit Larry adventure game (Sierra Online), 596

Letraset

ColorTag, 281

FontStudio 2.0, 394

ReadySetGo, 322

Levco Monster Mac upgrade, 152

Level 5 compliant twisted-pair wiring, 998

levers of handles in draw programs, 294

libraries

clip art, DrawArt, 383

downloading programs from, 930-932

forums, 923

graphics, America Online, 383

mediated, 757

online services, 930

utilities, 849

Life and Death simulation game (Software Toolworks), 605

LifeGuard program, 639

LifeTree Software, Correct Grammar, 427

ligatures, 98

lightning bolt icon, RSG (ReadySetGo), 306

line spacing, 306, 406

line tool, 304

linked-text objects, 306

linkers, 1087-1088

lint programs, C programming language, 1095

LipStick (McIntyre Computer Systems), 816

liquid crystal panels, 167

Lisa 2/10 PC, 145

Lisa 2/5 PC, 145

Lisa 7/7 Office System software, 146

Lisa PC, 145-146

LISP programming language, 1098

literature programs, 627-628

lithium batteries, 1064

lithographic background patterns, 389

Little Mouse (Mouse Systems), 255

Liveware, 24

Living Books program series (Brøderbund), 619

LLAP (LocalTalk Link Access Protocol), 970

local Mac user groups, 1042-1043

LocalSwitch (Tribe), 996

LocalTalk, 1120
- 230.4K baud speed, 193
- active star networking, 995
- bridged star networking, 996
- multiple routed backbone networking, 996-997
- networks, 968-971
- printer ports, 192

LocalTalk bridge (Tribe), 996

LocalTalk cards, PC/AppleTalk compatibility, 1010

LocalTalk connectors, PhoneNET (Farallon), 970

LocalTalk daisy-chain networking, 993-994

LocalTalk ports, PostScript LaserWriters, 1016

LocalTalk repeater, StarController (Farallon), 971

LocalTalk-to-Ethernet AppleTalk routers, 996

locked folder programs, 856

locking, 1120

lockup, 1120

log on, 1120

logging on online services with modems, 912-913

logic board terminators, 1066

logical addresses, 956

logical functions, spreadsheets, 460

logical volumes, partitioned disks, 57

LOGO programming language (Terrapin Software), 632, 1099

logos, 310

look and feel, 1120

Lookup feature, FileMaker Pro, 549-553

Lost Treasures of Infocom game set (Activision), 594

Lotus Jazz program, 458

Lotus 1-2-3/Mac program, 458, 467-468

Lotus Improv spreadsheets, 472-473

low-end dot-matrix printers, 239

low-end multimedia configuration, 795-796, 807

low-end office printers, 242

low-level languages, 1089

lpi (lines per inch), 274

Lucasfilm Games, Pipe Dream puzzle game, 602

luminance, video, 768

M

Mac 512, 147

Mac 512Ke, 148

Mac BIOS, 1093

Mac Classic, 150-151

Mac Classic II, 151, 174

Index

Mac Color Classic, 151-152, 174
Mac Daisy Link printer drivers (GDT Softworks), 213
Mac Guided Tour, 597
Mac II, 153-154, 198, 686
Mac IIci, 155-156
Mac IIcx, 155
Mac IIfx, 156-157
Mac IIsi, 158-159
Mac IIvx, 162-163, 174-175
Mac IIx, 154
Mac LC, 157-158, 174
Mac LCII, 162, 174
Mac LCIII, 163-164
Mac 'n Touch screen (MicroTouch Systems), 815
Mac Plus, 147-148, 1056-1057
Mac Portable, 167-168, 1061-1062
Mac resources, 1036
Mac SE, 148-149
   error codes, 1058
Mac SE/30, 150
Mac tutorials, 1048
Mac user groups, 1041-1044
Mac Utilities library (America Online), 927
Mac-in-DOS (PLI), 1004
Mac-infecting viruses, 874-887
Mac-to-PC cables, 1006
Mac/NTSC video conversion, 781-783
Mac/PC compatibility, 1002-1003
  compatibility
    EtherNet cards, 1010
    file differences, 1020-1022
    LaserJet 4M printers, 233
    LaserWriter Pro 630 printers, 233
    LocalTalk cards, 1010
    modem-to-modem connection procedure, 1006-1007
    networking, 1009-1012
    networking with AppleTalk, 1009-1011
    null modem interface procedure, 1006-1007
    null modem interfaces, 1006-1016
    printers, 232-235
    email sharing, 1016-1020
    serial cables, 1005-1006
  networks, 983-985
    Banyan VINES, 985
    Novell NetWare, 984-985
  resource sharing, 1016-1020
  translation of data, 1003
Mac/UNIX networks, 985
Mac286 NuBus boards (Orange Micro), 1013-1014

Everything You Wanted to Know About the Mac

Mac86 NuBus board (Orange Micro), 1013-1014

MacApp development system, 1105-1106

MacApp library (Apple), 1092

MacApp object-programming library, 1103

MacArc file compression freeware, 1031

MacBinary file format, 932

MacCalc program (Bravo Technologies), 468

MacDraw Pro program, 285

MacDraw program, 283

MACE, 92 (Mac Audio Compression Expansion), 789, 1032

MacEKG utility (MicroMAT Computer Systems), 1078

machine language, 1087

MacInker (Computer Friends), 213

MacinTalk, 93, 613, 686-687, 789, 1120

Macintosh II, 14

Macintosh models, 144-172

Macintosh Operating System, 27-54

Macintosh PC Exchange, 1004, 1026

   filters, 1028

   translation utility, 1022

Macintosh Programmer's Workshop development system, 1102

Macintosh programs, creating, 1085-1088

Macintosh User Interface, 1082, 1092

Macintosh XL PC, 146

MacIntyre WordWriter DA, 819

MacLabelPro (Avery), 387

MacLAN Connect program (Miramar), 1012

MacLink Plus/PC, 842

MacLinkPlus (Dataviz), 1005, 1026-1029, 1031

MacLinkPlus translation utility, 1022

MacLinkPlus/Translators

   Apple File Exchange, 1022

   Dataviz, 413

MacMag virus, 878

MacMainFrame emulator (Avatar), 991

MacNosy development system, 1104

MacPaint II program, 266

MacPaint program, 253-257, 300, 691

MacPalette II driver (Microspot), 213

MacPrint (Insight Development Corporation), 234

MacPrint (Insight Development Corporation), 234, 1017

MacRecorder

   Farallon, 92, 789, 1121

   Macromedia Paracomp, 788

Index

MacRecorder (MacroMind), 621, 645, 649
   sound box, 653-654
macro utilities, 847
MacroMaker program, 61, 415, 847
Macromedia
   Director, 766
   Director program, 756
   MediaMaker, 805
   MediaMaker program, 756
Macromedia Authorware, 806
Macromedia Director, 759, 801-805
Macromedia MediaMaker, 771
Macromedia Paracomp (MacRecorder), 788
Macromedia Player Toolkit, 760, 766
MacroMind
   MacRecorder digitizing program, 645, 649
   MacRecorder program, 621
   Windows Player accelerator board, 1032
macros, 414-415, 462, 818-819, 1121
Macs
   shutting off, 21-22
   special needs, 810-811
   starting, 18-19
   terms used in technology, 22-24
   troubleshooting, 1053-1057
MacsBug development system, 1103-1104
MacSki simulation game (XOR), 603
MacSprint II (Orchid Technology), 129
MacSwitch (Data Spec), 232
MacTCP (Apple), 953
MacTools Deluxe utilities, 859, 866
MacTOPS program (Sitka), 1010
MacTutor magazine, 1107
MacUser magazine, 1039
MacWEEK magazine, 1039
Macworld Expo convention, 1044-1045
Macworld magazine, 893, 1039
MacWrite 1.0, 402
MacWrite II, 115
MacWrite Pro (Claris), 412, 422
   sound integration, 427
   tables, 409
MacWrite program, 300
MacWrite version II, 421-422
magazines for Macintosh information, 1039-1040
Magic keyword (HyperCard), 700
Magic Typist (Tactic Software), 819

Everything You Wanted to Know About the Mac

Magic Wand tool (Adobe Photoshop), 265

magneto-optical cartridge drives, 798

mail, 917

mail merging, 388, 413

mailing lists of software updates, 1038-1039

main code segment of a resource, 1084

Mainstay (ClickPaste), 405

Make Alias command (File menu), 38

managers, software modules, 100

manuals for Mac, 1046

manufacturers of printers, 238-248

Map control panel, 33

Map icon, 33

MaraThon Multi-Comm NuBus card (Dove), 233

Marble and Granite textures (Artbeats), 389

margins, 306

Mariah multimedia organizer, 391

Mark of the Unicorn
    Mosaic score program, 685
    Performer program, 681
    Unisyn library editor, 684

marking features, 404

Markulla, Mike (Apple's first president), 9

Marquee tool (paint programs), 259

marquees, 1121

Martin, Tony (ASL FingerSpelling Tutor), 827

Mass Microsystems
    EasyVideo 8, 780
    QuickImage 24, 776

master backups (hard disks), 858

Master Juggler utility, 844

master page icon (PageMaker), 332

master pages, 330-340
    desktop publishing programs, 310
    PageMaker, 332-333
    overriding settings, 337
    QuarkXPress, 311
    whiting out items, 338

Master Switch box (Rose Electronics), 233

master synthesizers, 672

MasterJuggler (AlSoft), 81
    DAs, 91
    installing Fkeys, 89

materials for presentations, 800

Math Blaster Mystery program (Davidson), 624

Math Blaster Plus program (Davidson), 624

Index

math coprocessors, 121, 143-144
    68882, 137
    Motorola 68882, 121
    spreadsheets, 461

math programs, 624-626

Mathematica (Wolfram Research), 461

mathematics games, 624

matrices (worksheets), 459

Mavis Beacon Teaches Typing program (Software Toolworks), 637

Maxima (Connectix), 129, 132

Maxis
    games, 590
    RoboSport battle game, 592
    SimAnt simulation game, 608
    SimCity simulation game, 607
    SimEarth simulation game, 607
    SimLife simulation game, 608

Maxtor MXT hard drive series, 190

Mayer-Johnson Communication Board Builder, 828

MBDF virus, 883

MC68000 microprocessors (Motorola), 120

McCLint development system, 1105

McFarlane, Garrick (Sound Editor), 658

McGee program (Brøderbund), 618

MCI Mail, 1019-1020
    faxes/messages, 916

McIntyre Computer Systems LipStick, 816

McSink shareware, 423

MDEF virus, 881-882

MECC
    Easy Color Paint program, 268
    Number Munchers program, 625
    Time Share System, 630
    Word Munchers game, 623

media
    integration, 752
    interactive devices, 753
    interactivity, 753
    Macintosh networking, 968-983

MediaMaker (Macromedia), 756, 805

mediated libraries, 757

Mediator (VideoLogic), 781

megabytes, 1121

melodies in HyperCard, 732

memex device, 749

memory, 182-191, 1121
    32-bit cleanliness, 186-187
    allocation, 124-126
    architecture, 142-143

Everything You Wanted to Know About the Mac

caches, 184

failures, 187-188

model limitations, 187

packaging in SIMMs, 184-185

requirements for sampled sounds, 657

sound requirements, 654-657

sound storage, 656-657

speeds, 183-184

virtual, 130-131

wait states, 183-184

memory chips, 127

Memory control panel, 128-130

memory controllers (Centris 650), 165

menu bars, 18, 1121

menu items, 61

Menu Manager program, 102

menus, 56, 60-69, 1121

Mercer Mayer (Just Grandma and Me program), 619

Merchant's Row (Delphi), 921

merging documents, 447-450

see also traffic

message boxes, 1121

message rooms (forums), 923

messages

HyperCard scripts, 704

MIDI, 675-676

Out of Memory, 123

sysex, synthesizers, 676

Welcome to Macintosh, 1075

Metamorphosis Pro (Altsys), 394

Metamorphosis utility, 846

Metro (OSC), 679

ImageBase, 383

MetroLine City Search, 918

MFS (Macintosh File System), 1121

MHz (megahertz), 121

mice and ADB, 195

Microlytic Gofer, 411

MicroMAT Computer Systems MacEKG utility, 1078

MicroPhone (Software Venture), 1008

Microphone II communications program, 907-908

MicroPhone program (Software Ventures Corporation), 1006

microphone tips for recording, 650-653

microprocessors, *see* processors

Microsoft

Excel program, 458

database spreadsheets, 462

spreadsheets, 463-465, 476-477

Mail, 952, 1019

MultiPlan program, 458

PC operating system, 10

Word, 427, 432

built-in outliner, 409

Index

Command-Shift keys, 452
style sheets, 313
version 5.1, 415-417
WDBN native format, 115
Works, 422, 465, 573-577

Microspot MacPalette II driver, 213

MicroTouch Systems, Mac 'n Touch screen, 815

mid-range multimedia configuration, 796

MIDI (Musical Instrument Digital Interface), 669-686, 801, 1121
   advanced setups, 673
   Altech 1x3 interface, 670
   cables, 671-672
   channel standards, 676
   chooser names, 675-676
   clip music, 676
   Filters, 673
   General Sound Modules, 676
   interfaces, 670-671
   messages, 675-676
   note on or note off structure, 670
   Patchbays, 673
   programs, 676-681
   sequencers, 676-686
   sound, 790
   studio components, 670-676
   studio setup, 672
   synthesizers, 670-676

MIDI Interface (Apple), 670

MIDI Manager, 92, 685-686, 1121

MIDI System (Opcode), 686

MIDI Translator interface (Opcode Systems), 670

MindLink (Mindlink Software) word processor, 426

MindSet program, 639-640

Mini-DIN 8 connectors (modems), 147, 904

miniature keyboards, 815

minimal smart recalculation in spreadsheets, 461

Minimum System script Installer utility, 106

MiniWriter shareware, 423

mips (millions of instructions per second), 121

Miracle Piano System (Software Toolworks), 683

Miramar MacLAN Connect program, 1012

mirroring mode (PowerBook 160/180), 170

MIT (Massachusetts Institute of Technology)
   Professor Seymour Papert, 632
   Spacewars game, 588
   X-Windows, 987

mixing sound, 664-665

Mode 32, 132

Everything You Wanted to Know About the Mac

MODE32 software (Connectix), 187

MODE32 utility (Apple), 143, 150

modem ports, 192, 904

modem-to-modem connection procedure (Mac/PC interaction), 1006-1007

modems, 898-905, 1121
- communications programs, 906-916
- file transfers (Mac/PC), 1007-1008
- installing, 903-905
- logging on online services, 912-913
- placing calls, 910-916
- PowerBook internal expansion, 172
- purchasing, 900-901
- settings, 910-911
- TelePort (Global Village), 194

Modifier key, 1121

modifying sound, 660-665

Modula 2 programming language, 1099

Modula programming language, 1099

modular Macs, 152-166

modular phone jacks, 903

modules in databases, 514-515

monitors, 197-199, 1121
- 68000-based Mac, 198
- Centris 610, 176-177
- Centris 650, 176-177
- color video, 768
- enlarging, 824
- external video connectors, 177-178
- grayscale, 263-266
- Mac LC/LCII/Classic II/Color C, 174
- Quadra 700, 175
- Quadra 800, 176-177
- Quadra 900, 175
- Quadra 950, 176
- Radius external, 198
- sense codes, 178

Monitors control panel, 46, 173

Monitors icon, 263

Monster Mac upgrade (Levco), 152

MORE (Symantec), 409

MORE 4.0, 426

More After Dark screen savers, 614

Moriarty's Revenge simulation game (Mysterium Tremendum), 606

morse code switches for data entry, 816

Mosaic score program (Mark of the Unicorn), 685

Index

motherboards, 120-121

Motif (Open Software Foundation), 987

Motorola
- 68020 processor, 14
- Altair II wireless Ethernet, 981
- EMBARC, 981
- MC68000 microprocessors, 120
- processors, 6

Motorola 56001 digital signal processor, 122

Motorola 68000 processors, 141-142

Motorola 68020 processors, 14, 120, 142, 153

Motorola 68030 processors, 121, 154, 162, 169-170

Motorola 68040 processors, 121, 165

Motorola 68851 paged memory management, 143

Motorola 68881 math coprocessors, 143, 153

Motorola 68882 math coprocessors, 121, 143, 162

Motorola 68LC040 processors, 164-165

Mount 'Em program, 135

Mounty Extension program (QuicKeys), 135

mouse, 4, 19-20, 73, 1121
- head-controlled, 817
- numeric keypad substitution Mouse Keys (Easy Access utility), 812
- optical, 255
- painting with, 255-260
- problems, 1054

Mouse control panel, 73

Mouse Keys (Easy Access utility), 812

Mouse Systems (Little Mouse), 255

MousePenPro (Appoint), 256

mouthsticks, typing, 813-814

movies, 755

moving items in PageMaker with cursor keys, 364

MPEG (Motion Picture Experts Group), 785

MS-DOS (Microsoft Disk Operating System), 10, 27

MUG (Macintosh Users Group), 1041, 1122

multichannel sound, 92

MultiClip (Olduvai), 405

MultiFinder, 18, 30, 44, 56, 108, 123, 1122

multimedia, 748-751
- basic concepts, 751-755
- choosing systems, 792-799
- configurations, 807
- configuring systems, 795-797
- copyright laws, 800

1187

Everything You Wanted to Know About the Mac

elements, 762-770

organizers, 391-392

performance enhancements, 797

planning Macintosh platforms, 793-795

planning system, 807

presentations, 799-802

simulations, 757

storage, 797-799

toolkits, 805

uses, 756-758

multimedia engines, 758-760, 802-806

    configurations, 759-760

    integrated media presentations, 799-802

    types and complexity, 803

multimodule applications (integrated software), 584

MultiPlan program (Microsoft), 458

multiple clipboards, 405

multiple FDDI backbone networking (Ethernet), 997

multiple logical addresses, 956

multiple master fonts, 373, 379

multiple routed backbone networking (LocalTalk), 996-997

multiple routed backbone/star networking (Ethernet), 997

multiple screen shots, 89

multiple undo feature (Nisus), 404

multisystem databases, 515

multitasking in System 7, 424

multiuser databases, 515

multivendor networks (Macintosh), 983-992

MUMPS programming language, 1099

music, 644-645

    HyperCard, 728-732

    MIDI Manager (Apple), 685-686

    MIDI System (Opcode), 686

    professional, 684-685

    SoundEdit Pro (MacroMind), 656

    Voice Impact (Articulate Systems), 649

Musicshop (Opcode Systems), 678-679

MW2S native format (MacWrite II), 115

MyDiskLabeler (Williams & Macias), 848

Mysterium Tremendum (Moriarty's Revenge simulation game), 606

N

N.O.M.A.D. 1.0a1 program, 889

names of zones in networks, 961-964

native formats, 115

navigating stacks, 707-711

navigation icons (HyperCard), 711

Navigator, accessing CompuServe for file transfer, 1008

Navigator palette, HyperCard Version 2.0, 709-710

Navigator program, 1122

NBP (Name Binding Protocol), 965

NEC PC-VCR, 771

NEDA 1306A battery, 1064

Nekoosa printer paper (Georgia Pacific), 236

Nelson, Ted, hypertext/ hypermedia terms, 750

NetModem (Shiva), 1018

NetSerial peripheral interface (Shiva), 1018

NetWare for Macintosh (Novell), 1010-1012

network numbers, AppleTalk, 955

networking

    dynamic addressing, AppleTalk nodes, 959-961

    Ethernet

        daisy-chains, 994-995

        FDDI WAN, 998

        star, 995-996

    file formats, 952-953

    fundamentals/interaction of communication, 945-946

    LocalTalk, 993-997

    Mac/PC interaction, 1009-1012

    Macintosh, 943

    Macintosh/IBM, 991-992

    Macintosh/UNIX, 985-989

    Macintosh/Vax, 989-991

    Macs/PCs with AppleTalk, 1009-1011

    media, 968-983

    multiple Ethernet, 997

    multivendor, 983-992

    number assignments, AppleTalk Phase 2, 957-959

    print services, 949

    protocols, 953-968

    scenarios, 993-999

    services, 947-952

    structured wiring, 998-999

networks, 1122

    AlterNet, 941

    AppleTalk

        connecting PCs, 1016

        RoboSport battle game, 592

Index

1189

routing tables, 966-968

zones, 961-964

AppleTalk/LocalTalk, 232

EtherNet, 1011

Ethernet, 972-977

FDDI (Fiber Data Distributed Interface), 979-980

Fidonet, 941

gateways, 1012

Internet, 940

LocalTalk, 968-971

Mac/PC, 983-985

   Banyan VINES, 985

   Farallon PhoneNET PC, 983-984

Mac/UNIX (Xinet K-AShare), 985

Novell NetWare, 984-985, 1012

routers, 1012

serial, 980

sharing databases, 566-569

Token-Ring, 978-979, 1011-1012

virus prevention, 873-874

wireless, 981-982

New command, File menu

  Microsoft Excel, 488

  Microsoft Word, 448

New Layout command (Edit menu), FileMaker Pro, 555

New Layout dialog screen, 4th Dimension (ACIUS), 527

New Record command (Edit menu), FileMaker Pro, 543

New... command, File menu,

   FileMaker Pro, 549

   PageMaker, 332

news on online services, 917-918

NeXT computers, 14, 472

NFNT (New Font Numbering System), 377

NFS (Sun Microsystems), 986

NFS/Share (InterCon), 987

NHSMUG (National Home & School Mac User Group) shareware, 612

Nisus

   GREP functions, 411

   multiple undo feature, 404

Nisus Lite, 418

Nisus Professional, 417-418, 427

node numbers, AppleTalk, 954

nodes, 1122

non-block devices, 189

noninterlaced video scanning, 767

nonmalicious viruses, 871-872

nonrepeating keys, 814-816

Norstad, John, Disinfectant program, 611

Norton Utilities for the Macintosh, 106, 866

Index

DiskLight, 135

Speed Disk, 111

note on or note off structure of MIDI, 670

Note Pad command (Apple menu), 34

nouns used in Mac technology, 23-24

Novell NetWare, Mac/PC networks, 984-985, 1010-1012

Now Utilities (Now Software), 102, 849

   DeskPicture, 58

   extensions manager, 841

   Now Scrapbook, 392

NTSC (National Television Standards Committee)

   video conversion, 781-783

   video palette, 783

   video signal format, 767, 780-781

NuBus

   add-in cards

      Apple 8•24GC, 197

      Texas Instruments, 136-137

      Mac86/Mac286/Orange386, 1013-1014

   slots, 196-197

   video cards, 179

null modem interfaces, 1006-1016

number assignments on networks, AppleTalk Phase 2, 957-959

Number command (Format menu), Microsoft Excel, 483-485

number formats in spreadsheets, 482-484

Number Munchers program (MECC), 625

numeric keypads, 75, 813

NuVista+ video board (TrueVision), 767, 778-779

nView overhead projector panel, 756

nVIR virus, 114, 876

Nyquest Theorem, 655

O

OAG (Official Airline Guide) online travel service, 919

object code, 1087

Object Pascal programming language, 1094

object-oriented graphics, 282-283, 411, 1122

object-oriented programming, 742, 1090-1092, 1122

objects

   HyperCard, 704-707, 739

   in object-oriented programming, 1091

   linked-text, 306

OCR (Optical Character Recognition), 1122

Odesta TechConnect program, 526

Office of Special Education and Rehabilitation (Apple), 829

office printers, 241-243

Ohm Software, FormsProgrammer, 743-744

Ohtsuki Braille Printer (American Thermoform), 827

Okidata LED printer engines, 214

Old way chart command, Window menu (Microsoft Excel), 490

Olduvai MultiClip, 405

OLE (Object Linking and Embedding), 96

Omnis 7 (Blyth Software, Inc.), 535-537

On Location (On Technologies), 411

Once Upon a Time program series (Compu-Teach), 627

online services, 916-941, 1122
 electronic shopping, 920-921
 financial services, 922
 forums, 922-924
 GEnie call script, 912
 interactive games, 927-929
 libraries, 930
 logging on with modems, 912-913
 news, 917-918
 passwords, 914-915
 signing off, 915-916
 travel information, 918-919
 use guidelines, 915
 virus updates, 893

onscreen keyboards, 817

OnTrack, 771

Opcode Systems
 Audioshop music program, 645
 Audioshop playlist editor, 668
 Cue scoring program, 684
 Galaxy patch librarian, 683-684
 MIDI Translator interface, 670
 Musicshop, 678-679
 Studio Vision music program, 645
 Timecode Machine, 673
 Vision, 680-681

open font formats, 374

Open Software Foundation, Motif, 987

Open... command (File menu), Microsoft Word, 454

opening Story editor (PageMaker), 364

Operating System 6/7, 26-54

operating systems, 101-105

Optacon tactile output devices, 827

Index

optical mice, 73, 255

opticals, multimedia storage, 798

Optima TapeDisk utility, 798

optimizing compilers, 1087

optimizing hard disks, 859-865

Option key, 74

option-clicking, 23

Options menu commands

    Column guides... (PageMaker) 332, 337

    Workspace (Microsoft Excel), 478

Orange Micro

    Grappler 9-pin interface, 213, 233

    Grappler LX, 234

    NuBus boards, 1013-1014

Orchid Technology, MacSprint II, 129

Oregon Trail program (MECC Time Share System), 630

organization utilities, 854-855

organizing stacks, 703

organizing hard disks, 853-857

original fonts, 393-395

OSC Metro program, 679

Oscar the Grouch program, 94

OSPF (Open Shortest Path First) routing protocol, 998

Otari PD-464, 667

Out of Memory message, 123

outline fonts, 1122

Outline view, 59

outlining

    applications, MORE (Symantec), 409

    built-in, Microsoft Word, 409

    documents, 409

Outnumbered! program (Learning Company), 624

outSPOKEN program, 687, 825-826

overhead projector panels, 756

overlays in video signals, 778

overloading in sound recording, 650

overriding master pages settings, 337

overscan in video, 767

P

P-51 Mustang flight simulator (Bulleye Software), 604

PacificTalk (Pacific Data Products), 234

packets, 1122

Packit, .PIT file extensions, 934

PacMan game, 590

Page Composition Language (PCL) PDL (Hewlett-Packard), 207

Everything You Wanted to Know About the Mac

Page Down key, 75

page layout, word processors, 405-406

Page menu commands (PageMaker)
- Actual size, 333
- Fit in window, 335
- Insert pages…, 336

page numbers, 310
- adding with text tool (FileMaker Pro), 571
- master pages, PageMaker, 333

page preview features, 407-408

page set-up in desktop publishing programs, 309-311

Page Up key, 75

PageMaker (Aldus Corporation), 13, 115, 301, 321, 324-325
- AutoFlow feature, 313
- automatic threading text and graphics, 316
- kerning text, 314
- master pages, 330-340
- pages, adding, 336
- spell checking in Story Editor window, 317
- style palette, 313
- style-name tags, 314
- Styles, 354-357
- text placement symbol, 316
- version 4.2, 328

pages, printing
- Braille, 827
- color, 272-276

paging memory, 131

Paint menu, HyperCard, 715-717

paint programs, 266-272, 1123
- bitmapped images, 252
- colors/grayscales, 261-262
- paintbrushes, 256-260

painting
- by dragging in script, HyperCard, 719-722
- tools, HyperCard, 712-723
- with mouse, 255-260

palettes, 709, 1123

Pantone color Matching System, 265, 277-278

PAP (Printer Access Protocol), 949

paper for printers, 236

Paper Direct 28-pound Inkjet printer paper, 236

paragraphs
- attributes, 313
- margins, 406
- spacing, 306
- selecting in PageMaker, 364

parallel ports, SCSI, 134-136

parking the heads of hard drives, 1071, 1123

Index

partial screen shots, 89

partitioning hard disks, 109, 855-857, 865

Pascal programming language, 1094

passive matrix color display, PowerBook 165c, 171

passwords, online services, 914-915

Paste command (Edit menu), 29, 379

pasteboards, 1123
    PageMaker, 303-306

pasting, 1123
    documents, 28-30
    Scrapbook to Control Panel, 32-33

patch librarians, 683-684

Patchbays, MIDI, 673

patches
    extension managers, 840
    System file, 1092
    System software, 84

Pathway NFS (Wollongong), 987

PATHWORKS for Macintosh (DEC), 990

Pattern and Texture library (Adobe), 389

Pattern Mover, WetPaint clip art (DublClick), 389

patterns, 118, 388-389

Patterns command (Format menu), Microsoft Excel, 482

Patterns menu, HyperCard, 715

Patton Strikes Back battle game, 591

Paycheck database, FileMaker Pro, 549

Pazhitnov, Alexey, Tetris puzzle game, 598

PC floppy disks
    reading with FDHD SuperDrives, 1003
    reading with Finder, 1004

PC operating systems, Microsoft Corporation, 10

PC-DOS (Personal Computer Disk Operating System), 10

PC-Talk program, 1006

PC-VCR (NEC), 771

PCs (Personal Computers), 1123
    controlling from Macs, 1013-1016
    IBM Corporation, 10

PD-464 (Otari), 667

PDLs (page description languages), 204-208, 374

PDSs (processor direct slots), 149, 196-197

peer-to-peer file sharing, 1123

Penton VocabuLearn/ce program, 633

Performa series Macs, 145, 151, 162-164

Performer (Mark of the Unicorn), 681

peripherals, 192-199, 1123

permanent backups, 858-859

persistence of vision, 765

Personal Bibliographic Software, Por-Cite for the Macintosh, 428

personal printers, 240-241

Personal Press (Aldus), 322-323
- Broken Links icon, 305
- Equals tool, 306
- importing graphics, 311
- Links tool, 305
- spelling checker, 317

Personal Trainer for the SAT program (Davidson), 636

Personality! utility, 102

personalized Macs for those with special needs, 811-820

Persuasion program (Aldus), 756

phone use of sound, 668

PhoneNET (Farallon) LocalTalk connectors, 970

PhoneNET PC (Farallon), 983

PhoneNet PC II Network Interface Card (Farallon), 1010

PhoneNet PC program, Timbuktu for Windows, 1010

Photoshop (Adobe), 115, 264, 271

physics programs, 634-635

PICT files, 262, 383, 1024-1025, 1123

pictorial resources, 118

pictures, HyperCard, 733

Pie command (Gallery menu), Microsoft Excel, 490

Pioneer 2200 laser disc players, 773

Pioneer 8000 laser disc players, 774

Pipe Dream puzzle game (Lucasfilm Games), 590, 602

.PIT extensions, Packit files, 934

PixelMaster Braille printer (Howtek), 827

PixelPaint Professional, 257, 260-261, 271

pixels, 202, 252, 368, 1123

placeholder templates, 318, 386

placeholders, 404

placing calls on modems, 910-916

placing items in PageMaker documents, 340-353

placing text, 313-315

Planetfall adventure game (Activision), 594

planning multimedia presentations, 793-802

plastic coverings for keyboards, 815

Index

plastic magnifying lenses for screens, 822

playing sound in HyperCard, 731-732

playlist editor programs, 668-669

Playmaker Football simulation game (Brøderbund), 604

Playmate adventure game, 596

Playroom program (Brøderbund), 618

PLI Mac-in-DOS, 1004

plotters, 247

Pluma Capitalist Pig simulation game, 610

PMMUs (paged memory management units), 131, 143

PMS (Pantone Matching System), 238

PNTG files, 1024

Pointer Systems, Freewheel head-controlled mouse, 817

pointers, 58, 1123

pointing mouse, 19, 22

points

    fonts, 368

    handles, draw programs, 294

    typefaces, 366

Police Quest I & II adventure games (Sierra Online), 595

Polybus Systems Corp., Snooper utility, 1078

Pong (Atari), 5, 589

pop-up menus, 1123

PopChar shareware, 74

PopUp Funcs development system, 1104-1105

Por-Cite for the Macintosh (Personal Bibliographic Software), 428

portable inkjet printers, 217

portable Macs, 166-172

portable printers, 239

ports, 1123

    ADB, 133

    modem, 904

post-production sound, 644

Postcraft templates, 387

PostScript (Adobe Systems), 1123

    clones, 206-207

    files, 320

    fonts, 227, 366, 369-371, 375-376, 395, 1123

    LaserWriter printers, 1016

    Level 2 PDL, 207, 238

    PDL (page description language), 203-206, 370, 1024, 1100

    printer drivers, 1017

    printers, 232, 1016-1017

    Type 1/Type 3 fonts, 370

Power key, 75

Power Managers (PowerBooks), error codes, 1062-1063

power switches, 1064

PowerBooks

  integrated software, 574

  internal modem expansion, 172

  models, 168-171

  Power Manager error codes, 1062-1063

  trackballs, 73

  Wheelchair Battery Power Adapter, 815

PowerKey (Sophisticated Circuits), 134

PowerPad numeric keypad (Kensington), 813

PPP (Point-to-Point Protocol), 998

Practica Musica (Ars Nova), 682-683

Practical Solutions Strip Switch, 134

PRAM (Parameter RAM), 1064, 1076, 1124

Praxitel Read My Lips voice messaging, 427

Precision Bitmap Alignment, printing, 220

predictor programs, 819-820

Preferences command, Edit menu (PageMaker), 329

Preferences folder, System 7 folder, 79

Preferences... command (Edit menu/Tools menu), Microsoft Word, 439

Premiere (Adobe), 645, 668, 806

Prentke-Romich

  HeadMaster head-controlled mouse, 817

  keylatches/keyguards, 814

presentations, multimedia, 799-802

Preview mode, FileMaker II, 556

primitives, PDLs (page description languages), 205

print buffers, 225, 1124

Print command (File menu), 204

print controllers, 208

print merge documents, 447-450

Print Merge feature (Microsoft Word), 446-451

Print Merge... command (File menu), Microsoft Word, 450

Print Monitor print spooler, 845

Print Preview mode, Microsoft Word, 453-454

Print Preview... command (File menu), Microsoft Word, 453

print spoolers, 220, 223-225, 845, 1124

printer drivers, 84, 204, 209-210, 1124

  document scaling, 220

  files, 209

Index

Jetlink Express (GDT Softworks), 194
PostScript, 1017
printers, 238-248
- Apple LaserWriters, 13, 203, 300, 369, 1016
- as SCSI devices, 195
- bubblejet, 216-218
- color, 244-246, 320
- daisywheel, 202
- dot matrix, 202, 211-213, 239, 1116
- envelope, 246-247
- Hewlett Packard LaserJets, 1017
- high-end office, 242-243
- high-resolution, 243-244
- ImageWriter, 369
- inkjet, 203, 216-218
- label, 246-247
- laser, 203, 213-216, 240-241
- LED, 214
- Mac/PC compatibility, 232-235
- Ohtsuki Braille Printer (American Thermoform), 827
- paper, 236
- PixelMaster Braille (Howtek), 827
- portable, 239
- portable inkjet, 217
- ports, 192
- PostScript (Apple), 232, 240-241, 1016-1017
- QuickDraw, 240
- resolution, 230-231, 273
- Romeo Brailler (Enabling Technology), 827
- selecting with Chooser, 408
- solid-ink, 244-245, 248
- speeds, 229-230
- thermal transfer, 218-219
- thermal wax transfer, 203
- TrueImage laser, 240-241
- utilities, 845-846
- workgroup, 241

printing, 202-203, 320-321
- Braille pages, 827
- color, 236-238, 272-276
- from HyperCard, 723-728
- groups of cards (HyperCard), 724-726
- network services, 949
- PostScript files, 320
- Precision Bitmap Alignment, 220
- reports, 726-728
- sequence of events during, 204-205
- single cards, 723-724
- Text and Graphics Smoothing, 220

Everything You Wanted to Know About the Mac

printing engines, 211-219

printing terms in desktop publishing software, 306-309

PrintLink Collection (GDT SoftWorks), 213, 233

PrintMonitor Documents folder, System 7 folder, 79

PrintMonitor program, System 7, 223

PrintMonitor utility, 79

privacy switches, modems, 903

problems
- booting, 1054, 1075-1077
- dealer diagnosis, 1078
- fonts, 376-379
- hard drives, 1069-1071
- hardware, 1054
- INIT conflicts, 1072-1073
- keyboard, 1054
- mouse, 1054
- old software, 1073-1074
- rebooting, 1077
- SCSI chain rerouting, 1069
- SCSI devices, 1068-1069
- SCSI ports, 196
- software, 1072
- System file, 1074-1075
- troubleshooting, 1046-1047

procedural programming, 1090

procedures
- communications programs, 913
- databases, 517-518

processors, 6, 140-144
- 32-bit-wide internal registers, 141
- AMD 29000, 198
- clock signals, 142
- Input/Output, 122
- Intel, 6
- Motorola 68000, 141-142
- Motorola 68020, 14, 120
- Motorola 68030, 121, 131
- Motorola 68040, 121
- Motorola MC68000, 120
- RISC, 208

ProComm on the PC program, 1006

Prodigy, 1124
- bulletin boards, 924
- Catos, 924
- electronic shopping, 920
- features, 939
- financial service, 922
- interactive games, 927
- message monitoring, 924
- news, 917
- travel board, 919
- weather reports, 918

Index

program extensions, 85
program files, 1088
programmer's switch, 1124
programming, 1082-1083, 1106-1108
  books, 1107
  languages, 1093-1100
    alternatives, 1097-1099
    choosing, 1100
    LegoLOGO, 632
    LOGO, 632
  magazines, 1107
  object-oriented, 1090-1092
  procedural, 1090
  software packages, 1101-1106
programs, 1124
  32-bit QuickDraw, 261
  AccessPC, 1004
  Adobe Photoshop, 271
  Adventures in Musicland, 626
  Aldus PageMaker, 203
  Alge-Blaster Plus, 626
  AntiPan 1.5, 887
  AntiVirus 1.0E, 872, 887
  AppDisk, 130
  Assassin, 887
  At Ease, 620
  Audioshop playlist editor, 668
  BBSs
    FirstClass, 941
    TeleFinder, 941

BinHex (shareware), 1031
black and white paint, 266-267
Braille Display Processor, 827
Canvas, 269
Carmen Sandiego series, 628
Casper system, 94
Clear Access (Fairfield Software), 951
ClickChange, 102
Co:Writer, 820
Color MacCheese, 268
color-separation
  Aldus PrePress, 321
  PageMaker 5, 321
  Quark, 321
ColorFinder, 60
Communication Board Builder, 828
Communications Toolbox (Apple), 194
compiling, 1087-1088
ConcertWare, 678
ConcertWare Pro, 678
Copy II Mac, 859
Create (KE:nx), 815
creating Macintosh, 1085-1088
Cue, 684
DA Handler, 91
debugging, 1088

DECnet for Macintosh (Digital), 953
DeltaGraph Pro, 461
Deluxe Music Construction Set, 677
Desk Picture, 102
DeskPaint, 257, 270
DeskPicture, 58
desktop publishing, 303, 321-325
   Aldus PageMaker, 328-329
   creating graphics, 312-313
   importing graphics, 311
   importing style sheets, 313
   MacWrite, 300
   PageMaker (Aldus Corporation), 301
   Personal Press, 305, 311
   printing terms, 306-309
   Publish It! Easy, 306
   QuarkXPress, 311
   RSG (ReadySetGo), 306
   Ventura Publisher, 305, 311
Digital Darkroom, 264
Director, 756
Disinfectant, 872, 887-888
Disk Express II, 111
Disk First Aid, 106
DiskDoubler, 1031
DiskTool, 115
DiskTop, 115

DOS Mounter, 1004
DosTOPS, 1010
DoveFAX+, 667
draw, 283-291
Dyaxis, 667
Easy Color Paint, 268
Eco-Adventures, 635
educational, 618-632
   early grades, 621-623
   high school and higher, 633-637
Eradicat'Em 1.0, 888
errors, 1057-1058
Event Manager, 102
Excel, 458
Expert Color Paint, 268
Ferret 1.1, 888
File System, 102
FileMaker Pro, 539-572
FileMaster, 115
FileStar, 115
FKeys, 89-90, 115
Font Manager, 102
foreign language, 633
FormsProgrammer, 743-744
Fractal Design Painter, 271-272
Freedom of Press 3.0.1, 292
Freedom of Press Light, 292
FreeHand, 291

Index

freeware, ResEdit, 120
Full Impact 2.0, 458
FullPaint, 254
Gatekeeper, 872, 888
Gatekeeper Aid 1.2.1, 889
geography, 628-632
HD SC Setup, 191
HeapTool (CE Software), 126
HyperCard, 690-691
Hyperglot, 633
illustration, 291-298
Illustrator, 291
image processing, 264
inLARGE, 824-825
Interactive Physics, 634
Interferon 3.1, 889
inTouch, 827
Jazz, 458
KaleidaGraph, 461
KidArt, 621
KidPix, 268
KidPix Companion, 621
KillScores 1.0, 889
KillVirus, 889
Labview, 757
LapLink/Mac, 1026-1028
LifeGuard, 639
literature, 627-628
locked folder, 856
Lotus 1-2-3/Mac, 458, 467-468
Lotus Improv, 472-473
low-cost paint, 268-270
Mac-in-DOS, 1004
MacCalc, 468
MacDraw, 283
MacDraw Pro, 285
MacinTalk, 686-687
Macintosh components, 1083-1085
Macintosh PC Exchange, 1026
MacLAN Connect, 1012
MacLinkPlus, 1026
MacLinkPlus 7.0, 1028-1029
MacPaint, 253-254, 300, 691
MacPaint II, 266
MacRecorder, 92, 645, 649
MacroMaker, 61, 847
MacTCP (Apple), 953
MacTOPS, 1010
Magic Typist, 819
MasterJuggler, 81
math, 624-626
Math Blaster Mystery, 624
Math Blaster Plus, 624
Mathematica, 461
Mavis Beacon Teaches Typing, 637
Maxima, 129, 132
MediaMaker, 756
Menu Manager, 102
Metro, 679

MicroPhone, 1008

Microphone, 1006

Microsoft Excel, 463-465

Microsoft Mail for Macintosh, 952

Microsoft Works, 465

MIDI, 676-681

MIDI Manager (Apple), 685-686

MindSet, 639-640

Miracle Piano System, 683

modem communications, 906-916

Mosaic, 685

Motif, 987

Mount 'Em, 135

Mounty Extension, 135

MultiPlan, 458

music, 644-649, 656, 686

Musicshop, 678-679

MyDiskLabeler, 848

N.O.M.A.D. 1.0a1, 889

Navigator, 1122

NetWare, 1010

Norton Utilities, 106

Norton Utilities DiskLight, 135

NOW Utilities, 102

Number Munchers, 625

Once Upon a Time series, 627

Oregon Trail, 630

Oscar the Grouch, 94

Outnumbered!, 624

outSPOKEN, 825-826

PageMaker, 13, 115

Paint, 1123

paint, 252

PATHWORKS for Macintosh, 990

PC-Talk, 1006

PD-464, 667

Performer, 681

Personal Trainer for the SAT, 636

Personality!, 102

Persuasion, 756

Photoshop, 115, 264

PixelPaint, 257

PixelPaint Professional, 260-261, 271

playlist editor, 668-669

Practica Musica, 682-683

predictor, 819-820

printer drivers, 84

PrintMonitor, 223

problems, 1072

ProComm on the PC, 1006

professional music, 684-685

professional paint, 271-272

protecting from virus infection, 873-874

Index

Q-Sheet (DigiDesign), 684
QuickDraw, 101, 252, 1124
QuicKeys (CE Software), 61, 819
QuickMail (CE Software), 952
QuickScores, 890
RamDisk+, 130
RamStart, 130
registering, 1037-1038
Repair 1.5, 890
Resolve, 458, 467
Resource Manager, 102
RezSearch 1.0b, 890
RunPC, 1013-1016
RWatcher 1.0, 890
Sample Editor, 658
scanning, for data input, 816
science, 634-635
Script Editor, 98
SCSIProbe, 106
SCSITools, 106
See the U.S.A., 629
self-improvement, 637-640
SetFileKey, 115
shareware, 135
Silverlining, 110, 135
SoftPC for Windows, 109, 1015
Songworks, 682
sound, ResEdit, 687

Sound Master, 94
Sound Tools, 667
Speed Disk (Norton Utilities), 111
Stella, 757
Studio Vision, 680-681
Studio/1, 267
Studio/32, 271
Studio/8, 269-270
Stuffit Deluxe, 1031
Suitcase II, 81
SUM, 106, 111
Super Boomerang, 102
SuperCard, 744-746
SuperGlue, 849
SuperLaserSpool, 224
SuperPaint, 257, 266-267
Swamp Gas Visits the USA, 630
Symantec Tools (Symantec Utilities), 115
Synchronicity, 637-638
System 7 compatibility, 95
Talking Math Rabbit, 622
Talking Moose, 93-94
Talking Reader Rabbit, 622
Tappy Type, 94
TeachText, 1128
Tempo II, 61
test preparation, 635-636

TextEdit, 102
The Writing Center, 627
Timbuktu for Windows, 1010
Toucan Press, 623
tutorial, 757
Type Reunion (Adobe), 377
typing tutor, 637
Ultima Home Office, 667
updates on BBSs, 1038
upgrades, 1037-1040
Vaccination 1.1, 890
Vaccine 1.0.1, 891
Vaxene, 891
VCheck 1.3, 891
Virex, 872
Virex antivirus, 866
Virtual, 132
Virus Encyclopedia, 892
Virus Rx 1.6, 892
virus-detecting, 887-892
VirusBlockade II 1.0, 891
VirusDetective 4.0.4, 891
VirusWarning, 892
VisiCalc, 458
Vision, 680-681
VocabuLearn/ce, 633
vocal, 687
Voice Impact, 731
Voice Record, 731
Warning 1.1, 892

White Knight, 1008
White Knight on the Mac, 1006
Window Manager, 101
Wingz, 465
Word Munchers, 623
Write:OutLoud, 826
X-10, 820-821
see also utilities
progressive video scanning, 767
projection units, multimedia, 795, 807
projectors, 756
projects, SuperCard, 744-745
Prolog programming language, 1099
Prometheus Ultima Home Office, 667
prompts, 1124
proper technique for recording, 649-654
properties in HyperCard scripts, 722-723
Prosonus CD-ROM, 676
protecting against viruses, 872-874
protocols, 1124
    ASCII data format, 907
    baud rate, 906
    duplex mode, 906
    Fidonet network, 941
    half duplex, 907

Index

Macintosh networks, 953-968

modems, 906

public domain, 1124

public-domain stacks, 702

Publish and Subscribe feature, 35-37, 96, 425, 471, 758

Publish It! Easy (Timeworks), 321-322, 387

    kerned letters, 314

    Page Flipper palette, 310

    paint tools, 306

    Thesaurus Rex feature, 316

publishing forums, online services, 318

pull-down menus, 4, 60

Puzzle (Apple), 597

puzzle games, 597-603

Pyro! screen saver, 838

Q

Q-Sheet program (DigiDesign), 684

Quadra 700, 159-160, 175

Quadra 800, 165-166, 176-177

Quadra 840AV, 94

Quadra 900, 160-161, 175

Quadra 950, 161, 176

Quark color-separation programs, 321

QuarkXPress, 311, 325

Que Software RightWriter, 318, 427

Quick Report editor, 4th Dimension (ACIUS), 528

QuickDraw, 370

    graphics standard, 197

    PDL, 206

    printers, 226-227, 240, 1125

    program, 101, 252, 1124

QuicKeys (CE Software), 61, 135, 415, 819

QuickImage 24 (Mass Microsystems), 776

QuickMail (CE Software), 952, 1018-1019

QuickScores program, 890

QuickTime (Apple), 750, 766-770, 788, 1032

QuickTime compression manager, 784

QuickTime Tool Kit (Claris), 733

QuickTime Tools, 760

Quit command (File menu), 21, 29

quitting, 1125

quitting online services, 915-916

R

radio buttons, 1125

Radius VideoVision card, 779-781

Radius external monitors, 198

RAM (Random Access Memory), 24, 122, 183, 1125
- errors, 1056-1057, 1063
- installing, 127-128
- interleaved access, 185-186
- disk utilities, 130, 839-840
- disks, 129-130
- start-up loading, 108

RAM caches, 128-129, 865, 1125

RamDisk+ program, 130

RamStart program, 130

Rapport processor/drive controller (Kennect Technologies), 1005

raster calculation video coprocessors, 122

rasterizers, fonts, 375-376

RasterOps HyperCard Toolkit Stack, 777

RasterOps 24STV video board, 767, 777

RasterOps 364 video board, 767

RDEVs (resource drivers), 205, 1125

reactivity in multimedia applications, 791

Read Me! files, 854, 1125

Read My Lips (Praxitel), 427

read/write signal and memory, 183

reading
- enlarging screen views, 821-822
- PC floppy disks from Finder, 1004

ReadySetGo, 322

real-time conferences, 924-927

rebooting, 1077

rebuilding Desktop, 22, 113-114, 865

recharging toner cartridges, 215

recording concepts, 645-649

recording sound, 649-658, 728-731

records, 1125
- databases, 509
- in databases, 541
- sorting in FileMaker Pro, 559

redefining Styles in spreadsheets, 486-487

Reference Software, Grammatik Mac, 427

referential integrity in databases, 519

reformatting text, desktop publishing programs, 314

registering software, 1037-1038, 1046

registers, 32-bit-wide internal, 141

registers and memory, 182-183

reinforcement sounds, 787

Index

relational databases, 512-513, 1125

relative pointing devices, 73

Reliable Communications, Universal Print Buffer/Print Buffer Plus, 225

Relookup command (File menu), FileMaker Pro, 553

Remote Access (Apple), 981

removing from Desktop

    Bernoullis/CD-ROMs/SyQuest disks, 21

    floppy disks, 20

renaming icons, 60

Repair 1.5 program, 890

repairing hard drives, 1071

Repeat command (Edit menu)

    FileMaker Pro, 554

    Microsoft Excel, 500

replace features, 411-412

Report menu, 4th Dimension (ACIUS), 528

reports, printing in HyperCard, 726-728

rerouting SCSI chains to solve problems, 1069

ResEdit program (Apple), 120, 687, 843-844

    changing icons, 60

    development system, 1103

    examining file extensions, 1021

    file problems, 1074

    resource editor, 1102

Reset lines, 1068-1069

Resize boxes, windows, 71

resizing

    graphics, 311

    columns (Microsoft Excel), 499

resolution, 1125

    fonts, 371-373

    graphics, 262-266

    printers, 230-231, 273

resolution-dependent bitmapped images, 262

Resolve (Claris), 458, 467

Resorcerer development system, 1103

resource forks in files, 111, 1021

Resource Manager program, 102, 112

resources, 117-120

    Chooser, 1114

    CODE, 1084

    compilers, 1086

    editors, 843-844, 1085

    Font/DA Mover utility, 1083-1084

    hacking, 120

    Mac/PC sharing, 1016-1020, 1036

    programs, 1083-1085

    types, 118

restarting, 1125

ResumeWriter (Bootware Software), 428

RésumExpert (A Lasting Impression), 428

RET (Resolution Enhancement Technology), Hewlett-Packard, 207

Retrospect backup utility, 859

Return key, 75

reverb in sound, 663-664

reverse type, 290

Rez development system, 1103

RezSearch 1.0b program, 890

RF video signals, 769

RGB color scheme, 275

RGB video signals, 769

Ribbon, View menu (Microsoft Word), 433

right-hand master pages, PageMaker, 330

RightWriter (Que Software), 318, 427

RIPs (Raster Image Processors), 204, 1125

RISC (Reduced Instruction Set Computer), 208, 1125

RJ-11/RJ-14 phone jacks, 903

RoboSport battle game (Maxis), 592

ROM (Read Only Memory), 24, 100, 183, 1056, 1109, 1126

Romeo Brailler printer (Enabling Technology), 827

Rose Electronics, Master Switch box, 233

rotational delay of hard disks, 860

routed backbone networking, multiple LocalTalk setups, 996-997

routed backbone/star networking, multiple Ethernet setups, 997

routers, 1126
 AppleTalk, 954, 966
 for networks, 1012

routing tables, AppleTalk, 966-967

rows, inserting quickly in Microsoft Excel, 499

RS-232 ports, 192

RS-422 ports, 192

RSG (ReadySetGo), 306

RTF (Rich Text Format) text interchange format, 1023

RTMP (Routing Table Maintenance Protocol), 966

rubber stamps in paint programs, 256

Ruler, View menu (Microsoft Word), 433, 441

rulers
 document layout, 406
 draw programs, 291

rules, 308

RunPC (Argosy), 1013-1016

runtime editors in SuperCard, 746

RWatcher 1.0 program, 890

S

S Video component video type, 770

S.C.OUT puzzle game (Inline Design), 601

Sad Mac error codes, 1055

Sad Mac icon, 84, 1054-1057

SADE (Symbolic Application Debugging Environment), 1104

Sales Call Tracking stack, HyperCard, 705-706

Sample Editor (Garrick McFarlane), 658

Sample Layouts, Publish It! Easy, 387

sampled sound, memory requirements, 657

sampling (sound), 788, 1126
  music files, 645
  programs, 645
  rate of sound, 654-655

sans-serif typefaces, 367

Save As… command, 1126

saving, 1126
  HyperCard stacks, 697-698
  sound, 665-666

scanners, 195, 264, 1126

scanning software for data input, 816

scenarios for networking, 993-999

scheduled transmissions, fax modems, 902

Schwab Discount Brokerage service, GEnie, 922

science programs, 634-635

Scores virus, 874-875

Scrapbook, 31-32, 1126
  copying/pasting images, 29-33
  placing in PageMaker documents, 350-353

Scrapbook command (Apple menu), 31

screen burn-ins, 614

screen fonts, 1126

screen shots, 89, 1126

screens
  Boss key, Pipe Dream, 590
  enlarging views for ease of reading, 821-822
  splitting in Microsoft Excel, 454, 499

screensavers, 87, 613-616, 838, 1126

Index

Script Editor program, 98
scripting HyperCard stacks, 742
scripts, 1126
   databases, 518
   HyperCard, 701, 704, 719-723
   in spreadsheets, 462
   navigating stacks, 712
   spreadsheet programs, Heizer Software, 462
Scripts (FileMaker program), 553-565
scroll arrows, 71, 1126
scroll bars, 71, 1126
SCSI (Small Computer Systems Interface), 1126
   addresses, 1077
   bus, 189
   chains, 1069
   daisy-chaining, 134
   devices, 195
   ports, 195-196
      cable problems, 1067
      diagnosis of problems, 1065-1066
      hard drive connections, 189
      parallel, 134-136
      problems, 196, 1065-1068
      Quadra 900, 161
      terminators, 135
      problems, 1068-1069
      unit attention mode, 1068
SCSI DMA (Direct Memory Access) controllers, 122, 157
SCSI Evaluator shareware program, 135
SCSI IDs, internal drive, 1077
SCSI-1 standard, 196
SCSI-2 standard, 135, 196
SCSIProbe shareware program, 106, 135
SCSITools shareware program, 106, 135
Sculley, John, Apple's second president, 12
ScuzzyGraph, 199
SEA (Self Extracting Archive) files, 1031
.SEA extensions, self-extracting archives, 934
search features, 411-412
sectors of tracks on hard disks, 189
See the U.S.A. program (Compu-Teach), 629
Select All command (Edit menu), FileMaker Pro, 558
Select menu commands
   Define Fields (FileMaker Pro), 546
   Layout (FileMaker Pro), 555

Index

selecting
- items, 59-60
- text in Microsoft Word, 455

Selection command (Special menu), 72

selection marquees, 59

self-extracting archives, 934

self-improvement programs, Visionary Software, 637-640

self-study programming courses, 1106-1107

seminars
- Macintosh, 1048
- programming, 1106

sense codes for external displays, 178

Sensible Grammar (Sensible Software), 427

Sequence tile, Double Helix 3.5 (Helix), 525-526

sequencers, 1127
- MIDI, 676-686
- music programs, 644

serial cables and Mac/PC interaction, 1005-1006

serial networks, 980

serial port cards, 193-194

serial port switch boxes, 193-194

serial ports, 192-193, 1126-1027

serif typefaces, 367

servers, 947-948, 1127

service bureaus, 1127

services, Macintosh networking, 947-952

Set Startup... command (Special menu), 30, 44

SetFileKey program, 115

settings for modems, 910-911

shadows in charts, 495-496

shapes, filling, 287-289

shareware, 1038, 1127
- ADBProbe control panel, 133
- adult, 596
- BinHex, 1031
- Boomerang utility, 849
- clip art, 383
- ColorFinder program, 60
- FKey Manager, 89
- games, 610-611
- *Home & School Mac* disk magazine, 612
- Hunt the Wumpus maze, 597
- InUse program, 135
- libraries, 318, 930
- McSink, 423
- MiniWriter, 423
- NHSMUG (National Home & School Mac User Group), 612
- PopChar, 74
- RAM disk utilities, 840
- SCSI Evaluator/SCSIProbe/ SCSITools program, 135

Sound Converter, 83, 93

Stuffit Lite, 934

Sharing command (File menu), 60

Sherlock Holmes adventure game (ICOM), 595

Shift key, 74

shift-clicking, 23, 59, 1127

Shiva

NetModem/NetSerial peripheral interface, 1018

shortcuts

FileMaker Pro, 570-572

HyperCard painting tools, 714

userLevel five HyperCard objects, 739

shorthand real-time conferences, 926-927

Show Ruler command, Format menu (Microsoft Word), 434, 441

Shut Down command (Special menu), 21, 25, 1127

shutting off Macs, 21-22

Sierra Online games, 590, 595-596

signal types in video, 768-770

signing off online services, 915-916

SIGs (Special Interest Groups), 1043, 1127

Silicon Beach Software Digital Darkroom, 264

Silicon Beach Software SuperCard, 744-746

Silver Lining utility, 866

Silverlining program, 110, 135

SimAnt/City/Earth/Life simulation games (Maxis), 607-608

SIMMs (Single Inline Memory Modules), 127, 148, 182-185, 1056-1057, 1127

simulations, multimedia, 757

single cards (HyperCard), 723-724

.SIT extensions, Stuffit files, 934

Sitka DosTOPS/MacTOPS program, 1010

Smalltalk programming language, 1099

Smiley Face DA, Mac Utilities library (America Online), 927

Smiling Mac icon, 18

SmoothFont format, TypeStyler, 393

SMPTE (Society of Motion Picture and Television Engineers) Timecode, 674, 1127

SNA•ps 3270 emulators (Apple), 991

SND resource file format, 93

SNMP (Simple Network Management Protocol), 967

Snooper utility (Polybus Systems Corp.), 1078

socket numbers, AppleTalk, 955

Index

soft partitions in volumes, 855

SoftPC IBM PC emulator (Insignia Solutions), 109, 1014-1016

SoftSync Expert Color Paint program, 268

software, 24

    desktop publishing, 301, 306-309

    integrated, 573-574

    problems with older versions, 1072-1074

    registering, 1037-1038

    updates by mailing lists/on BBSs, 1038-1039

    see also programs

Software Bridge Macintosh (Systems Compatibility Corp.), 413

software module managers, 100

Software Toolworks

    Life and Death simulation game, 605

    Mavis Beacon Teaches Typing program, 637

    Miracle Piano System, 683

Software Venture, MicroPhone, 1006-1008

solid-ink printers, 244-245

Solutions International, SuperGlue, 849

Sonata laser font (Adobe), 685

Songworks, Ars Nova, 682

Sony Corp.

    .SONY driver, 193

    Trinitron picture tube, Mac Color Classic, 151

    Vbox, 771

    VISCA (Video System Control Architecture) machine control codes, 771

Sophisticated Circuits PowerKey, 134

sorting records in FileMaker Pro, 559

sound, 91-94, 644-649, 786-790

    adding to Apple menu, 41-43

    compressing, 656-657

    Compression pop-up menu (HyperCard), 730-731

    controlling, 658-667

    digitized, 787

    Doppler effect, 662

    editing, 649-667, 728-731

    equalizing, 662-663

    file formats, 93, 666

    files, 788

    HyperCard, 728-732

    memory, 654-657

    mixing, 664-665

    modifying, 660-665

    phone use, 668

    pitch effects, 660-662

    playlist editor programs, 668-669

professional editing, 667

recording, 649-658

saving final version, 665-666

SoundEdit Pro program, 658

sources, 787-790

speech, 686-687

Sound control panel, 46, 92

Sound Converter shareware, 83, 93

Sound Driver, 92

Sound Manager, 92, 788

Sound Master program, 94

Sound Tools (DigiDesign), 667

SoundEdit Pro (MacroMind), 656-658, 660-665

source programs, 1087

Space Invaders game, 590

Space Quest adventure games (Sierra Online), 595

Spacewars game, MIT (Massachusetts Institute of Technology), 588

special characters, 378-379

Special menu commands, 67-68

   Clean Up Window, 72

   Empty Trash, 57

   Selection, 72

   Set Startup..., 30, 44

   Shut Down, 21, 25, 1127

Spectrum puzzle games, 598-599

Speech Manager (Apple), 789

speech programs, 687

Speed Disk program, Norton Utilities, 111

speed of printing, 229-230

speed ratings, SIMMs, 127

spell checkers, 317, 405, 416, 427

spindle motor failure, hard drives, 1070

Spinnaker Plus multimedia engines, 759, 803-804

Spinning Beachball icon, 1129

SPLAsh (Symantec Programming Languages Association), 1108

splitting screens

   Microsoft Excel, 499

   Microsoft Word, 454

spot color separations, 280-281

spot-color printing, 320-321

spreadsheets, 458-463

   3-D, 459

   charting/graphing, 461

   DeltaGraph (DeltaPoint), 464

   designing, 468-470

   engines, 470-471

   files, 1025

   front-ends, 471

   KaleidaGraph, 464

   Lotus 1-2-3/Mac, 467-468

   Lotus Improv, 472-473

   MacCalc, 468

Index

macros, 462

Microsoft Excel, 463-465, 476-477

Microsoft Works, 465, 576

number formats, 482-484

redefining Styles, 486-487

Resolve 1.0, 467

scripts, 462

Styles feature, Microsoft Excel, 478-487

System 7, 471

templates, 473

Wingz, 465-466

words, 485

sprites in animation, 765

stacks, 123, 126, 1127

buttons, 737-738

customizing, 733-742

fields, 735-736

Heizer Software, 702

HyperCard, 696-698

accessing, 702

global variables, 741-742

moving to different cards, 707-712

printing cards, 724-726

scripting, 742

navigating

with arrow keys, 710-711

with buttons, 711

with menu commands, 707-709

with message box and scripts, 712

organizing, 703

starting, 734-735

userLevel four information, 734-738

Stanford Research Institute, home of the mouse, 73

star networking, Ethernet, 995-996

StarController (Farallon) LocalTalk repeater, 971

start-up disks, 105, 1127

start-up order of extensions, 87-88

Start-up screens, 1127

starting

stacks, 734-735

the Mac, 18-19

Startup Items folder, 43-45, 80, 106

static friction in hard drives, *see* stiction

static RAM, 123

Stationery, 1127

stationery files, 407

stationery pads, 386

statistical functions, spreadsheets, 460

status lights, modems, 905

Stella program, 757

Stereo Recording option, SoundEdit program, 654

Sticky Keys utility, special typing needs, 812

stiction, hard drive problems, 1070

still images in multimedia, 763-764

still video cameras, 772

Story editor (PageMaker), 364

straight-through cables, switch boxes, 193

StrataVision, 805

Strategic Conquest battle game (Delta Tao Software), 592

Streamline (Adobe), 385

stretched type, 290

Strip Switch (Practical Solutions), 134

Structure Editor screen, 4th Dimension (ACIUS), 526

structured wiring networks, 998-999

Studer Dyaxis, 667

Studio Vision (Opcode Systems), 645, 680-681

Studio/1 program, 267

Studio/32 program, 271

Studio/8 program, 269-270

studios, MIDI setup, 672

Stuffit compression utility (Raymond Lau), 934

Stuffit Deluxe (Aladdin Systems), 1031

Stuffit Lite compression utility, 934

style checkers, 405, 427

Style command (Format menu), Microsoft Excel, 485

style sheets, 407
- importing, 313
- Microsoft Word, 313
- Ventura Publisher, 311

style-name tags, 314

Style... command (Format menu), Microsoft Word, 435

styles
- fonts, 1127
- Microsoft Excel, 479-487
- PageMaker, 354-357
- redefining, 486-487
- templates (Excel), 498
- type, 295-296

Styles command, Format menu (Microsoft Excel), 479, 482

Styles feature
- Microsoft Excel, 478-487
- Microsoft Word, 432-437

subfiles, databases, 510

subheads, 308

submenus, 1128

subrecords, databases, 510

Index

Subscribe To... command (Edit menu), 36

substituting fonts, 373

Suitcase font manager, 377, 395, 1128

Suitcase 2 font manager, 89-91

Suitcase files, 81-82

Suitcase II program (Fifth Generation), 81, 844

SUM II (Symantec Utilities for Macintosh), 859, 866

SUM utility, 106, 111

Sun Systems Remarketing, Lisa PC support, 146

Super Boomerang program, 102, 849

SuperATM (Adobe), 372
- substituting fonts, 373
- typeface substitution, 397

SuperCard (Silicon Beach Software), 744-746, 759, 803

SuperDrive 1.44M floppy disk drive, 149, 153
- clones, 1005

SuperGlue (Solutions International), 849

SuperLaserSpool print spooler (Fifth Generation Systems), 224, 845

SuperMac VideoSpigot capture card, 776, 784

SuperPaint program, 266-267, 383

SuperSpool print spooler (Fifth Generation Systems), 845

SuperTetris puzzle game (Spectrum), 599

surface mount chips in SIMMs, 185

surge protectors for modems, 905

Surgeon 3: The Brain simulation game, 605

sustained transfer rate of hard disks, 190

SVHS video tape formats, 770

Swamp Gas Visits the USA program (Inline Design), 630

swap files, AppDisk, 130

switch boxes, serial ports, 193-194

switches
- for data input, 816
  - morse code, for data entry, 816

Swivel 3-D, 803, 805

SWM (Super Wozniak Machine) chip, 109

SYLK (Microsoft's SYmbolic LinK) interchange format, 115, 1025

Symantec
- Antivirus, 872
- GreatWorks, 422, 577-578
- MORE 4.0 outliner program, 409, 426

Everything You Wanted to Know About the Mac

Think Class Library, 1092

Tools (Symantec Utilities), 115

symmetrical video capture, 784

Symmetry Software, Acta DA outliners, 409, 426

Synchronicity (Visionary Software), 426, 637-638

Synergy Software KaleidaGraph, 464

synthesizers
  master, 672
  MIDI, 670-676
  sysex messages, 676

SyQuest disks, removing from desktop, 21

Sysop (System operator), 924, 1128

System 6
  Finder, 18
  Font/DA Mover, 837
  MultiFinder, 18
  NFNT (New Font Numbering System), 377
  Operating System, 28
  system resources, 80-82

System 7, 18, 1010
  aliases, 37-40
  and word processors, 424-426
  Apple Events, 758
  Apple Open Collaboration Environment, 758
  Control Panels folder, 835
  Data Access Manager, 757
  files, 80-83, 93, 1074-1075, 1128
  folder, 79-80
  Get Info window, 386
  icons, 113
  LaserWriter Font Utility, 225
  Operating System, 28
  PrintMonitor program, 223
  Publish and Subscribe, 758
  Sound Manager, 788
  spreadsheets, 471
  start-up loading, 106
  system resources, 82-83
  TrueType fonts, 376

System 7 Tune Up, 126

system clock and processors, 140

System Enabler files, 83-84, 106

System Extensions, 84-90

System file patches, 1092

System Font Manager, 375

System heap, 126

system modeling software, 757

System Picker freeware utility, 78

system resources
  System 6, 80-82
  System 7, 82-83

Index

System Tools floppy disk, 1076

Systems Compatibility Corp., Software Bridge Macintosh, 413

T

t-shirt transfers, Easy Transfer Cartridges, 216

T/Maker, WriteNow word processor, 420-421

T4 virus, 885-886

Tabby, Fidonet network protocol, 941

Table... command (Microsoft Word)
- Format menu, 440
- Insert menu, 438, 448

tables
- in documents, 409
- Microsoft Word, 438-445

tables of contents, 408-409

Tactic Software, Magic Typist, 819

tactile click feel on keyboards, 76

tactile output devices, 827

Talking Math Rabbit program (Learning Company), 622

Talking Moose program, 93-94, 687

Talking Reader Rabbit program (Learning Company), 622

tape drives, multimedia storage, 798

tape formats, video, 770

TapeDisk utility (Optima), 798

Tappy Type program, 94

TASH, Inc., keylatches/keyguards/mini-keyboards, 814-815

Taste (DeltaPoint), 412, 420

TeachText program, 1128

tear-off menus, 1128

tearing in animation, 765

TechConnect program (Odesta), 526

Teknosys Inc., Help! utility, 1078

Tektronix graphics terminals, 950

telecommuting, 810

TeleFinder BBS program, 941

TelePort modems (Global Village Communications), 194, 904

Telnet terminal services, 989

templates, 318-320, 385-388
- editors, 118
- grid, 319
- Icon, 60
- label, 320, 388
- placeholder, 318
- Postcraft, 387
- style, 498

Tempo II Plus (Affinity Microsystems), 61, 415
temporary resource files, 1086
terminal emulators, 911, 950, 989-991
terminals
   IBM, 950
   Tektronix graphics, 950
   VT (Digital), 950
terminators
   drive controller board, 1066
   external hard drives, 1066-1067
   IIfx, 1066
   logic board, 1066
   SCSI ports, problems, 1066
terminology of desktop publishing programs, 306
terms used in Macintosh technology, 22-24
Terrapin Software LOGO programming language, 632
Tesserae puzzle game (Inline Design), 599
test kits, databases, 520-521
test preparation programs, 635-636
Tetricycle Trojan horse, 883
Tetris puzzle game (Spectrum), 598
Texas Instruments NuBus, 136

text
   adding to master pages (PageMaker), 333
   automatic placement, 313
   editing
      creating CODE resources, 1087
      desktop publishing programs, 315-318
      word processors, 403-405
   greeking, 329
   holding with Text Box tool (Microsoft Excel), 500
   kerning
      PageMaker, 314
      Publish It! Easy, 314
   multimedia, 762
   paint programs, 258
   placing, 313-315, 341-345
   reformatting, 314
   threading automatically in PageMaker, 316
   tracking, 314
text blocks, 313
text fields (FileMaker Pro), 571
text files, 1128
   formats, 1022-1023
   importing, 313
text functions, spreadsheets, 460
TEXT interchange format, 115

Index

text layers in documents, 411

text placement symbols, 316

TextEdit program, 102

textures as backgrounds, 388

The Active Window newsletter (BCS•Mac), 1042

The Box (Voyager), 771, 774

The Printer Muffler (Kensington), 212

The Talking Moose (Baseline Publishing), 613

The Tinies puzzle game (Inline Design), 601

The Writing Center program (Learning Company), 627

thermal transfer printers, 218-219

thermal wax transfer printers, 203

thesaurus, 405, 418, 428

Thesaurus Rex feature, Publish It! Easy, 316

Thickwire Ethernet, 974

Think C development system, 1102-1103

Think Class Library (Symantec), 1102, 1092

Think Pascal development system, 1102-1103

Thinwire Ethernet, 975

thinwire Ethernet repeaters, 976

Thought I Could, Wallpaper program, 615

threading

    text, 313

    text and graphics automatically in PageMaker, 316

throughput of processors, 121

TidBITS electronic magazine, 1040

TIFF (Tagged Image File Format), 1128

    file formats, 262

    files, 1024

    interchange format, 115

Timbuktu for Windows program, 1010

Timecode Machine (Opcode Systems), 673

Timeworks Publish It! Easy, 387

Title bars, 70, 1128

titles in charts, 494

TMON Professional development system, 1104

Toby cards, Apple Macintosh Video Cards, 179

Token Ring networks, 978-979, 1011-1012

TokenTalk NuBus interface card (Apple), 957, 1011

toner cartridges, 215

tool palettes, 292-294, 305

toolboxes, 100, 283-284, 1092-1093

desktop publishing programs, 304

utilities, 834-835, 839-849

toolkits, multimedia engines, 759

Tools menu commands (Microsoft Word)

Commands..., 452

Preferences..., 439

Torx wrench tool, opening Mac cases, 127

Toucan Press program, 623

touch screens, Mac 'n Touch (MicroTouch Systems), 815

Trace Research and Development Center, 829

Track feature, 363

trackballs, 73, 195, 817

tracking text, 314

tracks, hard disks, 189

training skills on the Mac, 1048

transcendental functions, 143

transfer rate of hard disks, 190

transfer utilities, 841-843

transferring files, 1025-1027

translating files, 1020-1030

translation utilities, 841-843, 1022

translators in file formats, 412-413

transparent inks, 237

transparent rubber stamp tool, PixelPaint Professional, 260

trap patching, INITs, 1073

Trash, 1128

Trash Can icon, 57, 1128

Trash Zapper math game, 624

travel information, online services, 918-919

Traveling Software, LapLink/Mac, 1005, 1026-1028

Tribe LocalSwitch/LocalTalk bridge, 996

triggering Scripts, FileMaker Pro, 563

Trojan horses, 871, 883, 1128

troubleshooting

Mac, 1046-1047, 1053-1057

worksheets, 470

see also problems

TrueImage

fonts, 228

printer description language, 206, 374

TrueMatch color standard, 238

TrueType (Apple)

faxes, 903

fonts, 213, 366, 373-376, 380, 1128

rasterizers, 376

text standard, 207, 1024

Index

TrueVision NuVista+ video boards, 767, 778-779

Trumatch color-matching systems, 265

TTY (teletype) modem calls, 911

tuning hard disks, *see* optimizing hard disks

tutorials, 757, 1048

twisted-pair Ethernet, 976

two-color printing, *see* spot-color printing

type
- changing case in Microsoft Word, 455-456
- distorted/flipped/reversed/ stretched, 290
- effects in draw programs, 289-290
- kerning in PageMaker, 361-364
- styles, 295-296

Type 1/Type 3 fonts (Adobe), 206

type families, 366

Type menu, FoxBASE+/Mac 2.1 (Fox Software), 533

Type Reunion program (Adobe), 377, 396

typefaces, 366-367, 397

TypeStyler (Brøderbund), 393

typing
- expanded keyboards for limited movement, 814
- headpointers/wrist rests, 813
- keyguards/keylatches/ mouthsticks, 813-814
- special needs, Easy Access utilities, 811

typing tutor programs, 637

typography terminology, 366-367

U

U-Matic video tape formats, 770

UCB (University of California at Berkeley) Adventure game, 588

Ultima Home Office (Prometheus), 667

Undo command, 1128

Unicorn Adaptive keyboard, 814

Unisyn library editor (Mark of the Unicorn), 684

unit attention mode, SCSI devices, 1068

Universal Print Buffer/Print Buffer Plus (Reliable Communications), 225

University of Utah Computer Center, KeyMouse utility, 817

UNIX networking with Macintosh, 985-989

UnZip file compression freeware, 1031

upgrading hardware, 24

upgrading software, 583-584, 1037-1040

uploading files, 932-934, 1129

upper-end multimedia configuration, 796-797

USENET news groups, virus updates, 893

user functions in scripts, 721

user groups, 1129
- for Macs, 1041-1044
- local, 1042-1043
- teaching programming, 1107-1108
- virus updates, 893

user-defined fonts, 371

userLevels, 699-700
- defaults, 699
- userLevel five objects, 739
- userLevel four information stacks, 734-738

utilities, 833-850, 1129
- Adobe Type Align, 846
- Apple File Exchange, 841, 1003
- Apple HD SC setup, 1110
- AutoMac, 847
- automated diagnostic, 1078-1079
- Boomerang, 849
- ClickChange, 102
- Close View, 822-824
- compression
  - CompactPro, 934
  - DiskDoubler, 935
  - Stuffit, 934
  - Stuffit Deluxe, 934
  - Stuffit Lite, 934
- disk, 848
- disk doctor, 838
- Disk Express II, 111
- Disk First Aid, 106
- disk management, 866
  - 911 Utilities, 866
  - Hard Disk Toolkit, 866
  - Norton Utilities for the Macintosh, 866
  - Silver Lining, 866
- DOS Mounter, 842
- Easy Access, 848
- expanding toolbox, 839-849
- extension-managing, 840-841
- Extensions Manager, 841
- file translation
  - LapLink/Mac, 1022
  - Macintosh PC Exchange, 1022
  - MacLinkPlus, 1022
- font, 390-397, 846-847
  - Font/DA Juggler, 377
  - Suitcase, 377
- Font/DA Mover, 41, 80
- freeware, System Picker, 78

Index

Help!, 1078
Installer, 106, 837, 1073
Key Caps, 847
keyboard, 847-848
KeyMouse, 817
LapLink Mac, 842
LaserWriter Font, 225
libraries, 849
MacEKG, 1078
MacLink Plus/PC, 842
macro, 847
MacroMaker, 847
MacTools Deluxe, 859, 866
Master Juggler, 844
Metamorphosis, 846
MODE32, 143
organization, 854-855
Personality!, 102
printer, 845-846
PrintMonitor, 79
RAM disk, 130, 839-840
ResEdit, 843-844
Retrospect, 859
Screen saver, 838
Snooper, 1078
Sticky Keys, 812
suggested for the Mac, 835-838
SuitCase II, 844
SUM, 106, 111
Super Boomerang, 849
Symantec Utilities for Macintosh, 859, 866
TapeDisk, 798
toolboxes of, 834-835
transfer, 841-843
translation, 841-843
VideoSync, 780
virus, 837-838

V

Vaccination 1.1 program, 890-891
Vantage (Baseline Publishing), 423
vaporware, 1129
Varcon Diamonds/Jewelbox games, 599, 611
variables
    compression algorithms, 784
    HyperCard containers, 740
Vax networking with Macintosh, 989-991
Vaxene program, 891
VAXshare file servers, 989
Vbox (Sony), 771
VCheck 1.3 program, 891
vector calculation video coprocessors, 122
vector-mapped file formats, 763

Ventura Publisher (Xerox Corporation), 323-324
    Frame tool, 305
    style sheets, 311
    style-name tags, 314
    table editor, 305
    text placement symbol, 316
verbs used in Mac technology, 22-23
Versadapter (ConnExperts), 233
version numbers of software, 1129
versions of HyperCard, 694-696
'Vette simulation game, 603-610
VGA monitors, Mac LC, 174
VHS video tape formats, 770
video, 755
    analog, 766
    boards, 767
    cards, 173, 179
    conversion boxes, 780
    coprocessors, 122
    devices, 770-775
    digital, 767, 783-786
    hardware, 173-174
    high-resolution cameras, 772
    interlaced signals, 767
    Mac environment, 778-780
    Mac/NTSC conversion, 781-783
    media, 770-775
    noninterlaced scanning, 767
    outputting Mac to NTSC, 780-781
    overscan, 767
    progressive scanning, 767
    QuickTime, 766-770
    S Video component type, 770
    signal overlays, 778
    signal types, 768-770
    still cameras, 772
    tape formats, 770
    viewing, 775-778
    WORM, 773
video disc players, 772
video in a window, 777
video terminal (VT) modes, modem calls, 911
Videodisc toolkit, 760
VideoFusion (Diva), 806
VideoLogic DVA-4000 video board, 767, 778
VideoLogic Mediator, 781
VideoQuill, 782
VideoShop (Diva), 806
VideoSpigot capture card (SuperMac), 776, 784
VideoSync utility (Apple), 780
videotape recorders, interactive control, 771

Index

VideoVision card (Radius), 779, 781

View menu commands, 66

View window, FoxBASE+/Mac 2.1 (Fox Software), 532

viewing file attributes, Symantec Tools program, 115

Views control panel, 47-48, 71

VINES (Banyan) Mac/PC networks, 985

Virex antivirus program, 866, 872

Virtual (Connectix), 132

virtual memory, 130-131

Virtual Valerie adventure game, 596

Virus Encyclopedia program, 892

Virus Rx 1.6 program, 892

VIRUS-L distribution lists (BITNET), 893

VirusBlockade II 1.0 program, 891

VirusDetective 4.0.4 program, 891

viruses, 114, 865, 870-874, 1129
   Mac-infecting, 874-887
   updates through user groups, 893
   utilities, 837-838, 873-874, 887-892

VirusWarning program, 892

VISCA (Video System Control Architecture), Sony control codes, 771

VisiCalc program, 458

Visiflex Seels keyboard covers, 815

Vision (Opcode Systems), 680-681

Visionary Software
   self-improvement programs, 637-640
   Synchronicity word processor, 426

VocabuLearn/ce program (Penton), 633

Voice Impact (Articulate System), 649, 731

Voice Impact Pro sound box, 653-654

voice mail, 667

Voice Navigator (Articulate Systems), 818

Voice Record (Articulate System), 731

volatile memory, 1129

volume backups and incremental backups, 858

volumes, 109-111, 855

von Neumann, John, 869

Voyager, The Box, 771, 774

Voyager Expanded Books, 757

VT terminals (Digital), 950

W

Wacom graphics tablet, 256

wait states in memory, 183-184

wallpaper patterns, 389

Wallpaper program (Thought I Could), 615

WANs, Ethernet FDDI networking setups, 998

Warning 1.1 program, 892

Water Drop tool in paint programs, 259

Wave Maker program (Garry Galbreath), 647

waveform (sound), 646-648, 662-663

Wayne, Ron, original Apple logo, 7

WDBN native format (Microsoft Word), 115

WDEF virus, 878-880

weather reports in online services, 918

Welcome to Macintosh message, 1075

Welltris puzzle game (Spectrum), 599

WetPaint (DublClick), 383, 389

wetware, 1129

White Knight on the Mac (FreeSoft), 908, 1006-1008

white space, 306

white-out, electronic, 313

whiting out master page items, 338

Widget, Lisa PC hard drive, 145

width of columns, 333

Wild Magic control-panel extension, 784

wildcard searches, 411

Williams & Macias, MyDiskLabeler, 848

Window Format dialog box, Omnis 7 (Blyth Software, Inc.), 535

window headers, 70

Window Manager program, 101

Window menu commands
  Old way chart (Microsoft Excel), 490
  Zoom (Microsoft Excel), 505

window titles, 70

windows
  About the Finder, 30
  autoscrolling, 71
  Finder use, 56
  Get Info, System 7, 386
  in Finder, 70-72
  Views control panel, 71
  zoom boxes, Mac Plus, 148
  zooming in PageMaker, 360

Windows Player accelerator board (MacroMind), 1032

Wingz (Informix), 465-466

Index

wireless Ethernet, Altair II (Motorola), 981

wireless networks, 981-982

WMF files, 1024

Wolfram Research, Mathematica, 461

Wollongong, Pathway NFS, 987

Word Munchers game (MECC), 623

word processors, 402-429
   and System 7, 424-426
   evaluating, 415-422
   features, 402-404
   modules
      GreatWorks (Symantec), 577
      WordPerfect Works, 582
   selecting, 423-424
   text editing, 403-405

WordPerfect Corp.
   WordPerfect, 412, 419-420
   WordPerfect Works, 422, 581-582

words
   Macintosh technology, 22-24
   phonemes, 659
   spreadsheets, 485

WordTris puzzle game (Spectrum), 599

WordWriter DA (MacIntyre), 819

workarounds in HyperCard, 706-707

workgroup printers, 241

worksheets
   building, 469-470
   in spreadsheets, 459-460
   Microsoft Excel, 498
   troubleshooting, 470

Workspace command (Options menu), Microsoft Excel, 478

Workspace dialog box, Microsoft Excel, 478

World Builder adventure game (Aldus/Silicon Beach), 596

WorldLine Country Search, 918

WorldScript feature, System 7, 425

WorldWide Disability Solutions Group (Apple), 829

WORM (Write Once Read Many) video, 773

worms, 870-871, 1129

Wozniak, Steve, 3

wrist rests for typing, 813

Wristwatch, 1129

Write:OutLoud (Don Johnston Developmental Equipment), 826

WriteImpact dot-matrix printers (GCC), 212

WriteNow version 2.2, 420-421

WYSIWYG (What-You-See-Is-What-You-Get), 300, 367

X-Y

X-10 program (X-10 (USA), Inc.), 820-821

X-Window client/server windows (MIT), 987

Xante Accel-A-Writer controllers, 208

XCMDs (External Commands), 743-744, 1129

Xerox Corporation, Ventura Publisher, 323-324

XFCNs (External Functions), 743-744, 1129

Xinet K-AShare, Mac/UNIX networks, 985

XMODEM file transfer, 931

XOR MacSki simulation game, 603

XTND system, file translation (Claris), 115, 412, 1029-1030

YMODEM file transfer, 931

Z

zapping the PRAM, 1130

ZapShot (Canon), 772

ZIF (zero insertion force) connectors, 146

Zilog Z8530 Serial Communications Controller, 192

ZIP (AppleTalk Zone Information Protocol), 965

ZIP file format (PCs), 1031

ZMODEM file transfer, 931

zone names, networks, 961-964

Zoom boxes, 1130
    Mac Plus windows, 148
    windows, 71

Zoom command (Window menu), Microsoft Excel, 504-506

zooming windows in PageMaker, 360

Zork adventure game (Activision), 594

Zounds (Digital Eclipse), 616

ZTerm communication program, 909

ZUC virus, 880-881